The Science of Social Vision

Oxford Series In Visual Cognition

Series Editors

GILLIAN RHODES
MARY A. PETERSON

Perception of Faces, Objects, and Scenes: Analytic and Holistic Processes

Edited by MARY A. PETERSON AND GILLIAN RHODES

Fitting the Mind to the World: Adaptation and After-Effects in High-Level Vision

Edited by COLIN W. G. CLIFFORD AND GILLIAN RHODES

Human Body Perception from the Inside Out

Edited by GÜNTHER KNOBLICH, IAN M. THORNTON, MARC GROSJEAN, AND MAGGIE SHIFRAR

Understanding Events: From Perception to Action

Edited by THOMAS F. SHIPLEY AND JEFFREY M. ZACKS

Visual Memory

Edited by STEVEN J. LUCK AND ANDREW HOLLINGWORTH

Perceptual Expertise: Bridging Brain and Behavior

Edited by ISABEL GAUTHIER, MICHAEL J. TARR, AND DANIEL BUB

The Science of Social Vision

Edited by REGINALD B. ADAMS, Jr., NALINI AMBADY, KEN NAKAYAMA AND SHINSUKE SHIMOJO

The Science of Social Vision

Edited by

Reginald B. Adams, Jr.

Nalini Ambady

Ken Nakayama

Shinsuke Shimojo

UNIVERSITY PRESS

2011

OXFORD
UNIVERSITY PRESS

Oxford University Press, Inc., publishes works that further
Oxford University's objective of excellence
in research, scholarship, and education.

Oxford New York
Auckland Cape Town Dar es Salaam Hong Kong Karachi
Kuala Lumpur Madrid Melbourne Mexico City Nairobi
New Delhi Shanghai Taipei Toronto

With offices in
Argentina Austria Brazil Chile Czech Republic France Greece
Guatemala Hungary Italy Japan Poland Portugal Singapore
South Korea Switzerland Thailand Turkey Ukraine Vietnam

Published by Oxford University Press, Inc.
198 Madison Avenue, New York, New York 10016
www.oup.com

Library of Congress Cataloging-in-Publication Data

The science of social vision / edited by Reginald B. Adams, Jr. ... [et al.].
p. cm.—(Oxford series in visual cognition ; 7)
ISBN 978-0-19-533317-6
1. Visual perception—Psychological aspects.   2. Visual perception—Social aspects.
3. Social interaction.   4. Perception.   5. Cognition. I. Adams, Reginald B.
BF241.S366 2010
152.14—dc22
2009016075

9 8 7 6 5 4 3 2 1

Printed in China
on acid-free paper

PREFACE

Human beings are inherently communal, reliant in almost every aspect on others for survival. Not surprisingly, we have acquired an elaborate system of nonverbal communication and perception that helps us establish and maintain cohesive social interactions effortlessly. Notably, such social communication in everyday exchange is transmitted and received predominantly via the visual modality. The purpose of this book, therefore, is to underscore and explore this important intersection of social and visual perception.

More of the human brain is dedicated to visual processes than all other sensory modalities combined, and the visual system is particularly attuned to social cues in the environment. This anatomical fact reflects the central importance vision plays in both establishing and navigating us through our social worlds. As a result, we are able to see others' mental and emotional states, enabling us to understand their desires, intentions, motives, and beliefs. What we see informs our impressions and guides our ongoing interactions. In turn, these impressions influence the very way we process even low-level visual input. It is this reciprocal exchange that weds social and visual perception and from which future cross-disciplinary exchange will likely offer new and fruitful insights.

There is little doubt that our visual machinery evolved in the context of social demands. Similarly, given its important role in nonverbal communication and perception, the visual system undoubtedly shaped the evolution of social perception. Thus, in order to examine the interplay of visual and social processes, we must consider both what is innately prepared and what has emerged as the product of individual variation and cultural learning. Along these lines, four primary themes are explored in this book:

1. Vision plays a powerful role in moderating social interaction and perception;
2. Visual cues can also activate socially relevant knowledge stores, thereby guiding our impressions and social behavior toward others;
3. Social factors, in turn, play an important role in moderating basic visual processing;
4. Visual and social perception are in some cases functionally equivalent.

Social scientists are now recognizing the critical role of vision in the development and maintenance of social perception and cognition. As a result, these researchers are turning to known models of vision to better understand the functional and neuroanatomical mechanisms underlying social perception. Vision scientists are likewise increasingly attuned to the important role that people, as social agents, have played in shaping the structure and operation of the visual system. To fully understand the visual system, it is imperative to consider the socially adaptive functions it evolved to perform.

We believe that a substantial field already exists in which vision and social science overlap, and we are delighted to bring scientists together whose work naturally intersects in this regard. Although we treat social vision herein as an emerging field of study, the existing work that offers important insights into this interface is broadly interdisciplinary. Diverse fields such as cultural anthropology, ethology, developmental psychology, and neuroscience already lend important contributions to our understanding of the social vision interface.

This book opens with an introductory chapter delineating our overarching vision. Theoretical chapters that supply the framework for the concept of social vision follow this. The chapters that follow showcase cutting-edge research on this topic that unfolds from the micro- to macro-levels, opening first with chapters examining the language of the eyes, to face perception, then to body language and biological motion, and finally to the impact on and influences of social context and group memberships. Although insights from neuroscience are infused throughout these chapters, given its clear theoretical import and room for innovation, a final section is included that specifically addresses the neural underpinnings of social vision. This final section helps bridge the various preceding topics, addressing overarching questions such as the interplay of innate process and intra-/ intercultural variation.

ACKNOWLEDGMENTS

We would like to thank Catharine Carlin, our editor at Oxford University Press, whose initial insight led to this book, and whose encouragement saw it to fruition. We are also indebted to Jennifer Rappaport who initially approached us on behalf of Oxford University Press and who worked closely with us through the initial stages of the proposal process. We thank all the chapter writers, who gave of their valuable time to bring important insights and cutting-edge research to the topic of social vision. R.B.Adams Jr. appreciates the helpful comments received from his undergraduates and graduate students who read this book as part of a social vision seminar course, and to his colleagues who offered helpful input along the way. He thanks his co-editors for agreeing to embark upon this journey, offering wisdom and insight along the way to make this book truly exceptional. He thanks his friends and family, particularly Katharine Donnelly Adams, for their support, feedback, and encouragement throughout the process of putting this book together. N. Ambady appreciates the vision and generosity of her co-editors, students, and family. K. Nakayama appreciates the generosity of the contributing authors and the friendship and advice of his co-editors. S. Shimojo would like to thank his laboratory members at California Institute of Technology, and the members of JST.ERATO Shimojo Implicit Brain Function Project.

CONTENTS

Contributors   xi

Introduction: Vision Going Social   xv

Ken Nakayama

SECTION I THEORETICAL PERSPECTIVES ON SOCIAL VISION

1. **An Ecological Theory of Face Perception**   3

   *Leslie A. Zebrowitz, P. Matthew Bronstad,
   and Joann M. Montepare*

2. **The Cognitive Capitalist: Social Benefits of Perceptual
   Economy**   31

   Douglas Martin and C. Neil Macrae

3. **Faces, Bodies, Social Vision as Agent Vision, and Social
   Consciousness**   51

   Beatrice de Gelder and Marco Tamietto

4. **Perceiving Through Culture: The Socialized Attention
   Hypothesis**   75

   Hyekyung Park and Shinobu Kitayama

5. **Compound Social Cues in Human Face Processing**   90

   *Reginald B. Adams, Jr., Robert G. Franklin, Jr., Anthony J. Nelson,
   and Michael T. Stevenson*

SECTION II THE LANGUAGE OF THE EYES

6. **Gaze Perception and Visually Mediated Attention**   108

   Stephen R. H. Langton

7. Aging Eyes Facing an Emotional World: The Role of
    Motivated Gaze   133
    Derek M. Isaacowitz and Nora A. Murphy

8. Gaze and Preference-Orienting Behavior as a Somatic
    Precursor of Preference Decision   151
    Shinsuke Shimojo, Claude Simion, and Mark A. Changizi

SECTION III   SOCIAL VISION AT FACE VALUE

9. Facial Attractiveness   164
    Anthony C. Little and David I. Perrett

10. Why Cosmetics Work   186
    Richard Russell

11. Context-Specific Responses to Self-Resembling Faces   204
    Lisa M. DeBruine and Benedict C. Jones

12. In the Eyes of the Beholder: How Empathy Influences
    Emotion Perception   216
    Bhismadev Chakrabarti and Simon Baron-Cohen

SECTION IV   BODY LANGUAGE

13. Thin-Slice Vision   228
    Max Weisbuch and Nalini Ambady

14. Seeing Human Movement as Inherently Social   248
    Maggie Shiffrar, Martha D. Kaiser, and Areti Chouchourelou

15. Social Constraints on the Visual Perception of Biological
    Motion   264
    Kerri L. Johnson, Frank E. Pollick, and Lawrie S. McKay

16. Social Color Vision   278
    Mark A. Changizi and Shinsuke Shimojo

SECTION V   SOCIAL VISION IN CONTEXT

17. Mental Control and Visual Illusions: Errors of Action and
    Construal in Race-Based Weapon Misidentification   295
    Mark B. Stokes and B. Keith Payne

18. Afrocentric Facial Features and Stereotyping   306
    Irene V. Blair and Charles M. Judd

19. The Role of Racial Markers in Race Perception
    and Racial Categorization   321
    Otto H. MacLin and M. Kimberly MacLin

20. Aftereffects Reveal That Adaptive Face-Coding Mechanisms
    Are Selective for Race and Sex   347
    Gillian Rhodes and Emma Jaquet

SECTION VI   THE SOCIAL VISUAL BRAIN

21. Are People Special? A Brain's Eye View   363
    Anthony P. Atkinson, Andrea S. Heberlein, and Ralph Adolphs

22. Side Bias: Cerebral Hemispheric Asymmetry in
    Social Cognition and Emotion Perception   393
    Kimberley R. Savage, Joan C. Borod, and Lorraine O. Ramig

23. Biological Motion and Multisensory Integration: The Role
    of the Superior Temporal Sulcus   409
    Michael S. Beauchamp

24. Specialized Brain for the Social Vision: Perspectives from
    Typical and Atypical Development   421
    Teresa Farroni and Atsushi Senju

Author Index   445

Subject Index   459

CONTRIBUTORS

Reginald B. Adams, Jr
Department of Psychology
The Pennsylvania State University
University Park, PA

Ralph Adolphs
Division of the Humanities and
    Social Sciences
California Institute of Technology
Pasadena, CA

Nalini Ambady
Psychology Department
Tufts University
Medford, MA

Anthony P. Atkinson
Department of Psychology
Durham University
Durham, UK

Simon Baron-Cohen
Autism Research Centre
Psychiatry Department
University of Cambridge,
Cambridge, UK

Michael S. Beauchamp, Ph.D
Department of Neurobiology and Anatomy
University of Texas Medical School at Houston
Houston, TX

Irene V. Blair
Department of Psychology and
    Neuroscience
University of Colorado
Boulder, CO

Joan C. Borod
Department of Psychology
Queens College and The Graduate
    Center of the City University of New York
Flushing, NY
Department of Neurology
Mount Sinai School of Medicine
New York, NY

P. Matthew Bronstad
Schepens Eye Research Institute
Boston, MA

Bhismadev Chakrabarti
Department of Psychology
University of Reading
Reading, UK
Department of Psychiatry
University of Cambridge
Cambridge, UK

Mark A. Changizi
Department of Cognitive Science
Rensselaer Polytechnic Institute
Troy, NY

Areti Chouchourelou
The School of Humanities
and Social Sciences
European University Cyprus
Engomi, Nicosia-Cyprus

Lisa M. DeBruine
School of Psychology
University of Aberdeen
Scotland, UK

Teresa Farroni
Department of Developmental Psychology
University of Padua
Padua, IT
Centre for Brain and Cognitive Development
Birkbeck
University of London
London, UK

Robert G. Franklin, Jr
Department of Psychology
The Pennsylvania State University
University Park, PA

Beatrice de Gelder
Cognitive and Affective Neuroscience
    Laboratory
Tilburg University
Tilburg, The Netherlands
and
Athinoula A. Martinos Center for
    Biomedical Imaging
Harvard Medical School
Charlestown, MA

Andrea S. Heberlein
Department of Psychology
Harvard University
Cambridge, MA

Derek M. Isaacowitz
Brandeis University
Waltham, MA

Emma Jaquet
School of Psychology
University of Western Australia
Crawley, WA
Australia

Kerri L. Johnson
University of California
Los Angeles, California

Benedict C. Jones
School of Psychology
University of Aberdeen
Scotland, UK

Charles M. Judd
Department of Psychology
University of Colorado at Boulder
Boulder, CO

Martha D. Kaiser
Yale Child Study Center
Yale School of Medicine
New Haven, CT

Shinobu Kitayama
Professor of Psychology
Director, Culture and Cognition
Center for Culture, Mind, and the Brain
University of Michigan
Ann Arbor, MI

Stephen R. H. Langton
Department of Psychology
University of Stirling, Stirling
Scotland, UK

Anthony C. Little
Department of Psychology
University of Stirling
Scotland, UK

Dr. Otto H. MacLin
Department of Psychology
University of Northern Iowa
Cedar Falls, IA

M. Kimberly MacLin
Department of Psychology
University of Northern Iowa
Cedar Falls, IA

Douglas Martin
School of Psychology
University of Aberdeen
Scotland, UK

Lawrie S. McKay
University of Glasgow
Glasgow, Scotland

C. Neil Macrae
School of Psychology
University of Aberdeen
Scotland, UK

Joann M. Montepare
RoseMary B. Fuss Center for Research on
    Aging and Intergenerational Studies
Lasell College
Newton, MA

Nora A. Murphy
Brandeis University
New York, NY

Ken Nakayama
Vision Sciences Laboratory
Department of Psychology
Harvard University

Anthony J. Nelson
Department of Psychology
The Pennsylvania State University
University Park, PA

Hyekyung Park
Department of Psychology
Sungshin Women's University
Seoul, South Korea

Keith Payne
Department of Psychology
University of North Carolina
    at Chapel Hill
Chapel Hill, NC

David I. Perrett
School of Psychology
University of St Andrews
Scotland, UK

Frank E. Pollick
University of Glasgow
Glasgow, Scotland

Lorraine O. Ramig
Department of Speech, Language and Hearing
    Science
University of Colorado-Boulder
Boulder, CO
National Center for Voice and Speech
Denver, CO
Columbia University
New York, NY

Gillian Rhodes
School of Psychology
University of Western Australia
Crawley, WA
Australia

Richard Russell
Department of Psychology
Gettysburg College
Gettysburg, PA

Kimberley R. Savage
Department of Psychology
Queens College and The Graduate Center of
    the City University of New York
New York, NY

Atsushi Senju
Centre for Brain and Cognitive Development
Birkbeck
University of London
London, UK

Maggie Shiffrar
Department of Psychology
Rutgers University
Newark, NJ

Shinsuke Shimojo
Division of Biology, Computation and Neural
    Systems
California Institute of Technology
Pasadena, CA

Claude Simion
California Technical Institute
Pasadena, CA

Michael T. Stevenson
Department of Psychology
The Pennsylvania State University
University Park, PA

Mark B. Stokes
Department of Psychology
University of North Carolina
    at Chapel Hill
Chapel Hill, NC

Marco Tamietto
Department of Psychology
University of Torino
Torino, Italy

Max Weisbuch
Psychology Department
Tufts University
Medford, MA

Leslie A. Zebrowitz
Department of Psychology
Brandeis University
Waltham, MA

Introduction: Vision Going Social

Ken Nakayama

Vision is *"knowing* what *is* where *by looking"*
David Marr (1945-1980)
"There is no such thing as society … only individuals and families" Margaret Thatcher (b. 1925)
"All life is social" Steven A. Frank (2007 b. 1957)

Social psychology and vision science have stood as far apart as any two areas of psychology. At many universities, they are often in separate buildings: social psychology situated in the social sciences, vision research in the natural sciences. Yet, of late, there has been an emerging kinship between them, one that is exciting and propitious. This book provides a glimpse of this, and here we offer reasons for the likelihood of more lasting rewards.

First, it is clear from the chapters in this book and recent publications that vision scientists are using social stimuli, that is, *people*. Long-recognized are the point-light demonstrations of Gunnar Johansson, showing that simple movement of bright dots placed at the joints of figures against a dark background can provide vivid information about a human figure in motion. Later research has shown that these dots can easily convey gender, personal identity and other characteristics. More recently, vision and neuroscience journals have been studded with pictures of human faces. Vision scientists are abandoning their otherwise-featureless colored patches and sine wave gratings and exploring new visual stimuli. Social psychologists are poaching the field of vision, becoming interested in the basic perceptual processes that are involved in social

judgments, and showing that details of the stimulus are important (Langlois and Roggman, 1990; Martin and Macrae, this volume).

Is this just the opportunistic linking of two fields, related more to the availability of cheap computer graphics, or is it something more? Faces have replaced words as the most most-used stimulus in psychology, so it could be just be a fad, of no lasting consequence. Below, I review some trends that indicate a great broadening of the scope of both vision research and social psychology. This in turn indeed suggests more lasting opportunities.

A BRIEF HISTORY OF VISION SCIENCE

The study of vision has a long and illustrious history, but we restrict ourselves to a very short version, summarizing progress only over the past 100 years. There have been many developments in this time, but we mention just a few. Well known at the beginning of the twentieth century, were some very striking errors of vision. Estimates of length, area, color, brightness were dramatically changed by context. These were the classic visual illusions, including the Muller-Lyer, the Ponzo, the Ebbinghaus. These illusions have puzzled scientists to this day, and they grace textbooks of psychology. The elegant demonstrations of the Gestalt psychologists came next, showing compelling properties of the visual system, most importantly the phenomenon of figure ground and perceptual grouping. The visual system had rules of its own that were independent of higher-level processes, such as thinking.

Decades later, these views came to be supported in part by the revolutionary discoveries made by visual neurophysiologists. These scientists found that individual neurons in the visual system were selectively sensitive to patterns of visual input, not just light and dark. Thus, the work of early pioneers was able to show that neurons were sensitive to oriented bars, motion, and color. Some neurons were even selectively sensitive to things of interest to a particular organism: bugs for frogs, faces for humans and monkeys. Refined methods using the tools of psychophysics allowed researchers to make detailed and comparative assessments of the ability of humans, animals, and even individual cells to discriminate between different stimuli, motion, color, and so forth. This provided new methods to establish a causal link between the properties of neurons in animals and human perception.

At a theoretical level, there were many currents and crosscurrents. One broad theme stands out, addressing perhaps the most obvious but elusive question: What does the visual system do? It begins with Barlow's (1961) seminal article, which asks, "What are sensory systems for?" Barlow's answer, which borrowed from the newly emerging field of information theory, was that neurons of the sensory system are part of an efficient coding scheme. Thus, with a minimum number of spikes or impulses, the sensory system delivers *information* from the outside world to the brain. The efficiencies are obtained through redundancies in images, allowing complex recurring patterns to be coded with the fewest possible number of neural signals.

At about the same time, Gibson (1950, 1966) developed his theory of ecological optics. Like Barlow, Gibson claimed that information pickup is the function of the visual system. Gibson's genius was to specify many of the regularities in the optic array that convey useful information about the world. He identified previously unsuspected aspects of the optic array, such as patterns of motion, which delineated the layout of space. Thus, the coding of some simple, seemingly low-level optical variables conveyed very useful information for the organism. Gibson's theory ran parallel to that

of Barlow, with both emphasizing the need for information pickup; however, Barlow's theory emphasized neural mechanisms, whereas Gibson's delineated the rich source of information in the optic array. Gibson's emphasis on the coding of real-world properties de-emphasized the role of errors and illusions, hinting that preoccupation with such matters was a distraction and should be subordinated to the main effort.

Drawing heavily on Gibson, David Marr's (1980) most lasting contribution was theoretical. Familiar with the agenda of artificial intelligence, he came to vision with a broader perspective, less steeped in the physiology and psychology of vision. Vision at its simplest, according to Marr, is "knowing *what* is *where* by looking"; but he goes on to say that no single explanation can suffice to explain what constitutes vision. Of the many levels of explanation required, Marr argues, the most fundamental is the computational level—that is, the goal of the computation and the optical information required to arrive at it. Other explanatory levels, such as the formal properties of the computation (algorithmic) and the brain substrates (implementation), are subordinate to this main endeavor.

In the past 40 years, we have come to understand that the anatomical structures comprising the visual system are much larger than previously thought. Previously, the territory we believed to be devoted to vision was largely confined to the striate cortex, which occupies about 10 percent of the brain. Around 1970, however, almost overnight, a handful of neurophysiologists—John Allman, John Kaas, David van Essen—identified about a dozen distinct cortical areas that are visual and that occupy the posterior half of the brain in higher primates. Since then, and with help of high-resolution functional magnetic resonance imaging (fMRI), still more vision-related regions have been identified in both humans and monkeys.

This huge allocation of brain anatomy suggests that vision's role in the brain and mind is tremendous. It is arguably on a par with *all* other functions of the brain: language, thinking, planning, acting, and so on. The exciting implication is that vision must be many things, serving myriad functions, many of which are yet to be discovered.

Marr divides the visual system into a set of sequential stages, each with its own set of properties. At the earliest stage, the brain performs an analysis of the image, extracting statistical regularities with little or no reference to what these images might represent in the world. This is followed by a viewer-centered representation (a 2.5-D sketch) of surfaces. Finally, there is a view-independent stage for the representation of objects, the highest stage for Marr. Marr's theory that there is a sequence of stages is a viable one, but the idea that object recognition represents an ultimate stage has not gone unchallenged.

An alternative view was voiced by Gibson, who was more concerned with how animals, not just humans, deal with the world around them: According to Gibson, categorizing objects without reference to their usefulness to the animal is secondary to thinking about sheer everyday survival. When Gibson defined his theory of affordances 30 years ago, it seemed foreign, strange, and circular to some, but now it almost has the status of a household word in science. As stated by Gibson:

> The *affordances* of the environment are what it *offers* the animal, what it *provides* or *furnishes*, either for good or ill. The verb *to afford* is found in the dictionary, but the noun *affordance* is not. I have made it up. (Gibson, 1979, p. 127)

Thus for a weary traveler, a flat surface that will support his weight qualifies as "sittable," and for a frightened squirrel, a tree, a chain link fence, and telephone wire all afford travel to safety. Thus, Gibson identifies yet another fundamental role for vision: Its support of action.

These distinctions have anatomical underpinnings. Ungerleider and Mishkin's (1982) division of the visual system into a *what* system (ventral) and a *where* system (dorsal) was a landmark achievement, even if it was to be further refined by Milner and Goodale (1996) into a dorsal system (*how*, for motor behavior) and ventral system (*what*, for object recognition). Milner and Goodale's temporal lobe patient, DF, could hardly identify any object consciously, but showed an astounding ability to grasp complex objects appropriately. This demonstrated that there is indeed a separate nonconscious visuo-motor system that can act automatically outside the range of awareness. Conversely, patients with parietal lobe damage could easily recognize objects but could not make appropriate visuo-motor acts toward them. The parietal lobe, part of Milner and Goodale's dorsal system, is a possible substrate for Gibsonan affordances. This system is so important that it can function outside awareness.

The rise and current supremacy of faces as stimuli in the neurophysiological laboratory is also telling. Vision scientists had long studied cortical neurons' response to oriented bars, gratings, colored patches, moving dots. Each of these could selectively excite a class of cortical neurons with great reliability. Thanks to the pioneering work of Charles Gross, faces were added to this list because some neurons showed astonishing selectivity, firing only when a face appeared in the visual field. More recent studies have confirmed these findings, showing ever-greater selectivity for faces in discrete cortical areas (Tsao et al., 2008). These findings have also been corroborated by human fMRI studies, showing face-specific areas in many areas of the human brain, with further specializations for expression as opposed to identity.

ARGUMENT FOR AN EXPANDED SOCIAL PSYCHOLOGY

Vision's place in psychology has expanded dramatically in scope from a simple cortical image of the retina to the whole brain. There is a role for vision almost everywhere.

There has been a comparable or even greater expansion in fields relating to social psychology. However, this has yet to be fully recognized. From the beginnings of psychology, social psychology has not been linked strongly with mainstream experimental psychology, perhaps reflecting an early distinction between experimental and descriptive social sciences (Dilthey, 1883). Since the cognitive revolution, there has been some rapprochement, with social psychologists borrowing to some extent paradigms and concepts from cognitive psychology. But this has not been deemed by all to be entirely successful. Vision scientist and monkey researcher, Nick Humphrey, wrote that "Experimental psychologists in Britain have tended to regard social psychology as a poor country cousin of their subject ..." (Humphrey, 1976).

But in this same landmark essay, he made an astonishing case for the central role of social psychology. But, it was advocacy, not for the existing discipline, but a radically expanded one.

> ... the higher intellectual faculties of primates have evolved as an adaptation to the complexities of social living. For better or worse, styles of thinking which are primarily suited to social problem-solving colour the behaviour of man and other primates even towards the inanimate world. (N.K. Humphrey, "The social function of the intellect" (1976)

In this piece, Humphrey lays claim for the foundation of a new outlook, one that is intended to turn psychology upside down. Instead of social processes being derived from more basic cognitive processes, he argues it is the other way around. His main point is that (1) social life conferred enormous advantages to fledgling primates, (2) social life requires much more brain power, and (3) the brain mechanisms so evolved here form the foundation of our present intellect.

Although radical at the time, Humphrey's points find greater resonance today. That social life confers advantages to primates (and to other species) is almost self-evident. Of course there are the costs and benefits that have been arbitrated by the winnowing process of Darwinian natural selection. That social life requires more brain power seems likely or at least plausible. Dunbar (1998) has shown that brain size in primates and the size of the social group are strongly correlated. That, brain mechanisms evolved for social processing is the basis of our intellect is interesting and provocative.

In tandem with Humphrey's advocacy were the brilliant essays of Dan Dennett (1971, 1981), who provided an important philosophical underpinning for the study of social beings. He identified the *intentional stance*, part of an epistemological set of distinctions concerning the ways in which observers understand complex systems, including those of animals and people. Dennett argued that for social cognition, a causal system based on physics (the physical stance) or one based on design with purposes (for biological or manmade devices) was essentially useless. Only by adopting the intentional stance, a level of abstraction identifying the beliefs and desires of other minds, could social life as we know it, exist. More recently, psychologist Simon Baron Cohen made this view more accessible to psychologists with his monograph, Mindblindness (1995), drawing on the hypothesized deficits on the intentional stance in autism. See also Brothers, (2001).

It's obvious to those of us who make use of folk psychology in our everyday lives that we adopt the intentional stance, so much so that many academic psychologists have been troubled that our hard-won truths might not pass the "grandmother test." Does our new-found knowledge go beyond what Granny already knew? Mercifully, Granny didn't know about functional brain imaging, so we psychologists of the twenty-first century may rest assured that we do know something new. That aside, what about folk psychology for animals? To the extent that they are social beings, do animals share an awareness of the beliefs and desires of other animals?

Folk tales, from Aesop's fables to Walt Disney, suggest that they do: Folk traditions are replete with stories about the mental lives of animals, attributing Dennett's intentional states to them. Devoted pet owners such as Charles Darwin himself offered anecdotes about animals' awareness of the mental states of others. We have all heard them and we believed them with varying degrees of credulity. Some are clearly suspect but others are not easy to ignore. Thanks to modern technology (portable video cameras and the Internet), rare episodes can't be so easily relegated to the category of tall stories. One widely circulated video available on YouTube (called the Battle of Kruger) shows remarkable cooperation within a herd of African buffalo, surrounding and then charging a pride of female lions about to devour one of their captured calves. Such behavior is now preserved in one of the most watched YouTube videos in the world. In another video, the buffalo play offense by attacking poorly protected lion cubs, killing one of them (http://www.youtube.com/watch?v=8sdttH2Tq3E). In another video, it is hard to see anything other than a very small gibbon aware of the mental state of tiger cubs as he annoys them by risking his life in pulling their tail and ears (google "monkey taunts tiger").

Putting more flesh to the thoughts of Humphrey and Dennett is the fledgling field of *cognitive ethology*. Differing from the mechanistic ethology of Tinbergen, Lorenz and von Fries, this approach is open to thinking about the intentional stance. In cognitive ethology, the inner lives of animals as they deal with conspecifics, friend and foe, as well as prey and predator, are no longer considered to be taboo anthropomorphisms. Further, well-controlled observations support popular anecdotes suggesting that animals are indeed aware of the mental states of conspecifics; for instance, Emery and Clayton (2004) report that jays will move food that they have cached if they have been observed by other jays.

Although such studies indicate that animals have mental states and thus are likely to contribute to social living, they by themselves do not offer a rich portrait of the social behavior of a whole community. Such studies are inherently difficult because a community has many agents (animals), and most terrestrial animals are sleeping during the day (being nocturnal) or, if they are diurnal, they are under cover. Thus, one can only get glimpses of the social life by chance encounters. This underscores the importance of more serious efforts to live among social animals and to make continuous observations over a period of many years, using as much observational technology and efforts as possible. Fortunately, for us, there are dedicated scientists who have devoted their professional careers to providing information, with the richest detail possible, about the lives of animals

and how they interact socially. Some have been filmed for TV nature documentaries and for good reason. The richness and the drama of their social life is astonishing, so much so that humans spend many hours following these stories, much as they might watch other TV miniseries or soap operas.

MEERKAT MANOR

Meerkats (suricatta suricata) is one of the best examples. Not being primates, their social life is less complex and variable, yet their social existence has things that are in common with all primates, including ourselves. They have been featured on a four-year show on the BBC, called Meerkat Manor. Part behavioral ecology, part evolutionary psychology, the work was started by Timothy Clutton-Brock, a zoologist at the University of Cambridge.

Meerkats are very small slender burrowing animals related to the mongoose. They stand approximately 12 inches tall and weigh about 1.6 pounds. They are predators, catching small animals such as worms, millipedes, and scorpions, the poison of which is nontoxic to them. They live in family groups numbering somewhere between 10 and 40 individuals, under the dominance of an alpha female who reserves the exclusive right to bear offspring. If their daughters bear offspring, they are frequently killed or the daughters are banished from the group. They live in the Kalahari desert, which is not technically a true desert, there being some limited rainfall. Yet, there is much less vegetation than in forested areas, and conditions can be harsh. Food, while available, is not plentiful. Thus for a medium-size family, these tiny animals have a territory of approximately 1.5 square miles, which is jealously patrolled to ward off incursions by other meerkat families.

Each member has highly visible individual markings, rendering them identifiable to other family members and conspecifics. Clutton-Brock's outstanding research efforts took full advantage of the desert environment. With increased visibility, an unprecedented record of the activities of a whole family and rival families has been recorded. As a result of this fifteen-year-old continuing study, these animals are arguably the most studied social mammal in the wild.

Meerkats must face a number of challenging problems. I mention a few. First, is ever-present danger, mostly in the form of birds of prey but also from snakes. Mortality from predation is very high, over 20 percent per year. Against the desert, Meerkats are highly visible, particularly to birds who have excellent vision. Meerkats eat bugs and small animals that are buried deep underground. This requires digging deep into the sand so that their heads are buried while other parts of the body are dangerously exposed. Thus an individual Meerkat cannot forage for food and look out for predators at the same time. In addition all Meerkats have to go on very long foraging expeditions during the day, over an extended range, many hundreds of meters away from home. Young Meerkats, emerging from the burrows at three weeks of age, cannot go on foraging trips yet must learn to navigate the above-burrow terrain and eventually learn to forage. Finally, there is always the danger of hostile neighboring meerkat families, occupying neighboring territory.

To deal with the dangers during foraging expeditions, some family members take the posts as sentries. They stand on high ground or trees and, attentively scanning the environment for danger, give warning calls when needed. This comes at considerable sacrifice, for sentries must forgo eating on a sentry day. They appear to take turns insofar as sentry duty is usually for one day only. Similar considerations of individual versus group needs apply to child care. Daughters lactate and feed their alpha female mother's offspring. Adolescent Meerkats spend full days (on a rotating basis) supervising the play of younger siblings just outside the burrow.

Life and death social dramas are played out if a daughter becomes pregnant. This occurs when one of the daughters wanders slightly away from the group, say, during foraging, and meets a roving male from another family. After a brief courtship, mating can occur, often followed by pregnancy. On some occasions, the pregnancy

and subsequent birth is tolerated by the alpha female; in other cases it is not. Pregnant daughters make great efforts to gain the favor of the female leader, attempting to groom her and making otherwise supplicating movements. The errant offspring can develop normally if they are tolerated. If not, they are either killed or the daughter-mother is banished, which can lead to starvation and death from predators or exposure.

Meerkat families are territorial. Because food is often scarce there is inevitable conflict between families. If there are territorial infractions (and they are frequent), deadly warfare can be the result and territory in the border zones can be taken or lost. Its noteworthy that these conflicts have some hallmarks of human warfare: war dances, linear formations, and the rushing of each others lines into battle.

This brief description indicates a number of important features of social life that have been highlighted by Humphrey. First, is the obvious advantage of cooperation in this species. Childrearing, babysitting, sentry duty, as well as many other tasks keep the high mortality rate within bounds. Second, all is not smooth; there is plenty of evidence for conflicts between group versus individual interests. In times of warfare or when dealing with a common enemy (snakes), there is extreme group commitment, where individual family members will appear very unselfish and heroic, risking life for the group. At other times, however, there are intra-family conflicts, over food, over who can keep their babies, and so forth. These are mammals, not social insects, and the interplay between individual vs social needs becomes the stuff that makes their life resemble TV soap operas, so much so that Meerkat Manor was a very successful show.

There are many highly social animals, Meerkats being some of the most well studied. Thus, the requirements for social life exist not just in primates, although they may be more advanced here. There must also be brain mechanisms to regulate social life in many animals. The Meerkat colony is only one well-studied example.

CHIMPANZEE POLITICS

Closest to humans among primates are chimpanzees. The wel- known morphological criteria of similarity (teeth, bone structure) have been supported by DNA evidence. This latter evidence places Chimpanzees closer to humans than the other great apes. It indicates that we are the closest to chimpanzees in sharing a common ancestor, perhaps five to seven million years ago. Despite the 99 percent overlap in DNA, large differences can be concealed by this tiny 1 percent difference, explained mainly in terms of regulatory genes that can have huge effects in differently orchestrating sets of otherwise identical genes. Nevertheless, chimpanzees are the closest we have as animals, and if the social life of animals are to inform our own, they would seem to be *the* candidates. The comparison is greatly enriched by the existence of *two* very distinct chimpanzee species, the more familiar chimpanzee *pan troglodyte* and the *pan panicus*, the bonobos. The latter are now the subject of intense interest as they differ significantly from normal chimpanzees, which we will describe below.

Our understanding of Chimpanzee life was advanced significantly thanks to pioneering field work of Jane Goodall, who made many important discoveries in the course of describing the characteristics of their lives in their natural settings. First was her early discovery that chimpanzees were meat eaters, that they launched organized hunting parties for animals such as monkeys. Second was her discovery of their tool use and tool creation, the discovery of these animals fashioning a stick to get the termites in the hole. Third was the strong bonds between individual female animals (both related and unrelated) that were long lasting and which had great importance in regulating behavior, often determining which males would be dominant. Finally, and very shocking to her, was the existence of warfare between groups, where violence to outsiders could be deadly. Later research confirmed this, showing also that lone chimpanzees at the border of their own territory could be easily assaulted and killed by neighboring patrols.

These discoveries were consequential, each one of which was echoed in popular culture as well in the scientific community, overturning, repeatedly, various assumptions, not only about chimpanzees, but about ourselves, especially for those prone to use chimpanzee behavior to draw human lessons.

But, as mentioned before, studying the social life of animals is a very difficult undertaking, particularly when these animals have ranges over many miles and through thick vegetation. Too many interactions are just not visible. The Meerkats, described earlier, have the advantage of being desert animals and are visually evident. This is not possible for chimpanzees and so field work needed to be supplemented by closer observation, where countless daily encounters can be noted and recorded.

The pioneer here was Frans de Waal, who started his career with chimpanzees in the Arnheim Zoo in the Netherlands. Trained in the tradition of Dutch ethology, he became the beneficiary of the then-largest enclosed facility in the world, allowing free range over an outdoor two-acre area that housed approximately 20 chimpanzees. Initially, the many thousands of social exchanges involving vocalizations, displays, and gestures remained mysterious. Only after many months of observations, repeated viewings of videos and sound clips, was it possible for de Waal and colleagues to understand the complex dynamics of the group. Influenced by a political and evolutionary perspective, mindful of the importance of dominance relations in social groups, and explicitly taking Dennett's intentional stance, he gradually was able to piece together a more comprehensive picture of chimpanzee social life. After this, subtle gestures and behavior that were initially missed, were more clearly identified and were used in anticipating outcomes, such as upcoming hostile encounters. Thus, while the observations of human researchers had a subjective quality, they were often validated by their ability to predict future events repeatedly. Although, initially criticized for being anthropomorphic, especially by an older generation of behaviorally trained scientists, the general consensus is that de Waal has captured critical aspects of chimpanzee social life.

One of his first books, *Chimpanzee Politics*, was a riveting day-by-day, sometimes minute-by-minute, description of how various males in the group achieved dominance through often indirect social maneuvering. Although there is an acknowledged alpha male of the community, his power is clearly dependent on various alliances, both male and female within the group. Brute strength on the part of the males was important, but as important was how less-than-maximum force was deployed. Many examples were described. For example, an upstart male undermined the power of the alpha male without direct confrontation. More deviously, he intimidated females (one-by-one) who were friends of the dominant male. This coercion was successful—eventually leading to the over throw of the dominant male. There were dominance relations within females, but these were more stable and depended on age. While dominant animals afforded greater rewards (food, sex), it appeared that with these privileges came responsibilities, in particular conflict resolution. For example, he recounts the scene of two mothers whose quarreling children are getting out of hand, but the mothers don't intervene, lest this lead to hostility between them. After some time, one of mothers woke the dominant female. "Mama" was mildly disturbed, but she easily broke up the fighting. Similar, breakups of fighting between adults were often witnessed. One pattern seen repeatedly was the calming intervention of the alpha males who broke up fights in the community with impartiality.

Characteristic of male pan troglodyte society is its volatility and occasional shifts in power structure. Male-male hostile encounters are very frequent, with aggressive posturing, occasionally leading to fighting and consequent injuries. At the same time, continuing feuds are punctuated by moments of tender reconciliation between males, often fostered by females, male-male embraces, mutual grooming, and playfulness. These frequent examples of reconciliation are hypothesized mechanisms to dampen hostility that could lead the weakening of a particular chimpanzee group in relation to neighboring rival groups. Thus, de Waal indicates that peacemaking among chimpanzees is as ubiquitous as conflict.

Yet, there are high stakes within chimpanzee male society, and dominant ones have near-exclusive sexual rights with females and are first in line for food. As such, de Waal and others have seen clear links to observations of human politics. Harold Lasswell (1937), pioneer in the psychology of politics dubbed it as the study of "who gets what, when, and how." Machiavellian has been described as the characteristics of primate social life (Byrne and Whitten, 1990). The plots to overthrow kings and princes thus seem to have primate antecedents. De Waal describes in detail the lead-up and the results of a dramatic three-way power struggle where the outcome was the killing of the then-alpha male by his two closest rivals.

These anecdotes are mentioned to indicate to the reader that the social life of chimpanzees is very complicated and it can be a life and death struggle. Humphrey (1976) may indeed be correct, that all of this complex social interaction requires selection pressure to develop more brain power. He argues that in contrast to tool making or tool using, which is more of an incidental activity or at least a routinized one, social life requires constant vigilance, interpretation, and split second quick action.

BONOBOS, PAN PANISCUS

Were pan troglodytes our closest and only cousins, we might draw some hasty and possibly unwarranted conclusions. Fortunately, there is another species to consider. Bonobos are a separate species of chimpanzee, having been identified only fairly recently. Their isolation and their distinctiveness was maintained by the wide Congo river, with chimpanzees to the north, bonobos to the south. Bonobos are discriminated from the chimpanzee in having smaller heads, flared nostrils, thinner necks and longer legs. Although called pygmy chimpanzees, they are large, approximately 95 pounds for an adult make, 80 pounds for an adult female. In addition to this size difference, males have very large canines, which are lacking in females. Despite this sexual dimorphism, with its apparent advantage for male dominance, bonobo society is dominated by females (de Waal, 2005).

Female dominance is a further demonstration of the importance of more complex social factors and how they overshadow brute strength. Bonds between females are very strong in bonobo society, clearly offsetting the greater body size and lethality of male canine teeth. In distinction to baboons, where males leave their natal group, females are the ones to leave. In distinction to the volatility and violence associated with the maintenance of male dominance patterns in chimpanzees, female bonobo dominance, similar to that of female chimps, seems to be determined largely by seniority. There is also a male dominance hierarchy, but it is less contentiously established, being determined by the dominance of the mother's position in the female hierarchy. Thus, if the mother of the dominant male dies, her son's social position drops.

Perhaps the most striking aspect of bonobo society is the frequency and the varied forms of sexual behavior and expression. Distinct from all other animals, bonobos can engage in face-to-face sexual intercourse, with a mutuality afforded by gazing at each other's facial expressions. Homosexuality, adult-child sex, as well as extended kissing (French kissing) is common. Because, males are not dominant, there is little of the sexual exclusivity seen in chimpanzee society. Another aspect is the frequency of sex and its casualness. It is much more frequent than in chimpanzee (or in human) society. Some kind of overt sexual behavior can occur almost hourly among bonobos. But it is something that is not an activity apart, as it is in humans or chimpanzees, but it is woven into the fabric of everyday life. As an example, de Waal, describes an incident in which a male seems to be hogging food in the presence of a female. She briefly rubs her genitals against his arm, perhaps disarming him, and proceeds to get her food. This is part of a general use of sex to release tensions. Thus, when coming upon a large cache of sugar cane, which will be the basis of a long feast, bonobos commence with group sexual activities. Only, after a bout of this, with them more calmed down, will they proceed with eating. One curiosity, for those who observe the human male, is that male bonobos show more sexual attraction to older females than younger ones.

CHIMPS VS BONOBOS

Chimps and bonobos offer a stunning contrast in terms of their behavior and invite comparison to humans. A variety of measures suggest that humans and chimpanzees diverged approximately five to seven million years ago, whereas the genetic divergence that led to distinctiveness between modern chimps and bonobos occurred less than one million years ago. Thus, chimps and bonobos are five times more related to each other than they are to human beings. Neither is obviously closer to us genetically, yet differences between them in social behavior, particularly in terms of sex and aggression, is about as wide as we can imagine, wider than our human differences with either of these species. Tiny genetic differences, much smaller than those separating humans and these chimps, must be critical, but the mechanisms by which genes determine these very great differences remain unexplained.

Nevertheless, the comparison between such closely related species can lead to a greater appreciation of larger relationships that exist between conspecifics. One striking example is the relation between dominance, mating patterns, and infanticide. As with Meerkats, infanticide is prominent in chimpanzees. The argument is that it is advantageous in pan troglodytes for the survival of male genes when competition between males is intense and when dominant males have exclusive mating rights. However, there is little need for this in bonobos. Males don't have exclusive mating privileges, and so it follows that there is a lesser advantage for male genes to benefit from infanticide because there is no guarantee that any father would not be eliminating his own offspring.

COGNITIVE REQUIREMENTS FOR SOCIAL LIFE

Our nearest distant ape ancestors have very complex social lives, and they do so without the benefit of language. Now, much later, we humans are the only hominid species remaining. What happened during the past five to seven million years? Paleontological and archeological evidence is fragmentary, and a plausible single narrative is lacking. Our brains are three times larger than those of the great apes. Why do we have such large brains? Tool creation and tool use has been a favorite idea. Yet, the archeological record shows extremely long periods where brain size increased but tool technology did not advance. This is consistent with Humphrey's argument that the greatest advances in human evolution and brain development came with the greater need for social intelligence. But, what kind of social intelligence? We have already seen that chimpanzees and bonobos are both fairly sophisticated, having some of the key hallmarks of human social life.

Having a storehouse of episodic memories about individual events is something that would seem essential for our own lives. For us humans, it is frequently essential for us to know who did what to whom. Not having language, can apes conjure up episodes to guide their future behavior? The question about whether apes have episodic memory has no answer as yet. However, since their complex social life is simpler than ours, it's not inconceivable that it can be conducted without the ability to conjure up past events.

The scope of the mind relevant to human social living is enormous. We can recall social situations of the distant past and can plan and forecast for future events. These can take the form of complex scenarios, casts of characters, plots, and subplots. Thanks to print and other media, our store house of social knowledge, that is, knowledge about people, has exploded. It is likely we have some knowledge of tens of thousands, maybe hundreds of thousands of people, historical figures, literary figures in addition to the many thousands recognized through personal acquaintances. Yet, some of our social life does not depend on such vast knowledge stores in this area. We can also make important social decisions based on very quick judgments (Ambady et al., 2000) with little acquaintanceship of individuals, even doing so with little or no awareness (Bargh and Chartrand, 1999). Whether these particularly automatic routes constitute the main part of animal social cognition or whether animals have more extended

cognitive social scenarios is unclear. De Waal's observations, mentioned earlier, suggest that apes have these capacities but these conclusion are based to some extent on anecdotal reports.

We have surveyed several different species, Meerkats, very distant from ourselves, and two species of chimpanzees who are our nearest relatives. Compared to many other animals, the interdependence between conspecifics of these species is very high. What's surprising is that the social behavior between closely related species can vary tremendously. Chimps and bonobos are closely related, yet their social behavior is extremely different. The same holds for Meerkats and close mongoose relatives. The Egyptian mongoose, is almost solitary, clustering in groups whose average size is two or less (Palomares and Delibes, 1993).

The existence of large qualitative differences between closely related species has been a biological mystery for decades. How can closely related species be so different? This is a central question in the new field of evolutionary/developmental (evo devo) biology. Part of the answer lies in the now larger acknowledged size of the units of evolutionary variation. There exist control genes (Kirschner and Gerhart, 2005) or switches in noncoding parts of DNA (Carroll, 2005) that activate huge numbers of other genes such that very large jumps can be made. Genes and switches can control development at a very abstract level, more like a command language than a physical chain of events. As such, there is a single *eyeless* gene conserved over phyla for 500 million years, which leads to an eye no matter whether it be a single-chambered vertebrate eye, with one lens, or a compound eye with many separate facets and lenses. Similar levels of control are likely for brains; a single allele can determine whether a male vole will be monogamous or polygamous. Thus, it's not inconceivable that a finite number of genes can lead to the patterning of a whole constellation of social behaviors that are characteristic for a species. If the insights of evo-devo are applicable to the brain and to social behavior, it is possible that there is a finite number of processes that, when combined appropriately, will allow a species to have its uniquely stable characteristics.

If we are able to understand these hypothetical building blocks, it is possible that the basis of at least some human social characteristics could be better understood. For starters, it is likely that some prosocial behavior could develop out of parenting and pair-bonding mechanisms, present in most mammals, which are then generalized to other settings that would lead to larger-scale social cooperation.

Whatever the combination, it is very likely that we humans have been dealt a genetic deck of cards that is a given and can't be so easily changed. We are not chimps, nor are we bonobos, but we have some characteristics of each, and there is a combination and interaction that defines us as humans. What can't be changed, and what might be defined as human nature are characteristics that are shared by humans across all cultures, modern, premodern and aboriginal. This is presently the subject of intense inquiry by many, including anthropologists and evolutionary psychologists. Yet, it is obvious that, with the long childhood, the almost exclusive monopoly of a given society's influence, culture also has a decisive influence, shaping patterns of thought and possibly perception itself (Park & Kitayama, this volume). There is also the likelihood that, under selection pressure or perhaps by other mechanisms (genetic drift), different cultures have different genetic decks that could be consequential.

WHAT MORE HAVE WE LEARNED FROM ANIMALS?

Even if we remain skeptical about particular claims about intentionality or episodic memory in apes, it is clear that, for many species, the major events in their lives are social. Two broad groups of behaviors, common to our own society pertain: ones that promote pleasure and higher status for individual animals versus ones that promote well-being of others.

Many animals demonstrate the same selfishness we can witness in our own personal and political life: the endless efforts to raise one's status, to achieve dominance. Yet, besides competition, there is plenty of evidence for cooperation and selflessness. Of course, there is the

parent-offspring bond, where parents will sacrifice themselves to protect their own. Less obvious, but of great importance, is W.D. Hamilton's concept of inclusive fitness, later popularized as the selfish-gene hypothesis. Aiding one's cousins promulgates the survival of ones own genes (Dawkins, 1976). Yet, warm and affiliative behavior is not restricted to ones kin. Many unrelated animals will exhibit what we regard as sympathy and empathy toward each other, something less directly explainable by selfish genes.

Because each animal is an agent, looking for its share of resources, but also because they are part of a social group, the behavior of social animals can often very hard to predict. At one moment they are fighting, and later they may give succor to the same individual. Because of the importance of social life in many species, it is not unreasonable to assume that parts of the brain, not just in primates, could be devoted to negotiating the complexities of social life.

VISION AND THE SOCIAL WORLD

Nick Humphrey's (1976) essay "On the social origins of the intellect" was prescient, arguing that the benefits and complexity of primate social life led to the unprecedented evolutionary changes in brain size, from monkeys to the great apes, from apes to man. A likely selective pressure was on those structures that can respond adaptively to the delicate balancing between shifting coalitions in a society in which competition needs to be balanced by cooperation. Any individual's relation to any other individual in a given society is potentially relevant, so effective brain mechanisms to understand and also navigate these waters would surely be advantageous for a species. Thus, it is not entirely surprising that humans with their faculty of language and the benefits of cumulative culture became preeminent.

Yet, despite the large differences between, say, chimpanzee and human, it's also clear that there is continuity and that many of the key social processes evident in ourselves are present in chimpanzees and bonobos. An extremely complex social life can proceed without the benefit of language. Knowledge of the social world for apes comes almost exclusively from the senses: vision, hearing, touch, and smell, and communications come mainly through actions, gestures, and vocalizations.

Humans of course, with their much larger brains, communicate through spoken language, and this marks an obvious difference between us and the great apes. The sequence of phylogenetic/historic steps leading to our present spoken language ability is poorly understood, but it is likely that it has been in place for a hundred thousand years, perhaps more (Donald, 1991). In contrast, written language for most of humanity has only arrived in the past one hundred years with the advent of mass literacy. Traditional social psychology has benefited from the use of written verbal materials with its use of surveys and questionnaires. Yet, it should be recognized that this particular route toward furthering the understanding of our social lives, particularly as we have inherited basic social mechanisms from our ancestors, very is narrow.

To understand those basic brain mechanisms mediating our social life shared by our biological relatives (both close and distant), we need to consider the widest range of possible information available. All the senses are likely to be important. Hearing is important for primates who are arboreal, and are frequently unseen by their neighbors. Odors, both consciously and unconscious sensed, are increasingly recognized as playing a large role in both animals and humans (see McClintock, 2002). The sense of touch as physical contact is important for parenting and maintaining friendships. We single out vision, not only because it could be the most important, but because it has been the easiest of the senses to study and has received the greatest attention.

Several developments suggest that this endeavor is propitious and is likely repay dividends. First, as mentioned earlier, the notion of vision and visual perception has expanded greatly, and most researchers now agree that visual perception is more than just receiving an image but is clearly related to understanding an image. There is less agreement about what is to be understood, with most researchers preoccupied with object recognition.

Here is where Gibson's approach to perception is likely to provide some guidance. Rather than looking inward to the structure of the visual system or measuring its failures (as in characterizing illusions), he preferred to look outward to the real world, to see what aspects of the world were meaningful for an animal and how such information could be picked up most efficiently (see Nakayama, 1994). Twenty-five years ago, applying these ideas to social psychology, Leslie Zebrowitz MacArthur and Reuben Baron (1983) identified four distinguishing features of this approach:

> … First, it assumes that perception serves an *adaptive* function and that the external world must therefore provide information to guide biologically and socially functional behaviors. Second, it assumes that this information is typically revealed in objective physical *events*— dynamic, changing, multimodal stimulus information as opposed to static or unimodal displays. Third, it assumes that the information available in events specifies, among other things, environmental *affordances,* which are the opportunities for acting or being acted upon that are provided by environmental entities. Fourth, it assumes that the perception of these affordances depends upon the perceivers' *attunement,* that is, the particular stimulus invariants to which the perceiver attends. (McArthur and Baron, 1983)

A number of developments broadly based on these assumptions and represented in this volume should be mentioned. In, particular, neurophysiological studies of face selectivity amply confirm the *attunements* proposed by Gibson, that specific areas of the brain exist that mediate the detection and discrimination of faces just as there exist areas with neurons that can distinguish motion and color (Tsao and Livingstone, 2008). These attunements are built into the system and are robustly represented. For example, studies on infant monkeys, with enriched environments but deprived of seeing faces for six months, still show normal face processing (Sugita, 2008) after this period. In addition, they can be flexibly deployed, that is, they can pay attention to faces at one moment and ignore them at another.

Very subtle attunements can play a major role in our social life. We humans can draw conclusions about others not only from what they say and not only from their smiles but from many other aspects of their body movements. To fully understand humans, an anthropologist from Mars would need far more than a crash language course because he would also be faced with a problem similar to that initially posed to Frans de Waal observing gestures in the Arnheim Zoo. Although few of us are aware that we are reading subtle body movements, they can be decisive in everyday life. Subtle nonverbal information accompanying a verbal interchange can determine who will get the job, who will get sued (Ambady et al., 2000; Weisbuch & Ambady, this volume). This is perhaps reason why business executives travel so frequently with grueling schedules even in our age of phones, e-mail, and video conferencing. They need all the social channels of information to make key decisions regarding the motives, competence, and trustworthiness of their business partners.

There is no doubt that vision is important for our social life and it is clear that researchers have opened the door to get some first glimpses of pertinent psychological and neural mechanisms. We could be at the threshold of a new scientific adventure, part of a larger effort to understand human beings, making full use of the natural and the social sciences. If so, it is tempting to make some prescriptions and prognostications.

Vision science has a ready-made set of techniques, concepts that are presently being adopted to study elementary social processes. One advantage is experimental control, the ability to precisely manipulate the properties of stimulus so that it can be continuously or randomly varied along a chosen dimension (gender, race, distinctiveness) but not on others. Thanks to new mathematical techniques associated with image synthesis and generation, an essentially infinite metrical space of faces can be created. Such metrical spaces also provide the basis of quantitative theories of representation, such as norm based coding for faces (Rhodes & Jaquet, this volume). Thus, a given face can be seen as a point or vector in a multidimensional space, at a given distance from a neutral origin. This allows one to conduct experiments on high-level

social stimuli (faces) using essentially the same concepts and techniques that have been so successful in revealing the underlying mechanisms of color vision. This has also been accomplished for Johanson point-light walkers such that any individual can be continuously morphed into any other individual (Troje, 2002) and varied along chosen dimensions. Thus, adoption of these visual psychophysical techniques is beneficial to social psychology as well as for vision, furnishing social psychology new tools and ideas and in turn widening the scope of traditional vision research.

Yet, it's conceivable that there are even greater rewards, unseen for now, if vision researchers again revisit the functional question: What is the visual system for. Of course vision has many functions and some have been identified. But, if the social brain hypothesis is anywhere near correct, then our ideas regarding the function of the visual system needs to be re-evaluated. Rather than dividing the visual system into a dorsal ventral, actions versus objects, one may need to consider other meaningful subdivisions devoted to social stimuli. Many of the chapters in this book dwell on this, so it is clearly not a new idea (see Atkinson, Heberlein, Adolphs, this volume). Yet, it should be recognized that this outlook represents a major shift in understanding the functions of our visual system. It raises the possibility that eventually the current taxonomy of visual functions will widen significantly so that information about human social interactions and the social environment will be strongly represented.

Whether this will be a success is, of course, unknown but it is important for vision researchers to think more broadly about what events and features of the social world have the potential to be efficiently coded. Following Barlow's (1961) seminal paper, there is of late, much work on the optics and statistics of natural sciences, endeavoring to find those redundant features of natural images so that a more efficient image code can convey scene properties. An important yet daunting task is to do the same kind of analysis with the style and content of human gestures. These are obviously recognized by humans (either consciously or unconsciously), and there must exist mechanisms that are attuned to them. Underlying invariants here could thus act as building blocks for social perception and social cognition. Computer vision algorithms have made some limited progress in this area, identifying a small set of actions from larger subsets. Insights from computer graphics (the entertainment industry) could play a possible role, because the creators of such captivating characters have at least some implicit understanding of human social actions. Troje's (2002) parameterization of human action is also promising, providing a mathematical framework such that the movement patterns corresponding to perceived styles, actions, and actors can be understood.

What we have touched on and what lies ahead in this volume is just a tiny sample of a broad interdisciplinary effort to understand humans as evolved social beings, whose vision, together with other senses, will play a likely role in understanding our strong continuities with other species while also appreciating our uniquely human qualities.

REFERENCES

Ambady, N., Bernieri, F. J., & Richeson, J. A. (2000). Toward a histology of social behavior: Judgmental accuracy from thin slices of the behavioral stream. In M. P. Zanna (Ed.), *Advances in Experimental Social Psychology*, 32, 201–272.

Bargh, J. A. & Chartrand, T. L. (1999). The unbearable automaticity of being. *American Psychologist*, 54, 462–469.

Barlow, H. B. (1961). Possible principles underlying the transformation of sensory messages. In W. A. Rosenblith (Ed.), *Sensory communication: Contributions to the Symposium on Principles of Sensory Communication, July 19–August 1, 1959, Endicott House*. Cambridge, MA: MIT Press.

Baron-Cohen, S. (1995). *Mindblindness: An essay on autism and theory of mind*. Cambridge: MIT Press.

Brothers, L. (2001). *Friday's footprint: How society shapes the human mind*. New York: Oxford University Press.

Byrne, R. W. & Whiten, A. (1988). *Machiavellian intelligence. Social Expertise and the Evolution of Intellect in Monkeys, Apes, and Humans*. New York: Oxford University Press.

Carroll, S. B. (2005) *Endless forms most beautiful: the new science of evo devo and the making of the animal kingdom*. New York: W.W. Norton and Company.

Clutton-Brock, T. H., Gaynor, D., McIlrath, G. M., Maccoll, A. D. C., Kansky, R., Chadwick, P., Manser, M., Skinner, J. D., & Brotherton, P. N. M. (1999) Predation, group size and mortality in a cooperative mongoose, Suricata suricatta. *J. Animal Ecology*, 68, 672–683.

Clutton-Brock,T. (2008). *Meerkat manor: Flower of the Kalahari*, New York: Simon and Shuster.

Dawkins, R. (1976) *The selfish gene*. New York: Oxford University Press.

Dennett, D. (1971). Intentional systems. *J. Philosophy*, 68, 77–106.

Dennett, D. C. (1981). "True believers: The intentional strategy and why it works," Scientific Explanations: Papers based on Herbert Spencer Lectures Given in the University of Oxford, A. F. Heath (Ed.). Reprinted in *The Nature of Consciousness*, David Rosenthal (Ed.), 1991.

de Waal, F. B. M. (1982). *Chimpanzee politics: power and sex among apes*. London: Cape.

de Waal, F. B. M. (2005). *Our inner ape*, Riverhead, New York.

Dilthey, W (1883/1962/1988). Einleitung in die Geisteswissenschaften, in: Gesammelte Werke, Vol. 1, Stuttgart 1962. Dilthey, W., and Betanzos, R.J. (1962). *Introduction to the human sciences: An attempt to lay a foundation for the study of society and history*. Detroit: Wayne State University Press.

Donald, M. W. (1991). *Origins of the modern mind: Three stages in the evolution of culture and cognition*. Cambridge, MA: Harvard University Press.

Dunbar, R. I. M. (1998). The social brain hypothesis. *Evolutionary Anthropology* 6, 178–190.

Emery, N. and Clayton, N. S. (1903, 2004). The mentality of crows: Convergent evolution of intelligence in corvids and apes. *Science*, 306.

Frank, S. A. (2007). All of life is social. *Current Biology* 17, R648-R650.

Gibson, J. J. (1950). *The perception of the visual world*. Boston: Houghton-Mifflin.

Gibson, J. J. (1966). *The senses considered as perceptual systems*. Boston: Houghton-Mifflin.

Gibson, J. J. (1979). *The ecological approach to visual perception*. Boston: Houghton-Mifflin.

Humphrey, N. K., (1976). The social function of the intellect. In, P.P.G. Bateson and R.A. Hinde

(Eds.). *Growing points in ethology* (pp. 303–317). Cambridge, UK: Cambridge University Press.

Kirschner, M. W. & Gerhart, J. C. (2005). *The plausibility of life: resolving Darwin's dilemma.* New Haven: Yale University Press.

Langlois, J. H. & Roggman, L. A. (1990). Attractive faces are only average." *Psych.Sci.* 1, 115–121.

Lasswell, H. D. (1936). *Politics: who gets what, when, and how.* New York: McGraw Hill.

Marr, D. (1980) *Vision.* San Francisco: W.H. Freeman.

McClintock, M. K. (2002). The neuroendocrinology of social chemosignals in humans and animals: odors, pheromones and vasanas. In Pfaff, D., Arnold, A., Etgen, A., Rubin, R. and Fahrbach, S. (Eds.). *Hormones, Brain & Behavior* (pp. 797–870). San Diego: Academic Press.

Milner, A. D. & Goodale, M.A. (1996). The visual brain in action. New York: Oxford University Press.

Nakayama, K. (1994). James J. Gibson—An Appreciation. *Psychological Review*, 101, 329–335.

Palomares, F. and Delibes, M. (1993). Social organization of the Egyptian mongoose: group size, spatial behavior and inter-individual contacts between adults. *Animal Behavior*, 45, 917–925.

Sugita, Y. (2008). Face perception in monkeys reared with no exposure to faces. *Proc. National Academy of Sciences* 105, 394–398.

Troje, N. F. (2002). Decomposing biological motion: A framework for analysis and synthesis of human gait patterns. *Journal of Vision* 2: 371–387.

Tsao, D. Y., N. Schweers, et al. (2008). "Patches of face-selective cortex in the macaque frontal lobe." *Nat Neurosci* 11(8): 877–879.

Tsao, D. Y. and Livingstone, M.S. (2008). Mechanisms of face perception. *Ann. Rev. Neurosci.*, 31, 411–437.

Ungerleider, L. G. & Mishkin, M. (1982). Two cortical visual systems. In D.J. Ingle, M.A. Goodale & R.J.W. Mansfield (Eds). *Analysis of Visual Behavior* (pp. 549–586). Cambridge, MA: MIT Press.

Zebrowitz MacArther, Leslie A. with R. M. Baron. (1983). "Toward an ecological theory of social perception." Psychological Review 90: 215–238.

The Science of Social Vision

CHAPTER 1

An Ecological Theory of Face Perception

Leslie A. Zebrowitz, P. Matthew Bronstad, and Joann M. Montepare

AN ECOLOGICAL THEORY OF FACE PERCEPTION

Humans' fascination with faces dates to ancient times and spans diverse cultures (cf. Zebrowitz, 1997). Scientific attention to faces is more recent. Fifty years ago, an investigator interested in face perception could easily read all the extant research literature. However, the 590 citations to "face perception" found in PsycINFO in the quarter century from 1956 to 1980 swelled over 1,000 percent to 6,782 citations in the next 25 years. This burgeoning scientific interest has addressed a wide range of questions including the contents of face perception, influencing stimuli, individual differences, disorders, developmental trajectories, behavioral consequences, and neural mechanisms (for a review, see Zebrowitz, 2006). The rapid growth in the literature highlights the need for a theoretical framework that integrates what is known and directs future research.

A dominant model of face perception in the cognitive neuroscience literature is a dual process model that calls attention to dissociations between perceptions of identity and emotional expression in addition to changeable facial qualities such as eye gaze and head angle (Bruce & Young, 1998; Calder & Young, 2005; Haxby, Hoffman, & Gobbini, 2002). Although this model does not claim to be a comprehensive model of how face perception works, it has generated considerable support from both cognitive and neurological data demonstrating functional and neurological divisions in the processing of identity versus emotion information and other dynamic cues, such as speech movements, eye gaze direction, and head movements (but see Calder & Young, 2005 and the discussion of confluence below).

Another prominent face perception model holds that the information provided by faces is coded relative to an average face at the center of a mental face-space (Busey, Wenger, & Townsend, 2001; Lee, Byatt, & Rhodes, 2000; O'Toole, Wenger, & Townsend, 2001; Valentine, 1991). In this model, faces are represented as points, and the distance between faces represents the similarity in their appearance. The dimensions of the space are the features that differentiate faces. O'Toole, et al. (2001) discuss different instantiations of face space, from the empirical (e.g., the results of principal component analyses of face images) to the hypothetical (e.g., the assumption that similar facial expressions are located near one another in the face space). Although face space is anchored by physical appearance, the particular layout of the space is a function of

Preparation of this chapter was supported in part by NIH Grants MH066836 and K02MH72603 to the first author.

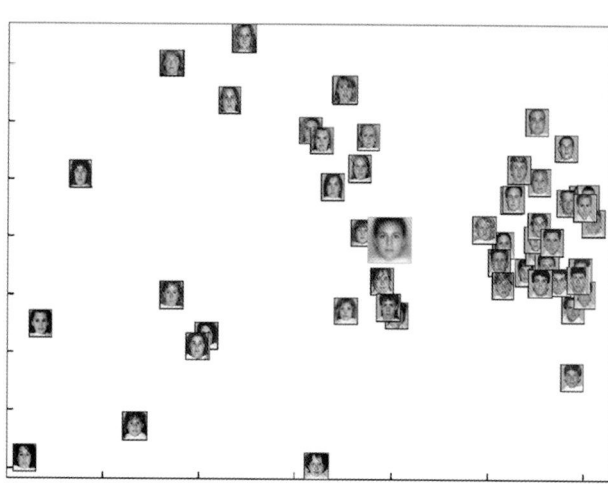

Figure 1.1 Example of a possible face space, where distance represents similarity among faces. Only two dimensions of facial variation are shown. Men's faces are on the right, women's are on the left. The horizontal dimension represents gender. The vertical dimension represents a different source of variation in faces, possibly hair color. The average face is the large face near the center.

an individual's perceptual experiences. Thus, the perceived similarity of two identical twins—their distance in the face space—depends on prior experiences with the twins (Stevenage, 1998). The face-space model has been applied primarily to the ease of recognizing different faces. However, it may also have relevance to other aspects of face perception. For example, faces with greater proximity in a face-space may be perceived to have similar psychological traits, as shown in early research demonstrating that people who looked alike were judged to be alike (Secord, 1958). (For an example of a face-space model, see Figure 1.1).

In this chapter we present an ecological theory of face perception (McArthur & Baron, 1983; Zebrowitz & Montepare, 2006), which draws on a Gibsonian approach to perception (Gibson, 1969; Gibson, 1966; Gibson, 1979). This theory is offered not as a hypothetico-deductive framework, but rather as a general conceptual model that can integrate existing research findings and guide future research questions. It adds to the dual process and face-space models by expanding the attributes perceived in faces, emphasizing the function of face perception to guide adaptive behavior, predicting face perceptions from the overgeneralization of adaptive responses, highlighting dynamic and multimodal cues to face perceptions, and considering the perceiver attunements that moderate face perceptions. In the following sections, we review the tenets of the ecological theory of face

perception and we consider how they inform the perception of four significant facial qualities: familiarity, age, emotion, and attractiveness. We also consider how ostensibly separate domains of face perception may be integrated through the ecological concept of perceived *affordances*.

PERCEIVED AFFORDANCES GUIDE ADAPTIVE BEHAVIOR

Ecological theory expands the facial attributes considered by the dual-process model to include the perception of *social affordances*—the opportunities for acting or being acted upon that are provided by other people. A vivid illustration of what Gibson meant by *affordance* is provided by his quotation from Koffka: "Each thing says what it is...a fruit says 'eat me'; water says 'drink me'; thunder says 'fear me'; and woman says 'love me'" (Gibson, 1979, p. 138). From an ecological perspective, face perception is not simply about recognizing a particular identity or emotion. Rather, it is about the function of the perceptual system to guide actions that serve to solve specific adaptive problems or to facilitate other goal attainments of individuals. As such, the affordance concept focuses attention on the behavioral responses linked to face perception.

The facial qualities highlighted in the dual-process model—identity, emotion expression, and gaze direction—each convey significant social affordances. We can expect different social interactions with people who have different identities, show different facial expressions, or look toward or away from us. Other attributes revealed in the face include familiarity, age, and attractiveness, and each is also associated with the perception of behavioral affordances.

Although affordances can be denoted by numerous descriptive trait adjectives (Beauvois & Dubois, 2000; Mignon & Mollaret, 2002), these traits are fairly well captured by the dimensions of likeability and power that correspond to the evaluative and potency dimensions on the semantic differential.[1] These dimensions underlie human judgments about a host of stimuli and decades of social psychology research reveal them to be the primary dimensions along which people evaluate others (Cuddy & Fiske, 2002; Rosenberg, Nelson, & Vivekananthan, 1968; Wiggins, 1996). Not surprisingly, likeability and power differentiate the perceived affordances of faces varying in familiarity, age, emotion, and attractiveness. Compared with unfamiliar faces, previously seen faces create impressions of high likeability (Bornstein, 1989; Bornstein, 1993; Zajonc, 1968), although there is no specific effect on perceived power. Compared with a neutral expression, angry expressions create impressions of low likeability and high power, fear expressions create impressions of moderate likeability and low power, happy expressions create impressions of high likeability and high power (Hess, Blairy, & Kleck, 2000; Knutson, 1996; Montepare & Dobish, 2003). Compared with young adult faces, faces of babies create impressions of high likeability and low power (Alley, 1983; Berry & McArthur, 1986; Zebrowitz, Fellous, Mignault, & Andreoletti, 2003), while faces of elderly adults create impressions of low likeability and

low power (Zebrowitz, et al., 2003).[2] Finally, attractive people are perceived as more likable as well as more powerful than those who are less attractive (Eagly, Ashmore, Makhijani, & Longo, 1991; Feingold, 1992; Langlois et al., 2000; Zebrowitz, Hall, Murphy, & Rhodes, 2002; Zebrowitz & Rhodes, 2004), effects that may be driven more by the perception that "ugly is bad" than by the perception that "beautiful is good" (Griffin & Langlois, 2006).

Consistent with the ecological theory tenet that perceiving is for doing, the affordances associated with different types of faces are linked to perceivers' behavior. Some behaviors are so obvious that they have received little research attention, such as those directed toward people whose faces vary in age, emotion expression, or familiarity. Nevertheless, there is empirical evidence that babies elicit different behavioral responses than do adults, although little work has focused on faces per se (Berry & McArthur, 1986; Eibl-Eibesfeldt, 1989; Zebrowitz, 1997). Considerable research has also documented preferential treatment of attractive people in interpersonal, occupational, judicial, and other domains (Langlois et al., 2000; Zebrowitz, 1997).

Other research has examined more subtle variations in behavioral responses to faces, with greater control over the stimulus information eliciting the response. For example, using evoked potentials, reaction time, and visual search measures, investigators have demonstrated more attention to faces than to other stimuli (Hershler & Hochstein, 2006; Ito & Cacioppo, 2000), as well as to particular types of faces, including the four facial qualities considered in this chapter: familiarity (Ito & Urland, 2003), age (Quinn & Macrae, 2005), emotional expression (Lundqvist, Ohman, Barrett, Niedenthal, & Winkielman, 2005) and attractiveness (Maner, Gailliot, & DeWall, 2007). (For a pertinent review, see Palermo & Rhodes, 2007).

---

[1] These dimensions are sometimes been labeled Warmth and Competence or Dominance, but the attributes that contribute are the same. Likablity/Warmth includes attributes such as warmth, approachability, and sociability; Power/Competence/Dominance includes attributes such as dominance, shrewdness, intelligence, and physical strength.

[2] In contrast, when people are making judgments in response to verbal probes rather than to faces, they rate elderly people as higher in likability than young adults (warmth), albeit still lower in power (competence) (Cuddy, Norton, & Fiske, 2005).

Faces also influence affective and approach/avoidance responses. For example, angry faces potentiate infant startle reactions to noise, a rudimentary defensive behavior (Balaban, 1995). Similarly, fearful or angry faces facilitate aversive classical conditioning and retard extinction as compared with happy faces (Lanzetta & Orr, 1981; Ohman & Dimberg, 1978; Orr & Lanzetta, 1984). Fearful or happy faces also speed hand movements that mimic approach responses, as do attractive faces, whereas angry or disfigured faces speed hand movements that mimic avoidant responses (Marsh, Ambady, & Kleck, 2005b; Zhang, 2007). Face race also influences hand movements that mimic approach/avoidance responses. Black faces, judged by white perceivers as more dangerous than own-race faces, speed avoidance responses in comparison with white faces; Asian faces, judged as less dangerous than own-race faces, speed approach (Zhang, 2007). Faces elicit motivational responses beyond approach or avoidance. Human perceivers exert more effort to see attractive faces (Aharon et al., 2001), and monkeys trade a favorite juice for a look at potential female mates or high-status conspecifics of either sex (Deaner, Khera, & Platt, 2005). Research on neural activation elicited by faces also suggests a link between face perception and behavior. Activity elicited when observing mouth and eye movements is differentiated within the superior temporal sulcus (STS), with the activation elicited by eye movements localized near areas involved in spatial attention and the activation elicited by mouth movements localized near areas involved in social communication (Pelphrey, Morris, Michelich, Allison, & McCarthy, 2005).

Not only does face perception influence behavior, but also behavior influences perception, as emphasized by Gibson (1966; 1979) and recent work on 'embodied cognition' (Niedenthal, 2007; Sommerville & Decety, 2006). For example, surreptitiously inducing people to smile or frown while viewing faces or other stimuli influences their evaluative responses (Ito, Chiao, Devine, Lorig, & Cacioppo, 2006; Laird, 1974). More research is clearly needed to conceptualize and specify the bidirectional relationships between behavior and face perception.

ACCURACY AND OVERGENERALIZATION

Ecological theory assumes that face perception functions to guide adaptive behavior, which raises the twin issues of accuracy and bias. Attention to accurate and biased face perceptions within the dual-process model has focused primarily on dissociations in the recognition of identity and emotions as evidenced in disorders of face perception, such as prosopagnosia or autism (Adolphs, Sears, & Piven, 2001; Damasio, Tranel, Rizzo, & Mesulam, 2000). A more comprehensive model of face perception requires attention to normally functioning individuals' accurate and biased perceptions of other socially relevant qualities that are revealed in the face.

In addition to recognizing obvious socially relevant attributes, such as familiarity, age, emotion, and sex, perceivers are also attuned to subtle qualities in faces such as ethnicity (Andrzejewski, Hall, & Salib, 2007) and sexual orientation (Rule, Ambady, Adams, & Macrae, 2007). Moreover, research using brief stimuli reveals how exquisitely sensitive perceivers are to functionally significant attributes. For instance, perceivers show rapid or automatic processing of facial emotion (Stenberg, Wiking, & Dahl, 1998), familiarity (Ellis, Young, & Koenken, 1993), and attractiveness (Olson & Marshuetz, 2005). Faces also activate spontaneous trait inferences (Mason, Cloutier, & Macrae, 2006) as well as rapid trait perceptions related to likeability and competence (Willis & Todorov, 2006), with judgments often showing above-chance accuracy (Zebrowitz & Collins, 1997).

The flipside of accuracy is biased face perception. A set of overgeneralization hypotheses derived from ecological theory codify biases that result from the preparedness to respond to adaptively significant facial qualities. These hypotheses hold that the affordances that are accurately revealed by the facial information that conveys familiarity, age, emotion, or low fitness also are perceived in people whose faces resemble one of these facial qualities (cf. Zebrowitz, 1996, 1997; Zebrowitz & Collins, 1997).[3] According to ecological theory, any errors yielded by overgeneralizations occur because they are less maladaptive than those that might result from failing to respond appropriately to people who vary in familiarity, age, emotion, or fitness.

Familiar face overgeneralization

In *familiar face overgeneralization*, faces that are similar in appearance to a known face will convey similar affordances (DeBruine, 2002; Lewicki, 1985). A broader familiar face overgeneralization effect is found in reactions to other-race faces. Faces of strangers from other racial groups appear less familiar than strangers from one's own group (Zebrowitz, Bronstad, & Lee, 2007). Moreover, consistent with evidence that unfamiliar stimuli are generally less liked (Bornstein, 1989; Bornstein, 1993; Hamm, Baum, & Nikels, 1975; Rhodes, Halberstadt, & Brajkovich, 2001; Zajonc, 1968), faces of other-race strangers are perceived as less likable, and this effect is partially mediated by their lower familiarity, quite apart from other contributing social factors. The lesser familiarity of other-race faces also contributes to the strength of culturally based race stereotypes, partially mediating negative stereotypes of other-race faces and partially suppressing positive ones (Zebrowitz, Bronstad, & Lee, 2007).

Other evidence that unfamiliarity influences a readiness to perceive particular affordances and to behave accordingly is provided by white judges' reactions to faces that are more prototypically black, regardless of their actual race. Such faces prime negative concepts more than do less prototypical black faces or white ones (Livingston & Brewer, 2002), and they are perceived to have more negative traits (Blair, Judd, Sadler, & Jenkins, 2002). Moreover, judges (mostly caucasian) give convicted criminals with a more prototypical black appearance longer prison terms (Blair, Judd, & Chapleau, 2004) and more frequent death sentences (Eberhardt, Davies, Purdie-Vaughns, & Johnson, 2006). Similarly, Koreans perceive

Korean or white faces with a more Asian appearance as more familiar, more likable, and less dangerous (Strom, Zhang, Zebrowitz, Bronstad, & Lee, 2008). Importantly, these effects were often found for faces that did not differ in race, indicating that they reflect a reaction to the deviation of the faces' similarity to the average face experienced by the judges rather than to face race per se.

Emotion face overgeneralization

In *emotion face overgeneralization*, responses to the actual affordances of people displaying emotion expressions generalize to impressions of people whose neutral expression resembles an emotion. For example, people whose neutral faces show some resemblance to an angry expression are perceived as less likable and more powerful (Montepare & Dobish, 2003; Said, Sebe, & Todorov, 2009; Zebrowitz, Kikuchi, & Fellous, in press). The lesser resemblance of female than male facial structure to anger expressions (Becker, Kenrick, Neuberg, Blackwell, & Smith, 2007; Hess, Adams, & Kleck, 2004, Zebrowitz et al., in press) may similarly contribute to impressions of greater likeability and lower power in women.

Baby-face overgeneralization

In *baby-face overgeneralization*, the actual affordances of babies are mirrored by impressions of baby-faced individuals as less powerful and more likable than their more mature-faced peers, an effect that holds true across age, sex, and race of faces and perceivers (Montepare & Zebrowitz, 1998; Zebrowitz, 1997). Supporting the overgeneralization hypothesis, research investigating the accuracy of such impressions has demonstrated that they are often inaccurate or even opposite to reality (Bachmann & Nurmoja, 2006; Zebrowitz, Andreoletti, Collins, Lee, & Blumenthal, 1998; Zebrowitz, Collins, & Dutta, 1998; Zebrowitz & Lee, 1999). Nevertheless, they are reflected in behavioral responses, consistent with the ecological tenet that perception guides behavior (Montepare & Zebrowitz, 1998; Zebrowitz, 1997). Baby-face overgeneralization also contributes to differences in the perceived affordances of female and male faces. Adult female faces typically retain more neotenous, babyish qualities than do adult male faces

---

[3] Another overgeneralization hypothesis is animal analogies, whereby people may be perceived to have traits that are associated with the animals that their features resemble (Zebrowitz, 1997, pp 58–61).

(Enlow, 1982), contributing to the perception of women as more likable and less powerful than men (Friedman & Zebrowitz, 1992). Although age overgeneralization in face perception has not been studied at the older end of the lifespan, young adults with more elderly gait qualities are perceived as less happy and less powerful than their more youthful-walking peers (Montepare & Zebrowitz-McArthur, 1988), and the same may be true for young adults with more elderly looking faces.

Anomalous face overgeneralization

In *anomalous face overgeneralization,* responses to the actual affordances of people whose faces are marked by disease or genetic anomalies generalize to people whose faces resemble an anomalous one. This hypothesis can explain the well-documented tendency for attractive people to be perceived as more likable and powerful than unattractive people—the attractiveness halo effect. Evidence for anomalous face overgeneralization is provided by the finding that the judged attractiveness, likability, and competence of normal faces were predicted by the extent to which a neural network confused them with those of people with craniofacial anomalies that mark syndromes characterized by various intellectual and social and physical deficits (Zebrowitz et al., 2003). Thus, accurate impressions of the deficiencies signaled by anomalous faces are overgeneralized to unattractive normal individuals. It is important to note that in this study, the people with more resemblance to anomalous faces were not less fit, as assessed by measures of their intelligence and health. Thus, the divergent impressions of them must be explained by overgeneralization, not accuracy.[4]

---

[4] Although impressions in this study were not accurate, other research using a sample of faces that was representative of the population revealed that lower-than-average facial attractiveness predicted lower health and intelligence, whereas higher-than-average attractiveness did not predict higher fitness. Nevertheless, consistent with the anomalous face overgeneralization hypothesis, intelligence and health were perceived to vary not only from low to moderate levels of attractiveness, but also from moderate to high levels (Zebrowitz & Rhodes, 2004).

STIMULUS INFORMATION

A pivotal feature of the ecological theory is an emphasis on identifying the *external stimulus environment* that informs perception. Gibson (1966, 1979) argued that multimodal, dynamic changes over space and time are features that provide the most useful information to perceivers in nonsocial perception, and McArthur and Baron (1983) suggested that the same is true for social perception. Thus, the dynamic and multifaceted facial information provided by facial structure, pigmentation, texture, and movement should provide the most useful information about all of the qualities gleaned from faces. Yet, research has often ignored the question of what stimulus information informs face perception or it has focused on facial structure revealed in two-dimensional black-and-white static facial images, ignoring dynamic and textural information. Research also has rarely considered face perception within the context of multimodal cues. However, the qualities that are conveyed by facial structure, be it familiarity, age, emotion, or attractiveness, may also be specified in voices, bodies, or gesture. Our perceptual systems have evolved to extract useful information from moving, talking faces attached to bodies, and we will learn more about how the face perception system works if we study it in more ecologically valid contexts.

Another significant shortcoming of efforts to identify the stimulus information that guides face perception is that much of the work has been data-driven or applied, although there are exceptions. Empirically driven investigations of cues to face perception tend to generate a laundry list that has no theoretical coherence, and such investigations have often failed to uncover the cues that perceivers actually utilize when perceiving various attributes in faces (Zebrowitz & Collins, 1997). The face overgeneralization hypotheses discussed earlier provide a theoretical rationale for examining the contribution of particular facial cues to perceived affordances.

Familiarity cues

Research examining the cues that facilitate the recognition of familiar faces indicates that face recognition relies on a large constellation of facial features (Gosselin & Schyns, 2001; Smith, Muir, Pascalis, & Slater, 2003) that are processed configurally (Myowa-Yamakoshi, Yamaguchi, Tomonaga, Tanaka, & Matsuzawa, 2005; Young, Hellawell, & Hay, 1987) with particular emphasis on the eye region (Prodan, Orbelo, Testa, & Ross, 2001; Sadr, Jarudi, & Sinha, 2003) and the left half of the face (Yovel, Levy, Grabowecky, & Paller, 2003). Research within the face-space conceptual framework that was discussed earlier also has revealed that accurate recognition of faces increases with their distance from the average face, located at the center of the face space (Rhodes, Brennan, & Carey, 1987), and, more importantly, with lower density of proximal faces (Caldara & Abdi, 2006; Furl, Phillips, & O'Toole, 2002).

The evidence that facial identity is coded relative to an average face and that face recognition depends on the spatial relations among facial features more than on isolated parts is consistent with the ecological emphasis on configural facial qualities. However, the ecological approach would also underscore the importance of studying three-dimensional, animated faces as well as multimodal presentations. Indeed, differentiating unfamiliar faces is better for the more three-dimensional, three-quarter view faces than it is for frontal or profile views (Bruce, Valentine, & Baddeley, 1987), and moving faces are recognized better than static ones (O'Toole, Roark, & Abdi, 2002; Pike, Kemp, Towell, & Phillips, 1997). In addition, identity can be revealed in facial movements alone, as shown using point-light displays (Bruce, Valentine, Gruneberg, Morris, & Sykes, 1988), and motion capture techniques (Bruce et al., 1988; Hill & Johnston, 2001). The recognition of familiar faces can also be influenced by multimodal cues as evidenced by the facilitatory effect of speech information on infants' discrimination of mother's and stranger's faces (Burnham, 1993). Moreover, the movement of the face and the sound of the voice provide equivalent information about identity, such that perceivers can match silent videotapes of talking faces with their corresponding voices at above-chance accuracy (Kamachi, Hill, Lander, & Vatikiotis-Bateson,

2003). It may be that movement cues beyond the face would also provide convergent information about identity. In sum, it seems likely that the similarity of faces within a face-space model and the deviations from an average face, with attendant variations in ease of recognition, may depend not only on similarities in their two-dimensional structure, but also on similarities in their three-dimensional and dynamic and multimodal qualities.

Identifying the face space underlying familiar face recognition requires, not only taking into account dynamic and multimodal cues when mapping similarities among faces, but also selecting an appropriately representative set of faces. Theoretically, the average face should depend on the set of faces to which a perceiver has been exposed most frequently. Since there may be nontrivial differences in the faces to which different perceivers are exposed, the average face and consequent ease of recognition of various faces is likely to differ across perceivers. Indeed, the well-documented other-race disadvantage in familiar face recognition (Meissner & Brigham, 2001) suggests that people attend less to the stimulus information that differentiates *among* other-race than own-race faces. This effect could reflect the fact other-race faces are more tightly clustered in the face space (Caldara & Abdi, 2006; Furl et al., 2002; Lewis, 2004) and/or it may occur because perceivers initially emphasize information specifying race category at the expense of individuating information (Levin, 2000).

The significant question remains as to what stimulus information actually differentiates less familiar other-race *from* own-race faces. Skin color is one salient difference. People report that it is the primary cue used to judge whether another person is African, Caucasian, or Hispanic, and that it is second only to eyes when judging whether another person is Asian (Brown, Dane, & Durham, 1998). Interestingly, however, three-dimensional shape was as important as surface color when participants were asked to categorize faces as European or Japanese on the basis of one cue or the other, and shape influenced racial categorization even in the context of contradictory color cues

(Hill, Bruce, & Akamatsu, 1995). Dynamic facial movements and textural cues besides skin color, such as eyebrows and facial and scalp hair may also contribute to race recognition, as may multimodal cues, such as vocal qualities (Walton & Orlikoff, 1994) and gesture (Johnson, 2006).

From an ecological theory perspective, the question is not only what stimulus information objectively or subjectively differentiates faces that vary in familiarity, but also what stimulus information influences their perceived affordances. Skin tone does not appear to be as univocal a cue as one may expect (Maddox, 2004). Consistent with familiar face overgeneralization, Black raters judged White faces that had been morphed to have darker skin as more likable than the original White faces, whose skin tone was less similar to own-race faces. However, White raters judged Black faces morphed to have lighter skin as less likable and less competent than the original Black faces, and the skin tone morphing had no effect on the perceived likeability or competence of own race faces for either Black or White raters (Zebrowitz, Barglow, Bronstad, & Lee, 2008). Other research has investigated the racial prototypicality of static two-dimensional faces, as subjectively defined. As noted earlier, this work reveals that a more prototypical other-race appearance, which can include a range of cues, elicits negative reactions at least in part due to its unfamiliarity (Blair et al., 2002; Eberhardt, Goff, Purdie, & Davies, 2004; Livingston & Brewer, 2002; Maddox, 2004; Strom et al., 2008). Although the influence of unfamiliar dynamic and multimodal cues has been little studied, evidence suggesting that these cues also influence perceived affordances is provided by the finding that hand gestures displayed more by black or hispanic than by white individuals tend to be perceived as suspicious by white police officers (Johnson, 2006).

Age cues

Anthropometric comparisons of the faces of babies and adults show that the facial structure of babies is characterized by a rounder face with bigger cheeks, a larger forehead with a more vertical slope, a larger cranium and a smaller,

less protrusive chin, a small, wide, and concave nose with a sunken bridge, thinner eyebrows, proportionately larger eyes and larger pupil size (Enlow, 1990; Todd, Mark, Shaw, & Pittenger, 1980). Strong evidence that at least some of these differences are sufficient to convey age is provided by research that has changed the shape of heads or automobiles using a mathematical formula (cardiodal strain transformation) that simulates changes produced by actual maturation. People are able to identify the older of two faces or two Volkswagen Beetles when the resultant difference in shape is only slightly greater than the smallest difference that can be detected (Mark, Todd, & Shaw, 1981; Pittenger, Shaw, & Mark, 1979; Shaw & Pittenger, 1977). Reliable relative age judgments were also made of 3-D heads to which the strain transformation was applied (Bruce, Burton, Doyle, & Dench, 1989; Mark & Todd, 1983).

Dynamic facial cues also vary with age, and perceivers can discern relative age from the facial movements of children, middle-aged adults, and elderly adults depicted in point-light displays (Berry, 1990). There are also age differences in textural cues (Frost, 1988; Zebrowitz, 1997), and age can be identified from facial information not only during the formative years, when there are pronounced structural variations in the face, but also with a fair degree of accuracy in adulthood when the variations are mostly textural (Henss, 1991). Although research has not investigated whether multimodal cues yield more accurate age recognition, as ecological theory would predict, relative age is specified not only by facial qualities, but also by voice qualities (Helfrich, 1979) and gait qualities (Montepare & Zebrowitz-McArthur, 1988).

Most interesting from an ecological perspective is the influence of age-related face cues on perceived affordances. Consistent with baby-face overgeneralization, the structural facial qualities that mark babies also mark adults who are judged to be baby-faced (Montepare & Zebrowitz, 1998; Zebrowitz, Fellous, Mignault, & Andreoletti, 2003). Moreover, faces of any age with more babyish structural qualities are perceived as more likable and less powerful (Berry & McArthur, 1985; McArthur & Apatow, 1983;

Montepare & Zebrowitz, 1998; Zebrowitz & Montepare, 1992). Age-related differences in movement patterns also reveal behavioral affordances, with children's faces shown in point-light displays eliciting impressions of lower power than adult faces even with perceived age controlled (Berry, 1990). It would be interesting to determine whether there is a baby-face overgeneralization effect shown in impressions of adults whose faces have more childlike textural cues or more childlike facial dynamics, and whether multimodal babyish cues elicit the strongest overgeneralization effects. Similar questions remain regarding the perceived affordances of young adult faces that resemble elderly ones.

Emotion cues

A prodigious body of research has identified specific two-dimensional static facial components that objectively *differentiate* the basic emotions of happy, angry, sad, fear, disgust, and surprise (Ekman, 1971; Izard, 1977). It has been further shown that these components differ from those that differentiate identity (Calder, Burton, Miller, Young, & Akamatsu, 2001). Research examining what two-dimensional static facial components effectively *communicate* an emotion reveals that perceivers use information in different regions to recognize different emotions (Smith, Cottrell, Gosselin, & Schyns, 2005). Nevertheless, emotion recognition, like identity recognition, is holistic (Calder, Young, Keane, & Dean, 2000).

Research investigating dynamic cues to emotion has identified the specific facial muscle movements that *differentiate* several basic emotions (Cohn, Ekman, Harrigan, Rosenthal, & Scherer, 2006). Other research has provided evidence for the contribution of dynamic facial information to the *communication* of emotion (Bassili, 1978, 1979; Sato & Yoshikawa, 2004; Wagner, MacDonald, & Manstead, 1986; Wehrle, Kaiser, Schmidt, & Scherer, 2000). The significance of dynamic cues is underscored by the finding that recognition of subtle emotion expressions is better from moving rather than static faces (Ambadar, Schooler, & Cohen, 2005), that people are highly sensitive to the temporal

progression of emotion displays (Edwards, 1998), and that dynamic facial expressions of emotion elicit stronger arousal in perceivers (Sato & Yoshikawa, 2007). Consistent with the ecological emphasis on multimodal stimulus information, there are vocal cues to emotion (Juslin & Scherer, 2005) as well as bodily cues (deGelder, 2006). Although not a focus of research, textural cues may also contribute to impressions of emotions which are marked by distinctive eyebrows and skin tone, with faces reddening in anger or embarrassment and paling in fear. Moreover, some research has demonstrated that when multimodal information is consistent, it can yield more effective communication of emotion than the face alone (DePaulo & Rosenthal, 1978; Vaish & Striano, 2004).

Research investigating the specific stimulus information for emotion perception has been more empirically than theoretically driven. A notable exception is provided by research that raised the question of why particular emotion expressions look the way they do (Marsh, Adams, & Kleck, 2005a). These authors suggested that both the morphology of emotion expressions and the impressions they elicit may derive from the adaptive utility of their mimicking variations in facial maturity. More specifically, they argued that fear and anger expressions evolved to mimic babies' faces and mature faces, respectively, because it is adaptive for those experiencing fear to elicit reactions paralleling those elicited by helpless babies and for those experiencing anger to elicit reactions paralleling those elicited by powerful adults. Consistent with this hypothesis, both *subjective ratings* of emotions' resemblance to babies as well as *objective indices* from connectionist models showed that fear expressions or closely related surprise expressions resemble babies more than do neutral expressions, while anger expressions resemble babies less (Marsh et al., 2005a; Zebrowitz, Kikuchi, & Fellous, 2007). As previously noted, anger expressions also resemble women less than they resemble men (Becker et al., 2007; Hess et al., 2004; Zebrowitz et al., in press), which is consistent with the fact that faces of adult women retain more neotenous qualities than those of men.

From an ecological theory perspective, the question is not only what stimulus information objectively or subjectively differentiates emotion expressions, but also what stimulus information influences perceived affordances. The previously cited research demonstrating the differential resemblance of emotion expressions to babies also showed effects on impressions. More baby-faced eye-region metrics in surprise than neutral faces mediated perceptions of surprise faces as less powerful and more likable, whereas the less baby-faced overall facial metrics in anger than neutral faces mediated perceptions of anger faces as more powerful and less likable. An ingenious program of research that examined primitive masks used for different rituals in a variety of cultures revealed that structural diagonality and angularity are higher order invariants that communicate, not only anger, but also threat, and other research suggests that angular structures or angular and diagonal movement patterns may communicate similar affordances in contrast to those communicated by rounded contours that are found in a baby's face (Aronoff, Barclay, & Stevenson, 1988; Aronoff, Woike, & Hyman, 1992; Bar & Neta, 2006, 2007).

Attractiveness

The research reviewed earlier indicates that unattractive faces resemble anomalous ones, but the question remains about exactly what stimulus information differentiates anomalous or normal unattractive faces from more attractive ones. Research motivated by evolutionary theory predictions concerning facial attributes that signal low fitness (Folstad & Karter, 1992; Scheib, Gangestad, & Thornhill, 1999; Thornhill & Gangestad, 1999) has identified several such qualities. These include low facial averageness (a facial configuration far from the population mean), low symmetry, poor skin quality, an older age, and low sexual dimorphism (a face less prototypical for its sex), (for a review, see Zebrowitz & Rhodes, 2002). Negative facial expressions also diminish attractiveness (Reis et al., 1990). For women, less prototypically female facial movements decrease attractiveness (Morrison,

Gralewski, Campbell, & Penton-Voak, 2007), and the dynamic quality of low expressiveness decreases attractiveness for both sexes (DePaulo, Blank, & Swaim, 1992; Riggio & Friedman, 1986). Although differences in the perceived affordances signaled by high versus low expressiveness provide a proximal explanation for this effect, it may also be influenced by anomalous face overgeneralization, since low facial expressiveness is a marker of physical and psychological disorders, such as Parkinson's disease (Pentland, Pitcairn, Gray, & Riddle, 1987) depression, and schizophrenia (Schneider, Heimann, Himer, & Huss, 1990). The fact that vocal cues vary in attractiveness (Miyake & Zuckerman, 1993), as do body cues (Peters, Rhodes, & Simmons, 2007) suggests that multimodal, dynamic stimulus information may have a more profound influence on judged facial attractiveness and than does the standard stimulus information of 2D faces. For example, judgments of speakers' facial attractiveness are influenced by their vocal attractiveness (Zuckerman, Miyake, & Hodgins, 1991).

Once again, from an ecological perspective, the influence of attractive or unattractive facial qualities on perceived affordances is of central interest. In addition to the enormous literature on the effects of global attractiveness (Eagly et al., 1991; Langlois et al., 2000; Zebrowitz, 1997), it has also been shown that the specific qualities of high facial symmetry and averageness each contribute to more positive impressions on traits related to likability and power as well as perceived health (Luevano, 2007; Zebrowitz et al., 2002; Zebrowitz & Rhodes, 2004; Zebrowitz, Voinescu, & Collins, 1996). Research investigating the influence of multimodal, dynamic stimulus information on perceived affordances is needed to better understand the contribution of facial attractiveness to real world social interactions.

NEURAL MECHANISMS

Although Gibson's ecological theory of perception did not focus on neural mechanisms per se (Gibson 1966, 1979), he argued that understanding the nature of the stimulus information to which organisms respond will elucidate how their perceptual systems operate. Thus, ecological theory implies that neural mechanisms may be elucidated by a deep understanding of the stimulus. Indeed, Gibson's specifications of the kinds of higher order stimulus information that informs adaptive action stimulated research that has identified neurons tuned to such information (Nakayama, 1994). Moreover, shortcomings of research on the neural mechanisms that guide face perception can be informed by ecological theory.

One shortcoming is that neural mechanisms have often been studied in a piecemeal fashion rather than as an integrated system. This certainly reflects our rudimentary understanding of neural systems and the difficult methodological and analytical task of assessing integration even in parts of the system that are fairly well understood. However, it may also reflect a mindset that was early criticized by Gibson (1966) in his landmark book *The Senses Considered as Perceptual Systems* when he wrote: "The question is not how the receptors work, or how the nerve cells work, or where the impulses go, but how the systems work as a whole" (p. 6). A systems analysis of face perception requires consideration of both the spatial and the temporal neural response to faces.

An excellent illustration of a systems approach is provided by research on taste perception in the rat (Katz, Nicolelis, & Simon, 2002). Whereas it was long believed that an animal identifies a taste on its tongue on the basis of which neurons are activated and how much they are activated, this research reveals that the story is much more complex. In the first 200 ms after a taste is applied to the tongue, neural responses in the cortex reflect the same somatosensory experience of fluid, regardless of taste. Between 250 and 800 ms, tastes with different identities, such as sweet, sour, salty, bitter, elicit unique neural responses. Still later, tastes of similar palatability (e.g., likable tastes of sweet and salty or disliked tastes of sour and bitter) elicit similar neural responses. Moreover,

manipulations of palatability, such as conditioned taste aversion, exclusively affect this late neural response to the taste's *affordance*, which may be the one associated with behavioral responses. This research provides a cautionary message to face perception researchers who search for neural mechanisms for the perception of certain face qualities in a particular brain region or even in a particular pattern of brain regions. Considering the temporal as well as the spatial pattern of activation is likely to be necessary to account for responses to different faces. For example, all faces may activate the fusiform face area (FFA), regardless of their identity. With some time lag, activation in other brain regions may be differentiated according to the identity or social category of the face, with the temporal delay varying across different types of faces. Indeed, research has documented temporal differences in the neural response to different face categories (Ito & Urland, 2003). The behavioral affordances of faces may be registered in yet other brain regions and perhaps with a different time stamp.

Research investigating the neural mechanisms for face perception has implicated several brain regions (Haxby et al., 2002). These include the FFA, involved in face recognition (Kanwisher, McDermott, & Chun, 1997; McKone, Kanwisher, & Duchaine, 2007); the superior temporal sulcus (STS), involved in the perception of changeable facial qualities, such as eye gaze and emotion expression (Hooker et al., 2003; LaBar, Crupain, Voyvodic, & McCarthy, 2003); the amygdala (AMG), activated by emotionally salient stimuli, including faces (Fitzgerald, Angstadt, Jelsone, Nathan, & Phan, 2006; Winston, O'Doherty, Kilner, Perrett, & Dolan, 2007); and the orbital frontal cortex (ORB) and other parts of the reward system, which are activated by positively and negatively reinforcing stimuli, including faces (Harris, van den Bos, Fiske, McClure, & Cohen, 2007; Liang, Zebrowitz, & Zhang, in press; Mitchell, Neil Macrae, & Banaji, 2005).

Consistent with the range of brain regions that are responsive to faces as well as with the ecological theory emphasis on a systems approach, there is considerable evidence that the neural mechanisms for the different facets of face perception are distributed rather than localized in a particular brain region. For example, FFA activation may be modulated by activation in other brain regions (Critchley et al., 2000; Lewis et al., 2003; Vuilleumier & Pourtois, 2007; Zebrowitz, Luevano, Bronstad, & Aharon, 2009; Zhang, Zebrowitz, & Aharon, 2007), and the pattern of neural activation to faces versus objects can be distinguished even when FFA activation is ignored (Haxby et al., 2001). Other evidence for a distributed processing of face perception is provided by the finding that the activation of brain reward regions by highly attractive faces (Aharon et al., 2001) is greater for faces that are looking directly at the observer (Kampe, Frith, Dolan, & Frith, 2001) or smiling (O'Doherty et al., 2003), thereby demonstrating that the brain regions that process both facial expression and eye gaze are also involved in the processing of facial attractiveness. Similarly, eye gaze moderates activation of the amgydala by emotion expressions (Adams, Gordon, Baird, Ambady, & Kleck, 2003). Consistent with this evidence that a single brain region may be involved in the perception of multiple facial qualities, investigations of face sensitive cells in macaques revealed that in addition to cells that responded to identity and others that responded to expression, some cells were sensitive to both qualities (Hasselmo, Rolls, & Baylis, 1989). Even the neural response to emotion expressions alone is distributed (Liang, Zebrowitz, & Aharon, 2009). A meta-analysis of brain areas consistently associated with particular emotional states identified six emotion networks that depend on the emotion and the category of eliciting stimuli (Wager et al., 2007).

There is temporal as well as spatial distribution in the neural substrates for face perception, as revealed in the neural response to facial stimuli in evoked response potentials (ERPs). ERPs are electrical activity measured at the scalp that reflect the neural activity of large populations of cortical neurons. They are negatively or positively charged and are measured over a very short timescale. For example, after initial attention to less racially

familiar faces shown in the N170 (a *negative-going* wave that peaks at approximately 170 milliseconds after stimulus), later ERP components indicated greater processing of more familiar own-race faces, with racially ambiguous faces treated like faces of one's own race. Slightly later, racially ambiguous faces are differentiated from both of the other groups, capturing the explicit categorizations provided by perceivers (Ito & Urland, 2003; Xiaohu, Yuejia, Xing, Guofeng, & Jinghan, 2003). ERP responses to emotion faces arise as early as 120 ms after presentation, and other, more sustained, ERP responses arise later, as do neural responses recorded intracranially (see Vuilleumier & Portois, 2007 for a review). A fuller understanding of the neural mechanisms for face perception will require considering both the temporal and spatial patterns of brain responses to faces, and the connectivity among brain regions across time.

A shortcoming in research on neural mechanisms for face perception is the frequent reliance on two-dimensional static facial images. Faces appear in a three-dimensional head on a body with a voice. A better understanding of neural mechanisms requires examining those involved in processing animated faces. Indeed, brain regions implicated in processing facial expressions of emotion showed stronger activation to dynamic than static expressions (LaBar et al., 2003; Yoshikawa & Sato, 2006). A related departure from ecological theory is the immobilization of perceivers in an MRI scanner. Gibson (1979) emphasized that we see things not with our eyes but with our "eyes-in-the-head-on-the-body-resting-on-the-ground" (p. 205), and that the process of picking up visual information involves, in part, head turning and walking around. Indeed, fixating the eye region while viewing faces facilitates emotion recognition (Adolphs, 2006), and conceptual representation of objects, as indexed by neural processing measures, depends on the sensory-motor interactions the perceiver has previously had with them (Kiefer, Sim, Liebich, Hauk, & Tanaka, 2007). Moreover, as noted earlier, the relationship between perception and action is bi-directional. Even immobilized perceivers show evidence of behavioral responses to faces. For example, there is greater activation in the motor cortex when viewing more attractive faces (Kawabata & Zeki, 2004), and research on mirror neurons shows neural activation to observed actions that mirrors activation to executed actions, suggesting that we may understand the affordances conveyed by another person's facial movement through its effect on our own incipient motor responses (Knoblich & Sebanz, 2006).

As in behavioral research on face perception, the dearth of work on multimodal stimulus information is another shortcoming of the research on neural mechanisms for face perception. Consistent with the suggestion that there will be intermodal neural mechanisms for face perception, neurons in the central nucleus of the monkey amygdala, which sends outputs to other-emotion-related brain areas, were activated either by facial or vocal emotion cues as well as both together (Kuraoka & Kakamura, 2007). In humans, bodily expressions of fear elicit similar patterns of neural activation to the facial expressions (Hadjikhani & de Gelder, 2003). Similarly, the posterior superior temporal sulcus (STSp), known to be activated by visual stimuli depicting biological motion, is similarly activated by the acoustic cues of a person walking (Bidet-Caulet, Voisin, Bertrand, & Fonlupt, 2005).

Not only are the same brain regions activated by information from multiple modalities, but also stimuli in other modalities can modulate the neural activation to faces. For example, late ERPs suggested enhanced attention to unpleasant faces that were preceded by an incongruous pleasant odor (Bensafi, Pierson, et al., 2002). Such multimodal influences on face perception can be adaptive. Animal research has demonstrated that in order for classical conditioning to occur, it is necessary that the conditioned stimulus and unconditioned stimulus activate the same neural regions (LeDoux, 2007). Extrapolating to humans, this suggests that learning functional associations to faces requires that the same neural regions be activated by the faces (CS) and the primary or secondary reinforcing stimuli with which they are paired, be they auditory, olfactory, or tactile.

Although current technology is not conducive to brain imaging of mobile human perceivers interacting with moving, talking people, a partial solution is to present dynamic facial images while scanning, as well as using virtual reality methods that allow perceivers to control their virtual position with respect to another person. Such methods, coupled with manipulations of perceivers' goals, can also accommodate the ecological dictum that perceiving is for doing. In particular, they may reveal that neural mechanisms for face perception significantly involve motor cortex and brain areas concerned with goal directed behavior, and that the mechanisms subserving perceptions of the same face may vary with the perceiver's goals and the concomitant affordances for that perceiver. In short, the neural mechanisms underlying face perception are likely to be more fully revealed when they can be studied in the context of dynamic social interactions.

PERCEIVER ATTUNEMENTS

A fundamental tenet of the ecological approach is that the detection of social affordances depends on the perceivers' *attunements*—their sensitivity to the stimulus information that reveals particular affordances. Although Gibson emphasized the objective reality of affordances ("Each thing says what it is...a fruit says 'eat me'... and woman says 'love me,'" Koffka, quoted in Gibson, 1979, p. 138), he also emphasized their emergence from the interaction of the environment and the perceiver. For example, *woman* does not communicate "love me" to heterosexual women or gay men. Indeed, neuroimage data reflects this; medial orbitofrontal cortex, activated when rewarding stimuli are viewed, is only active for facial stimuli of the appropriate sex for the perceiver's sexual orientation (Kranz & Ishai, 2006). In short, the concept of attunements captures the fact that what a person perceives in faces depends on what information exists, what information the person is able to detect, and what information is useful to that perceiver.

Attunements develop through a process of perceptual learning that spans a variety of mechanisms, including *imprinting, differentiation, unitization, attentional weighting, adaptation, prototype extraction,* and *stimulus generalization* (cf. Goldstone, 1998). These mechanisms, which may operate in concert, all reflect Gibson's idea of the education of attention (Gibson, 1966), and they may be modulated by perceivers' behavioral goals and capabilities (Zebrowitz & Montepare, 2006). Perceptual learning sensitizes neural mechanisms to particular object qualities (Quinn, Westerlund, & Nelson, 2006), a process that may create attunements that influence perceptions of face familiarity, emotion, age, attractiveness, and the associated affordances. Effects of the stimulus generalization mechanism have already been discussed in the context of the overgeneralization hypotheses. Illustrative examples of the other perceptual learning mechanisms are provided below.

Imprinting

In imprinting, specialized detectors rapidly become attuned after birth, and the stimuli subsequently shape the detectors' sensitivity (Goldstone, 1998). A notable example of this is that two-day old infants prefer their mother's face to a female stranger's (Bushnell, Sai, & Mullin, 1989; Walton, Bower, & Bower, 1992). Imprinting on the mother may be more critical to animals that are mobile soon after birth, such as Lorenz's geese, but it serves the problem of forming a lasting emotional bond between infant and caregiver. A generalization of infants' early preference for their parent's face is manifest also at three to four months of age, when they prefer faces of the same sex as their primary caregiver, whether male or female (Quinn, Yahr, Kuhn, Slater, & Pascalis, 2002). Imprinting may even affect mate preferences much later; men tend to facially resemble their wives' adoptive fathers (Bereczkai, Gyuris, & Weisfeld, 2004). That they prefer their adoptive fathers' appearance suggests that neither innate representations nor facial similarity to the self are involved, and gives some support to the imprinting hypothesis.

Differentiation, Unitization, and Attentional Weighting

Differentiation is the aspect of perceptual learning emphasized by Eleanor Gibson, who defined it as "extracting the information that specifies relevant events and narrowing down from a vast manifold of information to the minimal, optimal information that specifies the affordance…" (2003, p. 286). Given the vast amount of information in human faces, perceivers must extract that which is most useful for successful social interactions. Unitization and attentional weighting are two ways to reduce the manifold of stimulus information.

In *unitization,* perceptions that originally required detection of several parts are achieved by integrating the target features into a single unit. Face recognition is impaired when faces are inverted, suggesting that perceptual experience causes faces to be perceived as a configural unit that is disrupted by inversion (Bruce & Young, 1998). Interestingly, recognition of other-race faces is less impaired by inversion, indicating less unitization (Rhodes, Brake, Taylor, & Tan, 1989), which is already evident in preschoolers (Sangrigoli, Pallier, Argenti, Ventureyra, & de Schonen, 2005).

In *attentional weighting,* there is increased attention to relevant features, as well as a perceptual narrowing, whereby irrelevant features are not attended. This mechanism may contribute to unitization insofar as relational aspects of facial structure become weighted more than isolated features. Attentional weighting is illustrated by developmental changes in the ability to discriminate faces of monkeys and humans. Six-month-old human infants discriminate faces of different monkeys and different humans. However, nine-month-olds and adults ignore features that differentiate monkey faces and are only able to discriminate among human faces, which, of course, are the faces that need to be differentiated to successfully perceive social affordances (Dufour, Pascalis, & Petit, 2006; Quinn et al., 2002).

Attentional weighting also contributes to variations in differentiation among human faces. The other-race effect is a prime example of this. In adulthood, in childhood, and even by three months of age, people more easily recognize faces from familiar races, whereas those of an unfamiliar race tend to all look alike (Pezdek, Blandon-Gitlin, & Moore, 2003; Sangrigoli et al., 2005; Shapiro, 1986). This effect can be accounted for by greater *attentional weighting* of features that differentiate own-race faces (Furl et al., 2002; Rumelhart, Smolensky, McClelland, & Hinton, 1986). More specifically, Furl et al (2002) showed that the other-race effect can be simulated with a computational model that warps facial feature space as if it were a human with experience with one race. The greater weight given to features of familiar race A is reflected in face space by a local warping or expansion of the space that contains members of race A. Race B occupies relatively less volume in face space because the features that differentiate members of race B are either ignored or minimized. Such attentional weighting is flexible, as evidenced by a reversal of the other-race effect among Korean adults who were adopted into Caucasian families between the ages of three and nine (Sangrigoli et al., 2005). For these individuals, Korean faces are less differentiable than Caucasian ones. Moreover, reduced differentiation of other-race faces is somewhat penetrable; when attention is explicitly focused on variations in facial qualities, people are able to differentiate faces of outgroup members, although it unknown whether they do so using the same face processing mechanisms as for own-race faces (Hugenberg & Sczesny, 2006; Zebrowitz, Montepare, & Lee, 1993).

Just as people are better at differentiating among faces of their own race, so are they better at differentiating faces of their own age, sex, and sexual orientation. College-aged, middle-aged, and elderly participants, each showed better recognition of faces within their own age category (Anastasi & Rhodes, 2006), and men and women showed better recognition of own-sex faces (Cross, Cross, & Daly, 1971; Slone, Brigham, & Meissner, 2000). Men also better recall the faces of men who share their sexual orientation (Rule, Ambady, Adams, & Macrae, 2007). Like the own-race bias, these effects suggest that there is greater differentiation among faces of the types

of people with whom more social interaction occurs. However, research has not explicitly demonstrated greater *attentional weighting* of features that differentiate faces of one's own age, sex, or sexual orientation, like that suggested by the computational model of the face space that predicts own- and other-race recognition (Furl et al., 2002).

The own-race and own-age advantage in face recognition is also shown in emotion recognition. People are more accurate in judging the emotions of people from their own age group (Malatesta, Izard, Culver, & Nicolich, 1987). People also are more accurate in judging the emotions of people from racial and cultural groups with whom they have more perceptual experience. However, the attunements to emotional expression are more complex than a simple own-group advantage. Specifically, it appears that the own-group advantage is more marked when emotions are expressed differently in own- and other-group faces (Elfenbein, Beupré, Lévesque, & Hess, 2007), and it may derive in part from greater weighting of facial areas that are difficult to control by perceivers from cultures where concealing emotions is normative (Yuki, Maddux, & Masuda, 2007).

Differential attunement to the emotion information in own-race and own-age faces is consistent with the ecological theory emphasis on attunements in the service of perceiving adaptively relevant behavioral affordances, since it is most useful to perceive the emotions of those with whom we frequently interact. A nice illustration of the short-term development of attunements that reveal behavioral affordances is provided by research that exposed people to a series of faces, some of which were identified as "fair professors" and other of which were identified as "unfair professors." Subtle differences in face shape differentiated the fair and unfair professors. After viewing these faces, perceivers used facial shape to categorize new faces as fair or unfair although they were unaware of the facial cues that had differentiated the faces that served to develop their attunement (Hill, Lewicki, Czyzewska, & Schuller, 1990).

Prototype Extraction

In cognitive theories, a prototype is the mental representation of the central tendency of a category, which is like an average of the category members (Rosch, 1973). This differs from attentional weighting, since the central tendency of the category is an unweighted average of all of the feature dimensions. For example, many psychology researchers have an idea of what a greeble looks like (i.e., they have a greeble prototype), but cannot readily differentiate among greebles; those who are able to do so may differ from others in their attentional weighting of greeble features. Prototypes are important theoretical constructs in face perception, because they influence facial preferences, among other things. In particular, faces closer to the population prototype are judged more attractive (Bronstad, Langlois, & Russell, 2008a; Langlois & Roggman, 1990; Rhodes, 2006; Winkielman, Halberstadt, Fazendeiro, & Catty, 2006), and the own-race facial preferences that were discussed earlier (Zebrowitz, Bronstad, & Lee, 2007) may be explained, in part, by the fact that facial prototypes tend to differ for people of different races. Although the influence of prototypicality on preferences has been well documented, it is not clear why prototypes are preferred. Some candidate mechanisms include increased perceptual fluency for prototypes (Reber, Winkielman, & Schwarz, 1998), reduced negative affect, such as apprehension (Zajonc, 2001), and mate selection mechanisms (Halberstadt, 2006).

Research has demonstrated that we rapidly extract prototypes from the faces we view, contributing to flexible perceiver attunements. For example, after adults viewed several faces, they liked a prototype of these faces more than a prototype of faces they had not seen (Rhodes et al., 2001). Even infants appear to rapidly construct prototypes of faces they experience, reacting to an average of recently seen faces as if it were familiar (Rubenstein, Kalakanis, & Langlois, 1999). Different experiences with faces have noticeable influences early in life; infants prefer own-race faces only if they are living in a racially segregated environment (Bar-Haim, Ziv, Lamy, & Hodes, 2006). Long term effects of

experiences with particular faces also have been demonstrated. Specifically, affiliated individuals have more similar facial preferences than do strangers, presumably due in part to greater similarity in the prototypes extracted from the faces in their shared environment(Bronstad & Russell, 2007).

An interesting perceptual learning mechanism related to prototype extraction is the face adaptation aftereffect, which demonstrates a very rapid development of perceptual attunements. After briefly adapting to one face, perception of subsequent faces is biased relative to the adapting face. Adaptation effects can bias perception of face identity and sex (Leopold, O'Toole, Vetter, & Blanz, 2001; Webster, Kaping, Mizokami, & Duhamel, 2004), as well as preferences for faces. For example, when adults were briefly exposed to consistent distortions of normal faces, they experienced an aftereffect marked by a shift toward the distorted faces in which faces looked most normal and which faces looked most attractive (Rhodes, Jeffery, Watson, Clifford, & Nakayama, 2003). These aftereffects suggest that the average face—that is, the prototypical face—is used as a referent for coding facial appearance and that the prototype changes dynamically in response to external stimulation (cf. Clifford & Rhodes, 2005; Rhodes & Jeffery, 2006). The contribution of prototypicality to facial attractiveness is consistent with the previously cited evidence that averageness is one of the stimulus qualities that makes a face attractive. Short-term adaptation effects on face prototypicality also may explain the finding that short-term exposure to other-race faces increases the likability of other faces of that race (Zebrowitz, White, & Weineke, 2008). Although the prototypical face is malleable, the changes that short-term perceptual adaptation induces do not appear to be lasting.

Perceiver goals

There are other antecedents and consequences of attunements in addition to the effects of perceptual learning mechanisms. In particular, goal directed variations in attentional focus may attune perceivers to particular facial information, and these attunements may influence the perception of behavioral affordances. For example, dominant perceivers, with the goal of controlling others, may notice how assertive people are, whereas dependent perceivers, with the goal of eliciting support from others, may notice how affiliative the same individuals are (Battistich & Aronoff, 1985). People who live in cultures with a high incidence of parasites, who have a higher need to steer clear of unfit associates, show a stronger preference for physically attractive mates (Gangestad & Buss, 1993). Similarly, perceivers who feel more vulnerable to disease show more negative reactions to ethnic outgroups (Faulkner, Schaller, Park, & Duncan, 2004; Navarrete & Fessler, 2006). These studies have obvious implications for individual differences in the anomalous-face and familiar-face overgeneralization effects.

CONFLUENCE IN THE FACE PERCEPTION SYSTEM

The principal insight from ecological theory that face perception is focused on the detection of social affordances suggests that those faces that communicate similar affordances—be it due to their familiarity, emotion, or some other attribute—will elicit similar behavioral responses and be perceived via similar neural mechanisms. Interestingly, commonalities in responses to various types of faces are often tracked by commonalities in the stimulus information that defines them. As noted ealier, there are similarities in the facial configuration of faces varying in emotion and maturity, and these are paralleled by similarities in perceived affordances (Marsh et al., 2005a; Zebrowitz et al., 2007). There are also parallels in the facial structure and the behavioral affordances associated with emotion and sex (Becker et al., 2007; Zebrowitz et al., in press) and with sex and maturity (Friedman & Zebrowitz, 1992). Men, mature faces, and angry faces share similar facial structures and perceived affordances as do women, baby-faced, and fear or surprise faces. Similarities in perceived affordances may also track similarities in distance

from the average face. Principal components analysis (PCA) of the facial metrics of various face categories have shown that both disfigured and elderly faces are farther from the average face than are attractive faces (O'Toole et al., 1999; Bronstad, Zebrowitz, & Aharon, 2007). Own-race and less familiar other-race faces also are differently represented in face space (Caldara & Abdi, 2006; Furl et al., 2002), and it has been suggested that more familiar faces are closer to the average(Valentine, 1991). Thus, less likability is associated with faces that have facial metrics farther from the average in a perceiver's face space, be is due to attractiveness or familiarity or age.

Commonalities in the perceived affordances and stimulus information that differentiate various facial attributes have potential implications for the neural mechanisms involved in the perception of face familiarity, emotion, age, and attractiveness. To the extent that neural mechanisms have evolved to mirror the stimulus information provided in the perceiver's visual world, there may be mechanisms tuned to multiple facial attributes rather than a set of totally independent processes. Indeed, we have seen that, not only are the neural mechanisms for face perception spatially and temporally distributed, but also the mechanisms associated with perceiving some facial attributes have similar signatures. It would be interesting to determine whether perceiving the same behavioral affordance in faces marked by a particular emotion expression, age, familiarity or attractiveness level would give rise to a similar pattern of brain activation. Since babies, like fear expressions, are perceived as low in power, they may elicit similar patterns of activation as may happy faces and attractive faces, both of which are perceived as high in likability and power. Although some research suggests that emotion and personality trait judgments (of body movements) rely on at least partly distinct neural circuitry (Heberlein & Saxe, 2005), that research did not compare emotions and traits that specify the same affordances, such as fear and submissive or happy and likable. If basic facial qualities that share similar affordances elicit similar neural activation, then faces that resemble these basic qualities may do so as well, in keeping with the face overgeneralization hypotheses. Consistent with this suggestion, baby-faced men and babies, who communicate similar affordances, also elicit similar patterns of neural activation (Zebrowitz et al., 2009).

CONCLUSIONS

The ecological theory of face perception emphasizes the perception of behavioral *affordances*, and it views such perceptions as closely coupled to *action*. It predicts that reactions to faces that specify adaptively significant affordances will be *overgeneralized* to other faces that merely resemble them. It gives high priority to identifying the *stimulus information* to which perceivers respond, emphasizing the importance of dynamic and multimodal information. It also emphasizes the need to explain the development of perceivers' *attunements* to facial qualities. Research that embraces these ecological tenets can contribute much to our understanding of face perception.

The emphasis on perceiving affordances in faces suggests that many aspects of face perception are intertwined rather than independent, as suggested by the dual-process model. Placing a high priority on identifying the dynamic, multimodal stimulus information for face perception can enhance the face space model, and facilitate better prediction of evaluative and behavioral responses to particular faces. Focusing on the behavioral concomitants of face perception will move research into more ecologically valid settings, where the full breadth of attributes gleaned from faces can be better understood. Studying face perception in meaningful social interaction contexts also promises to provide a fuller understanding of the neural mechanisms that subserve this adaptively significant process. Finally, attention to perceiver differences in face perception beyond those accounted for by brain abnormalities will elucidate developmental processes that tune the perceptual system to particular facial qualities.

REFERENCES

Adams, R. B., Jr., Gordon, H. L., Baird, A. A., Ambady, N., & Kleck, R. E. (2003). Effects of gaze on amygdala sensitivity to anger and fear faces. *Science, 300*(5625), 1536.

Adolphs, R. (2006). Perception and emotion: How we recognize facial expressions. *Current Directions in Psychological Science, 15*(5), 222–226.

Adolphs, R., Sears, L., & Piven, J. (2001). Abnormal processing of social information from faces in autism. *Journal of Cognitive Neuroscience, 13*(2), 232–240.

Aharon, I., Etcoff, N., Ariely, D., Chabris, C. F., O'Connor, E., & Breiter, H. C. (2001). Beautiful faces have variable reward value: fMRI and behavioral evidence. *Neuron, 32*(3), 537–551.

Alley, T. R. (1983). Infant head shape as n elicitor of adult protection. *Merrill–Palmer Quarterly, 29*, 411–427.

Ambadar, Z., Schooler, J. W., & Cohen, J. F. (2005). Deciphering the enigmatic face: The importance of facial dynamics in interpreting subtle facial expressions. *Psychological Science, 16*, 403–410.

Anastasi, J. S., & Rhodes, M. G. (2006). Evidence for an own–age bias in face recognition. *North American Journal of Psychology, 8*, 237–252.

Andrzejewski, S. A., Hall, J. A., & Salib, E. R. (2007). Anti–semitism and identification of Jewish group membership from photographs. *Journal of Nonverbal Behavior, 33*(1), 47–58.

Aronoff, J., Barclay, A. M., & Stevenson, L. A. (1988). The recognition of threatening facial stimuli. *Journal of Personality and Social Psychology, 54*(4), 647–655.

Aronoff, J., Woike, B. A., & Hyman, L. M. (1992). Which are the stimuli in facial displays of anger and happiness? Configurational bases of emotion recognition. *Journal of Personality and Social Psychology, 62*, 1050–1066.

Bachmann, T., & Nurmoja, M. (2006). Are there affordances of suggestibility in facial appearance? *Journal of Nonverbal Behavior, 30*(2), 87–92.

Balaban, M. T. (1995). Affective influences on startle in five–month–old infants reactions to facial expressions of emotion. *Child Development, 58*, 28–36.

Bar–Haim, Y., Ziv, T., Lamy, D., & Hodes, R. M. (2006). Nature and Nurture in Own–Race Face Processing. *Psychological Science, 17*(2), 159–163.

Bar, M., & Neta, M. (2006). Humans Prefer Curved Visual Objects. *Psychological Science, 17*(8), 645–648.

Bar, M., & Neta, M. (2007). Visual elements of subjective preference modulate amygdala activation. *Neuropsychologia, 45*(10), 2191–2200.

Bassili, J. N. (1978). Facial motion in the perception of faces and of emotional expression. *Journal of Experimental Psychology: Human Perception and Performance, 4*(3), 373–379.

Bassili, J. N. (1979). Emotion recognition: The role of facial movement and the relative importance of upper and lower areas of the face. *Journal of Personality and Social Psychology, 37*(11), 2049–2058.

Battistich, V. A., & Aronoff, J. (1985). Perceiver, target, and situational influences on social cognition: An interactional analysis. *Journal of Personality and Social Psychology, 49*(3), 788–798.

Beauvois, J.-L., & Dubois, N. (2000). Affordances in social judgment: Experimental proof of why it is a mistake to ignore how others behave towards a target and look solely at how the target behaves. *Swiss Journal of Psychology – Zeitschrift fÄ¼r Psychologie – Revue Suisse de Psychologie, 59*(1), 16–33.

Becker, D. V., Kenrick, D. T., Neuberg, S. L., Blackwell, K. C., & Smith, D. M. (2007). The confounded nature of angry men and happy women. *Journal of Personality and Social Psychology, 92*(2), 179–190.

Bensafi, M., Pierson A., Rouby, C., Bertrand B., Vigouroux, M., Jouvent, R., & Holly, A. (2002). Modulation of visual event-related potentials by emotional olfactory stimuli. *Neurophysiologie Clinique-clinical Neurophysiology, 32*(6), 335–342.

Bereczkai, T., & Gyuris, Petra & Weisfeld, Glenn E. (2004). Sexual imprinting in human mate choice. *Proceedings of the Royal Society of London, Series B: Biological Sciences, 271*(1544), 1129–1134.

Berry, D. S. (1990). What can a moving face tell us? *Journal of Personality and Social Psychology, 58*(6), 1004–1014.

Berry, D. S., & McArthur, L. A. (1985). Some components and consequences of a babyface. *Journal of Personality and Social Psychology, 48*, 312–323.

Berry, D. S., & McArthur, L. A. (1986). Perceiving character in faces: The impact of age–related craniofacial changes on social perception. *Psychological Bulletin, 100*, 3–18.

Bidet–Caulet, A., Voisin, J., Bertrand, O., & Fonlupt, P. (2005). Listening to a walking human activates the temporal biological motion area *NeuroImage, 28*, 132–139.

Blair, I. V., Judd, C. M., & Chapleau, K. M. (2004). The influence of Afrocentric facial features in criminal sentencing. *Psychological Science, 15*(10), 674–679.

Blair, I. V., Judd, C. M., Sadler, M. S., & Jenkins, C. (2002). The role of Afrocentric features in person perception: Judging by features and categories. *Journal of Personality and Social Psychology, 83*(1), 5–25.

Bornstein, R. F. (1989). Exposure and affect: Overview and meta–analysis of research 1968–1987. *Psychological Bulletin, 106*, 265–289.

Bornstein, R. F. (1993). Mere exposure effects with outgroup stimuli. In D. M. Mackie & D. L. Hamilton (Eds.), *Affect, cognition, and stereotyping: Interactive processes in group perception.* (pp. 195–211). San Diego: Academic Press.

Bronstad, P. M., Langlois, J. H., & Russell, R. (2007). Classifying spatial patterns of brain activity associated with human face categories, poster presented at the Neural Systems of Social Behaviour Conference, Austin, Tx, May, 11–13.

Bronstad, P. M., & Russell, R. (2007). Beauty is in the "we" of the beholder: Greater agreement on facial attractiveness among close relations. *Perception, 36*, 1674–1681.

Bronstad, P. M., Zebrowitz, L. A., & Aharon, I. (2007). Classifying spatial patterns of brain activity associated with human face categories, poster presented at the Neural Systems of Social Behavior Conference, Austin, Tx, May, 11–13.

Brown, T. D., Jr., Dane, F. C., & Durham, M. D. (1998). Perception of race and ethnicity. *Journal of Social Behavior and Personality, 13*(2), 295–306.

Bruce, V., Burton, M., Doyle, T., & Dench, N. (1989). Further experiments on the perception of growth in three dimensions. *Perception and Psychophysics, 46*, 528–536.

Bruce, V., Valentine, T., & Baddeley, A. (1987). The basis of the 3/4 view advantage in face recognition. *Applied Cognitive Psychology, 1*(2), 109–120.

Bruce, V., Valentine, T., Gruneberg, M. M., Morris, P. E., & Sykes, R. N. (1988). When a nod's as good as a wink: The role of dynamic information in facial recognition. In *Practical aspects* of memory: Current research and issues, Vol. 1: Memory in everyday life. (pp. 169–174). New York: John Wiley & Sons.

Bruce, V., & Young, A. (1998). In the eye of the beholder: The science of face perception. New York: Oxford University Press.

Burnham, D. (1993). Visual recognition of mother by young infants: Facilitation by speech. Perception, 22(10), 1133–1153.

Busey, T. A., Wenger, M. J., & Townsend, J. T. (2001). Formal models of familiarity and memorability in face recognition. Mahwah, NJ: Erlbaum.

Bushnell, I. W., Sai, F., & Mullin, J. T. (1989). Neonatal recognition of the mother's face. British Journal of Developmental Psychology, 7(1), 3–15.

Caldara, R., & Abdi, H. (2006). Simulating the 'other–race' effect with autoassociative neural networks: Further evidence in favor of the face–space model. Perception, 35(5), 659–670.

Calder, A. J., Burton, A. M., Miller, P., Young, A. W., & Akamatsu, S. (2001). A principal component analysis of facial expressions. Vision Research, 41(9), 1179–1208.

Calder, A. J., & Young, A. W. (2005). Understanding the recognition of facial identity and facial expression. Nature Reviews Neuroscience, 6(8), 641–651.

Calder, A. J., Young, A. W., Keane, J., & Dean, M. (2000). Configural information in facial perception. Journal of Experimental Psychology: Human Perception and Performance, 26, 527–551.

Clifford, C. W. G. E., & Rhodes, G. E. (2005). Fitting the mind to the world : Adaptation and after-effects in high-level vision. Oxford: Oxford University Press.

Cohn, J. F., Ekman, P., Harrigan, J. A., Rosenthal, R., & Scherer, K. R. (2006). Measuring facial action. In The new handbook of methods in nonverbal behavior research. (pp. 9–64). New York: Oxford University Press.

Critchley, H., Daly, E., Phillips, M., Brammer, M., Bullmore, E., Williams, S., et al. (2000). Explicit and implicit neural mechanisms for processing of social information from facial expressions: a functional magnetic resonance imaging study. Human Brain Mapping, 9(2), 93–105.

Cross, J. F., Cross, J., & Daly, J. (1971). Sex, race, age, and beauty as factors in recognition of faces. Perception and Psychophysics, 10, 393–396.

Cuddy, A. J. C., & Fiske, S. T. (2002). Doddering but dear: Content, and functioning in stereotyping of older persons. In T. D. Nelson (Ed.), Ageism: Stereotyping and prejudice against older people (pp. 3–26). Cambridge, MA: MIT Press.

Cuddy, A. J. C., Norton, M. I., & Fiske, S. T. (2005). This Old Stereotype: The Pervasiveness and Persistence of the Elderly Stereotype. Journal of Social Issues, 61(2), 267–285.

Damasio, A. R., Tranel, D., Rizzo, M., & Mesulam, M. M. (2000). Disorders of complex visual processing. In Principles of behavioral and cognitive neurology (2nd ed.). (pp. 332–372): New York: Oxford University Press.

Deaner, R. O., Khera, A. V., & Platt, M. L. (2005). Monkeys pay per view: adaptive valuation of social images by rhesus macaques. Curr Biol, 15(6), 543–548.

DeBruine, L. (2002). Facial resemblance enhances trust. Proceedings of the Royal Society of London, Series B: Biological Sciences, 269, 1307–1312.

deGelder, B. (2006). Towards the neurobiology of emotional body language. Nature Reviews Neuroscience, 7, 242–249.

DePaulo, B. M., Blank, A. L., & Swaim, G. W. (1992). Expressiveness and expressive control. Personality and Social Psychology Bulletin, 18, 276–285.

DePaulo, B. M., & Rosenthal, R. (1978). Age changes in nonverbal decoding as a function of increasing amounts of information. Journal of Experimental Child Psychology, 26(2), 280–287.

Dufour, V., Pascalis, O., & Petit, O. (2006). Face processing limitation to own species in primates: a comparative study in brown capuchins, Tonkean macaques and humans. Behavioral Processes, 73, 107–113.

Eagly, A. H., Ashmore, R. D., Makhijani, M. G., & Longo, L. C. (1991). What is beautiful is good, but: A meta–analytic review of research on the physical attractiveness stereotype'. Psychological Bulletin, 110(1), 109–128.

Eberhardt, J. L., Davies, P. G., Purdie–Vaughns, V. J., & Johnson, S. L. (2006). Looking deathworthy: Perceived stereotypicality of black defendants predicts capital–sentencing outcomes. Psychological Science, 17(5), 383–386.

Eberhardt, J. L., Goff, P. A., Purdie, V. J., & Davies, P. G. (2004). Seeing Black: Race, Crime, and Visual Processing. Journal of Personality and Social Psychology, 87(6), 876–893.

Edwards, K. (1998). Temporal cues in facial expressions of emotion. *Psychological Science, 9,* 270–276.

Eibl–Eibesfeldt, I. (1989). *Human ethology.* New York: Aldine de Gruyter.

Ekman, P. (1971). Universals and cultural differences in facial expressions of emotion. *Nebraska Symposium on Motivation, 19,* 207–283.

Elfenbein, H. A., Beupré, M., Lévesque, M., & Hess, U. (2007). Toward a dialect theory: Cultural differences in the expression and recognition of posed facial expressions. *Emotion, 7,* 131–146.

Ellis, H. D., Young, A. W., & Koenken, G. (1993). Covert face recognition with prosopagnosia. *Behavioural Neurology, 6*(1), 27–32.

Enlow, D. H. (1990). *Facial Growth* (3rd ed.). philadelphia: Harcourt Brace.

Faulkner, J., Schaller, M., Park, J. H., & Duncan, L. A. (2004). Evolved disease–avoidance mechanisms and contemporary xenophobic attitudes. *Group Processes & Intergroup Relations, 7*(4), 333–353.

Feingold, A. (1992). Good–looking people are not what we think. *Psychological Bulletin, 111*(2).

Fitzgerald, D. A., Angstadt, M., Jelsone, L. M., Nathan, P. J., & Phan, K. L. (2006). Beyond threat: Amygdala reactivity across multiple expressions of facial affect. *NeuroImage, 30*(4), 1441–1448.

Folstad, I., & Karter, A. J. (1992). Parasites, bright males and the immunocompetence handicap. *American Naturalist, 139,* 603–622.

Friedman, H., & Zebrowitz, L. A. (1992). The contribution of typical sex differences in facial maturity to sex role stereotypes. *Personality & Social Psychology Bulletin, 18*(4), 430–438.

Frost, P. (1988). Human skin color: A possible relationship between its sexual dimorphism and its social perception. *Perspectives in Biology & Medicine, 32*(1), 38–58.

Furl, N., Phillips, P. J., & O'Toole, A. J. (2002). Face recognition algorithms and the other–race effect: Computational mechanisms for a developmental contact hypothesis. *Cognitive Science, 26*(6), 797–815.

Gangestad, S. W., & Buss, D. M. (1993). Pathogen prevalence and human mate preferences. *Ethology and Sociobiology, 14,* 89–96.

Gibson, E. J. (1969). *Principles of perceptual learning and development*: New York: Appleton–Century–Crofts.

Gibson, E. J. (2003). The world is so full of a number of things: On specification and perceptual learning. *Ecological Psychology, 15,* 283–287.

Gibson, J. J. (1966). *The senses considered as perceptual systems.* Oxford, England: Houghton Mifflin.

Gibson, J. J. (1979). *The ecological approach to visual perception.* Boston: Houghton Mifflin.

Goldstone, R. L. (1998). Perceptual learning. *Annual Review of Psychology, 49,* 585–612.

Gosselin, F., & Schyns, P. G. (2001). Bubbles: A technique to reveal the use of information in recognition tasks. *Perception, 41,* 2261–2271.

Griffin, A. M., & Langlois, J. H. (2006). Stereotype directionality and attractiveness stereotyping: Is beauty good or is ugly bad? *Social Cognition, 24*(2), 187–206.

Hadjikhani, N., & de Gelder, B. (2003). Seeing Fearful Body Expressions Activates the Fusiform Cortex and Amygdala. *Current Biology, 13*(24), 2201–2205.

Halberstadt, J. (2006). The Generality and Ultimate Origins of the Attractiveness of Prototypes. *Personality and Social Psychology Review, 10*(2), 166–183.

Hamm, N. H., Baum, M. R., & Nikels, K. W. (1975). Effects of race and exposure on judgments of interpersonal favorability. *Journal of Experimental Social Psychology, 11*(1), 14–24.

Harris, L., van den Bos, W., Fiske, S., McClure, S., & Cohen, J. (2007). *Neural Evidence for the Person Positivity Bias.* Paper presented at the Neural Systems of Social Behavior, Austin, Texas.

Hasselmo, M. E., Rolls, E. T., & Baylis, G. C. (1989). The role of expression and identity in the face-selective responses of neurons in the temporal visual cortex of the monkey. *Behavioural Brain Research, 32*(3), 203–218.

Haxby, J. V., Gobbini, M. I., Furey, M. L., Ishai, A., Schouten, J. L., & Pietrini, P. (2001). Distributed and overlapping representations of faces and objects in ventral temporal cortex. *Science, 293*(5539), 2425–2430.

Haxby, J. V., Hoffman, E. A., & Gobbini, M. I. (2002). Human neural systems for face recognition and social communication. *Biological Psychiatry, 51*(1), 59–67.

Heberlein, A. S., & Saxe, R. R. (2005). Dissociation between emotion and personality judgments: convergent evidence from functional neuroimaging. *NeuroImage,* 770–777.

Helfrich, H. (1979). Age markers in speech. In K. R. Scherer & H. Giles (Eds.), *Social markers in speech* (pp. 63–107). Cambridge: Cambridge University Press.

Henss, R. (1991). Perceiving age and attractiveness in facial photographs. *Journal of Applied Social Psychology, 21*(11), 933–946.

Hershler, O., & Hochstein, S. (2006). With a careful look: Still no low–level confound to face pop–out. *Vision Research, 46*(18), 3028–3035.

Hess, U., Adams, R. B., Jr., & Kleck, R. E. (2004). Facial Appearance, Gender, and Emotion Expression. *Emotion, 4*(4), 378–388.

Hess, U., Blairy, S., & Kleck, R. E. (2000). The influence of facial emotion displays, gender, and ethnicity on judgments of dominance and affiliation. *Journal of Nonverbal Behavior, 24,* 265–283.

Hill, H., Bruce, V., & Akamatsu, S. (1995). Perceiving the sex and race of faces: The role of shape and colour. *Proceedings of the Royal Society of London, Series B: Biological Sciences, 261,* 367–373.

Hill, H., & Johnston, A. (2001). Categorizing sex and identity from the biological motion of faces. *Current Biology, 11*(11), 880–885.

Hill, T., Lewicki, P., Czyzewska, M., & Schuller, G. (1990). The role of learned inferential encoding rules in the perception of faces: Effects of non-conscious self–perpetuation of a bias. *Journal of Experimental Social Psychology, 26,* 350–371.

Hooker, C. I., Paller, K. A., Gitelman, D. R., Parrish, T. B., Mesulam, M. M., & Reber, P. J. (2003). Brain networks for analyzing eye gaze. *Cognitive Brain Research, 17*(2), 406–418.

Hugenberg, K., & Sczesny, S. (2006). On wonderful women and seeing smiles: Social categorization moderates the happy face response latency advantage. *Social Cognition, 24*(5), 516–539.

Ito, T. A., & Cacioppo, J. T. (2000). Electrophysiological evidence of implicit and explicit categorization processes. *Journal of Experimental Social Psychology, 36*(6), 660–676.

Ito, T. A., Chiao, K. W., Devine, P. G., Lorig, T. S., & Cacioppo, T. (2006). The Influence of Facial Feedback on Race Bias. *Psychological Science, 17*(3), 256–261.

Ito, T. A., & Urland, G. R. (2003). Race and gender on the brain: Electrocortical measures of attention to the race and gender of multiply categorizable individuals. *Journal of Personality and Social Psychology, 85*(4), 616–626.

Izard, C. E. (1977). *Human emotions.* New York: Plenum Press.

Johnson, R. R. (2006). Confounding influences on police detection of suspiciousness. *Journal of Criminal Justice, 34*(4), 435–442.

Juslin, P. N., & Scherer, K. R. (2005). Vocal expression of affect. In J. A. Harrigan, R. Rosenthal & K. R. Scherer (Eds.), *The new handbook of methods in nonverbal behavior research.* (pp. 65–135). New York: Oxford University Press.

Kamachi, M., Hill, H., Lander, K., & Vatikiotis-Bateson, E. (2003). 'Putting the face to the voice': Matching identity across modality. *Current Biology, 13*(19), 1709–1714.

Kampe, K. K. W., Frith, C. D., Dolan, R. J., & Frith, U. (2001). Reward value of attractiveness and gaze. *Nature, 413*(6856), 589–590.

Kanwisher, N., McDermott, J., & Chun, M. M. (1997). The fusiform face area: A module in human extrastriate cortex specialized for face perception. *Journal of Neuroscience, 17*(11), 4302–4311.

Katz, D. B., Nicolelis, M. A., & Simon, S. A. (2002). Gustatory processing is dynamic and distributed. *Current Opinion in Neurobiology, 12*(4), 448–454.

Kawabata, H., & Zeki, S. (2004). Neural correlates of beauty. *Journal of Neurophysiology, 91*(4), 1699–1705.

Kiefer, M., Sim, E.-J., Liebich, S., Hauk, O., & Tanaka, J. (2007). Experience–dependent plasticity of conceptual representations in human sensory–motor areas. *Journal of Cognitive Neuroscience, 19*(3), 525–542.

Knoblich, G., & Sebanz, N. (2006). The social nature of perception and action. *Current Directions in Psychological Science, 15,* 99–104.

Knutson, B. (1996). Facial expressions of emotion influence interpersonal trait inferences. *Journal of Nonverbal Behavior, 20,* 165–182.

Kranz, F., & Ishai, A. (2006). Face perception is modulated by sexual preference. *Current Biology, 16,* 63–68.

Kuraoka, K. & Nakamura, K. (2007). Responses of single neurons in monkey amygdala to facial and vocal emotions. *Journal of Neurophysiology, 97*(2), 1379–1387.

LaBar, K. S., Crupain, M. J., Voyvodic, J. T., & McCarthy, G. (2003). Dynamic perception of facial affect and identity in the human brain. *Cerebral Cortex, 13*(10), 1023–1033.

Laird, J. D. (1974). Self–attribution of emotion: The effects of expressive behavior on the quality of emotional experience. *Journal of Personality and Social Psychology, 29*(4), 475–486.

Langlois, J. H., Kalakanis, L., Rubenstein, A. J., Larson, A., Hallam, M., & Smoot, M. (2000).

Maxims or myths of beauty? A meta-analytic and theoretical review. *Psychological Bulletin, 126,* 390–423.

Langlois, J. H., & Roggman, L. A. (1990). Attractive faces are only average. *Psychological Science, 1*(2), 115–121.

Lanzetta, J. T., & Orr, S. P. (1981). Stimulus properties of facial expressions and their influence on the classical conditioning of fear. *Motivation and Emotion, 5*(3), 225–234.

LeDoux, J. (2007, May 17). *Fearful brains in an anxious world.* Paper presented at the Eleventh International Conference on Cognitive and Neural Systems, Boston, MA.

Lee, K. J., Byatt, G., & Rhodes, G. (2000). Caricature effects, distinctiveness, and identification: Testing the face–space framework. *Psychological Science, 11,* 379–385.

Leopold, D. A., O'Toole, A. J., Vetter, T., & Blanz, V. (2001). Prototype-referenced shape encoding revealed by high–level aftereffects. *Nature Neuroscience, 4*(1), 89–94.

Levin, D. T. (2000). Race as a visual feature: Using visual search and perceptual discrimination tasks to understand face categories and the cross-race recognition deficit. *Journal of Experimental Psychology: General, 129*(4), 559–574.

Lewicki, P. (1985). Nonconscious biasing effects of single instances on subsequent judgments. *Journal of Personality and Social Psychology, 48,* 563–574.

Lewis, M. B. (2004). Face–space–R: Towards a unified account of face recognition. *Visual Cognition, 11*(1), 29–69.

Lewis, S., Thoma, R. J., Lanoue, M. D., Miller, G. A., Heller, W., Edgar, C., et al. (2003). Visual processing of facial affect. *Neuroreport, 14*(14), 1841–1845.

Liang, X., Zebrowitz, L. A., & Aharon, I. (2009). Effective connectivity between amygdala and orbitofrontal cortex differentiates the perception of facial expressions. *Social Neuroscience, 4,* 185–196.

Liang, X., Zebrowitz, L. A., & Zhang, Y. (in press). Neural Activation in the 'Reward Circuit' Shows a Nonlinear Response to Facial Attractiveness. *Social Neuroscience.*

Livingston, R. W., & Brewer, M. B. (2002). What are we really priming? Cue–based versus category–based processing of facial stimuli. *Journal of Personality and Social Psychology, 82*(1), 5–18.

Luevano, V. X. (2007). *Truth in Advertising: The Relationship of Facial Appearance to Apparent and Actual Health Across the Lifespan.* Unpublished Ph.D., Brandeis University, Waltham.

Lundqvist, D., Ohman, A., Barrett, L. F., Niedenthal, P. M., & Winkielman, P. (2005). *Caught by the Evil Eye: Nonconscious Information Processing, Emotion, and Attention to Facial Stimuli.* New York: Guilford Press.

Maddox, K. B. (2004). Perspectives on Racial Phenotypicality Bias. *Personality and Social Psychology Review, 8*(4), 383–401.

Malatesta, C. Z., Izard, C. E., Culver, C., & Nicolich, M. (1987). Emotion communication skills in young, middle–aged, and older women. *Psychology and Aging, 2,* 193–203.

Maner, J. K., Gailliot, M. T., & DeWall, C. N. (2007). Adaptive attentional attunement: evidence for mating–related perceptual bias. *Evolution and Human Behavior, 28*(1), 28–36.

Mark, L. E., & Todd, J. T. (1983). The perception of growth in three dimensions. *Perception and Psychophysics, 33,* 193–196.

Mark, L. S., Todd, J. T., & Shaw, R. E. (1981). Perception of growth: A geometric analysis of how different styles of change are distinguished. *Journal of Experimental Psychology: Human Perception and Performance, 7*(4), 855–868.

Marsh, A. A., Adams, R. B., Jr., & Kleck, R. E. (2005a). Why Do Fear and Anger Look the Way They Do? Form and Social Function in Facial Expressions. *Personality and Social Psychology Bulletin, 31*(1), 73–86.

Marsh, A. A., Ambady, N., & Kleck, R. E. (2005b). The effects of fear and anger facial expressions on approach and avoidance related behaviors. *Emotion, 5,* 119–124.

Mason, M. F., Cloutier, J., & Macrae, C. N. (2006). On construing others: Category and stereotype activation from facial cues. *Social Cognition, 24*(5), 540–562.

McArthur, L. Z., & Apatow, K. (1983). Impressions of baby-faced adults. *Social Cognition, 2,* 315–342.

McArthur, L. Z., & Baron, R. M. (1983). Toward an ecological theory of social perception. *Psychological Review, 90,* 215–238.

McKone, E., Kanwisher, N., & Duchaine, B. C. (2007). Can generic expertise explain special processing for faces? *Trends in Cognitive Sciences, 11*(1), 8–15.

Meissner, C. A., & Brigham, J. C. (2001). Thirty years of investigating the own–race bias in memory for faces: A meta-analytic review. *Psychology, Public Policy, and Law, 7*(1), 3–35.

Mignon, A., & Mollaret, P. (2002). Applying the affordance conception of traits: A person perception study. *Personality and Social Psychology Bulletin, 28*(10), 1327–1334.

Mitchell, J. P., Neil Macrae, C., & Banaji, M. R. (2005). Forming impressions of people versus inanimate objects: Social–cognitive processing in the medial prefrontal cortex. *NeuroImage, 26*(1), 251–257.

Miyake, K., & Zuckerman, M. (1993). Beyond Personality Impressions: Effects of Physical and Vocal Attractiveness on False Consensus, Social Comparison, Affiliation, and Assumed and perceived Similarity. *Journal of Personality, 61*(3), 411–437.

Montepare, J. M., & Dobish, H. (2003). The contribution of emotion perceptions and their over-generalizations to trait impressions. *Journal of Nonverbal Behavior, 27,* 237–254.

Montepare, J. M., & Zebrowitz–McArthur, L. (1988). Impressions of people created by age–related qualities of their gaits. *Journal of Personality and Social Psychology, 55*(4), 547–556.

Montepare, J. M., & Zebrowitz, L. A. (1998). "Person perception comes of age": The salience and significance of age in social judgments. In M. Zanna (Ed.), *Advances in Experimental Social Psychology* (vol. 30) (pp. 93–163). San Diego: Academic Press.

Morrison, E. R., Gralewski, L., Campbell, N., & Penton–Voak, I. S. (2007). Facial movement varies by sex and is related to attractiveness. *Evolution and Human Behavior, 28*(3), 186–192.

Myowa–Yamakoshi, M., Yamaguchi, M. K., Tomonaga, M., Tanaka, M., & Matsuzawa, T. (2005). Development of face recognition in infant chimpanzees (Pan troglodytes). *Cognitive Development, 20*(1), 49–63.

Nakayama, K. (1994). James J Gibson–An appreciation. *Psychological Review, 101,* 329–335.

Navarrete, C. D., & Fessler, D. M. T. (2006). Disease avoidance and ethnocentrism: the effects of disease vulnerability and disgust sensitivity on intergroup attitudes. *Evolution and Human Behavior, 27*(4), 270–282.

Niedenthal, P. M. (2007). Embodying emotion. *Science, 316,* 1002–1005.

O'Doherty, J., Winston, J., Critchley, H., Perrett, D., Burt, D. M., & Dolan, R. J. (2003). Beauty in a smile: The role of medial orbitofrontal cortex in facial attractiveness. *Neuropsychologia, 41*(2), 147–155.

O'Toole, A. J., Roark, D. A., & Abdi, H. (2002). Recognizing moving faces: A psychological and neural synthesis. *Trends in Cognitive Sciences, 6*(6), 261–266.

O'Toole, A. J., Wenger, M. J., & Townsend, J. T. (2001). Quantitative models of perceiving and remembering faces: Precedents and possibilities. In M. J. Wenger & J. T. Townsend (Eds.), *Computational, geometric, and process perspectives on facial cognition: Contexts and challenges.* (pp. 1–38). Mahwah, NJ: Erlbaum.

O'Toole, A. J., Price, T., Vetter T, Bartlett, J. C., & Blanz, V. (1999). 3D shape and 2D surface textures of human faces: The role of "averages" in attractiveness and age. *Imaging and Vision Computing, 18*(1), 9–19.

Ohman, A., & Dimberg, U. (1978). Facial expressions as conditioned stimuli for electrodermal responses: A case of 'preparedness'? *Journal of Personality and Social Psychology, 36*(11), 1251–1258.

Olson, I. R., & Marshuetz, C. (2005). Facial Attractiveness Is Appraised in a Glance. *Emotion, 5*(4), 498–502.

Orr, S. P., & Lanzetta, J. T. (1984). Extinction of an emotional response in the presence of facial expressions of emotion. *Motivation and Emotion, 8*(1), 55–66.

Palermo, R., & Rhodes, G. (2007). Are you always on my mind? A review of how face perception and attention interact. *Neuropsychologia, 45*(1), 75–92.

Pelphrey, K. A., Morris, J. P., Michelich, C. R., Allison, T., & McCarthy, G. (2005). Functional anatomy of biological motion perception in posterior temporal cortex: An fMRI study of eye, mouth and hand movements. *Cerebral Cortex, 15*(12), 1866–1876.

Pentland, B., Pitcairn, T. K., Gray, J. M., & Riddle, W. J. R. (1987). The effects of reduced expression in Parkinson's disease on impression formation by health professionals. *Clinical Rehabilitation, 1,* 307–313.

Peters, M., Rhodes, G., & Simmons, L. W. (2007). Contributions of the face and body to overall attractiveness. *Animal Behaviour, 73*(6), 937–942.

Pezdek, K., Blandon–Gitlin, Iris, & Moore, Catherine. (2003). Children's face recognition memory: More evidence for the cross–race effect. *Journal of Applied Psychology, 88*(4), 760–763.

Pike, G. E., Kemp, R. I., Towell, N. A., & Phillips, K. C. (1997). Recognizing moving faces: The relative contribution of motion and perspective view information. *Visual Cognition, 4*(4), 409–437.

Pittenger, J. B., Shaw, R. E., & Mark, L. S. (1979). Perceptual information for the age–level of faces as a higher order invariant of growth. *Journal of Experimental Psychology: Human Perception and Performance, 5*(478–493).

Prodan, C., Orbelo, D., Testa, J., & Ross, E. (2001). Hemispheric differences in recognizing upper and lower facial displays of emotion. *Neuropsychiatry, Neuropsychology, & Behavioral Neurology, 14*(4), 206–212.

Quinn, K. A., & Macrae, C. N. (2005). Categorizing Others: The Dynamics of Person Construal. *Journal of Personality and Social Psychology, 88*(3), 467–479.

Quinn, P. C., Westerlund, A., & Nelson, C. A. (2006). Neural Markers of Categorization in 6–Month–Old Infants. *Psychological Science, 17*(1), 59–66.

Quinn, P. C., Yahr, J., Kuhn, A., Slater, A. M., & Pascalis, O. (2002). Representation of the gender of human faces by infants: A preference for female. *Perception, 31*(9), 1109–1121.

Reber, R., Winkielman, P., & Schwarz, N. (1998). Effects of perceptual fluency on affective judgments. *Psychological Science, 9*(1), 45–48.

Reis, H. T., Wilson, I. M., Monestere, C., Bernstein, S., Clark, K., Seidl, E., et al. (1990). What is smiling is beautiful and good. *European Journal of Social Psychology, 20*, 259–267.

Rhodes, G. (2006). The evolutionary psychology of facial beauty. *Annual Review of Psychology, 57*, 199–226.

Rhodes, G., Brake, S., Taylor, K., Tan, S. (1989). Expertise and configural coding in face recognition. *British Journal of Psychology, 80*(3), 313–331.

Rhodes, G., Brennan, S., & Carey, S. (1987). Identification and ratings of caricatures: Implications for mental representations of faces. *Cognitive Psychology, 19*(4), 473–497.

Rhodes, G., Halberstadt, J., & Brajkovich, G. (2001). Generalization of mere exposure effects to averaged composite faces. *Social Cognition, 19*(1), 57–70.

Rhodes, G., & Jeffery, L. (2006). Adaptive norm-based coding of facial identity. *Vision Research, 46*(18), 2977–2987.

Rhodes, G., Jeffery, L., Watson, T. L., Clifford, C. W. G., & Nakayama, K. (2003). Fitting the mind to the world: Face adaptation and attractiveness aftereffects. *Psychological Science, 14*(6), 558–566.

Riggio, R. E., & Friedman, H. (1986). Impression formation:The role of expressive behavior. *Journal of Personality and Social Psychology, 50*, 421–427.

Rosch, E. H. (1973). Natural categories. *Cognitive Psychology, 4*, 328–350.

Rosenberg, S., Nelson, C., & Vivekananthan, P. S. (1968). A multidimensional approach to the structure of personality impressions *Journal of Personality and Social Psychology, 9*(4), 283–294.

Rubenstein, A. J., Kalakanis, L., & Langlois, J. H. (1999). Infant preferences for attractive faces: a cognitive explanation. *Developmental Psychology, 15*, 848–855.

Rule, N. O., Ambady, N., Adams, R. B., & Macrae, C. N. (2007). Us and them: Memory advantages in perceptually ambiguous groups. *Psychonomic Bulletin & Review, 14*, 687–692.

Rumelhart, D. E., Smolensky, P., McClelland, J. L., & Hinton, G. E. (1986). Schemata and sequential thought processes in PDP models. In D. E. R. J. L. McClelland & P. D. P. R. G. the (Eds.), *Parallel Distributed Processing* (Vol. 2). Cambridge, MA: MIT Press.

Sadr, J., Jarudi, I., & Sinha, P. (2003). The role of eyebrows in face recognition. *Perception, 32*(3), 285–293.

Said CP, Sebe N, Todorov A. (2009). Structural Resemblance to Emotional Expressions Predicts Evaluation of Emotionally Neutral Faces. *Emotion, 9*(2), 260–264.

Sangrigoli, S., Pallier, C., Argenti, A. M., Ventureyra, V. A. G., & de Schonen, S. (2005). Reversibility of the Other–Race Effect in Face Recognition During Childhood. *Psychological Science, 16*(6), 440–444.

Sato, W., & Yoshikawa, S. (2004). The dynamic aspects of emotional facial expressions. *Cognition & Emotion, 18*(5), 701–710.

Sato, W., & Yoshikawa, S. (2007). Enhanced experience of emotional arousal in response to dynamic facial expressions. *Journal of Nonverbal Behavior, 31*, 119–135.

Scheib, J. E., Gangestad, S. W., & Thornhill, R. (1999). Facial attractiveness, symmetry, and cues to good genes. *Proceedings of the Royal Society of London, Series B: Biological Sciences, 266*, 1913–1917.

Schneider, F., Heimann, H., Himer, W., & Huss, D. (1990). Computer-based analysis of facial action in schizophrenic and depressed patients. *European Archives of Psychiatry and Clinical Neuroscience, 240*(2), 67–76.

Secord, P. (1958). Facial features and inference processes in interpersonal perception. In R. Tagiuri & L. Petrullo (Eds.), *Person Perception and Interpersonal Behavior* (pp. 300–315). Stanford, CA: Stanford University Press.

Shapiro, P. P., S. (1986). Meta-analysis of facial identification studies. *Psychological bulletin, 100*(13), 156.

Shaw, R., & Pittenger, J. (Eds.). (1977). *Perceiving the face of change in changing faces: Implications for a theory of object perception.* Hillsdale, NJ: Erlbaum.

Slone, A., Brigham, J., & Meissner, C. (2000). Social and cognitive factors affecting the own-race bias in Whites. *Basic and Applied Social Psychology, 22*, 71–84.

Smith, M. L., Cottrell, G. W., Gosselin, F, & Schyns (2005). Transmitting and coding facial expressions. *Psychological Science, 16*(3) 184–189.

Smith, L., Muir, D., Pascalis, O., & Slater, A. (2003). Infant perception of dynamic faces: Emotion, inversion and eye direction effects. In *The development of face processing in infancy and early childhood: Current perspectives.* (pp. 119–130): Nova Science Publishers.

Sommerville, J. A., & Decety, J. (2006). Weaving the fabric of social interaction: Articulating developmental psychology and cognitive neuroscience in the domain of motor cognition. *Psychonomic Bulletin & Review, 13*(2), 179–200.

Stenberg, G., Wiking, S., & Dahl, M. (1998). Judging words at face value: Interference in a word processing task reveals automatic processing of affective facial expressions. *Cognition & Emotion, 12*(6), 755–782.

Stevenage, S. V. (1998). Which twin are you? A demonstration of induced categorical perception of identical twin faces. *British Journal of Psychology, 89*, 39–57.

Strom, M., Zhang, S., Zebrowitz, L. A., Bronstad, P. M., & Lee, H. K. (2008). *Race-related Facial Qualities Contribute to Stereotyping by White, Black, and Korean Judges.* Unpublished manuscript, Waltham, MA.

Thornhill, R., & Gangestad, S. W. (1999). Facial attractiveness. *Trends in Cognitive Sciences, 3*(12), 452–460.

Todd, J. T., Mark, L. S., Shaw, R. E., & Pittenger, J. B. (1980). The perception of human growth. *Scientific American, 24*, 106–114.

Vaish, A., & Striano, T. (2004). Is visual reference necessary? Contributions of facial versus vocal cues in 12-month-olds' social referencing behavior. *Developmental Science, 7*(3), 261–269.

Valentine, T. (1991). A unified account of the effects of distinctiveness, inversion, and race in face recognition. *The Quarterly Journal of Experimental Psychology A: Human Experimental Psychology, 43*(2), 161–204.

Vuilleumier, P., & Pourtois, G. (2007). Distributed and interactive brain mechanisms during emotion face perception: Evidence from functional neuroimaging. *Neuropsychologia, 45*(1), 174–194.

Wager, T. D., Barrett, L. F., Bliss-Moreau, E., Lindquist, K., Duncan, S., Kober, H., et al. (2007). *The neuroimaging of emotion.* New York: Columbia University.

Wagner, H. L., MacDonald, C. J., & Manstead, A. S. (1986). Communication of individual emotions by spontaneous facial expressions. *Journal of Personality and Social Psychology, 50*(4), 737–743.

Walton, G. E., Bower, N. J., & Bower, T. G. (1992). Recognition of familiar faces by newborns. *Infant Behavior & Development, 15*, 265–269.

Walton, J. H., & Orlikoff, R. F. (1994). Speaker race identification from acoustic cues in the vocal signal. *Journal of Speech & Hearing Research, 37*(4), 738–745.

Webster, M. A., Kaping, D., Mizokami, Y., Duhamel, P. (2004). Adaptation to natural facial categories. *Nature 428*(6982), 557–561.

Wehrle, T., Kaiser, S., Schmidt, S., & Scherer, K. R. (2000). Studying the dynamics of emotional expression using synthesized facial muscle movements. *Journal of Personality and Social Psychology, 78*(1), 105–119.

Wiggins, J. S. (1996). An informal history of the interpersonal circumplex tradition. *Journal of Personality Assessment, 66*, 217–233.

Willis, J., & Todorov, A. (2006). First Impressions: Making Up Your Mind After a 100-Ms Exposure to a Face. *Psychological Science, 17*(7), 592–598.

Winkielman, P., Halberstadt, J., Fazendeiro, T., & Catty, S. (2006). Prototypes are attractive because they are easy on the mind. *Psychological Science, 17*, 799–806.

Winston, J. S., O'Doherty, J., Kilner, J. M., Perrett, D. I., & Dolan, R. J. (2007). Brain systems for assessing facial attractiveness. *Neuropsychologia, 45*(1), 195–206.

Xiaohu, P., Yuejia, L., Xing, W., Guofeng, W., & Jinghan, W. (2003). The mechanism of other race effect between Eastern and Western faces revealed by electrophysiology study. *Acta Psychologica Sinica, 35*(1), 49–55.

Yoshikawa, S., & Sato, W. (2006). Enhanced perceptual, emotional, and motor processing in response to dynamic facial expressions of emotion. *Japanese Psychological Research, 48*(3), 213–222.

Young, A. W., Hellawell, D., & Hay, D. C. (1987). Configural information in face perception. *Perception, 28*, 141–145.

Yovel, G., Levy, J., Grabowecky, M., & Paller, K. A. (2003). Neural correlates of the left-visual-field superiority in face perception appear at multiple stages of face processing. *J Cogn Neurosci, 15*(3), 462–474.

Yuki, M., Maddux, W. W., & Masuda, T. (2007). Are the windows to the soul the same in the East and West? Cultural differences in using the eyes and mouth as cues to recognize emotions in Japan and the United States. *Journal of Experimental Social Psychology, 43*(2), 303–311.

Zajonc, R. B. (1968). Attitudinal effects of mere exposure. *Journal of Personality and Social Psychology, 9(2, PT. 2)*, 1–27.

Zajonc, R. B. (2001). Mere exposure: A gateway to the subliminal. *Current Directions in Psychological Science, 10*(6), 224–228.

Zebrowitz, L. A. (1996). Physical appearance as a basis of stereotyping. In N. MacRae, M. Hewstone, & C. Stangor (Eds.) *Foundations of stereotypes and stereotyping*, 79–120. New York: Guilford Press.

Zebrowitz, L. A. (1997). *Reading faces: Window to the soul?* Boulder, Colo.: Westview Press.

Zebrowitz, L. A. (2006). Finally, faces find favor. *Social Cognition, 24*(5), 657–701.

Zebrowitz, L. A., Andreoletti, C., Collins, M. A., Lee, S. Y., & Blumenthal, J. (1998). Bright, bad, babyfaced boys: appearance stereotypes do not always yield self–fulfilling prophecy effects. *J Pers Soc Psychol, 75*(5), 1300–1320.

Zebrowitz, L. A., Barglow, J., Bronstad, P. M., & Lee, H. K. (2008). Contribution of Skin Tone to White, Black, and Korean Judges' Impressions of Own and Other-Race Faces. Unpublished Manuscript. Brandeis University.

Zebrowitz, L. A., Bronstad, P. M., & Lee, H. K. (2007a). The contribution of face familiarity

to ingroup favoritism and stereotyping. *Social Cognition, 25*, 306–338.

Zebrowitz, L. A., & Collins, M. A. (1997). Accurate social perception at zero acquaintance: The affordances of a Gibsonian approach. *Personality and Social Psychology Review, 1*, 204–223.

Zebrowitz, L. A., Collins, M. A., & Dutta, R. (1998). The relationship between appearance and personality across the life span. *Personality & Social Psychology Bulletin, 24*(7), 736–749.

Zebrowitz, L. A., Kikuchi, M., & Fellous, J. M. (in press). Facial Resemblance to Emotions: Group Differences, Impression Effects, and Race Stereotypes. *Journal of Personality and Social Psychology*.

Zebrowitz, L. A., Fellous, J. M., Mignault, A., & Andreoletti, C. (2003). Trait impressions as overgeneralized responses to adaptively significant facial qualities: Evidence from connectionist modeling. *Personality and Social Psychology Review, 7*(3), 194–215.

Zebrowitz, L. A., Hall, J. A., Murphy, N. A., & Rhodes, G. (2002). Looking smart and looking good: Facial cues to intelligence and their origins. *Personality and Social Psychology Bulletin, 28*(2), 238–249.

Zebrowitz, L. A., Kikuchi, M., & Fellous, J.-M. (2007). Are effects of emotion expression on trait impressions mediated by babyfaceness? Evidence from connectionist modeling. *Personality and Social Psychology Bulletin, 33*(5), 648–662.

Zebrowitz, L. A., Kikuchi, M., & Fellous, J. M.(in press). Facial Resemblance to Emotions: Group Differences, Impression Effects, and Race Stereotypes. *Journal of Personality and Social Psychology*.

Zebrowitz, L. A., & Lee, S. Y. (1999). Appearance, stereotype incongruent behavior, and social relationships. *Personality and Social Psychology Bulletin, 25*, 569–584.

Zebrowitz, L. A., Luevano, V. X., Bronstad, P. M., & Aharon, I. (2009). Neural activation to babyfaced men matches activation to babies. *Journal of Social Neuroscience, 4*, 185–196.

Zebrowitz, L. A., & Montepare, J. M. (1992). Impressions of babyfaced individuals across the life span. *Developmental Psychology, 28*(6), 1143–1152.

Zebrowitz, L. A., & Montepare, J. M. (2006). The ecological approach to person perception: Evolutionary roots and contemporary offshoots. In M. Schaller, J. A. Simpson & D. T. Kenrick (Eds.), *Evolution and Social Psychology* (pp. 81–113). New York: Psychology Press.

Zebrowitz, L. A., Montepare, J. M., & Lee, H. K. (1993). They don't all look alike: Individual impressions of other racial groups. *Journal of Personality and Social Psychology, 65*(1), 85–101.

Zebrowitz, L. A., & Rhodes, G. (2002). Nature let a hundred flowers bloom: The multiple ways and wherefores of attractiveness. In G. Rhodes & L. A. Zebrowitz (Eds.), *Facial attractiveness: Evolutionary, cognitive, and social perspectives. Advances in visual cognition* (Vol. 1, pp. 261–293). Westport, CT: Ablex.

Zebrowitz, L. A., & Rhodes, G. (2004). Sensitivity to "Bad Genes" and the Anomalous Face Overgeneralization Effect: Cue Validity, Cue Utilization, and Accuracy in Judging Intelligence and Health. *Journal of Nonverbal Behavior, 28*(3), 167–185.

Zebrowitz, L. A., Voinescu, L., & Collins, M. A. (1996). "Wide-eyed" and "crooked-faced": Determinants of perceived and real honesty across the life span. *Personality and Social Psychology Bulletin, 22*(12), 1258–1269.

Zebrowitz, L. A., White, B., & Weineke, K. (2008). Mere exposure and racial prejudice: Exposure to other-race faces increases liking for strangers of that race. *Social Cognition, 26,* 259–275.

Zhang, Y. (2007). Perceiving is for doing: exploring the approach–avoidance predispositions of face perception. Unpublished Unpublished manuscript. Brandeis University.

Zhang, Y., Zebrowitz, L. A., & Aharon, I. (2007). *Neural Substrates of Perceiving Variations in Facial Attractiveness.* Paper presented at the Organization for Human Brain Mapping, Chicago, IL, June 10–14, 2007.

Zuckerman, M., Miyake, K., & Hodgins, H. S. (1991). Cross-Channel Effects of Vocal and Physical Attractiveness and Their Implications for Interpersonal Perception. *Journal of Personality & Social Psychology, 60*(4), 545–554.

CHAPTER 2

The Cognitive Capitalist: Social Benefits of Perceptual Economy

Douglas Martin and C. Neil Macrae

"While the miser is merely a capitalist gone mad, the capitalist is a rational miser." (Karl Marx, 1818-1883).

Of all the challenges we face as humans there is probably none more intricate than that of traversing the labyrinth of our social world. From the moment we are born until the moment we die, our social sphere becomes increasingly complex as we continually expand the sum of our social knowledge. Thankfully, we have an innate talent for processing all of this social information, and, without trying, we begin collecting, organizing, and storing it in order to guide our interactions with other people. That we are rarely aware of any of this is testament to the proficiency of our keenly evolved social brains. In this chapter we will explore the perceptual processes that support the extraction of social information from faces and how these fit within extant models of social cognition.

In the last 25 years, one of the most influential interpretations of the way we use social information in our everyday lives is the characterization of humans as social "cognitive misers" (Fiske & Taylor, 1984). The cognitive-miser interpretation of human behaviour is based on the premise that because we cannot possibly process every aspect of the perceptual array, we are forced instead to process a limited amount of information in a strategic manner. It is posited that we spend much of our time trying to save cognitive energy by using heuristics or cognitive shortcuts, only actually engaging in more substantial cognitive exertion in situations when we are particularly motivated to and have the spare capacity to do so.

One consequence of our status as cognitive misers is that, under certain circumstances, we engage in assiduous and elaborative attempts to understand other people based on their unique characteristics (individuation); whereas, in other situations, we are content to evaluate them based on our knowledge of information associated with the social categories to which we perceive they belong (categorization). There is broad consensus that we frequently rely on categorical information, often in the form of social stereotypes (e.g., Matt is a Scotsman, therefore, he eats haggis, drinks whisky, but never buys a drink for anyone else), rather than engaging in the more demanding process of individuation (e.g., Matt is a Scotsman who is vegan, is a tea-totaler, and is considered a generous and giving person by his friends). The very nature of our social experience is somewhat dependent on whether we employ categorical or individuated processing when construing other people because it not only affects the way we perceive others but also how we are perceived ourselves (see Brewer, 1988; Fiske & Neuberg, 1990). It is, therefore, unsurprising that understanding when and why we employ each strategy has become an issue of great theoretical and functional importance in social psychology.

The idea that we drift through large chunks of our social lives in a cognitive torpor, unwilling to view every person we encounter as a truly unique individual, is something that makes many of us feel uncomfortable. We do not like the idea that we are instinctively lazy, particularly if this means we tend to define other people in a crude manner based on characteristics associated with the groups they belong to, rather than building a more refined image based on the traits they actually possess. We would rather see ourselves as reasonable, egalitarian individuals, able to rise above any inclination to engage in processing based on such social stereotypes. It seems, however, even a nodding acceptance of the cognitive-miser metaphor means accepting that we all rely heavily on stereotypic categorical information; as Gilbert and Hixon (1991) succinctly state "A stereotype is the sluggard's best friend" (p. 509). Is it possible, however, that we are not driven to view people in a categorical manner because we are lazy but instead because we are capitalizing on a skill at which we excel? We believe this may indeed be the case and that the sheer efficiency and accuracy with which we extract social information from faces may be key in this regard.

Daily experience attests that even the briefest of glances at a face is sufficient to furnish information about the sex, age, race, and emotional status of its owner (Bruce & Young, 1986). We rarely expend time and energy in trying to understand the diverse array of perceptual signals we receive from viewing a face. Instead we expertly extract and use face information in a demonstrably automatic and often nonconscious fashion, leaving us free to deliberate other issues (Fiske & Taylor, 1984; Taylor, 1981). Imagine how demanding life would be if you had to spend your time consciously trying to extract information from the faces you encounter. What would your first week at university have been like if every time you encountered a new person you had to make deliberative judgements about their sex, age, race, attractiveness, and current mood? Just sitting in a lecture hall surrounded by other students would prove as cognitively demanding as even the most complex course in combined brain surgery and rocket science. But does our automatic face-processing expertise come at a high price? Certainly our ability to accurately perceptually construe other people is integrally entwined with our use of categorical (stereotyped) information. But does this mean that automatic face processing is another facet of the cognitive miser, whereby we have a propensity to perceptually categorize but not individuate people?

On the surface the manner in which we extract information from faces could be considered another example of humans behaving as social cognitive misers. Research into the efficacy of eye-witness testimony has demonstrated that while bystanders rarely make identification errors in the sex or race of perpetrators they often have considerable problems in making positive identity based judgements (Cutler & Penrod, 1995). It seems unlikely that one would ever see a reverse of this pattern, whereby an individual's identity would be recognized independent of whether they were male or female, or white or black. But why does this dissociation between categorical and individuated person perception occur? Why, when we have the ability to perceptually discriminate people as members of discrete categories and as distinct individuals are we so reliant on the former? Is it because at a perceptual level, as is suggested for higher order social cognition, we are often too niggardly to engage in individuated processing? Or are there perceptual efficiencies which benefit category-based face processing?

In order to answer these questions, we will assess the efficiency with which our perceptual system extracts visual information from faces to provide us with useful social cues. To this end, we are interested in the minimal perceptual requirements associated with categorization and individuation early in the person-construal process, rather than in the content of stereotypes and prejudices that occur further down the processing stream. Although we acknowledge that such higher-order influences cannot be ignored, they should in no way preclude examination of the critical role face processing plays in social cognition. Ultimately, we are interested in whether we really are being stingy with our cognitive resources or are actually investing them wisely? Put another way, when it comes to perceptually construing others are we really cognitive misers or merely very shrewd cognitive capitalists?

THE ROLE OF PERCEPTUAL DIFFERENCES IN CATEGORIZATION AND INDIVIDUATION

In assessing the role of visual perception in social cognition, it is of utmost importance to consider both the categorization and individuation processes that can occur as a result of viewing a face. Typically, the social-cognitive literature has differentiated the processes of categorization and individuation through their influence on memory retrieval (see Macrae & Bodenhausen, 2000). At a basic level, they are both examples of cue-driven memory recall; the main difference between the processes is that categorization relies mainly on recall from rule-based semantic memory, whereas individuation draws on specific episodic memory (Tulving, 1972). Thus, social cognition research has routinely examined how either semantic or episodic memory impact people's understanding of others (Macrae & Bodenhausen, 2000). Quite how these information-processing abilities are realized at a perceptual level, however, remains open to some debate.

In daily life, our social-cognitive functioning does not begin with the retrieval of information from long-term memory; we have usually conducted a considerable amount of related processing before we get to this stage. Most notably, perceivers have resolved the perceptual puzzle of identifying social agents from other available visual cues (i.e., object recognition). Capturing, as they do, different solutions or outcomes to the problem of person construal (i.e., group member vs. unique individual), categorization and individuation also operate at these early stages of person perception (Bruce & Young, 1986; Haxby, Hoffman, & Gobbini, 2000, 2002; Tarr & Cheng, 2003; Tarr & Gauthier, 2000). Any object, including a person, can be identified

at multiple levels of categorical abstraction (Jolicoeur, Gluck, & Kosslyn, 1984). To this end, for categorization to occur it requires that we are able to unambiguously identify a person as belonging to a specific category (e.g., male or female), whereas for individuation to occur we must be able to make an unequivocal determination of a person as a unique entity (e.g., Clint Eastwood or Elle McPherson). Is it possible that these discrete outcomes reflect the operation of different processing mechanisms or strategies early in the person-perception processing stream? There are certainly behavioral, neuroimaging, and neurological indicators that would suggest so.

There is considerable evidence to suggest the visual information we rely on to make categorical judgments differs from the information we use to make individuated judgments (Diamond & Carey, 1986; Gauthier & Tarr, 1997; Rhodes, Tan, Brake, & Taylor, 1989). Although many classes of objects can be recognized via relatively coarse analysis of distinguishing visual features (Marr, 1982), recognizing faces (i.e., individuating) appears markedly different. Accurately individuating requires fine-grained analysis of configural or relational face information, such as the relative distance between facial features (Gauthier & Tarr, 1997; Rhodes et al., 1989). As is the case for object recognition, however, person categorization is less dependent on configural processing and more reliant on feature-based processing (Rhodes et al., 1989; Diamond & Carey, 1986). It seems that when it comes to visually categorizing other people, single diagnostic cues are often sufficient for the purpose (e.g., hairstyle as a cue for sex categorization; Brown & Perret, 1993; Macrae & Martin, 2007; Martin & Macrae, 2007). But does this well-founded distinction in the minimum visual requirements to individuate and categorize faces (i.e., configural or featural information, respectively) impact our propensity to view an individual in an individuated or categorical manner later in the processing stream? If this were the case, then it would undoubtedly have enormous implications for extant models of social cognition.

One way of assessing whether categorization and individuation are functionally independent at a face-processing level is to assess the extent they are reliant on distinct perceptual and neurological processes. Support for such functional independence is provided by converging evidence from research demonstrating a disparate array of hemispheric asymmetries in perceptual processing (Marsolek, 1995; Marsolek, Kosslyn, & Squire, 1992; Martin & Macrae, unpublished manuscript; Mason & Macrae, 2004; Rhodes, 1993; Tarr & Cheng, 2003; Tarr & Gauthier, 2000). A number of studies have demonstrated that the right cerebral hemisphere (RH) is superior to the left cerebral hemisphere (LH) for tasks that involve processing the configural information contained in faces (Rhodes, 1985, 1993; Yin, 1969). These findings are supported by a growing body of neuroimaging research that suggest cerebral asymmetries in processes important for individuation. Specifically, there are regions in the right ventral temporal cortex (e.g., fusiform gyrus) that are functionally important for processing faces (Haxby et al., 2000; Kanwisher, McDermott, & Chun, 1997; Kanwisher, Stanley, & Harris, 1999). It appears these areas are implicated in processing the kind of fine-grained visual contrasts required to individuate faces, as well as other objects (Gauthier & Tarr, 1997; Gauthier, Tarr, Anderson, Skudlarski, & Gore, 1999; Tarr & Cheng, 2003; Tarr & Gauthier, 2000). That the right hemisphere localization of perceptual processes is specific to individuation but not categorization is an indication that, even at a very basic perceptual level, these socially important functions may be dissociated.

The apparent right hemisphere advantage for processing fine-grained face information is by no means the only example of cerebral asymmetry that may impact person construal. There is considerable evidence of functional and anatomical independence of other perceptual phenomena that may be directly or indirectly involved in categorization and individuation (e.g., Fink et al., 1996; Lamb, Roberston, & Knight, 1990; Martinez et al., 1997). There are substantive reports suggesting that in

"Navon"-type tasks (Navon, 1977), the LH preferentially processes local information from visual stimuli (i.e., individual features of a visual stimulus), whereas the RH preferentially processes global information (i.e., the overall configuration of a stimulus; see Roberston & Lamb, 1991, for an extensive review). The lateralization of global and local visual processing may have enormous implications for the functional independence of face categorization and individuation. Because efficiently discriminating the identity of a face requires configural analysis of the entire face, it is not unreasonable to suggest that if the RH preferentially processes global information, then it will also prove superior in individuating (Brown & Perrett, 1993; Bruce & Young, 1986; Burton, Bruce, & Dench, 1993). Similarly, as single local features (e.g., hair, skin-tone) are considerable cues for assigning category membership, it is plausible to suggest a LH specialization for processing local information would result in an advantage for categorization (Brown & Perrett, 1993; Bruce et al., 1993; Schyns, 1998; Schyns, Bonnar, & Gosselin, 2002). The functional and anatomical asymmetries described just suggest divergence between the processes of categorization and individuation at the earliest stages of perceptually processing face information.

There is also evidence of similar lateralized specialization of categorical and individuated information in the way that the visual percept is represented in memory (e.g., Marsolek, 1995; Marsolek, Nicholas, & Andresen, 2002; Marsolek, Schacter, Nicholas, 1996; Marsolek, Squire, Kosslyn, & Lulenski, 1994). Marsolek and colleagues posit that the right hemisphere (RH) is better able to encode information that is specific to individual exemplars, whereas, the left hemisphere (LH) is better able to encode information that is generic or prototypical of classes of objects. Marsolek (1995) trained participants to classify meaningless two-dimensional ideograms according to specific rules based on their visual form (see Posner & Keele, 1968). Participants were then presented with a selection of ideograms to their left and right visual hemifields independently, some of which were ideograms they had seen during the training phase, some of which were previously unseen but that were prototypical of previous examples, and some of which were entirely novel distortions of previous ideograms. Marsolek found that ideograms that had previously been seen were better recognized when presented to the left visual field (RH), whereas prototypical ideograms were better recognized when they were presented to the right visual field (LH). These results support the idea that the RH preferentially processes exemplar-based information and the LH preferentially processes category-based information, assertions that are supported by a number of similar divided-visual-field studies (e.g., Kosslyn, 1987; Laeng, Zarrinpar, & Kosslyn, 2003; Marsolek, Kosslyn, & Squire, 1992; Marsolek et al., 1996).

Although there are perceptual and conceptual cerebral asymmetries indicative of independent categorization and individuation early in the processing stream, these do not directly attest to whether this actually impacts our social cognition. Recent work, however, appears to show a more direct link between hemispheric specialization and person-based individuated processing (Macrae & Martin, unpublished manuscript; Mason & Macrae, 2004). In order to assess lateralization of categorization and individuation for face processing, Mason and Macrae (2004) report three studies in which they tested a split-brain patient and assessed undergraduates both behaviorally and using fMRI scans. In all three studies, the task involved participants completing a categorization task, in which they responded about whether two face images were of the same or different *sex*, and an individuation task, in which participants responded about whether two face images were of the same or different *identity*. Faces were presented side-by-side, simultaneously for 200ms, to either the right visual hemifield (left cerebral hemisphere—LH) or the left visual hemifield (right cerebral hemisphere—RH). The behavioral results from the study using healthy undergraduates showed that participants were more accurate at the individuation task when face images were presented to their RH relative to LH. There was no significant difference for

the categorization task. This pattern of results was identical when the study was conducted with the split-brain patient (JW). The RH dominance for the individuation task was further highlighted with results from a functional magnetic resonance imaging (fMRI) study, which showed greater levels of activation in the right fusiform and right inferior temporal gyri during the individuation than in the categorization task.

The results from the studies just described provide compelling empirical support for the idea of cerebral lateralization of individuated face processing (Mason & Macrae, 2004). In no sense, however, does this imply that areas of the right temporal cortex are dedicated to the task of individuation. Rather, as mentioned earlier, activity in these regions merely indexes fine-grained perceptual discrimination (Haxby et al., 2000; Tarr & Cheng, 2003; Tarr & Gauthier, 2000). As such, if the perceptual difficulty of person categorization was increased in some way, for example, by cropping the hair from the faces (Bruce & Young, 1986), then this task should also prompt increased activity in regions of the ventral temporal cortex. Put simply, whenever a social-cognitive task requires fine-grained perceptual processing (i.e., subordinate-level judgments), activity in regions of the ventral temporal cortex may be expected to emerge (Tarr & Cheng, 2003; Haxby et al., 2000, 2002). In reality, however, the majority of our categorizations are not made with perceptually challenging stimuli; instead we regularly use diagnostic featural cues as proxies for category membership.

At this point, it is pertinent to consider how our ability to extract information from faces, be it categorical or individuated, relates to our knowledge of how we extract information from other visual objects. According to Marr's theory of vision, visual perception is characterized by a timeline in which the information extracted by the visual system shifts from coarse to fine-grained aspects of the available perceptual inputs (Marr, 1982). Importantly, Marr's computational model proposes that major features are extracted at the earliest stage of visual perception (i.e., the primal sketch), whereas the relational layout of features does not come until greater processing of the image has occurred (i.e., 2.5-dimensional sketch or 3-dimensional model representation). When Marr's model is applied to the manner in which we extract information from faces, there is a strong argument to suggest the feature driven process of categorization occurs before the more visually complex process of individuation. Although any such differences in speed of access to categorical and individuated information would likely be very small, they would also be fundamental to the way we perceive every face we encounter.

If even small differences exist in the efficiency with which we are able to extract featural and configural information from faces, this may help explain some of the functional differences we see between face categorization and individuation. We conducted two experiments designed to try and gain a greater understanding of the time-line of person construal and its impacts on hemispheric specialization of face processing (Macrae & Martin, unpublished manuscript). Using a divided-visual-field paradigm and a task similar to that of Mason and Macrae (2004), we assessed the impact of altering presentation duration of face images on categorical and individuated processing in the hemispheres. The results of the two experiments revealed that, following brief face presentation durations (25 ms), there was a right- hemisphere advantage for individuated face processing (i.e., identity; see Figure 2.1, top panel), and a left-hemisphere advantage for categorical face processing (i.e., sex; see Figure 2.1, bottom panel). When faces were presented for longer durations any left-hemisphere advantage for categorization diminished. These results support the notion that, early in the processing stream, face categorization and individuation are, to some degree, functionally independent of one another due to the different visual- processing demands that each requires.

It seems there is growing support for some level of functional independence in the way we categorize and individuate faces (Mason & Macrae, 2004; Macrae & Martin, unpublished manuscript). At the same time, we would argue stalwartly against the idea that categorization and individuation are inexorably guided by distinct neural architecture. Instead, it seems the visual demands that each characteristically entails are undoubtedly different and, therefore, they are typically supported by divergent perceptual processes. It appears there are processing subsystems located in the left and right cerebral hemispheres, each of which overlaps with the particular perceptual demands of individuation and categorization. In the RH there are subsystems that efficiently extract fine-grained, configural, global information that results in more effective individuated face processing. In the LH there are subsystems that efficiently extract featural, local information resulting in more effective categorical face processing. Although these hemispheric face-processing asymmetries may only become apparent under specific processing task conditions, this does not undermine their potential significance.

Evidence of categorical and individuated processing independence at a perceptual level poses a number of questions for the way we consider social cognition as a whole. When we encounter other people, is the way we perceive them dependent on higher-order beliefs and attitudes or merely the relationship that exists between basic aspects of visual perception and our existing semantic knowledge and stereotypes? Are we driven to categorize people not because we are cognitively lazy but because, relative to individuating, we are more perceptually adept at this task? In other words, do we spend much of our time categorizing other people due to our perceptual efficiency?

THE PERCEPTUAL EFFICIENCY OF PERSON CATEGORIZATION

In the previous section, we outlined converging evidence highlighting the different perceptual demands required for categorization and individuation to occur and the impact this has for the way the information is represented neurally. Although it is acknowledged that the visual processing utilized for each task is in no way mutually exclusive, it seems likely that there will be

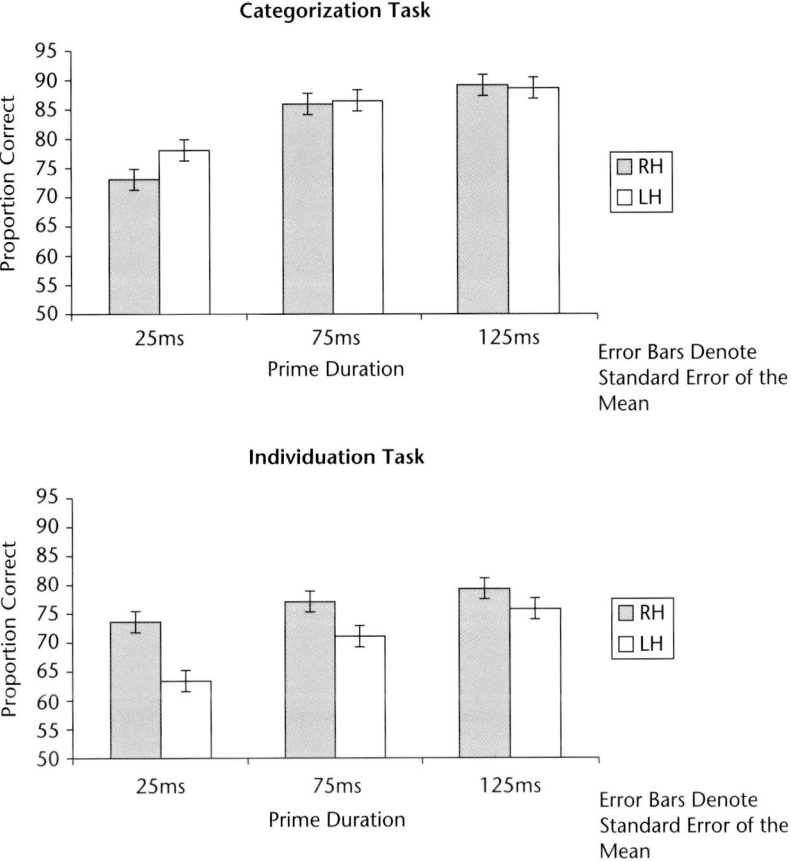

Figure 2.1 Percentage of Face Targets Correctly Identified as a Function of Presentation Duration and Cerebral Hemisphere (Categorization Task, top panel; Individuation Task, bottom panel). Macrae & Martin (unpublished manuscript).

perceptual and cognitive efficiencies associated with perceiving people in a particular manner. In this section we will explore just how proficient our perceptual system is at categorizing and individuating faces and discuss the impacts these efficiencies may have for higher-order social cognition.

Variability in the ease with which discrete information (i.e., featural vs. configural) is extracted from faces under different processing conditions, may provide a valuable insight into why category-based responding exerts such a dominant influence on person construal (Allport, 1954; Brewer, 1988; Fiske & Neuberg, 1990; Kunda & Spencer, 2003). There is evidence to suggest that category-specifying information may be the favored product of the perceptual operations that extract social knowledge from faces, particularly in challenging task environments. Relying as it does on facial configuration, individuation (i.e., identity-based processing) may be compromised by manipulations that impair the extraction of this information from stimuli, such as when faces are presented under suboptimal processing conditions (e.g., inverted faces; see Collishaw & Hole, 2002; Maurer, Le Grand, & Mondloch, 2002). As the extraction of featural information is less reliant on the quality of the available stimulus inputs (Leder & Bruce, 1998, 2000; Prkachin, 2003; Searcy & Bartlett, 1996), categorical thinking (i.e., person categorization) should not be impeded to the same degree by manipulations of this kind. In other words, category-based responding may dominate social-cognitive functioning because of the relative ease in which triggering information can be extracted from faces, especially in demanding task contexts (Cloutier, Mason, & Macrae, 2005).

To establish the functional characteristics of the perceptual processes that support categorization and individuation, Cloutier and colleagues (2005) assessed person-knowledge extraction both under normal viewing conditions and across a range of demanding processing contexts. Over three experiments, they assessed participants' ability to categorize and individuate faces that were inverted, degraded, or rapidly presented. In each experiment, the prediction was the same. When presented with faces in challenging task settings, perceivers should experience less difficulty extracting categorical than identity-related knowledge (Maurer et al., 2002). The data from all three experiments supported this supposition. It was apparent that the extraction of identity-based knowledge from faces (i.e., individuation) was less resistant to manipulations of processing difficulty (i.e., facial inversion, facial blurring, rapid presentation) than the extraction of categorical information (i.e., categorization), a finding that underscores the efficiency of the perceptual operations through which categorical thinking is initiated (Bruce & Young, 1986).

That substantial stimulus degradation, by inversion, blurring or rapidity of presentation, has only a minimal disruptive impact on the efficiency of person categorization suggests utilizing isolated features allows categorization to occur efficiently in circumstances when individuation is severely impaired. But does this categorical advantage persist across other non-standard viewing conditions? A number of studies have examined the effects of stimulus orientation on person *identification* and have demonstrated a monotonic decline in recognition performance as a result of within-plane rotation (Cochran, Pick, & Pick, 1983; Valentine & Bruce, 1988). If, however, categorization relies on the extraction of a single feature from the face (e.g., hairstyle as a featural cue of sex), then one might expect this process to be

resistant to the effects of facial disorientation (Leder & Bruce, 1998, 2000; Searcy & Bartlett, 1996). This idea is supported in recent work by Cloutier and Macrae (2007) which assessed the impact on categorization and individuation of increasing the degree of facial disorientation (i.e., increasing disorientation from a canonical viewpoint). On the one hand, their results demonstrate the expected monotonic decrement in the efficiency of person identification as a function of increased facial rotation (see Figure 2.2, top panel). On the other hand, although person categorization was also impaired by facial rotation, the resultant reaction-time costs were less pronounced than for person identification (see Figure 2.2, top panel). This suggests that the extraction of featural information is less dependent than the extraction of configural information, on the presentation of faces in a canonical orientation (Leder & Bruce, 1998). As such, at least for intact faces, it is easier for the face-processing system to extract featural than configural information, a perceptual effect that may contribute to perceivers' reliance on category-based responses during later stages of the person-perception process (Allport, 1954; Brewer, 1988; Fiske & Neuberg, 1990; Macrae & Bodenhausen, 2000).

Feature-based accounts of the categorization process are given further credence from investigations of the impact that specific featural cues may exert on the products of person construal (Schyns, 1998). Notable among these is the issue of just how potent category-cueing facial features may be in guiding the process of person categorization. For example, are facial features alone sufficient to trigger category (and stereotype) activation or must they be embedded in intact facial primes? Typically, researchers have manipulated the diagnosticity of category-cueing features that appear in intact facial stimuli (Blair, Judd, Sadler, & Jenkins, 2002; Livingston & Brewer, 2002; Locke, Macrae, & Eaton, 2005); thus it is possible that the effects of specific cues are supported by additional information (both featural and configural) that can be extracted from the face (Cloutier et al., 2005).

How an object is classified depends on a range of factors, including the quality of

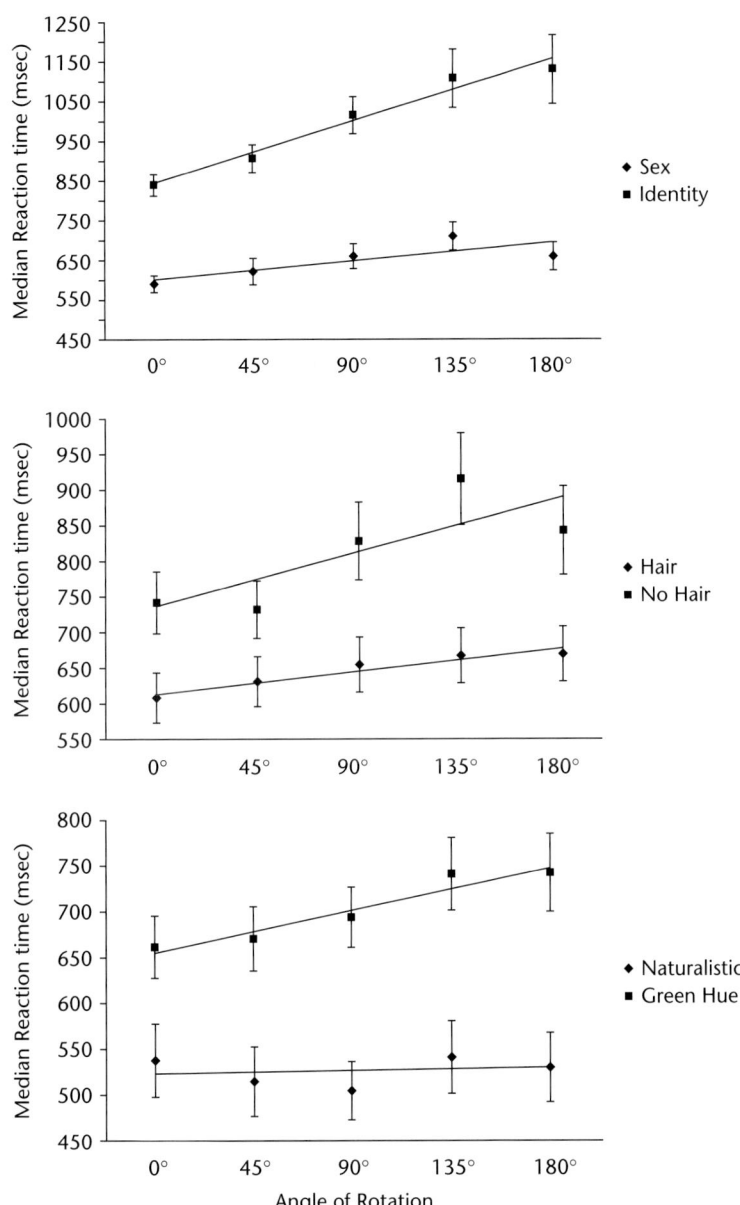

Figure 2.2 Task Performance as a Function of Facial Rotation (Sex and Identity Judgements - Intact-Faces, top panel; Sex Judgements - Cropped Vs Intact-Faces, middle panel; Race Judgements – Naturalistic Vs Green Hue, bottom panel). Cloutier & Macrae (2007).

available perceptual inputs and the particular processing goals or objectives that are operating during stimulus appraisal. Bound inexorably to basic perceptual operations, categorization is guided by the presence of diagnostic cues in the available visual inputs, cues that can support quite different categorical judgments (Schyns & Oliva, 1999; Schyns et al., 2002). When perceivers are charged with the task of explicitly classifying targets (i.e., overt categorization), then isolated featural cues are sufficient to drive the recognition process (Schyns et al., 2002). As Schyns et al. (2002) have noted, 'People who recognize visual events do not use all the information impinging on the retina, but instead use only the elements that are most useful (i.e., diagnostic) for the task at hand' (p. 402). But are these cues capable of triggering person categorization in task contexts in which perceivers are not instructed to categorize people? It is one thing to use a particular cue when overt classification is the task at hand; whether the cue spontaneously triggers person categorization, however, may be an entirely different matter (Macrae & Bodenhausen, 2000).

When confronted with other people, perceivers use a variety of physical cues to establish the sex of the individuals in question, including textural information (e.g., stubble) and specific facial features, such as the shape and thickness of the eyebrows (Bruce et al., 1993). By far the most useful and reliable cue when it comes to sexing a face, however, is a person's hairstyle (Brown & Perrett, 1993; Burton et al., 1993; Goshen-Gottstein & Ganel, 2000). This is something that was recently underlined in a study comparing the utility of intact faces and isolated hair cues in triggering activation of sex category knowledge (Macrae & Martin, 2007). Using a standard semantic priming methodology, we found that hair cues alone are sufficient to trigger category and stereotype activation. Whereas long hair triggered access to female knowledge, short hair primed the contents of generic beliefs about males. In fact, the effects observed for isolated hair cues were almost identical to those observed when intact faces served as the priming stimuli. These findings are noteworthy as they provide further evidence for the utility of feature-based accounts of the person construal (Schyns & Oliva, 1999; Schyns et al., 2002; Zebrowitz, 1997), demonstrating that category-specifying features need not be embedded in intact facial primes to moderate the process of person categorization (e.g., Blair, 2002; Blair, Judd, & Chapleau, 2004; Livingston & Brewer, 2002; Locke et al., 2005). They also highlight the impact that isolated facial cues exert in tasks in which perceivers are not explicitly required to identify the sex of targets (Schyns et al.)—mere registration of a featural cue is sufficient to trigger category activation.

If the registration of a diagnostic sex-specifying cue, such as a person's hairstyle, is sufficient to trigger category activation, a number of intriguing possibilities arise. In particular, could the presence of the cue ever prompt people to misconstrue the sex of a target (Schyns, 1998)? Consider, for example, two individuals, a woman with short, cropped hair and a man with long, flowing locks. Is it possible that these category-mismatching hair cues could induce people to assign the targets to the wrong sex (i.e., elicit a categorical sex change)? There is evidence to suspect that it is, but only temporarily and under conditions in which the processing of facial information is compromised or obstructed in some way (Macrae & Martin, 2007). Our recent study, which used prime images of male and female faces with non-sex-typed hairstyles (i.e., males with long hair and females with short hair) highlighted the importance of considering both featural cues and the time-course of person perception. When faces were presented very briefly (i.e., 25 ms), participants automatically categorized targets on the basis of their hair, even when this classification was at odds with other information conveyed by the face. For example, as indexed by the emergence of a reversed-priming effect, females with short hair triggered access to knowledge about men. When, however, additional time was available to extract additional sex-specifying information from faces (i.e., 200 ms), hair cues no longer led participants astray and veridical categorical responses were returned. Once again, it seems there is a two-tier system of person construal driven by the temporal constraints of extracting visual information from a face.

Person categorization is a puzzle for the perceptual system, a puzzle that can offer quite different categorical solutions (Schyns & Oliva, 1999; Schyns et al., 2002). Depending upon how much time is available to process a face, perceivers seemingly extract quite different solutions to the problem of person construal. Although rapid feature-driven categorizations may provide an initial response to a target, these can be easily overridden when additional sex-specifying information is extracted from the face. When sufficient time is available to process canonical facial representations, it is unlikely that errors of categorical construal will arise. In many settings, however, perceivers do not enjoy the luxury of these optimal processing conditions; instead target-related judgments are based on a rapid assessment of impoverished stimulus inputs (Cloutier et al., 2005).

There are a number of lines of evidence that point to perceptual efficiency as an important determinant of categorical thinking. First, perceivers can extract category-cueing material from faces more rapidly and accurately than identity-triggering information (Cloutier et al., 2005). Second, at least for intact stimuli, the operations that extract category-cueing information demonstrate a resistance to manipulations that impair face processing, such as stimulus orientation and degradation (Cloutier, & Macrae, 2007; Maurer et al., 2002; Valentine, 1988). Even when perceivers are presented with stimuli in suboptimal conditions, we are still capable of extracting categorical knowledge in a rapid and accurate manner (Cloutier & Macrae, 2007). Finally, when faces are presented under perceptually challenging circumstances, such as brief presentation durations, the perceptual system will efficiently extract category specifying featural information, which may dominate the way a person is initially perceived (Macrae & Martin, 2007).

It seems that when it comes to extracting visual information from a face, our perceptual system is more efficient at extracting information pertinent for making categorical relative to individuated person judgements. So much so, that under certain conditions, albeit the artificial manipulations of laboratory experiments, the efficiency of featural extraction results in categorical processing dominating person construal. What this suggests is that at a perceptual level, the dominant pattern of categorization appears to mirror models of higher order social cognition (Brewer, 1988; Fiske & Neuberg, 1990). There is, however, a major difference between the processes of perceptual and higher-order categorization. Notably, although saving cognitive energy by relying on group-based knowledge and stereotypes often provides misleading information about an individual, utilizing automatic perceptual categorizations seldom provides erroneous outcomes.

IS CATEGORIZATION INEVITABLE?

As the briefest of glances at a face allows our perceptual system the opportunity to extract the required featural information to automatically categorize individuals in a predominantly efficient and accurate manner, does this mean that person categorization is a wholly unconditional phenomenon? This is a question that taps into one of social psychology's fundamental theoretical disputes: whether category (and stereotype) activation is an unconditionally automatic mental process (see Bargh, 1999). The views expressed by the opposing camps in this debate have been decidedly polarized (see Bargh, 1999, Blair, 2002: Macrae & Bodenhausen, 2000). On the one hand, there is undoubtedly a wealth of evidence supporting Allport's (1954) account of the unconditional automaticity of category activation (see Bargh, 1999 for a review); within this chapter alone there are numerous examples of the seemingly automatic nature of category activation when one encounters a face. On the other hand, it would be unwise to view a large body of positive evidence in favor of automatic category activation as evidence that category activation is *unconditionally* automatic. The falsifiability of such inductive reasoning means the argument in favor of unconditional automatic categorization is founded on insecure ground and is subsequently in perpetual danger of collapse. Those opposed to the concept of unconditional category activation have seized on this point and argue that as there is positive evidence that automatic categorization can be moderated by a variety of top-down processes (e.g., Gilbert & Hixon, 1991; Lepore & Brown, 1997; Macrae et al., 1997), it cannot be considered unconditionally automatic. Is it possible, however, that, at a perceptual level, person categorization occurs as an unconditional consequence of viewing a face?

Guided by the assumption that categorical thinking is an inescapable facet of social cognitive functioning (Allport, 1954; Bargh, 1999; Brewer, 1988; Fiske & Neuberg, 1990), researchers have typically employed nonreactive experimental procedures (e.g., semantic priming) to explore the process of person categorization. The insights such techniques have allowed are impressive, with an extensive literature charting the determinants and consequences of category activation (Bargh, 1999; Blair, 2002; Macrae & Bodenhausen, 2000). Initial investigations provided support for Allport's (1954) conviction that it is impossible to encounter an individual without simultaneously triggering associated categorical representation in memory (i.e., unconditional automaticity, Bargh, 1999; Brewer, 1988; Devine, 1989; Dovidio, Evans, & Tyler, 1986). More recently, however, this assertion has been questioned through the identification of factors that reliably modulate category activation (i.e., conditional automaticity, Blair, 2002; Macrae & Bodenhausen, 2000). In a by no means exhaustive list, category activation has been shown to be attenuated or eliminated when: (1) person construal is irrelevant to people's current processing concerns (Macrae et al., 1997; Wheeler & Fiske, 2005); (2) attentional resources are depleted (Gilbert & Hixon, 1991); and (3) perceivers are motivated to avoid categorical thinking (Lepore & Brown, 1997; Locke, Macleod, & Walker, 1994; Wittenbrink, Judd, & Park, 1997). It is of note that, in all of these examples, category activation is moderated by the internal state of the perceiver (e.g., attentional capacity, processing goals, personal beliefs), but is it possible to show similar reductions in category activation by manipulating the perceptual characteristics of targets? Given the efficiency with which we process category-specifying featural cues, do they hold the key to spontaneous automatic categorization?

Research into the effects of facial typicality on person construal provides a revealing insight into the role specific features play in driving automatic categorization. It seems person categorization is remarkably sensitive to subtle differences in the features of people's facial appearance (Blair et al., 2005; Blair et al., 2004; Blair et al., 2002; Livingston & Brewer, 2002; Locke et al., 2005; Maddox & Gray, 2002; Uhlmann, Dasgupta, Elgueta, Greenwald, & Swanson, 2002). For example, targets with highly Afrocentric facial features are more likely to elicit associated negative evaluations and stereotype-based reactions than their less prototypical counterparts (Blair et al., 2004, 2005; Livingston & Brewer). That these effects are driven by the diagnosticity of category-cueing information is evident from the demonstration that European Americans trigger similar reactions, if these targets possess Afrocentric facial characteristics (Blair et al., 2002). In other words, featural cues can function independent of category membership in the generation of stereotype-based responses, at least for certain racial groups (Blair et al., 2002; Livingston & Brewer, 2002). Similarly, strength of category activation is modulated by the facial typicality of presented exemplars, such that typical targets facilitate access to category-related knowledge in memory (Locke et al., 2005). What these findings and others suggest is that feature-based information plays a pivotal role in the person-perception process (Schyns, 1998).

Although critical category-specifying facial cues undoubtedly have an important role to play in automatic categorization, is the role they play vital? Person categorization may occur even when the task confronting perceivers is challenging (cf. Gilbert & Hixon, 1991) and does not demand the explicit classification of a target (cf. Schyns et al., 2002). That is, cue registration may be sufficient to trigger category activation (Liu, Harris, & Kanwisher, 2002; Macrae & Martin, 2007). In the absence of these critical cues, however, it is possible that spontaneous person categorization may fail to occur, even under optimal face-processing conditions and despite the fact that perceivers are able to identify applicable target-relevant categories when explicitly probed. In other words, does cue availability determine whether category activation has the appearance of an unconditionally or conditionally automatic mental process (Bargh, 1999;

Blair, 2002)? Additionally, do the products of person construal depend on the manner in which person perception is probed?

If spontaneous automatic categorization is driven by the detection of a diagnostic featural cue in a face (Macrae & Martin, 2007; Schyns et al., 2002) then removal of the cue should impede the emergence of this effect. Paradoxically, however, as other category-specifying cues remain present in the face, removing that feature should not prevent perceivers from explicitly identifying the categories a particular target belongs to. For instance, if perceivers viewed a cropped face image under passive encoding, the lack of the sex-specifying featural cue of hairstyle may prevent automatic sex categorization of the target. If, however, the perceiver was asked to explicitly classify the sex of the target, it is likely they could do this with relative ease by utilizing other facial indicators of sex (e.g., eyebrow shape, textural information). As such, the overt (i.e., prompted-categorization) and covert (i.e., category-priming) products of person construal can be dissociated (Gilbert & Hixon, 1991).

Using a standard semantic priming procedure we investigated the effects of intact (i.e., hair-present) and cropped (i.e., hair-absent) faces on person construal (Martin & Macrae, 2007). By varying the ease with which information could be extracted from faces by perceptually degrading (i.e., blurring), the priming stimuli to varying degrees (Cloutier et al., 2005), it was possible to index the efficiency of person categorization. In order to contrast the processes of controlled and automatic person construal, following completion of the priming task, participants were also required to explicitly sex the blurred faces (i.e., priming stimuli). The results indicated that when hair cues were present (i.e., intact faces), automatic category activation (as indexed by priming effects) emerged, regardless of how blurred the target face images were (see Figure 2.3, top panel). These effects were eliminated, however, when hair cues were absent (i.e., cropped faces), even under optimal face-processing conditions (see Figure 2.3, bottom panel; Goshen-Gottstein & Ganel, 2000).

Scrutiny of the visual operations that drive person categorization may illuminate this issue.

Rather than characterizing category activation as an obligatory mental event (Brewer, 1988; Fiske & Neuberg, 1990), it may be more accurate to restrict this description to the perceptual processes that extract information from faces (Liu et al., 2002; Mouchetant-Rostaing & Giard, 2003). Operating in a mandatory fashion, these basic visual processes extract feature-based information from faces (e.g., hair cues, gaze direction), information that supports a range of person-related judgments, including sex categorization (Haxby et al., 2000, 2002). When, however, these visual operations are unable to detect critical sex specifying cues (i.e., hair cues) — as is the case when cropped faces are the stimuli of interest — category activation fails to occur. Thus, whether spontaneous category activation emerges is a function of feature availability.

But does failure to categorize a target imply that people are unable to identify the sex of the individual in question? The answer is a resounding no (Martin & Macrae, 2007). When required to report the sex of the facial primes, participants were remarkably adept at this task. Indeed, neither missing hair nor stimulus distortion alone did much to impair their classification accuracy (see Figure 2.4). Importantly, these findings corroborate Gilbert and Hixon's (1991) observation that, under certain processing conditions, category activation and category identification can be dissociated. That is, the ability to report the sex of an individual does not imply that the person has been spontaneously categorized as such; just as the ability to report the race of a card turner was not contingent on the spontaneous activation of that racial category when the individual was initially encountered (Gilbert & Hixon, 1991).

Although removing the diagnostic featural cues (e.g., hairstyle) impacts the overall *accuracy* with which people are able to explicitly categorise faces, there is evidence to suggest it also disrupts the *efficiency* with which they perform such tasks. In a further two experiments, using the same progressive face disorientation presentation method as described earlier (i.e., face-rotation paradigm), Cloutier and Macrae (2007) found monotonic disruption of face categorization performance when diagnostic category-specifying features

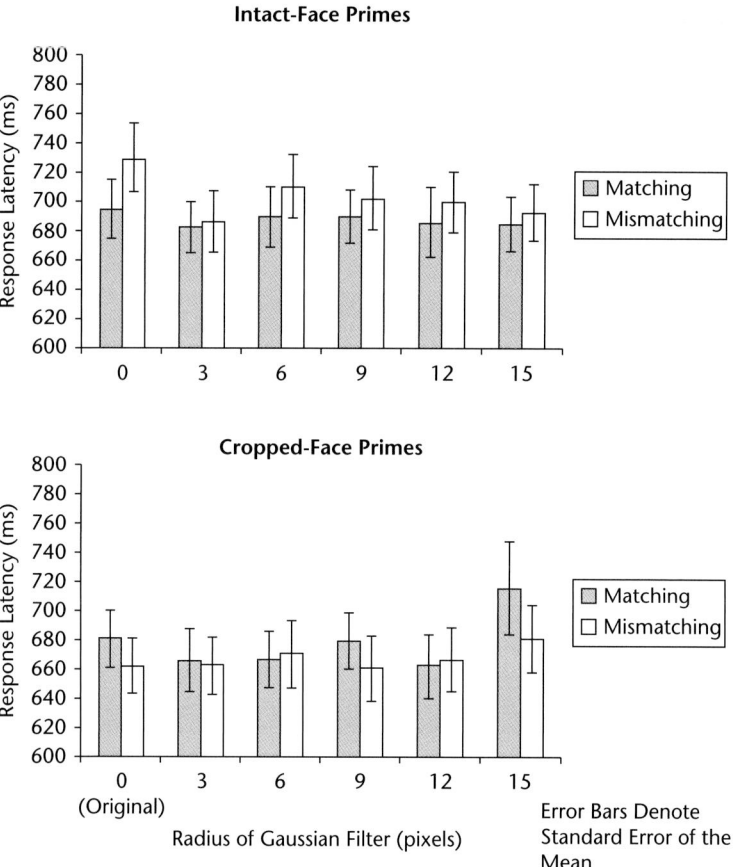

Figure 2.3 Task Performance as a Function of Prime, Blur and Trial Type (Intact-Face Primes, top panel; Cropped-Face Primes, bottom panel). Martin & Macrae (2007).

were removed. Specifically, when the prominent cues of hairstyle (i.e., by cropping hair from face images in a sex categorization task; see Figure 2.2, middle panel) and skin tone (i.e., by using a universal green tint on face images in a race categorization task; see Figure 2.2, bottom panel) were removed, performance on a categorization task resembled that of an individuation task. It seems that when we do not have the opportunity to categorize faces using featural cues, when we must instead rely on configural information, the relative efficiency of categorization over individuation effectively disappears. Therefore, although we have a perceptual advantage in our effectiveness at categorizing rather than individuating others, this is somewhat dependent on the

presence of highly prototypical category specifying features.

Although there is undoubtedly empirical evidence that category activation fails to emerge when critical categorical cues (e.g., hairstyle as a cue of sex) are absent, it is reasonable to question whether such conditions are encountered on a regular basis in life outside the laboratory. Apart from exchanges with bald people and individuals wearing hats, hair cues may rarely be unavailable to perceivers. In this respect, Bargh (1999) is probably accurate in his assertion that categorical thinking frequently dominates social interaction, or at least has the capacity to do so. Although, in a technical sense, category activation may be a conditionally automatic mental process (Blair, 2002;

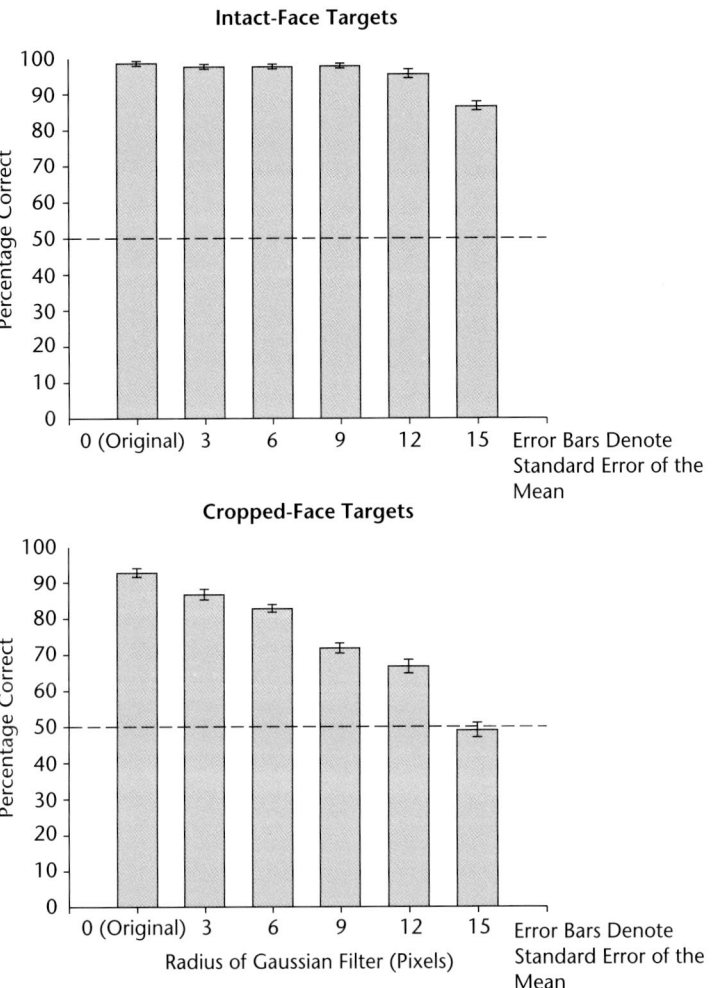

Intact-Face Targets

Cropped-Face Targets

Radius of Gaussian Filter (Pixels)

Error Bars Denote Standard Error of the Mean

Figure 2.4 Percentage of Intact and Cropped Face Targets Correctly Classified (Intact-Face Targets, top panel; Cropped-Face Targets, bottom panel). Martin & Macrae (2007).

Macrae & Bodenhausen, 2000), practically speaking, it may be the norm rather than the exception during most social interactions. It is perhaps no accident, therefore, that categorical thinking is most pronounced for groups that are characterized by the possession of a single salient feature (e.g., sex–hairstyle, race–skin tone, age–wrinkles). Through the operation of basic perceptual processes that extract featural information from faces (Liu et al., 2002; Mouchetant-Rostaing & Giard, 2003), these categories can be triggered with rapidity and ease. Although category activation may routinely follow the perceptual registration

of triggering featural cues, it is important to note that the impact of this activation is not identical across all processing episodes. Rather, categorical thinking is modulated by the facial typicality of encountered exemplars (Blair et al., 2002, 2004, 2005; Livingston & Brewer, 2002; Locke et al., 2005). So, while viewing a face does not inexorably mean it will be automatically categorized, the efficiency with which we perceptually process the presence of diagnostic featural cues associated with category membership, suggests that, in the vast majority of cases, categorization will occur.

CONCLUSION

The limited research that has investigated the role of face processing in social cognition suggests fundamental differences in the manner people can be construed before one even begins to consider the influence of higher order semantic knowledge, stereotypes or prejudice. However, is it apposite to view the way our perceptual system extracts categorical information from faces as an example of cognitive capitalism? We would argue, yes. The amount of cognitive effort required to process face information is so relatively small as to be considered negligible, yet we receive an excellent return from our meagre cognitive investment in terms of the information we glean directly, and importantly, for the information we infer. That is not to say our perceptual system isn't solving hugely complex processing tasks—it undoubtedly is—it is just that we extract information from faces in a remarkably effortless fashion. Crucially, however, there is inequity in the way our perceptual system extracts feature-based and configural face information, an inequality that means at a very early stage in our social encounters we have an advantage for categorical rather than individuated person processing.

As social cognitive misers, we rely on heuristics to guide our behaviour in a great many situations, therefore preventing the need to engage in more cognitively demanding novel evaluations. When it comes to construing other people, this often involves automatically attributing characteristics to an individual based on stereotypic information associated with specific features they posses (e.g., male = aggressive, competitive, loud; Bodenhausen & Macrae, 1998). One problem with using such cognitive shortcuts is that stereotypic attributions are very often erroneous (Judd & Park, 1993). As cognitive capitalists when viewing a face we also rely on specific features to guide the person construal process (e.g., long hair–female; Macrae & Martin, 2007), these attributions, however, are seldom wrong. We don't mistake black people for white people or eighty-year-olds for twenty-year-olds. Very occasionally we may misconstrue an individual's sex, but this occurrence is often a result of a female having very short hair or a male having very long hair. When it comes to perceptual economy, it would seem that accuracy is everything.

The accuracy with which we are able to perceptually categorize people is testament to the proficiency with which our visual system extracts diagnostic featural information from even suboptimal views of a face (Cloutier et al., 2005; Cloutier & Macrae, 2007; Macrae & Martin, 2007; Martin & Macrae, 2007). Although later in the processing stream utilizing categorical information is often considered a stringent or lazy strategy, at a perceptual level it is best characterized as efficient. It is not that we are too slothful to obtain identity-based perceptual information from faces, it is just that in many situations we are better able to extract categorical information. In circumstances when it is not necessarily possible to make a positive identity judgement, our superior categorization abilities allow us to glean a whole host of social information that we are able to use to guide our behaviour. Although the differential ability to extract categorical and identity-based information may be relatively small, they have potentially important implications for the inevitability of person categorization beyond the perceptual level.

Although person categorization is demonstrably not a wholly unconditional process, at either a perceptual or conceptual level, it seems it is often the predominant way that we construe other people (Brewer, 1988; Fiske & Neuberg, 1990). One reason for this may be the almost symbiotic relationship that exists between the perceptual demands of extracting prominent facial features and their salience as category cues. Many of the categories to which we commonly assign people to are also indexed by prominent visual cues[1] (e.g., Sex–hairstyle, Race–skin-tone, Age– wrinkles). The fact that our visual system extracts these prominent featural cues accurately and often more efficiently than configural information pertaining

---

[1] It is of note that, in addition to prominent visual cues of category membership, voice cues also trigger category assignment (e.g., Ko, Judd, & Blair, 2006).

to an individual's identity (Cloutier et al., 2005; Cloutier & Macrae, 2007; Macare & Martin, 2007) may contribute to the preponderance of these categories, the utility of such features as categorical cues, and ultimately to the apparent dominance of categorical thinking per se.

Demonstrating the relative accuracy, efficiency and dominance of categorical face perception as separate phenomena is of importance to better understand the process of person construal. When they are considered in concert they may have fundamental implications for the way we interpret social cognition. It is possible that one of the major conundrums for social psychology—why we have a propensity to engage in categorical rather than individuated thought—may be due in part to an advantage for perceptually decoding such information from our most salient social cue, the face. As faces are such a vital source of social information from the moment we are born, is it not possible any basic perceptual bias we possess may influence other aspects of our social cognition? Is it not feasible that our perceptual dominance for processing feature-based categorical face information is passed on down the line and results in a more generic dominance for categorical person processing? Although in one sense these questions are merely speculative musings, in another they represent a potentially vital line of future enquiry for social cognition researchers to tackle. No longer can we afford to ignore the manner in which we extract information from our most important social cue.

REFERENCES

Allport, G. W. (1954). *The nature of prejudice.* Reading, MA: Addison-Wesley.

Bargh, J. A. (1999). The cognitive monster: The case against controllability of automatic stereotype effects. In S. Chaiken, & Y. Trope (Eds.), *Dual process theories in social psychology.* New York: Guilford.

Blair, I. V. (2002). The malleability of automatic stereotypes and prejudice. *Personality and Social Psychology Bulletin, 6,* 242-261.Blair, I. V., Chapleau, K. M., & Judd, C. M. (2005). The use of afrocentric features as cues for judgment in the presence of diagnostic information. *European Journal of Social Psychology, 35,* 59–68.

Blair, I. V., Judd, C. M., & Chapleau, K. M. (2004). The influence of afrocentric facial features in criminal sentencing. *Psychological Science, 15,* 674–679.

Blair, I. V., Judd, C. M., Sadler, M. S., & Jenkins, C. (2002). The role of afrocentric facial features in person perception: Judging by features and categories. *Journal of Personality and Social Psychology, 83,* 5–25.

Bodenhausen, G. V., & Macrae, C. N. (1998). Stereotype activation and inhibition. In R. S. J. Wyer (Ed.), *Stereotype activation and inhibition: Advances in social cognition* (pp. 1–52). Hillsdale, NJ: Erlbaum.

Brewer, M. B. (1988). A dual process model of impression formation. In R. S. J. Wyer, & T. K. Srull (Eds.), *Advances in social cognition* (pp. 1–36). Hillsdale, NJ: Erlbaum.

Brown, E., & Perrett, D. I. (1993). What gives a face its gender? *Perception, 22,* 829–840.

Bruce, V., Burton, A. M., Hanna, E., Healey, P., Mason, O., Coombes, A., et al. (1993). Sex discrimination: How do we tell the difference between male and female faces? *Perception, 22,* 131–152.

Bruce, V., & Young, A. W. (1986). Understanding face recognition. *British Journal of Psychology, 77,* 305–327.

Burton, A. M., Bruce, V., & Dench, N. (1993). What's the difference between men and women?: Evidence from facial measurement. *Perception, 22,* 153–176.

Cloutier, J., Mason, M. F., & Macrae, C. N. (2005). The perceptual determinants of person construal: reopening the social-cognitive toolbox. *Journal of Personality and Social Psychology, 88,* 885–894.

Cloutier, J., & Macrae, C. N. (2007). Who or what are you? Facial orientation and person construal. *European Journal of Social Psychology, 37,* 1298–1309.

Cochran, E. L., Pick, A. D., & Pick, H. L. (1983). Task-specific strategies of mental 'rotation' of facial representations. *Memory & Cognition, 11,* 41–48.

Collishaw, S. M., & Hole, G. J. (2002). Is there a linear or a nonlinear relationship between rotation and configural processing of faces? *Perception, 31,* 287.

Cutler, B. L., & Penrod, S. D. (1995). *Mistaken identification: The eyewitness, psychology, and the law.* New York, NY, US: Cambridge University Press.

Devine, P. G. (1989). Stereotypes and prejudice: Their automatic and controlled components. *Journal of Personality and Social Psychology, 56,* 5–18.

Diamond, R., & Carey, S. (1986). Why faces are and are not special: An effect of expertise. *Journal of Experimental Psychology: General, 115,* 107–117.

Dovidio, J. F., Evans, N., & Tyler, R. B. (1986). Racial stereotypes: The contents of their cognitive representations. *Journal of Experimental Social Psychology, 22,* 22–37.

Fink, G. R., Halligan, P. W., Marshall, J. C., Frith, C. D., Frackowiak, R. S. J., & Dolan, R. J. (1996). Where in the brain does visual attention select the forest and the trees? *Nature, 382,* 626–628.

Fiske, S. T., & Neuberg, S. L. (1990). A continuum model of impression formation from category based to individuating processes: Influences of information and motivation on attention and interpretation. In M. P. Zanna (Ed.), *Advances in experimental social psychology* (pp. 1–74). San Diego, CA: Academic Press.

Fiske, S. T., & Taylor, S. E. (1984). *Social Cognition.* Reading, MA: Addison-Wesley.

Gauthier, I., Tarr, M. J., Anderson, A. W., Skudlarski, P., & Gore, J. C. (1999). Activation of the middle fusiform "face area" increases with expertise in recognizing novel objects. *Nature Neuroscience, 2,* 568–573.

Gauthier, I., & Tarr, M. J. (1997). Orientation priming of novel shapes in the context of viewpoint-dependent recognition. *Perception, 26,* 51–73.

Gilbert, D. T., & Hixon, J. G. (1991). The trouble of thinking: Activation and application of stereotypic beliefs. *Journal of Personality and Social Psychology, 60,* 509–517.

Goshen-Gottstein, Y., & Ganel, T. (2000). Repetition priming for familiar and unfamiliar faces in a sex-judgment task: Evidence for a common route for the processing of sex and identity. *Journal of Experimental Psychology: Learning, Memory, and Cognition, 26,* 1198–1214.

Haxby, J. V., Hoffman, E. A., & Gobbini, M. I. (2000). The distributed human neural system for face perception. *Trends in Cognitive Sciences, 4,* 223–233.

Haxby, J. V., Hoffman, E. A., & Gobbini, M. I. (2002). Human neural systems for face recognition and social communication. *Biological Psychiatry, 21,* 56–67.

Jolicoeur, P., Gluck, M., & Kosslyn, S. M. (1984). Pictures and names: Making the connection. *Cognitive Psychology, 16,* 243–275.

Judd, C. M., & Park, B. (1993). Definition and assessment of accuracy in social stereotypes. *Psychological Review, 100,* 109–128.

Kanwisher, N., McDermott, J., & Chun, M. M. (1997). The fusiform face area: A module in human extrastriate cortex specialized for face perception. *Journal of Neuroscience, 17,* 4302–4311.

Kanwisher, N., Stanley, D., & Harris, A. (1999). The fusiform face area is selective for faces not animals. *Neuroreport, 10,* 183–187.

Ko, S. J., Judd, C. M., & Blair, I. V. (2006). What the voice reveals: Within- and between-category stereotyping on the basis of voice. *Personality and Social Psychology Bulletin, 32,* 806–819.

Kosslyn, S. M. (1987). Seeing and imagining in the cerebral hemispheres: A computational approach. *Psychological Review, 94,* 148–175.

Kunda, Z., & Spencer, S. J. (2003). When do stereotypes come to mind and when do they color judgment? A goal-based theoretical framework for stereotype activation and application. *Psychological Bulletin, 129,* 522–544.

Laeng, B., Zarrinpar, A., & Kosslyn, S. M. (2003). Do separate processes identify objects as exemplars versus members of basic-level categories? evidence from hemispheric specialization. *Brain and Cognition, 53,* 15–27.

Lamb, M. R., Robertson, L. C., & Knight, R. T. (1990). Component mechanisms underlying the processing of hierarchically organized patterns: Inferences from patients with unilateral cortical lesions. *Journal of Experimental Psychology: Learning, Memory, & Cognition, 16,* 471–483.

Leder, H., & Bruce, V. (1998). Local and relational aspects of face distinctiveness. *Quarterly Journal of Experimental Psychology: Human Experimental Psychology, 51,* 449.

Leder, H., & Bruce, V. (2000). When inverted faces are recognized: The role of configural information in face recognition. *Quarterly Journal of Experimental Psychology: Human Experimental Psychology, 53,* 513–536.

Lepore, L., & Brown, R. (1997). Category and stereotype activation: Is prejudice inevitable? *Journal of Personality and Social Psychology, 72,* 275–287.

Liu, J., Harris, A., & Kanwisher, N. (2002). Stages of processing in face perception: An MEG study. *Nature Neuroscience, 5,* 910–916.

Livingston, R. W., & Brewer, M. B. (2002). What are we really priming? cue-based versus category based processing of facial stimuli. *Journal of Personality and Social Psychology, 82,* 5–18.

Locke, V., MacLeod, C., & Walker, I. (1994). Automatic activation of stereotypes: Individual differences associated with prejudice. *British Journal of Social Psychology, 33,* 29–46.

Locke, V., Macrae, C. N., & Eaton, J. L. (2005). Is person categorization modulated by goodness-of-category fit? *Social Cognition, 23,* 417–428.

Macrae, C. N., & Bodenhausen, G. V. (2000). Social cognition: Thinking categorically about others. *Annual Review of Psychology, 51,* 93–120.

Macrae, C. N., Bodenhausen, G. V., Milne, A. B., Thorn, T. M. J., & Castelli, L. (1997). On the activation of social stereotypes: The moderating role of processing objectives. *Journal of Experimental Social Psychology, 22,* 471–489.

Macrae, C. N., & Martin, D. (2007). A boy primed sue: Feature-based processing and person construal. *European Journal of Social Psychology, 37,* 793–805.

Maddox, K. B., & Gray, S. A. (2002). Cognitive representations of black americans: Re-exploring the role of skin tone. *Personality and Social Psychology Bulletin, 28,* 250–259.

Marr, D. (1982). *Vision: A computational investigation into the human representation and processing of visual information.* San Francisco: W.H. Freeman and Company.

Marsolek, C. J. (1995). Abstract visual-form representations in the left cerebral hemisphere. *Journal of Experimental Psychology: Human Perception and Performance, 21,* 375–386.

Marsolek, C. J., Kosslyn, S. M., & Squire, L. R. (1992). Form-specific visual priming in the right cerebral hemisphere. *Journal of Experimental Psychology: Learning, Memory, and Cognition, 18,* 492–508.

Marsolek, C. J., Nicholas, C. D., & Andresen, D. R. (2002). Interhemispheric communication of abstract and specific visual-form information. *Neuropsychologia, 40,* 1983–1999.

Marsolek, C. J., Schacter, D. L., & Nicholas, C. D. (1996). Form-specific visual priming for new associations in the right cerebral hemisphere. *Memory & Cognition, 24,* 539–556.

Marsolek, C. J., Squire, L. R., Kosslyn, S. M., & Lulenski, M. E. (1994). Form-specific explicit and implicit memory in the right cerebral hemisphere. *Neuropsychology, 8,* 588–597.

Martin, D., & Macrae, C. N. *Time changes everything: The temporal constraints of lateralized categorical and individuated face processing.* Unpublished manuscript.

Martin, D., & Macrae, C. N. (2007). A face with a cue: Exploring the inevitability of person categorization. *European Journal of Social Psychology, 37,* 806–816.

Martinez, A., Moses, P., Frank, L., Buxton, R., Wong, E., & Stiles, L. (1997). Hemispheric asymmetries in global and local processing: Evidence from fMRI. *Neuroreport, 8,* 1685–1689.

Mason, M. F., & Macrae, C. N. (2004). Categorizing and individuating others: The neural substrates of person perception. *Journal of Cognitive Neuroscience, 16,* 1785–1795.

Maurer, D., Le Grand, R., & Mondloch, C. J. (2002). The many faces of configural processing. *Trends in Cognitive Sciences, 6,* 255–260.

Mouchetant-Rostaing, Y., & Giard, M. H. (2003). Electrophysiological correlates of age and gender perception on human faces. *Journal of Cognitive Neuroscience, 15,* 900–910.

Navon, D. (1977). Forest before trees: The precedence of global features in visual perception. *Cognitive Psychology, 9,* 353–383.

Posner, M. I., & Keele, S. W. (1968). On the genesis of abstract ideas. *Journal of Experimental Psychology, 77,* 353–363.

Prkachin, G. C. (2003). The effects of orientation on detection and identification of facial expressions of emotion. *British Journal of Psychology, 94,* 45–62.

Rhodes, G., Tan, S., Brake, S., & Taylor, K. (1989). Expertise and configural coding in face recognition. *British Journal of Psychology, 80,* 313–331.

Rhodes, G. (1985). Lateralized processes in face recognition. *British Journal of Psychology, 76,* 249–271.

Rhodes, G. (1993). Configural coding, expertise, and the right hemisphere advantage for face recognition. *Brain and Cognition, 22,* 19–41.

Robertson, L. C., & Lamb, M. R. (1991). Neuropsychological contributions to theories of part/whole organization. *Cognitive Psychology, 23,* 299–330.

Schyns, P. G. (1998). Diagnostic recognition: Task constraints, object information and their interactions. *Cognition, 67,* 147–179.

Schyns, P. G., Bonnar, L., & Gosselin, F. (2002). Show me the features! understanding recognition from the use of visual information. *Psychological Science, 13,* 402–409.

Schyns, P. G., & Oliva, A. (1999). Dr. angry and mr. smile: When categorization flexibly modifies the perception of faces in rapid visual presentations. *Cognition, 69,* 243–265.

Searcy, J., & Bartlett, J. (1996). Inversion and processing of component and spatial-relational information in faces. *Journal of Experimental Psychology: Human Perception and Performance, 22,* 904–915.

Tarr, M. J., & Cheng, Y. D. (2003). Learning to see faces and objects. *Psychological Science, 7,* 23–30.

Tarr, M. J., & Gauthier, I. (2000). FFA: A flexible fusiform area for subordinate-level visual processing automatized by expertise. *Nature Neuroscience, 3,* 764–769.

Taylor, S. E. (1981). The interface of cognitive and social psychology. In J. Harvey (Ed.), *Cognition, social behavior and the environment* (pp. 189–211). Hillsdale, NJ: Erlbaum.

Tulving, E. (1972). Episodic and semantic memory. In E. Tulving, & W. Donaldson (Eds.), *Organization of memory.* New York: Academic Press.

Uhlmann, E., Dasgupta, N., Elgueta, A., Greenwald, A. G., & Swanson, J. (2002). Subgroup prejudice based on skin color among hispanics in the united states and latin america. *Social Cognition, 20,* 198–226.

Valentine, T. (1988). Upside-down faces: A review of the effect of inversion upon face recognition. *British Journal of Psychology, 79,* 471.

Valentine, T., & Bruce, V. (1988). Mental rotation of faces. *Memory & Cognition, 16,* 556–566.

Wheeler, M. E., & Fiske, S. T. (2005). Controlling racial prejudice: Social-cognitive goals affect amygdala and stereotype activation. *Psychological Science, 16,* 55–63.

Wittenbrink, B., Judd, C. M., & Park, B. (1997). Evidence for racial prejudice at the implicit level and its relationship with questionnaire measures. *Journal of Personality and Social Psychology, 72,* 262–274.

Yin, R. K. (1969). Looking at upside-down faces. *Journal of Experimental Psychology, 81,* 141–145.

Zebrowitz, L. A. (1997). *Reading faces: Window to the soul?* Boulder, CO: Westview Press.

CHAPTER 3

Faces, Bodies, Social Vision as Agent Vision, and Social Consciousness

Beatrice de Gelder and Marco Tamietto

This chapter discusses recent findings from our own research on face and body perception with special attention to the implications of the findings for social vision. The first section is devoted to similarities between the processes underlying face and body perception. In the second section we discuss how the perception of faces and bodies is integrated. The third section tackles issues on conscious and nonconscious perception of socially meaningful signals and their neuroanatomical underpinnings. Finally, the relation between social vision and awareness is explored and notion of social consciousness is developed. Throughout this chapter we use the notions of agent vision and social vision in the sense made familiar by the expression 'night vision' to refer to various devices that expand the normal visual abilities and allows the observer to see in the dark, outside the spotlight of consciousness. Night vision is a metaphor for the enhanced abilities that allow the viewer to take advantage of nonvisible sources of information in the enviroment. For example, some animals can see well into the infrared and/or ultraviolet compared to humans, enough to help them see in conditions humans cannot.

A familiar claim in the cognitive neuroscience literature of the last decade is that many cognitive abilities have a social dimension and can usefully be grouped together under the umbrella of the social brain hypothesis. Often this notion refers to a subset of cognitive abilities that are concerned with perception of and reasoning about social objects and agents. For example, we perceive objects as we perceive people, we reason about objects as we reason about people, and, in the latter cases, the perceptual skills and reasoning abilities are labeled as social because the domain in which they are exercised is that of the social as opposed to the physical reality. In the classical hierarchical models of vision, the social dimension of object cognition is associated with the later stages of processing in temporal cortex and in prefrontal cortex.

A more radical meaning of the social dimension of perceptual and cognitive abilities is that they have a social origin. Seen in an evolutionary perspective, this amounts to the thesis that the social brain evolved in the process of and as a consequence of the demands of the social environment. The hypothesis that consciousness may have a social origin was initially put forward by Humphrey (Humphrey, 1983). He argues that our ability to be conscious of ourselves and others may have its evolutionary origin in the increasing need to collaborate with others, and the interdependence between agents created by living in extended communities.

We would like to argue that this broad social-evolutionary perspective on consciousness may also be applied to the visual system, at least as a heuristic principle, and may orient the search for specific hypotheses about phylogenetically ancient social properties of the visual system of higher organisms. Indeed, if the latter evolved as part of this evolutionary adaptation to, and specialization for, the social environment, it makes sense to look for traces of social tuning in the brain's visual abilities, including in the early stages. In other words, a specialization for social objects may be present at different stages throughout the visual system, starting with early vision in posterior brain regions and including later and more familiar processes in temporal cortex. This chapter discusses to what extent the evolutionary social vision framework is substantiated by a discussion on similarities between processing of faces and bodies, and by the investigation of nonconscious vision abilities reported for both classes of stimuli.

Conversely, as we propose in concluding the chapter, the evolutionary relation between consciousness and vision may also obtain in the other direction, that is, from social vision to consciousness. The co-evolution of consciousness and social-vision abilities suggests that the two may have a privileged relationship, so that social species may have a specialized ability for being aware of their co-specifics. In other words, like vision, our ability to be conscious may not be a *tabula rasa*, but may come with an evolutionary disposition to be aware of others. This social consciousness may have a strong emotional component, and it may, in part, be mediated by mechanisms on which our own body awareness is based. Our approach in this chapter is to take the issue of the functional similarities between faces and bodies as a privileged access road for clarifying social vision. The functional similarity of face and body signals challenges theories exclusively concerned with analysis of the specific visual features, and instead suggests an approach that cuts across gross physical stimulus differences, as there exist between facial and bodily expressions, to focus more on the functional and semantic properties of visual signals.

IS THERE A COMMON SOCIAL VISION ABILITY FOR FACES AND BODIES?

To act effectively and adaptively, social species must rapidly perceive relevant signals about intentions and actions provided by the social environment. In the visual domain, facial expressions and body language are among the most frequent signals routinely exchanged. Because faces are parts of bodies, they often communicate the same message; their individual cues can be cumulated, increasing the changes for adaptive reactions from the observer. For example, as observers we experience similarly the negative impact of an angry face and that of an angry fist, or of an aggressive posture. The few studies that have compared explicit recognition and verbal labeling of facial expressions and bodily expressions each presented on their own, have shown, not surprisingly, that, in neurologically intact observers, both are recognized equally well.

Because facial expressions and signals provided by emotional body language are physically so different, we are interested to explore their similar functional status and significance for the observer. If there are indications that similarities in functional significance between faces and bodies already exists in the relatively early stages, then this may have some consequences for theories of social vision.

Our review of current evidence for similarities between face and body perception includes findings about overlap in the neural basis and in the temporal dynamics of face and body processes in neurologically intact observers. Furthermore, a very valuable source of evidence in favor of the notion that faces and body perception share common neural resources comes from findings that deficits in face and body processing are possibly associated in some neurological populations. These include developmental prosopagnosics and patients with Huntington disease, as well as populations with affective-communicative disorders like autism and schizophrenia.

Functional Neuroanatomy

A mainstream approach to understanding functional neuroanatomy (certainly it was in

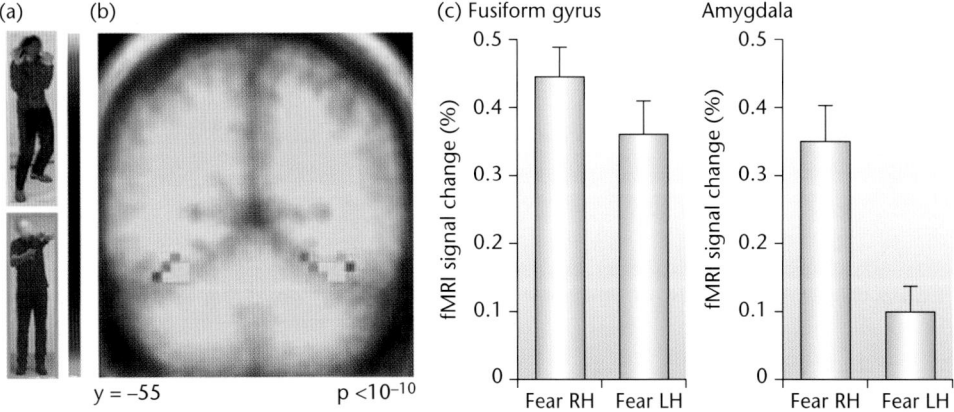

Figure 3.1 The fusiform gyrus and the amygdala show increased activation in response to bodily expressions of fear. (a) Example of the stimuli used: top, body expression of fear; bottom, emotionally neutral body posture (pouring liquid into a container). (b) Functional MRI (fMRI) activation associated with fearful compared with neutral bodies. Activation shown is in response to the fearful bodies (yellow) in the fusiform face area (FFA). No activation is seen for the neutral bodies (blue). (c) Average percentage signal change in functionally defined regions of interest in the FFA and amygdala in fearful compared with neutral body postures. From de Gelder 2006.

the early days of human brain imaging) is to look for distinct brain areas that more or less uniquely represent a given stimulus category. Because functional similarities are typically considered to be secondary from this perspective, they are not the focus of attention, whereas considerations about functions would possibly lead to a different cross-categorization, as recently argued (Mahon et al., 2007). Faces, objects, tools, places and, more recently, bodies have so far been prime candidates of discrete stimulus categories represented by distinct brain areas, with faces and bodies as the candidates for social vision. We first review this work before returning to the issue of functional similarities that cross category boundaries.

Many studies have reported that an area in the midfusiform cortex is selectively sensitive to faces (the fusiform face area, FFA) (Haxby et al., 1994). Another cortical area, near the middle occipital gyrus has come to the foreground because it appeared selectively activated during presentation of body stimuli and was named the extrastriate body area (EBA) (Downing, Jiang, Shuman, & Kanwisher, 2001; Grossman & Blake, 2002; Peelen & Downing, 2005; Sakreida, Schubotz, Wolfensteller, & von

Cramon, 2005; Spiridon, Fischl, & Kanwisher, 2006). More recently, however, it has been shown that an area in the midfusiform cortex is also selectively activated in response to whole bodies, and this led the authors to propose a division of the midfusiform cortex in a face vs. body sensitive set of voxels (fusiform body area, FBA) (Peelen & Downing, 2005; Schwarzlose, Baker, & Kanwisher, 2005; Spiridon et al., 2006). The latter result is consistent with our previous findings on the role of the fusiform cortex in body processing (Figure 3.1) (Hadjikhani & de Gelder, 2003).

At present, it is an open question whether novel theoretical and methodological developments will allow even more fine-grained category specificity, and even more detailed charts of cortical specialization. It is worth noting though, that most of the studies that have predominantly reported on the role for the midfusiform cortex for faces, also provided systematic evidence for face-specific activation on other cortical areas, mainly the inferior occipital gyrus (I. Gauthier, Behrmann, & Tarr, 1999; I. Gauthier, Tarr, Anderson, Skudlarski, & Gore, 1999; I. I. Gauthier, 2000; Hadjikhani & de Gelder, 2003; Kanwisher & Moscovitch, 2000) and the superior temporal sulcus (STS). Interestingly, these three areas also figure in recent reports on body representation in the brain (de Gelder, 2006a; Peelen & Downing, 2007).

It is important to note that the results about category specificity just mentioned mostly concern studies that have used neutral face and body images. Moreover, lots of these studies have contrasted faces or bodies to artifact objects, like houses or chairs, rather than to other stimuli of similar ecological and natural salience. A more challenging picture for the notion of discrete category representations emerges, however, when we turn to results obtained using facial and bodily expressions of emotion, a perspective that introduces functional considerations based on the fact that faces and bodies may convey the same affective information.

With respect to the functional neuroanatomy we found that the fusiform cortex and amygdala play an important role in processing fearful bodily expressions (de Gelder, 2006a; de Gelder, Snyder, Greve, Gerard, & Hadjikhani, 2004; Hadjikhani & de Gelder, 2003), as was previously shown for fearful facial expressions (Dolan, Morris, & de Gelder, 2001; Morris, Friston et al., 1998; Morris, Ohman, & Dolan, 1998; Rotshtein, Malach, Hadar, Graif, & Hendler, 2001a, 2001b). The original finding has now been confirmed in other studies using upper body parts (Grosbras & Paus, 2006) and whole bodies (Grèzes, Pichon, & de Gelder, 2007; Pichon, De Gelder, & Grèzes, 2007; van de Riet, Grèzes, & de Gelder, in press).

Another avenue for exploring the functional similarity between seeing faces and bodies is to measure the observers' spontaneous muscle reaction triggered by seeing facial or bodily expressions, as can be done with the tools of facial electromyography (EMG). It has been showed that observing facial expressions automatically prompts spontaneous imitation (Dimberg, 1982, 1990; Dimberg & Thunberg, 1998; Dimberg, Thunberg, & Elmehed, 2000). To investigate whether this muscle reaction is driven by automatic mimicry of the visual stimulus only, or if it implies some degree of understanding and resonance to the emotion displayed, we recorded and compared responses to presentations of different stimulus categories with the same meaning; facial expressions, face-voice combinations, and bodily expressions communicating either fear or happiness (Magnée, de Gelder, van Engeland, & Kemner, 2007). We observed the same emotion-specific facial muscle activity (zygomaticus for happiness, corrugator for fear) for all three stimulus categories. This indicates that spontaneous facial expression is more akin to an emotional reaction than to facial mimicry and imitation of the seen face stimulus. Most notably, these emotionally congruent facial reactions occur also when the bodily expressions presented as stimuli are backwardly masked, and thus invisible to the observers (Tamietto & de Gelder, 2008b). A possible explanation for this similarity is that, for a given emotion, seeing a facial expression, a body expression, or hearing an emotional tone of voice all activate the same affect program (Frijda, 2007). The latter notion figures prominently in many evolutionary-inspired approaches to emotion. Of course this similarity in reactions across different emotion triggers begs the question of the embedding of affect programs in the brains' evolutionary history.

Clearly, none of these facts amount to claiming that any signal from the face is interchangeable with its equivalent from the body. Stimulus equivalence depends on a number of factors. It likely depends on the kind of emotion one focuses on. For example, disgust is obviously predominantly shown by facial movements and seldom involves the rest of body. Distance between agents is another factor playing an important role, as bodily expressions can communicate emotional intentions from a greater distance than facial expressions. The nature of the social relation is another dimension of intersubjective perception, and still other factors like hierarchical relation, familiarity, common goals, and friendship all determine, to some extent, the display of facial and bodily expressions (de Waal, 2005). Finally, there may be major differences in the voluntary cognitive control we have over facial and bodily expressions. In this context it is often assumed that facial expressions do come more easily under voluntary control than emotional body language does (Argyle, 1988).

Temporal Dynamics of Face and Body Processing

Do these correspondences in neurofunctional bases of face and body perception also extend to the time course of such processing? Important similarities in the temporal dynamics associated with the perception of faces and bodies have already been revealed in their electrophysiological correlates. The N170 is a well-known negative ERP-component, peaking around 170 ms at occipito-temporal sites, and is often linked to the stage of the structural encoding of faces (Bentin, Allison, Puce, Perez, & et al., 1996; Bruce & Young, 1986; Eimer, 2000b). Yet this component is also elicited by images of whole bodies (Gliga & Dehaene-Lambertz, 2005; Meeren, van Heijnsbergen, & de Gelder, 2005; Stekelenburg & de Gelder, 2004; Thierry et al., 2006). Most importantly, the electrophysiological inversion effect (Eimer, 2000a; Itier & Taylor, 2002; Watanabe, Kakigi, & Puce, 2003), consisting of a delayed and enhanced N170 deflection for inverted stimulus presentation, was elicited by both faces and bodies in contrast to control objects (Stekelenburg & de Gelder, 2004). This latter finding suggests that the recognition of both bodies and faces relies more on global perceptual processing and structural encoding, rather than on extensive analysis of individual details of the stimuli. In keeping with these results, behavioral data (Slaughter, Stone, & Reed, 2004) have recently been obtained showing sensitivity for the canonical properties of faces and bodies alike at around 18 months. These results are supported by ERP recordings providing evidence that the configuration of faces and bodies is already processed at thrre months of age (Gliga & Dehaene-Lambertz, 2005).

Although our first EEG study (Stekelenburg & de Gelder, 2004) revealed effects of fearful expressions for face (left N170 amplitude enhanced for fear) and body stimuli (VPP amplitude enhanced for fear), in the same time window we did not obtain an effect of emotional body expression on the P1, an earlier waveform that recent studies have reported to be sensitive to emotion. A possible confounding variable may, however, have accounted for this. This previous study presented still images of fearful and neutral bodies (faces blurred) in which the fearful bodies were rather dynamic (i.e., a defensive retreating body movement), whereas the neutral instrumental actions were rather static (i.e., the action entailed only the upper body) (e.g., combing hair, drinking from a glass, holding a telephone), but the actor did not show any forward or backward whole body movement, known to induce ERP effects (Wheaton, Pipingas, Silberstein, & Puce, 2001). A follow-up study was set up to exclude the possible confounding effects of perceiving implicit body action by controlling explicitly for the instrumental action aspect (van Heijnsbergen, Meeren, Grezes, & de Gelder, 2007). Participants viewed images of whole-body actions presented either in a neutral or a fearful version. We observed an early emotion effect on the P1 peak latency around 112 ms post stimulus onset, hitherto only found for facial expressions. Moreover, consistent with the majority of facial expression studies, the N170 component elicited by perceiving bodies proved not to be sensitive for the expressed fear. In line with previous work, its vertex positive counterpart, the VPP, did show a condition-specific influence for fearful body expression. Thus, our results indicate that the information provided by fearful body expressions is already encoded in the early stages of visual processing, and suggest that similar early-processing mechanisms are involved in the perception of fear from faces and bodies.

Mageneto-encephalography (MEG) has also been used for pinning down the earliest time window of face-specific processing. First, it has been reported that the M170 is obtaned for faces, which is presumably similar to the N170 described in EEG recording (Linkenkaer-Hansen et al., 1998). More recently, an earlier component in the 100 ms time-window has been described for faces and localizes in the midoccipital region (Halgren, Raij, Marinkovic, Jousmaki, & Hari, 2000; Linkenkaer-Hansen et al., 1998). In a study using fMRI constrained MEG we investigated for the first time the very early stages of visual processing for faces and bodies conjointly (Meeren, Hadjikhani, Ahlfors, Hamalainen,

& de Gelder, 2008). We observed that, when compared to inverted faces, upright faces elicited stronger responses in a distinct area in the lingual gyrus at 55–60 ms after stimulus presentation, which was followed by a response decrease in the calcarine sulcus and the lingual gyrus starting at around 65 ms. On the other hand, upright bodies elicited smaller responses compared to inverted bodies during the 80–90 ms latency window, in a small area in the calcarine sulcus and in a larger area involving precuneus and posterior cingulate gyrus. This category-specific sensitivity to orientation suggests that the extraction of the overall stimulus configuration of biologically salient stimuli already takes place in cortical areas V1/V2 earlier in the visual processing stream than hitherto assumed. If this would indeed be the case, such early category specificity may plead in favor of social specialization of the visual system, indicating that the early stages of this system are not a *tabula rasa* in the sense of being insensitive to the stimulus category until much later.

Findings from face and body perception and the associated speed of processing are in line with recent psychophysical and electro-physiological findings suggesting that visual categorization processes can already take place at even early latencies. In fact, Thorpe and colleagues (Kirchner & Thorpe, 2006; Thorpe, Fize, & Marlot, 1996) have found evidence for rapid visual categorization (i.e., the detection of animals versus nonanimals in natural images) to take place within the first 100–150 ms after stimulus onset.

Associated Deficits of Face and Body Processing

Valuable insight into functional association of physically different stimulus categories, like bodies and faces, are traditionally obtained from clinical populations, and this continues to be the case. For instance, do patients with face-recognition deficits also exhibit subtle body-recognition deficits and vice versa?

Prosopagnosia is a deficit in face recognition in the presence of relatively normal object recognition and may be due to brain damage in adulthood or to abnormal development of face-recognition skills. Accumulating evidence for closely related representations of faces and bodies, and overlapping brain areas sensitive to faces and bodies, raise the issue of whether developmental prosopagnosics may also be impaired in encoding bodies. We investigated the first stages of face, body, and object perception in four developmental prosopagnosics by comparing event-related brain potentials (ERPs) to canonically and upside-down presented stimuli (Righart & de Gelder, 2007) and by using fMRI. Normal configural encoding, as measured by the inversion effect was absent in three out of four developmental prosopagnosics for faces at the P1, and for both faces and bodies at the N170 component. The neural underpinnings of behavioral inversion effect explored with fMRI methods seem to underscore that the midfusiform face area is the most sensitive to face inversion and thereby the most likely candidate to subserve normal configural face processing (Yovel & Kanwisher, 2005).

Our results provide clear indications that prosopagnosics do not have this normal processing routine readily available neither for faces nor for some aspects of body perception. Yet one should not conclude, in line with the findings just quoted, that abnormal functioning of the midfusiform gyrus is the only determinant of configural processing of faces or bodies. Notably, however, a pronounced face recognition deficit characteristic of developmental prosopagnosia may not necessarily have its origin in a deficit in the initial stages of development. It may also or even exclusively be rooted in a general anomalous processing of the configuration that is important for other stimuli besides faces, which require similar visual strategies for initial encoding and bootstraps the acquisition of visual skill that progressively build up in the course of development. Fluent processing of faces as well as of bodies mobilizes form- as well as movement-processing abilities. More importantly, they seem to require a smooth translation back and forth between form- and movement-based recognition routines and integration of the two (Figure 3.2). Thus, the notion that faces and bodies have a similar developmental course needs further study, and findings about

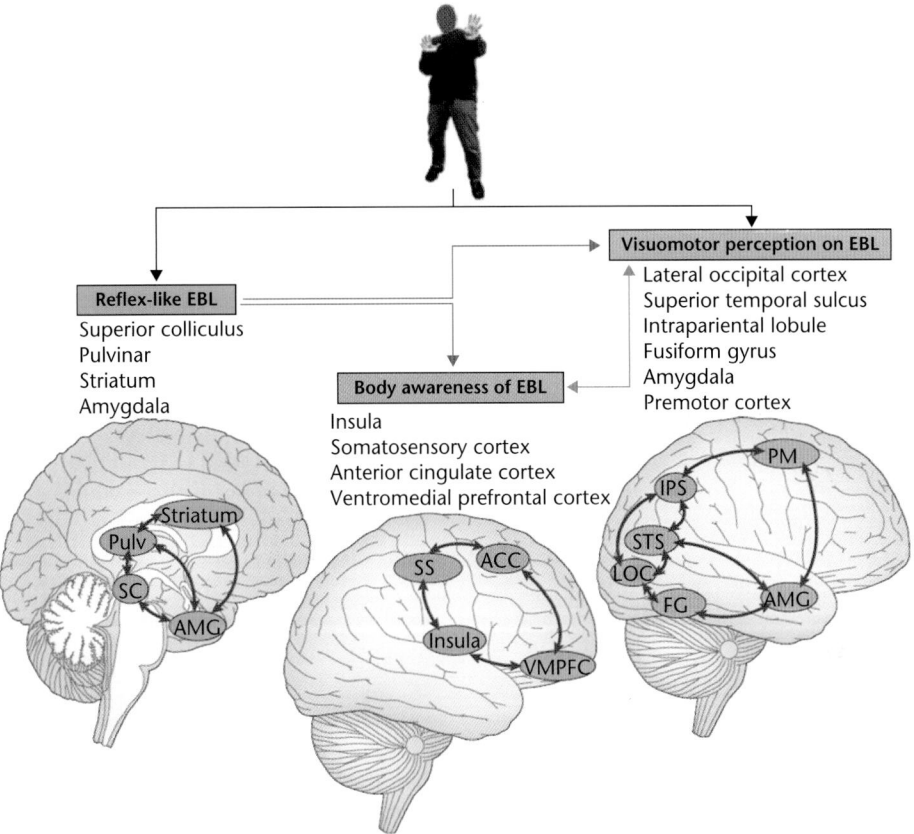

Figure 3.2 The three interrelated brain networks involved in emotional body language. (a) Reflex-like EBL (orange) involves the superior colliculus (SC), pulvinar (Pulv), striatum and amygdala (AMG). (b) Body awareness of EBL (green) involves the insula, somatosensory cortex (SS), anterior cingulate cortex (ACC) and ventromedial prefrontal cortex (VMPFC). (c) Visuomotor perception of EBL (blue) involves the lateral occipital complex (LOC), superior temporal sulcus (STS), intraparietal sulcus (IPS), fusiform gyrus (FG), amygdala (AMG) and premotor cortex (PM). Visual information from EBL enters in parallel via a subcortical (red) and a cortical (blue) input system. Feedforward connections from the subcortical to the cortical system and body awareness system are shown in red, reciprocal interactions between cortical system and body awareness system are shown in blue. From de Gelder 2006.

associated deficits may still fundamentally be related to the fact that they present similar challenges to the visual system.

Recent studies investigating emotional body perception in individuals with autism are providing evidence that emotional body perception is impaired, partly due to the anomalous functioning of the amygdala (Grezes, Wicker, Berthoz, & de Gelder, 2009; Hadjikhani et al., 2009). Another clinical population, patients with Huntington's disease (HD), provides very valuable insights into functional similarities

between facial and emotional body expressions because HD patients exhibit motor impairments as well as cognitive and emotional deficits. So far, impairments in the ability to recognize emotional stimuli have only been investigated by using facial expressions and emotional voices. To investigate the relation between motor disorders and emotion deficits, we tested recognition of emotional body language in 19 HD patients and their matched controls with a nonverbal whole-body-expression matching task (Van den Stock, de Gelder, De Diego

Balaguer, & Bachoud-Lévi, 2005). Results indicate that HD patients are impaired in recognizing both instrumental and angry whole-body postures. Furthermore, the body-language deficits are correlated with measures of motor deficit. Taken together, the results suggest a close relationship between emotion recognition and motor abilities, and this provide an element for the explanation of the perceptual deficit previously observed for facial expressions.

The findings mentioned so far allow us to compare the neurofunctional bases and time course of faces and bodies, and to document similarities and overlaps that may testify the existence of functional commonalities between these two classes of visual signals. Note though that not all studies have tried to control for low-level visual differences, which misleadingly may acerbate category differences (Thierry, Martin, Downing, & Pegna, 2007). The way around the major differences in visual properties we opted for in our own studies has been to compare systematically scrambled, inverted, and normally presented stimuli of faces, bodies, and objects, as a means to control for low-level differences when directly comparing stimuli belonging to different categories (Meeren et al., 2008). Some caution is also required concerning the use of localizers, because often these consist of a set of faces contrasted with a set of objects where the latter consists of a variety of different objects (e.g., in the study by Yovel & Kanwisher, 2005).

INTEGRATED PROCESSING OF INFORMATION FROM FACES AND BODIES

Obviously, in real life faces and bodies are simultaneously present and it makes sense to assume that we react to both together and at the same time, even if we focus more on one than on the other. On the other hand, depending on a whole set of context factors and also on which specific emotion is communicated at a given moment, either the face or the body may be the privileged medium to convey that particular meaning and set the emotional tone of the interaction. There are, at present, very few empirical data that throw light on this issue.

Nonetheless, it seems clear enough that context does influence how strongly the facial expression (Righart & de Gelder, 2006) and the emotional body language is appraised (Van den Stock, Righart, & de Gelder, 2007). It may well be the case that in one-to-one interactions, attention is, or appears to be, absorbed by the face. This may also be due to the fact that, by watching the face, one attends better to what is said. On the other hand, facial expressions are to some extent under intentional control because we are more used to attend to and monitor our facial expression and because they are more under our voluntary control.

These considerations were the starting point of some recent experiments in which we investigated the impact of the unattended body expression on how observers rate the emotion in the face. In the first behavioral study, we used a continuum of facial expressions created by morphing between two anchor points consisting of a happy and a fearful facial expression, while the bodily expression remained always the same (always happy or always fearful) (Van den Stock et al., 2007). The results provided clear evidence that recognition of facial expressions is influenced by the accompanying body language. A happy face combined with a happy body is categorized as more happy, compared to when the same happy face appears on a fearful body. Likewise, a fearful face on a fearful body is categorized as more fearful, compared to when it appears in combination with a happy body expression. It should be stressed that the instructions explicitly stated to categorize the facial expression, so there was no ambiguity regarding the target for attention and classification. Moreover, the interaction and trend analysis reported in this study indicate that the influence of the body expression is a function of the ambiguity of the facial expression: the whole-body expression has the strongest influence when the face ambiguity is highest, and decreases with reduced facial ambiguity. This indicates that the merging of information across stimulus categories is driven by the perception of the meaning irrespective of the medium through which the meaning is conveyed.

The same questions of whether and how multiple emotional expressions are integrated were addressed using a very different paradigm, which excludes potential confounds from attention and carefully controls for task demands. We used the redundant target paradigm and measured redundancy gain when two facial expressions, which could have either congruent or incongruent expressions, were presented at the same time (Tamietto, Adenzato, Geminiani, & de Gelder, 2007; Tamietto & de Gelder, 2008a; Tamietto, Geminiani, & de Gelder, 2005; Tamietto, Latini Corazzini, de Gelder, & Geminiani, 2006). Even more interestingly, we used this approach when emotional congruency was provided by the simultaneous presentation of a fearful face in one visual field and a fearful body in the opposite field, a situation in which there is no perceptual similarity between stimuli (Tamietto, Geminiani, & De Gelder, 2006). We consistently found that expressions of fear or happiness are more readily recognized when they are paired with a congruent expression, regardless of whether this is a face or a body. The fact that interhemispheric integration of emotions does not seem sensitive to the physical properties of the stimuli suggests that the emotional significance of different stimuli is extracted quite early on in the visual-processing stream and raises the possibility that body and face perception share partly overlapping neurofunctional resources.

These questions were explored in follow-up studies with methods that provide a better insight in the temporal dynamics. In a first investigation of the time course, EEG was used (Meeren et al., 2005). The combined processing of facial and bodily expressions revealed behavioral and rapid electrophysiological effects of emotional congruency. Already at 110 ms post stimulus onset, the P1, a positive ERP component found at occipital electrode sites, significantly distinguished between matching and nonmatching angry and fearful facial and bodily expressions (Figure 3.3).

Besides emphasizing the close relationship between processing of facial and bodily expressions, these findings additionally suggest that emotional expressions in both faces and bodies are encoded within a very early stage of processing, even before the visual categorization of a stimulus as a face or a body and the recognition of the personal identity has taken place, as indexed by the time course of the N170/M170 component (Bentin et al., 1996; Eimer, 2000b; Gliga & Dehaene-Lambertz, 2005; Kloth et al., 2006; Liu, Harris, & Kanwisher, 2002; Stekelenburg & de Gelder, 2004; Thierry et al., 2006). In fact, faces or bodies that were presented in isolation as control conditions did not elicit early emotion effects on the P1-component.

Neurofunctional Basis of Face-Body Congruence Effects

In a fMRI study, we presented compound stimuli consisting of a face and a body with a fearful, happy, or neutral expression, using a task that required judging the emotion of either the face or body, as indicated by a response screen directly following the stimulus. We focused on the hemodynamic response to these stimuli in the fusiform face and body area, the amygdala, and the extrastriate body area. Significant effects, for the fusiform face and body area, and near-significant effects for the amygdala, were found with larger activity for the fearful body in contrast to the happy and/or neutral body when this expression was combined with a nonfearful facial expression, that is, happy or neutral expression. When the emotion of the body had to be judged, we observed that a fearful body elicited a larger hemodynamic response than a happy body in the right extrastriate body area regardless of which facial expression was coupled to it (van de Riet, Grezes & de Gelder, 2009).

SUBCORTICAL SOCIAL VISION

As we remarked at the start, the notion of a brain with social-vision abilities most often reflects the notion that social skills may be attributed to some brain areas possibly reflecting the distinction between social and nonsocial categories of objects. Functionalist considerations like those already mentioned, which lump together faces and bodies carrying the same meaning, challenges a categorization based on such object properties and favors functional over physical categories. A different line of arguments in favor

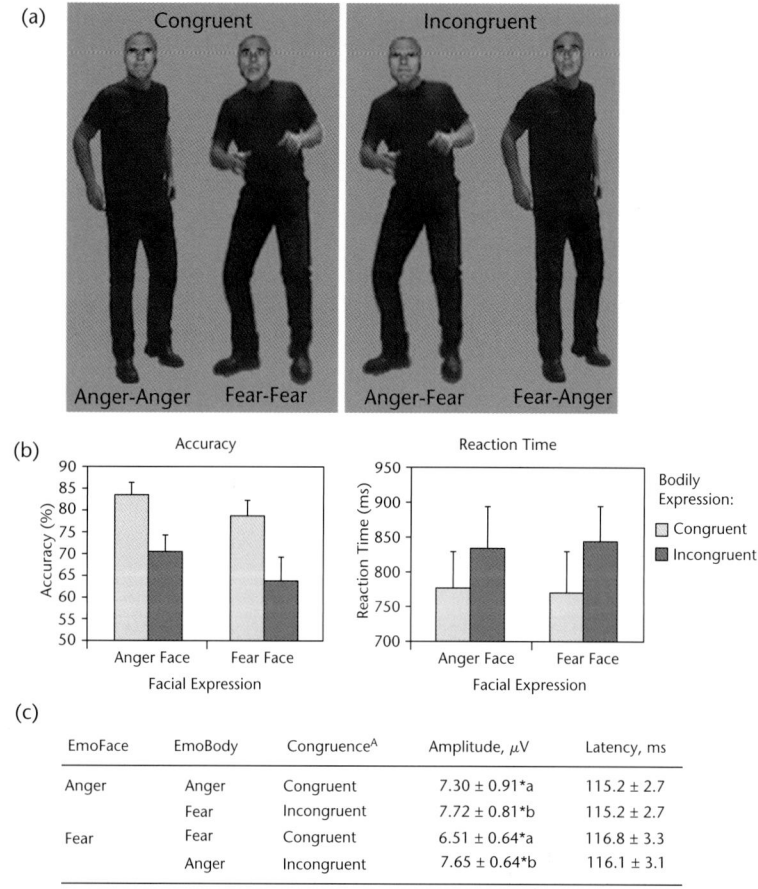

Figure 3.3 Examples of the four different categories of face–body compound stimuli used. Congruent and incongruent stimuli consisted of the same material in different combinations. The bodies of the two congruent stimulus conditions were swapped to create a mismatch between the emotion expressed by the face and that expressed by the body. (b) Behavioural results of the facial expression task for the compound stimuli. Participants had to judge the expression of faces that were accompanied by either a congruent or incongruent bodily expression. Categorization of facial expressions in the presence of an incongruent body emotion significantly reduces accuracy and increases observers' reaction times. (c) Mean event-related potentials at occipital electrodes at scalp sites O1, Oz and O2 for the face–body compound stimuli. This so-called P1 scalp site component is sensitive for the mismatch between the facial expression and the emotional body language. Asterisks denote corresponding P values (*, P < 0.05; **, P < 0.01; and ***, P < 0.001), with symbols a and b, indicating the contrasting conditions. The A in column heading denotes main effects for amplitudes. Modified from Meeren et al., 2005.

of functional analysis comes from evolutionary considerations, which draw attention away from strictly cortical taxonomies to processes in midbrain and in phylogenetically older subcortical structures. This is the area in which the notion of a brain equipped with social vision may be best implemented. In this section we review current evidence for the notion that humans have a brain with social-vision abilities and that subcortical structures are an important part of this. Comparing this to the night-vision abilities of some cameras, one might say that a brain with social vision can perceive social information "in the dark" and act under control of subcortical structures outside the realm of the light of explicit thought, deliberate reflection, and awareness.

In human social neuroscience research, the contribution of subcortical structures has come to the foreground through recent discoveries of nonconscious affective perception, first in studies of so called subliminal perception in healthy observers, and, more recently, in studies on nonconscious perception in neurological patients.

There are now many studies in normal observers and in brain-damaged patients showing that reactions to emotional stimuli do not depend on normal visual awareness. The latter may have become impossible due to brain damage, as in the rare cases of selective striate cortex damage, or because awareness is prevented by experimental manipulation; most typically visual masking (Dimberg et al., 2000; Esteves, Dimberg, & Öhman, 1994; Jolij & Lamme, 2005; Killgore & Yurgelun-Todd, 2004; Liddell et al., 2005; Morris, Ohman et al., 1998; Murphy & Zajonc, 1993; Niedenthal, 1990; Pessoa, Japee, Sturman, & Ungerleider, 2006; Pessoa, Japee, & Ungerleider, 2005; Tamietto & de Gelder, 2008a; Whalen et al., 2004; Whalen et al., 1998b; Williams et al., 2006; Williams et al., 2004). This suggests that there might be a nonconscious perceptual subsystem for visually based affect experience and cognition. To the extent that this system is an integral part of the brain, it may also be functional, though dormant, in normal observers and not only in patients with cortical blindness (affective blindsight) (de Gelder et al. 2000). This nonconscious system seems to operate in parallel with the normal, predominantly cortical, processing routes and may have characteristics that are possibly different from that of conscious emotion recognition. The extent to which the involvement of cortical routes can be ruled out in healthy observers is still controversial, as it is still a matter of debate whether masking or other techniques, like TMS, create a situation that is a functional equivalent of blindsight or of affective blindsight (Marzi, Minelli, & Savazzi, 2004).

Nonconscious or Unattended Perception

Findings about subliminal perception in the 1950s raised the question of whether unseen information influences our conscious perception of the seen world. The most radical indications are provided by studies of patients with striate cortex lesion, which we review first. A number of studies have been devoted to similar observations in neurologically intact observers discussed next.

New experiments on affective blindsight investigated possible online interaction between the aware and the unaware modes of emotional processing, as well as the influence exerted by unseen emotions over ongoing recognition of other consciously perceived stimuli (de Gelder, Morris, & Dolan, 2005; de Gelder, Pourtois, van Raamsdonk, Vroomen, & Weiskrantz, 2001; de Gelder, Pourtois, & Weiskrantz, 2002; Tamietto, Weiskrantz, Geminiani, & de Gelder, 2007). This series of studies took advantage of indirect methods of testing which, as compared to direct "guessing" methods, cannot be influenced by deliberate response strategies used by the patient. In these methods, two stimuli are simultaneously presented, one projected to the blind field, and thus unseen by the patient, while the other stimulus is projected to the normal field and hence consciously perceived. The patient is asked to respond to the normally perceived stimulus, and conclusions about nonconscious processing are based on evidence that conscious evaluation of the former stimulus is biased by the presence of the latter unseen stimulus (Marzi, Tassinari, Aglioti, & Lutzemberger, 1986). This approach has been successful in demonstrating both visual/visual as well as cross-modal interactions (visual/auditory) between consciously and nonconsciously perceived emotional stimuli. For instance, conscious recognition of facial expressions is speeded up if another face showing the same expression is presented in the blind field (de Gelder et al., 2005; de Gelder et al., 2001). Interestingly, the influence of nonconscious processing over conscious perception does not seem related to the physical/perceptual similarities between stimuli, but rather appears to be driven by the emotional information conveyed by the stimuli. Indeed, a bias from unseen to seen stimulus is also present when two stimuli have very different physical properties, such as a facial and a bodily expression, but represent congruent or incongruent information like, for example, a happy face paired with a fearful body expression (Tamietto, Weiskrantz et al., 2007).

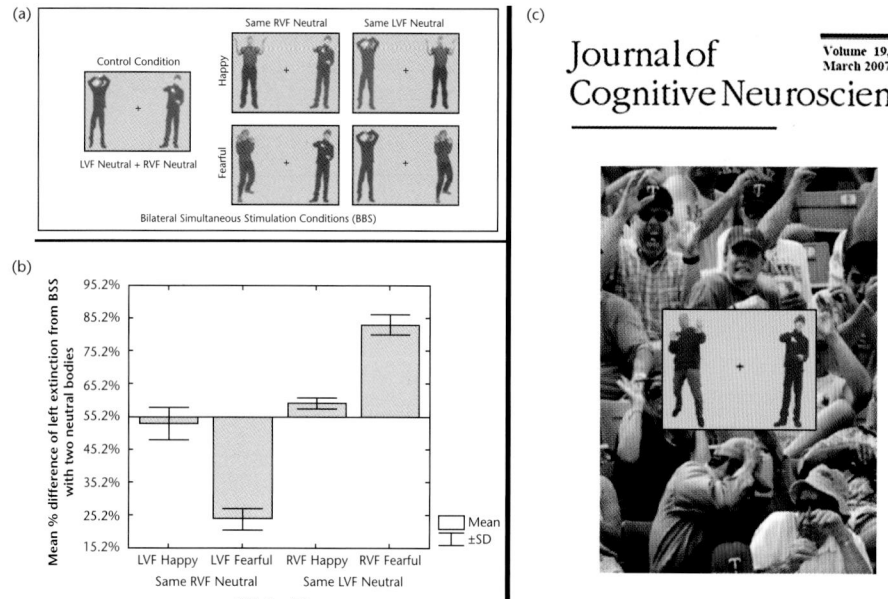

Figure 3.4 (a) Examples of the five bilateral simultaneous stimulation (BSS) displays presented to patients with hemispatial neglect and visual extinction. The five BSS conditions consisted of two neutral expressions (control condition) one left-side happy plus one right-side neutral, one left-side fearful plus one right-side neutral, one left-side neutral plus one right-side happy, and one left-side fearful plus one right-side neutral bodily expression. (b) Mean difference in the percentage of contralesional left extinction from the BSS control condition with left-side neutral plus right-side neutral bodily images. (c) cover of the *Journal of Cognitive Neuroscience* illustrating the fact that emotional bodily expression automatically summon attention and triggers similar and coordinated responses. Modified from Tamietto et al., 2007.

Similar findings have been reported by studies that investigate perceptual recognition of emotions in the absence of stimulus awareness in neurological populations with lesions to brain areas that are not primarily visual. For instance, a striking dissociation between the loss of conscious perception and the preservation of residual, nonconscious processing of some stimulus attributes (included emotional valence) is present also in conditions such as hemispatial neglect or visual extinction that follow from injury to the parietal lobe in the right cerebral hemisphere (Figure 3.4) (Tamietto, Geminiani, Genero, & de Gelder, 2007; Tamietto, Latini Corazzini et al., 2005; Vuilleumier, 2005; Vuilleumier & Schwartz, 2001). In these cases, however, the deficit of visual awareness is remarkably different from that shown by blindsight patients and arises at later stages of stimulus processing that are

most likely related to the ability to orient attention toward stimuli presented in a portion of the space, rather than to a defect directly due to visual perception (Driver & Mattingley, 1998).

A longstanding debate in all the areas where nonconscious perception has been reported is whether the difference with conscious vision is qualitative or only quantitative. In the latter case the difference between the conscious and the nonconscious mode is one of degree. This argument has been made in a number of studies by Pessoa and Ungerleider (Pessoa, 2005; Pessoa et al., 2006; Pessoa et al., 2005; Pessoa, McKenna, Gutierrez, & Ungerleider, 2002; Pessoa & Padmala, 2005; Pessoa, Padmala, & Morland, 2005; Pessoa & Ungerleider, 2004). Pessoa and collaborators (2005) paid attention to individual difference and discounted these in their fMRI analysis. Using a trial-by-trial analysis they observed that masked fear expressions only triggered amygdala activation in the study participants. However, when individual differences were taken into account and data were analysed separately for the subpopulation that had seen some of the masked stimuli, the amygdala only showed a response to these "seen" trials. Pessoa and collaborators concluded that nonconscious processing of emotional expressions may be the effect of weakly conscious processing. Of course, results like these do not settle the debate in favor of consciousness as a prerequisite for processing visual stimuli, but they indicate how difficult it is for the researcher to implement conditions in which the stimulus is completely unseen.

Nonconscious Perception in Cortical Blindness

For the time being, research on affective blindsight in cortically blind persons thus presents the clearest window on nonconscious emotion perception because, when visual parameters like luminance are carefully controlled, the patients literally cannot see nor visually acknowledge the presence of a stimulus. Investigation of this condition offers a unique opportunity to understand the neurofunctional bases of emotion perception without awareness. Its importance is directly related to the fact that emotional processing in the absence of stimulus awareness is an important component of the emotional capabilities of neurologically intact individuals. Thus, studies of nonconscious vision in healthy observers can thus provide only partial support for nonconscious emotional processing and its neural underpinnings.

Until recently, investigation of nonconscious perception in blindsight had focused predominantly on basic psychophysical properties, such as discrimination of simple shapes, gratings, movement, or color (Weiskrantz, 1986, 2000). The first report that a patient with blindsight could discriminate, with a reliability exceeding chance level, the emotion of stimuli he could not consciously perceive was published by de Gelder and co-workers in 1999 (de Gelder, Vroomen, Pourtois, & Weiskrantz, 1999). It involved patient GY with blindness in his right visual field following damage to his left occipital lobe, and consisted of four different experiments in which short video fragments and still images showing different facial expressions were used as stimuli. This first exploration used a conventional method requiring the patient to guess the emotion conveyed by stimuli he remained unaware of. At that time, there was some evidence from animal and human studies that subcortical structures (like amygdale in the medial temporal lobe) were able to survey for emotionally laden stimuli in the environment and to initiate appropriate responses toward them, even before a detailed perceptual analysis in occipito-temporal cortices (LeDoux, 1996; Morris, Ohman et al., 1998; Morris, Ohman, & Dolan, 1999; Whalen et al., 1998a). The finding that blindsight subjects can discriminate something as subtle as facial expressions without the contribution of primary visual cortex is, however, less puzzling when viewed against a broader biological context. Indeed, behavioral manifestations of emotion in the face or by whatever other means, including vocalizations and body language, have a high communicative function in many species (Darwin, 1872; de Gelder, 2006b; Hatfield, Cacioppo, & Rapson, 1994).

Over the years alternative explanations that do not need to invoke a noncortical route have been put forth (Cowey, 2004; de Gelder, Vroomen, Pourtois, & Weiskrantz, 2000; Heywood & Kentridge, 2000; Pessoa, 2005). One possibility may be that simple and easily discriminated visual features (e.g., eyes wide open) are systematically associated with a specific facial expression. When this simple feature is first shown in the intact field and then in the blind one, correct responses may be based on the association of the single and easiest feature to the correct response. This possibility of interhemispheric transfer has been conclusively discarded when evidence of affective blindsight emerged in patients with total bilateral cortical blindness who are, by definition, unable to use visual information perceived in the intact field (Hamm et al., 2003; Pegna, Khateb, Lazeyras, & Seghier, 2005).

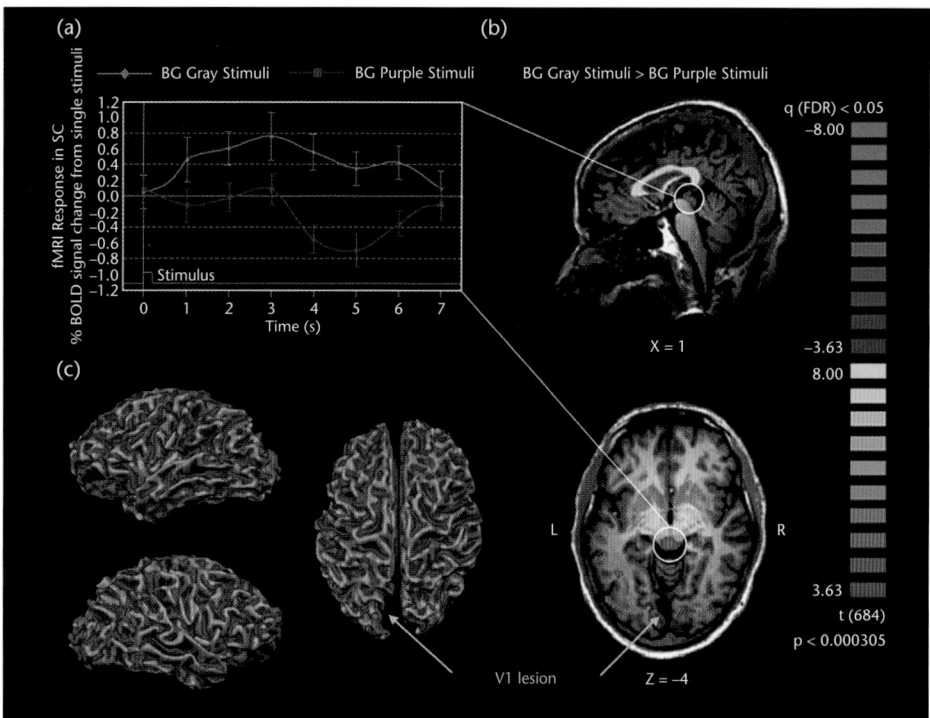

Figure 3.5 Neural correlates of the bilateral gain in blindsight patient G. Y. indicating a critical role of the superior colliculus in visuo-motor integration. Activation maps and mean percent of BOLD response in the SC for the contrast between bilateral gain for gray versus purple stimuli. Areas colored from yellow to red are significantly more activated in the bilateral gain for gray stimuli, whereas areas from blue to green are significantly more activated in the bilateral gain for purple stimuli. (a) mean percent of BOLD signal change (±SEM) for the voxels in the activated clusters as a function of stimulus color and position. (b) Sagittal and transversal slices of G. Y.'s brain showing significant activations in the left and right SC and in extrastriate visual areas corresponding to higher responses to the condition of bilateral gain for gray stimuli. (c) Three-dimensional reconstruction of G. Y.'s brain from lateral and top view showing the occipito-temporal extrastriate areas significantly more activated by the bilateral gain for gray stimuli. The dorsal portion of the lesion to V1 is visible in top view. BG = bilateral gain; BVF = both visual fields; FDR = false discovery rate; LVF = left visual field; RVF = right visual field; SC = superior colliculus. Modified from Tamietto et al., 2010.

The critical role of the superior colliculus (SC) was shown in a direct demonstration that in the absence of V1, the SC in the midbrain is essential to translate into motor outputs visual signals that cannot be consciously perceived (Figure 3.5). We showed that a stimulus in the blind field of a patient with a unilateral V1 lesion, although not consciously seen, can influence his behavioral and pupillary responses to consciously perceived stimuli in the intact field, and this is accompanied by activation in the SC. However, when the stimulus was colored purple,

and was hence rendered selectively invisible to the SC that is insensitive to short wavelength light, it no longer modulated visuo-motor or pupillary responses, and the activation in the SC dropped significantly. These findings show that the SC acts as an interface between sensory and motor processing in the human brain, thereby providing an essential contribution to visually guided behavior that may remain anatomically segregated from the major geniculo-striate pathway and entirely outside conscious visual experience (Tamietto, Cauda et al., 2010).

Is There a Subcortical Social Vision Only for Faces?

Until very recently, most investigations of human emotions predominately concentrated on perception of facial expressions (Adolphs, 2002). So, it is not surprising that affective blindsight was initially tested with facial expressions. Other facial attributes, such as personal identity or gender, were also tested with negative results, thereby suggesting that neither movement or nonemotional facial attributes are *per se* the determinant of the phenomenon. More directly, in later research, affective blindsight also emerged very clearly when still images of facial expressions were used, especially if the patients were tested with indirect methodologies that typically do not require the subjects to make guesses about visual events they do not perceive consciously (Anders et al., 2004; de Gelder et al., 2005; de Gelder et al., 2001; de Gelder et al., 2002; Pegna et al., 2005). Still unanswered is the issue of whether affective blindsight is induced by nonconscious processing of overall face configuration or by individual key features in the face. There is evidence that the eye region is particularly salient in conveying emotion information (namely of fear), and that the most ancient parts of our visual and emotion systems in the brain seem tuned to detect this simple signal rather than the whole face configuration (Morris, deBonis, & Dolan, 2002; Whalen et al., 2004). Nonetheless, a direct test of this issue in blindsight patients is still missing.

The functional notion of social vision we put forward here suggests that other stimulus categories with very different physical visual properties and/or attributes can also give rise to affective blindsight. Under the assumption that the special role of faces is not fixed by their physical properties but by their functional ones, it can be assumed that affective blindsight is possible for physically different stimuli with similar functional properties, such as bodily expressions.

Aside from facial expressions, other stimulus categories have been used to test whether affective blindsight could be extended to stimuli other than faces. Thus far, the most studied categories are affective scenes and bodily expressions of emotions. Generally, negative results have been reported for scenes with both direct and indirect methods, suggesting that the appraisal of the emotional content of complex pictures requires cognitive and semantic processing that depend critically on conscious visual perception, which is prevented by V1 damage in blindsight patients (de Gelder et al., 2005; de Gelder et al., 2002). On the other hand, behavioral and neuroimaging results have shown that affective blindsight for bodily expressions may be at least as clearly established as that previously reported for facial expressions, and sustained by a partly overlapping neural pathway (de Gelder & Hadjikhani, 2006; Tamietto, Weiskrantz et al., 2007). This indicates that implicit processing of emotions in blindsight does not seem to be specific for faces but rather, and more generically, for biologically primitive emotional expressions that are clearly associated with action tendencies.

The use of brainimaging techniques, mainly fMRI, provided direct evidence regarding the functional areas and pathways sustaining affective blindsight and the neural structures involved in it (Anders et al., 2004; de Gelder & Hadjikhani, 2006; de Gelder et al., 2005; Morris, DeGelder, Weiskrantz, & Dolan, 2001; Pegna et al., 2005). With the use of electroencephalography and its temporal resolution of the order of milliseconds, one also gets a better idea of the temporal dimension (de Gelder et al., 2002; Rossion, de Gelder, Pourtois, Guerit, & Weiskrantz, 2000).

A source of information used less often, but eminently complementing others, is provided by measuring the peripheral physiological changes that may be induced in blindsight patients by the presentation of unseen emotions. There is initial evidence that nonconsciously perceived emotions may elicit arousal and expressive reactions in the patients that are consistent with the affective valence of the unseen stimuli, as measured by electromyography and pupillometry (Figure 3.6) (Tamietto, Castelli et al., 2009).

The neuro-anatomical underpinnings of affective blindsight are still not fully understood. Yet, in the case of nonconscious social vision, as in that of affective blindsight, theories and hypotheses are enriched by the numerous findings on affective processing derived from animal studies, the information about pathways, and the

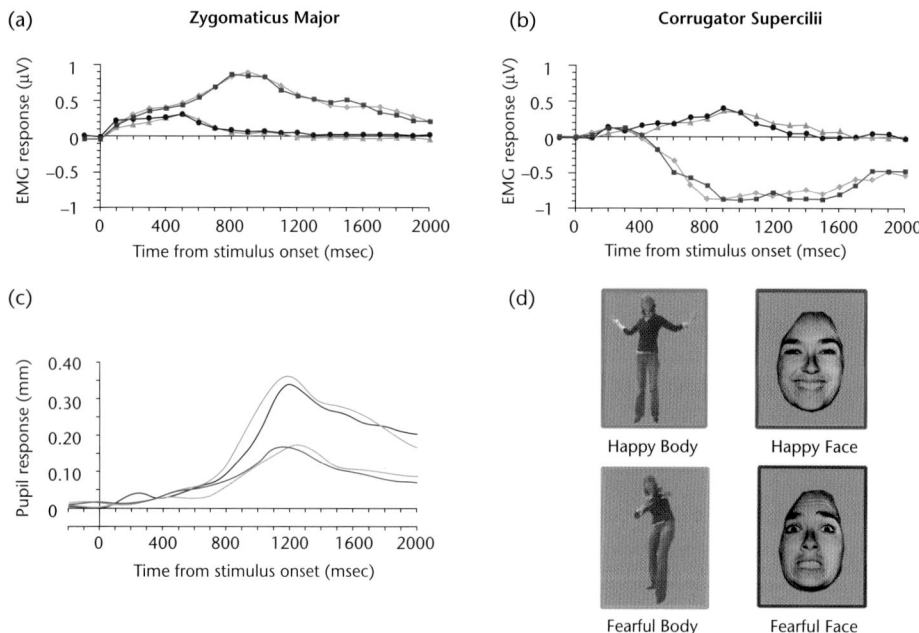

Figure 3.6 EMG and pupil responses in blindsight patient DB for unseen facial and bodily expressions of happiness and fear (a) Mean responses in the Zigomaticus Major. (b) Mean responses in the Corrugator Supercilii. (c) Mean pupil responses. (d). Examples of the stimuli used. Frame color on the stimuli corresponds to coding of EMG and pupil response waveforms to the same class of stimuli. Modified from Tamietto et al., 2009.

theoretical models they have produced. Earlier animal studies in rats underlined the role of midbrain structures in providing a rapid but coarse analysis of the affective value of auditory as well as visual stimuli, even without the contribution of the primary sensory cortices (Campeau & Davis, 1995; Doron & Ledoux, 1999; Jones & Burton, 1976; LeDoux, 1996; Linke, De Lima, Schwegler, & Pape, 1999; Shi & Davis, 2001). A similar subcortical pathway was also envisaged in a healthy human observer when facial expressions were subliminally presented (Morris et al., 1999). Thus, attention was suddenly focused on the functional integrity of this subcortical visual pathway in patients with affective blindsight and, indeed, the activation of subcortical structures composing this pathway has been repeatedly shown in different neuroimaging studies (de Gelder & Hadjikhani, 2006; de Gelder et al., 2005; Morris et al., 2001; Pegna et al., 2005).

The involvement of the subcortical pathway in affective and, before that, nonaffective blindsight has been mostly documented in patient GY, who suffered an occipital lesion very early in life (at age 7) (de Gelder et al., 2005; Morris et al., 2001; Sahraie et al., 1997). Thus, it is possible that postlesion and experience-dependent plasticity have taken place in this patient. In this case the role of the subcortical pathway would not generalize to all patients showing affective blindsight. Even though the presentation of affective stimuli to the blind fields of other patients also activated subcortical structures like the amygdala, the functional or anatomical connectivity of the different structures putatively implicated along this route have not been directly tested in patients different from GY. Interestingly, however, subliminal emotional expressions activate in healthy subjects the same subcortical pathway that is the most likely candidate in affective blindsight following striate cortex lesions (Liddell et al., 2005; Morris et al., 1999; Williams et al., 2006). Studies that will trace the pathways involved in noncortical processing are now under way using tractography methods like diffusion tensor imaging (DTI).

FROM SOCIAL VISION TO SOCIAL CONSCIOUSNESS

Is there a specialization of consciousness that corresponds to the brains' specialization for social vision? This is a bold question in view of the fact that our common sense notion of consciousness balks at the idea of fragmented, local, or regional subprocesses and sees consciousness as one and indivisible. Mainstream philosophical analyses are also built upon the notion that consciousness is not many but one, and almost by definition linked to constitutive singularity of the subject of consciousness (Galati, Tamietto, & Tinti, 2001). Yet, an a priori weak version of the social consciousness hypothesis is that social vision has a privileged entry into consciousness. It may be that by looking into the mechanism whereby this is made possible, we get support for the strong notion of social consciousness or at least a better understanding of what the strong notion would imply.

As a matter of fact there are multiple indications in the clinical neuroscience literature on dissociated consciousness phenomena (Marcel & Bisiach, 1988). A strong example that is relevant here concerns anosognosia. When central neurological damage yields paralysis (plegia) and/or loss of sensation, a variety of psychological phenomena related to the affected limbs may occur, whether separately or in combination, and one of them is anosognosia (Babinski, 1914). The term refers to the lack of awareness for a neurological symptom like hemiplegia following an acute brain lesion, and most often follows a right hemisphere damage. Anosognosia is also of great clinical importance because it is closely linked with successful rehabilitation, which is often ineffective as long as patients are unaware of or fail to explicitly acknowledge that their deficit exists and that they are not aware of it (Marcel, Tegner, & Nimmo-Smith, 2004). The manifestations of anosognosia are diverse. Often the patients simply ignore the plegic limb and do not recognize it as theirs. The lack of awareness may also have a variety of positive correlates going from delusions like denial of the existence or ownership of the limb to hatred of the alien object, but also, as we saw in a recent case, to admiration of scientific achievements of having been given a beautiful robotic arm.

The debate is still open whether anosognosia is a single phenomenon or a collection of loosely related ones. While the link with sensory loss, motor loss, or both is traceable, the terms *aware* and *conscious* or *unaware* are often used loosely. Marcel et al. (2004) list a deficit in afferent proprioceptive information, absence of proprioceptive phenomenal experience, or of awareness of such experience possibly due to an attentional failure; a failure to update long-term bodily knowledge (e.g., that one cannot move one's left arm); a delusory experience of limb movement.

The aspect of interest here is that the unawareness may be limited to, and specific for, the functional loss, and thereby specifically relates to the functional role of a damaged brain area (Bisiach, Vallar, & Geminiani, 1989). That is, awareness of having a sensory/motor deficit is not inferred from immediate experience of one's performance (Marcel et al., 2004). Two recent studies have investigated what brain areas may be credited specifically (Karnath, Baier, & Nagele, 2005) or even exclusively with the loss of awareness (Berti et al., 2005). Karnath and collaborators (2005) compared lesions in a large group of hemiplegic patents following right-hemisphere lesions. They show that the right posterior insula is the most critical structure in the contrast between hemiplegic/hemiparetic patients with anosognosia vs. patients without anosognosia. The functional significance of the insula is consistent with neuroimaging results in healthy subjects, which have revealed the specific involvement of this area in the subject's feeling of being or not being involved in a movement. Thus, taken together, the normal and the anosognosic patient data underscore the role of the insular cortex for one's awareness and beliefs about the functioning of body parts. A study by Berti and collaborators (2005) adds a further dimension to this by providing information on the motor structures involved in anosognosia. They focused on the critical lesion difference associated with anosognosia. By computing the difference in focal brain damage between two groups of patients with similar left side spatial neglect and hemiplegia, one with and one without anosognosia for motor deficit, the brain damage specific to anosognosia may be revealed. Interestingly they report that motor deficit denial was associated with lesions in areas related to the programming of motor acts, specifically Brodmann's premotor areas 6 and 44, motor area 4, and the somatosensory cortex. They conclude from this that the movement monitoring systems and the function it monitors may be implemented within the same cortical network. Provided one identifies this failure in monitoring function with what is the core phenomenon of anosognosia, we can tentatively and speculatively find support here for the notion of fragmented modular awareness. Action recognition and self-recognition may be closely related, and the role of the insula and that of motor monitoring/execution may be complementary, and both may be needed for clarifying anosognosia. For example, in a neuroimaging study in neurologically intact observers Farrer and collaborators measured brain activation as a function of whether the hand actions the subjects observed matched the movements the subjects themselves actually performed (Farrer et al., 2003). They found a modulation of activation level in two main brain areas by the degree of discrepancy between the movement executed and the movement seen on the screen. Activation in the right posterior insula decreased with a decreasing feeling of controlling the movement. When there was a mismatch between the hand actions they performed and what they saw, activity in the right posterior insula was low, whereas the activity was high when the afferent input matched the action. In contrast, in the inferior part of the parietal lobe, specifically on the right side, the less the subject felt in control of the movements of the virtual hand, the higher the level of activation was. These results suggest that action perception and awareness of execution are intimately linked, with action awareness requiring that the action is represented.

Affective Blindsight and the Mechanism Linking Social Vision and Consciousness

As we noted already, blindsight offers a unique window into the vestigial social abilities implemented in part in subcortical structures, which in neurologically intact subjects tend to be overruled by cortical processes. Nevertheless, blindsight continues to fascinate philosophers not so much because of what we may learn from it about the visual and the social visual system, but mainly because it appears as a critical test case for theories of consciousness. Affective blindsight raises issues that may be more specific than those of blindsight. One reason is that it provides a window into the brain's primitive social-vision abilities as described earlier. The other reason is that the presence of an unseen affective stimulus may give rise to a chain of affective reactions in the organism that provide the blindsight subject with nonvisual cues about the stimulus attributes. These nonvisual cues triggered by social vision may usefully complement the impoverished visual cues. For example, if emotions are characterized by the action tendencies they are associated with (Frijda, 2007), then the blindsight viewer may *sense and feel*, in a way to be described, the affective qualities of the stimulus he is presented with. This nonvisual sensation may determine his response independently of any visual awareness of it. Alternatively, for the more sceptical readers of affective blindsight findings, it may boost his weak or below-threshold input to the visually based response.

Unlike presentation of gratings or dot patterns to the blind field, presentation of affective images presumably resonates in the perceiving organism in other ways than by sending ripples through the visual system only. In future developments the scope of the debate on consciousness in perception will probably be broadened, because attention needs to be paid to the affective resonance of nonvisual stimulus processing and the ways in which this provides an indirect but efficient basis for guessing the meaning of unseen stimuli. This is already suggested by the findings about the role parietal somatosensory cortex plays in affective blindsight (Anders et al., 2004) and by similar mimicry reactions to unseen facial as well as bodily expressions (Tamietto, Castelli et al., 2009).

An evolutionary perspective on vision and emotion suggests that environmental events relevant for survival, such as affective stimuli, should be susceptible to preferential processing. Since a major constraint of sensory systems is their limited capacity to process incoming information, one means to cope with this limitation is by emotion enhancing attention, thus leading to increased detection of salient events. Indeed, normal vision depends critically on selective attention as many stimuli often escape awareness if unattended. Numerous studies on healthy subjects using different paradigms like visual search, attentional blink, or spatial orienting tasks, have shown that people more readily pay attention to emotional than neutral stimuli, especially when they communicate possible danger (Anderson & Phelps, 2001; Compton, 2003; Dolan, 2002; Eastwood, Smilek, & Merikle, 2003; Esteves, Dimberg, & Ohman, 1994).

Studies on brain-damaged patients with neurological deficits affecting visuo-spatial attentional selection may provide additional information and further elucidate how emotion influences attention and contributes to the making of consciousness. Following an injury to the right parietal cortex, patients frequently show a rightward attentional bias accompanied by loss of awareness for contralesional left stimuli (hemispatial neglect), especially when competing stimuli appear further to the right (visual extinction) (Driver & Mattingley, 1998). Nonetheless, the presence of emotional bodily expressions can reduce this attentional bias and help patients to temporarily regain awareness of the stimuli in the neglected (right) side of the space, as previously shown for facial expressions (Tamietto, Geminiani et al., 2007; Vuilleumier & Schwartz, 2001). This further strengthens the role played by the functional significance of the stimuli over and above their specific visual attributes, and suggests that many previous findings on emotional face processing might extend also to body processing. In this latter case, the effect of integrating facial and bodily expressions of fear across hemispheres is associated to specific peripheral psychophysiological changes, as indexed by phasic pupil-size changes. Pupillary dilation is indeed enhanced and fastened in the situation of emotional congruency between faces and bodies, whereas the effect of emotional incongruence is evident at longer latencies in the pupillary waveform.

Consistent with this perspective, preliminary data from our group indicate that emotional information is equally available from bodies and faces alike, with differences between the two possibly depending on the specific context and conditions in which they appear. For instance, facial expressions seem to be more effective in summoning attention when presented in the near (peri-personal) space of neglect patients, consistent with the prevailing role played by facial information when social interactions take place between individuals in close proximity. Conversely, however, bodily expressions have a privileged role when other people are perceived from a distance that does not allow recognition of specific facials traits, so that bodily expressions more readily recruit attention when shown in the far (extra-personal, out-of-reach) space (Geminiani, Tamietto, Rusconi, & De Gelder, in preparation).

REFERENCES

Adolphs, R. (2002). Neural systems for recognizing emotion. *Curr Opin Neurobiol, 12,* 169–177.

Anders, S., Birbaumer, N., Sadowski, B., Erb, M., Mader, I., Grodd, W., et al. (2004). Parietal somatosensory association cortex mediates affective blindsight. *Nature Neuroscience, 7,* 339–340.

Anderson, A. K., & Phelps, E. A. (2001). Lesions of the human amygdala impair enhanced perception of emotionally salient events. *Nature, 411,* 305–309.

Argyle, M. (1988). *Bodily communication.* London: Methuen.

Babinski, J. (1914). Contribution à l'étude des trobles mentaux dans l'hemiplégie organique cérébrale (anosognosie). *Revue Neurologique, 27,* 845–848.

Bentin, S., Allison, T., Puce, A., Perez, E., & et al. (1996). Electrophysiological studies of face perception in humans. *Journal of Cognitive Neuroscience, 8,* 551–565.

Berti, A., Bottini, G., Gandola, M., Pia, L., Smania, N., Stracciari, A., et al. (2005). Shared cortical anatomy for motor awareness and motor control. *Science, 309,* 488–491.

Bisiach, E., Vallar, G., & Geminiani, G. (1989). Influence of response modality on perceptual awareness of contralesional visual stimuli. *Brain, 112 (Pt 6),* 1627–1636.

Bruce, V., & Young, A. (1986). Understanding face recognition. *Br J Psychol, 77 (Pt 3),* 305–327.

Campeau, S., & Davis, M. (1995). Involvement of subcortical and cortical afferents to the lateral nucleus of the amygdala in fear conditioning measured with fear-potentiated startle in rats trained concurrently with auditory and visual conditioned stimuli. *J Neurosci, 15,* 2312–2327.

Compton, R. J. (2003). The interface between emotion and attention: a review of evidence from psychology and neuroscience. *Behavioral and Cognitive Neuroscience Reviews, 2,* 115–129.

Cowey, A. (2004). The 30th Sir Frederick Bartlett lecture. Fact, artefact, and myth about blindsight. *Quarterly Journal of Experimental Psychology A, 57,* 577–609.

Darwin, C. (1872). *The Expression of Emotions in Man and Animals* (third edition ed.). Oxford, UK: Oxford University Press, 1998.

de Gelder, B. (2006a). Towards the neurobiology of emotional body language. *Nat Rev Neurosci, 7,* 242–249.

de Gelder, B. (2006b). Towards the neurobiology of emotional body language. *Nature Reviews Neuroscience, 7,* 242–249.

de Gelder, B., & Hadjikhani, N. (2006). Nonconscious recognition of emotional body language. *Neuroreport, 17,* 583–586.

de Gelder, B., Morris, J. S., & Dolan, R. J. (2005). Unconscious fear influences emotional awareness of faces and voices. *Proceedings of the National Academy of Sciences, U.S.A., 102,* 18682–18687.

de Gelder, B., Pourtois, G., van Raamsdonk, M., Vroomen, J., & Weiskrantz, L. (2001). Unseen stimuli modulate conscious visual experience: evidence from inter-hemispheric summation. *Neuroreport, 12,* 385–391.

de Gelder, B., Pourtois, G., & Weiskrantz, L. (2002). Fear recognition in the voice is modulated by unconsciously recognized facial expressions but not by unconsciously recognized affective pictures. *Proceedings of the National Academy of Sciences, U.S.A., 99,* 4121–4126.

de Gelder, B., Snyder, J., Greve, D., Gerard, G., & Hadjikhani, N. (2004). Fear fosters flight: A mechanism for fear contagion when perceiving emotion expressed by a whole body. *Proc Natl Acad Sci U S A, 101,* 16701–16706.

de Gelder, B., Vroomen, J., Pourtois, G., & Weiskrantz, L. (1999). Non-conscious recognition of affect in the absence of striate cortex. *Neuroreport, 10,* 3759–3763.

de Gelder, B., Vroomen, J., Pourtois, G., & Weiskrantz, L. (2000). Affective blindsight: are we blindly led by emotions? Response to Heywood and Kentridge (2000). *Trends in Cognitive Sciences, 4,* 126–127.

de Waal, F. (2005). *Our Inner Ape: A Leading Primatologist Explains Why We Are Who We Are.* Tantor Media.

Dimberg, U. (1982). Facial reactions to facial expressions. *Psychophysiology, 19,* 643–647.

Dimberg, U. (1990). Facial electromyography and emotional reactions. *Psychophysiology, 27,* 481–494.

Dimberg, U., & Thunberg, M. (1998). Rapid facial reactions to emotional facial expressions. *Scand J Psychol, 39,* 39–45.

Dimberg, U., Thunberg, M., & Elmehed, K. (2000). Unconscious facial reactions to emotional facial expressions. *Psychol Sci, 11,* 86–89.

Dolan, R. J. (2002). Emotion, cognition, and behavior. *Science, 298,* 1191–1194.

Dolan, R. J., Morris, J. S., & de Gelder, B. (2001). Crossmodal binding of fear in voice and face. *Proc Natl Acad Sci U S A, 98,* 10006–10010.

Doron, N. N., & Ledoux, J. E. (1999). Organization of projections to the lateral amygdala from auditory and visual areas of the thalamus in the rat. *J Comp Neurol, 412,* 383–409.

Downing, P. E., Jiang, Y., Shuman, M., & Kanwisher, N. (2001). A cortical area selective for visual processing of the human body. *Science, 293,* 2470–2473.

Driver, J., & Mattingley, J. B. (1998). Parietal neglect and visual awareness. *Nature Neuroscience, 1,* 17–22.

Eastwood, J. D., Smilek, D., & Merikle, P. M. (2003). Negative facial expression captures attention and disrupts performance. *Perception & Psychophysics, 65,* 352–358.

Eimer, M. (2000a). Effects of face inversion on the structural encoding and recognition of faces. Evidence from event-related brain potentials. *Brain Res Cogn Brain Res, 10,* 145–158.

Eimer, M. (2000b). The face-specific N170 component reflects late stages in the structural encoding of faces. *Neuroreport, 11,* 2319–2324.

Esteves, F., Dimberg, U., & Ohman, A. (1994). Automatically elicited fear: conditioned skin conductance responses to masked facial expressions. *Cognition & Emotion, 8,* 99–108.

Esteves, F., Dimberg, U., & Öhman, A. (1994). Automatically elicited fear: conditioned skin conductance responses to masked facial expressions. *Cognition and Emotion, 9,* 99–108.

Farrer, C., Franck, N., Georgieff, N., Frith, C. D., Decety, J., & Jeannerod, M. (2003). Modulating the experience of agency: a positron emission tomography study. *Neuroimage, 18,* 324–333.

Frijda, N. H. (2007). *The Laws of Emotion*. Lawrence Erlbaum Associates.

Galati, D., Tamietto, M., & Tinti, C. (2001). La coscienza tra filosofia e scienza. *Rivista di Estetica, 18,* 8–36.

Gauthier, I., Behrmann, M., & Tarr, M. J. (1999). Can face recognition really be dissociated from object recognition? *J Cogn Neurosci, 11,* 349–370.

Gauthier, I., Tarr, M. J., Anderson, A. W., Skudlarski, P., & Gore, J. C. (1999). Activation of the middle fusiform 'face area' increases with expertise in recognizing novel objects. *Nat Neurosci, 2,* 568–573.

Gauthier, I. I. (2000). What constrains the organization of the ventral temporal cortex? *Trends Cogn Sci, 4,* 1–2.

Geminiani, G., Tamietto, M., Rusconi, M., & De Gelder, B. (in preparation). Diffential modulation of attention for facial expressions and emotional body language presented in the near and far space of neglect patients.

Gliga, T., & Dehaene-Lambertz, G. (2005). Structural encoding of body and face in human infants and adults. *J Cogn Neurosci, 17,* 1328–1340.

Grèzes, J., Pichon, S., & de Gelder, B. (2007). Perceiving fear in dynamic body expressions. *Neuroimage,* in press.

Grezes, J., Wicker, B., Berthoz, S., & de Gelder, B. (2009). A failure to grasp the affective meaning of actions in autism spectrum disorder subjects. *Neuropsychologia, 47,* 1816–1825.

Grosbras, M. H., & Paus, T. (2006). Brain networks involved in viewing angry hands or faces. *Cereb Cortex, 16,* 1087–1096.

Grossman, E. D., & Blake, R. (2002). Brain Areas Active during Visual Perception of Biological Motion. *Neuron, 35,* 1167–1175.

Hadjikhani, N., & de Gelder, B. (2003). Seeing fearful body expressions activates the fusiform cortex and amygdala. *Curr Biol, 13,* 2201–2205.

Hadjikhani, N., Joseph, R. M., Manoach, D. S., Naik, P., Snyder, J., Dominick, K., et al. (2009). Body expressions of emotion do not trigger fear contagion in autism spectrum disorder. *Soc Cogn Affect Neurosci, 4,* 70–78.

Halgren, E., Raij, T., Marinkovic, K., Jousmaki, V., & Hari, R. (2000). Cognitive response profile of the human fusiform face area as determined by MEG. *Cereb Cortex, 10,* 69–81.

Hamm, A. O., Weike, A. I., Schupp, H. T., Treig, T., Dressel, A., & Kessler, C. (2003). Affective blindsight: intact fear conditioning to a visual cue in a cortically blind patient. *Brain, 126,* 267–275.

Hatfield, H., Cacioppo, J. T., & Rapson, R. L. (1994). *Emotional Contagion*. Cambridge, MA: Cambridge University Press.

Haxby, J. V., Horwitz, B., Ungerleider, L. G., Maisog, J. M., Pietrini, P., & Grady, C. L. (1994). The functional organization of human extrastriate cortex: a PET-rCBF study of selective attention to faces and locations. *J Neurosci, 14,* 6336–6353.

Heywood, C. A., & Kentridge, R. W. (2000). Affective blindsight? *Trends Cogn Sci, 4,* 125–126.

Humphrey, N. K. (1983). *Consciousness Regained: Chapters in the Development of Mind*. Oxford: Oxford University Press.

Itier, R. J., & Taylor, M. J. (2002). Inversion and contrast polarity reversal affect both encoding and recognition processes of unfamiliar faces: a repetition study using ERPs. *Neuroimage, 15,* 353–372.

Jolij, J., & Lamme, V. A. (2005). Repression of unconscious information by conscious processing: evidence from affective blindsight induced by transcranial magnetic stimulation. *Proceedings of the National Academy of Sciences, U.S.A., 102,* 10747–10751.

Jones, E. G., & Burton, H. (1976). A projection from the medial pulvinar to the amygdala in primates. *Brain Res, 104,* 142–147.

Kanwisher, N., & Moscovitch, M. (2000). The cognitive neuroscience of face processing. *Cognitive Neuropsychology, 17,* 1–12.

Karnath, H. O., Baier, B., & Nagele, T. (2005). Awareness of the functioning of one's own limbs mediated by the insular cortex? *J Neurosci, 25,* 7134–7138.

Killgore, W. D., & Yurgelun-Todd, D. A. (2004). Activation of the amygdala and anterior cingulate during nonconscious processing of sad versus happy faces. *Neuroimage, 21,* 1215–1223.

Kirchner, H., & Thorpe, S. J. (2006). Ultra-rapid object detection with saccadic eye movements: Visual processing speed revisited. *Vision Res, 46,* 1762–1776.

Kloth, N., Dobel, C., Schweinberger, S. R., Zwitserlood, P., Bolte, J., & Junghofer, M. (2006). Effects of personal familiarity on early neuromagnetic correlates of face perception. *Eur J Neurosci, 24,* 3317–3321.

LeDoux, J. E. (1996). *The emotional brain.* New York: Simon & Shuster.

Liddell, B. J., Brown, K. J., Kemp, A. H., Barton, M. J., Das, P., Peduto, A., et al. (2005). A direct brainstem-amygdala-cortical 'alarm' system for subliminal signals of fear. *Neuroimage, 24,* 235–243.

Linke, R., De Lima, A. D., Schwegler, H., & Pape, H. C. (1999). Direct synaptic connections of axons from superior colliculus with identified thalamo-amygdaloid projection neurons in the rat: possible substrates of a subcortical visual pathway to the amygdala. *J Comp Neurol, 403,* 158–170.

Linkenkaer-Hansen, K., Palva, J. M., Sams, M., Hietanen, J. K., Aronen, H. J., & Ilmoniemi, R. J. (1998). Face-selective processing in human extrastriate cortex around 120 ms after stimulus onset revealed by magneto- and electroencephalography. *Neurosci Lett, 253,* 147–150.

Liu, J., Harris, A., & Kanwisher, N. (2002). Stages of processing in face perception: an MEG study. *Nat Neurosci, 5,* 910–916.

Magnée, M. J., de Gelder, B., van Engeland, H., & Kemner, C. (2007). Facial electromyographic responses to emotional information from faces and voices in individuals with pervasive developmental disorder. *J Child Psychol Psychiatry, 48,* 1122–1130.

Mahon, B. Z., Milleville, S. C., Negri, G. A., Rumiati, R. I., Caramazza, A., & Martin, A. (2007). Action-related properties shape object representations in the ventral stream. *Neuron, 55,* 507–520.

Marcel, A. J., & Bisiach, E. (1988). *Consciousness in Contemporary Science.* Oxford: Oxford University Press.

Marcel, A. J., Tegner, R., & Nimmo-Smith, I. (2004). Anosognosia for plegia: specificity, extension, partiality and disunity of bodily unawareness. *Cortex, 40,* 19–40.

Marzi, C. A., Minelli, A., & Savazzi, S. (2004). Is blindsight in normals akin to blindsight following brain damage? *Progress in Brain Research, 144,* 295–303.

Marzi, C. A., Tassinari, G., Aglioti, S., & Lutzemberger, L. (1986). Spatial summation across the vertical meridian in hemianopics: a test of blindsight. *Neuropsychologia, 24,* 749–758.

Meeren, H. K., van Heijnsbergen, C. C., & de Gelder, B. (2005). Rapid perceptual integration of facial expression and emotional body language. *Proc Natl Acad Sci USA, 102,* 16518–16523.

Meeren, H. K. M., Hadjikhani, N., Ahlfors, S. P., Hamalainen, M. S., & de Gelder, B. (2008). Early category-specific cortical activation revealed by visual stimulus inversion. *PLoS One, 3,* e3503.

Morris, J. S., deBonis, M., & Dolan, R. J. (2002). Human amygdala responses to fearful eyes. *Neuroimage, 17,* 214–222.

Morris, J. S., DeGelder, B., Weiskrantz, L., & Dolan, R. J. (2001). Differential extrageniculo-striate and amygdala responses to presentation of emotional faces in a cortically blind field. *Brain, 124,* 1241–1252.

Morris, J. S., Friston, K. J., Buchel, C., Frith, C. D., Young, A. W., Calder, A. J., et al. (1998). A neuromodulatory role for the human amygdala in processing emotional facial expressions. *Brain, 121 (Pt 1),* 47–57.

Morris, J. S., Ohman, A., & Dolan, R. J. (1998). Conscious and unconscious emotional learning in the human amygdala. *Nature, 393,* 467–470.

Morris, J. S., Ohman, A., & Dolan, R. J. (1999). A subcortical pathway to the right amygdala mediating "unseen" fear. *Proceedings of the National Academy of Sciences, U.S.A., 96,* 1680–1685.

Murphy, S. T., & Zajonc, R. B. (1993). Affect, cognition, and awareness: affective priming with optimal and suboptimal stimulus exposures. *J Pers Soc Psychol, 64,* 723–739.

Niedenthal, P. M. (1990). Implicit perception of affective information. *Journal of Experimental Social Psychology, 26,* 505–527.

Peelen, M. V., & Downing, P. E. (2005). Selectivity for the human body in the fusiform gyrus. *J Neurophysiol, 93,* 603–608.

Peelen, M. V., & Downing, P. E. (2007). The neural basis of visual body perception. *Nat Rev Neurosci, 8,* 636–648.

Pegna, A. J., Khateb, A., Lazeyras, F., & Seghier, M. L. (2005). Discriminating emotional faces without primary visual cortices involves the right amygdala. *Nature Neuroscience, 8,* 24–25.

Pessoa, L. (2005). To what extent are emotional visual stimuli processed without attention and awareness? *Current Opinion in Neurobiology, 15,* 188–196.

Pessoa, L., Japee, S., Sturman, D., & Ungerleider, L. G. (2006). Target visibility and visual awareness modulate amygdala responses to fearful faces. *Cereb Cortex, 16,* 366–375.

Pessoa, L., Japee, S., & Ungerleider, L. G. (2005). Visual awareness and the detection of fearful faces. *Emotion, 5,* 243–247.

Pessoa, L., McKenna, M., Gutierrez, E., & Ungerleider, L. G. (2002). Neural processing of emotional faces requires attention. *Proc Natl Acad Sci U S A, 99,* 11458–11463.

Pessoa, L., & Padmala, S. (2005). Quantitative prediction of perceptual decisions during near-threshold fear detection. *Proc Natl Acad Sci U S A, 102,* 5612–5617.

Pessoa, L., Padmala, S., & Morland, T. (2005). Fate of unattended fearful faces in the amygdala is determined by both attentional resources and cognitive modulation. *Neuroimage, 28,* 249–255.

Pessoa, L., & Ungerleider, L. G. (2004). Neuroimaging studies of attention and the processing of emotion-laden stimuli. *Prog Brain Res, 144,* 171–182.

Pichon, S., De Gelder, B., & Grèzes, J. (2007). Emotional modulation of visual and motor areas by still and dynamic body expressions of anger. *Social Neuroscience In Press.*

Righart, R., & de Gelder, B. (2006). Context influences early perceptual analysis of faces--an electrophysiological study. *Cereb Cortex, 16,* 1249–1257.

Righart, R., & de Gelder, B. (2007). Impaired face and body perception in developmental prosopagnosia. *Proceedings of the National Acedemy of Sciences of the USA,* (in press).

Rossion, B., de Gelder, B., Pourtois, G., Guerit, J. M., & Weiskrantz, L. (2000). Early extrastriate activity without primary visual cortex in humans. *Neurosci Lett, 279,* 25–28.

Rotshtein, P., Malach, R., Hadar, U., Graif, M., & Hendler, T. (2001a). Feeling or features: different sensitivity to emotion in high-order visual cortex and amygdala. *Neuron, 32,* 747–757.

Rotshtein, P., Malach, R., Hadar, U., Graif, M., & Hendler, T. (2001b). Feeling or features: different sensitivity to emotion in high-order visual cortex and amygdala. *Neuron, 32,* 747–757.

Sahraie, A., Weiskrantz, L., Barbur, J. L., Simmons, A., Williams, S. C., & Brammer, M. J. (1997). Pattern of neuronal activity associated with conscious and unconscious processing of visual signals. *Proc Natl Acad Sci U S A, 94,* 9406–9411.

Sakreida, K., Schubotz, R. I., Wolfensteller, U., & von Cramon, D. Y. (2005). Motion class dependency in observers' motor areas revealed by functional magnetic resonance imaging. *J Neurosci, 25,* 1335–1342.

Schwarzlose, R. F., Baker, C. I., & Kanwisher, N. (2005). Separate face and body selectivity on the fusiform gyrus. *J Neurosci, 25,* 11055–11059.

Shi, C., & Davis, M. (2001). Visual pathways involved in fear conditioning measured with fear-potentiated startle: behavioral and anatomic studies. *J Neurosci, 21,* 9844–9855.

Slaughter, V., Stone, V. E., & Reed, C. (2004). Perception of faces and bodies - Similar or different? *Current Directions in Psychological Science, 13,* 219–223.

Spiridon, M., Fischl, B., & Kanwisher, N. (2006). Location and spatial profile of category-specific regions in human extrastriate cortex. *Hum Brain Mapp, 27,* 77–89.

Stekelenburg, J. J., & de Gelder, B. (2004). The neural correlates of perceiving human bodies: an ERP study on the body-inversion effect. *Neuroreport, 15,* 777–780.

Tamietto, M., Adenzato, M., Geminiani, G., & de Gelder, B. (2007). Fast recognition of social emotions takes the whole brain: Interhemispheric cooperation in the absence of cerebral asymmetry. *Neuropsychologia, 45,* 836–843.

Tamietto, M., Castelli, L., Vighetti, S., Perozzo, P., Geminiani, G., Weiskrantz, L., et al. (2009). Unseen facial and bodily expressions trigger fast emotional reactions. *Proc Natl Acad Sci USA, 106,* 17661–17666.

Tamietto, M., Cauda, F., Corazzini, L. L., Savazzi, S., Marzi, C. A., Goebel, R., et al. (2010). Collicular Vision Guides Nonconscious Behavior. *Journal of Cognitive Neuroscience, 22,* 888–902.

Tamietto, M., & de Gelder, B. (2008a). Affective blindsight in the intact brain: Neural interhemispheric summation for unseen fearful expressions. *Neuropsychologia, 46,* 820–828.

Tamietto, M., & de Gelder, B. (2008b). Emotional contagion for unseen bodily expressions: evidence from facial EMG. *2008 8th IEEE International Conference on Automatic Face and Gesture Recognition, FG 2008,* Article number 4813317.

Tamietto, M., Geminiani, G., & de Gelder, B. (2005). Inter-hemispheric interaction for bodily emotional expressions: Is the right-hemisphere superiority related to facial rather than emotional processing? *Perception, 34 Supp.,* 205–206.

Tamietto, M., Geminiani, G., & De Gelder, B. (2006). Inter-hemispheric cooperation for facial and bodily emotional expressions is independent of visual similarities between stimuli. *Journal of Vision, 6,* 1063a.

Tamietto, M., Geminiani, G., Genero, R., & de Gelder, B. (2007). Seeing fearful body language overcomes attentional deficits in patients with neglect. *Journal of Cognitive Neuroscience, 19,* 445–454.

Tamietto, M., Latini Corazzini, L., de Gelder, B., & Geminiani, G. (2006). Functional asymmetry and interhemispheric cooperation in the perception of emotions from facial expressions. *Experimental Brain Research, 171,* 389–404.

Tamietto, M., Latini Corazzini, L., Pia, L., Zettin, M., Gionco, M., & Geminiani, G. (2005). Effects of emotional face cueing on line bisection in neglect: a single case study. *Neurocase, 11,* 399–404.

Tamietto, M., Weiskrantz, L., Geminiani, G., & de Gelder, B. (2007). *The Medium and the Message: Non-conscious processing of emotions from facial expressions and body language in blindsight.* Paper presented at the Cognitive Neuroscience Society Annual Meeting, New York, NY.

Thierry, G., Martin, C. D., Downing, P., & Pegna, A. J. (2007). Controlling for interstimulus perceptual variance abolishes N170 face selectivity. *Nat Neurosci, 10,* 505–511.

Thierry, G., Pegna, A. J., Dodds, C., Roberts, M., Basan, S., & Downing, P. (2006). An event-related potential component sensitive to images of the human body. *Neuroimage, 32,* 871–879.

Thorpe, S., Fize, D., & Marlot, C. (1996). Speed of processing in the human visual system. *Nature, 381,* 520–522.

van de Riet, W. A. C., Grèzes, J., & de Gelder, B. (2009). Specific and common brain regions involved in the perception of faces and bodies and the representation of their emotional expressions. *Social Neuroscience, 4,* 101–120.

Van den Stock, J., de Gelder, B., De Diego Balaguer, R., & Bachoud-Lévi, A.-C. (2005). *Huntington's disease impairs recognition of facial expression but also of body language. Paper presented at the 14th Conference of the European Society for Cognitive Psychology, Leiden, The Netherlands, 31 August-3 September.*

Van den Stock, J., Righart, R., & de Gelder, B. (2007). Body expressions influence recognition of emotions in the face and voice. *Emotion, 7,* 487–494.

van Heijnsbergen, C. C., Meeren, H. K., Grezes, J., & de Gelder, B. (2007). Rapid detection of fear in body expressions, an ERP study. *Brain Res, 1186,* 233–241.

Vuilleumier, P. (2005). How brains beware: neural mechanisms of emotional attention. *Trends Cogn Sci, 9,* 585–594.

Vuilleumier, P., & Schwartz, S. (2001). Emotional facial expressions capture attention. *Neurology, 56,* 153–158.

Watanabe, S., Kakigi, R., & Puce, A. (2003). The spatiotemporal dynamics of the face inversion effect: a magneto- and electro-encephalographic study. *Neuroscience, 116,* 879–895.

Weiskrantz, L. (1986). *Blindsight: a case study and implications.* Oxford: Clarendon Press.

Weiskrantz, L. (2000). *Blindsight: Implications for the conscious experience of emotion.* (Vol. Cognitive Neuroscience of Emotion.). Oxford: Oxford University Press.

Whalen, P. J., Kagan, J., Cook, R. G., Davis, F. C., Kim, H., Polis, S., et al. (2004). Human amygdala responsivity to masked fearful eye whites. *Science, 306,* 2061.

Whalen, P. J., Rauch, S. L., Etcoff, N. L., McInerney, S. C., Lee, M. B., & Jenike, M. A. (1998a). Masked presentations of emotional facial expressions modulate amygdala activity without explicit knowledge. *The Journal of Neuroscience, 18,* 411–418.

Whalen, P. J., Rauch, S. L., Etcoff, N. L., McInerney, S. C., Lee, M. B., & Jenike, M. A. (1998b). Masked presentations of emotional facial expressions modulate amygdala activity without explicit knowledge. *J Neurosci, 18,* 411–418.

Wheaton, K. J., Pipingas, A., Silberstein, R. B., & Puce, A. (2001). Human neural responses elicited to observing the actions of others. *Vis Neurosci, 18,* 401–406.

Williams, L. M., Das, P., Liddell, B. J., Kemp, A. H., Rennie, C. J., & Gordon, E. (2006). Mode of functional connectivity in amygdala pathways dissociates level of awareness for signals of fear. *The Journal of Neuroscience, 26,* 9264–9271.

Williams, L. M., Liddell, B. J., Rathjen, J., Brown, K. J., Gray, J., Phillips, M., et al. (2004). Mapping the time course of nonconscious and conscious perception of fear: an integration of central and peripheral measures. *Human Brain Mapping, 21,* 64–74.

Yovel, G., & Kanwisher, N. (2005). The neural basis of the behavioral face-inversion effect. *Current Biology, 15,* 2256–2262.

CHAPTER 4

Perceiving Through Culture:
The Socialized Attention Hypothesis

Hyekyung Park and Shinobu Kitayama

INTRODUCTION

One of the most important insights of modern psychology is that conscious perception is a culmination of a series of active, constructive processes of encoding and elaboration on information that impinges on sensory receptors (Bruner, 1957). Although conscious percepts almost always correspond to stimulus patterns and configurations (Gibson, 1979), they are also influenced by an assortment of factors that pertain to the perceiver him or herself. These factors include personality, motivation, need, cognitive sets, expectations, and most importantly for this chapter, culture.

The insight that perception can vary as a function of the perceiver factors was initially brought forward by Bruner and colleagues during the 1950s under the rubric of "New Look". This was followed up by a number of social cognition researchers who tested schematic effects in information processing (e.g., Higgins & Bargh, 1987). Among others, in a series of studies published during the 1970s and 1980s Higgins, Wyer, Bargh, and their colleagues convincingly demonstrated that perception and thought are powerfully influenced by cognitive categories that are made accessible during stimulus encoding and retrieval. More recently, a host of new studies have been conducted on perceptual and social judgmental consequences of racial stereotypes (Correll, Park, Judd, & Wittenbrink, 2002;

Eberhardt, Goff, Purdie, & Davies, 2004). Although the basic idea remains the same, it is elaborated with remarkable methodological sophistications.

So far, however, the research on constructive processes in perception has largely ignored culture. Culture is a constellation of ideational resources such as schemas, icons, images, discourses, and ideologies as well as their realization in daily practices, routines, and social institutions (Adams & Markus, 2004; Kitayama, Duffy, & Uchida, 2007). It is reasonable to anticipate, then, that different cultures offer very different categories and schemas even when impinging stimulus configurations remain identical, with substantial consequences in perception, judgment, and memory. For example, making a conciliatory statement could be seen as Machiavellian maneuver for political manipulation. Alternatively, it can also signify loss of face or honor. And, of course, such a statement may just be a genuine expression of defeat. Which of these and potentially many other meanings are activated and applied will depend on categories that are made available in a given socio-cultural context. This basic point, indeed, has been a major source of theoretical inspirations in socio-cultural psychology of the recent years. An increasing number of studies on cultural priming are premised on this basic idea (Oyserman & Lee, 2007). Furthermore, many cross-cultural variations in psychological processes can be interpreted in similar terms. For example, Uchida, Kitayama, and colleagues (2008) have argued that emotional support, such as compassion and encouragement, can either affirm interdependence or pose a threat to one's independence, depending, among other things, on the predominant cultural views of the self as independent or interdependent.

Although available categories constitute one major way in which culture can influence perception and thought, it is not the only way. In fact, as we shall argue later, it may not even be the primary way. In this chapter, we propose that culture influences perception and cognition by encouraging different attention strategies (Kitayama & Duffy, 2004). Attention is a gateway for information processing, determining what is taken up and what is neglected for further processing. Moreover, attention is also a set of resources for this processing. Depending on specific strategies used to allocate attention to incoming stimuli, the nature of processing can be quite different. This will have important consequences in the final percept and judgment. Furthermore, once acquired, attention strategies may prove to be relatively stable across time. Such is likely because, as we shall see, a variety of more sophisticated cognitive structures are built on the initial strategies that are acquired. Attention strategies may thus provide an anchor for cultural continuity and can even function as a stabilizer of cultural practices and meanings.

In what follows, we present a socialized attention hypothesis and argue that people in different cultures are bound to acquire attention strategies that vary in attentional breadth. People engaging in European American cultures are bound to form a strategy of focusing attention on one object at a time. Multiple objects can be attended to, but this is done only sequentially. In contrast, those engaging in East Asian cultures are bound to form a strategy of simultaneously dividing attention to multiple objects and holistically allocating it to the entire field. In line with earlier theorizing in this area (e.g., Markus & Kitayama, 1991: Nisbett, Peng, Choi, & Norenzayan, 2001), we contend that the cultural difference in attention is derived

from corresponding differences in practices and public meanings. Focused strategies are fostered by independent practices and meanings, whereas holistic strategies are encouraged by interdependent practices and meanings. In the main body of this chapter, we review this evidence, with an emphasis on cross-cultural, sub-cultural, or regional variations. We will conclude by reiterating the significance of attention as a central corner stone of both information processing and cultural transmission and reproduction.

SOCIALIZED ATTENTION AND CULTURE

Hypothesis

Our theoretical framework is presented in Figure 4.1. The general idea is quite straight-forward.

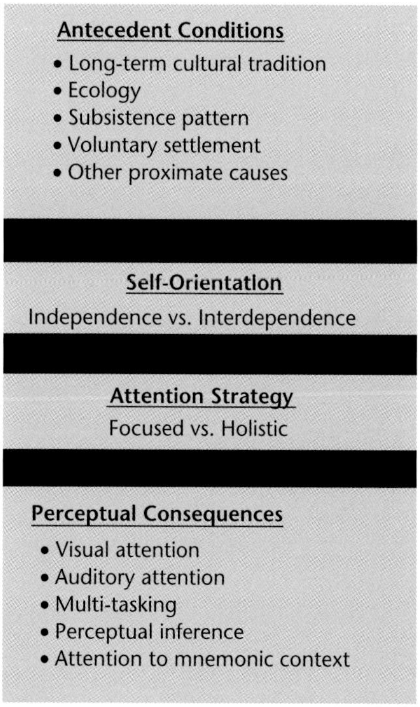

Antecedent Conditions
- Long-term cultural tradition
- Ecology
- Subsistence pattern
- Voluntary settlement
- Other proximate causes

Self-Orientation
Independence vs. Interdependence

Attention Strategy
Focused vs. Holistic

Perceptual Consequences
- Visual attention
- Auditory attention
- Multi-tasking
- Perceptual inference
- Attention to mnemonic context

Figure 4.1 The socialized attention hypothesis: A variety of antecedent conditions are expected to influence the degree of independence or interdependence, which in turn fosters different attention strategies. These strategies, varying in width, are assumed to entail various perceptual consequences.

A variety of antecedent conditions, including long-term cultural traditions, encourage different self-orientations, called here *independence* and *interdependence*, which, in turn, foster different strategies of attention. These strategies vary in the breadth of attention that is deployed to the external environment and internal memory representations. As such, they have a variety of perceptual consequences.

In some cultures social relations are tight, relatively closed, and emotionally bound, and mutual dependencies are socially sanctioned and normatively encouraged. These cultures may be called interdependent. In interdependent cultures it is important for people to pay close attention to social relations and other contextual factors. As a consequence, children are typically socialized to be attentive to multiple elements in the social surrounding (Chavajay & Rogoff, 1999; Correa-Chavez, Rogoff, & Arauz, 2005). For example, Miller, Wiley, Fung, and Liang (1997) studied socialization practices in Taiwan and found that Taiwanese parents constantly remind their children of what others might be thinking of them. This practice of shaming is wide-spread across East Asia. Correspondingly, cultural lay theories are also holistic, emphasizing interconnections of elements in the world, whether the elements are people or nonsocial objects (e.g., Ji, Peng, & Nisbett, 2000; Morris & Peng, 1994). Once brought up in these cultures, individuals are likely to acquire a strategy of dividing their attention simultaneously to potentially available stimulus elements. Kitayama and Duffy (2004) referred to this strategy of attention allocation as the dispersed (or *D*) strategy.

In contrast, in some other cultures social relations are relatively voluntary, formed or disbanded depending on each individual's goals and desires. Instead of social relations, the primary value is placed on each distinct self. Thus, mutual independence of people is emphasized, often taken for granted, and, normatively encouraged in a social group. These cultures may be called independent. In independent cultures, children are socialized to be attentive to their own preferences, desires, and intentions that are separate from those of others. They are thus encouraged to pay focused attention to the object that is most relevant to their desires and preferences. They can attend multiple objects, of course. But they tend to do so sequentially (Chavajay & Rogoff, 1999; Correa-Chavez et al., 2005). Correspondingly, cultural lay theories are also individualistic, emphasizing dispositions and traits of each separate individual (e.g., Morris & Peng, 1994). Once brought up and socialized in these cultures, individuals are likely to acquire a strategy of focusing their attention on one object at a time and sequentially attending multiple objects. Kitayama and Duffy (2004) referred to this strategy of attention as the focused (or *F*) strategy.

Precursors of Independence and Interdependence

Long-term Cultural Traditions

There are many different factors that influence independence or interdependence of a given cultural group. In their original formulation, Markus and Kitayama (1991) focused on independent, European American cultures and interdependent, East Asian cultures. They argued that the primary precursor of independence and interdependence involve very different traditions of culture that are relatively long-term, which have provided their members with opportunities to develop the type of attentional strategy that is most adaptive in their cultural contexts.

Independence of European American cultures can be traced back to a variety of philosophical ideas, political thoughts, and epistemologies of the modern West, some of which in turn may have origins in the ancient Greek civilization (Nisbett, 2003). Kitayama et al. (2007) argued that these cultural traditions form an important basis of socio-cultural practices and public meanings of the cultural context today. These practices and meanings emphasize the independence of the self. By regulating one's actions in accordance with these cultural practices and meanings, individuals will tend to gradually develop an *F* strategy of attention allocation.

In contrast, interdependence of East Asian cultures can be traced back to a number of Asian traditions of thought including Confucianism, Buddhist, Taoism, among others. Again these cultural traditions form a significant basis of socio-cultural practices and public meanings of many Asian cultures. Because these practices and meanings highlight interdependence and connectedness of individuals in a social whole, they encourage the individuals to pay close and simultaneous attention to various elements in the social setting. By regulating one's actions in accordance with the practices and meanings of interdependent cultures, individuals tend to gradually develop a *D* strategy of attention allocation.

Ecology, Subsistence Patterns, and Voluntary Settlement

Numerous other variables can systematically influence independence and interdependence, but what stands out as most plausible involve different ecological conditions and subsistence patterns and a process of voluntary settlement. In particular, different ecological conditions and associated subsistence systems may encourage very different views of self. Edgerton (1971) showed in his studies of four East African tribes that a greater degree of personal independence is characteristic of pastoralists as compared to farmers. He maintained that pastoralists, relative to farmers, tend to be more independent minded in their behaviors and that they have stronger and more clearly defined values including independence, self-control, and bravery. As noted by Goldschmidt (1971), "this independence of action is a characteristic of pastoral peoples (both as an institution and as a personality trait), and that it is structured into the social situation by the requirements of the pastoral economy" (pp. 133). If independence is related to focused attention, herders may be more focused in attention than more sedentary communities that live, for example, on agriculture or in-shore fishing. In fact, Uskul, Kitayama, and Nisbett (2008) have recently shown that herders are more focused in attention than farmers and small-scale fishermen in rural Turkey.

The role of eco-cultural conditions has also been emphasized in a recent proposal that voluntary settlement in frontiers is an important precursor to ethos of independence (Kitayama & Bowman, in press; Kitayama, Ishii, Imada, Takemura, & Ramaswamy, 2006). These researchers argue that the harsh ecology in frontier environments, together with primitive infrastructure, low population density, and high social mobility of the frontier is likely to foster self-reliance and independence. This consideration may prove to be especially important in understanding the cultural ethos of the mainstream U.S. culture, which is unique in its history of voluntary settlement in the frontier.

Proximate Causes

The factors just discussed are quite distal, largely operating over a long period of time. In addition to these factors, a host of more proximate causes can influence the degree of independence or interdependence. Although independence and interdependence refer primarily to patterns of self and social relations, they are also stored in memory as schematic forms of practical knowledge. There is growing evidence that once activated, these cognitive schemas of independence or interdependence regulate the person's behavior in the corresponding fashion (see e.g., Oyserman & Lee, 2007, for a review.).

Charting the Domains

In sum, our overarching hypothesis is that people vary in attentional breadth. Whereas independence encourages more focused strategies of attention, interdependence fosters more holistic strategies of attention. Given the foregoing considerations regarding the antecedents of independence and interdependence, we may expect sizable cross-cultural variations in strategies of attention. Those engaging in Western cultural contexts may be expected to be more focused or less holistic in attention than those engaging in Asian cultural contexts. In the remainder of this chapter, we will review existing evidence in support of this notion. Much of the evidence pertains to visual attention. But substantive evidence exists in the auditory channel as well. Moreover, attention to context has been observed not only for spatial context, but also for mnemonic context. Finally, much of evidence comes from behavioral data, but we attempt to review more recent studies that have tested physiological or neural correlates of attention by using electroencephalography (EEG) and fMRI.

CULTURAL VARIATION IN ATTENTION AND PERCEPTION

Visual Attention

A number of recent studies have demonstrated substantial cultural variation in the width of attention. People engaging in Asian cultures are bound to be more holistic in attention than those engaging in Western cultures. One of the first demonstrations came from research by Masuda and Nisbett (2001). These researchers presented participants with video vignettes of underwater scenes. Shortly afterward, participants were asked to describe what they saw in the video vignettes. American participants started out their descriptions by mentioning focal fish or moving objects in the scenes (i.e., information on salient objects) far more frequently than did Japanese participants. In contrast, Japanese participants tended to start out their responses by mentioning inert objects or background (i.e., field information). The researchers also examined recognition performance. In a second phase of the study, participants were given a surprise recognition task in which the objects they had previously seen were presented in one of the following conditions: with the original background, with no background, or with a novel background. Recognition performance of Americans was relatively impervious to the background manipulation. As may be expected, however, recognition performance of Japanese varied significantly as a function of the background conditions. Accuracy was highest when the target objects were presented with the original background, and it was lowest when presented with a novel background.

In a subsequent study, Masuda and Nisbett (2006) adopted a paradigm of change blindness (Rensink, O'Regan, & Clark, 1997).

Participants with either Western or East Asian cultural backgrounds were presented with an animated vignette that depicted various focal objects (e.g., airplanes) in the background of many contextual stimuli. Shortly afterward, they were presented with another vignette that depicted the very scene. In the second vignette, however, some details of the scene changed. Some changes occurred in the focal objects, but the remaining changes occurred in the background. Participants were to detect as many changes as possible. As may be expected, Americans were more likely to detect changes in the focal objects than changes in the background whereas East Asians were more likely to detect contextual changes than focal changes.

The foregoing studies indicate that even when exposed to physically identical stimuli, Americans and Asians tend to look at different aspects of the stimuli. Chua and colleagues (Chua, Boland, & Nisbett, 2005) directly examined this cultural variation with eye tracking. American and Chinese participants were recruited at an American university, and their eye movements were tracked as they were exposed to a series of pictures of a focal object (e.g., train) in a background scene. Each picture was presented for three seconds. During the first 400 ms after the stimulus presentation, both Americans and Chinese tended to focus on the focal object. Interestingly, however, during the next half second, Chinese made frequent saccades to the context, whereas Americans tended to continuously look at the focal object. Approximately 1 sec after the stimulus onset, Americans also moved their eyes to the context, but this effect remained more pronounced for Chinese than for Americans. Overall, Chinese looked more at the background than did the Americans. Conversely, Americans were more likely to look at focal objects than Chinese.

If Americans are more likely to look at a focal object than Asians do, the brain regions involved in object processing should activate to a greater degree for Americans than for Asians. Gutchess, Welsh, Boduroglu, and Park (2006) monitored brain activation patterns of Americans and East Asians while they were looking at everyday objects and background scenes. The visual stimuli were presented in one of the following forms: a central target object with white background (object only), a background scene without any central object (background only), and the target object combined with the background (combined). The researchers first identified brain areas that are more involved in either object processing (i.e., the areas showing greater activation in the object-only condition than in the background-only condition) or background processing (i.e., the areas showing greater activation in the background-only condition than in the object-only condition). For each of these two sets of areas, further analysis was conducted to determine cultural differences in the processing of an object plus background.

For the areas that are associated with object processing, there were some sizable cross-cultural differences. Overall, greater activations were found for Americans than for Asians. These areas included the left middle temporal gyrus (which is involved in retrieval of semantic knowledge about objects) and the angular gyrus (which is involved in processing of cross-modal information), and the right superior temporal/supramarginal and superior parietal gyrus (which is involved in processing of object location). These results are consistent with the hypothesis that Americans are focusing more on objects than Asians. Cultural differences were less pronounced for areas involved in background processing. Although the difference did not reach statistical significance, the culturally varied patterns in brain activation were consistent with the suggestion that East Asians pay more attention to background information than Americans.

In another relevant study, participants were shown realistic drawings of a target person who is surrounded by four people (Masuda, Ellsworth, Mesquita, Leu, Tamida, & Van de Veerdonk, 2008). Emotion displays of the stimulus people were varied in such a way that, in some trials, the emotion display of the target person was congruous with the emotion display of the background people (e.g., both looking happy) and in some other trials they were incongruous with each other (e.g., target person looks happy while the background people look sad).

Participants were instructed to make a judgment about the genuine emotion displayed by the target person. It was observed that, for participants with Western cultural backgrounds, the judgment of the target emotion was uninfluenced by congruence or incongruence of the emotions displayed by the surrounding faces. The finding suggests that people with Western cultural backgrounds tacitly believe that emotions are properties of an individual and separate from those of social others. In contrast, Japanese participants showed a strong halo effect. For example, when the target face shows happiness, it was perceived as happier when the surrounding faces also showed happiness than when those faces showed sadness. Supposedly, this judgmental bias reflects a Japanese cultural lay theory that emotions are to be socially shared. This speculation was indeed supported by behavioral data. These researchers tracked eye movements when participants were making judgments, which showed that Japanese were more likely than Americans to direct gazes to contextual faces.

So far, all studies reviewed here used naturalistic stimuli such as persons, animals, and objects from everyday life. Yet, one of the first tasks used to test cognitive styles in different cultural and ethnic groups involved very abstract geometric stimuli. In a rod and frame test (RFT) invented by Asch and Witkin (1948), participants are seated at one end of a tilted rectangular tube. At the other end of the tube, there is a line. Participants' job is to rotate the line and align it vertically while ignoring the tilted frame. As it turned out, many individuals have difficulties in completely ignoring the tilted rectangular frame, resulting in errors in the vertical alignment of the line. If the alignment error results from attention paid to the tilted rectangle, it should be larger for people with holistic attention (or equivalently, field-dependent as opposed to field-independent people). Consistent with this reasoning, Ji and colleagues (2000) have shown that European Americans made fewer errors in performing the RFT than did East Asians.

One ambiguity in interpretation of the RFT results, however, stems from the fact that, in this task, field independence or focused attention is indicated by superior performance. The RFT performance can be confounded with an assortment of other factors including intelligence and motivation. If people are more skillful (or intelligent) and/or more motivated, both of which are quite independent of their attentional characteristics, they may perform the task better. In fact, a number of studies have demonstrated that RFT performance is often correlated with IQ (Tinajero & Paramo, 1997; Witkin, 1962).

To get around this problem, it is imperative to use both a task that indicates holistic attention with improved performance and another task (like RFT) that indicates focused attention with improved performance. Moreover, the two tasks should be comparable in terms of difficulty. In addition, given that the RFT typically is assessed with equipment that is quite sizable, which has been a crucial setback as a tool for cross-cultural research, it should be desirable to have an equivalent task that is portable and thus lends itself to testing people in different cultures and locales.

These requirements have been met by a recently devised Framed-Line Test (FLT; Kitayama, Duffy, Kawamura, & Larsen, 2003). In this task participants are briefly presented with a square frame with a vertical line drawn in it. Participants are then shown another square frame of different size, and asked to reproduce in the second square frame either a line that is identical in the absolute length to the first line (*absolute* task) or a line that is proportionally the same as the first line (*relative* task). The absolute task requires people to focus on the target line while ignoring the square frame, so better performance in this task indicates focused attention. In contrast, the relative task requires people to pay divided attention to both the target line and the square frame; thus better performance in the relative task indicates holistic attention.

In the original study, Kitayama and colleagues (2003, Study 1) tested American and Japanese undergraduates and found, as predicted, that Americans performed better than Japanese in the FLT absolute task. Replicating the Ji et al. finding (2000), this could indicate

either that Americans are more focused in attention than Japanese, that Americans are more motivated than Japanese, or both. Importantly, a completely reversed pattern was observed for the relative task. In this task, Japanese performed better than Americans. It is clear, then, that the cross-cultural differences in the performance of the two FLT tasks reflect culture-specific attention tendencies, with attention more focused for Americans and more holistic for Japanese.

Although reliable, the cultural difference described here must not be overdrawn. Americans can carry out the relative task. They are just somewhat less effective in this task than Asians are. Conversely, Asians can carry out the absolute task, but the effectiveness or ease with which they do so is somewhat less than it is for Americans. This point was nicely made by Hedden, Ketay, Aron, Markus, and Gabrieli (2007) in a recent fMRI study. These researchers observed neural activities of the brain as Caucasian Americans and East Asians who recently moved to the United States, worked on a modified version of the FLT. Participants were presented with a series of framed lines. Their task was to judge whether the length of the current framed line is the same or different from the preceding one, according to either the absolute or the relative criterion. On "easy" sequences, stimuli were set up in such a way that the correct answer was identical for both criteria; on "difficult" sequences they were set up in such a way that the correct answer was different, depending on the criterion to be adopted. The researchers subtracted the activation patterns produced during the easy sequences from the patterns produced during the difficult sequences. The expectation was that the difficult sequences would pose especially dire problems, thereby demanding a greater degree of attention control when the task at hand requires attention operations that were not culturally sanctioned.

The findings were consistent with this reasoning. A reliably greater activation was found in brain regions associated with attentional control (frontal and parietal regions) (Wager & Smith, 2003) both when Caucasian Americans performed the relative judgment and when East Asians performed the absolute judgment.

The results suggest that when participants performed the culturally nonpreferred task (the relative task for Caucasian Americans and the absolute task for East Asians), they expended more effort.

Auditory Attention

The previous section described cultural variations in visual attention. If people over time set their attention in some range that varies in width, they may show corresponding variations in using auditory channels as well. Although this possibility has yet to be fully investigated, available data provide some support. In linguistic communication, word content carries primary information in all known languages. This information, however, is qualified or supplemented by various paralinguistic cues, such as vocal tones, facial expressions, and speech speed. People with more focused attention may attend more exclusively to word content in lieu of such paralinguistic cues, whereas those with more holistic attention may extend their attention more to those paralinguistic cues.

Kitayama and Ishii (2002) used a modified Stroop paradigm to investigate this possibility. Participants listened to a number of spoken words. The words varied in evaluative meanings. Some were positive (e.g., lucky, enjoy) and some others were negative (ugly, fault). Importantly, voice varied in tones. Some words were read in round tones, which are typically perceived as positive and some others were read in harsh tones, which are typically perceived as negative (Scherer, 1986). In a study like this, it is crucial to ensure that the vocal tones were manipulated in the same way across cultures or languages. To address this issue, Kitayama and Ishii low-pass filtered the vocal stimuli so that only vocal rhythms could be discerned. They then pretested these stimuli. Specifically, they had both Japanese and Americans rate the intensity of positive and negative emotions expressed by the rhythms. This data showed that the vocal tones were equally positive or negative across the two cultures.

In a critical condition, participants were asked to judge the meaning of the word as positive or negative while ignoring the vocal tone. To the extent that the contextual, paralinguistic information (vocal tone) is automatically attended to, it should influence the ease of judging the word meaning depending on the congruence between the two. Thus, the speed needed to judge the word meaning should be faster when the insignificant vocal tone is consistent with the word meaning than when it is inconsistent with the word meaning. The results confirmed this prediction. For Americans, the response time for word-meaning judgment was no slower when the attendant vocal tone was incongruous than when it was congruous, indicating that they are fully capable of filtering out the insignificant contextual information. In contrast, for Japanese, the response time for word-meaning judgment was much slower when the attendant vocal tone was incongruous than when it was congruous, meaning that they spontaneously paid attention to the insignificant contextual channel of information.

It might seem remarkable that Americans in the Kitayama and Ishii study (2002) were capable of completely ignoring the insignificant vocal tone information. This, however, may have been partly due to the fact that the vocal tone in this study was quite moderate and, thus, easy to ignore. Of course, given this fact it would seem quite surprising that Japanese were so completely thrown off by the vocal tone that was too weak to be even noted by Americans. Nevertheless, it remains to be seen whether Americans might in fact take note of vocal tone if it is more intense. In a subsequent experiment, Ishii, Reyes and Kitayama (2003) created Japanese and English stimuli such that vocal tones were substantially stronger than the ones used in the previous study. As may be expected, with this new set of stimuli, even Americans failed to completely ignore vocal tones. Thus, the time taken to make meaning judgments was longer when the attendant vocal tone was incongruous than when it was congruous. Importantly, however, this interference effect was still more pronounced for Japanese than for Americans, providing strong evidence that Japanese are more attuned to contextual (i.e., paralinguistic, vocal) information than Americans are.

In this series of studies, other participants were asked to make a judgment of vocal tone as positive or negative while ignoring word meaning. Consistent with the hypothesis that, as compared to Japanese, Americans are more attuned to focal, verbal information in lieu of contextual vocal tone information, an interference effect observed in this condition tended to be reliably greater for Americans than for Japanese.

Multitasking

If Asian attention is relatively more holistic, will Asians be able to simultaneously process multiple channels of information? Conversely, if American attention is relatively more focused, will they find it more difficult to do so at least as effectively as Asians do?

Kopecky, Kitayama, Saiki, and Meyer (2007, Study 2) had American and Japanese participants perform two tasks. In one task, participants were shown one of four colors (green, yellow, blue, or red) and asked to indicate which color was presented by pressing one of four keys that corresponded to that color (color task). In another task, they were presented with one of three tones that varied in pitch (low, medium, or high) and asked to indicate which tone was presented by announcing 1, 2, or 3 (tone task). Participants were extensively trained to perform each task alone or to perform the two tasks simultaneously. After the training, performance in the dual task condition was compared to performance in the single task condition. Accuracy was quite high for both Americans and Japanese, perhaps due to the extensive training. But response time (RT) showed quite substantial variations. Of particular interest is the difference in the RT in the dual task condition relative to the RT in the single task condition. To the extent that people can perform the two tasks without any difficulty, the RT difference should be close to zero. However, to the extent that there is an attentional bottleneck in the simultaneous processing of two channels of information, RT should be longer in the dual task condition than in the single task condition.

Kopecky and colleagues have found that, overall, the RT difference between the dual task condition and the single task condition was much greater than zero, indicating that there existed an important bottleneck in attention. As may be predicted, however, this difference was significantly greater for Americans than for Japanese. This data is consistent with the hypothesis that Japanese are more capable than Americans to simultaneously attend to and process two channels of information.

Further scrutiny of RT patterns revealed that the cross-cultural difference is due, in large part, to cultural variations in the choice of multitasking strategies. Specifically, when the RT difference between the dual task condition and the single color task condition and the RT difference between the dual task condition and the single tone task condition were examined in combination, it was possible to identify three different groups of participants. First, there was a group of participants who showed an equally good performance in both the tone task and the color task (with the RT difference very small). These participants put equal weights to both tasks and optimized the performance of both. In other words, they successfully carried out the two tasks simultaneously. As may be predicted, there were more Japanese than Americans in this group. Second, there was another group of participants who showed a very small RT difference for the tone task, but greater for the color task. Third, the remaining participants showed a reversed pattern, with the RT difference very small for the color task, but greater for the tone task. It is likely that these two groups of participants carried out the two tasks sequentially even when they were asked to do so simultaneously. As may be expected, there were more Americans than Japanese in these two groups. The finding is consistent with the notion that Japanese are better than Americans at handling information coming from dual channels.

Perceptual Inference

The two strategies of attention discussed here may also influence perceptual inference. Perceptual inference comes into play when people have to figure out the identity of an object that is presented under less than optimal conditions. It can happen, for example, when you see some beastlike object moving very quickly in front of you. In addition to such an overall, gestalt image, you may also recognize some distinct features, say, yellow and black stripes. In combination, you might conclude that the moving object must have been a tiger.

As in the tiger example, various visual cues are associated with the identity of the object at hand. Thus, in order to identify it correctly, we should draw systematic inferences from those available cues. Some cues may be quite holistic, pertaining to an overall shape or a degraded image of the object at hand; whereas some other cues may be much more local, pertaining to certain features of the object.

Ishii, Tsukasaki, and Kitayama (2009) have proposed that the ease with which detection and use of the two types of cues might vary systematically across cultures. Specifically, local cues should be easier to detect if attention is focused on them than if it is holistically dispersed on the entire image. In contrast, gestalt cues should be easier to detect if attention is holistically applied to the entire scene. It is important to note, however, that, once these cues have been detected, they must be analyzed to systematically garner relevant prior knowledge from memory and produce valid inferences. Because this type of linear inference requires careful analysis of the particular cues that are detected, it may be better served by focused attention than by holistic attention. It is, therefore, quite apt that Nisbett and colleagues referred to focused attention as "analytic." Overall, then, when only local cues are available, those with habitually focused mode of attention (e.g., Caucasian Americans) should be more capable than those with habitually holistic mode of attention (e.g., Asians and Asian Americans) to perform perceptual inference. In contrast, when only global, gestalt cues are available, people with holistic attention (e.g., Asians) may have an advantage in detecting the cues. However, as suggested by cross-cultural studies on logical reasoning (Norenzayan), they may be somewhat disadvantaged by virtue of the fact that holistic attention does not lend

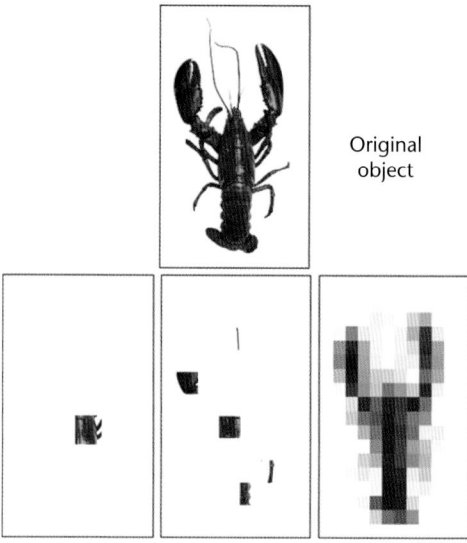

Figure 4.2 An example (lobster) of stimulus pictures in the Ishii et al. (2009) study. For each object, three types of stimuli (single-part, multipart, and gestalt picture) were used.

itself to systematic linear inference. In balance there may be no advantage for them under such conditions.

Ishii and colleagues prepared a number of visual images of common objects. Pilot data was used to ensure that the objects were equally familiar to both Americans and Japanese. From each image (e.g., lobster), two types of cue were created. As shown in Figure 4.2, a local cue for the object consisted of several distinct features of the object at hand (e.g., different parts of red armor); whereas a global cue was created by degrading the entire image. Participants were shown each cue and asked to identify the original object. As was predicted, performance in this perceptual identification task depended on both the cue type and cultural background of participants. Thus, in the local cue condition Caucasian Americans significantly outperformed both Japanese (Study 1) and Asian Americans (Study 2). Importantly, however, in the gestalt cue condition, as also expected, the cross-cultural difference was negligible.

Mnemonic Context Effect

From the research reviewed so far, it is fair to conclude that Asians are more sensitive or more attuned to contextual or background information than Americans are. Conversely, Americans are more sensitive to or attuned to object information than Asians are. However, one limitation of this conclusion comes from the fact that all the studies reviewed tested spatial context or background. Contexts can also be internal and mnemonic. For example, when observing another person, individuals may recollect previous experiences with this person, when and where they met him or her, what happened, and so on. Such information constitutes mnemonic context for the processing of the information about the target person. Individuals may then simultaneously attend to this mnemonic context along with the focal information about the person in order to form impressions or make judgments about the individual. Extrapolating from the previous evidence for the attention difference in the processing of external context, we may predict that Asians will be more likely than Americans to attend to the mnemonic context when processing focal objects.

To test this possibility, Duffy and Kitayama (2007) used a sequential stimulus estimation task. In this task, participants observe and reproduce a set of items that vary along a dimension (i.e., stimulus size). Over time, individual estimates of focal stimuli are assimilated with the average size of the set of stimuli that preceded the focal one and are thus available only in memory. The memory representations of the preceding stimuli serve as a context that helps inform judgments about the particular stimulus estimated on any given trial. This combination of prior information with present information results in a contraction bias, such that objects are remembered as being more typical of the set of which they are a member. In order for this mnemonic context effect (MCE) to occur when people are faced with the task of estimating a particular stimulus, they must divide their attention between the stimulus in question and their representations of previous instances stored in memory. Because a propensity

toward simultaneously processing context is likely to apply regardless of the nature of context being external or internal, it may be expected that the extent to which people attend to either a focal stimulus or its mnemonic context would vary as a function of their attention strategy, with Asians more likely than Caucasian Americans to attend to previous instances. If so, the MCE should be more pronounced for Asians than for Americans.

American and Japanese college students were presented with a series of 192 lines that vary in length. A target line was presented for 1.5 seconds, and the participants were to reproduce the length of the line by pressing keys of the computer keyboard. After they registered the response, the next target line was presented. Results are summarized in Figure 4.3, which depicts the extent of either overestimation or underestimation of line length as a function of the objective length of stimulus lines. As can be seen, when the stimulus lines were relatively long, underestimation tended to occur, whereas when they were relatively short, overestimation tended to occur. Thus, the perceived length was judged as a combination of the length of the current line and the average representation of the previously presented lines. As predicted by the notion that Asians are more likely than Americans to pay attend to the mnemonic context (i.e., the average representation of the previous instances), the assimilation effect was significantly stronger for Japanese than for Americans.

A conceptually similar effect has been shown by Lewis, Goto, Kong, and Lowenberg (2008) with an EEG measure. Within a so-called oddball paradigm, participants are exposed to a series of identical distracters ("8"). With a very low likelihood, however, a target ("6") is presented. When the target occurs, participants are to press a key. The target oddball causes a positive peak of EEG approximately 300 ms after the stimulus presentation. This effect is called novelty P300 or simply novelty P3. This P3 response tends to be observed in the relatively posterior regions of the brain, indicating that the signal is caused by relatively early stages of attentional processing. Within the same sequence of the

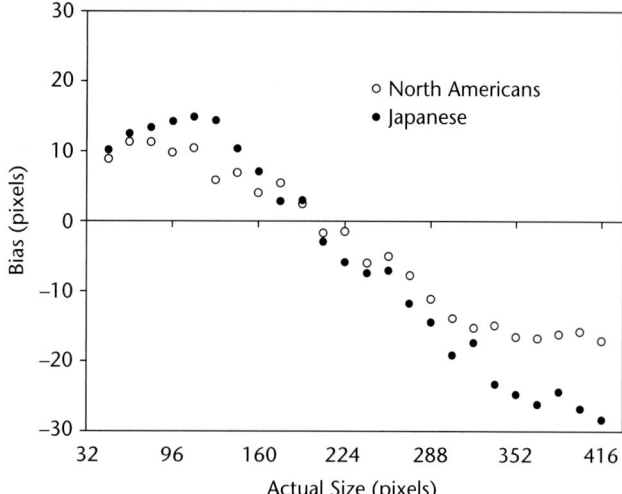

Figure 4.3 Mnemonic context effect for North Americans and Japanese: Generally, people overestimate line length for shorter lines and underestimate it for longer lines, but this effect is reliably larger for Japanese than for North Americans (Adapted from Duffy & Kitayama, 2007).

distracters, yet another completely novel stimulus ("DOG") may be inserted. This distracter oddball also results in P3 response. This P3 response tends to be observed in the relatively anterior regions of the brain, indicating that the response is caused by a relatively late stage of attentional processing.

Lewis and colleagues hypothesized that the novelty P3 responding to a target oddball is caused by attention focus on the target and, thus, it should be larger for Americans than for Asians. In contrast, the novelty P3 response responding to a distracter oddball is caused by a disruption of a mnemonic context created by a sequence of regular distracters. Thus, this P3 response should be larger for those who chronically allocate more attention to mnemonic context. The results were in line with the hypothesis. Lewis and colleagues found both the target oddball P3 response and the distracter oddball P3 response. As predicted, the target oddball P3 tended to be larger for Caucasian Americans than for Asian Americans, but the distracter oddball P3 response was reliably larger for Asian Americans than for Caucasian Americans.

CONCLUSIONS

In this chapter, we reviewed accumulating evidence for cultural variation in attention strategies. Evidence consistently shows that Asians tend to be more holistic in attention, dispersing it more broadly and simultaneously to multiple stimuli, whereas Caucasian Americans tend to be more focused on a single object. Evidence is particularly strong in respect to visual attention. However, evidence has also been found in respect to auditory attention, multitasking, perceptual inference, and attention to mnemonic context.

Causal Role of Self-Orientation in Attention Regulation

Future work should examine causal links between self-orientations of the self as independent versus interdependent and the attention strategies. Some initial evidence is quite promising. First, some studies have observed reliable correlations between individual difference measures of independence versus interdependence and indicators of attention. For example, in an aforementioned neuro-imaging study, Hedden and colleagues (2007) found that Asian Americans showed an especially strong frontal activation (indicative of greater attention control) when they engage in culturally nonsanctioned FLT absolute task. This effect, of importance, was stronger for nonacculturated Asian Americans. Likewise, Lewis and colleagues (2008) found that a novelty P3 caused by a distracter oddball is stronger for Asians than for Caucasians. Furthermore, this ethnic difference was largely explained by cultural collectivism as assessed by a collectivism scale developed by Triandis (1995).

A second line of evidence for the causal role of self-orientations on attention comes from some small number of studies showing a reliable priming effect on attention (see Oyserman & Lee, 2007, for a review). It is commonly assumed that personal self is primed when participants are asked to circle a number of singular first-person pronouns (i.e., I, my, me). Under these conditions, attention tends to be more focused. In contrast, it is also assumed that collective self is primed when participants are asked to circle a number of plural first-person pronouns (i.e., we, our, us). Under these conditions, attention tends to be more holistic and dispersed. At present, however, this evidence is somewhat limited because (1) only a small number of priming methods have so far been used in respect to a relatively small range of attention tasks, and (2) nearly all published data come from Europe and North America. The extent to which attention strategies can be primed by pronoun priming or other priming methods must be further tested in future work.

A third method that is highly promising in testing a causal role of self-orientations in attention is to examine different subgroups that vary in the form of social relationship. Following an earlier work by Edgerton (1971), Uskul and colleagues (2008) hypothesized and found that herders are likely to be more independent than farmers and small-scale fishermen in a rural traditional society. Much more effort along this line is warranted in future work.

Socialization of Attention Strategy

Another important agenda for future work is to trace the trajectory of the development of attention strategies (Keller, 2007). One important piece of research is reported by Chavajay and Rogoff (1999). They videotaped 14–20-month-old toddlers and their caregivers in both a Guatemalan Mayan community and a middle-class, European American community. In home visits, caregivers were interviewed and in the middle of the interview, they were provided with novel toys and asked to get their toddlers to operate them. In each of the home visits, there were at least five people present including a caregiver, a toddler, an older sibling, the interviewer, and the camera operator. The researchers then observed both child-focused activities (e.g., caregivers aiding toddlers to explore those novel toys) and adult-focused activities (e.g., caregivers interacting with other adults). Consistent with the notion that attention is more dispersed or holistic in traditional, farming communities, it was found that Guatemalan Mayan caregivers and toddlers were more likely than European American counterparts to attend to multiple events simultaneously.

In another effort along this line, Duffy, Toriyama, Itakura, and Kitayama (2007) developed a kid version of the FLT and tested 4–5 – year-olds, 6–8-year-olds, and 8–13-year-olds in both Japan and the United States. Children older than 6 years of age in the United States and Japan showed the culturally divergent patterns of attention that are highly analogous to the one found in adult samples. However, 4–5 year olds in both cultures were more similar than different. Both American and Japanese children tended to perform better in the relative than in the absolute FLT task. The cultural difference at this age was negligible, but it became significant for the 6- year-olds. Much more effort along this line is required in future work to gain more detailed information about the development of the culturally specific attention strategies.

Attention, Self, and Social Behavior

Attention is a gateway to all information processing. Thus, the fact that culture has a profound effect on attention may be taken to suggest that the nature of information that is brought to bear on all sort of psychological processing is systematically different across cultures. We believe that future research may benefit from concerted research attention paid to this possibility. It may well be the case, then, that once formed, habits of focused attention lead to more independent self or, alternatively, holistic attention results in more interdependent self because of constraints the attention patterns pose on the kind of self-relevant processes. At present, we are aware of no direct evidence. Nevertheless, as Kitayama and Duffy (2004) argued, to the extent that effects like these exist, socialized attention may well have quite significant roles in perpetuation, transmission, and maintenance of cultural patterns of both self and social behaviors.

REFERENCES

Adams, G., & Markus, H. R. (2004). Toward a conception of culture suitable for a social psychology of culture. In M. Schaller and C. S. Crandall (Eds.), *The psychological foundations of culture* (pp. 335–360). Mahwah, NJ: Erlbaum.

Asch, S. E., & Witkin, H. A. (1948). Studies in space orientation: II. Perception of the upright with displaced visual fields and with body tilted. *Journal of Experimental Psychology, 38,* 455–475.

Bruner, J. S. (1957). On perceptual readiness. *Psychological Review, 64,* 123–152.

Chavajay, P., & Rogoff, B. (1999). Cultural variation in management of attention by children and their caregivers. *Developmental Psychology, 35,* 1079–1090.

Chua, H. F., Boland, J. E., & Nisbett, R. E. (2005). Cultural variation in eye movements during scene perception. *Proceedings of the National Academy of Sciences, 102,* 12629–12633.

Correa–Chavez, M., Rogoff, B., & Arauz, R. M. (2005). Cultural patterns in attending to two events at once. *Child Development, 76,* 664–678.

Correll, J., Park, B., Judd, C. M., & Wittenbrink, B. (2002). The police officer's dilemma: Using ethnicity to disambiguate potentially threatening individuals. *Journal of Personality and Social Psychology, 83,* 1314–1329.

Duffy, S., & Kitayama, S. (2007). Mnemonic context effect in two cultures: Attention to memory representations? *Cognitive Science, 31,* 1–12.

Duffy, S., Toriyama, R., Itakura, S., & Kitayama, S. (2007). *When culture comes to mind: The development of culturally contingent strategies of attention in children.* Unpublished manuscript, Rutgers University.

Eberhardt, J. L., Goff, P. A., Purdie, V. J., & Davies, P. G. (2004). Seeing black: Race, crime, and visual processing. *Journal of Personality and Social Psychology, 87,* 876–893.

Edgerton, R. B. (1971). *The individual in cultural adaptation: A study of four East African peoples.* Berkeley, CA: University of California Press.

Gibson, J. J. (1979). *The ecological approach to visual perception.* Boston: Houghton Mifflin.

Goldschmidt, W. (1971). Independence as an element in pastoral social systems. *Anthropological Quarterly, 44,* 132–142.

Gutchess, A. H., Welsh, R. C., Boduroglu, A., & Park, D. C. (2006). Cultural differences in neural function associated with object processing. *Cognitive, Affective, and Behavioral Neuroscience, 6,* 102–109.

Hedden, T., Ketay, S., Aron, A., Markus, H., & Gabrieli, J. (2007). *Cultural influences on neural substrates of attention control.* Unpublished manuscript. Stanford University.

Higgins, E. T., & Bargh, J. A. (1987). Social cognition and social perception. *Annual review of psychology, 38,* 369–425.

Ishii, K., Reyes, J. A., & Kitayama, S. (2003). Spontaneous attention to word content versus emotional tone: Differences among three cultures. *Psychological Science, 14,* 39–46.

Ishii, K., Tsukasaki, T., & Kitayama, S. (2009). Cultural and visual perception: Does perceptual inference depend on culture? *Japanese Phychological Research, 51,* 103–109.

Ji, L–J., Peng, K., & Nisbett, R. E. (2000). Culture, control, and perception of relationships in the environment. *Journal of Personality and Social Psychology, 78,* 943–955.

Keller, H. (2007). *Cultures of infancy.* Erlbaum.

Kitayama, S., & Bowman, N. A. (in press). Cultural consequences of voluntary settlement in the frontier: Evidence and implications. In M. Schaller, A. Norenzayan, S. J. Heine, T. Yamagishi and T. Kameda (Eds.), *Evolution, culture, and the human mind.* Mahwah, NJ: Erlbaum.

Kitayama, S., & Duffy, S. (2004). Cultural competence – tacit, yet fundamental: Self, social relations, and cognition in the United States and Japan. In R. J. Stenberg and E. L. Grigorenko (Eds.), *Culture and competence: Contexts of life success* (pp. 55–87). Washington, DC: American Psychological Association.

Kitayama, S., Duffy, S., Kawamura, T., & Larsen, J. T. (2003). Perceiving an object and its context in different cultures: A cultural look at New Look. *Psychological Science, 14*, 201–206.

Kitayama, S., Duffy, S., & Uchida, Y. (2007). Self as cultural mode of being. In S. Kitayama and D. Cohen (Eds.), *Handbook of cultural psychology* (pp. 136–174). New York: Guilford Press.

Kitayama, S., & Ishii, K. (2002). Word and voice: Spontaneous attention to emotional utterances in two languages. *Cognition and Emotion, 16*, 29–59.

Kitayama, S., Ishii, K., Imada, T., Takemura, K., & Ramaswamy, J. (2006). Voluntary settlement and the spirit of independence: Evidence from Japan's 'Northern Frontier.' *Journal of Personality and Social Psychology, 91*, 369–384.

Kopecky, J., Kitayama, S., Saiki, J. & Meyer, D. E. (2007). *Cross-cultural differences in multi-tasking by East Asians and North Americans*. Unpublished manuscript. University of Michigan.

Lewis, R. S., Goto, S. G., & Kong, L, & Lowenberg, K. (2008). *Culture and context: East Asian American and European American Differences in P3 event-related potentials*. Personality and Social Psychology Bulletin, *34*, 623–634.

Markus, H. R., & Kitayama, S. (1991). Culture and the self: Implications for cognition, emotion, and motivation. *Psychological Review, 98*, 224–253.

Masuda, T., Ellsworth, P. C., Mesquita, B., Leu, J., Tanida, S., & Van de Veerdonk, E. (2008). Placing the face in context: Cultural differences in the perception of facial emotion. *Journal of Personality and Social Psychology, 94*, 365–381.

Masuda, T., & Nisbett, R. E. (2001). Attending holistically versus analytically: Comparing the context sensitivity of Japanese and Americans. *Journal of Personality and Social Psychology, 81*, 922–934.

Masuda, T., & Nisbett, R. E. (2006). Culture and change blindness. *Cognitive Science, 30*, 381–399.

Miller, P. J., Wiley, A., Fung, H., & Liang, C. H. (1997). Personal storytelling as a medium of socialization in Chinese and American families. *Child Development, 68*, 557–568.

Morris, M. W., & Peng, K. (1994). Culture and cause: American and Chinese attributions for social and physical events. *Journal of Personality and Social Psychology, 67*, 949–971.

Nisbett, R. E. (2003). *The geography of thought: How Asians and Westerners think differently … and why*. New York: Free Press.

Nisbett, R. E., Peng, K., Choi, I. & Norenzayan, A. (2001). Culture and systems of thought: Holistic versus analytic cognition. *Psychological Review, 108*, 291–310.

Oyserman, D., & Lee, S. W–S. (2007). Priming 'culture': Culture as situated cognition. In S. Kitayama and D. Cohen (Eds.) *Handbook of Cultural Psychology*. New York: Guilford Press.

Rensink, R. A., O'Regan, J. K., & Clark, J. J. (1997). To see or not to see: The need for attention to perceive changes in scenes. *Psychological Science, 8*, 368–373.

Scherer, K. R. (1986). Vocal affect expression: A review and a model for future research. *Psychological Bulletin, 99*, 143–165.

Tinajero, C., & Paramo, M. F. (1997). Field dependence-independence and academic achievement: A re–examination of their relationship. *British Journal of Educational Psychology, 67*, 199–212.

Triandis, H. C. (1995). *Individualism and collectivism*. Boulder, CO: Westview Press.

Uchida, Y., Kitayama, S., Mesquita, B. Reyes, J., & Morling, B. (2008). Is perceived emotional support beneficial: Well–being and health in independent and interdependent cultures. *Personality and Social Psychology Bulletin, 34*, 741–754.

Uskul, A. K., Kitayama, S., & Nisbett, R. E. (2008), Ecocultural basis of cognition: Farmers and fishermen are more holistic than herders. *Proceedings of the National Academy of Sciences of the USA, 105*, 8552–8556.

Wager, T. D., & Smith, E. E. (2001). Neuroimaging studies of working memory: A meta-analysis. *Cognitive Affective Behavioral Neuroscience, 3*, 255–274.

Witkin, H. A. (1962). *Psychological differentiation*. Wiley.

CHAPTER 5

Compound Social Cues in Human Face Processing

Reginald B. Adams, Jr., Robert G. Franklin, Jr., Anthony J. Nelson, and Michael T. Stevenson

---

"we respond to gestures…in accordance with an elaborate and secret code that is written nowhere, known by none and understood by all" (Sapir, 1927, p. 892)

INTRODUCTION

The face is the most richly informative and pervasive social stimulus we encounter in our daily lives and by far the most thoroughly researched. The proverbial warning "don't judge a book by its cover" notwithstanding, it is with such ease that we draw inferences about others' personalities, inner thoughts, beliefs, and intentions from facial appearance, that not to do so can be beyond our conscious control. Snap judgments such as these from faces are effortless, nonreflective, highly consensual, and the tendency toward making them is arguably hardwired (Kenny, Horner, Kashy, & Chu, 1992; Van Overwalle, Drenth, & Marsman, 1999; Willis & Todorov, 2006). We draw these inferences both from invariant aspects of the face, such as features indicating social category membership (i.e., race and gender), facial maturity, and attractiveness, as well as from changeable aspects of the face, such as eye-gaze direction and facial expression. As such, the human face conveys a wide variety of social information within a finite and overlapping array of features, making our ability to effortlessly draw social meaning from it quite a remarkable feat.

Although the quote at the outset of this chapter implies that nonverbal communication is "understood by all," there is wide variability in how well people understand nonverbal language. The inability to decipher the nuances of nonverbal language is associated with a host of psychological disorders (Rosenthal, Hall, DiMatteo, Rogers, & Archer, 1979; Russell, Stokes, Jones, Czogalik, & Rohleder, 1993). Indeed, certain psychopathologies such as autism, schizophrenia, and prosopagnosia, as well as brain lesions, such as temporal lobectomy and amygdalotomy, are marked by—and in some cases defined by—deficits in socioemotional perception (Emery, 2000). Yet most of us do share an innate capacity to communicate in what seems to be a universal nonverbal language. The natural laws governing this language, however, remain almost entirely unknown. That this language is "an elaborate and secret code…known by none," therefore, remains quite accurate. Although our focus here is on the human face, the conceptual framework represented herein can be applied to nonverbal communication more broadly defined.

To date, research involving the face has led to several separate and relatively nonoverlapping lines of inquiry including visually mediated attention, emotion recognition, and face memory. Such subspecialties generally treat the foci of the respective other areas as noise, thus failing to systematically examine how each type of cue might impact the processing of and meaning derived from the other cues. This "parallel" approach to the study of face perception is consistent with and likely spurred on by contemporary face-processing models, which contend that functionally distinct sources of facial information are processed via functionally distinct neural underpinnings (e.g., Bruce & Young, 1986; Haxby, Hoffman, & Gobbini, 2000; LeGal & Bruce, 2002). The underlying notion is not without its logic. Given the abundance of visual information bombarding the perceptual system, parsing such visual processing arguably avoids perceptual overload.

This traditional approach to face processing, however, overlooks the importance of social meaning signaled in tandem by various facial cues. As a result, the compound nature of social perception has largely been neglected. In social psychology, most of the work examining the intersection of social cues has focused on multiple identities, in particular on the conditions under which one identity dominates another (Crisp, Hewstone, & Rubin, 2001; Shih, Pittinsky, & Ambady, 1999; Vescio, Judd, & Kwan, 2004). Vision cognition has been focused on whether various facial cues interfere with the perceptual processing of one another, with little regard to the underlying social factors. Even simple demonstrations of perceptual interference, however, suggest interdependence in the processing of various facial cues, something not currently accounted for in existing face-processing models.

We argue here that, in order to fully understand both the visual and social aspects of face processing, it is necessary to consider the social factors that guide vision, as well as the boundary conditions vision imposes on social perception. Only in this way will the complex interplay between these two systems be fully understood. As we work toward a more comprehensive model of face processing, we recognize that some aspects of this interplay are innately prepared, whereas others are the product of individual variation and cultural learning. The approach we advocate draws from ecological theory, and emphasizes the co-evolution of social signaling and social perception. From this perspective, because the perceiver is as important to social perception as the stimulus being perceived, we argue that individual and situational variation in the perceiver, whether stable or transient, whether due to brain chemistry or culture, will meaningfully impact social perception. Herein we treat the social meaning signaled by the face and the perceiver's capacity to extract such meaning as critical features in face processing. Taking this approach, we must consider the shared meanings or signals conveyed by various facial cues. We believe this approach will offer new insights to the origin, adaptive purpose, and cognitive, behavioral, cultural, and biological underpinnings of social perception. We feel these efforts represent the next critical step toward establishing a more integrative approach to the study of face processing, and more generally to social perception.

CURRENT FACE-PROCESSING MODELS

Bruce and Young (1986) proposed a widely cited dual-process model of face processing. It delineates a dual process for extracting identity versus expressive information from the face. Multiple sources of evidence suggest that the processing of invariant facial cues such as facial identity and changeable facial cues such as emotional expression are functionally and neurologically separable. Evidence for such a claim includes: (1) behavioral data (e.g., Etcoff, 1984), (2) clinical cases showing a dissociation between prosopagnosia (i.e., face blindness) and expressive agnosia (e.g., Tranel & Damasio, 1988), (3) single-cell recordings in primates (e.g., Hasselmo, Rolls, & Baylis, 1989), and (4) brain-imaging studies in humans (e.g., Hoffman & Haxby, 2000). Although the fusiform gyrus and the superior temporal sulcus (STS) have both been shown to have cells preferentially responsive to facial stimuli (Kanwisher McDermott, & Chun, 1997; Kanwisher, Tong, & Nakayama, 1998; Perrett, Rolls, & Caan, 1982), the former appears to be predominant in processing static-appearance relevant aspects of the face, whereas the latter appears predominant in processing changeable aspects of the face, including but not limited to emotional expression and eye gaze (Hasselmo et al., 1989; Perrett et al., 1985; Phillips et al., 1998; Puce et al., 1998). Building on these findings Haxby et al. (2000) proposed a neurological model of face perception that delineates a dual-pathway system where the processing of invariant facial information travels primarily through the fusiform gyrus and the processing of changeable aspects of the face travel primarily through the STS. This model is loosely associated with an earlier model of basic vision proposed by Mishkin, Ungerleider, and Macko (1983), which also proposed a dual pathway (the "what" and "where" pathways) in which visual information splits into a dorsal pathway specialized for object information (roughly the facial identity route) and a ventral pathway specialized for spatial information (roughly the facial-expression route).

From the perspective of this model, the dissociation between facial-expression recognition and facial identification is believed to reflect the important but independent roles each played in our evolutionary past. The contention that facial identity and emotion are fully dissociable, however, is a strong claim. Defined in the cognitive-processing literature, independence demands that the two cues have *no* influence on the processing of each other (Ashby & Townsend, 1986). Essentially, if two cues are processed independently, varying one cue should, by definition, not exert any influence on the perception of the other cue. Yet, a growing number of studies reviewed later in this chapter, using a variety of methodologies, reveal quite the opposite. Various facial cues do appear to influence one another in perceptual processing, including those proposed to involve complete neurological separation, namely facial identity and expression (see Calder & Young, 2005; Zebrowitz, 2006 for reviews). We suggest that, given their shared social functions, facial cues give rise to fundamentally interdependent processes, and that such interdependence is inherently adaptive.

To clarify our assumptions, we begin with an illustrative example. A person with an extremely mature and hypermasculine face conveys high dominance and low affiliation through neutral facial appearance (Adams & Kleck, 2002), thereby signaling a heightened probability of threat to an observer. A person displaying a prototypical expression of anger similarly signals a heightened probability of threat (particularly when coupled with direct gaze; Adams & Kleck, 2003, 2005). In addition, the specific facial muscle patterning associated with at least some emotion expressions (e.g., low knitted brows, compressed lips, and jutted jaw shown in anger; Ekman & Friesen, 1978) strike a close resemblance to the structural appearance related to facial maturity. Marsh, Adams, and Kleck (2005) demonstrated, for instance, that anger and fear eyes (i.e., cues including large, wide eyes and high eyebrows versus small, beady eyes and low eyebrows) influence person construal (i.e., inferences made regarding warmth, naivety, honesty etc.) in a manner consistent with that previously found for neutral baby-faced versus mature-faced individuals (see Zebrowitz, 1997). Just low- versus high-eyebrow placement alone on otherwise neutral faces has been found to vary perceived dominance and submissiveness, *and* perceived anger and fear, respectively (Keating, Mazur, & Segall, 1977; Laser & Mathie, 1982). Given that we are innately prepared to process potential threat in our environment (LeDoux, 1996), mutually informative signals from different facial cues such as these should be integrated in the detection of threat. Such a response would afford a clear adaptive advantage allowing for a more timely behavioral response to threat. From this perspective, we, therefore, propose that facial cues exert their greatest influence on threat detection when they are combined (see also Hess, Sabourin, & Kleck, 2007).

TOWARD A NEW LOOK AT FACE PROCESSING

One of the foundational tenets of social vision put forth in this book is that the people who fill our social worlds represent a prominent computational factor, one that has likely influenced the very evolution of our visual system. In other words social vision implies a social brain. In the 1970s primatologists ignited a frenzy of research and theory based on this premise (Brothers, 1997; Byrne & Whiten, 1988, 1997; Premack & Woodruff, 1978). The more recent social-brain hypothesis tested this premise (Dunbar, 1998) by correlating average neocortex size with the average communal group size of a variety of primates, revealing a strong positive relationship. Notably, the primary visual cortex was excluded from this analysis given that it is relatively large and stable across primates. Dunbar argued that a shift from nocturnal to diurnal living marked a dramatic shift from primary reliance on olfaction to vision, offering, in the process, a gateway to social intelligence. Also included in this thinking was that color vision, which likely initially evolved to support dietary demands, eventually became implicated in the evolution of complex social signaling (see Barton & Dunbar, 1997; also see Changizi & Shimojo, this volume). The implication of this finding is that brain evolution has been directly influenced by social factors. We take this insight to heart as we build toward a social visual model of face processing, believing that to fully understand how the brain processes facial information, it is first imperative to consider the socially adaptive functions it evolved to perform.

Thus, in formulating a compound social cue approach to face processing, we draw heavily on a functional account, borrowing insights from neo-Darwinian perspectives on the co-evolution of emotional expression and recognition and on the ecological approach to vision perception (see Zebrowitz, Bronstad, & Montepare, this volume). Current evolutionary theory of socio-emotional cuing suggests a co-evolution of social expression and perception. Perhaps the most studied example of this in face processing is between the proposed universal-affect program underlying experience and expression of emotion and our corresponding capacity to universally recognize such emotions expressed by others (e.g., Ekman & Friesen, 1971). Although Darwin strongly resisted the notion that facial expressions evolved specifically in response to socio-communicative pressures (1872/1965), today's evolutionary theorists, both ethologists and psychologists alike, for the most part accept such a claim (e.g., Redican, 1982). Current opinion holds that although emotional expressions may have originally developed due to nonsocial

pressures as Darwin contended, members of a group likely benefited from being able to recognize facial expressions and predict behavior from them, as well as from being able to use facial expressions to convey mental and emotional states to others. These abilities would have thus conferred a survival advantage on any individual who possessed them, leading to the greater propagation of their genes and spurring on the socio-emotional co-evolution of expression and recognition.

Evidence for this logic is necessarily indirect, but nevertheless compelling. For instance, Redican (1982) drew upon research on the facial expressivity of New versus Old World monkeys. If the ability to produce and recognize facial expressions co-evolved due to socio-communicative pressures, then facial expressivity should not be nearly as evident in an environment in which visual cues are obscured, such as in a forest environment where vision is obstructed by dense foliage. If, however facial expression is not linked to such a socio-communicative advantage, then whether it is visually obscured or not should have no bearing on the evolution of facial expression. Supporting the former argument, Redican found that Old World monkeys, which are characteristically terrestrial, relative to New World monkeys, which are characteristically arboreal, show a greater repertoire of facial muscle patterning and consequent expression. In this same vein, Moynihan (1964; also cited by Redican) found that platyrrhine night monkeys, which are both arboreal and nocturnal, exhibit virtually no facial muscle patterning and thus no facial expression.

The ecological approach to visual perception similarly assumes an interplay between stimulus and perceiver through the notions of behavioral affordances and perceiver attunements (Gibson, 1979). Affordances are defined as opportunities to act on or be acted upon by a stimulus. Gibson argued that affordances influence perception in a direct and nonreflective manner, requiring no need for symbolic representation or cognitive appraisal. Although originally characterized as behavioral in nature, thereby bypassing any in-termediate processes, the notion of direct perception is expanded here to include social, cognitive, and affective outcomes as well. Perceiver attunements on the other hand are defined as the observer's sensitivity to such stimulus features. The affordances signaled by water (drinkable) or food (edible), for example, should not be as likely to yield direct perception in a person who has recently gorged on a feast compared to a person who is fasting. Thus, although certain perceiver attunements are thought to be innately prepared, they can vary within and across individuals in meaningful ways (see also Zebrowitz et al., this volume). Indeed, top-down influences have been shown to affect even the earliest stages of visual perception underscoring just how tightly bound bottom-up and top-downs processes can be, particularly in vision (Kveraga, Boshyan, & Bar, 2008, Schyns & Oliva, 1999).

Both the neo-Darwinian and ecological accounts assume a link between stimulus features and the perceiver's sensitivity to such features. Perhaps such a link is intuitive, but underscoring it leads to some important new insights regarding the link between facial features and perception and allows bridges between individual differences, context, culture, and basic face processing, which are now missing from face-processing models. Furthermore, neither of the aforementioned accounts, neo-Darwinian or Gibsonian, nor contemporary face-processing models adequately address the combinatorial nature of social perception and the tightly bound influences of top-down versus bottom-up processing in visual perception. In a recent review, Zebrowitz (2006) does note: "A perceived identity, social category, emotion, or psychological trait may each specify the same behavioral affordance" (p. 668). This notion is consistent with Adams and colleagues' shared-signal approach to examining compound social cues (see also Adams, Ambady, Macrae, & Kleck, 2006; Adams & Kleck, 2003, 2005). Here we draw together these two notions by focusing on core dimensions of social perception. In doing so we break down the essential nature of social affordances into shared component parts. Because various social cues share fundamental meanings (i.e., *shared signal value*), we assume, too, that the social affordances they confer on an observer will likewise share fundamental functions.

EVIDENCE FOR PERCEPTUAL INTERFERENCE AND INTEGRATION

One of the most common paradigms used to examine perceptual interference between two facial cues is the Garner selective attention paradigm (Garner, 1974). In this paradigm, performance on judgments of one stimulus dimension are examined by comparing two essential treatment conditions, one examining responses to a facial cue while holding a second cue constant (the baseline condition), the other while allowing both stimulus cues to randomly vary (the "orthogonal" condition). Consider the case of emotional expression and eye gaze. The baseline condition would involve, for example, making eye gaze (direct versus averted) judgments from faces blocked by emotion expressed (e.g., either anger or fear, but not both). The orthogonal condition, on the other hand, would involve the same eye-gaze judgments in faces in which emotional displays randomly vary. The assumption of this paradigm is that, if performance is slower in the orthogonal compared to the baseline condition, at least one cue has caused perceptual interference in the processing of the other cue. This interference may be symmetric, whereby both facial cues mutually influence the processing of the other, or asymmetric, whereby only one cue influences the other but not vice versa. Using the Garner paradigm Ganel and colleagues (2005) provided evidence for symmetric interference of gaze and emotion expression when faces were presented upright. In other words, participants took longer to accurately decode both gaze direction and emotion when both cues were allowed to randomly vary (orthogonal condition) than when they were not (baseline condition). However, when faces were inverted, only gaze processing was slowed, not emotion, thereby indicating asymmetric interference.

In the face-processing literature, the Garner paradigm was originally used to support the notion of perceptual independence between facial identity and expression processing (Etcoff, 1984). This conclusion was drawn, however, based on a null effect (no evidence of slowed processing in the orthogonal condition), and has since been countered by a growing number of studies demonstrating perceptual interference involving a growing number of facial cues including: (1) speech patterns and identity (Schweinberger & Soukup, 1998), (2) gender and emotion (Atkinson, Tipples, Burt, & Young, 2005; cf., Le Gal & Bruce, 2002), (3) gender and age judgments (Quinn & Macrae, 2005), (4) gaze and emotion (Ganel et al., 2005; Graham & LaBar, 2007), (5) familiarity and gender judgments (Ganel & Goshen-Gottstein, 2004; Ganel & Goshen-Gottstein, 2002), as well as (6) identity and expression at both the behavioral (Baudouin, Martin, Tiberghien, Verlut, & Franck, 2002; Levy & Bentin, 2008; Schweinberger, Burton, & Kelley, 1999) and (7) neural activation (Ganel et al., 2005). This body of work, therefore, questions the strong assumption of independence currently put forth by face-processing models (e.g., Bruce & Young, 1986; Burton, Bruce & Johnson, 1990).

Additional evidence supports interdependent processing. Single-cell recordings in monkeys have revealed patches of neurons responsive to the combination of invariant identity and expressive facial cues (Hasselmo et al., 1989), as well as between eye-gaze direction and expression (Perrett & Mistlin, 1990), suggesting a neural mechanism for perceptual integration. In addition, based on potential measurement error inherent in certain tests and lack of systematic control, Calder and Young (2005) recently questioned previous evidence for double dissociations between perceived expression and identity demonstrated in patient populations. Further, simply finding that facial cues *can* be processed independently of one another is also not tantamount to concluding that, in typically functioning brains, they *are* processed in an independent manner (cf. Townsend's & Wenger's 2004 theory of interactive parallel processing). Further although the fusiform gyrus appears to be more involved in processing identity and the STS in the processing of expression, both regions nonetheless meaningfully respond to both types of cues. For instance, a number of studies have reported greater fusiform activation to expressive than to neutral faces (e.g., Critchley et al.,

2000), while in another recent study greater STS activation was found when judging attraction versus age (Winston, O'Doherty, Kilner, Perrett, & Dolan, 2007).

It is important to note here that the work just mentioned—although challenging the strong notion of independence—still does not address the more essential question of why various facial cues influence one another in the first place. A primary assumption motivating the current work is that social visual cues differ fundamentally from other types of visual information in that they share inherent and underlying social meaning and physical resemblance, and thus cannot be construed as orthogonal. Thus distinct social cues, even expressive-versus identity-based cues, can signal similar behavioral tendencies to approach-avoid, dominate, and/or affiliate. Such cues do not simply influence one another in an incidental manner, but rather meaningfully interact to enhance or inhibit processing based on congruent (shared signals such as hypermasculine appearance and anger expression) or incongruent (mixed signals such as baby-face appearance and anger expression) pairings. Such shared meaning should, therefore, be reflected in the mental and neural operations involved in perceiving such cues.

Our proposition for shared signals is not meant to argue that all facial cues interact in face processing, nor do we suggest that when one cue influences the processing of another it is always in an interactive manner. For instance, observing direct eye contact is known to capture attention (Senju & Hasegawa, 2005), whereas observing averted eyes shifts attention away from the face (Driver et al., 1999; Langton, Watt, & Bruce, 2000). Such attentional cuing effects are thought to be exogenous and thus triggered reflexively (see Langton, this volume). Because direct gaze draws attention toward a face and averted gaze away from a face, one might then predict a main effect, rather than interaction, for the role of eye gaze in emotion perception, an effect that is independent of any shared social meaning per se (e.g., Juth, Lundqvist, Karlsson, & Öhman, 2005; see also Bindeman, Burton, & Langton, 2008). A survey of the literature on eye gaze and emotion from the last five years reveals that although eye gaze and emotion do appear to share social meaning and thus yield interactive effects, under some circumstances eye gaze also exerts a main effect on emotion perception due to such attention-allocation effects. Thus, adding to the complexity of compound social cues are potential competing social processes.

Adams and colleagues' work (Adams & Kleck, 2002, 2003; Adams et al., 2003) on eye gaze and emotion represents an initial inquiry into the shared signal approach to examining compound facial cues. In this work, we examined a hypothesized connection between the processing of eye gaze direction and emotion in terms of underlying congruent (e.g., direct gaze anger) versus incongruent signals (e.g., averted gaze anger) of approach and avoidance (*shared signal hypothesis*). It is important to emphasize, however, that we are not alone in the quest for a functional account of compound social cues. In the last five years, several papers have been published that similarly predict and demonstrate functional interactions among various social cues in the face, including race and emotion (Ackerman et al. 2006; Hugenberg, 2005), gender and emotion (Becker et al., 2007 cf. LeGal & Bruce, 2002), gender and age (Quinn & Macrae, 2005), and body and face (deGelder, 2006).

PUTTING THE "SOCIAL" BACK INTO FACE PROCESSING

Soon after Gibson proposed the ecological approach to understanding basic visual perception, it was extended and applied to visual perception of the social world (Baron & Boudreau, 1987; Baron & Misovich, 1993; McArthur & Baron, 1983). The ecological approach applied to social perception maintains that certain social features, such as facial maturity, emotion, health, gender, and familiarity are associated with adaptive social affordances and thus give rise to direct perception. Seeing a baby affords us an opportunity to provide care for and to protect it. Babyish facial appearance, even in adult faces, yields perceptions of dependence, submission, naivety,

warmth, weakness, and femininity compared to perceptions made from mature faces (see Zebrowitz, 1997). Such attributions appear to be culturally consistent (Keating, Mazur, & Segall, 1977; Keating, Mazur, & Segall, 1981; McArthur & Berry, 1987; Zebrowitz, Montepare, & Lee, 1993), and influence profound life outcomes, such as job promotions and length of criminal sentencing (Zebrowitz, 1997). More transient and short-lived influences on social perception include the expression of mental (e.g., Baron-Cohen, 1995) and emotional states (e.g., Ekman & Friesen, 1971). As noted earlier, we appear to have co-evolved both a complex signaling system and a propensity to read such signals in one another. Common to each of these approaches is the underlying assumption that facial features convey universal meaning, and that we are innately prepared to respond to such meaning. Later we extend this understanding by considering shared meanings across different types of facial features and what they can tell us about basic face processing.

Across several fields of study, including social, personality, and developmental sciences, sociology, cultural anthropology, ethology, and sociolinguistics, similar dimensions of social meaning repeatedly arise, namely, those related to *dominance* and *affiliation* (Brown, Dovidio, & Ellyson, 1990; Brown & Levinson, 1987; Judd, Fiske, Cuddy, & Glick, 2007; see also Ken Nakayama's introduction to this volume). Dominance is a judgment of the apparent status, power, or competence of an individual, or an underlying motivation to seek it, whereas affiliation is a judgment of the apparent solidarity, friendliness, or warmth of an individual, or an underlying motivation to seek it. Little work to date has examined the neural underpinnings of dominance and affiliation perception from social cues (though see Chiao et al., 2008 on dominance perception). What has been done in nonhuman primates (Pineda, Sebestyen, & Nava 1994) suggests distinct neural mechanisms.

In humans, the dimensions of dominance and affiliation repeatedly emerge as key factors in social perception (Wiggins & Broughton, 1991;

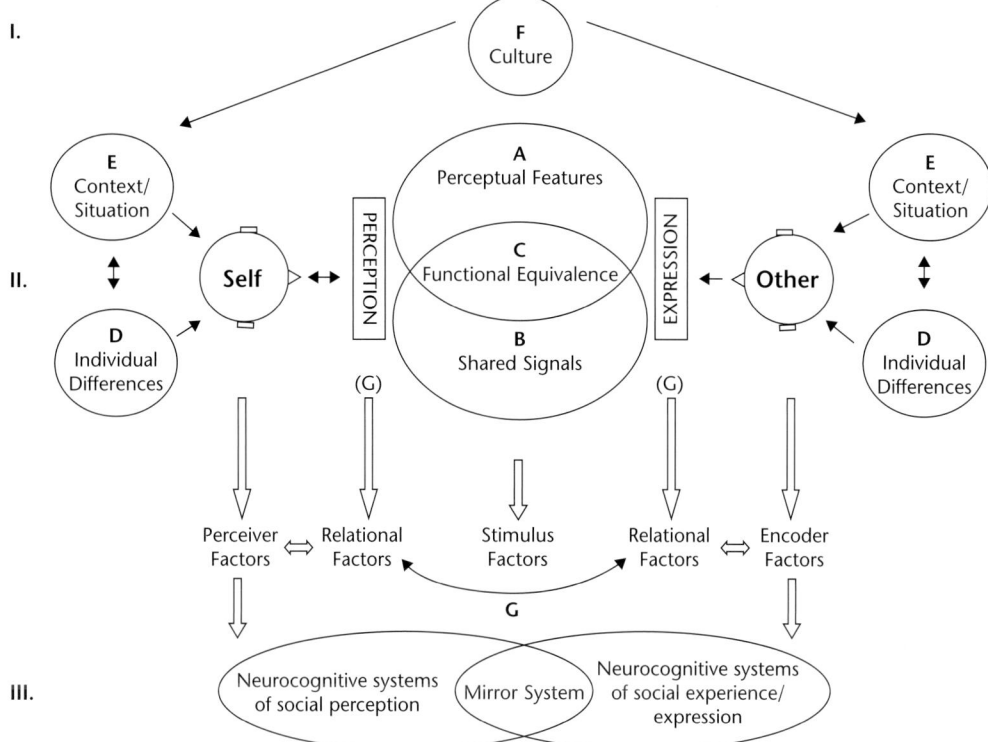

Figure 5.1 Represented here are three levels of analysis of compound social cues including: I. Cultural, II. Individual, and III. Neurocognitive. Proposed factors involving stimulus and perceiver include: (A) *Perceptual resemblance*, which refers to two or more social cues (e.g., race, facial maturity, emotional expression) that share physical characteristics but not necessarily meaning; (B) *Shared signals,* which refer to two or more social cues (e.g., gaze direction and emotional expression) that share a common meaning (approach-avoidance) but do not necessarily physically resemble one another; (C) *Functional equivalence,* which refers to two or more social cues (e.g., gender, facial maturity, emotional expression) with physical resemblance *and* shared meaning; (D) *Individual differences,* which refer to observer-based differences that influence attunements to certain social cues, such as trait anxiety; (E) *Context/Situation,* which refers to situational circumstances that influence attunements to certain social cues, such as danger; (F) *Culture,* which refers to learned social ideology and attentional gating mechanisms that influence perceiver attunements to certain social cues; and (G) *Relational factors,* which refer to stimulus cues that take on certain meanings only in relation to the observer (e.g., social group memberships such as same versus other race, sex, etc.). Although the influence of such factors on the decoding of social information is highlighted earlier (illustrated in left side of the figure), the model also highlights the important role these factors exert on the encoding of social information (illustrated in right side of the figure).

Schaefer & Plutchik, 1966). Movements of the head, hands, and legs during social interaction convey these basic signals (Gifford, 1991). Gender stereotypes cross-culturally yield these same core dimensions (Williams & Best, 1990). They arise based on perceptions of facial appearance and expression, such as from perceived facial maturity (Zebrowitz, 1997), gender perception (Friedman & Zebrowitz, 1992), eye-gaze behavior (Argyle & Cook, 1976), and basic emotional displays (Knutson, 1996; see also Hess, Blairy, & Kleck, 2000). Thus, it should not be at all surprising to find that the perception of social cues that share these signals are systematically intertwined, that is, that they interact and combine to influence perception.

Underlying both dominance and affiliation is the even more basic behavioral tendency to *approach* or *avoid* (Baron-Cohen, 1995; Davidson & Hugdahl, 1995). Someone who is dominant, affiliative, or both has a higher probability of approaching others socially than someone who is submissive, socially aloof, or both. The processing of this behavioral tendency also appears to have a distinct neural basis in nonhuman primates (Brothers & Ring, 1993), and humans (Davidson & Hugdahl, 1995; Harmon-Jones, 2003). Davidson and Hugdahl (1995) suggest that "approach and withdrawal are fundamental motivational dimensions that are present at any level of phylogeny where behavior itself is present" (page 362). As such, shared signals of approach-avoidance are likely to be inherent in all forms of social communication as well.

Borrowing from the ecological and co-evolutionary approaches then, we argue that social features in the face innately signal basic behavioral tendencies. We will also argue that the social features we attend to, and from which we derive such meaning, can vary from individual to individual, situation to situation, culture to culture. That some of the meanings derived from facial cues may be learned, however, does not undermine the proposition that as humans we possess the innate propensity to extract such meaning from the human face. It makes adaptive sense that certain cues—such as an angry, staring, hypermasculine face—would combine to influence cognitive, behavioral, cultural, and biological correlates of social perception.

Given how tightly bound stimulus features are within perception, Gibson (1979) also argued that we can learn much about the perceptual system by first inspecting stimulus features. We readily agree and apply this insight to the shared signal approach delineated here. In doing so, we draw attention to shared perceptual properties of various social cues conveyed by the face (i.e., the actual physical resemblance of various cues). That the shared signal values and physical resemblances of facial cues are often confounded suggests some interesting insights into how they may be processed and perceived as well.

Gender, emotion, and facial maturity offer such a case in point. Gender appearance is associated with facial features, which perceptually overlaps with facial maturity (see Zebrowitz, 1997), in that "babyish" features (e.g., large, round eyes, full lips) are more typical in women, and "mature" features (e.g., square jaw, pronounced brow) are more typical in men. Such facial appearance is so strongly associated with gender, in fact, that inconsistent pairings of these features can override normal gender stereotypic attributions (Friedman & Zebrowitz, 1992). A similar confound has been demonstrated between gender and emotion cues (Becker et al., 2007; Hess, Adams, & Kleck, 2005), as well as between facial maturity and emotion (see Marsh, Adams, & Kleck, 2005, Zebrowitz, 2006). Perhaps not surprising then are the similar patterns of social perception that are also derived from these cues, namely, those of dominance and affiliation. It stands to reason that any two social cues in a space so finite and overlapping as the face that signal similar meaning would likewise recruit similar physical properties in which to do so, because often form follows function. Thus, such physical overlap in stimulus features may also be expected to reflect perceptual and possibly neurological overlap as well.

That facial emotion and appearance can both look alike and yield similar social perceptions invites the notion of functional equivalence (see also Hess, Adams, & Kleck, 2008; see Figure 5.1[1]). One example proposed by Darwin (1872/1965) in support of this supposition that some expressive behaviors mimic stable appearance features is piloerection, which, when used in animals, makes them appear larger (see for example, p.95 and p.104). Other examples include eye-spot configurations on lower-order animals thought to mimic the eyes of larger animals to ward off potential predators (Argyle & Cook, 1976), and the porcupine fish that becomes both enlarged and pointy when threatened. Indeed, humans appear innately prepared to perceive threat in angular versus round visual stimuli (Aronoff, Woike, & Hyman, 1992; Bar & Neta, 2006).

Initial tests of this rationale in the human-face literature were conducted by Adams and

---

[1] Figure 5.1 graphically represents various social factors propsed here to be involved in face processing.

Kleck (2002) and Marsh, Adams, & Kleck (2005), who demonstrated an intrinsic link between emotional expressions and appearance cues related to facial maturity and babyfacedness. Adams and Kleck (2002) demonstrated facial maturity extremes (hyper- vs. hypomaturity) yield systematic differences in perceived emotion in faces, similar to common gender-emotion stereotypes. Marsh, Adams, & Kleck (2005) argued that facial expressions (particularly anger and fear) may have evolved to mimic more stable appearance cues to exploit their underlying affordances. Anger, with its low and bulging brow ridge and narrowed eyes takes on a perceptual resemblance to a mature face, while fear with its raised and arched brow ridge, and widened eyes takes on a perceptual resemblance to a baby-face. In this way gender cues, facial maturity, and the expressions of anger and fear appear to possess functionally equivalent forms in that they share similar configurations by which they perform a similar functions.

PUTTING THE "PERSON" BACK INTO FACE PROCESSING

Assuming that perceiver attunements to stimulus features are a necessary component of social visual perception—that stimulus features only take on social meaning when perceived by another—it is increasingly important to treat perceiver factors as pivotal to understanding face perception. This insight allows us to consider individual differences, as well as context and culture as primary factors in face processing. The focus in current face-processing models, as well as co-evolutionary and functional approaches, tends to be on delineating the universals across individuals, rather than explicating intra- and interpersonal variation. There are a multitude of factors highlighted throughout this book including changes in brain chemistry (i.e., hormones; see DeBruine & Jones, this volume), state and trait anxiety, developmental (see Faronni & Senju, this volume), cultural influences and situational priming (see Park & Kitayama, this volume), age (Isaacowitz & Murphy, this volume), goal states and social learning (see MacLin & MacLin, and Stokes & Payne, this volume) that

can all influence visual perception in dramatic ways. We need not be bound to consider perceiver attunements as purely innate complements to stimulus affordances. In fact, only by considering socially varying attunements can such recent evidence for modulation in visual experience due to learned stereotypes and cultural priming be properly understood.

It is becoming increasingly apparent just how tightly bound top-down and bottom-up processes are in perception. For example, specific facial features (hairstyle) are potent social categorization cues (e.g., Macrae & Martin, 2007). When race-typical hairstyles are placed on race-ambiguous faces, social categorization exerts a powerful top-down influence on even low-level visual perception, changing how deeply a face is encoded and remembered, and influencing self-reported impressions of facial appearance such as skin tone and fullness of lips (MacLin & Malpass, 2001; see also MacLin & MacLin, this volume). Likewise Schyns and Oliva (1999) found that processing goals related to extracting socio-emotional information from faces influence perceiver attunements to certain visual information (i.e., high versus low spatial frequencies), and that such processing attunements can carry over to subsequent unrelated categorization tasks.

Bruce and Young's (1986) original face-processing model, which is primarily focused on a bottom-up stream of face processing, includes goal-directed visual processing as a central characteristic. Their notion of directed visual processing assumes that we can be selectively attuned to different aspects of visual encoding that are congruent with our search goals. In this framework, it is not far fetched to presume a whole host of top-down influences on low-level visual perception including perceiver's motivation, situational primes, learned stereotypes, and cultural exposure. Further, though the cues from which we derive such meaning may change from individual to individual, context to context, culture to culture, the basic information being sought need not.

A number of person-level factors have already been shown to influence basic face processing. Some of these factors include individual differences in brain chemistry, level of prejudice, and trait anxiety, and transient differences, such hormonal cycles, current goal states, and state anxiety. As an example, threat cues are found to be more salient for high- versus low- anxiety individuals (Mogg, Garner, & Bradley, 2007), an effect likely due to increased amygdalar responsivity (Schwartz, Wright, Shin, Kagan, & Rauch, 2003). Trait anxiety also plays an important role in attentional shifting towards threatening stimuli (MacLeod, Mathews, & Tata, 1986; Mathews & MacLeod, 1985; Mogg, Millar, & Bradley, 2000). Hormonal shifts during the menstrual cycle have also been found to influence how heterosexual women perceive male faces. During the follicular phase, reward is more salient, and women appear more attuned to hyper-masculine faces, rating them as more attractive (Dreher et al., 2007). Conversely, during the luteal phase of menstruation, when progesterone is higher, attunement to kinship cues in the face increases (DeBruine & Jones, this volume). Such shifts in attunement to reward, threat, and affiliation conveyed by a face suggest individually tuned responses.

Individual differences should also influence which compound cues are attended to and how and to what extent compound cues are visually integrated. Work on the compound cues of eye gaze and emotion has begun to corroborate this notion, both when examining high and low anxiety, and women during different phases of the menstrual cycle. Individuals who are high versus low in trait anxiety (Fox et al., 2007; Mathews, Fox, Yiend, & Calder, 2003; Putman, Hermans, & van Honk, 2006) and trait fearfulness (Tipples, 2006) show enhanced attentional shifts toward targets of fearful gaze. Fox and colleagues (2007) also found greater attentional capture in high- versus low-anxiety individuals to direct anger faces. This provides evidence that high-anxiety individuals may be more sensitive to integrating threat-related facial cues. The pattern of these results are consistent with that predicted by the shared signal hypothesis, in that high-anxiety individuals, for whom threat is more salient, appear to integrate compound threat cues more readily than low-anxiety individuals. Conway et al. (2008) also demonstrated that trait anxiety influences the extent to which eye gaze and expression are integrated in judgments of facial preference. Hormonal changes have also been implicated as moderating the expression-gaze interaction. Conway et al. (2007), for instance, found that women during the luteal phase of menstruation integrate eye-gaze direction in fear and disgust face perception more readily than women in the follicular phase of menstruation.

Recent research is revealing that context matters as well, even in simple object perception (e.g., Davenport & Potter 2004). A number of contextual cues come into play in face perception. The context can be the face itself. For instance, perceiving direct gaze in an anger face is clearly different from perceiving the same gaze in a happy face. Context may also represent the processing of a facial expression when combined with congruent or incongruent body language (see also de Gelder et al., this volume). We propose here that individual difference factors as discussed earlier, such as trait anxiety and hormonal rhythms, will thus interact with contextual factors as well to impact perceiver attunements. For example, we would predict that an anxious person put in a dangerous situation would be particularly likely to integrate threat-related facial cues, such as the staring, hypermasculine, angry face.

Finally, culture represents a powerful influence on perceiver attunements that may be influenced by learned attentional gating (Park & Kitayama, this volume), chronic accessibility of certain semantic knowledge and stereotypes, or through learning and exposure. For instance, although Ekman proposed the *universal-affect program* described earlier (the idea that emotional communication is largely dictated and predetermined) a meta-analysis conducted by Elfenbein and Ambady (2002) revealed intracultural advantages in basic emotion recognition. Thus, Elfenbein and Ambady (2003a, 2003b) posited the existence of a *specific-affect program,* one that represents subtle variation (like verbal accents). In this way, culture appears to leak through nonverbal expression (see Marsh, Elfenbein, & Ambady, 2003), and perceivers from the same culture appear specifically attuned to these variations, arguably due to perceptual experience and expertise. When considering face processing more broadly, such learned attunements influence the stimulus features one attends to (Beaupré & Hess, 2005; Hess & Thibault, 2009) and likely the way various social cues are combined in perception. Although the core social signals extracted from the face may remain the same (e.g., dominance and affiliation, approach-avoidance), the facial features from which they are extracted can vary from one culture to another. The relative importance of such signals, however, may also be modulated by culture (Ambady, Bernieri, & Richeson, 2000; see, also, Weisbuch & Ambady, this volume).

The social categories to which one belongs also affect compound cue processing. A prevailing example of this type of influence is the ubiquitously reported own-race bias for better memory of faces of one's own racial group versus other racial groups, the putative cross-race effect (Malpass & Kravitz, 1969; Meissner & Brigham, 2001). In terms of compound cues, we recently found that the own-race bias in memory only appears to occur when black and white faces are paired with direct versus averted gaze (Adams, Pauker, & Weisbuch, 2010), arguably because direct gaze facilitates social relevance and categorization, thereby exerting a top-down influence on basic face processing. In addition, eye gaze influences amygdalar response to black and white faces as well, revealing greater response to black than white faces in white participants, but again only when coupled with direct versus averted gaze (Richeson Todd, Tralwater, & Baird, 2008). Perceiver factors such as one's current situational context, cultural influences, sexual orientation, or internalized stereotypes can all clearly impact the extent to which one identifies a stimulus person as same versus other. Similarly the extent to which one categorizes others as same versus other will influence the activation of learned stereotypes, showing the complexity and importance of considering such compound factors.

Necessarily underlying all of the operations previously discussed are neuro-cognitive systems related to socio-emotional perception (Adolphs, 2002) and socio-emotional experience/ expression (Davidson & Irwin, 1999). We argue herein that the clear link between stimulus and perception has implications for making predictions about neural processing. This link also creates a natural bridge for connecting individual differences, social context, and cultural influences to neural underpinnings (see also Chiao & Ambady, 2007). We have argued here that social perception and communication are tightly bound. This assumption is supported by recent evidence of overlap in neural systems underlying both the experience and expression of mental and emotional states and those involved in the perception of mental and emotional states (i.e., the putative mirror system; see Iacoboni, 2005; see also Chakrabarti & Baron-Cohen, this volume). Discoveries like these will likely give rise to important new insights for our understanding of the broader aspects of social perception.

CONCLUDING REMARKS

The current chapter describes a rationale for understanding compound social cue processing in the face. This approach comes with a number of assumptions. The first assumption is that facial features fundamentally signal social information. The second is that humans possess an innate propensity to extract this information from the face. The third assumption is that facial communication—both encoding and decoding—is innately, individually, socially, and culturally tuned.

From these assumptions we argue that visual features can perceptually determine social perception, both in terms of innate signaling (e.g., basic emotion) and learned stereotypes (e.g., racial and gender social category memberships). Vision can, in turn, moderate social interaction, arguably even playing a pivotal role in the development of complex social cognition (Baron-Cohen, 1995). Also, social factors can exert powerful influences on even low-level visual processing through attentional gating and stereotypic expectations.

Finally, although this chapter focused on face processing, it is clear that the same social information is readily available via other visual channels, such as biological motion (see Atkinson,

Heberlein, & Adolphs; Johnson Pollick, & McKay; and Shiffrar, Kaisar, & Chouchourelou, this volume), as well as via different modalities (see Weisbuch & Ambady, this volume). In addition, social meaning can be integrated across different visual channels, such as facial expression and body expression of basic emotion (see deGelder, this volume). Finally, as it becomes increasingly apparent that the brain is equipped for early polymodal perceptual integration involving areas also known to be involved in social intelligence (see Beauchamp, this volume), we believe that the current approach to compound social cues will also allow for a basic understanding of how these various types of sources of information will combine. We focused our attention on the face primarily given its clear role in complex social communication and the existence of well-established models and extensive empirical work readily available. Future research efforts will clearly build on and extend these issues. Our hope is that establishing an approach that considers both the social value of the stimulus and perceiver attunements, which can vary across and within the individual, social context, and culture, will help guide future efforts to fill existing gaps in our knowledge. Considering the compound nature of social perception represents the next essential step toward constructing a theoretical model of face processing that grapples with the compound nature of nonverbal language, with the ultimate goal of putting both the social back into the face as well as the person back into the perceiver.

REFERENCES

Ackerman, J. M., Shapiro, J. R., Neuberg, S. L., Kenrick, D. T., Becker, D. V., Griskevicius, V., Maner, J. K., & Schaller, M. (2006). They all look the same to me (unless they're angry): From out-group homogeneity to out-group heterogeneity. *Psychological Science, 17*, 836–840.

Adams, R. B., Jr., Ambady, N., Macrae, C. N., & Kleck, R. E. (2006). Emotional Expressions Forecast Approach-Avoidance Behavior. *Motivation & Emotion, 30*, 177–186.

Adams, R.B., Jr., Gordon, H.L., Baird, A.A., Ambady, N., & Kleck, R.E. (2003). Gaze

differentially modulates amygdala sensitivity to anger and fear faces. *Science, 300*, 1536.

Adams, R.B. Jr., & Kleck, R.E. (2002). Differences in perceived emotional disposition based on static facial structure. Poster presented at the annual meeting of the *Society for Personality and Social Psychology*, Savannah, GA.

Adams, R.B., Jr., & Kleck, R.E. (2003). Perceived gaze direction and the processing of facial displays of emotion. *Psychological Science, 14*, 644–647.

Adams, R.B., Jr., & Kleck, R.E. (2005). The effects of direct and averted gaze on the perception of facially communicated emotion. *Emotion, 5*, 3–11.

Adams, R. B., Jr., Pauker, K., & Weisbuch, M. (2010). Looking the other way: The role of gaze direction in the cross-race memory effect. *Journal of Experimental Social Psychology, 46*, 478–481.

Adolphs, R. (2002). Neural systems for recognizing emotion. *Current Opinion in Neurobiology, 12*, 169–177.

Ambady, N., Bernieri, F. J., & Richeson, J. A. (2000). Toward a histology of social behavior: Judgmental accuracy from thin slices of the behavioral stream. In M. P. Zanna (Ed.), *Advances in Experimental Social Psychology, 32* (pp. 201–272). San Diego: Academic Press.

Argyle, M., & Cook, M. (1976). *Gaze and mutual gaze*. New York: Cambridge University Press.

Aronoff, J., Woike, B.A., & Hyman, L.M. (1992). Which are the stimuli in facial displays of anger and happiness? Configurational bases of emotion recognition. *Journal of Personality and Social Psychology, 62*, 1050–1066.

Ashby, F. G. & Townsend, J. T. (1986). Varieties of perceptual independence. *Psychological Review, 93*, 154–179.

Atkinson, A.P., Tipples, J., Burt, D.M., & Young, A.W. (2005). Asymmetric interference between sex and emotion in face perception. *Perception and Psychophysics, 67*, 1199–1213.

Bar, M. & Neta, M. (2006). Humans prefer curved visual objects. *Psychological Science, 17*, 645–648.

Baron, R. M. & Boudreau, L. A. (1987). An ecological perspective on integrating personality and social psychology. *Journal of Personality and Social Psychology, 53*, 1222–1228.

Baron, R. M. & Misovich, S. J. (1993). Dispositional knowing from an ecological perspective. *Personality and Social Psychology Bulletin, 19*, 541–552.

Baron–Cohen, S. (1995). *Theory of mind and face-processing: How do they interact in development and psychopathology?* New York: John Wiley & Sons.

Barton, R. A., & Dunbar, R. I. M. (1997). Evolution of the social brain. In *Machiavellian intelligence II: Extensions and evaluations* (pp. 240–263). Cambridge, UK: Cambridge University Press.

Barton RA, Dunbar RLM (1997) Evolution of the social brain. In Whiten A, Byrne R (Eds.), *Machiavellian Intelligence,* Vol. II. Cambridge: Cambridge University Press.

Baudouin, J., Martin, F., Tiberghien, G., Verlut, I., & Franck, N. (2002). Selective attention to facial emotion and identity in schizophrenia. *Neuropsychologia, 40,* 503–511.

Beaupre, M. G. & Hess, U. (2005). Cross–cultural emotion recognition among canadian ethnic groups. *Journal of Cross–Cultural Psychology, 36,* 355–370.

Becker, D. V., Kenrick, D. T., Neuberg, S. L., Blackwell, K. C., & Smith, D. M. (2007). The confounded nature of angery men and happy women. *Journal of Personality and Social Psychology, 92,* 179–190.

Bindemann, M., Burton, A. M., & Langton, S. R. H. (2008). How do eye gaze and facial expression interact? *Visual Cognition, 16,* 708–733.

Brothers, L., & Ring, B. (1993). Mesial temporal neurons in the macaque monkey with responses selective for aspects of social stimuli. *Behavioural Brain Research, 57,* 53–61.

Brothers, L., & Ring, B. (1992). A neuroethological framework for the representation of minds. *Journal of Cognitive Neuroscience, 4,* 107–118.

Brown, C. E., Dovidio, J. F., & Ellyson, S. L. (1990). Reducing sex differences in visual displays of dominance: Knowledge is power. *Personality and Social Psychology Bulletin, 16,* 358–368.

Brown, P. & Levinson, S. C. (1987). *Politeness: Some universals in language usage.* New York: Cambridge University Press.

Bruce, V., & Young, A. (1986). Understanding face recognition. *British Journal of Psychology, 77,* 305–327.

Burton, A. M., Bruce, V., & Johnson, R. A. (1990). Understanding face recognition with an interactive activation and competition model. *British Journal of Psychology, 81,* 361–380.

Byrne, R.W., Whiten, A. (eds.) (1988) Machiavellian Intelligence: Social Expertise and the Evolution of Intellect in Monkeys, Apes and Humans, Oxford: Clarendon Press.

Byrne, R. W., Whiten, A. (eds.) (1997) Machiavellian Intelligence II: Extensions and Evaluations, Cambridge: Cambridge University Press.

Brothers, L. (1997). *Friday's Footprint: How Society Shapes the Human Mind.* Oxford: Oxford University Press.

Calder, A. J. & Young, A. W. (2005). Understanding the recognition of facial identity and facial expressions. *Nature Reviews Neuroscience, 6,* 641–651.

Chiao, J. Y., & Ambady, N. (2007). Cultural neuroscience: Parsing universality and diversity across levels of analysis. In S. Kitayama & D. Cohen (Eds.), *Handbook of cultural psychology.* New York: Guilford Press.

Chiao, J. Y., Adams, R. B., Jr., Tse, P., Lowenthal, & W., Richeson, J. A., Ambady, N. (2008). Distinct neural systems underlying the perception of social dominance from facial cues. *Group Processes and Intergroup Relations, 11,* 201–214.

Conway, C.A., Jones, B.C., DeBruine, Welling, L.L.M., Law Smith, M.J., Perrett, D.I., Sharp M., & Al-Dujaili, E.A.S. (2007). Salience of emotional displays of danger and contagion in faces is enhanced when progesterone levels are raised. *Hormones and Behavior, 51,* 202–206.

Conway, C.A., Jones, B.C., DeBruine, L.M., Little, A.C., Hay, J., Welling, L.L.M., Perrett, D.I., & Feinberg, D.R. (2008). Integrating physical and social cues when forming face preferences: Differences among low and high anxiety individuals. *Social Neuroscience, 3,* 89–95.

Crisp, R. J., Hewstone, M., & Rubin, M. (2001). Does multiple categorization reduce intergroupbias? *Personality and Social Psychology Bulletin, 27,* 76–89.

Critchley, H., Daly, E., Phillips, M., Brammer, M., Bullmore, E., Williams, S., Van Amelsvoort, T., Robertson, D., David, A., & Murphy, D. (2000). Explicit and implicit neural mechanisms for processing social information from facial expressions: A functional magnetic resonance imaging study. *Human Brain Mapping, 9,* 93–105.

Darwin, C. (1872; 1965). *The expression of the emotions in man and animals.* Chicago: University of Chicago Press.

Davidson, R. J., & Hugdahl, K., (Eds.). (1995). *Brain asymmetry.* Cambridge, MA: Mit Press.

Davidson R. J. & Irwin W. (1999). The functional neuroanatomy of emotion and affective style. *Trends in Cognitive Science, 3,* 11–21.

Davenport J.L., Potter M.C. (2004). Scene consistency in object and background perception. *Psychological Science, 15*, 559–564.

de Gelder (2006). Towards a neurobiology of emotional body language. *Nature Reviews Neuroscience, 7*, 242–249.

Dreher, J. C., Schmidt, P. J., Kohn, P., Furman, D., Rubinow, D., & Berman, K. F. (2007). Menstrual cycle phase modulates reward-related neural function in women. *PNAS Proceedings of the National Academy of Sciences of the United States of America, 104*, 2465– 2470.

Driver, J., Davis, G., Ricciardelli, P., Kidd, P., Maxwell, E., & Baron–Cohen, S. (1999). Gaze perception triggers reflexive visuospatial orienting. *Visual Cogntion, 6*, 509–540.

Dunbar, R. I. M. (1998). The social brain hypothesis. *Evolutionary Anthropology, 6*, 178–190.

Ekman, P., & Friesen, W. V. (1971). Constants across cultures in the face and emotion. *Journal of Personality and Social Psychology, 17*, 124–129.

Ekman, P. F., & Friesen, W. V. (1978). *The Facial Action Coding System: A technique for the measurement of facial movement.* Palo Alto, CA: Consulting Psychologists Press.

Elfenbein, H. A. & Ambady, N. (2002). On the universality and cultural specificity of emotion recognition: A meta–analysis. *Psychological Bulletin, 128(2)*, 203–235.

Elfenbein, H. A. & Ambady, N. (2003a). Universals and cultural differences in recognizing emotions. *Current Directions in Psychological Science, 12(5)*, 159–164.

Elfenbein, H. A. & Ambady, N. (2003b). When familiarity breeds accuracy: Cultural exposure and facial emotion recognition. *Journal of Personality and Social Psychology, 85(2)*, 276–290.

Emery, N. J. (2000). The eyes have it: The neuroethology, function and evolution of social gaze. *Neuroscience and Biobehavioral Reviews, 24*, 581–604.

Etcoff, N. L. (1984). Selective attention to facial identity and facial emotion. *Neuropsychologia, 22*, 281–295.

Fiske, S. T., Cuddy, A. J. C., & Glick, P. (2007). Universal dimensions of social cognition: Warmth and competence. *Trends in Cognitive Sciences, 11*, 77–83.

Fox, E., Mathews, A., Calder, A., & Yiend, J. (2007). Anxiety and sensitivity to gaze direction in emotionally expressive faces. *Emotion, 7*, 478–486.

Fox, E., Lester, V., Russo, R., Bowles, R. J., Pichler, A., & Dutton, K. (2000). Facial expressions of emotion: Are angry faces detected more efficiently? *Cognition and Emotion, 14*, 61–92.

Friedman, H., & Zebrowitz, L. A. (1992). The contribution of typical sex differences in facial maturity to sex role stereotypes. *Personality and Psychological Bulletin, 18*, 430–438.

Ganel, T. & Goshen-Gottstein, Y., (2002). The perceptual integrality of sex and identity of faces: Further evidence for the single-route hypothesis. *Journal of Experimental Psychology: Human Perception and Performance, 28*, 854–867.

Ganel, T. & Goshen–Gottstein, Y., (2004). Effects of familiarity on the perceptual integrality of the identity and expression of faces: The parallel-route hypothesis revisited. *Journal of Experimental Psychology: Human Perception and Performance, 30*, 583–597.

Ganel, Valyear, Goshen-Gottstein, & Goodale (2005). The involvement of the "fusiform face area" in processing facial expression. *Neuropsychologia, 43*, 1645–1654.

Garner, W. R. (1974). *The Processing of Information and Structure,* Potomac, Md. Lawrence Erlbaum Associates.

Gibson, J. J. (1979). *The ecological approach to visual perception,* Boston: Houghton–Mifflin.

Gifford, R. (1991). Mapping nonverbal behavior on the interpersonal circle. *Journal of Personality and Social Psychology, 61*, 279–288.

Graham, R. & LaBar, K. S. (2007). Garner interference reveals dependencies between emotional expression and gaze in face perception. *Emotion, 7*, 296–313.

Harmon–Jones, E. (2003). Clarifying the emotive functions of asymmetrical frontal cortical activity. *Psychophysiology, 40*, 838–848.

Hasselmo, M. E., Rolls, E. T., & Baylis, G. C. (1989). The role of expression and identity in the face–selective responses of neurons in the temporal visual cortex of the monkey. *Behavioural Brain Research, 32*, 203–218.

Haxby, J. V., Hoffman, E. A., & Gobbini, M. I. (2000). The distributed human neural system for face perception. *Trends in Cognitive Sciences, 4*, 223–233.

Hess, U., Adams, R. B., Jr., & Kleck, R. E. (2008). The role of perceived emotion in person perception, 234–254. J. Skowronski and N. Ambady (Eds.), *First Impressions.* Guilford Press.

Hess, U., Adams, R. B., Jr., & Kleck, R. E. (2005). Who may frown and who should smile? Dominance, affiliation, and the display of happiness and anger. *Cognition & Emotion, 19,* 515–536.

Hess, U., Blairy, S., & Kleck, R. E. (2000). The influence of expression intensity, gender, and ethnicity on judgments of dominance and affiliation. *Journal of Nonverbal Behavior, 24,* 265–283.

Hess, U., Sabourin, G., & Kleck, R. E. (2007). Postauricular and eyeblink startle responses to facial expressions. *Psychophysiology, 44,* 431–435.

Hess, U., & Thibault, P. (2009). Darwin and emotion expression. *American Psychologist, 64,* 120–128.

Hoffman, E. A., & Haxby, J. V. (2000). Distinct representations of eye gaze and identity in the distributed human neural system for face perception. *Nature Neuroscience, 3,* 80–84.

Hugenberg, K. (2005). Social categorization and the perception of facial affect: Target race moderates the response latency advantage for happy faces. *Emotion, 5,* 267–276.

Iacoboni, M. (2005). Neural mechanisms of imitation. *Current Opinion in Neurobiology, 15,* 632–637.

Juth, P., Lundqvist, D., Karlsson, A., & Öhman, A. (2005). Looking for foes and friends: Perceptual and emotional factors when finding a face in the crowd. *Emotion, 5,* 379–395.

Kanwisher, N., McDermott, J., & Chun, M. M. (1997). The fusiform face area: A module in human extrastriate cortex specialized for face perception. *Journal of Neuroscience, 17,* 4302–4311.

Kanwisher, N., Tong, F., & Nakayama, K. (1998). The effect of face inversion on the human fusiform face area. *Cognition, 68,* 1–11.

Keating, C. F., Mazur, A., & Segall, M. H. (1981). A cross-cultural exploration of physiognomic traits of dominance and happiness. *Ethology & Sociobiology, 2,* 41–48.

Keating, C. F., Mazur, A., & Segall, M. H. (1977). Facial gestures which influence the perception of status. *Social Psychology Quarterly, 40,* 374–378.

Kenny, D. A., Horner, C., Kashy, D. A., & Chu, L. (1992). Consensus at zero acquaintance: Replication, behavioral cues, and stability. *Journal of Personality and Social Psychology, 62,* 88–97.

Knutson, B. (1996). Facial expressions of emotion influence interpersonal trait inferences. *Journal of Nonverbal Behavior, 20,* 165–182.

Kveraga, K., Boshyan, J., & Bar, M. (2008). Magnocellular projections as the trigger of top–down facilitation in recognition. *Journal of Neuroscience, 27,* 13232–13240.

Langton, S. R. H., Watt. R., & Bruce, V. (2000). Do the eyes have it? Cues to the direction of social attention. *Trends in cognitive neuroscience, 4,* 50–59.

Laser, P. S., & Mathie, V. A. (1982). Face facts: An unbidden role for features in communication. *Journal of Nonverbal Behavior, 7,* 3–19.

LeDoux, J. (1996). *The emotional brain: The mysterious underpinnings of emotional life,* New York: Simon and Schuster.

Le Gal, P. M., & Bruce, V. (2002). Evaluating the independence of sex and expression in judgments of faces. *Perception and Psychophysics, 2,* 230–243.

Levy, Y. & Bentin, S. (2008). Interactive processes in matching identity and expressions of unfamiliar faces: Evidence for mutual facilitation effects. *Perception, 37,* 915–930.

MacLeod, C., Mathews, A., & Tata, P. (1986). Attentional bias in emotional disorders. *Journal of Abnormal Psychology, 95,* 15–20.

MacLin, O. H. & Malpass, R. S. (2001). Racial categorization of faces: The ambiguous race face effect. *Psychology, Public Policy, and Law, 7,* 98–118.

Macrae, C. N. & Martin, D. (2007). A boy primed sue: Feature-based processing and person construal. *European Journal of Social Psychology, 37,* 793–805.

Malpass, R. S. & Kravitz, J. (1969). Recognition for faces of own and other race. *Journal of Personality and Social Psychology, 13,* 330–334.

Marsh, A. A., Adams, R.B., Jr., & Kleck, R.E. (2005). Why do fear and anger look the way they do? Form and social function in facial expressions. *Personality and Social Psychological Bulletin, 31(1),* 73–86.

Marsh, A. A., Elfenbein, H. A., & Ambady, N. (2003). Nonverbal "accents": Cultural differences in facial expressions of emotion. *Psychological Science, 14,* 373–376.

Mathews, A. & MacLeod, C. (1985). Selective processing of threat cues in anxiety states. *Behaviour Research and Therapy, 23,* 563–569.

Mathews, A., Fox, E. Yiend, J. & Calder, A. (2003). The face of fear: Effects of eye gaze and emotion on visual attention. *Visual Cognition, 10,* 823–835.

McArthur, L. Z. & Berry, D. S. (1987). Cross-cultural agreement in perceptions of babyfaced adults. *Journal of Cross-Cultural Psychology, 18*, 165–192.

McArthur, L. Z. & Baron, R. M. (1983). Toward an ecological theory of social perception. *Psychological Review, 90*, 215–238.

Meissner, C. A., & Brigham, J. C. (2001). Thirty years of investigating the own-race bias in memory for faces: A meta-analytic review. *Psychology, Public Policy, and Law, 7*, 3–35.

Mishkin, M., Ungerleider, L. G., & Macko, K. A. (1983). Object vision and spatial vision: Two cortical pathways. *Trends in Neurosciences, 6*, 414–417.

Mogg, K., Millar, N., & Bradley, B. P. (2000). Biases in eye movements to threatening facial expressions in generalized anxiety disorder and depressive disorder. *Journal of Abnormal Psychology, 109*, 695–704.

Mogg, K., Garner. M., & Bradley, B. P. (2007). Anxiety and orienting of gaze to angry and fearful faces. *Biological Psychology, 76*, 163–169.

Moynihan, M. (1964). Some behavior patterns of platyrrhine monkeys I. The night monkeys (*Aotus trivirgatus*). *Smithsonian Miscellaneous Collections. 146*, 1–84.

Perrett, D. I., & Mistlin, A. J. (1990). Perception of facial characteristics by monkeys. In W. C. Stebbins, & M. A. Berkley (Eds.), *Comparative perception.* (pp. 187–215). New York: John Wiley.

Perret, D. I., Rolls, E. T., & Caan, W. (1982). Visual neurons responsive to faces in the monkey temporal cortex. *Experimental Brain Research, 47*, 329–342.

Perrett, D. I., Smith, P. A. J., Mistlin, A. J., Chitty, A. J., Head, A. S., Potter, D. D., Broennimann, R., Milner, A. D., & Jeeves, M. A. (1985). Visual analysis of body movements by neurones in the temporal cortex of the macaque monkey: A preliminary report. *Behavioural Brain Research, 16*, 153–170.

Phillips, M. L., Bullmore, E. T., Howard, R., Woodruff, P. W. R., Wright, I. C., Williams, S. C. R., Simmons, A., Andrew, C., Brammer, M., & David, A. S. (1998). Investigation of facial recognition memory and happy and sad facial expression perception: An fMRI study. *Psychiatry Research: Neuroimaging, 83*, 127–138.

Pineda, J.A., Sebestyen, G., Nava, C. (1994). Face recognition as a function of social attention in non-human primates: an ERP study. *Brain Res Cogn Brain Res, 2*, 1–12.

Premack, D. & Woodruff, G. (1978). Does the chimpanzee have a theory of mind? *Behavioral Brain. Science. 1*, 515–526.

Puce, A., Allison, T., Bentin, S., Gore, J. C., & McCarthy, G. (1998). Temporal cortex activation in humans viewing eye and mouth movements. *Journal of Neuroscience, 18*, 2188–2199.

Putnam, P. Hermans, E. & van Honk, J. (2006). Anxiety meets fear in perception of dynamic expressive gaze. *Emotion, 6*, 94–102.

Quinn, K. A., & Macrae, C. N. (2005). Categorizing others: The dynamics of person construal. *Journal of Personality and Social Psychology, 88*, 467–479.

Redican, W. K. (1982). An evolutionary perspective on human facial displays. In P. Ekman (Ed.). Emotion in the human face, 2nd ed. (pp. 212–280) Cambridge, UK: Cambridge University Press.

Richeson, J. A., Todd, A. R., Trawalter, S. & Baird, A. A. (2008). Eye–gaze direction modulates race–related amygdala activity. *Group Processes and Intergroup Relations, 11*, 233–246.

Rosenthal, R., Hall, A., DiMatteo, M., Rogers, P., Archer, D. (1979). *Sensitivity to nonverbal communication: The PONS test.* Baltimore: Johns Hopkins University Press.

Russell, R. L., Stokes, J. M., Jones, M. E., Czogalik, D., & Rohleder, L. (1993). The role of nonverbal sensitivity in children psychopathology. *Journal of Nonverbal Behavior, 17*, 69–83.

Sapir, E. (1927). Speech as a personality trait. *American Journal of Sociology, 32*, 892–905.

Schaefer, E. S. & Plutchik, R. (1966). Interrelationships of emotions, traits, and diagnostic constructs. *Psychological Reports, 18*, 399–410.

Schwartz, C. E., Wright, C. I., Shin, L. M., Kagan, J. & Rauch, S. L. (2003). Inhibited and uninhibited infants "grown up": adult amygdalar response to novelty. *Science, 300*, 1952–3.

Schweinberger, S. R., Burton, A. M., & Kelly, S. W. (1999). Asymmetric dependencies in perceiving identity and emotion: Experiments with morphed faces. *Perception & Psychophysics*, 61, 1102–1115.

Schweinberger, S. R., & Soukup, G. R. (1998). Asymmetric relationships among perceptions of facial identity, emotion, and facial speech. *Journal of Experimental Psychology: Human Perception & Performance, 24*, 1748–1765.

Schyns, P. G., & Oliva, A. (1999). Dr. angry and mr. smile: When categorization flexibly modifies the perception of faces in rapid visual presentations. *Cognition, 69,* 243–265.

Senju, A. & Hasegawa, T. (2005). Direct gaze captures visuospatial attention. *Visual Cognition, 12,* 127–144.

Shih, M., Pittinsky, T. L., & Ambady, N. (1999). Stereotype susceptibility: Identity salience and shifts in quantitative performance. *Psychological Science, 10,* 80–83.

Tipples, J. (2006). Fear and fearlessness potentiate automatic orienting to eye gaze. *Cognition and Emotion, 20,* 309–320.

Townsend J. T. & Wenger, M. J. (2004). A theory of interactive parallel processing: New capacity measures and predictions for a response time inequality series. *Psychological Review, 111,* 1003–1035.

Tranel, D., & Damasio, A. R. (1988). Non-conscious face recognition in patients with face agnosia. *Behavioural Brain Research, 30,* 235–249.

Van Overwalle, F., Drenth, T., & Marsman, G. (1999). Spontaneous trait interferences: Are they linked to the actor or to the action? *Personality & Social Psychology Bulletin, 25,* 450–462.

Vescio, T. K., Judd, C. M., & Kwan, S. Y. (2004). The cross–categorization hypothesis: Evidence of reductions in the strength of categorization, but not intergroup bias. *Journal of Experimental Social Psychology, 40,* 478–496.

Wiggins, J. S. & Broughton, R. (1991). A geometric taxonomy of personality scales. *European Journal of Personality, 5,* 343–365.

Williams, J. E., & Best, D. L. (1990). Measuring sex stereotypes: A multination study. Newbury Park, CA: Sage.

Willis, J. & Todorov, A. (2006). First impressions: Making up your mind after a 100-ms exposure to a face. *Psychological Science, 17,* 592–598.

Winston, J. S., O'Doherty, J., Kilner, J. M., Perrett, D. I., & Dolan, R. J. (2007). Brain systems for assessing facial attractiveness. *Neuropsychologia, 45,* 195–206.

Zebrowitz, L. A. (1997). *Reading faces: window to the soul?* Boulder, CO: Westview Press.

Zebrowitz, L. A. (2006). Finally, faces find favor. *Social Cognition, 24,* 657–701.

Zebrowitz, L. A., Montepare, J. M., & Lee, H. K. (1993). They don't all look alike: Individual impressions of other racial groups. *Journal of Personality and Social Psychology, 65,* 85–101.

CHAPTER 6

Gaze Perception and Visually Mediated Attention

Stephen R. H. Langton

Among all of the nonverbal social signals that humans use, eye gaze is arguably the most important in terms of conveying something about the current contents of the gazer's inner world. This is because people tend to look at things that are relevant to their immediate ongoing behavior —things they are about to act upon, things in which they are interested, or things about which they are thinking or talking. Once we come to understand that gazing at something brings about an inner experience of the gazed-at object, and that other people experience something similar when their eyes point toward the same object, then perceiving another's gaze and following their line of regard to the gazed-at object actually brings about a meeting of minds; at one level, both people will share a similar visual experience of one aspect of the world. This kind of joint or shared attention is considered by some to be an important milestone in developing the full range of mental state concepts known as a Theory of Mind (e.g., Baron-Cohen, 1995). However, as well as telling us something about the content of another person's mind, the person's gaze direction influences our judgements about how they are feeling (Adams & Kleck, 2003, 2005; Bindemann, Burton & Langton, in press), whether the person is likable or attractive (Mason, Tatkow & Macrae, 2005), and whether we are likely to remember the person's face in the future (Mason, Hood & Macrae, 2004). Keeping track of someone's gaze during a social interaction also helps

us to judge when it is our turn to speak or when we should leave the conversational stage to the speaker (Kendon, 1967). In assimilating all of this information, we are, therefore, able to make predictions about what someone is likely to do next so that we can prepare appropriate behavioral responses in return.

Eye gaze, therefore, serves as a useful guide through the complexities of the social world, one that evolution has made all the clearer by rendering it, not quite in black and white, but at least in relatively dark (the iris and pupil) and light (the whites of the eyes). Effective use of this conveniently clear signal seems to require the smooth operation of at least two core mechanisms. First of all, we must be able to figure out the angle of rotation of the eyes in their head in order to determine gaze direction. Second, on the basis of this information, we need to re-deploy our own attention along the same line of regard so as to facilitate the processing of whatever it is that is being gazed at. In this chapter I summarize and review some of the work that has investigated these two core mechanisms. I begin by discussing some of the studies that have investigated the accuracy of gaze judgements and then go on to consider the perceptual mechanisms that support these judgements. In the second half of the chapter, the discussion switches to the discovery that viewing someone else's eye gaze tends to trigger a shift in attention on the part of the observer.

GAZE PERCEPTION

The first task faced by the visual system is to compute the angle of rotation of the eyes in the head. Before considering how the brain might tackle this task—what visual cues does the system use to derive another's gaze direction and how might the computation be achieved at a neural level—it is useful to understand the scale of the problem to be faced. In other words, just how accurately can we perceive another's gaze direction?

Psychophysical Studies of Gaze Perception?

Interest in the perception of gaze direction began in earnest in the late 1960s with the classic psychophysical studies of Gibson and Pick (1963); Cline (1967); and Anstis, Mayhew, and Morley (1969). These studies employed live "lookers" who were trained to gaze at various points on or around an observer's face, or at targets that were actually or—through the use of a half-silvered mirror—effectively positioned at eye-level between themselves and an observer. On each trial, the looker fixated one of the targets and observers were either asked to indicate whether this corresponded with a fixation directed into their own eyes—a direct gaze (Gibson & Pick, 1963)—or to indicate on a target board where they thought the looker was looking (Cline, 1967; Anstis et al., 1969). From the data collected using these procedures, the authors used various methods to estimate constant errors and threshold values for direct gazes (sometimes called dyadic gaze), or for gazes directed toward any number of other targets (sometimes called triadic gaze). Threshold values represent the smallest deviation of gaze away from the target that the observer is able to perceive (i.e., acuity) and constant errors reflect any tendency to overestimate or underestimate gaze direction. Thresholds and constant errors can be expressed in several ways; for example, as a lateral displacement of the looker's iris or as a distance from the specified target, both of which are usually represented as the visual angle such distances subtend at the observer's eye (see Figure 6.1). So a threshold of 1 minute of arc (a complete circle is

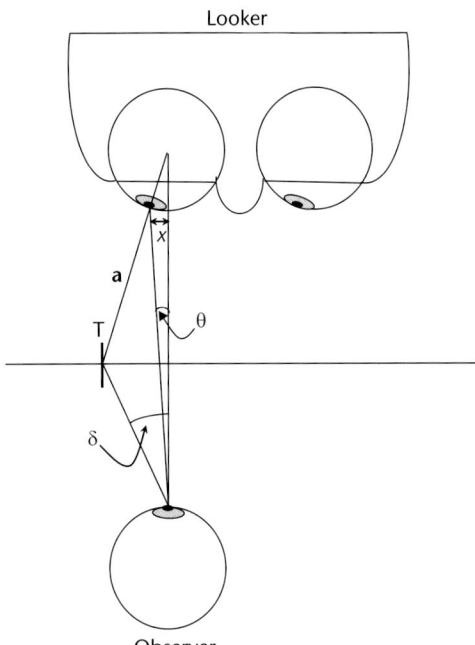

Figure 6.1 When a looker deviates their gaze away from an observer toward a target (T) along line of regard **a**, this gaze can be expressed as the angle through which the observer will have to turn their eye in order to fixate the same target (δ) or in terms of the lateral distance through which the looker's iris has moved in fixating the target (x). This lateral displacement is usually expressed by the angle it subtends at the observer's eye (θ).

60 minutes of arc) in the former sense means that the observer will just about be able to perceive a lateral shift of the looker's iris, which subtends 1 min. of arc (i.e., one-sixtieth of a degree.) at the observer's eye. A 2-degree threshold in the latter sense means that lookers will have to move their gaze from the target by a distance that subtends 2 degrees of visual angle at the observer's eye before it can be detected.

So what conclusions can we draw from these studies? First, it seems as though people are very good at judging when they are being looked at by someone who is facing them; there is very little in the way of systematic error for direct gazes, and we can detect very small shifts of the iris away from the central position. For instance, Gibson and Pick (1963) report their threshold as representing a shift of the looker's iris by 1 min. of arc, whereas the average figure

Figure 6.2 The face on the left has a direct gaze. In the right panel the same gazer has rotated her eyes to her left by 1.06° (i.e. a linear displacement of the iris of 0.25 mm). This corresponds to the average threshold measured by Cline (1967) in his experiments.

in Cline's experiments was just 0.71 min. of arc. The latter would allow you to discriminate between someone gazing at the bridge of your nose and the edge of your face when they are facing you from a distance of roughly 5 m (See Figure 6.2). This is beyond the finest discrimination that is required for social purposes, where most interactions probably take place over distances of around 2 m. Second, our ability to determine where in space another person is looking rather depends on the location of the target relative to the gazer and the observer; results generally indicate that acuity is worse for laterally averted targets—around 2 min. of arc in Cline's studies—compared to acuity for direct gaze, coupled with which we tend to slightly overestimate the deviation of another's gaze directed at laterally averted targets (Anstis et al, 1969).

The findings of these original studies were, however, challenged by a number of authors (Vine, 1971; Lord & Haith, 1974; von Cranach & Ellgring, 1973). Von Cranach and Ellgring questioned the use made by both Gibson and Pick (1963) and Cline (1967) of standard deviations of error responses in calculating thresholds values. Moreover, they argued that the yes/no "are you looking at me or not," response used by Gibson and Pick might be subject to a response bias, where observers, when uncertain of the actual point of fixation, will default to guessing that the gaze is directed at them (see Martin & Rovira, 1981 for supporting evidence using the Signal Detection Theory). Ellgring's own data (1970, cited in von Cranach & Ellgring, 1973) suggest that observers are

actually quite poor at judging where on their face a looker's gaze is directed. Their participants correctly judged only 49 percent of gazes directed into the eye region from a distance of 80 cm (this would correspond to a threshold of about 2 min. of arc) and, when taking into account the direct gaze response bias, were no better at judging gazes directed toward the eye region than those directed toward other regions of the face. Lord and Haith's (1974) observers also made more errors in this kind of task than one would expect if thresholds were as good as those estimated by Cline; on average they missed 35 percent of gazes directed toward their eye region from a looker just 1 m away and misjudged 46 percent of gazes directed at the mouth as being directed in the eyes.

How can these findings be reconciled with the earlier psychophysical studies? Direct comparisons are rather difficult because of methodological differences and because it is not possible to compute equivalent thresholds from all of the studies. One notable difference is that, in the studies in which performance is relatively poor (Lord & Haith, 1974; Ellgring, 1970), observers were asked to make judgements about gazes directed toward their own faces, whereas in Cline's (1967) study, in which performance was markedly better, observers were making judgements about gazes directed toward a target board positioned in front of them. Given that the task involves extrapolating an invisible line of regard from the looker's eyes to the target, more error might be expected with increasing distance between the looker and target. Moreover, the task may simply be intrinsically harder when the target is actually invisible to the observer than it is when the looker's gaze is directed toward a point on their face rather than an external target. However, although this may be true for triadic gazes (Anstis et al, 1969; Cline, 1967; Ellgring, 1970), intuitively it would not seem to be so for judgements about whether a gaze is dyadic or not (e.g., Gibson & Pick, 1963; Lord & Haith, 1974). Judgements of this kind would simply seem to involve monitoring the relative symmetry of the two eyes (Symons, Lee, Cedrone, & Nisimura, 2004), and so issues concerning the relative locations of the target and observer become irrelevant. Thus, the different results from the Lord & Haith (1974) and Gibson and Pick (1963) studies may well be due to the latter's failure to take response bias into account and hence find an inflated estimate of discrimination performance.

The difficulties in comparing studies may thus be summarized as follows. First, in studies in which participants are asked to make judgements about direct gaze (e.g., Gibson & Pick, 1963; Lord & Haith, 1974), a bias for guessing that a gaze is self-directed is not always taken into account (von Cranach & Ellgring, 1973). Second, the measures of performance differ between studies; some report threshold values, but these are not necessarily computed in a standard fashion, whereas others report percentage-correct scores. Finally, some studies assessing triadic gaze involve gazes at external targets (i.e., between looker and observer; e.g., Anstis et al., 1969; Cline, 1967) whereas others involve on-face targets (Lord & Haith, 1974; Ellgring, 1970).

Two more recent studies take into account at least the first two of these problems. Jenkins and Langton (2003) asked observers to make left/right judgements to digitized greyscale images of faces gazing to the left or right by varying degrees, a procedure likely to produce unbiased responding. From the psychophysical function relating the probability of making one or other of the responses to the angle of gaze, we obtained an estimate of the discrimination threshold that was equivalent to a lateral shift of the looker's iris, which subtended 0.6 min. of arc at the observers' eyes, which is certainly

in line with the figure obtained in Cline's original study. Symons et al (2004) employed a similar method with digitized images to estimate observers' ability to judge gazes directed toward various targets situated below eye-level on a table between the looker and the observer. They, too, used psychophysical functions to estimate discrimination thresholds. The threshold for the central position (i.e., on a line between looker and observer) was again very good (0.41 min. of arc) but tended to worsen slightly as the target moved laterally away from the looker and the observer before recovering for more eccentric targets.

Thus, two recent studies that used standard psychophysical methods, conventional, well-established methods of computing thresholds, and, what are very probably unbiased responses, yielded estimates that are very similar to those measured by Gibson and Pick (1963) and Cline (1967). Under ideal but somewhat artificial conditions, then, it seems as though human gaze perception is roughly as good as visual acuity would theoretically permit, although whether it is as good in practice remains unclear. From the studies reviewed, it is still not clear how to resolve the issue between those showing good acuity for off-face gazes and those showing relatively poor performance for on-face gazes; however, it is fair to say that acuity is sufficient to permit one to judge whether someone is gazing at your face or not over distances where social interactions usually take place. Indeed, in his review Vine (1971) speculated that when people look at one another, they tend to look toward the eye region rather than at other targets in the head region so that observers need only be able to discriminate on-face from off-face gazes. In support of this, recordings of eye movements of people inspecting faces indicate that the eyes are fixated many more times than other face regions (e.g., Yarbus, 1967).

It should also be remembered that, in real-world conditions, we are able to rely on a host of other contextual cues to support judgements about whether someone's gaze is directed at us. For example, a change in someone's facial expression as their gaze is oriented in your direction may reinforce a judgement that you are the target of their attention. Similarly, the more subtle gestures people make in greeting or acknowledging someone's presence, such as the raise of the eyebrows or the nod of the head, may also make it clear that you are recipient of the greeter's attention. In addition, eye-gaze signals are often supported by concomitant changes in head angle and body posture, which also serve as strong signals of attention direction (see below), as do certain verbal utterances they might make. If another's gaze is directed elsewhere, these same cues can help resolve any ambiguity about the target of their fixation as can the target itself; Lobmier, Fischer and Schwaninger (2006) recently demonstrated that the presence of an object near someone's line of regard causes an observer's judgement of that person's gaze to be drawn toward the object. In view of all this, it appears that our acuity for gaze probably exceeds that which is absolutely necessary for social purposes.

MECHANISMS OF GAZE PERCEPTION

How might our perceptual machinery bring about this high degree of accuracy in judgements of gaze direction? First, the task is aided by the morphology of the human eye, which, uniquely among primates, has a widely exposed sclera (the white part of the eye) surrounding a much darker iris (Kobayashi & Kohshima, 1997). In most other primate species the color of the sclera is rather similar to that of the skin around the eyes so that, compared with humans, the direction of gaze will be relatively camouflaged, perhaps in order to deceive predators, prey, or even fellow primates who might be in competition for scarce resources. We humans may have evolved eyes with a greater contrast between iris and sclera precisely because the risk of predation is minimal, and the benefits of an enhanced gaze signal in terms of communication and cooperation far outweigh the cost of an inability to deceive. The unique morphology of the human eye may have evolved to exploit preexisting perceptual structures that function to detect edges and luminance contrast and that support each of the mechanisms that

have been suggested to contribute to gaze perception, which I've labeled the geometric and luminance mechanisms. However, as we shall see, there is also evidence that we have evolved more specialized neural circuitry to support the task of determining where another's attention is directed.

The Geometric Mechanism

The direction of gaze is defined by an invisible line drawn from the fovea through the center of the pupil to the gazed at spot (denoted a in Figure 6.1).[1] All one needs to do in order to determine where someone is looking is to recover this vector. Luckily, the visible features of the eye provide some potentially useful cues, which may facilitate this process. The human eye is roughly spherical and the vector defining gaze direction passes through its center. Because it also rotates in its socket around this central point, the line of regard can be estimated by locating the position of the pupil on the surface of the eye relative to some fixed point, such as the corner of the eye (the canthus). Given the relatively small diameter of the pupil, this might be a fairly tricky job were it not for the fact that, in the human eye, the pupil is positioned in the center of a circular shaped pigmented region called the iris, which is itself surrounded by the lighter colored area called the sclera. Extracting gaze direction then becomes a somewhat simpler job of segmenting the large dark iris from the much brighter background of the sclera and measuring its location relative to the canthus which, of course, must itself be identified and localized. This kind of geometric account was emphasized, or at least implied, by the early accounts of gaze perception (Anstis et al., 1969; Cline, 1967; Gibson & Pick, 1963).

Indirect support for the geometric account comes from the fact that judgements of gaze direction are impaired by turning upside-down either the whole face (Campbell, Heywood, Cowey, Regard and Landis, 1990; Vecera & Johnson, 1995) or just the eye region in the context of an upright

---

[1] Normally this involves two eyes (binocular looking) so the actual direction of gaze involves the convergence of two such lines, but for simplicity the fact that these lines are slightly different will be ignored.

face (Jenkins & Langton, 2003). According to this line of reasoning, the geometric account of gaze perception is effectively an exercise in configural processing: gaze direction is given by the *configuration* of features in the eye and face. Now, configural processing is known to be disrupted by face inversion, and because gaze perception is also impaired by face inversion, it is also likely to be a configural, and hence a geometrical, process.

The Luminance Mechanism

However, several authors have pointed out that there is another plausible account of gaze perception that does not involve the computationally demanding processes of locating and identifying various face features and then measuring their relative spatial positions (Ando, 2002, 2004; Watt, 1999, see Langton, Watt & Bruce, 2000). This alternative mechanism relies on the fact that, as the eye turns, the gross luminance distribution within the eye changes in a way that is predicted by the degree of rotation of the eye. For example, when someone facing you is gazing straight at you, the amount of light reflected by the portions of the sclera on either side of the iris of either eye will be roughly equal. When the eye turns, the area of sclera on the side to which the darker iris moves will be reduced whereas the area of sclera on the other side of the iris increases. The amount of light reflected by the sclera on the side to which the eye turns will, therefore, be reduced, relative to the light reflected by the portion of the sclera on the other side of the iris. The gross difference in luminance on either side of the iris might, therefore, be a useful cue to gaze direction.[2] Watt

(1999) called this cue "scleral contrast" whereas Ando (2002, 2004) labeled it "luminance ratio."

In support of this luminance-based account, Watt found that sensitivity to gaze direction did not vary with viewing distance up to a cut-off point beyond which, presumably, the relevant luminance cues could not be resolved. An account based on the geometry of the eye, on the other hand, would predict that performance should deteriorate with increased viewing distance. The results of a study by Ricciardelli, Baylis and Driver (2000) could also be interpreted as offering support for a luminance-based mechanism. They showed that judgements of gaze direction were highly impaired when the normal contrast polarity of the eyes was reversed so that the sclera appeared to be much darker than the iris. In a similar way, Sinha (2000) contrived the "Bogart Illusion" where contrast negation of a photograph of the eponymous actor's face caused an apparent reversal of his gaze direction. Finally, in Ando's "bloodshot illusion" a bias in participants' gaze judgements was induced by darkening one side of the sclera without shifting the actual location of the iris (e.g., Ando, 2002). Of course, neither contrast negation nor the darkening of the sclera affect the spatial relationships between the features of the eye, suggesting that a geometrical mechanism cannot be entirely responsible for normal judgements of gaze direction.

Clearly, however, we are able to judge where someone is looking from line-drawn images containing no luminance difference between the iris and sclera (see Figure 6.3). Ando (2002), therefore, suggested that *both* the geometric and luminance mechanisms may be involved in recovering eye direction. He argued that the luminance mechanism may operate on information provided at coarse spatial scales whereas the geometric mechanism would be governed by higher spatial frequency information. Assuming visual processing operates in a coarse-to-fine fashion (e.g., Watt, 1987), the luminance mechanism would yield information regarding gaze direction more rapidly than the geometric mechanism. Furthermore, it would continue to operate when viewing conditions are too poor for the geometric mechanism to extract

---

[2] Ando (2004) has convincingly argued that the actual cue to gaze direction must the ratio of "normalised" values of luminance on either side of the sclera; that is, the amount of light reflected by the portion of the sclera relative to the surrounding luminance. This is to take into account of the fact that gaze perception is not impaired by, say, the shadow of the nose falling across one side of the eye region. This would induce a perceived shift in gaze if only the ratio of gross luminance values were used as the cue to gaze direction. However, as long as the shadow covers the sclera and the area immediately surrounding it, the normalised luminance value would remain unchanged

Figure 6.3 Even though these images contain no luminance cues to gaze direction we can nevertheless perceive where they are looking

explicit information about the location of the iris. The luminance mechanism would, therefore, be useful in extracting gaze information if the gazer was standing some distance away, if they were viewed in dim light, or their eyes were only briefly visible. The geometric mechanism, on the other hand, would operate more slowly; it would be much less tolerant to noise, but it would yield more accurate information about gaze direction. Normal gaze perception may then rely on some combination of the output of these two mechanisms, which together operate to make another's gaze direction explicit under a variety of viewing conditions.

The Contribution of Head Orientation

The discussion so far has concerned the extraction of gaze direction from someone who is facing you or, more precisely, someone whose head is oriented frontally with respect to the observer. Under these circumstances the geometric cue concerning the location of the iris in the eye opening provides a good estimate of gaze direction with respect to both the gazer and the observer. However, the gazer might move the head slightly while maintaining fixation on the same spot. When this happens, the geometric arrangement of eye features changes, although the direction of gaze with respect to the observer does not. The simple geometric cue of iris location is, therefore, not in itself sufficient to specify gaze direction. The problem is that location of the iris in the eye opening yields an estimate of the angle of gaze in relation to the gazer's head orientation when what is most useful to the perceiver is the direction of gaze with respect to themselves or, better still, with respect to some environmental reference frame (Todorovic, 2006). Todorovic (2006) explains how, geometrically speaking,

environment-related gaze direction can be specified by adding together the orientation of the gazer's eyes with respect to their head and the orientation of the gazer's head with respect to the observer (see Figure 6.4). It, therefore, follows that the perception of where someone is looking must also involve some consideration of the gazer's head angle.

The authors of the original psychophysical studies of gaze perception (see earlier) all attempted to assess whether the ability to judge gaze direction was influenced by variations in head orientation. In general these studies revealed two kinds of biases. First, under certain circumstances, the perceived direction of gaze can be "towed" toward the orientation of the head. Imagine a situation in which a gazer's head is angled toward, say, your right shoulder and their eyes are directed at a point that is also to your right, but less extreme than their head angle—your right ear, perhaps. In this case the direction of gaze is perceived to be somewhere between the angle of the head and the true line of regard of the eyes (Anstis et al., 1969; Cline, 1967; see also Maruyama & Endo, 1983, 1984); the gaze directed toward your ear will now be seen as directed over your shoulder. The second kind of influence of head angle on the perception of gaze is a kind of overshoot or repulsion effect, where an error in gaze perception is introduced in the *opposite* direction to the angle of rotation of the head. For example, imagine someone standing in front of you with their head 30° or so to your right and with their eyes either staring straight back at you, or back toward your left shoulder. Apparently, under these conditions, you might perceive their eyes to be gazing a little further to the left than they actually are (Anstis et al., 1969; Cline, 1967).

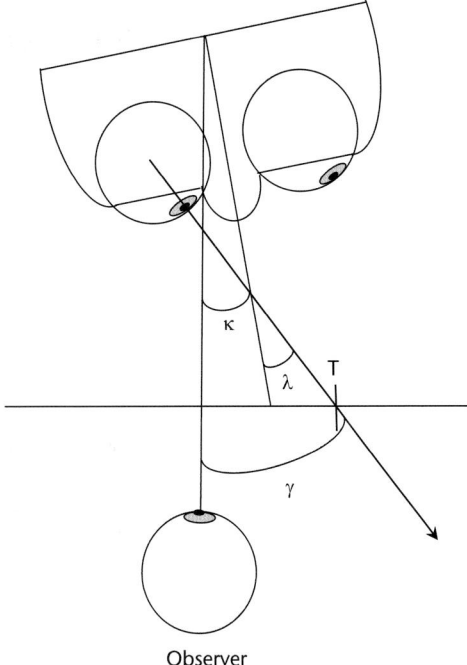

Figure 6.4 A looker's gaze toward target T in the environment is at an angle γ with respect to the observer. This angle can be computed by adding together the looker's gaze with respect to their head orientation (λ) and the angle in which their head is pointing with respect to the observer (κ) (See Todorovic, 2006).

What are the origins of these biases and what do they tell us about the contribution of head orientation to the perception of gaze direction? The repulsion or overshoot bias may actually arise because a rotated head projects a foreshortened view of the eyes to an observer, which, in turn, results in a misjudgement of the actual location of the iris in the eye socket. Figure 6.5 illustrates how the projected image of the eye region changes as the head rotates to the left and right of the observer while the eyes remain fixed on the same point in the environment. The image of the eye as it is projected to the observer for each of the head angles is represented in the figure by the diagrams below each eyeball, with the white and grey bars illustrating the extent of the visible portions of the sclera and iris, respectively. The numbers at the bottom represent a numerical expression of the gaze direction computed by subtracting the area of sclera to the right of each iris from the corresponding area on the left and dividing this by their sum. A value of 0 will, therefore, correspond to the situation in which the iris is flanked by equal areas of sclera, -1 where there is no visible sclera on the left hand side of the iris and +1 where there is no visible sclera to the left of the iris. This might be thought of as either the outcome of a mechanism that compares luminance on either side of the iris or one that measures the relative distances between each edge of the iris and the visible extent of each portion of sclera. When the head is pointing straight toward the observer (Figure 6.5D), the scleral contrast measure is − 0.54, which corresponds to a leftward gaze. As the head rotates to the observer's right (Figures 6.5E and 6.5D) a little more sclera becomes visible on the right-hand side of the iris and progressively less on the left-hand side resulting in more negative scleral contrast measures. If the gaze perception mechanism treated scleral contrast as a measure of observer-related gaze direction, then the effect of a head turn to the right is that the gaze direction will be judged to be more to the left than is actually the case. Conversely, a head turn to the left (Figures 6.5C – 6.5D) reveals progressively less sclera on the right of the iris relative to the left so that gaze direction is judged to be a little more to the right than the true line of regard (the contrast measures are less negative than when the head is viewed straight on). The overshoot bias can, therefore, be explained if the gaze perception mechanism actually ignores the orientation of the head and makes its computation on what it can see of the eye region.

It is also worth considering what the scleral contrast measures in Figure 6.5 actually compute. Those in Figures 6.5D and 6.5E are a good representation of gaze direction with respect to the gazer—from their point of view, their gaze becomes more extreme as they turn their head and this is signaled by the more negative scleral contrast measures. However, this is not the case in Figures 6.5A–6.5C. In Figure 6.5C, for example, the eye is pointing in roughly the same direction as the head—the gazer is looking

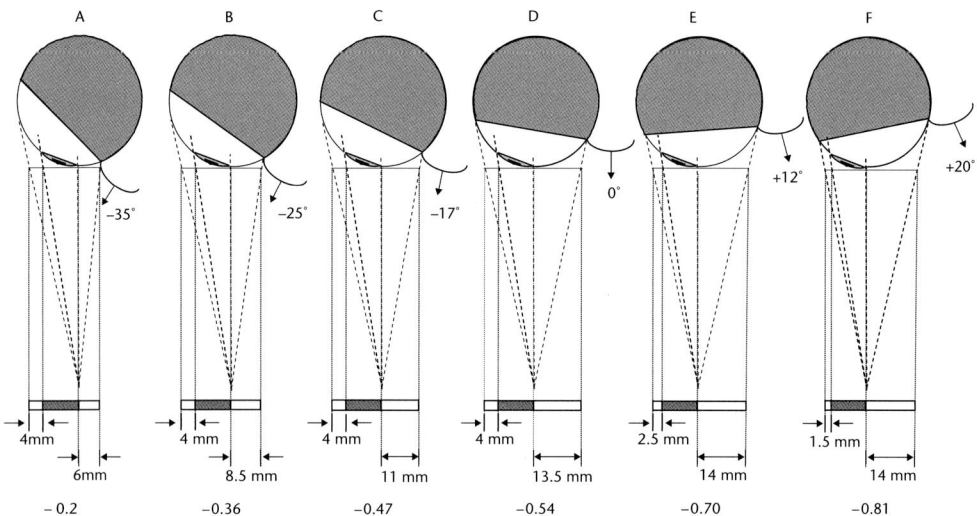

Figure 6.5 An illustration of how the projection of the visible area of the eye changes as the gazer's head rotates. Figures A–D are schematic representations of someone's right eye as seen from above with the pupil rotated 20° from straight ahead (i.e. from vertical in the figure). In D the head is also directed straight ahead (denoted by the arrow pointing from the nose with a label indicating the angle from straight ahead). In A–C the head is rotated clockwise to the viewer's left and in a counter-clockwise direction in E and F. The figures below each eye provide a schematic representation of the proportions of sclera and iris visible to the observer at each head angle and the figures in the bottom row indicate the relative amount of sclera visible on the left compared to the right of the iris as a proportion of the total area of visible sclera. See text for more detail.

straight ahead—and yet the scleral contrast figure is negative; in Figures 6.5B and 6.5A the gaze becomes more extreme in relation to the head angle, but this does not seem to be signaled by the contrast measures. The reason for this is that, for the head angles represented in Figures 6.5A–6.5C, the corner of the eye is out of sight around the eyeball. In these cases, the scleral contrast measure—the computation that reflects the location of the iris in the projectively foreshortened view of the eye—actually signals something that is closer to the absolute gaze direction in space (i.e., gaze with respect to the observer). Treating the iris location as a measure of absolute eye gaze may, therefore, produce a quick solution to the problem of detecting gaze direction in a head that moves, but one that is subject to the kind of overshoot bias reported by Anstis et al. (1969) and Cline (1967).

Does this mean that we do not actually have to worry about head orientation in considering the mechanisms by which gaze direction is computed? The observation of the other kind of bias—the effect where the perceived gaze direction is "towed" toward the angle of the head—suggests that perhaps we do. The effect is perhaps best illustrated by William Wollaston's (1824) drawings and our own greyscale images (see Figure 6.6). The eyes in the bottom two images of Figure 6.6 are absolutely identical. An analysis of the gaze directions in the two images would, therefore, yield identical outputs, regardless of whether it was based on luminance contrast or a spatial measurement of iris location, and yet the gaze directions in the two images appear to be different. The effect, therefore, seems to suggest that the system that computes another's attention direction accesses some information about the rotation of the head as well as the configuration of the visible features of the eye.

If the human visual system uses iris location as a cue to gaze direction (whether computed geometrically or by scleral contrast), what is the equivalent cue for head orientation? Wilson,

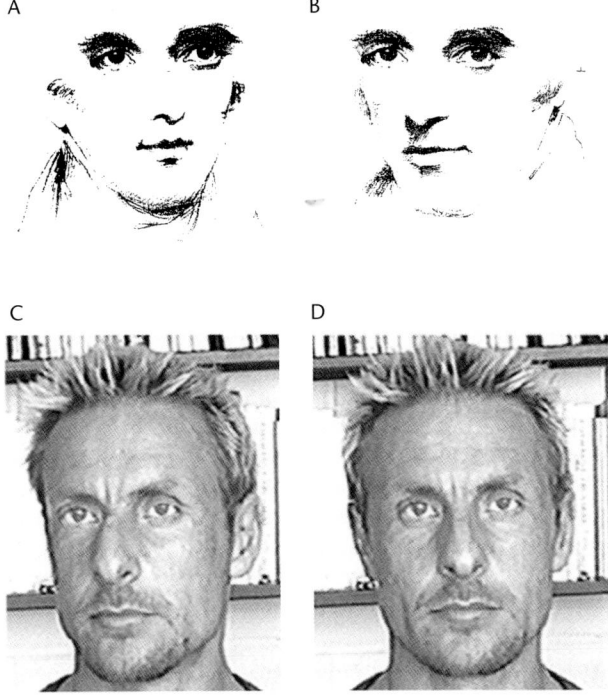

Figure 6.6 Head orientation influences the perceived direction of gaze. The top two pictures are taken from Wollaston's original paper. Face B seems to be gazing directly at the viewer whereas Face A appears to be looking slightly to the viewer's right. By covering the lower and upper parts of each face you can see that the eye regions of both are, in fact, identical. The lower two faces illustrate a similar effect with greyscale images. The eye region from D has been pasted onto C where the head is rotated slightly to the viewer's left.

Wilkinson, Lin, & Castillo (2000) measured their participants' thresholds for discriminating rotations of the head and found that they were not significantly affected by removal of either the internal features of the face or the outline head contour, suggesting that head orientation can be discriminated using either of these two equal-strength cues. By using surrogate nose and head shapes, Wilson and colleagues established that, for the internal features, the deviation of nose angle from vertical is the likely source of head orientation information, and that the external cue is the deviation of the head contour from bilateral symmetry. To elaborate, when the head is oriented directly at you, its outline contour projects an approximately symmetrical shape about the vertical midline, and a line drawn from the bridge to the tip of the nose will be roughly vertical. As the head rotates, its shape becomes increasingly asymmetrical and the nose angle shifts away from vertical. Wilson et al.'s evidence suggests that the visual system is able to compute these deviations from bilateral symmetry and vertical angle, respectively,

and use them as cues to the orientation of the head.

We (Langton, Honeyman & Tessler, 2004) wondered whether these cues were actually those used in practice to influence the perception of gaze. In a series of experiments we first established that participants' ability to discriminate direct from averted gaze in brief, masked presentations of digitized images of faces was significantly reduced when the same pair of eyes appeared on a face with an incongruent as compared to a congruent head orientation (see Figure 6.7). We then removed the internal features of the faces (apart from the eyes) and repeated the experiment. The findings were identical to the first experiment: the outline profile of the head was sufficient to produce an effect on gaze discrimination and did so even when we controlled for the lateral displacement of the eyes that occurs with a head turn. More surprisingly, in another experiment we found that nose angle was also able to influence participants' ability to discriminate direct from averted gaze, although the magnitude of

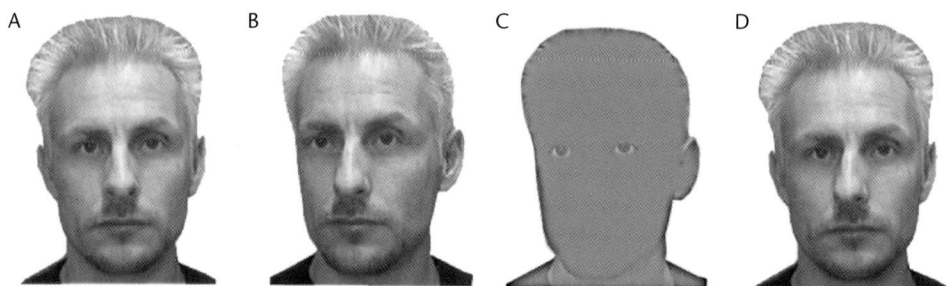

Figure 6.7 Examples of the stimuli used in Langton et al's (2004) experiments. In each case the eyes are identical and looking straight ahead. In A the head is congruent with the gaze direction and in B it is incongruent. The internal features have been removed from the incongruent head/gaze image in C. In D the nose angle and gaze are incongruent.

the effect was very much smaller. Together the results of these experiments confirmed that the cues to head orientation suggested by Wilson et al. (2000) are also those used in the perception of eye-gaze direction, although the mechanisms by which they do so may well be different (see Langton et al., 2004).

Clearly then we need to amend our account of gaze perception. The evidence just reviewed suggests that it involves a combination of both iris location and head orientation. However, there are at least two ways in which this might be achieved (e.g., see Todorovic. 2006). First, independent mechanisms may compute eye direction (e.g., from eye geometry) and head orientation (e.g., from asymmetry of head profile), and then this information may be somehow combined to yield a representation of attention direction. Second, a more holistic account may involve a kind of matching of the whole input pattern to a set of template representations that specify different observer- or environment-related attention directions. Each of these templates may embody some combination of head orientation and eye direction and the gazer's attention direction would be given by the most activated template or, if the input does not exactly correspond with one of the templates, an interpolation between two such discrete entities. Under this account there is no need for the system to derive separate estimates of iris location or degree of head turn; the input is instead a representation of the whole face configuration.

Some evidence from our laboratory favors the independent mechanisms account. First of all, in the experiments described earlier (Langton et al., 2004) the influence of the shape of the head profile on gaze discrimination was found to be unaffected by turning faces upside down. Inversion ought to make it difficult for the input pattern to be matched to any existing template or set of templates, so the fact that it didn't rather argues against this type of account. Instead we suggested that head orientation and eye direction are extracted fairly early in processing by mechanisms that would be insensitive to inversion. (For example, detection of asymmetry by units in area V4 might signal head turn while scleral contrast can, in principal, be signaled by V1 units. Both of these areas are toward the back of the brain and are early recipients of visual information from the eyes.) Second, in another set of experiments (Langton, 2000), participants were asked to make speeded decisions about spoken directional words (up, down, left, and right) while viewing photographs of faces with various combinations of head and gaze directions. The key independent variables in this experiment were the congruent/incongruent relationships between, on the one hand, the head orientation and the spoken word and, on the other, the eye-gaze direction and the spoken word. Results indicated that participants' responses to the spoken words were additively affected by both head and gaze direction, findings that are consistent with a model in which head and gaze are analyzed in parallel by separate systems with the output of each exerting an effect on the processing of the auditory information.

Experimental work, therefore, converges on the suggestion that gaze direction—computed via geometry and/or luminance contrast—and head orientation are processed independently and then integrated to yield a representation of another's direction of attention. Support for the idea of separate eye-gaze and head-orientation analyzers also comes from cognitive neuroscience and neuropsychology.

Neural Mechanisms of Social Attention Perception

When it is discovered that the brain does something very well, such as recognize faces or understand language, and that something seems to have biological and social importance, then it is tempting to look for evidence that the brain contains neural machinery dedicated to performing that function. This is no less true of the processing of eye gaze and head orientation. In fact, evidence from neurophysiology, neuropsychology, neuroimaging, and experimental cognitive psychology is converging on the suggestion that such dedicated circuitry exists in the superior temporal sulcus (STS) region of the primate brain.

Using a technique that enables the activity of a single nerve cell to be recorded, Perrett and his co-workers have identified certain cells in the STS region of the macaque temporal lobe that respond maximally to the particular direction in which the eyes in that face are looking. For example, one population of cells fire with maximum frequency when the monkey sees another individual gazing upward, and another population of cells respond well to gazes directed downward (e.g., Perrett, Hietanen, Oram & Benson, 1992; Perrett et al., 1985). Moreover, when this region of the macaque cortex is removed, these monkeys are unable to make gaze-direction judgements, but nevertheless perform well on a number of other face-processing tasks (Heywood & Cowey, 1992). Humans suffering damage to the equivalent part of the brain have also been shown to be impaired in gaze recognition (Campbell et al., 1990; Heywood & Cowey, 1992).

More recently, several functional imaging studies have supported the proposal that the STS plays an important role in human gaze perception. For example, Puce et al. (1998) showed that the posterior region of the STS was activated by movements of the eyes and mouth but not by moving control patterns. In another study, a similar region of the STS was found to respond strongly when participants were paying attention to a gaze-matching task, but less so when the same faces were being matched for identity (Hoffman & Haxby, 2000). However, subsequent work has suggested that, rather than coding particular gaze directions, the posterior STS is actually sensitive to the goal-directed nature, or *intentionality*, of gaze signals. For example, Pelphrey, Viola and McCarthy (2004) found that the same physical shift in gaze produced greater posterior STS activity when it was directed toward the participant than when it was directed away from the participant. In another study, STS activation was found to persist for longer when participants viewed someone shifting his or her gaze away from a target—a violation of the expected intentionality—than when the gaze was shifted toward the target (Pelphrey, Singerman, Allison & McCarthy, 2003). Thus, the posterior region of the STS seems to play a role in processing the goal of a gaze shift rather than simply coding its direction per se.

The functional imaging studies, then, do not quite tally with the single-cell recordings. The latter point to a role for specialization in the STS for gaze-direction perception whereas the former implicate the STS in the rather higher-level task of analyzing gaze and other biological movements, such as reaching-to-grasp (e.g., Pelphrey, Morris & McCarthy, 2004) in terms of their intentions. The difficulty may be that the invasive single-cell recording technique is a much more precise instrument than is functional imaging, which indirectly samples the activity of many neurons engaged in a particular behavior. It is entirely possible, therefore, that the STS region in humans contains cells that are specialized for analyzing gaze direction as well as others that are more concerned with the goal-directed nature of gaze behavior. Indeed, recent work by Calder, Jenkins and colleagues supports this conclusion (Calder et al., 2007; Jenkins, Beaver, & Calder, 2006). Jenkins et al. (2006) showed that repeated exposure to faces displaying a particular gaze direction in an adaptation block of trials virtually eliminated participants' ability to perceive that type of gaze in a subsequent run of test trials. For example, repeated exposure to leftward gaze resulted in subsequent presentations of a leftward gaze to be misperceived as looking straight ahead, while judgements of rightward gazes were unaffected. This kind of stimulus-specific aftereffect is widely considered to reveal the existence of cell populations that are selectively tuned to that particular stimulus. The data of Jenkins et al., therefore, suggest the existence of populations of neurons that are selectively responsive to particular directions of gaze. Calder et al. (2007) have replicated and extended these findings using fMRI adaptation. They showed that adapting to leftward gaze produced a reduction in activation in the anterior STS to left relative to right gazes. Similarly, adapting to rightward gaze produced a corresponding reduction in activation to right versus left gazes. Together these adaptation studies suggest that there are separate populations of cells in the anterior STS that code, respectively, left and right gazes. As Jenkins et al. explain, having two such populations broadly tuned to left and right gaze is sufficient to represent a range of gaze directions, including direct gaze. For example, in a so-called opponent coding system the perceived gaze direction is signaled by the relative activation of the two pools of cells with the perception of direct gaze arising from equivalent activation in these two channels. On the other hand, rather than two distinct cell populations, the data are also consistent with a multichannel coding system in which many pools of cells exist, each coding for a different direction of gaze. Recent research seems to favor the latter system (Calder, Jenkins, Cassel, & Clifford, 2008).

Therefore, there seems to be some evidence for a kind of functionally distinct gaze analysis system, at least in the sense that there is neural circuitry devoted to the perception of gaze direction. Whatever the precise nature of the neural mechanism involved in the perception of particular gaze angles, it seems that the anterior region of the STS is involved in this task, whereas the posterior region of the STS is involved in encoding something about the meaning of these gazes—the intention or goal that elicited them in the first place.

In the preceding section, I suggested that both gaze direction and head orientation might be computed by separate systems. We have seen some evidence in support of a gaze analysis system but what of an equivalent system for processing head orientation? Again, there is some evidence for this from single cell recordings and from at least one adaptation study. Perrett and colleagues' single cell recording studies also identified cells in the STS region that were selective for different views of the head. For example, one class of cells responded more to full face than to profile views, whereas other cells showed the opposite pattern of selectivity. Some cells seem to be selective for heads angled at approximately 45°, some were sensitive to heads oriented upwards, whereas others preferred views of the head looking downward. Recent adaptation studies suggest that the human visual system may contain similarly selective neurons. For example, Fang and He (2005) repeatedly presented their participants with heads angled at either 15° or 30°. When subsequently presented with a head facing forward, participants tended to misperceive it as directed in the opposite direction to the stimuli to which they were adapted. As with the gaze adaptation studies described earlier, this result supports the existence of neurons tuned to the adapted head angles, probably also coded by multichannel system (see Calder et al., 2008).

So far then, there is some evidence in favor of the idea that separate neural mechanisms code for, respectively, gaze and head orientation. The experimental evidence discussed earlier suggests that these two sources of information are integrated somehow to yield a representation of attention direction. It turns out that the STS region may also be responsible for this. Perrett's work (Perrett, et al., 1985, 1992) showed that at least some of the cells in the STS respond to *both* head and gaze direction. For example, there are down cells, which respond maximally to either downward-directed gaze or to a head tilted downward. Perrett et al (1992) suggested that these cells pool information from separate analyzers for gaze, head, and body posture in a kind of hierarchical arrangement, which would ensure that eye gaze would always override head orientation and that both of these would override body posture. For example, if the head were oriented downward but gaze was directed upward the output of eye-direction analyzers would activate an up STS cell while preventing head orientation analyzers from activating a down cell through presynaptic inhibition. This kind of arrangement would also allow attention direction to be specified under a number of other viewing conditions, such as when the eyes are invisible (e.g., concealed by sunglasses), if lighting conditions are poor, or when viewing distances are large.

As yet, however, there is little in the way of behavioral evidence from studies with human participants that directly supports the kind of model suggested by Perrett et al (1992). For instance, it is clear that an incorrect head orientation is not completely inhibited when social-attention direction is assessed; we have already seen how head orientation can influence perceptual judgements of gaze direction, but decisions about gaze direction are also slower when the head is pointing in an incongruent, as opposed to a congruent, direction to the eyes (Langton, 2000; Ricciardelli & Driver, 2008; Seyama & Nagayama, 2005). The model can incorporate these data by allowing the output from eye-gaze detectors to attenuate, as opposed to completely inhibit, head orientation analyzers. If there are cells that pool information from head and eyes, it ought to be possible to influence gaze discrimination by repeated exposure to heads oriented in the same direction. Indeed, it is possible that the adaptation effects already described operate at this level. However, Calder et al (2008) site evidence from an unpublished study by Jenkins, Keane and Calder, which showed that gaze discrimination was unaffected by adapting to heads (with gaze masked) oriented in the same direction, suggesting that gaze adaptation occurs in cells coding gaze alone. Of course, this is effectively a null result, so it remains possible

that future studies will find evidence of the kind of cross-cue adaptation that would constitute evidence of social-attention cells.

To summarize so far, it is clear that we are very good indeed at judging where someone is looking, and this ability seems to be underpinned by two putative mechanisms: one aimed at assessing the luminance configuration in the eye and the other segmenting the eye into its constituent features before performing a spatial analysis in order to determine gaze direction. The output of the eye-direction analysis must somehow be integrated with information from a system that extracts head orientation, and there is growing evidence from behavioral studies, supported by single-cell recordings, that eye gaze and head orientation are processed by separate systems. Precisely how information from the two systems is combined is as yet unclear and awaits future research.

GAZE CUEING OF ATTENTION

People tend to look at things that are behaviorally important to them. Another's shift in gaze might signify the approach of something threatening, or the opposite—a potential mate. It might indicate the subject of their last remark, or the location of the object they are about to act upon. More generally, the focus of another's visual attention is often the thing that is currently occupying their thoughts. Observing and acting upon this kind of behavior in another individual can, therefore, give us an insight into their mental lives, which—in the case of an approaching threat or attractive member of the opposite sex—might be of some adaptive advantage. In the preceding sections I have discussed how we might go about perceiving the direction of another's attention, but this is really only half of the story. To have a chance of accessing their thoughts on the basis of their social attention, we need to be able to re-align our attention with a shift in theirs. If we can do this effortlessly and rapidly, then so much the better. In the remainder of this chapter I discuss research that has examined these claims. Rather than provide an exhaustive review of the literature (for a recent, more comprehensive account see Frischen,

Bayliss & Tipper, 2007), I will concentrate on the question of whether we have evolved a special system for directing attention in response to another's gaze before attempting to link what we know about gaze perception with this gaze cueing effect.

Anecdotally, at least, we do seem to feel some kind of compulsion to follow other people's shifts in gaze. Think how irritating it is when someone to whom you are talking keeps looking over your shoulder toward the door or how someone standing in a street looking upward into the sky seems to induce others into doing the same. Of course, we are actually able to suppress this urge, and so we do not always shift our gaze every time our conversant looks around the room for someone more interesting to talk to. However, just because we do not make an *overt* shift of attention—a movement of the eyes and/or head—this does not preclude the possibility that a *covert* shift of attention has been made (Posner, 1980). An overt shift of attention occurs when we move our eyes and head toward an object of interest so that light reflected from this object will be directed toward the most sensitive part of the retina—the fovea. A covert shift, on the other hand, directs some kind of internal mechanism at a mental representation of the sensory input, which facilitates further processing of this input. So the question is whether a shift in another's gaze tends to trigger a shift in the observer's covert attention.

Over the last 10 years, a wealth of research has suggested that social attention cues from the head and/or the eyes do indeed induce this kind of attention shift (e.g., Driver et al., 1999; Friesen & Kingstone, 1998; Hietanen, 1999; Langton & Bruce, 1999). In a typical study, participants are asked to make a speeded detection, discrimination, or localization response to a target letter, which can appear on either the left- or the right-hand side of a computer screen. Shortly before the presentation of the target, a face appears on the screen, which, on a cued or valid trial, is gazing toward the side of the screen where the target is about to appear, and, on an uncued or invalid trial, is gazing in the opposite direction. When the delay between the appearance of the gaze cue and the onset of the target is short (i.e.,

stimulus onset asynchronies [SOAs] of around 100–700 ms) reaction time (RT) to cued targets is faster than to uncued targets. This cueing effect occurs despite the fact that participants do not move their eyes (eye tracking can be used to eliminate data from trials where eye movements occur) and that they are informed that the gaze cue is completely uninformative of the location, identity, or time of onset of the target. The widely accepted explanation for this effect is that the gaze cue induces a covert shift of participants' attention, which facilitates the processing of cued relative to uncued targets. There are also indications that this shift in attention occurs automatically: the cueing effect emerges rapidly (i.e., at short SOAs), dissipates at longer SOAs (Friesen & Kingstone, 1998) and even occurs when gazes are known by participants to be counterpredictive of the likely location of the target (Driver et al., 1999).

IS GAZE CUEING SPECIAL?

One of the reasons attention researchers became interested in gaze cueing was that it seemed to represent a rather special kind of attention shifting effect. Early studies by Eriksen and Hoffman (1973), Posner (1980) and Jonides (1981) suggested that people are able to deploy visual attention to different regions of space in two ways. First, certain events in the periphery of vision, such as sudden changes in luminance or motion, attract attention automatically to their location. Attention seems to be pulled toward these events by the stimuli themselves so that it is said to be bottom-up, stimulus-driven, reflexive, or exogenous. Second, attention can be shifted voluntarily on the basis of an informative visual cue such as an arrow or by any other visual information that has become associated with the location of a target stimulus. In this case, attention is pushed toward the cued location by the force of will; it is top-down, goal-driven, voluntary, or endogenous. Exogenous shifts are triggered by events in the periphery of vision and occur regardless of whether the event itself is relevant to ongoing activity or is informative of the likely location of a target event. Endogenous shifts are prompted by symbolic information that is usually presented centrally at fixation and that must first be interpreted before attention can be shifted. Importantly, endogenous shifts do not generally occur if the symbolic cue is uninformative of a target's location. Gaze cueing, therefore, seems to represent a special category of attention shift insofar as it is produced by a central, symbolic cue yet bears many hallmarks of one that has been exogenously triggered. Indeed, both Friesen and Kingstone (1998) and Langton and Bruce (1999) speculated that gaze cueing might represent a kind of special social-orienting response, perhaps subserved by dedicated neural circuitry.

In the years since the initial demonstration of the gaze-cueing effect, several groups established that, contrary to what had hitherto been received wisdom since Jonides's (1981) work, arrows and other symbolic cues also produce attention-cueing effects that are similar to those triggered by gaze and head cues (e.g., Hommel, Pratt, Colzato, & Godjin, 2001; Ristic, Friesen & Kingstone, 2002; Tipples, 2002). Along similar lines, Downing, Dodds and Bray (2004) found that an attention-cueing effect could be induced from a face where the tongue was extended laterally to the left or right. On the face of it, these observations would seem to weaken the argument for gaze cueing representing a special social-orienting mechanism. However, while many different symbolic cues might be capable of triggering reflexive shifts, it seems that there are qualitative differences in the behavioral effects produced by gazes and these symbolic cues. For example, at short cue-target SOAs (up to 500–600 ms), gaze cues produce attention shifts even when participants are attempting to shift their attention voluntarily in the opposite direction; however, the same is not true of arrows (Friesen, Ristic & Kingstone, 2004) or tongues (Downing et al., 2004). Gaze-cued attention shifts might, therefore, be special in the sense of being uniquely resistant to top-down suppression. Langdon and Smith (2005) also demonstrated a dissociation between gaze-cued and arrow-cued attention. They compared target-detection performance at cued and uncued locations with performance following the appearance of a neutral cue (i.e., for gazes: eyes directed straight ahead; for arrows: a straight line with short vertical lines at either end). Both gaze-cued and arrow-cued attention were associated with performance benefits for targets whose locations were cued relative to those that received a neutral cue, whereas only shifts triggered by eye gaze were associated with performance costs at the uncued location. Following Posner, Nissen and Ogden (1978), Langdon and Smith argued that only when performance benefits are paired with performance costs should we invoke an attentional explanation. According to the argument, performance benefits in the absence of costs suggests the operation of automatic but nonattentional processes, such as the priming of mechanisms used to produce the response. The implication is that although gaze cues actually trigger shifts of spatial attention, arrows exert their effects perhaps through some kind of spatial stimulus-response compatibility. Whatever the merits of this kind of interpretation, the fact that, in several studies, gaze- and arrow-cued attention produce qualitatively different effects, suggests that reflexive shifting of attention in response to seen gaze might represent a rather special form of symbolic orienting.

There are also indications that different brain systems subserve reflexive attention cueing from gazes and arrows. Kingstone's group (Kingstone, Friesen & Gazzaniga, 2000; Ristic et al., 2002) studied gaze cueing in a split-brain patient, JW—an individual who, because of intractable epilepsy, had the structures connecting his cerebral hemispheres severed through surgery. Kingstone et al. (2000) found that reflexive gaze cueing was only produced when the gaze cues were presented to JW's right hemisphere whereas nonpredictive arrows triggered reflexive attention cueing in both of his cerebral hemispheres (Ristic et al., 2002). More recently, Akiyama et al. (2006) studied a patient who had a lesion confined to the right superior temporal gyrus, part of the STS which, as we have seen, has been implicated in gaze perception. This patient showed normal reflexive cueing effects from nonpredictive arrows but showed no such effect for gaze. These studies, therefore, suggest that rather different brain mechanisms are involved in cueing from gaze and arrows with gaze cueing likely to be lateralized to the STS region of the face-processing hemisphere (usually the right). Indeed, before the demonstrations of the gaze-cueing effect, Harries and Perrett (1991) noted that the STS supplies heavy output projections to the parietal cortex, which is implicated in attention orienting. Perrett et al. (1992) speculated that this link may provide the channel through which another's attention direction might influence the attentional orientation of an observer. Subsequent research is, therefore, beginning to support this idea.

Notice, however, that the argument about whether gaze cueing is special has really been reduced to a claim about whether gaze perception is special, for which there is a good deal of supporting evidence. There do, indeed, appear to be neurons that are involved in the perception of gaze direction, which otherwise do nothing else. Whether the same can be said for arrows is unlikely, but whatever circuitry is involved in categorizing something as an arrow (and it must exist somewhere), it must also be connected to structures that control the allocation of attention. The fact that connections exist between structures encoding gaze and those involved in attention orienting does not, therefore, constitute strong evidence that gaze-cueing per se is somehow special.

More persuasive evidence that gaze cueing involves some dedicated neural circuitry comes from a recent study by Hietanen et al. (2006). They measured brain activity using fMRI while participants performed standard cueing tasks with gazes and with arrows. For each type of cue, they looked at the difference between activity in cued and uncued conditions and the activity produced by corresponding neutral cues (a straight-ahead gaze and, for a neutral arrow, a horizontal line with vertical bars at each end). The idea here is that the residual activity represents stages of processing *after* the visual analysis of the directional cues; in other words, activity pertaining to the shifting of attention produced by either cue and the subsequent processing of the target stimuli. Results indicated that gaze-cued orienting and arrow-cued orienting were associated with activity in different regions of the brain. Gaze-cued orienting

involved activity in areas that are generally thought to be involved in the reflexive orienting of attention, whereas arrow-cued orienting activated a much more extensive network that included areas such as the frontal eye fields, which are associated with voluntary shifts of attention. This study, therefore, suggests that eye gaze may well represent a special kind of symbolic cue that triggers attention shifts through different neural circuitry compared to the shifts of attention triggered by arrows.

In summary, converging evidence from imaging studies and purely behavioral work suggest that gaze cueing is special in the following sense: Biologically or socially relevant directional cues (e.g., from the head and eyes) seem to represent a unique class of symbolic cue that trigger shifts of attention with all the hallmarks of reflexive or exogenous orienting via a separate mechanism to that engaged by arrows—the standard comparison nonbiological directional cue. What I do not think is clear from the research conducted so far is whether eye gaze and head orientation actually engage a dedicated attentional resource (i.e., one that is somehow reserved for deployment by only these kinds of cues). At present the evidence suggests that social directional cues offer a unique mode of control over an otherwise nonspecial exogenous orienting system.

Another thorny issue is the extent to which social directional cues have acquired their special attention-shifting status by virtue of an innate predisposition or by experiential learning. The difficulty is that we obviously have a good deal more experience at following gazes and head turns than we do with following arrows. If we were able to control for this, it is possible that arrows, like gazes, would begin to recruit the mechanisms associated with reflexive orienting and produce orienting effects that are qualitatively indistinguishable to those produced by eye gaze (e.g., costs plus benefits, resistance to top-down control, etc.). On the other hand, studies by Hood, Willen, and Driver (1998) and Farroni, Johnson, Brockbank, and Simion (2000), showing that neonates and two-month-olds show a form of gaze-cueing behavior, might be taken to indicate that this is an innate ability. There are, however, indications that this early ability requires the eyes to be moving so that infants may simply be responding to the movement of a highly discriminable (particularly to the developing neonate) features of the face. Thus, rather than evolving a dedicated gaze-following system, it is possible that the eyes have evolved to provide a clear social directional signal that exploits the relatively rudimentary perceptual and attentional abilities of newborns. Clearly this is a very difficult issue to resolve; however, as Liu and Chaudhuri (2003) have pointed out, "specialness" might be evaluated along three separate and orthogonal dimensions: domain specificity, innateness, and neural representations. On this view, gaze cueing might not be special in the sense that, like arrow cueing, it is learned rather than innate, but it may be special in the sense of involving separate neural mechanisms to those involved in orienting attention in response to other kinds of symbolic cue.

LINKING GAZE PERCEPTION AND GAZE CUEING

In an earlier section, I described how gaze perception might be based on separate mechanisms that use, respectively, geometric and luminance information to compute gaze angle. I also discussed research that reveals how the perception of where someone is looking is influenced by both the angle of eye-gaze and the orientation of the head. The perception of another's attention direction, therefore, seems to involve a fairly complex integration of information from a variety of different sources. All this presumably takes some time, and yet gaze cueing has been shown to occur very rapidly (within 100 ms of the presentation of the gaze cue). This prompts several questions about the nature of gaze cueing, one of which concerns the actual perceptual basis for the orienting effect; is an attention shift generated on the basis of a rich, detailed representation of gaze direction based on the integration of the various sources of information, or does its rapidity suggest a rather simpler mechanism, perhaps one based on a "quick and dirty" analysis of luminance contrast? In principal, at least, the ratio of light reflected by the portions of the sclera on either side of the iris (a possible cue to gaze direction) can be computed very early in visual processing by V1 units (see Watt, 1999) so perhaps this information, rather than an analysis of the geometry of the eye, is what triggers the attention shift.

A recent experiment conducted in our lab was aimed at addressing this issue. The idea was simply to examine whether the gaze-cueing effect was influenced by the removal of either geometric or luminance information in the face (see Figure 6.8). In a standard cueing procedure, 39 participants performed a speeded localization task to a target that could appear on the left or right of a computer monitor. Two hundred milliseconds before the appearance of the target, a face appeared, which, on cued trials, was

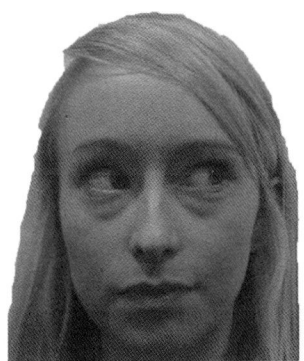

Figure 6.8 The stimuli used in the experiment described in the text. A normal cue is illustrated in the left panel, a luminance cue containing minimal geometric information in the center, and a geometric cue containing no luminance information is shown in the right panel.

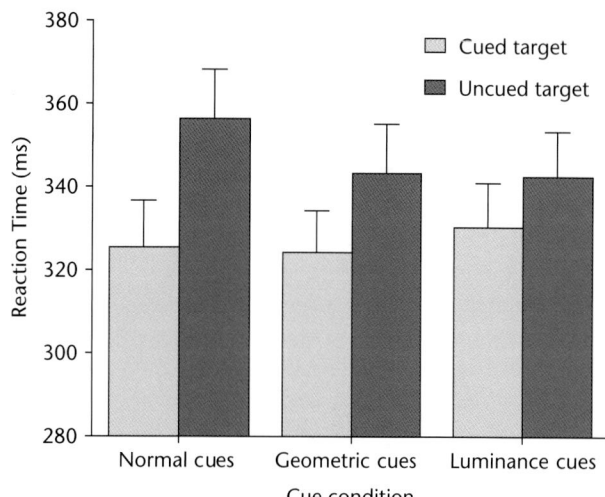

Figure 6.9 Mean reaction times in milliseconds (with error bars of ± 1 standard error) to localise target stimuli in each of the conditions of the experiment described in the text.

gazing toward the target location or toward the opposite location on uncued trials. In one block of trials, the cues were either normal faces, in another they were blurred faces with only luminance information (i.e. geometry removed), and in a third block they were faces containing only geometric information (i.e., with luminance information removed). The order of blocks was counterbalanced across participants. Median reaction times (RTs) were computed for each participant in each of the cue conditions, and the overall mean RTs are illustrated in Figure 6.9. As can be seen from this figure, RTs were faster in cued compared to uncued conditions for each type of cue. However, the difference between RTs in uncued and cued conditions (i.e., the cueing effect) was much larger for the normal cues (those containing both luminance and geometric information) than for cues containing only luminance or geometrical information, which were fairly similar. In other words, removal of either type of information reduced, but did not eliminate, the cueing effect. It seems, then, that both the luminance and geometric cues in the eye contribute to gaze cueing. This could be achieved by the separate putative mechanisms (geometric and luminance), each contributing outputs to the attention system, or through a single representation of gaze direction that combines geometric and luminance information. Further research is necessary to

investigate these possibilities; however, the results of our preliminary experiment allow us to reject the notion that gaze cueing operates only via a coarse-scale analysis of luminance cues in the eye.

Indeed, a number of other studies have suggested that the representation of gaze direction underpinning gaze cueing is actually quite sophisticated. For example, Bayliss and Tipper (2006) showed that a rotated face (e.g., clockwise by 90° so that it's lying on its side) will induce attention shifts both at the spatial location toward which the eyes are actually looking and at the location toward which the eyes would be looking if the face were actually in its normal upright orientation. As well as creating an environment-centered gaze representation (where is this person looking in the environment?) which caused attention to be deployed at this location, participants also seem to create a kind of gazer-centered representation of gaze direction (where is this person's gaze oriented with respect to themselves?), which also triggers an attention shift. Hietanen's (1999) findings also imply that, at least in certain cases, attention is shifted on the basis of a kind of gazer-centered representation. Although both faces are gazing to your (the observer's) left in Figure 6.10, only a face like the one in the right panel of the figure triggered an attention shift. Hietanen (1999) argued that, because the person in the left panel

 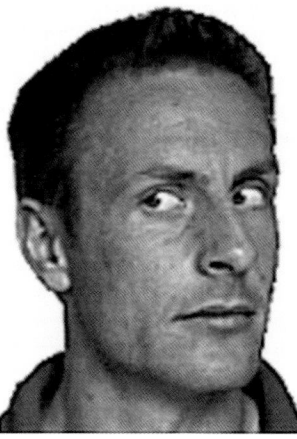

Figure 6.10 Both of these faces are gazing at roughly the same point somewhere on the left of the page. However, with respect to the gazer's own frame of reference, the face on the left is staring straight ahead whereas the face on the right is gazing to his right. Only a face like the one on the right triggered an attention shift in Hietanen's (1999) study.

is actually looking straight ahead with respect to his own reference frame, no shift of attention was induced on the part of the viewer. The face in the other panel is actually averted in both a viewer-centered and gazer-centered frame of reference, so an attention shift is programmed and executed (see also Hietanen, 2002; Seyama & Nagayama, 2005). What this study broadly shows is that the representation that underpins gaze-cued shifts of attention is actually relatively complex and must include some information about head orientation.

CONCLUDING REMARKS

The aim of this chapter was to introduce and review some of the work on the perception of gaze direction and shifting of attention, which is triggered by eye gaze. The evidence suggests that the excellent accuracy we display in perceiving gaze is underpinned by at least two mechanisms—one analyzing luminance contrast, the other performing a spatial computation on the eye's features—and must take into account the orientation of the gazer's head. Both of the mechanisms for perceiving gaze also seem to be involved in the generation of shifts of attention in the direction in which another's eyes are pointing and do so via dedicated neural circuitry.

As Frischen et al. (2007) pointed out in their recent review, a good deal of research in this area has been directed toward discovering such things as whether attention cueing from eye

gaze is stimulus driven or wilfully produced and whether cueing from arrows and eyes are driven by the same mechanisms. They suggest that rather than attempt to categorisze cueing effects in this way, we should focus on the "boundary conditions…and specific circumstances under which certain effects are observed" (p.713). Frischen et al. emphasize research in this vein that has explored individual differences in gaze cueing—females showing larger effects than males (Bayliss, di Pellegrino, & Tipper, 2005), gaze cueing in anxious but not nonanxious individuals being modulated by fearful expressions (Fox, Mathews, Calder & Yiend, 2007; Mathews, Fox, Yiend & Calder, 2003)—and they recommend manipulating the nature of the target object in cueing studies. However, to their list I would like to suggest that researchers examine how gaze cueing operates or does not operate in everyday social interactions. For instance, it is hard to believe that during a face-to-face conversation between two people, shifts in one person's gaze—for example when a speaker is taking their conversational turn—will continually trigger shifts in the listener's visual attention. If effective communication requires an integration of verbal information with visual signals, such as facial expressions and other facial gestures (e.g., eyebrow raises), eye gaze, head nods, hand gestures, body movements, and so forth. (Langton, O'Malley & Bruce, 1996), attention ought not to be averted from the speaker unless absolutely necessary or unless some benefit to the listener would accrue from doing so. Perhaps, then, viewers are sensitive to the type of eye turns that a speaker tends to make so that the only gazes that are likely to trigger a redeployment of a listener's attention are large angle shifts, faster shifts, or shifts in which the speaker's gaze dwells on a target.

On the other side of the coin, it may be that people are aware that their gazing behavior has the potential to influence a listener's attention and implicitly moderate this behavior accordingly. People do indeed tend to look away from their conversational partner's face while they are speaking—perhaps to reduce cognitive demand while dealing with the tricky business of planning and executing their utterance—but they may do so using the type of gaze shifts that are less likely to trigger distracting attention shifts on the part of the listener. However, when the speaker actually wants to redirect the listener's attention to the referent of some remark or when something has captured the speaker's attention, he or she may make the kind of gaze shift that is most likely to induce the listener to follow. An explicit awareness of the kind of gazing behavior that is likely to induce an observer to shift their attention provides the magician with one of many techniques for misdirecting their audience's attention away from the business end of a trick, and is frequently exploited by soccer players in attempting to send goalkeepers the wrong way when taking penalties.

The implication of all this is that research should be aimed at examining how the gaze-cueing effect is modulated by various parameters of gazing behavior, such as the duration of the shift and dwell time. A challenge for researchers will also be to link this with real life gazing behavior so we can discover whether a speaker's goal-directed gazes—those directed toward an object because it has captured their attention or because it is the referent of a remark—will trigger an attention shift on the part of a listener, whereas the more random nongoal oriented gazes made by speakers will not.

The fact that magicians are able to misdirect people's attention with their eyes illustrates how the mechanisms of gaze perception and gaze cueing discussed earlier are considered to be "dumb" processes that support higher level inferences involved in reading people's behavior in terms of mental states. So, detecting and analyzing someone's gaze direction will allow you to bring your own attention into line with the object toward which they are looking, which will, in turn, help you to figure out that this is something they want or something they're about to kick, and so on. An assumption often made because of this, and one alluded to in the opening paragraph of this chapter is that, developmentally speaking, the ability to read people's behavior in terms of mental states arises *after* we have acquired expertise with gaze-perception and gaze-following behaviors. Indeed, infants as young as four months are able to discriminate direct from averted gaze (Vecera & Johnson, 1995), and children can turn their heads to follow shifts in their mothers' gazes by around 18 months of age (Butterworth & Jarrett, 1991; Moore & Corkum, 1998). Therefore, these abilities do seem to predate the acquisition of a more sophisticated understanding of mental states (i.e., a Theory of Mind), which happens at around three to four years of age. However, it is clear that despite possessing these gaze-perception and gaze-following skills, as well as at least a rudimentary understanding of mental states, three- to four-year-old children still have something to learn as far as using eye gaze is concerned. In particular, Doherty and Anderson (1999) showed that it is not until around this age that children are able to make explicit judgements about what someone is looking at. This suggests that there may be a more reciprocal relationship between gaze skills and Theory of Mind abilities. For example, one idea is that the gaze discrimination and gaze following skills displayed by 18-month-olds are underpinned by a relatively crude gaze-perception mechanism—perhaps one based on the gross luminance configuration in the eye (e.g., "if I turn in roughly the direction of the dark part of mummy's eye I'm likely to find something interesting"); however, once they realize that eyes provide important clues about the state of people's knowledge and the current content of their thoughts, children become motivated to develop a more accurate means of determining where other people are looking—perhaps using the detailed geometry of the eye —which is capable of supporting explicit judgements about another's direction of gaze. At present this is just a speculative story that links Theory of Mind with the development of the two gaze-perception mechanisms discussed earlier in this chapter, and, clearly, further research is needed to test some of the predictions that arise from it. However, along with the research I have discussed in this chapter, it serves to illustrate how the study of eye gaze and attention brings together work from a broad range of disciplines within the psychological sciences.

ACKNOWLEDGMENTS

The author would like to thank Paul Borthwick, Alistair Cernik, Laura Cumming, Stephen Graham, Flora, Lecuyer, Amy Murphy, Pamela Renfrew and Linzi Brown who contributed to the data collection for the experiment described in the text.

REFERENCES

Adams, R. B., & Kleck, R. E. (2003). Perceived gaze direction and the processing of facial displays of emotion. *Psychological Science, 14,* 644–647.

Adams, R. B., & Kleck, R. E. (2005). Effects of direct and averted gaze on the perception of facially communicated emotion. *Emotion, 5,* 3–11.

Akiyama, T., Kato, M., Muramatsu, T., Saito, F., Umeda, S., & Kashima, H. (2006). Gaze but not arrows: A dissociative impairment after right superior temporal gyrus damage. *Neuropsychologia, 44,* 1804–1810.

Ando S. (2002). Luminance–induced shift in the apparent direction of gaze. *Perception, 31,* 657–674.

Ando, S. (2004). Perception of gaze direction based on luminance ratio. *Perception, 33,* 1173–1184.

Anstis, S. M., Mayhew, J. W. & Morley, T. (1969). The perception of where a face or television 'portrait' is looking. *American Journal of Psychology, 82,* 474–489.

Baron–Cohen, S. (1995). *Mindblindness: An essay on autism and theory of mind.* Cambridge, MA: MIT Press/Bradford Books.

Bayliss, A. P., di Pellegrino, G., & Tipper, S. P. (2005). Sex differences in eye gaze and symbolic cueing of attention. *Quarterly Journal of Experimental Psychology, 58A,* 631–650.

Bayliss, A. P., & Tipper, S. P. (2006). Gaze cues evoke both spatial and object–centred shifts of attention. *Perception & Psychophysics, 68,* 310–318.

Bindemann, M., Burton, A. M., & Langton, S. R. H. (in press). How do eye-gaze and facial expression interact? *Visual Cognition.*

Butterworth G, Jarrett N. (1991). What minds have in common is space: spacial mechanisms serving joint visual attention in infancy. *British Journal of Developmental Psychology, 9,* 55–72.

Calder, A. J., Jenkins, R., Cassel, A., & Clifford, C. W. G. (2008). Visual representation of eye gaze is coded by a nonopponent multichannel system. *Journal of Experimental Psychology: General, 137,* 244–261.

Calder, A. J., Beaver, J. D., Winston, J. S., Dolan, R. J., Jenkins, R., Eger, E., & Henson, R. N. A. (2007). Separate coding of different gaze directions in the superior temporal sulcus and inferior parietal lobe. *Current Biology, 17,* 20–25.

Campbell, R., Heywood, C. A., Cowey, A., Regard, M., & Landis, T. (1990). Sensitivity to eye gaze in prosopagnosic patients and monkeys with superior temporal sulcus ablation. *Neuropsychologia, 28,* 1123–1142.

Cline, M. G. (1967). The perception of where a person is looking. *American Journal of Psychology, 80,* 41–50.

Doherty, M. J., & Anderson, J. R. (1999). A new look at gaze: preschool children's understanding of eye–direction. *Cognitive Development, 14,* 549–571.

Downing, P., Dodds, C. M., & Bray, D. (2004). Why does the eye gaze of others direct visual attention? *Visual Cognition, 11,* 71–79.

Driver, J., Davis, G., Ricciardelli, P., Kidd, P., Maxwell, E., & Baron–Cohen, S. (1999). Shared attention and the social brain: Gaze perception triggers automatic visuospatial orienting in adults. *Visual Cognition, 6,* 509–540.

Ellgring, J. H. (1970). Die Beurteilung des Blicks auf Punkte innerhalb des Gesichtes. [Estimation of gazes directed at points within the face]. *Zeitschrift fr Experimentelle und Angewandte Psychologie, 17,* 600–607. Cited in Von Cranach, M., & Ellgring, J. H. (1973). Problems in the recognition of gaze direction. In M. von Cranach and I. Vine (Eds.), *Social*

communication and movement: Studies of interaction and expression in man and chimpanzee
(pp. 419–443). London: Academic Press.

Eiksen, C. W., & Hoffman, J. E. (1973). Extent of
processing of noise elements during selective
encoding from visual-displays. *Perception &
Psychophysics, 14,* 155–160.

Eriksen, C. W., & Hoffman, J. E. (1974). Selective
attention: Noise suppression or signal enhancement? *Bulletin of the Psychonomic Society, 4,*
587–589.

Fang, F., & He, S. (2005). Viewer–centerd object
representation in the human visual system
revealed by viewpoint aftereffects. *Neuron, 45,*
793–800.

Farroni, T., Johnson, M. H., Brockbank, M.,
Simion, F. (2000). Infants' use of gaze direction
to cue attention: The importance of perceived
motion. *Visual Cognition, 7,* 705–718.

Fox, E., Mathews, A., Calder, A. J., & Yiend, J. (2007).
Anxiety and sensitivity to gaze direction in emotionally expressive faces, *Emotion, 7,* 478–486.

Friesen, C. K. & Kingstone, A. (1998). The eyes
have it!: reflexive orienting is triggered by
nonpredictive gaze. *Psychonomic Bulletin and
Review, 5,* 490–495.

Friesen, C. K. Ristic, J., & Kingstone, A. (2004).
Attentional effects of counterpredictive gaze
and arrow cues. Journal of Experimental
Psychology: *Human   Perception   and
Performance, 30,* 319–329.

Frischen, A., Bayliss, A. P., & Tipper, S. P. (2007).
Gaze cueing of attention: Visual attention,
social cognition and individual differences.
Psychological Bulletin, 133, 694–724.

Gibson, J. J., & Pick, A. (1963). Perception of
another person's looking. *American Journal of
Psychology, 76,* 86–94.

Harries, M. H., & Perrett, D. I. (1991). Visual
processing of faces in the temporal cortex:
Physiological evidence for a modular organisation and possible anatomical correlates.
Journal of Cognitive Neuroscience, 3, 9–24.

Heywood, C. A., & Cowey, A. (1992). The role of
the 'face cell' area in the discrimination and
recognition of faces by monkeys. *Philosophical
Transactions of the Royal Society of London,
Series B., 335,* 31–38.

Hietanen, J. K. (1999). Does your gaze direction
and head orientation shift my visual attention?
NeuroReport, 10, 3443–3447.

Hietanen, J. K. (2002). Social attention orienting
integrates visual information from head and

body orientation. *Psychological Research, 66,*
174–179.

Hietanen, J. K., Nummenmaa, L., Nyman, M.
J., Parkkola, R., & Hämäläinen, H. (2006).
Automatic orienting of attention by social
and symbolic cues activates different neural
networks: An fMRI study. *NeuroImage, 33,*
406–413.

Hoffman, E. A., & Haxby, J. V. (2000). Distinct
representations of eye gaze and identity in the
distributed human neural system for face perception. *Nature Neuroscience, 3,* 80–84.

Hommel, B., Pratt, J., Colzato, L., & Godijn, R.
(2001). Symbolic control of visual attention.
Psychological Science, 12, 360–365.

Hood, B. M, Willen, J. D, & Driver, J. (1998). Adult's
eyes trigger shifts of visual attention in human
infants. *Psychological Science, 9,* 131–134.

Jenkins, J., & Langton, S. R. H. (2003). Configural
processing in the perception of eye–gaze direction. *Perception 32,* 1117–1125.

Jenkins, R., Beaver, J. D., & Calder, A. J. (2006).
I thought you were looking at me: Direction-
specific aftereffects in gaze perception.
Psychological Science, 17, 506–513.

Jonides, J. (1981). Voluntary versus automatic con-
trol over the mind's eye's movement. In J. B.
Long & A. D. Baddeley (Eds.), *Attention and
Performance IX* (pp. 187–203). Hillsdale, NJ:
Lawrence Erlbaum Associates.

Kendon, A. (1967). Some functions of gaze direction in social interaction. *Acta Psychologica,
26,* 22–63.

Kingstone, A., Friesen, C. K., & Gazzaniga, M. S.
(2000). Reflexive joint attention depends on
lateralized cortical connections. *Psychological
Science, 11,* 159–166.

Kobayashi, H., & Kohshima, S. (1997). Unique
morphology of the human eye. *Nature, 383,*
767–768.

Langdon, R., & Smith, P. (2005). Spatial cueing
by social versus non-social directional signals.
Visual Cognition, 12, 1497–1527.

Langton, S. R. H. (2000). The mutual influence of
gaze and head orientation in the analysis of
social attention direction. *Quarterly Journal of
Experimental Psychology.53,* 825–845.

Langton, S. R. H., & Bruce, V. (1999). Reflexive
visual orienting in response to the social
attention of others. *Visual Cognition, 6,*
541–567.

Langton, S. R. H., Honeyman, H., & Tessler, E.
(2004). The influence of head contour and nose

angle on the perception of eye–gaze direction. *Perception & Psychophysics, 66, 752–771.*

Langton, S. R. H., O'Malley, C., & Bruce, V. (1996). Actions speak no louder than words: Symmetrical cross-modal interference effects in the processing of verbal and gestural information. *Journal of Experimental Psychology: Human Perception and Performance, 22,* 1357–1375.

Langton, S. R. H., Watt, R. J., & Bruce, V. (2000). Do the eyes have it? Cues to the direction of social attention. *Trends in Cognitive Sciences, 4,* 50–59.

Liu, C. H., & Chaudhuri, A. (2003). What determines whether faces are special? *Visual Cognition, 10,* 385–408.

Lobmaier, J. S., Fischer, M. H., & Schwaninger, A. (2006). Objects capture perceived gaze direction. *Experimental Psychology, 53,* 117–122.

Lord, C., & Haith, M. M. (1974). *Perception & Psychophysics, 16,* 413–416.

Maruyama, K., & Endo, M. (1983). The effect of face orientation upon apparent direction of gaze. *Tohoku Psychologica Folia, 42,* 126–138.

Maruyama, K., & Endo, M. (1984). The illusory face dislocation effect and configurational integration in the inverted face. *Tohoku Psychologica Folia, 43,* 150–160.

Martin, W. W., & Rovira, M. L. (1981). An experimental analysis of discriminability and bias in eye-gaze judgment. *Journal of Nonverbal Behavior, 5,* 155–163.

Mason, M. F., Hood, B. M., & Macrae, C. N. (2004). Look into my eyes: Gaze direction and person memory. *Memory, 12,* 637–643.

Mason, M. F., Tatkow, E. P., & Macrae, C. N. (2005). The look of love: Gaze shifts and person perception. *Psychological Science, 16,* 236–239.

Mathews, A., Fox, E., Yiend, J., & Calder, A. J. (2003). The face of fear: Effects of eye gaze and emotion on visual attention. *Visual Cognition, 7,* 823–836.

Moore, C., & Corkum, V. (1998). Infant gaze following based on eye direction. *British Journal of Developmental Psychology, 16,* 495–503.

Pelphrey, K. A., Morris, J. P., & McCarthy, G. (2004). Grasping the intentions of others: The perceived intentionality of an action influences activity in the superior temporal sulcus during social perception. *Journal of Cognitive Neuroscience, 16,* 1706–1716.

Pelphrey, K. A, Singerman, J. D., Allison, T., & McCarthy, G. (2003). Brain activation evoked by perception of gaze shifts: The influence of context. *Neuropsychologia, 41,* 156–170.

Pelphrey, K. A., Viola, R. J., & McCarthy, G. (2004). When strangers pass: Processing of mutual and averted social gaze in the superior temporal sulcus. *Psychological Science, 15,* 598–603.

Perrett, D. I., Hietanen, J. K., Oram, M. W., & Benson, P. J. (1992). Organisation and functions of cells responsive to faces in the temporal cortex. *Philosophical Transactions of the Royal Society of London, Series B., 335,* 23–30.

Perrett, D. I., Smith, P. A. J., Potter, D. D., Mistlin, A. J., Head, A. S., Milner, A. D., & Jeeves, M. A. (1985). Visual cells in the temporal cortex sensitive to face view and gaze direction. *Proceedings of the Royal Society of London, B223,* 293–317.

Posner, M. I. (1980). Orienting of attention. *Quarterly Journal of Experimental Psychology, 32,* 3–25.

Posner, M. I., Nissen, M. J., & Ogden, W. C., (1978). Attended and unattended processing modes: The role of spatial set for location. In J. Requin (Ed.), *Attention and performance VII* (pp 137–157). Hillsdale, NJ: Erlbaum.

Puce, A., Allison, T., Bentin, S., Gore, J. C., & McCarthy, G. (1998). Temporal cortex activation in humans viewing eye and mouth movements. *Journal of Neuroscience, 18,* 2188–2199.

Ricciardelli, P., Baylis, G., & Driver, J. (2000). The positive and negative of human expertise in gaze perception. *Cognition, 77,* B1–B14.

Ricciardelli, P., & Driver, J. (2008). Effects of head orientation on gaze perception: How positive congruency effects can be reversed. *Quarterly Journal of Experimental Psychology, 61,* 491–504.

Ristic, J., Friesen, C. K., & Kingstone, A. (2002). Are the eyes special? It depends on how you look at it. *Psychonomic Bulletin & Review, 9,* 507–513.

Seyama, J., & Nagayama, R. S. (2005). The effect of torso direction on the judgement of eye direction. *Visual Cognition, 12,* 103–116.

Sinha, P. (2000). Here's looking at you, kid. *Perception, 29,* 1005–1008.

Symons L. A., Lee, K., Cedrone, C. C., & Nishimura, M. (2004). What are you looking at? Acuity for triadic eye–gaze. *Journal of General Psychology, 131,* 451–469.

Tipples, J. (2002). Eye gaze is not unique: Automatic orienting in response to uninformative arrows. *Psychonomic Bulletin & Review, 9*, 314–318.

Todorovic, D. (2006). Geometrical basis of perception of gaze direction. *Vision Research, 46*, 3349–3362.

Vecera, S. P., & Johnson, M. H. (1995). Gaze detection and the cortical processing of faces: Evidence from infants and adults. *Visual Cognition, 2*, 59–87.

Vine, I. (1971). Judgement of the direction of gaze: An interpretation of discrepant results. *British Journal of Social and Clinical Psychology, 10*, 320–331.

Von Cranach, M., & Ellgring, J. H. (1973). Problems in the recognition of gaze direction. In M. von Cranach and I. Vine (Eds.), Social communication and movement. London: Academic Press.

Watt, R. J. (1987). Scanning from coarse to fine spatial scales in the human visual–system after the onset of a stimulus. *Journal Of The Optical Society Of America A–Optics Image Science And Vision, 4*, 2006–2021.

Watt, R. J. (1999). What your eyes tell my eyes, and how your eyebrows try to stop them. Paper presented at Tenth International Conference on Perception and Action – ICPA–X, University of Edinburgh, August 1999

Wilson, H. R., Wilkinson, F., Lin, L–M., & Castillo, M. (2000). Perception of head orientation. *Vision Research, 40*, 459–472.

Wollaston, W. H. (1824). On the apparent direction of eyes in a portrait. *Philosophical Transactions of the Royal Society, London*, 247–256. Cited in Bruce, V., & Young, A. (1998). *In the eye of the Beholder: The science of face perception*. Oxford: Oxford University Press.

Yarbus, A. L. (1967). *Eye movements and vision*. New York: Plenum.

CHAPTER 7

Aging Eyes Facing an Emotional World: The Role of Motivated Gaze

Derek M. Isaacowitz and Nora A. Murphy

What do aging eyes look at, and why is their visual attention directed there? By definition, top-down influences on attention refer to goal-directed processing by the perceiver. Top-down perspectives would consider what older adults *want* to look at and would use goals of the perceiver to explain looking patterns. Much of the research in the field of vision on such top-down influences has focused on goals related to a specific cognitive task that a perceiver is trying to complete—for example, when participants instructed to conduct a visual search for one type of stimuli are distracted by other stimulus types. A standard top-down explanation might consider the instructions given to the perceiver, assuming the goal of the perceiver was to follow those instructions as well as possible. In this chapter, we broaden the consideration of goal-directed, or top-down, influences on vision to include motivation of the perceiver more generally, such as the goals they prioritize in their everyday lives. As we will show, these more general motivational states appear to influence patterns of visual attention even in non-task-relevant contexts. Moreover, consideration of such top-down influences of motivation on vision appear to help explain interesting age differences in visual processing of emotional information; in other words, motivation may hold the key to understanding where older eyes look.

We propose in this chapter that motivation may be one framework for considering how the perceiver and the target of perception can be connected, and that this may be a particularly useful way of understanding how certain types of perceiver-stimulus interactions shift across the adult lifespan. In other words, perceivers may bring motivation with them to the task of perceiving, separate from any goal states specific to the task, and these person-level motivational states appear to influence how visual attention is deployed. Later, we provide evidence that such motivational influences on vision reflect developmental processes.

We use a general definition of motivation to include any goal-directed psychological properties of the perceiving individual, whether these goals are explicit (e.g., the individual could report that they are pursuing that goal) or implicit (e.g., the individual might not report having that goal, but is a member of a group that has been shown in other work to have certain goal-relevant tendencies in their cognition and behavior). For example, a young adult may not indicate that they are focused on pursuing future-oriented goals such as gaining information, and an older adult might not explicitly state that they are motivated to regulate their emotions. However, various studies in the socioemotional aging literature, such as those on age changes in social choices, have been interpreted as reflecting such age-related motivational states (see Carstensen, Isaacowitz & Charles, 1999 for a review). Similarly, individuals in a positive mood seem to behave in ways suggesting that they are motivated to maintain that good mood (Handley, Lassiter, & Nickell, 2004; Wegener & Petty, 1994), even if they do not explicitly state that as their main goal at the time.

In this chapter, we focus primarily on research from our laboratory that has directly investigated motivational effects on gaze and has generally focused on age effects, using eye tracking as a methodology to study these processes. However, we have endeavored to also identify evidence from different research groups and using different methodologies that also bears on how motivation can influence looking. This allows us to consider not just explicitly lifespan-oriented motivational states (such as motivation to maintain control), but also to widen the net to include some consideration of motivation in contexts not explicitly related to aging.

Most of the work described in this chapter centers on one class of stimuli: those that are emotionally valenced. We focus on emotional processing both for theoretical and pragmatic reasons. The fact is that much of the work on motivational influences on gaze have centered on stimuli that are emotional in nature. We do not believe that this is a mere coincidence. On the one hand, emotional stimuli are thought to grab attention, as a way of communicating to a perceiver that something relevant is happening in the environment (Nummenma, Hyönä, & Calvo, 2006). On the other hand, there are clear individual differences in how emotional material in the environment is processed, and these differences appear to relate to the emotional state of the perceiver (Williams, Watts, MacLeod, & Matthews, 1997). The relationship between emotional processing and mood would appear to be reciprocal: certain mood states may guide processing (e.g., Isen, 2004), but processing can impact mood as well (John & Gross, 2004). Findings that preferential attention to or memory for emotional stimuli can change mood begs the question as to what perceivers are trying to do as they process emotional information in their environment, thus making motivation an obvious topic of interest.

GAZE: A REAL-TIME MEASURE OF LOOKING

Where in a visual array a perceiver is looking has been of interest in the social psychological literature dating back to early research on the role of attention in attributions. For example, individuals engaged in moderate gazing are viewed more positively than individuals with high or low gazing patterns (see Kleinke, 1986 for a review). Other research has shown that gazing influences impressions such as extraversion and intelligence (Borkenau & Liebler, 1995; Murphy, Hall, & Colvin, 2003). Much of this work used an observer-based approach to assess gaze: target's heads were videotaped and raters judged which way their eyes were looking. If stimuli were clearly placed in the left and right visual fields, then these ratings could reliably be used to determine the basic direction of gaze to one stimuli or the other. Obviously, only overt gaze can be assessed this way.

Other research has employed more indirect measures for assessing visual attention. Such measures use reaction time rather than direct gaze recording. In a dot-probe paradigm, a pair of stimuli, typically one picture of neutral valence and one emotionally valenced picture, appears on a computer screen. Immediately following the stimuli, a dot probe appears; a participant's reaction time is measured when s/he indicates which side of the screen the dot probe appears (left or right; top or bottom). If the participant's reaction time is faster when the dot probe appears behind the emotionally valenced pictures than neutral pictures, s/he is presumed to have a bias or preference for emotionally valenced material. Similarly, emotional Stroop paradigms measure reaction time when reading target (i.e., emotional) or nontarget (i.e., unrelated, nonemotional) words. Words are presented in different colored ink, and participants are instructed to name the color of the ink. Longer color-naming latencies are interpreted as reflecting attention being grabbed by the content of the word; thus, longer latencies for color naming when the word is emotional would indicate that the emotional content is attracting attention and making it harder to ignore the content and name the color. Dot-probe and emotional Stroop paradigms lend support toward the link between motivation and eye gaze but do not provide direct evidence because these paradigms measure reaction time rather than gaze patterns directly.

While researchers studying (dys)regulation of emotion were using dot-probe and emotional Stroop methodologies to better understand the role of information processing in emotional disorders (see Williams et al., 1997), reading researchers started using eye tracking to assess gaze in ways that better approximate real time. Specifically, they used eye tracking to study saccades (eye movements from one place to another) and fixations (eye movements directed at a particular point). This work led reading researchers to estimate that it takes approximately 150 ms to plan and execute an eye movement, whereas the fixation resulting from that eye movement can last from 100 ms to 750 ms or more (Manor & Gordon, 2003; Reichle, Pollatsek, Fisher, & Rayner, 1998). Clearly, observer-based techniques that relied on coding gaze direction from videotape would be limited in their ability to identify rapid, subtle shifts in gaze, or to differentiate saccades from fixations. Therefore, in order to investigate gaze patterns to real-world visual arrays with possible emotional content, a more subtle measure is needed. Eye tracking allows for the recording of gaze fixation toward visually presented stimuli in real time. Although it is possible to dissociate fixation from the target of visual attention, in most cases the two are identical (Parkhust, Law, & Niebur, 2002). This makes eye tracking a valuable measure for assessing visual attention.

Eye tracking as a measure of gaze and attention has been used across a variety of domains including the study of autism (e.g., Dalton et al., 2005), causal reasoning in children (Sobel & Kirkham, 2006), language comprehension (Gordon, Hendrick, Johnson, & Lee, 2006), and threat responses in phobic individuals (Rinck & Becker, 2006). The wide range of research areas employing eye-tracking technology speaks to the power of this methodology to understand processes related to attention

and gaze. Eye tracking is a noninvasive procedure in which a camera is positioned toward one or both eyes of a participant. In a typical lab-based paradigm, stimuli are presented on a computer monitor and participants' eye movements are recorded as they view the stimuli on the monitor. Eye-tracker software provides data such as the number of fixations and time spent fixated on a particular stimulus; these areas-of-interest (AOIs) of the stimuli are designated by the experimenter. For instance, in one study, participant's reaction to cancer images was measured via eye tracking (Isaacowitz, 2005b). AOIs for these images included the melanoma of the skin cancer image; attention was measured in terms of gaze patterns toward the AOIs in comparison to other areas of the skin. For the eye-tracking studies conducted in our lab and described in this chapter, each participant's left pupil was recorded at a rate of 60 Hz (i.e., 60 times per second) using a remote tracker. A fixation is defined as eye gaze directed to within 1° visual angle of a predetermined AOI for at least 100 ms (Manor & Gordon, 2003).

Later, we describe research using eye tracking to assess differences in gaze toward emotional stimuli between young and older adults. Most of this work uses an extreme-age design, comparing individuals in the 18-25 age range (younger adults) to those 60 or 65 and above (older adults). Some previous work had investigated age differences in attention using indirect approaches: for example, Mather and Carstensen (2003) used a dot-probe paradigm to study age and visual processing of emotional stimuli, and found some evidence that older adults attended more to positive and less to negative faces. It seemed to us that eye tracking could be used to clarify such potential age effects, by allowing us to focus directly on the actual gaze of older and younger perceivers as they viewed emotionally valenced stimuli. Previous research had found that eye tracking could provide information about intentions not apparent using other behavioral measures (Griffin, 2004), so it seemed that such a direct measure of visual processing could elucidate whether older adults actually do show positive preferences in their real-time transactions with their environment.

AGE DIFFERENCES: POSITIVITY IN VISUAL ATTENTION?

In several studies using eye tracking to investigate age differences in attention toward emotional faces, we have found that older adults tend to gaze away from some types of negative stimuli. Each of the studies involved young adult and older adult participants viewing synthetic faces that varied in emotional valence: in each pair, a face displaying an emotional expression was paired with the same individual's face in a nonemotional/neutral expression. Participants had their left eye tracked as they viewed the faces on a computer screen. In one study of emotional-nonemotional face pairs, including the emotions of happiness, sadness, fear, and anger, results showed that older adults tended to look away from angry faces and toward a neutral face (Isaacowitz, Wadlinger, Goren, & Wilson, 2006b). In a second study, which focused only on sad and happy faces paired with neutral ones, older adults looked more toward happy faces and away from neutral faces, as well as looking away from sad faces (Isaacowitz, Wadlinger, Goren, & Wilson, 2006a). (These studies are described in more detail in subsequent sections.) Thus, community-dwelling older adults, whose gaze was captured with the direct method of eye tracking, appear to gaze away from some types of negative stimuli and toward positive stimuli as well.

Below, we consider whether motivation can explain age differences in fixation, and what models of motivation might account for such findings. We focus primarily on links between motivation and gaze in the context of aging because we have done more work on mechanisms involved in the age differences, and because of the prominence of motivational theories in the life-span developmental literature (cf. Balcetis & Dunning, 2006). The rise of the "motivational approach" in the lifespan literature likely is due to multiple factors, such as the action-theoretical framework utilized in much lifespan theory and research (e.g., Freund & Baltes, 1998) in which the goal-directedness of behavior is emphasized. In addition, the aging literature has been concerned with plasticity in

performance and the functional adaptiveness of behaviors, as well as compensatory strategies older individuals use to contend with declines in physical and cognitive functioning (Baltes & Baltes, 1990). This type of work implicates motivation as psychologists struggle to understand what abilities are selected for preservation and compensation and which are allowed to deteriorate, as the systems in general decline. For older adults to accomplish any goals given declines in their information processing speed (Salthouse, 2000) and increased working memory clutter (Hasher & Zacks, 1988) requires strong goal-driven mechanisms that must be robust despite these influences, which could impair goal-directed processes.

MOTIVATIONAL ACCOUNTS OF AGE-RELATED FINDINGS

What motivational framework can account for findings indicating some groups looking less at negative and/or more toward positive stimuli than are other groups? One straightforward possibility, suggested by the Hedonic Contingency Model (Wegener & Petty, 1994), is that individuals are simply motivated to maintain good moods. Indeed, mood has been linked to gaze patterns: in one study, we found that young adults who had just experienced a positive mood induction showed looking patterns suggesting that they were scanning their environment for positively valenced stimuli that would serve to support their good mood (Wadlinger & Isaacowitz, 2006). In other work, we have found that young adults high in dispositional optimism, a construct highly correlated with happiness (e.g., Isaacowitz, 2005a), tend to gaze less than their peers at unpleasant images than their peers lower in optimism (Isaacowitz, 2005b). That finding can be interpreted as reflecting optimists' "rose-colored glasses" that allows them to see the world in a way that maintains the good moods they tend to be experiencing (see also Luo & Isaacowitz, 2007). Thus, the good mood spurs a motivational state most concerned with preserving the good mood.

Why, though, should mood be linked to motivation and gaze in the context of aging?

Hedonic contingency may indeed be relevant to findings of age differences, as some recent research has indicated that older adults tend to experience positive affective lives, perhaps more so than younger adults. For example, in a nationally representative sample of American adults aged 25–74 years, the older individuals reported higher levels of positive affect and lower levels of negative affect than did their younger counterparts (Mrozcek & Kolarz, 1998). In an experience-sampling study of naturalistic affect over a seven-day period in adults aged 17–94 years, age was unrelated to the frequency and intensity of positive affect and to the intensity of negative affect, but older adults showed less frequent negative affect (Carstensen, Pasupathi, Mayr, & Nesselroade, 2000). These results are consistent with epidemiological studies of psychopathology, which have found low rates of diagnosable depression in older adults (Regier et al., 1988) and older adults have been shown in numerous studies to display fairly positive affective profiles (e.g., Carstensen et al., 2000; Mrozcek & Kolarz, 1998). Findings have not been entirely consistent: for example, no unique effect of age on affect is found among individuals age 70 and above (Isaacowitz & Smith, 2003). However, given the bulk of evidence suggesting that older adults tend to feel good, it could be the case that older adults are simply motivated to maintain the good moods that they are already in, and show gaze patterns away from negative stimuli that might threaten that good mood.

A related possibility about how motivation may explain the observed pattern of age differences in gaze toward emotional stimuli is derived from socioemotional selectivity theory (Carstensen et al., 1999). Socioemotional selectivity theory is a lifespan motivational account linking goals to social and emotional functioning. The theory purports that goals shift as a function of time perspective, making this a general motivational theory applicable across the lifespan rather than an aging theory per se. According to the theory, individuals who perceive their time as open ended and the future as unlimited are motivated to pursue knowledge-based goals, such as gaining information, that will benefit them in the future. In contrast,

those who perceive their future as limited are motivated to pursue goals associated with present benefits; chief among these present-focused goals is regulating emotion and optimizing feeling state (Carstensen et al.). Advancing age, possibly the life context in which time is more limited, has thus been associated with the motivation to pursue emotional goals (Fredrickson & Carstensen, 1990); however, this motivational state has also been demonstrated in younger individuals whose time perspective is also limited (e.g., Carstensen & Fredrickson, 1998; Fredrickson & Carstensen, 1990).

More recently, older adults' motivation to regulate their emotions has been linked to a so-called positivity effect in which positive rather than negatively valenced material receives preferential processing, presumably to facilitate emotion regulation (Carstensen & Mikels, 2005). Indeed, a variety of findings from the memory literature provide support for this positivity effect. For instance, older adults tended to recognize more positive words than negative words from a previously presented list of emotionally valenced words (which were matched in valence, frequency, and length) (Leigland, Schulz, & Janowsky, 2004). Charles and colleagues (2003) found that older adults recalled more positive images than negative images, whereas younger adults recalled equal numbers of positive and negative images (Study 1). Mather and Knight (2005) found that older adults recalled proportionally more positive images than negative images whereas younger adults showed the reverse pattern (full attention condition, Study 3). However, not all findings are so unequivocal. In one study, older adults recalled the same number of positive, negative, and neutral words (Grühn, Smith, & Baltes, 2005). As younger adults demonstrate a robust negativity bias (Baumeister, Bratslavsky, Finkenauer, & Vohs, 2001; Murphy & Isaacowitz, 2008; Rozin & Royzman, 2001), perhaps older adults are curbing their attention or memory for negative information rather than paying more attention to (or remembering more of) positive information; in other words, there may be a negativity suppression effect in addition to, or instead of, a positivity enhancement effect. This distinction may depend upon the comparison stimuli; is the positive stimuli response being compared to a negative stimuli response or to a neutral stimuli response? A recent meta-analysis showed that both older and younger adults exhibit negativity and positivity preferences that are similar in magnitude (Murphy & Isaacowitz, 2008). That is, both older and younger adults attend more toward and remember more negatively valenced information than neutrally valenced information (i.e., negativity preference) and attend more toward and remember more positive information than neutral information (positivity preference). Thus, an age-related positivity effect may emerge when comparing positive to negative information, but there is not yet strong evidence to suggest that positivity preferences are age-dependent or that older adults are suppressing responses to negative stimuli in comparison to younger adults. Regardless of how ubiquitous it is, though, studies that do find age-related positivity effects (or negativity suppression effects) have been interpreted as reflecting information processing that takes place "under the influence" of motivated goals toward optimizing positive feelings and minimizing negative ones (Carstensen & Mikels, 2005). It is important to note, though, that the theory is that older adults are using information processing to regulate their moods, rather than their gaze simply reflecting the mood they are already experiencing (Carstensen, Mather, & Mikels, 2006; Isaacowitz, Toner, Goren, & Wilson, 2008).

HOW CAN WE BE CERTAIN THAT AGE EFFECTS ARE MOTIVATED?

The eye-tracking work just described, in which older adults gaze toward positive and away from some types of negative stimuli, is generally consistent with the positivity effect, but age differences in valenced processing raises an important question: How can it be demonstrated that these processes are motivated rather than simply a side effect of cognitive aging? Although we made efforts to use stimuli that would minimize psychophysical properties that might elicit differential attention in different age groups (such as luminance and

contour: see description of the creation of the synthetic faces in Isaacowitz et al., 2006b), there remained the possibility that other *general* age-related cognitive changes could nonetheless account for the *specific* valenced preferences we had observed. We have used two approaches to this important issue. The first has involved matching age groups on performance using a variety of cognitive measures, to determine if the age differences in fixation survive controlling for other, more general cognitive and perceptual processes that vary by age as well (the *rule-out* approach). The second approach has been to attempt to use young adults to mimic the motivational patterns of older adults, thus eliminating the cognitive aging confound altogether (the *rule-in* approach). We review these two approaches in more detail next.

Rule out: A statistical approach

The first approach we used to discern whether the observed age differences in gaze toward emotional stimuli could be attributed to more general age-related changes in cognition and perception was to use matching strategies — both person-matching and statistical-matching. In one eye-tracking study, young and older adults viewed pairs of synthetic faces displaying nonemotional faces paired with facial expressions associated with four discrete emotions (Isaacowitz et al., 2006b). We predicted that older adults would spend more time attending toward positive emotional faces, and away from negative emotional faces, in comparison to younger adults. Results confirmed our hypotheses: older adults showed preferential looking patterns toward happy faces and away from angry faces in comparison to younger adults. Younger adults only showed preferential attention toward afraid faces. Thus, in this high-functioning sample of older adults, we provided support that older adults' attention toward positive emotional information may be motivated rather than an effect of age-related general cognitive or perceptual factors.

In the second study, in which a dot-probe task was paired with eye tracking of happy-neutral and sad-neutral face pairs, the age groups showed differences in a predictable direction (Isaacowitz et al., 2006a). That is, older adults oriented more toward happy faces, and away from sad faces, than younger adults. Although younger adults paid more attention to sad faces, they did not pay more attention to happy faces. This general pattern of results was true when attention was measured indirectly by a dot-probe paradigm or more directly by eye tracking, though the pattern of results was stronger for the eye-tracking technique, suggesting the added utility of the eye-tracking method in terms of sensitivity to age differences.

Results of the aforementioned studies (Isaacowitz et al., 2006a; 2006b) were not attributable to cognitive effects of aging. In the first study, the samples of older and younger adults did not significantly differ across a number of cognitive and perceptual functioning indicators, though older adults (not surprisingly) had higher levels of education and vocabulary scores (Isaacowitz et al., 2006b). However, in the second study, the younger and older adult samples differed significantly on a number of fluid intelligence measures and perceptual variables. Yet, when controlling for such differences, the pattern of results remained the same: older adult oriented more toward positive faces and away from negative faces (Isaacowitz et al., 2006a). Essentially, controlling for cognitive and perceptual variables did not make a difference in terms of attentional preferences in older adults.

These results suggest that the observed age differences in gaze are not attributable to general age-related changes in perceptual or cognitive systems. That is, age-related changes in perception and cognition were ruled-out as explanations for differences in gaze patterns between younger and older adults. In more recent work, we have added another measure of general attentional abilities, the Attention Network Test (ANT: Fan, McCandliss, Sommer, Raz, & Posner, 2002), to be even more conservative in our attempts to show that age effects are specific and motivated rather than general. The ANT tests the efficiency of three independent attentional networks: alerting attention, orienting attention, and executive attention. Research indicates that each network is an important facet in general attention but that each operates relatively independently of one another (Fan et al.). By using the ANT to measure these three types of attention, we aim to test in a more comprehensive manner whether the specific age-related attentional preferences we have documented in gaze toward emotional stimuli are really unrelated to general attentional abilities. This will also allow us to answer questions about mechanisms related to cognitive control abilities, as detailed below.

Rule in: A laboratory manipulation approach

Next, we turn to the other approach we have taken to determine whether motivation can explain age-related gaze preference patterns: using young adults in laboratory manipulations of motivations to test whether we can see age-related patterns in these experimental groups. Although the preceding statistical approaches can at best rule out alternative interpretations, suggesting motivation as the cause of observed age differences in gaze toward emotional images by elimination of other possible causes, the laboratory manipulation approach described here actually allows us to "rule in" motivation as a cause for observed age differences.

The first manipulation we conducted to determine whether motivation could produce the same gaze patterns observed in older adults used a naturalistic paradigm developed by Fredrickson (1995) in early work on the social aspects of socioemotional selectivity theory. She observed that college seniors facing graduation were in a naturalistic condition of limited time and an impending ending, especially as compared to college freshmen. Moreover, Fredrickson found that college seniors showed socioemotional choices akin to older adults, due to their shared limited-time perspective. We reasoned that, if graduating college seniors showed looking patterns similar to those of older adults, that such a finding would also support a motivational account of age-related gaze preferences. Therefore, we conducted a study in which college freshmen and graduating seniors were asked to "look naturally" as they viewed pairs of real faces that varied in valence (Pruzan & Isaacowitz, 2006). Participants were shown a pair of pictures featuring the same individual. In one picture, the individual had a neutral facial expression; in the paired picture, the individual's expression was happy or sad. We found that the college seniors in part mimicked the looking patterns of older adults, in that they gazed less at the negative faces than did the first-year students. Although we replicated the avoidance of negative stimuli found in older adults, we did not find increased engagement with positive stimuli: both groups looked equally at the happy faces.

Next, we tried to create these motivational states in the lab by randomly assigning a sample of young adults to various instructional conditions before viewing emotional images (Xing & Isaacowitz, 2006). This time emotional stimuli were culled from the International Affective Picture System (IAPS) (Lang, Bradley, & Cuthbert, 1999). One group was instructed to manage their emotions as they viewed the stimuli ("the most important thing is to try to manage how you feel as you see the images"); the goal of this was to create a manipulation that would mimic the presumed motivational state of older adults. A second group was instructed to try to gather as much information as possible ("the most important thing is to try to get as much information as possible from each image"); this instruction was designed to try to mimic the information-gathering motivational state of groups with an unlimited future, such as young adults. The third group was instructed to "look naturally, as if at home watching television." Findings were similar to the previous motivational manipulation study. There was an overall main effect of condition, such that those participants instructed to regulate their emotions looked less at all stimuli than did the participants in the other groups. However, this main effect was qualified by a Group X Emotion Type interaction, such that the individuals in the emotion- regulation group especially looked less at negative stimuli. Individuals motivated to regulate how they felt appeared to be pursuing a general avoidance strategy, combined with a particular focus away from negative

information or a negative suppression effect, to regulate their emotions.

Using our rule-in approach via experimental manipulations, the studies just described suggest that motivation can, at least in part, explain age differences in gaze toward emotional stimuli. To some degree, the findings of Xing and Isaacowitz (2006) are compatible both with the hedonic contingency model as well as with the socioemotional selectivity theory, though the Pruzan and Isaacowitz (2006) findings are more compatible with the socioemotional selectivity theory.

It is notable though that our laboratory manipulations of motivation successfully reproduced the observed age-related lessening of fixation to negative stimuli but not the heightened gaze toward positive stimuli. In other words, the negativity avoidance of older adults' attentional patterns was recreated in the lab, but their positivity engagement was not. This was the case even though the stimuli were equated on arousal across valences in the Xing and Isaacowitz (2006) study. Of note, several recent studies of possible positivity effects in older adults' neural responding have failed to find effects for positive stimuli, even when age differences were found for negative ones (Williams et al., 2006; Wood & Kisley, 2006). Some behavioral data have also suggested an age-related negativity suppression rather than a positivity enhancement effect per se (e.g., Grühn et al., 2005). This may not be surprising in light of evidence for "negativity dominance"—an apparently general human property in which negatively valenced stimuli exert stronger influences on processing than do positively valenced ones (Baumeister et al., 2001; Rozin & Royzman, 2001). Perhaps the processing of negative stimuli is simply more amenable to motivational manipulations? One recent paper has found negatively valenced stimuli have more widespread influence on cognition and memory than positively valenced stimuli, and this negative emotion effect operated independently of semantic relatedness (Talmi, Schimmack, Paterson, & Moscovitch, 2007); thus asymmetric valence effects may need to be anticipated, and future work will need to delineate how these asymmetric effects relate to motivation and to aging.

Do these gaze biases work?

In our account of gaze thus far, gaze preferences toward positive and away from negative stimuli are argued to reflect an underlying motivation to regulate emotions in a positive direction. However, none of the evidence reviewed thus far has demonstrated that such motivated gaze preferences actually facilitate accomplishing the affective goal. Below, we explain two approaches that we are currently using to explicitly test whether gaze preferences serve to help regulate emotions in real time.

The first approach involves using training paradigms to test causal relationships between attention and feeling states. If gaze can be used strategically for regulating feelings, then changing gaze patterns should change feeling states as well. In one study (Wadlinger & Isaacowitz, 2008), we found that a single-session attentional training using a constrained dot-probe paradigm with positive words can indeed shift gaze patterns in a more positively oriented direction. This shows that training can move gaze patterns to make them more similar to the gaze shown by happy, optimistic individuals. However, that study did not directly show an effect of gaze training on actual mood states, so future work will need to evaluate whether attentional training can change mood in addition to changing gaze. The second approach we have introduced to determine whether gaze actually does work for emotion regulation is to induce mood states in our participants that need to be regulated, and then to assess in real time whether mood changes as attentional preferences for emotional stimuli are displayed. Results will tell us if age-related gaze preferences actually serve to help regulate feelings when there is a mood state that warrants regulation.

Summary: Age effects in gaze appear to be motivated

In this section, we have presented several lines of empirical evidence suggesting that differences between younger and older adults in gaze toward emotional stimuli are due to motivational factors rather than other factors, such as general cognitive decline. Despite ruling out some other possible causes and ruling in some parts of the motivational story, we have noted that several parts of this motivational account of age differences remain to be clarified: for example, whether these gaze preferences are activated in contexts in which emotion regulatory goals are made relevant (e.g., trying to get out of a bad mood) and whether using gaze biases do actually work in producing and maintaining positive mood states. Next, we turn to larger issues related to what these motivated gaze preferences mean for behavior, and how they may develop.

THE SOCIAL CONTEXT OF MOTIVATED GAZE TO EMOTIONAL STIMULI

So far, the discussion of motivational links to gaze has focused on task contexts in which a perceiver is observing a stimulus that has some emotionally valenced content embedded within it, such as when someone is watching television. However, gaze toward emotionally valenced information often takes place in a much more interpersonal context, such as when a perceiver tries to determine the emotional response of someone they are interacting with (*did I upset him or not?*) or someone they might interact with (*does he look angry?*).

Emotion recognition serves a crucial function in social life. Accurately recognizing another's affective state, particularly through facial expressions, guides social behavior and effective communication. Faces are particularly important for social interaction and show distinct age-related effects in social cognition (Keightley, Winocur, Burianova, Hongwanishkul, & Grady, 2006). Studies of emotion-recognition accuracy involving various nationalities and ethnicities of the participants found broad consistency among such judgments (Ekman, 1999; Ekman et al., 1987). Yet, these studies primarily studied younger adults. Older adults do not seem to show the same robust recognition abilities as younger adults. In fact, older adults appear to be distinctly disadvantaged at accurately recognizing certain types of emotional states including anger, fear, and sadness (Isaacowitz et al., 2007; Murphy & Isaacowitz, 2010).

Studies using eye-tracking to examine emotion recognition in older adults suggest that older adults may not be correctly allocating their attention to different parts of the face (Sullivan, Ruffman, & Hutton, 2007; Wong, Cronin-Golomb, & Neargarder, 2005) In a study designed to thoroughly investigate the cognitive, affective, and visual components associated with negative emotion recognition, we tracked gaze patterns in older and younger adult participants while they completed an emotion recognition task (Murphy & Isaacowitz, 2010). Participants also completed a battery of cognitive and affective questionnaires in order to test whether such variables affected gaze patterns and/or emotion recognition. Behavioral results replicated previous findings; older adults were worse at recognizing emotions than younger adults. However, age effects in gaze patterns depended on specific emotions. For instance, younger adults paid more attention toward the eye region of anger expressions than did older adults. Yet, better anger recognition was negatively correlated with attention toward the eyes for younger adults but not for older adults. In older adults, better anger recognition was associated with more attention toward the mouth. Some research suggests that particular emotions are better recognized by attending toward the mouth region (e.g., happy), whereas other emotions are better recognized by attending toward the eye region (e.g., anger and fear) (Sullivan et al., 2007). Perhaps older adults' attentional bias toward the mouth indicates older adults' inclination toward positive information, which would be a smiling mouth on a happy face (see figure 7.1).

In regression analysis including the aforementioned cognitive and affective measures, as well as age-related gaze patterns, age remained a significant predictor of negative emotion recognition accuracy beyond the aforementioned variables. Along the lines of the rule-out approach explained earlier, we ruled out the possibility of cognitive, affective, and age-related factors that may account for the decline in negative emotion recognition for older adults. The pattern of age-related emotion recognition declines may depend on the specific emotion being recognized (Murphy & Isaacowitz, 2010).

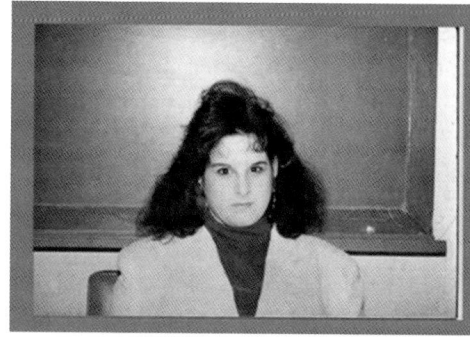

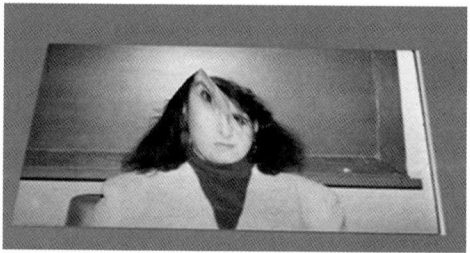

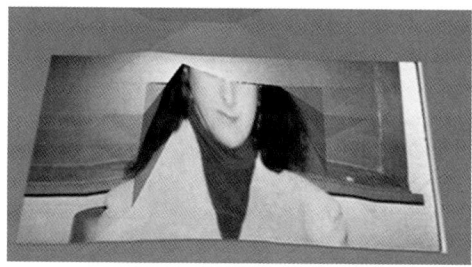

Figure 7.1 Gaze Patterns While Viewing an Anger Expression. The top panel, featuring an angry expression by a young female, is a stimulus slide from the DANVA2-AF (Nowicki & Carton, 1993). The center and bottom panels are contoured illustrations of the same slide while tilted on a horizontal axis with higher peaks indicating more attention towards that facial region. The center panel is the gaze pattern of a younger adult (age = 18 years) while viewing the anger expression; the bottom panel is an older adult's gaze pattern (age = 71 years) while viewing the same slide. A comparison between the center and bottom panel illustrates how younger adults tend to pay more attention towards the eye region when viewing anger expressions whereas older tend to pay more attention towards the mouth region (Murphy & Isaacowitz, 2010).

This interpretation is compelling, given that different emotions are processed distinctly in the brain (e.g., Adolphs, 2006). Perhaps the most illuminating finding of this study was the fact that age remained a (very) significant predictor of negative emotion recognition accuracy; there appear to be factors beyond cognitive, affective, and age-related gaze patterns that account for negative emotion recognition differences between older and younger adults. When we look more closely at the processes underlying age differences, it is hard not to think of motivational influences—why is this age effect not eliminated by controlling for gaze patterns? What else could play a role? One thought is that motivational processes (such as those described earlier) interfere with accurate recognition of emotions, though this hypothesis remains to be directly investigated in future research.

WHAT ARE THE MECHANISMS BY WHICH MOTIVATION AFFECTS EMOTIONAL GAZE?

How exactly does motivation affect aspects of information processing, such as attention? Motivational influences on processing are, by definition, top-down, in that processing is considered to be a function of the goal states of the perceiver. Below, we consider two aspects of these mechanisms: first, do these processes conform to what would be expected of top-down influences; and second, if they are indeed top-down in nature, is the influence of motivation on attention controlled or automatic?

With regard to the first issue, in addition to the motivational manipulations described earlier, we have recently conducted an in-depth temporal analysis of, more precisely, the point at which gaze preferences begin after stimulus presentation (Isaacowitz, Allard, Murphy & Schlangel, 2009). Preferences in gaze did not emerge in either young or older adults for any of the four emotional stimulus types (happy, angry, afraid, and sad) until after the first 500 ms post-stimulus onset. This time course is consistent with what would be expected from top-down rather than bottom-up influences, given that bottom-up stimulus-driven properties are thought to happen more rapidly than top-down influences (van Zoest, Donk, & Theeuwes, 2004) as well as to constrain top-down processing (Kosslyn, 1995). Although it

may take some time for participants to scan two faces when both are presented simultaneously, a strong bottom-up influence on processing could be detected before multiple fixations had happened. For instance, if emotional faces had extremely strong bottom-up influence, this could lead all attention to be directed toward the emotional face rapidly in an emotional-neutral face pair rather than there being multiple fixations scattered spatially across both faces before any preference emerges. However, our results indicated that attention toward emotionally-valenced faces (and away from neutral) did not occur immediately but rather emerged later (post 500 ms stimulus onset) and there was evidence that the bias toward happy faces in older adults increased over time. Such findings are more in line with a top-down processing trajectory than bottom-up processing.

Although it may seem that top-down is synonymous with controlled processing, and bottom-up the same as automatic, in reality this distinction is not quite so clear-cut (e.g., Madden, 2007; Okon-Singer, Tzelgov, & Henik, 2007; Pessoa, 2005). Not surprisingly then, the issue of the controlled vs. automatic nature of age-related gaze preferences toward emotional stimuli is much more thorny than simply establishing that they are top-down in nature. Mather and colleagues have recently argued (e.g., Mather & Knight, 2005) that it requires cognitive control for older adults to display positivity effects in their processing of emotional information. In three studies, Mather and Knight provide evidence that positivity effects relate to cognitive control. For example, positivity effects are observed in a memory task when older adults can perform the task in full attention, free from distraction (Study 1). However, when distracted, both young and older adults appear to actually show negativity effects in memory (Study 3). Additionally, individual differences in cognitive control were measured (Study 2); older adults who were high in cognitive control showed better memory for positive material than older adults low in cognitive control. These findings suggest that cognitive control resources need to be available for older adults to display a motivated shift toward posi-tivity in their information processing.

Other evidence has not been entirely consis-tent with a cognitive control account of positivity effects. Kennedy and O'Hara (2005) found that older individuals with mild cognitive impair-ment (MCI) showed positivity effects in their memory. Individuals with MCI are presumed to have deficient cognitive control. Moreover, while some aspects of visual attention appear maintained with age, and there is evidence that older adults may show greater use of top-down processes in visual attention (Madden, 2007), it is nonetheless the case that age-related declines in executive control are well-documented (Verhaegen & Cerella, 2002), raising questions about how a positivity effect that both requires executive control and increases with age could be possible.

Another methodology for investigating how much cognitive control is required for older adults to display a positivity effect or even a neg-ativity suppression effect in their information processing is to utilize divided-attention para-digms. Although Mather and Knight (2005) used a divided-attention paradigm in their original study on the role of cognitive control (Study 2), divided attention was investigated as a between-subjects factor in that particular work. Investigating divided attention as a with-in-subjects factor allows for the calculation of within-subject divided-attention costs; it also permits the investigation of divided-attention costs separately for whether attention is divided at encoding or at retrieval. This is important given past work that has found greater mem-ory costs associated with divided attention at encoding than when attention is divided at retrieval (Naveh-Benjamin, Craik, Guez, & Krueger, 2005).

In one study of divided attention conducted in our lab (Allard & Isaacowitz, 2007), older and younger adults performed a memory task involving emotional synthetic faces (determin-ing whether they had previously been seen or not) either under conditions of full attention, as well as with attention divided either at encod-ing or at retrieval. The secondary task in those conditions involved making a simple number

judgment. Although accuracy scores were not informative in that study due to floor effects in the data, reaction time data yielded interesting findings. Both young and older adults showed an apparent positivity effect in their responding when attention was divided at encoding: they were more disrupted in their responding to the secondary task when the primary task involved encoding a positive face than when it involved encoding a negative face. No such valenced costs were apparent for older adults when attention was divided at retrieval, though young adults showed evidence of a negativity effect in that condition. Results from this study suggest that positivity effects may be observed even under conditions in which attention is divided.

These findings raise the question about whether motivated influences on gaze must necessarily be controlled or whether they could, at least in theory, ever be automatic. The time course data may suggest a controlled process, but there is no particular moment at which a process goes from being automatic to becoming controlled. Instead, the time course of a pro-cess can change as it goes from being fully con-trolled to becoming more automatic (Shiffrin & Schneider, 1977). Human-factors research abounds with examples of controlled processes becoming faster and more efficient with experi-ence, such as has been shown with expert pilots, drivers, and mail sorters (Polk & Farah, 1995; Williams, 1995). Other research also distin-guishes between effortful control and other less voluntary (i.e., more automatic) cognitive pro-cesses, particularly in relation to self-regulation and emotion regulation (e.g., Eisenberg, Hofer, & Vaughan, 2007). Gross and Thompson (2007) note that emotion regulation may initially be "deliberate but later occurs without conscious awareness … [We believe in] a continuum from conscious, effortful, and controlled regulation to unconscious, effortless, and automatic reg-ulation" (p. 8). Could aging perceivers follow such a trajectory in terms of gaze patterns and emotional processing? With repeated episodes of controlled attempts to use gaze to regulate emotions, could that become automatic?

This possibility is in line with the prop-osition that goal pursuits can be automatic;

unconscious motives, including emotion reg- ulation, may be the result of long-standing chronic accessibility of that motive that devel- ops because of extended experience (Bargh & Williams, 2007; Gollwitzer & Bargh, 2005). In terms of aging, nonconscious emotion regula- tion may be operating at the attentional level when older adults pay more attention to positive stimuli than negative stimuli. Over time, older adults' attempts to regulate their own emotions may become automatic as they learn to attend more toward positive information than negative information.

Research on threat detection among phobic individuals may be informative in regards to automatic gaze motives. In Öhman's (Öhman, Flykt, & Esteves, 2001) work on threatening stimuli detection, everyone (including non- phobics) showed a preference for detecting fear- relevant stimuli, but phobic participants showed even more of it. This is interpreted as reflecting these individuals becoming sensitized to these stimuli.

If emotions are understood as action sets, which presume a set of goals, it could be sug- gested that emotion involves "attention control settings" (Folk, Remington & Johnson, 1992) that make goal-relevant stimuli salient for the person. As a result, these stimuli may then automatically capture attention (Yantis, 1998). Similarly, one would expect motivational states to involve different attention control settings (Öhman et al., 2001, p. 475).

Could older adults develop more auto- matic motivated gaze preferences, akin to the development of visual preferences for threat- relevant stimuli among phobic individuals? Interestingly, two recent studies have found that rapid threat detection is maintained in older adults (Hahn, Carlson Singer, & Gronlund, 2006; Mather & Knight, 2006). Hahn et al. also found evidence that older adults were more efficient in inhibiting task-irrelevant angry faces from influencing their processing than were younger adults, which the authors inter- pret as reflecting age invariance in automatic processing (the threat detection effect) but age differences in controlled processing (the threat inhibition effect).

To some degree, the answer to whether motivated gaze preferences can ever be auto- matic depends on the definition of automatic- ity. Pessoa (2005) defines "strong automaticity" as involving processes that are independent of nonstimulus-based factors such as attention and instructions. In strong automaticity, top- down influences play no role at all in processing. In contrast, "weak automaticity" entails "task- irrelevant or involuntary processing" (Pessoa, 2005, p. 193) and thus may involve some top- down influence. More recently, Okon-Singer and colleagues (2007) have found evidence that general emotional processing is weakly auto- matic: it requires some attention to be initiated but can then proceed even if not task-relevant and no further effort is put into it. In their stud- ies, participants' performance was affected by emotionally valenced stimuli even when those stimuli were not relevant to their primary task, but such interference only took place in condi- tions in which participants had at least some attentional resources available (i.e., their atten- tion was not totally consumed by the primary task). Even so, there was no evidence that basic emotion processing met the "strong automa- ticity" criteria in that study, and Pessoa (2005) describes the challenge of ever showing strong automaticity for emotional processing.

Thus, in response to the question of whether motivated influences on gaze, such as the seem- ing age-related positivity effect in visual atten- tion, are controlled, automatic, or both, the answer seems as though it will be a complex one. Certainly, such effects *can* be controlled in the sense that, in a particular situation (such as a novel one), an individual can, by effort and volition, modulate his ir her gaze in a motiva- tion-consistent way in this situation. Recent evidence linking cognitive control capabil- ity to the demonstration of positivity effects supports this position (e.g., Mather & Knight, 2005). Motivated effects on gaze likely can- not be strongly automatic, because they could not operate in an entirely bottom-up manner in the absence of any attention whatsoever. However, we believe that motivated effects on gaze could become weakly automatic, in the sense that it always requires some attention or effort to initiate, but once initiated can proceed without additional effort and even when task-irrelevant. It seems unlikely that this would be the case in a novel situation, but with repeated experience enacting controlled processes, motivated gaze for similar and/or familiar situations could become automatic, such that enacting it takes minimal cognitive resources and can proceed without effort once initiated even if not relevant to the task. Top-down influences on gaze do not necessarily have to be a product of executive control (Madden, 2007), and future research should not take this as a given. Work aimed specifically at determining the presence or absence of positivity effects when the task and motivation are at odds, given variations in situation novelty and changes with experience, can best test these propositions. Further consideration must be given to the neural substrates of gaze preferences (van Reekum et al., 2007) and to research designs that can delineate to what extent such processes are implicit or explicit. Research indicates that age-related emotional preferences in attention and memory can differ depending on the research design (Murphy & Isaacowitz, 2008). Thus, additional research and related analyses could clarify how top-down motivated processing goals can influence gaze along a controlled automatic continuum across adulthood.

SUMMARY AND FUTURE DIRECTIONS

Here, we presented evidence that motivation affects gaze, especially in the context of human aging, and we have considered the mechanisms by which motivation could affect gaze across the adult lifespan. Perhaps not surprisingly, given evidence that top-down influences on visual processing may increase with age (Madden, 2007), we have found in other work that gaze is quite malleable to diverse motivational influences: in a study of childless women (Light & Isaacowitz, 2006), gaze was linked to motivation to maintain control, consistent with Schulz and Heckhausen's (1996) life-span theory of control motivation. Thus, it appears that motivation is a concept richly tied to gaze and vision. Future

research could delineate how and when the various motivational theories can best account for attentional findings, especially age-related ones, by developing paradigms that focus on specific rather than general motivational effects on gaze patterns. Then, it will be time to document mechanisms by which specific motivational processes can impact gaze to specific stimulus types. That way, researchers will fully understand how aging eyes view the emotional world, and what goals are best accomplished by "looking old."

AUTHOR NOTES

Derek M. Isaacowitz, Department of Psychology, Brandeis University; Nora A. Murphy, Department of Psychology, Brandeis University.

This research described in this chapter was funded in part by National Institute on Aging grants R03 AG022168, R01 AG026323 (to the first author) and T32 AG00204. We thank Michaela Riediger for her helpful feedback on an earlier version of this chapter, and Stephen Nowicki for permission to reprint a stimulus slide from the DANVA2-AF.

Address correspondence to Derek M. Isaacowitz at Brandeis University, Department of Psychology MS 062, P.O. Box 549110, Waltham, MA 02454-9110. E-mail: dmi@brandeis.edu.

REFERENCES

Adolphs, R. (2006). Perception and emotion: How we recognize facial expressions. *Current Directions in Psychological Science, 15,* 222–226.

Allard, E., & Isaacowitz, D.M. (2007). *Dual-task costs and emotional memory for younger and older adults.* Unpublished manuscript, Waltham, MA.

Balcetis, E., & Dunning, D. (2006). See what you want to see: Motivational influences on visual perception. *Journal of Personality and Social Psychology, 91,* 612–625.

Baltes, P. B., & Baltes, M. M. (1990). Psychological perspectives on successful aging: The model of selective optimization with compensation. In P. B. Baltes & M. M. Baltes (Eds.), *Successful aging: Perspectives from the behavioral sciences* (pp. 1–34). New York: Cambridge University Press.

Bargh, J. A., & Williams, L. E. (2007). The non-conscious regulation of emotion. In J. J. Gross (Ed.), *Handbook of emotion regulation* (pp. 429–445). New York: Guilford Press.

Baumeister, R. F., Bratslavsky, E., Finkenauer, C., & Vohs, K. D. (2001). Bad is stronger than good. *Review of General Psychology, 5*, 323–373.

Borkenau, P., & Liebler, A. (1995). Observable attributes a manifestations and cues of personality and intelligence. *Journal of Personality, 63*, 1–25.

Carstensen, L. L., & Fredrickson, B. L. (1998). The influence of HIV-status and age on cognitive representations of others. *Health Psychology, 17*, 494–503.

Carstensen, L. L., Isaacowitz, D. M., & Charles, S. T. (1999). Taking time seriously: A theory of socioemotional selectivity. *American Psychologist, 54*, 165–181.

Carstensen, L. L., & Mikels, J. A. (2005). At the intersection of emotion and cognition: Aging and the positivity effect. *Current Directions in Psychological Science, 14*, 117–121.

Carstensen, L. L., Mather, M., & Mikels, J. A. (2006). Aging and the intersection of cognition, motivation, and emotion. In J. E. Birren & K. W. Schaire (Eds.), *Handbook of the psychology of aging* (6th ed.) (pp. 343–362). Amsterdam: Elsevier.

Carstensen, L. L., Pasupathi, M., Mayr, U., & Nesselroade, J. (2000). Emotion experience in everyday life across the adult life span. *Journal of Personality and Social Psychology, 79*, 644–655.

Charles, S., Mather, M., & Carstensen, L. L. (2003). Aging and emotional memory: The forgettable nature of negative images for older adults. *Journal of Experimental Psychology: General, 132*, 310–324.

Dalton, K. M., Nacewicz, B. M., Johnstone, T., Schaefer, H. S., Gernsbacher, M. A., Goldsmith, H. H., et al. (2005). Gaze fixation and the neural circuitry of face processing in autism. *Nature Neuroscience, 8*, 519–526.

Eisenberg, N., Hofer, C., & Vaughan, J. (2007). Effortful control and its socioemotional consequences. In J. J. Gross (Ed.), *Handbook of emotion regulation* (pp. 287–306). New York: Guilford Press.

Ekman, P. (1999). Facial expressions. In T. Dalgleish & T. Power (Eds.), *The handbook of cognition and emotion* (pp. 301–320). Sussex, UK: John Wiley & Sons.

Ekman, P., Friesen, W. V., O'Sullivan, M., Chan, A., Diacoyanni-Tarlatzis, I., Heider, K., et al. (1987). Universals and cultural differences in the judgments of facial expressions of emotion. *Journal of Personality and Social Psychology, 53*, 712–717.

Fan, J., McCandliss, B. D., Sommer, T., Raz, M., & Posner, M. I. (2002). Testing the efficiency and independence of attentional networks. *Journal of Cognitive Neuroscience, 14*, 340–347.

Folk, C. L., Remington, R. W., & Johnson, J. C. (1992). Involuntary covert orienting is contingent on attention control setting. *Journal of Experimental Psychology: Human Perception and Performance, 113*, 501–517.

Fredrickson, B. L. (1995). Socioemotional behavior at the end of college life. *Journal of Social and Personal Relationships, 12*, 261–276.

Fredrickson, B. L., & Carstensen, L. L. (1990). Choosing social partners: How old age and anticipated endings make people more selective. *Psychology and Aging, 5*, 335–347.

Freund, A. M., & Baltes, P. B. (1999). The orchestration of selection, optimization, and compensation: An action-theoretical conceptualization of a theory of developmental regulation. In W. J. Perrig & A. Grob (Eds.), *Control of human behaviour, mental processes, and consciousness* (pp. 35–58). Mahwah, NJ: Erlbaum.

Gollwitzer, P. M., & Bargh, J. A. (2005). Automaticity in goal pursuit. In A. Elliot & C. Dweck (Eds.), *Handbook of competence and motivation* (pp. 624–646). New York: Guilford Press.

Gordon, P. C., Hendrick, R., Johnson, M., & Lee, Y. (2006). Similarity-based interference during language comprehension: Evidence from eye tracking during reading. *Journal of Experimental Psychology: Learning, Memory, and Cognition, 32*, 1304–1321.

Griffin, Z. M. (2004). The eyes are right when the mouth is wrong. *Psychological Science, 15*, 814–821.

Gross, J. J., & Thompson, R. A. (2007). Emotion regulation: Conceptual foundations. In J. J. Gross (Ed.), *Handbook of emotion regulation* (pp. 3–24). New York: Guildford Press.

Grühn, D., Smith, J., & Baltes, P. B. (2005). No aging bias favoring memory for positive material: Evidence from a heterogeneity-homogeneity list paradigm using emotionally toned words. *Psychology and Aging, 20*, 579–588.

Hahn, S., Carlson, C., Singer, S., & Gronlund, S. D. (2006). Aging and visual search: Automatic and controlled attentional bias to threat faces. *Acta Psychologica, 123*, 312–336.

Handley, I. M., Lassiter, G. D., & Nickell, E. F. (2004). Affect and automatic mood maintenance. *Journal of Experimental Social Psychology, 40*, 106–112.

Hasher, L., & Zacks, R. T. (1988). Working memory, comprehension, and aging: A review and a new view. In G. H. Bower (Ed.), *The psychology of learning and motivation, Vol. 22* (pp. 193–225). New York: Academic Press.

Isaacowitz, D. M. (2005a). Correlates of well-being in adulthood and old age: A tale of two optimisms. *Journal of Research in Personality, 39*, 224–244.

Isaacowitz, D. M. (2005b). The gaze of the optimist. *Personality and Social Psychology Bulletin, 3*, 407–415.

Isaacowitz, D. M., Allard, E., Murphy, N. M., & Schlangel, M. (2009). The time course of age-related preferences toward positive and negative stimuli. *Journals of Gerontology Series B: Psychological Sciences and Social Sciences, 64*, 188–192.

Isaacowitz, D. M., Löckenhoff, C., Wright, R., Sechrest, L., Riedel, R., Lane, R. A., & Costa, P. T. (2007). Age differences in recognition of emotion in lexical stimuli and facial expressions. *Psychology and Aging, 22*, 147–159.

Isaacowitz, D. M., & Smith, J. (2003). Positive and negative affect in very old age. *Journal of Gerontology: Psychological Sciences, 58B*, 143–152.

Isaacowitz, D. M., Toner, K., Goren, D., & Wilson, H. R. (2008). Looking while unhappy: Mood congruent gaze in young adults, positive gaze in older adults. *Psychological Science, 19*, 848–853.

Isaacowitz, D. M., Wadlinger, H. A., Goren, D., & Wilson, H. R. (2006a). Is there an age-related positivity effect in visual attention? A comparison of two methodologies. *Emotion, 6*, 511–516.

Isaacowitz, D. M., Wadlinger, H. A., Goren, D., & Wilson, H. R. (2006b). Selective preference in visual fixation away from negative images in old age? An eye tracking study. *Psychology and Aging, 21*, 40–48.

Isen, A. M. (2004). Some perspectives on positive feelings and emotions: Positive affect facilitates thinking and problem solving. In A. S. R. Manstead, N. Frijda, & A. Fischer (Eds.), *Feelings and emotions: The Amsterdam symposium* (pp. 263–281). New York: Cambridge.

John, O. P., & Gross, J. J. (2004). Healthy and unhealthy emotion regulation: Personality processes, individual differences, and life span development. *Journal of Personality, 72*, 1301–1333.

Keightley, M. L., Winocur, G., Burianova, H., Hongwanishkul, D., & Grady, C. L. (2006). Age effects on social cognition: Faces tell a different story. *Psychology and Aging, 21*, 558–572.

Kennedy, Q., & O'Hara, R. (2005). *Individual differences in emotional memory: The role of memory ability.* Paper presented at Gerontological Society of America annual convention, Orlando, FL.

Kleinke, C. L. (1986). Gaze and eye contact: A research review. *Psychological Bulletin, 100*, 78–100.

Kosslyn, S. M. (1995). Freud returns? In R. L. Solso & D. W. Massaro (Eds.), *The science of the mind: 2001 and beyond* (pp. 90–106). New York: Oxford University Press.

Lang, P. J., Bradley, M. M., & Cuthbert, B. N. (1999). *International affective picture system (IAPS): Technical manual and affective ratings.* Gainesville, FL: University of Florida, Center for Research in Psychophysiology.

Leigland, L. A., Schulz, L. E., & Janowsky, J. S. (2004). Age related changes in emotional memory. *Neurobiology of Aging, 25*, 1117–1124.

Light, J., & Isaacowitz, D. M. (2006). The effect of developmental regulation on visual attention: The example of the "Biological Clock." *Cognition and Emotion, 20*, 623–645.

Luo, J., & Isaacowitz, D. M. (2007). How optimists face skin cancer: Risk assessment, attention, memory, and behavior. *Psychology and Health, 22*, 963–984.

Madden, D. J. (2007). Aging and visual attention. *Current Directions in Psychological Science, 16*, 70–74.

Manor, B. R., & Gordon, E. (2003). Defining the temporal threshold for ocular fixation in free-viewing visuocognitive tasks. *Journal of Neuroscience Methods, 128*, 85–93.

Mather, M., & Carstensen, L. L. (2003). Aging and attentional biases for emotional faces. *Psychological Science, 14*, 409–415.

Mather, M., & Knight, M. (2005). Goal-directed memory: The role of cognitive control in older adults' emotional memory. *Psychology and Aging, 20*, 554–570.

Mather, M., & Knight, M. (2006). Angry faces get noticed quickly: Threat detection is not impaired among older adults. *Journals of Gerontology Series B: Psychological Sciences and Social Sciences, 61*, 54–57.

Mroczek, D. K., & Kolarz, C. M. (1998). The effect of age on positive and negative affect: A developmental perspective on happiness. *Journal of Personality and Social Psychology, 75*, 1333–1349.

Murphy, N. A., Hall, J. A., & Colvin, C. R. (2003). Accurate intelligence assessments in social interactions: Mediators and gender effects. *Journal of Personality, 71*, 465–493.

Murphy, N. A., & Isaacowitz, D. M. (2010). Age effects and gaze patterns in recognising emotional expressions: An in-depth look at gaze measures and covariates. *Cognition and Emotion, 24*, 436–452.

Murphy, N. A., & Isaacowitz, D. M. (2008). Preferences for emotional information in younger and older adults: A meta-analysis of memory and attention tasks. *Psychology and Aging, 23*, 263–286.

Naveh–Benjamin, M., Craik, F. I. M., Guez, J., & Krueger, S. (2005). Divided attention in younger and older adults: Effects of strategy and relatedness on memory performance and secondary task costs. *Journal of Experimental Psychology: Learning, Memory, and Cognition, 31*, 520–537.

Nowicki, S., Jr., & Carton, J. S. (1993). The measurement of emotional intensity from facial expressions. *Journal of Social Psychology, 133*, 749–750.

Nummenmaa, L., Hyönä, J., & Calvo, M. G. (2006). Eye movement assessment of selective attentional capture by emotional pictures. *Emotion, 6*, 257–268.

Öhman, A., Flykt, A., & Esteves, F. (2001). Emotion drives attention: Detecting the snake in the grass. *Journal of Experimental Psychology: General, 130*, 466–479.

Okon–Singer, H., Tzelgov, J., & Henik, A. (2007). Distinguishing between automaticity and attention in the processing of emotionally significant stimuli. *Emotion, 7*, 147–157.

Parkhurst, D., Law, K., & Niebur, E. (2002). Modeling the role of salience in the allocation of overt visual selective attention. *Vision Research, 42*, 107–123.

Pessoa, L. (2005) To what extent are emotional visual stimuli processed without attention and awareness? *Current Opinion in Neurobiology, 15*, 188–196.

Polk, T. A., & Farah, M. J. (1995). Late experience alters vision. *Nature, 376*, 648–649.

Pruzan, K., & Isaacowitz, D. M. (2006). An attentional application of socioemotional selectivity theory in college students. *Social Development, 15*, 326–338.

Reichle, E. D., Pollatsek, A., Fisher, D. L., & Rayner, K. (1998). Toward a model of eye movement control in reading. *Psychological Review, 105*, 125–157.

Regier, D. A., Boyd, J. H., Burke, J. D., Rae, D. S., Myers, J. K., et al. (1988). One-month prevalence of mental disorders in the United States. *Archives of General Psychiatry, 45*, 977–986.

Rinck, M., & Becker, E. S. (2006). Spider fearful individuals attend to threat, then quickly avoid it: Evidence from eye movements. *Journal of Abnormal Psychology, 115*, 231–238.

Rozin, P., & Royzman, E. B. (2001). Negativity bias, negativity dominance, and contagion. *Personality and Social Psychology Review, 5*, 296–320.

Salthouse, T. A. (2000). Aging and measures of processing speed. *Biological Psychology, 54*, 35–54.

Schulz, R. & Heckhausen, J. (1996). A life span model of successful aging. *American Psychologist, 51*, 702–714.

Shiffrin, R. M., & Schneider, W. (1977). Controlled and automatic human information processing: II. Perceptual learning, automatic attending, and a general theory. *Psychological Review, 84*, 127–190.

Sobel, D. M., & Kirkham, N. Z. (2006). Blickets and babies: The development of causal reasoning in toddlers and infants. *Developmental Psychology, 42*, 1103–1115.

Sullivan, S., Ruffman, T., & Hutton, S. B. (2007). Age differences in emotion recognition skills and the visual scanning of emotion faces. *Journals of Gerontology: Psychological Sciences and Social Sciences, 62B*, 53–60.

Talmi, D., Schimmack, U., Paterson, T., & Moscovitch, M. (2007). The role of attention in emotional memory enhancement. *Emotion, 7*, 89–102.

van Reekum, C. M., Johnstone, T., Urry, H. L., Thurow, M. T., Schaefer, H. S., Alexander, A. L., & Davidson, R. J. (2007). Gaze fixations predict brain activation during the voluntary regulation of picture-induced negative affect. *Neuroimage, 36*, 1041–1055.

van Zoest, W., Donk, M., & Theeuwes, J. (2004). The role of stimulus-driven and goal–driven control in saccadic visual selection. *Journal of Experimental Psychology: Human Perception and Performance, 30,* 746–759.

Verhaeghen, P., & Cerella, J. (2002). Aging, executive control, and attention: A review of meta-analyses. *Neuroscience and Biobehavioral Reviews, 26,* 849–857.

Wadlinger, H. A., & Isaacowitz, D. M. (2006). Positive mood broadens visual attention to positive stimuli. *Motivation and Emotion, 30,* 89–101.

Wadlinger, H. A., & Isaacowitz, D. M. (2008). Looking happy: The experimental manipulation of a positive visual attention bias. *Emotion, 8,* 121–126.

Wegener, D. T., & Petty, R. E. (1994). Mood management across affective states: The hedonic contingency hypothesis. *Journal of Personality and Social Psychology, 66,* 1034–1048.

Williams, L. J. (1995). Peripheral target recognition and visual field narrowing in aviators and nonaviators. *The International Journal of Aviation Psychology, 5,* 215–232.

Williams, L. M., Brown, K. J., Palmer, D., Liddell, B. J., Kemp, A. H., Olivieri, G.,

Peduto, A., & Gordon, E. (2006). The mellow years? Neural basis of improving emotional stability over age. *Journal of Neuroscience, 26,* 6422–6430.

Williams, J. M.G., Watts, F. N., MacLeod, C., & Mathews, A. (1997). *Cognitive psychology and emotional disorders (2nd ed.).* New York: Wiley.

Wong, B., Cronin-Golomb, A., & Neargarder, S. (2005). Patterns of visual scanning as predictors of emotion identification in normal aging. *Neuropsychology, 19,* 739–749.

Wood, S., & Kisley, M. A. (2006). The negativity bias is eliminated in older adults: Age-related reduction in event-related brain potentials associated with evaluative categorization. *Psychology and Aging, 21,* 815–820.

Xing, C., & Isaacowitz, D. M. (2006). Aiming at happiness: How motivation affects attention to and memory for emotional images. *Motivation and Emotion, 30,* 249–256.

Yantis, S. (1998). Control of visual attention. In H. Pashler (Ed.), *Attention* (pp. 223–256). London: Psychology Press.

CHAPTER 8

Gaze and Preference-Orienting Behavior as a Somatic Precursor of Preference Decision

Shinsuke Shimojo, Claude Simion, and Mark A. Changizi

INTRODUCTION—GAZE, ORIENTING, AND PREFERENCE

Eye gaze has some distinctive functions in a variety of species, even among monkeys and great apes in the wilderness. Prolonged gaze, for instance, is often used by dominants as a mild form of threat in most of group-living primate species. By contrast, in some great apes, it may be used to signal a request for social sharing of food (see Yamagiwa, 2004 for a review). In the case of humans, the social role of gaze becomes even more significant and variable (Emery, 2000). Eye gaze is considered the "window to the soul" across various cultures (Baron-Cohen, 1995), and often used as a sign of curse ("evil eye") or warning. Most importantly, it is one of the first points of contact between infants and mothers (Haith, Bergman, & Moore, 1977).

In fact, gaze and gaze shifts are critical elements in the newborn's sensory-motor repertoire. Preferential looking, or selective gaze, can be easily observed from several-hour to year-old infants (including monkey infants as well). It serves as a basis for sensory-motor coordination on the one hand and social-cognitive development on the other hand. Mimicking, joint visual attention, and social referencing are some examples of social-cognitive functions that requires gaze as the primary basis.

Gaze shifting is just one example of bodily orienting mechanism. Other examples may include head turn, body turn, turning of toes, and weight shift. Such orienting mechanism may be one of the earliest sensory-motor functions ontogenetically, as mentioned earlier. It may also be found in most primitive species, and is thus considered very old evolutionarily.

Considering such a long phylogenetic history and functional significance, one may speculate that gaze is still the basis of and an indispensable condition for sensory-motor coordination and attention, as well as for memory and learning in the human adult. In this chapter, we will step even further arguing that gaze orienting is an implicit somatic precursor of even higher cognitive functions such as preference and decision making.

To be more specific, let us raise three questions. First, does infantlike preferential looking (i.e., gaze bias) in adults have anything to do with their cognitive/ conscious decision of preference? And to be more specific, does implicit gaze orienting precede and determine conscious preference decisions in adults? Finally, is emotional decision making (preference, in our case) unique with this regard, relative to other types of decision making, both behaviorally and neurologically? Note that these questions may also be considered in line with James-Lange's classical question (e.g., "One cries because (s)he is sad, or one feels sad because (s)he cries?)", more recently the "somatic precursor" hypothesis postulated by Antonio Damasio, and the "mind first, or body first" question in general. The following in this chapter aims to address these issues.

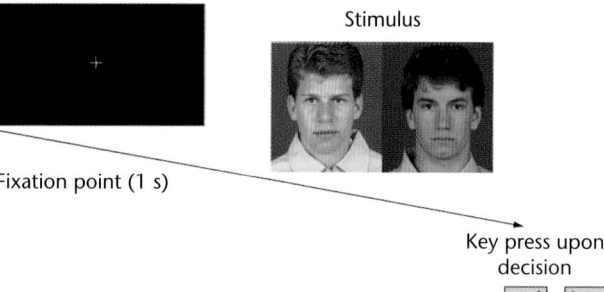

Figure 8.1 The gaze cascade experiment. A pair of faces were presented after a fixation point. The subject was allowed free inspection without time limit, but asked to press one of the two keys to indicate the decision as soon as (s)he was consciously aware of it.

THE GAZE CASCADE EFFECT— GAZE BIAS PRECEDING PREFERENCE

To address these issues, we performed a two-alternative forced-choice (2AFC) experiment in which the subject was asked to observe two faces presented on a CRT monitor to make a preference judgment (see Figure 8.1) (Shimojo, Simion, Shimojo, et al., 2003). There was no fixed time limit, and the subject can freely move his or her eyes to compare the two faces. The subject was also asked to press one of two buttons to indicate his or her preference as soon as (s)he was consciously aware of the choice. The faces were kept on the screen until the subject made a response. Attractiveness was matched within pairs based on pre-ratings to remove any inessential effects, and to make the decision relatively hard. Eye movements were recorded with an eye tracker (EyeLink2) to examine whether gaze could predict preference choices.

When we time-locked the eye-movement data to the stimulus onset and averaged across trials, we did not find any significant bias, other than the strong general tendency of the initial gaze toward left (which was expected among typical readers of English and most other languages with few exceptions, such as Hebrew and Arabic). The lack of effects may be partly because the performance time greatly varied across trials and subjects. A very intriguing gaze pattern was found only when we time-locked the eye-movement data to the moment of response. The data were divided into 200-ms time bin and the likelihood of the gaze toward the preferred face was calculated for each bin.

The likelihood of the gaze was roughly .50 as expected until approximately 1,000 ms prior to subject response, when the probability jumped past .80 (Figure 8.2a; the solid curve in the figure is the best-fit sigmoid function). The baseline attractiveness within pairs were minimized in the initial experiment, thus the preference task was difficult. Figure 8.2b (solid curve) represents the result when baseline differences were maximized, thereby simplifying the task (to be discussed later).

When the subjects performed other tasks, such as choosing the rounder of two faces or the less attractive face (dislike task), the gaze likelihood curves are elevated somewhat, but level off at 55–65 percent, in contrast to the preference task (Figure 8.3). Note that task difficulty did not differ significantly among the tasks, as estimated from the means of performance time (data not shown). Therefore, such a plateaulike elevation in the control tasks may be interpreted as reflecting preparation for the response (i.e., the subject tended to fixate on the chosen face before choosing it). The extremity and the distinctive pattern of elevation in the preference task, on the other hand, indicate that the gaze cascade is unique to relative attractiveness.

THE GAZE CASCADE IS A ROBUST EFFECT

The gaze cascade effect, which had turned out to be a distinctively unique characteristic of the preference-decision process, raised an important question. How generalizable and robust is the gaze cascade effect, across various conditions and stimuli?

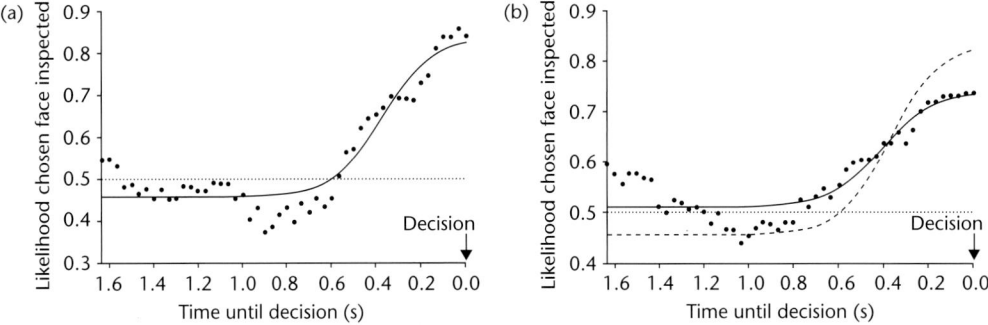

Figure 8.2 The results in the attractiveness/preference task. The likelihood that an observer's gaze was directed toward the chosen stimulus is plotted against the time left until decision (key press), and a four-parameter sigmoid function was fit. When the baseline attractiveness difference within the pair was maximized, and thus the task was difficult (a); and minimized, thus easy (b). (The figure is adopted from Shimojo, et al., 2003)) The dashed curve in (b) was replotted from (a) (preference, difficult) for a comparison.

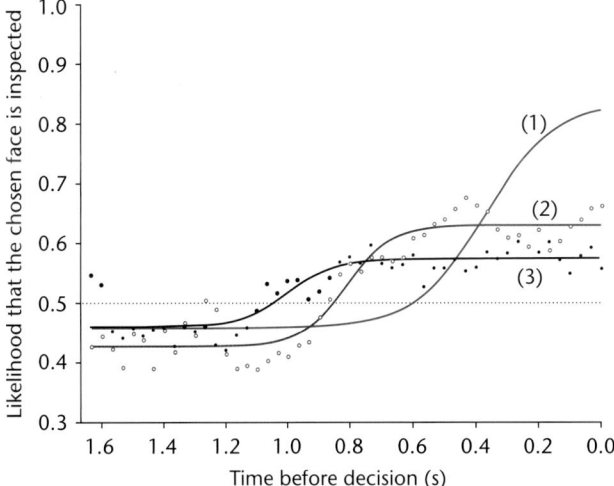

Figure 8.3 The results in control tasks: (1) face attractiveness, difficult (replotted), (2) face roundness. (3) face dislike.

A series of studies indicates generality and robustness of the gaze-cascade effect. In our initial experiment (discussed earlier), for instance, we matched the baseline attractiveness within a pair of faces, thus making the preference decision inevitably more difficult. One may ask if the gaze cascade occurs only in such a difficult preference decision. Intuitively, it may not occur if the attractiveness difference is obvious, even at the first glance of the pair.

To address this issue, we repeated the experiment while maximizing the average difference in attractiveness within pairs. As a result, we obtained a very similar gaze cascade curve (see Figure 8.2b, the solid curve; the dashed curve is the same as that in Figure 8.2a, replotted

for a comparison). The amplitude of elevation (to 74 percent) was significantly weaker than (83 percent) in the original experiment with minimum attractiveness differences, yet the other parameters to fit a sigmoid function (such as the onset timing) were highly similar.

People are highly sensitive to others' gaze directions, and this has been interpreted in relation to the significant social functions of gaze in communication (which will be discussed later). Thus, one may ask if either the gaze cascade effect itself or its characteristics may be susceptible to direct/averted gaze in stimulus faces. To address this, we manipulated the gaze direction in the face stimuli in the following three ways; (1) direct gaze (to the observer) in both faces, (2) averted

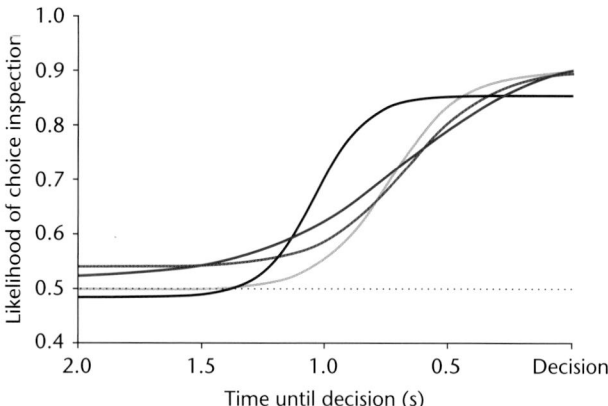

Figure 8.4 The results with gaze manipulation in face stimuli. Again, the likelihood of inspecting the chosen face is plotted against time till the decision response in the three conditions. The eye movement data in the gaze mixed condition (i.e., one face with its gaze straight in vs. the other with its gaze away) were further analyzed separately, depending on which face (gaze in or out) the subject chose. Thus the four conditions/situations are color coded. Light blue: both-away, red: both-forward, pink: mixed-forward, dark blue: mixed-away.

gaze in both faces, and (3) one face with direct gaze and the other with averted gaze (Simion & Shimojo, unpublished data). The procedures were otherwise the same as our original experiment. In the latter condition (3), we analyzed the gaze data separately for the trials in which the subject had chosen the gaze-toward face as more attractive (this happened in roughly 70 percent of trials) and for the trials in which the subject had chosen the gaze-away face (30 percent).

As a result, we obtained qualitatively similar gaze biases in all the conditions (Figure 8.4). Although the exact shape of the gaze likelihood curves varies to some extent, the likelihood curve reached 85–90 percent before the response in all conditions. What is particularly noticeable is the curve in the case in which the stimulus pair included both direct and averted gazes and subjects chose the face with averted gaze. The curve seems to have a steeper slope to reach an asymptote earlier than in the other three conditions/situation. It appears that the decision requires additional cognitive assessment based on the gaze in/out cues in the stimulus face, even after the sensory-motor system reached previously adequate thresholds.

So far, the gaze cascade effect was demonstrated only with face stimuli. One expectation, based on the robustness of the effect across a variety of gaze conditions, would be that the effect is intrinsically related to gaze contact or social interaction with gaze, thus limited to faces only. Faces are also massively experienced stimuli, and perhaps such massive experience may be necessary for the gaze cascade effect to occur. If so, the gaze cascade or any gaze bias should disappear with complex stimuli that subjects have never been exposed to. Interestingly, our results show quite the opposite: a similar gaze-cascade effect was found with geometric shapes (Fourier descriptors; see Figure 8.5). In fact, the amplitude of the effect is larger (up to 93 percent), while the other parameters are comparable. Unlike faces, these are highly-artificial stimuli, which the majority of the subjects had limited experience with, thus the subjects could not rely on their past experience to make the preference decision. Likewise, we found gaze cascade effects in commercial products, such as jewelry and watches, where parameters are similar to those in the original gaze cascade effect that is shown in Figure 8.2.

The other limitation in our initial paradigm was that it was only 2AFC. Most of our real-world choice decisions have more than two alternatives. Perhaps the gaze cascade may be tied to this severely constrained situation. To examine this issue, we ran another experiment with a 4AFC task in which the subject was asked to choose the most preferable one out of four faces. As a result, we found a qualitatively

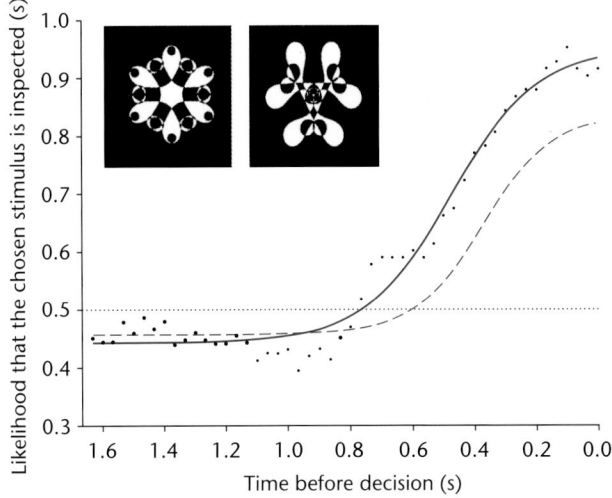

Figure 8.5 The results with complex geometrical figures (fourier descriptors). The way of analysis and plotting is the same as in the previous figures. The dashed curve is again replotted from Figure 8.2 (preference, difficult) for a comparison.

similar gaze bias, although it went up only to 38 percent of likelihood (as opposed to 25 percent at chance level) before the subject made a response (Figure 8.6a). To quantify how the subject proceeded to select the final choice from the four alternatives to begin with, we rank-ordered the four faces and defined gaze entropy as:

$$H = \sum -p_i \log_2 p_i$$

where p_i (*i* from 1 to 4) are the likelihood measures. As shown in Figure 8.6b, the gaze entropy measure explicitly quantifies how some face stimuli were gradually selected in (as well as out) over the time course to finally reach one choice. The subject assessed all four faces equally at the beginning, but toward the end of the trial he or she appeared to narrow the focus to two or three faces before making a choice.

Another issue that is theoretically significant is whether it is the orienting eye movement itself, or rather attention shift in general, not specific to eyes, that drive these effects. Although more studies may be needed to dissociate between overt and covert attention, we do have preliminary data that suggests that general orienting or attention shift is responsible for this cascadelike bias. The idea was to devise a comparable preference task in purely tactile domain, and we found a cascadelike bias of hand exploration that was qualitatively similar to the gaze cascade effect (Park & Shimojo, unpublished). So in short, eye

gaze is not a critical necessity for the effect, but rather, it is a combination of orientation, attention, and motor exploration that is critical.

To summarize, the gaze cascade effect is a very robust and general effect across a variety of stimuli and conditions.

IS THE GAZE BIAS A CRITICAL PART OF THE DECISION-MAKING PROCESS OF PREFERENCE?

The second main issue that was raised by the initial finding was whether orienting mechanisms (such as that for gaze shift) underlies, precedes, and plays an indispensable role in the preference decision-making process. If orienting mechanisms turn out to be a necessary component (at least under a natural free-view condition), it would be a very intriguing finding, particularly from the evolutionary and the developmental viewpoints.

As an alternative, however, it could rather be some kind of epiphenomenon that is not necessary or intrinsic to the decision-making process. To be more specific, for instance, one may argue that the subject perhaps makes a tentative decision subconsciously at one moment, and the subsequent gaze bias merely reflects their implicit efforts to gather more evidence for the decision.

This account has several logical problems. First, the task is a relative one, so to gather more evidence (for the tentative decision) one needs to compare both of the stimuli, not just the one to

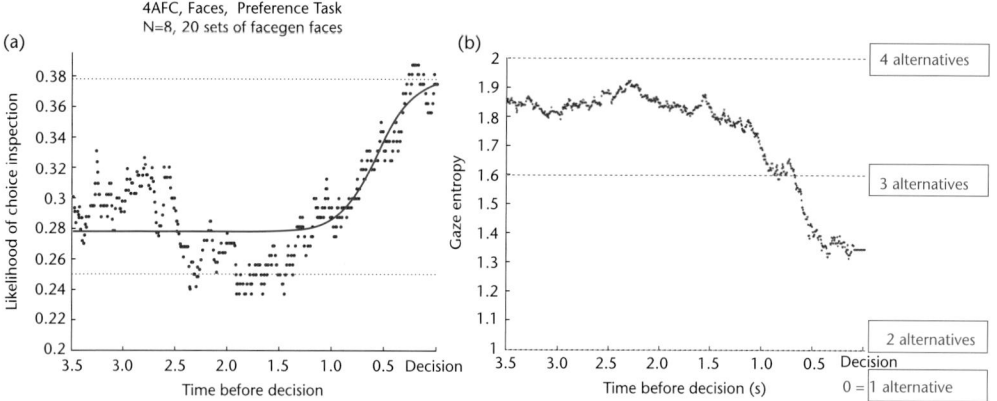

Figure 8.6 The results in 4-alternative, forced-choice, preference task. (a) The likelihood of inspecting the chosen face against time till the decision response. The way of analysis and plotting is the same as in the previous figures. Note, however, that the chance level is 25 percent in this case, and the scale of the ordinate is very different. (b) Gaze entropy, as defined in the text, is plotted against time till the decision response. Horizontal dashed lines indicate levels of the entropy for comparisons of 4, 3, 2, and 1 alternative(s), respectively.

be chosen. Second, there is no empirical way to nail down when this moment occurs, particularly considering that it is implicit by definition. As such, this account is based upon an assumption that is nearly impossible to prove or disprove empirically, Third, there is no *a priori* reason to assume that there is a single moment, as opposed to a dynamic process evolving over a substantial temporal scale during which all the relevant processing happens. Indeed, our data, which will be summarized next, strongly argue for the latter.

To some, this account may still be intuitively appealing. Thus in this section, we will summarize our follow-up findings, which strongly argue against such an explanation and in support for gaze as an important part of a dynamic process toward preference decision.

In what we call the peep-hole experiment (Simion & Shimojo, 2006), we presented two faces side by side on the display, as before. The task was the same, 2AFC preference decision. This time, however, the faces were mostly occluded, except for a small window that moves contingently with the gaze. The size of the visibility widow was adjusted such that only one facial feature (such as an eye, or a nose; see Figure 8.7a) could be seen at a time. Needless to say, this makes the task more laborious, and the subjects inevitably made large numbers of saccades within and across faces (the average performance time extended up to 29–31 sec, from 3.1–3.6 sec in the original experiment).

There were several possible outcomes. The gaze cascade effect would be entirely abolished if the distinctively holistic nature of face perception and initial matching of such a holistic input with an internally stored template of attractiveness (e.g., Perett, et al., 2002) is necessary for the effect to occur (although this possibility had been already refuted by the gaze cascade effect obtained with Fourier descriptors as mentioned earlier). Alternatively, there would be the same gaze cascade effect, again time-locked to the response within 1 sec, even though the overall performance time is significantly extended. This would be interpreted in terms of a response preparation because it would be natural for the subject to orient the gaze toward the responding side. Finally, the same gaze cascade would be observed but in extended timescale in accordance with the extension of the performance time.

The last possibility was indeed consistent with the result, as illustrated in Figure 8.7b. As can be seen, the onset time of the bias (according to the best fit with a sigmoid function) was 7.5 sec, as opposed to 0.8 sec in the original experiment. This finding has an indirect but significant implication with regard to our main question (i.e., whether the orienting mechanism is intrinsically involved in the decision-making process of preference). More than several seconds before the final response, the subjects were still vigorously

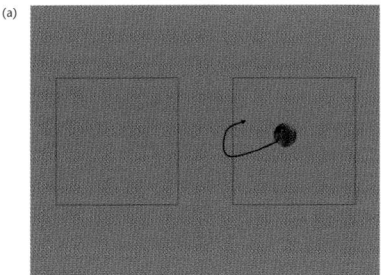

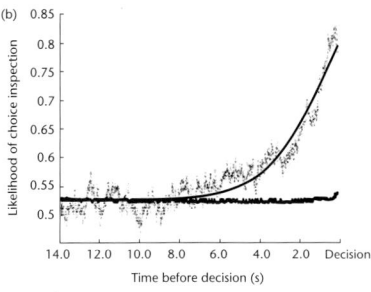

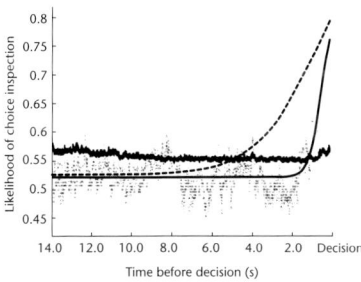

Figure 8.7 The peep-hole experiment. (a) Stimulus display (a snapshot). Only the foveal part was visible at a time, and the window of visibility moves with gaze. (b) gaze cascade curves for the face preference task (top), and the face roundness task (bottom). The thin dots are the likelihood data (time-binned), whereas the thick curve is a sigmoid function fit with four parameters in each graph. The corresponding significance thresholds are also plotted (and are variable because of changes in sample size due to blinks, saccades, or trial shorter than 14s). (modified from Simion and Shimojo, 2006, Figure 8.1 and 8.2)

collecting local sensory information (perhaps to construct internal representations of the two faces that are detailed enough for preference decision). However, such local sensory sampling was already starting to show bias toward the final choice.

The core aspect of the alternative account was that gaze was shifted more toward the to-be-chosen face *in order to* gather more sensory evidence for the tentative decision. For this purpose, needless to say, the face had to be present there when accessed with a gaze, and this gave us another opportunity to test this account. In yet another experiment, we first measured variation of performance time in each subject. Then, in the main experiment, we erased the two faces from the display altogether, at various times with regard to the mean performance time of the subject. As a result, we had two types of trials: early-decision trials, in which the subject made a response before the display became blank, and late-decision trials in which it made a response only after the display was turned off. The critical question was whether or not the gaze likelihood (on the to-be-chosen face) would still increase after the disappearance of faces, particularly in the late-decision trials. The gathering-evidence account would not predict this in late-decision trials, whereas if the increase is still seen in the late-decision trials, it may indicate that gaze is a part of the dynamic process toward the conscious decision.

The results were consistent with the latter prediction, as shown in Figure 8.8. The oblique ellipse underscores the critical finding here, that is, the likelihood of gaze to the chosen face kept increasing even after it was removed from the display in the late-decision trials. The curve was certainly slower and noisier, but it was also predicted because the subject had already responded by the time of the disappearance in some trials. Thus the results are consistent only with the idea that gaze shift is an inevitable part of the dynamic process over time toward the conscious decision making of preference.

CAN PREFERENCE BE MANIPULATED BY MANIPULATING GAZE?

If the gaze shift is an intrinsic component of the process toward preference decision making, then we may be able to manipulate preference decisions to some extent by manipulating their gaze behavior. This would be even stronger evidence for gaze as an intrinsic component of the preference-decision-making process.

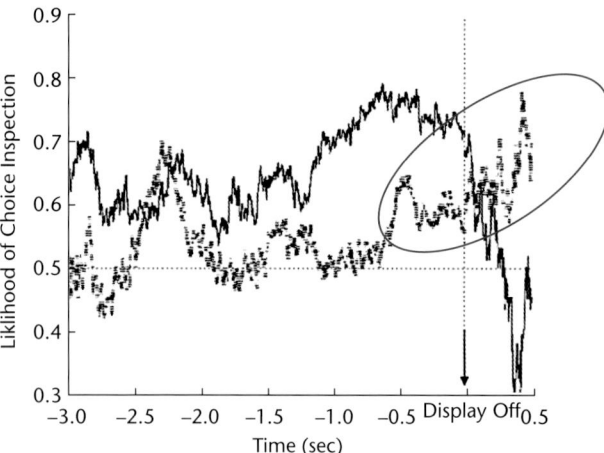

Figure 8.8 The result of the display-off experiment. Likelihood of choice inspection is plotted against time to the moment when the display was blanked. The arrow indicates the moment when the display was off (not the moment of key pressing, unlike the previous figures). The thick curve represents the result in early-decision trials in which the subject responded before the display was turned off. The thin curve represents that in late-decision trials in which the subject responded only after the display was turned off. The oblique ellipse underscores the critical finding here, that is, the likelihood of gaze to the chosen face kept increasing even after the display off in the late trials (but not in early trials, as expected). (modified from Simion and Shimojo, 2007, Figure 8.2)

We again presented two faces side by side, but unlike our original paradigm, we presented one face and the other alternately with different durations (900 ms vs. 300 ms) (Shimojo et al., 2003). This cycle of presentation was repeated twice, 6 times, or 12 times. Note that the same face was presented always on the same side (right or left) of the screen, but never presented simultaneously. Thus, the subject naturally followed one face and then the other with their gaze. Toward the end of each trial, the two faces are briefly presented simultaneously (500 ms), and the subject had to indicate which face was more preferable by pressing a button.

The preference was at chance level between the longer- and the shorter-duration faces after 2 cycles of repetition, but significantly above chance level after 6 and 12 cycles (59.0 percent, $p < 0.001$ for 6 cycle, and 59.2 percent, $p < 0.005$ for 12 cycle, respectively). The same qualitative result was obtained when the faces were presented top and bottom of the screen (60.2 percent, $p < 0.0001$); thus the manipulation effect is not related to the specific layout of the faces.

It has long been known, however, that repeated mere exposure to the same object/stimulus increases attractiveness of it monotonously (Zajonc, 1968). In order to see if the manipulation effect on preference was due to the mere exposure effect, or if the spontaneous engagement of the subjects with their gaze was critical, we performed two follow-up experiments. In the first, we repeated the same procedure with identical stimulus sequences, but did not allow the subject's to make eye movements away from the fixation point which stayed at the center until the subject's choice response. In the second, we again asked the subject to maintain their eye fixation and presented the two faces with different durations alternately at the fixation/fovea (thus, two faces looked as if superimposed on top of each other). In either case, we did not observe a preference rate significantly different from the chance level (45.8 and 49.8 percent, respectively). Finally, to see if this manipulation is specific to the preference task or more general, we tried the same gaze manipulation in the round-face task (to choose the face which is rounder). Again, we were not successful in creating a significant bias in the subject's judgment (51.8 percent).

It may also be worth mentioning that, when interviewing subjects after the session, the majority of the subjects did not notice the bias in presentation durations (and thus their gaze bias), and even those who did notice denied any causal relationship of it to their final preference decision. At the 6-repetition level, 2 out of the 11 subjects reported that they were vaguely aware. At the 12-repetition level, more than half (7 of 10) were aware. However, none of them admitted that the gaze bias had anything to do with their final preference decision. We found basically the same in the original gaze-cascade experiment (with free inspection) in general. Thus, the role of gaze shift in preference decision is indeed implicit in two distinctive senses; first, they are often not aware of the gaze bias itself, and second, they actively deny the causal link to the final cognitive decision.

To consistently interpret both the gaze cascade findings and the gaze manipulation findings, the gaze as an intrinsic component seems to be the only simple and feasible account. One may still ask how strong this manipulation could be. To address this, we prepared a series of face pairs, whose baseline difference in attractiveness had systematically varied from minimal to maximal. The expectation was that perhaps minimal differences in attractiveness might be easily reversed by gaze manipulation, but maximal difference may be more difficult. Against this expectation, our results suggest that even the largest baseline differences can be partly reversed by gaze manipulation, approximately at the same frequency (15 percent of trials) as minimal differences (Simion & Shimojo, unpublished data). Thus, the gaze manipulation turned out to have a substantial influence on the subject's preference decision.

NEURAL CORRELATES OF PREFERENCE DECISION

To identify the neural correlates of processes (including the gaze bias) that precede the conscious preference decision, we recorded EEG (32 channels) while the subject performed the preference tasks (on faces or Fourier descriptors), control tasks (roundness, or dislike of face), or passively viewing the stimuli.

Our preliminary data (Bhattacharya, Simion, & Shimojo, unpublished data) indicated that there was stronger neural activity in the frontal channels in the preference tasks, regardless of the stimuli, relative to the control tasks or the passive viewing. Such a task-specific increase of activity was particularly noticeable in the final 1 sec before the key-pressing response, which roughly corresponds to the duration of the gaze cascade. Thus, the EEG data are consistent with the behavioral finding of the gaze cascade effect.

To localize the brain regions that are relevant to the preference-decision task, fMRI may be more preferable. There are, however, a couple of factors that made the original gaze cascade paradigm unsuitable to obtain meaningful fMRI data. First, presenting two faces prevents us from contrasting brain response to one face (say, chosen as more attractive) against that to the other. Second, allowing free inspection, thus eye movements, add extra noise to the MRI signals. For these reasons, we abandoned the original paradigm, and devised another behavioral paradigm of preference decision, which was, in our opinion, much more suitable for fMRI (Kim, Adolphs, O'Doherty, & Shimojo, 2007).

Figure 8.9a illustrates the procedures. While it was still a 2AFC preference decision task, only one face was presented briefly (50 ms) at a time, then the other, sequentially with a random variable interval (1–3 sec.). The same two faces were thus repeatedly presented sequentially until the subject made a choice. Note that this procedure allows us to isolate the brain responses to each face, and to search for neural signals that predict the conscious preference decision later. Also, it was expected to enable us to overcome the limitation in the temporal resolution of fMRI, and to identify dynamic changes of activity in the brain, from the initial stimulus presentation to the final response. Thus we call it the temporally extended decision–making (TED) paradigm. Owing to this paradigm, we expected to see an earlier contrast (e.g., more neural activation to the to-be-chosen face) at a subcortical level, and a later contrast at a cortical level.

Figure 8.9b shows the fMRI results. Since most of the subjects responded during the second cycle in the vast majority of the trials, our analysis concentrated on the second-cycle trials. As shown in the figure, there are three distinctive areas that were activated during the preference decision between faces: the nucleus accumbens

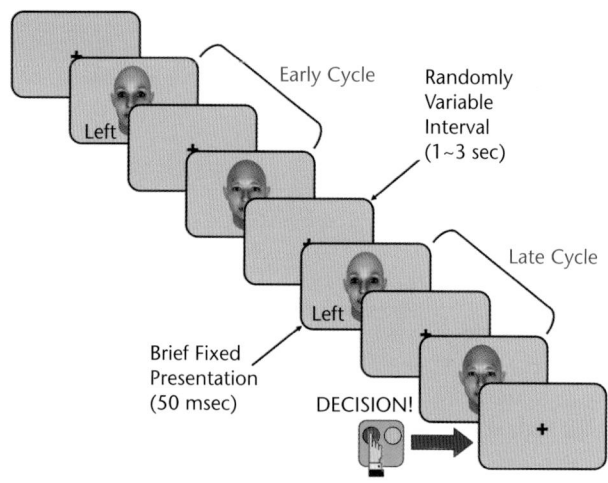

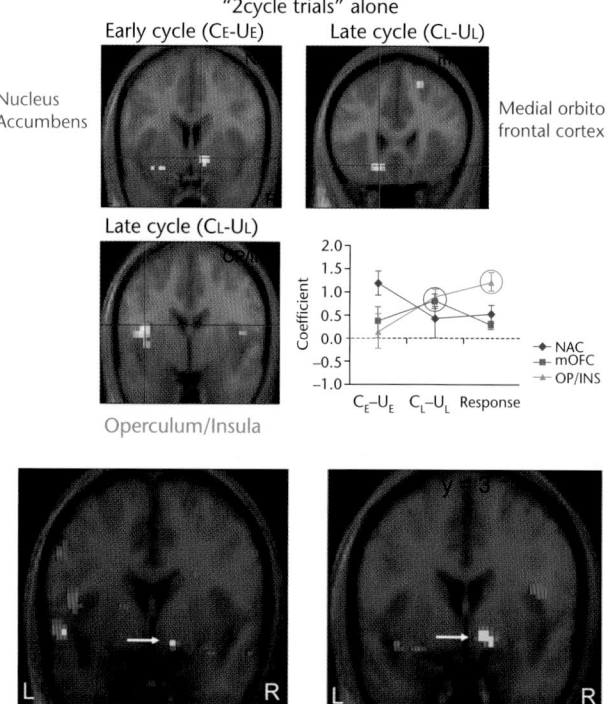

Figure 8.9 The fMRI study of preference decision. (a) The TED (Temporally Extended Decision) paradigm. The same face pair was presented sequentially and repeatedly till the subject made a decision response. We call the initial presentations of the two faces "early cycle", and the second presentations "late cycle". (b) The results: three areas, the nucleus accumbens (NAC; top left), the medial orbitofrontal cortex (mOFC; top right), and the operculum/insula (OP/INS), were more activated in response to the to-be-chosen face, in this time order. As shown in the bottom right graph, in which relative neural activity is plotted against time (early cycle, late cycle, and immediately before the response), each of the three areas has its own activity peak at a distinctively different timing. (c) The fMRI result of the implicit preference task (left; the brain signals during the roundness task, analyzed with regard to the preference decisions later), in comparison with that of the explicit preference task (same as b, shown again for a comparison). The white arrows both indicate activation of the NAC. (modified from Kim, et al., 2007)

(NAC), the medial orbito-frontal cortex (mOFC), and the operculum/insula (OP/INS).

The dynamic changes of neural activity in these areas were of particular interest. As shown in the graph at the bottom right in the figure, where we plotted the contrast between the to-be-chosen and the not-to-be-chosen faces, the three areas had different peak timings: the NAC showed a very early difference in the first cycle, while the mOFC had its activity peak in the second cycle. Interestingly, activity in these areas decreased toward the response, and instead, the OP/INS increased their activity presumably to prepare for the motor response. The overall pattern of the results was highly consistent with our expectation in that (1) there were early differential signals in subcortical regions that predict the conscious preference decision, but (2) it was replaced by differential signals in cortical areas before the motor response.

Since the NAC is a subcortical area known to be activated during reward-related learning, preference decision and affective aspects (see Kim et al., 2007 for original references), it may be reasonable to assume that activation of this area may be the implicit precursor of conscious preference decision. However, is it really implicit, and in what specific sense?

We came up with yet another set of experimental designs to address these issues. Another group of subjects (n = 11) performed the preference and the control (face-roundness) tasks in a reversed order relative to those performed by the first group; that is, this time the new group performed the control task first, and then the preference task in the scanner. We then examined whether the NAC during the roundness task would still show the same contrast between the preferable and the nonpreferable faces, even though the subjects were not asked for it in the first session. Thus we analyzed the fMRI data during the roundness task in the first session, while utilizing the preference decision data on the same face pairs that were taken during the preference task in the second session in this group of subjects.

Figure 8.9c shows the results of this analysis of group 2 is on the left side, and those of the original analysis in group 1 (explicit preference-decision task in the first session) on the right side, for a comparison. The NAC was again activated more for the preferable face (indicated by the white arrows), even when the task was irrelevant. Note that this means that NAC activity during the first session with an irrelevant task predicts (at least in a statistical sense) which face the subject will choose as more attractive in future. Thus, the NAC responds to attractiveness of faces, regardless of task (thus implicit and reflexive/automatic), although the differential signals were limited to the first encounters to the faces (thus we may call it "the first impression" activity).

Note again that the results of the fMRI study cannot be directly compared with the behavioral gaze-cascade findings because of the different ways of stimulus presentation and the observation conditions (whether free eye movements are allowed). Nonetheless, together they strongly point to a conclusion that even though preference decision is seemingly based on free will, an implicit stimulus-driven process more or less determines it, and this process is reflected both in orienting behavior (e.g., eye movements) as well as subcortical neural activity.

SUMMARY AND IMPLICATIONS

In this chapter, we reviewed our recent series of findings that link eye orienting (saccade) mechanism to conscious preference judgment.

First, we found a systematic gaze bias preceding a cognitive preference decision (the gaze cascade effect), but such bias was very specific to preference (i.e., relative attractiveness) judgment. Second, the effect turned out to be very robust across a variety of conditions, including when the preference task was easy, when gaze direction in the face stimulus was manipulated, when the preference was on objects other than faces (such as geometric figures or commercial products), when the preference was not 2-alternative, but rather 4-alternative, and so on. Third, we raised a question as to whether the gaze bias is a critical part of the decision-making process of preference. The results of the peep-hole and the display-off experiments were inconsistent with the prediction from an alternative hypothesis (the gathering-more-evidence hypothesis; see earlier), but were consistent with our account that the gaze cascade is a natural and indispensable precursor of cognitive preference decision. Fourth, if the latter explanation is true, we should be able to manipulate people's preference decision by merely manipulating their gaze-shift pattern. The results of a gaze-manipulation experiment support this notion. Moreover, we were able to reverse the preference decision even when baseline attractiveness differences were maximized within the face pair. Fifth, our EEG data are largely consistent with the behavioral findings, indicating frontal-lobe activity specific to the preference decision approximately 1 sec. ahead of the decision response. For technical reasons, we could not use the same paradigm (with two faces presented simultaneously while allowing free inspection) in thefMRI session. Yet, the data strongly suggest that implicit neural process, most likely at a subcortical level, precedes and determines the conscious preference decision.

As explained in the introduction, these findings strongly implicate such implicit orienting mechanisms as the developmental origin of conscious emotional decision; implicit bodily preference precedes explicit conscious preference, not vice versa, both in the developmental sense as well as in the on-line process leading to preference decision in adults.

COEVOLUTION SCENARIO?

In group-living primates that typically have rigid social hierarchies, gaze is frequently used by dominants as a mild form of threat to subordinates (Redican, 1975). By contrast, in all great apes, prolonged gazing or eye contact between conspecifics is often used for different social purposes, such as for sharing of food (Bard, 1990; van Schaik, van Deaner,& Merrill, 1999). For example, social staring accompanied by begging behavior is used to solicit food sharing, which is a unique foraging behavior of chimps and bonobos (Idani, 1995). Similar observations have been made in orangutans (Bard, 1990). Food sharing rarely occurs in gorillas, but subordinates use gaze staring to dominants as a request for withdrawal from feeding spots, and this is usually successful (Yamagiwa, 2004).

Thus, in a broader scope of evolution, gaze most likely had social functions even before the human species. And needless to say, the social significance of gaze became even more important in humans (Emery, 2000). Since eye contact has a critical role in a variety of human societies and cultures, the findings that we have reviewed here may have substantial relevance for nonverbal implicit communications. However, we need to be careful when attempting to make connections because we have also found that the same type of gaze cascade occurs when one makes a preference decision over nonface objects, such as geometric shapes or commercial products (see earlier).

Since preference for objects should have preceded preference for faces in the history of mammalian evolution, it may be highly *unlikely* that the gaze cascade mechanism has originally evolved from social communication skills, which are unique to the human species. Rather, it may have its origin in the links across attention, orienting, and liking in general. Nonetheless, one may still argue that the orienting mechanisms that had originally developed to search for food and a better environment for survival may later be highjacked by a relatively new function of gaze as a social signal.

There is abundant evidence in the psychophysics literature that human observers are very sensitive to gaze direction. When somebody stares at you among a crowd, he or she sticks out of the crowd and effortlessly draws your attention (e.g., von Grunau & Anston, 1995). Why we are so sensitive to this particular aspect of visual face information has been left unanswered, except for a vague speculation that perhaps it is useful for social life. The series of findings that we reported in this chapter may possibly be the first to answer this question. In short, if gaze shift is a necessary modulator of the dynamic mind-body system that generates conscious preference (at least in natural social situation), then carefully observing the gaze direction of one's communication partner would be highly beneficial because that is indeed a reliable indicator of generating an affective decision in the person.

One could further speculate that there may have been a co-evolution process, that is, a sort of mutual facilitation process between the two—the gaze-orienting mechanism that modulates/generates preference decisions on one hand, and the perceptual mechanism to be very sensitive to others' gaze direction and shift on the other hand. In short, presence of one mechanism among the other group members may have provided a selection pressure to the other mechanism to evolve faster, and vice versa.

Although this remains purely speculative, some studies on patients with emotional disorders are consistent with this. Patients with amygdala damage typically have social problems because they often have difficulty in reading emotion in others' faces. This no doubt creates difficulties with spouses, family members, and caretakers as well, to deal with patients in their daily social interactions. Adolphs and his colleagues (Adolphs et al., 2005) found that amygdala patients rarely looked at the eyes in face photos. They further demonstrated that this was the fundamental cause of their problems in judging emotion from facial expressions by showing a remarkable improvement once the patients were trained to look at the eyes.

Eye gaze and orienting seem to be a promising key to reveal interface between the implicit and the explicit processes, and relationship between body and mind in general. Although the findings that are reviewed here have some philosophical implications (in relation to the James-Lange claim, as mentioned in the introduction), they may have more pragmatic implications in medicine (rehabilitation in particular), education, BMI (Brain-Machine-Interface) technology, consumer behavior, and marketing.

REFERENCES

Adolphs, R., Gosselin, F., Buchanan, T. W., Tranel, D., Schyns, P., & Damasio, A. R. (2005). A mechanism for impaired fear recognition after amygdala damage. *Nature, 433*, 68–72.

Bard, K. (1992). Intentional behavior and intentional communication in young free-ranging orangutans. *Child Development, 63*, 1186–1197.

Baron-Cohen, S. (1995). *Mindblindness: An essay on autism and theory of mind.* Cambridge, MA: MIT Press.

Emery, N. J. (2000). The eyes have it: The neuroethology, function and evolution of social gaze.

Neuroscience & Biobehavioral Reviews, 24, 581–604.

Idani, G. (1995). Function of peering behavior among bonobos (Pan Paniscus) at Wamba, Zaire. *Primates, 36*, 377–383.

Kim, H., Adolphs, R., O'Doherty, J. P., & Shimojo, S. (2007). Temporal isolation of neural processes underlying face preference decision. *Proceedings of the National Academy of Sciences, 104*, 18253–18258.

Haith, M. M., Bergman, T., & Moore, M. J. (1977). Eye contact and face scanning in early infancy. *Science, 198*, 853–855.

Perret, D. I., Penton-Voak, I. S., Little, A. C., Tiddeman, B. P., Burt, D. M., Schmidt, N., Oxley, R., Kinloch, N., & Barrett, L. (2002). Facial attractiveness judgments reflect learning of parental age characteristics. *Proceedings of the Royal Society B, 269*, 873–880.

Redican, W. K. (1975). Facial expressions in nonhuman primates. In Rosenblum, L. A. (ed.), *Primate Behavior: Developments in Field and Laboratory Research* (Vol. 4). Academic Press, 104–194.

Shimojo, S., Simion, C., Shimojo, E., et al. (2003). Gaze bias both reflects and influences preference. *Nature Neuroscience, 6*, 1317–1322.

Simion, C., & Shimojo, S. (2006). Early interactions between orienting, visual sampling and decision making in facial preference. *Vision Research, 46*, 3331–3335.

Simion, C., & Shimojo, S. (2007). Interrupting the cascade:Orienting contributes to decision making even in the absence of visual stimulation. *Perception and Psychophysics, 69*, 591–595.

Van Schaik, C. P., Deaner, R. O., & Merrill, M. Y. (1999). The conditions for tool use in primates: implications for the evolution of material culture. *Journal of Human Evolution, 36*, 719–741.

Von Grunau, M., & Anston, C. (1995). The detection of gaze direction: A stare-in-the-crowd effect. *Perception, 24*, 1297–1313.

Yamagiwa, J. (2004). Diet and foraging of the great apes: Ecological constraints on their social organizations and implications for their divergence. In Russon, A. E. & Begun, D. R. (Eds.), *The Evolution of Thought Evolutionary Origins of Great Ape Intelligence.* Cambridge Univ. Press, 210–233.

Zajonc, R. B. (1968). Attitudinal effects of mere exposure. *Journal of Personality and Social Psychology Monograph,* Supplement, *9*, 1–27.

CHAPTER 9

Facial Attractiveness

Anthony C. Little and David I. Perrett

THE POWER OF FACIAL BEAUTY

The human face has been a source of great interest to psychologists and other scientists in recent years because of the extraordinarily well-developed ability of humans to process, recognize, and draw information from others' faces. Scientists are not alone in their interest in human faces; human beings generally appear to be fascinated by the faces of others. Faces cover our magazines and posters, television and movie cameras focus our attention on the face, and a portrait without a face is a very odd thing indeed. Faces dominate our works of art, ancient and modern, and our sensitivity to faces is highlighted when we see faces in many everyday shapes under ambiguous conditions, such as in clouds or the face of the man in the moon. Human infants only minutes old attend particularly to face like stimuli compared to equally complicated non-face stimuli (Goren, Sarty, & Wu, 1975; Johnson, Dziurawiec, Ellis, & Morton, 1991).

Our magazines and television screens are not just filled with any faces; they are filled with attractive faces, and both women and men are highly concerned with good looks in a potential partner. Beauty impacts our lives in many ways not only because we are attempting to attract the attention of beautiful people to be our partners, but also because our attractiveness affects the way that people behave toward us.

Physical attractiveness is a major asset in sexual exchange. Beauty is associated with upward economic mobility, especially for females (Elder 1969; Holmes & Hatch 1938). Attractive people have more dates than less attractive people. Berscheid and colleagues (1971) and Walster, Aronson, Abrahams, & Rottman (1966) found that after random pairing for a computer-date dance the main determinant of whether participants would like to date their partner again was that partner's independently rated physical attractiveness. In a more ecologically valid setting the same result has been found using real dating frequencies from a computer dating agency, with independently rated attractiveness being the best predictor of those selected most often by others for dates (Riggio & Woll 1984).

Experimental studies have also demonstrated the many advantages of attractiveness. It has long been noted that there exists a "What is beautiful is good" stereotype (Dion, Berscheid, & Walster, 1972), whereby attractive individuals are perceived to possess a variety of positive personality attributions. For example, in Dion et al.'s study, attractive individuals were thought to be able to achieve more prestigious occupations, be more competent spouses with happier marriages, and have better prospects for personal fulfilment (Dion et al. 1972). There have been a wealth of studies examining this attractiveness stereotype, mainly demonstrating that attractive people are seen in positive light for a wide range of attributes compared to unattractive people (although some negative attributes, such as vanity, do get attributed to attractive individuals, e.g., Dermer & Thiel 1975). In mock interviews attractive people are more likely to be hired than less attractive individuals (Cash & Kilcullen 1985) and attractiveness can also influence judgements about the seriousness of committed crimes (Sigall & Ostrove 1975). Feingold (1992) reports that, for both males and females, attractive individuals report more satisfying and more pleasurable interactions with others than less attractive individuals. Outside the laboratory, attractive people also appear to lead favorable lives; attractive individuals pay lower bail (Downs & Lyons 1991) and are more likely to be hired for jobs (Chiu & Babcock 2002; Marlowe, Schneider, & Nelson, 1996) than less attractive individuals. On the basis of such studies it has been suggested that there exists a positive stereotype associated with physical attractiveness (see Eagly, Ashmore, Makhijani, & Longo, 1991; Feingold 1992; Langlois et al. 2000 for meta-analytic reviews of research on physical attractiveness stereotypes).

The social impact of facial appearance is not restricted to adulthood; attractiveness appears to elicit more positive reaction from infancy. Langlois, Ritter, Casey, & Solwin (1995) found that mothers are more nurturing to attractive babies than unattractive babies, using both self-report and observational methods, and Barden, Ford, Jensen, & Salyer (1989) found a similar pattern in facially deformed babies, with deformed babies receiving less loving behavior than a control group. In both of these cases the mothers were unaware that their behavior was less nurturing. In preschoolers it has been found that both boys and girls preferred pictures of attractive peers as potential friends and rejected unattractive children, and that attractive peers were expected to behave prosocially and unattractive peers to exhibit antisocial behavior (Dion & Berscheid 1974). In natural situations, experiments on group membership in children have also shown a positive correlation between facial attractiveness and acceptance by groups (Krebs & Adinolfi 1975).

In a classic study, Snyder, Tanke, & Berscheid (1977) found evidence that beauty may impact

on the behavior of the perceived. In a telephone conversation, males who believed the female they were conversing with was attractive were judged to be more positive and socially interested in the person on the phone by independent judges than those who thought they were interacting with an unattractive person. The behavior of the women interacting with the men also changed according to whether the person talking to them thought they were attractive or unattractive. Those women that had a partner who thought that they were attractive behaved in a more confident way and also believed that the partnered male liked them more than those in the group where the partnered male was told the woman was less attractive. Thus, not only does attractiveness change the way others interact with us, it also changes the way we interact with them.

The data just reviewed indicates that attractive people appear to be treated differently than unattractive people despite a prevalent belief, at least in Western society, that one should not judge a book by its cover. This highlights the influence that facial attractiveness can have on our social interactions as well as our mating behavior. Despite the findings of what facial attractiveness can influence, there is still much debate about what is attractive about attractive faces and what is unattractive about unattractive faces.

Beauty has major social consequences, but exactly what it is that makes a face beautiful is poorly defined. One of the major deterrents in determining the features of an attractive face lies in the widespread belief that standards of attractiveness are learned gradually through exposure to culturally presented ideals (e.g., through the media in western society) and this has also led to a general belief that cultures vary dramatically in what they perceive to be attractive. If this were true it would mean that attractiveness was arbitrary and what is beautiful now could, in a different time or place, be considered unattractive. The well-known phrase "beauty is in the eye of the beholder" is a testament to our belief that attractiveness is ephemeral. For example, the philosopher David Hume is often quoted for making the argument

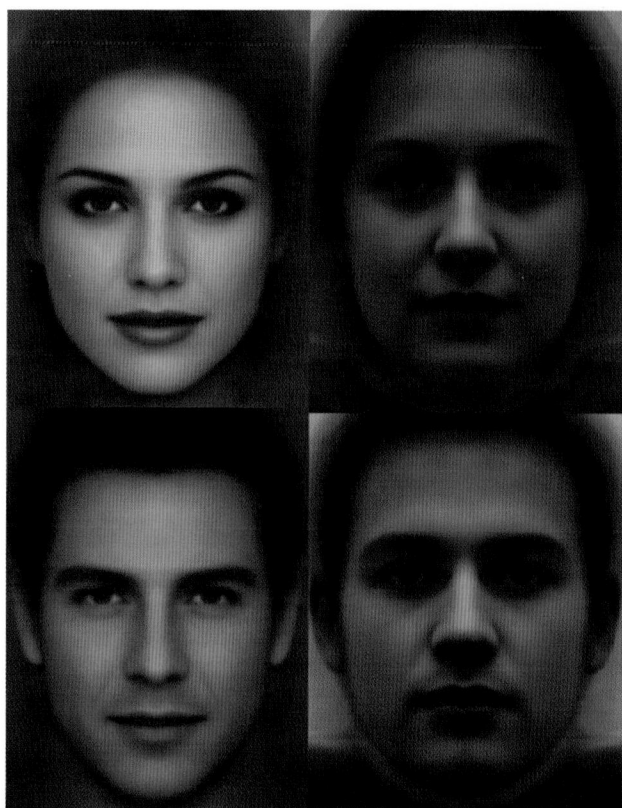

Figure 9.1 Male and female students versus model composites. The pictures on the left are composite images of celebrities whereas the images in the right are composite images of students. People usually agree on which of each pair is the most attractive.

that beauty, "is no quality in things themselves: it exists merely in the mind which contemplates them; and each mind contemplates a different beauty" (Hume, 1757, pp. 208–209).

Darwin (1871) was also struck by cultural differences, such as preferences for skin color, body hair, body fat, and practices such as lip ornamentation and teeth filing, "*It is certainly not true that there is in the mind of man any universal standards of beauty with respect to the human body.*" (Darwin cited by Berscheid & Walster 1974). Such convictions were supported by early cross-cultural work by Ford and Beach (1951) who catalogued differences between cultures in preferences for body weight, breast size, and other aspects of female physique and suggested little consensus.

Although individual and cross-cultural differences exist (see later) something in this politically correct view of beauty just does not ring true. Admittedly the latest movie star is not everyone's favorite pinup but it is undeniable that, on average,

Hollywood stars are generally more attractive than the people we meet in the street. You may disagree over your best friend's choice of partner, but there are countless individuals that you and your friend could agree were more or less attractive than each particular partner (e.g., Figure 9.1). So this is the problem with beauty being only in the eye of the beholder: some people are beautiful and some people are not, and most people agree on who is and is not beautiful.

It appears then that there are certain features of faces that are attractive to all (or at least the majority of) judges. In fact, agreement between individuals is one of the best-documented and most robust findings in facial attractiveness research since the 1970s. Across many studies, it has been found that there is a high degree of agreement from individuals within a particular culture and also high agreement between individuals from different cultures (e.g., Cunningham, Roberts Barbee, & Druen, 1995; see Langlois et al. 2000 for a meta-analytic review). If different people can agree on which faces are attractive and which faces are not attractive when judging faces of varying ethnic background, then this suggests that people everywhere are all using the same, or at least similar, criteria in their judgements.

Further evidence for universal attractiveness criteria comes from studies of infants. When infants (3–6 months of age) are shown faces that have been judged by adults for attractiveness, they prefer to look at faces that are rated more highly for attractiveness than at those faces rated lower (Langlois et al. 1987; Samuels et al. 1994). Langlois, Ritter, Roggman, & Vaughn (1991) have demonstrated that this preference in infants for attractive faces also holds across cultures (using Caucasian and non-Caucasian faces). It, therefore, appears that before any substantial exposure to cultural standards of attractiveness infants demonstrate a preference for attractive faces that are in agreement with adult judgements. Again, this suggests a set of criteria for attractiveness that are possessed by attractive faces and possessed by less attractive faces.

From the studies outlined in this section it has been suggested that there is something innate about attractiveness, that human children (and adults) have a biologically based, universal attractiveness detector (Langlois & Roggman 1990). A different explanation also put forward by Langlois & Roggman (1990) is that the visual system is able to extract average or prototypic characteristics from, for example, the faces that an individual is exposed to. Such prototype formation in the visual system, forms the basis of many models of face processing (see Bruce & Young 1986). Comparing encountered faces to a stored face prototype may then influence our preferences. Faces that appear more typical or closer to the average of the category of faces may be judged more positively because they look familiar or normal (see the discussion of the attractiveness of averageness later)." At the very least, the studies reviewed suggest that attractiveness is recognized at a much earlier age than most would expect and that, contrary to popular belief, there is much agreement in what is and what is not attractive about faces across

human cultures. Both early developmental and cross-cultural agreement on attractiveness are evidence against the notion that attractiveness ideals are slowly absorbed by those growing up within a particular culture, and this suggests that there is something universal about attractive faces (and unattractive faces) that is recognized both across individuals and cultures, and in adults and very early in infancy. In the next section we discuss three traits that are proposed to be attractive, based on evolutionary theoretical reasoning, but we will return to the notion of individual variation later.

FACE TRAITS ASSOCIATED WITH ATTRACTION

Physical appearance is important to humans, and there appear to be certain features that are found attractive across individuals and cultures. The same holds true across the animal kingdom: most nonhuman species rely on external factors, such as the size, shape, and color of adornments (e.g., feathers, fur, and fins) to attract mates. Research on animals has focused on individual traits that are attractive across individuals, and even species, such as symmetry (e.g., Møller & Thornhill 1998a). An evolutionary view assumes that perception and preferences serve an adaptive function: The external world provides information to guide biologically and socially functional behaviors (Zebrowitz-McArthur & Baron 1983). If, in our evolutionary past, information was present about a person's value (e.g., genetic quality) in any way, then an advantage would accrue for those who utilized these signs and those individuals would leave more genes behind in the next generation. Theoretically then, preferences guide us to choose mates that will provide the best chance of our genes surviving.

In many studies, this evolutionary view of attractiveness has been used to predict the specific characteristics of attractive faces (Thornhill & Gangestad 1999 for review). The three main factors that have been proposed to advertise the biological quality of an individual via the human face, and hence to influence attractiveness as a mate, are averageness, symmetry, and secondary sexual characteristics (see also Rhodes 2006 for meta-analysis).

Facial Averageness

The averageness of a face is related to how closely it resembles the majority of other faces within a population. Average faces are not distinctive and nonaverage faces have more extreme and recognizable characteristics.

Evolutionary View

Average faces are proposed to be attractive because the possession of features that are close to a population average in shape, size, or configuration is potentially linked to genetic heterozygosity/diversity (Mitton & Grant 1984; Thornhill & Gangestad 1993). Thornhill and Gangestad (1993) have argued that average faces may be attractive because the owners of average faces possess a diverse set of genes. Such genetic diversity may result in the owner producing less common proteins to which common pathogens are poorly adapted. Parasites are generally best adapted to proteins that are common in the host population, hence parasites are adapted to the genes that code for the production of these proteins. This would mean that those possessing average faces would be less susceptible to parasitism than those with less average features. A second evolutionary-based theory is that extreme (nonaverage) genotypes are more likely to be homozygous for deleterious alleles, that is, to be more likely to possess genes that are detrimental to an individual than those with more average genotypes (Thornhill & Gangestad 1993). Both of these theories propose evolutionary benefits to mating with those possessing average faces.

Averageness and Actual Quality

There is only limited evidence that averageness in faces is linked to health and/or fertility, though there are very few studies that address this question. Following the preceding logic on genetic diversity, it has been shown that heterozygosity in the major histocompatibility complex (MHC) is positively related to male facial attractiveness (Roberts et al. 2005). MHC genes code for proteins involved in immune response and

so choice of heterozygous individuals, via facial cues, is consistent with choosing mates that are likely to pass on a diverse immune response to the chooser's offspring. As noted earlier genetic heterozygosity/diversity could be related to average features (Mitton & Grant 1984; Thornhill & Gangestad 1993). More directly, another study has shown that facial averageness is positively related to medical health as measured from actual medical records in both men and women (Rhodes et al. 2001b). In this study, facial distinctiveness was negatively correlated with health (Rhodes et al. 2001b).

Is Averageness Attractive in Human Faces?

Averageness has been found to be attractive in real faces. For example, Light, Hollander, and Kayra-Stuart (1981) found that in real male faces, more-attractive faces were rated as less distinctive. A second line of evidence comes from studies that manipulate the averageness of faces. Francis Galton (1878) was one of the first to propose that facial attractiveness may relate to facial averageness. When using photographic superimposing techniques to combine facial images, he noted that the faces created from this blending were more attractive than the constituent faces. Recent studies have improved upon these techniques using computer graphic techniques. Classic early work by Langlois and colleagues (Langlois & Roggman 1990; Langlois, Roggman, & Musselman, 1994) has shown that these composite faces are judged to be more attractive than the individual faces that they are made up from (see Figure 9.2). Caricaturing has also been used to study the attractiveness of averageness. A caricature exaggerates the differences between an individual face and an average face, thereby reducing the averageness of the original, and Rhodes and Tremewan (1996), using this technique, found that higher averageness was associated with higher attractiveness.

Dissociating facial averageness from other factors is somewhat problematic. Alley and Cunningham (1991) have pointed out that composite faces possess a high degree of bilateral symmetry as well as possessing features that are close to a population average. Average faces are, by definition, symmetric, and symmetry is

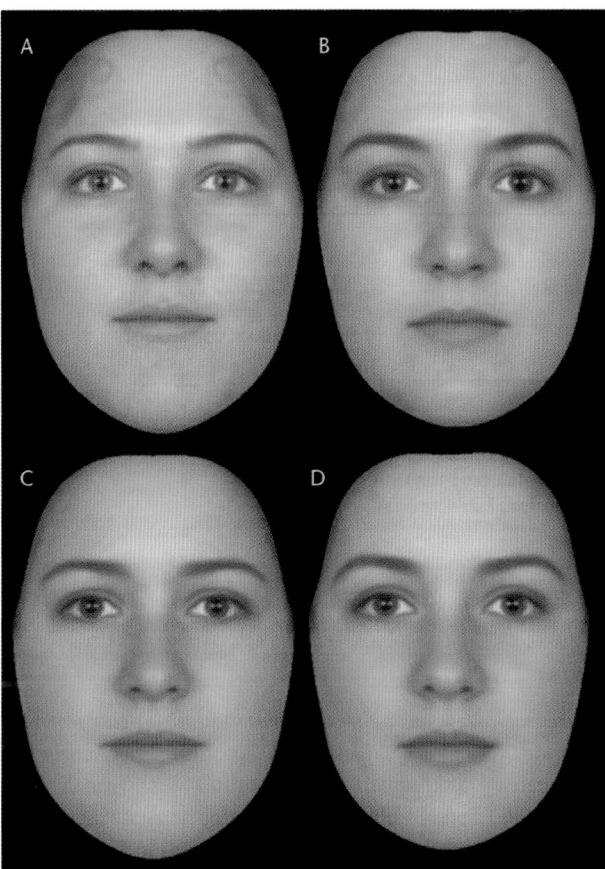

Figure 9.2 The attractiveness of averageness. All faces have been made perfectly symmetric. Face A is a composite made from two images and Face B is made from five images. As Face B is more average in shape and color it should be seen as more attractive than Face A. Faces C and D are the same images with the same averaged skin color. Again Face D should be seen as more attractive than Face C as it is more average in shape.

proposed to be found attractive in faces (discussed in more detail later). Several studies have controlled for this confound of the original studies. In one study, when independently manipulated averageness and symmetry, it was found that both positively and independently influenced attractiveness judgments. (Rhodes, Sumich, & Byatt, 1999). Other studies have used perfectly symmetric images manipulated in averageness and still have demonstrated preferences for averageness (Apicella, Little, & Marlowe, 2007; Jones, deBruine, & Little, 2007a). A study using faces manipulated in averageness of shape in profile view, where bilateral symmetry is irrelevant, also found that average is attractive (Valentine, Darling, & Donnelly, 2004). It has also been noted that, in the original composite studies, the more images that are blended together, the more the skin texture becomes smoother as imperfections, such as lines or blemishes, are averaged also (Alley & Cunningham 1991). Skin color/texture has been controlled in studies which normalize the texture/color of all the faces seen, and these studies all demonstrate average is attractive (Apicella et al. 2007; Jones et al. 2007a; Little & Hancock 2002; Rhodes & Tremewan 1996).

Although the majority of the work already described has been carried out in North America, Britain, and Australia, averageness has also been found to be attractive across different cultures. For example, averageness is also found attractive in Japanese participants (Rhodes et al. 2001a) and in African hunter-gatherers (Apicella et al. 2007). Overall, then, there is clear evidence that averageness is an important determinant of facial attractiveness.

Cognitive Explanations for Averageness Preferences

The attractiveness of average faces is consistent with certain theories of cognitive processing. The human visual system may develop an individual representation, or prototype, made up of an average of the characteristics of all the different stimuli that have been seen. This could mean that individuals may compare a seen face with their stored average representation, and greater similarity to the stored representation could lead to greater liking for average faces because they appear familiar (Langlois & Roggman 1990; Langlois et al. 1994). In this view averageness might be preferred in many domains and indeed averageness is preferred in a variety of stimuli, such as birds, fish and cars (Halberstadt & Rhodes 2003). It is interesting to note that such studies have supported the idea that part of the attraction to averageness is a general preference for familiar stimuli but that preferences for averageness can be found when controlling for familiarly, at least for biological stimuli, demonstrating a preference for averageness independent of familiarity (Halberstadt & Rhodes 2003).

Attraction to average representations formed from experience with faces is consistent with studies demonstrating that exposure, or adaptation, to faces that possess certain characteristics can increase the perceived normality, conceptually similar to averageness, and attractiveness of these characteristics (Little, DeBruine, & Jones, 2005; Rhodes et al. 2003b). For example, if exposed to faces that look like a particular person, then faces that also resemble that person are subsequently seen as more attractive than faces that do not (Little et al. 2005). Further support for the role of experience in generating averageness preferences is found in a cross-cultural study noted previously. When examining preferences for facial averageness in Europeans and African hunter-gatherers, using both European and African faces, Apicella et al. (2007) found that there were preferences for averageness in both types of faces for European judges but only in African faces for the African judges. The European judges are likely to have much experience of both types of face. In

contrast, the hunter-gathers were the Hadza of Northern Tanzania, a group who are relatively isolated and who have only a limited experience of European faces. Potentially the limited experience of European faces may have lead to a lack of preference for averageness in European faces for the Hadza (Apicella et al. 2007).

Beyond Averageness

Although it is clear that increasing averageness increases attractiveness, some have argued that there is more to facial attractiveness than just averageness and that very attractive faces may be, in some ways, more extreme (e.g., Alley & Cunningham, 1991). One study has demonstrated that the characteristics of highly attractive faces are more attractive than average characteristics (Perrett, May, & Yoshikawa, 1994). In a population of female faces, it was found that if a composite was made of all the faces and a composite was made of just the faces that were rated as the most attractive, then the attractive composite was seen as more attractive than the composite of all faces in the population (Perrett et al. 1994). This suggests some characteristics that are not average in attractive faces. In another study, DeBruine and colleagues (2007) found that if individuals are exposed to sets of attractive faces, then attractive faces are seen as more normal, and if exposed to unattractive faces, then attractive faces are seen as less normal. In contrast, when asked about attractiveness, if individuals are exposed to sets of attractive faces, then attractive faces are seen as less attractive, and if exposed to unattractive faces, then attractive faces are seen as more attractive (DeBruine et al. 2007). As normality judgments move in the opposite direction to attractiveness judgments, this data suggests that individuals judging attractiveness are comparing the faces to some dimension of attractiveness that is independent of averageness (DeBruine et al. 2007).

Facial Symmetry

Symmetry refers to the extent that one half of an image (organism, etc.) is the same as the other half. Much work has been done on morphological symmetry and sexual selection in other animals, and this forms the basis of theories of symmetry preferences in humans.

Evolutionary View

Individuals differ in their ability to maintain the stable development of their morphology under the prevailing environmental conditions under which that development is taking place (Møller & Swaddle 1997). The ability of an individual to develop successfully in the face of environmental pressures is, therefore, one proposed indicator of genetic quality. A character demonstrates fluctuating asymmetry (FA) when symmetry reflects the normal development and deviations from this symmetry are randomly distributed with respect to side (Ludwig 1932; Valen 1962). Fluctuating asymmetry is a particularly useful measure of developmental control ability, because we know the optimal development outcome is symmetry. Therefore, any deviation from perfect symmetry can be considered a suboptimal solution that will result in performance problems in the future. Fluctuating asymmetry is also a useful measure because it subsumes a huge amount of individual variation in development, being the outcome of differences in genetic (e.g., inbreeding, mutation, and homozygosity) and environmental (e.g., nutrient intake, parasite load) factors (Møller 1997; Møller & Swaddle 1997).

Symmetry and Actual Quality

Whether symmetry is actually related to quality in other animals and humans is an issue addressed by a large literature, and a complete review is beyond the scope of this discussion. Although the issue is divided, and there is evidence that symmetry is not associated with quality (e.g., see Dufour & Weatherhead 1998), many studies do show links between symmetry and quality (Møller 1997; Møller & Swaddle 1997). For example, in nonhuman animals, antler symmetry positively related to immune measures in reindeer (Lagesen & Folstad 1998) and symmetry is associated with ejaculate quality in three different species of ungulate (Gomendio, Cassinello, & Roldan, 2000). In humans, male body symmetry is positively

related to sperm number per ejaculate and sperm speed (Manning, Scutt, & Lewis-Jones, 1998), and in human females, breast symmetry is positively correlated with fecundity (Manning, Scutt, Whitehouse, & Leinster, 1997; Møller, Soller, & Thornhill, 1995). Relating to faces, one study has demonstrated that facial asymmetry is positively related to self-reported number of occurrences of respiratory disease (Thornhill & Gangestad 2006). The relationship between symmetry and quality is not reviewed in detail here, but it should be noted that fitness-related characteristics, such as growth rate, fecundity, and survivability, are positively associated with symmetry across a number of species and taxa (see Møller 1997; see Møller & Swaddle 1997 for reviews), and ultimately, any link between symmetry and quality, no matter how weak, is sufficient to create a selection pressure on the opposite sex to choose symmetric mates in order to provide genetic quality benefits to their offspring.

Is Symmetry Attractive in Human Faces?

In human males, Thornhill and Gangestad (1994) found that the total number of sexual partners a man reported having was positively related to skeletal symmetry. Studies of naturally occurring human facial asymmetries also provide evidence that symmetry is found attractive, though such studies can be confounded by potential correlates. Grammer & Thornhill (1994) measured overall asymmetry, using points marked on facial images (Figure 9.3), and found that the horizontal symmetry of the faces was positively correlated with attractiveness judgments of both male and female faces. Using a similar technique, Scheib, Gangestad, and Thornhill (1999) also found that measured symmetry and rated attractiveness correlated in male faces. Interestingly, the relationship between symmetry and facial attractiveness was still observed when only the left or right half of each face was presented. Although this technique does not remove all cues to symmetry, the authors note that some covariant of symmetry that can be ascertained from half-faces may influence attractiveness judgements. A third study has also shown that attractiveness ratings of women

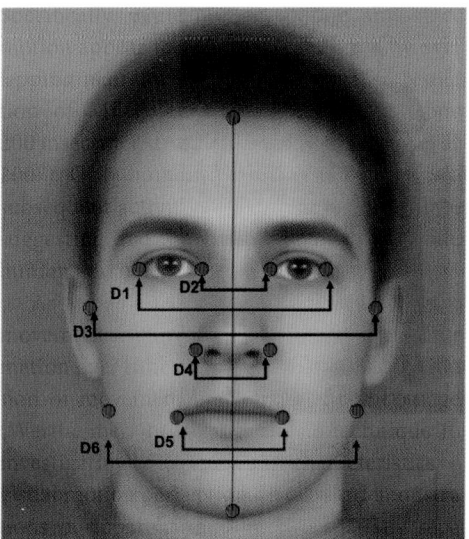

Figure 9.3 Measurements for symmetry. Symmetry was calculated by summing the left and right deviation from the midline for points D1–D6.

positively correlate with measured symmetry (Penton-Voak et al. 2001). Symmetry measurements used in these studies can be seen in Figure 9.3. Mealey, Bridgestock, and Townsend, (1999) studied symmetry and attractiveness in monozygotic twin pairs. Such twins are genetically but not developmentally identical, and hence manifest differing levels of facial symmetry when adult. A significant correlation was found between ratings of symmetry and attractiveness for both male and female twins. These four studies of real faces, therefore, support the notion that symmetry in faces is attractive though they do not discount the notion that it is in fact a correlate of symmetry that is attractive in studies of measured facial symmetry.

Given positive results for real faces is surprising that several studies directly manipulating human facial images have found that asymmetry is generally preferred to symmetry (Kowner, 1996; Langlois et al., 1994; Samuels et al., 1994; Swaddle & Cuthill, 1995). Most of these studies have created symmetric chimeric face images by aligning one vertically bisected half-face with its mirror reflection (Kowner 1996; Langlois et al., 1994; Samuels et al., 1994).

These techniques may induce additional stimulus differences unrelated to symmetry. For example, a mouth of normal width displaced to the right of the midline will assume atypical widths in left-mirrored and right-mirrored chimera face images (Perrett et al. 1999).

Despite results from experiments that used chimeric stimuli failing to detect a preference for symmetry, several studies have demonstrated that symmetry can have a positive influence on attractiveness. Rhodes, Proffitt, Grady, and Sumich (1998) have examined symmetry preference by blending an original face and a mirror image to create more symmetrical versions of original faces (the symmetrical images were retouched to remove artefacts). Symmetry was found attractive in these faces.

Perrett et al. (1999) have also examined the role of symmetry in facial attractiveness. In one experiment, symmetry in face shape was improved without changing the symmetry of face textures; natural asymmetries in skin pigmentation were present in both the original and more symmetric remapped versions of the same face (see Figure 9.4). Adults' responses to paired presentation of these two versions of each face indicated a clear preference for the symmetrically remapped stimuli. In a second experiment, stimuli with average texture information were generated from a set of faces. This average texture was rendered into both the original face shapes and symmetrically remapped shapes of the set of individual faces, giving perfect symmetry in the remapped version. Paired presentation showed a preference for perfectly symmetrical face stimuli.

Thus the methodologically superior computer graphic studies (Perrett et al. 1999; Rhodes et al. 1998) parallel the findings of investigations into naturally occurring facial asymmetries (Grammer & Thornhill 1994; Mealey et al. 1999; Scheib et al. 1999). The computer graphic studies demonstrate that increasing symmetry alone is sufficient to increase attractiveness. Subsequently, other studies have replicated preferences for symmetry using manipulated stimuli in different Western samples (e.g., Little & Jones 2003; Little & Jones 2006). Preferences for symmetry using manipulated faces have also been

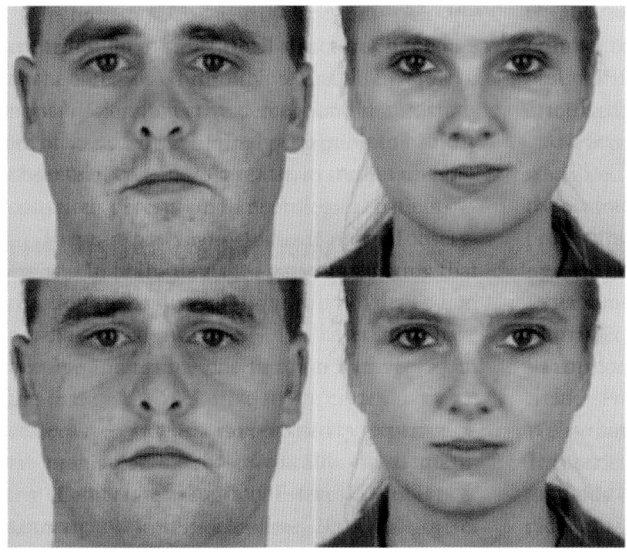

Figure 9.4 Asymmetric (top) versus symmetric faces (bottom). Symmetric images are usually found more attractive (e.g., Perrett et al., 1999).

found in samples of African hunter-gatherers (Little, Apicella, & Marlowe, 2007a), and macaque monkeys have also been found to gaze longer at symmetrical than asymmetrical face images of conspecifics (Waitt & Little 2006).

Cognitive Explanations for Symmetry Preferences

Some authors have argued that a preference for symmetry reflects a general sensory bias in perception toward symmetric shapes (Enquist & Arak 1994). Such a view implies that symmetry preferences are arbitrary and arise only because of the way in which the visual system operates. If an organism encounters asymmetric stimuli in which asymmetry is random, then the average of all seen stimuli will be symmetric. If an organism then compares stimuli to its stored representation, then symmetric stimuli will be closer. For example, computer-based neural networks trained to recognize asymmetric stimuli (stimuli with random asymmetry) respond most strongly to novel symmetric stimuli that are the average of training stimuli (Johnstone, 1994). Preferences for symmetry can arise in a similar manner in bird species as well. Jansson, Forkman, and Enquist, (2002) trained chickens to discriminate between rewarded and nonrewarded stimuli. The stimuli were two asymmetric crosses that were mirror images of each

other. On subsequent testing, chickens preferred a novel symmetric cross to either asymmetric cross, despite the fact it was never associated with reward. So symmetry preference can arise as by-product of the visual system via perceptual experience. There are studies that present data inconsistent with this view however. Although this version of the perceptual-bias view predicts that novel faces may be compared to a symmetric prototype, real known faces are asymmetric. If individuals prefer faces that are closest to their stored representation, then they should prefer original asymmetric versions. Symmetry preferences, however, are found for symmetric versions of familiar faces despite experience being closest to naturally asymmetric versions (Little & Jones 2003).

In a simpler perceptual bias view, the symmetry of a given stimuli could generate preference via ease of processing (e.g., because one half of the stimuli is more similar to the other half). This view also appears unsupported for faces as inversion, which maintains identical information and symmetry, disrupts facial symmetry preferences (Little & Jones 2003). Together these findings suggest there is more behind symmetry preferences than ease of processing or comparison to learned stimuli. Finally, there is also variability in facial-symmetry preference according to the perceivers self-rated attractiveness (Little, Burk,

Penton-Voak, & Perrett, 2001) and in relation to the menstrual cycle (Little, Jones, Burt, & Perrett, 2007c), which are difficult to accommodate in such perceptual-bias views (see Section 3 later for a discussion of these factors in regard to sexual dimorphism).

Secondary Sexual Characteristics in Faces

Male and female faces differ in their shape. Mature features in adult human faces reflect the masculinization or feminization of secondary sexual characteristics that occurs at puberty. These face shape differences in part arise because of the action of hormones such as testosterone. Larger jawbones, more prominent cheekbones, and thinner cheeks are all features of male faces that differentiate them from female faces (e.g., Enlow 1982).

Evolutionary View

From an evolutionary view, extremes of secondary sexual characteristics (more female for women, more male for men) are proposed to be attractive because they advertise the quality of an individual in terms of heritable benefits: they indicate that the owners of such characteristics possess good genes. The favored explanation of the importance of these facial traits is that they represent a handicap to an organism (Zahavi 1975) and the costs of growing the trait means that only healthy individuals can produce them. In this way, these "honest" handicaps are proposed to indicate the fitness of the owner. For example, secondary sexual characteristics are proposed to be linked to parasite resistance because the sex hormones that influence their growth, particularly testosterone, lower immuno-competence. Testosterone has been linked to the suppression of immune function in many species (Hillgarth & Wingfield, 1997), including humans (Kanda, Tsuchida, & Tamaki, 1996; Yesilova et al. 2000). Larger secondary sexual characteristics should be related to a healthier immune system because only healthy organisms can afford the high sex hormone handicap on the immune system that is necessary to produce these characteristics (Folstad & Karter, 1992). For example, in roaches (*Rutilus*

rutilus) it has been shown that the size of certain sexual characteristics varies according to parasitic infection, and infection in turn is related to immune system quality (Wedekind 1992). Female roaches may use sexually dimorphic features to accurately judge infection and immune-system quality in males.

Sexual Dimorphism and Actual Quality

In many nonhuman animal studies, there is a positive association between secondary sexual trait expression and immunocompetence (see e.g., Møller, Christe, & Lux, 1999). Peafowls (*Pavo cristatus*) are a good example of an extremely sexual dimorphic species. Peahens are not very colorful and prefer (the much more colorful) peacocks with the most elaborate trains (Petrie, Halliday, & Sanders, 1991). There appears to be an indirect benefit with this choice because the offspring of peacocks with more elaborate trains have greater survival chances (Petrie 1994), and so preferences for sexual dimorphism in peafowl can be said to lead peahens to acquire males with good genes. The relationship between sexual-dimorphism and good genes in humans is less clear. A study by Rhodes, Chan, Zebrowitz, & Simmons (2003a), however, has shown that perceived masculinity correlated positively (if weakly, $r = .17$ $n = 154$) with actual measures of health in male adolescents. No relationship was found between femininity and actual health in female faces though (Rhodes et al. 2003a). Another study has demonstrated that men's facial masculinity and women's facial femininity are negatively related to self-reports of respiratory disease (Thornhill & Gangestad, 2006). If health is heritable, then female preferences for masculinity and male preferences for femininity may indeed also reflect the choice of males with good genes. There is also a link between hormonal profile and face shape. Women with higher circulating estrogen have more feminine faces (Law-Smith et al., 2006) whereas men with high testosterone have more masculine faces (Penton-Voak & Chen 2004). Potentially, preferences for hormonal profile, if women with high oestrogen and men with high testosterone are valued as mates, could also drive preferences for sexually dimorphic face shape.

Is Sexual Dimorphism Attractive in Human Faces?

There is considerable evidence that feminine female faces are considered attractive. Studies measuring facial features from photographs of women (Cunningham 1986; Grammer & Thornhill 1994; Jones & Hill 1993) and studies manipulating facial composites (Perrett et al. 1998, discussed in more detail later) all indicate that feminine features increase the attractiveness of female faces across different cultures. If estrogenized female faces provide cues to fertility and health, then male preferences for such features are potentially adaptive. This reasoning does not require estrogen to be immunosuppressive or part of a handicap.

The link between sexual dimorphism and attractiveness in male faces is less clear. Cunningham, Barbee, & Pike (1990) and Grammer and Thornhill (1994) used facial measurements and found that females preferred large jaws in males. Masculine features, such as a large jaw and a prominent brow ridge are reliably associated with ratings of dominance in photographic, identi-kit, and composite stimuli (Berry & Brownlow 1989; Keating 1985; McArthur 1983–1984; McArthur & Berry 1987; Perrett et al. 1998). Despite findings showing a preference for more masculine and dominant faces, several studies have shown that feminine characteristics and faces of low dominance are of increased attractiveness (Berry & McArthur 1985; Cunningham et al. 1990; Little & Hancock 2002; Perrett et al. 1998; Rhodes, Hickford, & Jeffrey, 2000; Swaddle & Reierson 2003).

Cunningham et al. (1990) have suggested that, because both masculine and feminine faces are only rated as moderately attractive, a resolution to this conflict could be that very attractive male faces possess a combination of factors and so reflect multiple motives in female mate choice (i.e., the desire for a dominant and a co-operative partner, as advertised by a combination of masculine and feminine features). They found that attractive male faces possessed the more infantile/feminine traits of large eyes and a small nose area and the mature features of prominent cheekbones and large chins which

indeed may combine both co-operative and dominant signals.

Computer graphic techniques can be used to construct average male and female faces by digitally blending photographs of individuals of one sex. Sexual dimorphism in face shape can then be enhanced or diminished by taking the geometrical differences between male and female face shapes and either exaggerating or decreasing them (Perrett et al. 1998). This process simultaneously changes all dimorphic shape characteristics in the face. For example, masculinizing a male face shape by increasing the differences between a male and female average increases the size of the jaw and reduces lip thickness because male jaws are larger than female jaws and the lips of men are thinner than those of women.

The shape differences between male and female faces can be described by a set of vectors between marked delineation points on the features of the male and female averages (Perrett et al. 1998). Transforms are expressed as a percentage of the distance travelled along these vectors: in a 25 percent feminized male face shape, each delineation point is moved 25 percent of the way along the vector to the female average face. The color information from the original male average is then warped into this new shape. To masculinize male face shapes, the direction of the male-female vector is reversed before the points are moved along it (see Figure 9.5 for examples of masculinized and feminized male and female face stimuli).

Perrett et al. (1998) presented both Japanese and Caucasian faces in their country of origin. Participants could alter the appearance of a face (increasing the masculinity or femininity of the shape) on a computer monitor by using a computer mouse. For the male face stimuli, the shape selected by Caucasians as most attractive was significantly feminized for both the Caucasian male face and the Japanese male face continua. Similarly, Japanese participants also selected significantly feminized versions of the male stimuli for both the Japanese and Caucasian male face continua. Thus, in both cultures it was found that participants showed a preference for feminized male faces. Several studies have also documented

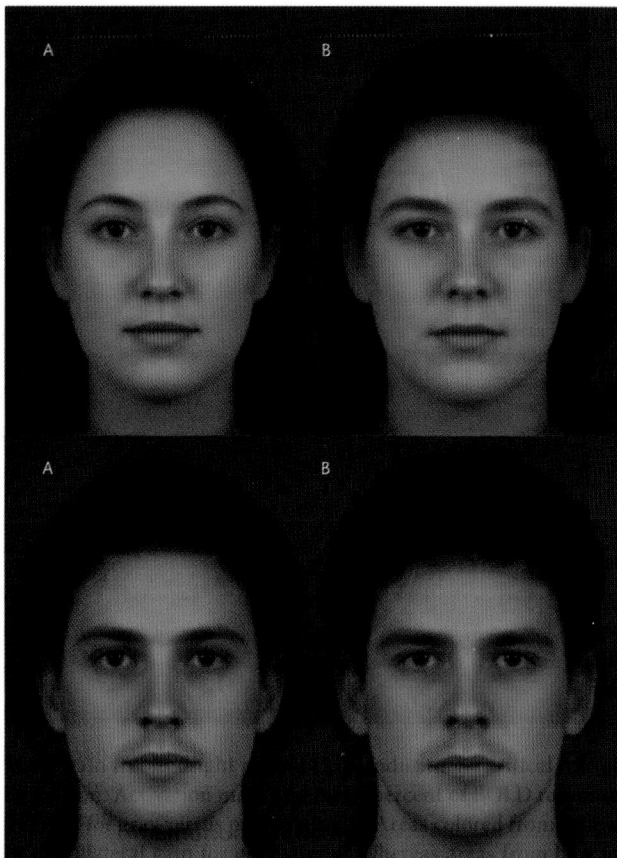

Figure 9.5 Feminized faces (A) versus masculinized faces (B). Feminized images are usually found more attractive (e.g., Perrett et al., 1998) though some studies show preferences for masculine images (e.g., DeBruine at al. 2006).

preferences for femininity (Little et al. 2001; Little & Hancock 2002; Little, Jones, Penton-Voak, Burt, & Perrett, 2002; Rhodes et al. 2000) but some similar computer graphic studies have also reported preferences for masculinity (DeBruine et al. 2006; Little & Mannion 2006). Preferences for sexual dimorphism then appear variable and we discuss this in the next section.

Masculinity May Represent a Trade-off in Male Attractiveness

A preference for feminized male faces seems contrary to predictions from a good-gene view of sexual selection and to some other published studies of male facial attractiveness already reviewed briefly. Rather than preferring typically masculine faces (with prominent brow ridges and large jaws), which are associated with possible immuno-competence benefits, both male and female adults appear to favor

a small amount of femininity in men's faces. The explanation may lie in the personality traits masculine- and feminine-faced males are assumed to possess. Increasing the masculinity of face shape increased perceptions of dominance, masculinity, and age but decreased perceptions of warmth, emotionality, honesty, cooperativeness, and quality as a parent (Perrett et al. 1998).

It appears then that socially valued traits such as honesty, warmth, cooperation, and skill as a parent are associated with feminized versions of male faces, whereas traits such as dominance are associated with masculinized face shapes. Feminization of male face shape may increase attractiveness because it softens particular features that are perceived to be associated with negative personality traits. Female-face choice may thus represent a trade-off between the desire for good genes and the desire for a cooperative partner. This trade-off means that masculinity may be more or less attractive under certain contexts and to certain individuals and we discuss this in Section 3.

Attractive or Dominant?

Although various studies have linked sexual dimorphism to attractiveness, it is plausible that facial masculinity is also related to intrasexual selection, or competition within a sex to compete for mates. An association between sexual-dimorphism and quality would enable masculine men and feminine women to be better able to compete with others of their own sex, for example, high-quality sexually dimorphic individuals may be better able to physically fight off competitors than lower quality, less sexually dimorphic members of the same sex. Swaddle and Reierson (2003) have shown that when using slightly different morphing techniques to those just outlined (focusing on traits under the action of testosterone) that, as masculinity increases in male faces, they are perceived as more dominant but not more attractive. On this basis they suggest that masculinity in male faces is more related to competition between males than attractiveness to females. One issue with this conclusion is that a recent study has demonstrated that preferences for masculinity are seen when manipulating faces in various different ways, including a similar manipulation than that employed by Swaddle and Reierson (DeBruine et al. 2006). Also, given that preferences for masculinity are variable (see later) it appears likely that measuring absolute preferences for masculinity in a population can be misleading in determining its importance to attractiveness judgements. Sexual dimorphism of face shape has been found to be linked to attractiveness in many studies and alongside this may also play an important role in signaling dominance.

Cognitive Explanations for Masculinity Preferences

Preferences for sexual dimorphism may also arise in the same way as perceptual bias may account for symmetry preference. Enquist and Arak (1993) used computer neural networks to examine the mechanisms involved in signal recognition. They used these neural networks to model the evolution of female preferences for long-tailed conspecifics. Simulated female birds were trained to recognize different patterns that represented males. When shown new patterns, it was found that females recognized patterns that were similar to patterns that were first presented, but these females also preferred patterns similar to those first presented but exaggerated in size. This result was proposed to suggest that recognition systems could contain hidden preferences, that is, that training on discrimination between the category male and female may result in preferences for extremes of sexual dimorphism. Again there is some evidence that the visual systems of real birds behave as predicted by computer modeling. Chickens trained to discriminate between human male and female faces show just such an effect: after training chickens respond most strongly to faces that differ most greatly in sexual dimorphism, more than the original rewarded more average male and female stimuli (Jansson et al. 2002). One problem with this view is that preferences for femininity in male faces are not predicted from this view. The individual differences in preferences for masculinity discussed in the next section are also problematic for a simple perceptual bias view of preferences for sexual dimorphism.

INDIVIDUAL DIFFERENCES IN PREFERENCES FOR SEXUAL DIMORPHISM

Having argued for the universality of attractive traits earlier in this chapter, we now examine some factors that may lead to individual differences in the perception of facial attractiveness and speculate about how such differences may arise from learning and differences in life history. Across the animal kingdom not all members of a given species engage in the same mating behavior. Indeed, there may be a range of mating strategies within a species that can be employed, based on both the environmental cues and the body that an individual finds him or herself in. In humans, although individuals may share certain basic criteria for finding faces attractive, many factors may influence the specific types of face they find attractive.

As noted earlier, there appears disagreement among studies about whether masculinity is attractive in male faces. The explanation may lie in a potential trade-off between the genetic quality of the male and the investment he makes in the relationship and toward any resultant offspring; high quality males may invest less in each partner (and offspring) and so may not make ideal long-term partners in a species, such as humans, with extended parental investment (Burley 1986; Møller & Thornhill 1998b). Such arguments may also apply to preferences for female faces because highly attractive women may be more likely to stray from their partners. This trade-off between attractiveness and investment has led to a hypothesis concerning how attractiveness may mediate the trade-off and variability under conditions in which quality may be favored over investment. Although we focus on studies of women's preferences, there are, of course, also individual differences and variation by context in men's preferences for female face femininity, but in such studies males overall consistently prefer feminine face shapes (Jones et al. 2007b; Little et al. 2007b). Also, as noted above, the effects of perceiver attractiveness (Little et al. 2001) and cycle (Little et al. 2007c) have also been found for symmetry preferences.

Perceiver Attractiveness

The attractiveness of the bodies that men and women find themselves inhabiting will influence the mate they may acquire and so it is likely to impact on their mating strategy. Nancy Burley's work (Burley, 1986) with Zebra finches has demonstrated that manipulating the attractiveness of individuals using colored leg bands changes the mating strategy they employ. The attractiveness of the bands was measured by their impact on the other birds; some bands decreased the sexual attention received from opposite-sex birds and some bands increased the amount of sexual attention received from opposite-sex birds. Zebra finches mate monogamously (both in the wild and in captivity) with both males and females equally sharing parental duties. Males given attractive leg bands engaged in polygynous mating, whereas those males given unattractive green bands continued to attempt to mate monogamously (Burley 1986). Females made attractive with colored leg bands were found to spend less time carrying out parental duties than both those typical of their sex and unattractive females but still had higher reproductive success, possibly because mates of attractive females spent more time than those typical of their sex carrying out parental duties (Burley 1986). Again, higher attractiveness allowed females to adjust their strategy and induced partners to behave differently. Condition may also influence an individual's preferences as well as their perceived attractiveness. For example, the red coloration of male sticklebacks decreases in intensity with parasite load, and female sticklebacks demonstrate a preference for intense male coloration. Females in poor condition, however, show an unexpected preference for less intensely colored (i.e., poorer condition) males (Bakker, Künsler, & Mazzi, 1999).

In humans, Little et al. (2001) examined how women's self-rated attractiveness influenced male face preference. Using faces manipulated with computer graphics, we found that there is an increased preference for masculinity and symmetry in male faces for women who regard themselves as attractive (Little et al., 2001). This finding may reflect a condition-dependent mating strategy analogous to behavior found in other species. It is possible that women who are of high mate value (or who believe their mate value to be high) may be more likely to attract and retain a high mate value male (i.e., a masculine male) than a lower mate value female. It is also worth noting that self-perceived attractiveness is variable, even for one individual, and that exposure to members of the opposite-sex of low attractiveness increases self-esteem and leads to stronger preferences for masculinity (Little & Mannion, 2006). The perceiver's attractiveness then is one important between-individual variable in judgements of facial attractiveness.

Relationship Context and Partnership Status

Depending on the type of relationship sought, masculine and feminine faces may differ in their attractiveness to females. In the context of a short-term sexual relationship, the perceived cues to high paternal investment in the feminine-faced male are of little value to a female. The perceived cues to low parental investment in masculine-faced males should have little negative influence on attractiveness in this relationship context. Females should, therefore, seek to maximize the genetic fitness of potential offspring if they are not extracting any other benefits from their mates, and thus may prefer more masculine males. In the context of a long-term relationship, the perceived better parenting and increased cooperation of the feminine-faced male should be of increased importance, enhancing a feminine-faced male's attractiveness. The lower perceived levels of cooperation and decreased value as a parent will detract from a masculine-faced male's attractiveness in a long-term relationship. In line with such predictions, for short-term relationships, women are more likely to choose an attractive male, who is less cooperative and appears to have poorer parenting qualities, over a less attractive male, who is more co-operative and with better parenting qualities (Scheib, 2001). By contrast, for long-term contexts, women may choose the less attractive but more co-operative man more often (Scheib 2001). In face-preference tasks, women judging for short-term relationships prefer more masculinity in faces than those judging for long-term relationships (Little et al. 2002). In a similar vein to relationship context, once a person has acquired an investing partner, issues of investment are presumably relaxed. Women who have a partner prefer more masculine faces than those who do not (Little et al. 2002). Potentially, women in relationships are more attractive than their unpartnered peers, which could lead to different preferences in women with and without partners. Women may also have different social experiences while in a relationship, which could also lead to differences in preferences. Because individuals may find themselves looking for both short- and long-term relationships and may be with or without a partner at different points in their lives, these studies highlight how flexible preferences are according to personal circumstances.

Peak Fertility

The proposed genetic quality of masculine males is mainly of benefit if a female is likely to conceive. Women with a main sexual partner are more likely to engage in extra-pair copulations at a point in the menstrual cycle when they are most likely to conceive (Baker & Bellis 1995), which suggests that women may pursue extra-pair copulations to gain genetic benefits that they will not receive from their current partner. Research into male facial attractiveness has revealed that female preferences for male faces vary over the menstrual cycle. During the follicular phase of the menstrual cycle, when conception is most likely, women show increased preferences for facial masculinity (Frost 1994; Johnston et al. 2001; Penton-Voak & Perrett 2000; Penton-Voak et al. 1999a). It appears that during the high-risk conception phase females become more influenced by the potential good-gene benefits to their offspring advertised by masculine-faced males than the higher perceived investment of feminine faces (Johnston et al. 2001; Penton-Voak & Perrett 2000; Penton-Voak, Perrett, & Pierce, 1999b). Shifts across the menstrual cycle further highlight a potentially strategic aspect to face preferences (see also Gangestad & Thornhill 2008; Jones et al. 2008 for reviews).

SUMMARY AND CONCLUSIONS

Being more or less attractive has important social consequences and people do generally agree on who is and who is not attractive. Beauty is not just a simple social construct; attractiveness appears to be ingrained in our biology. Although some aspects of face perception appear innate, other aspects are clearly influenced by experience; it seems unlikely that individuals are born with a representation of what a perfect partner looks like. Hard-wired propensities to attend to face-like stimuli early in life provide the opportunity to learn the details of facial appearance, and, hence, experience will shape facial aesthetic judgements.

Some structural aspects of human facial appearance are linked to preferences. If a trait reliably advertises mate quality, then we would expect individuals in a population to find that trait attractive. Averageness, symmetry, and sexual dimorphism are all traits in human faces that are linked to preferences and also to potentially good genes. We might expect, then, that all humans will prefer masculine male faces, feminine female faces and average and symmetrical faces of both sexes. This chapter, for example, presents data that is in line with the notion that averageness, sexual dimorphism, and symmetry may all advertise quality in human faces and are, hence, found attractive.

Having argued for an overall preference for certain traits advertising quality, it is clear that individual differences in preferences for some traits will prove adaptive and so can be consistent with evolutionary theory. This chapter also documents several potentially adaptive individual differences in human face preferences. For humans, as with other species, there is no optimal strategy for mate-choice and parenting that applies to all individuals. Indeed the range of personal circumstances (physical, environmental, social) will guarantee that what is a good or adequate strategy, and, therefore, what is attractive, will depend on the individual. In this way facial beauty can be said to be both in the face of the beheld and in the eye of beholder.

ACKNOWLEDGMENTS

Anthony Little is supported by a Royal Society University Research Fellowship.

REFERENCES

Alley, T. R. & Cunningham, M. R. (1991). Averaged faces are attractive, but very attractive faces are not average. *Psychological Science 2*, 123–125.

Apicella, C. L., Little, A. C. & Marlowe, F. W. (2007). Facial averageness and attractiveness in an isolated population of hunter-gatherers. *Perception 36*, 1813–1820.

Baker, R. R. & Bellis, M. A. (1995). *Human sperm competition: Copulation, masturbation and infidelity.* London: Chapman & Hall.

Bakker, T. C. M., Künzler, R. & Mazzi, D. (1999). Condition-related mate-choice in sticklebacks. *Nature 401*, 234.

Barden, C. R., Ford, M. E., Jensen, A. & Salyer, K. (1989). Effects of craniofacial deformity in infancy on the quality of mother-infant interactions. *Child Development 60*, 819–824.

Berry, D. S. & Brownlow, S. (1989). Were the physiognomists right? Personality correlates of facial babyishness. *Personality and Social Psychology Bulletin 15*, 266–279.

Berry, D. S. & McArthur, L. Z. (1985). Some components and consequences of a babyface. *Journal of Personality and Social Psychology 48*, 312–323.

Berscheid, E., Dion, K., Walster, E. & Walster, G. W. (1971). Physical attractiveness and dating choice: A test of the matching hypothesis. *Journal of Experimental and Social Psychology 7*, 173–189.

Berscheid, E. & Walster, E. (1974). Physical attractiveness. In L. Berkowitz (Ed.). *Advances in Experimental Social Psychology*, vol. 7, pp. 157–215. New York: Academic Press.

Bruce, V. & Young, A. W. (1986). Understanding face recognition. *British Journal of Psychology 77*, 307–327.

Burley, N. (1986). Sexual selection for aesthetic traits in species with biparental care. *American Naturalist 127*, 415–445.

Cash, T. F. & Kilcullen, R. N. (1985). The Aye of the Beholder—Susceptibility to Sexism and Beautyism in the Evaluation of Managerial Applicants. *Journal of Applied Social Psychology 15*, 591–605.

Chiu, R. K. & Babcock, R. D. (2002). The relative importance of facial attractiveness and gender in Hong Kong selection decisions. *International Journal of Human Resource Management 13*, 141–155.

Cunningham, M. R. (1986). Measuring the physical in physical attractiveness: quasi-experiments on the sociobiology of female facial beauty. *Journal of Personality and Social Psychology 50*, 925–935.

Cunningham, M. R., Barbee, A. P. & Pike, C. L. (1990). What do women want? Facialmetric assessment of multiple motives in the perception of male facial physical attractiveness. *Journal of Personality and Social Psychology 59*, 61–72.

Cunningham, M. R., Roberts, A. R., Barbee, A. P. & Druen, P. B. (1995). "Their ideas of beauty are, on the whole, the same as ours": Consistency and variability in the cross-cultural perception of female attractiveness. *Journal of Personality and Social Psychology 68*, 261–279.

Darwin, C. (1871). *The Descent of Man, and Selection in Relation to Sex*. London: John Murray.

DeBruine, L. M., Jones, B. C., Little, A. C., Boothroyd, L. G., Perrett, D. I., Penton-Voak, I. S., Cooper, P. A., Penke, L., Feinberg, D. R. & Tiddeman, B. P. (2006). Correlated preferences for facial masculinity and ideal or actual partner's masculinity. *Proceedings of the Royal Society B–Biological Sciences 273*, 1355–1360.

DeBruine, L. M., Jones, B. C., Unger, L., Little, A. C. & Feinberg, D. R. (2007). Dissociating averageness and attractiveness: Attractive faces are not always average. *Journal of Experimental Psychology–Human Perception and Performance 33*, 1420–1430.

Dermer, M. & Thiel, D. L. (1975). When beauty may fail. *Journal of Personality and Social Psychology 31*, 1168–1176.

Dion, K., Berscheid, E. & Walster, E. (1972). What is beautiful is good. *Journal of Personality and Social Psychology 24*, 285–290.

Dion, K. K. & Berscheid, E. (1974). Physical attractiveness and peer perception among children. *Sociometry 37*, 1–12.

Downs, A. C. & Lyons, P. M. (1991). Natural observations of the links between attractiveness and initial legal judgments. *Personality and Social Psychology Bulletin 17*, 541–547.

Dufour, K. W. & Weatherhead, P. J. (1998). Bilateral symmetry and social dominance in captive male red-winged blackbirds. *Behavioural Ecology and Sociobiology 42*, 71–76.

Eagly, A. H., Ashmore, R. D., Makhijani, M. G. & Longo, L. C. (1991). What is beautiful is good, but …: A meta-analytic review of research on the physical attractiveness stereotype. *Psychological Bulletin 110*, 109–128.

Elder, G. H. J. (1969). Appearance and education in marriage mobility. *American Sociological Review 34*, 519–533.

Enlow, D. M. (1982). *Handbook of facial growth*. Philadelphia: Saunders.

Enquist, M. & Arak, A. (1993). Selection of exaggerated male traits by female aesthetic senses. *Nature 361*, 446–448.

Enquist, M. & Arak, A. (1994). Symmetry, beauty and evolution. *Nature 372*, 169–172.

Feingold, A. (1992). Good-looking people are not what we think. *Psychological Bulletin 111*, 304–341.

Folstad, I. & Karter, A. J. (1992). Parasites, bright males and the immunocompetence handicap. *American Naturalist 139*, 603–622.

Ford, C. S. & Beach, F. A. (1951). *Patterns of sexual behaviour*. New York: Harper & Row.

Frost, P. (1994). Preference for darker faces in photographs at different phases of the menstrual cycle: preliminary assessment of evidence for a hormonal relationship. *Perceptual and Motor Skills 79*, 507–514.

Galton, F. J. (1878). Composite portraits. *Nature 18*, 97–100.

Gangestad, S. W. & Thornhill, R. (2008). Human oestrus. *Proceedings of the Royal Society B–Biological Sciences 275*, 991–1000.

Gomendio, M., Cassinello, J. & Roldan, E. R. S. (2000). A comparative study of ejaculate traits in three endangered ungulates with different levels of inbreeding: fluctuating asymmetry as an indicator of reproductive and genetic stress. *Proceedings of the Royal Society of London, B 267*, 875–882.

Goren, C. C., Sarty, M. & Wu, P. Y. K. (1975). Visual following and pattern discrimination of face like stimuli by newborn infants. *Paediatrics 56*, 544–549.

Grammer, K. & Thornhill, R. (1994). Human (*Homo sapiens*) facial attractiveness and sexual selection: the role of symmetry and averageness. *Journal of Comparative Psychology 108*, 233–242.

Halberstadt, J. & Rhodes, G. (2003). It's not just average faces that are attractive: Computer-manipulated averageness makes birds, fish, and automobiles attractive. *Psychonomic Bulletin and Review 10*, 149–156.

Hillgarth, N. & Wingfield, J. C. (1997). Testosterone and Immunosuppression in vertebrates: implications for parasite mediated sexual selection. In N. E. Beckage (Ed.). *Parasites and Pathogens*. New York: Chapman & Hall.

Holmes, S. J. & Hatch, C. E. (1938). Personal appearance as related to scholastic records and marriage selection in college women. *Human Biology 10*, 65–76.

Hume, D. (1757). *Four dissertations. IV: Of the standard of taste*. London: Millar.

Jansson, L., Forkman, B. & Enquist, M. (2002). Experimental evidence of receiver bias for symmetry. *Animal Behaviour 63*, 617–621.

Johnson, M. H., Dziurawiec, S., Ellis, H. & Morton, J. (1991). Newborns' preferential tracking of face–like stimuli and its subsequent decline. *Cognition 40*, 1–19.

Johnston, V. S., Hagel, R., Franklin, M., Fink, B. & Grammer, K. (2001). Male facial attractiveness: evidence for a hormone-mediated adaptive design. *Evolution and Human Behavior 22*, 251–267.

Johnstone, R. A. (1994). Female preference for symmetrical males as a by-product of selection for mate recognition. *Nature 372*, 172–175.

Jones, B. C., DeBruine, L. M. & Little, A. C. (2007a). The role of symmetry in attraction to average faces. *Perception & Psychophysics 69*, 1273–1277.

Jones, B. C., DeBruine, L. M., Little, A. C., Conway, C. A., Welling, L. L. M. & Smith, F. (2007b). Sensation seeking and men's face preferences. *Evolution and Human Behavior 28*, 439–446.

Jones, B. C., DeBruine, L. M., Perrett, D. I., Little, A. C., Feinberg, D. R. & Smith, M. J. L. (2008). Effects of menstrual cycle phase on face preferences. *Archives of Sexual Behavior 37*, 78–84.

Jones, D. & Hill, K. (1993). Criteria of facial attractiveness in five populations. *Human Nature 4*, 271–296.

Kanda, N., Tsuchida, T. & Tamaki, K. (1996). Testosterone inhibits immunoglobulin production by human peripheral blood mononuclear cells. *Clinical and Experimental Immunology 106*, 410–415.

Keating, C. F. (1985). Gender and the physiognomy of dominance and attractiveness. *Social Psychology Quarterly 48*, 61–70.

Kowner, R. (1996). Facial asymmetry and attractiveness judgment in developmental perspective. *Journal of Experimental Psychology: Human Perception and Performance. 22*, 662–675.

Krebs, D. & Adinolfi, A. A. (1975). Physical attractiveness, social relations, and personality style. *Journal of Personality and Social Psychology 31*, 245–253.

Lagesen, K. & Folstad, I. (1998). Antler asymmetry and immunity in reindeer. *Behavioural Ecology and Sociobiology 44*, 135–142.

Langlois, J., Ritter, J., Casey, J. & Solwin, D. (1995). Infant attractiveness predicts maternal behaviors and attitudes. *Developmental Psychology 31*, 464–472.

Langlois, J. H., Kalakanis, L., Rubenstein, A. J., Larson, A., Hallamm, M. & Smoot, M. 2000 Maxims or myths of beauty? A meta–analytic and theoretical review. *Psychological Bulletin 126*, 390–423.

Langlois, J. H., Ritter, J. M., Roggman, L. A. & Vaughn, L. S. (1991). Facial diversity and infant preferences for attractive faces. *Developmental Psychology 27*, 79–84.

Langlois, J. H. & Roggman, L. A. (1990). Attractive faces are only average. *Psychological Science 1*, 115–121.

Langlois, J. H., Roggman, L. A., Casey, R. J., Ritter, J. M., Riser-Danner, L. A. & Jenkins, V. Y. (1987). Infant preferences for attractive faces: Rudiments of a stereotype? *Developmental Psychology 23*, 363–369.

Langlois, J. H., Roggman, L. A. & Musselman, L. (1994). What is average and what is not average about attractive faces. *Psychological Science 5*, 214–220.

Law–Smith, M. J., Perrett, D. I., Jones, B. C., Cornwell, R. E., Moore, F. R., Feinberg, D. R., Boothroyd, L. G., Durrani, S. J., Stirrat, M. R., Whiten, S., Pitman, R. M. & Hillier, S. G. (2006). Facial appearance is a cue to oestrogen levels in women. *Proceedings of the Royal Society B–Biological Sciences 273*, 135–140.

Light, L. L., Hollander, S. & Kayra-Stuart, F. (1981). Why attractive people are harder to remember. *Personality and Social Psychology Bulletin 7*, 269–276.

Little, A. C., Apicella, C. L. & Marlowe, F. W. (2007a). Preferences for symmetry in human faces in two cultures: data from the UK and the Hadza, an isolated group of hunter-gatherers. *Proceedings of the Royal Society B–Biological Sciences 274*, 3113–3117.

Little, A. C., Burt, D. M., Penton-Voak, I. S. & Perrett, D. I. (2001). Self-perceived attractiveness influences human female preferences for sexual dimorphism and symmetry in male faces. *Proceedings of the Royal Society of London, B 268*, 39–44.

Little, A. C., Cohen, D. L., Jones, B. C. & Belsky, J. (2007b). Human preferences for facial masculinity change with relationship type and environmental harshness. *Behavioral Ecology and Sociobiology 61*, 967–973.

Little, A. C., DeBruine, L. M. & Jones, B. C. (2005). Sex-contingent face after-effects suggest distinct neural populations code male and female faces. *Proceedings of the Royal Society B-Biological Sciences 272*, 2283–2287.

Little, A. C. & Hancock, P. J. B. (2002). The role of masculinity and distinctiveness in judgments of human male facial attractiveness. *British Journal of Psychology 93*, 451–464.

Little, A. C. & Jones, B. C. (2003). Evidence against perceptual bias views for symmetry preferences in human faces. *Proceedings of the Royal Society of London Series B–Biological Sciences 270*, 1759–1763.

Little, A. C. & Jones, B. C. (2006). Attraction independent of detection suggests special mechanisms for symmetry preferences in human face perception. *Proceedings of the Royal Society B-Biological Sciences 273*, 3093–3099.

Little, A. C., Jones, B. C., Burt, D. M. & Perrett, D. I. (2007c). Preferences for symmetry in faces change across the menstrual cycle. *Biological Psychology 76*, 209–216.

Little, A. C., Jones, B. C., Penton-Voak, I. S., Burt, D. M. & Perrett, D. I. (2002). Partnership status and the temporal context of relationships influence human female preferences for sexual dimorphism in male face shape. *Proceedings of the Royal Society of London, B 269*, 1095–1100.

Little, A. C. & Mannion, H. (2006). Viewing attractive or unattractive same-sex individuals changes self-rated attractiveness and face preferences in women. *Animal Behaviour 72*, 981–987.

Ludwig, W. (1932). *Das Rechts-links problem im tierreich und beim menschen*. Berlin: Springer-Verlag.

Manning, J. T., Scutt, D. & Lewis-Jones, D. I. (1998). Developmental stability, ejaculate size, and sperm quality in men. *Evolution and Human Behavior 19*, 273–282.

Manning, J. T., Scutt, D., Whitehouse, G. H. & Leinster, S. J. (1997). Breast asymmetry and phenotypic quality in women. *Evolution and Human Behavior 18*, 223–236.

Marlowe, C. M., Schneider, S. L. & Nelson, C. E. (1996). Gender and attractiveness biases in hiring decisions: Are more experienced managers less biased? *Journal of Applied Psychology 81*, 11–21.

McArthur, L. A., K. (1983–1984). Impressions of baby-faced adults. *Social Cognition 2*, 315–342.

McArthur, L. Z. & Berry, D. S. (1987). Cross-cultural agreement in perceptions of babyfaced adults. *Journal of Cross–cultural Psychology 18*, 165–192.

Mealey, L., Bridgestock, R. & Townsend, G. (1999). Symmetry and perceived facial attractiveness. *Journal of Personality and Social Psychology 76*, 151–158.

Mitton, J. B. & Grant, M. C. (1984). Associations among proteins heterozygosity, growth rate, and developmental homeostasis. *Annual Review of Ecology and Systematics 15*, 479–499.

Møller, A. P. (1997). Developmental stability and fitness: A review. *American Naturalist* **149**, 916–942.

Møller, A. P., Christe, P. & Lux, E. (1999). Parasitism, host immune function, and sexual selection. *Quarterly Review of Biology 74*, 3–20.

Møller, A. P., Soler, M. & Thornhill, R. (1995). Breast asymmetry, sexual selection, and human reproductive success. *Ethology and Sociobiology 16*, 207–219.

Møller, A. P. & Swaddle, J. P. (1997). *Asymmetry, Developmental Stability, and Evolution*. Oxford: Oxford University Press.

Møller, A. P. & Thornhill, R. (1998a). Bilateral symmetry and sexual selection: A meta-analysis. *American Naturalist 151*, 174–192.

Møller, A. P. & Thornhill, R. (1998b). Male parental care, differential parental investment by females and sexual selection. *Animal Behaviour 55*, 1507–1515.

Penton-Voak, I. S. & Chen, J. Y. (2004). High salivary testosterone is linked to masculine male facial appearance in humans. *Evolution and Human Behavior 25*, 229–241.

Penton-Voak, I. S., Jones, B. C., Little, A. C., Baker, S., Tiddeman, B., Burt, D. M. & Perrett, D. I. (2001). Symmetry, sexual dimorphism in facial proportions, and male facial attractiveness. *Proceedings of the Royal Society of London, B 268*, 1617–1623.

Penton-Voak, I. S. & Perrett, D. I. (2000). Female preference for male faces changes cyclically—further evidence. *Evolution and Human Behavior 21*, 39–48.

Penton-Voak, I. S., Perrett, D. I., Castles, D. L., Kobayashi, T., Burt, D. M., Murray, L. K. & Minamisawa, R. (1999a). Menstrual cycle alters face preference. *Nature 399*, 741–742.

Penton-Voak, I. S., Perrett, D. I. & Pierce, J. (1999b). Computer graphic studies of the role of facial similarity in attractiveness judgements. *Current Psychology 18*, 104–117.

Perrett, D. I., Burt, D. M., Penton-Voak, I. S., Lee, K. J., Rowland, D. A. & Edwards, R. (1999). Symmetry and human facial attractiveness. *Evolution and Human Behavior 20*, 295–307.

Perrett, D. I., Lee, K. J., Penton-Voak, I. S., Rowland, D. R., Yoshikawa, S., Burt, D. M., Henzi, S. P.,

Castles, D. L. & Akamatsu, S. (1998). Effects of sexual dimorphism on facial attractiveness. *Nature 394*, 884–887.

Perrett, D. I., May, K. A. & Yoshikawa, S. (1994). Facial shape and judgments of female attractiveness. *Nature 368*, 239–242.

Petrie, M. (1994). Improved growth and survival of offspring of peacocks with more elaborate trains. *Nature 371*, 598–599.

Petrie, M., Halliday, T. & Sanders, C. (1991). Peahens prefer peacocks with more elaborate trains. *Animal Behaviour 41*, 323–331.

Rhodes, G. (2006). The evolutionary psychology of facial beauty. *Annual Review of Psychology 57*, 199–226.

Rhodes, G., Chan, J., Zebrowitz, L. A. & Simmons, L. W. (2003a). Does sexual dimorphism in human faces signal health? *Proceedings of the Royal Society of London B 270*, S93–S95.

Rhodes, G., Hickford, C. & Jeffery, L. (2000). Sex-typicality and attractiveness: Are supermale and superfemale faces super-attractive. *British Journal of Psychology 91*, 125–140.

Rhodes, G., Jeffery, L., Watson, T. L., Clifford, C. W. G. & Nakayama, K. (2003b). Fitting the mind to the world: Face adaptation and attractiveness aftereffects. *Psychological Science 14*, 558–566.

Rhodes, G., Proffitt, F., Grady, J. & Sumich, A. (1998). Facial symmetry and the perception of beauty. *Psychonomic Bulletin Review 5*, 659–669.

Rhodes, G., Sumich, A. & Byatt, G. (1999). Are average facial configurations attractive only because of their symmetry? *Psychological Science 10*, 52–58.

Rhodes, G. & Tremewan, T. (1996). Averageness, exaggeration, and facial attractiveness. *Psychological Science 7*, 105–110.

Rhodes, G., Yoshikawa, S., Clark, A., Lee, K., McKay, R. & Akamatsu, S. (2001a). Attractiveness of facial averageness and symmetry in non-Western populations: In search of biologically based standards of beauty. *Perception 30*, 611–625.

Rhodes, G., Zebrowitz, L. A., Clark, A., Kalick, S. M., Hightower, A. & McKay, R. (2001b). Do facial averageness and symmetry signal health? *Evolution and Human Behaviour 22*, 31–46.

Riggio, R. & Woll, S. 1984 The role of non-verbal and physical attractiveness in the selection of dating partners. *Journal of Social and Personal Relations 1*, 347–357.

Roberts, S. C., Little, A. C., Gosling, L. M., Perrett, D. I., Carter, V., Jones, B. C., Penton-Voak, I. & Petrie, M. 2005 MHC-heterozygosity and human facial attractiveness. *Evolution and Human Behavior 26*, 213–226.

Samuels, C. A., Butterworth, G., Roberts, T., Graupner, L. & Hoyle, G. 1994 Facial aesthetics: babies prefer attractiveness to symmetry. *Perception 23*, 823–831.

Scheib, J. E. 2001 Context–specific mate choice criteria: women's trade-offs in the contexts of long–term and extra-pair mateships. *Personal Relationships 8*, 371–389.

Scheib, J. E., Gangestad, S. W. & Thornhill, R. 1999 Facial attractiveness, symmetry, and cues to good genes. *Proceedings of the Royal Society of London, B 266*, 1913–1917.

Sigall, H. & Ostrove, N. 1975 Beautiful but dangerous: Effects of offender attractiveness and nature of the crime on juridical judgement. *Journal of Personality and Social Psychology 31*, 410–414.

Snyder, M., Tanke, E. D. & Berscheid, E. 1977 Social perception and interpersonal behaviour: On the self-fulfilling nature of social stereotypes. *Journal of Personality and Social Psychology 35*, 656–666.

Swaddle, J. P. & Cuthill, I. C. 1995 Asymmetry and human facial attractiveness: symmetry may not always be beautiful. *Proceedings of the Royal Society of London, B 261*, 111–116.

Swaddle, J. P. & Reierson, G. W. 2003 Testosterone increases perceived dominance but not attractiveness in human males. *Proceedings of the Royal Society of London, B 269*, 2285–2289.

Thornhill, R. & Gangestad, S. W. 1993 Human facial beauty: averageness, symmetry, and parasite resistance. *Human Nature 4*, 237–269.

Thornhill, R. & Gangestad, S. W. 1994 Human fluctuating asymmetry and sexual behaviour. *Psychological Science 5*, 297–302.

Thornhill, R. & Gangestad, S. W. 1999 Facial attractiveness. *Trends in Cognitive Sciences 3*, 452–460.

Thornhill, R. & Gangestad, S. W. 2006 Facial sexual dimorphism, developmental stability, and susceptibility to disease in men and women. *Evolution and Human Behavior 27*, 131–144.

Valen, L. V. 1962 A study of fluctuating asymmetry. *Evolution 16*, 125–142.

Valentine, T., Darling, S. & Donnelly, M. 2004 Why are average faces attractive? The effect of view and averageness on the attractiveness of female faces. *Psychonomic Bulletin & Review 11*, 482–487.

Waitt, C. & Little, A. C. 2006 Preferences for symmetry in conspecific facial shape among Macaca mulatta. *International Journal of Primatology 27*, 133–145.

Walster, E., Aronson, V., Abrahams, D. & Rottman, L. 1966 Importance of physical attractiveness in dating behaviour. *Journal of Personality and Social Psychology 4*, 508–516.

Wedekind, C. 1992 Detailed information about parasites as revealed by sexual ornamentation. *Proceedings of the Royal Society of London, B 147*, 169–174.

Yesilova, Z., Ozata, M., Kocar, I. H., Turan, M., Pekel, A., Sengul, A. & Ozdemir, I. C. 2000 The effects of gonadotropin treatment on the immunological features of male patients with idiopathic hypogonadotropic hypogonadism. *Journal of Clinical Endocrinology and Metabolism, 85*, 66–70.

Zahavi, A. 1975 Mate selection: A selection for a handicap. *Journal of Theoretical Biology 53*, 205–214.

Zebrowitz–McArthur, L. & Baron, R. M. 1983 Toward and ecological approach to social perception. *Psychological Review 90*, 215–238.

CHAPTER 10

Why Cosmetics Work

Richard Russell

COSMETICS AND BEAUTY

The Power of Cosmetics

Decorating the face and body is an activity that is among the oldest, most widespread, and persistent of human behaviors. Paint pigments have been found in archeological contexts over 75,000 years old, indicating that people may have decorated themselves with body paint before they covered their bodies with clothing (Jablonski, 2006). The practice has continued since, and people in all societies decorate the face and body. In his cross-cultural description of the decoration of the human body, Robert Brain marvels that "body decoration in some societies is the most important of the arts, and in many cases may justly be termed a fine art. However, for myself as an anthropologist, the most interesting fact to have emerged from researching and writing this book is that the transformation through art of the human body is a basic need which is universally practiced among the peoples of the world, even the most puritanical or the most simple." (Brain, 1979, p. 185)

Cosmetic practices are as difficult to eradicate as they are widespread. During the Victorian era in the English-speaking world, the use of cosmetics was strongly discouraged, and viewed as morally unsound. Nevertheless, women found ways to change the apparent coloration of their face, using techniques such as pinching their cheeks and biting their lips to create a rosy hue,

and wearing colors in their bonnet linings to produce the optical effect of lightening their skin (Peiss, 1998). More recently, attempts in communist countries to ban cosmetics were unsuccessful because they resulted in a black market (Brain, 1979). In the most industrialized societies of the current era, cosmetics are neither discouraged nor banned, and their use is widespread. In 2007 the worldwide retail value of color cosmetics alone[1] was more than $37 billion (source: ©Euromonitor International).

Cosmetics and other decorations of the body are widespread and persistent because they are a part of what defines us as individuals and as humans. Cosmetics help to give us our identity, and people cling to them in even the most extreme of circumstances. Nancy Etcoff argues that the fashion designer Betsey Johnson's statement "If I were dying, I would be in the hospital wearing lipstick," expressed a timeless sentiment, as evidenced by the pots of red iron oxide for the lips left in ancient Sumerian and Egyptian tombs (Etcoff, 1999). Lieutenant Colonel Mervin Willett Gonin, who was in the

---

[1] *Color cosmetics* refers to products intended to alter the user's appearance, and is what is typically meant by colloquial use of the term *make-up*. For example, this would include lipstick and eyeliner, but not soap, moisturizer, or perfume. *Cosmetics* can refer to all these products and more. The 2007 worldwide retail value of all cosmetics and toiletries was more than $290 billion (source: ©Euromonitor International).

British Army unit that liberated the concentration camp Bergen-Belsen in 1945 wrote "It was shortly after the B.R.C.S. teams arrived, though it may have no connection, that a very large quantity of lipstick arrived. This was not at all what we men wanted, we were screaming for hundreds and thousands of other things and I don't know who asked for lipstick. I wish so much that I could discover who did it, it was the action of genius, sheer unadulterated brilliance. I believe nothing did more for those internees than the lipstick. Women lay in bed with no sheets and no nightie but with scarlet lips, you saw them wandering about with nothing but a blanket over their shoulders, but with scarlet lips. I saw a woman dead on the post mortem table and clutched in her hand was a piece of lipstick. Do you see what I mean? At last someone had done something to make them individuals again, they were someone, no longer merely the number tattooed on the arm. At last they could take an interest in their appearance. That lipstick started to give them back their humanity" (Gonin, 1945, final page).

A Universal Practice with Parochial Forms

Charles Darwin argued that the practices of personal decoration found among all different peoples of the world was an argument for the unity of the human race "They rather indicate the close similarity of the mind of man, to whatever race he may belong, in the same manner as the almost universal habits of dancing, masquerading, and making rude pictures" (Darwin, 1871, Ch. XIX, p.339). However, in the same text, he also wrote that "Savages at the present day everywhere deck themselves with plumes, necklaces, armlets, earrings, &c. They paint themselves in the most diversified manner" (Ch. XIX, p.343). These two observations illustrate the paradoxical nature of personal decoration: it is a timeless and universal human pursuit, but there is immense variety in the specific ways in which it is performed. This situation was not confined to Darwin's era, and anthropologists continue to record an immense diversity of the forms that cosmetic decoration can take. From the toes to the scalp, every part of the body is painted, tattooed, scarred, or ornamented by one culture or another, in a dazzling variety of styles (Brain, 1979; Ebin, 1979). Even within a given culture, cosmetic practices change rapidly, as they are a primary object of fashion. There can even be multiple, conflicting fashions in the same culture at the same time. In the 1990s, two of the most popular lines of cosmetics in the United States were M.A.C. (which had a bold, theatrical style and a famous drag queen as its spokesmodel) and Bobbi Brown (which had a minimal, natural style and sold 10 different neutral shades of lipstick) (Berg, 2001).

Though the practice of personal decoration is a human universal, the *forms* that these practices impart on the body are diverse. There seem to be few if any universal preferences for particular styles. Given that fashions change and cultural variation is enormous, it would seem that there is no place for a scientific approach to understanding cosmetics. Perhaps for this reason, scientists have not taken significant interest in studying cosmetics. However, science has taken an intense interest in the question of whether there are consistent factors that result in particular faces being considered more or less attractive.

Universal Beauty

In the past several decades, the social, evolutionary, developmental, and perceptual psychology communities have taken up the study of facial attractiveness. An important conceptual shift occurred during this period, with researchers moving from the belief that notions of beauty are arbitrary cultural conventions, to the belief that there exist biologically based universal factors influencing perceptions of attractiveness (Etcoff, 1999; Fink & Neave, 2005; Langlois et al., 2000; Little & Perrett, this volume; Rhodes, 2006; Thornhill & Gangestad, 1999; Zebrowitz, 1997). The main evidence for the idea that attractiveness has some basis in biology are the observations of agreement between adults in different cultures (Cunningham et al. 1995; D. M. Jones & Hill, 1993; Langlois et al., 2000) and between adults and very young infants (who are too young to have learned cultural standards) (Langlois et al., 1987; Samuels & Ewy, 1985; Slater et al., 1998) on the relative attractiveness of different faces. Together, these lines of evidence suggest that there is at least some agreement on facial attractiveness that is not culturally or socially determined, and hence is biological in origin.

A consequence of the belief in universal agreement on attractiveness is that it has become more meaningful to consider the question, "What is considered attractive?" There are now considered to be several reasonably consistent factors of facial attractiveness, including youthfulness (Zebrowitz, Olson, & Hoffman, 1993), skin homogeneity (Fink, Grammer, & Thornhill, 2001), averageness (similarity of the face to the population average) (Langlois & Roggman, 1990), sexual dimorphism (masculinity or femininity) (Cunningham, 1986; Perrett et al., 1998), and bilateral symmetry of the face (Thornhill & Gangestad, 1993). However, none of these factors alone is either sufficient or necessary for a face to be attractive (Zebrowitz & Rhodes, 2002).

The Paradox of Cosmetics

Given that universal preferences for beauty exist and are structured around biologically based factors of attractiveness, there should also be universal approaches to practices of personal decoration. If there is agreement on what is attractive in a face, there should also be agreement on how the attractiveness of a face can be enhanced. Yet the beautification practices used by the full range of human societies are incredibly varied.

This chapter addresses the question of whether personal decoration practices are arbitrary or follow discernable rules. The primary focus of investigation is the practice of color cosmetics (make-up). I begin by demonstrating the existence of a sex difference in facial contrast, then present evidence that cosmetics are used in precisely the correct way to exaggerate this sex difference, making the face appear more feminine, and hence attractive. I then describe ways in which cosmetics are used to manipulate other factors of beauty in addition to sexual dimorphism. I propose that cosmetics can be viewed as a kind of technology for manipulating these universal factors of facial attractiveness. Finally I discuss how this account of cosmetics may relate to personal decoration in general.

EXAGGERATION OF SEX DIFFERENCES BY COSMETICS

Sex Differences in Pigmentation

As described earlier, sex differences in facial appearance play an important role in facial attractiveness. However, there is not at present a complete understanding of how male and female faces differ in their appearance. Sex differences in the shape of the face have been well described using traditional caliper-based anthropometric methods (Enlow, 1990; Farkas & Munro, 1987), photographic methods (Burton, Bruce, & Dench, 1993), and laser-scanning methods (Bruce et al., 1993; Burton et al., 1993). The differences between male and female facial pigmentation are less well characterized, despite the fact that pigmentation (i.e., surface reflectance properties) is known to be important for sex classification (Bruce & Langton, 1994; Hill, Bruce, & Akamatsu, 1995; O'Toole et al., 1998; O'Toole, Vetter, Troje, & Bulthoff, 1997).

Known sex differences in pigmentation are limited to differences in the overall brightness and hue of the skin. Female skin is lighter than male skin, a sex difference that has been consistently found in human populations around the world (reviewed by Frost, 1988; Jablonski & Chaplin, 2000). Peter Frost has also provided historical and archeological evidence that this sex difference is well known to ethnically homogenous populations, for whom it is the primary source of skin color variation (Frost, 2005). Female skin is also more green than male skin, which is more red in appearance (Edwards & Duntley, 1939). This is likely due to males having higher concentrations of hemoglobin.[2] This difference is perceptible, and can be used to classify faces by sex (Tarr, Kersten, Cheng, & Rossion, 2001). Little is known about whether

---

[2] Variations in hemoglobin, including transitory within-individual changes, are visible through even the darkest skin. It has been hypothesized that color vision in primates evolved in order to perceive these fluctuations in hemoglobin concentrations of the blood (Changizi, Zhang, & Shimojo, 2006; Changizi & Shimojo, this volume).

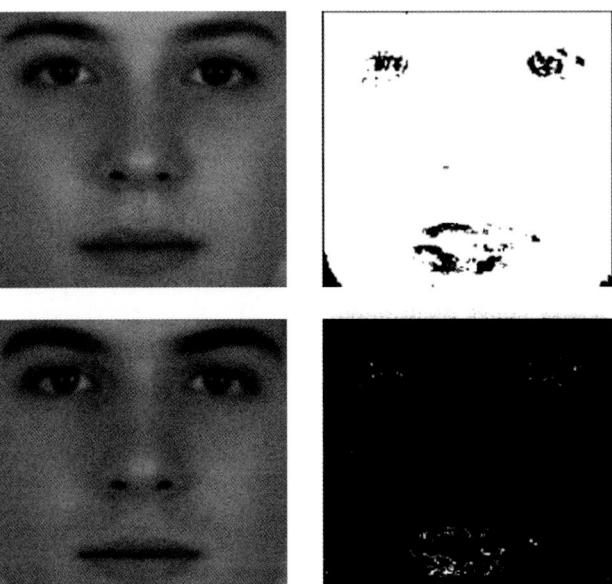

Figure 10.1 The upper left image was produced by morphing together 22 Caucasian female faces, then warping the averaged image into an androgynous shape. The lower left image was produced by morphing together 22 Caucasian male faces, then warping the averaged image into the same androgynous shape as the female averaged face, above. In the upper right image, white pixels correspond to regions of the female average that are lighter than the male average. In the lower right image, white pixels correspond to regions of the male average that are lighter than the female average.

and how male and female facial skin differs beyond these one-dimensional differences in overall brightness or redness. For example, are the sex differences in pigmentation consistent across different parts of the face?

An agnostic approach toward determining whether there are spatially organized sex differences in pigmentation is to compare the morphed averages of photographs of many male faces and many female faces taken under controlled lighting conditions. Toward this end, I averaged together 22 female and 22 male Caucasian faces. I then warped these two averages into the same androgynous shape, so that all the features were in the same locations. This produced two images in which the outline of the face and the contours of the internal features were spatially registered. These two images are shown on the left of Figure 10.1. The locations of all the features in these two images are the same, and yet the top left image appears female, and the bottom left image appears male. That the two faces appear male or female despite having the same

shapes indicates that pigmentation alone can drive sex classification. However, the specific nature of the differences in pigmentation is not immediately apparent.

To explore the differences between the two images, we can subtract one from the other to see which regions of the face are darker or lighter in one sex than the other. The two images on the right of Figure 10.1 show which pixels are lighter in the female or male averages. In the top right image, the white pixels indicate regions in which the female average is lighter than the male average. In the bottom right image, the white pixels indicate regions in which the male average is lighter than the female average. Consistent with the literature showing that female skin is lighter than male skin, the female average is lighter in all parts of the face besides the eyes and lips. However, in the regions of the eyes and lips, some pixels are lighter in the female average, while others are lighter in the male average. All the pixels that are equally light in the two images are found in the eyes and lips (not shown). This suggests that, although the skin of the female average is lighter than that of the male average, the eyes and lips of the male and female averages are about equally dark.

A Sex Difference in Facial Contrast

If female skin is lighter than male skin, but female eyes and lips are not lighter than male eyes and lips, there should be greater luminance contrast surrounding female eyes and lips than male eyes and lips. This would be important, because the visual system is sensitive to contrast rather than to absolute luminance differences. Indeed, luminance contrast is the cue to which most neurons in the early visual cortex respond. Moreover, contrast internal to the face would be robust to changes in illumination. The black ink of this text under direct midday sun reflects more light than does the white page under dim indoor lighting, yet in both contexts the text appears black and the page appears white because the contrast between the two is constant. In the same way, a sex difference in contrast could be a particularly robust cue for sex classification. If there is a sex difference in contrast it would also mean that the femaleness of the face could be increased by lightening the skin or by darkening the eyes and lips—either change would increase the contrast.

To determine whether there exists a sex difference in luminance contrast between the eyes and lips and the rest of the face—which I term *facial contrast*—I photographed sets of males and females (Russell, 2009). These sets consisted of 118 clean-shaven and cosmetics-free MIT students, including 51 East Asians and 67 Caucasians. The photos were taken under standardized lighting conditions in order to avoid systematic differences in illumination.

Grayscale versions of each image were individually hand labeled to define regions corresponding to the eyes (including the skin between the epicanthal fold and the eye, and the skin immediately below the eye), the lips, annuli surrounding the eyes (with the approximate width of the eyes but not including the

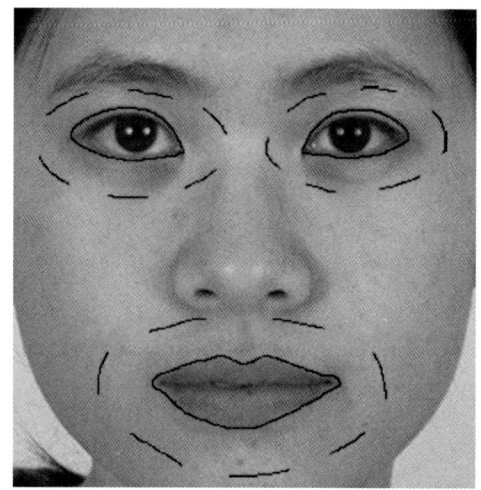

Figure 10.2 Illustration of feature labeling. Solid lines demonstrate how the boundaries of the eyes and lips were defined. Dashed lines indicate how the boundaries of the annuli surrounding those features were defined.

eyebrow), and an annulus surrounding the lips (with the approximate width of the mouth). The definition of these regions is illustrated in Figure 10.2. The luminance values of all pixels within the eyes were averaged, as were all the pixels in the lips, the annuli surrounding the eyes, and the annulus surrounding the lips. This yielded mean luminance values for each of the four regions (eyes, skin surrounding eyes, lips, skin surrounding lips). Mean luminance values for the eyes and lips were averaged to produce the mean feature luminance. Similarly, mean luminance values for the eye annuli and lip annulus were averaged to produce the mean skin luminance. Skin and feature luminance, both being the averages of 8-bit pixel values, could range from 0 (black) to 255 (white). Facial contrast was calculated as C_F = (feature luminance − skin luminance) / (feature luminance + skin luminance). This is a kind of Michelson contrast, which varies from 0 to 1, with higher values indicating greater contrast, and 0 indicating no contrast.

In both the East Asian and Caucasian samples, the female faces had greater facial contrast than male faces. The East Asian faces (with

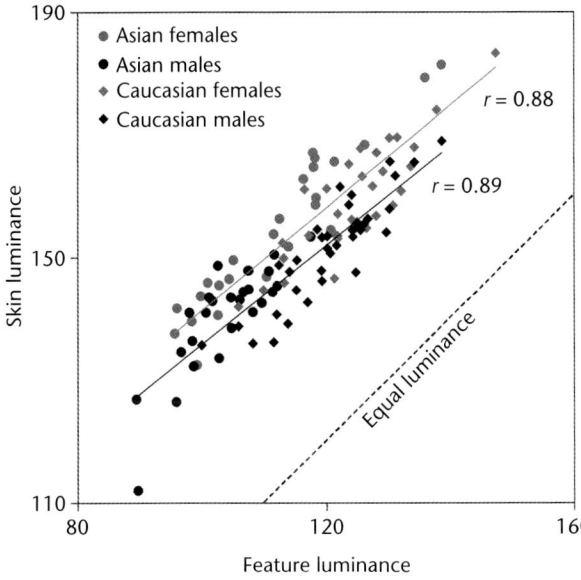

Figure 10.3 Skin luminance plotted against feature luminance, with each point representing a single face image. Larger values on either axis indicate brighter regions. The regression line for female faces is above that for the male faces, due to female faces having lighter skin than male faces. Female eyes and lips are also lighter, but to a much smaller degree.

dark eyes) had greater facial contrast than the Caucasian faces (with lighter eyes), but the sex difference in facial contrast did not differ between East Asian and Caucasian faces. Contrast around the eyes or mouth alone can also be calculated, with eye contrast as $C_E =$ (eye luminance − eye skin luminance) / (eye luminance + eye skin luminance) and mouth contrast as $C_M =$ (mouth luminance − mouth skin luminance) / (mouth luminance + mouth skin luminance). Females had greater eye contrast than males in both the East Asian and Caucasian samples. The East Asians (with dark eyes) had much greater eye contrast than the Caucasians (with lighter eyes), but the sex difference was the same in both ethnic groups. There was also a sex difference in the mouth contrast, but it was almost nonexistent for the East Asian faces. Of the two features, the sex difference in contrast was larger for the eyes than the mouth, particularly for East Asians.

Figure 10.3 shows skin luminance plotted against eye and lip (feature) luminance for each face. The sex difference in facial contrast can be appreciated by noting that the regression line for female faces lies further from the line of equal luminance (along which the skin and features are equally dark) than does the regression line for male faces. Female skin was lighter than

male skin. Female eyes and lips were also lighter than male eyes and lips, but the difference was much smaller than the difference between male and female skin. The sex difference in facial contrast is a result of the sex difference in feature (eye and lip) luminance being much smaller than the sex difference in skin luminance.

Although the lighting was diffuse and standardized across faces, a potential concern is that this sex difference in facial contrast could be caused by a sex difference in the shape of the face. Light reflected by a surface is a product not only of the illumination and reflectance properties of the surface, but also of the three-dimensional shape of the surface. In the context of facial contrast, the concern is that eyes and lips that recede more from the facial surface will appear darker than eyes and lips that recede less from the facial surface. However, male eyes recede more than female eyes, and male brows are more protuberant than female brows (lip protuberance does not differ between the sexes) (Bruce et al., 1993). This means that sex differences in face shape may actually *reduce* the apparent sex difference in eye contrast, because male eyes are further recessed and shaded by the brow, which may result in less illumination falling on male eyes than female eyes.

It is unclear why the sex difference in eye and lip reflectance is smaller than the sex difference for the skin more generally. A recent account of the evolution of skin pigmentation (Jablonski & Chaplin, 2000) may suggest a possible answer. This account argues that the amount of melanin in the skin represents a compromise between the costs and benefits of exposure to solar UV radiation. Melanin regulates the penetration of UV radiation into the skin; darker skin with more melanin permits less UV radiation. There are several dangers of UV exposure; the benefit is that it leads to the synthesis of vitamin D_3, which enhances calcium absorption. According to this account, natural selection has resulted in females having lighter skin and increased vitamin D_3 production to meet the greater calcium needs of pregnancy and lactation. This account does not discuss eye and lip pigmentation, and it is possible that there is a different balance between costs and benefits of UV exposure in the eyes and lips than in the rest of the skin. These features (particularly the eyes) have greater sensitivity to light, yet cannot significantly contribute to vitamin D_3 production because they form a miniscule portion of the body area exposed to the sun. Thus, it may be that female eyes and lips are not much lighter than male eyes and lips because they are too small to play a significant role in vitamin D_3 production, but could be damaged by greater UV exposure.

There was not a significant correlation between skin tone and facial contrast when sex and race were included as control variables. This indicates that facial contrast is not a simple function of skin tone, which suggests that the sex difference in facial contrast should also exist in ethnic groups with darker skin. However, this relationship may not extrapolate, and because only Caucasian and East Asian faces were actually measured, it cannot be stated with certainty that the sex difference in facial contrast will generalize to other ethnic groups. This represents an important avenue for further research.

Perceptual Relevance of Facial Contrast

Though luminance contrast is a robust visual cue, the effect size of the sex difference in facial contrast ($d = 0.55$ for East Asians and $d = 0.60$

for Caucasians) is much smaller than effect sizes for well known sexual dimorphisms such as waist-to-hip ratio $d = 1.7$ (Dobbelsteyn, Joffres, MacLean, & Flowerdew, 2001). The smaller effect size is likely the reason people are not aware of the sex difference in facial contrast, while they are aware of the sex difference in waist-to-hip ratio. Though people are not conscious of the sex difference in facial contrast, they may nevertheless use it as a cue in making judgments of facial masculinity or femininity and to determine the sex of a face.

In order to determine whether the magnitude of facial contrast is related to judgments of masculinity and femininity, we had 29 subjects (15 female) give Likert scale ratings of masculinity (for male faces) or femininity (for female faces) to the images described earlier. Facial contrast was positively correlated with rated femininity of female faces but negatively correlated with rated masculinity of male faces. After controlling for skin luminance (which is also sexually dimorphic) and ethnicity (there were both Caucasian and East Asian faces), facial contrast was still positively correlated with rated femininity of female faces and negatively correlated with rated masculinity of male faces, though the relationship was very weak for male faces. In summary, greater facial contrast was considered more feminine in female faces and less masculine in male faces. This effect was also found when looking at eye contrast or mouth contrast alone.

The ability of facial contrast to determine the apparent sex of a face is demonstrated in Figure 10.4. Both images were created by manipulating the same original image—a perceptually androgynous face that was made by morphing together male and female average faces. To make both images, the eyes and lips were left unchanged, but the rest of the image was darkened to produce the left image, and lightened to produce the right image. Because the eyes and lips were unchanged while the rest of the face was made darker or lighter, facial contrast was decreased or increased. Though a subtle manipulation, it has a powerful effect— making the image with decreased contrast appear male and the image with increased

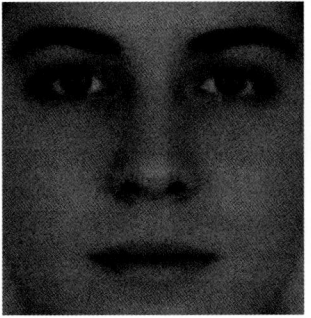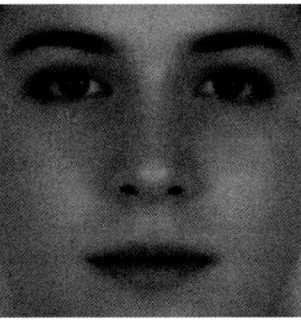

Figure 10.4 The illusion of Sex. The left face appears male, while the right face appears female, yet both images were produced by making slight alterations of the same original image. The eyes and lips were unchanged, and hence equally dark in both images. The remainder of the image was darkened in the left image, and lightened in the right image. The eyes and lips may appear darker in the right than the left image, but are not—it is an example of simultaneous contrast.

contrast appear female. A similar effect is achieved if facial contrast is manipulated by darkening or lightening the eyes and lips but keeping the rest of the face unchanged (Russell, 2009, Figure 4). However, darkening or lightening the entire face (leaving facial contrast unchanged) has no effect on perceived gender (Russell, 2009, Figure A2), indicating that it is the magnitude of the facial contrast and not the overall lightness or darkness of the face that affects the apparent gender. Though people are not consciously aware of the sex difference in facial contrast, this illusion demonstrates that they nevertheless use facial contrast as a cue in perceiving the sex of a face.

Relevance of Facial Contrast to Attractiveness

Of the factors of facial attractiveness, sexual dimorphism is among the most important but also one of the most complex (Rhodes, 2006). For female faces, the relationship between attractiveness and femininity is straightforward. Evidence from many studies using a variety of methods supports the notion that more feminine female faces are considered more attractive. However, for males there is conflicting evidence about whether a more or less masculine face is considered attractive, and there are systematic individual differences in preference for masculine or feminine faces

(Little & Perrett this volume). Setting aside the individual differences, the best evidence currently supports a weak but positive relationship between masculinity and attractiveness, as found by a recent meta-analysis (Rhodes, 2006). Regardless, it is undisputed that femininity is much more attractive in female faces than in male faces.

Because facial contrast is sexually dimorphic, and there is a relationship between sexual dimorphism and facial attractiveness, we might expect to find some relationship between facial contrast and facial attractiveness. In an earlier study, I investigated this question by manipulating the facial contrast of male and female faces, and having subjects rate the faces for attractiveness (Russell, 2003). Whether contrast was manipulated by changing the darkness of the eyes and lips while keeping the rest of the face constant (Experiment 1), or by keeping the eyes and lips constant while changing the darkness of the rest of the face (Experiment 2), the manipulation had opposite effects on male and female faces. Example stimuli from Experiment 1 of Russell (2003) are presented here in Figure 10.5. However, changing the darkness of the *entire* face had no effect on ratings of male or female attractiveness (Experiment 4), indicating that it is not the overall darkness of the face, but the magnitude of the facial contrast that affects the perceived attractiveness.

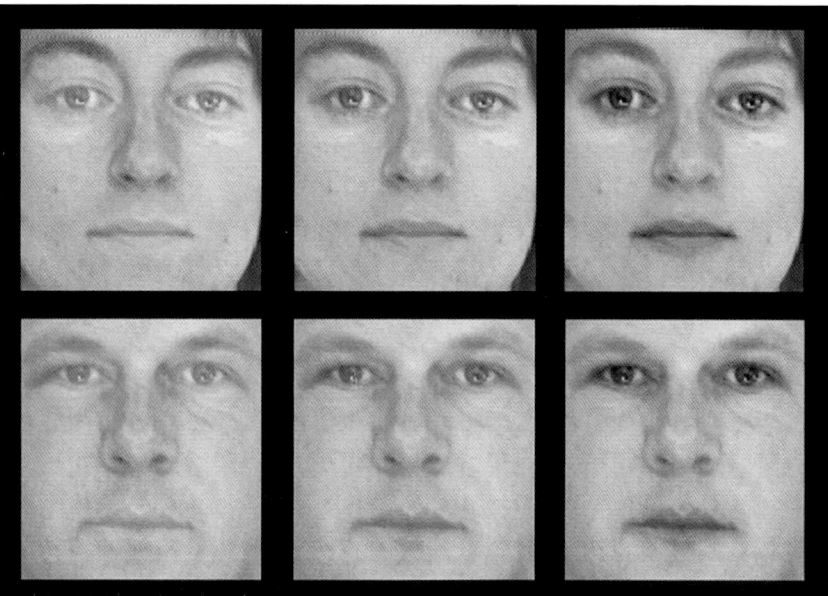

Figure 10.5 Examples of female (top row) and male (bottom row) stimuli from Experiment 1 of Russell (2003). Faces in the middle column are original photos that have not been manipulated. Faces in the left column have had the eyes and lips lightened, while the rest of the face remains constant. Faces in the right column have had the eyes and lips darkened, while the rest of the face remains constant. Female faces with greater facial contrast were rated more attractive than those with lesser facial contrast, while the opposite was found with the male faces.

Received Cosmetics

Before specifically discussing how facial contrast relates to cosmetic use, let us first consider how cosmetics are used. One approach toward understanding how cosmetics are used is to compare 'before and after' images (i.e. a photograph taken 'before' cosmetics have been applied paired with another taken 'after' cosmetics have been applied), as illustrated in Figure 10.6. On the left is the morphed average of 12 Caucasian females (18–21 years, mean 19.6 years) photographed under controlled lighting conditions wearing no cosmetics. On the right is the morphed average of the same 12 females photographed under the same lighting conditions wearing cosmetics that they applied themselves, with the instruction to "apply cosmetics as you would when going out at night." The most obvious difference between the two images is the darkening of the eyes and lips in the image of the faces with cosmetics. This is not surprising—lipstick and eyeliner are among the most commonly used cosmetics.

The general style of cosmetics seen in Figure 10.6 will be familiar to the readers of this chapter. The primary constituents of this style are: eyeliner, eye-shadow, and mascara for darkening the eyes and lashes, lipstick for darkening the lips, blush for making the cheeks pink, and foundation for making the skin tone more even, and sometimes lighter.[3] I call this the "received style" of cosmetics, or simply "received cosmetics," to indicate the common or generally accepted use of this style in industrialized societies.

Why do received cosmetics exist in the form that they do? Why are the eyes and lips darkened

---

[3] Though it reflects the vision of a particular make-up artist, the book *Makeup Your Mind* by François Nars (Nars, 2001) is an excellent resource for understanding how cosmetics affect the appearance of the face. It contains tightly controlled before-and-after images on facing pages with clear plastic overlays to indicate the specific cosmetics applied to different parts of the face in the 'after' images.

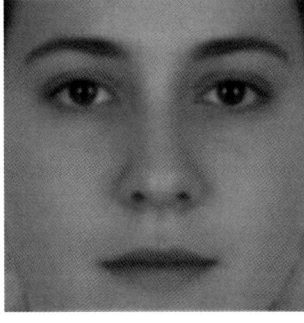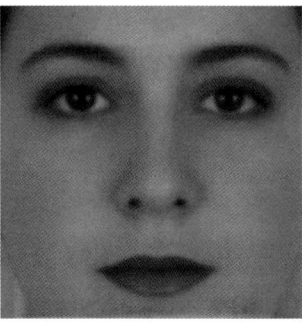

Figure 10.6 Averages of the same 12 females wearing no cosmetics (left) and wearing cosmetics as they would "when going out at night."

instead of the nose and eyebrows? And why are they darkened and not lightened? Of the hundreds of possible patterns of modification by color cosmetics, why was this pattern chosen? It should be clear by now that this pattern of cosmetic use is almost certainly not accidental; that it precisely exaggerates the sex difference in facial contrast.

Exaggeration of Facial Contrast by Cosmetics

The received style of cosmetics involves darkening the eyes and lips while leaving the rest of the face largely unchanged. This is one of two patterns of cosmetic application that could increase facial contrast (the other being to significantly lighten the entire face, except for the eyes and lips). To confirm that cosmetic application increases facial contrast, we measured the facial contrast of the set of 12 Caucasian faces that were photographed with and without cosmetics (Russell, 2009). On average, facial contrast was much larger with cosmetics than without cosmetics, and greater facial contrast was found in each of the 12 faces when they were wearing cosmetics than when they were not. Both eye contrast and mouth contrast were increased by cosmetics. The large and consistent increase in facial contrast achieved with cosmetics more clearly differentiates male and female faces. The effect size of the sex difference in facial contrast comparing the 36 male Caucasian faces and the 12 female Caucasian faces wearing cosmetics, $d = 1.85$, is similar to the effect size of the sex differences in waist-to-hip ratio.

Application of cosmetics increases facial contrast—precisely the manipulation capable of making the face appear more feminine. It is highly unlikely that this would happen by chance. Different parts of the face could be lightened or darkened in many ways, but only this particular pattern is related to how male and female faces differ. Moreover, there is a direction to the pattern—increasing the contrast makes the face appear more feminine, but decreasing it makes the face appear more masculine. Yet cosmetics are used consistently to increase facial contrast. Faces are rated more feminine when they are wearing cosmetics than when they are not wearing cosmetics (Cox & Glick, 1986), and are also rated more attractive, whether the cosmetics are self-applied (Cash, Dawson, Davis, Bowen, & Galumbeck, 1989) or professionally-applied (Cox & Glick, 1986; Graham & Jouhar, 1980; Huguet, Croizet, & Richetin, 2004; Mulhern, Fieldman, Hussey, Leveque, & Pineau, 2003). Taken together, this suggests that an important function of the received style of cosmetics is to increase the apparent femininity—and hence attractiveness—of the female face by increasing facial contrast.

Cosmetics Manipulate Biologically Based Factors of Attractiveness

The use of color cosmetics to increase facial contrast is not the only situation in which cosmetics are used to accentuate a sex difference to make the female face appear more feminine and hence more attractive. Another such manipulation of a sexually dimorphic facial feature is eyebrow plucking. Both eyebrow thickness and eyebrow-to-eye distance are sexually dimorphic (Burton, Bruce, & Dench, 1993; Farkas & Munro, 1987), with females having thinner brows that are higher above the eye. Accordingly, these sex differences of the eyebrow are important cues for perceiving the sex of a face (Bruce et al., 1993; Sadr, Jarudi, & Sinha, 2003). Eyebrows are routinely plucked from the bottom rather than the top of the brow (Aucoin, 1997; Brown & Iverson, 1997), resulting in a thinner brow that is also further from the eye, making the face appear more feminine. Thus, trimming the bottom of the eyebrow exaggerates two sexually dimorphic features at once. The exaggeration of sex differences in facial appearance to make the female face appear more feminine and hence more attractive is likely a major principle of cosmetic use, albeit an implicit rather than explicit principle.

As was already described, in addition to sexual dimorphism there are several other factors of facial attractiveness, including youthfulness, skin homogeneity, averageness (proximity to the population average), and bilateral symmetry of the face. Several cosmetic practices involve manipulations to make the face appear more youthful, including lip plumping and rhytidectomy (face lift). Among the more common of cosmetic practices are the application of foundation and the covering of blemishes, both of which increase the homogeneity of the appearance of the skin (Mulhern, Fieldman, Hussey, Leveque, & Pineau, 2003), which is known to be related to the perceived age, health, and beauty of a face (Fink, Grammer, & Matts, 2006; Fink, Grammer, & Thornhill, 2001; B. C. Jones, Little, Burt, & Perret, 2004; Matts, Fink, Grammer, & Burquest, 2007). Facial averageness is perhaps the factor of attractiveness that is the least well understood outside the scientific community, and so there are few direct references to practices that aim to increase it. However, popular women's magazines and other guides to cosmetic practice advise identifying "problem features"—typically meaning distinctive or unusual features (e.g., very wide-set eyes or a large nose)—and learning how to make them appear less distinctive. For more sophisticated practitioners, this may even involve the use of techniques designed to change the apparent shape of the face by acting on the brain's

shape-from-shading heuristics for visual perception (Pearl, 2004). Symmetry at the least is generally not violated by cosmetics; it is rare to find a cosmetic technique that involves asymmetric manipulation. The application of foundation also reduces the asymmetry of skin pigmentation (Mulhern, Fieldman, Hussey, Leveque, & Pineau, 2003), and presumably makes the pigmentation appear closer to the population average.

Collectively, these practices indicate that cosmetics are applied in ways that manipulate many of the factors of attractiveness that have been discovered by the scientific community in recent decades. Though cosmetics are used in ways that affect these factors, there is not necessarily conscious awareness of these factors. With some factors there is explicit knowledge (as in treatments to make the face appear more youthful and the skin tone more homogenous) whereas with other factors the knowledge is implicit (as in treatments to make the face appear more feminine or more average).

Cosmetics as Technology

We have seen here that cosmetic use is not arbitrary, but instead follows discernible patterns. In particular, it is organized in such a way as to manipulate known factors of attractiveness. Could this be an accident that cosmetics just happen to be used in such ways as to manipulate these factors of beauty? Though possible, it is extraordinarily improbable. It is even more improbable given that this style of cosmetics developed independently in different locations, as I will describe later in the chapter. This poses a problem for accounts of cosmetics as arbitrary cultural phenomena. However, it is consistent with the notion that the manipulation of these factors of beauty is an integral function of cosmetics.

The idea that cosmetics have the function of manipulating the appearance of the face to affect universal factors of beauty suggests that cosmetics can be viewed as a kind of technology for making the face more attractive. In this account, cosmetics function by manipulating biologically based factors of attractiveness (including those that have been recently discovered and perhaps other undiscovered factors). The technology consists of applying implicit knowledge of facial attractiveness in order to alter the appearance of the face to make it more attractive to the perceptual systems of other people.[4]

Though cosmetics are applied to the face of the wearer, they are designed to operate on the visual system of the perceiver—it is how the face will be perceived that is relevant. For example, darkening the eyes and lips does not make the face more feminine in a physical sense (female eyes and lips are actually slightly lighter than male eyes and lips), but it does increase facial contrast, which makes the face more feminine in a perceptual sense. Thus it is necessary to consider cosmetics in terms of the visual system of the intended perceiver.

Indeed, different people have different visual systems, and different visual experiences. The ability of cosmetics to enhance facial attractiveness is greater for some observers than others, and greater for some groups of observers than others (e.g., psychology students vs. aesthetic (cosmetology) students (Huguet, Croizet, & Richetin, 2004). This may be due to differing attitudes about cosmetics and who wears them. Alternatively (or additionally) it may be due to people having had different visual experiences. Though there is ample evidence for universal agreement on facial attractiveness, this agreement is not complete. There are substantial individual differences in attractiveness

preferences (Cornwell et al., 2006; Honekopp, 2006; Little & Perrett, 2002), and attractiveness preferences are socially organized (Bronstad & Russell, 2007) and socially transmitted (B. C. Jones, DeBruine, Little, Burriss, & Feinberg, 2007). Some of the variation in the use of cosmetics may be caused by these individual and group differences in facial attractiveness preferences.

An account of cosmetics as technology need not deny the possibility for functions that cosmetics can play, including stylistic and cultural functions. The application of cosmetics can have a functional or technological goal (making the face more attractive), as well as a stylistic goal. Cosmetics—like houses, clothing, and cars—can be objects of fashion and at the same time have a functional purpose. With their position front and center on the face, cosmetics have the ability to serve multiple functions. They allow for different self-presentations in different contexts. A woman may want to convey competence and maturity while at work during the day, but romantic availability and youthfulness at night. Though the facial qualities associated with these traits are not the same, cosmetics in the hands of a skilled practitioner can be used to emphasize the relevant traits to convey these impressions. More subtly, there is evidence for different *kinds* of beauty (Franklin & Adams, this volume; Zebrowitz & Rhodes, 2002), which may not involve the same factors as beauty for mate selection. Consistent with this idea, cosmetics can be used to emphasize different kinds of looks (Aucoin, 1997). Cosmetics can also communicate where the wearer sees herself fitting into society. This connection between cosmetics and identity will be taken up at length later in this chapter.

From Cosmetics to Personal Decoration

Careful study demonstrates that cosmetic use is not arbitrary, but rather is used to manipulate biologically based factors of beauty. But what about other kinds of personal decoration? Personal decoration in all its forms is much more diverse than received cosmetics, and so contemplating how it works is inherently more

[4] There is another sense in which cosmetics can be considered a technology. Cosmetic science (or cosmetic chemistry) is an active field of research devoted to advancing the development of cosmetics, toiletries, and perfumery, with its own specialized degrees, societies, and journals. The focus of this field is the development and safety testing of chemicals and materials to be used as cosmetics, and is allied with other branches of chemistry and dermatology. The development of substances for use as cosmetics is unambiguously a technology; however, it is not what I am describing here. The idea of cosmetics as technology that I am describing is focused on the process of choosing how to manipulate the visual appearance of the face. Though there is overlap in these endeavors, they are also easily discernable.

speculative. But can we at least formulate a systematic approach to understanding patterns of decoration?

A critical step toward a universal account of personal decoration lies in recognizing that not all styles exist for the purpose of making the wearer appear more attractive. For the present purposes, decoration can be divided into two primary types: beautification and signification. Beautification refers to adornment intended to make the wearer more attractive, without affecting their location within society. Signification refers to adornment that places an individual within society, wherein the specific adornments are signs that stand for something else. In the words of Victoria Ebin, body decorations can amount to "...a statement made by the individual about himself and his society," and are "part of a signaling system, communicating information not because of any mechanical link between means and ends, but because of the existence of a culturally defined communication code." (Ebin, 1979, p.10) This kind of adornment can be used to mark the culture, class, religion, or other social group to which a person belongs. It can also be used to indicate status, rank, or wealth within a group, as well as other personal information, such as age, gender, or reproductive status. Adornment can also signal more subtle information, such as rebellion against social norms. Like clothing (Barnard, 1996; Davis, 1992), marks of signification are involved in the *visual representation of identity*, and have enormous scope and range (Brain, 1979; Ebin, 1979).

This classification is not binary; specific decorations may play both beautification and signification roles. A particular hairstyle, item of clothing, or style of cosmetics may signal that the wearer is from a particular cultural group, of a certain age, and so on, but also enhance the beauty of the wearer. For example, tattoos and face paint are often used to indicate group identity or social position, but they may also be used in ways that manipulate biological beauty factors; there are systematic sex differences in the anatomical locations of scarification and tattooing (Singh & Bronstad,

1997) and symmetrically applied decorations can enhance facial attractiveness (Cárdenas & Harris, 2006). Conversely, lipstick and other cosmetics are often forbidden to girls, and so their use can mark the passage from girlhood to womanhood (Ragas & Kozlowski, 1998). Decoration for signification may also develop beauty connotations via *overgeneralization* (Zebrowitz et al. this volume). For example, a particular decoration may become associated with beauty precisely because it signifies an attractive group such as nubile women or the wealthy or powerful.

The set of possible forms of decoration that could work for signification is much larger than the array of possible forms of decoration that could work for beautification, because the visual constraints on beautification are much stronger than on signification. Any pattern, color, or shape can potentially be used as a sign, but only a small set of alterations to the face or body are capable of acting on the biological factors of beauty. For this reason, signification most likely predated beautification as a function of adornment. Decoration for beautification (e.g., cosmetics) may have developed by accident at multiple locations and times when it was noticed that a signifying decoration had the effect of making the wearer more beautiful. Or it may have been an entirely unconscious process. Adornments for signification (or other functional purposes, such as medicinal) that happened to make the wearer more beautiful may have simply been more likely to withstand changes in fashion.

Insofar as adornment or markings for signification have a symbolic nature, their surface forms are inherently arbitrary. In this light it is not surprising that there is diversity in the specific forms that this kind of decoration takes. It would not make sense to look for universal *forms* for signification. Instead, we might expect to find universal *functions* (categories) of signification. For example, most, if not all, cultures use adornment to communicate marital or mating status. However, this status is conveyed by a wide variety of forms, including tattoos, jewelry, hairstyle, and body painting.

Cultural Variation

Returning to the question of why there is so much variation in styles of personal decoration, we can see that much of it can be attributed to adornment for signification. Although there may well be universals regarding the *functions* of this kind decoration, we cannot expect the *forms* to follow rules, beyond that they must be perceptible by the relevant people under the relevant conditions (a sign works only if the intended viewers can see it). Thus, much of the variation in the forms of personal decoration—probably the majority of the variation—does not need to be explained.

Yet even if we restrict ourselves to decoration whose purpose is to make the person more beautiful, there is still significant variation. However, this problem largely disappears when we take the viewpoint that cosmetics are a kind of technology. Technology is not consistently developed across all cultures. It is taken as a given that different cultures have differently developed practices of agriculture, medicine, and communication, for example. Similarly, there is no reason to expect cosmetic practices to be equally developed in all cultures. A reasonable assumption is that the development of cosmetic technology is roughly correlated with the development of other technologies in a given society.

Consistent with the idea that development of cosmetics is associated with other technologies is the evidence that the received style of cosmetics developed in early centers of civilization—the same locations where many other technologies were first developed. Ancient Egypt was an early center for the development of cosmetics (Dayagi-Mendels, 1989). Indeed, the Egyptians "had most of the cosmetic aids which have ever been devised" (Corson, 1972, p.8), including rouge for the lips and cheeks, eyeliner (kohl), eyeshadows, and foundation, all of which were produced by professional cosmetics makers. The painted limestone bust of the famously beautiful Queen Nefertiti, attributed to the sculptor Thutmose in the fourteenth century B.C.E., demonstrates cosmetic use that appears strikingly modern (Figure 10.7). In Mesopotamia,

Figure 10.7 Bust of Nefertiti displayed in Altes Museum in Berlin.

pots of colored paints for the eyes, and rouges for the lips have been found in Sumerian tombs near Ur from 5,000 years ago.

However, the received style of cosmetics did not develop in only a single civilization or even adjacent civilizations. Another early center of technological and cosmetic development was the Indus Valley Civilization. Excavations at Harappa and Mohenjo-daro have found kohl pots and sticks for lining the eyes, as well as red iron oxides and white lead-based compounds that have been surmised to be rouge for the lips and cheeks and foundation for lightening the skin (Chandra, 1973; Subbarayappa, 1999). These uses of cosmetics persisted into historical times in the Indian subcontinent, and can be seen in the eleventh century C.E. temple sculpture from the Khajuraho temples in Madhya Pradesh (Figure 10.8). Evidence for ancient uses of received cosmetics in the East Asia is less clear, though there is a long history of the

Figure 10.8 Eleventh century sculpture from Khajuraho temples of a woman applying eyeliner.

Figure 10.9 Traditional Geisha apprentice cosmetics.

use of white face paint and rouge for the lips in China and Japan (Corson, 1972). Overall, there is evidence for the idea that the received style of cosmetics developed in multiple centers of early technology development, and spread outward to peripheral areas such as Europe and Southeast Asia, analogous to the spread of other technologies like agriculture and writing.

As at the present, the early societies who wore the received style of cosmetics would have been relatively wealthy and powerful in comparison with neighboring societies who wore other styles. Wealth and power are always desirable, regardless of other aesthetic considerations. An alternative possibility is that the received cosmetic style spread outward from early technology centers simply because it represented the appearance of the dominant people in the region, and not because it was a more advanced technology for personal decoration. An argument against this alternative possibility comes from the development of cosmetics during Edo (Tokugawa) period Japan (1603–1868). During this period Japan was marked by seclusion, with very limited political, economic and cultural influences from external sources. It was during this time of isolation that witnessed the development of Geisha, whose style of cosmetics has remained unchanged to the present day (Corson, 1972). The cosmetics worn

by the Geisha are perhaps the most exaggerated version of received cosmetics (it is actually the Geisha apprentice, or *Maiko*, who wears this style). With virtually white skin, black eyeliner, and bright red lips, a Geisha apprentice has exceptionally high facial contrast (Figure 10.9). That this style developed during a period of extreme isolation contradicts the notion that use of the received style of cosmetics has expanded only as a result of subordinate groups wishing to look like dominant groups.

The Future of Cosmetics

A possible critique of this analysis is that it is a new version of the traditional assumption that "what we do is better than what they do." Specifically, it could be argued that it is simply an invented justification for why the customs of the author's society are superior to those of other societies. This would be similar to what Elaine Hatfield and Susan Sprecher have named "Finckism," after the Victorian psychologist Henry Finck, who argued that humankind reached it's pinnacle of attractiveness in the upper-class English gentleman (Finck was such an individual) (Hatfield & Sprecher, 1986). However, the idea presented here of cosmetics as a kind of technology suggests that the received style of cosmetics is itself underdeveloped.

Technology can be defined as the application of a body of knowledge toward a practical problem. In that sense received cosmetics may best be described as an implicit or primitive technology, because it is applied without explicit knowledge of many of the factors of beauty. Rather, it has developed over a long period of time through trial and error in order to meet the desire of people to appear more attractive. The organizing factors of beauty are only now being discovered, and their systematic application will allow cosmetics to become a technology in the full sense. In this regard, the idea that cosmetics are a kind of technology contains a testable hypothesis—that the effectiveness of cosmetics could be enhanced through the application of scientifically discovered factors of beauty.

ACKNOWLEDGMENTS

This work was supported by a NRSA fellowship from the U.S. National Eye Institute. The studies of sex differences in facial contrast and judgments of facial attractiveness are described more fully in Russell (2003) and Russell (2009). I thank the book editors and P. Matt Bronstad for helpful comments on this chapter.

REFERENCES

Aucoin, K. (1997). *Making faces.* Boston: Little, Brown and Company.

Barnard, M. (1996). *Fashion as communication.* London: Routledge.

Berg, R. (2001). *Beauty : the new basics.* New York: Workman.

Brain, R. (1979). *The decorated body.* London: Hutchinson & Co.

Bronstad, P. M., & Russell, R. (2007). Beauty is in the 'we' of the beholder: Greater agreement on facial attractiveness among close relations. *Perception, 36,* 1674–1681.

Brown, B., & Iverson, A. (1997). *Bobbi Brown beauty.* New York: HarperCollins.

Bruce, V., Burton, A. M., Hanna, E., Healey, P., Mason, O., Coombes, A., et al. (1993). Sex discrimination: How do we tell the difference between male and female faces? *Perception, 22,* 131–152.

Bruce, V., & Langton, S. (1994). The use of pigmentation and shading information in recognizing the sex and identities of faces. *Perception, 23,* 803–822.

Burton, A. M., Bruce, V., & Dench, N. (1993). What's the difference between men and women? Evidence from facial measurement. *Perception, 22,* 153–176.

Cárdenas, R. A., & Harris, L. J. (2006). Symmetrical decorations enhance the attractiveness of faces and abstract designs. *Evolution and Human Behavior, 27,* 1–18.

Cash, T. F., Dawson, K., Davis, P., Bowen, M., & Galumbeck, C. (1989). Effects of cosmetics use on the physical attractiveness and body image of American college women. *Journal of Social Psychology, 129*(3), 349–355.

Chandra, M. (1973). *Costumes textiles cosmetics & coiffure in ancient and mediaeval India.* Delhi: Oriental.

Changizi, M. A., Zhang, Q., & Shimojo, S. (2006). Bare skin, blood and the evolution of primate colour vision. *Biology Letters, 2,* 217–221.

Cornwell, R. E., Law Smith, M. J., Boothroyd, L. G., Moore, F. R., Davis, H. P., Stirrat, M. R., et al. (2006). Reproductive strategy, sexual development and attraction to facial characteristics. *Philosophical Transactions of the Royal Society B, 361,* 2143–2154.

Corson, R. (1972). *Fashions in makeup: From ancient to modern times.* London: Peter Owen.

Cox, C. L., & Glick, W. H. (1986). Resume evaluations and cosmetics use: When more is not better. *Sex Roles, 14,* 51–58.

Cunningham, M. R. (1986). Measuring the physical in physical attractiveness: Quasi-experiments on the sociobiology of female facial beauty. *Journal of Personality and Social Psychology, 50,* 925–935.

Cunningham, M. R., Roberts, A. R., Barbee, A. P., Druen, P. B., & Wu, C. H. (1995). "Their ideas of beauty are, on the whole, the same as ours": Consistency and variability in the cross-cultural perception of female physical attractiveness. *Journal of Personality and Social Psychology, 68,* 261–279.

Darwin, C. (1871). *The descent of man, and selection in relation to sex.* London: John Murray.

Davis, F. (1992). *Fashion, culture, and identity.* Chicago: University of Chicago Press.

Dayagi-Mendels, M. (1989). *Perfumes and Cosmetics in the Ancient World.* Jerusalem: The Israel Museum.

Dobbelsteyn, C., Joffres, M., MacLean, D., & Flowerdew, G. (2001). A comparative evaluation of waist circumference, waist-to-hip ratio and body mass index as indicators of cardiovascular risk factors. The Canadian Heart Health Surveys. *International Journal of Obesity, 25*, 652–661.

Ebin, V. (1979). *The body decorated*. London: Thames & Hudson.

Edwards, E. A., & Duntley, S. Q. (1939). The pigments and color of living human skin. *American Journal of Anatomy, 65*, 1–33.

Enlow, D. H. (1990). *Facial Growth* (3rd ed.). Philadelphia: W.B. Saunders.

Etcoff, N. (1999). *Survival of the prettiest: the science of beauty*. New York: Doubleday.

Farkas, L. G., & Munro, I. R. (Eds.). (1987). *Anthropometric facial proportions in medicine*. Springfield, IL: Charles C Thomas.

Fink, B., Grammer, K., & Matts, P. J. (2006). Visible skin color distribution plays a role in the perception of age, attractiveness, and health in female faces. *Evolution and Human Behavior, 27*, 433–442.

Fink, B., Grammer, K., & Thornhill, R. (2001). Human (*Homo sapiens*) facial attractiveness in relation to skin texture and color. *Journal of Comparative Psychology, 115*(1), 92–99.

Fink, B., & Neave, N. (2005). The biology of facial beauty. *International Journal of Cosmetic Science, 27*, 317–325.

Frost, P. (1988). Human skin color: A possible relationship between its sexual dimorphism and its social perception. *Perspectives in Biology and Medicine, 32*(1), 38–58.

Frost, P. (2005). *Fair Women, Dark Men*. Christchurch: Cybereditions.

Gonin, L.-C. M. W. (1945). 'Report on the Liberation of Belsen', Imperial War Museum, Department of Documents, File 85/38/1.

Graham, J. A., & Jouhar, A. J. (1980). Cosmetics considered in the context of physical attractiveness: a review. *International Journal of Cosmetic Science*(2), 77–101.

Hatfield, E., & Sprecher, S. (1986). *Mirror, mirror... The importance of looks in everyday life*. Albany, New York: State University of New York Press.

Hill, H., Bruce, V., & Akamatsu, S. (1995). Perceiving the sex and race of faces: the role of shape and colour. *Proceedings of the Royal Society of London B, 261*, 367–373.

Honekopp, J. (2006). Once More: Is Beauty in the Eye of the Beholder? Relative Contributions of Private and Shared Taste to Judgments of Facial Attractiveness. *Journal of Experimental Psychology: Human Perception and Performance, 32*(2), 199–209.

Huguet, P., Croizet, J.-C., & Richetin, J. (2004). Is "What has been cared for" necessarily good? Further evidence for the negative impact of cosmetics use on impression formation. *Journal of Applied Social Psychology, 34*(8), 1752–1771.

Jablonski, N. G. (2006). *Skin: a natural history*. Berkeley: University of California Press.

Jablonski, N. G., & Chaplin, G. (2000). The evolution of human skin coloration. *Journal of Human Evolution, 39*, 57–106.

Jones, B. C., DeBruine, L. M., Little, A. C., Burriss, R. P., & Feinberg, D. R. (2007). Social transmission of face preferences among humans. *Proceedings of the Royal Society B, 274*, 899–903.

Jones, B. C., Little, A. C., Burt, D. M., & Perret, D. I. (2004). When facial attractiveness is only skin deep. *Perception, 33*, 569–576.

Jones, D. M., & Hill, K. (1993). Criteria of facial attractiveness in five populations. *Human Nature, 4*, 271–296.

Langlois, J. H., Kalakanis, L., Rubenstein, A. J., Larson, A., Hallam, M., & Smoot, M. (2000). Maxims or myths of beauty? A meta-analytic and theoretical review. *Psychological Bulletin, 126*(3), 390–423.

Langlois, J. H., & Roggman, L. A. (1990). Attractive faces are only average. *Psychological Science, 1*, 115–121.

Langlois, J. H., Roggman, L. A., Casey, R. J., Ritter, J. M., Rieser-Danner, L. A., & Jenkins, V. Y. (1987). Infant preferences for attractive faces: Rudiments of a stereotype?. *Developmental Psychology, 23*, 363–369.

Little, A., C., & Perrett, D. I. (2002). Putting beauty back in the eye of the beholder. *The Psychologist, 15*(1), 28–32.

Matts, P. J., Fink, B., Grammer, K., & Burquest, M. (2007). Color homogeneity and visual perception of age, health, and attractiveness of female facial skin. *Journal of the American Academy of Dermatology, 57*, 977–984.

Mulhern, R., Fieldman, G., Hussey, T., Leveque, J.-L., & Pineau, P. (2003). Do cosmetics enhance female Caucasian facial attractiveness? *International Journal of Cosmetic Science, 25*, 199–205.

Nars, F. (2001). *Makeup your mind*. New York: powerHouse Books.

O'Toole, A. J., Deffenbacher, K. A., Valentin, D., McKee, K., Huff, D., & Abdi, H. (1998). The perception of face gender: The role of stimulus structure in recognition and classification. *Memory & Cognition, 26*, 146–160.

O'Toole, A. J., Vetter, T., Troje, N. F., & Bulthoff, H. H. (1997). Sex classification is better with three-dimensional head structure than with image intensity information. *Perception, 26*, 75–84.

Pearl, E. (2004). *Plastic surgery without the surgery: The miracle of makeup techniques*. New York: Warner Books.

Peiss, K. (1998). *Hope in a jar: The making of America's beauty culture*. New York: Henry Holt and Company.

Perrett, D. I., Lee, K. J., Penton-Voak, I., Rowland, D., Yoshikawa, S., Burt, D. M., et al. (1998). Effects of sexual dimorphism on facial attractiveness. *Nature, 394*, 884–887.

Ragas, M. C., & Kozlowski, K. (1998). *Read my lips: a cultural history of lipstick*. San Francisco: Chronicle Books.

Rhodes, G. (2006). The evolutionary psychology of facial beauty. *Annual Review of Psychology, 57*(1), 199–226.

Russell, R. (2003). Sex, beauty, and the relative luminance of facial features. *Perception, 32*, 1093–1107.

Russell, R. (2009). A sex difference in facial contrast and its exaggeration by cosmetics. *Perception, 38*, 1211–1219.

Sadr, J., Jarudi, I., & Sinha, P. (2003). The role of eyebrows in face recognition. *Perception, 32*, 285–293.

Samuels, C. A., & Ewy, R. (1985). Aesthetic perception of faces during infancy. *British Journal of Developmental Psychology, 3*, 221–228.

Singh, D., & Bronstad, P. M. (1997). Sex differences in the anatomical locations of human body scarification and tattooing as a function of pathogen prevalence. *Evolution and Human Behavior, 18*, 403–416.

Slater, A., Von der Schulenberg, C., Brown, E., Badenoch, M., Butterworth, G., Parsons, S., et al. (1998). Newborn infants prefer attractive faces. *Infant Behavior and Development, 21*(2), 345–354.

Subbarayappa, B. V. (Ed.). (1999). *Chemistry and chemical techniques in India*. New Delhi: Pauls Press.

Tarr, M. J., Kersten, D., Cheng, Y., & Rossion, B. (2001). It's Pat! Sexing faces using only red and green. *Journal of Vision, 1*(3), 337.

Thornhill, R., & Gangestad, S. W. (1993). Human facial beauty: Averageness, symmetry, and parasite resistance. *Human Nature, 4*, 237–269.

Thornhill, R., & Gangestad, S. W. (1999). Facial Attractiveness. *Trends in Cognitive Sciences, 3*(12), 452–460.

Zebrowitz, L. A. (1997). *Reading faces: Window to the soul?* Boulder, CO: Westview Press.

Zebrowitz, L. A., Olson, K., & Hoffman, K. (1993). Stability of babyfaceness and attractiveness across the life span. *Journal of Personality and Social Psychology, 64*(3), 453–466.

Zebrowitz, L. A., & Rhodes, G. (2002). Nature let a hundred flowers bloom: The multiple ways and wherefores of attractiveness. In G. Rhodes & L. A. Zebrowitz (Eds.), *Facial attractiveness : Evolutionary, cognitive, and social perspectives* (pp. 261–293). Westport, CT: Ablex.

CHAPTER 11

Context-Specific Responses to Self-Resembling Faces

Lisa M. DeBruine and Benedict C. Jones

How do people determine who is related enough to help and who is too closely related to mate with? Phenotype matching, the assessment of relatedness through the comparison of an individual's physical cues to a self- or family template, is one possible mechanism. For humans, the most obvious physical cue indicating genetic relatedness is facial resemblance. In fact, judgments of facial similarity have been shown to be practically synonymous with judgments of perceived kinship (Maloney & Dal Martello, 2006, Dal Martello & Maloney, 2006). The social perception of facial resemblance can be investigated experimentally using computer-graphic image transformation techniques that can manipulate facial similarity in a realistic and objective manner (Rowland & Perrett, 1995, Tiddeman, Perrett, & Burt, 2001). In this chapter we will detail the methodological issues surrounding the experimental study of human facial resemblance and review experimental evidence from studies using such methods.

METHODOLOGICAL ISSUES

The studies we will review are experimental in nature and use computer-imaging techniques to manipulate facial resemblance between subjects and the faces they viewed during the experiments. Two different methods are used: averaging and transforming. The general procedures are as follows.

Averaging Faces

The basic procedure for averaging images is illustrated in Figure 11.1a–d. A number of corresponding points, such as the center of the pupils and the corners of the lips, are defined on two images. These images are termed endpoint images because they can be conceptualized as the 0 percent and 100 percent endpoints of a continuum. An algorithm is used to divide the endpoint images into triangular sections with the points as vertices (Fig. 1a,b). Two images can be combined (also termed averaged or morphed) by calculating the weighted average of the point coordinates. This results in new coordinates that are a specified percent of the distance between corresponding points along a vector connecting those points (Fig. 1c). This percent can be positive or negative: Positive values move the points from the first image toward those from the second and negative values move them away. The triangular sections of the original images are warped into the shape of the new triangular sections defined by these calculated points. Color values of corresponding pixels from the resulting warped images are combined in a specified ratio to make the finished morph (also termed average or composite, Fig. 1d). If the color values from only one image are used, it is termed a shape-only morph.

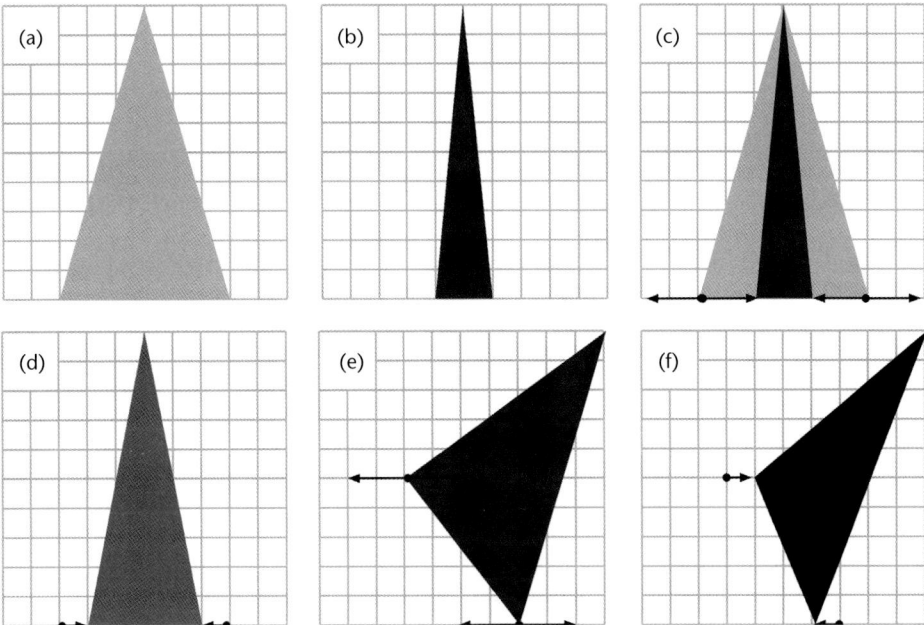

Figure 11.1 Averaging and transforming procedure examples. Averaging combines endpoint images (a, b) by calculating vectors through corresponding points (c), warping the endpoint images by moving these points to a specified position along the vector, and/or averaging color values to make a morph (d). Transforming applies a percentage of the shape and/or color differences between the two endpoint images to a third base image (e) to make a transform (f). These examples use 50 percent values for both shape and color of each of the endpoint images. Notice that the morph (c) is a color that is halfway between the endpoint images (a, b), but the transform (f) is darker than its base image (e) to 50 percent of the extent that the second endpoint image (b) is darker than the first (a).

Transforming Faces

Transforming images involves calculating the differences between two endpoint images and applying those differences to a base image. The basic procedure is much like morphing (see Tiddeman, Perrett, & Burt, 2001, for computational details); the same corresponding points are defined on each of the three images, and these images are divided into triangular sections. The base image (Fig. 1e) can be transformed by moving the points on the base image a percentage of the distance between corresponding points on the endpoint images along the vector defined by the corresponding points on the endpoint images (Fig. 1c). Color can also be transformed by changing the pixel color values of the base image by a percentage of the difference between the corresponding pixel color values of the endpoint images. The resulting transformation

(Fig. 1f) is different from the base image in the same way that the second endpoint image is different from the first endpoint image. For example, if the second endpoint image (Fig. 1b) is thinner and darker than the first endpoint image (Fig. 1a), the transformed image (Fig. 1f) will be thinner and darker than its base image (Fig. 1e).

Although the averaging technique is useful under certain conditions and software for averaging images is readily available, the transforming technique has several advantages for testing reactions to self-resemblance. First, averaging makes the resulting face more symmetrical and prototypical than either of the endpoint faces. Increasing averageness increases perceptions of attractiveness (Langlois & Roggman, 1990) and using averaged faces could cause ceiling effects for attractiveness judgments. More importantly, the transforming technique

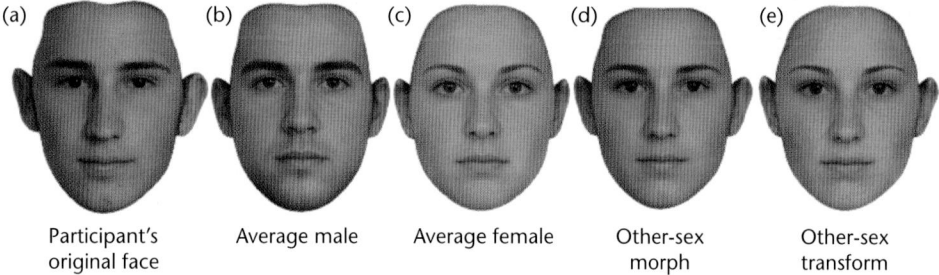

(a) Participant's original face (b) Average male (c) Average female (d) Other-sex morph (e) Other-sex transform

Figure 11.2 Other-sex morph versus other-sex transform. The other sex morph (d) was made by averaging the shape and color of the participant's face (a) and an average female face (c). The other-sex transform (e) was made by applying 100 percent of the difference in shape and color between the participant's face (a) and the average male face (b) to the average female face (c). Notice how androgynous the morph (d) appears compared to the transform (e).

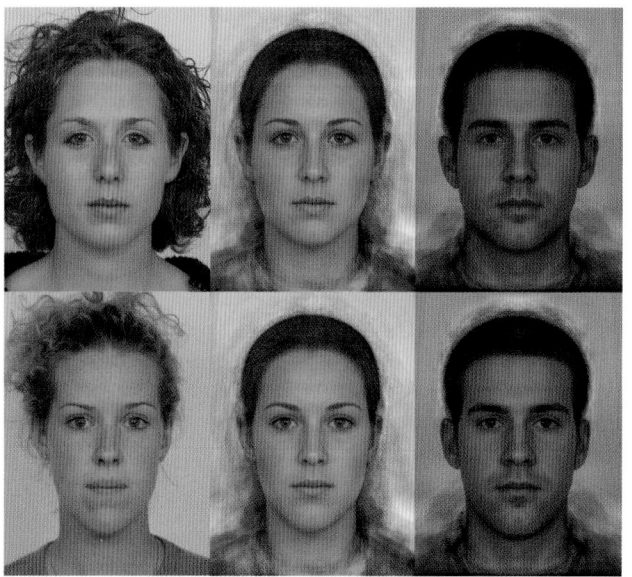

Figure 11.3 Example stimuli. 50 percent of the shape differences between the participants (left) and a same-sex composite face were applied to a same-sex composite (center) and an other-sex composite face (right).

makes the production of other-sex self-resembling faces possible (Figure 11.2). Averaging participants with other-sex faces would produce androgynous, unrealistic morphs (e.g. Fig. 2d). Transforming other-sex faces to the extent that the participant faces differ from a prototypical same-sex face does not masculinize or feminize the resulting other-sex transformation (Fig. 2e).

Additionally, the use of shape-only transformations is required to eliminate unnatural color artifacts caused by transforming female faces using male endpoint faces with differing amounts of facial hair. A man with more facial hair than the male average will have a female

transformation with the appearance of stubble, whereas a man with less facial hair than average will have a female transformation with light blotches in the areas where facial hair differs on the endpoint faces.

EXPERIMENTAL EVIDENCE

Next, we will review experimental evidence that humans use facial resemblance to respond to others in a context-dependent manner that is consistent with facial resemblance functioning as a cue of genetic kinship. First, we will review evidence that facial resemblance has a positive effect on prosocial behavior.

FACIAL RESEMBLANCE INCREASES PROSOCIAL BEHAVIOR

DeBruine (2002) used the "trust game," an interactive investment game common to experimental economic research, to investigate how facial resemblance affects prosocial behavior. This trust game gave the first player a choice between evenly splitting a small sum of money between self and a second player or entrusting a larger sum of money to the second player, who could divide it equally or selfishly. Interactions were made via computer and the opponent's face was pictured on screen. Participants played the game once with each of 12 opponents, half of whom had been subtly manipulated to resemble the experimental participant and half of whom had been equally manipulated to resemble an unfamiliar other. When participants were in the role of the first player, they showed more trusting behavior toward self-resembling opponents than other-resembling opponents. When participants were in the role of the second player, they showed no difference in selfish behavior toward self-resembling and other-resembling opponents (Figure 11.4). Control participants who interacted with the same faces as the experimental participants showed no bias

of more trusting or unselfish behavior toward the faces that resembled the experimental participants, indicating that the effect observed on trusting behavior reflected the influence of self-resemblance rather than possible influences of other facial cues (e.g., physical attractiveness). These results were replicated across two samples using slightly different techniques for manipulating the resemblance of the opponents' faces: one that included both shape and color information from the participants' faces and one that included only shape information. DeBruine (2002) did not find equivalent effects when faces resembling the experimental participants were replaced with faces that had been manipulated to resemble familiar celebrities. This latter finding suggests that the effect of self-resemblance on trusting behavior was not simply due to familiarity alone.

In a more recent study, Krupp, DeBruine, and Barclay (2008) found that cooperation in a "tragedy of the commons" game increased as the proportion of self-resembling players in the game increased. In this economics game, participants were grouped with three other players, and each player was given a $10 endowment. Each player could choose to donate any whole-dollar amount of this endowment to the

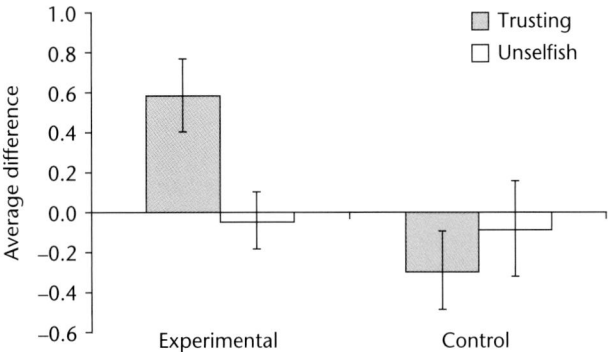

Figure 11.4 Average difference (±SEM) between number of prosocial responses to self-resembling and other-resembling opponents for experimental and control subjects. Scores are the number of trusting or unselfish responses to self-resembling faces (out of 3) minus those to other-resembling faces (out of 3), so that positive scores indicate more prosocial responses toward self-resembling opponents and negative scores indicate more prosocial responses toward other-resembling opponents. An additional set of control subjects saw the same face stimuli as the experimental subjects. These control players showed no significant differences in either trusting or unselfish behaviour, while experimental subjects were significantly more trusting of self-resembling than other-resembling opponents.

public good. Donations were then doubled and re-distributed equally to all four players, regardless of their individual contributions. Although the best strategy for the group is for all players to donate all of their endowment, the best strategy for any individual is to keep their endowment and free ride on the other players. Thus, donations to the public good are a measure of group altruism or cooperation. Participants donated increasing amounts to the public good as the number of self-resembling other players in their groups increased from zero to two. This latter finding demonstrates that increasing the number of self-resembling faces in a group increases the extent to which individuals behave in a manner that is beneficial to the group. As was the case in DeBruine (2002), Krupp et al.'s findings suggest that facial cues of self-resemblance function as a cue of kinship.

Although DeBruine's (2002) and Krupp et al.'s (2008) findings suggest that responses to self-resemblance are consistent with inclusive fitness theory, studies of the effects of self-resemblance on attractiveness judgments suggest that responses to self-resemblance are also influenced by inbreeding avoidance. In the experiments described in the rest of this chapter (DeBruine, 2004b, 2005, DeBruine, Jones, & Perrett, 2005, Penton-Voak, Perrett, Castles, et al., 1999), facial resemblance was manipulated by using a computer-graphic technique called transforming (Tiddeman et al., 2001). Because simply morphing a male and female face together causes those faces to be unnaturally androgynous, the method of transforming is used to produce more realistic opposite-sex self-resembling faces (Figure 11.3). See DeBruine, Jones, Little, and Perrett (2008) for an in-depth discussion of this method.

Facial Resemblance Is Less Attractive in a Mating Context

Considering facial resemblance when making decisions about mating partners can help to regulate the genetic relatedness of mates. Mating between close relatives is associated with the risk of autosomal recessive genetic disorders and miscarriage (Bittles, 2001), although a positive association between consanguinity

and fertility has been found due to other factors associated with consanguineous marriages, such as earlier age at first reproduction and longer duration of marriage (Bittles et al., 2002).

Although some studies have found evidence for greater-than-expected facial resemblance between engaged and married partners (Hinsz, 1989, Griffiths & Kunz, 1973), others have found that similarity was only present after many years of marriage and not at engagement (Zajonc, Adelmann, Murphy, & Niendenthal, 1987). Couples may grow more alike over time due to shared experience, or because those who look alike in personality stay together longer (Zajonc et al., 1987). This was supported by a study showing that, when age and similarity in attractiveness were controlled, the faces of couples were perceived as more similar on a variety of personality traits and that couples with longer relationships were perceived as more similar in personality. Although these studies attempted to control for factors, such as similarities in attractiveness, health, and ethnicity, that could account for the above-chance matching of couples' faces, experimental studies using computer-graphic manipulations allow for a more direct investigation of perceptions of facial self-resemblance.

Penton-Voak, Perrett, and Peirce (1999) first investigated the attractiveness of facial resemblance in opposite-sex faces by manufacturing opposite-sex versions of a group of female participants and correlating each woman's attractiveness ratings of the manufactured male faces with the independently rated similarity of those manufactured faces to her own. This study found a positive effect of facial resemblance on attractiveness ratings, which disappeared after controlling for general attractiveness. In a second study, male and female participants chose the most attractive face from a continuum that ranged from their opposite-sex version through average to a face that was perceptually opposite to their self-resembling opposite-sex version. Participants chose faces that were, on average, not significantly different from the midpoint face. However, in this study self-resemblance and averageness were confounded and, thus, strong preferences for averageness (DeBruine, Jones, Unger, Little, & Feinberg, 2007) could

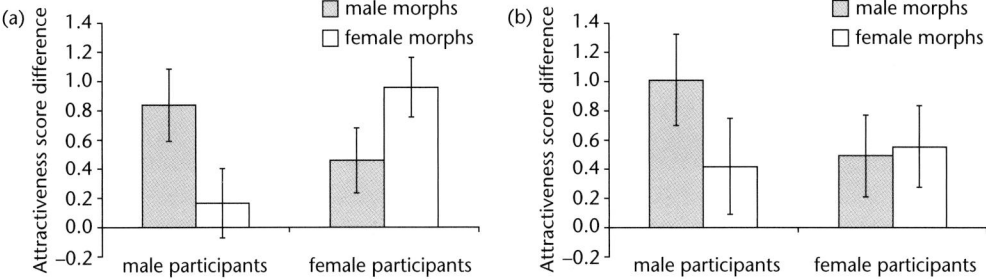

Figure 11.5 Mean attractiveness (a) and averageness (b) score differences (± SEM) were calculated from the number of times a participant chose his or her own transformed image (own-preference) minus the average number of times other participants chose that image (other-preference). Self-resemblance increased the attractiveness of same-sex faces more than opposite-sex faces. In contrast, self-resemblance increased the perceived averageness of same-sex faces no more than opposite-sex faces.

have masked any preferences for or aversions to self-resembling faces.

DeBruine (2004b) addressed some limitations to these early studies by comparing perceptions of the attractiveness of self-resembling male and female faces. Male and female versions of both male and female participants were manufactured using methods similar to those used by Penton-Voak, Perrett, and Peirce (1999). Participants were then grouped with eight other participants of the same sex, age, and ethnicity, and each participant viewed all possible pairings of the faces manufactured for that group. Participants chose the more attractive face from each pair, resulting in a measure of the extent to which they preferred self-resembling faces more than others preferred these same faces. Analyses of these scores indicated that participants demonstrated preferences for self-resemblance in own-sex faces that were significantly greater than for opposite-sex faces (Figure 11.5a). This own-sex bias in preferences for self-resemblance indicates that while self-resemblance is attractive in an exclusively prosocial (i.e., nonsexual) context, it is considerably less attractive in a mating context. Stronger attraction to cues of kinship in own-sex faces than in opposite-sex faces will promote prosocial behavior toward own-sex kin, while minimizing occurrences of inbreeding. Thus, DeBruine's (2004) findings are consistent with both inclusive fitness and inbreeding avoidance theories. Importantly, DeBruine (2004) found that while

self-resembling faces of both sexes were perceived as more average (i.e., typical) than other-resembling faces, no own-sex bias occurred for these averageness judgments (Figure 11.5b). These findings for averageness judgments, therefore, suggest that equivalent cues of self-resemblance were contained in both own-sex and opposite-sex faces and that the own-sex bias in attractiveness judgments was not simply a consequence of own-sex faces capturing cues of self-resemblance better than opposite-sex faces.

DeBruine's findings for an own-sex bias in attraction to facial cues of self-resemblance point to context-sensitivity in responses to phenotypic cues of kinship (as predicted by both inclusive fitness and inbreeding avoidance theories). DeBruine (2005) presented further evidence for such context-sensitivity by comparing men's and women's preferences for self-resemblance in opposite-sex faces in three different contexts. These contexts were short-term relationships that were predominantly sexual, long-term relationships, and that contained both prosocial and sexual aspects and the prosocial attribution of trustworthiness. Although self-resemblance in opposite-sex faces increased perceptions of trustworthiness, it decreased attractiveness for short-term relationships and had a no significant effect on attractiveness for long-term relationships (Figure 11.6). The fact that self-resemblance in opposite-sex faces was found to be trustworthy but not lustworthy is, again, consistent with

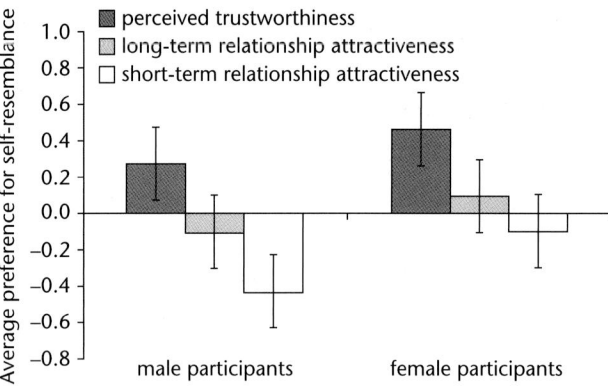

Figure 11.6 The average (±SEM) preference for self-resemblance in response to the trustworthiness, long-term and short-term relationship questions for men and women.

both inclusive fitness and inbreeding avoidance theories, and it emphasizes the context-sensitivity of responses to self-resemblance. Importantly, this context-sensitivity is very difficult to explain if responses to self-resemblance occur simply because of familiarty alone (i.e., the mere exposure effect, Zajonc, 1968). Indeed, familiarity has been shown to increase judgments of both attractiveness and trustworthiness (Buckingham et al., 2006).

Although the previous section focused on context-sensitive responses to self-resemblance in adult faces, other research has tested for responses to self-resemblance in children's faces. The next section will review this research.

DOES FACIAL RESEMBLANCE OF CHILDREN MATTER MORE TO FATHERS THAN MOTHERS?

In certain situations, the costs and benefits of kin discrimination are different for different categories of individuals. To the degree that males and females both invest parentally in offspring, both should direct parental care preferentially toward genetically related young. However, the reliability of the association between kinship cues and genetic relatedness can differ according to sex. Male mammals face much greater uncertainty about their paternity than female mammals do about their maternity, and thus males have greater utility for indirect cues of relatedness, such as facial resemblance. Consistent with this, matrilateral kin, who have

relatively high certainty of relatedness, invest more in children than patrilateral kin, who have greater reason to doubt their relatedness (Gaulin, McBurney, & Wartell, 1997, Euler & Weitzel, 1999).

Thus, mammalian mothers are predicted to use kin recognition methods, such as regarding any infant who is present after childbirth as one's own child, and to be less affected by other, even conflicting, cues of relatedness, such as lack of resemblance to self. On the other hand, fathers are predicted to rely on different cues, such as phenotypic similarity, to evaluate genetic relatedness. As a consequence, one might anticipate that men's investment in and relationships with offspring will vary with phenotypic similarity when other indicators of paternity (such as suspected maternal infidelity) are held constant, but women's investment will be relatively unaffected by phenotypic similarity. Consistent with this proposal, perceptions of children's resemblance to self predicts men's reported investment and family violence (Apicella & Marlowe, 2004, Burch & Gallup, 2000). However, self-reports of resemblance may be inaccurate. Studies investigating sex differences in the effect of computer-graphic manipulations of adults' resemblance to child faces have produced mixed results.

Several studies of men's and women's responses to self-resembling child faces have shown that men report a greater preference for and willingness to invest in self-resembling children than women do (Platek, Burch, Panyavin, Wasserman, & Gallup, 2002, Platek et al., 2003).

In the first study (Platek et al., 2002), five child faces were displayed, one of which had been manipulated to resemble the participant and the other four to resemble random male or female adults, and participants were asked to choose one face in response to each of several questions about investment and preferences. Although both sexes showed some bias toward the self-resembling faces, men were much more likely than women to choose the self-resembling child faces in response to positive investment questions. The second study (Platek et al., 2003) replicated and extended these findings, showing the sex difference for a lower level of resemblance (child faces made using 25 percent as opposed to 50 percent of the participant's image) and that men, but not women, preferred children with a greater degree of resemblance to self than expected by chance. A sex difference has also been reported for neural responses to self-resembling children (Platek et al., 2004, Platek, Keenan, & Mohamedc, 2005).

Despite consistent significant sex differences in the two separate experiments, several methodological issues have been raised about these studies. DeBruine (2004a) extended the behavioral experiments just described by (1) constraining the other-resembling child faces to be made using adult faces of the same sex as the participant, rather than from random adult faces of either sex, (2) ensuring that self-resembling faces were seen no more frequently than other-resembling faces, (3) using a different set of child faces for each question in order to ensure that established sex differences in preferences for equitable treatment (Austin & McGinn, 1977, Kahn, O'Leary, Krulewitz, & Lamm, 1980) did not bias the results, and (4) using a morphing procedure that produced more realistic child faces. In this study, participants chose the self-resembling child faces significantly more than expected by chance and this bias was no greater for men than for women. In a further experiment, independent participants were asked to match the self-resembling child faces to the adult faces from which they had been made. Men's and women's ability to do this was equivalent for child faces made using the method from Platek et al. (2002), 2003) and the method from DeBruine (2004a).

Women were slightly, but not significantly better than men at detecting resemblance for faces made using both methods, eliminating the possibility that previous findings were an artifact of sex differences in the ability to detect facial resemblance. Additionally, the accuracy of these independent judges' matching was correlated with the extent to which experimental participants preferred self-resembling child faces, and this correlation was not significantly different between men and women.

Bressan, Bertamini, Nalli, and Zanutto (2008) digitally manipulated child faces to resemble experimental participants, their acquaintances, and strangers. Participants were shown sets of six images, comprising one self-resembling face, one acquaintance-resembling face, and four stranger-resembling faces, and asked to rank these faces for attractiveness, adoptability, and familiarity. The self-resembling faces were ranked higher than chance for attractiveness and adoptability by female but not by male participants, and this effect was not mediated by either perceived familiarity or conscious self-recognition. Although these women showed greater preferences for acquaintance-resembling faces than stranger-resembling faces, they also showed stronger preferences for self-resembling faces than for acquaintance-resembling faces. They proposed that the previously reported sex difference (Platek et al., 2002, 2003) was an artifact of the fast-response, multiple-question procedure used in these studies.

Although the studies described in this section have consistently shown that self-resemblance increases positive responses to children's faces, findings for a sex-difference in this effect are inconsistent. One possibility is that the sex differences reported in various studies by Platek and colleagues are artifacts of the paradigm that they have used. Alternatively, there may be individual differences in the extent to which people value self-resemblance in children's faces. Although individual differences in responses to self-resembling children's faces remain to be investigated, individual differences in women's responses for self-resemblance in adults' faces have been investigated. The next section reviews findings for

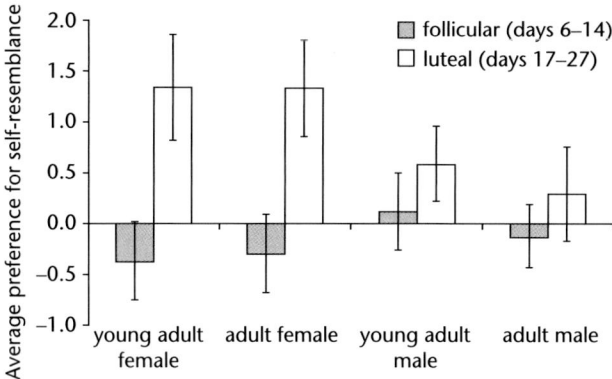

Figure 11.7 Average preferences for self-resemblance (± SEM) were greater in the luteal phase (21 women) than the late follicular phase (22 women). This shift was greater for female faces than for male faces.

effects of menstrual cycle phase on women's preferences for self-resemblance in adult faces and in face preferences more generally.

Hormone-Mediated Preferences for Facial Resemblance

The costs and benefits of recognizing kin can change under different circumstances. Several studies have shown that women's preferences for male masculinity in many domains increase near ovulation (Feinberg et al., 2006, Gangestad, Simpson, Cousins, Garver-Apgar, & Christensen, 2004, Havlicek, Roberts, & Flegr, 2005, Johnston, Hagel, Franklin, Fink, & Grammer, 2001, Jones, Little, et al., 2005, Little, Jones, & Burriss, 2007, Penton-Voak, Perrett, Castles, et al., 1999, Penton-Voak & Perrett, 2000, Welling et al., 2007). This cyclic shift in preferences is consistent with women having a greater motivation to mate with men displaying cues to good genes when most likely to become pregnant (see Jones et al., 2008, for a review). Aversions to facial cues of illness also increase during pregnancy, presumably to protect the mother and developing fetus from potential infection (Jones, Perrett, et al., 2005, Jones, Little, et al., 2005). Kin recognition functioning to avoid inbreeding may be stronger close to women's most fertile times or kin recognition functioning to promote prosocial behavior may be stronger when women are pregnant (or when raised progesterone prepares the body for pregnancy).

DeBruine et al. (2005) assessed women's preferences for male and female self-resembling faces at different points in the menstrual cycle. Women preferred self-resemblance in both male and female faces more during the luteal phase than during the fertile late follicular phase (Figure 11.7). The size of the preference for self-resemblance correlated with estimated progesterone levels (the pregnancy hormone) but not with conception risk, and the effect was larger for female than male faces. This suggests that cyclic shifts in preference for self-resemblance in faces function to motivate women to seek kin, who are likely to provide social and material support, when pregnant (and when the body is in a hormonal state similar to pregnancy), rather than to prevent inbreeding when most fertile.

CONCLUSIONS

In line with theoretical predictions, facial resemblance was found to increase prosocial behavior (DeBruine, 2002, Krupp et al., 2008) and attributions (DeBruine, 2005) consistent with the kinds of contexts in which favoring kin would have been adaptive. Moreover, resemblance had a less positive effect on the general attractiveness of opposite-sex faces than same-sex faces (DeBruine, 2004b) and had a detrimental effect on judgments of sexual attractiveness (DeBruine, 2005), consistent with inbreeding avoidance. Facial resemblance was shown to increase preferences for child faces (Bressan et al., 2008, DeBruine, 2004a) and may do so more for men than women (Platek et al., 2002,

2003). Additionally, preferences for self-resemblance are sensitive to cyclic hormone changes, with self-resemblance being preferred more during the luteal phase than during the fertile late follicular phase, especially in female faces (DeBruine et al., 2005).

These effects provide evidence that responses to facial resemblance are more specialized than would be expected if they were mere byproducts of general face-processing mechanisms (Little, DeBruine, & Jones, 2005). The context specificity of responses to facial resemblance are key to this conclusion. Although hypotheses based on familiarity, such as mere exposure (Rhodes, Halberstadt, & Brajkovich, 2001) or visual adaptation (Buckingham et al., 2006, Rhodes, Jeffery, Watson, Clifford, & Nakayama, 2003) predict that visual experience with a face will result in increased preferences for similar faces, regardless of the context in which the face is judged, preferences for facial resemblance are highly sensitive to context. The experiments reviewed in this chapter show that experience with one's own face influences face processing. However, the context-specific nature of responses to resemblance cannot be explained as byproducts of mechanisms, such as visual adaptation, or mere exposure.

REFERENCES

Apicella, C. L., & Marlowe, F. W. (2004). Perceived mate fidelity and paternal resemblance predict men's investment in children. *Evolution and Human Behavior, 25*, 371–378.

Austin, W., & McGinn, N. C. (1977). Sex differences in choice of distribution rules. *Journal of Personality, 45*, 379–394.

Bateson, P. (1983). Optimal outbreeding. In P. Bateson (Ed.), *Mate choice* (p. 257–278). Cambridge University Press.

Bittles, A. H. (2001). Consanguinity and its relevance to clinical genetics. *Clinical Genetics, 60*, 89–98.

Bittles, A. H., Grant, J. C., Sullivan, S. G., & Hussain, R. (2002). Does inbreeding lead to decreased human fertility? *Annals of Human Biology, 29*, 111–130.

Bressan, P., Bertamini, M., Nalli, A., & Zanutto, A. (2008). How men and women respond to self-resemblance in child faces. *Archives of Sexual Behavior, in press.*

Buckingham, G., DeBruine, L. M., Little, A. C., Welling, L. L. M., Conway, C. A., Tiddeman, B. P., (2006). Visual adaptation to masculine and feminine faces influences generalized preferences and perceptions of trustworthiness. *Evolution and Human Behavior, 27*, 381–389.

Burch, R. L., & Gallup, G. G., Jr. (2000). Perceptions of paternal resemblance predict family violence. *Evolution and Human Behavior, 21*, 429–435.

Dal Martello, M. F., & Maloney, L. T. (2006). Where are kin recognition signals in the human face? *Journal of Vision, 6*, 1356–1366.

DeBruine, L. M. (2002). Facial resemblance enhances trust. *Proceedings of the Royal Society of London B, 269*, 1307–1312.

DeBruine, L. M. (2004a). Facial resemblance increases the attractiveness of same-sex faces more than other-sex faces. *Proceedings of the Royal Society of London B, 271*, 2085–90.

DeBruine, L. M. (2004b). Resemblance to self increases the appeal of child faces to both men and women. *Evolution and Human Behavior, 25*, 142–154.

DeBruine, L. M. (2005). Trustworthy but not lust-worthy: Context-specific effects of facial resemblance. *Proceedings of the Royal Society of London B, 272*, 919–922.

DeBruine, L. M., Jones, B. C., Little, A. C., & Perrett, D. I. (2008). Social perception of facial resemblance in humans. *Archives of Sexual Behavior, 37*, 64–77.

DeBruine, L. M., Jones, B. C., & Perrett, D. I. (2005). Women's attractiveness judgments of self-resembling faces change across the menstrual cycle. *Hormones and Behavior, 47*, 379–383.

DeBruine, L. M., Jones, B. C., Unger, L., Little, A. C., & Feinberg, D. R. (2007). Dissociating averageness and attractiveness: Attractive faces are not always average. *Journal of Experimental Psychology: Human Perception and Performance, 33*, 1420–1430.

Euler, H. A., & Weitzel, B. (1999). Grandparental caregiving and intergenerational relations reflect reproductive strategies. In J. M. van der Dennen, D. Smillie, & D. R. Wilson (Eds.), *The Darwinian heritage and sociobiology: Human evolution, behavior, and intelligence* (p. 243–252). Westport, CT: Praeger Publishers.

Feinberg, D. R., Jones, B. C., Law Smith, M. J., Moore, F. R., DeBruine, L. M., Cornwell, R. E., (2006). Menstrual cycle, trait estrogen level and masculinity preferences in the human voice. *Hormones and Behavior, 49,* 215–222.

Gangestad, S. W., Simpson, J. A., Cousins, A. J., Garver–Apgar, C. E., & Christensen, P. N. (2004). Women's preferences for male behavioral displays change across the menstrual cycle. *Psychological Science, 15,* 203–207.

Gaulin, S. J. C., McBurney, D. H., & Wartell, S. L. B. (1997). Matrilateral biases in the investment of aunts and uncles: A consequence and measure of paternity uncertainty. *Human Nature, 8,* 139–151.

Griffiths, R., & Kunz, P. (1973). Assortative mating: A study of physiognomic homogamy. *Social Biology, 20,* 448–453.

Hamilton, W. D. (1964). The genetical evolution of social behaviour, I. *Journal of Theoretical Biology, 7,* 1–16.

Havlicek, J., Roberts, S. C., & Flegr, J. (2005). Women's preference for dominant male odour: effects of menstrual cycle and relationship status. *Biology Letters, 1,* 256–259.

Hinsz, V. B. (1989). Facial resemblance in engaged and married couples. *Journal of Social and Personal Relationships, 6,* 223–229.

Johnston, V. S., Hagel, R., Franklin, M., Fink, B., & Grammer, K. (2001). Male facial attractiveness: evidence for a hormone–mediated adaptive design. *Evolution and Human Behavior, 22,* 251–267.

Jones, B. C., DeBruine, L. M., Perrett, D. I., Little, A. C., Feinberg, D. R., & Law Smith, M. J. (2008). Effects of menstrual cycle on face preferences. *Archives of Sexual Behavior, 37,* 78–84.

Jones, B. C., Little, A. C., Boothroyd, L., DeBruine, L. M., Feinberg, D. R., Law Smith, M. J., (2005). Commitment to relationships and preferences for femininity and apparent health in faces are strongest on days of the menstrual cycle when progesterone level is high. *Hormones and Behavior, 48,* 283–290.

Jones, B. C., Perrett, D. I., Little, A. C., Boothroyd, L., Cornwell, R. E., Feinberg, D. R., (2005). Menstrual cycle, pregnancy and oral contraceptive use alter attraction to apparent health in faces. *Proceedings of the Royal Society of London B, 272,* 347–354.

Kahn, A., O'Leary, V. E., Krulewitz, J. E., & Lamm, H. (1980). Equity and equality: Male and female

means to a just end. *Basic and Applied Social Psychology, 1,* 173–197.

Krupp, D. B., DeBruine, L. M., & Barclay, P. (2008). A cue of kinship promotes cooperation for the public good. *Evolution and Human Behavior, 29,* 49–55.

Langlois, J. H., & Roggman, L. A. (1990). Attractive faces are only average. *Psychological Science, 1,* 115–121.

Little, A. C., DeBruine, L. M., & Jones, B. C. (2005). Sex-contingent face aftereffects suggest distinct neural populations code male and female faces. *Proceedings of the Royal Society of London B, 272,* 2283–2287.

Little, A. C., Jones, B. C., & Burriss, R. P. (2007). Preferences for masculinity in male bodies change across the menstrual cycle. *Hormones and Behavior, 52,* 633–639.

Maloney, L. T., & Dal Martello, M. F. (2006). Kin recognition and the perceived facial similarity of children. *Journal of Vision, 6,* 1047–1056.

Penton–Voak, I. S., & Perrett, D. I. (2000). Female preference for male faces changes cyclically: Further evidence. *Evolution and Human Behavior, 21,* 39–48.

Penton–Voak, I. S., Perrett, D. I., Castles, D. L., Kobayashi, T., Burt, D. M., Murray, L. K., (1999). Menstrual cycle alters face preference. *Nature, 399,* 741–742.

Penton–Voak, I. S., Perrett, D. I., & Peirce, J. W. (1999). Computer graphic studies of the role of facial similarity in judgments of attractiveness. *Current Psychology, 18,* 104–117.

Platek, S. M., Burch, R. L., Panyavin, I. S., Wasserman, B. H., & Gallup, G. G., Jr. (2002). Reactions to children's faces: Resemblance affects males more than females. *Evolution and Human Behavior, 23,* 159–166.

Platek, S. M., Critton, S. R., Burch, R. L., Frederick, D. A., Meyers, T. E., & Gallup, G. G., Jr. (2003). How much paternal resemblance is enough? Sex differences in hypothetical investment decisions but not in the detection of resemblance. *Evolution and Human Behavior, 24,* 81–87.

Platek, S. M., Keenan, J. P., & Mohamedc, F. B. (2005). Sex differences in the neural correlates of child facial resemblance: an event-related fMRI study. *NeuroImage, 25,* 1336–1344.

Platek, S. M., Raines, D. M., Gallup, G. G., Jr., Mohamed, F. B., Thomson, J. W., Myers, T. E., (2004). Reactions to children's faces: Males are more affected by resemblance than females are, and so are their brains. *Evolution and Human Behavior, 25,* 394–405.

Rhodes, G., Halberstadt, J., & Brajkovich, G. (2001). Generalization of mere exposure effects to averaged composite faces. *Social Cognition, 19,* 57–70.

Rhodes, G., Jeffery, L., Watson, T., Clifford, C. W. G., & Nakayama, K. (2003). Fitting the mind to the world: Face adaptation and attractiveness aftereffects. *Psychological Science, 14,* 558–566.

Rowland, D., & Perrett, D. I. (1995). Manipulating facial appearance through shape and color. *IEEE Computer Graphics and Applications, 15,* 70–76.

Tiddeman, B. P., Perrett, D. I., & Burt, D. M. (2001). Prototyping and transforming facial textures for perception research. *IEEE Computer Graphics and Applications, 21,* 42–50.

Welling, L. L. M., Jones, B. C., DeBruine, L. M., Conway, C. A., Law Smith, M. J., Little, A. C., (2007). Raised salivary testosterone in women is associated with increased attraction to masculine faces. *Hormones and Behavior, 52,* 156–161.

Zajonc, R. B. (1968). Attitudinal effects of mere exposure. *Journal of Personality and Social Psychology, 9,* 1S–27S.

Zajonc, R. B., Adelmann, P. K., Murphy, S. T., & Niendenthal, P. M. (1987). Convergence in the physical appearance of spouses. *Motivation and Emotion, 11,* 335–346.

CHAPTER 12

In the Eyes of the Beholder: How Empathy Influences Emotion Perception

Bhismadev Chakrabarti and Simon Baron-Cohen

One of the points of agreement among neurobiologists, psychologists, and philosophers studying the emotions is that, as well as being mental states that we experience, these are also essential tools for social communication. Expressions of emotion from conspecifics are informative signals, coding salient events in the external environment such as potential rewards and threats. In higher primates, and especially humans, facial expressions form a large part of the repertoire of emotion expressions (Darwin, 1998). In addition to being the response output of emotions, facial expressions serve as highly salient emotional stimuli in their own right. Social referencing is seen in infants when they check their primary care-giver's facial expression, influencing whether they approach or avoid an object (Sorce, Emde, Campos, & Klinnert, 1985; Walden & Ogan, 1988). Beyond infancy, facial expressions remain salient emotional stimuli throughout life. This suggests strong links between perception, recognition, and experience of emotions.

What determines how we perceive others' facial expressions of emotion? In this chapter we explore the role of empathy (Smith, 1759) in relation to emotion perception, considering it in terms of individual differences as a quantitative trait. We then review the literature from neuroimaging studies that suggest that discrete basic emotions are processed in different neural regions and networks. Finally, we describe a recent study that reconciles these two approaches to empathy by investigating whether empathy affects how the brain processes discrete emotions.

WHAT IS EMPATHIZING?

Empathizing is the drive to identify another person's emotions and thoughts, and to respond to these with an appropriate emotion (Davis, 1994). We use the term *drive* but recognize that it also overlaps with the concept of a skill or an ability. We also focus on the definition of empathy given by Davis while recognizing that other authors may have a slightly different definition. Empathizing doesn't just entail the cold calculation of what someone else thinks and feels (or what is sometimes called mindreading). Psychopaths can do that much. Empathizing is also about having an appropriate emotional reaction, an emotion triggered by the other person's emotion. Empathizing occurs in order to understand other people, predict their behaviors, and to connect with them emotionally. Empathy is a skill (or a set of skills). As with any other skill, we all vary in it. In the same way that we can think about why someone is talented or average or even disabled in these other areas, so we can think about individual differences in empathy.

FRACTIONATING EMPATHY

Philosophical (Stein, 1989) and evolutionary (Brothers, 1990; Levenson, 1996; Preston & de Waal, 2002) accounts have suggested that empathizing is not a unitary construct. Possible constituent "fractions" of empathy include (1) cognitive empathy, (2) emotional contagion/affective empathy, and (3) sympathy.

Cognitive empathy is involved in explicit understanding of another's feelings and switching to take their perspective. Piaget referred to empathy as "decentering," or responding non-egocentrically (Piaget & Inhelder, 1956). More recent developmental psychologists refer to this aspect of empathy in terms of using a "theory of mind," or "mindreading" (Astington, Harris, & Olson, 1988; Whiten, 1991). Essentially, the cognitive component of empathizing entails setting aside your own current perspective, attributing a mental state (sometimes called an attitude) to the other person, and then inferring the likely content of their mental state, given their experience. The cognitive element also allows you to predict the other person's mental state or behavior.

The second aspect to empathy is the affective component (Hobson, 1993). A similar component in other accounts has been called "emotional contagion," defined as the tendency to automatically mimic and synchronize facial expressions, vocalizations, postures, and movements with those of another person, and, consequently, to converge emotionally (Hatfield, Cacioppo, & Rapson, 1992). This may be the most primitive component of empathy. For example, when witnessing someone else in a state of fear, if one "catches" a similar state of fear, this acts as a quick-and-easy route to alerting oneself to environmental dangers without having to face the dangers oneself.

A third component involves a concern mechanism (Nichols, 2001) often associated with a prosocial/altruistic component, also termed *sympathy*. This is distinct from emotional contagion in not necessarily involving matched states between the observer and the person experiencing the emotion. It also seems to be specific to a certain class of emotions (sadness and pain, but not disgust or happiness) in the other person. It represents a case in which the observer feels both an emotional response to someone else's distress, and a desire to alleviate their suffering.

SEX DIFFERENCES IN EMPATHIZING

Some of the best evidence for individual differences in empathizing comes from the study of sex differences, where many studies converge on the conclusion that there is a female superiority in empathizing. Sex differences are best viewed as summated individual differences, on multiple dimensions that include genetic and epigenetic factors. Some of the observed behavioral differences are reviewed here:

1. Sharing and turn taking. On average, girls show more concern for fairness, whereas boys share less. In one study, boys showed 50 times more competition, whereas girls showed 20 times more turn-taking (Charlesworth & Dzur, 1987).
2. Rough-and-tumble play or roughhousing (wrestling, mock fighting, etc). Boys show more of this than girls do. Although there's a playful component, this can hurt or be intrusive, so it involves lower levels of empathy (Maccoby, 1999).
3. Responding empathically to the distress of other people. Girls from 1 year old show greater concern through more sad looks, sympathetic vocalizations, and comforting. More women than men also report frequently sharing the emotional distress of their friends. Women also show more comforting, even of strangers, than do men (Hoffman, 1977).
4. Using a "theory of mind." By 3 years old, little girls are already ahead of boys in their ability to infer what people might be thinking or intending (Happe, 1995). This sex difference appears in some but not all studies (Charman, Ruffman, & Clements, 2002).
5. Sensitivity to facial expressions. Women are better at decoding nonverbal communication, picking up subtle nuances from tone of voice or facial expression, or judging a person's character (Hall, 1978).

6. Questionnaires measuring empathy. Many of these find that women score higher than men (Davis, 1994).

7. Values in relationships. More women value the development of altruistic, reciprocal relationships, which require empathizing. In contrast, more men value power, politics, and competition (Ahlgren & Johnson, 1979). Girls are more likely to endorse cooperative items on a questionnaire and to rate the establishment of intimacy as more important than the establishment of dominance. Boys are more likely than girls to endorse competitive items and to rate social status as more important than intimacy (Knight, Fabes, & Higgins, 1989).

8. Disorders of empathy (such as psychopathic personality disorder, or conduct disorder) are far more common among males (R. J. Blair, 1995; Dodge, 1980).

9. Aggression can only occur with reduced empathizing. Here again, there is a clear sex difference. Males tend to show far more direct aggression (pushing, hitting, punching, etc.,) whereas females tend to show more indirect (or relational, covert) aggression (gossip, exclusion, bitchy remarks, etc.). Direct aggression may require an even lower level of empathy than indirect aggression. Indirect aggression needs better mindreading skills than does direct aggression, because its impact is strategic (Crick & Grotpeter, 1995).

10. Murder is the ultimate example of a lack of empathy. Daly and Wilson (Daly & Wilson, 1988) analyzed homicide records dating back over 700 years, from a range of different societies. They found that male-on-male homicide was 30–40 times more frequent than female-on-female homicide.

11. Establishing a dominance hierarchy. Males are quicker to establish these. This in part may reflect their lower empathizing skills, because often a hierarchy is established by one person pushing others around, to become the leader (Strayer, 1980).

12. Language style. Girls' speech is more cooperative, reciprocal, and collaborative. In concrete terms, this is also reflected in girls being able to keep a conversational exchange with a partner going for longer. When girls disagree, they are more likely to express their different opinion sensitively, in the form of a question, rather than an assertion. Boys' talk is more single-voiced discourse (the speaker presents their own perspective alone). The female speech style is more double-voiced discourse (girls spend more time negotiating with the other person, trying to take the other person's wishes into account) (P. M. Smith, 1985).

13. Talk about emotions. Women's conversation involves much more talk about feelings, whereas men's conversation with each other tends to be more object- or activity-focused (Tannen, 1991).

14. Parenting style. Fathers are less likely than mothers to hold their infant in a face-to-face position. Mothers are more likely to follow through the child's choice of topic in play, whereas fathers are more likely to impose their own topic. And mothers fine-tune their speech more often to match what the child can understand (Power, 1985).

15. Face preference and eye contact. From birth, females look longer at faces, and particularly at people's eyes, and males are more likely to look at inanimate objects (Connellan, Baron-Cohen, Wheelwright, Ba'tki, & Ahluwalia, 2001).

16. Finally, females have also been shown to have better language ability than males. It seems likely that good empathizing might promote language development (Baron-Cohen, Baldwin, & Crowson, 1997) and vice versa, so these may not be independent.

Leaving aside sex differences as one source of evidence for individual differences, one can see that empathy is continuously distributed within the population. Figure 12.1 below shows the data from the Empathy Quotient (EQ), a validated 60–item self-report questionnaire (Baron-Cohen and Wheelwright, 2004). It has been factor-analyzed to suggest the existence of three distinct components, which roughly correspond to the three-component model of empathy (Lawrence, Shaw, Baker, Baron-Cohen, &

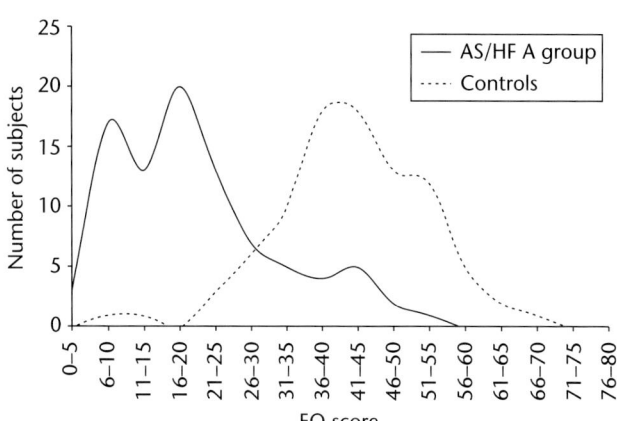

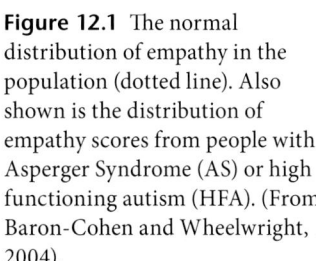

Figure 12.1 The normal distribution of empathy in the population (dotted line). Also shown is the distribution of empathy scores from people with Asperger Syndrome (AS) or high functioning autism (HFA). (From Baron-Cohen and Wheelwright, 2004).

David, 2004; Muncer & Ling, 2006). Scores on the EQ show a normal distribution in several populations, with scores from people with autism spectrum conditions (ASCs) clustering toward the lower end (see Figure 12.1). The EQ shows significant sex differences (Goldenfeld, Baron-Cohen, Wheelwright, Ashwin, & Chakrabarti, 2007).

On finding increasing evidence of sex differences on the EQ in the typical population, we sought to investigate the neural correlates of this trait measure of empathizing across the population. Since empathizing can be viewed as a lens through which we perceive emotions, we attempted to marry the two fields of emotion perception and empathizing. The following section briefly summarizes the current state of the literature concerning the neural bases of basic emotions and the results of a recent study from our lab.

NEUROIMAGING EMPATHY

Neuroimaging studies have implicated the following different brain areas for performing tasks that tap components of the model of empathy proposed earlier, presented in order of their development.

1. Studies of emotional contagion have demonstrated involuntary facial mimicry (Dimberg, Thunberg, & Elmehead, 2000) as well as activity in regions of the brain where the existence of "mirror" neurons has been suggested. (Carr, Iacoboni, Dubeau, Mazziotta, & Lenzi, 2003; Jackson, Meltzoff, & Decety, 2005; Wicker et al., 2003).

2. Intentionality detection (ID) has been tested (Brunet, Sarfati, Hardy-Bayle, & Decety, 2000) in a PET study in a task involving attribution of intentions to cartoon characters. Reported activation clusters included the right medial prefrontal (BA 9), inferior frontal (BA 47) cortices, superior temporal gyrus (BA42) and bilateral anterior cingulate cortex. In an elegant set of experiments that required participants to attribute intentions to animations of simple geometric shapes (Castelli, Happe, Frith, & Frith, 2000), it was found that the intentionality score attributed by the participants to individual animations was positively correlated to the activity in superior temporal sulcus (STS), the temporo-parietal junction and the medial prefrontal cortex. A subsequent study (Castelli, Frith, Happe, & Frith, 2002), demonstrated a group difference in activity in the same set of structures between people with Autism/Asperger's Syndrome and neurotypical controls.

3. Eye direction detection (EDD) has been studied in several neuroimaging studies on gaze direction perception (A. Calder et al., 2002; Pelphrey, Singerman, Allison, & McCarthy,

2003) (see Grosbras, Laird, & Paus, 2005 for a review), and have implicated the posterior STS bilaterally. This evidence, taken together with similar findings from primate literature (Perrett & Emery, 1994) suggests this area to be a strong candidate for the anatomical equivalent of the EDD.

4. A recent imaging study (Williams, Waiter, Perra, Perrett, & Whiten, 2005) investigated the neural correlates of joint attention reported bilateral activation in anterior cingulate (BA 32,24), and medial prefrontal cortex (BA 9,10) and the body of caudate nucleus in a joint-attention task, when compared to a control task involving nonjoint attention. (See Frith & Frith, 2003 for a review).

5. Traditional "theory of mind" (cognitive-empathy) tasks have consistently shown activity in medial prefrontal cortex, superior temporal gyrus and the temporo-parietal junctions (Frith & Frith, 2003; Saxe, Carey, & Kanwisher, 2004). This could be equated to the brain basis of "theory of mind" (ToMM).

6. Sympathy has been relatively less investigated, with one study implicating the left inferior frontal gyrus, among a network of other structures (Decety & Chaminade, 2003). Work on "moral" emotions has suggested the involvement of a network comprising the medial frontal gyrus, the medial orbitofrontal cortex and the STS (Moll et al., 2002).

NEUROIMAGING BASIC EMOTIONS

An increasing body of evidence from lesion, neuroimaging, and electrophysiological studies suggest that emotions might have discrete neural bases (Calder, Lawrence, & Young, 2001), and are best viewed as affect programs (stereotypical facial-bodily action patterns that originate in response to different elicitors) that constitute natural kinds (Griffiths, 1997). Fear is possibly the most well investigated of the basic emotions. Passive viewing of fear expressions as well as experiencing fear (as induced through recalling a fear memory, or seeing fear stimuli) reliably activates the amygdala, orbitofrontal cortex,

and the anterior cingulate cortex (Blair, Morris, Frith, Perrett, & Dolan, 1999; Hariri, Mattay, Tessitore, Fera, & Weinberger, 2003). There is considerable evidence from nonhuman primates (Kalin, Shelton, & Davidson, 2001) and rats (LeDoux, 2000) to suggest a crucial role for these regions in processing fear. Passive viewing of disgust faces as well as experiencing disgust oneself is known to evoke a response in the anterior insula and globus pallidus as reported in several studies (Calder, 2001; Wicker et al., 2003). An increasing consensus on the role of the ventral striatum in processing reward from different sensory domains [receiving food rewards (O'Doherty, Deichmann,w Critchley, & Dolan, 2002), viewing funny cartoons (Mobbs, Greicius, Abdel-Azim, Menon, & Reiss, 2003), remembering happy events (Damasio et al., 2000)] concurs well with studies that report activation of this region in response to viewing happy faces (Lawrence, Shaw, Baker, Baron-Cohen, & David, 2004; Phillips, Baron-Cohen, & Rutter, 1998).

Perception of angry expressions have been shown to evoke a response in the premotor cortex and the striatum (Grosbras & Paus, 2006) as well as the lateral orbitofrontal cortex (Blair & Cipolotti, 2000; Blair, Morris, Frith, Perrett, & Dolan, 1999). The results of studies on the processing of sad expressions are comparatively less consistent. Perception of sad face and induction of sad mood are both known to be associated with an increased response in the subgenual cingulate cortex (Liotti et al., 2000; Mayberg et al., 1999), the hypothalamus in humans (Malhi et al., 2004) and in rats (Shumake, Edwards, & Gonzalez-Lima, 2001), as well as in the middle temporal gyrus (Eugene et al., 2003). There have been very few studies on the passive viewing of surprise. One study by (Schroeder et al., 2004) has reported bilateral activation in the parahippocampal region, which is known for its role in novelty detection from animal literature.

Although the discrete-emotions model holds well for these relatively simple emotions, the dimensional models (e.g., see Rolls, 2002) become increasingly relevant as we consider the more socially complex emotions (e.g., pride,

shame and guilt) because it would not be very economical to have discrete neural substrates for the whole gamut of emotions. There are, however, some recent reports that suggest a degree of functional regionalization even within these emotions (Zahn et al., 2008). These two models, however, need not be in conflict, since the more complex emotions can be conceptualized as being formed of a combination of the basic ones (i.e., with each of the basic emotions representing a dimension in emotion space).

Two major meta-analytic studies of neuroimaging literature on emotions highlight the role of discrete regions in primarily visual processing of different basic emotions (Murphy, Nimmo-Smith, & Lawrence, 2003; Phan, Wager, Taylor, & Liberzon, 2002). Some studies using other sensory stimuli: olfactory (Anderson et al., 2003), gustatory (Small et al., 2003), and auditory (Lewis, Critchley, Rotshtein, & Dolan, 2005)) have shown the possibly dissociable role for the amygdala and the orbitofrontal cortex in processing emotions along the two dimensions of valence and arousal.

The relative absence of neuroimaging studies on complex emotions could be due to the increased cultural variability of the elicitors, as well as the display rules that these expressions entail. Among the few exceptions, guilt and embarrassment have been investigated by Takahashi et al. (2004), and more recently by Zahn et al. (2008) who reported consistent regional activations in the ventromedial prefrontal cortex. This, taken together with the areas underlying theory of mind (ToMM) could point to an increased role of the "theory of mind" in making sense of these emotions.

EMPATHIZING WITH DISCRETE EMOTIONS?

The notion of individual differences in empathizing poses an interesting question regarding the brain basis of perception of discrete emotions. Do we use a centralized empathy circuit to make sense of all emotions? If so, can one detect differences in how discrete emotions are processed in individuals who are at different points on the EQ continuum?

An indirect approach to investigate individual differences in empathizing has been to test for sex differences in the perception of emotions. Females perform better in several measures of empathy (as discussed before), and Helland (2005) used facial electromyography (EMG) to observe that females showed a greater degree of facial mimicry to facial expressions of happiness and anger, compared to males. In a meta-analysis of neuroimaging results on sex differences on emotion perception, (Wager, Phan, Liberzon, & Taylor, 2003) reported that females show increased bilaterality in emotion-relevant activation compared to males. However, this is not always found (Lee et al., 2002; Schienle, Schafer, Stark, Walter, & Vaitl, 2005). One of the reasons for this might have been the fact that sex differences are summated individual differences. Instead of such a broad category-based approach (as in sex-difference studies), a more direct approach might be based on individual differences in self-report personality scores (Canli, Sivers, SL, Gotlib, & Gabrieli, 2002) or genetics (e.g., Hariri et al., 2002).

To test the influence of individual variability in empathy on emotion perception, we examined whether an individual's score on the EQ predicted his/her brain response to four basic emotions (happy, sad, angry, disgust). If empathizing was modulated by a unitary circuit, then individual differences in empathizing would correlate with activity in the same structures for all basic emotions. Twenty-five volunteers (13 female, 12 male) selected across the EQ space were scanned in a 3T fMRI scanner on a passive viewing task using dynamic facial expressions as stimuli. We generated a correlation map for each (emotion-neutral) contrast vs (EQ scores), and performed two sets of analysis.

1. A region-of-interest (ROI) analysis on the conjunction of all four correlation maps, to determine if any/all of the regions correlated with EQ across the four different emotions. The regions chosen for this analysis are known for their involvement in the ToMM paradigms as well as those suggested to be part of the mirror-system for action

observation (specifically, the inferior frontal gyrus, premotor cortex, medial prefrontal cortex, inferior parietal lobule, posterior superior temporal sulcus/temporo-parietal junction) (Buccino et al., 2001; Fletcher et al., 1995; Gusnard, Akbudak, Shulman, & Raichle, 2001; Hynes, Baird, & Grafton, 2006; Johnson-Frey et al., 2003; Leslie, Johnson-Frey, & Grafton, 2004).

2. Additionally, we used nonparametric cluster-based methods (Bullmore et al., 1999) to determine brain regions that are maximally correlated with EQ for each (emotion-neutral) contrast, that survive whole-brain correction for multiple comparisons.

The ROI analysis on the conjunction of the four correlation maps showed a region in the left inferior frontal gyrus-premotor cortex that correlated positively with EQ for all emotions, confirming earlier reports that suggests a fundamental role of this region in action perception (Hamzei et al., 2003; Johnson-Frey et al., 2003; Rizzolatti, Fadiga, Gallese, & Fogassi, 1996). Around the same time as we published this study, Lee, Josephs, Dolan, & Critchley (1996) reported results from a study that involved active imitation or observation of different facial expressions of emotion. This found a similar pattern of results with a cluster centered on the inferior frontal gyrus, which was activated during imitation of facial expressions, across different emotions. The second analysis tested which brain regions correlated maximally with EQ for each of the four emotions, when compared to neutral expressions. A whole-brain cluster-based nonparametric analysis revealed discrete regional patterns of correlation of EQ with the different emotions that are described in detail elsewhere (Chakrabarti, Bullmore, & Baron- Cohen, 2006).

COMMON AND DISCRETE NEURAL SUBSTRATES OF EMPATHY

Comparing the results from the conjunction analysis (showing a common neural substrate of EQ across different emotions) with those from the whole brain analysis (showing varying spatial patterns of correlation of EQ with different emotions) shows that there are both common regions that underlie empathy across different emotions, and there are regions that are more involved in modulating the response to specific emotions.

We interpret this using a model of face processing (Haxby, Hoffman, & Ida Gobbini, 2000) applied to a discrete-emotions framework (see Figure 12.2a). At its simplest, the model proposes a core visual system for face perception. This constitutes the inferior occipital gyrus (for low-level facial feature analysis), the lateral fusiform gyrus (for higher-order invariant aspects of faces such as identity) and the superior temporal sulcus (for variable aspects of faces such as lip movement and speech comprehension). This then interacts with an extended system, which involves different structures for different emotions (Haxby, Hoffman, & Ida-Gobbini, 2002). Focusing specifically on perception of dynamic facial expressions of emotion, we propose the involvement of an intermediate module for action perception, in line with similar suggestions from others (Gallese, 2003; Keysers & Perrett, 2004; Preston & de Waal, 2002); (Rizzolatti & Craighero, 2004) (see Figure 12.2b).

Focusing on the left of the dotted line in Figure 12.2b shows the processes that are equally influenced by trait empathy across all emotions. This includes the regions involved in face perception and the fundamental mirror systems used for action perception. This is revealed by the conjunction analysis, which shows a cluster that includes the inferior frontal gyrus/premotor cortex. The common element between different facial expressions of emotion is the fact that they involve movement of eyes and mouth, which are possibly coded for by generic mirror systems used for action perception. However, on investigating the interaction of each emotion with empathy, we move over to the right hand side of the dotted line, which gives us emotion-specific correlation maps, in accordance with the discrete-emotions model. We have interpreted these in light of their evolutionary function. It is worth noting though that

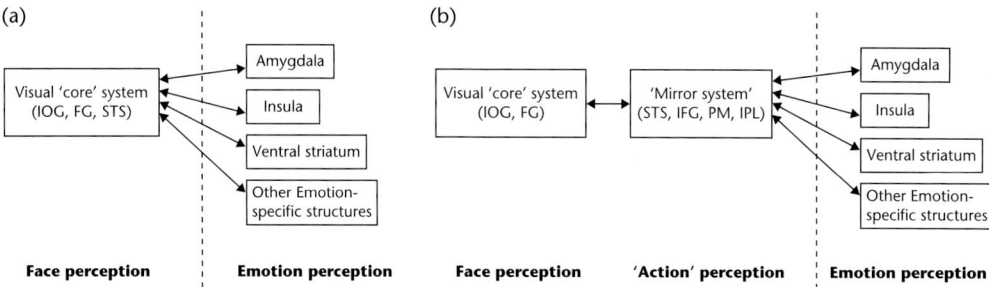

Figure 12.2 (a) The original model for face perception proposed by (Haxby, Hoffman, & Ida Gobbini, 2000) applied to a discrete-emotions framework (adapted from (Haxby, Hoffman, & Ida Gobbini, 2000). (b) Suggested modifications to the model, specifically for perception of facial expressions of emotion, incorporating a module for action perception. See text for discussion.

we do not propose a strict temporal sequence of activation from left to right of this model, nor do we represent subcortical pathways from the visual areas to the emotion-related structures. As in the original model, several of these regions are reciprocally connected, and the temporal progression of activation could be mediated through reafferent projections (Iacoboni et al., 2001). These can be investigated through methods that allow better temporal resolution (e.g., MEG) and forward-model based connectivity analysis (e.g., dynamic causal modeling) (Friston, Harrison, & Penny, 2003).

CONCLUSIONS

The biological basis of individual differences in empathy still remains to be fully delineated. These could include a variety of factors, such as fetal testosterone (Castelli, Happe, Frith, & Frith, 2000; Chapman et al., 2006), genetic variation (Chakrabarti et al., 2007; Skuse et al., 1997), as well as early care or neglect (Fonagy, Steele, Steele, & Holder, 1997). We expect that some of these biological factors underlying empathy may be linked to sex differences (e.g., genes related to sex steroid synthesis and transport), thus accounting for the observed gender differences in this trait. We end by encouraging more basic research into empathy, both for its own sake and for its potential relevance to understanding medical conditions in which empathy is compromised.

ACKNOWLEDGMENTS

The authors were supported by the MRC, and the Shirley Foundation during the period of this work. Parts of this article are taken from elsewhere (Baron-Cohen, 2005; Chakrabarti & Baron-Cohen, 2006; Chakrabarti, Bullmore, & Baron-Cohen, 2006; Goldenfeld, Baron-Cohen, & Wheelwright, 2005).

REFERENCES

Ahlgren, A., & Johnson, D. W. (1979). Sex differences in cooperative and competitive attitudes from the 2nd to the 12th grades. *Developmental Psychology, 15,* 45–49.

Anderson, A., Christoff, K., Stappen, I., Panitz, D., Ghahremani, D., Glover, G., et al. (2003). Dissociated neural representations of intensity and valence in human olfaction. *Nature Neuroscience, 6,* 196–202.

Astington, J., Harris, P., & Olson, D. (1988). *Developing theories of mind.* New York: Cambridge University Press.

Baron–Cohen, S. (2005). The empathizing system: a revision of the 1994 model of the Mindreading system. In B. Ellis & D. Bjorklund (Eds.), *Origins of the Social Mind*: Guilford Press.

Baron–Cohen, S., Baldwin, D., & Crowson, M. (1997). Do children with autism use the Speaker's Direction of Gaze (SDG) strategy to crack the code of language? *Child Development, 68,* 48–57.

Baron–Cohen, S., & Wheelwright, S. (2004). The Empathy Quotient. *Journal of Autism and Developmental Disorders, 34,* 163–175.

Blair, R., & Cipolotti, L. (2000). Impaired social response reversal —a case of "acquired" sociopathy. *Brain, 123*, 1122–1141.

Blair, R. J. (1995). A cognitive developmental approach to morality: investigating the psychopath. *Cognition, 57*, 1–29.

Blair, R., Morris, J., Frith, C., Perrett, D. I., & Dolan, R. J. (1999). Dissociable neural responses to facial expressions of sadness and anger. *Brain, 122*, 883–893.

Brothers, L. (1990). The neural basis of primate social communication. *Motivation and Emotion, 14*(2), 81–91.

Brunet, E., Sarfati, Y., Hardy-Bayle, M.-C., & Decety, J. (2000). A PET investigation of the attribution of intentions with a non-verbal task. *NeuroImage, 11*, 157–166.

Buccino, G., Binkofski, F., Fink, G., Fadiga, L., Fogassi, L., Gallese, V., et al. (2001). Action observation activates premotor and parietal areas in a somatotopic manner: an fMRI study. *European Journal of Neuroscience, 13*, 400–404.

Bullmore, E. T., Suckling, J., Overmeyer, S., Rabe–Hesketh, S., Taylor, E., & Brammer, M. J. (1999). Global, voxel and cluster tests, by theory and permutation, for a difference between two groups of structural MR images of the brain. *IEEE Trans Med Imaging, 18*, 32–42.

Calder, A., Lawrence, A., Keane, J., Scott, S., Owen, A., Christoffels, I., et al. (2002). Reading the mind from eye gaze. *Neuropsychologia, 40*, 1129–1138.

Calder, A. J., Lawrence, A. D., & Young, A. W. (2001). Neuropsychology of fear and loathing. *Nature Reviews Neuroscience, 2*, 352–363.

Canli, T., Sivers, H., SL, W., Gotlib, I., & Gabrieli, J. (2002). Amygdala response to happy faces as a function of extraversion. *Science, 296*, 2191.

Carr, L., Iacoboni, M., Dubeau, M.-C., Mazziotta, J., & Lenzi, G. (2003). Neural mechanisms of empathy in humans: A relay from neural systems for imitation to limbic areas. *PNAS, 100*(9), 5497–5502.

Castelli, F., Frith, C., Happe, F., & Frith, U. (2002). Autism, Asperger syndrome and brain mechanisms for the attribution of mental states to animated shapes. *Brain, 125*, 1839–1849.

Castelli, F., Happe, F., Frith, U., & Frith, C. (2000). Movement and mind: a functional imaging study of perception and interpretation of complex intentional movement patterns. *NeuroImage, 12*, 314–325.

Chakrabarti, B., & Baron-Cohen, S. (2006). Empathizing: Neurocognitive developmental mechanisms and individual differences. *Progress in Brain Research, 156* (Special issue on Understanding Emotions), 406–417.

Chakrabarti, B., Bullmore, E. T., & Baron-Cohen, S. (2006). Empathising with basic emotions: common and discrete neural substrates. *Social Neuroscience, 1*(3–4), 364–384.

Chakrabarti B., Dudbridge F., Kent L., Hill-Cawthorne G., Wheelwright S., Allison C., Banerjee-Basu S., Baron-Cohen S. (2009). Genes related to sex steroids, neural growth and social-emotional behaviour are associated with autistic traits and Asperger Syndrome, *Autism Research, 2*(3), 157–177.

Chapman, E., Baron-Cohen, S., Auyeung, B., Knickmeyer, R., Hackett, G., & Taylor, K. (2006). Foetal testosterone and empathy: Evidence from the Empathy Quotient (EQ) and the 'Reading the mind in the Eyes Test'. *Social Neuroscience, 1*, 135–148.

Charlesworth, W. R., & Dzur, C. (1987). Gender comparisons of preschoolers' behavior and resource utilization in group problem–solving. *Child Development, 58*, 191–200.

Charman, T., Ruffman, T., & Clements, W. (2002). Is there a gender difference in false belief development. *Social Development, 11*, 1–10.

Connellan, J., Baron-Cohen, S., Wheelwright, S., Ba'tki, A., & Ahluwalia, J. (2001). Sex differences in human neonatal social perception. *Infant Behavior and Development, 23*, 113–118.

Crick, N. R., & Grotpeter, J. K. (1995). Relational aggression, gender, and social–psychological adjustment. *Child Development, 66*, 710–722.

Daly, M., & Wilson, M. (1988). *Homicide.* New York: Aldine de Gruyter.

Damasio, A., R, Grabowski, T., J, Bechara, A., Damasio, H., Ponto, L., L, B, Parvizi, J., et al. (2000). Subcortical and cortical brain activity during the feeling of self-generated emotions. *Nature Neuroscience, 3*, 1049–1056.

Darwin, C. (1998). *The expression of emotions in man and animals(1872)*: Harper Collins.

Davis, M. H. (1994). *Empathy: A social psychological approach.* Colorado: Westview Press.

Decety, J., & Chaminade, T. (2003). Neural correlates of feeling sympathy. *Neuropsychologia, 41*, 127–138.

Dimberg, U., Thunberg, M., & Elmehead, K. (2000). Unconscious facial reactions to emotional facial expressions. *Psychological Science, 11*, 86–89.

Dodge, K. (1980). Social cognition and children's aggressive behaviour. *Child Development, 51*, 162–170.

Eugene, F., Levesque, J., Mensour, B., Leroux, J.-M., Beaudoin, G., Bourgouin, P., et al. (2003). The impact of individual differences on the neural circuitry underlying sadness. *Neuroimage, 19*, 354–364.

Fletcher, P. C., Happe, F., Frith, U., Baker, S. C., Dolan, R. J., Frackowiak, R. S. J., et al. (1995). Other minds in the brain: a functional imaging study of "theory of mind" in story comprehension. *Cognition, 57*, 109–128.

Fonagy, P., Steele, H., Steele, M., & Holder, J. (1997). Attachment and theory of mind: Overlapping constructs? *ACPP Occasional Papers, 14*, 31–40.

Friston, K., Harrison, L., & Penny, W. (2003). Dynamic causal modelling. *NeuroImage, 19*(4), 1273–1302.

Frith, U., & Frith, C. (2003). Development and neurophysiology of mentalizing. *Philosophical Transactions of the Royal Society, 358*, 459–473.

Gallese, V. (2003). The roots of empathy: The shared manifold hypothesis and the neural basis of intersubjectivity. *Psychopathology, 36*, 171–180.

Goldenfeld, N., Baron-Cohen, S., Wheelwright, S., Ashwin, C., & Chakrabarti, B. (2007). Empathizing and systemizing in males and females, and in autism spectrum conditions. In T. Farrow & P. W. R. Woodruff (Eds.), *Empathy and mental illness*. Cambridge: Cambridge University Press.

Goldenfeld, N., Baron-Cohen, S., & Wheelwright, S. (2005). Empathizing and systemizing in males, females, and autism. *Clinical Neuropsychiatry, 2*, 338–345

Griffiths, P. E. (1997). *What emotions really are: The problem of psychological categories*. Chicago: University of Chicago Press.

Grosbras, M.-H., Laird, A. R., & Paus, T. (2005). Cortical regions involved in eye movements, shifts of attention and gaze perception. *Hum Brain Mapp, 25*, 140–154.

Grosbras, M.-H., & Paus, T. (2006). Brain networks involved in viewing angry hands or faces. *Cereb Cortex, 16*(8), 1087–1096.

Gusnard, D., Akbudak, E., Shulman, G., & Raichle, M. (2001). Medial prefrontal cortex and self-referential mental activity: Relation to a default mode of brain function. *PNAS, 98*(7), 4259–4264.

Hall, J. A. (1978). Gender effects in decoding nonverbal cues. *Psychological Bulletin, 85*, 845–858.

Hamzei, F., Rijntjes, M., Dettmers, C., Glauche, V., Weiller, C., & Buchel, C. (2003). The human action recognition system and its relationship to Broca's area: An fMRI study. *Neuroimage, 19*(3), 637–644.

Happe, F. (1995). The role of age and verbal ability in the theory of mind task performance of subjects with autism. *Child Development, 66*, 843–855.

Hariri, A., R, Mattay, V., S, Tessitore, A., Fera, F., & Weinberger, D. R. (2003). Neocortical modulation of the amygdala response to fearful stimuli. *Biol Psychiatry, 53*, 494–501.

Hariri, A., R, Mattay, V., S, Tessitore, A., Kolachana, B., Fera, F., Goldman, D., et al. (2002). Serotonin transporter genetic variation and the response of the human amygdala. *Science, 297*, 400–403.

Hatfield, E., Cacioppo, J. T., & Rapson, R. (1992). Primitive emotional contagion. In M. Clark (Ed.), *Review of personality and social psychology: emotion and behavior* (pp. 151–177). Newbury Park, CA: Sage Publications.

Haxby, J., Hoffman, E., & Ida-Gobbini, M. (2002). Human neural systems for face recognition and social communication. *Society of Biological Psychiatry, 51*, 59–67.

Haxby, J. V., Hoffman, E. A., & Ida Gobbini, M. (2000). The distributed human neural system for face perception. *Trends in Cognitive Sciences, 4*, 223–233.

Helland, S. (2005). *Gender differences in facial imitation*. Unpublished Bachelor's Thesis, University of Lund.

Hobson, R. P. (1993). *Autism and the development of mind*: Lawrence Erlbaum Associates.

Hoffman, M. L. (1977). Sex differences in empathy and related behaviors. *Psychological Bulletin, 84*, 712–722.

Hynes, C., Baird, A., & Grafton, S. (2006). Differential role of the orbital frontal lobe in emotional versus cognitive perspective-taking. *Neuropsychologia, 44*(3), 374–383.

Iacoboni, M., Koski, L., Brass, M., Bekkering, H., Woods, R., Dubeau, M., et al. (2001). Reafferent copies of imitated actions in the right superior temporal cortex. *Proceedings of the National Academy of Sciences, 98*(24), 13995–13999.

Jackson, P., Meltzoff, A., & Decety, J. (2005). How do we perceive the pain of others? A window into the neural processes involved in empathy. *NeuroImage, 24*(3), 771–779.

Johnson-Frey, S., Maloof, F., Newman-Norlund, R., Farrer, C., Inati, S., & Grafton, S. (2003). Actions or hand-object interactions? Human inferior frontal cortex and action observation. *Neuron, 39*(6), 1053–1058.

Kalin, N., H, Shelton, S., E, & Davidson, R. J. (2001). The primate amygdala mediates acute fear but not the behavioral and physiological components of anxious temperament. *J Neurosci, 21*(6), 2067–2074.

Keysers, C., & Perrett, D. I. (2004). Demystifying social cognition: a Hebbian perspective. *Trends Cogn Sci, 8*(11), 501–507.

Knight, G. P., Fabes, R. A., & Higgins, D. A. (1989). Gender differences in the cooperative, competitive, and individualistic social values of children. *Motivation and Emotion, 13*, 125–141.

Lawrence, E. J., Shaw, P., Baker, D., Baron-Cohen, S., & David, A. S. (2004). Measuring Empathy—Reliability and validity of the empathy quotient. *Psychological Medicine, 34*, 911–919.

LeDoux, J. (2000). Emotion circuits in the brain. *Annual Review of Neuroscience, 23*, 155–184.

Lee, T.-W., Josephs, O., Dolan, R. J., & Critchley, H. D. (2006). Imitating expressions: emotion-specific neural substrates in facial mimicry. *Soc Cogn Affect Neurosci, 1*(2), 122–135.

Lee, T., Liu, H.-L., Hoosain, R., Liao, W.-T., Wu, C.-T., Yuan, K., et al. (2002). Gender differences in neural correlates of recognition of happy and sad faces in humans assessed by functional magnetic resonance imaging. *Neuroscience Letters, 333*, 13–16.

Leslie, K., Johnson-Frey, S., & Grafton, S. (2004). Functional imaging of face and hand imitation: toward a motor theory of empathy. *Neuroimage, 21*, 601–607.

Levenson, R. (1996). Biological substrates of empathy and facial modulation of emotion: two facets of the scientific legacy of John Lanzetta. *Motivation and Emotion, 20*, 185–204.

Lewis, P., Critchley, H. D., Rotshtein, P., & Dolan, R. J. (2005). *Processing valence and arousal in affective words.* Paper presented at the SFN Annual Conference, Washington DC, USA.

Liotti, M., Mayberg, H., Brannan, S., McGinnis, S., Jerabek, P., & Fox, P. (2000). Differential limbic-cortical correlates of sadness and anxiety in healthy subjects: Implications for affective disorders. *Biol Psychiatry, 48*, 30–42.

Maccoby, E. (1999). *The two sexes: growing up apart, coming together*: Harvard University Press.

Malhi, G., Lagopoulos, J., Ward, P., Kumari, V., Mitchell, D., Parker, G., et al. (2004). Cognitive generation of affect in bipolar depression: an fMRI study. *Eur J Neurosci, 19*(3), 741–754.

Mayberg, H., Liotti, M., Brannan, S., McGinnis, M. Y., Mahurin, R., Jerabek, P., et al. (1999). Reciprocal limbic-cortical function and negative mood: Converging PET findings in depression and normal sadness. *Am J Psychiatry, 156*, 675–682.

Mobbs, D., Greicius, M. D., Abdel-Azim, E., Menon, V., & Reiss, A. L. (2003). Humor modulates the mesolimbic reward centres. *Neuron, 40*, 1041–1048.

Moll, J., de Oliveira-Souza, R., Eslinger, P., Bramati, I., Mourao-Miranda, J., Andreiuolo, P., et al. (2002). The neural correlates of moral sensitivity: A functional magnetic resonance imaging investigation of basic and moral emotions. *J Neurosci, 22*(7), 2730–2736.

Muncer, S., & Ling, J. (2006). Psychometric analysis of the empathy quotient (EQ) scale. *Person. Individ.Diff, 40*, 1111–1119.

Murphy, F. C., Nimmo-Smith, I., & Lawrence, A. D. (2003). Functional neuroanatomy of emotions: a meta-analysis. *Cognitive, Affective & Behavioral Neuroscience, 3*(3), 207–233.

Nichols, S. (2001). Mindreading and the cognitive architecture underlying altruistic motivation. *Mind and Language, 16*, 425–455.

O'Doherty, J., Deichmann, R., Critchley, H. D., & Dolan, R. J. (2002). Neural responses during anticipation of a primary taste reward. *Neuron, 33*, 815–826.

Pelphrey, K. A., Singerman, J. D., Allison, T., & McCarthy, G. (2003). Brain activation evoked by perception of gaze shifts: the influence of context. *Neuropsychologia, 41*, 156–170.

Perrett, D. I., & Emery, N. (1994). Understanding the intentions of others from visual signals: neurophysiological evidence. *Curr Psychol Cogn, 13*, 683–694.

Phan, K. L., Wager, T., Taylor, S. F., & Liberzon, I. (2002). Functional neuroanatomy of emotion: A meta-analysis of emotion activation studies in PET and fMRI. *Neuroimage, 16*, 331–348.

Phillips, W., Baron-Cohen, S., & Rutter, M. (1998). Understanding intention in normal development and in autism. *British Journal of Developmental Psychology, 16*, 337–348.

Piaget, J., & Inhelder, B. (1956). *The child's conception of space.* London: Routledge and Kegan Paul.

Power, T. G. (1985). Mother- and father-infant play: A developmental analysis. *Child Development, 56,* 1514–1524.

Preston, S., D, & de Waal, F., B, M,. (2002). Empathy: Its ultimate and proximate bases. *Behavioural and Brain Sciences, 25,* 1–72.

Rizzolatti, G., & Craighero, L. (2004). The mirror-neuron system. *Annual Review of Neuroscience, 27,* 169–192.

Rizzolatti, G., Fadiga, L., Gallese, V., & Fogassi, L. (1996). Premotor cortex and the recognition of motor actions. *Cognitive Brain Research, 3,* 131–141.

Rolls, E., T. (2002). Neural basis of emotions. In N. Smelsner & P. Baltes (Eds.), *International encyclopedia of the social and behavioral sciences* (pp. 4444–4449). Amsterdam: Elsevier.

Saxe, R., Carey, S., & Kanwisher, N. (2004). Understanding other minds: linking developmental psychology and functional neuroimaging. *Annual Review of Psychology, 55,* 87–124.

Schienle, A., Schafer, A., Stark, R., Walter, B., & Vaitl, D. (2005). Gender differences in the processing of disgust- and fear-inducing pictures: an fMRI study. *Neuroreport, 16*(3), 277–280.

Schroeder, U., Hennenlotter, A., Erhard, P., Haslinger, B., Stahl, R., Lange, K., et al. (2004). Functional neuroanatomy of perceiving suprised faces. *Hum Brain Mapp, 23,* 181–187.

Shumake, J., Edwards, E., & Gonzalez–Lima, F. (2001). Hypermetabolism of paraventricular hypothalamus in the congenitally helpless rat. *Neuroscience Letters, 311*(1), 45–48.

Skuse, D., H, James, R., S, Bishop, D., V, M, Coppins, B., Dalton, P., Aamodt-Leeper, G., et al. (1997). Evidence from Turner's syndrome of the imprinted x-linked locus affecting cognitive function. *Nature, 287,* 705–708.

Small, D., Gregory, M., Mak, Y., Gitelman, D., Mesulam, M., & Parrish, T. (2003). Dissociation of neural representation of intensity and affective valuation in human gustation. *Neuron, 39,* 701–711.

Smith, A. (1759). *The theory of moral sentiments* (Republished 1976 ed.). Oxford: Clarendon Press.

Smith, P. M. (1985). *Language, the sexes and society.* Oxford: Basil Blackwell.

Sorce, J., Emde, R., Campos, J., & Klinnert, M. (1985). Maternal emotional signalling: its effect on the visual cliff behavior of 1 year olds. *Developmental Psychology, 21,* 195–200.

Stein, E. (1989). *On the problem of empathy (1917)* (W. Stein, Trans. 3rd ed.). Washington, D.C.: ICS Publications.

Strayer, F. F. (1980). Child ethology and the study of preschool soical relations. In H. C. Foot, A. J. Chapman & J. R. Smith (Eds.), *Friendship and social relations in children* (pp. 235–266). New York: John Wiley.

Takahashi, H., Yahata, N., Koeda, M., Matsuda, T., Asai, K., & Okubo, Y. (2004). Brain activation associated with evaluative process of guilt and embarrassment: an fMRI study. *Neuroimage, 23*(3), 967–974.

Tannen, D. (1991). *You just don't understand: Women and men in conversation.* London: Virago.

Wager, T., Phan, K. L., Liberzon, I., & Taylor, S. (2003). Valence gender and lateralization of functional brain anatomy: a meta-analysis of findings from neuroimaging. *Neuroimage, 19,* 513–531.

Walden, T., & Ogan, T. (1988). The development of social referencing. *Child Development, 59*(5), 1230–1240.

Whiten, A. (1991). *Natural theories of mind.* Oxford: Basil Blackwell.

Wicker, B., Keysers, C., Plailly, J., Royet, J.-P., Gallese, V., & Rizzolatti, G. (2003). Both of us disgusted in *my* insula: The common neural basis of seeing and feeling disgust. *Neuron, 40,* 655–664.

Williams, J. H. G., Waiter, G. D., Perra, O., Perrett, D. I., & Whiten, A. (2005). An fMRI study of joint attention experience. *Neuroimage, 25,* 133–140.

Zahn, R., Moll, J., Paiva, M., Garrido, G., Krueger, F., Huey, E. D., et al. (2008). The neural basis of human social values: Evidence from functional MRI. *Cereb. Cortex,* bhn080.

CHAPTER 13

Thin-Slice Vision

Max Weisbuch and Nalini Ambady

People might not feel comfortable revealing internal states, personality traits, and personal relationships to complete strangers. It may, therefore, be disturbing to learn that complete strangers often need less than 10-seconds to make nonrandom inferences about others personality traits, sexual orientation, popularity, vulnerability, and so on. In other words, aspects of the psychological self are visible to complete strangers who are only briefly exposed to one's nonverbal behavior.

Fortunately, there are limits to the thin-slice vision of strangers, just as there are limits to traditional vision. For example, just as the accuracy of traditional vision is limited by physical distance, the accuracy of social vision is limited by context. In the same way that inferences about object texture may be inaccurate when judged from several miles, inferences of mathematical prowess may be inaccurate when judged from visual exposure to a 10-second social interaction. And although we are not always successful in our efforts to mislead others about the psychological self, such camouflage may sometimes impair the accuracy of strangers' inferences. Finally, strangers will differ in their ability to see the psychological self from 10 seconds of visual exposure. In summary, the visibility of the psychological self depends on several factors.

This chapter reviews the nuances involved in inferring personal characteristics from exposure to thin slices of nonverbal behavior. Consistent with the theme of this volume, our review is framed within the perspective of social vision. The first section establishes that thin slices provide a visual peephole to the self. The second section reviews factors that enhance or limit such thin-slice vision, including factors such as the importance of the sampled context and the role of camouflage. The focus in the second section is on establishing analogues between traditional and social vision. The final section is a short review of individual differences in thin-slice vision.

THIN-SLICE VISION: ON USING THE VISUAL PEEPHOLE

A visual thin slice is a brief silent excerpt of expressive behavior sampled from the behavioral stream. Thin slices are always less than 5 minutes and typically closer to 30 seconds. Thin-slice research utilizes perceivers with (1) no prior history with the thin slice target and (2) little or no knowledge of the global context in which the behavior takes place. That these perceivers require little time to make (often) accurate inferences about others may seem both unintuitive and unremarkable. Two clichés best

This work was supported in part by National Institute of Mental Health National Research Service Award to the first author (#5F32MH078350–02).

describe these opposing sentiments: "bigger is better" and "a picture is worth a thousand words."

Bigger Is Better

Intuition would compel most reasonable people to suspect that larger slices will be more representative and more useful to judge. By definition, larger slices contain more information and should, therefore, provide a more reliable sample. Psychologists have conducted tens of thousands of studies over the last century in an attempt to understand the complexity of human beings—it seems unreasonable and perhaps offensive to suggest that a layperson could obtain some of this same knowledge in 30 silent seconds. The history of psychology would suggest that a sampling of personal history, an understanding of situational context, and self-reports of the individual would be necessary for a confident evaluation of another person. Yet in one meta-analytic study, the effect size for accuracy from visual thin slices was $r = .45$ (see Ambady & Rosenthal, 1992, Table IV). Moreover, the addition of verbal information to thin slices did not improve accuracy—the effect size for visual + verbal information was actually lower than that of visual alone. Finally, the relationship between length of thin slice and accuracy was not a clear positive or negative linear function—hence, length of thin slice did not influence accuracy. Indeed, specific nonverbal cues (e.g., nods) coded from a single thin-slice appear to be highly correlated with the same cues coded from a longer, 15 minute segment (Murphy, 2005).

A Picture Is Worth a Thousand Words

Research reviewed in several chapters in this volume suggests that accurate inferences can be made without dynamic behavioral information. For example, there is widespread agreement among perceivers on the emotional meaning of static posed facial images (see Adams, Franklin, Nelson, & Stevonson, and Zebrowitz, Montepare, & Bronstadt this volume) and ratings of pictures can be used to predict a variety of outcomes, including elections (Todorov, Mandisodza, Goren, & Hall,

2005). If static images are all that is necessary for accurate inferences, is there any reason to suggest that thin slices are uniquely informative? Indeed, there is.

The focus here is on expressive movement. In their classic book, *Studies in Expressive Movement,* Allport and Vernon (1933) defined expressive movement as "individual differences in the manner of performing adaptive acts, considered as dependent less upon external and temporary conditions than upon enduring qualities of personality" (p. 23). Expressive behavior conveys important information about the cultural, social, interpersonal, and behavioral ecology—information regarding affect and emotions, personality and dispositions, internal goals and motives, and, finally, information about social relationships (Ambady, Bernieri, & Richeson, 2000). And DePaulo (1992) has argued that expressive nonverbal behaviors are both more difficult to suppress relative to verbal behavior and more accessible to observers than actors. One implication of the lack of control and the presence of accessibility in expressive behavior is that such behavior provides observers with a relatively valid source of information regarding the true internal states and dispositions of another. By sampling expressive behavior, thin slices capture chronic, reliable, and stylistic psychological information not subject to conscious control and monitoring (DePaulo, 1992; Ekman & Friesen, 1969, 1974; Rime & Schiaratura, 1991).

One might argue that static images contain expressive behavior. And they certainly *can* contain expressive behavior. Part of the problem, however, is that most "accuracy" research using static images has used posed faces. In this sense, the displays in most static image studies lack some degree of expressivity. The prototypical and intense emotion expressions typically used in this research are the real-life exception rather than the rule. Notably, there is less evidence for the accuracy of emotion recognition from more ecologically valid and spontaneous expressions (e.g., Carroll & Russell, 1997). Indeed, recent research using more ecologically valid and subtle emotional displays has shown that accuracy was greater for minimal but dynamic displays than it was for static displays (Ambadar, Schooler, & Cohn, 2005). By using random-noise interstimulus intervals, Ambadar and colleagues were able to show that the benefit of the dynamic displays did not reside simply in providing more information than static images, but instead resided in the dynamic unfolding of the emotion display. This is not to say that posed static images are uninformative in their own right—we only wish to argue that dynamic motion provides a unique peephole into individuals' minds.

Is Looking Through the Visual Peephole Different from Hearing a Whisper?

Some scholars may argue that the vision analogy breaks down because thin-slice vision, hearing, and feeling (e.g., handshakes) are likely to reveal qualitatively similar information, whereas traditional vision, hearing, and touch are clearly distinct. In fact, visual thin-slice impressions are often quite distinct from auditory thin-slice impressions. In their wide-ranging work on nonverbal sensitivity, Rosenthal and colleagues (Rosenthal, Hall, DiMatteo, Rogers, & Archer, 1979) provided strong evidence for the discriminant validity of visual and auditory forms of thin-slice decoding. This monograph described studies with uncommonly diverse samples, including cognitively impaired samples, samples of a variety of ages, a thorough examination of gendered samples, culturally distinct samples, samples with heterogenous and measured personality traits, and so on. All of these samples were asked to make a forced-choice decision about the predicament of an actor across a number of scenarios. Each scenario was presented in one of 11 modalities, with each modality presenting a slightly different type of information (e.g., facial and bodily but no audio, face plus prosodic audio). In factor-analyses on subsets of this data, independent factors emerged, which clearly distinguished visual channels (face or body) from vocal channels. Moreover, the predictive validity of visual versus auditory channels was well-differentiated. Finally, analyses of test-retest reliability showed that

modality-specific patterns of decoding accuracy remained stable over several weeks.

Additionally attesting to the distinction in sensory modality is that nonverbal behavior that is seen has a much different impact than nonverbal (paraverbal) behavior that is heard (Elfenbein & Ambady 2002a, Puccinelli & Tickle-Degnen, 2004), with differential implications for both targets and observers. Moreover, certain characteristics are better observed on the visual channel (e.g., traits) than on the vocal channel, whereas others are not (Harrigan, Wilson, & Rosenthal, 2004).

In summary, there is ample reason to consider thin-slice vision a unique modality of social perception, separate from auditory perception and perception of static stimuli. Visual thin slices provide perceivers with dynamic expressive behavior that allow for relatively accurate inferences into the psychological and social life of target. Inferences made from thin slices are empirically related to inferences from "thicker" slices, are theoretically and empirically superior to inferences made from static images, and are theoretically and empirically distinct from other thin-slice modalities. This review will focus on studies in which visual channel was the *only* channel of communication open to observers. Thin-slice studies were excluded when observers had access to auditory information or any other type of information. Specifically, our review is limited to *thin-slice vision*.

Like traditional vision, there are domains in which thin-slice vision may be better or worse. In the next section, we detail the domains in which people clearly have thin-slice vision.

DOMAINS OF THIN-SLICE VISION

Thin-slice vision might reasonably be limited to socially valued characteristics. For example, you might not mind if a stranger can see that you are outgoing but you might mind if that stranger can see that you have a personality disorder. If so, you might be more forthcoming with your extraversion than your personality disorder. As will become apparent, however, a host of desirable *and* undesirable characteristics are visible through the visual peephole of thin slices.

Personality

Personality is visible via silent thin slices. For example, in one study (Gangestad, Simpson, DiGeronimo, & Biek, 1992), target participants completed measures of extraversion, interpersonal warmth, and sociosexuality. Naïve judges exposed to silent thin slices (an interview) of these targets were able to make accurate personality inferences on all three variables, especially with male targets. In another study, Borkenau and Liebler (1992) showed that perceivers could make accurate inferences about masculinity, extraversion, conscientiousness, and neuroticism from silent thin slices. Of particular interest is that these visual thin slices were of a largely asocial situation—target participants simply entered an empty room, read a weather report, and exited the room. It is rather remarkable that such a minimal context was sufficient for naïve judges to "see" a target's enduring personality. Yet Borkenau and Liebler (1993) replicated these findings and showed that complete strangers' thin-slice ratings correlated not only with target self-ratings but also with acquaintance ratings. More recent research (Yeagley, Morling, & Nelson, 2007) replicated accuracy effects for extraversion and masculinity and additionally showed that satisfaction with life was visible via thin-slices. Thus, there seems to be considerable evidence that people can "see" at least some personality traits in thin slices.

Internal States

In Western culture, it is undesirable to be an anxious or depressed person (Corrigan, 2005). In fact, trait anxious and depressed people often try to conceal their enduringly negative emotional state (Corrigan, 2005). It would, therefore, be reasonable if such states were not visually observable, at least in a thin slice. Yet a meta-analysis comparing detection of anxiety from either visual or auditory channels demonstrated that both state and trait anxiety could be revealed via silent behavior alone—the vast majority of studies in this meta-analysis were thin slice studies (Harrigan et al., 2004). As an example of one of these studies, 20 psychiatric

inpatient participants were videotaped as they engaged in a clinical interview (Waxer, 1977). These patients differed considerably in self-reported trait anxiety, yet naïve judges were able to accurately infer trait anxiety from one-minute silent thin slices.

The same meta-analysis suggested that inferences of trait anxiety from thin-slices are *especially* reliable when the visual (nonverbal) channel is isolated (Harrigan et al., 2004). In one study with a nonclinical sample, people differing in trait anxiety were videotaped while discussing a variety of events (Harrigan, Harrigan, Sale, & Rosenthal, 1996). For each of these target participants, a variety of 30-second silent video segments were created. Subsequently, naïve judges rated the anxiety level of each target participant's clips. Naïve judges viewing silent videos readily discriminated between high and low trait anxious participants. Yet judges given auditory information alone could *not* accurately discriminate between high and low trait anxiety, a pattern also observed in the meta-analysis. Thus, both state and trait anxiety can become visible via thin slices. Indeed, the visual modality appears to be uniquely sensitive to dispositional anxiety.

Depression can also become visible via silent thin slices. For example, in one study (Waxer, 1974), videotapes of admission interviews at a psychiatric hospital were reduced to silent thin-slice segments and presented to naïve judges. Half of the thin slices included patients admitted for depression, and the other half included patients admitted for other reasons (these patients scored low on a depression inventory). Naïve nonexpert and expert judges were asked to make categorical judgments as to whether each clip was of a depressed or nondepressed person. These judgments were correct 88 percent of the time on average, though the thin-slice vision of experts was greater than that of nonexperts (see also, Waxer, 1976). A more recent study utilized a non-clinical sample videotaped during a non-clinical interview (Clarke, Weisbuch, & Ambady, 2007). Judges were presented with a 10-second silent thin-slice from the interview and asked to rate the extent to which the participant was depressed. Despite the brevity of the interview and the nonclinical nature of the context, the ratings of naïve judges were positively correlated with participants' self-reported levels of depression.

In summary, enduring emotional states, including those meeting criteria for clinical diagnosis, can be accurately inferred by naïve judges from nonverbal thin slices.

Sexuality

In most of Western culture, sexuality is a highly personal topic and sexual preferences are rarely disclosed to strangers. Yet some of these sexual preferences can be visible in silent thin slices.

For example, Ambady, Hallahan, and Conner (1999) conducted a series of studies to examine the accuracy of judgments of sexual orientation from extremely brief (10- and 1-second) and silent thin slices. Heterosexual and homosexual participants were videotaped as they discussed the demands of academic and extracurricular activities. In none of these clips was reference made to participant's sexual orientation. Accuracy was significantly greater than chance for 1-second and 10-second nonverbal thin slice clips but did not exceed chance for still images captured from the behavioral stream. This pattern of findings was replicated in a study in which the visual images were digitally degraded such that only an outlined figure was observable. Thus, brief but dynamic nonverbal social behavior was sufficient for making accurate inferences into sexual orientation. Sexual orientation can become visible via silent thin slices.

Building on these findings, a recent set of studies examined a set of dynamic body cues that may be important for revealing sexuality (Johnson, Gill, Reichman, & Tassinary, 2007). The results suggested that thin-slice vision for sexual orientation is facilitated by perceptions of gait. Men who walk with swaying hips (a gait more typical of *women*) but not swaggering shoulders (a gait more typical of *men*) were more likely to be perceived as homosexual, as compared to men with a gender-typical gait.

Moreover, to the extent that perceivers used this information in their overall judgments of sexuality, the more likely that perceivers were to be correct.

Sexual orientation is not the only sex-related preference visible to the thin-slice observer. For example, sociosexuality is the degree to which people are willing to and likely to engage in sex without commitment—a reliable and valid self-report measure of this construct has been developed (Simpson & Gangestad, 1991). In one study, naïve judges were shown silent thin slices of people who were speaking to a video-camera during a first-date interview. Judges rated participants on several components of sociosexuality (e.g., sexual permissiveness). These ratings were positively correlated with participants' self-ratings, and this correlation held even after controlling for the physical attractiveness of the target.

Finally, certain men are more likely to sexually harass than are others, and this potential is visible via thin slices. In one set of studies, male participants varying on a likelihood-to-sexually-harass (LSH) scale were interviewed by an attractive and subordinate woman. Hidden video captured the nonverbal behavior of the male. Naïve judges were shown a short (several minutes) silent video clip of this interview—from these nonverbal thin slices, judges were able to discriminate between men who were likely to sexually harass from those who were unlikely to do so (Craig, Kelly, & Driscoll, 2001; Driscoll, Kelly, & Henderson, 1998).

In summary, visual exposure to thin slices can be sufficient for strangers to make accurate (above-chance) inferences about certain aspects of sexuality. This relationship holds for sexual orientation, sexual permissiveness, and likelihood of sexual harassment.

Biased Attitudes

Most people would prefer to appear unbiased in their judgments (e.g., Gaertner & Dovidio, 1986). One form of bias that people often go to pains to cover up is racial bias. It has become unacceptable to express race-based prejudice in Western culture, especially prejudice against

African-Americans (Blanchard, Lilly, & Vaughn, 1991; Monteith, Deneen, & Tooman, 1996). Richeson and Shelton (2005) examined the degree to which this undesirable characteristic is visible via thin slices. In this study, naïve judges rated the affect of white participants whilst the latter interacted with a white confederate or a black confederate. Importantly, the race of the confederate was not visible to judges and judges rated silent thin slices of both interactions. Racial bias of the white participants was examined with an implicit reaction-time measure. To the extent that white participants were racially biased, they were judged as expressing little positive affect during the interracial interaction. This same pattern did not hold for judgments of same-race interactions. Hence, white racial bias against black people was visible in a 20-second silent thin slice.

Another form of bias is based not on social category but on personal expectations. People in positions of authority often have differing expectations for particular subordinates or students yet in many contexts, including the classroom, authority figures are expected to treat all people equally. In fact, teachers with positive expectations for certain students have been shown to have more positive nonverbal styles with those students (e.g., Babad, Bernieri, & Rosenthal, 1989) than with others. Of course, teachers differ in the extent to which they exhibit bias. Can naïve judges accurately infer—from a silent thin-slice—whether a teacher is likely to be biased? In an attempt to answer this question, Babad (2005) asked high school students to view 10-second silent thin slices of unfamiliar teachers giving a public lecture to an entire classroom. Judges rated the extent to which each teacher could be expected to treat high- and low-achieving students with equality during a dyadic (one-on-one) interaction. The ratings of these naïve (unfamiliar high school student) judges were positively correlated with teachers' actual bias, as indicated by ratings of each teacher's own students.

The biases of *actual* trial judges are also visible via silent thin slices. For example, trial judges in one study (Blanck, Rosenthal, & Cordell, 1985) were videotaped while giving standardized final instructions to a jury. These trial judges self-reported their expectations for the trial outcome (innocent or guilty). Raters unfamiliar with the judges viewed thin slices of the final jury instructions and rated the judge on a variety of characteristics. Trial judges were seen as less warm, less competent, less wise, and more anxious when they expected the defendant to be found guilty than when they did not.

Personality Disorders

Just as certain types of enduring affect, sexuality, and bias can be undesirable, some aspects of personality are socially stigmatized and likely to be concealed. For example, a person with a personality disorder may not want others to know about the disorder. One study has examined the extent to which personality disorders are visible to the thin-slice observer (Friedman, Oltmanns, Gleason, & Turkheimer, 2006). Although many personality disorders were not well predicted by thin-slice ratings, such ratings were predictive of avoidant personality disorder, histrionic personality disorder, and obsessive-compulsive personality disorder. Hence, there is preliminary evidence that certain personality disorders can be seen via thin slices.

Intelligence

From one-minute or less of strictly visual exposure, strangers can make above-chance inferences about the IQ of a target person, even when viewing a target in an informal social interaction (Murphy, Hall, & Colvin, 2003). Murphy and colleagues observed that several visual cues were related to both actual intelligence and inferred intelligence. Greater eye gaze with a partner was associated with greater intelligence *and* greater perceived intelligence; this appeared to be especially true with regard eye gaze while speaking (Murphy et al., 2003). Hence, thin-slice vision for intelligence may be facilitated by focusing on targets' eye gaze behavior.

Power

People can have feelings of power or dominance and people can have actual power or status—often feelings of power and actual power will coincide but often they do not. Most of the evidence regarding thin-slice vision concerns actual power. In one study (Hall & Friedman, 1999) employees of a company engaged in a videotaped conversation or a puzzle task. The relative status of each employee within the company was visible to naïve judges via silent thin-slices. This finding is somewhat inconsistent with a later meta-analysis (Hall, Coats, & LeBeau, 2005), which focused on nonverbal *cues* rather than on thin-slice accuracy. In this meta-analysis, there was substantial heterogeneity in the nonverbal cues perceived to be and actually related to power. Nonetheless, the meta-analysis did show that perceivers' beliefs about power-related nonverbal cues showed an overall kernel of truth. The cues perceived to be associated with power actually were associated with power; however, perceivers believed the cues to be much more closely related to power than was actually the case. In summary, evidence suggests that actual power can be accurately inferred from silent thin slices, whereas nonverbal cues to power are difficult to identify.

Relationships

In addition to effectively judging characteristics of individuals, strangers can accurately judge relationship type and quality from silent thin slices. For example, target participants in one study were videotaped as they sat side by side and had a brief discussion. Naïve judges were able to see, from a 15-second silent thin slice, whether the pair of target participants were (1) involved in a romantic relationship, (2) were platonic friends, or (c) were strangers (Ambady & Gray, 2002). Given a particular type of relationship, the quality of that relationship is also visible via thin slices. In one study (Grahe & Bernieri, 1999), for example, previously unfamiliar student pairs planned a trip around the world together—these videotaped planning sessions lasted up to 15 minutes. Afterwards, each student completed a questionnaire assessing the quality (rapport) of the interaction. Naive judges' ratings of rapport (from 30-second silent thin slices) were significantly associated with

the targets' self-reported ratings of rapport. Of special note is that four other groups of judges also rated the pairs, with each group of judges rating from a different channel. Judges whose thin slice ratings came from a verbal transcript had the lowest accuracy, and judges whose thin slice ratings came from only visual information had the greatest accuracy, even greater than judges who had access to both visual and verbal information. In summary, there is evidence that both relationship type and quality can literally be "seen" in silent thin slices.

Future Behavior

Perhaps the most compelling evidence for vision through thin slices is the fact that naïve visual thin slice judgments can predict a broad spectrum of behavior, including teacher effectiveness, jury behavior, criminal behavior, and the effectiveness of health practitioners.

First, teacher effectiveness is visible via silent thin slices. In one set of studies, college professors and high school teachers were videotaped while teaching classes (Ambady & Rosenthal, 1993). Silent thin slices were created from these videotaped sessions, and naïve judges rated the instructors on a variety of characteristics (e.g., competent, empathic). The single factor that emerged from these ratings predicted both end-of-semester student evaluations and supervisor (i.e., principal) evaluations, independent of physical attractiveness ratings. Hence, a full semester's worth of teaching performance was presaged by naïve strangers who viewed only 30-seconds of teacher nonverbal behavior.

Second, future outcomes of criminal trials (i.e., jury behavior) are visible via thin slices. Specifically, in one study, raters unfamiliar with the trial judges viewed nonverbal thin slices of trial judges' final instructions to the jury—these instructions were standardized (Blanck et al., 1985). The extent to which the trial judge was rated as dominant predicted the likelihood that the jury would find the defendant innocent.

Third, future crime is visible via nonverbal thin slices. In a study with remarkable ecological validity, closed-circuit television (CCTV) cameras provided the thin-slice materials (Trosianko et al., 2004). Eighteen silent thin slice clips depicted the lead-up to a crime but not the crime itself. Eighteen carefully matched clips depicted nearly identical lead-ups that did not lead to a crime. All judges were unfamiliar with the targets, but half of the judges were novices (college students) and half of the judges were experts (employed as CCTV monitors). Both novice and expert judges were able to see into the future. Specifically, novice and expert judges accurately discriminated silent clips that led to bad (criminal) behaviors from nonverbal clips that led to not bad (noncriminal) behaviors. A signal-detection analysis confirmed that these patterns were not simply due to response biases. Further descriptive analyses suggested that vision for future criminal behavior relied heavily on the perception of gait and gestures.

Fourth, the future performance (effectiveness) of health practitioners is visible via nonverbal thin slices. For example, 15-second silent thin-slice judgments of occupational therapy students predicted those students' clinical performance (Tickle-Degnen & Puccinelli, 1999). If negative thin-slice judgments of health practitioners predict poor clinical performance, then it may also be true that negative thin-slice judgments of health practitioners predict poor patient outcomes. This is indeed the case. Specifically, physical therapists in one study (Ambady, Koo, Rosenthal, & Winograd, 2002) were videotaped during an interaction with an elderly inpatient. The patients had multiple physical-therapy sessions over an average inpatient stay of nine days. Despite the fact that each patient had multiple physical-therapy sessions, each lasting 30 minutes, ratings made by naïve judges from a one-minute silent thin slice predicted patients' clinical improvement (or decrement) immediately following and three months following discharge. Specifically, to the extent that naïve judges rated the practitioner as distant, patients had decreases in activities of daily living (e.g., grooming, bathing, walking by oneself) after discharge. Moreover, naïve

judgments of physician distance predicted increased patient confusion immediately following discharge. Hence, the future health of hospital inpatients can become visible via thin slices of practitioner behavior.

CONTEXT AND CAMOUFLAGE: BOUNDARIES FOR THIN-SLICE VISION

From the preceding review, one could conclude that silent thin slices are analogous to a large microscopic lens that magnifies and makes visible all dispositions, internal states, and future behavior. In fact, thin-slice vision is more like normal vision than a magical microscope. With normal vision, not all physical objects are equally visible and the visibility of any individual object may change. Deer ticks are more difficult to see than black Labrador Retrievers and the latter are easier to see during the day than at night. These same principles can be applied to thin-slice vision. For example, soft drink preferences are more difficult to see than extraversion, and the latter is easier to see within social than asocial contexts.

Additionally, normal observers can have difficulty seeing purposely concealed stimuli; for example, certain animals camouflage themselves by changing the color of their skin and cannot be easily seen. In combat, military personnel wear clothing to camouflage themselves. In a similar fashion, people have learned to conceal their internal states. Just as normal camouflage may fail, so too may thin-slice camouflage, as when perceivers are able to detect deception from nonverbal behavior. These analogues—of physical visibility to thin-slice visibility—will be examined in what follows.

Of Size and Context

Many visual judgments can be extremely difficult to make, except under certain conditions. For example, determining the extent to which a line on a wall is exactly parallel to the floor can be extremely difficult. However, when the line is only an inch above the floor, the judgment becomes much easier. The potential for a lack of visual clarity applies to other types of judgments as well—for example, visual judgments of the presence or absence of an object may be extremely difficult for tiny objects unless those objects are quite close to one's eyes. And judgments of texture, contour, and even color are often difficult without appropriate frames of reference. These examples illustrate that certain stimuli are difficult to see but that the visibility of these stimuli can be enhanced by contextual factors. The same principles apply to visual thin-slice judgments.

First, the most visible characteristics should be those that have a pervasive impact on physical behavior. This principle is similar to the principle of size in normal vision. Just as a larger object is more likely to enter the visual field than a smaller object, a characteristic with a broad impact on behavior is more likely to enter the visual field than is a characteristic with a narrow impact on visible behavior. Certain characteristics manifest themselves behaviorally across many contexts but others do not. Much, if not most, of the behavioral stream occurs in public, in the presence of others. Consequently, the behavioral stream will often reflect the target individual's level of extraversion, a trait that reflects (in part) the individual's tendency to engage others and respond to others. Observable behavior should thus be influenced by extraversion in many or most situations. Indeed, extraversion is quite visible by thin-slice standards (e.g., Gangestad et al., 1992). In contrast, trait hostility is likely to be directly observable only in social situations that also have the potential for conflict.

Another reason to expect context effects in thin-slice vision is that people don't exhibit the same nonverbal cues across situations. For example, people engaged in a competitive task are especially likely to gaze at each other, as compared to some other types of tasks (Knapp & Hall, 2002). The effect of these situational constraints on nonverbal behavior can be illustrated with a thin-slice study. Target participants in one experiment (Ambady et al., 1996) role-played each of six different scenarios in which they gave supervisors, peers, or subordinates good or bad news. As expected, judges' thin-slice judgments of targets' communication style depended on the particular situation viewed by those judges, even though judges were unaware of the target's role-play scenario.

Indeed, there is now direct evidence that context can influence thin-slice visual acuity. For example, we noted earlier that naïve judges could assess the quality of a relationship from silent thin slices. One study (Puccinelli, Tickle-Degnen, & Rosenthal, 2003) examined the consistency of such judgments across context by having target dyads first complete a puzzle task together and then interview each other one month later. Based on the idea that less valid cues to rapport exist in internally focused interactions (Bernieri & Gillis, 2001), the authors hypothesized and found that rapport between the dyad members was less visible during the interview than during the puzzle task. Likewise, recall that racial bias was visible when White targets were interacting with a black person but not when they were interacting with a white person (Richeson & Shelton, 2005). These findings suggest that racial bias may only be visible in cross-race interactions. Finally, recall that teacher performance (as assessed with student evaluations) could be predicted via visual thin slices of lecturing. Later research (Babad, Avni-Babad, & Rosenthal, 2004) showed that thin-slice ratings based on individual teacher-student interactions were *negatively* related to end of semester evaluations, whereas lecture-based thin-slice ratings were *positively* related to end of semester evaluations. In summary, there is evidence for the idea that context influences thin-slice visual acuity.

Beyond the three studies mentioned above (Babad et al., 2004; Puccinelli et al., 2003; Richeson & Shelton, 2005), the role of context in thin-slice vision is woefully understudied. Given the many reasons to believe that visual acuity depends on context, it is surprising that most research to date has largely examined thin-slices within a single context. Even the studies reviewed earlier that *have* examined thin-slice judgments across tasks have done so only for individual characteristics. Indeed, Puccinelli and colleagues (2003) argued that contexts constrained by implicit social norms may reduce thin-slice visibility *in general*, much as a dark room would reduce normal vision.

So does context influence the visibility of particular characteristics or all characteristics? A recent study, remarkable for its breadth, has attempted to answer this question though the answer is not specific to the visual modality (Borkenau, Mauer, Riemann, Spinath, & Angleitner, 2004). Target participants in this study engaged in 15 different tasks, ranging from reading newspaper headlines aloud to rigging up a paper tower to introducing oneself to a confederate. Self- and acquaintance reports of personality were taken and IQ was assessed. Naïve judges observed only one task per target and rated targets on a variety of characteristics, including personality and intelligence. Consistent with the idea that context can influence diagnosticity, openness to experience and intelligence were more accurately judged in some tasks than in others. To the contrary, other personality traits (e.g., agreeableness) were not terribly sensitive to context. The abundance of data yielded from this study prevented a full published description so the conclusions should be more closely examined. Nonetheless, the methodology of Borkenau and colleagues (2004) provides an excellent template for researchers interested in examining effects of context on thin-slice visual acuity.

Of Camouflage, Obstruction, and Magnification

People who you do not know would, in general, rather not let you see them naked. Government intelligence agencies often prefer that you not see important statements in government documents. And, if you are a military enemy engaged in battle, people would rather not let you see them at all. Toward these ends, people usually wear clothes in public, intelligence agencies routinely obscure sentences with black marker, and soldiers wear camouflage that allows them to blend in to the background. Similarly, there are some personal characteristics that people do not want you to see. Although we have seen that some of these characteristics are visible via thin-slices, people can try to obstruct others' view of many personal characteristics.

The philanderer can try to camouflage his infidelity, the nervous interviewee may try to conceal her anxiety, and the gay soldier might dine with women to promote the view that he is heterosexual.

Given that silent thin-slices *can* reveal undesirable sexual proclivities, psychological disorders, and politically incorrect biases, it seems likely that thin-slice vision is resistant to camouflage. Yet it is also possible that thin-slice vision is only accurate when people do not try to conceal those stigmatized identities—for example, gay men who have come out of the closet may assume that others can see their sexual preference and hence don't try to conceal their sexual orientation (cf., Ambady et al., 1999). And perhaps depressed people simply don't have the energy to conceal their emotional state (cf., Clarke et al., 1999). For these reasons the effects of purposive obstruction are best understood in studies that experimentally vary the obstructive motives of target persons. We review such studies in what follows.

At first glance, it appears that perceivers *can* be visually deceived; research on deception detection has revealed that perceivers are unable to detect deceit from visual information alone—a meta-analysis revealed that perceivers were correct in visual lie/truth classification 50.35 percent of the time (about as accurate as a coin flip; Bond & DePaulo, 2006). A closer look reveals, however, that when target deceivers are highly motivated to conceal the truth, perceivers' deception detection accuracy is actually *increased*. This is especially true of the visual channel, via which motivated liars are especially likely to be perceived as liars. Thus, the research on deception detection suggests that purposefully placed thin-slice obstructions (nonverbal deceptions) are neither transparent (ineffective) or opaque (100 percent effective): instead, such obstructions are translucent (somewhat effective).

But can the research on deception detection be applied to thin-slice vision? The former requires explicit judgments of truth/falsity whereas thin-slice vision requires only judgments of personality, emotions, and so forth. A recent study on thin-slice judgments of intelligence is instructive. In this study (Murphy, 2007), naïve judges had access to both the visual and auditory channel, so conclusions from this study can only be taken as preliminary with regard to thin-slice vision. Nonetheless, the findings are provocative. Although this study failed to replicate previous studies in that the intelligence of naturally behaving targets was inaccurately judged, thin-slice judges *were* accurate in assessing the intelligence of targets *who were trying to appear especially intelligent.* In other words, targets who tried to mislead perceivers were especially likely to be judged accurately. Moreover, it appears that accurate inferences of intelligence were based largely on thin-slice vision—in particular, eye gaze while speaking appeared to be the main cue that both distinguished (1) real from fake intelligence and (2) contributed to judges' ratings.

Given the reviewed findings, it appears as if conscious strategies of targets for obscuring thin-slice vision can be successful but usually are not. That is, many of the domains in which thin-slice vision clearly exist (e.g., sexuality, negative affective states, personality flaws) are domains in which targets are (1) likely aware of their standing and (2) likely motivated to conceal their standing. Moreover, motivated concealment among targets appears to *increase* accuracy among perceivers in some domains (Bond & DePaulo, 2006; Murphy, 2007). To the extent that conscious concealment of personal characteristics in the real world is highly motivated, such concealed personal characteristics may be visible to the thin-slice observer.

On the other end of the spectrum, certain targets may be magnifying lenses for thin-slice vision. That is, the characteristics of certain people may be especially likely to be visible to thin-slice perceivers. Although this hypothesis seems reasonable, there is actually little research on what types of individuals are most visible. The best evidence that certain people are magnifying lenses for thin-slice vision is evidence that expressive personalities do appear to be more visible from thin-slices. Specifically, individuals scoring high on a self-report measure of expressiveness were more accurately judged by silent thin-slice judges on

several traits (Gangestad et al., 1992). Beyond silent thin-slice studies (i.e., studies examining multiple modalities or "thick" slices), there is evidence that some individuals are more legible than others. For example, in one study (Ambady, Hallahan, & Rosenthal, 1995) targets completed a series of personality questionnaires while in a group. Members of the group then rated each other on a variety of personality characteristics. Extraverted participants were more legible than introverted participants and participants who scored higher on a measure of expressiveness were more legible than those who scored low on this measure. In general, extraverted and expressive individuals are consistently more legible than their introverted and unexpressive counterparts (Riggio, 2006), though it is important to bear in mind that these studies provide more information to judges, either temporally (with more time) or spatially (with more modalities). In any case, it seems reasonable to suggest that extraverted and/or expressive individuals are especially likely to serve as magnifying lenses for visible thin-slices.

In summary, existing empirical evidence suggests that it is difficult, though not impossible for targets to camouflage themselves from thin-slice judges. Moreover, certain types of targets do appear to magnify thin-slice vision, though research on this topic is lacking.

FACTORS THAT INCREASE OR DIMINISH INDIVIDUAL THIN-SLICE VISION

Just as environmental factors can impair vision, factors that reside inside the viewer can impair vision as well. Although some individuals have 20/20 vision, others have considerably worse vision. And even those individuals with 20/20 vision can fail to see objects when they are otherwise engaged (e.g., Simons & Chabris, 1999) or have blind spots for certain properties of stimuli, such as color. Likewise, some individuals have especially accurate thin-slice vision. But even individuals who generally tend to be accurate may fail to see certain types of psychological characteristics. This section reviews vision-limiting and vision-enhancing features that reside within the individual.

A great deal of empirical research has been conducted on individual differences in decoding nonverbal and paraverbal (e.g., vocal prosody and tone) behavior. This review will be confined to individual differences in thin-slice vision—specifically, it will be confined to individual differences in the ability to accurately see others' psychological characteristics from several seconds or minutes of exposure to behavior that does *not* include any vocal behavior. Consequently, research that utilizes both visual and auditory channels in measuring decoding ability (e.g., the Interpersonal Perception Test; IPT, see Archer, Costanzo, & Akert, 2001) will not be heavily reviewed. Moreover, research that relies on still images in measuring nonverbal accuracy (the Diagnostic Analysis of Nonverbal Accuracy; Nowicki & Duke, 1994) will not be reviewed here, nor will research that relies on "thick" (longer than 5 minute) slices.

Much of the individual differences evidence is drawn from an expansive set of studies described in a monograph (Rosenthal et al., 1979). The studies described in this monograph used the heavily validated Profile of Nonverbal Sensitivity (PONS). With the PONS, participants make a forced-choice judgment about an actor from two seconds of exposure. Rosenthal and colleagues describe their findings within each channel (e.g., among participants who *only* had visual exposure to the body) such that it is possible to isolate individual differences in thin-slice vision. Moreover, the relevance of these studies is as great today for thin-slice vision as it was several decades ago. Subsequent interpersonal-sensitivity instruments do not isolate thin-slice vision (see earlier) and recent studies using the PONS have generally used the auditory channels (e.g., Lieberman & Rosenthal, 2001) or combined auditory and visual. Finally, the studies described by Rosenthal and colleagues are remarkable for the variety of populations studied, including children, teenagers, and adults, men and women, blind and deaf individuals, over 20 countries, a variety of personality traits, and a variety of psychiatric disorders. Combined with several visual channels

(face, body, face and body) these studies provide a wealth of information.

First, women appear to have better thin-slice vision than men. Despite the abundant evidence that females are more accurate than males in decoding nonverbal behavior in general (see Hall & Andrzejewski, in press), the size of this gender difference is small in thin-slice vision. As compared to males, the female advantage in PONS thin-slice accuracy was 2.7 percent for dynamic facial stimuli, 4.2 percent for dynamic body stimuli, and 3.6 percent for face + body (Rosenthal et al., 1979). Moreover, these gender differences hold throughout childhood and adulthood. Among adults, recent replications support both the statistical significance and relative size of the gender differences (e.g., Rosip & Hall, 2004).

Second, thin-slice vision appears to improve with age, up to a certain point. Rosenthal and colleagues used an uncommonly age-diverse sample to demonstrate developmental changes in thin-slice vision. For example, third-graders' thin-slice vision accuracy was approximately 58 percent for the body, whereas fourth-graders' accuracy was approximately 68 percent. This same general pattern (10 percent improvement from third to fourth grade) also occurred with thin-slice vision for face and for face + body. Interestingly, there were few differences from fourth to sixth grade, suggesting that a qualitative change occurred for many of the sampled children between third and fourth grade. Such specific age-related patterns can also be observed for teenagers (junior high school), college students, and adults. Of particular interest is that thin-slice vision continues to improve in a linear fashion after sixth grade, with vision jumps occurring from sixth grade to junior high and from high school to college. Moreover, this improvement appears to be much greater than similar improvement in thin-slice judgments form auditory channels. It does appear that performance levels off at around age 25.

Third, there is some evidence that psychological impairment is associated with impairment in thin-slice vision. For psychologically impaired individuals, thin-slice judgment difficulties may be related to difficulties in processing substantial amounts of configural information. For example, among alcoholic and psychiatric inpatients, thin-slice vision was consistently reduced (for face, for body, and for face + body; Rosenthal et al., 1979), as compared to "normals." The corresponding impairment in thin-slice hearing was quite limited. One explanation is that these groups found it especially difficult to integrate the many visible aspects of nonverbal communication into a coherent whole—indeed, these groups purposely skipped more items than the normals, and skipping differences were especially pronounced when items contained a diversity of information. Similarly, learning-disabled children were impaired in thin-slice vision as compared to nondisabled children of the same age. Indeed, the thin-slice vision of the learning disabled children was especially impaired for the face, where configural arrangements are particularly important for interpersonal judgment (Zebrowitz, 1997). The evidence for concomitant impairment in cognitive function and thin-slice vision is clearly quite general—just as all psychiatric patients should not be grouped together as a meaningful cohort, neither should learning disabled children and alcoholic adults. Yet, because all these groups appeared to share some level of difficulty in integrating nonverbal cues, it seems reasonable to speculate that when cognitive impairment reduces configural processing, thin-slice vision may also be reduced.

Other evidence supports alternative mechanisms for impairment in thin-slice vision. A recent study provides preliminary evidence that the frontal regions of the cerebral cortex—implicated in many psychiatric disorders, organic dementia, and learning disorders—play an important role in thin-slice vision (Heberlein, Adolphs, Tranel, & Damasio, 2004). Specifically, 37 brain-damaged participants were compared to normal participants in their judgments of emotion and personality from thin-slices of body movement. Heberlein and colleagues examined the discrepancy between normal participants' consensus judgments and individual brain-damaged participants' judgments. By examining these discrepancies in relation to the focal area of damage for each participant, the

researchers were able to model the areas of the cortex most heavily involved in thin-slice vision. The frontal cortex, especially areas of the frontal cortex associated with simulating movement, was heavily implicated in thin-slice vision. It, therefore, seems reasonable to speculate that the thin-slice vision of cognitively impaired individuals is reduced to the extent that cognitive impairments include changes to frontal lobe activity, and perhaps especially frontal lobe activity involved in simulating others' behavior.

A different type of impairment with particularly interesting implications for thin-slice vision is deafness. Rosenthal and colleagues found that across childhood, deaf children had significantly worse thin-slice vision than did hearing children. Adding to the peculiarity of the differences between deaf and hearing children is that facial expressions play an important role in American sign language. Hence, people who can read sign language (e.g., the deaf) should be especially proficient in reading facial expressions. Indeed, as compared to adults who do not know sign language, *hearing* adults who were fluent in sign-language had superior thin-slice vision with regard to dynamic facial expressions (Goldstein & Feldman, 1996). Why then do deaf children have such poor thin-slice vision? Rosenthal and colleagues have argued that nondeaf individuals may avoid the deaf such that deaf individuals may not have sufficient experience with others' nonverbal behavior. Indeed, among deaf individuals, thin-slice vision appears to be more positively related to social functioning (Weisel & Hagit, 1992).

Finally, a variety of theories suggest that individuals who are especially focused on engaging in social life (e.g., extraverts) should have especially good thin-slice vision (e.g., Allport, 1924; Eysenck, 1990). A number of other personality traits have also been proposed as important associates of interpersonal perception in general (see Riggio, 2006). Yet there is considerable debate about the *actual* relationship of almost any personality trait to interpersonal perception. For example, whereas several studies suggest that there is a positive relationship between extraversion and nonverbal/paraverbal decoding (Akert & Panter, 1988; Funder & Harris, 1996), others have observed a negative relationship or no relationship at all (Cunningham, 1977; Rosenthal et al., 1979). A recent meta-analysis (Davis & Kraus, 1997) tried to make sense of all of these conflicting findings. Unfortunately, this meta-analysis included a variety of irrelevant paradigms (for our purposes) and a second meta-analysis (Lieberman & Rosenthal, 2001) limited to more relevant paradigms observed contradictory results. The evidence for thin-slice vision in particular is unclear because of the limited number of vision-only findings. For example, although Rosenthal and colleagues failed to demonstrate a relationship between extraversion and PONS scores (visual or audio), Funder & Harris (1986) did observe a positive relationship between extraversion and overall PONS scores.

One line of research provides a promising framework for investigating characteristics that distinguish those with good from those with poor thin-slice vision. Although not technically a personality trait, *knowledge* of appropriate nonverbal cues may be especially likely to play an important role in thin-slice vision. Specifically, people usually have beliefs about the meaning of different nonverbal cues. For example, an individual may believe that posture is indicative of self-esteem. But people also differ in the degree to which their beliefs are correct or incorrect. Thus, there is logic to the idea that people with accurate nonverbal cue knowledge will have especially clear thin-slice vision. There is some evidence to suggest that this is the case: Rosip and Hall (2004) developed the Test of Nonverbal Cue Knowledge (TONCK), an 81-item true-false self-report measure. Examples of items included "someone who blinks a lot may be anxious" and "under stress, the pitch of the human voice gets lower." These items were based on a review of the relevant literature on nonverbal cues. In an initial set of studies, participants achieved about 74 percent accuracy, and scores on the TONCK were modestly correlated with thin-slice vision. This work indicates that the assessment of explicit knowledge of nonverbal cues may be a fruitful starting point for examining individual differences in thin-slice vision. Most notably, the relationship between personality and thin-slice vision

may be moderated by accuracy in everyday knowledge of nonverbal cues—the people with the most motivation *and* knowledge should be best at decoding nonverbal behavior and have superior thin-slice vision.

In summary, individual differences in thin-slice vision are most clear for gender, age, and cognitive impairment. There is scant evidence that personality plays a reliable role in thin-slice vision. Knowledge of nonverbal cues is one promising potential moderator of the relationship between personality and thin-slice vision.

VISUAL PROCESSES IN THIN-SLICE VISION

Thus far, our discussion of thin-slice vision has been relatively abstract with respect to visual processes. The many chapters in this volume attest to a burgeoning literature on the role of visual processes in social perception and there are aspects of this literature that have considerable import for understanding thin-slice vision. Yet there is surprisingly little research directly examining the relationship between basic visual processes and the ability to make accurate inferences from thin-slices of behavior. Building on the extant literature, we speculate about the importance of several visual mechanisms and cues to thin-slice accuracy.

Processes occurring early in visual processing are likely to influence thin-slice accuracy. One illustration refers to the phenomenon of visual masking, which occurs when a briefly presented but identifiable stimulus is immediately preceded or followed by a second stimulus, preventing visual identification of the former stimulus. Visual masking is thought to occur because the masking stimulus interferes with the formation of a detailed visual representation of the target stimulus (e.g., Breitmeyer, 1984). Resistance to visual masking may enhance thin-slice vision. Early *interference-resistant* visual processes would efficiently build detailed visual representations of behavior unencumbered by irrelevant aspects of the stimulus environment, thus providing thin-slice judgments with a solid visual foundation. Such clarity and specificity would seem to be especially important for thin-slice vision, given the potential for visual interference in a brief but stimulus-rich social environment. Indeed, one recent study with a clinical population demonstrated that *decreases* in susceptibility to visual masking were associated with *increases* in thin-slice vision (measured via the PONS; Sergi, Rassovsky, Nuechterlein, & Green, 2006). Because participants were equated for unmasked recognition ability, the relationship could not be explained as simple differences in visual acuity. Future research could examine the extent to which resistance to visual masking is predictive of visual representations (of thin-slice targets) that are especially rich and detailed yet unbiased by irrelevant stimuli. In this way, resistance to visual masking may be an important foundation for thin-slice vision.

Another visual substrate of thin-slice accuracy may be the location of eye fixations during the thin slice. Preferential attention to social stimuli and to the socially revealing parts of the face mark normal social development but is relatively absent in autism, suggesting that such visual focus is important to making accurate and socially functional inferences (Baron-Cohen, Wheelwright, & Joliffe, 1997; Haith, Bergman, & Moore, 1977; see also Spelke, Phillips, & Woodward, 1995). The eyes are especially important for revealing internal states, including emotion and intention (e.g., Baron-Cohen et al., 1997). Notably, a recent study used eye-tracking technology to examine normal and autistic adults' eye fixations during several thin-slice video clips (Klin, Jones, Schultz, Volkmar, & Cohen, 2002). Normal adults focused on targets' eye regions about 65 percent of the time, whereas autistic adults looked at the eyes only about 25 percent of the time. Although thin-slice vision (accuracy) was not measured in this study, it seems reasonable to suggest that a visual focus on targets' eye region may enhance thin-slice accuracy (cf. Murphy et al., 2007). Focal attention directed toward the eyes can provide the perceiver with detailed visual representations of targets' ocular behavior; such representations may form the foundation of thin-slice judgments by providing a basis for inferring targets' intentions and emotions. In the absence of focal attention directed at targets' eye region, perceivers may lack the visual representations most pertinent to thin-slice vision.

By the same token, an exclusive focus on the eyes is unlikely to yield accurate thin-slice vision because a focus on only one aspect of the face is associated with poor social function (e.g., Hobson, Ouston, & Lee, 1988). Most people must integrate visual information from various parts of the face and body to come to reasonable and accurate conclusions about a social target (Farah, Wilson, Drain, & Tanaka, 1998). Hence, a quadratic function may characterize the relationship between visual attention to targets' eyes and thin-slice accuracy: a focus on the eye region may enhance thin-slice vision up to a certain point, after which such focus becomes detrimental.

Finally, unlike still images, thin slices include ongoing and dynamic behavior. This property of thin slices has important considerations for the visual substrates of thin-slice vision. Clearly, it is not just the frequency of eye fixations that should be important for thin-slice accuracy but also the degree to which perceivers' *sustain* eye fixations on a social target. That is, social judgment accuracy is markedly reduced when dynamic behavior occurs on the periphery of one's visual field (see Ikeda, Blake, & Watanabe, 2005). Relatedly, visual attention to movement may be a crucial component of thin-slice vision. From movement alone, people are capable of recognizing the identity, emotion, gender, sexuality, and activity of a social target (e.g., Clarke, Bradshaw, Field, Hampson, & Rose, 2005; Cutting & Kozlowski, 1977; Johnson et al., 2007; Kozlowski & Cutting, 1977; Norman, Payton, Long, & Hawkes, 2004). Although the visual detection of meaningful social action is remarkably robust to the presence of distracting cues (e.g., Ahlstrom, Blake, & Ahlstrom, 1997; Cutting, Moore, & Morrison, 1988), disturbances in the temporal continuity of behavior appear to eliminate or greatly reduce individuals' ability to make social judgments from movement (e.g., Ambadar et al., 2005; Bertenthal & Pinto, 1993; Mather, Radford, & West, 1992). For this reason, and because *focal* attention to movement appears to be critical for social judgments, it seems likely that continuous and focal visual attention to the movement of the social target is an important aspect of thin-slice vision.

In this section, we have highlighted several of the many visual processes likely to be involved in thin-slice accuracy. Our focus has been on the broad visual processes and cues that may be relevant across several judgment domains, as we have described thin-slice vision as domain-general. It is likely, though, that a number of visual processes are important to specific domains of thin-slice vision. For example, facial contrast in the eye and mouth region may be important to judgments of femininity and hence sexuality (Russell, this volume) but irrelevant to thin-slice judgments of intelligence. Nonetheless, identifying the visual processes and cues relevant to thin-slice accuracy *in general* is likely to be crucial to establishing thin-slice vision as a social construct unique from other types of social vision.

SUMMARY AND CONCLUSION: THIN-SLICE VISION AS A SOCIAL PERCEPTION MODALITY

Thin-slice vision has been defined as an observer's ability to accurately extract personal information about target individuals from brief visual exposure to those target individuals. We reviewed the domains in which thin-slice vision is known to be acute across observers. Moreover, we reviewed the parallels in limitations to normal vision and thin-slice vision and followed that with a discussion of the basic visual substrates of thin-slice accuracy. Finally, we reviewed the evidence that people differ in their thin-slice vision.

On the whole, the last several decades have brought a great deal of research on thin-slices. Although much of this research is specific to thin-slice vision, much is not. The auditory channel, in particular, has received considerable attention and some have argued that vocal cues are more revealing than are visual cues (e.g., Rosenthal & DePaulo, 1979). The analogue of thin-slice vision to traditional vision may prove quite fruitful for all modalities of thin-slice perception.

REFERENCES

Ahlstrom, V., Blake, R., & Ahlstrom, U. (1997). Perception of biological motion. *Perception, 26,* 1539–1548.

Akert, R. M., & Panter, A. T. (1988). Extraversion and the ability to decode nonverbal communication. *Personality and Individual Differences, 9,* 965–972.

Allport, G. W. (1924). *Social Psychology.* New York: Houghton Mifflin.

Allport, G. W., Vernon, P. E. (1933). *Studies in Expressive Movement* New York:. The MacMillan Company.

Ambadar, Z., Schooler, J. W., Cohn, J. F. (2005). Deciphering the enigmatic face: The importance of facial dynamics in interpreting subtle facial expressions. *Psychological Science, 16,* 403–410.

Ambady, N., Bernieri, F. J., & Richeson, J. A. (2000). Toward a histology of social behavior: Judgmental accuracy from thin slices of the behavioral stream. In M. Zanna (Ed.), *Advances in experimental social psychology* (Vol. 32, pp. 201–271). San Diego, CA: Academic Press.

Ambady, N., & Gray, H. M. (2002). On being sad and mistaken: Mood effects on the accuracy of thin–slice judgments. *Journal of Personality and Social Psychology,* 947–961.

Ambady, N., Hallahan, M., & Conner, B. (1999). Accuracy of judgments of sexual orientation from thin slices of behavior. *Journal of Personality and Social Psychology, 77,* 538–547.

Ambady, N., Hallahan, M., & Rosenthal, R. (1995). On judging and being judged accurately in zero acquaintance situations. *Journal of Personality and Social Psychology, 69,* 518–529.

Ambady, N., Koo, J., Lee, F., & Rosenthal, R. (1996). More than words: Linguistic and nonlinguistic politeness in two cultures. *Journal of Personality and Social Psychology, 70,* 996–1011.

Ambady, N., Koo, J., Rosenthal, R., & Winograd, C. H. (2002). Physical therapists' nonverbal communication predicts geriatric patients' health outcomes. *Psychology and Aging, 17,* 443–452.

Ambady, N., & Rosenthal, R. (1992). Thin slices of expressive behavior as predictors of interpersonal consequences: A meta-analysis. *Psychological Bulletin, 111,* 256–274.

Ambady, N., & Rosenthal, R. (1993). Half a minute: Predicting teacher evaluations from thin slices of nonverbal behavior and physical attractiveness. *Journal of Personality and Social Psychology, 64,* 431–441.

Archer, D., Costanzo, M., & Akert, R. (2001). The Interpersonal Perception Task (IPT): Alternative approaches to problems of theory and design. In J. A. Hall & F. J. Bernieri (Eds.), *Interpersonal sensitivity: Theory and measurement* (pp. 135–148). Prospect Heights, IL: Waveland Press.

Babad, E. (2005). Guessing teachers differential treatment of high- and low-achievers from thin slices of their lecturing behavior. *Journal of Nonverbal Behavior, 29,* 125–134.

Babad, E., Avni–Babad, D., & Rosenthal, R. (2004). Prediction of students evaluations from brief instances of professors nonverbal behavior in defined instructional situations. *Social Psychology of Education, 7,* 3–33.

Babad, E., Bernieri, F., & Rosenthal, R. (1989). Nonverbal communication and leakage in the behavior of biased and unbiased teachers. *Journal of Personality and Social Psychology, 56,* 89–94.

Baron–Cohen, S., Wheelwright, S., & Joliffe, T. (1997). Is there a "language of the eyes?" Evidence from normal adults and adults with autism or Asperger syndrome. *Visual Cognition,4,* 311–331.

Bernieri, F. J., & Gillis, J. S. (2001). Judging rapport: Employing Brunswik's lens model to study interpersonal sensitivity. In J. A. Hall & F. J. Bernieri, *Interpersonal sensitivity: Theory and measurement* (pp. 67–88). Mahwah, NJ : Erlbaum.

Bertenthal, B. I., & Pinto, J. (1994). Global processing of biological motions. *Psychological Science, 5,* 221–225.

Blanchard, F. A., Lilly, T., & Vaghn, L. A. (1991). Condemning and condoning racism: A social context approach to interracial settings. *Journal of Applied Psychology, 79,* 993–997.

Blanck, P. D., Rosenthal, R., & Cordell, L. D. H. (1985). The appearance of justice: Judges verbal and nonverbal behaviour in criminal jury trials. *Stanford Law Review, 38,* 89–164.

Bond, C. F. Jr., & DePaulo, B. M. (2006). Accuracy of deception judgments. *Personality and Social Psychology Review, 10,* 214–234.

Borkenau, P., & Liebler, A. (1992). Trait inferences: Sources of validity at zero acquaintance. *Journal of Personality and Social Psychology, 62,* 645–657.

Borkenau, P., & Liebler, A. (1993). Convergence of stranger ratings of personality and intelligence with self–ratings, partner ratings, and measured intelligence. *Journal of Personality and Social Psychology, 65,* 546–553.

Borkenau, P., Mauer, N., Riemann, R., Spinath, F. M., Angleitner, A. (2004). Thin slices of behavior as cues of personality and intelligence. *Journal of Personality and Social Psychology, 86,* 599–614.

Breitmeyer, B. G. (1984). *Visual masking: An integrative approach.* New York: Oxford University Press.

Carroll, J. M., Russell, J. A. (1997). Facial expressions in Hollywood's portrayal of emotion. *Journal of Personality and Social Psychology, 72,* 164–176.

Clarke, T. J., Bradshaw, M. F., Field, D. T., Hampson, S. E., & Rose, D. (2005). The perception of emotion from body movement in point-light displays of interpersonal dialogue. *Perception, 34,* 1171–80.

Clarke, A., Weisbuch, M., & Ambady, N. (2007). Thin-slices of depression: The visibility of enduring affect to the lay perceiver. *Unpublished manuscript.*

Craig, T. Y., Kelly, J. R., & Driscoll, D. (2001). Participant perceptions of potential employers. *Sex Roles, 44,* 389–400.

Corrigan, P. W. (2005). *On the stigma of mental illness: Practical strategies for research and social change* (Ed.). Washington, DC: American Psychological Association.

Cunningham, M. R. (1977). Personality and the structure of nonverbal communication of emotion. *Journal of Personality, 45,* 564–584.

Cutting, J. E., & Kozlowski, L. T. (1977). Recognition of friends by their walk: Gait perception without familiarity cues. *Bulletin of the Psychonomic Society, 9,* 353–356.

Cutting, J. E., Moore, C., & Morrison, R. (1988). Masking the motions of human gait. *Perception and Psychophysics, 44,* 339–347.

Davis, M. H., & Kraus, L. A. (1997). Personality and empathic accuracy. In W. Ickes (Ed.), *Empathic accuracy* (pp. 144–168). New York: Guilford.

DePaulo, B. M. (1992). Nonverbal behavior and self-representation. *Psychological Bulletin, 111,* 203–243.

Driscoll, D. M., Kelly, J. R., & Henderson, W. L. (1998). Can perceivers identify likelihood to sexually harass? *Sex Roles, 38,* 557–588.

Elfenbein, H. A., & Ambady, N. A. (2002a). Predicting workplace outcomes from the ability to eavesdrop on feelings. *Journal of Applied Psychology, 87,* 963–971.

Ekman, P., & Friesen, W. V. (1969). Nonverbal leakage and clues to deception. *Psychiatry: Journal for the Study of Interpersonal Processes, 32,* 88–106.

Ekman, P., & Friesen, W. V. (1974). Detecting deception from the body or face. *Journal of Personality and Social Psychology, 29,* 288–298.

Eysenck, H. J. (1990). Biological dimensions of personality. In L. A. Pervin (Ed.), *Handbook of personality: Theory and research* (pp. 244–276). New York: Guilford Press.

Farah, M. J., Wilson, D., Drain, M., Tanaka, J. N. (1998). What is "special" about face perception? *Psychological Review, 105,* 482–498.

Friedman, J. N. W., Oltmanns, T. F., Gleason, M. E. J., & Turkheimer, E. (2004). Mixed impressions: Reactions of strangers to people with pathological personality traits. *Journal of Personality, 40,* 395–410.

Funder, D. C., & Harris, M. J. (1986). On the several facets of personality assessment: The case of social acuity. *Journal of Personality, 54,* 528–550.

Gaertner, S. L., & Dovidio, J., F. (1986). The aversive form of racism. In J. F. Dovidio & S. L. Gaertner (Eds.), *Prejudice, discrimination, and racism* (pp. 61–89). New York: Academic Press.

Gangestad, S. W., Simpson, J. A., DiGeronimo, K, & Biek,. M. (1992). Differential accuracy in person perception across traits: Examination of a functional hypothesis. *Journal of Personality and Social Psychology, 62,* 688–698.

Goldstein, N. E., & Feldman, R. S. (1996). Knowledge of American sign-language and the ability of hearing individuals to decode facial expressions of emotion. *Journal of Nonverbal Behavior, 20,* 111–122.

Grahe, J. E., & Bernieri, F. J. (1999). The importance of nonverbal cues in judging rapport. *Journal of Nonverbal Behavior, 23,* 253–269.

Haith, M. M., Bergman, T., & Moore, M. J. (1977). Eye contact and face scanning in early infancy. *Science, 198,* 853–855.

Hall, J. A., & Andrzejewski, S. A. (in press). Who draws accurate first impressions? Personal correlates of sensitivity to nonverbal cues. In N. Ambady & J. Skowronski (Eds.), *First impressions.* New York: Guilford.

Hall, J. A., Coats, E. J., & LeBeau, L. S. (2005). Nonverbal behavior and the vertical dimension of social relations: A meta-analysis. *Psychological Bulletin, 131,* 898–924.

Hall, J. A., & Friedman, G. B. (1999). Status, gender and nonverbal behavior: A study of structured interactions between employees of a company. *Personality and Social Psychology Bulletin, 25,* 1082–1091.

Harrigan, J. A., Harrigan, K. M., Sale, B. A., & Rosenthal, R. (1996). Detecting anxiety and defensiveness from visual and auditory cues. *Journal of Personality, 64,* 675–709.

Harrigan, J. A., Wilson, K., & Rosenthal, R. (2004). Detecting state and trait anxiety from auditory and visual cues: A meta-analysis. *Personality and Social Psychology Bulletin, 30,* 56–66.

Heberlein, A. S., Adolphs, R., Tranel, D., & Damasio, H. (2004). Cortical regions for judgments of emotions and personality traits from point-light walkers. *Journal of Cognitive Neuroscience, 16,* 1143–1158.

Hobson, R. P., Ouston, J., & Lee, A. (1988). What in a face? The case of autism. *British Journal of Psychology, 79,* 441–453.

Ikeda, H., Blake, R., & Watanabe, K. (2005). Eccentric perception of biological motion is unscalably poor. *Vision Research, 45,* 1935–1943.

Johnson, K. L., Gill, S., Reichman, V., & Tassinary, L. G. (2007). Swagger, sway, and sexuality: Judging sexual orientation from body motion and morphology. *Journal of Personality and Social Psychology, 93,* 321–334.

Klin, A., Jones, W., Schultz, R., Volkmar, F., & Cohen, D. (2002). Visual fixation patterns during viewing of naturalistic social situations as predictors of social competence in individuals with autism. *Archives of General Psychiatry, 59,* 809–816.

Knapp, M. L., & Hall, J. (2002). *Nonverbal behavior in human interaction.* Wadsworth: New York.

Kozlowski, L. T., & Cutting, J. E. (1977). Recognizing the sex of a walker from a dynamic point light display. *Perception and Psychophysics, 21,* 575–580.

Lieberman, M. D., & Rosenthal, R. (2001). Why introverts can't always tell who likes them: Multitasking and nonverbal decoding. *Journal of Personality and Social Psychology, 80,* 294–310.

Mather, G., Radford, K., & West, S. (1992). Low level visual processing of biological motion. *Proceedings of the Royal Society of London: Section B, Biological Sciences, 249,* 149–155.

Monteith, Deneen, N. E., & Tooman, G. D. (1996). The effect of social norm activation on the expression of opinions concerning gay men and blacks. *Basic and Applied Social Psychology, 18,* 267–288.

Murphy, N. A. (2005). Using thin slices for behavioral coding. *Journal of Nonverbal Behavior, 29,* 235–246.

Murphy, N. A. (2007). Appearing smart: The impression management of intelligence, person perception accuracy, and behavior in social interaction. *Personality and Social Psychology Bulletin, 33,* 325–339.

Murphy, N. A., Hall, J. A., & Colvin, C. R. (2003). Accurate intelligence assessments in social interactions: Mediators and gender effects. *Journal of Personality, 71,* 465–493.

Norman, J. F., Payton, S. M., Long, J. R., & Hawkes, L. M. (2004). Aging and perception of biological motion. *Psychology and Aging, 19,* 219–225.

Nowicki, S., & Duke, M. P. (1994). Individual differences in the nonverbal communication of affect: The Diagnostic Analysis of Nonverbal Accuracy scale. *Journal of Nonverbal Behavior, 18,* 9–35.

Puccinelli, N. M., & Tickle–Degnen, L. (2004). Knowing too much about others: Moderators of the relationship between eavesdropping and rapport in social interaction. *Journal of Nonverbal Behavior, 28,* 223–243.

Puccinelli, N. M., Tickle–Degnen, L., & Rosenthal, R. (2003). Effect of dyadic context on judgments of rapport: Dyad task and partner presence. *Journal of Nonverbal Behavior, 27,* 211–236.

Richeson, J. A., & Shelton, J. N. (2005). Thin slices of racial bias. *Journal of Nonverbal Behavior, 29,* 75–86.

Riggio, R. E. (2006). Nonverbal skills and abilities. In V. Manusov & M. L. Patterson (Eds.), *The Sage handbook of nonverbal communication,* (pp. 79–96). Thousand Oaks, CA: Sage.

Rime, B., Schiaratura, L. (1991). Gesture and speech. In R. S. Feldman, B. Rime, (Eds.), *Fundamentals of Nonverbal Behavior* (pp. 239–281). New York: Cambridge University Press.

Rosenthal, R., & DePaulo, B. M. (1979). Sex differences in eavesdropping on nonverbal cues. *Journal of Personality and Social Psychology, 37,* 273–285.

Rosenthal, R., Hall, J. A., DiMatteo, M. R., Rogers, P. L., & Archer, D. (1979). *Sensitivity to nonverbal communication.* Baltimore, MD: Johns Hopkins University Press.

Rosip, J. C., & Hall, J. A. (2004). Knowledge of nonverbal cues, gender, and decoding accuracy. *Journal of Nonverbal Behavior, 28,* 267–286.

Sergi, M. J., Rassovsky, Y., Nuechterlein, K. H., & Green, M. F. (2006). Social perception as a mediator of the influence of early visual processing on functional status in schizophrenia. *American Journal of Psychiatry, 163,* 448–454.

Simons, D. J., & Chabris, C. F. (1999). Gorillas in our midst: Sustained inattentional blindness for dynamic events. *Perception, 28,* 1059–1074.

Simpson, J. A., & Gangestad, S. W. (1991). Individual differences in sociosexuality: Evidence for convergent and discriminant validity. *Journal of Personality and Social Psychology, 60,* 870–883.

Spelke, E. S., Phillips, A., Woodward, A. L. (1995). Infants knowledge of object motion and human action. In D. Sperper, D. Premack, & A. J. Premack (Eds.), *Causal cognition: A multidisciplinary debate* (pp. 44–78). Oxford, England: Oxford University Press.

Tickle–Degnen, L., & Puccinelli, N. M. (1999). The nonverbal expression of negative emotions: Peer and supervisor responses to occupational therapy students' emotional attributes. *Occupational Therapy Journal of Research, 19,* 18–29.

Todorov, A., Mandisodza, A. N., Goren, A., & Hall, C. C. (2005). Inferences of competence from faces predict election outcomes. *Science, 308,* 1623–1626.

Troscianko, T., Holmes, A., Stillman, J., Mirmehdi, M., Wright, D., & Wilson, A. (2004). What happens next? The predictability of natural behaviour viewed through CCTV cameras. *Perception, 33,* 87–101.

Waxer, P. H., (1974). Nonverbal cues for depression. *Journal of Abnormal Psychology, 83,* 319–322.

Waxer, P. H. (1976). Nonverbal cues for depth of depression: Set versus no set. *Journal of Consulting and Clinical Psychology, 44,* 493.

Waxer, P. H. (1977). Nonverbal cues for anxiety: An examination of emotional leakage. *Journal of Abnormal Psychology, 86,* 306–314.

Weisel, A. & Hagit, B. L. (1992). Role–taking ability, nonverbal sensitivity, language and social adjustment of deaf adolescents. *Educational Psychology, 12,* 3–13.

Yeagley, E., Morling, B., & Nelson, M. (2007). Nonverbal zero-acquaintance accuracy of self-esteem, social dominance orientation, and satisfaction with life. *Journal of Research in Personality, 41,* 1099–1106.

Zebrowitz, L. (1997). *Reading faces: Window to the soul?* Boulder, CO: Westview Press.

CHAPTER 14

Seeing Human Movement as Inherently Social

Maggie Shiffrar, Martha D. Kaiser, and Areti Chouchourelou

THE OBJECTIFICATION OF HUMAN MOVEMENT

For many decades, vision scientists objectified the human body. That is, studies of the perception of the human body, in motion and in static postures, adopted the same theoretical approaches and experimental methodologies as those used in the study of object perception. There are certainly several reasons for this, one being historical. Gunnar Johansson, the researcher who first captured the attention of vision scientists with point-light displays of human movement (see Figure 14.1), does not appear to have been particularly interested in the visual perception of human motion, *per se*. Instead, his primary goal was to define the motion processing algorithms that direct grouping for all categories of visual motion (Johannson, 1976). Nonetheless, Johansson (1973; 1976) discovered that in as little as 200 msec, observers could identify specific human actions from the movements of a few points depicting the dynamic locations of a moving person's major joints and head. Johansson (1973) attributed the especially vivid percepts that observers of point-light displays of human movement readily experience to observers' extensive prior visual experience with those movements. Such a conclusion suggests that, at least in terms of visual processing, there is nothing particularly special or distinctive about human action other than its prevalence. Thus, the study of human motion perception started with the assumption that the human body is just another complex object.

Johansson was certainly not alone in his approach to the human visual system as a general purpose processor that processes all categories of the visual stimuli in the same way. Indeed, many classic models of the visual system have made the same assumption. For example, David Marr (1982) developed a very influential model of the visual system as a hierarchical system that applies a fixed set of visual processes to all retinal images. Roger Shepard (1984) targeted visual motion perception directly and argued that all types of visual motion are similarly analyzed. This argument continues to the present day as evidence is interpreted as suggesting that the visual perception of human movement does not differ from the visual perception of moving objects and surfaces (e.g., Hiris, 2007).

Of course, not all scientists understood the visual system in this way. J. J. and Eleanor Gibson conceptualized the visual system in functional terms. According to their approaches, perception and action are intrinsically coupled such that visual perception depends upon the observer's motor activities and capabilities (e.g., E. Gibson, 1969; J.J. Gibson, 1986). Thus, Gibsonian theories emphasize the functional relationships between what a person sees and what that person can do, or is doing. On a functional level, human movement must be defined as social, especially when compared to the

(a)

(b)

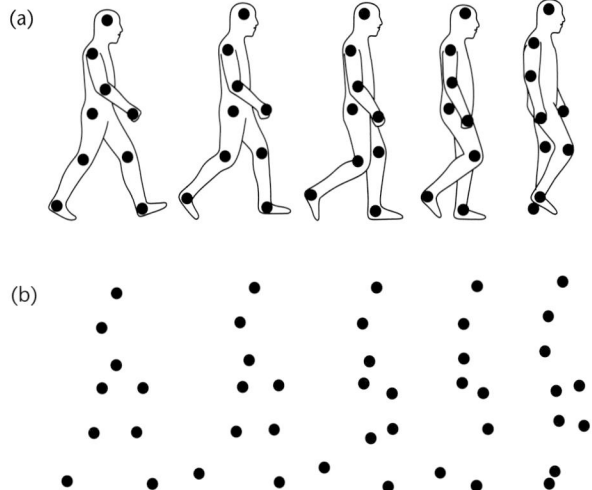

Figure 14.1 (a) A series of static outlines depicting the changing shape of a walking person's body with points positioned on the major joints and head. (b) A point light walker is constructed by removing everything from each image except the points. When static, these displays are difficult to interpret. However, once set in motion, observers readily detect the presence of a walking person.

movements of objects such as wind blown trees and crashing waves. Because social processes drive much of human behavior, social psychologists with a Gibsonian approach began to study the relationships between social processes and visual perception (e.g., McArthur & Baron, 1983; Zebrowitz & Collins, 1997). The field of social neuroscience emerged around this same time and one of the field's pioneering researchers, Leslie Brothers (1997), convincingly argued that neural systems could not be understood independently of the social processes that shaped them. Indeed, she predicted that neuroscientists are doomed to failure in their quest to understand neuronal processing as long as they ignore social constraints on the development and evolution of the brain.

The ways in which individuals hold and move their facial features conveys extensive social information and, as several of the chapters in this text have beautifully demonstrated, the human visual system is finely tuned for the detection and analysis of facial information. However, social cues are not limited to the face and the visibility of a social partner's facial features is not guaranteed. The high spatial frequency content of a face become less detectable and face perception becomes difficult, for example, when light levels decrease, individuals turn their heads, and distance between the observer and an observed face increases (e.g.,

Fiorentini, Maffei, & Sandini, 1983; Goffaux & Rossion, 2006). Yet, social interaction certainly doesn't stop in the evening or when heads turn. Because bodies are bigger than faces, observers can detect social information from bodily motions whenever facial cues are difficult to detect. As will be described later in this chapter and in the chapter by Kerri Johnson (this volume), such large-scale signals convey a surprising array of socially relevant information. Of course, faces are almost always attached to bodies. As the chapter by Beatrice de Gelder (this volume) makes clear, visual percepts of faces and bodies are interdependent. Nonetheless, this chapter will focus on the visual perception of whole body actions.

To better understand how the visual system processes the movements of the human body, four topics will be addressed. Section 2 describes differences between the perceptual and neurophysiological analyses of moving people and moving objects. The goal of this section will be to make a convincing argument against vision scientists' general tendency to objectify human movement. Indeed, evidence will be reviewed that suggests that the human visual system uses distinct mechanisms during the perception of objects and people in motion. Next, Section 3 will briefly describe some of the social and emotion information that observers can detect from highly degraded displays of human motion. For a more extensive discussion of this topic, the reader should consult the chapter by Kerri Johnson in this volume. Section 4 focuses on an argument that classically trained vision scientists may find disagreeable. That is, classic models of the visual system are largely modular in that visual perception depends exclusively upon visual processes (e.g., Fodor & Pylyshyn, 1981). The output of visual processes may be passed onto higher-level mechanisms that process social and cognitive information, but those higher-level processes cannot feed back to change visual processes. Instead, social and cognitive processes can only change the decisions that observers make about their percepts. In conflict with this traditionally bottom-up approach, this section will review evidence suggesting that social and emotional processes change the visual perception, per se, of human movement. Section 5 describes investigations of the relationships between observers' social capabilities and their visual sensitivity to other people's actions.

DIFFERENCES IN THE VISUAL ANALYSIS OF HUMAN AND OBJECT MOVEMENT

Movement, by definition, is a change in location over time. Therefore, the visual perception of motion depends upon analyses of luminance across both space and time. Evidence from several studies, summarized below, indicates that these processes of spatio-temporal integration differ during the perception of object movement and physically possible human movement.

The integration of visual motion information over space has been studied with point-light displays and multiple-aperture displays. The point-light technique that Gunnar Johansson made famous in the vision sciences during the 1970s was a modification of a technique developed by Etienne Jules Marey in the 1890s for the study of locomotion in animals and humans (Marey, 1895/1972). Working during the same period as Eadweard Muybridge (1830–1904), Marey developed a system for achieving multiple photographic exposures on a single plate. The resulting images were too blurry for

Marey's measurement needs so he added luminous markings or small lights to the actor whose movements he wanted to measure (Verfaillie, 2000). In this way, measurements of limb displacements over time became more accurate. Johansson (1976) adapted this technique for the study of visual motion perception and over the subsequent decades, scientists from around the world used point-light displays to study the perception of human motion (see Blake & Shiffrar, 2007 for review). Such research has shown that the visual perception of point-light depictions of human motion depends upon analyses that are spatially global, rather than local or point-by-point. For example, when a point-light defined person appears to walk within a point-light mask, as shown in Figure 14.2, observers can reliably detect the walking person (e.g., Bertenthal & Pinto, 1994; Cutting, Moore, & Morrison, 1988). Because the points in the mask have the same size, luminance, and velocities as the points defining the walker (indeed, masks are generally made by duplicating the point-light walker and then scrambling the starting locations of that walker's points), local analyses of the motions of individual points cannot be used to detect the walker. Instead, only the global spatiotemporal configuration of the points distinguishes the walker from the mask. As a result, detection of point-light walkers in a mask depends upon on the integration of motion cues over space (Bertenthal & Pinto 1994). When the same masking technique is used with complex, nonhuman motions (Hiris, Krebeck, Edmonds, & Stout, 2005), detection sensitivity drops significantly. This combination of results suggests that visual sensitivity to human and object movements differ. We'll return to this point in Section 4.

Studies using multiple aperture displays provide additional evidence that the human visual system analyzes human motion over larger spatial extents than object motion. All visual systems measure motion through spatially limited receptors. Yet, motion information falling outside of the receptive fields cannot be measured. This produces inherently ambiguous motion measurements. Integrating individually ambiguous motion signals across different

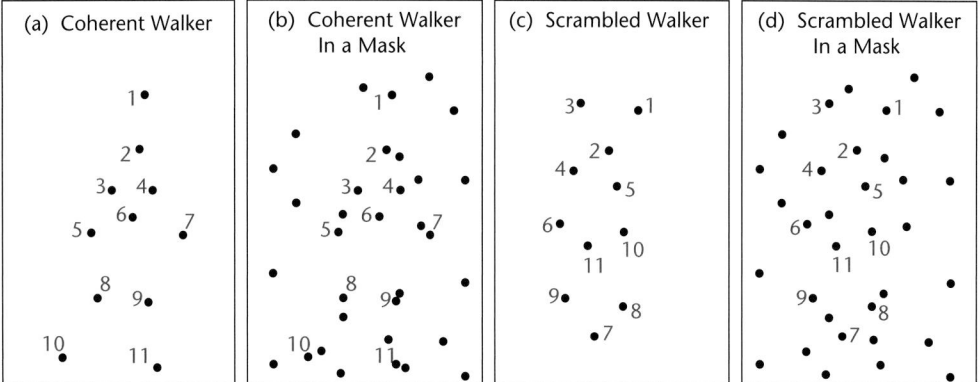

Figure 14.2 (a) Visual sensitivity to point-light displays of human motion is frequently measured with motion coherence discrimination tasks. Within the tasks, half of the trials depict a coherent point light walker. (c) In the other half of the trials, the starting locations of the points are scrambled. (b,d) Then, these scrambled and coherent point-light walkers are presented within point-light masks. The masks are usually constructed by duplicating the walker and then scrambling that duplicate walker(s). As a result, the same motion energy is present in the mask and walkers (whether coherent or scrambled).

spatial locations provides one solution to this so-called aperture problem (Hildreth, 1984). However, this solution comes with its own set of problems because while motion integration may be needed to integrate motion measurements within an object, it must often be inhibited across different objects (Shiffrar & Lorenceau, 1996). As a result, the visual system must strike a delicate balance between motion integration and motion segmentation. Interestingly, the visual system does not appear to adopt the same balance point for human motion and object motion. When observers view a walking person through a set of apertures, they perceive coherent motion, suggesting that they have integrated motion information across the disconnected regions of space. However, when observers view complex objects, such as cars or scissors, through apertures, they perceive incoherent motion that indicates a lack of integration across space (Shiffrar, Lichtey, & Heptulla-Chatterjee, 1997). Interestingly, only physically possible human motions appear to be integrated across such spatially extended windows. Human movements that are impossibly slow, fast, or oriented appear to be analyzed by local motion mechanisms (Shiffrar et al., 1997).

Neurophysiological evidence further supports the hypothesis that the perception of human movement depends upon the global integration of motion measurements. For example, the perception of point-light displays of human motion is associated with elevated activity in the posterior region of the superior temporal sulcus or STSp (e.g., Bonda, Petrides, Ostry, & Evans, 1996, Beauchamp, this volume, Puce & Perrett, 2003). If STSp activity simply depended upon the movements of any individual points, then shuffling the locations of those points should have no impact on STSp activity. Instead, when the point-lights that define a moving person are scrambled, so that the individual velocity trajectories remain unchanged while the hierarchical structure of the points is broken, STSp activity drops significantly (Grossman et al., 2000). Thus, the neural processes underlying action perception in point-light displays appear to depend upon the global relationships between moving points.

Magnetoencephalography (MEG), a brain imaging technique with high temporal resolution, has been used to directly compare neural activity during the perception of point-light displays of human motion and object motion. Resultant analyses have identified both overlapping and divergent areas of neural activity.

Specifically, while human motion and object motion appear to be initially analyzed by overlapping neural areas (given the spatial resolution of MEG), their analyses diverge about 200 msec after stimulus onset (Virji-Babul et al., 2007). Only human motion is associated with subsequent activity in the right temporal lobe, suggesting that the visual system differentiates human and object motion.

As stated earlier, the visual perception of movement also involves the integration of information over time. Apparent motion, or the illusion of movement between brief static images (Wertheimer, 1912), is a classic technique for investigating the temporal characteristics of visual motion perception. In classic demonstrations of apparent motion, two spatially separated objects are sequentially presented. Within certain temporal parameters, this sequential presentation of static objects gives rise to the perception of a single moving object. While there are an infinite number of paths that might connect any two object locations, perceived paths of apparent motion usually follow the shortest possible path (Burt & Sperling, 1981). Because human limbs follow approximately pendular trajectories (because we are jointed), human movement cannot follow direct, rectilinear trajectories. Consistent with this conflict, something interesting can happen when images of people replace images of objects in apparent motion displays.

When observers view apparent motion displays depicting a person with a limb in two different positions (Figure 14.3), their apparent motion percepts depend upon the display rate. When pictures of the human body are presented at temporal rates that fall within the temporal range for the production of normal human actions, observers tend to perceive paths of apparent motion that are consistent with the biomechanical constraints on human movement (Shiffrar & Freyd, 1990; 1993). That is, they perceive physically possible paths of apparent human motion rather than the shortest, physically impossible path of human movement. When these same pictures are presented at rates that are inconsistent with the possible speeds of human movement, then observers perceive the shortest possible paths of apparent motion, even if those paths are physically impossible. Conversely, when control objects are shown at different apparent motion display rates, observers always perceive the shortest possible paths of apparent motion. This pattern of results suggests that human movement is analyzed by motion processes that operate over relatively large temporal windows and that take into account the biomechanical limitations of the human body. Brain imaging data support this conclusion (Stevens, Fonlupt, Shiffrar, Decety, 2000). When observers of apparent motion displays perceive physically possible paths of limb movement (slower display rates), neural activity increases in motor planning areas and body representation areas. When display rates increase, so that observers perceive physically impossible paths of apparent human motion, neural activity does not increase in these areas. Furthermore, these areas remain relatively inactive during

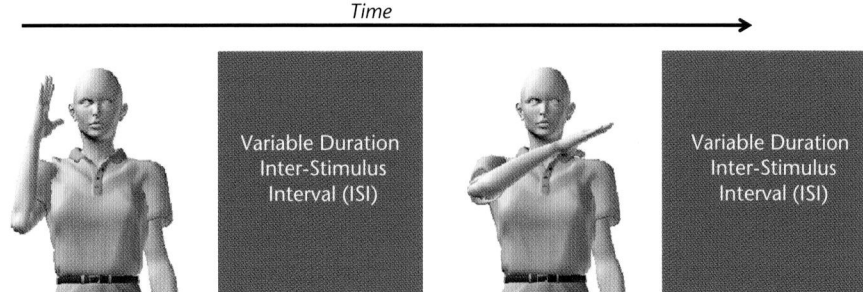

Figure 14.3 An apparent motion display of an arm on either side of a person's head. At long ISIs, the arm appears to move around the head. At short ISIs, the arm appears to move through the head following the shortest possible path of apparent motion.

the perception of objects in apparent motion. Such results suggest that the visual perception of physically possible human movement relies upon some neural mechanisms that are not involved in the visual perception of object movement or impossible human movement.

THE VISUAL DETECTION OF SOCIAL AND EMOTIONAL INFORMATION FROM HUMAN MOVEMENT

Most studies of the visual perception of human movement have focused on the detection of physical features. Given the traditional assumption that object movement and human body movement are similarly, if not identically, processed, it is not surprising that the perception of physical features (shared by objects and humans) has been emphasized. For example, participants viewing point-light displays of human movement are frequently asked to discriminate the location, presence, coherence, or direction of their moving target. A few studies have asked observers to categorize the actions that a point-light actor performs (e.g., Dittrich, 1993).

Importantly, an impressive variety of social features can also be detected from degraded displays of human movement. For example, naïve observers are above chance in their ability to detect a walking person's gender from point-light displays (Barclay, Cutting, & Kozlowski, 1978; Pollick, Kay, Heim, & Stringer, 2005; Johnson, this volume). An individual's sexual orientation can be detected at above chance levels (Ambady, Haallan, & Connor, 1999; Weisbuch & Ambady, this volume, Johnson, Gill, Reichman, & Tassinary, 2007; Johnson, Pollick & Mckay, this volume). Numerous studies have shown that observers can recognize the identities of other people, as well as themselves from dynamic, but not static, point-light displays (Cutting & Kozlowski, 1977; Jacobs, Pinto, & Shiffrar, 2004; Jokisch, Daum, & Troje, 2006; Loula, Prasad, Harber, & Shiffrar, 2005). Other studies have demonstrated that untrained observers can detect another person's potential reproductive fitness (Brown et al., 2005), degree of psychological openness (Brownlow, Dixon, Egbert, & Radcliffe,

1997), age and social dominance (Montepare & Zebrowitz-McArthur, 1988), and vulnerability to attack (Gunns, Johnston, & Hudson, 2002) in point-light displays. Such findings indicate that when people move, their movements express extensive social information that the human visual system is capable of detecting.

Intentionality is another complex psychological state that naïve observers can detect in point-light displays of human movement. In a now classic study, individuals were asked to move in a manner that was either consistent or inconsistent with their own gender. When naïve observers viewed point-light displays of these deceptive actions, they readily detected the deceptive intentions (Runeson & Frykholm, 1983). In this same set of studies, point-light displays were created of people who lifted an empty box normally and in a manner that erroneously suggested that the box was heavy. Again, observers accurately detected the deceitful lifts. Visual sensitivity to the intention to deceive is experience dependent. For example, the accuracy with which a stationary observer can determine whether a point-light defined basketball player intends to pass a basketball or to fake a pass depends upon the observer's motor and visual experience playing the game of basketball (Sebanz & Shiffrar, 2009).

Affective state can also be reliably detected in point-light displays of human movement. Observers can readily identify the emotions felt by point-light defined individuals who move their entire bodies (Atkinson, Dittrich, Gemmell, & Young, 2004; Dittrich et al., 1996). Even more impressively, naïve observers can identify the emotional state of a person knocking on a door when only the knocking, point-light arm is visible (Pollick, Paterson, Bruderlin, & Sanford, 2001). The affective states of point-light defined individuals appear to be most recognizable when they are presented within a consistent social context. For example, when a point-light defined person expresses some emotional state during an interaction with another person, that emotional state is most accurately detected when point-light displays show both individuals rather than only the emotional individual (Clarke, Bradshaw, Field, Hampson,

& Rose, 2005). Thus, social and emotional cues appear to be integrated during the visual analysis of human movement. Neurophysiological evidence supports this conclusion. The STSp is required for the visual perception of point-light displays of human movement (Saygin, 2007). Interestingly, the STSp responds more strongly during the perception of emotional than instrumental actions (Gallagher & Frith, 2004). Furthermore, STSp activity is clearly involved in the analysis of visual cues to socially relevant information (e.g., Allison, Puce, & McCarthy, 2000). Thus, overlapping neural circuitry is involved in the visual perception of emotion, social cues, and human action (Puce & Perrett, 2003). Because people express emotional states and behave socially, whereas physical objects do not, these results provide additional evidence that the human visual system differentiates its analyses of human and object motion.

To interact successfully with other people, it would be helpful if one could detect other people's social, affective, and intentional states. The results summarized earlier indicate that such detection is possible with only a few moving points. Sensitivity to social and emotional cues in significantly degraded visual stimuli suggests that the human visual system is well tuned for the detection and analyses of essentially human information. Thus, the results summarized here suggest that the visual system plays a critical role in allowing and promoting human interaction.

SOCIAL AND EMOTIONAL PROCESSES CHANGE HUMAN MOVEMENT PERCEPTION

The previous section focused on the types of social and affective information that naïve human observers can detect from whole body human movements, especially those depicted in point-light displays. The ability to detect such high-level information presents no challenge to traditional models of the visual system. According to such modular, feed-forward models, the outputs of low-level visual processes are simply passed along to subsequent social and affective mechanisms that extract socially relevant information. However, although the

visual system has been traditionally understood as a feed-forward system, neurophysiological support for feedback processes has long been available (e.g., Rockland & Pandya, 1979). At least within the visual system, feedback connections appear to be more extensive than feed-forward connections (Salin & Bullier, 1995). Interestingly, and contrary to many long held assumptions, feedback connections can modify lower level visual processes very quickly, indeed, in as little as 10 msec (Hupe et al., 2001). Recent researchers have made significant advances in understanding core visual processes, such as object recognition, by taking feedback or top-down processing into account (e.g., Kveraga, Ghuman, & Bar, 2007). The visual area that is critical for the perception of point-light displays of human motion—namely, the STSp (Saygin, 2007)—is tightly connected with the neural areas involved in social and emotional processes (e.g., Adolphs, 1999; Allison et al., 2000). If feedback from social and emotional mechanisms can rapidly modify lower-level visual analyses, then one would expect to find that social and emotional information can change visual sensitivity to human movement. This proposal was tested in the following experiments.

Social Processes

Does the visual perception of human movement change as a function of the social context within which that movement appears? Recall that social context enhances visual sensitivity to a point-light actor's emotional state (Clarke et al., 2005). Furthermore, fMRI data suggest that people spontaneously and continuously monitor visual scenes for their social content. When people passively observe a human action within a social context, increases in neural activity are found in the medial parietal and medial prefrontal cortices, areas that are interconnected with the STS (Iacoboni et al., 2004). However, when that same human action is presented in social isolation, that is, in the absence of another person, no activation increases are found. Thus, something changes when human actions are presented within social contexts. But, does visual sensitivity to human movement change, per se?

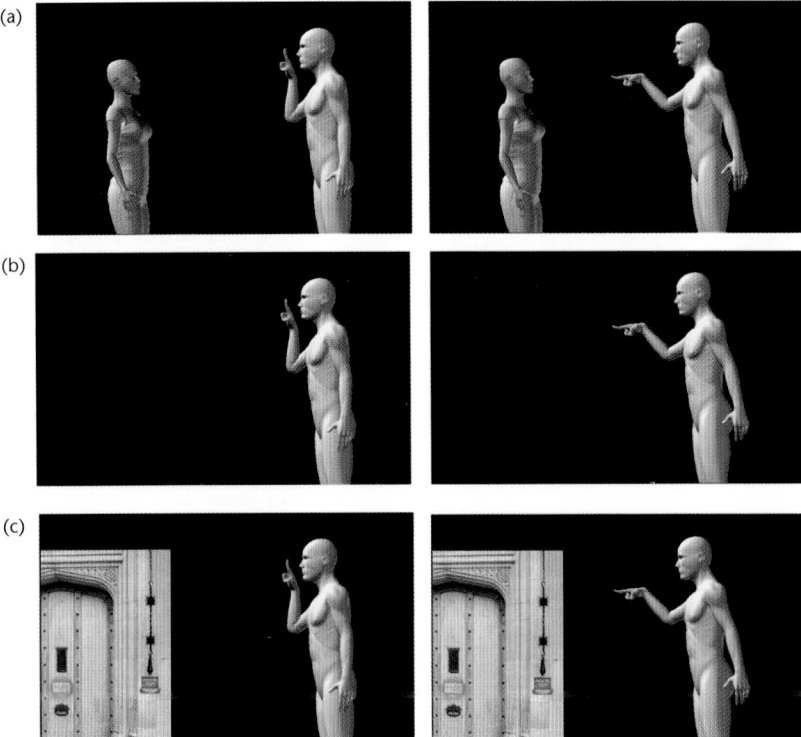

Figure 14.4 Apparent motion stimuli adapted from Chouchourelou & Shiffrar (2011). The same human movement appears in three different static contexts. (a) On the top row, two frames of an apparent motion sequence depict a person on the right gesturing towards a static person. Notice that the person on the left remains stationary while there is a displacement of the right arm of the other person. (b) The same human gesture appears in isolation or (c) within the context of a stationary object. When asked to judge how much motion is depicted in these apparent motion displays, observers who view the movements within social contexts, as in (a), report the perception of significantly more motion than observers who view the identical displacements in non-social contexts, as in b and c.

To determine whether social context influences the visual perception of human movement, Areti Chouchourelou conducted the following studies of apparent motion perception. In the first study, naïve participants viewed a set of two-frame apparent motion stimuli depicting a woman performing various simple actions, such as reaching, pointing, or kicking (Figure 14.4). These stimuli were constructed by filming two people interacting with each other. The resulting digital video clips were systematically edited. First, two static frames, separated by 150 msec, were pulled from the video clip of each action. These static frames were edited so that everything from each frame was removed except the person performing the action. Then, graphic editing was used so that each two-frame action sequence appeared in isolation, directed toward a static object, or directed toward a static person. The assumption was made that the presence of another person created a social context, whereas the presence of an object did not.

Each participant saw all of the actions presented in one of the different contexts. Across trials, the display rate of the apparent motion stimuli was varied. Each picture in an apparent motion stimulus pair was displayed for a 100 msec and the time between each picture, or inter-stimulus-interval, ranged from 10 to 600 msec. Participants were lead to believe that they were taking part in a study of the dynamic image quality of various computer monitors. That is, the phenomenon of apparent motion was explained to them. Then participants were told that monitors vary in the quality of apparent motion that they produce. Participants were then asked to watch various apparent motion sequences for 5 seconds each and to rate how much motion they saw on a scale from 1 (no motion) to 7 (smooth motion) in each apparent motion sequence. Participants who viewed the actions within a social context rated the apparent motion displays as conveying significantly more motion than participants who viewed the same actions in the non-social contexts (Chouchourelou & Shiffrar, 2011). That is, even though participants viewed identical physical displacements, because the same human displacements appeared in every context, motion percepts were enhanced for social human actions relative to isolated actions or actions directed toward objects. This result is consistent with the hypothesis that social processes change fundamental aspects of the visual perception of human movement.

There is, however, an alternative interpretation of the these results. That is, all of the apparent motion stimuli were constructed from human actions that were originally directed toward another person. So maybe more compelling motion percepts were reported in the social context simply because the actions made the most sense within that context. To address this confound, another study was conducted. Stimulus construction began with the digital videotaping of human actions directed toward objects and toward people. As before, two static frames were pulled from the video depicting each action. These frames were edited so that only the central moving person was visible. Then, a pilot study was conducted with these two sets of isolated actions. As before, naïve observers rated the amount of movement (as compared to stationary flashing) they perceived when they viewed each action in isolation. The

resulting judgments were used to equate stimuli for the amount of perceived movement they produced. Once the stimuli were equated, graphic editing was used to reintroduce the stationary images of the original object or person toward which each action had been directed. Then a new group of participants rated the amount of movement they observed in the two types of apparent motion sequences. The results of this experiment showed that naïve observers saw significantly more motion when apparent motion displays depicted actions directed toward another person than actions directed toward an object (Chouchourelou & Shiffrar, 2011). This finding is consistent with the hypothesis that the neural analysis of object-directed actions differs from the analysis of person-directed actions (Jacobs & Jeannerod, 2003). Indeed, the results of these two studies suggest that social processes, per se, spontaneously enhance the visual analysis of human motion. Given that human movement is an inherently social stimulus, it certainly makes sense that social context would contribute to its analysis.

Emotional Processes

Is the visual analysis of human action similarly modulated by the emotional content of that action? Neuroanatomical connections between visual and emotional areas suggest that such modulation is possible. The STSp, a visual area that plays a critical role in the perception of human movement (e.g., Grossman et al., 2000; Saygin, 2007), is extensively interconnected with the amygdala, a region of the limbic system that is involved in the analysis of the emotional content of sensory information (Brothers, 1997; Amaral, 2003). Recurrent processing between the amygdala and the STSp (Amaral, 2003) raises the possibility that the visual analysis of human movement is systematically modified by the emotional content of that movement. A series of psychophysical studies by Chouchourelou and her colleagues (2006) produced data that are consistent with this prediction. Stimulus construction began when trained actors walked within a motion capture system while expressing five different emotional states: happy, sad, angry, fearful, and neutral. The motion-capture data were converted into point-light displays. In the first study, naïve observers viewed the emotional point-light walkers one by one and reported each walker's emotional state. Performance in this emotion recognition task was well above chance, confirming previous findings (Atkinson et al., 2004; Dittrich et al., 1996). Then, point-light movies with at least 83 percent interparticipant agreement in this emotion recognition task were selected for use in subsequent studies.

In the main study, point-light walkers with readily recognizable emotional states were placed within specially constructed point-light masks. Each walker was presented within its own mask. Each mask was constructed by scrambling the starting locations of the points defining the walker that appeared within that mask. Thus, a happy walker was presented within its own happy mask and a sad walker was presented within its own sad mask. As a result, for each stimulus, there was no net velocity difference between the points defining the walker and the points defining the mask. This manipulation is important because different emotions are associated with different patterns of movement (Pollick et al., 2001). For example, sad people tend to move slowly whereas happy people move more quickly. The technique described ensured that walker detection performance could not be driven by the differences in gait velocity associated with different emotional states.

In one half of the trials, a coherent point-light walker was present within its point-light mask. On the other half of the trials, the walker was scrambled, like the mask, so that no coherent walker was present. Participants viewed each masked display and reported whether a coherent point-light walker was present within the mask. No feedback was provided. Importantly, participants were not asked to judge any emotional information. Indeed, the experimenter never mentioned emotion. Participants simply reported whether a walker was present or absent. The results showed that walker detection was systematically modulated by the emotional content of the walkers' gaits. Specifically, participants demonstrated the greatest visual

sensitivity to the presence of angry walkers (Chouchourelou, Matsuka, Harber, & Shiffrar, 2006). This finding is particularly interesting because researchers have argued that the amygdala is most responsive to potentially threatening stimuli (Amaral, 2003; Whalen et al., 2004). An angry person is clearly a threatening stimulus. Thus, these results suggest that emotional processes automatically contribute to and indeed help to define visual sensitivity to the actions of other people.

SOCIAL BEHAVIOR AND THE DETECTION OF HUMAN MOVEMENT

Most researchers who study the visual perception of human movement motivate their experiments with the argument that successful social behavior requires the rapid and accurate perception of other people's actions (e.g., Blake & Shiffrar, 2007). Although this assertion seems simple enough, it nonetheless predicts that there is a direct relationship between visual sensitivity to human movement and social behavior. This prediction has been tested with studies of the perceptual capabilities of people with Autism Spectrum Disorder (ASD). ASD is an inherently social disorder that affects, to varying degrees, an individual's ability to communicate and interact with other people (DSM-IV TR, 2000). If visual sensitivity to human action is directly related to successful social behavior, then observers with ASD should show deficits, relative to typical observers, in their visual sensitivity to human movement. Yet, previously published studies have not resolved whether observers with ASD are compromised in their visual sensitivity to point-light displays of human movement (Kaiser & Shiffrar, 2009).

Autism Spectrum Disorder

Moore, Hobson, and Lee (1997) were the first to examine the visual perception of human movement by observers with ASD. In their studies, children and adolescents with autism or non-autistic retardation viewed variable-duration point-light displays of people and objects and verbally described each display. No significant differences were found in the amount of time that observers with ASD and controls needed to accurately describe each movie's content. Observers with ASD did show, however, a nonsignificant trend toward delayed recognition of moving people when defined by only 5 point lights. Children with ASD were significantly less likely to describe a point-light person's emotional state (e.g., happy, sad) than nonautistic control observers, but those with ASD showed no difference from controls in their tendency to describe the type of action being performed (e.g., walking, running). This finding was replicated with observers with Asperger's Syndrome (Hubert et al., 2007). These researchers concluded that young observers with ASD exhibit normal perceptual sensitivity to human movement, *per se*, but they exhibit impairments in the attribution of mental states to human movement. However, because autism is strongly associated with language deficits (DSM-IV-TR, 2000), it is difficult to interpret the results of verbal measures.

Motivated by concerns about the sensitivity of descriptive measures, Blake and his colleagues (2003) conducted a two-alternative forced-choice study of visual sensitivity to point-light displays of human motion by young observers with ASD and matched controls. On half of the trials, observers viewed brief point-light movies of a person performing some action such as running, throwing or jumping. On the other half of the trials, the points defining the point-light actors were temporally scrambled to disrupt the hierarchy of pendular motions that define the human body. Children viewed these point-light movies in random order and reported whether the dots moved like a person. As a control for grouping processes, these same observers also performed a global form task by pointing to which of four quadrants contained a static, circular target shape among an array of distractor line segments. These researchers found that children with ASD performed the human motion detection task more poorly than matched controls and the global form detection task as well as controls. Impressively, a significant correlation was found between children's severity of autism and their performance on the human motion detection task. These researchers concluded that children with ASD are

compromised in their ability to perceive coherent human motion. However, alternative interpretations remain. Given the diagnostic language and communication impairments in ASD, children with ASD may have performed relatively poorly on the human motion task compared to the static form task because the first required a verbal response whereas the second did not. Furthermore, because a static control task was used, the results of this experiment are consistent with the hypothesis that observers with ASD show deficits in global motion processing, in general, and not in human motion processing, in specific. Consistent with this alternative explanation, several studies have reported that observers with ASD show deficits in their ability to perceive global motion in random dot cinematograms (Milne et al., 2002; Pellicano et al., 2005; Spencer et al., 2000).

There is, nonetheless, neurophysiological evidence suggesting that autism does impact the visual analysis of human movement. Recent studies have identified associations between ASD and abnormalities in the STSp (e.g., Boddaert et al., 2004; Pelphrey, Morris, McCarthy, & LaBar, 2007). If abnormalities in the STSp impact the visual analysis of human movement, then observers with ASD should show selective deficits in their visual perception of human movement.

Martha Kaiser and her colleagues recently began a series of experiments designed to avoid the pitfalls that have complicated previous studies. In these studies, observers with ASD and controls are asked to perform a motion coherence discrimination task with point-light depictions of human motion and object motion. The human stimuli depict a point-light-defined person walking and/or reaching over to pick up an object. The object stimuli depict a point-light-defined tractor with a front bucket that moves forward while the bucket does or does not reach down to pick up an object. Across trials, these stimuli are presented as either coherent or scrambled by a rearrangement of the starting positions of the point-lights. In the human condition, participants report with a button press whether the point lights were stuck to a person. In the object condition, participants similarly report whether the point lights were stuck to a tractor. The preliminary results (Kaiser et al., 2010) indicate that observers with ASD and controls show no significant difference in their visual sensitivity to the presence of coherent object motion. Conversely, in the human motion condition, task performance by control observers is significantly better than performance by observers with ASD. These results suggest that observers with ASD have a specific deficit in their visual sensitivity to human motion. This deficit in visual sensitivity to human movement cannot be attributed to a general deficit in global motion perception because observers with ASD performed as well as typical observers in the tractor motion detection task. Furthermore, task performance in the human motion condition cannot be attributed to cognitive deficits in task comprehension or response production because the same task and response were used in the object motion condition where observers with ASD performed as well as controls. Such evidence supports the hypothesis that visual sensitivity to human movement is related to, or may even be a precursor to, successful social behavior.

Typical Observers

Although the described results are useful for understanding perceptual processing in autism, they do not inform us about the relationships between action perception and social behavior in typical observers. To address that issue, Kaiser took advantage of the fact that autistic symptoms appear in both clinical and nonclinical populations (Baron-Cohen et al., 2001). In other words, autistic traits are present among typical, non-autistic individuals. Interestingly, nonautistic scientists, mathematicians, and engineers exhibit more autistic traits than scholars in the humanities and social sciences (Baron-Cohen et al., 2001). The Autism-Spectrum Quotient or AQ is a short questionnaire that measures the extent to which individuals with normal IQs exhibit autistic traits (Baron-Cohen et al., 2001). To investigate the relationship, if any, between visual sensitivity to human movement and social behavior, typical university students performed the same point-light human-

motion- and tractor-motion-detection tasks already described and then completed the AQ questionnaire. The results showed that as scores on the AQ increased, indicating the increasing presence of autistic traits, performance on the human motion detection task decreased. Importantly, performance on the tractor motion detection task did not vary with scores on the AQ (Kaiser, Fermano, & Shiffrar, 2008). These data suggest that visual sensitivity to human motion is indeed related to social behavior in the typical population. The directionality of that relationship remains to be determined. That is, we do not yet know whether enhanced visual sensitivity to human movement promotes more successful social behavior or whether successful social behavior leads to improvements in visual sensitivity to human movement, or both.

GENERAL CONCLUSION

In conclusion, the results of the studies summarized here indicate that the visual perception of human motion differs in fundamental ways from the visual perception of object motion. First, multiple psychophysical measures indicate that visual analyses of human motion involve the integration of information over greater spatiotemporal extents than the visual analysis of complex object motion. One result of such expanded integration capacities may be the ability to tolerate more noise during action perception. The lifetime of visual experience that observers gain from watching the actions of other people likely enhances noise tolerance (Bulthoff, Bulthoff, & Sinha, 1998), as does disambiguating input from motor, social and emotional centers (see Blake & Shiffrar, 2007 for review). Second, neurophysiological evidence shows that distinct neural areas are involved in the visual analysis of human motion. Although the perception of meaningful objects and people in motion initially rely on overlapping mechanisms, divergent processing is found soon thereafter (Virji-Babul et al., 2007). Third, naïve observers are able to detect an impressive variety of surprisingly complex and subtle types of socially relevant information from the movements of the human body. Obviously, the detection of such information in object motion is not possible because objects, unlike people, do not vary, for example, in their social dominance, sexual orientation, psychological openness, or affective state. Instead, the visual perception of dynamic stimuli that are structurally and/or biomechanically consistent with an observer's own body appears to trigger social, emotional, and motor analyses that help to define visual sensitivity to those stimuli (Shiffrar, 2006). This is not to say that objects cannot be interpreted as having human-like characteristics (Hieder & Simmel, 1944). Indeed, perception of geometric figures can trigger activity in the STSp (Castelli, Frith, Happe, & Frith, 2002). Fourth, social and emotional processes significantly modify visual sensitivity to human movement. The dynamic cues to emotion that are produced by an individual's bodily actions alter an observer's ability to detect the presence of that person's moving body. Furthermore, the ability to detect the presence of human motion within apparent motion displays depends upon the social context within which that motion is presented. And finally, visual sensitivity to the presence of coherent human movement, but not coherent object movement, correlates with observers' autistic tendencies. Because autism is an inherently social disorder (Schultz, 2005), this result suggests that an observer's social abilities are related to that observer's visual sensitivity to the actions of other people.

For the past several decades, vision scientists and psychologists have been fascinated by point-light displays of human movement. These displays are surprisingly engaging. The results of the studies described in this chapter suggest that point-light displays of human motion may be especially compelling because their visual analysis is deeply intertwined with human social behavior. Indeed, the human visual system appears to detect, reflect, and promote the complex social behaviors that define us as human.

ACKNOWLEDGMENT

The authors wish to the thank the Simons Foundation (grant#94915) and the National Science Foundation (EXP–SA 0730985) for support.

REFERENCES

Adolphs, R. (1999). Social cognition and the human brain. *Trends in Cognitive Science, 3,* 469–479.

Allison, T., Puce, A., & McCarthy, G. (2000). Social perception from visual cues: Role of the STS region. *Trends in Cognitive Science, 4,* 267–278.

Amaral, D. G. (2003). The amygdala, social behavior, and danger detection. *Annals of the New York Academy of Science, 1000,* 337–347.

Ambady, N., Hallahan, M., & Conner, B. (1999). Accuracy of judgments of sexual orientation from thin slices of behavior. *Journal of Personality and Social Psychology, 77,* 538–547.

Atkinson, A.P., Dittrich, W.H., Gemmell, A.J., & Young, A.W. (2004). Emotion perception from dynamic and static body expressions in point–light and full–light displays. *Perception, 33,* 717–746.

Barclay, C., Cutting, J., & Kozlowski, L. (1978). Temporal and spatial factors in gait perception that influence gender recognition. *Perception & Psychophysics, 23,* 145–152.

Baron–Cohen, S., Wheelwright, S., Skinner, R., Martin, J., & Clubley, E. (2001). The Autism–Spectrum Quotient (AQ): Evidence from Asperger syndrome/high functioning autism, males and females, scientists and mathematicians. *Journal of Autism and Developmental Disorders, 31,* 5–17.

Bertenthal, B.I., & Pinto, J. (1994). Global processing of biological motions. *Psychological Science, 5,* 221–225.

Blake, R., & Shiffrar, M. (2007). Perception of human motion. *Annual Review of Psychology, 58, 47–74.*

Blake, R., Turner, L., Smoski, M., Pozdol, S., & Stone, W. (2003). Visual recognition of biological motion is impaired in children with autism. *Psychological Science, 14,* 151–157.

Boddaert, N., Chabane, N., Gervais, H., Good, C. D., Bourgeois, M., Plumet, M. H., et al. (2004). Superior temporal sulcus anatomical abnormalities in childhood autism: A voxel based morphometry MRI study. *Neuroimage, 23,* 364–369.

Bonda, E., Petrides, M., Ostry, D., & Evans, A. (1996). Specific involvement of human parietal systems and the amygdala in the perception of biological motion. *Journal of Neuroscience, 16,* 3737 – 3744.

Brothers, L. (1997). *Friday's footprint: How society shapes the human mind.* London: Oxford University Press.

Brown, W.M., Cronk, L., Grochow, K., Jacobson, A., Liu, C.K., et al. (2005). Dance reveals symmetry especially in young men. *Nature,* 438, 148–150.

Brownlow, S., Dixon, A.R., Egbert, C.A., & Radcliffe, R.D. (1997). Perception of movement and dancer characteristics from point–light displays of dance. *Psychological Record,* 47, 411–421.

Bulthoff, I., Bulthoff, H., & Sinha, P. (1998). Top-down influences on stereoscopic depth–perception. *Nature Neuroscience, 1,* 254–257.

Burt, P., & Sperling, G. (1981). Time, distance, and feature trade–offs in visual apparent motion. *Psychological Review, 88,* 171–195.

Castelli, F., Frith, C., Happe, F., & Frith, U. (2002). Autism, Asperger syndrome and brain mechanisms for the attribution of mental states to animated shapes. *Brain, 125,* 1839–1849.

Chouchourelou, A., Matsuka, T., Harber, K., & Shiffrar, M. (2006). The visual analysis of emotional actions. *Social Neuroscience, 1,* 63–74.

Chouchourelou, A., & Shiffrar, M. (2011). Social context influences the visual perception of apparent human motion. *Manuscript under revision.*

Clarke, T.J., Bradshaw, M.F., Field, D.T., Hampson, S.E., & Rose, D. (2005). The perception of emotion from body movement in point–light displays of interpersonal dialogue. *Perception, 34,* 1171–1180.

Cutting, J., & Kozlowski, L. (1977). Recognizing friends by their walk: Gait perception without familiarity cues. *Bulletin of the Psychonomic Society, 9,* 353–356.

Cutting, J. E., Moore, C., & Morrison, R. (1988). Masking the motions of human gait. *Perception & Psychophysics, 44,* 339–347.

Diagnostic and statistical manual of mental disorders (DSM–IV–TR). (2000). Washington, DC.: American Psychiatric Association.

Dittrich, W.H. (1993). Action categories and the perception of biological motion. *Perception, 22,* 15–22.

Dittrich, W.H., Troscianko, T., Lea, S.E.G., & Morgan, D. (1996). Perception of emotion from dynamic point–light displays represented in dance. *Perception, 25,* 727–738.

Fiorentini, A., Maffei, L., & Sandini, G. (1983). The role of high spatial frequencies in face perception. *Perception, 12,* 195–201.

Fodor, J.A., & Pylyshyn, Z. (1981). How direct is visual perception? *Cognition, 9,* 139–196.

Gallagher, H.L., & Frith, C.D. (2004). Dissociable neural pathways for the perception and recognition of expressive and instrumental gestures. *Neuropsychologia,* 42, 1725–1736.

Gibson, E. (1969). *Principles of perceptual learning and development.* New York: Meredith Corporation.

Gibson, J.J. (1986). *The ecological approach to visual perception.* Hillsdale, NJ: Lawrence Erlbaum Associates.

Goffaux, V., & Rossion, B. (2006). Faces are "spatial"–Holistic face perception is supported by low spatial frequencies. *Journal of Experimental Psychology: Human Perception & Performance, 32,* 1023–1039.

Grossman, E., Donnelly, M., Price, R., Pickens, D., Morgan, V., *et al.* (2000). Brain areas involved in perception of biological motion. *Journal of Cognitive Neuroscience, 12,* 711–720.

Gunns, R.E., Johnston, L., & Hudson, S. (2002). Victim selection and kinematics: A point–light investigation of vulnerability to attack. *Journal of Nonverbal Behavior, 26,* 129–158.

Heider, F., & Simmel, M. (1944). An experimental study of apparent behavior. *American Journal of Psychology, 57,* 243–259.

Hildreth, E. (1984). *The measurement of visual motion.* Cambridge, MA: MIT Press.

Hiris, E., Krebeck, A., Edmonds, J., & Stout, A. (2005). What learning to see arbitrary motion tells us about biological motion perception. *Journal of Experimental Psychology: Human Perception & Performance, 31,* 1096–1106.

Hiris, E. (2007). Detection of biological and non-biological motion. *Journal of Vision, 7,* 1–16.

Hubert, B., Wicker, B., Moore, D.G., Monfardini, E., Duverger, H., Da Fonseca, D., et al. (2007). Recognition of emotional and non–emotional biological motion in individuals with autistic spectrum disorders. *Journal of Autism and Developmental Disorders, 37,* 1386–1392.

Hupe, J.M., James, A.C., Girard, P., Lomber, S.G., Payne, B.R., & Bullier, J. (2001). Feedback connections act on the early part of the responses in monkey visual cortex. *Journal of Neurophysiology, 85,* 134–145.

Iacoboni, M., Lieberman, M., Knowlton, B., Molnar–Szakacs, I., Moritz, M., Throop, J. et al. (2004). Watching social interactions produces dorsomedial prefrontal and medial parietal BOLD fMRI signal increases compared to a resting baseline. *Neuroimage, 21,* 1167–1173.

Jacobs, A., & Jeannerod, M. (2003). *Ways of seeing.* New York: Oxford University Press.

Jacobs, A., Pinto, J., & Shiffrar, M. (2004). Experience, context, and the visual perception of human movement. *Journal of Experimental Psychology: Human Perception & Performance, 30*, 822–835.

Johansson, G. (1973). Visual perception of biological motion and a model for its analysis. *Perception & Psychophysics, 14*, 201–211.

Johansson, G. (1976). Spatio–temporal differentiation and integration in visual motion perception: An experimental and theoretical analysis of calculus–like functions in visual data processing. *Psychological Research, 38*, 379–393.

Johnson, K.L., Gill, S., Reichman, V., & Tassinary, L.G. (2007). Swagger, sway, and sexuality: Judging sexual orientation from body motion and morphology. *Journal of Personality and Social Psychology, 93*, 321–334.

Jokisch, D., Daum, I., & Troje, N. (2006). Self–recognition versus recognition of others by biological motion: Viewpoint–dependent effects. *Perception, 35*, 911–920.

Kaiser, M.D., & Shiffrar, M. (2009). The visual perception of motion by observers with autism spectrum disorder: A review and synthesis. *Psychonomic Bulletin & Review, 16*, 761–777.

Kaiser, M.D., Delmolino, L., Tanaka, J., & Shiffrar, M. (2010). Comparison of Visual Sensitivity to Human and Object Motion in Autism Spectrum Disorder, Autism Research, in press.

Kaiser, M., Fermano, Z., & Shiffrar, M. (2008, May). *Visual sensitivity to human movement and the magnitude of autistic traits.* Paper presented at the 7th International Meeting for Autism Research, London, England.

Kveraga, K., Ghuman, A. S., & Bar, M. (2007). Top–down predictions in the cognitive brain. *Brain and Cognition, 65*, 145–168.

Loula, F., Prasad, S., Harber, K., & Shiffrar, M. (2005). Recognizing people from their movement. *Journal of Experimental Psychology: Human Perception & Performance, 31*, 210–220.

Marey, E. J. (1895/1972). *Movement.* New York: Arno Press & New York Times. (Originally published in 1895).

Marr, D. (1982). *Vision: A computational investigation into the human representation and processing of visual information.* San Francisco: W. H. Freeman.

McArthur, L.Z., & Baron, R. M. (1983). Toward an ecological theory of social perception. *Psychological Review, 90*, 215–238.

Milne, E., Swettenham, J. Hansen, P., Campbell, R., Jeffries, H., & Plaisted, K. (2002). High motion coherence thresholds in children with autism. *Journal of Child Psychology and Psychiatry, 43*, 255–263.

Montepare, J.M., & Zebrowitz–McArthur, L.A. (1988). Impressions of people created by age–related qualities of their gaits. *Journal of Personality and Social Psychology, 55*, 547–556.

Moore, D. G., Hobson, R. P., & Lee, A. (1997). Components of person perception: An investigation with autistic, non–autistic retarded and typically developing children and adolescents. *British Journal of Developmental Psychology, 15*, 401–423.

Pellicano, E., Gibson, L., Maybery, M., Kevin, D., & Badcock, D. (2005). Abnormal global processing along the dorsal visual pathway in autism: A possible mechanism for weak visuospatial coherence? *Neuropsychologia, 43*, 1044–1053.

Pelphrey, K. A., Morris, J.P., McCarthy, G., & LaBar, K.S. (2007). Perception of dynamic changes in facial affect and identity in autism. *Social, Cognitive and Affective Neuroscience, 2*, 140–149.

Pollick, F.E., Paterson, H.M., Bruderlin, A., & Sanford, A.J. (2001). Perceiving affect from arm movement. *Cognition, 82*, 51–61.

Pollick, F.E., Kay, J.W., Heim, K., & Stringer, R. (2005). Gender recognition from point–light walkers. *Journal of Experimental Psychology: Human Perception & Performance, 31*, 1247–1265.

Puce, A., & Perrett, D. (2003). Electrophysiological and brain imaging of biological motion. *Philosophical Transactions of the Royal Society, London B, 358*, 435–445.

Rockland, K. S., & Pandya, D. N. (1979). Laminar origins and terminations of cortical connections of the occipital lobe in the rhesus monkey. *Brain Research, 179*, 3–20.

Runeson, S., & Frykholm, G. (1983). Kinematic specification of dynamics as an informational bias for person–and–action perception: Expectation, gender recognition, and deceptive intent. *Journal of Experimental Psychology: General, 112*, 585–615.

Salin, P–A., & Bullier, J. (1995). Corticocortical connections in the visual system: Structure and function. *Physiological Review, 75*, 107–154.

Saygin, A. P. (2007). Superior temporal and premotor brain areas are necessary for biological motion perception. *Brain, 130*, 2452–2461.

Schultz, R. (2005). Developmental deficits in social perception in autism: The role of the amygdala and fusiform face area. *International Journal of Developmental Neuroscience, 23,* 125–141.

Sebanz, N., & Shiffrar, M. (2009). Detecting deception in a bluffing body: The role of expertise. *Psychonomic Bulletin & Review, 16,* 170–175.

Shepard, R.N. (1984). Ecological constraints on internal representation: Resonant kinematics of perceiving, imagining, thinking, and dreaming. *Psychological Review, 91,* 417–447.

Shiffrar, M. (2006). Body–based views of the world. In G. Knoblich, M. Grosjean, I. Thornton, & M. Shiffrar (Eds.), *Perception of the human body from the inside out.* Oxford University Press, 135–146.

Shiffrar, M., & Freyd, J.J. (1990). Apparent motion of the human body. *Psychological Science, 1,* 257–264.

Shiffrar, M., & Freyd, J. (1993). Timing and apparent motion path choice with human body photographs. *Psychological Science, 4,* 379–384.

Shiffrar, M., Lichtey, L., & Heptulla–Chatterjee, S. (1997). The perception of biological motion across apertures. *Perception & Psychophysics, 59,* 51–59.

Shiffrar, M., & Lorenceau, J. (1996). Increased motion linking across edges with decreased luminance contrast, edge width and duration. *Vision Research, 36,* 2061–2067.

Spencer, J., O'Brien, J., Riggs, K., Braddick, O., Atkinson, J., & Wattam–Bell, J. (2000). Motion processing in autism: Evidence for a dorsal stream deficiency. *Cognitive Neuroscience and Neuropsychology, 11,* 2765–2767.

Stevens, J.A., Fonlupt, P., Shiffrar, M., & Decety, J. (2000). New aspects of motion perception: Selective neural encoding of apparent human movements. *NeuroReport, 11,* 109–115.

Verfaillie, K. (2000). Perceiving human locomotion: Priming effects in direction discrimination. *Brain and Cognition, 44,* 192–213.

Virji–Babul, N., Cheung, T., Weeks, D., Kerns, K., & Shiffrar, M. (2007). Neural activity involved in the perception of human and meaningful object motion. *NeuroReport, 18,* 1125–1128.

Wertheimer, M. (1912). Experimentelle stuidien uber das Sehen von Beuegung. *Zeitschrift fuer Psychologie, 61,* 161–265.

Whalen, P. J., Kagan, J., Cook, R. G., Davis, F. C., Kim, H., Polis, S., et al. (2004). Human amygdala responsivity to masked fearful eye whites. *Science, 306,* 2061.

Zebrowitz, L. A., & Collins, M. A. (1997). Accurate social perception at zero acquaintance: The affordances of a Gibsonian approach. *Personality and Social Psychology Review, 1,* 203–222.

CHAPTER 15

Social Constraints on the Visual Perception of Biological Motion

Kerri L. Johnson, Frank E. Pollick, and Lawrie S. McKay

The importance of the human face as a cue for person construal has been well established by decades of research. Its privileged status, however, has been rivaled by a growing literature that identifies the dynamic human body as a potent cue to meaningful social information. In fact, some (here and elsewhere) have even argued that under some circumstances, perception of the body may be the primary means of social perception (see de Gelder this volume and 2005). The body, for example, can be perceived at a physical distance or a visual vantage point that precludes face perception. Moreover, the body is unique in its ability not only to convey an emotional state elicited by a certain circumstance, but also to suggest an appropriate behavioral response to a given context. For these reasons among others, an emerging consensus is developing carving a special role for body perception as a vehicle to social perception.

Studies investigating the perception of the body in motion were once the exclusive domain of vision scholars (for a review of this history, see Shiffrar, Chapter 14, this volume). These researchers sought to understand either the physical parameters that enabled observers to distinguish between biological and nonbiological motion or the cues that led observers to accurately categorize biological motion displays according to social categories, personal identities, and psychological states (e.g., emotional state). Although such questions necessarily involved social judgments, the vast majority of

this work treated such social categorizations as perceptual endpoints, not as a part of social perception more generally.

In a largely independent field of research, social psychologists were at the same time appreciating the profound consequences of perceiving the social categories that vision scholars had long sought to understand. These social researchers examined the effects of social categorization on interpersonal processes including stereotyping, evaluation, and person construal more generally. By and large, these scholars treated social categorization as a given, and used category knowledge as a beginning point to understand its effect on other aspects of person perception, with little concern for how the categorization emerged in the first place. Thus, social psychologists and vision scholars used categorization quite differently in their pursuit to understand social perception.

This chapter aims to shed light on how the once-clear distinctions between the visual and social approaches to social categorization of the human body have begun to blur. First, we will review findings from classic studies of biological motion perception that bear directly on domains that social psychologists care deeply about—the perception of social categories, identities, and psychological states. Then we describe two ways in which these basic patterns are constrained by social psychological processes. First, we review evidence that social category knowledge constrains the interpretation and evaluation of dynamic body motion for evaluative social judgments. Then, we present data that highlight how knowledge structures (i.e., stereotypes) can bias one's basic perception of the human body in motion.

SOMETHING (IN THE WAY SHE MOVES)

The scientific study of biological motion perception grew to its current level within the vision sciences with the development of an elegant technique to isolate body motion in visual displays. Borrowing from early observations of filmed motion (e.g., Marey 1884), Johannsson (1973) created what came to be known as point-light or biological-motion displays. These quickly became a mainstay of modern biological-motion-perception research. In its most primitive form, illuminated bulbs (or reflective markers) were affixed to the body's major joints, and the person was filmed engaging in a variety of activities. When replayed, the resulting film depicted the action as a coordinated set of lights against a dark background (see Figure 15.1). In spite of their impoverished nature, early reports suggested that point-light displays compelled reliable perceptions among observers. In fact, observers readily reported the clips to depict human motion and also accurately identified the depicted activities (Johansson, 1973; 1975). Thus, Johansson's work could be characterized as one of the first empirical demonstrations of observers' remarkable ability to recover the human form from motion cues alone. Building on this basic foundation, a considerable amount of research has sought to understand the perceptual mechanisms that enable observers to discriminate human from nonhuman motion, and much of that work focused on understanding low-level aspects of visual perception.

Other researchers quickly sought to determine which categories of information could be perceived from biological motion displays. These next steps examined whether and how identity-relevant information could be conveyed by body motion. This shift in focus from distinguishing between human and nonhuman to a focus on the perception of social identities

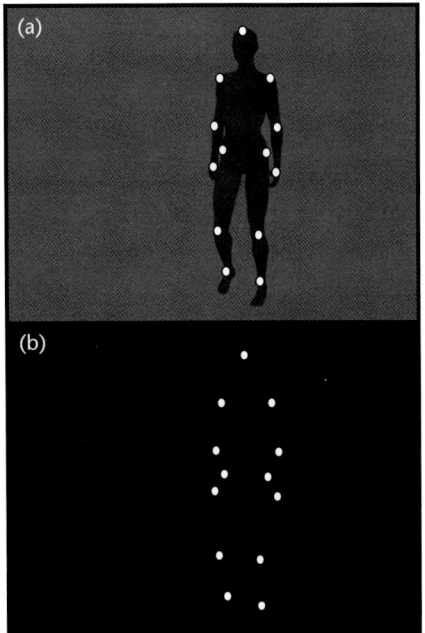

Figure 15.1 Point-Light Display. (a) When generating point-light displays, researchers affix reflective or infrared markers to the body's major joints, depicted here superimposed over a computer animated body. (b) When presented to participants, only the points of light are visible. Though static here, these lights would depict the dynamic motion of each light over time.

paved the way for a yoking between vision and social processes, in part because vision scholars were asking observers to make judgments that carry interpersonal consequences.

Three domains of percepts that are supported by biological motion, for example, have a long-standing tradition of research in social psychology. These include social categorization, the identification of others (i.e., personal identities), and the appreciation of another's psychological state. For each domain, we describe their theoretical and interpersonal significance from a social perspective and briefly review evidence that biological motion is a potent cue for its perception.

Perceiving Social Categories

Social categorization has long been characterized as a central factor in how observers perceive others. Among all of the possible categories into which an individual might fall, three in particular tend to dominate social perception: sex, race, and age. Categorizing others along these dimensions has been argued to be an efficient cognitive strategy (e.g., Allport, 1954), and it unleashes a cascade of subsequent interpersonal events. Social category knowledge, for example, evokes applicable stereotypes. This can ease person perception by providing rough-and-ready expectations that are specified by the stereotype. Such category-based expectations have been shown to carry profound implications for subsequent interactions and evaluations (Brewer, 1988; Devine, 1989; Fiske & Neuberg, 1990). Because of this widespread importance, such categories have been labeled *master status categories*, and many have argued that categorization of others according to sex, race, and age is an obligatory and automatic process (Bargh, 1999; Brewer, 1988; Devine, 1989; Dovidio, Evans, & Tyler, 1986). Much of this work has measured social categorization indirectly by assessing the activation of category-relevant knowledge structures (i.e., stereotypes) after a target is visually perceived. Though the tendency to perceive social categories may remain strong, some evidence suggests that the activation of category stereotypes may be moderated by experimental manipulations that either change a perceiver's goals or restrict category-relevant visual cues (e.g., Blair, 2002; Gilbert & Hixon, 1991; Kurzban, Tooby, & Cosmides, 2001; Macrae & Bodenhausen, 2000). Such demonstrations of moderation notwithstanding, social categorization retains a central role in person construal. Martin and Macrae (2007) noted, "…it [social categorization] may be the norm rather than the exception during most social interactions (p. 814)." Cues to sex category, in particular, are visually apparent in the face and body and thus appear to be highly likely to elicit compulsory categorization (Martin & Macrae, 2007).

Perhaps it is unsurprising; therefore, that a range of sexually dimorphic body cues support the perception of sex category membership. Body motion is diagnostic of sex category membership, and it is the category that has received the most attention within the perceptual literature. In a collection of studies, James Cutting and colleagues examined the extent to which observers could identify the sex category membership of point-light walkers. In an initial report, Kozlowski & Cutting (1977) found that sex category judgments of point-light walkers exceeded chance responding, even when judgments were based on few points of light. Moreover, observers' accuracy was highly correlated with self-reported confidence, implying a systematic appreciation of sexually dimorphic body motion. Indeed, later work corroborated the supposition that the *production* of biological motion is inextricably tied to the morphological differences among individuals. Because men's and women's bodies differ, not only in absolute, but also in relative proportions, body motion is also likely to vary accordingly (Mather & Murdoch, 1994). This perspective implicated motion as a potentially stable and reliable cue to sex category membership. Indeed, a biomechanical invariant, the *center of moment*, was later established as a sexually dimorphic cue in reality, and a potent determinant of perceptual accuracy (Cutting, Proffitt, & Kozlowski, 1978).

Subsequent research in this area has applied more sophisticated modeling techniques to identify the spatio-temporal parameters that compel observers' accuracy. Work by Cutting and colleagues, for example, identified the temporal boundaries (Barclay, Cutting, & Kozlowski, 1978) and the spatial parameters that affect observers' perception of sex category (Cutting, 1978). Troje (2002) developed a linear classifier that reliably extracts category-diagnostic gait parameters and demonstrated its performance on perception of sex category. Pollick, Kay, Heim, and Stringer (2005) reviewed all previous data on judging sex category and coupled this with modeling the distributions of male and female centers of moment to calculate how efficiently observers use the available structural information to make sex category judgments. These results indicated that although the proportion correct for sex categorization is not typically very high, observers do appear to be very efficient at extracting the relevant information.

Collectively, these data highlight a privileged role of body motion for the perception of at least one social category—biological sex— that has profound interpersonal implications. The extent to which other social categories (e.g., race and age) can be discerned from bio- logical- motion displays has not been explored as extensively. Some evidence suggests, how- ever, that gait may support the identification of both factors. Age-related aspects of gait, for example, lead observers to draw stereotype- consistent inferences about targets (Montepare & Zebrowitz-McArthur, 1988), and this ten- dency is cross-culturally consistent (Montepare & Zebrowitz, 1993). These findings suggest that motion parameters can support age recognition and elicit group-based normative judgments.

Likewise, race category membership may also be conveyed via biological motion. Korean and American women exhibit different walk- ing speeds relative to their male counterparts. Whereas American women appear to compen- sate for shorter stride lengths with an increased walking cadence, Korean women do not and thus walk more slowly than Koren men, sug- gesting that this category distinction might be cued by body motion. Additionally, preliminary evidence suggests that the race categories black and white are apparent in silhouetted images depicting a dynamic human body, again sug- gesting that biological motion may play a role in observers' ability to identify race category membership from a distance (Eberhardt, Goff, Ambady, Toosi, & Choi, 2010).

Perceiving Identities

Many social psychological theories of person perception identify distinct processes for social categorization, described earlier, and the pro- cess of individuation (see Brewer, 1988; Fiske & Neuberg, 1990). Whereas social categorization involves general processes of perception that are theorized to be efficient because of their ability to evoke category-based expectations, individu- ation entails a finer discrimination of a person's unique qualities which, at times, may contra- dict common assumptions about their social category membership. Therefore, individuation is presumed to be a more complex and effort- ful process in social perception. In spite of the effort required for individuation, it remains an

important component of interpersonal inter- actions because it permits people to overcome biased assumptions based on social categoriza- tion alone.

The same basic logic that underscored research on perceiving sex categories from bio- logical motion also led researchers to speculate that individual identities might be specified by unique motion patterns as well. If correct, such patterns should be appreciable in point- light displays. Early studies investigated this possibility by inviting groups of friends to the lab who were each filmed while walking. Researchers transformed the films into point- light displays and showed them to each member of the group with the task of correctly identi- fying the depicted individual. This research found that observers of point-light walkers could identify oneself and others with accuracy that exceeded chance (Cutting & Kozlowski, 1977; see also Beardsworth & Buckner, 1981; Richardson & Johnston, 2005), presumably due to stable individual differences in movement (Troje, Westhoff, & Lavrov, 2005; Westhoff & Troje, 2007). Moreover, confidence and accu- racy were highly correlated. Observers seemed to know what they were doing. Subsequent research established that recognition ability is due both to the perceiver's extensive visual experience with the body motions of close oth- ers (Jacobs, Pinto, & Shiffrar, 2004) and to the perceiver's own prior motor experiences (Loula, Prasad, Harber, & Shiffrar, 2005). Furthermore, exaggerating the spatiotemporal parameters of point-light motion enhanced observer's abil- ity to identify general motion styles (Pollick, Fidopiastis, & Braden, 2001) and to recognize individual identities (Hill & Pollick, 2000).

Perceiving Psychological States

An ability to discern information about another individual's internal state is extremely impor- tant for interpersonal interactions. Of all pos- sible internal states, emotion has long been theorized to be elemental in social perception (Darwin, 1872; Ekman & Friesen, 1975). The ability to discern anger from sadness, for exam- ple, can help one determine whether it would be most appropriate to avoid or approach another person. Misreading such information can be catastrophic. Moreover, though the vast majority of emotion-recognition studies have involved face perception (see chapters in this volume), the distinction between facial and bodily expressions of emotions has long been recognized (e.g., Ekman, 1965) and has received increasing attention in recent years. Moreover, some scholars have suggested that the perception of emotion from the body is more important than other forms of emotion perception because of its informative value. De Gelder (2005), for example, argued for the primacy of body perception in emotion recognition stating, "When we see a bodily expression of emotion, we immediately know what specific action is associated with a particular emotion, leaving little need for interpretation of the signal, as is the case for facial expressions (p. 583)." Put simply, emotion detection is an important perceptual skill, and it may be supported by multiple visual cues.

Like other domains of social relevance, body motion supports accurate emotion perception. In an early demonstration of this, actors were asked to convey various emotional states while being filmed. Later, participants judged the emotional state depicted in the resulting videos of body motions (but not facial expressions). The accuracy of the judgments highlighted a profound sensitivity to perceiving emotional state from body cues (Montepare, Goldstein, & Clausen, 1987). These data provided a glimpse into the influence of body cues for emotion recognition, but they could not fully disentangle the relative impact of body motion and body form or postural information because the full body videos contained both types of information. Indeed, static images of body postures tend to affect emotion processing across domains (e.g., Van den Stock, Righart, & de Gelder, 2007), leaving open the question of how body motion may uniquely serve emotion recognition.

A growing body of evidence suggests that body motion does, in fact, play an important role in the perception of emotion. By decoupling body form from body motion through the use of point-light techniques, researchers isolated the motion associated with distinct emotions and assessed their potency for emotion recognition. Across a variety of motions including both full body (Atkinson, Dittrich, Gemmell, & Young, 2004; Atkinson, Tunstall, & Dittrich, 2007; Chouchourelou, Matsuka, Harber, & Shiffrar, 2007; Dittrich, Troscianko, Lea, & Morgan, 1996) and partial body motions (Pollick, Paterson, Bruderlin, & Sanford, 2001; Sawada, Suda, & Ishii, 2003), observers of point-light displays depicting emotional body motions discern the emotional state of others with surprising accuracy from such sparse displays. This success is due in part to systematic encoding of the distinct emotions with the underlying dynamic motion patterns (Pollick et al., 2001). Some evidence suggests that these perceptual skills are highly tuned to perceive anger or fear in others, arguably due to its importance for one's own physical well-being (Chouchourelou et al., 2007; Dittrich et al., 1996; Walk & Homan, 1984; see also; Grèzes, Pichon, & de Gelder, 2007). Furthermore, such perceptions can occur without conscious intent (de Gelder & Hadjikhani, 2006) and appear to be the product of both kinematic and configural information (Atkinson et al., 2007). Chapter 14 by Shiffrar (this volume) reviews this evidence extensively.

In addition to emotion states, biological motion reveals information about other internal states, such as intention. After viewing a point-light display of an actor lifting a box, for example, observers can estimate the relative weight of the box based solely on the dynamic information specified by the motion (Runeson & Frykholm, 1981). These weight estimates that are based on the passive viewing of point-light displays rival estimates made by participants who had actual physical experience with the box. Observers can also identify a target's deceptive intent in such actions. For example, when actors in point-light displays were asked to appear as though the weight of the box differed from its actual weight, observers accurately perceived this intent to deceive (Runeson & Frykholm, 1983). In other studies, actors were asked to convey a particular social category. Observers of these displays accurately distinguished between sequences in which the actor's goal was to exaggerate their own sex-typical walk pattern and sequences in which the actor's goal was to feign an opposite-sex walk pattern (Runeson & Frykholm, 1983)—the actual sex of the target and the sex-typed walk motion being conveyed—permitting them to ascertain that a target was a man who was walking with feminine motion. Finally, the perception of motion cues can be used as a foundation for future interactions based on the perceptions they engender. Observers of point-light displays are quite adept at evaluating a target's vulnerability to attack based solely on motion cues (Gunns, Johnston, & Hudson, 2002), and people can be trained to alter their gait to convey less vulnerability to others (Johnston, Hudson, Richardson, Gunns, & Garner, 2004).

In sum, the body's dynamic motion provides sufficient information for observers to render judgments about domains that have been and remain central to social psychology. These include the perception of social categories, personal identity, and internal states. With few exceptions, studies in the visual perception of biological motion have focused heavily on the stimulus parameters that give rise to these perceptual ends. As such, they treated the judgment as the final point in their investigations. Social psychologists, in contrast, have tended to begin their investigations with these factors as a starting rather than an ending point, and subsequently explored the downstream consequences thereof. Yet the simple fact remains that person construal occupies the entire spectrum of the perceptual process—from the apprehension of visual cues to the ultimate effects of the judgments and interactions that they affect. Although some scholars have historically treated social judgments as dependent variables, and other scholars have treated social judgments as independent variables, a comprehensive understanding of social perception requires substantial integration of these seemingly different approaches.

COME TOGETHER

Person-perception research conducted by vision and social psychologists has historically shown little overlap, in part due to methodological and theoretical gaps. Yet these gaps are slowly beginning to close due to research conducted at the boundary of social and cognitive science. The Shiffrar Chapter 14 in this volume, for example, reviews neurophysiological evidence highlighting considerable anatomical links between social and visual brain regions. Additionally, she and her colleagues describe behavioral studies in which the perception that a body is in motion depends on social context. Thus, a growing body of boundary-crossing work demonstrates that the visual and social psychologists will continue to come together in meaningful ways.

Though undoubtedly merely two of many (see chapters by de Gelder and Shiffrar), we now turn our attention to ways in which the visual perception of motion might be constrained by social processes. First, the perception of a social category is likely to constrain the way that other cues are interpreted and evaluated. Second, prior expectations are likely to constrain the perception of cues that can bias fundamental social perception.

Categorization Constrains Other Social Judgments

One way that social processes constrain the perception of biological motion is in observers' interpretation of motion cues. Social categorization has been described as a likely, if not inevitable aspect of person construal, and it can be appreciated from a variety of sexually dimorphic cues that appear in the face and body. Though biological motion displays isolate the body's motion, some have argued that observers' ability to discern sex category from such displays is due primarily to the ability to recover structural information about the target's body. The extent to which structural mediation accounts for sex categorization ability in observers of point-light displays remains hotly debated, but the notion that body shape conveys meaningful information to observers is unassailable.

In some ways, this debate is purely theoretical. "In the wild," observers typically perceive body motion combined with its shape. Therefore, body shape need not be *recovered from* body motion but can be perceived

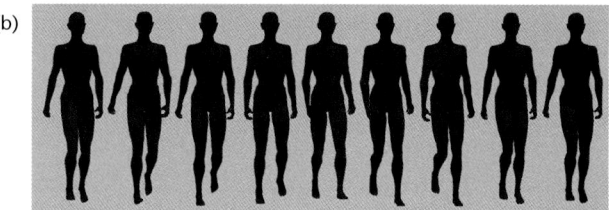

Figure 15.2 Waist-to-Hip Ratio and Walk Motion in Animated Stimuli. (a) Five waist to hip ratios and (b) keyframes from a neutral walk cycle used in Johnson & Tassinary (2005; 2007) and Johnson, Gill, Reichman, & Tassinary (2007).

directly. The question of whether structural or dynamic factors determine social perception changes substantially when observers are viewing full bodies in motion, and modern technology makes it possible to manipulate independently the body shape and motion of computer-generated human animations. Therefore, the direct impact of both structure and motion for social perception can be measured independently.

Johnson and Tassinary (2005) examined the relative importance for body shape and motion. They asked observers to judge the sex category membership of animations that varied orthogonally in two sexually dimorphic cues (see Figure 15.2). Walkers varied statically in body shape (waist-to-hip ratios from 0.5 to 0.9) and dynamically in gait (from a masculine shoulder swagger to a feminine shoulder sway). When this was done, body shape proved to be a more compelling cue to sex category membership; body motion was a potent cue for the perceived degree of masculinity/femininity (Johnson & Tassinary, 2005). A final study in this same set found that sex-category judgments that relied on body motion were the product of inference. Observers first perceived body motion in terms of masculinity/femininity and then inferred the appropriate sex-category label. Moreover, the ability to infer sex category from body shape emerges by age 5 (Johnson, Murphy, & Tassinary, in press).

The primacy of body shape for sex-category judgments has important implications for other social perceptions. Once sex categorization has

occurred, sexually dimorphic body motion is likely to be perceived, not only as masculine or feminine, but also as either gender-typical or gender-atypical, given the perceived sex category of the target. Additionally, sex categorization based on body shape will constrain the expected range of body motions within what is normative for the sex category. Thus, as in other domains (see Biernat & Manis, 1994; Biernat, Manis, & Nelson, 1991), the perception and evaluation of body motion will be highly dependent upon the sex-category judgment that precedes it. Early judgments of sex category from body shape, therefore, constrain both evaluative judgments and related social categorizations that incorporate body motion.

The perception of sex category from a sex diagnostic cue such as body shape, therefore, determines precisely how body motion will be evaluated (e.g., in the perception of attractiveness). Johnson and Tassinary (2007) examined how body shape and motion combined to determine perceived attractiveness. As before, participants viewed computer-generated animations that varied systematically in two sexually dimorphic cues—body shape and body motion. Observers judged the sex, masculinity, femininity, and attractiveness of each walker. Relative to body motion, body shape carried considerably more weight for sex category judgments, again reinforcing it's importance for foundational social categorizations. Once this judgment was made, the perception of masculinity/femininity strongly impacted perceived attractiveness. As seen in Figure 15.3a, when walkers were judged

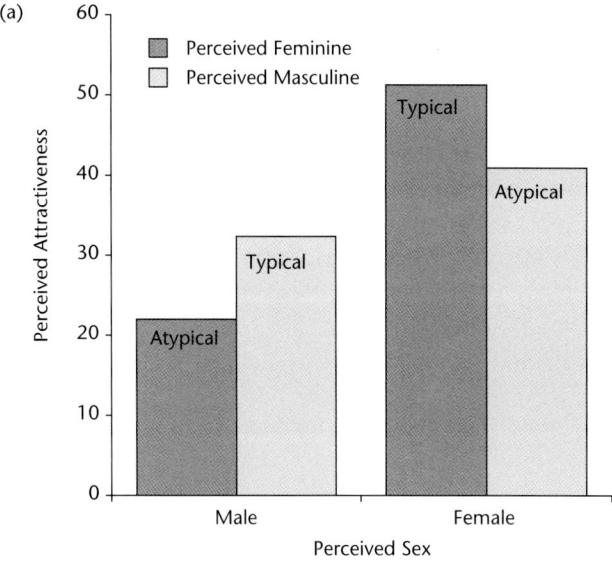

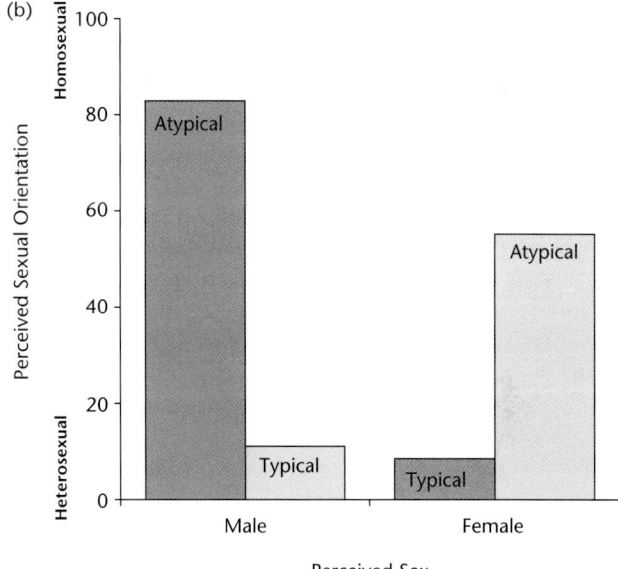

Figure 15.3 Effects of Social Categorization on Evaluative and Categorical Social Judgments. Once sex category judgments were made, body motion affected perceived attractiveness (a) and perceived sexual orientation (b) of men and women differently. Figures adapted from Johnson & Tassinary (2007) and Johnson, Gill, Reichman, & Tassinary, (2007).

to be women, they were deemed more attractive when walking with feminine hip sway; but when walkers were judged to be men, they were deemed more attractive when walking with masculine shoulder swagger. Thus, the perception of sex category determined how body motion was perceived and evaluated.

Importantly, social categorization provides the critical foundation for higher level evaluative judgments. In the case of attractiveness,

for example, there is little reason to expect evaluative judgments to favor either masculine or feminine walk motions. Once such motions become contextualized by the apparent sex of the target, however, the motion is perceived to be not only masculine or feminine, but also typical or atypical for the given sex, and it, therefore, becomes valenced. Although we have focused primarily on mechanisms that affect evaluative judgments through social processes, others have highlighted the critical role that perceptual fluency plays in evaluative judgments of visual patterns (Winkielman, Halberstadt, Fazendeiro, & Catty, 2006).

The contextualized effects of sex category and typicality in walk motion can also constrain the impact of body motion for other social categorizations that are gender relevant, such as perceived sexual orientation. Johnson, Gill, Reichman, and Tassinary (2007) applied the same experimental paradigm just described to determine whether (and how) judgments of sexual orientation relate to body motion. Across three studies, including both animations and real human targets, observers' judgments of sexual orientation reflected the degree of perceived gender atypicality in walk motion. That is, targets judged to be men were perceived to be gay when they moved with a feminine gait, and targets judged to be women were perceived to be gay when they moved with a masculine gait (see Figure 15.3b). These effects were independent of the effects of attractiveness already described.

These basic perceptions of sex and masculinity/femininity that arise from perceiving the dynamic human body can also help us understand some biases against homosexuality (Johnson & Gill, 2010). One may predict, for example, that gender atypicality in gait would be perceived generally to be intentional and flaunting one's sexuality. From this perspective, evaluative judgments of gay men and lesbian women who exhibit gender atypical body motions should be harsh *because of* the perceived intent of the individual to convey their sexuality to observers. Indeed, Johnson & Gill (2010) found that gender atypical body motion among gay men and lesbians was perceived by observers to be intentional, with goal to communicate one's sexual identity to others. Instead, Johnson, Gill, & and Reichman (2008) found that *feminine* motion, whether exhibited by a man or a woman, was perceived by observers to be intentional with a goal to communicate one's sexuality to others. This perceived communicative act was also judged to be untoward. Therefore, harsh social judgments were not the result of perceived gender atypicality or the perception of membership in a stigmatized social category,

per se, but rather a product of perceived communicative intent.

These data shed light on the process by which sex categorization constrains the perception and evaluation of the dynamic human body. Sex categorization is a highly probable, if not inevitable, social judgment that occurs in the earliest stages of person construal. Although undoubtedly supported by multiple physical cues, body shape appears to be a potent determinant of sex category judgments. These judgments set the stage for perceptions of masculinity/femininity, or gender typicality, to affect both evaluative and categorical social judgments. Thus, the perception of biological motion is likely to be constrained by social categorizations that occur early in the perception process.

Stereotyped Knowledge Constrains Social Perception

Another way that social processes constrain the perception of biological motion is through the use of stereotypes. The vast majority of work examining the relation between categorization and stereotypes has presumed a particular directional arrow. Following the lead of Allport (1954), prior work examined the role that categorization plays in unleashing the deleterious effects of stereotypes on judgments, attitudes, and expectations (Brewer, 1988; Devine, 1989; Fiske & Neuberg, 1990). The central argument in much of this work rested in the assumption that stereotypes, even when not personally endorsed, are widely known nevertheless. That knowledge, once activated by perceiving a social category, was argued to be sufficient to trigger stereotype-based behavior and judgments (Bargh, 1999). Because cues to social categories (not necessarily the perception of the category, per se) may set such effects in motion (Martin & Macrae, 2007), understanding the cues from both face and body that support those categorizations was and continues to be important. Yet we propose that the opposite directional arrow is also important, and is another way in which social processes constrain visual perception, especially in the perception of emotion from biological motion.

Sex stereotypes are arguably the most pervasive stereotypes for social categories. The distinction between the sexes has a powerful impact from birth on, and biological sex becomes the first meaningful social category that young children learn (see Ruble, Martin, & Berenbaum, 2006, for a review). Expectations for gender-normative behavior are pervasive by early childhood, and violations of such expectations receive harsh social penalties from childhood on (Fagot, 1977; Fagot & Hagan, 1991; Fagot, Leinbach, & O'Boyle, 1992; Martin, 1990; Sandnabba & Ahlberg, 1999).

One facet of sex-based stereotypes involves the experience and expression of emotion. In one early study, participants made judgments about an infant who was crying (Condry & Condry, 1976). When the infant was described as male, "his" crying was perceived to be due to anger; when the infant was described as female, "her" crying was perceived to be due to sadness. This basic demonstration reflects what has been found more generally, lay theories lead people to assume that, relative to men, women feel and express emotions more intensely (Grossman & Wood, 1993; Hess, Blairy, & Kleck, 1997; Fisher, 1993; Johnson & Schulman, 1988; Plant, Hyde, Keltner, & Devine, 2000; Plant, Kling, & Smith, 2004). The experience and expression of anger and pride, however, prove to be exceptions to this general sex-typed lay theory (Plant et al., 2000). Men are presumed to both feel and express these emotions more than women. Judgments of facial expressions tend to reflect these gender-based assumptions (Grossman & Wood, 1993), and such judgments are also underscored by phenotypic confounding between men's faces and an anger expression (Becker, Kenrick, Neuberg, Blackwell, & Smith, 2007) and physical markers of dominance (Hess, Adams, & Kleck, 2007). Though a theoretical debate persists concerning whether stereotypes or phenotypes better explain observed differences in perceptions of expressiveness for men's and women's displays of anger, sadness, and happiness, the existence of gender stereotypes for emotional displays are widespread (Plant et al., 2000).

We have argued elsewhere (Johnson, McKay, & Pollick, 2010) that although the effect of stereotypes on the perception of facial expressions may be debatable, their effect on the perception of biological motion displays is more straightforward. We reasoned that gender stereotypes for emotional displays, specifically for sadness and anger, might bias observers' ability to discern the sex category membership from motion cues.

We tested this idea in a series of studies that examined how gender-stereotyped emotions affect observers' perceptions of sex-category membership. Actors were filmed throwing a ball in different emotional states while the three-dimensional coordinates of their bodies were recorded (Ma, Paterson, & Pollick, 2006). Specifically, their shoulder, elbow, wrist, and hand coordinates were used to generate point-light displays for each throw. Using these coordinates, we generated point-light displays for each throw. Later, naïve observers judged each point-light display for sex-category membership. Our results stood in stark contrast to prior findings that suggested that sex category membership can be discerned from biological motion displays. Instead of demonstrating a high degree of decoding competence, our observers' judgments hovered near chance. We examined the pattern of accuracy by both sex and emotion categories. When broken down in this way, an intriguing pattern was evident. As seen in Figure 15.4, displays depicting angry throws were overwhelmingly judged to be men, and displays depicting sad throws were overwhelmingly judged to be women. In both cases, observers' confidence was remarkably high —in spite of the fact that approximately half of their judgments yielded errors.

As in face-perception studies, the possibility that the categories male and angry and the categories female and sad bear kinematic similarity cannot be ignored. The nature of our stimuli (point-light displays generated via motion capture) enabled us to remove the most likely parameter that may exhibit such confounding. Specifically, we equated all throws for velocity, a cue that varies reliably with both the sex and emotion of thrower. These studies replicated the prior effects, thus ruling out the possibility that

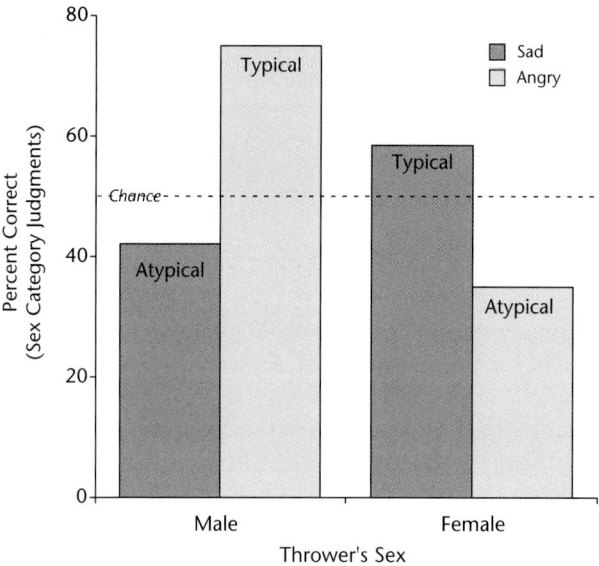

Figure 15.4 Accuracy of Sex Category Judgments from Emotional Arm Movements. Participants' judgments of sex category varied greatly for judgments of sex-typed emotional displays, specifically anger and sadness. Data depicted here represent a portion of those reported in Johnson, McKay, & Pollick (2010).

variation in average velocity across the emotions biased judgments due to analogous sex differences in velocity. Instead, perceived sex was highly dependent on the perceived emotion of the display. When observers perceived a throw to be angry, they also judged the actor to be a man; when observers perceived a throw to be sad, they also judged the actor to be a woman. This pattern of perceptions impacted accuracy (see Figure 15.4).

This pattern of results is consistent with a stereotype, but not a cue overlap, interpretation. Observers perceived the emotion depicted in a point-light throw, and this affected other judgments as well. Because the emotions of sadness and anger correspond to sex-typed lay theories, observers used prior knowledge structures—sex stereotypes for emotion—to help disambiguate the sex of point-light throwing displays. Thus, angry throws were judged to be men, and sad throws were judged to be women due to stereotyped expectations. In sum, the findings from this set of studies highlight an important way in which a traditionally social process, the use of stereotypes, can bias the visual perception of biological motion.

CONCLUSION

Rudyard Kipling famously lamented about the East and the West, questioning whether "Never the twain shall meet." For decades, a similar charge could have been levied to describe the gulf that separated person perception research conducted by vision scholars and social psychologists. We hope that this chapter, and the work described in it, convinces readers that the visual perception of biological motion is indeed a social process and that interdisciplinary work is beginning to realize this potential. Kipling ended his poem with optimistic speculation about what could emerge when "two strong men (or women!) stand face to face." Similarly, we end our chapter with optimism about the future of a social-vision approach to the study of biological motion. It is indeed backed by the strength of many.

ACKNOWLEDGMENTS

Section titles *Something* and *Come Together* are from the Beatles album, *Abbey Road* (1969). Part of the research described in this chapter was supported the ESRC and the EPSRC, both awarded to Frank Pollick.

REFERENCES

Allport, G. (1954). *The nature of prejudice.* Reading, MA: Addison-Wesley.

Atkinson, A.P., Dittrich, W.H., Gemmell, A.J., & Young, A.W. (2004). Emotion perception from dynamic and static body expressions in point-light and full-light displays. *Perception, 33,* 717–746.

Atkinson, A.P., Tunstall, M.L., & Dittrich, W.H. (2007). Evidence for distinct contributions of form and motion information to the recognition of emotions from body gestures. *Cognition, 104,* 59–72.

Barclay, C.D., Cutting, J.E., & Kozlowski, L.T. (1978). Temporal and spatial factors in gait perception that influence gender recognition. *Perception and Psychophysics, 23,* 145– 152.

Bargh, J.A. (1999). The cognitive monster: The case against controllability of automatic stereotype effects. In S. Chaiken and Y. Trope (Eds.), *Dual process theories in social psychology.* New York: Guilford Press.

Becker, D.V., Kenrick, D.T., Neuberg, S.L, Blackwell, K.C., & Smith, D.M. (2007). The confounded nature of angry men and happy women. *Journal of Personality and Social Psychology, 92,* 179–190.

Beardsworth, T., & Buckner, T. (1981). The ability to recognize oneself from a video recording of one's movements without seeing one's body. *Bulletin of the Psychonomic Society, 18,* 19–22.

Biernat, M., & Manis, M. (1994). Shifting standards and stereotype-based judgments. *Journal of Personality and Social Psychology, 66,* 5–20.

Biernat, M., Manis, M., & Nelson, T.E. (1991). Stereotypes and standards of judgment. *Journal of Personality and Social Psychology, 60,* 485–499.

Blair, I.V. (2002). The malleability of automatic stereotypes and prejudice. *Personality and Social Psychology Bulletin, 6,* 242–261.

Brewer, M.B. (1988). A dual process model of impression formation. In T.K. Srull & R.S. Wyer (Eds.) *Advances in Social Cognition* (Vol 1, pp. 1–36). Hillsdale, NJ: Erlbaum.

Chouchourelou, A., Matsuka, T., Harber, K., & Shiffrar, M. (2007). The visual analysis of emotional actions. *Social Neuroscience, 1,* 63–74.

Condry, J., & Condry, S. (1976). Sex differences: A study of the eye of the beholder. *Child Development, 47,* 812–819.

Cutting, J.E. (1978). A program to generate synthetic walkers as dynamic point-light displays. *Behavior Research Methods & Instrumentation, 10,* 91–94.

Cutting, J.E., & Kozlowski, L.T. (1977). Recognizing friends by their walk: Gait perception without familiarity cues. *Bulletin of the Psychonomic Society, 9,* 353–356.

Cutting, J.E., Proffitt, D.R., & Kozlowski, L.T. (1978). A biomechanical invariant for gait perception. *Journal of Experimental Psychology: Human Perception and Performance, 4,* 357–372.

Darwin, C. (1872). *The expression of the emotions in man and animals.* London: John Murray.

De Gelder, B. (2005). Toward a neurobiology of emotional body language. *Nature Reviews Neuroscience, 7,* 242–249.

De Gelder, B., & Hadjikhani, N. (2006). Nonconscious recognition of emotional body language. *NeuroReport, 17,* 583–586.

Devine, P. (1989). Stereotypes and prejudice: Their automatic and controlled components. *Journal of Personality and Social Psychology, 56,* 5–18.

Dittrich, W.H., Troscianko, T., Lea, S.E.G., & Morgan, D. (1996). Perception of emotion from dynamic point light displays represented in dance. *Perception, 25,* 727–738.

Dovidio, J.F., Evans, N., & Tyler, R.B. (1986). Racial stereotypes: The contents of their cognitive representations. *Journal of Experimental Social Psychology, 22,* 22–37.

Eberhardt, J.L., Goff, P.A., Ambady, N., Toosi, N., & Choi, S. (2010). Race in motion: Perceived body movement cues racial identity and threat. *Manuscript in preparation.*

Ekman, P. (1965). Differential communication of affect by head and body cues. *Journal of Personality and Social Psychology, 2,* 726–735.

Ekman, P., & Friesen, W.V. (1975). *Unmasking the Face.* Englewood Cliffs, NJ: Prentice-Hall.

Fagot, B. I. (1977). Consequences of moderate cross-gender behavior in preschool children. *Child Development, 48,* 902–907.

Fagot, B. I., & Hagan, R. (1991). Observations of parent reactions to sex-stereotyped behaviors: Age and sex effects. *Child Development, 62,* 617–628.

Fagot, B. I., Leinbach, M. D., & O'Boyle, C. (1992). Gender labeling, gender stereotyping, and parenting behaviors. *Developmental Psychology, 28,* 225–230.

Fisher, A.H. (1993). Sex differences in emotionality: Fact or stereotype? *Feminism & Psychology, 3,* 303–318.

Fiske, S.T., & Neuberg, S.L. (1990). A continuum of impression formation from category-based to individuating processes: Influences of information and motivation on attention and interpretation. In M. Zanna (Ed.), *Advances in experimental social psychology* (Vol. 23, pp. 1–74). New York: Academic Press.

Gilbert, D.T., & Hixon, J.G. (1991). The trouble of thinking: Activation and application of stereotypic beliefs. *Journal of Personality and Social Psychology, 60,* 509–517.

Grèzes, J., Pichon, S., & de Gelder, B. (2007). Perceiving fear in dynamic body expressions. *Neuroimage, 35,* 959–967.

Grossman, M., & Wood, W. (1993). Sex differences in intensity of emotional experience: A social role interpretation. *Journal of Personality and Social Psychology, 65,* 1010–1022

Gunns, R.E., Johnston, L., & Hudson, S.M. (2002). Victim selection and kinematics: A point-light investigation of vulnerability to attack. *Journal of Nonverbal Behavior, 26,* 129–158.

Hess, U., Adams, R., & Kleck, R. E. (2007). Who may frown and who should smile? Dominance, affiliation, and the display of happiness and anger. *Cognition & Emotion, 19,* 515–536.

Hess, U., Blairy, S., & Kleck, R. E. (1997). The intensity of emotional facial expressions and decoding accuracy. *Journal of Nonverbal Behavior, 21,* 241–257.

Hill, H., & Pollick, F.E. (2000). Exaggerating temporal differences enhances recognition of individuals from point light displays, *Psychological Science, 11,* 223–228.

Jacobs, A., Pinto, J., & Shiffrar, M. (2004). Frequency, context, and human motion perception. *Journal of Vision, 2,* 338.

Johansson, G. (1973). Visual perception of biological motion and a model for its analysis. *Perception and Psychophysics, 14,* 201–211.

Johansson, G. (1975). Visual motion perception. *Scientific American, 232,* 76–89.

Johansson, G. (1976). Spatio-temporal differentiation and integration in visual motion perception. *Psychological Research, 38,* 379–393.

Johnson, K.L., & Gill, S. (2010). The role of gender atypical body motion in perceptions of others' intent to communicate sexuality. Manuscript submitted for publication.

Johnson, K.L., Gill, S., Reichman, V., & Tassinary, L.G. (2007). Swagger, sway, and sexuality:

Judging sexual orientation from body motion and morphology. *Journal of Personality and Social Psychology, 93,* 321–334.

Johnson, K.L., McKay, L., & Pollick, F. (2010). *He throws like a girl (but only when he's sad): Gender stereotypes affect the perception of biological motion displays.* Manuscript submitted for publication, *University of California, Los Angeles.*

Johnson, K.L., Murphy, L.L., & Tassinary, L.G. (in press). Sex categorization among preschool children: Increasing sensitivity to sexually dimorphic cues. *Child Development.*

Johnson, J. T., & Schulman, G. A. (1988). More alike than meets the eye: Perceived gender differences in subjective experience and its display. *Sex Roles, 19,* 67–79.

Johnson, K.L., & Tassinary, L.G. (2005). Perceiving sex directly and indirectly: Meaning in motion and morphology. *Psychological Science, 16,* 890–897.

Johnson, K.L., & Tassinary, L.G. (2007). Compatibility of basic social perceptions determines perceived attractiveness. *Proceedings of the National Academy of Sciences, USA, 104,* 5246–5251.

Johnston, L., Hudson, S.M., Richardson, M.J., Gunns, R.E., & Garner, M. (2004). Changing kinematics as a means of reducing vulnerability to physical attack. *Journal of Applied Social Psychology, 34,* 514–537.

Kozlowski, L.T., & Cutting, J.E. (1977). Recognizing the sex of a walker from a dynamic point-light display. *Perception and Psychophysics, 21,* 575–580.

Kurzban, R., Tooby, J., & Cosmides, L. (2001). Can race be erased? Coalitional computation and social categorization. *Proceedings of the National Academy of Sciences, USA, 98,* 15387–15392.

Loula, F., Prasad, S., Harber, K., & Shiffrar, M. (2005). Recognizing people from their movement. *Journal of Experimental Psychology: Human Perception and Performance, 31,* 210–220.

Ma, Y., Paterson, E., & Pollick, F.E. (2006). A motion-capture library for the study of indentity, gender, and emotion perception from biological motion. *Behavior Research Methods, 38,* 134–141.

Macrae, C.N., & Bodenhausen, G.V. (2000). Social cognition: Thinking categorically about others. *Annual Review of Psychology, 51,* 93–120.

Martin, C.L. (1990). Attitudes and expectations about children with nontraditional and traditional gender roles. *Sex Roles, 22,* 151–166.

Martin, D., & Macrae, C.N. (2007). A face with a cue: Exploring the inevitability of person categorization. *European Journal of Social Psychology, 37,* 806–816.

Mather, G., & Murdoch, L. (1994). Gender discrimination in biological motion displays based on dynamic cues. *Proceedings of the Royal Society of London: Biological Sciences, 258,* 273–279.

Montepare, J.M., Goldstein, S.B., & Clausen, A. (1987). The identification of emotions from gait information. *Journal of Nonverbal Behaviour, 11,* 33–42.

Montepare, J.M., & Zebrowitz, L.A. (1993). A cross-cultural comparison of impressions created by age-related variations in gait. *Journal of Nonverbal Behaviour, 17,* 55– 68.

Montepare, J.M., & Zebrowitz-McArthur, L. (1988). Impressions of people created by age-related qualities of their gaits. *Journal of Personality and Social Psychology, 55,* 547–556.

Plant, E. A., Hyde, J. S., Keltner, D., & Devine, P. G. (2000). The gender stereotyping of emotion. *Psychology of Women Quarterly, 24,* 81–92.

Plant, E. A., Kling, K. C., & Smith, G. L. (2004). The influence of gender and social role on the interpretation of facial expressions. *Sex Roles, 51,* 187–196.

Pollick, F.E., Fidopiastis, C., & Braden, V. (2001). Recognising the style of spatially exaggerated tennis serves. *Perception, 30,* 323–338.

Pollick, F.E., Kay, J., Heim, K., & Stringer, R. (2005). Gender recognition from point-light walkers. *Journal of Experimental Psychology: Human Perception and Performance, 31,* 1247–1265.

Pollick, F.E., Paterson, H.M., Bruderlin, A., & Sanford, A.J. (2001). Perceiving affect from arm movement. *Cognition, 82,* B51–B61.

Richardson, M.J., & Johnston, L. (2005). Person recognition from dynamic events: The kinematic specification of individual identity in walking style. *Journal of Nonverbal Behavior, 29,* 25–44.

Ruble, D. N., Martin, C. L., & Berenbaum, S. A. (2006). Gender development. In W. Damon (Ed.), *Handbook of child psychology* (6th Edition, Vol. 3, pp. 858–932). New York: J. Wiley.

Runeson, S., & Frykholm, G. (1981). Visual perception of lifted weight. *Journal of Experimental Psychology: Human Perception and Performance, 7,* 733–740.

Runeson, S., & Frykholm, G. (1983). Kinematic specification of dynamics as an informational basis for person-and-action perception: Expectation, gender recognition, and deceptive intention. *Journal of Experimental Psychology: General, 112,* 585–615.

Sawada, M., Suda, K., & Ishii, M. (2003). Expression of emotions in dance: Relation between arm movement characteristics and emotion. *Perceptual and Motor Skills, 97,* 697–708.

Sandnabba, N. K., & Ahlberg, C. (1999). Parents' attitudes and expectations about children's cross-gender behavior. *Sex Roles, 40,* 249–263.

Troje, N.F. (2002). Decomposing biological motion: A framework for analysis and synthesis of human gait patterns. *Journal of Vision, 2,* 371–387.

Troje, N.F., Westhoff, C., & Lavrov, M. (2005). Person identification from biological motion: Effects of structural and kinematic cues. *Perception and Psychophysics, 67,* 667–675.

Van den Stock, J., Righart, R., & de Gelder, B. (2007). Body expressions influence recognition of emotions in the face and voice. *Emotion, 7,* 487–494.

Walk, R.D., & Homan, C.P. (1984). Emotion and dance in dynamic light displays. *Bulletin of the Psychonomic Society, 22,* 437–440.

Westhoff, C., & Troje, N.F. (2007). Kinematic cues for person identification from biological motion. *Perception and Psychophysics, 69,* 241–253.

Winkielman, P., Halberstadt, J., Fazendeiro, T., & Catty, S. (2006). Prototypes are attractive because they are easy on the mind. *Psychological Science, 17,* 799–806.

CHAPTER 16

Social Color Vision

Mark A. Changizi and Shinsuke Shimojo

INTRODUCTION

In psychophysics-oriented, nonevolutionary vision circles, the function of color vision is often implicitly assumed to provide perceptions representative of the surface reflectances of objects in one's environment. Although our color vision can be used as a general-purpose spectrometer, it is a poor-man's spectrometer, selectively measuring wavelengths of light at only three parts of the spectrum. Within evolutionary circles, on the other hand, color vision has been thought to be about foraging for fruit or leaves (Allen 1879; Mollon 1989; Lucas et al. 2003; Osorio & Vorobyev 1996; Regan et al. 2001; Surridge & Mundy 2002). These antiseptic roles for color vision may be missing out on one of its main functions...a *social* function. Recent research suggests that one of the central selection pressures for trichromatic color vision in primates concerns the perception of the emotional and physiological states of others. Here we review evidence supporting this hypothesis, and take up some of its implications.

COLOR ACCENT

If chameleons wore clothes, it wouldn't be surprising to find that they preferred colorful clothing. Chameleons engage in color signaling, and they could perhaps choose clothing colors that help indicate their mood. But why do *we* wear colored clothing? Our skin tends to

be dull and uncolored, and yet our clothing is not (Figure 16.1). The short answer is, of course, that our skin *does* change color. We blush with embarrassment (e.g., Crozier, 2006), redden with anger, yellow or whiten with fear, go green with sickness, and become purplish with muscular effort (Darwin, 1899). Crying changes the color of our skin, as does sexual excitement. And these are almost certainly color *signals*, not simply inexorable physiological side effects of our emotions; for example, there is evidence that when we blush, the cheek facing other individuals blushes more than the unseen cheek (Drummond, 2004).

Why, though, is our own skin often so dull and uncolorful, and so difficult to describe? Caucasions may use *peach* and *tan,* but will admit they aren't quite right; and the same is the case for *chocolate* or *brown* as used by those of African descent. We tend to think the *other* skin colors are categorizably colorful (e.g., skin that is *red, white, black, yellow, brown*), but not our own. Human skin colors, in fact, fall in a region of color space that is the most difficult to describe with the eleven basic color terms (black, gray, white, blue, green, yellow, orange, red, pink, purple, brown). Robert Boynton found that nearly every part of color space is close to one of these color terms, except for a conspicuous hole in color space where none of these apply well (Boynton & Olson 1987, Boynton 1997). For the most uncategorizable

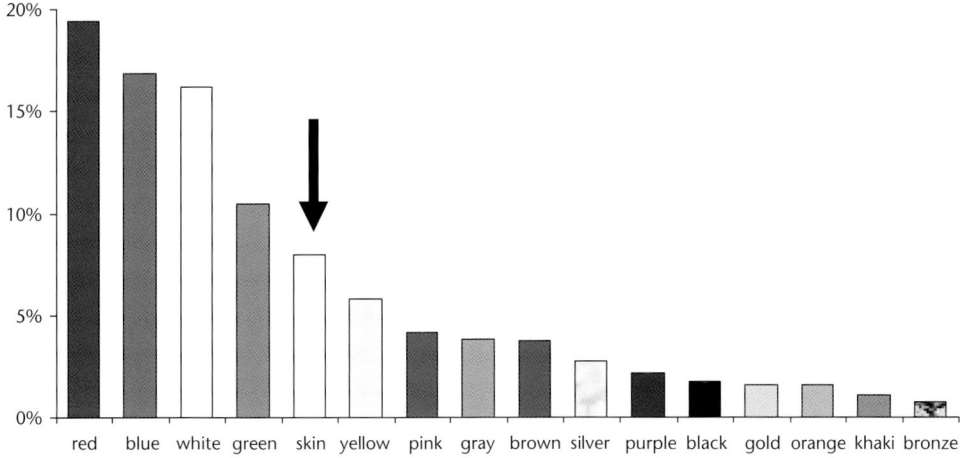

Figure 16.1 Proportions of colors measured from 1,813 pieces of clothing from Racinet (1987). The arrow points to the data point for broadly skin-toned clothes.

color in this hole, among 18 people asked to name its color, 5 responded with *peach,* 4 with *tan,* 3 with *brown,* 3 with *salmon,* 2 used *orange,* and 1 person called it *pink.* Why should this be? Skin is on one of the most important objects in our lives (when looking at other people, and especially their faces), and yet it is one of the few things that is so hard to color name! It was in pondering over the strange uncategorizable nature of our skin color that the hypothesis that color vision may be for seeing skin color modulations was motivated.

A great way to understand the uncolorfulness of our skin is by considering, as an analogy, our perception of the accent of the voiced speech of others. Notice that each of us tends to think we have no accent. Our own accent does not sound accented at all. Other accents (e.g., English, Irish, New York, Boston, Texas), however, sound categorizably accented. There is a good reason for our perception to be like this, and it is connected to the fact that greater categorizability tends to mean lower discriminability (Honig & Urcuioli, 1981; Kalish, 1958). Intuitively, this is because to categorize is to gloss over differences, and so having our own accent be perceptually nonaccented to ourselves aids us in discriminating the voice variations that occur around the baseline accent of those around us, especially variations due to

emotional overtones. That is, when a perceptual system is designed to be highly sensitive to discriminations in one stimulus regime—in this case baseline accent—then one expects a lack of perceptual quality in that regime, but expects stimuli outside of that regime to fall into a perceptual category. This is not only true for accent, but for nearly every sensory modality undergoing adaptation of some kind. The temperature of your own skin, for example, does not feel hot (or cold) to you, but another person's skin will feel hot even if it is only one degree Fahrenheit warmer. You don't taste your own saliva, but more easily taste others. Your nose and body doesn't smell like anything to you, but it definitely does to others. And so on.

In this light, the uncolorful and uncategorizable nature of our skin—and the categorizably colorful nature of the skin of those of different color—is just what we'd expect if our perception of color was organized to be maximally sensitive to spectral changes around the baseline skin color of those around us. That was the original motivation for supposing that color vision may be intrinsically about emotion, because, presumably, our greater sensitivity to skin spectral changes is in order to gather information about the emotion or state of others. That is, it suggested that perhaps color vision is intrinsically a socio-emotional perception.

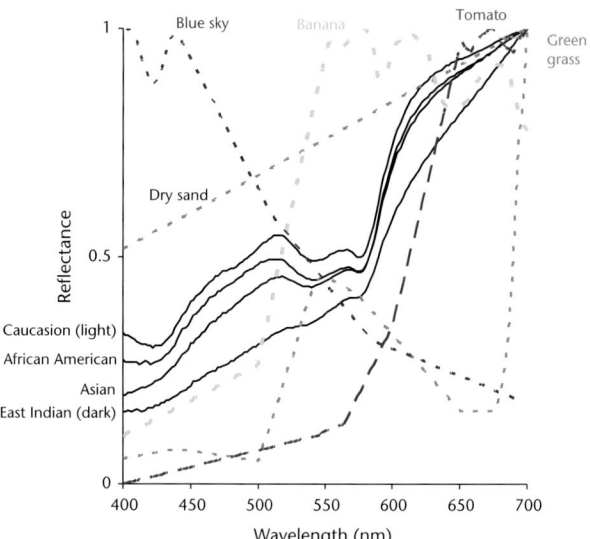

Figure 16.2 Reflectance spectra from a variety of human skin (data from North Carolina State University [NCSU] spectral database). Notice how similar they are, compared to a variety of other spectra.

As just discussed, the need to be more sensitive to skin spectral changes around the baseline skin color of one's community leads one to seeing baseline skin as uncolorful, but seeing other skin colors as colorful. This probably contributes to prejudice against other ethnicities, for it engenders (1) the illusion that one's own ethnicity is not colorful but others are, (2) the illusion that one's own skin color is vastly different from that of other ethnicities ("they *must* be different, because one is colorful and the other is not") even though their spectra are not so different (see Figure 16.2), and (3) the illusion that one's own ethnicity consists of a wider variety of skin colors than that of other ethnicities ("they're all alike").

It also leads to a fourth illusion, that whereas one can see the color signs of emotions on the face of others of one's own ethnicity, one cannot as well see these color signs on the faces of other ethnicities (which might suggest to one that other ethnicities don't have the same feelings as one's own ethnicity). This last illusion probably underlies why many who hear about this new hypothesis for color vision ask whether skin spectral changes are visible on humans with the darkest skin—and color signals *are* visible even on dark skinned people, as has been observed long ago by Darwin and his informants, many

of whom were even "color handicapped" by the previously mentioned illusion because their own baseline skin color differed from that of the darker-skinned population.

Skin-color changes that occur with mood, then, appear to be visible on all humans, especially to those accustomed to the same baseline skin color. As we will see next, the important determinant of these color modulations is invariant across people—and primates—namely, our shared blood and physiology.

BLOOD IN THE EYE

When our skin changes color, it is due to modulations of our blood. Modulating the oxygen saturation of the blood in the skin changes color along a red-green axis (more oxygenated is more red), and modulating the concentration of blood in the skin changes color along a blue-yellow axis (more concentrated is more blue). See Figure 16.3. Something amazing follows from this: because every hue is a combination of these two opponent axes (red-green and yellow-blue), it follows that our skin can, in principle, take on any hue at all. For example, skin with underlying veins has deoxygenated, high-concentration blood, and so is greenish-blue. And skin with a greater volume of oxygenated

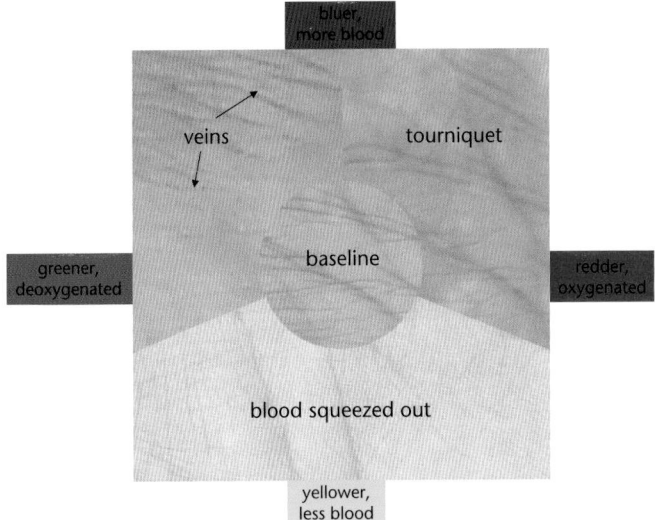

Figure 16.3 Photographs of skin helping to illustrate skin-color changes from baseline as a function of hemoglobin oxygenation and concentration. Skin with underlying veins is deoxygenated and has high concentration (upper left), whereas applying a tourniquet to the skin leads to an accumulation of relatively oxygenated blood (upper right). Each of these is bluish (because of the high concentration), but the former has a greenish component (and so green-blue veins) and the latter a reddish (so reddish-blue, or purple), so that the difference between these two skin colors is a along a red-green axis. Skin with blood pushed out (bottom) is yellowish, whereas the other two skin samples (upper left and right) are blueish, meaning that the difference between the top skin samples and the bottom one is along a yellow-blue axis.

blood will be purple. Not only can our skin in principle obtain every hue in the color circle, but it can also return to uncolorful baseline skin color—it can turn off.

Our primate skin and blood are not fundamentally different from that found among mammals generally; all but some of us primates are color blind, having only two cones, and seeing only color modulations along a yellow-blue axis. So it is mysterious why the two major dimensions of skin reflectance modulation (oxygenation and concentration) should map so well onto the two opponent dimensions of color. That is, why should phylogenetically ancient mammalian skin happen to be capable of eliciting any hue (and also capable of returning to baseline uncolorfulness) for trichromatic primate observers?

The answer is that our skin didn't evolve to be colorful, but, instead, our eyes evolved to have a kind of color vision, turning run-of-the-mill mammalian skin into a full color monitor.

The source of our color-signaling power is in the eye, not in the skin. In fact, our cone sensitivities have to be *just so* in order to make this work, in large part because the spectral modulations due to oxygenation changes are highly subtle. Figure 16.4 shows a generic reflectance distribution for baseline skin, and notice the W-shaped feature centered at around 550 nm. This feature is due to the presence of oxygenated hemoglobin, and it turns into a U shape when hemoglobin becomes deoxygenated. Note also in Figure 16.4 the maximal wavelength sensitivities of our three cones, and specifically at how the middle- and long-wavelength sensitive cones (M and L) are at the left-trough and center-peak of the W, respectively.

Figure 16.5 shows the spectrum of skin for four modulations around baseline, namely, as oxygenation is raised and lowered, and as hemoglobin concentration under the skin is raised and lowered. (The spectra in this figure are after having been filtered by the eye.)

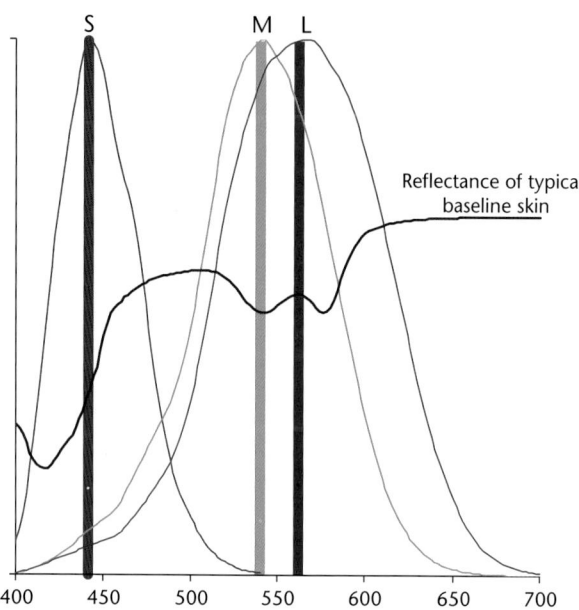

Figure 16.4 The wavelength sensitivities of our three-color cone types, S, M, and L. One can see that M and L have very similar sensitivities (maximum sensitivies are about 535 nm and 562 nm. Also shown is a model spectrum from human skin. A characteristic feature of skin is the W feature at about 550 nm, and note how the left trough of the W and the peak of the W are near the maximum sensitivities of the M and L cones, respectively. The W feature is due to hemoglobin in the skin, and having the M and L cone sensitivities where they are is what gives us our empath power. (This reflectance spectrum, and those in Figures 5 and 6, are obtained via a model of Zonios et al., 2001.)

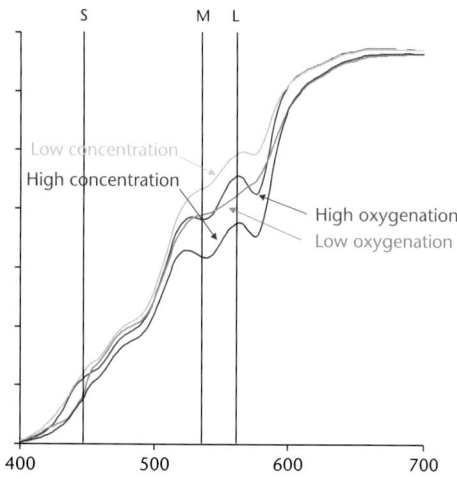

Figure 16.5 The spectrum of skin as seen by the retina (i.e., after having been filtered by the eye) varies depending on the underlying blood. The blue and yellow plots show skin when blood (hemoglobin) concentration is high and low, respectively. One can see that greater blood concentration lowers the W region, and lower concentration raises it. The red and green plots show skin when blood oxygenation is high and low, respectively. One can see that the only region of the spectrum that varies is the W region. By computing the difference between the activation of L and M it is possible to sense the oxygenation of the blood; and note that the overall height of the W region doesn't much change as oxygenation changes, meaning there will be relatively little yellow-blue changes with oxygenation. By computing the average of M and L and comparing this average to the activation of the S cone, our brain can determine the concentration of blood in the skin.

First, consider how the spectrum varies with oxygenation modulations. There is very little change in the spectrum of skin in these two cases, and the most salient change occurs in the W region, which, as was already mentioned, becomes obliterated when blood deoxygenates. Being sensitive to oxygenation modulation requires having two cones in this part of the spectrum that can sense this modulation, and one can see that having M and L with these maximal sensitivities serves this purpose well (see also Changizi, Zhang, & Shimojo, 2006 and Changizi, 2009). Furthermore, the pair of M and L cones together act as a single M/L average to be compared with the activation of the S cone for the yellow-blue channel, just as was the case for our nontrichromatic mammalian ancestors. Thus, the new cone type in trichromatic primates was presumably constrained to be near that of the single ancestral M/L cone, which was maximally sensitive at 543 nm (Surridge, Osorio, & Mundy, 2003). And, preferably, the sensitivities of the M and L cones would straddle the ancestral value. And, indeed, this is the case. That is, the maximal wavelength sensitivities of M and L are not only able to sense oxygenation changes, but they do so while straddling and staying close to the ancestral M/L cone sensitivity (namely, to have maximal sensitivites for M and L of, respectively, about 535 nm and 560 nm) (Jacobs & Deegan 1999). Our M and L wavelength sensitivities appear, then, to be optimized for seeing oxygenation changes in hemoglobin, and we find the same wavelength sensitivities across all primates with routine trichromacy. *That's* why our M and L cone sensitivities are so similar to one another, something sometimes referred to as a case of poor design.

Furthermore, the resultant M and L sensitivities together, when contrasted with that of the S cone, allow near-optimal sensitivity to the concentration of hemoglobin under the skin. One can see this in Figure 16.5, where the entire W region raises and lowers with modulations in hemoglobin concentration, so that more blood leads to bluer skin, less blood leads to yellow (as we saw earlier in Figure 16.3). That is, greater and lower oxygenation leads to modulations in the relative activation of L and M, which is why these modulations lead to red-green modulations; and greater and lower hemoglobin concentration leads to modulations in the relative activation of S and M/L, which is why these modulations lead to blue-yellow modulations. Figure 16.6 shows the same four skin spectra from Figure 16.5, but now places them in the hue circle.

With an appreciation of the tight link between color, emotion, skin, and blood, the associations that colors are imbued with become less enigmatic. Why should red have an emotional association? Perhaps because one *literally looks red* when having that emotion.

For example, Internet forums sometimes utilize colorful faces (emoticons) to help writers better express their emotion. Figure 16.7a shows the frequency distribution of blue, green, yellow, and red faces, for happy, sad, sick, and angry emotional states. Relative to happy faces, sad faces tend to be bluer, sick faces greener, and angry faces redder (Figure 16.7b). Color terms in the English language have a tendency to have meanings related to emotion, skin, and blood. For example, the meaning of *red* in the *Oxford English Dictionary* mentions blood and skin, such as "of the cheeks (or complexion) and lips (as a natural healthy colour)," and "of the face, or of persons in respect of it: Temporarily suffused with blood, esp. as the result of some sudden feeling or emotion; flushed or blushing with (anger, shame, etc.); esp. in phr. red face, a sign of embarrassment or shame." *Blue* has meanings in English such as, "livid, leaden-coloured, as the skin becomes after a blow, from severe cold, from alarm, etc." One of the definitions of purple is, "of this colour as being the hue of mourning." The meaning of *green* even includes, "of the complexion (often green and wan, green and pale): Having a pale, sickly, or bilious hue, indicative of fear, jealousy, ill-humour, or sickness." The definition of *yellow* includes, "craven, cowardly." See Figure 16.8. And, more generally, colors appear to have strong cross-cultural associations with emotions (Osgood, 1960). Figure 16.9 helps organize some of the stronger associations.

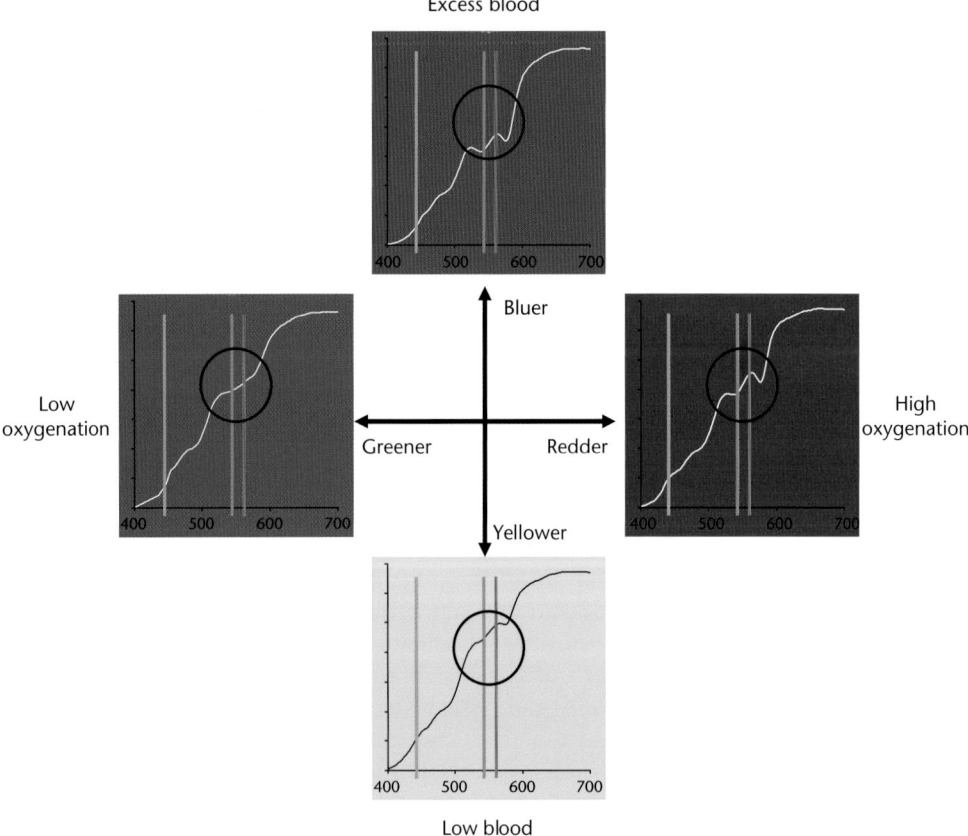

Figure 16.6 Each of the plots shows the spectrum of light from skin after it has gone through the eye; that is, just before the cones see it. By examining the blue and yellow plots, one can learn how the spectrum changes as the concentration of blood changes. The main change is in the 550 nm region, where the W feature is, and the entire skin spectrum there lowers as blood accumulates. The result is that more blood in the skin is seen as bluer because the pair of M and L cones are less activated relative to the S cone. The red and green plots can help us grasp how the spectrum changes as the oxygenation of blood in the skin changes. The main change now is that the W becomes more accentuated with greater oxygenation, and disappears with greater deoxygenation. Because the center peak of the W lies at approximately the maximum sensitive wavelength for the L cone, as the W becomes more accentuated the L cone becomes more activated compared to the M cone, leading to increased redness. Having the color cones we have allows our red-green dimension of color to map approximately onto changes of blood oxygenation, while still allowing the ancestral mammalian blue-yellow opponent channel to behave as usual. And the blue-yellow channel also has a considerable ability to sense changes in blood concentration, being at the maximally sensitive wavelength band to capture this. (See Changizi et al. [2006] for methods.)

Colors are also associated with warmth and lightness (Kay & Regier 2003), where the blue-green hues are cold and dark but the yellow-red hues are warm and light. One potential explanation for this three-way association (color-temperature-lightness) is that it correlates with the overall temperature and luminance of the skin. Of the two dimensions of blood modulation, only the hemoglobin volume affects the temperature of the skin. A greater volume of

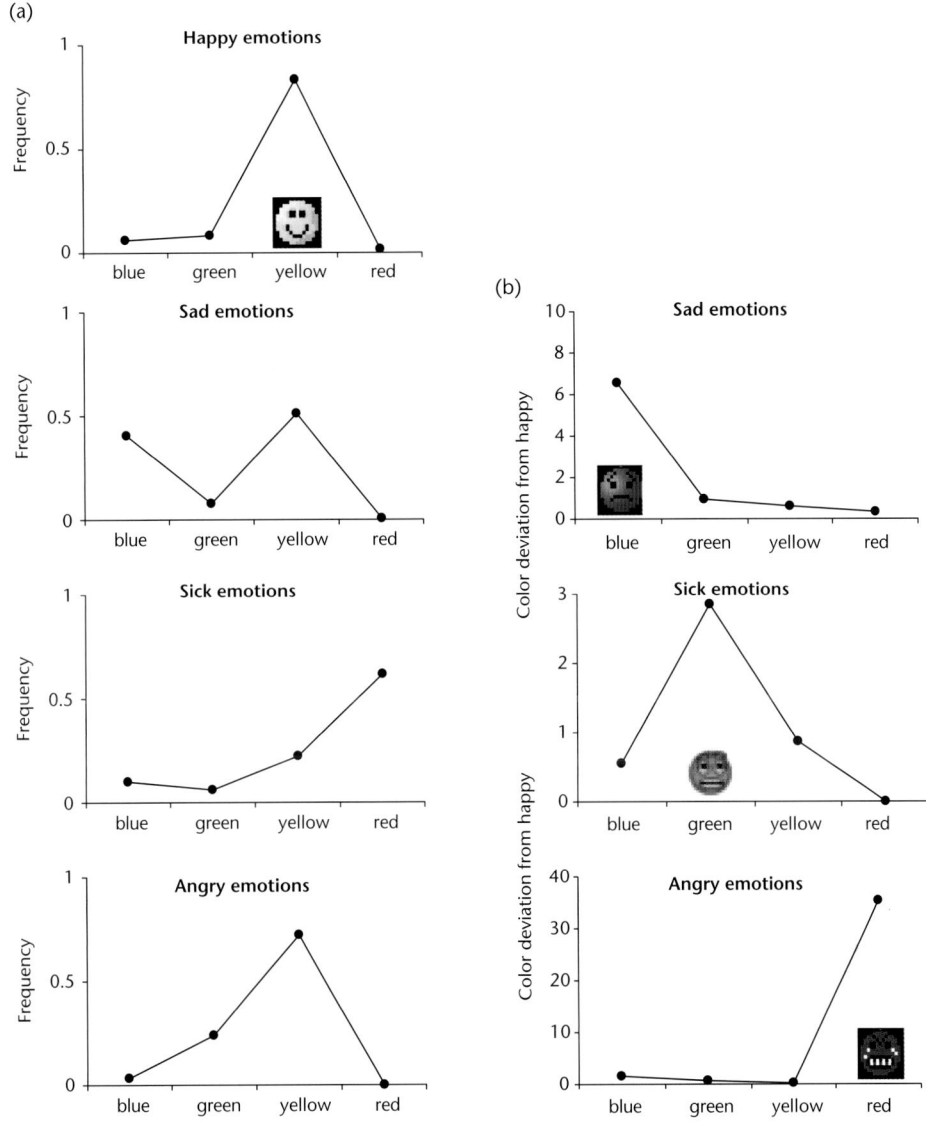

Figure 16.7 (a) Frequency distribution of the use of colors on cartoon smileys on the web (used in forums), for happy, sad, sick, and angry. Data are from two companies: allemoticons.com (the face colors were obtained from 90 happy faces, 83 sad faces, 85 angry faces, and 29 sick faces) and smileycentral. com (the face colors were measured from 42 happy faces, 22 sad faces, 25 angry faces, and no sick faces). Average frequency distributions across the four colors were computed, for the four emotions. (b) The baseline color and emotion of smiley faces tends to be yellow and happy, and for each emotion I calculated the color deviation relative to the distribution of happy face colors, which is the frequency that the color is used on a face for that emotion, divided by the baseline frequency that the color is used (in happy faces). That is, each of the distributions is now normalized by the happy distribution. One can see that sad faces have a tendency to be colored blue, that angry faces tend to be colored red, and that sick faces tend to be colored green.

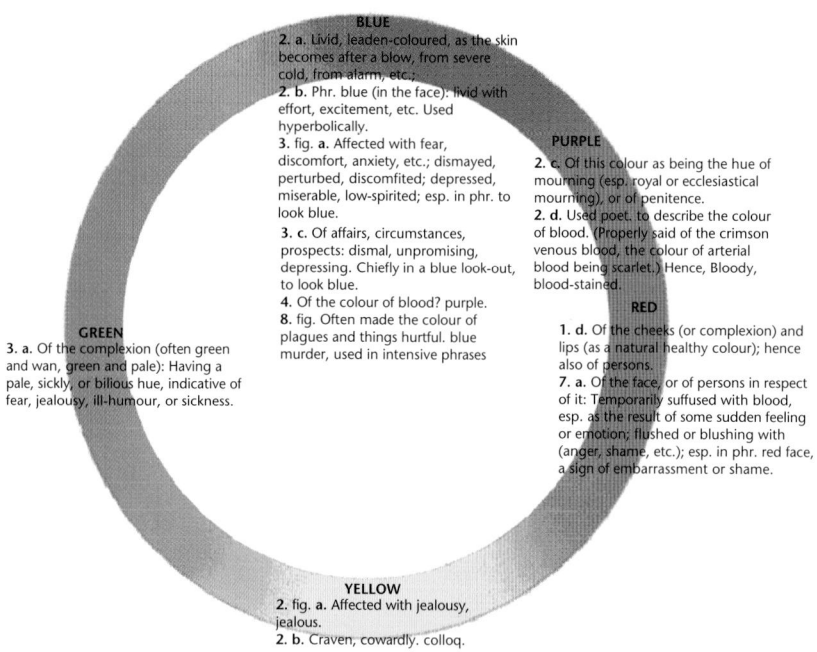

Figure 16.8 Oxford English Dictionary definitions for color terms related to blood, skin and emotion.

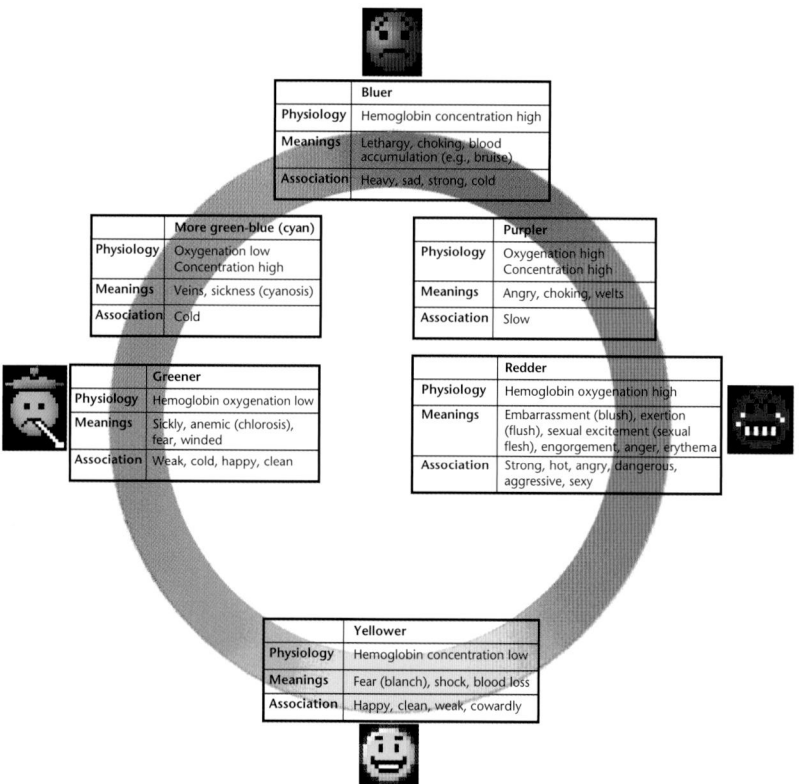

Figure 16.9 Summary of the manner in which skin color changes with blood, what those colors can sometimes mean to observers, and common associations of these colors.

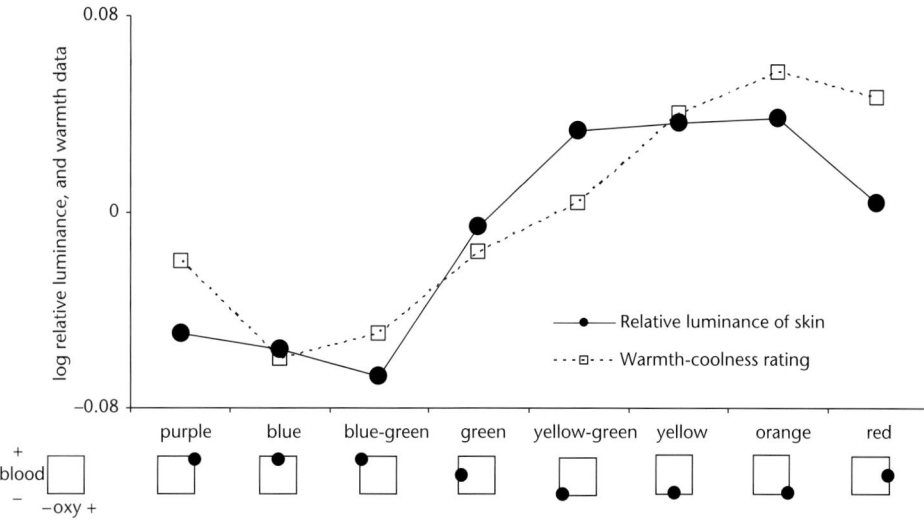

Figure 16.10 Plot of logarithm (base 10) of the luminance of skin, and also ratings of warmth or coolness of the hues (or light and dark hues). The color names on the bottom correspond roughly to the direction of the color deviation away from baseline skin. Warmth data are from Katra & Wooten (1996) and published in Hardin (2005), and show observer judgements of the warmth (positive) versus coolness (negative) of the colors. One can see a close similarity between the relative luminance of skin and judgments of the warm or light hues, suggesting a conjecture that perhaps light (or warm) and dark (cool) are given these terms because of the typical luminance modulations of skin when skin moves in those hue directions.

blood in the skin—which looks bluer—is due to a slowing of blood flow, and there is consequently a greater reduction of temperature. But there is also a concomitant lowering of oxygenation when this occurs, because there is more oxygen uptake by the cells. Also, a greater volume of blood significantly lowers the luminance of skin, so that skin not only becomes bluer, but darker. Modulations of oxygenation have only a meager effect on skin luminance, with deoxygenated blood slightly lower in luminance. The result is that skin is often at its darkest and coldest when blue-green and blue, whereas it is at its lightest and warmest when orange and yellow. See Figure 16.10.

BARING YOUR EMOTIONS

If color vision is for seeing skin, then a central prediction is that primates with color vision should have bare skin. Consistent with this prediction, the primates with color vision have bare faces (Figure 16.11), and sometimes other bare spots (rumps, chest, genitalia), with which they

color signal [Darwin, 1899 (e.g., red with anger on p. 137, pale with terror on p. 144); Hingston, 1933; Wickler, 1967; Waitt et al., 2003]; primates without color vision do not tend to have bare spots. Interestingly, although the prosimians are mostly color blind (i.e., monochromatic or dichromatic) and furry-faced, there are two species that have color vision (of the polymorphic kind), *Varecia* and *Propithecus* (the top two photographs in the center column of Figure 16.11b), and they each have substantial bare spots on the face.

In light of the idea that color vision is for seeing skin, one might wonder whether color may be the key to understanding why we are the "naked apes" (Morris, 1967). One might speculate that our upright posture more easily allows color signaling on our fronts and backs, and so they have become largely bare. But could all our naked spots really be for color signaling? (Not counting the parts that were naked well before primates acquired color vision, such as the palms.) Notice that the color-signaling hypothesis predicts that "if bare, then visible."

(a)   **Color blind**

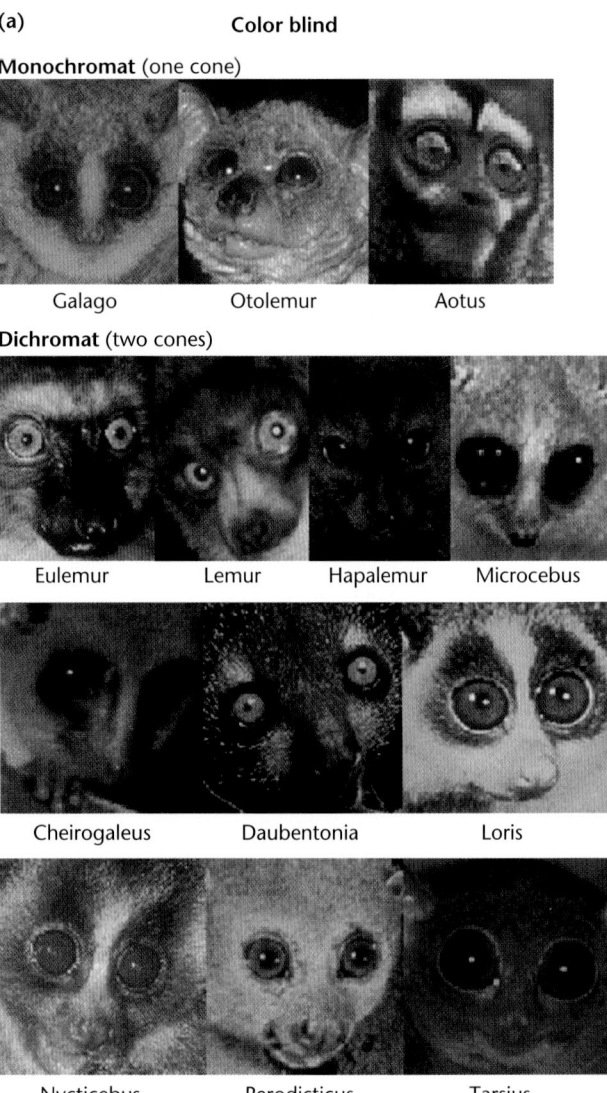

Figure 16.11 Sample photos from the National Primate Research Center, University of Wisconsin, Madison (http://pin.primate.wisc.edu/av/images/) for (a) color blind primate genera (monochromats or dichromats), (b) polymorphic trichromats (where only the females have color vision), and (c) routine trichromats (like old world primates, great apes, and us).

That is, if a body part has bare skin, then, as it is for color signaling, it must be a part of the body that other animals can actually see. Such a conditional is equivalent to "if not visible, then furry," and let us now ask which of our body parts are unlikely to be visible in normal circumstances to conspecifics. Three body parts immediately leap to mind. First is the top of the head, which faces upward and will tend to be difficult to see. And it is typically furry, consistent with the conditional. Second are the underarms, where the arms occlude the skin. Underarms, too, are furry. And third is the groin, which tends to be occluded by the legs. Again, furry. That is, the three main human body parts that are not easily visible do tend to be the most universally furry parts for humans, consistent with the hypothesis that all our naked skin is for color signaling. (Note that, concerning the groin, one might object that there is bare skin there, especially on the engorged genitalia. But when the genitalia are engorged, they are no longer occluded by the legs.)

(b)   **Color vision in females only**

Prosimians

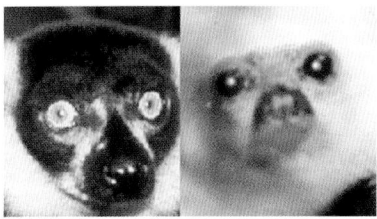

Varecia   Propithecus

New World Monkeys

Callithrix   Cebuella   Callimico   Leontopithecus

Saguinus   Saimiri   Cebus

Lagothrix   Ateles   Callicebus

Figure 16.11 Continued.

And it should be emphasized that "if not visible, then furry" does *not* imply "if visible, then bare." There are many potential advantages to fur, and a part of the body may be visible by conspecifics, and yet it is still advantageous to place fur there. Beards and eyebrows, then, are not counterexamples to the empirical conformance to the "if not visible, then furry" rule. In fact, it is interesting that as furry and bearded as a man might become, the remaining bare skin is still sufficient to easily display color signals (see Figure 16.12a) such as Santa's rosy cheeks. It clearly never looks like a case of hypertrichosis (Figure 16.12b).

Color vision in males and females

New World Monkeys

Alouatta

Old World Monkeys

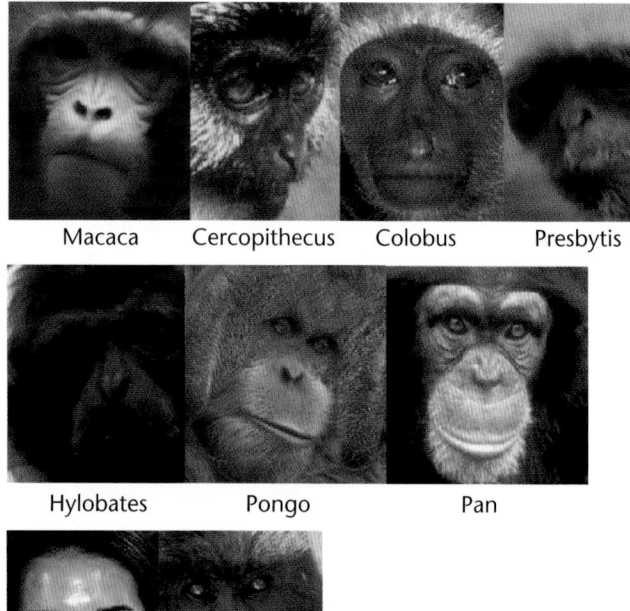

Macaca   Cercopithecus   Colobus   Presbytis

Hylobates   Pongo   Pan

Figure 16.11 Continued.

Homo   Gorilla

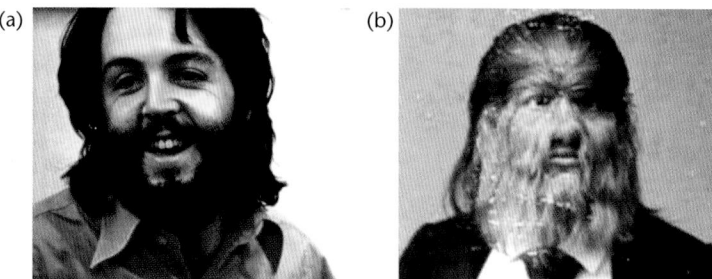

(a)   (b)

Figure 16.12 (a) A normal male beard doesn't cover up our color signals, whereas (b) the signals are obliterated in cases of hypertrichosis.

DISCUSSION

One question we have thus far left unanswered is why would primates evolve *color* signaling? Why not just communicate the signal via a facial expression or gesture? First, colors can be signaled without muscular activity, and so they thereby do not hinder our behavior. Second, color can be displayed on parts of the body where muscular gestures are not possible, like on the chest or rump. This provides us with more surface area for signals, and sometimes allows us to put our color signals where they matter, like on genitalia. Third, color signals more directly inform others about our physiological state. This is useful, not only because it may provide a more direct view into the state of others, but also because these physiological blood variables are intrinsically difficult to consciously manipulate, whereas muscular expressions are much easier to consciously manipulate. A red signal can't be faked, for example, because it requires good oxygenation. (This may underly why red clothing in certain sports appears to enigmatically increase the chances of success) (Hill & Barton, 2005). Color signals are more honest signals: you are more likely to be forgiven an ethical breach if others believe your contriteness emotion is honest, and so a pink blush serves to communicate true forgiveness better than a bowed head.

Another issue we have skirted around concerns whether the important color signals are primarily emotional or whether they could also be due to clinical coloration changes. Some clinical color changes could even be, in part, signals. For example, choking babies who possessed mechanisms that enhanced their blueness would be more likely to alert their mothers. Whether a clinical color change is selected for or just a side effect of a clinical disorder, our color vision has long been an asset for clinicians, able to see blanching, cyanosis, erythema and many other skin-color changes in clinical settings. In fact, for those among us who are dichromats—most of whom have lost one of the M or L cones—there is a long history of complaints about their inability to see skin coloration changes (Table 16.1). It would be surprising if these clinical color changes were not

part of the selective advantage of color vision. After all, hospitals find oximeters (which measure hemoglobin volume and oxygenation) so useful that they are next to every bed, and so the fact that we've had oximeters in our eyes for millions of years must have been put to use in ways that affected our evolution.

To sum up, in our three main sections of this chapter we have presented three of the main lines of evidence supporting our new hypothesis that color vision is a kind of social vision, about the emotional states and moods of others. The argument from the first of these sections (Section 2, "Color Accent") centered on evidence that our perception of skin is organized so that we are maximally able to discriminate spectral changes around baseline skin color, akin to the way in which we are maximally able to discriminate temperature changes of skin around baseline skin temperature. Key to that discussion was that our own skin (or that of our community) tends to appear uncategorizably colorful, but other skin colors appear categorizably colorful. This is just what we would expect if color perception was about sensing emotions off the skin. The argument from the second of the three sections (Section 3, Blood in the Eye) concerned evidence that our primate cone sensitivities have been designed by natural selection to sense the subtle spectrum changes that occur with modulations of hemoglobin oxygenation. In particular, the single ancestral M/L cone split into two cone types having sensitivities that simultaneously capture the spectrally difficult-to-detect oxygenation changes, preserve the ancestral yellow-blue channel, and also allow us to see changes in blood volume in the skin. Eyes are unlikely to have become oximeters by chance, and thus this provides strong evidence that our color vision has been selected for seeing skin. And, finally, in the third of these sections (Section 4, Baring Your Emotions) we presented evidence that it is the primates with color vision that are bare-skinned; the nontrichromatic primates are furry faced, like a typical mammal. This is just as our hypothesis would predict if color vision is about skin.

Table 16.1. Evidence That Human Dichromats Have Difficulty Perceiving Skin Modulations.

Citation	Difficulty for color deficient observer
PERSONAL OBSERVATIONS	
Dalton (1794) [discussed in Anthony & Spalding (2004)]	could scarcely distinguish mud from blood on his stockings.
Wilson (1855) [discussed in Anthony & Spalding (1999, 2004)]	Problems recognizing redness in the lips, cheeks, nose, and inflammation, all which looked like blue. [A physician interviewed by Wilson.]
Best & Haenel (1880) [discussed in Anthony & Spalding (1999, 2004)]	Most struck by the change in normal people's complexion. Skin appeared waxen pale, with a hint of icterus, their lips and cheeks cyanosed and their optic discs very pale. [Haenel, a physician, induced temporary color deficiency in himself via snowblindness through snow skiing.]
Little (1881) [discussed in Anthony & Spalding (1999, 2004)	Difficulty recognizing inflammation in the eyes. Red appeared to him bluish; for example, in kerato-conjunctivitis and the retinal reflex. [An ophthalmologist.]
Ahlenstiel (1951)	"Slight reddening of the skin, as in blushing, is overlooked by the red-green blind. Growing pale is also overlooked, as is a very slight scarlet rash. Stronger reddening of the skin is labeled as dark grey shadow by the red-green blind. … Reddening of the interior parts of the body, in the throat, nose, ears and epiglottis, are more difficult to recognise. The bluish discolouration of the lips and nails in circulatory disorders remains imperceptible. Blood spots are imperceptible to the red-green blind on dark materials."
Logan (1977), Spalding (1993), Currier (1994) [discussed in Anthony & Spalding (1999, 2004)]	Difficulty recognizing blushing, pallor, faint rashes, cyanosis, erythema, blood in body products. Difficulties common to four congenital color-deficient doctors.]
Jeffries (1983) [discussed in Anthony & Spalding (1999, 2004)]	Trouble recognizing the colour of throats ulcers, gangrene, and some sores. [A physician.]
Voke (1980) [discussed in Anthony & Spalding (1999)]	Identifying organs, the presence of pus, blood, cyanosis, jaundice, and facial discolouration. [Medical professionals.]
Cockburn (2004)	"As a child I could not understand what people meant when they said someone was blushing…" [first sentence of this paper!]. "…embarrassment when a patient complained of a red eye but the offending side…was not specified. …most severe problem was in differentiating between blood and pigment in the retina" [p. 351]. [An optometrist.]
Anthony & Spalding (2004), p. 345	"I had failed to see the extreme pallor of a woman waiting for surgery. 'Anyone could see it,' the gynaecologist said but I could not. The operation was delayed for a week while the patient received a blood transfusion."

Table 16.1. Continued.

Citation	Difficulty for color deficient observer
STUDIES	
Steward & Cole (1989), Cole (2004)	Difficulties recognizing skin rashes and sunburn. [17% of color deficient patients queried.]
Campbell et al. (1999)	Recognizing skin rashes, erythema, cyanosis, jaundice, blood in stool. [Among doctors.]
Spalding (1997, 1999)	Most common difficulties were recognizing body color changes of pallor, cyanosis, jaundice, and cherry red. Second commonest difficulty concerned recognizing rashes and erythema of skin. [Among doctors.]
Reiss et al. (2001)	Problems detecting blood in body fluids. [Among doctors.]

Changizi, Zhang, & Shimojo. 2006.

REFERENCES

Ahlenstiel, H. (1951). *Red-green blindness as a personal experience.* (Kodak Research Library, London).

Allen, G. (1879). *The Colour-Sense: Its Origin and Development* (London, Trubner & Co.).

Anthony, J. & Spalding, B. (1999). Colour vision deficiency in the medical profession. *Br J Gen Pract* 49, 469–475.

Anthony, J. & Spalding, B. (2004). Confessions of a colour blind physician. *Clin Exp Opt* 87, 344–349.

Best, F. & Haenel, H. (1880). Rotgrün blindheit nach schneeblendung. *Kin Monatsbl Augenheilkd. Beilagen* 45, 88–105.

Boynton R.M. & Olson C.X. (1987). Locating basic colors in OSA space. *Color Research and Applications 12*, 94–105.

Campbell, J.L., Spalding, A.J., Mir, F.A., & Birch, J. (1999). Doctors and the assessment of clinical photographs—does colour blindness matter? *Br J Gen Pract* 49, 459–461.

Changizi, M.A., Zhang, Q., & Shimojo S. (2006). Bare skin, blood, and the evolution of primate color vision. *Biology Letters* 2: 217–221.

Changizi M.A. (2009). *The Vision Revolution.* Dallas: Benbella Books.

Cockburn, D.M. (2004). Confessions of a colour blind optometrist. *Clin Exp Opt* 87, 350–352.

Cole, B.L. (2004). The handicap of abnormal colour vision. *Clin Exp Opt* 87, 258–275.

Crozier, R.W. (2006). *Blushing and the Social Emotions.* Basingstoke, UK: Palgrave Macmillan.

Currier, J.D. (1994). A two and a half colour rainbow. *Arch Neurol* 51, 1090–1092.

Dalton, J. (1798). Extraordinary facts relating to the vision of colours. *Memoirs of the Manchester Literary and Philosophical Society* 5, 28–45.

Darwin C (1899). *The Expression of the Emotions in Man and Animals* (D. Appleton and Company, New York and London). [Reprinted by University of Chicago Press, Chicago, 1965.]

Drummond PD & Mirco N (2004) Staring at one side of the face increases blood flow on that side of the face. *Psychophysiology* 41: 281-287.

Hardin, C.L. (2005) Explaining basic color categories. *Cross-Cultural Research* 39, 72-87.

Hill, R.A. & Barton, R.A. (2005). Red enhances human performance in contests: signals biologically attributed to red coloration in males may operate in the arena of combat sports. *Nature* 435, 293.

Hingston R.W.G. (1933). *The Meaning of Animal Colour and Adornment.* Edward Arnold, London.

Honig W.K. & Urcuioli P.J. (1981). The legacy of Guttman and Kalish (1956): 25 years of research on stimulus generalization. *J Exp Anal Behav* 36: 405–445.

Jacobs G.H., & Deegan, J.F. (1999) Uniformity of colour vision in Old World monkeys. *Proc R Soc Lond* B 266: 2023–2028.

Jeffries, B.J. (1983). *Colour blindness—its dangers and detection.* Cambridge, MA: Riverside Press.

Kalish, H.I. (1958). The relationship between discriminability and generalization: A re-evaluation. *J Exp Psychol* 55: 637–644.

Katra, E. & Wooten, B.R. (1996). Perceived lightness/darkness and warmth/coolness in chromatic experience. Unpublished MA thesis, Brown University.

Kay, P. & Regier, T. (2003). Resolving the question of color naming universals. *Proc Natl Acad Sci* 100: 9085–9089.

Little, W.S. (1881). Experience of a red-blind physician with one ophthalmoscope. Practical advantage of colour-blindness with a case. *Arch Ophthalm* 10, 20–22.

Logan, J.S. (1977). The disability in so-called red-green blindness. An account based on many years of self-observation. *Ulster Med J* 46, 41–45.

Lucas, P.W., Dominy, N.J., Riba-Hernandez, P., Stoner, K.E., Yamashita, N/, Loria-Calderon, E/, Petersen-Pereira. W/, Rojas-Duran. Y/, Salas-Pena. R/, Solis-Madrigal, S., Osorio, D. & Darvell, B.W. (2003). Evolution and function of routine trichromatic vision in primates. *Evolution* 57: 2636–2643.

Morris, D. (1967). *The Naked Ape: A Zoologist's Study of the Human Animal.* New York: McGraw-Hill.

Osgood, C.E. (1960). The cross-cultural generality of visual-verbal synesthetic tendencies. *Behav Sci* 5: 146–169.

Osorio, D. & Vorobyev, M. (1996). Colour vision as an adaptation to frugivory in primates. *Proc R Soc Lond B* 263: 593–599.

Racinet, Augusta (1987). *Racinet's Full-Color Pictorial History of Western Costume: With 92 Plates Showing Over 950 Authentic Costumes from the Middle Ages to 1800.* New York: Dover.

Regan BC, Julliot C, Simmen B, Vienot F, Charles-Dominque P & Mollon JD (2001) Fruits, foliage and the evolution of primate colour vision. *Phil Trans R Soc Lond* B 356: 229–283.

Reiss MJ, Labowitz DA, Forman S & Wormser GP (2001) Impact of color blindness on recognition of blood in body fluids. *Arch Int Med* 161: 461-465.

Spalding, J.A.B. (1993). The doctor with an inherited defect of colour vision: The effect on clinical skills. *Br J Gen Pract* 43, 32–33.

Spalding, J.A.B. (1997). Doctor with inherited colour vision deficiency: Their difficulties with clinical work. In C. R. Cavonius (Ed.) *Colour Vision Deficiencies XIII* (pp. 483–489). Dordrecht: Kluwer.

Spalding, J.A.B. (1999). Medical students and congenital colour vision deficiency: Unnoticed problems and the cases for screening. *Occup Med* 49, 247–252.

Steward, S.M., & Cole, B.L. (1989). What do colour vision defectives say about everyday tasks? *Optom Vis Sci* 66, 288–295.

Surridge, A.K. & Mundy, N.I. (2002). Trans-specific evolution of opsin alleles and the maintenance of trichromatic colour vision in Callitrichine primates. *Molecular Ecology* 11: 2157–2169.

Surridge, A.K., Osorio, D. & Mundy, N.I. (2003). Evolution and selection of trichromatic vision in primates. *Trends in Ecology and Evolution* 18: 198–205.

Voke, J. (1980). *Colour vision testing in specific industries and professions.* London: Keller.

Waitt, C., Little, A.C., Wolfensohn, S., Honess, P., Brown, A.P., Buchanan-Smith, H.M., & Perrett, D.I. (2003). Evidence from rhesus macaques suggests that male coloration plays a role in female primate choice. *Proc R Soc Lond B* (Suppl) 270: S144–S146.

Wickler, W. (1967). Socio-sexual signals and their intra-specific imitation among primates. In Morris D (Ed.) *Primate Ethology* (pp. 69–147). London: Weidenfeld and Nicolsonpp.

Wilson, G. (1855). *Research on colour blindness with a supplement.* Edinburgh: Southerland and Knox.

Zonios, G., Bykowski, J. & Kollias, N. (2001). Skin melanin, hemoglobin, and light scattering properties can be quantitatively assessed in vivo using diffuse reflectance spectroscopy. *J Invest Dermatol* 117:1452–1457.

CHAPTER 17

Mental Control and Visual Illusions: Errors of Action and Construal in Race-Based Weapon Misidentification

Mark B. Stokes and B. Keith Payne

If social psychology could teach everyone in the world only one lesson, it would be that the power of the situation is immense, though often invisible. And if a second lesson were allowed it would be that construals—subjective interpretations of the world—are at least as important for human behavior as objective facts about the world. The power of the situation and the mediating role of subjective construal can be used to explain many of the classic and contemporary findings in psychology. This volume draws together these themes at several levels of analysis and from many interesting perspectives. In our chapter we will examine research on automatic race biases from the perspectives of the social situation and subjective construal. The broad question addressed in this research is this: How, and under what conditions do racial stereotypes alter how people construe the world? We outline some conditions under which social contexts, including racial stereotypes, can be expected to bias construals. We distinguish those from conditions in which stereotypes might bias behavior directly, without altering construals at all. The question is important because it speaks to the mechanisms by which racial biases have their effects. It also suggests ways that race bias might be ameliorated. We begin by considering some examples of how social context and construal have been treated in social psychology.

A classic study by Duncan (1976) investigated how subjects interpret behaviors based on the races of the actors involved. In the experiment, children viewed videotapes of fellow students arguing, finally resulting in one of the students shoving the other. Each of the scenes was scripted so that the only variation was the race of the two actors. In one video, a white child shoved a black child. In another, a black child shoved a white child. And in two other versions, both children were white or both were black. Subjects rated the behavior as more violent when a black child, rather than a white child, did the pushing, regardless of the race of the child being pushed. When the white child did the pushing, subjects interpreted it as playing.

Does this study demonstrate social stereotypes influencing "perception"? Probably not in the sense of "perception" that is typically studied by many vision scientists. If asked, subjects could probably discriminate the event they saw from other events. If perceptions were altered, it was in a broader sense of the term—the sense in which social psychologists often discuss social perception. In this sense, perception means a person's construal or interpretation of an event. The object being perceived here is the social situation as a gestalt. It is the meaning attached to the event rather than the features of the scene.

Although these two senses of *perception* can be distinguished conceptually, they are not always easy to separate empirically.

Consider, for example, another classic study by Bruner and Goodman (1947). In this study, wealthy and poor children were asked to adjust a circle of light to match the size of U.S. coins of increasing value. As the value of the coin moved from a penny to a quarter, all children adjusted the size of the light beam larger than the appropriate size. However, the poor children increased the circle of light substantially more than the rich children, and the difference grew greater as they moved from pennies to quarters. Bruner and Goodman interpreted this finding as evidence that the value people place on an object influences the perception of physical objects. Here the two senses of *perception* seem to merge, with the ability to perceptually discriminate an object and the meaning attached to it blurring together.

In this chapter we describe a program of research examining the influence of race bias on visual perception, and we focus on disentangling the various ways in which we can describe these biases as perceptual. Unfortunately, the objects in question are sometimes more important and dangerous than pennies and quarters. Shortly after midnight on February 4, 1999, an African immigrant named Amadou Diallo was shot to death outside his apartment building by four New York City police officers. Suspecting that was reaching for a weapon, the policemen fired 41 rounds before discovering that the unarmed victim had simply been reaching for his wallet.

The aftermath of this shooting resulted in public outcry against racial profiling and police brutality. But it also sparked various lines of research aimed at discovering why such a tragedy may have taken place. Can the race of a person holding a harmless object make it seem to morph into a gun? What are the factors contributing to such a bias? And if the bias exists, how do we understand the psychological mechanisms involved?

WEAPON MISIDENTIFICATION

There is no way to know what went through the minds of those police officers on that night in 1999. And there is no way to know whether the outcome would have been the same if Diallo had been white. The scientific questions at stake, though, go beyond the specifics of this case. In the studies we describe later, we sought to understand how the typical person responds when faced with the kind of split-second decision these officers had to make. Does race influence those decisions? And, if so, how?

We developed a laboratory study to investigate people's ability to distinguish innocuous items, such as hand tools, from dangerous ones such as handguns (Payne, 2001). The task simply presented pictures of various tools and guns on a computer monitor, and subjects were asked to identify each item by pressing one of two keys. Before the items were presented, we also showed the participants a black or white face, flashed for a fraction of a second. Subjects were instructed to ignore the face and to only identify the object that they had seen. In our first study using this task, two versions of this experiment were run: one in which participants had unlimited time to respond, and another in which they were forced to respond within a half a second.

When participants were given plenty of time to make their decision, they made few errors, and the number of errors did not differ based on the race of the prime. However, the amount of time required to identify a gun was significantly shorter when it followed a black face compared to a white face. Likewise, identifying a tool was faster when it was preceded by a white face as opposed to a black face. This pattern of response times provided preliminary evidence that race could influence identification of weapons, but it did not show that it altered perceptions.

In the second version of the study, when participants were under time pressure, they more frequently misperceived innocuous items as guns when they were paired with black faces than with white faces. In this case, the race cues actually shaped subjects' decisions. Other studies have found similar results using more complex and realistic scenes, noncollege samples, and African-American samples (Correll, Park, Judd, & Wittenbrink, 2002).

This research suggests that weapon bias is replicable and generalizes to numerous situations. However, the findings by themselves can be interpreted in multiple ways. One question is whether the bias reflects intentional racial animus. The available evidence suggests that it does not. One study tested whether intentional use of race was necessary to produce bias (Payne, Lambert, & Jacoby, 2002). In a baseline condition, participants completed the weapon task under instructions to ignore the faces altogether. A second group was told that the faces might bias them, and was instructed to try to avoid being influenced by race. Finally, a third group was told about the biasing potential of the faces, but was urged to intentionally use the race of the faces as a cue to help them identify guns.

Although participants' goals affected their self-reported intentions, they did not significantly alter their performance. Reliable race bias emerged in all three conditions, and was, in fact, greater in both the avoid-race-bias and the use-race-bias conditions than in the baseline condition. Ironically, directing attention to race had exactly the same effect whether participants attended to race with the intent to discriminate, or the intent to avoid discrimination. In these studies, the weapon bias seems largely independent of intent. This is important because it means that the bias can coexist with conscious intentions to be fair and unbiased.

How can this race bias co-exist with fair-minded intentions? One way would be that race stereotypes might exert a top-down influence on perceptions and/or responses regardless of whether subjects agree with the stereotypes. Studies examining individual differences in weapon bias provide mixed evidence. In one study, the degree of race bias correlated with perceptions of racial stereotypes in the culture, but not with personally endorsed stereotypes (Correll et al., 2002). In other studies, however, the race bias has been found to correlate with

measures of racial attitudes. Payne (2001) found that the bias was associated with more negative racial attitudes on a self-report questionnaire. And another study found that the bias was associated with racial attitudes measured using an affective priming procedure (Payne, 2005). Thus far, the evidence suggests that negative racial stereotypes and attitudes may be sufficient to produce the weapon bias, but they are not necessary. That is, some proportion of people showing the bias may not endorse negative attitudes or stereotypes at all.

The research reviewed so far suggests that a race bias in weapon perception exists, that it is difficult to intentionally control, and that it is not likely to depend on hostile racial intentions. But the question remains whether the bias can truly be said to be an error of perception. When a person mistakes a harmless object for a weapon because it is associated with a black person, should we understand that error as a visual illusion, in the sense that the perceiver experienced seeing the item as a weapon? Alternatively, people might misidentify objects because of mistakes in the response process, even though they see the item clearly. In this latter case, people perceive the object accurately, but nonetheless make errors because they have difficulty controlling their response. In the following section, we discuss the importance of understanding the difference between errors that result from illusions and those that result from response errors.

CONSTRUAL ERRORS AND ACTION ERRORS

Illusions are typically understood as distortions of perception. A well-known example is the Müller-Lyer illusion (see Figure 17.1). For most viewers, there is a compelling perception that the two horizontal lines are of different lengths.

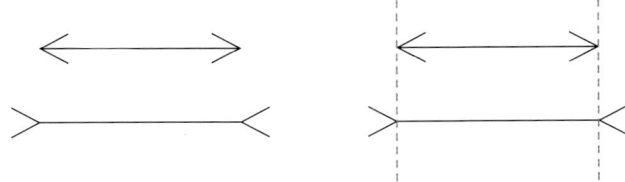

Figure 17.1 The Muller-Lyer illusion illustrates a construal error.

Although the precise mechanisms behind the illusion are debated, it is clear that the arrows attached to the ends of the lines create a context that changes how people interpret the length of the line. We describe this kind of error as a *construal error* because people misconstrue or misinterpret the visual cues. The result is that the subjective impression of the object is distorted, and people seem convinced that their misperception is true. One way to understand the weapon bias is as a construal error. By this account, race provides a context that changes how people interpret the object. As a result, a harmless object in the hand of a black person might genuinely look like a gun to the perceiver.

On the other hand, not all errors of visual discrimination are subjectively compelling illusions. Some are simply guesses, in which a person does not know what an object is. And others are mistakes in which the subject knows the correct answer, but fails to respond correctly. We describe this latter kind of error as an *action error*, because correct perceptions fail to be translated into correct responses. Action errors are especially likely when cognitive capacity is diminished, as when making split-second decisions or when distracted.

One popular example of this type of error can be observed in the Stroop color-naming task (Stroop, 1935). In this task, a participant is asked to look at a set of words and name the ink color of each word. The catch is that the words themselves are color words (see Figure 17.2). The task is very difficult when the ink color does not correspond with the color the word describes. Response times are longer, and errors are more common when the ink color and the word meaning are incompatible. Quickly naming the ink colors of the words in Figure 17.2 would probably lead to one or more errors. However, these errors do not result from perceptual illusions. Anyone who took the time to carefully examine each word before responding would be able to accurately identify the color. Rather, it is the failure to fully control responses that results in the action error of saying "red" when we meant to say "blue."

Action errors and construal errors are important to social vision because they represent two distinct interactions between social contexts

PURPLE

WHITE

BLUE

GREEN

YELLOW

RED

Figure 17.2 The Stroop color naming test. Errors made when naming the ink or font color in this task illustrate action errors.

and perceptual judgments. With action errors, visual perception may be accurate, but people still make behavioral errors. They are influenced despite what they see. On the other hand, social context may produce a visual illusion, influencing what people see to begin with. If people can be influenced in both ways, it is important to identify when each is likely to explain people's mistakes.

The distinction is important when explaining the mechanisms behind the weapon bias. If a construal error is the culprit, then it would suggest that the biasing influence of race stereotypes takes place preconsciously. That is, stereotypes shape what kind of representation people become conscious of. In such a case, people are aware only of the final product of the perceptual process, and any top-down constructive processes that have shaped that product are invisible. In contrast, if action errors drive the weapon bias, then the bias may not distort conscious perceptions at all. Instead, the bias could be traced to decision and response processes. As a result, by this account a person could fall prey to the weapon bias even as they correctly perceive the object and know that they are making a mistake.

These two explanations are not mutually exclusive; both may operate at the same time or under different conditions. We consider next the conditions under which construal errors and action errors are each likely to explain the weapon bias. Several lines of research show that context alters the interpretation of events only when the events are ambiguous, in the sense that they can be plausibly construed to have more than one meaning (e.g., Kunda & Sherman-Williams, 1993; Trope, 1986). The studies of weapon bias described earlier did not measure or manipulate the ambiguity of the target items. On the one hand, there was a correct or incorrect answer for each item. In that sense, there would seem to be little ambiguity. On the other hand, the guns and tools were presented briefly and masked, which would contribute to a sense of ambiguity when subjects viewed them. It is possible that some of the items appeared ambiguous, at least to some subjects. But the extent of ambiguity in those studies is unclear. In the studies we describe below we systematically took visual ambiguity into account.

Though ambiguity is an important precondition for construal errors, the factors affecting action errors are likely different. Specifically, we suggest that action errors happen when the stimulus is not ambiguous, but cognitive resources are strained in some way. In the weapon bias studies, most of the experiments that have observed race bias in error rates (as opposed to response times) have required subjects to respond quickly. Such quick responses are a potent way to limit the contribution of controlled cognitive resources in a decision.

Avoiding action errors and responding as intended may depend on cognitive control resources. Cognitive control refers to a set of processes by which people direct their thoughts and actions in order to keep them consistent with their goals (this term is used generally interchangeably with *executive control* or *executive functioning*). These processes include planning and monitoring behavior; coordinating behavior in complex, novel, or uncertain situations; selectively activating information that facilitate one's goal, while actively inhibiting information that interferes; and overriding impulsive or automatic responses when they clash with goals

(see Baddeley, 1986; Norman & Shallice, 1986). We consider below the conditions in which cognitive control is likely to play an important role in causing weapon bias.

AMBIGUITY AND COGNITIVE CONTROL

Visual ambiguity and cognitive control thus appear to be two critical factors that might determine when weapon bias is driven by construal errors, leading to visual illusions versus action errors. Any situation might be high or low in ambiguity or in the degree that it allows carefully controlled responding. Figure 17.3 shows a heuristic framework useful for framing the issue. First, we consider situations that allow high cognitive control and where ambiguity is low. Imagine walking down a street in no particular hurry and in broad daylight, and seeing a person with a cell phone clearly in his hand. Under such conditions, there is little reason for errors or biases of any kind. Responses are expected to be accurate.

In contrast, when cognitive control is high but ambiguity is also high, there is a potential for errors. Imagine looking carefully to examine what is in the hand of someone who is far away under bad light. Even though cognitive resources are not strained—attention and concentration can be recruited—there is still room for error. Although there may be a correct answer for what is in the person's hand, to the

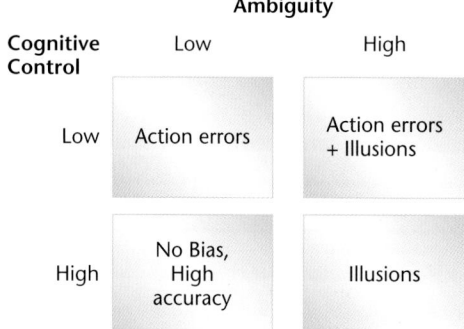

Figure 17.3 Errors in the weapons task may result from action errors, construal errors, or both, depending on such factors as cognitive control and visual ambiguity.

perceiver the object is ambiguous. In this case, we propose that the ambiguity of the situation may lead to construal errors. Stereotypes about the target person might distort the way the object is interpreted, producing a subjectively compelling belief that in the hand of a black man, the object looks like a gun.

Next we address conditions of low cognitive control. A common, although certainly not the only, way of reducing cognitive resources is to put participants under time pressure. These time constraints force people to make quick judgments that don't allow for complete processing of the situation. As a result, people fall back on their automatic biases (Payne, 2001). However, under the same circumstances, highly ambiguous items should provoke both action errors (since cognitive capacity is low) and construal errors (since the item is difficult to discern). This case is not very informative to our argument because it is impossible to differentiate if an error is a result of action or construal. Therefore, the cases of most interest are those in which action errors and illusions are separated from one another, namely, the low-capacity low-ambiguity case and the high-capacity high-ambiguity case. These two instances are of interest because each one uniquely targets action errors and construal errors, and by tackling each of these two conditions in turn, we can distinguish between failures in action and failures in construal.

Low Ambiguity, Low Cognitive Control

We know from previous studies (discussed earlier, e.g., Payne, 2001) that when participants have low cognitive capacity (time pressure) they make errors in identification. Yet, are participants making errors because they misconstrue the item or because they are relying on automatic racial biases due to a lack of cognitive control?

In order to rule out the possibility that these errors are the result of illusions, we implemented a modified design (Payne, Shimizu, & Jacoby, 2005). As before, participants viewed either a black or white face followed by a gun or a tool. The presentation rates were pretested to ensure that when presented alone and without

time pressure, subjects could correctly identify all the items. Subjects completed the weapon identification task using these presentation rates, and they were then given a half a second to respond whether they had seen a gun or a tool. By the time subjects made the first response, the target item had been replaced by a visual mask to prevent further viewing and to disrupt after-images. Immediately after this first response, they were prompted for a second response about whether they had *actually* seen a gun or a tool. This second response did not have a time limit.

We expected that if participants were misperceiving the target item there would be no differences between response one and response two. After all, if they formed an illusory representation of the item, it should not matter how much time they are given to respond. The Muller-Lyer illusion, for example, does not depend on fast responding. On the other hand, if participants correctly perceived the target, there would be close to perfect identification at the second response, made with no time pressure. When under time pressure (response one), we expected racial bias to be expressed as action errors, but when under no time pressure (response two) full cognitive control was expected to result in no bias.

Figure 17.4 shows the results. The kinds of errors subjects made are shown separately for black and white prime conditions and for the first response and second response. The first thing to notice is that there was a large decline in error rates between response 1 and response 2. When provided with ample time, participants were able to correctly identify the target item, with no race bias. Under the time pressure of response 1, however, results replicated previous studies, showing a significant degree of racial bias. Subjects were more likely to mistakenly call a tool a gun when it was primed with a black face than a white face. And they were somewhat more likely to call a gun a tool if it was preceded by a white face. This pattern suggests that with unambiguous items, the main reason for race-biased misidentifications may be the limitations on cognitive control imposed by fast responding. Under these conditions, the bias may be more like errors in the Stroop task than a visual

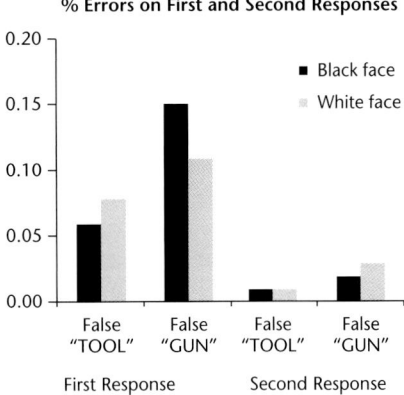

% Errors on First and Second Responses

- Black face
- White face

First Response / Second Response

Figure 17.4 Proportion of false "tool" and false "gun" responses as a function of racial primes and first versus second response attempts. Adapted from Payne, Shimizu, & Jacoby (2005).

illusion. However, police officers are not likely to face only conditions of low ambiguity, where the items they perceive are presented clearly. In the next section we consider how the processes underlying race bias may change when faced with highly ambiguous circumstances.

High Ambiguity, High Cognitive Control

The study just summarized showed that when given ample time to respond to unambiguous items, subjects showed nearly perfect performance and no race bias. What happens when subjects have ample time to respond, but the items are ambiguous? We conducted a study to investigate conditions of high cognitive capacity coupled with high item ambiguity (Shimizu, Payne, & Jacoby, 2007). Again, participants saw on each trial a black or white face followed by a gun or a tool. In this study they had unlimited time to respond, affording high cognitive control over their responses. We made the target items ambiguous by presenting them so briefly that they were just on the threshold of accurate perception. Because individuals vary widely in perceptual acuity, the presentation rates were set for each subject individually. Each subject completed practice trials, where only guns and tools were presented. During these practice

trials, the speed of presentation was periodically increased until the participant correctly identified the object 65 percent of the time. Performance at this level is better than chance (50 percent), but certainly far from perfect. Once the presentation rate was determined, the participant began the experiment, and, as in previous experiments, was asked to identify the item after each trial.

In addition to identifying the item, participants were also asked to categorize their subjective experience of the item on each trial. They were instructed to indicate after each response whether they *saw* the item, *knew* what the item was, or *guessed* what the item was. These three terms were defined for the subjects. They were told to respond "see" if they were confident in their answer and saw the perceptual details of the item, such as a gun barrel or the handles of pliers. They were told to respond "know" if they were confident that their response was correct, but they did not see specific perceptual details. Finally, they were told to respond "guess" if they were not confident that their response was correct, and were simply making a best guess. These subjective reports helped determine subjects' subjective experiences of the items.

We used these subjective categories rather than a second gun/tool response as in the first study because they provide an additional level of detail about subjects' experiences. If a subject falsely called a tool a gun, and claimed that they saw it in perceptual detail, it would suggest an illusion-like error. Not only did they make a mistake, but they believed it to be true and experienced the visual features that supported the error. False responses described as "known" are also of interest, because they also reveal an error that the subject believes to be correct. Although "known" errors provide weaker evidence of a visual illusion than "seen" errors, they nonetheless suggest an interesting type of construal error. Finally, "guess" responses would not suggest a construal error, but instead a form of strategic responding. For example, if subjects intentionally used race as a cue to the item's identity when they did not see anything at all, they might be expected to make race-biased errors and describe them as guesses.

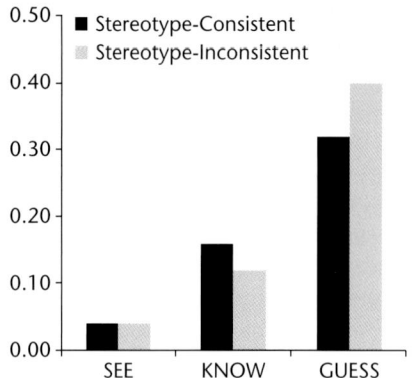

Figure 17.5 Proportion of stereotype-congruent errors and stereotype-incongruent errors as a function of subjective experience reports. Adapted from Shimizu, Payne, & Jacoby (2007).

Figure 17.5 displays the results, with stereotype-consistent errors and stereotype-inconsistent errors plotted as a function of each subjective report. Notice first that when subjects reported "seeing" the object they made very few errors, and there was no difference between stereotype-consistent versus inconsistent errors. However, race stereotypes did have other effects. A stereotype-consistent pattern of misidentifications occurred for the "know" responses. Tools were significantly mistaken for guns more often when paired with a black prime than a white prime. Conversely, guns were more often mistaken for tools after a White prime than a black prime. This stereotyping pattern among "known" responses is interesting because it suggests that subjects believed their errors were correct. Under these conditions, stereotypes influenced responses in a way that is consistent with an error of construal. Although subjects did not believe they saw the perceptual details of illusory objects, they did seem to believe their responses.

Of course, the relationship between errors and subjective reports is correlational. Therefore, we cannot tell whether subjects' subjective experience led them to respond in stereotypical ways, or whether responding in stereotypical ways shaped their subjective experiences. Nonetheless, the finding that stereotype-based errors were associated primarily with "know"

responses suggests that under some conditions, stereotypes can distort the construal of an ambiguous object in ways that lead subjects to believe that their mistakes are reality.

For those trials in which participants reported "guessing," performance was markedly different. The trend for "guess" responses was in a stereotype-inconsistent direction (although not statistically significant). Tools were more often mistaken for guns when paired with a white prime than a black prime. Conversely, guns were more often mistaken for tools when paired with black primes than with white primes. Such a pattern indicates two distinct and opposite influences of social context. In the "know" condition, subjects had ambiguous or partial information, and they respond in a stereotype-consistent way. However, in the "guess" condition, subjects likely felt that they had no information. Consistent with this interpretation, errors were highest in the "guess" condition, although they were significantly more accurate than chance. Participants may have made an effort to correct their responses so as to avoid being influenced by stereotypes. The different patterns among responses described as "seen," "known," and "guessed" are important because they clearly differentiate the ways that stereotypes may influence perceptions, depending on the level of ambiguity and subjective experience.

SUMMARY

In the two studies reported here, the weapon misidentification paradigm was modified so that we could examine the contributions of action errors and construal errors independently from each other. The first study examined cognitive control while the second study examined ambiguity and subjective experience. We predicted that the effect of action errors could be differentiated based on levels of cognitive control, whereas the effect of illusions could be differentiated based on changes in target ambiguity. The results from study 1 show that a lack of cognitive control, due to a hastened response, resulted in weapon bias. Participants showed stereotype-consistent errors in identification when required to respond within one-half second after seeing the target item. However, when given another, untimed attempt to identify the item immediately after the first identification, the errors almost completely disappeared.

In study 2, cognitive control was not impaired in any way as there was unlimited time to respond. However, items were made ambiguous by presenting them near the threshold of perceptual identification. When participants reported "seeing" an item, racial primes had no effect on responses. But when subjects reported "knowing" that their response was correct, they showed significant race bias. One way to interpret this pattern is that only "know" responses reflected truly ambiguous items. Items that were "seen" may have been perceived clearly enough that there was no ambiguity. And items that were "guessed" may have been perceived so poorly that there was little or no perceptual information available. In fact, subjects may have overcorrected in an effort to avoid appearing biased by stereotypes. In contrast, items whose identity was "known" provide the most interesting and potentially ambiguous case. Subjects felt that they had enough information to make a confident response, but not enough to see details. In this subjective "window" between clear perception and no perception, there may have been enough ambiguity for stereotypes to alter construals.

The studies we described here indicate how these two different interplays between social context and perception can both occur depending on the factors of the situation, specifically ambiguity and cognitive control, leading to either action errors or construal errors. Although these two types of errors are by no means exhaustive of all potential interactions, they do demonstrate that not only do social factors influence perceptual judgments, but they can do so in a variety of ways under different circumstances. Action errors and illusions are both integral components of the relationship between social context and perception. Sometimes social context influences what we see, as in the case of ambiguity. In these circumstances, we may actually believe that we have seen someone holding a gun rather than a wallet. Other times, social context influences our behavior despite what we see. Here, we see the wallet, but we act as though we have seen a gun.

IMPLICATIONS FOR VISION, SOCIAL AND OTHERWISE

We have distinguished between construal errors and action errors as bases for racial biases in detecting weapons. But this distinction may have broader utility in understanding a number of phenomena. Consider, for instance, the job of an airport screener who is inspecting x-rays of baggage for threats. Actual threatening targets will be exceedingly rare, but it is critically important that screeners detect them when they appear. The same situation is faced by radiologists screening for rare malignancies (Berlin, 1994). Research suggests that in visual searches for rare targets, targets are missed at an alarmingly high rate. For example, in one study, when the target was present on 50 percent of trials it was missed less that 10 percent of the time, but when it was present on only 1 percent of trials, it was missed about 30 percent of the time (Wolfe, Horowitz, & Kenner, 2005).

When targets were rare, did observers not see them at all, or did they make an action error? Wolfe and colleagues (2005) interpreted their findings to mean that subjects terminated their search before the target was found, and, therefore, never saw the missed targets. In contrast, a recent study suggests that action errors may be responsible (Fleck & Mitroff, 2007). The study gave subjects a chance to correct their responses. The logic was the same as in our studies described earlier. Observers can presumably correct action errors—but not perceptual errors—by saying they made a mistake. Subjects searched arrays varying from 3 to 18 pictures to identify whether a target was present. If it was not, they pressed a key to advance to the next array. Interestingly, the target in these studies was a tool, not a gun. When subjects had no chance to correct their mistakes, they missed the target at much higher rates when it was rare than when it was common. But when they had the chance to correct their responses by pressing a key to reverse their responses, the miss rate fell dramatically. In this condition, rare and common targets were missed at the same (low) rate.

This pattern of findings suggests that the impact of rare targets is not to impair vision, but to cause action errors. When the targets were rare, observers advanced impulsively to the next trial despite having seen the target. There are doubtless many factors that influence hit-and-miss rates in visual searches of all kinds. This research highlights the importance of considering both perceptual construals and action errors in these situations, and the conditions under which each may prevail. It also suggests different kinds of remedies for construal errors versus action errors. In the case of radiologists or baggage screeners, this research suggests that importance of being able to correct oneself. We discuss next some of the implications for correcting social biases.

IMPLICATIONS FOR MINIMIZING BIAS

Action errors and construal errors suggest different approaches to preventing or reducing race bias. If action errors are caused by poor cognitive control, as we have suggested, then any factors that promote good cognitive control should be effective at reducing biases driven by action errors. For example, situations that minimize speeded responses and distraction can be expected to reduce action errors. In addition to situational factors, dispositional factors such as cognitive skills and attention-related training might be expected to play an important role. For example, in one study, individual differences in executive control as measured by an attention-demanding antisaccade task correlated with performance on the weapons task (Payne, 2005). Individuals with better attentional control made fewer stereotyped errors.

In cases in which construal errors are at work, recommendations for reducing bias would be quite different. Situations that minimize perceptual ambiguity should be important in these cases. Simple interventions ranging from correcting vision with eye glasses to good lighting, for example, could be effective.

Some interventions might be expected to target both action errors and construal errors. Take, for example, recent studies showing that race biases in weapon identification can be reduced by training (Correll, Park, Judd, Wittenbrink, Sadler, & Keesee, 2007; Plant, Peruche, & Butz, 2005). Both police officers and civilians benefited from practice at distinguishing weapons from harmless items. In one study, officers who had completed more live firearms training on the job showed less race bias in laboratory tasks (Correll et al., 2007). Training effects like these could reduce both action errors and construal errors. On the one hand, training could reduce action errors by building cognitive skills, such as attention and executive control used in controlling responses. On the other hand, training could reduce construal errors by improving the ability to visually discriminate between weapons and other objects. In either case, training does indeed seem to increase accuracy and attenuate bias, and to generalize across tasks and time. Future research might be able to distinguish training's impressive effects on action errors and construal errors, shedding light on how we may modify effects of race on both mental control and visual illusions.

REFERENCES

Baddeley, A. D. (1986). *Working memory*. London: Oxford University Press.

Berlin, L. (1994). Reporting the "missed" radiologic diagnosis: Medicolegal and ethical considerations. *Radiology, 192,* 183–187.

Bruner, J.S., & Goodman, C.C. (1947). Value and need as organizing factors in perception. *The Journal of Abnormal and Social Psychology, 42,* 33–44.

Correll, J., Park, B., Judd, C.M., & Wittenbrink, B. (2002). The police officers' dilemma: Using ethnicity to disambiguate potentially threatening individuals. *Journal of Personality and Social Psychology, 83,* 1314–1329.

Correll, J., Park, B., Judd, C.M., Wittenbrink, B., Sadler, M. S., & Keesee, T. (2007). Across the thin blue line: Police officers and racial bias in the decision to shoot. *Journal of Personality and Social Psychology, 92,* 1006–1023.

Duncan, B.L. (1976). Differential social perception and attribution of intergroup violence: Testing the lower limits of stereotyping of Blacks. *Journal of Personality and Social Psychology, 34*, 590–598.

Fleck, M. S., & Mitroff, S. R. (2007). Rare targets are rarely missed in correctable visual search. *Psychological Science, 18*, 943–947.

Kunda, Z., & Sherman-Williams, B. (1993). Stereotype and the construal of individuating information. *Personality and Social Psychology Bulletin, 19*, 90–99.

Norman, D. A., & Shallice, T. (1986). Attention to action: Willed and automatic control of behavior. In R. J. Davidson, G. E. Schwartz, & D. Shapiro (Eds.), *Consciousness and self-regulation: Advances in research and theory* (Vol. 4, pp. 1–18). New York: Plenum Press.

Payne, B.K. (2001). Prejudice and perception: The role of automatic and controlled processes in misperceiving a weapon. *Journal of Personality and Social Psychology, 81*, 181–192.

Payne, B.K. (2005). Conceptualizing control in social cognition: How executive functioning modulates the expression of automatic stereotyping. *Journal of Personality and Social Psychology, 89*, 488–503.

Payne, B.K., Lambert, A.J, & Jacoby, L.L., (2002). Best laid plans: Effects of goals on accessibility bias and cognitive control in race-based misperceptions of weapons. *Journal of Experimental Social Psychology, 38*, 384–396.

Payne, B.K., Shimzu, Y., & Jacoby, L.L. (2005). Mental control and visual illusions: Toward explaining race-based weapon misidentifications. *Journal of Experimental Social Psychology, 41*, 36–47.

Plant, E. A., Peruche, B. M., & Butz, D. A. (2005). Eliminating Automatic Racial Bias: Making Race Non-Diagnostic for Responses to Criminal Suspects. *Journal of Experimental Social Psychology, 41*, 141–156.

Shimizu, Y., Payne, B. K., & Jacoby, L. L. (2007). *The experience of misperceiving a weapon.* Unpublished manuscript, Washington University.

Stroop, J.R. (1935). Studies of interference in serial verbal reactions. *Journal of Experimental Psychology, 18*, 643–662.

Trope, Y. (1986). Identification and inferential processes in dispositional attribution. *Psychological Review, 93*, 239–257.

Wolfe, J.M., Horowitz, T.S., & Kenner, N.M. (2005). Rare items often missed in visual searches. *Nature, 435*, 439–440.

CHAPTER 18

Afrocentric Facial Features and Stereotyping

Irene V. Blair and Charles M. Judd

I have a dream that my four children will one day live in a nation where they will not be judged by the color of their skin but by the content of their character. Martin Luther King, Jr.

In this line of his landmark speech, King expresses the troubling reality faced by thousands of people who are judged by the "color of their skin" instead of by more valid attributes. His reference to a specific, seemingly innocuous physical feature makes the injustice of the situation all the more apparent. Why would anyone use skin color as a basis for serious judgment? What, if anything, makes this specific feature so special? In this chapter, we consider two, nonopposing perspectives on these questions: Category-based stereotyping and feature-based stereotyping.

CATEGORY-BASED STEREOTYPING: FEATURES → CATEGORY → STEREOTYPES

For stereotype scholars, the questions raised previously are elementary: Skin color serves the well-known function of helping perceivers identify and categorize individuals as members of specific racial/ethnic groups. It—and a handful of other salient features—is merely a cue for social-group membership and otherwise has no inherent meaning. A person with dark skin, full lips, and coarse hair *is an African American*,

making available all associated attributes (stereotypes) for judgment. Skin color is special because values on this dimension are strongly associated with specific, socially significant groups, and it is highly visible.

Walter Lippmann (1922) was the first to make note of the social importance of certain group-related physical features when he characterized stereotypes as "pictures in our heads." He argued that because people must be able to see group differences to treat them differently, mental pictures are an important mechanism for maintaining social inequality. Although Lippmann's ideas had little impact on research at the time, later work showed that people do indeed have mental pictures that are central to stereotypes (Anderson & Klatzky, 1987; Ashmore & Del Boca, 1979; Bodenhausen & Macrae, 1998; Brewer, 1988; Fiske & Neuberg, 1990; Green & Ashmore, 1998). For example, physical features and other observable characteristics are frequently mentioned in open-ended descriptions of social groups, and such features may be one of the ways that social groups differ from other social categories (e.g., Anderson & Klatzky, 1987; Aube, Norcliffe, & Koestner, 1995; Six & Eckes, 1991; for a review, see Green & Ashmore, 1998). Furthermore, multidimensional scaling of descriptions of individuals shows that social group labels are mentally represented in closer proximity to physical appearance information than to trait, evaluative, or behavioral information (Carlston, 1994). Similarly, participants' group-based picture sorts are strikingly similar to those based on physical features (Brewer & Lui, 1989).[1]

Thus, the more individuals possess the features related to a group, the easier it is for perceivers to categorize them and make use of associated stereotypes (Blair, Judd, Sadler, & Jenkins, 2002; Bodenhausen & Macrae, 1998; Brewer, 1988; Corneille Huart, Becquart, & Brédart, 2004; Eberhardt, Goff, Purdie, & Davies, 2004; Fiske & Neuberg, 1990; Livingston & Brewer, 2002; Maddox & Gray, 2002). Once categorization has occurred, however, the importance of those features has been assumed to cease, as made clear in the following quote, "Once a person is categorized as Black or White, male or female, young or old, the stereotypic content of the schema is likely to apply regardless of how much or how little the person looks like the typical category member" (Fiske & Taylor, 1991, p. 121).

FEATURE-BASED STEREOTYPING: FEATURES → STEREOTYPES

The second perspective on the role of group-related features in judgment accepts the critical function of such features for social categorization, but extends their role beyond categorization. That is, skin color not only signals that a target belongs to a specific racial group, but it may also serve as a direct cue for associated traits. The argument is that stereotypes provide the opportunity and social context for certain

physical features to become associated with specific traits. Because those features serve as the primary cues for social categorization, and categorization leads to the activation of stereotypes, the features end up being frequently and consistently paired with the traits—through their shared association to a social group. Based on associative-learning principles (Anderson & Bower, 1973; Hayes-Roth, 1977; Hebb, 1948), direct feature-trait links are likely to form, allowing for "feature-based stereotyping" to occur unmediated by social categorization (Blair et al., 2002). To continue our example, dark skin may become directly associated with the traits lazy and musical, due to their shared association with the concept *African American* (see Figure 18.1), and consequently, dark skin may lead to stereotypic trait inferences *over and above* any inferences that result from categorization on the basis of those features. In other words, category-based and feature-based stereotyping may occur simultaneously as well as independently.

In one of the first demonstrations of this effect, Blair et al. (2002) asked participants to read biographic descriptions and, following each description, rate facial photographs (targets) for the probability that each photo shows the person previously described. The descriptions varied in the degree to which they were consistent with African-American stereotypes (e.g., musical versus intelligent), and in their valence; the target faces varied in the degree to which they had been judged by other participants as possessing *Afrocentric features* (i.e., looking more strongly African American). As predicted, targets with more Afrocentric facial features were judged as more likely the person previously described when the descriptions were stereotypic of African Americans, and these same targets were judged as less likely the person previously described in the counterstereotypic descriptions (see also Eberhardt et al., 2004; Maddox & Gray, 2002). As an indication that these feature-based inferences were occurring independently of racial categorization, Blair et al. found that they occurred when all of the targets were clearly categorized as members of the same racial group: all African Americans or all European

---

[1] The link between physical features and social group categorization is further reinforced by evidence showing that one's perception and memory for specific features are distorted by social categorization. Specifically, an individual who is categorized as a member of a group is perceived to have more group-related physical features and is (mis)remembered to possess more of those features (Corneille et al., 2004; Eberhardt, Dasgupta, & Banaszynski, 2003; Huart, Corneille, & Becquart, 2005; Levin & Banaji, 2006; Oliver, Jackson, Moses, & Dangerfield, 2004).

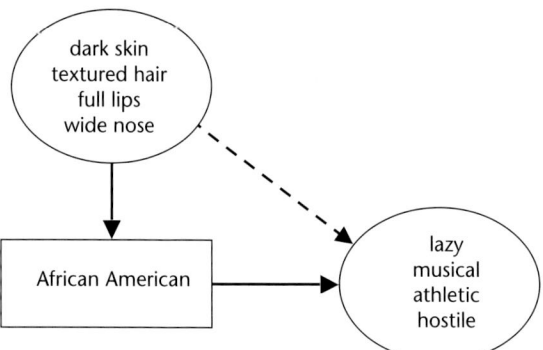

Figure 18.1 Example of the direct associations that may form between physical features and traits through their shared association to the category concept.

Americans.[2] When the participants were asked to make judgments of faces that included both African Americans and European Americans, stereotypic inferences were found on the basis of both category and (within each category) feature distinctions. Thus, the African-American faces, as a group, were considered more likely than the European American faces in the stereotypic than the counterstereotypic descriptions, but within each racial group, targets with relatively more Afrocentric features were judged as more likely in the stereotypic than the counterstereotypic descriptions. Other research has shown that Afrocentric-feature-based stereotyping occurs even in the presence of highly diagnostic information. In a study by Blair, Chapleau, and Judd (2005), participants were asked to judge the probability that each of a series of targets had performed a particular (aggressive) behavior, given four pieces of diagnostic behavioral information and a facial photograph for each target. Although the participants' judgments demonstrated their attention to and reliance on the diagnostic behavioral information, still the more Afrocentric the facial features of a target, the more probable the aggressive behavior was judged.

---

[2] The influence that category membership may have on judgment can be measured in at least two ways, (a) as the effect of a dichotomous variable (member vs. non-member), or (b) as the effect of a continuous variable (the ease or speed which a target can be categorized as a group member). We have used both measures and in both cases, we continue to find effects of Afrocentric features over and above any effects due to category membership (e.g., Blair et al., 2002).

These findings are of great interest because they suggest that stereotyping may be both more fine-grained and prevalent than previously understood. If stereotyping occurs exclusively via categorization, then only those individuals who are categorized as group members will be judged according to that group's presumed attributes—and generally to the same extent (Bodenhausen & Macrae, 1998; Brewer, 1988; Fiske & Neuberg, 1990). With direct feature-based stereotyping also possible, individuals who are categorized as members of a group may be stereotyped and discriminated against to different degrees, depending on the extent to which they manifest their group's physical features. Furthermore, there is the possibility that members of other groups can be stereotyped and discriminated against to the extent that they have some of those physical features. Individuals with full lips and a wide nose may be presumed to be musical and aggressive, for example, even though they are clearly categorized as European American (Blair et al., 2002).

Of further importance is the finding that category-based and feature-based stereotyping may differ in their operation. Consider, for example, a study conducted by Blair, Judd, and Chapleau (2004) in which the public records of felony offenders incarcerated in the state of Florida were examined. As expected, the inmates' sentences were largely based on criminally relevant factors (e.g., the number and seriousness of crimes committed), and once these were controlled there was no overall sentencing difference between African-American and European-American inmates. However, when the cases were examined within each racial category, it was found that inmates with more Afrocentric facial features had been given longer sentences than those with less Afrocentric features, controlling for criminally relevant variables. Thus, although judges in Florida had avoided sentencing bias due to racial category, they had not eliminated bias within each racial category due to Afrocentric features. Similar findings have been obtained with death-penalty cases (Eberhardt, Davies, Purdie-Vaughns, & Johnson, 2006).

We believe that there are at least two reasons that category-based and feature-based stereotyping may surface in different ways. First, a lot of public attention has been focused on category-based stereotyping, sensitizing people to the problem and motivating them to avoid such bias. In contrast, there seems to be little awareness of the potential for feature-based stereotyping (Blair et al., 2002; see also Sczesny & Kühnen, 2004). Second, feature-based stereotyping appears to be a very efficient process—similar to category-based stereotyping—with some unique challenges to controlling it. We will review the evidence for efficiency, first, and then the issue of control.

The Efficiency of Feature-Based Stereotyping

An efficient process is capable of operating even when processing is made difficult, thus increasing its overall likelihood of occurring and the difficulty of controlling it (Bargh, 1994). There is growing evidence that feature-based stereotyping is an efficient process. Using a dual-task manipulation, Blair, Judd, and Fallman (2004) found that participants who were required to monitor a random series of letters, stereotyped individuals on the basis of their (within category) Afrocentric features to the same degree as participants not under that constraint. Similarly, Sczesny and Kühnen (2004) found that stereotyping based on targets' masculine facial features, within gender category, was unaltered when participants' attentional resources were compromised by a nine-digit memory task.

Using a somewhat different procedure, Blair (2006) provided additional support for the efficiency of feature-based stereotyping by using inverted faces, a manipulation that has been shown to disrupt normal face processing. In this study, participants were asked to complete the same probability rating task used in Blair et al. (2002), but, for half of the participants, the faces appeared upside-down. Replicating the prior effect, targets with more Afrocentric facial features were given higher probabilities in the stereotypic than the counterstereotypic descriptions. Attesting to the efficiency of this form of stereotyping, face inversion did not disrupt nor modify the outcome in any way.

Unique Challenges for Control

As noted earlier, one of the reasons that feature-based stereotyping may be difficult to control is that people are not generally aware of the potential for bias and thus are unmotivated to control it. For example, in all three of the prior studies on the efficiency of feature-based stereotyping, category-based stereotyping actually increased when participants were under cognitive constraints (dual-task or inverted faces), a reliable effect documented by others (Bodenhausen, 1990; Gilbert & Hixon, 1991; Kruglanski & Freund, 1983; Macrae, Hewstone, & Griffiths, 1993; Pendry & Macrae, 1994, 1999; Pratto & Bargh, 1991). The most plausible account of the data is that because people are sensitized to race-based stereotyping, they attempt to suppress or otherwise counter it under normal processing conditions in an effort to avoid bias. The disruption in processing caused by a dual task or by inversion interferes with this strategy, allowing greater race-based stereotyping to emerge under these conditions. The complete lack of a similar effect on feature-based stereotyping suggests that people are not aware of this form of stereotyping and do not spontaneously attempt to control it under the best of circumstances, as they do for race-based stereotyping.

More direct evidence on the controllability of feature-based stereotyping comes from a recent series of studies, in which Blair, Judd, and Fallman (2004) showed that a general instruction to avoid stereotyping was entirely unsuccessful in reducing participants' reliance on Afrocentric facial features in judgment. Even when participants were given explicit information about how Afrocentric features could influence them, and they demonstrated that they could easily and reliably identify the relevant features, they were unable to avoid making stereotypic inferences on the basis of those features. Again, these findings are made all the more interesting when compared to those obtained in the same studies on racial category-based judgments. In the latter case, both the general instruction to avoid stereotyping and the more explicit instructions significantly reduced participants' reliance on target race as a cue for judgment. Thus, participants appeared more aware of racial stereotypes and they were better able to avoid the influence of those stereotypes, compared to their awareness of and ability to control Afrocentric feature-based stereotyping.

DEFINING AFROCENTRIC FACIAL FEATURES: A MEASUREMENT STUDY

As reviewed thus far, there now exists strong documentation of greater stereotyping of faces perceived as more Afrocentric. Until now, however, there has been little research on the specific physical features that underlie this dimension. We sought to fill this gap using the pool of photographs we had been drawing upon for our research (Blair, 2006; Blair et al., 2005; Blair et al., 2004; Blair et al., 2004; Blair et al., 2002). Specifically, we selected a set of 167 facial photographs of young males,[3] all with reliable ratings on our Afrocentric scale, that met the following criteria: (1) these individuals had been clearly identified as African American ($n = 58$) or

European American ($n = 109$) by pretest participants (99 percent agreement, on average; Blair et al., 2002), (2) they had neutral facial expressions, (3) there were no visible accessories (e.g., no glasses or jewelry), and (4) they were in a forward-facing pose. The background and any visible clothing were digitally altered to be uniform across the photographs, and the photographs were cropped so that the faces would be approximately the same size (4 × 6 inches).

Face Measurements

There are hundreds if not thousands of measures that one might take of a human face. The measures we took were based primarily on the features that have been associated with African Americans in the literature (Zebrowitz, 1998; Oliver, Jackson, Moses, & Dangerfield, 2004; Cartmill, 1998). These sources suggested that there are four primary features: dark skin, a broad nose, full lips, and coarse or textured hair, with dark skin often assumed to be the most dominant. We took a number of additional measurements that would provide a more comprehensive assessment of a person's facial appearance, such as the length and shape of the face, height of forehead, height of cheekbones, prominence of cheeks, eye and hair color, quantity of hair, type of eyebrows, and both the shape and size of the eyes (see Table 18.1).

In taking these measurements, we attempted to eliminate subjectivity to the extent possible. For example, instead of relying on subjective judgments of skin tone, we used a computer program (Adobe Photoshop) to determine the luminance of each digitized face.[4] Such objectivity provides more precision and, importantly, avoids the possible cross-influence that one feature may have on another in subjective judgments. That is, assuming people have naive theories about what features ought to go together, perceptions of one feature may influence perceptions of another feature (e.g., a person with a wider nose may be perceived to have darker skin). However, for a limited number of

---

[3] All of our research on Afrocentric feature-based stereotyping has been conducted solely with male targets, and thus its conclusions may or may not generalize to female targets. We used only male targets in large part to simplify the materials (e.g., stereotypes of African American women may not be exactly the same as those of African American men, and the relation between Afrocentrism and attractiveness may differ for women and men, as noted by Blair et al., 2002). We look forward to extensions of this work with female targets, that could uncover new insights into the process of feature-based stereotyping.

[4] We thank Jennifer Fallman for the countless hours she spent taking the many face measurements.

Table 18.1. Face Measurements.

Feature (higher numbers indicate)	Measurement
Luminance (lighter skin)	Median luminance of face without hair, measured by Adobe Photoshop
Nose shape (wider, shorter nose)*	Nose width[a] ÷ Nose length[b]
Lip fullness (fuller lips)*	Lip thickness[c] ÷ Face length[d]
Eye shape (rounder eyes)*	Avg eye height[e] ÷ Avg eye width[f]
Eye size (larger eyes)*	Avg eye height x Avg eye width ÷ Face length x Face width at cheeks[g]
Upper head length (longer upper head)*	Distance between pupil center to top of head ÷ Face length
Midface length (longer midface)*	Distance between pupil center and top edge of lips ÷ Face length
Chin length (longer chin)*	Distance from bottom edge of lips to base of chin ÷ Face length
Forehead height (higher forehead)*	Distance from mid eyebrow to hairline ÷ Face length
Cheekbone height (higher cheekbones)*	Distance between midcheek and bottom of chin ÷ Face length
Cheekbone prominence (more prominent)*	Face width at cheekbones – face width at mouth[h] ÷ Face length
Face shape (rounder face)*	Face width at mouth ÷ Face length
Prominence of nose bridge[‡]	Subject Rating: 1 = *Very flat*, 7 = *Very prominent*
Hair texture[‡]	Subject Rating: 1 = *Very straight*, 7 = *Very curly/coarse*
Hair quantity[‡]	Subject Rating: 1 = *No hair*, 7 = *A lot of hair*
Hair color[‡]	Subject Rating: 1 = *Very light*, 7 = *Very dark*
Eye color[‡]	Subject Rating: 1 = *Very light*, 7 = *Very dark*
Eyebrow type[‡]	Subject Rating: 1 = *Very small & thin*, 7 = *Very big & bushy*

*Measurement was taken using a dial caliper, accurate to .1 mm (inter-rater reliability, $r = .91$). Minor variations in image size were controlled by using ratios, with the target measurement divided by the indicated horizontal or vertical axis.
[‡]Photos were rated by nine subjects with the mean rating for each photo used in our analysis (α = .65, .76, .94, .89, .88, .91, respectively, for ratings of nose, hair texture, hair quantity, hair color, eye color, & eyebrows).
[a]Distance between outer edges of nostrils at widest point; [b]Distance between forehead bridge at level of upper edge of visible eye to nose tip; [c]Distance between uppermost and lowermost point of lips. If lips were separated, upper lip and lower lip were measured separately; [d]Distance between hairline and base of chin; [e] Distance between upper and lower edge of visible eye within eyelids at center of pupil; [f]Distance between inner and outer corner of eye; [g]Distance between outer edges of cheeks at most prominent points; [h]Distance between outer edges of cheeks at level of mid-mouth.

features, we had to rely on subjective ratings. Table 18.1 contains a description of all the measurements taken of each face, and the method used for each.

Selection of Afrocentric Features

Three statistical methods were used to determine the set of features that best represents the degree to which a face is perceived as being Afrocentric, trading off number of features with variance accounted for. The first method was the "all possible subsets" approach in which all possible subsets of features (of size p) were used to predict perceived Afrocentrism, and from these the best possible subset was selected for that value of p. For instance, when $p = 1$, this

Table 18.2.   Standardized Parameter Estimates from a Simultaneous
Multiple Regression of Faces' Perceived Afrocentrism on all 18
Measured Facial Features (Face set N = 167).

Measured Feature	Standardized Parameter Estimate	t-value
Intercept	0	1.82
Skin Luminance	**−0.23159**	**4.42*****
Nose shape	**0.12866**	**3.16****
Lip fullness	**0.36072**	**4.34*****
Eye shape	−0.05957	1.56
Eye size	0.01568	0.33
Upper head length	−0.02686	0.65
Midface length	−0.05031	0.66
Chin length	−0.03179	0.60
Forehead height	−0.05105	0.79
Cheekbone height	−0.00396	0.07
Cheekbone prominence	−0.05364	1.48
Face shape	−0.04025	0.99
Prominence of nose bridge	0.00613	0.20
Hair texture	**0.13716**	**3.40****
Hair quantity	**−0.16878**	**4.71*****
Hair color	0.06076	1.61
Eye color	0.04408	1.02
Eyebrow type	−0.00228	0.07

**$p < .01$ ***$p < .0001$

approach reveals the single best predictor (in terms of maximizing R^2). When $p = 2$, it reveals the best possible pair of predictors, again with the goal of maximizing R^2. Using this approach it appeared that while the best possible set of five predictors explained more variance than the best possible set of four predictors, there was not a substantial improvement when this best possible set of five predictors was compared to the best possible set of six predictors. Accordingly, this approach suggested that perceived Afrocentrism is best predicted by a set of five features, including *skin luminance, lip fullness, nose shape, hair texture, and hair quantity*. This set explained 87 percent of the variance in perceived Afrocentrism.

The second selection method was stepwise regression, in which face measurements were added one by one to a model predicting Afrocentric ratings, with the constraint that the F-statistic for a measure to be added must be significant at the .05 level and that each measure must remain significant at that level to remain in the model. This method of selection also returned the five measured features listed previously.

Finally, the third selection method was simultaneous multiple regression, in which all face measurements were used to predict Afrocentric ratings, and we examined the measures that explained a significant ($p < .05$), unique portion of the variance. Again, the same five features were returned, as shown in Table 18.2. Thus, all three methods converged on the same best set of features as predictive of perceived Afrocentrism. Table 18.3 provides the intercorrelations among these five features across the full set of faces.

Table 18.3.   Correlations among the Five Facial Features Most Predictive of Faces' Perceived Afrocentricism (Face set N = 167).

	Skin Luminance	Lip Fullness	Nose Shape	Hair Texture
Lip Fullness	−.77***			
Nose Shape	−.37***	.32***		
Hair Texture	−.53***	.59***	.28**	
Hair Quantity	.34***	−.40***	−.17*	−.01

*p < .05, **p < .01, ***p < .0001

From Features to Stereotyping

Now that we have identified a set of facial features that seem to be consistently related to the degree to which a face is judged as Afrocentric, we wanted to examine the role of these in subsequent stereotyping. Of the 167 faces used to select the set of Afrocentric features, 75 had been used in one or more of our 7 studies that had used similar methodology to assess the degree to which each face was stereotyped by participants (Blair et al., 2002; Blair, Judd, & Fallman, 2004). In other words, for each of these 75 faces (39 African American and 36 European American) we could calculate the mean probability that a face had been assigned in the stereotypically African-American scenarios minus the mean probability assigned to that face in the counter-stereotypic scenarios —averaged across studies for faces used in more than one study. For each of these faces, we obviously also have the mean judgment of the degree to which the face is seen as Afrocentric in its features (scale values between 1 and 9). Additionally, we have for each face two other measures, average speed of racial categorization and mean rated attractiveness (scale values between 1 and 7). Because all these faces were consensually categorized as either African American or European American by virtually all participants, the reaction time measure can be seen as a measure of the ease with which each face is correctly assigned to its (presumed) racial category. These mean categorization times were log transformed and then, to distinguish the category to which

the face was consensually assigned, the transformed latencies for the African American faces were divided by +1 while the latencies for the European American faces were divided by −1. Thus, larger positive numbers indicate an easier or more confident categorization of the face as African American, and lower (negative) numbers indicate an easier or more confident categorization of the face as European American. The bivariate correlations among the measured facial features and these more global assessments of the faces are presented in Table 18.4.

Our theoretical interest is in the association between actual (measured) facial features and the extent to which a face is stereotyped. Additionally, we wanted to examine how the measured facial features relate to perceived Afrocentrism and ease of racial categorization. We consider these latter two variables to be more global reactions to faces that may in turn mediate the degree to which specific facial features result in stereotyping of the individuals. That is, we wish to examine a mediational model in which facial features are associated with greater stereotyping *because* those features determine the degree to which a face is perceived as Afrocentric *and* the ease with which the face can be categorized into a racial group. And these latter two variables—Afrocentrism and categorization—are the two routes to stereotyping. Because facial attractiveness has been shown to be an important dimension of face-based judgment (and Table 18.4 shows that it is correlated with both Afrocentrism and stereotyping), we controlled for this variable in

Table 18.4. Correlations Among Five Measured Facial Features (Face set N = 75).

	Skin Luminance	Lip Fullness	Nose Shape	Hair Texture	Hair Quantity	Afrocentric	Category RT	Attractive
Lip Fullness	-.81***							
Nose Shape	-.37**	.32**						
Hair Texture	-.58***	.62***	.28*					
Hair Quantity	.29**	-.39**	-.34**	.01				
Afrocentric	-.85***	.87***	.55***	.64***	-.43***			
Category RT	-.87***	.88***	.39**	.73***	-.32**	.86***		
Attractiveness	-.15	.12	.33**	.04	-.18	.36**	.10	
Stereotyping	-.75***	.77***	.50***	.56***	-.43***	.89***	.82***	.40**

*p < .05, ** p < .01, *** p < .0001

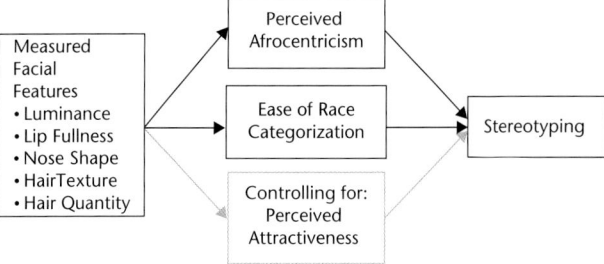

Figure 18.2 Schematic Mediational Model.

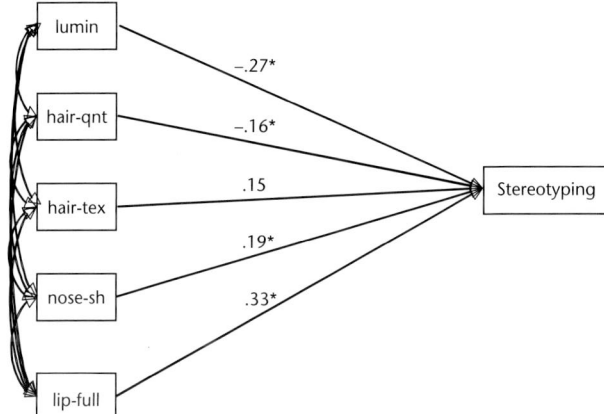

Figure 18.3 Overall or Unmediated Measured Facial Features of Stereotyping.

the mediational analysis. Figure 18.2 presents a schematic of the mediational model.

The first step in evaluating this mediational model was to examine the overall or unmediated effects of the five measured features on stereotyping. To do this, we regressed the stereotyping measure on the five measured features. These explained a full 71 percent of the variance in stereotyping, $F_{5,69} = 33.34$, $p < 0.001$. Their partial effects were all significant, with the exception of *hair texture*. The standardized partial regression coefficients for each feature, controlling for the others, are given in Figure 18.3 and in the second column of Table 18.5.

Next, to examine the effects of these five measured features on the potential mediators (Afrocentrism and categorization ease, and also facial attractiveness as a control), each mediator was in turn regressed on the set of five measured features. For Afrocentrism (Afro), the features explained 88 percent of the variance

in perceptions, and all five predictors had significant standardized partial regression coefficients, given in the third column of Table 18.5. This result is unsurprising since, in fact, these five features were chosen based on their ability to predict perceptions of Afrocentrism.

The five measured facial features explained 89 percent of the variance in mean categorization latencies (*Cat RT*). As indicated in the fourth column of Table 18.5, *skin luminance*, *hair texture*, and *lip fullness* all had significant standardized partial standardized regression coefficients. Finally, for the control variable, attractiveness, the overall model did not explain a significant amount of variance and only *nose shape* had a significant standardized partial regression coefficient (see column 5 of Table 18.5).

Next, to examine whether the measured facial features continued to predict stereotyping, once we controlled for the hypothesized mediators (Afrocentrism and categorization ease, and

Table 18.5.   Results of Regression Models Estimated.

Predictors	Feature Effects on Stereotyping	Feature Effects on Mediators			Feature and Mediator Effects on Stereotyping
		Afro	Cat RT	Attract	
Skin Luminance	−.27*	−.32*	−.37*	−.07	.13
Lip Fullness	.33*	.40*	.37*	−.01	−.12
Nose Shape	.19*	.22*	.04	.31*	−.02
Hair Texture	.15	.14*	.28*	−.08	−.07
Hair Quantity	−.16*	−.10*	−.06	−.06	−.05
Afrocentrism					.51*
Category RT					.65*
Attractiveness (control)					.15*
Model R²	**.71***	**.88***	**.89***	**.12**	**.83***

*p < .05

controlling for attractiveness) and to examine the effects of these mediators on stereotyping, we estimated a model in which stereotyping was regressed on all five measured features as well as the three mediating variables. The results of this model are presented in Figure 18.4 and the last column of Table 18.5.

Figure 18.4 presents the full mediational model, in that the measured facial features affect the mediators (these standardized regression coefficients were given in the third, fourth, and fifth columns of Table 18.5, and are represented here only by the three arrows from these features to the mediators, omitting the other 12 effects for presentational clarity), the mediators affect the stereotyping outcome, controlling for the physical features, and the physical features are allowed to affect the stereotyping outcome, controlling for the mediators. As expected, this model explained a very large percentage of the variance in stereotyping of this set of targets (83 percent) and did a significantly better job than the model that just used the measured facial features to predict stereotyping (column 2 model of Table 18.5), $F_{3,66} = 16.91$, $p < .0001$. In other words, as a set the mediators significantly explained variation in stereotyping controlling for the measured facial features. Additionally, all three standardized partial regression coefficients

for the mediators were significant over and above the measured features and over and above the other mediators. Most importantly for our argument, however, is that none of the measured facial features exerted a significant residual direct effect on stereotyping once we controlled for the three mediators (Afrocentrism, categorization ease, and attractiveness). Additionally, when we compared this full model to a model with just the mediators (model not presented), the five measured facial features, as a set, did not influence stereotyping, once the mediators were controlled, $F_{5,65} = 0.87$, $p > .20$.

In sum, it appears that the set of five measured facial features are highly predictive of the degree to which faces are stereotyped along the dimensions associated with African Americans. But the reason that they are so predictive is that they allow for inferences of Afrocentrism and for racial categorization. And it is these two global variables—Afrocentrism and categorization—that ultimately lead to stereotyping. Most importantly, these two routes to stereotyping—one through perceived Afrocentrism and one through categorization—co-occur, with each accounting for unique variance in judgment. There are thus two nonredundant routes to stereotyping from discrete physical

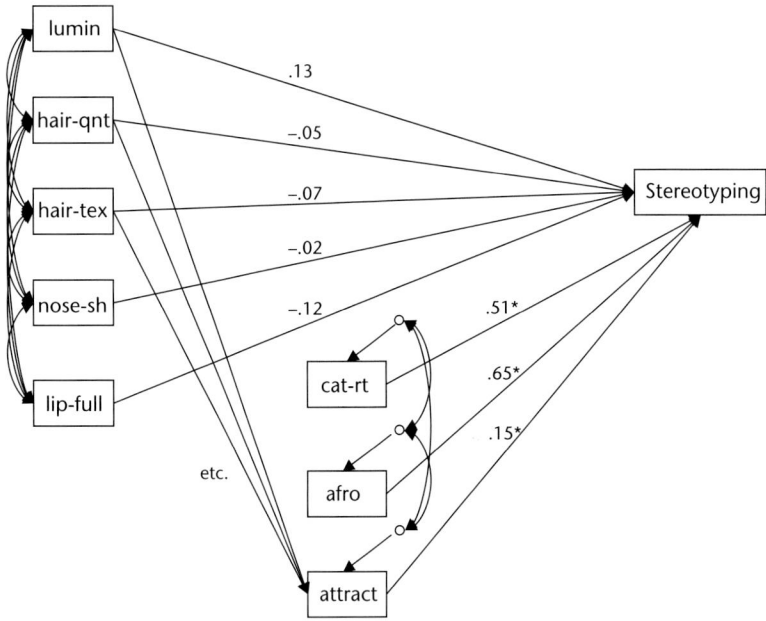

Figure 18.4 Measured Features and Mediators Predicting Stereotyping.

Table 18.6.   Calculated Indirect Effects of Measured Features on Stereotyping.

Measured Feature	Effect via Perceived Afrocentrism	Effect via Categorization Ease
Skin luminance	−.16	−.24
Lip fullness	.20	.24
Nose shape	.11	.03
Hair texture	.07	.18
Hair quantity	−.05	−.04

features: certain features prompt categorization of a face and stereotyping ensues from that, and other features lead to inferences of Afrocentrism and stereotyping ensues from that.

In the preceding sentence we implied that different features are responsible for stereotyping through categorization and through perceived Afrocentrism. In fact, this is only partly the case. It is possible to calculate from the standardized partial regression coefficients given in Table 18.5 the indirect effects of each feature on stereotyping via the two routes, one via perceived Afrocentrism as the mediator and

one via (ease of) categorization as the mediator. These indirect effects are calculated as the products of the partial coefficients for the measured feature effect on each mediator times the partial effect of that mediator on stereotyping controlling for measured features and the other mediators. In Table 18.6, we give these calculated partial indirect effects. These suggest that the substantial effects of both *skin luminance* and *lip fullness* on stereotyping are through both routes, although they are larger through categorization than through perceived Afrocentrism. On the other hand, *nose shape* leads to stereotyping more strongly through its effects on perceived Afrocentrism than its effects on categorization.[5]

One final piece of data is of some interest. Unsurprisingly the zero-order correlation between ease of racial categorization and perceived Afrocentrism is very large and highly significant, $r = .86$. However, once we control for the five measured facial features, this correlation is reduced to a nonsignificant value, $r = .16$. Thus, it seems that these five measured facial features are largely responsible for the substantial correlation between categorization ease and perceived Afrocentrism of these faces. This seems a further confirmation that these facial features really do capture the cues that participants rely upon both for racial categorization and for inferences of Afrocentrism within racial category.

CONCLUSIONS

There is now convincing evidence that stereotyping from visual information such as facial features proceeds in two different manners. On the one hand, and consistent with most existing models of stereotyping, these features give rise to categorization of an individual into a social group. As a result of this, the stereotypic attributes associated with the group may then be applied to the individual. On the other hand, and this is a rather different perspective that is represented in our work and other emerging work, physical features can also lead to stereotyping more directly, through their impact on inferences about the extent to which a face has those features that are associated with a group (e.g., Afrocentric features). Such features vary within categories as well as between them. Accordingly, to the extent that stereotyping ensues directly from features, varying within categories as well as between them, stereotypic inference will be made within groups as well as between them.

---

[5] The results presented in Table 18.6 might also suggest that *hair texture* has a greater influence on stereotyping through categorization than Afrocentrism. However, caution is warranted in this case since *hair texture* did not show a significant direct relation with stereotyping.

Our prior work has demonstrated this second route to stereotyping. Additionally, it has explored the extent to which people are aware of and can control stereotyping based on features or categories. It appears that while many are motivated and able to control category-based stereotyping, most perceivers are not aware of the extent to which they engage in within-category, feature-based stereotyping. Additionally, we have shown that explicit instructions to avoid such stereotyping meet with little success. Accordingly, our work on the role of Afrocentric features in criminal sentencing suggests that these stereotypic differences can be of considerable importance, even though judges and the legal system are well aware of and intent on eliminating racial biases in sentencing.

The empirical work reported for the first time in this chapter explores the specific facial features that lead to stereotyping via one or both of the two routes. Specifically we examined a large number of facial features that might be used in inferring category membership and a face's Afrocentrism. Across a large sample of African American and European American faces, we found five specific physical features that predicted the degree to which a face was judged to have Afrocentric features: *skin luminance, nose shape, lip fullness, hair texture*, and *hair quantity*. And these were, unsurprisingly, strongly predictive of the degree to which stereotypic inferences were made about the face, i.e., judging that the person depicted was more likely to engage in behaviors stereotypic of African Americans and less likely to engage in counter-stereotypic behaviors. Importantly these very same features were strongly predictive of the ease with which the faces were categorized as members of one racial group or the other. Thus, the very same features that determine racial group membership largely determine perceptions of Afrocentrism within racial groups. Given our theoretical understanding of how features acquire the ability to directly lead to stereotypic inferences, this is hardly surprising. Stereotypes are fundamentally category-based. But the features that are used to determine category membership become directly associated with category-based stereotypic inferences.

Accordingly, the features themselves invoke the stereotypic inferences within category.

Given this theoretical perspective, what is interesting, then, about the present analysis of the physical features that guide stereotyping via categorization or perceived Afrocentrism is that some physical features lead to stereotyping more through categorization, whereas other features lead to stereotyping more through perceived Afrocentrism. Obviously, as we would predict, most physical features are important in both categorization and perceived Afrocentrism. And the five physical features we have identified appear to be crucial in both sorts of judgments. The important point, however, is that there are two paths to stereotyping based on facial features. Although the same physical features play a role in both, the paths are discriminable and so are the features that line each path.

REFERENCES

Anderson, J. R., & Bower, G. H. (1973). *Human associative memory.* Washington: V. H. Winston: distributed by the Halsted Press Division of Wiley, New York.

Anderson, S., & Klatzky, R. (1987). Traits and social stereotypes: Levels of categorization in person perception. *Journal of Personality and Social Psychology, 53*, 235–246.

Ashmore, R., & Del Boca, F. (1979). Sex stereotypes and implicit personality theory: Toward a cognitive-social psychological conceptualization. *Sex Roles, 5*, 219–248.

Aube, J., Norcliffe, H., & Koestner, R. (1995). Physical characteristics and the multifactorial approach to the study of gender characteristics. *Social Behavior and Personality, 23*, 69–82.

Bargh, J. A. (1994). The four horsemen of automaticity: Awareness, intention, efficiency, and control in social cognition. In R. S. Wyer & T. K. Srull (Eds.), *Handbook of social cognition, 2nd edition* (pp. 1–40). Hillsdale, NJ: Erlbaum.

Blair, I. V., Chapleau, K. M., & Judd, C. M. (2005). The use of Afrocentric features as cues for Judgment in the presence of diagnostic information. *European Journal of Social Psychology, 35*, 59–68.

Blair, I. V., Judd, C. M., & Chapleau, K. M. (2004). The influence of Afrocentric facial features in criminal sentencing. *Psychological Science, 15*, 674–679.

Blair, I. V., Judd, C. M., & Fallman, J. L. (2004). The automaticity of race and Afrocentric facial features in social judgments. *Journal of Personality and Social Psychology, 87, 6* 763–778.

Blair, I. V., Judd, C. M., Sadler, M. S., & Jenkins, C. (2002). The role of Afrocentric features in person perception: Judging by features and categories. *Journal of Personality and Social Psychology, 83*(1), 5–25.

Blair, I. V. (2006). The efficient use of race and Afrocentric features in inverted faces. *Social Cognition, 24*, 563–579.

Bodenhausen, G. V. (1990). Stereotypes as judgmental heuristics: Evidence of circadian variations in discrimination. *Psychological Science, 1*, 319–322.

Bodenhausen, G., & Macrae, N. (1998). Stereotype activation and inhibition. In J. R. Wyer (Ed.), *Advances in Social Cognition* (Vol. 11, pp. 1-52). Mahwah, NJ: Erlbaum.

Brewer, M. (1988). A dual process model of impression formation. *Advances in Social Cognition, 1*, 1–36.

Brewer, M., & Lui, L. (1989). The primacy of age and sex in the structure of person categories. *Social Cognition, 7*, 262–274.

Carlston, D. (1994). Associated systems theory: A systematic approach to cognitive representations of persons. In R. W. Wyer (Ed.), *Advances in Social Cognition* (Vol. 7, pp. 1-78). Hillsdale, NJ: Erlbaum.

Cartmill, M. (1998). The status of the race concept in physical anthropology. *American Anthropologist, 100*, 651–660.

Corneille, O., Huart, J., Becquart, E., & Brédart, S. (2004). When memory shifts toward more typical category exemplars: Accentuation effects in the recollection of ethnically ambiguous faces. *Journal of Personality and Social Psychology, 86*, 236–250.

Eberhardt, J. L., Dasgupta, N., & Banaszynski, T. L. (2003). Believing is seeing: The effects of racial labels and implicit beliefs on face perception. *Personality and Social Psychology Bulletin, 29*, 360–370.

Eberhardt, J. L., Davies, P. G., Purdie-Vaughns, V. J., Johnson, S. L. (2006). Looking deathworthy: perceived stereotypicality of Black defendants predicts capital-sentencing outcomes. *Psychological Science, 17*, 383–386.

Eberhardt, J. L., Goff, P. A., Purdie, V. J., & Davies, P. G., (2004). Seeing Black: Race, crime, and visual processing. *Journal of Personality and Social Psychology, 87,* 876–893.

Fiske, S. T., & Taylor, S. E. (1991). *Social cognition* (second ed.). New York: McGraw-Hill.

Fiske, S., & Neuberg, S. (1990). A continuum of impression formation, from category-based to individuating processes: Influences of information and motivation on attention and interpretation. *Advances in Experimental Social Psychology, 23,* 1–74.

Gilbert, D. T., & Hixon, J. G. (1991). The trouble of thinking: Activation and application of stereotypic beliefs. *Journal of Personality and Social Psychology, 60,* 509–517.

Green, R., & Ashmore, R. (1998). Taking and developing pictures in the head: Assessing the physical stereotypes of eight gender types. *Journal of Applied Social Psychology, 28,* 1609–1636.

Hayes-Roth, B. (1977). Evolution of cognitive structures and processes. *Psychological Review, 84,* 260–278.

Hebb, D. A. (1948). *Organization of behavior.* New York: Wiley.

Huart, J., Corneille, O., & Becquart, E. (2005). Face-based categorization, context-based categorization, and distortions in the recollection of gender ambiguous faces. *Journal of Experimental Social Psychology, 41,* 598–608.

Kruglanski, A., & Freund, T. (1983). The freezing and unfreezing of lay-inferences: Effects of impressional primacy, ethnic stereotyping, and numerical anchoring. *Journal of Experimental Social Psychology, 19,* 448–468.

Levin, D. T., & Banaji, M. R., (2006). Distortions in the perceived lightness of faces: The role of race categories. *Journal of Experimental Psychology: General, 135,* 501–512.

Lippmann, W. (1922). *Public Opinion.* New York: Harcourt, Brace and Company.

Livingston, R. W., & Brewer, M. B. (2002). What are we really priming?: Cue-based versus category-based processing of facial stimuli. *Journal of Personality & Social Psychology, 82,* 5–18.

Macrae, C. N., Hewstone, M., & Griffiths, R. J. (1993). Processing load and memory for stereotype-based information. *European Journal of Social Psychology, 23,* 77–87.

Maddox, K. B., & Gray, S. A. (2002). Cognitive representations of Black Americans: Re-exploring the role of skin tone. *Personality and Social Psychology Bulletin, 28,* 250–259.

Oliver, M. B., Jackson, R. L., II, Moses, N. N., & Dangerfield, C. L. (2004). The face of crime: Viewers' memory of race-related facial features of individuals pictured in the news. *Journal of Communication, 54,* 88–104.

Pendry, L. F., & Macrae, C. N. (1994). Stereotypes and mental life: The case of the motivated but thwarted tactician. *Journal of Experimental Social Psychology, 30,* 303–325.

Pendry, L. F., & Macrae, C. N. (1999). Cognitive load and person memory: The role of perceived group variability. *European Journal of Social Psychology, 29,* 925–942.

Pratto, F., & Bargh, J. (1991). Stereotyping based on apparently individuating information: Trait and global components of sex stereotypes under attention overload. *Journal of Experimental Social Psychology, 27,* 26–47.

Sczesny, S., & Kühnen, U. (2004). Meta-cognition about biological sex and gender-stereotypic physical appearance: Consequences for the assessment of leadership competence. *Personality and Social Psychology Bulletin, 30,* 13–21.

Six, B., & Eckes, T. (1991). A closer look at the complex structure of gender stereotypes. *Sex Roles, 24,* 57–71.

Zebrowitz, L. A. (1998). *Reading faces.* Boulder. CO: Westview Press.

CHAPTER 19

The Role of Racial Markers in Race Perception and Racial Categorization

Otto H. MacLin and M. Kimberly MacLin

Most people would agree that race plays an important role in our social lives. However, some might be surprised to learn that race also plays an important role in our basic perceptual processes. In this chapter we present the argument that race is so important socially, that a special cognitive mechanism sensitive to race via racial markers has been selected out through adaptive pressures within the evolutionary process. We will present a model representing how we believe the mechanism integrates with other cognitive processes. And finally, we will discuss how this model might be useful in examining other face-related phenomena such as the inversion effect. In this light then, a phenomenon such as the cross-race effect (being less able to recognize faces of other races compared to our own), is adaptive, and not a social or cognitive deficit as most, if not all, theories attempting to explain the cross-race effect would have it. We draw these conclusions based on a review of the growing body of research on race detection, ambiguous race faces, and on pilot studies conducted recently in our lab to test our theory.

Based on previous research and on current neurophysiological data, we believe that the mechanisms involved in the cross-race effect are linked to a cognitive gating mechanism associated with the N100 event-related potential (ERP) component, which signals, among other things, threat (Correll, Urland, & Ito, 2006) and possibly emotional processing in the amygdala (Phelps & Thomas, 2003), although many brain areas likely play a role in the process. Racial markers, such as hair and skin tone, change the state of the gating mechanism, and depending on the state, differential perceptual and cognitive processing occurs for the perception of other-race faces (outgroup members) relative to same-race faces (ingroup members). We further propose that the underlying perceptual processes serve to reduce, refine, and calibrate the racial boundaries delineating same-race and other-race faces. The perception of a racial marker of another race serves to shift the racial boundary to reduce the number of acceptable same-race faces in similar fashion as occurs with adaptation to faces (MacLin & Webster, 2001; MacLin & Webster, 1998; Webster, Kaping, Mizokami, & Dunamel, 2004) to further protect us from possible threats from outgroup members.

This chapter provides (1) a discussion of the relevance and impact of cross-racial issues; (2) a brief overview of the cross-race effect itself and the theories attempting to explain it; (3) a proposal for an ecological explanation for the cross-race effect; (4) an overview of methodology useful for studying these issues, broadly defined as social psychophysics; (5) data from two pilot studies examining how racial markers affect the gating mechanism; and (6) a presentation of a gating mechanism model for processing other-race faces.

THE IMPORTANCE OF RACE AND THE CROSS-RACE EFFECT

Race plays a large role in society that impacts personal relationships, politics, and the legal system. For example, problems associated with a witness of one race attempting to identify a suspect of another race has been shown to be prone to misidentifications, in particular false identification where the suspect is erroneously identified as the culprit. Nationally, with the advances in DNA testing, over 250 prisoners serving an average of 13 years in jail have been exonerated postconviction from America's prisons. More than 75 percent of these convictions were due to faulty eyewitness identification (www.innocenceproject.org). Data from these exonerations, along with other archival data (Behrman & Davey, 2001), provide legal scholars and psychological researchers a window into the legal system revealing a disproportionate number of minorities being released through exonerations (Gross et al., 2002; Scheck, Nuefeld, & Dwyer, 2000).

Unfortunately, this comes as no surprise to the research community studying what is known as the cross-race effect (also known as the own-race bias; Malpass & Kravitz, 1969). While cross-race identifications refer to legal circumstances in which the witness/victim is of a different race than the perpetrator (Wells & Olson, 2001), the cross-race effect is more generally a phenomenon in which people of one race typically have greater difficulty recognizing those of another race (Malpass & Kravitz, 1969). This difficulty manifests itself by people erroneously believing they have seen a face before when they have not (called a false alarm).

There are many theories as to why the cross-race effect occurs, however, after almost 40 years of empirical study, we still know very little about the underlying causes of this extremely robust phenomenon (Meissner & Brigham, 2001). The Malpass and Kravitz (1969) study set off a plethora of research examining the cross-race effect. In 2001, Meissner and Brigham conducted a meta-analysis on the cross-race effect based on over 90 independent samples (almost 5,000 participants) and concluded that indeed the cross-race effect exists with, in signal detection terms, a greater number of hits for same-race and a greater number of false alarms for other-race faces (also see Sporer, 2001). The problem being, when people see an other-race face they error in thinking that they have seen it before, when in fact they have not. This is exactly how it plays out in our legal system with a disproportionate number of exonerations being of cases where an African American man is falsely identified by a Caucasian woman in a rape case (rape cases are more likely to yield usable biological evidence, which can then be used during post-conviction appeals to determine actual innocence) (Gross et al., 2005).

The cross-race effect is not limited to African Americans and Caucasians; in fact, it occurs across borders and across-races (see Meissner & Brigham, 2001; Sporer, 2001). The cross-race effect has been and continues to be a robust phenomenon in and out of the laboratory, with no firm answers about its cause. There are, however, several social and cognitive theories attempting to explain the effect that we will briefly review.

EXPLANATIONS FOR THE CROSS-RACE EFFECT

Social Theories—Attitudes and Contact

Empirical examinations of racial issues have been extensively studied within social psychologists (e.g., Allport & Kramer, 1946; Secord, Bevan, & Katz, 1954), and thus it was a logical step for social psychologists to examine the relationship between recognition performance, attitudes toward racial groups, and contact with members of racial groups as potential explanations for the cross-race effect.

Contact with members of other racial groups and attitudes toward them are related in that those reporting stronger prejudices also report less contact with members of other races (Brigham & Meissner, 2000; Slone, Brigham, & Meissner, 2000; Swope, 1994). Thus, it was thought that increased contact with members of other races would reduce the cross-race effect. However, researchers have met with little success in finding a relationship between the cross-race effect and contact (Cross, Cross, & Daly, 1971; Malpass & Kravitz, 1969; Brigham & Barkowitz, 1978; Ng & Lindsay, 1994; Platz & Hosch, 1988; Shepherd, 1981; Slone et al., 2000; Walker & Hewstone, 2006). Some limited support for the contact hypothesis, however, has been found in some recent studies (Carroo, 1986; Chiroro & Valentine, 1995; MacLin, van Sickler, MacLin, & Li, 2004; Wright, Boyd, & Tredoux, 1999). Why would this be? In his Utilitarian Hypothesis account for differential recognition of other-race faces, Malpass (1990) proposed that contact by itself is insufficient; there must be a reason or need to individuate members of another race before the cross-race effect is reduced. Take for example a city dweller with no desire to own a car who relies on taxi cabs to get around town. Even though the city dweller is in contact with thousands of cars on a daily basis, there is no utility in being able to recognize different type of cars. Categorically, the only class of car this person must recognize is a taxi, which is discriminated by its markings or color, rather than the particular make or model. Thus, if people have no need to individuate other-race members, they will continue to make errors when attempting to recognize them (Malpass, 1990).

Race as a Feature

Researchers have examined perceptual features such as orientation, color, and size, using a visual search paradigm. In these studies, features will "pop out" in that they are noticed almost instantly when surrounded by objects lacking these features (see Carter, 1948; Cavanagh, Arguin, & Treisman, 1990; von Gruenau, Dube, & Kwas, 1996). For example, a horizontal line amidst a background of vertical lines will "pop out" supporting orientation as a feature. Similarly, Levin (2000) used a visual search task to examine whether race functions as a perceptual feature. He found that when Caucasian participants viewed an African-American face amidst a background of Caucasian faces, the African-American face

"popped-out." However, a Caucasian face did not "pop-out" when African-American faces were used as the background, suggesting that race is a salient feature. Using a speeded classification task with same-race and other-race faces, Levin (1996) found an advantage with other-race faces being classified more quickly than same-race faces. Levin suggested that racial information was automatically coded at the expense of individuating information. He also found that those individuals who were better at classifying other race faces, were also subject to a greater cross-race effect in a face memory task (Levin, 1996; Levin & Lacruz, 1999). Therefore, it would appear that these participants were processing race information, which had little value for determining if each face had been seen before or not. It has been proposed that only "other-race" functions as a feature because same-race is the "cultural default" and is not encoded as a perceptual dimension (Zárate & Smith, 1990) which is consistent with Levin's overall pattern of data.

Given that Levin posits that race is encoded at the expense of other individuating information (for outgroup members) (Levin, 2000), he is in essence framing race as a feature in what we label a deficit model. Results from fMRI appear to support a deficit model because activation in the right fusiform face area, which processes facial information, is reduced when viewing other-race faces for a majority of participants (Golby, Gabrieli, Chiao, & Eberhardt, 2001; for a review see Phelps & Thomas, 2003). However, we will argue later that race as a feature actually supports an optimal processing, ecologically valid model in that the brain is making use of exactly what information it needs in processing facial information from ingroup and outgroup members. We will further argue that measuring how we process other-race faces using a memory test will naturally result in a deficit interpretation of the data and the processes involved.

Perceptual Learning: Race as a Stimulus Class

One can also consider race as a stimulus class with individual faces of that race comprising the stimulus exemplars. Stimulus classes consist of exemplars sharing a common function or common physical properties. Considering race as a stimulus class (with individual faces as exemplars) makes sense, given that faces of different races vary on physiognomic facial features (Ellis et al., 1975; Shepherd, 1981; Shepherd & Deregowski, 1981), but the features themselves (e.g., eyes, nose, mouth) are of course Constant Features of a face regardless of racial membership. Goldstein (1979) measured the physiognomic variability across different racial groups (African American, white, and Asian) and found qualitative differences, but no quantitative difference (also see Milord, 1978). These differences, however, do not give any particular race an advantage of being more memorable because the variance within each race is roughly equivalent. Thus, observable physical differences between races (e.g., hair type, nose, eye and lip shape, skin tone) serve to create racial stimulus classes with variation within them, and, therefore, although members of another racial group may be perceived as looking "all alike" to an outgroup member, they are all uniquely different and show as much variation as is found in Caucasian faces.

According to Valentine (1991), a facial stimulus class should develop as a person gains experience with individual facial exemplars, thus building a representational system based on same-race faces (also see Valentine, Chiroro, & Dixon, 1994; Valentine & Endo, 1992). Most people grow up exposed to a primary race, therefore, they develop an expertise with same-race faces and form a representational system based on the invariant features of these ingroup faces. Invariant features refer to those that are relatively unchanging over time and circumstances (e.g., distance between the eyes, shape of nose); whereas variant features such as hair color, facial hair, and facial weight (gain or loss) do change over time and circumstances. People exposed to a primary race are best able to discriminate individual members of their own race. Given that other-race members belong to a separate facial stimulus class based on entirely different physical properties, it becomes difficult to encode and discriminate other-race faces. Once expertise with same-race faces is acquired, even training designed to perceptually discriminate

other-race faces has met with only some success (Goldstein & Chance, 1985), but most have not been successful at all (Elliott, Wills, & Goldstein, 1973; Malpass, Lavigueur, & Weldon, 1973; for review see Malpass, 1981).

Valentine's (1991) exemplar-based model accounts for how a facial stimulus class is developed through the acquisition of new faces. The exemplar model posits that through experience with a sufficient number of faces (typically same-race), a representational system develops. Multiple dimensions representing the invariant properties of the faces emerge with one dimension for each invariant property. Existing faces are stored as exemplars along each dimension in a continuum. When a new face is encoded, it becomes located near previously stored exemplars sharing similar properties. For example, a dimension representing nose length likely exists. On this nose length dimension, short noses might be located at one end of the continuum and long noses at the other end of the continuum. Valentine and Endo (1992) proposed that within any dimension, nose length for example, exemplars will be normally distributed along a Gaussian distribution with noses expressing the average length located in the center of the distribution. When a new face is to be accommodated into the existing structure, it is encoded relative to other faces with similar properties (or dimensions). This model supports the reality of multiple dimensions. Thus, for example, if a face has a long nose and close-set eyes, it will be located near other faces with similar close-set eyes and similarly long noses. Valentine's (1991) model is often referred to as an n-dimensional face-space model, given that the actual number of dimensions is unknown. Additionally, few researchers have as yet defined what the actual perceptual dimensions are, although eye width and nose length are known to be important (Hosie, Ellis, & Haig, 1988) as well as eyebrows (Sadr, Jarudi & Sinha, 2003). Valentine's model can also be viewed as a deficit model since he and his colleagues view it as a problem which occurs encoding.

We should note that we can examine facial dimensions in two ways. We can first examine the physical or mathematical properties of faces to determine how many dimensions are available to perceive if we were "ideal observers" and able to extract all possible information (Geisler, 2003). Computers are ideal observers to some extent and have been designed to recognize faces by decomposing a facial image into pixel values and then using principle components analysis to evaluate their commonality by creating a large set of facial dimensions called Eigenfaces (Turk & Pentland, 1991). Individual faces can then be compared to Eigenface values stored in databases for potential matches, where a "match" would be the equivalent of recognition. Although Eigenfaces represent the physical dimensions of faces, they are limited to the number of faces used in the stimulus set to conduct the initial factor analysis (these stimulus sets are small relative to the number of faces humans naturally encounter). Another limitation with Eigenfaces is that it is often difficult to interpret just what the dimension represents (O'Toole, Abdi, Deffenbacher, & Valentine, 1993; Tredoux, 2002).

Facial dimensions can also be examined using multidimensional scaling (MDS). Researchers have made use of statistical procedures such as MDS to evaluate the perceptual dimensions of small facial stimulus sets (Rhodes, 1988; Sergent, 1984; Shepherd, 1981). With the MDS procedure, participants make a series of similarity ratings for each possible pair of faces in the stimulus set. The similarity ratings are used to construct a proximity matrix that is then analyzed using MDS. The problem with MDS is that only very small stimulus sets can be used because the addition of each new face increases exponentially the number of comparisons required. Additionally, with a small number of faces, the dimensions that emerge from the MDS solution are limited to those found in the initial stimulus set. One solution to the problem of being able to examine only the physical dimensions of faces (using Eigenfaces) or the perceptual dimensions of faces (using MDS) would be to use the method of adaptation (MacLin & Webster, 2001, MacLin & Webster, 1998; Webster, Werner & Field, 2005), which is addressed elsewhere in this chapter.

Although Valentine's model provides a theoretical structure for a same-race stimulus class, he has also extended the face-space model to account for other-race faces. Chiroro and Valentine (1995) contend that by the time most people begin to experience a sufficient number of other-race exemplars, the structure of the face space is rather complete, already populated with thousands of same-race exemplars, making it difficult to encode other-race faces, which now must be encoded based on same-race feature dimensions inadequate for other-race faces, and thus this too is a deficit model explanation. Further, other-race faces have a high likelihood of being poorly encoded on dimensions that do not adequately preserve the featural dimensions required to differentiate them from one another. Chiroro and Valentine (1995) posit that other-race faces ultimately become tightly clustered in one area of the face space, which accounts for a higher number of false alarms. However, some researchers contend that, as experience is gained through prolonged, meaningful contact with people of another race, other-race faces can be better discriminated. However, even under these circumstances the cross-race effect is not eliminated (Cross et al., 1971; Feinman & Entwisle, 1976; Malpass, 1993). To summarize the cross-race effect model of race as a stimulus class, the face space is formed and calibrated to same-race faces. Other-race faces represent a different stimulus class and are poorly encoded in the face space in high density clusters leading to the cross-race effect.

To test Chiroro and Valentine's (1995) account of how other-race faces are encoded in face space, MacLin and Malpass (2001) developed a stimulus set of faces using a facial composite construction program used in law enforcement. The composite program allows the operator to construct a facial composite feature by feature. Composite faces were constructed such that faces were created using features that were non-race specific (ears and chin) and overlapping across racial (African-American and Hispanic) lines (e.g., dark eyebrows, dark eyes, broad nose, and full lips are features that are common in both African-American and Hispanic faces). These composites were termed ambiguous race faces

Figure 19.1 Ambiguous Race
Faces. A. Unique face without
racial marker (hair); B. Same face
with Hispanic racial marker;
C. Same face with African-
American racial marker.

(ARFs) because racial identity was not apparent. When a key feature functioning as a racial
marker (in this case hair), was added to the face,
it was perceived as a person of that race (see
Figure 19.1). By manipulating the racial marker,
they were able to manipulate the perception of
racial categorization. It should be noted that
skin tone was not manipulated with the composites, and the faces had the same pixel value
for the areas of the face that would account for
skin. MacLin and Malpass (2001) had Hispanic
participants classify the faces as either African
American, Hispanic, or Other and found that
approximately 70 percent of the faces with the
African-American racial marker were classified
as African American, and about 70 percent of
the faces with the Hispanic racial marker were
classified as Hispanic. Additionally, participants rated the faces with the African-American
marker as more assertive, cold, with a wider
mouth and darker skin among other attributes
(keeping in mind that these are identical faces
with the exception of the racial marker, hair).
Levin and Banaji (2006) later replicated the
finding of perceived skin tone difference using
morphed facial images, demonstrating that the
effect transfers to other types of facial stimuli,
stimuli depicting other races, and, Caucasian
participants. Further, we found that the ARFs
(with the appropriate racial marker) also successfully elicited race-congruent implicit attitudes using the Implicit Attitude Test (IAT)
indicating that they are processed similarly to
"real" faces (MacLin & MacLin, 2002; MacLin,
MacLin, & Malpass, 2001).

Additionally, MacLin and Malpass (2001)
used the ARFs, with half having a Hispanic
racial marker (hair), and half having an

African-American racial marker as stimuli in
a study examining the cross-race effect. They
found an increase in false alarms when an
African- American racial marker was in place,
thus replicating the cross-race effect. The significance of the MacLin and Malpass (2001)
study is that they demonstrated the ability of a
single feature functioning as a racial marker to
change the perception of the otherwise identical
faces to the extent they were able to produce the
cross-race effect in participants.

These findings with ARF faces, however, present a problem for the Valentine's (1991) face-
space model. Imagine two identical twins with
different hair cuts. Without a doubt, the faces
would be encoded in close proximity to each
other and near other exemplars with similar
features because they are encoded on the same
physical dimensions, and vary on only one
of the n-dimensions (hair). However, when a
racial marker (hair) acts as a signal for race, the
face is perceived as entirely different and stored
elsewhere, underutilizing other featural information needed to later recognize the face. It is
possible that multiple face spaces exist (MacLin
& Malpass, 2001), with a well-developed space
for same-race faces and a less-developed space
for the representation of other-race faces. In this
case, the racial marker might signal the cognitive system to encode the face in a different face
space.

Some support for a separate face space comes
from McClure, Maddox, and Sanders (under
revision) who found that participants performed
better at recognizing other-race faces when the
faces had either a dark skin tone or a light skin
tone as compared to a medium skin tone. This
suggests that skin tone, too, may be represented

on a Gaussian continuum with the average skin tone faces more difficult to recognize because they are located in the center of the perceptual dimension and, therefore, cluster more closely. Rather than all of the other-race faces being clustered together as Valentine's model would have it, they suggest that a well-defined distribution for skin tone exists, possibly located in a separate face space developed for other-race faces.

AN ECOLOGICAL EXPLANATION FOR THE CROSS-RACE EFFECT— NEUROPHYSIOLOGICAL EVIDENCE

Most if not all explanations of the cross-race effect are deficit based (see Sporer, 2001). MacLin and Malpass (2001, 2003) disagree with these deficit models arguing that race functions to alter the perceptual process indicating that information from other-race faces is used for different purposes than is the information from same-race faces. This process, however, did not evolve to optimize other-race recognition; this process instead serves to evaluate facial information such as threat from outgroup members (cf. Ito & Urland, 2003; 2005). Support comes from data examining the role of the amygdala in face recognition. Recognizing faces of other races results in more activity in the amygdala, suggesting greater emotional processing associated with threat (Hart, et al., 2000; Phelps, et al., 2000). These findings are further supported by data from physiological studies (Correll, et al., 2006; Ito & Urland, 2003; 2005).

With this in mind, we argue from an ecological perspective that the brain did not evolve to be good at recognizing members of other races. Moreover, the brain evolved to quickly categorize a face as ingroup or outgroup based on the presence or absence of racial markers and to direct the facial information to appropriate brain areas once categorization has occurred. This theory is supported by physiological data from racial categorization studies (Ito & Urland, 2003, 2005) and by fMRI studies (Hart et al., 2000; Phelps et al., 2000) indicating separate neural regions for processing same-race and other-race faces. Ito and colleagues use electroencephalogram (EEG) to evaluate the time to process objects and faces by measuring event-related brain potentials (ERPs). ERPs are "changes in brain electrical activity that occur in response to discrete events such as a stimulus…they can be recorded noninvasively from the surface of the scalp and are thought to reflect summated postsynaptic potentials from large sets of synchronously firing neurons in the cerebral cortex" (Fabiani, Gratton, & Coles, 2000; p. 401, Ito, Willadsen-Jensen, & Correll, 2007). Kubota and Ito (2007) provide a nice review of the research findings as they relate to the brain's sensitivity to race. The N100, P200, and P300 all show larger amplitudes for angry faces and outgroup faces, with the N100 and P200 orienting the brain to threatening information in the environment; and the P300 being responsive to highly arousing stimuli. The N200 (250 ms) exhibits larger amplitudes for ingroup faces indicating individuating processes at work. Figure 19.2 shows a timeline for the perception of faces. Time 1 shows the presentation of a face at 0 ms. Time 2 shows the earliest activation indicated by the N100 waveform responsive to angry faces and outgroup faces. Time 3, also in the N100 range, shows increased activity for black faces and male faces. Time 4 continues to show increased activity for angry faces and out-group members. Time 5 is the point at which individuating processes occur. Time 6 is when arousing stimuli increase activation of the P300 waveform. And finally Time 7, while still represented by the P300 waveform, is the first point in time where explicit processing occurs (overt judgments). Next, we provide some details regarding the studies behind these findings.

Ito and colleagues have concluded that social category information (including race) is encoded automatically, and particularly, that race is detected as early as 120 ms, with greater attention paid initially to black faces and male faces (as indicated by increased N100s) and later to whites and females (as indicated by increased N200s) (Ito & Urland, 2003; Ito et al., 2007). Interestingly, by the 170 ms marker participants were able to classify an object as a face or nonface, and, by 250 ms ingroup members

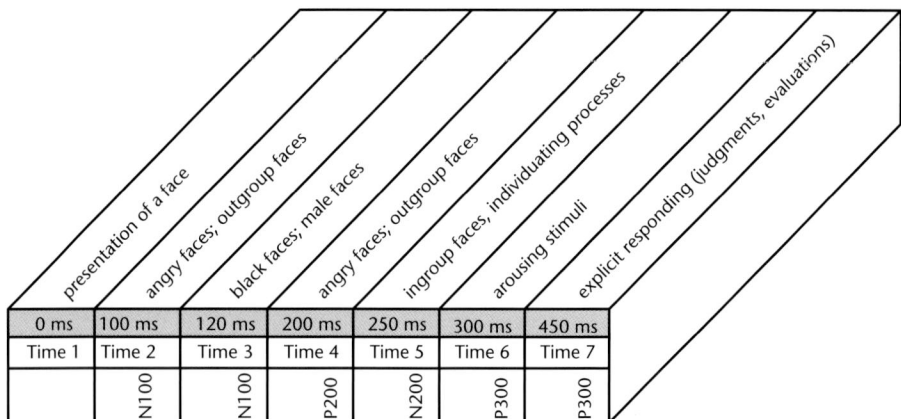

Figure 19.2 Perceptual Timeline for Detecting Faces Based on ERP data.

were differentiated from outgroup members (Ito, Thompson, & Cacioppo, 2004). At 250 ms, processing was greater for Caucasian faces than for African-American faces (indicating that greater cognitive resources are being devoted to Caucasian faces, due to individuation processes). We believe that, at the 120 ms marker, the additional cognitive processing is possibly the result of a cognitive gating mechanism sensitive to the presence of an outgroup member and signaling the brain to route some of the facial information to different areas of the brain (some information is still directed to same-race face processing areas). Next, more resources are provided to same-race faces. Based on fMRI data, Golby et al., (2001) found that 84 percent of their participants showed reduced activation for other-race faces in the fusiform face area, indicating that some of the other-race facial information is processed in the same area with same-race faces.

Willadsen-Jensen and Ito (2006) conducted an ERP study using cross-racial stimuli and ambiguous race faces (similar to MacLin and Malpass, 2001). They created their ambiguous race faces, however, using a morphing program by mathematically averaging a same-race face (Caucasian) and an other-race face. The ambiguous race face was represented by the morph at the half way point (50 percent) which is the mathematical average of the two faces. Whereas Willadsen-Jensen and Ito (2006) pilot tested the ambiguous faces they used to confirm that

they were indeed perceived as ambiguous to race, other research shows that the mathematical midpoint is not always the perceptual midpoint (Chowdhry, et al., 2008). Willadsen-Jensen, and Ito (2006) found similar results as Ito et al. (2004), in that same-race faces are processed with greater attention. With ambiguous-race faces, the classification took longer (500 ms) suggesting, we would say, that ambiguous-race faces are being processed more akin to Caucasian faces due to the absence of a racial marker.

Correll and colleagues (Correll, Urland, & Ito, 2006; Correll, Park, Judd, & Wittenbrink, 2002) found evidence that African-American faces are perceived as threatening as measured by ERPs. They studied this by having participants make a shoot/don't shoot judgment while viewing armed and unarmed African-American or Caucasian targets. Using behavioral data and ERP, they found that armed African-American targets were shot more quickly and more accurately than armed Caucasians; participants more quickly and more accurately decided *not* to shoot unarmed Caucasians compared to unarmed African Americans.

We know that the brain has a propensity to detect very early in the time course of perception, the presence of threat; and even an African American without a weapon is perceived as threatening. This threat arises in part out of pervasive personal and cultural stereotypes that are activated in the brain (prior to conscious awareness) when seeing a black person (Ito et al., 2007). However, these effects are not limited to African-American faces, and are not entirely a result of negative stereotypes. Other outgroup members (such as Asians) elicit the same effects in Caucasian participants as do African American faces (Willadsen-Jensen, & Ito, 2006).

Ito et al. (2007) refer to a "course level of analysis that scans the environment for more threatening and/or more novel stimuli" (p. 416). Threatening objects (or faces) are processed differently, we argue, for an evolutionarily adaptive purpose. Survival and reproductive success may be enhanced by avoiding threat in the environment, including potential threat from outgroup members. Threatening objects are thus important information in the environment and we need to be able to reliably detect them (Cacioppo & Berntson, 1994; Ohman, Lundqvist, & Esteves, 2001; Correll et al., 2006). These ERP studies demonstrate that outgroup members are perceived by the brain as threatening, and that ingroup members are individuated more. Thus, we argue, threat alters how the face information is processed, such that the information is gated to other parts of the brain not associated with individuation and later recognition, resulting in the cross-race effect.

These results combined with those from Levin's (1996; 2000) race as a feature work, and MacLin and Malpass's (2001; 2003) work with racial markers, suggest to us that racial markers (or "features") are detected by a cognitive gating mechanism that signals the brain to process other-race faces differently. Therefore, we can reconsider previous findings and conceptualize them not as evidence of a cognitive or social deficit, but rather, as an indication of how the brain optimally processes facial information for survival value. For example, early in the time course of face perception (Ito & Urland, 2003), if the face is of another race, the brain is activated by a racial feature (as evidenced by greater ERP activation at 120 ms) signaling the brain to gate facial information to areas of the brain other than those involved in same-race face processing. At the 250 ms mark, we see less ERP activation for other-race faces indicating less attention

and fewer cognitive resources being allocated to those stimuli. Although this could be a result of a lack of information encoded, we believe that, instead, it is the case that the need for individuating information is reduced. Same-race faces, on the other hand, show less processing at the 120 ms mark relative to other-race faces, suggesting that same-race faces are default (Zárate & Smith, 1990) and the perceptual system is not picking up on any racial marker. This also supports Levin's (1996) data that same-race faces lack a feature and thus do not "pop out." At 250 ms however, we see greater ERP activation for same-race faces relative to other-race faces, suggesting that greater cognitive resources are being devoted to same-race faces, leading to greater information gain, individuation, and better recognition.

METHODOLOGY OVERVIEW

In our lab, we have used several methodologies to assist in empirically evaluating the effect of racial markers on racial categorization. We use the term *social psychophysics* as an umbrella term encompassing psychophysical methods applied to 'social' questions (MacLin, MacLin, Peterson, Chowdhry, & Joshi, 2008). We will provide justification for their use and an overview of the techniques involved.

Social Psychophysics

Social psychology has a rich theoretical and methodological history. Triplett (1898) was the first to transpose social psychological phenomena to the lab when he studied the competitive nature of the cyclist to peddle faster when near other cyclists. By having participants spin reels (and they indeed spun them faster when with others than when alone), he was able to scientifically verify his observation of cyclists. As a result of studies such as Triplett's, social psychologists have established a set of creative and useful research methodologies grounded in the laboratory. However, there are other methods available, and social psychologists have begun adopting these methodologies. Social psychologists have borrowed methodology from other content areas in psychology when their use will assist in uncovering new aspects of social thought or behavior, particularly when those psychological processes typically studied from one perspective (e.g., memory, attention, perception) are relevant to social psychology (Ito et al., 2007). Methodological contributions from cognitive psychology and neuroscience in particular have led to the areas of social cognition and social neuroscience, respectively. (e.g., MacLin, et al., 2008; Blair & Banaji, 1996; Mandel & Lehman, 1996; Smith, 1996; Ito, Urland, Willadsen-Jensen, & Correll, 2006).

Another area that could prove very useful for social psychologists is psychophysics. Given that psychophysics is the study of how humans (in particular) detect events and stimuli in their environment, one can imagine that psychophysical methods could be used to study how humans detect social events and stimuli in the environment (Gescheider, 1997). Instead of lights, tones, and colors, social stimuli (such as faces) can be studied using psychophysics. Faces are one of the most important ways that we gather social information about other people (Zebrowitz, 1998). Physically identifiable factors such as race, gender, and age, as well as more abstract factors like attractiveness and personality characteristics are often presumed from the face (MacLin et al., 2008; Zebrowitz, 1998). Using psychophysics to answer 'social' questions provides yet another dimension of experimental manipulation and control to the diverse array of methodologies already used by social psychologists—a "social psychophysics" as it were (MacLin et al., 2008).

Psychophysical Methods

Data from the experiments presented later in this chapter rely on the use of psychophysics to examine the perception of race. A brief overview of psychophysical methodology thus follows. Psychophysics examines the relationship between the physical world and our perception of it. It is one of the oldest areas of psychology established by Gustav Fechner in the mid 1800s and brought forward by Wilhelm Wundt in Leipzig, Germany in 1879 when he established the first psychological laboratory. As such,

psychophysics became the basis of early experimental psychology. Early emphasis in psychophysics was determining sensory thresholds (Snodgrass, 1975). Thresholds are the point at which the presence of a stimulus is detected (absolute threshold) or the point at which one stimulus is reliability discriminated from a similar one (differential threshold). The point at which a change in the stimulus is detected is a difference threshold, also known as just noticeable difference or JND (Fechner, 1860/1966). Different threshold values will occur for ascending or descending trials.

Psychophysicists have developed several experimental methods to evaluate perceptual experiences: method of limits, method of constant, stimuli method of adjustment, staircase procedure, the discrimination task, and perceptual adaptation (Snodgrass, 1975). A simple example for measuring thresholds would be luminance intensity. At what point can a light be detected? At what point can a light no longer be detected? There are several psychophysical methods that can be used to answer these questions.

With method of limits, the experimenter adjusts the stimulus intensity down until the observer reports no longer detecting it (descending trials). With ascending trials the experimenter begins with a stimulus value that cannot be detected and systematically adjusts it upward until it is detected. Data points from ascending and descending trials can then be averaged to determine a threshold value. The method of adjustment is similar to the method of limits; however, the observer (rather than the experimenter) adjusts the stimulus properties. One problem with the method of limits and the method of adjustment is that observers can bias their reporting by anticipating the approaching threshold. This is overcome by the method of constant stimuli where there is no systematic presentation of the various stimulus properties, so participants cannot anticipate the nearing threshold. With the method of constant stimuli, stimulus values are presented randomly and the observer reports the stimulus presence or absence. From these data a monotonic frequency of "seeing curve" or psychometric function is determined using curve-fitting methods (Finney, 1947). One problem with the constant stimuli method is that many observations are often required in comparison to the method of adjustment.

The staircase procedure on the other hand, involves sampling points on either side of the threshold and then averaging those values to derive the threshold. The staircase procedure is similar to the method of limits in that by using a staircase, stimulus values are presented for the observer to report. With the light intensity example, if the observer reports the stimulus presence, its value is adjusted downward. If the observer cannot report the stimulus presence, its value is adjusted upward. Each change in the direction of adjustment is a reversal. The point at which the reversal occurred is recorded. After a fixed number of reversals, the experiment terminates and the reversal points are averaged to determine the stimulus threshold. The discrimination task involves the presentation of two stimulus values and determining the value where they are reliably discriminated (the JND).

Walker and Tanaka (2003) used a discrimination task to evaluate encoding for same-race and other-race faces. The researchers created a continuum of morphed faces using an East Asian face (0 percent) and a Caucasian face (100 percent) as starting images. Hair was removed from the starting images that were then converted to grey-scale. Control points located at 10 percent intervals along the morphed continuum were created. Observers were presented with one of the starting images, followed by a visual mask (Sperling, 1963), temporally followed by either the same starting image or a morph. Observers were required to report Same or Different for each stimulus pair presentation. The researchers found that Caucasian observers were more sensitive to differences with Caucasian faces (smaller JNDs), whereas East-Asian observers were more sensitive to differences with East-Asian faces supporting a same-race encoding advantage.

Facial Adaptation

Another psychophysical method is perceptual adaptation. Perceptual adaptation occurs as the perceptual system adjusts to new environmental conditions (Wade & Verstraten, 2005). Psychophysicists have long used the noninvasive technique of adaptation to examine the neural processes underlying low level perception, such as the motion aftereffect underlying the waterfall illusion (see Mather & Harris,1998 for review), optical distortion (Welch, 1978), and orientation (Gibson & Radner, 1937), for example.

Researchers suggest that we are under a constant state of adaptation with our perception of faces dynamically altered by experience with the environment. Thus, our perception of faces and face space is altered by the faces we see (MacLin & Webster, 1996; Rhodes, et al., 2005; Webster et al., 2004). Referring to Figure 19.3, the morphed image in the center appears to be a cross between President Bush and Senator Kerry (images courtesy of Michael Webster). Now cover the morph and the senator, fixating only on the president for a minute or so. Move your hand to view the morph; it will not look much like the president because the unique features used to individuate the president have been adapted out.

Adaptation works by altering the neuronal activity underlying the specific perceptual experience. The first study to demonstrate that adaptation could be used to study complex visual patterns such as faces was carried out by Webster and MacLin (1999) (also see MacLin & Webster, 1996, 1998, 2001). In this study, observers viewed distorted faces (see Figure 19.4) to temporarily alter hypothesized face-selective units (Perrett, Rolls, & Caan, 1982) causing the subsequently viewed face to appear distorted in the opposite direction of the adapting stimulus. Others have since demonstrated facial aftereffects for size (Zhao & Chubb, 2001), orientation (Watson & Clifford, 2003), attractiveness and distinctiveness (Nelson, MacLin, & Radeke, 1996; Rhodes et al., 2005), as well as race (Webster et al., 2004), and identity (Leopold, O'Toole, Vetter, & Blanz, 2001).

A staircase method was used by MacLin and Webster (2001) to evaluate how adaptation affects the perception of face space. In this study, the face images were distorted by

Figure 19.3 Creating a Morph from Two Starting Images.

expanding or contracting the frontal-view image of the face relative to a midpoint on the nose. The distortion was weighted by a circular Gaussian envelope so that the largest changes were near the midpoint and so that there were only small changes in the outline of the head. Images were created by remapping pixel values from a location within the original image (xj, yj) to a given location in the new image (xi, yi) (see Figure 19.4). Observers were presented with a facial image and asked to report whether the face was Normal or Distorted. If the observation report was Normal, a face located farther out in the Cartesian space was presented. However, if the image was reported as Distorted, an image closer to the center of the space was presented. So that all X, Y, and diagonal dimensions were represented, an eight-spoke staircase was used. Webster and MacLin (1999) also measured the same face space using the method of adjustment in a matching procedure where the observer was presented with a distorted face and had the task of adjusting the horizontal and vertical dimensions until the face appeared normal.

MacLin and Webster (2001) found that the perceptual space shifts away from the adapting stimulus in a manner similar to the way adapting to color shifts the perceptual color space (Webster & Mollon, 1995). In color space,

adapting to the color white produces no shift because it represents the center of the perceptual space. MacLin and Webster (2001) found similar results with little to no adaptation occurring for the average, nondistorted face (see Figure 19.5), and Leopold et al., (2001) found reduced neural firing for average faces than other faces presented to a nonhuman primate. Additionally, MacLin and Webster (2001) found that, after adaptation, the area of faces perceived as normal increased in size forming an elliptical shape oriented toward the adapting stimulus indicating much more than a simple shift in perceptual space. If Zárate and Smith (1990) are correct and same-race represents the default, and is not processed by the perceptual system, then we should see less adaptation to same-race faces when adapting to race as seen in the center grid in Figure 19.5, where observers adapted to the undistorted face.

Morphing Faces

One critical point relevant to applying psychophysical methodology to social psychological research questions is that psychophysics is reliant on stimuli that can be expressed on a continuum (e.g., light, sound, etc.). To use psychophysics, social stimuli of interest must also be expressed on a continuum. Faces are of course typically considered to be unique, categorical stimuli; however, it is possible to create facial continua using morphing techniques. Beale and

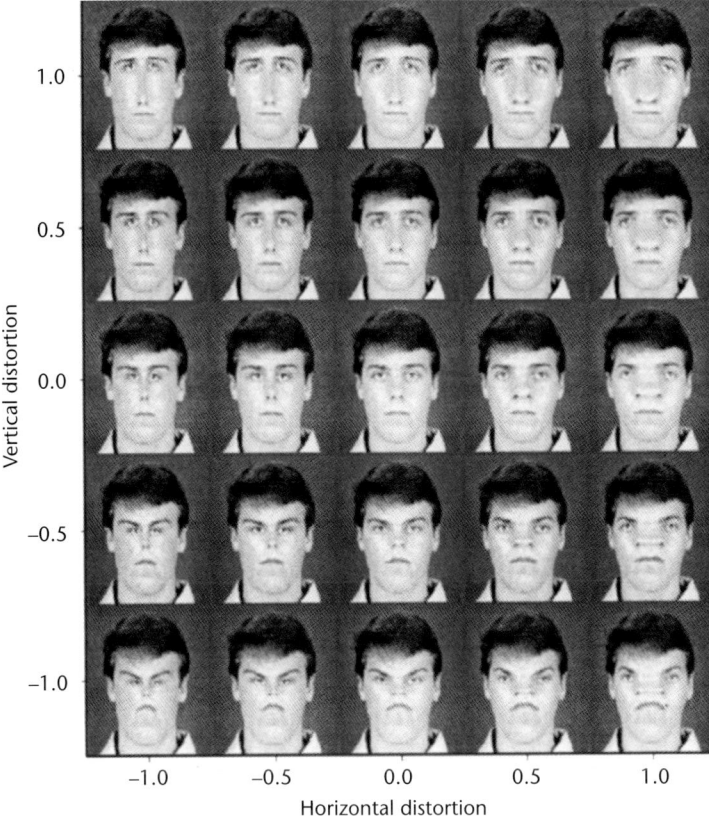

Figure 19.4 Face Space. Normal face (Starting Stimulus) Is in the Center of the Array, Surrounded by Distorted Faces.

Influence of adaptation

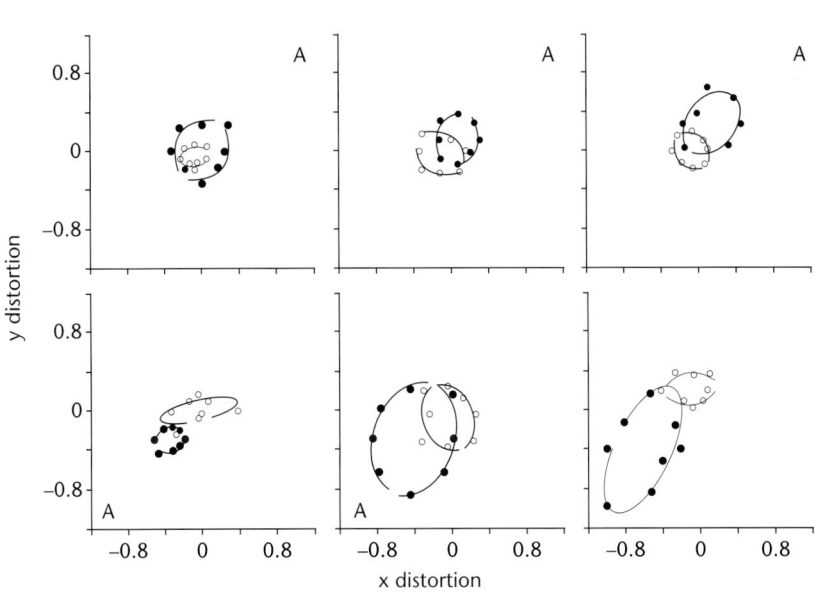

Figure 19.5 Mean Ratings Showing Perceptual Shift Due to Adaptation. Thin ellipse: prior to adaptation; Thick ellipse: after adaptation; A: location of single adapting image.

Keil (1995) used a morphing distortion technique based on mathematically manipulating the pixel properties of two facial images used as starting points. The output of the morphing process is either a digital video of the process or separate images representing discrete intervals representing a mathematical percentage, based on the two starting images (see also, Walker & Tanaka, 2003).

An interesting aside, is that much of the research examining race using morphed stimuli presume that the mathematical properties of the morph continuum are isomorphic to our perception of race. This is akin to our earlier discussion regarding face space and the differences between mathematical and perceptual models. Studies using ambiguous faces often designate the 50 percent morph to be the ambiguous race face (cf. Willadsen-Jensen & Ito, 2006). Our data (Chowdhry et al., 2008) show that the morph at the 50 percent point of the continuum is often classified as African American (not ambiguous at all) with the ARF (perceptual midpoint) occurring at a location closer to the Caucasian face. Furthermore, our data suggest that often a true continuum between the starting images does not exist, because we find a third race emerging when we modify our classification task to include a response of Other (these data will be discussed later).

USING PSYCHOPHYSICS TO EXAMINE RACE CATEGORIZATION

Stimulus Development—Ambiguous Race Faces

As mentioned previously, MacLin and Malpass (2001, 2003) developed a set of facial stimuli to examine the cross-race effect and racial categorization. One of the major problems in studying the cross-race effect has been stimulus control. Simply put, faces are unique, and while the use of actual photographic images of faces seems desirable, their very uniqueness poses control problems in experimental research. We reasoned that a stimulus set that could be perceived as either same-race or other-race by changing a single facial feature functioning as a racial

marker would go a long way toward solving the problem of stimulus control. We referred to the faces created as ARFs. With these stimuli, race was ambiguous until the addition of a feature (hair) acting as a racial marker. Using hair we could make the faces appear to be either Hispanic or African American. The resulting stimuli were ideal because we were conducting the research at the University of Texas at El Paso where the majority of students are Hispanic; thus the faces served as both same-race and other-race faces simply by changing the racial marker.

These faces proved to be extremely useful. Not only were we able to demonstrate the cross-race effect using these ARFs, but we also discovered that by simply changing the racial marker on the face, the perceptual processes were altered. Identical faces looked like completely different individuals. What came as a surprise was that faces with the African American racial marker actually looked darker relative to the faces with the Hispanic racial marker. Essentially, the hair feature acted as a racial marker, which signaled the brain to use different perceptual processes to rate, categorize, respond to, and recognize the once ambiguous face. This suggests that the mechanisms involved in the cross-race effect use a top-down process that affects our perception of virtually identical stimuli in a manner similar to the Müller-Lyer illusion in which identical lines are perceived as being different lengths depending on which way the arrow heads are pointing (see Figure 19.6). As with the Müller-Lyer illusion, the racial marker has such a profound effect that it forces us to view identical faces differently! As such, this creates problems for some leading theories attempting to explain the cross-race effect.

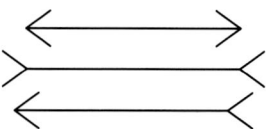

Figure 19.6 Müller-Lyer Illusion.

One problem with the original ARF stimuli was that it was time consuming to create realistic faces using the composite program. We wanted to develop a technique using morphing that would allow us to create a stimulus continuum so psychophysical methodology could be used, and, where racial markers could be manipulated. We accomplished this in the following manner. Initial face stimuli were obtained from the Meissner, Brigham, and Butz (2005) face database that contains facial stimuli of African Americans, Hispanics, and Caucasians. These faces were used as starting images in a morphing process (see Beale & Keil, 1995; Steyvers, 1999). A series of 49 morphed images were generated using an image-morphing program (FantaMorph 3) that produced new images along a linear continuum based on two starting images (see Figure 19.7). Each of the 49 morphs represent a 2 percent change along a 0 percent to 100 percent continuum. Faces at the 0 percent and 100 percent are the actual starting-point images. The African-American starting images are located

to the left of the continuum, and Caucasian starting images are located to the right. For consistency in our studies, as any given morph value increases, it is being shifted toward the Caucasian end of the continuum.

To study racial markers, we used Adobe Photoshop to manipulate the images. When a Caucasian racial marker (hair) is being used, the hair is selected and copied from the Caucasian starting image, sized and pasted onto the African-American starting image. This allows for the racial marker to remain constant across the morph continuum with each of the 51 faces (49 morphs + 2 starting images) having the identical racial marker. By manipulating the racial marker, the perception of the morphed faces is altered, as can be seen with the 50 percent morphs located at the center of the continuum in Figure 19.7.

We then created a Windows-based program designed in Visual Basic 2008 (MacLin et al., 2008; Peterson, et al., 2007; MacLin, Dixon, & James, 2007) to display images and collect observer responses using psychophysical

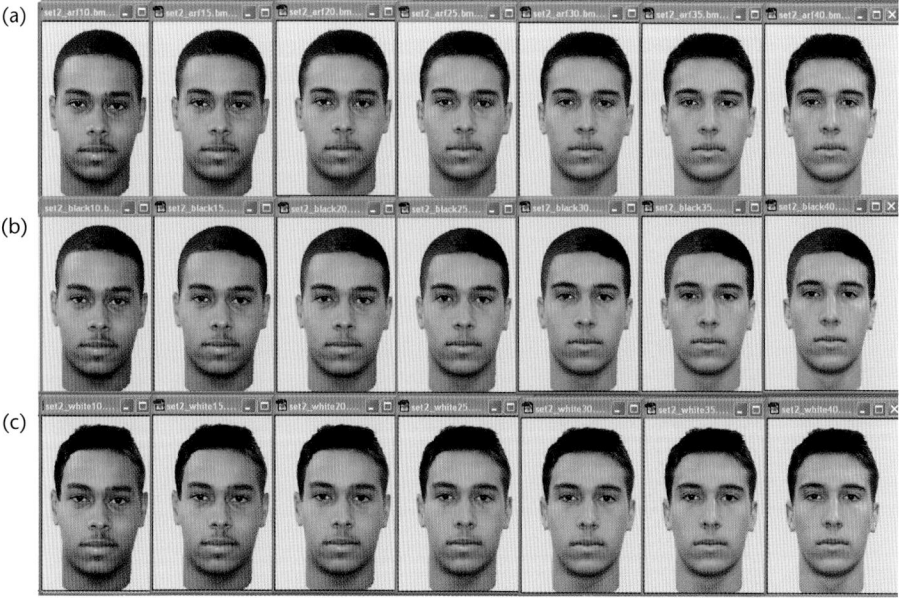

Figure 19.7 Morph Array. Row A. Regular morph using African American (far left) and Caucasian (far right) starting images; Row B. Morph using African American racial marker (hair is held constant); Row C. Morph using Caucasian racial marker (hair is held constant). Columns are identical faces with varying racial marker (morphed hair, African American hair, Caucasian hair).

methods such as constant stimuli, method of adjustment, and the staircase method using these stimuli.

Study 1

Our first question of interest was to examine how the racial marker affects the cognitive gating mechanism by shifting the racial boundaries to either increase or decrease the number of faces categorized as African American or Caucasian. Although other studies typically use a forced categorization task (e.g., Asian/Caucasian) (Webster et al., 2004), we found it easier for the participants to make two sets of categorizations (African American/Other and Caucasian/Other). We used Other because when we used the forced choice, as other studies have typically done, (African American/Caucasian) we found that for some stimulus sets there were faces that appeared neither African American nor Caucasian. Some of the faces actually were perceived as Hispanic or South Asian. A staircase method was used to collect the data.

Based on our cognitive gating mechanism (CGM) theory, we predicted that the perceptual boundaries for race would shift away from the Caucasian starting image (toward the African-American starting image) when a Caucasian racial marker was used because the CGM is sensitive to the racial marker. The result was a greater number of faces being classified as Caucasian. A similar shift away from the African-American starting image should occur when the African-American marker is used, resulting in a greater number of faces being classified as African American. Data from three Caucasian observers support our theory (small n is not uncommon in psychophysical studies, given the number of data points generated per observer). We found that, when an African-American racial marker was used (Figure 19.8, yellow line), the racial boundary was shifted away from the African-American starting image and toward the Caucasian starting image, relative to the ARF stimulus that did not have a specific racial marker. As a result, the number of faces classified as Caucasian decreased. Furthermore, when the Caucasian racial marker was used, the racial boundary shifted away from the Caucasian starting image. Clearly, the racial markers affect the perception of the faces. This is reflected as a systematic shift in racial categorization boundaries (see Figure 19.8).

We did not predict, however, the emergence of a third race. With two of our other stimulus sets with which we had difficulty in making

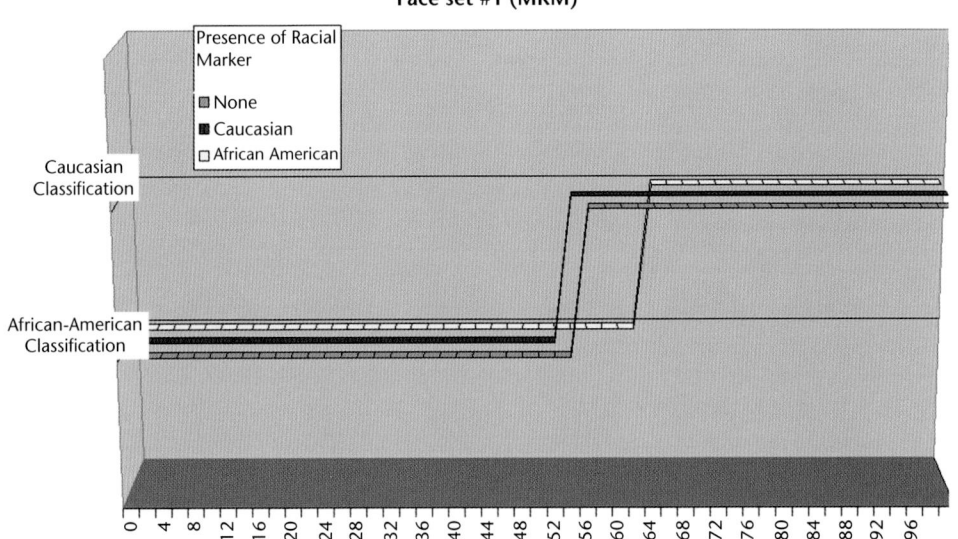

Figure 19.8 Racial Categorization Boundaries for Morphs.

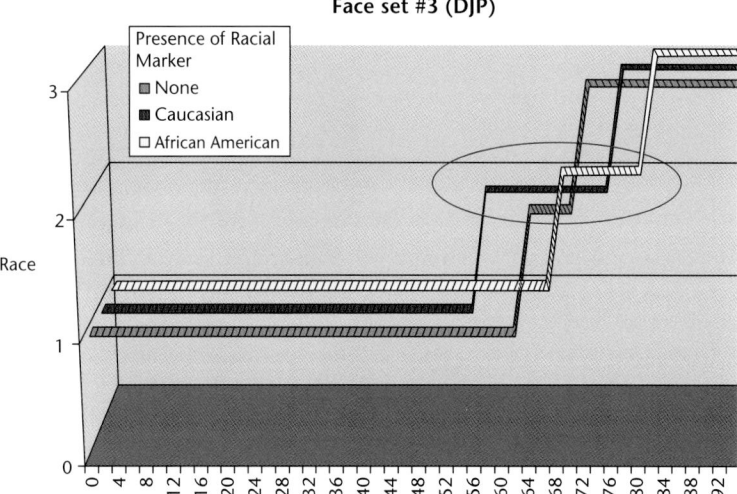

Figure 19.9 Racial Categorization Boundaries for Morphs: Emergent Third Race.

the forced decision task, we noticed that faces toward the center did not look African American or Caucasian. Our pilot data suggest the emergence of a third race as depicted in Figure 19.9. As seen in Figure 19.8, a systematic shift occurs for each of the racial markers. However, the racial boundaries are spaced apart from one another. For example, when using the Caucasian racial marker, the boundary for African American faces is located at 56 percent whereas the boundary for the Caucasian faces is located at about 76 percent, indicating that about 20 percent of the faces along the continuum are not classified in accordance to either race category.

This surprising finding is consistent across all three observers and suggests that the perception of race does not follow the mathematical continuum generated by the morphing program. Also, notice that the racial marker affects the number of faces categorized in the emergent third race. More faces are included in this Other category when the Caucasian racial marker is used relative to when the African-American racial marker is used.

Other studies have not found this emergent race because they tend to use a forced classification task and they often remove important features functioning as racial markers such as

hair (usually in an effort for stimulus control). We believe the third race emerges because of the introduction of a unique set of features created along the morphing continuum with the addition of the racial marker. At this point, the faces no longer look African American, nor do they look Caucasian (see Figure 19.10).

The main purpose of Study 1 was to evaluate the effects racial markers have on the perception of race. We used hair as a racial marker and found it to systematically shift the racial boundaries away from the starting image originally possessing that feature. Interestingly, this shift is similar to that found with perceptual adaptation to faces (MacLin & Webster, 2001; Webster & MacLin, 1998). Unexpectedly, a third race emerged, which suggests that race may not be located on a continuum in face space, and that it is likely categorical in nature. We are currently examining the effects of multiple racial markers. For example, what happens when a second racial marker (perhaps blue eyes) is added? Is the shift the equivalent of a main effect, or is there an interaction?

Study 2

Previous research has established that the visual system is dynamic and is under a constant state of adaptation. MacLin and Webster

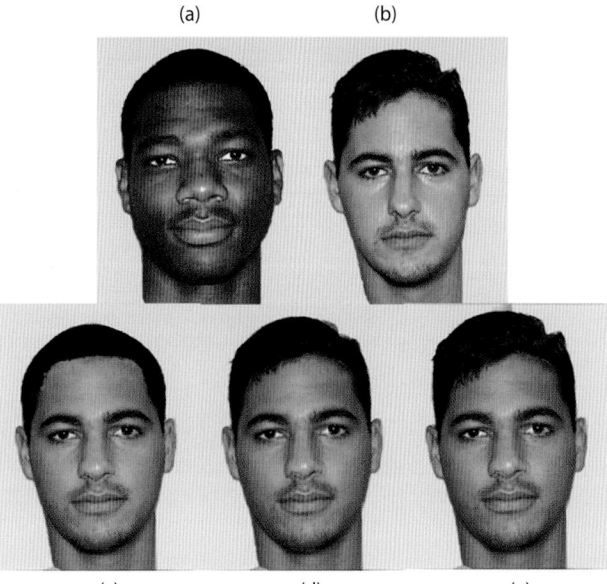

Figure 19.10 Emergent Third Race. Faces A and B are the original starting images for the morph array. Faces C, D, and E are the midpoints for the emergent race when: the African American racial marker is used (C; yellow line-74 percent), no racial marker is used (D; blue line-64 percent), and when the Caucasian racial marker is used (E; red line-64 percent) (See Figure 19.9).

(2001) demonstrated a perceptual shift for a two-dimensional face space where face space is shifted away from the adapting stimulus after a brief three-minute exposure to the adapting stimulus. Webster et al. (2004) demonstrated that we are also under a state of adaptation for race. One problem with the Webster et al. study was that the racial marker (hair) was masked out so only the face was viewed. Faces were converted to grey-scale reducing the ability to use skin tone as a racial marker. Additionally, they used a forced categorization task eliminating the potential of an emergent third race. Understanding how adaptation calibrates our perceptual system to adjust the number of allowable same-race faces is important.

The following data were collected using the method of adaptation to alter the face space and to examine the shift in racial boundaries due to adaptation. We were interested not only in the boundary shift, but also in how the shape of the seeing curve would be altered. In particular, would adaptation reduce the variance in the observations thus creating a steeper slope in the curve? The method constant stimuli was used to obtain a "frequency of seeing curve" (Boynton, 1984) to evaluate the slope of

frequency curve to determine if adaptation not only shifts the racial boundary, but additionally sharpens/defines the racial boundary by reducing the variance surrounding the racial boundary as well. Each face was categorized 10 times in blocks of 51 resulting in 510 observations. Faces within blocks were randomized for each presentation. Only faces with the Caucasian racial marker were used in the experiment presented here.

The procedure for Study 2 was as follows. In Phase one (pre-adapt), baseline data were collected to evaluate perceptual racial thresholds prior to adapting. In Phase two (adapt), the observer was presented with an adapting stimulus consisting of the African-American starting image. Both phases were identical with the exception that a uniform grey image was substituted for the adapting stimulus in Phase 1. In Phase 2, the observer was presented with the adapting stimulus for three minutes and kept his attention to the faces on the monitor at all times. A brief visual mask was presented following the adapting stimulus. A randomly selected face appeared on the screen for the observer to classify race as either Caucasian or Other. Once the face was rated, the adapting stimulus was

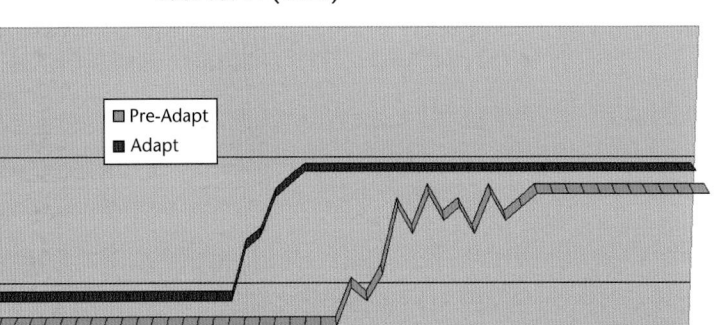

Figure 19.11 Racial Categorization Boundaries Before and After Adaptation.

presented for 5 seconds to top-up and maintain the state of adaptation. The test faces, adapt faces, and visual mask were separated by a 250 ms interval where only the uniform grey background was present.

As can be seen in Figure 19.11, the pre-adapt data (blue) indicate that approximately 25 percent of the faces were consistently classified as Caucasian, with about 25 percent of the faces defining the racial boundary by being classified as Other between one and nine times. Once the observers were adapted to the African-American starting image, the entire face space shifts away from the adapting stimulus (see MacLin & Webster, 2001), which, in effect, calibrates the perceptual system to allow for more faces to be categorized as Caucasian (about 52 percent). Additionally, as hypothesized, the faces representing the racial boundary (or area of ambiguity) are fewer in number (about 12 percent) indicating a sharper delineation between the racial categories. These data support our hypothesis that adaptation not only shifts the racial boundary to adjust the number of acceptable same-race faces, it also reduces the boundary area substantially, suggesting that adaptation calibrates the racial boundaries by reducing variance surrounding the racial threshold evidenced by a steeper

slope on the frequency of the seeing curve (see Figure 19.11).

THE COGNITIVE GATING MECHANISM

In this section we present a model based on our cognitive gating theory. Previous research using racial markers has demonstrated that virtually identical faces are processed differently once they have been classified as same-race or other-race faces (MacLin & Malpass, 2001). For example, faces with other-race racial markers are perceived as being darker than are same-race faces. This has been demonstrated with Hispanic participants (MacLin & Malpass, 2001) and later with Caucasian participants (Levin & Banaji, 2006). Results from these studies showing changes in perceptual processes make it difficult to support theories for the cross-race effect such as the contact hypothesis and perceptual expertise.

Based on existing data from our lab (and elsewhere) we believe that the racial marker is detected by a gating mechanism to direct same-race and other-race facial information to different areas of the brain. Once routed, the other-race faces are processed differently than same-race faces with less emphasis on encoding

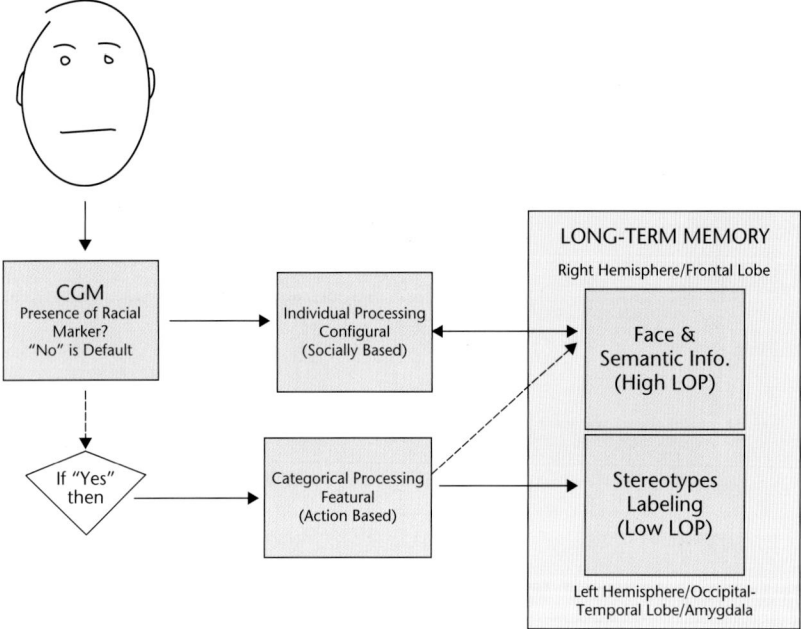

Figure 19.12 Cognitive Gating Mechanism.

for later identification purposes. Yet how does this mechanism work? We posit that the CGM is sensitive to racial markers because the markers signal outgroup membership. Upon seeing a person, facial information is routed based on the presence or absence of a racial marker.

Sufficient data exist to indicate that same-race (ingroup) faces are considered default. With the absence of a racial marker, faces are processed configurally for individuation leading to greater recognition relative to other-race (outgroup) faces. However, if a racial marker is detected by the CGM indicating other-race (outgroup) members, facial information is processed featurally often leading to an action-based (fight or flight) response. Both same-race and other-race faces then activate information in long-term memory. Differential processing continues to occur in long term memory systems as well. Same-race faces are encoded for facial and semantic information involving a high level of processing (Bruce & Young, 1986), and involving brain areas such as the right hemisphere and frontal lobe (Perrett, Hietanen, Oram, & Benson, 1992). Other-race faces activate stereotype information stored in long-term

memory requiring a lower level, rapid processing. As indicated by the broken line in Figure 19.12, other-race faces can ultimately tap into higher-level processing operations, including accessing semantic information. This line can be strengthened via meaningful, extended contact with that individual (e.g., the recognition of celebrities, political figures, and friends of other races). However, we believe that the other-race faces are still initially gated for other-race processing due to the presence of a racial marker (see Figure 19.12). Our model, in fact, predicts that it will take longer to classify an other-race face as famous, than it would to classify a same-race face as famous. Since both classifications require the access of semantic information, the other-race face must take a circuitous route (via the broken line) to access that information.

We propose that the CGM is dynamic and is constantly adjusting to the environment through perceptual adaptation such that it self-calibrates to the available same-race or other-race faces to determine the allowable range of same-race faces. Early brain activation in detecting other race as indicated by ERP studies demonstrates a state of neural readiness (cf. Ito

& Cacioppo, 2007) for processing threat, indicating the critical importance of detecting and assessing threat in the environment.

Our data are problematic for existing explanations for the cross-race effect, because most of these are deficit-processing models that refer to problems associated with processing to explain the cross-race effect. On the other hand, we propose an optimal-processing model whereby, in actuality, we are really good at processing facial information based on how that information is likely to be used and thus the processing needs are different for same- as compared to other-race faces. It is fairly well agreed upon that we have two types of face processing, configural and featural. Evidence for these two types of processing comes from research examining the inversion effect (Yin, 1969). Inverted faces, as with other-race faces, involve a greater number of false alarms for inverted faces relative to upright faces (MacLin et al., 2004). It has been argued that the decrement in recognition performance with inverted faces is a result of a shift from configural processing to featural processing, which is less efficient. Note that this, too, is a deficit theory. But why would evolutionary pressures support inferior featural processing? From an ecological perspective there must be some utility or function for when the brain switches to a featural-processing strategy. Just as race is a feature that activates the CGM, inversion acts as a feature that also activates the CGM signaling that this face is not like me, (not ingroup), resulting in featural processing.

We believe that faces are processed for different evolutionary purposes, such that social category information is initially critically important (to determine ingroup or outgroup membership). From an ecological perspective, this makes intuitive sense. Same-race faces are likely evaluated for social content and properly stored for later recognition. Other-race faces are evaluated for potential threat and not for subsequent recognition. With this function in mind, incoming perceptual information must be gated to relevant brain areas for specialized processing. This gating mechanism would need to be sensitive to features (such as racial markers) to determine the appropriate route for processing.

Support for this idea comes from the ERP studies reviewed previously. Outgroup members (as are other threatening objects) are detected automatically, and early, in the time course of perceiving faces (Correll et al., 2006). We also know that the amygdala plays a role in processing other-race faces as well as threat (Phelps et al., 2000; Phelps & Thomas, 2003), and that there is evidence of differential processing of other-race faces such that activity in the right fusiform area, which is essential in processing facial information, is actually reduced when processing other-race faces (Golby et al., 2001). In our lab, we have recently found that adaptation to threatening stimuli, such as a vicious dog, will cause a similar shift in the classification, as would adaptation to an African American face for Caucasian observers. This suggests that areas involving threat are similarly affected by the presence of outgroup members as they are when exposed to images of vicious dogs.

The CGM also explains why featural information is more important than configural information when processing other-race faces. Some features act as racial markers, gating the information; additionally, same-race faces are known to be processed configurally, which aids in later recognition. Racial markers are easy to attend to as they have been found to pop-out (Levin, 2000) and this is consistent with the presence of the N100 signal (Correll, Urland, & Ito, 2006). If this is the case, individuals who are socially oriented might shift their racial boundary to include more same-race faces, whereas those who are more racist may shift their boundaries to reduce the number of acceptable same-race faces, as Blascovich, Wyer, Swart, and Kibler, (1997) found.

DEFICIT- VERSUS OPTIMAL-PROCESSING MODELS

After over 40 years, there is no unified explanation for the cross-race effect. One of the problems in arriving at a unified explanation of why the cross-race effect (and for that matter, the inversion effect) occurs has generally been a result of the how we measure the effect. Given that other-race faces are processed for information that does not necessarily result in better recognition, by using a memory test to study how we process cross-race faces, researchers have put themselves in the position to interpret the data using a deficit explanation as though there is a problem with how the brain processes other-race faces. When we then conclude that other-race faces are processed featurally, these data are interpreted as though there was a problem with featural processing, which is often described as inferior as a result. Different research questions arise from the different perspectives. Researchers adopting a deficit perspective ask, "Why are we bad at recognizing other-race faces?" One answer has been, "Because we process them featurally." This then leads us to the conclusion that featural processing is inferior.

From an optimal-processing perspective we ask, "How are other-race faces processed?" What is the advantage of featural processing for other-race faces? What is gained? Our answer is, to extract the necessary information from the stimulus in order to respond to outgroup members. This can even be extended to the inversion effect. Why are inverted faces processed featurally? Our answer is that inverted faces are also processed as outgroup members because the inverted orientation acts as a marker, which the CGM responds to by gating the information accordingly. An optimal-processing perspective using the CGM model ultimately provides a more parsimonious explanation for these two seemingly distinct phenomena (the cross-race and inversion effects).

CONCLUSION

We have begun examining this gating mechanism using a variety of psychophysical techniques using morphed facial stimuli. We have demonstrated and reviewed other research that indicates that the perceptual system is highly responsive to racial markers, such as hair; supports featural processing; is dynamic; and adjusts to stimuli in the environment (providing some support for the contact hypothesis). We further propose that these and other important research questions can be studied scientifically using what we call social psychophysics—a marriage of well-established psychophysical methods to the

important empirical and applied questions regarding race that are of interest to researchers and the public alike. We have provided what we hope is a convincing argument and a model that readily lends itself to testable hypotheses for an ecological explanation for face-processing deficits. Instead, detecting outgroup membership is in fact optimal from an evolutionary perspective. Although the automaticity of detecting outgroup members has empirical support, and the CGM provides an explanation for how and why it occurs, that in no way condones discriminatory and prejudiced behavior that is clearly under conscious control, nor does it resolve problems associated with misidentifications in a legal context.

REFERENCES

Allport, G. W., & Kramer, B. M. (1946). Some roots of prejudice. *Journal of Psychology, 22*, 9–39.

Beale, J. M., & Keil, F. C. (1995). Categorical effects in the perception of faces. *Cognition, 57*, 217–239.

Behrman, B. W., & Davey, S. L. (2001). Eyewitness identification in actual criminal cases: An archival analysis. *Law & Human Behavior, 25*, 475–489.

Blair, I. V., & Banaji, M. (1996). Automatic and controlled processes in stereotype priming. *Journal of Personality and Social Psychology, 70*, 1142–1163.

Blascovich, J., Wyer, N. A., Swart, L. A., & Kibler, J. L. (1997). Racism and racial categorization. *Journal of Personality and Social Psychology, 72*, 1364–1372.

Boynton, R M. (1984). Psychophysics. In F. Grum & C. J. Bartleson (Eds.) *Optic radiation measurements* Volume 5: *Visual measurements.* San Diego: Academic.

Brigham, J. C., & Barkowitz, P. (1978). The effect of race, sex, experience and attitude on the ability to recognize faces. Do "they all look alike?" *Journal of Applied Social Psychology, 8*, 306–318.

Brigham, J. C., & Meissner, C. A. (2000). *Representation and memory for same and other-race faces.* Symposium Presentation, American Psychology–Law Society.

Bruce, V. & Young, A. (1986). Understanding face recognition. *British Journal of Psychology, 77*(3), 305–327.

Cacioppo, J. T., & Berntson, G. G. (1994). Relationship between attitudes and evaluative space: A critical review, with emphasis on the separability of positive and negative substrates. *Psychological Bulletin, 115*, 401–423.

Carroo, A. W. (1986). Other race recognition: A comparison of Black American and African subjects. *Perceptual & Motor Skills, 62*, 135–138.

Carter, L. F. (1948). The identification of "racial membership." *Journal of Abnormal & Social Psychology*, 51, 339–341.

Cavanagh, P., Arguin, M., & Treisman, A., (1990). Effect of surface medium on visual search for orientation and size features. *Journal of Experimental Psychology: Human Perception and Performance 16*, 479–491.

Chiroro, P., & Valentine, T. (1995). An investigation of the contact hypothesis of the own–race bias in face recognition. *Quarterly Journal of Experimental Psychology*, 48A, 879–894.

Chowdhry, O., Joshi, P., Fantroy, E., Peterson, D., MacLin, M. K., & MacLin, O. (2008). *Perceptual discontinuities in the perception of other race faces: Implications for examining the cross-race effect.* Paper presented at the American Psychology–Law Society Annual Conference, Jacksonville, FL.

Correll, J., Park, B., Judd, C. M., & Wittenbrink, B. (2002). The police officer's dilemma: Using ethnicity to disambiguate potentially threatening individuals. *Journal of Personality and Social Psychology, 38*, 315–322.

Correll, J., Urland, G. R., & Ito, T. A. (2006). Event-related potentials and the decision to shoot: The role of threat perception and cognitive control. *Journal of Experimental Social Psychology, 42*, 120–128.

Cross, J. F., Cross, J. & Daly, J. (1971). Sex, race, age, and beauty as factors in recognition of faces. *Perception and Psychophysics, 10*, 393–396.

Elliott, E. S., Wills, E. J., & Goldstein, A. G. (1973). The effects of discrimination training on the recognition of white and oriental faces. *Bulletin of the Psychonomic Society, 2*, 71–73.

Ellis, H. D., Deregowski, J. G., & Shepherd, J. W. (1975). Descriptions of White and Black faces by White and Black subjects. *International Journal of Psychology, 10*, 119–123.

Fabiani, M., Gratton, G., & Cole, M. G. H. (2000). Event-related potentials. In J. T. Cacioppo, L. G. Tassinary, & G. G. Berntson (Eds.), *Handbook of psychophysiology* (2nd ed., pp. 53–84). Cambridge, UK: Cambridge University Press.

Fechner, G. (1860/1966). *Elements of psychophysics:* Volume I. H. E. Adler, D. H. Howes, & E. G. Boring (Trans.), New York: Holt.

Feinman, S., & Entwistle, D. R. (1976). Children's ability to recognize other children's faces. *Child Development*, 47, 506–570.

Finney, D.J. (1947), *Probit Analysis*. (1st ed.). Cambridge, UK: Cambridge University Press.

Geisler, W. S. (2003). Ideal observer analysis. In L. M. Chalupa & J. S. Werner (Eds.), *Visual neurosciences*. Cambridge, MA: MIT Press.

Gescheider, G. A. (1997). *Psychophysics: The fundamentals*, (3rd ed). Mahwah, NJ: Erlbaum.

Gibson, J. J., & Radner, M. (1937). Adaptation, after–effect, and contrast in the perception of tilted lines. I. Quantitative studies. *Journal of Experimental Psychology, 20*, 453–467.

Golby, A. J., Gabrieli, J. D. E., Chiao, J. Y., & Eberhardt, J. L. (2001). Differential responses in the fusiform region to same–race and other–race faces. *Nature Neuroscience, 4*, 845–850.

Goldstein, A. G. (1979). Race-related variation of facial features: Anthropometric data I. *Bulletin of the Psychonomic Society, 13*(3), 187–190.

Goldstein, A. G., & Chance, J. E. (1985). Effects of training on Japanese faces recognition: Reduction of the other-race effect. *Bulletin of the Psychonomic Society, 23*, 211–214.

Gross, S. R., Hacoby, K., Matheson, D. J., Montgomery, N., & Patil, S. (2005) Exonerations in the United States 1989 through 2003. *The Journal of Criminal Law & Criminology, 95*(2), 523–560.

Hart A. J., Whalen P. J., Shin L. M., McInerney, S. C., Fischer H., & Rauch S. L. (2000). Differential response in the human amygdala to racial outgroup vs ingroup face stimuli. *Neuroreport, 11*(11), 2351–2355.

Hosie, J. A., Ellis, H. D., & Haig, N. D. (1988). The effect of feature displacement on the perception of well-known faces. *Perception, 17*, 461–474.

Ito, T. A., & Cacioppo, J. T. (2007). Attitudes as mental and neural states of readiness: Using Physiological measures to study implicit attitudes. In N. Schwarz, & B. Wittenbrink (Eds), *Implicit measures of attitudes*. New York: Guilford Press.

Ito, T. A., & Urland, G. R. (2003). Race and gender on the brain: Electrocortical measures of attention to the race and gender of multiply categorizable individuals. *Journal of Personality and Social Psychology, 85*, 616–626.

Ito, T. A., Thompson, E., & Cacioppo, J. T. (2004). Tracking the timecourse of social perception: The effects of racial cues on event-related brain potentials. *Personality and Social Psychology Bulletin, 30*(10), 1267–1280.

Ito, T. A., and Urland, G. R. (2005). The Influence of proccessing objectives on the perception faces: An ERP study of race and gender perception. *Cognitive, Affective, and Behavioral Neuroscience, 5,* 21–36.

Ito, T. A., Urland, G. R., Willadsen–Jensen, E., & Correll, J. (2006). The social neuroscience of stereotyping and prejudice: Using event-related brain potentials to study social perception. In C. L. Pickett, J. T. Cacioppo, & P. S. Visser (Eds), *Social neuroscience: People thinking about thinking people.* Cambridge, MA: MIT Press.

Ito, T. A., Willadsen–Jensen, E., & Correll, J. (2007). Social neuroscience and social perception: New perspectives on categorization, prejudice, and stereotyping. In P. Winkielman and E. Harmon-Jones (Eds), *Social neuroscience: Integrating biological and psychological explanations of social behavior,* New York: Guilford Press.

Kubota, J. T. & Ito, T. A. (2007). Multiple cues in social perception: The time course of processing race and facial expression. *Journal of Experimental Social Psychology, 43,* 738–752.

Leopold, D. A., O'Toole, A. J., Vetter, T., & Blanz, V. (2001). Prototype-referenced shape encoding revealed by high-level aftereffect. *Nature Neuroscience, 4,* 89–94.

Levin, D. T. (1996). Classifying faces by race: The structure of face categories. *Journal of Experimental Psychology: Learning, Memory, and Cognition, 22*(6), 1364–1382.

Levin, D. T. (2000). Race as visual feature: Using visual search and perceptual discrimination tasks to understand face categories and the cross-race recognition deficit. *Journal of Experimental Psychology: General, 129*(4), 559–574.

Levin, D. T., & Banaji, M. R. (2006). Distortions in the perceived lightness of faces: The role of race categories. *Journal of Experimental Psychology: General, 135*(4), 501–512.

Levin, D.T., & Lacruz, I. (1999). *An alternative to the encoding expertise explanation for the cross–race recognition deficit.* Poster presentation at the Psychonomics conference, Los Angeles, CA.

MacLin, M. K., & MacLin, O. H. (February, 2002). *Assessing the social properties of ambiguous race faces using the IAT.* Poster presented at the Annual Meeting of the Society for Personality and Social Psychology, Savannah, GA.

MacLin, M. K., MacLin, O. H., & Malpass, R. S. (April, 2001). *Using the implicit association test to assess ambiguous race faces.* Poster presented at the Rocky Mountain Psychological Association Convention. Reno, NV.

MacLin, O. H. & Malpass, R. S. (2001). Racial categorization of faces: The ambiguous race face effect. *Psychology, Public Policy, and Law, 7,* 98–118.

MacLin, O. H., & Malpass, R. S. (2003). The ambiguous–race face illusion. *Perception, 32,* 249–252.

MacLin, O. H., van Sickler, B. R., MacLin, M. K., & Li, A. (2004). A re-examination of the cross-race effect: The role of race, inversion, and basketball trivia. *North American Journal of Psychology, 6*(2), 189–204.

MacLin, O. H., & Webster M. A. (1998). Visual adaptation and the perception of distortions in natural images. In B. E. Rogowitz and T. N. Pappas (Eds.) *Human vision and electronic imaging III, SPIE 3299,* 264–273.

MacLin, O. H., & Webster, M. A. (2001). The influence of adaptation on the perception of distortions in natural images. *Journal of Electronic Imaging special section on Human Vision and Electronic Imaging,* 10, 100–109.

MacLin, O. H., & Webster, M. A. (June, 1996). *Adaptation and face recognition.* Proceedings of the 77th Annual Conference of the American Association for the Advancement of Science – Pacific Division, San Jose, CA. [Abstract published in proceedings].

MacLin, O. H., Dixon, M. A., James, A. (2007). *Visual Basic 2005 for behavioral psychologists.* Reno, NV: Context Press.

MacLin, O. H., MacLin, M. K., Peterson, D. J., Chowdhry, O., & Joshi, P. (2008). Social psychophysics: Using psychophysics to answer "social" questions with *PsychoPro. Behavior Research Methods, 41,* 623–632.

Malpass, R. S. (1990). An excursion into utilitarian analyses, with side trips. *Behavioral Science Research, 24,* 1–15.

Malpass, R. S. (1993). They all look alike to me. In G. Brannigan and M. Merrens (Eds). *The undaunted psychologist: Adventures in research.* New York: McGraw–Hill.

Malpass, R.S. (1981). Training in face recognition. In G. Davies, H. Ellis, & J. Shepherd (Eds.), *Perceiving and remembering faces* (pp. 271–285). London: Academic Press.

Malpass, R.S., & Kravitz, J. (1969). Recognition for faces of own- and other-race faces. *Journal of Personality and Social Psychology, 13*, 330–334.

Malpass, R.S., Lavigueur, H., & Weldon, D.E. (1973). Verbal and visual training in face recognition. *Perception & Psychophysics, 14*, 283–292.

Mandel, D. R., & Lehman, D. R. (1996). Counterfactual thinking and ascriptions of cause and preventability. *Journal of Personality and Social Psychology, 71*, 450–463.

Mather, G., & Harris, J. (1998). Theoretical models of the motion aftereffect. In G. Mather, F. Verstraten, & S. Anstis (Eds.). *The motion aftereffect: A modern perspective* (pp. 157–185). Cambridge, MA: MIT Press.

McClure, K. A., Maddox, K. B., & Sanders, J. D. (under revision). *Are out-group members destined to be undifferentiated? The effects of skin tone on other-race face recognition.*

Meissner, C. A., & Brigham, J. C. (2001). Thirty years of investigating the own-race bias in memory for faces: A meta-analytic review. *Psychology, Public Policy, and Law, 7*, 3–35.

Meissner, C. A., Brigham, J. C., & Butz, D. A. (2005). Memory for own- and other-race faces: A dual-process approach. *Applied Cognitive Psychology, 19*, 545–567.

Milord, J. (1978). Aesthetics of faces: A (somewhat) phenomenological analysis using multidimensional scaling methods. *Journal of Personality and Social Psychology, 36*, 205–216.

Nelson, H., MacLin, O. H., & Radeke, M. K. (April, 1996). *Systematic changes in second-order facial configurations as determinants of attractiveness and distinctiveness.* Presented at the 66th Annual Convention of the Rocky Mountain Psychological Association, Park City, UT.

Ng, W., & Lindsay, R.C.L. (1994). Cross-race facial recognition: Failure of the contact hypothesis. *Journal of Cross-Cultural Psychology, 25*, 217–232.

Ohman, A., Lundqvist, D., & Esteves, F. (2001). The face in the crowd revisited: A threat advantage with schematic stimuli. *Journal of Personality and Social Psychology, 81*, 181–192.

O'Toole, A.J., Abdi, H., Deffenbacher, K.A., & Valentine, D. (1993). A low-dimensional representation of faces in the higher dimensions of the space. *Journal of the Optical Society of America, A:10*: 405–411.

Perrett, D. I., Rolls, E. T., & Caan, W. (1982). Visual neurons responsive to faces in the monkey temporal cortex. *Experimental Brain Research, 47*, 329–342.

Perrett, D. I., Hietanen, J. K., Oram, M. W., & Benson, P. J. (1992). Organization and functions of cells responsive to faces in the temporal cortex. *Philosophical Transactions of the Royal Society of London Series B, 335*(1273), 23–30.

Peterson, D., Stone, B., Joshi, P., MacLin, M. K., & MacLin, O. H. (November, 2007). *PsychoPro: A Visual Basic program to collect psychophysical ratings using morphed stimuli.* Paper presented at the 37th annual meeting of the Society for Computers in Psychology, Long Beach, CA.

Phelps, E. A., & Thomas, L. A. (2003). Race, behavior, and the brain: The role of neuron imaging in understanding complex social behaviors. *Political Psychology, 24*(4), 747–758.

Phelps, E. A., O'Connor, K.J., Cunningham, W.A., Funayma, E.S., Gatenby, J.C., Gore, J.C., Banaji, M.R. (2000). Performance on indirect measures of race evaluation predicts amygdala activity. *Journal of Cognitive Neuroscience, 12*, 1–10

Platz, S.J., & Hosch, H.M. (1988). Cross-racial/ethnic eyewitness identification: A field study. *Journal of Applied Social Psychology, 18*, 972–984.

Rhodes, G. (1988). Looking at faces: First-order and second order features as determinates of facial appearance. *Perception, 17*, 43–63.

Rhodes, G., Robbins, R., Jaquet, E., McKone, E., Jeffery, L., & Clifford, W. G. (2005). Adaptation and face perception – How aftereffects implicate norm-based coding for faces. In C. Clifford, & G. Rhodes (Eds.). *Fitting the mind to the world.* Oxford, UK: Oxford University Press.

Scheck, B.C., Neufeld, P. & Dwyer, J. (2000). *Actual innocence: Five days to execution and other dispatches from the wrongly convicted.* New York: Doubleday.

Secord, P. F., Bevan, W., & Katz, B. (1956). The Negro stereotype and perceptual accentuation. *Journal of Abnormal & Social Psychology, 53*, 78–83.

Sergent, J. (1984). An investigation into component and configural processes underlying face perception. *British Journal of Psychology, 75*, 221–242.

Shepherd, J. W. (1981). Social factors in face recognition. In G. Davies, H. Ellis, & J. Shepherd (Eds.), *Perceiving and remembering faces* (pp. 55–79). London: Academic Press.

Shepherd, J.W., & Deregowski, J.B. (1981). Races and faces: A comparison of the responses of Africans and Europeans to faces of the same and different races. British *Journal of Social Psychology, 20*, 125–133.

Slone, A.E., Brigham, J.C., & Meissner, C.A. (2000). Social and cognitive factors affecting the own-race bias in Whites. *Basic & Applied Social Psychology, 22*, 71–84.

Smith, E. R. (1996). What do connectionism and social psychology offer each other? *Journal of Personality and Social Psychology, 70*, 893–912.

Snodgrass, J. G. (1975). Psychophysics. In: *Experimental Sensory Psychology.* B Scharf. (Ed.) pp. 17–67.

Sperling, G. (1963). A model for visual memory tasks. *Human Factors, 5*, 19–31.

Sporer, S. L. (2001). Recognizing faces of other ethnic groups: An integration of theories. *Psychology, Public Policy, and Law, 7*, 36–97.

Steyvers, M. (1999). Morphing techniques for manipulating face images. *Behavior Research Methods, Instruments, & Computers, 31*(2), 359–369.

Swope, T. M. (1994). *Social experience, illusory correlation and facial recognition ability.* Unpublished master's thesis, Florida State University.

Tredoux, C.G. (2002). A direct measure of facial similarity and its relation to human similarity perceptions. *Journal of Experimental Psychology: Applied, 8*(3), 180–193.

Triplett, N. (1898). The dynamogenic factors in pacemaking and competition. *American Journal of Psychology, 9*, 507–533.

Turk, M., & Pentland. A. (1991). Eigenfaces for recognition. *Journal of Cognitive Neuroscience, 3*(1), 71–86.

Valentine, T. (1991). A unified account of the effects of distinctiveness, inversion and race on face recognition. *Quarterly Journal of Experimental Psychology, 43A*, 161–204.

Valentine, T., & Endo, M. (1992). Towards an exemplar model of face processing: The effects of race and distinctiveness. *Quarterly Journal of Experimental Psychology, 44A*, 671–703.

Valentine, T., Chiroro, P., & Dixon, R. (1994). An account of the own-race bias and the contact hypothesis based on a 'face space' model of face recognition. In T. Valentine (Ed.), *Cognitive and computational aspects of face recognition*, (pp. 69–94). London: Routledge.

von Grunau, M., Dube, S., & Kwas, M. (1994). Visual search asymmetry for viewing direction. *Perception & Psychophysics, 56*, 211–220.

Wade, N.J. & Verstraten, F.A.J. (2005). Accommodating the past: a selective history of adaptation. In C. Clifford & G. Rhodes (Eds.) *Fitting the Mind to the World: Adaptation and Aftereffects in High-Level Vision. Volume 2,*

Advances in Visual Cognition Series. Oxford, UK: Oxford University Press.

Walker, P. M., & Hewstone, M. (2006) A perceptual discrimination investigation of the own-race effect and intergroup experience. *Applied Cognitive Psychology, 20*(4), 461–475.

Walker, P. M., & Tanaka, J. W. (2003). An encoding advantage for own-race versus other-race faces. *Perception, 32*(2), 1117–1125.

Watson, T. L., & Clifford, C. W. G. (2003). Pulling faces: An investigation of the face-distortion aftereffect. *Perception, 32*, 1109–1116.

Webster M. A., & Mollon, J. D. (1995). Color constancy influenced by contrast adaptation. *Nature, 373*(23), 694–698.

Webster, M. A., & MacLin, O. H. (1999). Figural after-effects in the perception of faces. *Psychonomic Bulletin and Review, 6*, 647–653.

Webster, M. A., Kaping, D., Mizokami, Y., & Dunamel, P. (2004). Adaptation to natural facial categories. *Nature, 428*, 557–561.

Webster, M. A., Werner, J. S., & Field, D. J. (2005). Adaptation and the phenomenology of perception. In C. Clifford, & G. Rhodes (Eds.). *Fitting the mind to the world.* Oxford, UK: Oxford University Press.

Welch, R. B. (1978). *Perceptual modification: Adapting to altered sensory environments.* New York: Academic Press.

Wells, G. L., & Olson, E. A. (2001). The other-race effect in eyewitness identification: What do we do about it? *Psychology, Public Policy, and Law, 7*(1), 23–246.

Willadsen-Jensen, E. C. & Ito, T. A. (2006). Ambiguity and the timecourse of racial perception. *Social Cognition, 24*(5), 580–606.

Wright, D.B., Boyd, C.E., & Tredoux, C.G. (1999, June). *Own-race bias in South Africa and England.* Paper presented at the biennial meeting of the Society of Applied Research in Memory & Cognition, Boulder, CO.

Yin, R. K. (1969). Looking at upside-down faces. *Journal of Experimental Psychology, 81*, 141–145.

Zárate, M. A., & Smith, E. R. (1990). Person categorization and stereotyping. *Social Cognition, 8*, 161–185.

Zebrowitz, L. A. (1998). *Reading faces: Window to the soul?* Boulder, CO: Westview Press.

Zhao, L., & Chubb, C. (2001). The size-tuning of the face-distortion after-effect. *Vision Research, 41*, 2979–2994.

CHAPTER 20

Aftereffects Reveal That Adaptive Face-Coding Mechanisms Are Selective for Race and Sex

Gillian Rhodes and Emma Jaquet

Adaptive processes, which alter the operating characteristics of a system in response to changing inputs, can have dramatic effects on perceptual experience in the form of perceptual aftereffects (Barlow, 1990; Clifford & Rhodes, 2005; Frisby, 1990). A classic example is the waterfall illusion in which stationary objects appear to move upward after viewing a downward-flowing waterfall (Mather, Verstraten & Anstis, 1998). Aftereffects can also alter the appearance of faces, affecting judgments of identity, sex, race, expression, normality, attractiveness, and eye gaze direction (Jenkins, Beaver & Calder, 2006; O'Leary & McMahon, 1991; Leopold, O'Toole, Vetter & Blanz, 2001; MacLin & Webster, 2001; Rhodes, et al., 2003; Rhodes & Jeffery, 2006; Watson & Clifford, 2003; Webster & MacLin, 1999; Webster, Kaping, Mizokami & Duhamel, 2004). These aftereffects highlight the dynamic nature of perception, including face perception.

Aftereffects have been widely used to study the coding of simple visual attributes, leading them to be dubbed, "the psychologist's microelectrode" (Frisby, 1980). In this chapter we use face aftereffects to examine the role of adaptive mechanisms in forming visual representations of faces. We suggest that such mechanisms may underlie our remarkable ability to distinguish thousands of faces, despite their similarity, as visual patterns, an ability that is fundamental

to human social interaction. We also demonstrate that these mechanisms are sensitive to important social dimensions of faces, such as their sex and race. This selectivity may increase our capacity to discriminate faces relative to a system that codes the same visual information for all faces.

ADAPTIVE NORM-BASED CODING OF IDENTITY

Faces can be thought of as represented in a multidimensional space, whose dimensions correspond to whatever information is used to discriminate faces (Valentine, 1991, 2001). An average face lies at the center of face-space, with typical faces located nearby and more distinctive faces located further away. Many face-perception phenomena can be accounted for in the face-space framework, including better recognition of distinctive than typical faces, better recognition of own-race than other-race faces, and better recognition of caricatures than undistorted faces (for reviews, see Valentine, 1991; 2001; Valentine & Endo, 1992).

We begin by considering whether the average face might function as a perceptual norm against which faces are coded. Rather than coding an absolute value for each dimension of face space, the visual system may code deviations from (above or below) the average value

348

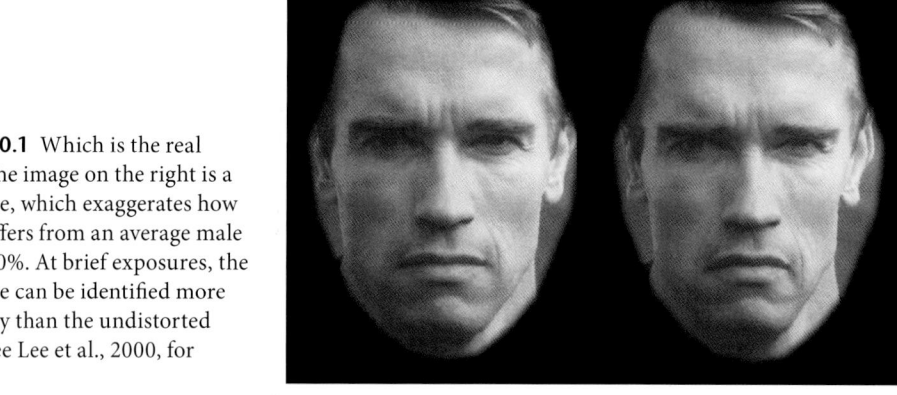

Figure 20.1 Which is the real Arnie? The image on the right is a caricature, which exaggerates how Arnie differs from an average male face by 50%. At brief exposures, the caricature can be identified more accurately than the undistorted image (see Lee et al., 2000, for details).

on each dimension. Such norm-based coding is widely used in low-level vision to code simple attributes like brightness, contrast, and color (Bartlett, 2007; MacLeod & Von der Twer, 2003) and a central function of adaptation may be to abstract and update perceptual norms (Barlow, 1990; Bartlett, 2007; Blakemore & Sutton, 1969; Helson, 1964; Hosoya, Baccus & Meister, 2005; Webster, 2003; Werblin, 1973).

Norm-based coding is efficient because it calibrates a limited range of neural responses to the range of inputs experienced (Barlow, 1990; Bartlett, 2007; Webster, Werner, & Field, 2005). It can also facilitate discrimination in low-level vision (e.g., Clifford, Ma Wyatt, Arnold, Smith, & Wenderoth, 2001; Phinney, Bowd, & Patterson, 1997; Regan & Beverley, 1985; Werblin, 1973) and could potentially help us discriminate thousands of faces despite their similarity as visual patterns (Wilson, Loffler & Wilkinson, 2002; but see Rhodes, Maloney, Turner & Ewing, 2007). Not surprisingly, several theorists have proposed that the average face may function as a perceptual norm against which faces are coded (Diamond & Carey, 1986; Goldstein & Chance, 1980; Hebb, 1949; Hochberg, 1978; Leopold et al., 2001; Rhodes, Brennan & Carey, 1987; Rhodes, 1996; Valentine, 1991).

Several lines of evidence are consistent with norm-based coding of faces. People can abstract an average face from experience, which they update in response to a consistent change in the diet of faces experienced (Bruce, Doyle, Dench &

Burton, 1991; Cabeza, Bruce, Kato & Oda, 1999; Cabeza & Kato, 2000; De Haan, Johnson, Maurer & Perrett, 2001; Inn, Walden & Solso, 1993; MacLin & Webster, 2001; Reed, 1972; Rhodes et al., 2003, 2004; Solso & McCarthy, 1981a,b; Strauss, 1979; Walton & Bower, 1993; Webster & MacLin, 1999). In addition, exaggerating how a face differs from the average, by caricaturing, can facilitate identification (Benson & Perrett, 1994; Byatt & Rhodes, 2004; Lee, Byatt & Rhodes, 2000; Rhodes, 1996; Rhodes, Brennan & Carey, 1987). The effectiveness of caricatures as representations of individuals (Figure 20.1), despite their obvious distortions, suggests that the way a face differs from the average provides important information for identification.

The most compelling evidence for norm-based coding of faces comes from a face aftereffect, in which perceived identity changes when the average changes (Anderson & Wilson, 2005; Leopold et al., 2001; Leopold, Rhodes, Muller, & Jeffery, 2005; Loffler, Yourganov, Wilkinson, & Wilson, 2005; Rhodes & Jeffery, 2006). To understand this identity aftereffect, consider Figure 20.2, which shows two identities in a simplified two-dimensional face-space. Each identity has a computationally opposite identity, or antiface, which occupies the opposite location in face-space, relative to the average. A face and its antiface have opposite properties. For example, Dan has large eyes and thick eyebrows, whereas anti-Dan has small eyes and thin eyebrows. Adaptation to a face (e.g., anti-Dan) biases perception toward

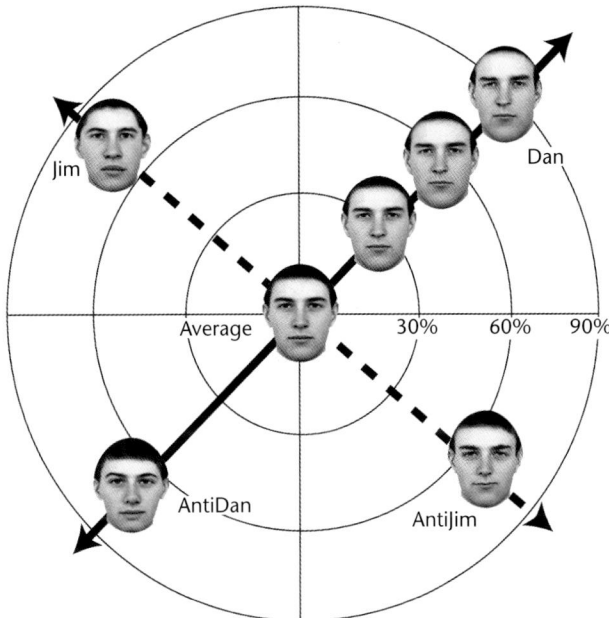

Figure 20.2 A simple two-dimensional face-space showing two identities, Dan and Jim, represented as vectors from the origin. Each face has a corresponding antiface (anti-Dan and anti-Jim), which is constructed by morphing the original face toward the average (norm) and beyond. The average face was constructed from 20 male Caucasian faces. Reduced identity strength versions of Dan are also shown.

the opposite identity (Dan), due to a temporary shift in the average toward the adapting identity. As a result, the old average is now located on the Dan side of the average, and so this previously identity-neutral average now looks like Dan. Clearly, this aftereffect implicates the average face in coding identity, because a change in the average has changed the perception of identity.

The identity aftereffect supports a norm-based, opponent-coding model in which identity is coded by pairs of neural populations tuned to above-average and below-average values, respectively, of each dimension in face-space (Figure 20.3) (Rhodes et al., 2005; Rhodes & Jeffery, 2006; Tsao & Freiwald, 2006). A face's value on each dimension is signaled by the relative activation of the relevant pair of populations. Figure 20.3 also illustrates how the model explains the identity aftereffect. Viewing a face temporarily suppresses activity in the member of each population pair that responds more strongly to that face. For example, a face with large eyes will more strongly activate, and so more strongly suppress, neurons that respond to above-average eye size. As a result, a face with average-sized eyes, which previously activated the paired populations equally, now selectively activates the below-average population.

Similarly, for all the other dimensions of the face, so that viewing a face biases perception toward the opposite identity (see also Robbins, McKone, & Edwards, 2007).

Splitting the coding of inputs, as illustrated in Figure 20.3, effectively doubles the precision of representation possible, and may provide an optimal code for representing sensory inputs with a limited neural response range in the presence of noise (MacLeod & von der Twer, 2003). In this context an optimal code is defined as one that minimizes the average error in the estimate of the input. Under this optimality criterion (and others are certainly possible), norm-based opponent coding is optimal for unidimensional domains and multidimensional domains with independent dimensions (MacLeod & von der Twer, 2003). Therefore, if the dimensions of face-space are independent, such a coding scheme may be optimal for face coding. It would also be neurally and computationally efficient because it focuses neural responses on relatively uncommon, nonaverage inputs, with little response to more common, average inputs.

Recent neuroimaging and neurophysiological findings are consistent with norm-based coding of faces. Both fMRI-activation in the human fusiform face area (Loffler, et al., 2005)

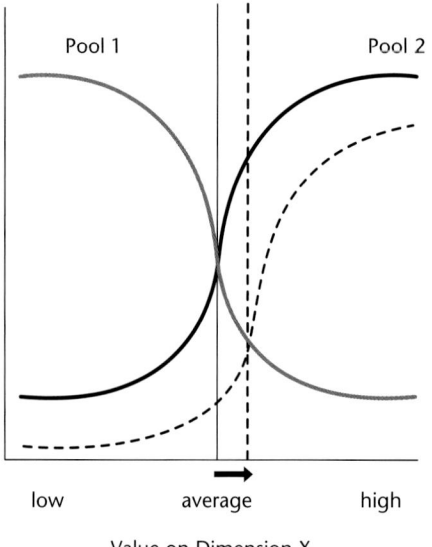

Value on Dimension X

Figure 20.3 Adaptive norm-based coding model for facial identity (adapted from Rhodes et al., 2005). For each dimension of face-space, there are two populations of neurons, as illustrated. Pool 1 codes below-average, and Pool 2 codes above-average values on dimension X. Average values are coded implicitly, by equal activation of the two populations. Exposure to an adapting face with a high value on dimension X shifts the perceived average toward the adapting face (dotted line) and make a previously neutral, average face take on the opposite identity. The identity aftereffect results from a temporary reduction in responsivity of Pool 2 neurons, which respond strongly to the adapting face. (Reprinted from Rhodes & Jeffery, 2006, with permission).

and firing rates of many face-selective neurons in monkey anterior inferotemporal cortex increase with increasing identity strength, and respond weakly to average faces (Leopold, Bondar & Giese, 2006). These response properties are precisely what one would expect if the average face functions as a perceptual norm for coding facial identity, with face-coding neurons tuned to deviations from average values.

A FACE IS A FACE IS A FACE, OR IS IT?

So far we have talked as if faces form a single class of stimuli, with a single average or norm.

However, faces of different races and sexes form important social categories and are visually distinct. They could, therefore, have different norms. The optimality of norm-based opponent coding, as described earlier, depends on splitting coding at the average stimulus value (MacLeod & von der Twer, 2003). Therefore, it would not be optimal to code faces from visually distinct and socially relevant populations, using a single face norm that is not average for either population. Rather, it would be advantageous to use the average of each population as the norm for coding faces from that population. Prima facie support for this hypothesis comes from evidence that caricatures of Caucasian and Chinese faces are recognized better when they exaggerate differences from Caucasian and Chinese averages, respectively (Byatt & Rhodes, 1998).[1] In this section, we consider further the evidence for race-selective and/or sex-selective coding mechanisms and their implications for face-space models of face perception.

Are Face-Coding Mechanisms Race-Selective?

Neuroimaging evidence indicates some neural sensitivity to race. Areas in and around the face-selective fusiform face area (Kanwisher, McDermott & Chun, 1997) respond more strongly to own- than other-race faces (Golby, Gabrieli, Chiao & Eberhardt, 2001), at least for unfamiliar faces (Kim, Yoon, Kim, Juen, Jung & Choe, 2006). These results are consistent with several kinds of race-selectivity. Faces from one race could generate more activity in an area than faces from another race, because they activate more neurons in that area or because they activate those neurons more strongly than faces from the other race. In both cases, there would be selectivity for own race faces, but not for faces from the other race. Alternatively, there may be selectivity for both races, but with more neurons tuned to own-race than other-race faces. The fMRI techniques, which average

[1] Byatt and Rhodes' (1998) original interpretation of these results, as evidence against norm-based coding, was based on the assumption that a single own-race norm was used to code all faces. However, the research reviewed in this chapter suggests that this assumption is incorrect.

activity over large numbers of neurons, cannot differentiate between these various patterns of neural organization and are poorly suited for assessing the selectivity of face-coding mechanisms (Kourtzi & Grill-Spector, 2005; Rhodes et al., 2004). Adaptation methods may be more revealing, and we consider those next.

Adaptive processes ensure that what looks normal or average in a face is dynamically updated by the diet of faces we experience. If we introduce a systematic change in the diet of faces, the average is updated accordingly. As a result we experience figural aftereffects in which perception is biased toward opposite figural properties to those in the adapting faces (MacLin & Webster, 2001; Rhodes et al., 2003, 2004; Robbins, McKone & Edwards, 2007; Watson & Clifford, 2003; Webster & MacLin, 1999). These aftereffects have been demonstrated by adapting people to consistently distorted faces, which shifts what looks normal toward the adapting distortion, resulting in a bias to perceive the opposite distortion in undistorted faces (Rhodes et al., 2003). For example, after adapting to faces with internal features "contracted" into the center of the face, slightly contracted faces look normal, and undistorted faces appear slightly "expanded." Similarly, after adapting to "expanded" faces, slightly expanded faces look normal and undistorted faces appear slightly "contracted."

We have used these aftereffects to investigate whether faces of different races have different norms, and more generally, whether face-coding mechanisms are race-selective (Jaquet, Rhodes & Hayward, 2007, 2008). We reasoned that, if it is possible to induce opposite aftereffects at the same time in faces of different races, (i.e., *race-contingent aftereffects*), then there must be different norms for faces of different races. If there is only a single face norm, then adapting concurrently to opposite distortions will pull the norm in opposite directions, resulting in no net aftereffect. Only if there are different norms for faces of different races will it be possible to change these in opposite ways at the same time. More generally, race-contingent aftereffects would indicate that there are race-selective face-coding mechanisms.

We attempted to induce opposite aftereffects concurrently in faces of different races, by adapting participants to Caucasian faces with one distortion (e.g., –60 percent contracted) and Chinese faces with the opposite distortion (e.g., +60 percent expanded) (Jaquet, et al., 2008). Participants rated the perceived normality of 16 female faces (8 Caucasian, 8 Chinese), shown at a range of distortion levels ($N = 17$) from extremely contracted to extremely expanded (–60, –50, –40, –30, –20, –15, –10, –5, 0, +5, +10, +15, +20, +30, +40, +50, +60) (Figure 20.4),

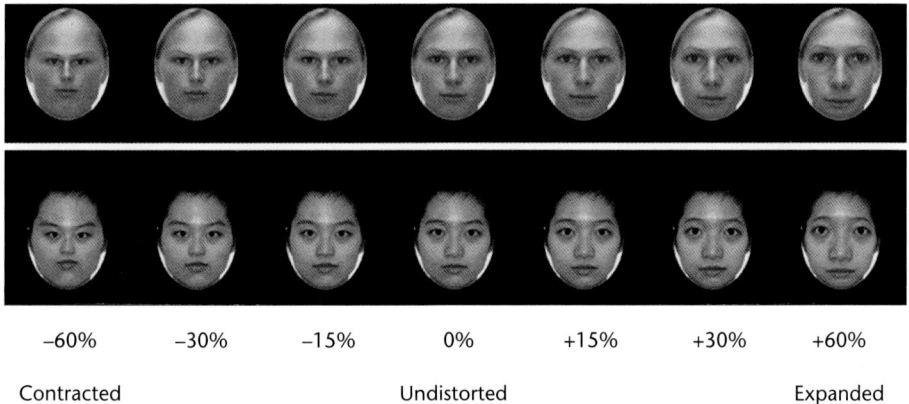

| −60% | −30% | −15% | 0% | +15% | +30% | +60% |

Contracted   Undistorted   Expanded

Figure 20.4 A Caucasian (top) and Chinese (bottom) face shown at seven distortion levels, selected from the 17 distortion levels (−60%, −50%, −40%, −30%, −20%, −15%, −10%, −5%, 0%, +5%, +10%, +15%, +20%, +30%, +40%, +50%, and +60%) used to measure race-contingent aftereffects. (Reprinted from Jaquet et al., 2008, with permission).

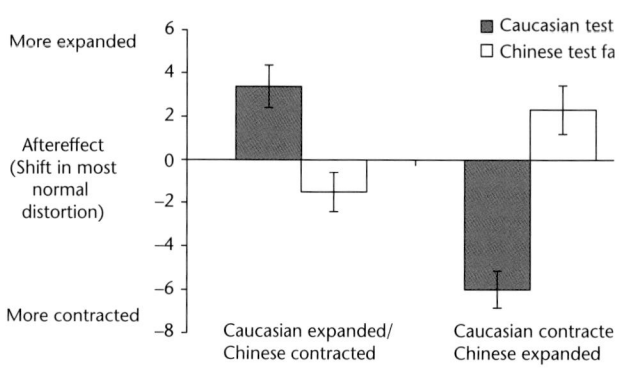

Figure 20.5 Size of aftereffect as a function of adapting condition and race of test face. The aftereffect is measured as the mean difference (postadaptation vs pre-adaptation) in the most normal-looking distortion. Data are collapsed across participant race. SE bars are shown. (This figure replots data from Figure 4, Jaquet, et al., 2008).

before and after adapting. Twenty additional faces (10 Caucasian, 10 Chinese) were used as adapting stimuli. During adaptation, participants viewed oppositely distorted Caucasian and Chinese faces for two minutes. Adapting and test blocks were alternated. We tested both Caucasian ($N = 43$) and Chinese ($N = 40$) participants in order to see whether there were any race expertise effects, but there were not, so the results will be presented collapsed across these groups (see Jaquet et al., 2008 for details).

For each participant, we plotted normality ratings as a function of distortion level before and after adapting and determined the most normal looking distortion before and after adapting, by finding the peaks of third-order polynomials fitted to each function (see Jaquet et al., 2008 for details). The prepost adaptation difference in most normal looking distortion is our measure of the size of the aftereffect. The results are shown in Figure 20.5. Clearly, we were able to induce opposite aftereffects at the same time for each race. Participants who adapted to expanded Caucasian and contracted Chinese faces selected more expanded Caucasian faces and more contracted Chinese faces as most normal after adapting than before. In contrast, participants who adapted to contracted Caucasian and expanded Chinese faces, showed the opposite pattern. These race-contingent aftereffects show that people have different norms for faces of different races, at least in the case of Caucasian and Chinese faces.

Our Caucasian and Chinese participants lived in Australia and Hong Kong, respectively,

and had greater expertise with own-race than other-race faces. However, we found no expertise effects. In retrospect, this should not be surprising, given that similar sized aftereffects occur for upright and inverted faces, despite the substantial difference in expertise (Rhodes, et al., 2004). Moreover, humans and monkeys show similar-sized identity aftereffects for human faces, despite obvious differences in expertise (Leopold & Bondar, 2005). Therefore, differences in expertise do not appear to be associated with differences in adaptability for different kinds of faces.

Implications for Coding Faces of Different Races

Race-contingent aftereffects suggest that there are different norms for faces of different races. They are also consistent with a functional architecture in which faces of different races are represented in distinct face-spaces with no common dimensions (cf., Little, DeBruine, & Jones, 2005), and a neural architecture in which they are coded by distinct (although not necessarily spatially separated) neural populations. However, such a scheme seems implausible because all faces share many properties. Instead, we propose a dissociable coding model in which all faces are represented in a single face-space that contains both common and race-selective dimensions. Common dimensions code faces of both races, whereas race-selective dimensions code faces from one race or the other. A similar model has been proposed to handle the dissociable coding of facial identity and

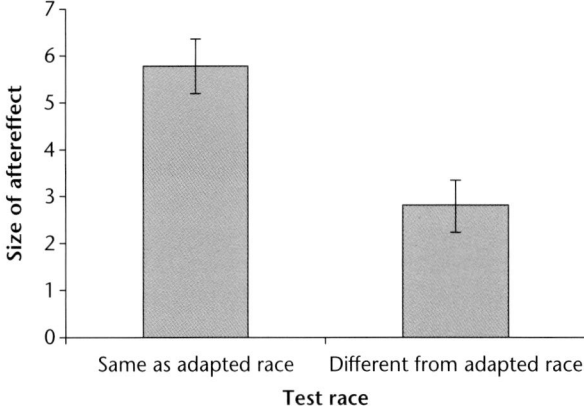

Figure 20.6 Size of aftereffect, measured as the mean shift (in the expected direction) of the most normal-looking distortion, for faces from the adapted and unadapted races. Data are collapsed across race of face and race of participants, because neither affected the results. SE bars are shown. (This figure replots data from Figure 3, Jaquet, et al., 2008).

expression (Calder & Young, 2005). Neurally, this would mean that both common (race-generic) and race-selective neurons contribute to face coding.

The dissociable coding model explains the race-contingent aftereffects obtained earlier as mediated by opposite adaptation of dimensions/neurons that are selective for each adapting race. The distribution of inputs on Chinese-selective and Caucasian-selective dimensions will shift in opposite directions, resulting in opposite shifts in the average (norm) for each.[2] However, exposure to any face will also adapt common dimensions/neurons that code properties common to all faces. The dissociable coding model, therefore, predicts that face aftereffects should show some transfer across face race. Jaquet, et al. (2008) tested this prediction by adapting Caucasian ($N = 80$) and Chinese ($N = 40$) participants to distorted faces of one race (e.g., contracted Chinese faces) and testing aftereffects in faces of both races. Otherwise the procedure was identical to that described earlier for generating race-contingent aftereffects.

The results are shown in Figure 20.6. Not surprisingly, the aftereffect was larger for faces from the adapted than the unadapted race. However, a significant aftereffect still occurred for the face from the unadapted race, as predicted by the

dissociable coding model. This "transferred" aftereffect presumably reflects the adaptation of common mechanisms. It is smaller than the aftereffect for faces from the adapted race, because there is no contribution from adaptation of race-selective mechanisms. The size of this *reduction* should, therefore, predict the size of the race-contingent aftereffects (i.e., differences from zero in Figure 20.5), which reflect adaptation of just those race-selective mechanisms. Comparing Figures 20.6 and 20.5, we can see that this is indeed the case, with a reduction of 3.0 for the "transferred" aftereffect (test race matches adapt race minus test match does not match adapt race) and a mean difference from zero of 3.3 for the race-contingent aftereffects (see Watson & Clifford, 2006 for a similar analysis in the case of orientation-selective aftereffects). Taken together, the race-contingent aftereffects demonstrated earlier and the transfer results described here, suggest that there are common, as well as race-selective, face-coding neurons.

Are Face-Coding Mechanisms Sex-Selective?

If we have race-selective coding mechanisms and norms, might we also have sex-selective coding mechanisms and norms? Given that male and female faces, like faces of different races, are visually distinct, we hypothesized that different norms might be used to code male and female faces. The results of a recent adaptation study suggest that this is indeed the case

[2] This assumes that the distortion used affects both Chinese- and Caucasian-selective dimensions. Given that these dimensions code different information, this will not be the case for all distortions.

(Little et al., 2005). After adapting participants to male faces with eyes moved apart and female faces with eyes moved inwards, participants judged male faces with wide-set eyes and female faces with close-set eyes as most normal looking. These sex-contingent aftereffects suggest that there are different norms for male and female faces, and that there are sex-selective face-coding mechanisms. More generally, these results seem consistent with a dissociable coding model, analogous to that described earlier for race, in which both sex-selective and common mechanisms are used to code faces of different sexes. However, the results of two subsequent studies led Little and colleagues (2005) to a more extreme conclusion. In those studies, there was no transfer at all of aftereffects across sex, prompting the conclusion that completely distinct neural populations code faces of different sexes. In computational terms, male and female faces would be coded in separate face-spaces, with completely distinct sets of dimensions.

Failure to find transfer across sex is surprising on several counts. First, male and female faces are very similar as visual patterns and share many common properties. Second, face aftereffects consistently show transfer, even between classes of faces that differ at least as much as male and female faces. These include Caucasian and Chinese faces, as described earlier (Jaquet et al., 2007a,b), upright and inverted faces (Rhodes et al., 2004; Watson & Clifford, 2006; Webster & MacLin, 1999), faces seen from different view-points (Jeffery, Rhodes & Busey, 2006), faces shown at different sizes (Zhao & Chubb, 2001), and many other face groups differing on low-level visual attributes (Yamashita, Hardy, DeValois, & Webster, 2005).

We conjectured that Little et al.'s (2005) failure to observe transfer might reflect the choice of adapting distortions used. Participants were adapted to faces from one sex only, which were transformed to look either more or less like a particular male identity or more or less masculine. They found, for example, that adapting to a masculinized male face increased subsequent preference for masculine male faces, but preference for masculine female faces did not change.

Perhaps by using distortions that altered masculine traits, they adapted primarily male face dimensions and not shared face dimensions. In this case, little transfer would be seen. To test the generality of their findings we re-examined whether face aftereffects transfer across sex, using figural distortions that globally distort faces and which should affect many common dimensions. Such distortions have been widely used in face-adaptation research and transfer across different kinds of faces (e.g., Yamashita et al., 2005).

To measure the aftereffect, participants were asked to choose the more normal-looking face from test pairs consisting of a slightly contracted (–10 percent) and slightly expanded (+10 percent) version of the same face (similar to the procedure used by Little et al., 2005) (Jaquet & Rhodes, 2008). After adapting to contracted faces, the more contracted face in each pair should be selected, and after adapting to expanded faces the more expanded face should be selected. The size of the aftereffect was measured as the change (postadaptation versus preadaptation) in percent of test trials on which the adapting distortion was chosen as most normal. The results, shown in Figure 20.7, are clear. In contrast to Little et al. (2005), we found substantial transfer across sex. Indeed, there was no significant reduction in the aftereffect for test faces of a different sex to the adapting faces. This result indicates substantial common coding mechanisms for male and female faces.

Somewhat paradoxically, given the strong transfer of aftereffects across face sex, we also found sex-contingent aftereffects, indicating some sex-selective mechanisms. These small, but significant, sex-contingent aftereffects are shown in Figure 20.8. For this figure we measured the aftereffect as the change (postadaptation versus pre-adaptation) in percent of test trials on which the expanded face was chosen as more normal, rather than the percent on which the adapting distortion was chosen, to illustrate that opposite aftereffects were obtained for each sex of face. Taken together, these results rule out a model in which male and female faces are coded by entirely distinct neural populations and face-spaces. Rather they are consistent

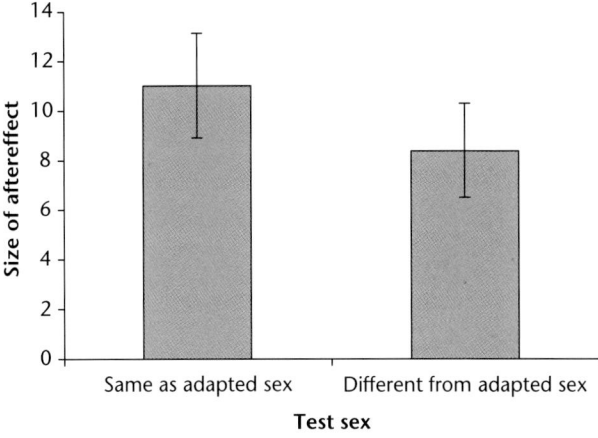

Figure 20.7 Size of aftereffect for faces from the adapted and unadapted sex. The aftereffect is measured as the difference (postadaptation vs pre-adaptation) in percentage of trials on which the adapting distortion was chosen as more normal. Data are collapsed across sex of face and sex of participants, because neither affected the results. SE bars are shown.

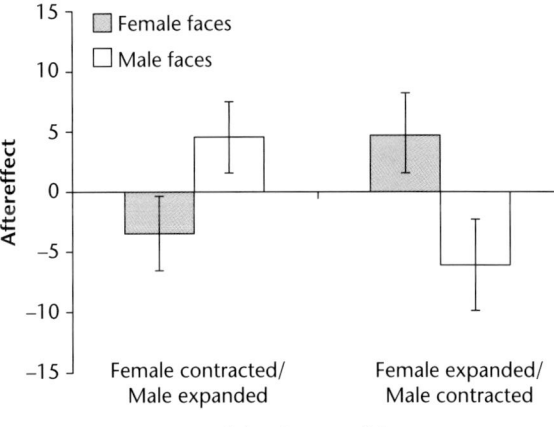

Figure 20.8 Size of aftereffect as a function of adapting condition and sex of test face. The aftereffect is measured as the difference (postadaptation vs pre-adaptation) in percentage of trials on which the expanded face was chosen as more normal, to highlight that opposite aftereffects are obtained for male and female faces. SE bars are shown. (Reprinted from Jaquet & Rhodes, 2008, with permission).

with a dissociable coding model, analogous to that proposed earlier for faces of different races, which contains both common and sex-selective dimensions.

The existence of race-contingent and sex-contingent aftereffects indicates that there are both race-selective and sex-selective face-coding mechanisms. It is also possible that some face-coding mechanisms, or dimensions in face space, may also be selective for both race and gender. Such joint selectivity would be plausible if different information distinguished male and female faces in different races. Although male-female category boundaries can be independently adapted for faces of different races, and vice versa, suggesting that judgments of sex show some selectivity for race, and vice versa (Ng, Ciaramitaro, Anstis, Boynton, & Fine, 2006), it remains an open question whether any mechanisms that code the appearance of faces (e.g., dimensions of face-space) are jointly selective for both race and gender.

The Locus of Race-Selective Coding Mechanisms

We have argued that race-contingent aftereffects reflect the adaptation of race-selective face-coding mechanisms. We would expect such mechanisms to be located in higher-level face-selective areas, such as the fusiform face area (FFA), or the occipital face area (OFA) (Gauthier et al., 2000; Grill-Spector, Knouf & Kanwisher, 2004;

Kanwisher et al.,1997; Kanwisher & Yovel, 2006). Evidence that race-contingent aftereffects are robust to a size change between adapt and test faces shows that they are generated beyond low-level, retinoptically organized areas such as V1 (Jaquet et al., 2008). But can we locate them more precisely than that?

We asked whether the mechanisms underlying race-contingent aftereffects are located in higher cortical areas that are sensitive to social category information in faces or in lower areas that are sensitive only to physical differences between faces (cf. Rotshtein, Henson, Treves, Driver & Dolan, 2005) (Jaquet, et al., 2007).[3] To address this question, we created face continua that ranged from extreme (caricatured) Caucasian faces ("SuperCaucasian" faces) to extreme (caricatured) Chinese faces ("SuperChinese" faces) (cf., Rotshtein et al., 2005). These continua were created by linear interpolation between pairs of faces using standard morphing procedures, and they are assumed to be physically, but not necessarily perceptually, linear. The linearity assumption is supported by the results of a functional-imaging study using similar identity continua (made from same-race face pairs) (Rothstein et al., 2005). During brain imaging, participants made same-different responses to face pairs selected from these continua. Face pairs were morphed images that either crossed the identity category boundary between Marilyn Monroe and Margaret (Maggie) Thatcher (e.g., 40 percent Maggie and 70 percent Maggie), or were within an identity category (e.g., 100 petcent Maggie and 70 percent Maggie). Responses in the face-selective fusiform face area were higher for pairs that spanned a perceptual identity-category boundary than pairs (equally far apart on the continua) that did not, indicating a perceptual nonlinearity. Physical nonlinearities in the continua were ruled out, because earlier, face-selective cortex, in the inferior occipital gyrus, did not show a differential response to these two kinds of pairs.

For our study, we reasoned that if race-contingent aftereffects are generated in areas that are sensitive to race, then we should be able to induce larger opposite (contingent) aftereffects for faces perceived as being from different races (Caucasian or Chinese) than for faces the same distance apart on the race continua that were not perceived as being from different races. Caucasian and Chinese participants were adapted and tested with oppositely distorted faces that were perceived as different races (contracted Chinese and expanded Caucasian faces) or as the same race (e.g., contracted SuperChinese and expanded Chinese faces). We coded these same-race conditions as either own-race or other-race, to test for expertise effects.

To measure the aftereffect, we presented participants with pairs consisting of a slightly contracted (-10 percent) and a slightly expanded (+10 percent) distortion of the same face. They were asked to choose the more normal-looking face. We measured the proportion of trials on which the expanded face was chosen as more normal before and after two minutes of adaptation (with 6 seconds of top-up adaptation before each postadaptation test trial to maintain adaptation). Positive values are expected for faces from the group shown with expanded distortions during adaptation and negative values are expected for faces from the group shown with contracted distortions. We calculated a set selectivity (contingency) score for each adaptation type (cross-race, within-own-race and within-other race) by subtracting the score for the contracted-adaptation set from the score from the expanded-adaptation set.[4] Selectivity scores greater than zero indicate group-selective aftereffects.

The results are shown in Figure 20.9 (and see Jaquet & Rhodes, 2008). The selectivity scores were much larger for the cross-race condition, in which the adapting faces were perceived as belonging to different races, than for the same-race conditions, in which they were not. These results clearly show that race-contingent aftereffects reflect adaptation of face-coding

---

[3] The study described here and reported in Jaquet, et al., (2007) was conducted after, and follows logically from, those reported in Jaquet, et al. (2008). The reversal in publication dates resulted from different publication lags for the two journals.

[4] This was done separately for two assignments of distortion to set (e.g., contacted own-race and expanded other-race or vice versa), and the mean value used.

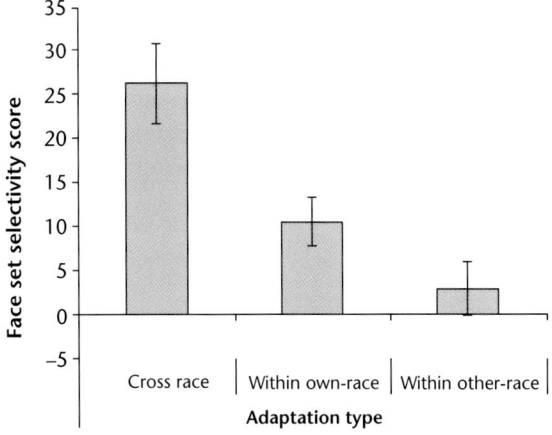

Figure 20.9 Set selectivity scores for the cross-race, within own-race and within other-race adapting conditions. Scores reflect the extent to which aftereffects for the two face sets differed from one another. A score of 0 indicates that there was no difference, and hence no selectivity for the face sets. SE bars are shown. (Reprinted from Jaquet et al., 2007, with permission).

mechanisms that are sensitive to, not just any difference between faces, but to differences associated with semantic category information in faces, in this case, their race. Such race-selective mechanisms are likely to be relatively high in the visual cortical hierarchy.

The selectivity results are consistent with adaptation of preexisting race-selective coding mechanisms, because the selectivity scores were higher when the oppositely adapted sets came from different preexisting categories than when they did not. The alternative possibility, that selectivity is generated on-line, by pairing different face properties (e.g., race) with different distortions, must be taken seriously, however, given the wide range of properties for which contingent face aftereffects can be obtained (Yamashita, et al., 2005). These include some quite arbitrary properties (e.g., red versus green faces) for which preexisting selectivity seems implausible (Yamashita et al., 2005). The idea that contingent aftereffects might be generated during adaptation, by associative learning or retuning of neural selectivity, has been suggested in several other domains (e.g., Dong, Sindale, & Cyander, 1999; Krizay, Vul, Shubel, & MacLeod, 2007; Skowbo, Timney, Gentry & Morant, 1975).

On a learning account, we should have obtained similar selectivity scores in all three conditions, but we did not. However, an advocate of the learning account might counter that the difference occurs because selectivity can be induced more readily for more visually distinct groups.

On this view, larger selectivity scores for cross-race than same-race conditions would reflect the greater perceived difference of faces that cross a race category boundary than those that do not, due to categorical perception of race (Levin & Beale, 2000; Levin & Angelone, 2002). Similarly, the larger selectivity scores for the same-race condition with two groups of own-race than with two groups of other-race faces could reflect the greater discriminability of own- than other-race faces (Walker & Tanaka, 2003).[5] Therefore, we do not rule out a "learning" account of these aftereffects, and consider the extent to which selectivity can be generated by pairing visually distinct groups of faces with different distortions to be an intriguing question for future research. The results may reveal an important role for adaptive processes in perceptual learning.

SUMMARY AND CONCLUSIONS

People are sensitive not only to the identity of a face, but also to its race and sex. This kind of social category information is rapidly encoded (Ito & Urland, 2004; Montepare

[5] We note, however, although there was a significant selectivity score for the two own-race sets (Caucasian and SuperCaucasian), this may not reflect genuine selectivity. Inspection of Figure 5b in Jaquet et al. (2007) shows that there was no significant aftereffect following expanded adaptation for either group, and hence that selectivity has not been demonstrated. This was not a problem for the cross-race selectivity score.

& Opeyo, 2004) and can have powerful consequences for interpersonal behaviour and the
treatment of others (e.g., Blair, Judd & Chapleau,
2004; Devine, 1989; Eagly, Beall & Sternberg,
2004). The results of our aftereffect studies
reviewed earlier suggest that faces of different
races and sexes also form dissociable visual categories (Jaquet et al., 2007, 2008; Jaquet & Rhodes,
2008). Specifically, the race-contingent and sex-
contingent aftereffects that we found implicate
race-selective and sex-selective mechanisms in
coding facial appearance. Not surprisingly, more
generic face-coding mechanisms also contribute,
as indicated by the substantial transfer of aftereffects from one race or sex to another (Jaquet,
et al., 2007, 2008; Jaquet & Rhodes, 2008).

Our results are consistent with a functional
architecture in which faces are represented in
a single face-space, with some dimensions that
code all faces (common or generic dimensions)
and others that code faces of a particular race or
sex. Such selectivity may increase the capacity
of the face-coding system to discriminate faces,
compared with a system in which all faces must
be coded on the same dimensions. A similar
architecture has been proposed to account for
dissociable coding of identity and expression,
analogous to the dissociable coding of faces of
different races (or sexes) seen here (Calder &
Young, 2005).

Selectivity could be implemented by generating dimensions that are specific to a particular race or sex. Alternatively, it could be
implemented by adjusting the weights given to
dimensions according to what kind of face one
is looking at. For example, following an initial
early categorization of a face's race and/or sex,
weights could be adjusted accordingly for more
detailed subsequent coding of appearance. Such
adjustment is possible given that information
about a face's race and sex is available early in
perceptual processing (e.g., Ito & Urland, 2004).
The question of how much exposure to a particular race (or sex) is needed to generate selectivity for that race (or sex) is an interesting topic
for future research.

More generally, we have argued that the
average face functions as a perceptual norm for
coding facial identity. By this, we mean that the

important information for coding facial appearance is how a face deviates from the average.
Specifically, we have proposed a norm-based,
opponent-coding model, in which the value of a
face on each dimension of face space is signaled
by the relative activity of two neural populations,
which are tuned to above-average and below-
average values, respectively, on the dimension.
Such a coding scheme may be optimal for coding inputs with a limited neural response range
in the presence of noise (MacLeod & von der
Twer, 2003). To the extent that different dimensions are used to code faces of different races (or
sexes), different norms would be used for faces
of different races and sexes.

We have demonstrated race-contingent aftereffects, and, therefore, race-selective coding, for
Chinese and Caucasian faces only. However,
there is no reason to think that similar results
would not be found for other races of faces. Nor
do we think that race-contingent aftereffects
require differential expertise with the races
involved. We found no difference in the size of
simple figural aftereffects for own- and other-
race faces, and contingent aftereffects occurred
for sex as well as race, despite little, if any, differential expertise for own- and other-sex faces.
Furthermore, contingent aftereffects occur for
many other facial attributes that are not associated with differences in expertise (Yamashita
et al., 2005). Nevertheless, the visual system
does not develop equivalent selectivity for all
visually distinct groups. For example, we found
that selectivity was greater for visual differences
that were associated with a difference in perceived race than for physically equivalent differences that were not (Jaquet, et al., 2007).

Why should greater selectivity develop for
some groups of faces than others? We suggest
that the degree of selectivity may reflect both the
degree of visual difference between the groups
and the relevance of those differences for social
and behavioral outcomes. Sex and race are highly
relevant to social interactions, and successful
social interaction requires attention to cues to sex
and gender. We speculate that attention to visual
cues to sex and race in the face may promote the
development of distinct norms, and hence visual
selectivity, for these categories of faces.

We hope that our studies have demonstrated how the psychologist's microelectrode, aftereffects, can reveal some of the coding mechanisms underlying the perception of faces. Studies with real microelectrodes will be needed to reveal how these mechanisms are implemented in the brain.

ACKNOWLEDGMENTS

This work was supported by a professorial fellowship grant to the first author from the Australian Research Council, and an Australian postgraduate scholarship and UWA completion scholarship to the second author. The race- and sex-contingent aftereffect studies discussed here form part of a doctoral dissertation by the second author and are described more fully in Jaquet, et al. (2007, 2008) and Jaquet and Rhodes (2008). We thank Linda Jeffery and Larry Maloney for helpful comments on this chapter. Correspondence should be addressed to Gillian Rhodes, School of Psychology, University of Western Australia, 35 Stirling Highway, Crawley, Perth, WA 6009, Australia, or emailed to gill@psy.uwa.edu.au.

REFERENCES

Anderson, N. D., & Wilson, H. R. (2005). The nature of synthetic face adaptation. *Vision Research, 45*, 1815–1828.

Barlow, H. B. (1990). A theory about the functional role and synaptic mechanism of visual aftereffects. In C. Blakemore (Ed.). *Vision: Coding and efficiency.* Cambridge, UK: Cambridge University Press.

Bartlett, M. S. (2007). Information maximization in face processing. Neurocomputing, in press.

Benson, P. J., & Perrett, D. I. (1994). Visual processing of facial distinctiveness. *Perception, 23*, 75–93.

Blair, I. V., Judd, C. M., & Chapleau, K. M. (2004). The influence of Afrocentric facial features in criminal sentencing. *Psychological Science, 15*, 674–679.

Blakemore, C. & Sutton, P. (1969). Size adaptation: a new aftereffect. *Science, 166*, 245–247.

Bruce, V., Doyle, T., Dench, N., & Burton, M. (1991). Remembering facial configurations. *Cognition, 38*, 109–144.

Byatt, G., & Rhodes, G. (1998). Recognition of own–race and other–race caricatures: Implications for models of face recognition. *Vision Research, 38*, 2455–2468.

Byatt, G., & Rhodes, G. (2004). Identification of own–race and other–race faces: Implications for the representation of race in face–space. *Psychonomic Bulletin & Review, 11(40)*, 735–741.

Cabeza, R., & Kato, T. (2000). Features are also important: Contribution of featural and configural processing to face recognition. *Psychological Science, 11*, 429–433.

Cabeza, R., Bruce, V., Kato, T., & Oda, M. (1999). The prototype effect in face recognition: Extension and limits. *Memory & Cognition, 27*, 139–151.

Calder, A. J., & Young, A. W. (2005). Understanding the recognition of facial identity and facial expression. *Nature Reviews Neuroscience, 6*, 641–651

Calder AJ, Young AW (2005), Understanding facial identity and facial expression recognition. *Nature Neuroscience Reviews, 6(8)*:641–653.

Clifford, C.W.G., Ma Wyatt, A., Arnold, D.H., Smith, S.T., & Wenderoth, P. (2001). Orthogonal adaptation improves orientation discrimination. *Vision Research, 41*, 151–159.

Clifford, C. W. G., & Rhodes, G. (Eds.) (2005). *Fitting the mind to the world: Adaptation and aftereffects in high-level vision.* Oxford, UK: Oxford University Press.

De Haan, M., Johnson, M. H., Maurer, D., & Perrett, D. I. (2001). Recognition of individual faces and average face prototypes by 1- and 3-month-old infants. *Cognitive Development, 16*, 659–678.

Devine, P. G. (1989). Stereotypes and prejudice: Their automatic and controlled components. *Journal of Personality and Social Psychology, 56*, 5–18.

Diamond, R., & Carey, S. (1986). Why faces are and are not special: An effect of expertise. *Journal of Experimental Psychology: General, 115*, 107–117.

Dong, C. –J., Sindale, N. V., & Cynader, M. S. (1999). A contingent aftereffect in the auditory system. *Nature Neuroscience, 2*, 863–865.

Eagly, A. H., Beall, A. E., Sternberg, R. J. (Eds.). (2004). *The psychology of gender.* New York: Guilford Press.

Frisby, J. P. (1980). *Seeing: Illusion, mind and brain.* Oxford, UK: Oxford University Press.

Gauthier, I., Tarr, M. J., Moylan, J., Skudlarski, P., Gore, J. C. & Anderson, A. W. (2000). The fusiform "face area" is part of a network that processes faces at the individual level. *Journal of Cognitive Neuroscience, 12*, 495–504.

Golby, A. J., Gabrieli, J. D. E., Chiao, J. Y., & Eberhardt, J. L. (2001). Differential responses in the fusiform region to same-race and other-race faces. *Nature Neuroscience, 4*, 845–850.

Goldstein, A. G., & Chance, J. E. (1980). Memory for faces and schema theory. *Journal of Psychology, 105*, 47–59.

Grill–Spector, K., Knouf, N., & Kanwisher, N. (2004). The fusiform area subserves face perception, not generic within-category discrimination. *Nature Neuroscience, 7*, 555–562.

Hebb, D. O. (1949). *The organization of behavior.* New York: Wiley.

Hochberg, J. E. (1978). *Perception* (2nd ed.). Englewood Cliffs, NJ: Prentice–Hall.

Helson, H. (1964). *Adaptation level theory.* New York: Harper & Row.

Hosoya, T., Baccus, S. A., & Meister, M. (2005). Dynamic predictive coding by the retina. *Nature, 436*, 71–77.

Inn, D., Walden, K. J., & Solso, R. L. (1993). Facial prototype formation in children. *Bulletin of the Psychonomic Society, 31*, 197–200.

Ito, T. A., & Urland, G. R. (2004). Race and gender on the brain: Electrocortical measures of attention to the race and gender of multiply categorizable individuals. *Journal of Personality & Social Psychology, 85*, 616–626.

Jaquet, E. & Rhodes, G. (2008). Face aftereffects indicate dissociable, but not distinct, coding of male and female faces. *Journal of Experimental Psychology: Human Perception & Performance, 34*, 101–112.

Jaquet, E., Rhodes, G., & Hayward, W. G. (2007). Opposite aftereffects for Chinese and Caucasian faces are selective for social category information and not just physical face differences. *Quarterly Journal of Experimental Psychology, 60*, 1457–1467.

Jaquet, E., Rhodes, G., & Hayward, W. G. (2008). Race-contingent aftereffects suggest distinct perceptual norms for different race faces. *Visual Cognition, 16*, 734–753.

Jenkins, R., Beaver, J. D., & Calder, A. J. (2006). I thought you were looking at me: Direction specific aftereffects in gaze perception. *Psychological Science, 17*, 506–513.

Jeffery, L., Rhodes, G., & Busey, T. (2006). View-specific norms code face shape. *Psychological Science, 17*, 501–505.

Kanwisher, N., McDermott, J., & Chun, M. (1997). The fusiform face area: A module in human extrastriate cortex specialized for face perception. *Journal of Neuroscience, 17*, 4302–4311.

Kanwisher, N., & Yovel, G. (2006). The fusiform face area: a cortical region specialized for the perception of faces. *Philosophical Transactions of the Royal Society of London, Series B, 361*, 2109–2128.

Kim, J. S., Yoon, H. W., Kim, B. S., Jeun, S. S., Jung, S. L., & Choe, B. Y. (2006). Racial distinction of the unknown facial identity recognition mechanism by event-related fMRI. *Neuroscience Letters, 397*, 279–284.

Krizay, E., Vul, E., Shubel, E. & MacLeod, D. I. A. (2007). Two timescales of orientation–contingent color adaptation. *Journal of Vision. 7*, 271.

Kourtzi, Z & Grill-Spector, K. (2005). fMRI Adaptation: A tool for studying visual representations in the primate brain. In C.W.G. Clifford & G. Rhodes (eds.), *Fitting the Mind to the World: Adaptation and Aftereffects in High Level Vision.* Oxford: Oxford University Press, 47–82.

Lee, K., Byatt, G., & Rhodes, G. (2000). Caricature effects, distinctiveness and identification: Testing the face–space framework. *Psychological Science, 11*, 379–385.

Leopold, D. A. & Bondar, I. (2005). Adaptation to complex visual patterns in humans and monkeys. In Fitting the mind to the world: adaptation and aftereffects in high-level vision (ed. C. W. Clifford & G. Rhodes). Oxford University Press, 189–211.

Leopold, D. A., Bondar, I., & Giese, M. A. (2006). Norm-based face encoding by single neurons in the monkey inferotemporal cortex. *Nature, 442*, 572–575.

Leopold, D. A., O'Toole, A. J., Vetter, T., & Blanz, V. (2001). Prototype–referenced shape encoding revealed by high-level aftereffects. *Nature Neuroscience, 4*, 89–94.

Leopold, D. A., Rhodes, G., Müller, K-M & Jeffery, L. (2005). The dynamics of visual adaptation to faces. *Proceedings of the Royal Society of London, Series B, 272*, 897–904.

Levin, D. T. & Beale, J. M. (2000). Categorical perception occurs in newly learned faces, other-race faces, and inverted faces. *Perception & Psychophysics, 62*, 386–401.

Levin, D. T. & Angelone, B. L. (2002). Categorical perception of race. *Perception, 31,* 567–578.

Little, A. C., DeBruine, L. M., & Jones, B. C. (2005). Sex-contingent face aftereffects suggest distinct neural populations code male and female faces. *Proceedings of the Royal Society of London, Series B, 272,* 2283–2287.

Loffler, G., Yourganov, G., Wilkinson, F., & Wilson, H. (2005). fMRI evidence for the neural representation of faces. *Nature Neuroscience, 8,* 1386–1391.

MacLeod, D. I. A., & von der Twer, T. (2003). The pleistochrome: Optimal opponent codes for natural colours. In Mausfield, R. & Heyer, D. (Eds.), *Color perception: Mind and the physical world.* Oxford, UK: Oxford University Press. (pp. 155–184).

MacLin, O. H. & Webster, M. A. (2001). Influence of adaptation on the perception of distortions in natural images. *Journal of Electronic Imaging, 10,* 100–109.

Mather, G., Verstraten, F., & Anstis, S. (Eds.). (1998). *The Motion Aftereffect: A Modern Perspective.* Cambridge, MA: MIT Press.

Montepare, J. M., & Opeyo, A. (2004). The relative salience of physiognomic cues in differentiating faces: A methodological tool. *Journal of Nonverbal Behaviour, 26,* 43–59.

Ng, M., Ciaramitaro, V. M., Anstis, S., Boynton, G. M., & Fine, I. (2006). Selectivity for the configural cues that identify the gender, ethnicity and identity of face in the human cortex. *Proceedings of the National Academy of Sciences of the United States of America, 103,* 19552–19557.

O'Leary, A., & McMahon, M. (1991). Adaptation to form distortion of a familiar shape. *Perception & Psychophysics, 49,* 328–332.

Phinney, R.E., Bowd, C., & Patterson, R. (1997). Direction–selective coding of stereoscopic (cyclopean) motion. *Vision Research, 37,* 865–869.

Regan, D., & Beverley, K.I. (1985). Postadaptation orientation discrimination. *Journal of the Optical Society of America A, 2,* 147–155.

Reed, S. K. (1972). Pattern recognition and categorization. *Cognitive Psychology, 3,* 382–407.

Rhodes, G. (1996). *Superportraits: Caricatures and recognition.* Hove, UK: The Psychology Press.

Rhodes, G., Brennan, S., & Carey, S. (1987). Identification and ratings of caricatures: Implications for mental representations of faces. *Cognitive Psychology, 19,* 473–497.

Rhodes, G., & Jeffery, L. (2006). Adaptive norm-based coding of facial identity. *Vision Research, 46,* 2977–2987.

Rhodes, G., Jeffery, L., Watson, T. L., Clifford, C. W. G., & Nakayama, K. (2003). Fitting the mind to the world: Face adaptation and attractiveness aftereffects. *Psychological Science, 14,* 558–566.

Rhodes, G., Jeffery, L., Watson, T., Jaquet, E., Winkler, C., Clifford, C. W. G. (2004). Orientation-contingent face aftereffects and implications for face coding mechanisms. *Current Biology, 14,* 2119–2123.

Rhodes, G., Maloney, L. T., Turner, J., & Ewing, L. (2007). Adaptive face coding and discrimination around the average face. *Vision Research, 47,* 974–989.

Rhodes, G., Robbins, R., Jaquet, E., McKone, E., Jeffery, L., & Clifford, C. W. G., (2005). Adaptation and face perception: How aftereffects implicate norm–based coding of faces. In C. W. G. Clifford & G. Rhodes (Eds.), *Fitting the mind to the world: Adaptation and aftereffects in high–level vision.* Oxford, UK: Oxford University Press.

Robbins, R., McKone, E., & Edwards, M. (2007). Aftereffects for face attributes with different natural variability: Adaptor position effects and neural models. *Journal of Experimental Psychology: Human Perception & Performance, 33,* 570–592.

Rotshtein, P., Henson, R. N. A., Treves, A., Driver, J., & Dolan, R. J. (2005). Morphing Marilyn into Maggie dissociates physical and identity representations in the brain. *Nature Neuroscience, 8,* 107–113.

Skowbo, D., Timney, B. N., Gentry, T. A., & Morant, R. B. (1975). McCollough effects: Experimental findings and theoretical accounts. *Psychological Bulletin, 82,* 497–510.

Solso, R. L., & McCarthy, J. E. (1981a). Prototype formation of faces: A case of pseudomemory. *British Journal of Psychology, 72,* 499–503.

Solso, R. L., & McCarthy, J. E. (1981b). Prototype formation: Central tendency models vs. attribute frequency model. *Bulletin of the Psychonomic Society, 17,* 10–11.

Strauss, M. S., (1979). Abstraction of prototype information by adults and 10-month-old infants. *Journal of Experimental Psychology: Human Learning & Memory, 5,* 618–632.

Tsao, D. Y., & Freiwald, W. A. (2006). What's so special about the average face? *Trends in Cognitive Sciences, 10,* 391–393.

Valentine, T. (1991). A unified account of the effects of distinctiveness, inversion and race on face recognition. *Quarterly Journal of Experimental Psychology, 43A*, 161–204.

Valentine, T. (2001). Face-space models of face recognition. In M. J. Wenger & J. T. Townsend (Eds.). *Computational, geometric, and process perspectives on facial cognition: Contexts and challenges.* Hillsdale, NJ: Erlbaum.

Valentine, T., & Endo, M. (1992). Towards an exemplar model of face processing: The effects of race and distinctiveness. *The Quarterly Journal of Experimental Psychology, 44,* 671–703.

Walker, P. M. & Tanaka, J. W. (2003). An encoding advantage for own–race versus other–race faces. *Perception, 32,* 1117–1125.

Walton, G. E., & Bower, T. G. R. (1993). Newborns form "prototypes" in less than 1 minute. *Psychological Science, 4,* 203–205.

Watson, T. L., & Clifford, C. W. G. (2006). Orientation dependence of the orientation contingent face aftereffect. *Vision Research, 46,* 3422–3429.

Watson, T.L., & Clifford, C.W.G. (2003). Pulling faces: An investigation of the face-distortion aftereffect. *Perception, 32,* 1109–1116.

Webster, M. A. (2003). Light adaptation, contrast adaptation, and human vision. In. R. Mausfeld & D. Heyer (Eds.), *Colour Perception: Mind and the Physical World.* Oxford, UK: Oxford University Press.

Webster, M. A., Kaping, D., Mizokami, Y., & Duhamel, P. (2004). Adaptation to natural face categories. *Nature, 428,* 557–560.

Webster, M. A., & MacLin, O. H. (1999). Figural aftereffects in the perception of faces. *Psychonomic Bulletin & Review, 6*(4), 647–653.

Webster, M.A., Werner, J.S., & Field, D.J. (2005). Adaptation and the phenomenology of perception. In Clifford, C. & Rhodes, G. (Eds.) *Fitting the Mind to the World: Adaptation and Aftereffects in High-Level Vision* (pp. 241–277). Oxford, UK: Oxford University Press.

Werblin, F. S. (1973). The control of sensitivity in the retina. *Scientific American, 228,* 70–79.

Wilson, H. R., Loffler, G., & Wilkinson, F. (2002). Synthetic faces, face cubes, and the geometry of face space. *Vision Research, 42,* 2909–2923.

Yamashita, J. A., Hardy, J. L., De Valois, K. K., & Webster, M. A. (2005). Stimulus selectivity of figural aftereffects for faces. *Journal of Experimental Psychology: Human Perception and Performance, 31,* 420–437.

Zhao, L., & Chubb, C. (2001). The size–tuning of the face–distortion after–effect. *Vision Research, 41,* 2979–2994.

CHAPTER 21

Are People Special? A Brain's Eye View

Anthony P. Atkinson, Andrea S. Heberlein, and Ralph Adolphs

INTRODUCTION

In this chapter our focus will be on people as visual stimuli, that is, objects that have a certain appearance and that move in a certain way, and whose said visual properties we can use as the basis for attributing the states and traits, intentions and actions of other people. By focusing on the visuoperceptual aspects of social cognition, we acknowledge of course that people are much more than visual objects: they have characteristic auditory, olfactory, and tactile properties, and they are also social agents, who act, react, and interact, and with whom we talk, cooperate, fight, and fall in love. Studying people *qua* visual objects will by no means tell us all there is to know about ourselves as social creatures or even about how we understand others as social agents, but as we shall illustrate, important advances have been made in particular at this level of information processing. And one of those important advances is that we are now beginning to understand, at the level of brain function, how *being* a social agent may be at the very core of *perceiving* others as social agents. In part, this is a reflection of the fact that processes central to being a person, to having emotions, intentions, and the ability to act in certain ways, are intrinsic to the act of perceiving another person. That is not all, however. First, persons and their brains are necessarily located within bodies, and there

is growing evidence that we can use our own bodily responses and their neural representations to model the states of others. Second, human social life is both active and interactive. We actively explore our social environments and engage with other people. It is not just our brains that enable and structure our skillful engagements with others, but also those people themselves. Yet those other people are not just passive sensory objects; they are also engaging with us. There is a dynamic interplay among social agents, whose thoughts, feelings, and judgments about one another will thus evolve over time. These interactive aspects of human social life have long been central to social psychology and other social sciences, but have not been fully appreciated in social neuroscience. Nonetheless, as we shall see, inroads into how brain mechanisms contribute to enactivate social perception and cognition are increasingly evident, with important implications for claims about the functional specialization of brain mechanisms for social perception and cognition.

WHAT DOES IT MEAN FOR SOCIAL PERCEPTION AND COGNITION TO BE SPECIAL?

The question of whether social perception and cognition are special can be pitched at two levels.

On the one hand there is the question of whether perception and cognition can be carved into at least two parts, the social and nonsocial. Do we perceive and think about the social world any differently from the way we perceive and think about the nonsocial or physical world? Social psychology is replete with examples supporting an affirmative answer to this question, even if there are commonalities between our engagements with the social and physical realms. On the other hand, there is the question of whether there are psychological processes and neural structures that are specialized for social perception and cognition. An affirmative answer to the first question need not imply an affirmative answer to the second. Social perception and cognition might be special without drawing upon psychological processes and neural structures specialized for social perception and cognition. That is, we might engage with the social and physical worlds using only machinery specialized for engaging with the physical world, but nonetheless engage that machinery in a particular way. In some sense, this is trivially true in that social perception and cognition would be necessarily social just by virtue of the stimuli that are being processed—but here it would be the stimuli that drive the specialness of social cognition, not anything in the brain as such. Clearly, then, a lot hangs on the term *specialized*.

Claims about what a particular mechanism is specialized for are claims about its function. Yet claims about a mechanism's function might refer to one or other of at least two distinct but nevertheless potentially overlapping senses of function. There is the evolutionary sense of function, namely, a role that a mechanism evolved to fulfill and which explains why that mechanism is there in the first place, that is, the mechanism's 'proper function' (Millikan, 1989; Wright, 1973). There is also the sense of function that relates to more proximal causal roles by referring to what a mechanism and its constituent components currently do and how those components and the effects of their interactions contribute to a given capacity of the overall system. This is sometimes known

as the containing-system sense of function (Cummins, 1975).[1] Thus, for example, a claim that a region of fusiform gyrus is specialized for a certain class of social stimuli, such as faces or bodies, might mean that it evolved for processing just that class of visual stimuli. Alternatively, a claim that a region of fusiform gyrus is specialized for processing faces or bodies might refer simply to the fact it processes certain visual properties of faces or bodies and is thus a crucial component in the brain's face or body processing system, without any commitment to whether it evolved for the purpose of processing faces. Although there is more to the distinction between the proper and containing-system senses of function than the distinction between evolved and current function, we should nevertheless note that it is, of course, possible that a mechanism's current and evolved functions either may or may not be the same or overlap. For example, a mechanism that evolved for processing faces may be co-opted for processing other stimulus classes.

In the preceding paragraph we spoke of a neural structure's function as being to process a certain specific body of information. In the case of perceptual mechanisms, this specialization might be conceived as the capacity to process a particular class of stimuli. However, this is only part of the story, for functions are specified in terms of their effects. A neural structure's function is what it does with a specific body of information, what input-output operations it performs. Consider, for example, the debate over the "specialness" of faces and face processing. The debate is often characterized in terms of two opposing sets of hypotheses: those that argue that the neural mechanisms engaged by faces are specific for that particular stimulus class (i.e., faces), and the more domain-general hypotheses, which argue that these mechanisms are, instead, specific for a particular process that

---

[1] These seminal essays by Cummins, Millikan, and Wright are collected together in Allen, Bekoff, and Lauder (1998), along with a number of more recent discussions of the two notions of function. We highly recommend this collection of essays to the interested reader.

may operate on multiple stimulus classes (e.g., Kanwisher & Yovel, 2006; McKone, Kanwisher, & Duchaine, 2007). Examples of the latter class of hypotheses are the claims that faces recruit a mechanism whose function is the individuation of exemplars within a category (the individuation hypothesis: Gauthier et al., 1997; Gauthier et al., 2000a) or within a category for which observers have substantial expertise (the expertise-individuation hypothesis: Gauthier, Behrmann, & Tarr, 1999; Gauthier et al., 2000b; Tarr & Gauthier, 2000). According to these characterizations, a domain is a specific body of information that constitutes the input to some perceptual mechanism or process (e.g., Fodor, 1983) (note that we are not attributing any additional properties to such input domains, such as those historically associated with strong modularity claims).

Notwithstanding the fact that there are several other valid interpretations of domain in the psychological literature (Hirschfeld & Gelman, 1994; Wheeler & Atkinson, 2001), domains conceived as bodies of information are inseparable from the processes that operate over those inputs. This is illustrated in Figure 21.1, which depicts the in-principle design possibilities for cognitive systems. Here we have distinguished relatively special-purpose from relatively general-purpose mechanisms, and relatively domain-specific from relatively domain-general information. A mechanism might have relatively few (minimally one) particular information processing jobs to do, and those operations might be carried out over only one stimulus class (region 1 in Figure 21.1) or over multiple stimulus classes (region 2). Alternatively, a mechanism might have multiple information-processing jobs to perform, and those operations might be carried out over only one stimulus class (region 3 in Figure 21.1) or over multiple stimulus classes (region 4). As an illustration, consider the in-principle cognitive architectures for face processing in the brain in terms of the conceptual map depicted in Figure 21.1. A putative face region might individuate exemplars of only faces (region 1 in Figure 21.1), or of a variety of objects including faces (region 2),

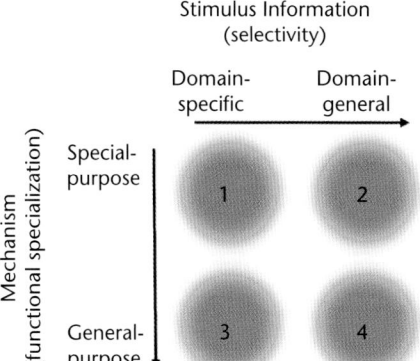

Figure 21.1 In-principle design possibilities for cognitive systems (after Wheeler & Atkinson, 2001).

or it might perform multiple operations, one of which might be the individuation of exemplars on only faces (region 3) or on a variety of objects including faces (region 4). As an aid to preserving the distinction between the two dimensions in this conceptual map, in the discussion that follows we shall refer to a mechanism's specificity for a stimulus class, such as faces or bodies, in terms of its *selectivity*, and to a mechanism's specificity for performing a particular process in terms of its *functional specialization* (or *function* for short).

FACES, BODIES AND BIOLOGICAL MOTION

The human brain contains regions that are disproportionately selective for faces and bodies, and that are specialized for processing their visual form and motion. Our task in this section is to summarize the evidence and draw some conclusions about the more specific functional roles of these regions. The same regions are also implicated in the perception of emotions expressed by the face and body, and our task in subsequent sections is to explore the roles of these regions and their interaction with each other and with additional neural systems in the perception and identification of emotional states and personality traits.

Face Perception

Here we review the neural mechanisms underlying face perception. We begin with a summary of cortical face selectivity, followed by a summary of the functional specialization of these cortical regions for face processing. Additional reviews of face processing can be found elsewhere in this volume (e.g., the chapters by Adams, Franklin, Nelson and Stevenson, de Gelder and Tamietto, and Rhodes and Jaquet).

An initial feed-forward sweep of activity selective for faces compared to nonface objects occurs along the ventral visual stream. A first face-selective response peaks at around 100 ms after stimulus onset, as indicated by a positive deflection of the evoked response potential (ERP) recorded using electroencephalography (EEG) (the P1 or P100: e.g., Herrmann Ehlis, Ellgring, & Fallgatter, 2005a; Itier & Taylor, 2004; Thierry, Martin, Downing, Pegna, 2007) or magnetoencephalography (the M100: Liu, Harris, & Kanwisher, 2002). This is followed by a negative peak of face-selective activity at around 140–170 ms after stimulus onset, the so-called N170 (e.g., Bentin et al., 1996; Bentin & Deouell, 2000; Eimer, 2000; Zion-Golumbic & Bentin, 2007) (although see Thierry et al., 2007) or M170 (e.g., Ewbank, Smith, Hancock, & Andrews, 2007; Furey et al., 2006; Harris & Nakayama, 2007; Liu et al., 2002; Tanskanen, Nasanen, Montez, & Paallysaho, 2005). It is probable that these two early face-selective responses reflect a gradient of face specificity, with the N/M170 being more selective for faces than its predecessor (Liu & Ioannides, 2006). Depth electrode studies in humans have shown selectivity for faces over objects in prefrontal cortex at around the same time as the occipitotemporal N/M170 (Marinkovic, Trebon, Chauvel, & Halgren, 2000), and intracranial surface electrode studies have shown later face-selective responses in ventral temporal cortex at various time points beyond about 290 ms from stimulus onset (Allison, Puce, Spencer, & McCarthy, 1999; Puce, Allison, & McCarthy, 1999).

The sources of the early occipitotemporal face-selective responses have been localized to the fusiform gyrus (Deffke et al., 2007; Furl et al., 2007; Herrmann, Ehlis, Muehlberger, & Fallgatter, 2005b), with the N/M170 indexing activation in a more distributed network than the earlier P/M100, including the occipital cortex (Herrmann et al., 2005b) and perhaps also the superior temporal cortex (Henson et al., 2003; Puce et al., 2003). Evidence from intracranial recordings on the cortical surface (e.g., Allison et al., 1994a; Allison et al., 1994b; Allison et al., 1999) and from functional neuroimaging studies (e.g., Hoffman & Haxby, 2000; Kanwisher, McDermott, & Chun, 1997; McCarthy, Puce, Gore, & Allison, 1997; Puce, Allison, Gore, & McCarthy, 1995) also shows that faces preferentially activate patches of cortex in these regions, specifically, in the occipital and fusiform gyri (Figure 21.2) and the superior temporal sulcus/gyrus (STS/STG) (Figure 21.3). These regions have been dubbed, respectively, the occipital face area (OFA), the fusiform face area (FFA), and the face-selective STS (fSTS) (reviewed by Kanwisher & Yovel, 2006). However, the neural activity indicated by the M170 (and probably also the N170) does not correspond to the face-selective responses in occipital and fusiform cortices recorded using fMRI (Furey et al., 2006). Rather, the face-selective activity assayed by the haemodynamic fMRI response corresponds to a later stage of processing, greater than about 230 ms poststimulus onset, which can be modulated by attention and which may be more closely associated with face identification (Furey et al., 2006).

Face-selectivity is also evident at the level of individual neurons. Early studies in monkeys showed face-selective responses of single neurons located in both superior and inferior aspects of temporal cortex (e.g., Desimone, Albright, Gross, & Bruce, 1984; Perrett et al., 1988). More recent functional neuroimaging studies have confirmed, not only that monkeys have a small number of discrete face-selective regions similar in relative size to those in humans (Pinsk et al., 2005; Tsao et al., 2003), but also that the great majority of neurons in at least one of these face-selective regions (one of the face patches in STS) are themselves face selective (Tsao, Freiwald, Tootell, & Livingstone, 2006).

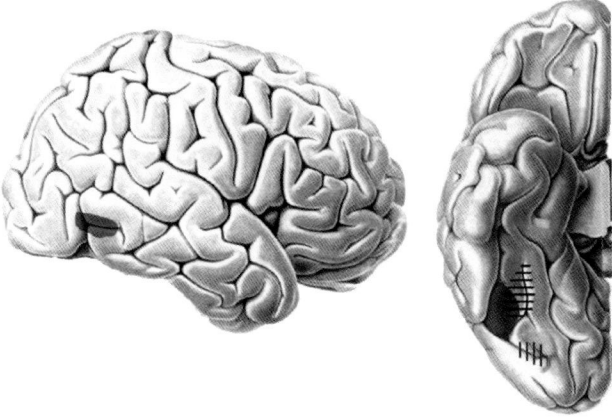

Figure 21.2 The locations of the extrastriate body area (EBA, highlighted in gray on the lateral view), fusiform face and body areas (FFA and FBA, respectively in horizontal stripes and gray on the ventral view) and occipital face area (OFA, in vertical stripes on the ventral view).

The early face-selective responses are associated primarily with face detection and categorization, prior to higher-level semantic processes associated with, for example, identity and emotion recognition. Face detection and categorization are underpinned by the *structural encoding of face stimuli,* a term that refers to the perceptual processing of the features of faces and their configural relations (Bruce & Young, 1986). The N170 and M170 are generally considered

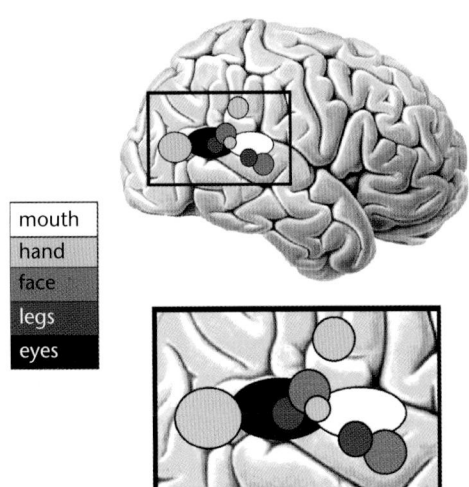

Figure 21.3 Regions activated during the viewing of body movements. Note that the posterior STS region in which there's a significant overlap of activations for viewing multiple different body movements is also active during viewing whole-body depictions of biological motion.

to reflect the later stages of structural encoding of faces, and the P/M100 presumably reflects earlier stages. For example, whereas the M100 is positively correlated with the ability to discriminate faces from nonface objects but not with the ability to identify the faces, the M170 is correlated with both the discrimination and identification of faces (Liu et al., 2002).

Exactly what structural encoding of faces consists in is a matter of ongoing debate. A common view is that separate processes extract facial features (e.g., the eyes, mouth, and nose) and their configuration (i.e., arrangement and spacing), and that this information is then integrated into representations suitable for enabling face perception and identification (e.g., Bruce & Young, 1986; Farah, Wilson, Drain, & Tanaka, 1998; Mondloch, LeGrand, & Maurer, 2002; Rhodes, Brake, & Atkinson, 1993; Valentine, 1991; Young, 1998). Several proposals have been made about how such face-specific processes might be implemented, but the consensus is that distinct but overlapping populations of neurons in occipital and fusiform gyri encode separable aspects of faces, including information about isolated features and second-order relations between features, such as their spacing (Betts & Wilson, 2007; Maurer et al., 2007; Mazard, Schlitz, & Rossion, 2006; Rhodes et al., 2004; Rotshtein et al., 2007a; Schiltz & Rossion, 2006; Yovel & Kanwisher, 2004). The processing of featural information principally underpins relatively low-level face perception abilities such as the discrimination of faces from non-face objects, whereas the processing of second-order spatial relations principally underpins the ability to discriminate and recognize faces on the basis of their identity (Grill-Spector, Knouf, & Kanwisher, 2004; Leder & Bruce, 2000; Peterson & Rhodes, 2003; Rhodes et al., 1993; Rotshtein, Geng, Driver, & Dolan, 2007a; Schiltz et al., 2006; Steeves et al., 2006). A recent repetitive transcranial magnetic stimulation (rTMS) study has confirmed a critical role for the right (but not left) OFA in the discrimination of individual facial features but not of the spacing between those features, within a window of 60–100 ms from stimulus onset (Pitcher, Walsh, Yovel, & Duchaine, 2007). Extraction of a unique identity from facial stimuli may well involve an integration of featural and second-order relational cues, occurring principally in the FFA (Rotshtein et al., 2007a). Nonetheless, neuroimaging evidence from brain lesion subjects indicates that the ability to discriminate between different facial identities requires the operation of both the OFA and FFA, perhaps mediated by re-entrant connections between them (Rossion et al., 2003; Schiltz et al., 2006; Steeves et al., 2006).

In contrast to theories that posit face-specific processes, some theorists have been proposing models of the structural encoding of faces based on the extraction of face shape, similar to the mechanisms used to discriminate nonface objects. These alternative models do not posit separate encoding of featural and configural information, but can nevertheless account for at least some of the behavioral and neuroimaging evidence taken to be indicative of such face-specific processes (e.g., Jiang et al., 2006; Riesenhuber, Jarudi, Gilad, & Sinha, 2004). For example, it is possible that facial identity-related FFA activation is due to top-down identity-based modulation of earlier, bottom-up shape-based processing (Jiang et al., 2006). These proposals are related to more general accounts of object perception that postulate an initial, rapid, feed-forward sweep of coarse visual processing, the outputs of which are then integrated with or otherwise influence the results of a later (but temporally overlapping) stage of more detailed local processing in occipital and temporal cortices (Bar, 2003; Bar et al., 2006a; Blakemore & Campbell, 1969; Bullier, 2001; Buschman & Miller, 2007; Furey et al., 2006; Hughes, Nozawa, & Kitterle, 1996; Sugase, Yamane, Ueno, & Kawano, 1999; Tanskanen et al., 2005; Tanskanen, Nasanen, Ojanpaa, & Hari, et al., 2007). Such coarse-to-fine hypotheses propose that the initial coarse perceptual analysis involves extraction of global aspects of the scene, such as the overall shape, orientation and proportions of stimuli, and a basic configuration of parts. Such an analysis most probably relies on low spatial frequencies of the image (Bar, 2003; Bullier, 2001) (although see Rotshtein et al., 2007b for a note of caution on this association).

As we have mentioned, an area of superior temporal cortex, especially in posterior STS, is selective for faces beginning in the same time frame as initial fusiform face activation, that is, 140–200 ms from stimulus onset (Puce et al., 2003; Watanabe, Kakigi, & Puce, 2003). Yet whereas the ventral stream's role is in the analysis of facial form relating to the more invariant aspects of faces such as their identity, superior temporal regions are involved in processing more changeable aspects of faces, such as expression and eye gaze (Haxby, Hoffman, & Gobini, 2000), or in the integration of motion, form, and auditory information related to such changeable social signals (Calder & Young, 2005). Evidence for these dissociable functions comes principally from lesion studies in humans (e.g., Damasio, Tranel, & Damasio, 1990; Humphreys, Donnelly, & Riddoch, 1993; Parry, Young, Saul, & Moss, 1991; Vaina, 1994; Young et al., 1993) and monkeys (e.g., Heywood & Cowey, 1992) and functional imaging studies in humans (e.g., Grill-Spector et al., 2004; Hoffman & Haxby, 2000; Winston et al., 2003). Nonetheless, there is also evidence of sensitivity to facial identity in posterior STS (Winston, Henson, Fine-Goulden, & Dolan, et al., 2004), and other evidence indicating that monkey STS contains individual neurons (Perrett et al., 1991) or populations of neurons (Baylis, Rolls, & Leonard, 1985; Tsao et al., 2006) that code for information related to identity. Thus, though Haxby et al. (2000) posit a clear separation between processing of invariant vs. changeable facial features, these features may not be processed entirely separately. A more accurate characterization may be that different and perhaps overlapping populations along the STS contribute to different aspects of face perception (Calder & Young, 2005). Consistent with this latter idea is evidence from functional MR adaptation studies showing that facial expression and gaze direction are encoded in regions of STS more anterior than the typical face-selective posterior STS. For example, Winston et al. (2004) found adaptation to repeated presentations of a given emotional expression, compared to repeated presentations of different expressions, in a region of mid-STS. And Calder et al. (2007) report fMR adaptation evidence for separate coding of leftward and rightward eye gaze directions in anterior STS. In the section *Biological Motion Perception*, we discuss additional evidence for the role of superior temporal cortices in processing facial and other bodily motion.

Body Perception

The form of the human (or, more generally, primate) body is another category of visual object for which there appears to be both selectivity and functional specialization in higher-level visual cortices (see Figure 21.2). Evidence for body-selective visual mechanisms comes from studies of both humans and nonhuman primates (reviewed by Peelen & Downing, 2007). In humans, the evidence points to two distinct regions, dubbed the extrastriate body area (EBA), located in lateral occipitotemporal cortex, usually in posterior inferior temporal sulcus (Downing, Jiang, Shuman, & Kanwisher, 2001), and the fusiform body area (FBA), located in fusiform gyrus (Peelen & Downing, 2005; Schwarzlose, Baker, & Kanwisher, 2005). The EBA and FBA respond selectively to human bodies and body parts compared with objects, faces, and other control stimuli, despite considerable anatomical overlap between the FBA and the face-selective FFA (Peelen & Downing, 2005; Peelen, Wiggett, & Downing, 2006; Schwarzlose et al., 2005) and between the EBA, motion processing area V5/MT, and

object-form-selective lateral occipital complex (Downing, Wiggett, & Peelen, 2007; Peelen et al., 2006).

With respect to functional specialization, the EBA represents the static structure of viewed bodies (Downing, Peelen, Wiggett, & Tew, 2006; Michels, Lappe, & Vaina, 2005; Peelen et al., 2006), although these representations appear to be at the level of individual body parts rather than at the level of whole-body configuration (Taylor, Wiggett, & Downing, 2007; Urgesi, Calvo-Merino, Haggard, & Aglioti, 2007a). Configural cues in body perception include the relative positions of body parts and the positions of those parts with respect to the whole body (Reed, Stone, Grubb, & McGoldrick, 2006), and there is evidence indicating that the processing of one or other or both of these configural cues is more a function of the FBA than of the EBA (Taylor et al., 2007). Another region implicated as having a critical role in processing configural body cues is the left ventral premotor cortex (Urgesi et al., 2007a), which also has a crucial role in the visual discrimination of body actions (Pobric & Hamilton, 2006; Urgesi, Candidi, Ionta, & Aglioti, 2007b).

The EBA appears to constitute a critical early stage in the perception of other people (Chan, Peelen, & Downing, 2004), rather than a later processing stage via, for example, top-down effects related to imaginary gestures and movement (de Gelder, 2006). Evidence in support of this claim comes from recent studies using either intracranial recordings or TMS. Pourtois et al. (2007) recorded highly body-selective visual evoked potentials over the EBA of a patient that started approximately 190 ms and peaked 260 ms after stimulus onset. Consistent with this finding are reports of selectively impaired perception of body form following application of TMS over EBA at 150–250 ms (Urgesi, Berlucchi, & Aglioti, 2004; Urgesi et al., 2007a) and at 150–350 ms (Urgesi et al., 2007b) poststimulus onset. Despite this evidence, however, it is entirely possible that, in addition to its role in the early visual processing of body form, the EBA also plays a role in later processing stages of person perception. We shall point to some relevant suggestions in a later section. Little is yet known about the timing of the FBA and ventral premotor cortex involvement in body and person perception, although, given that they preferentially represent configural over body-part cues, it is likely that their initial involvement occurs subsequent to that of the EBA. Nonetheless, as Taylor et al. (2007) comment, a strictly serial model is probably too simplistic, given the widespread bidirectional connectivity in visual cortex. Because the FBA is on the ventral-medial surface of the temporal lobes, it is inaccessible to TMS, and so studies of when it is involved in body and person perception will have to rely on other methods, such as MEG or combined fMRI-TMS investigations that measure the effect of TMS-induced deactivation of the EBA on the activity of FBA and ventral premotor cortex.

Biological Motion Perception

Our brains contain systems specialized for processing the movements of faces, bodies, and their parts, in addition to those systems specialized for processing facial and bodily form. (Although as we shall soon see, the computations performed by these biological motion-processing systems may well draw on form information.) Important early evidence came from neuropsychological lesion studies, which demonstrated spared ability to discriminate biological motion stimuli despite severe impairments in discriminating other types of motion (McLeod et al., 1996; Vaina et al., 1990). However, not all aspects of biological motion perception are normal in such "motion-blind" patients. For example, McLeod et al. (1996) reported a case of a subject who was able to describe accurately a variety of actions from whole-body movements represented in point-light displays, in which static body form information is minimal or absent (Johansson, 1973), but was unable to report in which direction the figure was facing, or whether it was approaching or retreating from her. Furthermore, this same patient was severely impaired at identifying natural speech from point-light or fully illuminated facial movements, despite being unimpaired in recognizing speech-patterns from face photographs (Campbell et al., 1997).

In patients with relatively spared biological motion perception despite deficits in perceiving other sorts of motion, the lesions are restricted to ventral and middle occipitotemporal cortices, sparing superior temporal and parietal areas. Electrophysiological and neuroimaging studies confirm a particularly important role for superior temporal cortex in the perception of body and facial movement (Allison, Puce, & McCarthy, 2000; Puce & Perrett, 2003). Single-cell recording studies in monkeys revealed neurons in STS and superior temporal gyrus (STG), especially in the anterior portion of the superior temporal polysensory area (STPa), selective for various types of face, limb and whole body motion (Jellema, Baker, Wicker, & Perrett, 2000; Jellema & Perrett, 2003; Oram & Perrett, 1994; Perrett et al., 1985). Functional imaging studies in humans show that whole-body movements as represented in pointlight displays elicit activation in pSTS compared to a variety of nonbiological movements (e.g., Bonda, Petrides, Ostry, & Evans, 1996; Grossman et al., 2000; Grossman & Blake, 2001; Grossman & Blake, 2002; Pelphrey et al., 2003; Peuskens, Vanrie, Verfaillie, & Orban, 2005; Vaina et al., 2001). Regions of posterior and middle STS and surrounding superior and middle temporal gyri are also selectively activated by movements of the face or other body parts, as represented in fully-illuminated displays, compared to static images of the same body parts (Wheaton et al., 2004) and to nonbiological motion (Puce et al., 1998). Disruption of the activity of right pSTS using transcranial magnetic stimulation has confirmed a critical role for this region in perceiving body movement (Grossman, Batelli, Pascual-Leone, 2005). More recently, a study with 60 brain-damaged subjects showed that the ability to discriminate whole-body from nonbiological motion in point-light displays was most impaired by lesions in posterior temporal and ventral premotor cortices, which corresponded with the regions whose activity in neurologically intact subjects was selective for the same point-light whole-body movements; moreover, the effects of lesions in these two areas were independent (Saygin, 2007). The critical involvement of ventral premotor cortex in this study confirms earlier studies showing selectivity in this region for point-light whole-body movements (Pelphrey et al., 2003; Saygin et al., 2004).

Selectivity for biological (whole-body) motion has also been reported in the lingual gyrus (in the medial occipital lobe), especially at the cuneus border (Santi et al., 2003; Servos, Osu, Santi, Kawato, 2002). There are also reports of selectivity to biological motion, in the form of whole-body movements, in the posterior inferior temporal sulcus/middle temporal gyrus (Grossman & Blake, 2002; Michels et al., 2005; Peuskens et al., 2005; Saygin et al., 2004), which might reflect activation of body-selective neurons in the EBA or motion-selective neurons in the overlapping V5/MT. There is even a report of selectivity to whole-body movements in the face-selective FFA (Grossman & Blake, 2002), which might reflect activation of body-selective or face-selective neurons, or of both body- and face-selective neurons. These last two issues have been resolved by a recent study: selectivity for biological (whole-body) motion in the occipitotemporal cortex was correlated on a voxel-by-voxel basis to body selectivity (i.e., EBA and FBA activation) but not to face selectivity (i.e., FFA activation) or to nonbiological motion selectivity (i.e., V5/MT activation) (Peelen et al., 2006).[2]

Neuroimaging studies in humans have also revealed distinct regions of STS selective for the movements of different body parts. While face, hand, mouth, and leg movements activate substantially overlapping regions of right pSTS (Pelphrey et al., 2005; Thompson et al., 2007; Wheaton et al., 2004), movements of the face

(Thompson et al., 2007; Wheaton et al., 2004) and mouth (Pelphrey et al., 2005) are also associated with activity along the midposterior STS, as are leg movements (Wheaton et al., 2004). Moreover, whereas both facial speech (principally mouth) and visually similar but linguistically meaningless facial movements activate right pSTS, speech and nonspeech facial movements also elicit dissociable patterns of temporal cortex activation, with speech movements activating traditional language processing areas in both hemispheres, including auditory cortex (Calvert et al., 1997; Campbell et al., 2001). In addition to activating pSTS, hand motion is associated with activity in inferior right pSTS and inferior parietal lobule (Thompson et al., 2007), extending into middle occipital and lingual gyri (Pelphrey et al., 2005), whereas eye movements are associated with activity in more superior and posterior portions of the right pSTS (Pelphrey et al., 2005) and elicit stronger responses in these pSTS regions for mutual than for averted gaze (Pelphrey, Viola, & McCarthy, 2004). Other areas, including ventral premotor and intraparietal cortex, also show differential selectivity to the motion of different body parts, in a somatotopic manner (Buccino et al., 2001; Wheaton et al., 2004). Figure 21.3 shows a summary of the different sectors of the STS that are involved in processing the motion of body parts.

Selectivity to whole-body movements relative to nonbiological motion is evident as early as 80–100 ms poststimulus onset over the left parieto-occipital region, as measured with MEG (Pavlova et al., 2006; Pavlova et al., 2004), a response that is not modulated by attention (Pavlova et al., 2006). Subsequent selectivity for whole-body motion is evident at latencies of 120–130 ms over the right medial parietal cortex and at 155–170 ms over the right posterior temporal cortex, including temporal-parietal junction (Pavlova, Birbaumer, & Sokolov, 2006; Pavlova, Lutzenberger, Sokolov, & Birbaumer, 2004; Pavlova et al., 2007), but only when the stimuli are attended (Pavlova et al., 2006). ERPs recorded using EEG show negative peaks selective for whole-body motion at latencies of 170–210 ms and again at 230–360 ms (Hirai &

---

[2] Interestingly, viewing simple geometric shapes animated so that their movements are interpreted in intentional or social terms elicits greater activity in, among other regions, lateral fusiform cortex (Castelli et al., 2000; Martin & Weisberg, 2003), including FFA (Schultz et al., 2003), as compared with mechanical movements or random motion. These tasks do not involve visual perception of faces or bodies, but do involve perception of animacy and thinking about simple shapes as though they were (human) bodies. No study has yet examined whether viewing such simple animations is associated specifically with body selectivity (i.e., of FBA or EBA).

Hiraki, 2006; Hirai, Senju, Fukushima, & Hiraki, 2005; Jokisch, Daum, Suchan, & Troje, 2005). The earlier ERP component is associated with orbitofrontal brain areas (anterior cingulate and medial frontal gyri), whereas the later ERP component is associated with right fusiform and right superior temporal cortex (Jokisch et al., 2005). Facial movements also elicit a negative deflection of the ERP over posterior temporal regions, compared to motion control stimuli, at latencies of 170–200 ms (Puce et al., 2003).

The distribution of responses in STS and surrounding cortex to the motion of different body parts suggests a functional organization in which distinct but overlapping patches of cortex extract body-part specific representations of biological motion, with a posterior region of STS, especially in the right hemisphere, encoding a higher-level representation of biological motion that is not dependent on the particular body part generating that motion. Consistent with the first part of this hypothesis is the considerable evidence for an important role for areas of STS in the integration of motion and form information, especially that related to social perception (Beauchamp, 2005; Campbell et al., 1997; e.g., Oram & Perrett, 1996; Puce et al., 2003; Vaina et al., 2001). With respect to the second part of this hypothesis, there is some debate over whether pSTS analyzes local image motion (optic flow) or some more global motion of the whole figure (Beintema & Lappe, 2002; Giese & Poggio, 2003; Lange, Georg, & Lappe, 2006; Lange & Lappe, 2006; Thompson, Clarke, Stewart, & Puce, 2005). Although this issue has yet to be fully resolved, recent evidence is building up in favor of the latter proposal. Two computational models of biological motion perception (Giese & Poggio, 2003; Lange & Lappe, 2006) propose that a ventral form pathway derives "snapshots" that represent the various static postures comprising a movement sequence. Neuroimaging evidence indicates these snapshots are derived by the EBA and FBA (Peelen et al., 2006). In one model (Giese & Poggio, 2003), these snapshots are summed and temporally smoothed in ventral visual areas on the basis of local image motion information derived in separate areas,

including pSTS. The other model (Lange & Lappe, 2006) proposes that more superior cortical areas, especially pSTS, temporally integrate sequences of intact body configurations, a suggestion also supported by neuroimaging evidence (Peuskens et al., 2005; Thompson et al., 2005). Nonetheless, it is possible that pSTS both analyzes local image motion, at an early stage, and, at later stage, the more global motion information related to changes in body and body part configurations over time, subsequent to the analysis of individual configurations of body form in the EBA and FBA and facial form in the OFA and FFA and perhaps also fSTS.

PERCEIVING AND IDENTIFYING EMOTIONAL STATES

We have discussed the functions of regions specialized for the representation and analysis of faces, bodies, and biological motion. In this section we detail how these neural regions are involved in the perception and identification of other people's emotional states. We will highlight the ways in which these regions interact or might interact with each other and with other brain regions, such as the amygdala, so as to enable emotion perception and recognition. We will also highlight recent evidence suggesting an important role for the amygdala in allowing us to explore the social environment and to probe it interactively.

The Role of the Amygdala in Emotion Perception

The amygdala has long been implicated in two domains whose investigation has defined largely parallel research agenda: social behavior and emotional memory. The first is exemplified in historical (Klüver & Bucy, 1939) and modern (Emery et al., 2001; Machado & Bachevalier, 2006; Meunier et al., 1999) lesion studies of the amygdala in monkeys, which have shown that such damage results in context-sensitive impairments in social behavior; the latter is exemplified in demonstrations that the amygdala is critical for fear conditioning (LeDoux, 2000) and declarative memory modulation (McGaugh, 2004). Studies of the amygdala in humans are more recent, and began with initial studies of rare patients who had selective amygdala lesions; nowadays, there is an industry devoted to fMRI studies of the structure.

Bilateral amygdala lesions impair the ability to recognize fear, and to a more variable extent anger and other negatively valenced emotions, from static facial expressions (e.g., Adolphs, Tranel, Damasio, & Damasio, 1994; Adolphs et al., 1999; Calder et al., 1996). The amygdala is also activated by fearful facial expressions in neuroimaging studies, although this finding is more variable and appears to be less specific to fear (e.g., Breiter et al., 1996; Morris et al., 1996; Whalen et al., 2001; Winston et al., 2003), and does not require conscious perception of the emotion (Morris, Ohman, & Dolan, 1999) or even of the face (Jiang & He, 2006; Morris, deGelder, Weiskrantz, Dolan, 2001; Williams et al., 2004).[3] For instance, Jiang and He (2006) used continuous flash suppression to render face stimuli completely invisible to subjects. The technique involves presenting rapidly flashing patterns to the dominant eye while the target face stimulus is presented into the nondominant eye, resulting in suppression of the conscious percept for a relatively long duration (longer and more controlled than with standard binocular rivalry). They found that activation of the amygdala did not show any decrement to invisible fear faces compared to when they were visible, but this effect was specific to fear (neutral faces did show a decrement).[4]

Although other visual stimuli have been less investigated, greater amygdala activation has been recorded also for fearful versus neutral whole-body postures and movements (de Gelder et al., 2004; Hadjikhani & de Gelder, 2003; Pichon, deGelder, & Grézes, 2008). However, this finding is variable, because, as is the case with facial expressions, fear is not the only emotion to activate the amygdala when expressed by body movements, and such fearful movements do not always activate the amygdala (Grézes, Pichon, & deGelder, 2007; Peelen, Atkinson, Anderson, & Vuilleumier, 2007).

Amygdala damage particularly affects the ability to recognize emotions from faces more so than from other visual stimuli. Adolphs and Tranel (2003), for example, demonstrated that bilateral (but not unilateral) amygdala damage reduced the ability to recognize emotions from static images of complex social scenes when subjects utilized information from facial expressions, but not for negative emotions when the faces were obscured such that the participants had to rely on other cues including body posture, hand gestures, and interpersonal stances. The eye region of the face is especially diagnostic for the discrimination of fearful expressions (Smith, Cottrell, Gosselin, & Schyns, 2005), although it also appears to be primary in feature-integration processing for all emotional expressions (Schyns, Petro, & Smith, 2007). Functional imaging studies have shown that the amygdala participates in processing information about the eyes (Kawashima et al., 1999), especially when they relate to threat, i.e., fear or anger (Adams et al., 2003; Morris, deBonis, & Dolan, 2002; Whalen et al., 2004). An impairment in processing information from the eye region is at the heart of the fear recognition deficit following bilateral amygdala damage: Adolphs et al. (2005) showed that a patient (SM) with complete bilateral amygdala lesions is severely impaired at perceiving fear in faces because she fails to spontaneously fixate on the eyes of viewed faces and consequently lacks the ability to use information from the eye region when judging emotions (Figure 21.4). This suggests a failure by the amygdala to direct her

---

[3] Nonetheless, some evidence indicates that amygdala activation to fearful faces is not unconditionally automatic (e.g., Pessoa, McKenna, Gutierrez, & Ungerleider, 2002).

[4] It has been suggested that amygdala activation to unconsciously presented fearful faces may be due to input from a subcortical pathway, from the superior colliculus to the pulvinar and thus to the amygdala, that provides rapid, coarse sensory inputs (e.g., Morris et al., 2001; Morris et al., 1999; Pegna, Khateb, Lazeyras, & Seghier, 2005). This proposal remains controversial, however (e.g., Pessoa, 2005), not least because the relevant projections from the superior colliculus to the pulvinar and from the pulvinar to the amygdala seem to form separate and distinct neural circuits (Jones & Burton, 1976; Romanski, Giguere, Bates, & Golman-Rakic, 1997).

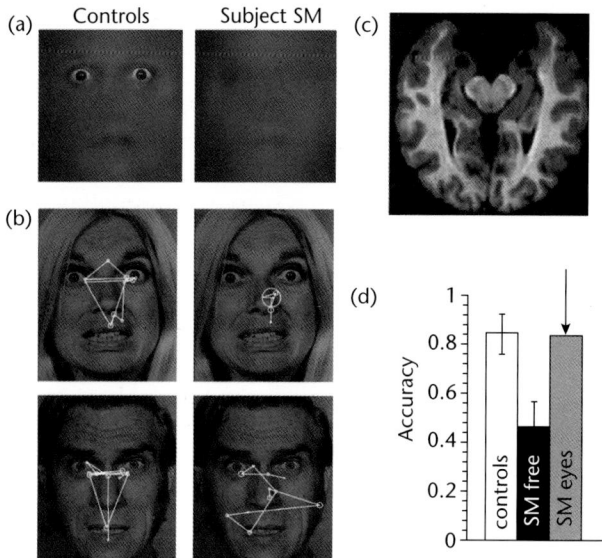

Figure 21.4 Bilateral amygdala lesions impair the use of the eyes and gaze to the eyes during emotion judgment. Using the Bubbles method (see Adolphs et al., 2005) to identify face areas used during emotion judgment, patient SM (brain shown in c) differed from controls such that controls exhibited much greater use of the eyes than SM, while SM did not rely more on any area of the face than did controls (a). While looking at whole faces, SM exhibited abnormal face gaze (b), making far fewer fixations to the eyes than did controls. This was observed across emotions (free viewing, emotion judgment, gender discrimination). When SM was instructed to look at the eyes (d, "SM eyes") in a whole face, she could do this, resulting in a remarkable recovery in ability to recognize the facial expression of fear. Modified from Adolphs et al. (2005).

visual system to seek out, fixate, pay attention to, and make use of such information to identify emotions. The findings are in line with other studies that argue that the amygdala is important in order to assign saliency to stimuli in the environment, or to the features of stimuli (Whalen, 1999). Whether it is relatively selective for processing the salience of social stimuli as opposed to stimuli in general (Herry et al., 2007) is an open question; we suggest assigning the amygdala's function to sectors 1 or 2 (the top row) in Figure 21.1 without making any present commitments about further selectivity at this stage.

Recently we reported a study assessing SM's ability to judge bodily expressed emotions (Atkinson, Heberlein, & Adolphs, 2007). SM completed a battery of tasks involving forced-choice labeling and rating of the emotions in two sets of dynamic body-movement

stimuli, as well as in a set of static body postures. Unexpectedly, SM's performance was completely normal. We replicated the finding in a second rare subject with bilateral lesions entirely confined to the amygdala. Compared to healthy comparison subjects, neither of the amygdala-lesion subjects was impaired in identifying fear from any of these displays. Thus, while the amygdala may sometimes be involved in processing whole-body fear cues, it is not necessary for the normal recognition of fear from either static or dynamic body expressions. Nevertheless, the amygdala's role in social perception, including the recognition of emotions, is not restricted to the eyes or even to faces. For instance, SM's descriptions of the movements of the Heider and Simmel (1944) stimulus, which depicts simple geometric shapes moving on a plain background, are abnormal. Solely on the basis of the movements of these shapes, normal and brain-damaged control subjects attribute social and emotional states to the objects. SM, however, failed to describe these movements spontaneously in social terms, an impairment that was not the result of a global inability to describe social stimuli or of a bias in language use (Heberlein & Adolphs, 2004).

Emotional Modulation of Face, Body, and Biological Motion-Selective Visual Regions

A consistent finding from functional imaging studies of emotional face perception is an enhanced activation of occipital and temporal regions, including the FFA, in response to faces expressing emotions, relative to emotionally neutral faces (for reviews, see Vuilleumier & Driver, 2007; Vuilleumier & Pourtois, 2007). Emotional enhancement of FFA activation has been shown to correlate with activity in the amygdala (e.g., Morris et al., 1998), which is consistent with findings from animal studies demonstrating substantial bidirectional connections between the amygdala and much of ventral temporal cortex (Amaral, Behniea, & Kelly, 2003; Freese & Amaral, 2005), and thus implicates the amygdala as the source of the emotional modulation of visual cortex. More direct evidence of the amygdala's role as the source of the emotional modulation comes from a combined lesion and fMRI study. Vuilleumier et al. (2004) found that individuals with hippocampal damage but spared amygdala showed the normal modulation of fusiform cortex by fearful compared to neutral facial expressions, whereas individuals with amygdala and hippocampal damage did not; furthermore, in an important control condition, the fusiform cortex was modulated by attention to faces as opposed to houses in both groups of patients.

EEG and MEG studies show that the modulation of cortical activity by emotional relative to neutral faces-occurs first over fronto-central areas at latencies of around 120 ms. This is prior to the enhancements of activity in occipital and temporal face-selective regions indexed by amplitude modulations of the N/M170, which

have been recorded in some but by no means all studies (for reviews, see Eimer & Holmes, 2007; Vuilleumier & Pourtois, 2007). It has recently been reported that, not only does the N170 show different latencies for different facial emotions, but it also reflects an integration of visual information specific to each expression, beginning 50 ms prior to and ending at the peak of this ERP (Schyns et al., 2007). For all facial expressions tested, this integration begins at the eyes and moves down the face, stopping once the diagnostic information for the relevant expression has been resolved (e.g., at the eyes for fear expressions, the corners of the nose for disgust, and the mouth for happiness). It is the behavioral goal of emotion classification that determines when the integration of facial information ceases, which suggests top-down cognitive control of processing in occipitotemporal cortex, perhaps from prefrontal regions (Schyns et al., 2007).

EEG studies have also revealed emotional enhancements of activity over more central areas (posterior to the earlier responses), beginning at latencies of around 250 ms and extending to at least 1,000 ms. Intracranial recordings in humans have revealed late emotional enhancements of cortical activity specific to fearful faces in orbitofrontal cortex and anterior STS/middle temporal gyrus after approximately 500 ms and 600 ms from stimulus onset, respectively, as well as in the occipitotemporal cortex after 300 ms (Krolak-Salmon et al., 2004), and specific to disgust in the ventral anterior insula cortex from 300–500 ms (Krolak-Salmon et al., 2003). Given that the amygdala response to emotional, especially fearful, faces does not begin until around 200 ms from stimulus onset (Krolak-Salmon et al., 2004), it is probably only the later modulations of cortical activity that is the result of feedback from the amygdala, whereas the earliest emotional enhancements of visual cortical activity, at around 120 ms, might have other sources, probably related to attention (Eimer & Holmes, 2007; Vuilleumier & Driver, 2007; Vuilleumier & Pourtois, 2007).

Research on the perception of bodily expressed emotions and its neural substrates is relatively young but burgeoning (de Gelder,

2006). Although some of this work is showing that the processing of bodily expressed emotions has a lot in common with the processing of facially expressed emotions, some important differences are coming to light. The first studies of neural responses to emotional bodily expressions found greater amygdala activity to fearful than to neutral or happy static whole-body postures (de Gelder et al., 2004; Hadjikhani & de Gelder, 2003), paralleling the findings with facial expressions of fear. Subsequent studies with dynamic or static displays of bodily expressions have produced mixed findings regarding amygdala activation, however. In one study, angry compared to neutral bodies activated right amygdala irrespective of whether they were presented in static or dynamic displays (Pichon et al., 2008). Yet in another study amygdala activation did not distinguish between fearful and neutral bodies in either static or dynamic displays (Grézes et al., 2007), which is surprising given this group's earlier results with static fearful postures; nonetheless, the right amygdala was activated more by body stimuli per se (a mixture of static and dynamic fearful and emotionally neutral bodies) than by scrambled control images.

Paralleling the findings with facial expressions, research on emotional body perception has similarly reported enhanced activation in visual cortex for emotional bodies and body parts. Such modulation by emotional bodies was consistently reported in the fusiform gyrus (de Gelder et al., 2004; Grosbras & Paus, 2006; Hadjikhani & de Gelder, 2003; Pichon et al., 2008), the lateral occipitotemporal cortex (Grézes et al., 2007; Grosbras & Paus, 2006) and STS (Grézes et al., 2007; Pichon et al., 2008). For example, de Gelder and colleagues have shown that the fusiform and occipital gyri, as well as the amygdala, are activated by static whole-body postures of fear, relative to emotionally neutral postures (de Gelder et al., 2004; Hadjikhani & de Gelder, 2003). More recently they demonstrated that fearful (Grézes et al., 2007) and angry (Pichon et al., 2008) body actions activated, among other regions, bilateral pSTS, irrespective of whether they were presented in static or dynamic displays. Activation specific to dynamic displays of emotional body actions

was evident along the length of STS in the right hemisphere for expressions of anger (Pichon et al., 2008), but only in posterior STS in both hemispheres for expressions of fear (Grézes et al., 2007). Another region activated by fearful body actions irrespective of static or dynamic information was the right middle temporal gyrus, in the region of the EBA and overlapping MT/V5 (Grézes et al., 2007).

In sum, prominent among the regions modulated by the observation of emotional body actions are areas of cortex selective for bodies, faces, and biological motion. This raises the intriguing possibility that emotion signals from the body might modulate precisely those populations of neurons that code for the viewed stimulus category (see Sugase et al., 1999), instead of reflecting synergies between the perception of facial and bodily expressions (de Gelder et al., 2004), or a global boost to all visual processing in extrastriate visual cortex. Evidence of just such category-specific emotional modulation has recently been reported. Peelen Atkinson, Andersson & Vuileumier (2007) found increased activation in the EBA for angry, disgusted, happy, and fearful (but not sad) body movements, compared to neutral controls, and increased activation in the FBA for angry, disgusted, and happy (but not fearful or sad) body movements. Importantly, multivoxel pattern analysis showed that the strength of this emotional modulation was related, on a voxel-by-voxel basis, to the degree of body selectivity, whereas there was no relation with the degree of selectivity for faces, supporting the idea that emotional cues from body movements produce topographically selective influences on category-specific populations of neurons in visual cortex. Furthermore, across subjects, amygdala responses to emotional bodies positively correlated with the modulation of the EBA and FBA but not the FFA. This result parallels the findings of correlations between amygdala and fusiform activity to facially expressed emotions, discussed above, and thus implicates feedback modulatory influences on visual cortex from the amygdala, but in addition suggests that this modulatory feedback is category specific.

What, then, does the increased activity of category-specific regions of visual cortex by emotional stimuli reflect about the functions of those areas in emotion perception? Does this emotional modulation reflect qualitatively different functions or just more of the same, such as enhanced processing of the features, configuration, and motion of faces, bodies, and their parts? Vuilleumier and colleagues (Vuilleumier, 2005; Vuilleumier & Driver, 2007; Vuilleumier & Pourtois, 2007) have suggested the latter, specifically, that feedback modulatory influences from the amygdala serve to prioritize visual processing of emotionally salient events, and argue that such enhanced activity does not simply reflect attentional modulation. With respect to emotion perception, emotional modulation of regions specialized for processing faces, bodies, and biological motion suggests prioritized or enhanced visual processing of the stimulus features so as to allow more efficient or accurate discrimination of others' emotions. To the extent that the discrimination and identification of others' expressions depends on the features of the stimuli conveying the expressions, the regions specialized for processing faces, bodies, and biological motion are likely to be involved. There is, however, surprisingly little work to date demonstrating critical roles for these regions in emotion perception. Furthermore, it is not yet clear whether the roles of these visual regions in social communication are restricted to the processing of stimulus features, although there is recent evidence suggestive of a wider role for at least the STS than mere sensory representation of visual information. For example, a region of right pSTS is involved in the representation of the intentional actions of agents and not just their biological movements (Castelli, Happe, Frith, & Frith, 2000; Saxe et al., 2004; Schultz et al., 2003), and STS activity is modulated by the observer's own facial expression as well as the expressions of others (Carr et al., 2003; Lee, Dolan, & Critchley, 2007; Lee, Josephs, Dolan, & Critchley, 2006), perhaps reflecting a role of this region in mirroring or simulating the viewed facial expression (a topic we take up next).

Emotion Recognition via Emotional Contagion and Simulation

One way in which we might be able to recognize the emotional state of another is via our perception of an emotional response within ourselves (Adolphs, 2002; Atkinson, 2007; Atkinson & Adolphs, 2005; Gallese, Keysers, & Rizzolatti, 2004; Heberlein & Adolphs, 2007). One version of this idea is that emotion recognition involves simulating the viewed emotional state via the generation of a somatosensory image of the associated body state (Adolphs, 2002). Consistent with this proposal are data from several studies implicating right somatosensory-related cortices as an important part of a neural system for recognizing emotions.

Using lesion overlap analyses with large groups of brain-damaged subjects, three separate studies found that impaired recognition of a range of emotions in static faces (Adolphs et al., 2000), prosody (Adolphs, Damasio, & Tranel, 2002), and body movements represented in point-light stimuli (Heberlein, Adolphs, Tranel, & Damasio, 2004) correlated best with lesions in right somatosensory cortex. Given that the lesion method can reveal critical roles for structures only when lesions are confined to those structures, it is significant that in two of these studies (Adolphs et al., 2002; Heberlein et al., 2004) a small number of people had lesions restricted to right SSC and were impaired at recognizing emotions, whereas people with lesions that spared right SSC tended not to have impaired emotion recognition.

Two studies using functional neuroimaging have corroborated these lesion-based findings. Winston et al. (2003) found that the activity of SSC, as well as the ventromedial prefrontal cortex (which also represents somatic states), was enhanced when participants were judging the emotion as compared to the masculinity of faces. Heberlein and Saxe (2005) found converging evidence for the involvement of right SSC in emotion judgments from point-light walkers. In addition, two studies using TMS have confirmed the critical role of right SSC in emotion recognition in the healthy brain. Pourtois et al. (2004) found that reaction times (RTs) for discriminating facial emotion were slowed by single pulse TMS over right SSC compared to stimulation of the superior lateral temporal cortex, whereas the converse pattern was observed for discriminations of eye gaze. Moreover, stimulation of right SSC slowed RTs for judgments of fearful but not happy expressions, which contrasts with the lack of emotion-specific effects for SSC in the lesion and neuroimaging studies. Van Rijn et al. (2005) delivered repetitive pulse TMS to participants' right frontoparietal operculum, a region of SSC where the lips, tongue and jaw are represented. Immediately afterward, the participants judged the emotion of heard sentences with respect to prosody or meaning. For the prosody task, detection of withdrawal emotions (fear plus sadness) was significantly slowed when the right frontoparietal operculum was stimulated compared to sham stimulation. No effect was observed for the approach emotions (happiness plus anger). This differential effect of emotions was not evident in the emotion semantics task. It is interesting that both of these TMS studies found emotion-specific laterality effects, which van Rijn et al (2005) interpret in the light of Davidson and colleagues' (e.g., Davidson, 1992; Sutton & Davidson, 1997) theories regarding differential left/right hemispheric engagement in approach vs. withdrawal emotion experience. It is unclear how to reconcile these findings with the lesion and functional-imaging studies implicating right somatosensory regions for emotion recognition across categories; further studies using TMS on the right and left somatosensory regions will help to establish the role of somatosensory cortices in emotion recognition based on facial or bodily expressions.

A more general question concerns why a region of the brain named for its role in representing bodily sensations, such as touch and pressure, should be critical for recognizing *others'* emotional expressions? We have previously interpreted this involvement in light of simulation models of emotion recognition. Specifically, at least one component of emotion recognition may require internal representations of the body state associated with an observed emotion, in other words, what it *feels like* to be

experiencing the emotion that we view another person *expressing* (Adolphs, 2002; Atkinson, 2007; Atkinson & Adolphs, 2005; Heberlein & Adolphs, 2007). Somatosensory cortices, perhaps especially on the right or perhaps lateralized, depending on the emotion, may play a role in the representation of a somatosensory image associated with an experienced emotion (Adolphs, 2002).

PERCEIVING AND IDENTIFYING PERSONALITY TRAITS

In addition to attributing emotional states to others on the basis of the way they look and behave, we also use cues from their faces and bodies to effortlessly and often automatically attribute to them more stable personality traits, such as trustworthiness, approachability, and competence. Many studies of such processes focus on facial appearance (the form and surface properties of faces), using as stimuli static images of people in a relaxed or neutral pose or snapshots of facial expressions or actions. For example, people are able to rank order faces in terms of how trustworthy and approachable they appear to be, and there is considerable agreement among raters on those rank orderings (e.g., Adolphs, Tranel, & Damasio, 1998). People are also better than chance in guessing others' self-assessed personality from photographs of their faces, particularly for the traits conscientiousness and extraversion (Little & Perrett, 2007), and personality ratings based on photographs are positively correlated with self-report scores for extraversion, and, at least for male faces, emotional stability and openness to experience (Penton-Voak, Pound, Little, & Perrett, 2006). Personality judgments can be made even after only very brief exposure to the faces (Bar et al., 2006b; Willis & Todorov, 2006), and people often make these judgments spontaneously (for a review, see Todorov, Harris, & Fiske, 2006). Trait judgments get associated with or attached to our representations of those peoples' faces in memory (Todorov & Uleman, 2002) in a fairly automatic fashion (Todorov & Uleman, 2003), and are spontaneously retrieved when the face is seen again later (Todorov, Gobbini,

Evans, & Haxby, 2007). Moreover, these rapid, unreflective trait inferences can unconsciously influence subsequent behavior related to that person. For example, inferences of competence from faces predict election outcomes (Todorov, Mandisodza, Goren, & Hall, 2005) and judged attractiveness influences how positively other people are treated (Langlois et al., 2000).

Although the investigation of the neural substrates of personality judgments from visual cues is relatively nascent (especially in comparison to a sizeable literature concerned with such judgments from words that describe people), studies to date have implicated the involvement of four regions: the amygdala, insula, pSTS, and left frontal operculum. As we discuss later, the amygdala and insula appear to be involved in both the simple perception and explicit judgment of at least some personality traits. This involvement probably reflects the roles of these neural structures in emotion perception and emotional response, which fits with the reasonable assumption that at least some personality judgments rely on emotion-related processes (Todorov et al., 2006). The involvement of pSTS and frontal operculum, in contrast, may be limited to explicit judgments, probably reflecting higher-level processes related to understanding other peoples' intentions and other mental states. It remains to be seen whether the involvement of pSTS is related to its involvement in processing faces or biological motion, or indeed whether the face- and body-selective regions of the occipitotemporal cortex are involved in perceiving and judging personality traits from faces and bodies.

Subjects with bilateral amygdala damage are able to judge trustworthy and approachable-looking faces normally, both in terms of absolute ratings and in terms of their relative rank order. Yet they also rate as highly trustworthy and approachable those faces that are normally judged to look the least trustworthy and approachable, and are unable to rank or discriminate those faces in terms of their perceived trustworthiness and approachability, deficits that are not apparent in people with unilateral amygdala lesions (Adolphs et al., 1998). These findings confirm a critical role for the amygdala in the perception of the trustworthiness and approachability of people from their facial appearance. Furthermore, these findings support clinical (Tranel, Gullickson, Koch, & Adolphs 2006) and anecdotal (e.g., Buchanan, Tranel, & Adolphs, 2009) evidence that, in their everyday lives, people with bilateral amygdala lesions are very friendly and forthcoming in their social interactions and are overly trusting of other people.

Adolphs et al.'s (1998) amygdala-lesion study has been corroborated by a functional neuroimaging study showing that activation of both left and right amygdalae to static faces correlates with the judged untrustworthiness of the face (Winston et al., 2002). The amygdala activation to untrustworthy faces was automatic, in the sense that it was evident irrespective of whether participants were explicitly judging the trustworthiness of the individual or making an unrelated age assessment; furthermore, this amygdala activation was not a function of the emotional expression of the face. That study also found activation to perceived untrustworthiness in the right insula regardless of whether participants were judging trustworthiness or age. In the light of the insula's known role in representing somato-visceral states (Craig, 2002), the authors suggested that the observed insular activation to untrustworthy faces might signify the representation of a bodily emotional response to the untrustworthy faces triggered by the amygdala. Activation was also observed in right posterior superior temporal sulcus (pSTS), but only when participants made explicit judgments of trustworthiness. Activation of pSTS and the adjacent temporo-parietal junction has been associated with tasks requiring theory-of-mind inferences (Fletcher et al., 1995; Gallagher et al., 2000; Saxe & Powell, 2006; Saxe & Wexler, 2005), leading some of these same authors to propose STS involvement in the detection of people's intentions (Frith & Frith, 1999) (although this may be more a function of the TPJ: Saxe, 2006a; Saxe, 2006b). As Winston, Strange, O'Doherty, & Dolan, (2002) suggest, given that decisions about someone's trustworthiness are bound up with judgments about their intentions, the involvement of right pSTS in intention detection might explain the activation of this region for explicit trustworthiness judgments.

In contrast to the studies examining personality trait attribution based on face stimuli, studies implicating the left frontal operculum (or left inferior frontal regions more generally) in trait judgments have used whole-body cues as well as verbal tasks. Work examining trait attribution based on thin slices has shown that people make remarkably consistent judgments about traits from very short (e.g., 5 s) segments of nonverbal behavior (Ambady, Hallahan, & Rosenthal, 1995). A lesion overlap study examining personality-trait attributions based on point-light walker stimuli implicated left inferior frontal gyrus, at the frontal operculum, in such judgments (Heberlein et al., 2004); notably, several of these patients were unimpaired at making emotion judgments based on the same stimuli. This finding was corroborated by an fMRI study in which the region of maximal lesion overlap was used as a region of interest. Activity in this region was significantly greater when neurologically normal subjects made personality trait, as compared to emotion, judgments from point-light walkers (Heberlein & Saxe, 2005). Other functional-imaging studies have also reported left inferior frontal activation during personality- trait attributions, though based on verbal tasks. For example, Mitchell and colleagues (Mitchell, Macrae, & Banaji 2005) found activity in this region, as well as in medial PFC, when subjects formed impressions of individual people based on a series of statements about them. Amodio and colleagues (Potanina, Pfeifer, Lieberman, & Amodio, in prep.) reported activity in left inferior frontal regions when subjects performed tasks requiring attribution of nonevaluative stereotypic traits from verbal stimuli (interestingly, tasks requiring attribution of evaluative traits elicited amygdala activity).

In sum, a handful of recent studies have begun to investigate the neural substrates underlying personality trait judgments based on facial and body cues. Due to the very early nature of this work, it is difficult to draw any conclusions. For example, research on trait inferences from faces has focused mostly on facial appearance (the form and surface properties of faces). However, very little is yet known about how the way people move their faces affects our judgments of their personalities, or how facial motion and appearance cues combine to influence trait judgments, or what neural mechanisms underpin trait judgments from facial motion cues. Research in our laboratories is beginning to pursue these issues. Additional questions for future research focus on the relationships between how we perceive or attribute emotional vs. nonemotional traits, as well as the relationships between visual/nonverbal cues and verbal or conceptual information in these judgments.

CONCLUSION

We began with the question of what it means for social perception and cognition to be special. At one level this is the question of whether we perceive and think about the social world any differently from the way we perceive and think about the nonsocial or physical world. At another level, the question of what it means for social perception and cognition to be special is the question of whether there are psychological processes and neural structures that are specialized for social perception and cognition. This chapter has been about the second of these more specific questions but also sheds light on the first.

We have illustrated how the human brain treats other people as special visual categories. There are visual regions selective for faces, bodies, and biological motion, and these are functionally specialized for processing visual cues that underpin our abilities to perceive and understand other peoples' states and traits, intentions and actions. Such abilities depend on a complex interaction of these regions of occipital and temporal cortices with a number of other cortical and subcortical structures, in a way that we are only just beginning to understand. The amygdala, for example, has roles in linking information about the visual world received from these regions to our emotional responses, prioritizing or otherwise enhancing the activity of these and other visual regions via feedback connections, and directing our attention or gaze to emotionally or otherwise socially salient areas of the visual world. The findings we have reviewed emphasize an attentional role for the amygdala—a role that we believe applies not only to sensory input selection, but also operates on internally generated and simulation-related representations (Adolphs & Spezio, 2006). Important interactions also exist between these areas of visual cortex and frontal regions, and between frontal regions and the amygdala. The full extent of processes in which these networks participate is still very unclear, but at a minimum it involves social perception, social inference ('mentalizing'), and aspects of executive functioning. It will be of paramount importance for the adequate interpretation of current and future data to parse out these different processes and to understand their interactions.

Thus it is not simply the stimuli that drive the "specialness" of social perception and cognition; the human brain contains mechanisms that are both selectively activated by and functionally specialized for processing certain types of social stimuli. We perceive the social world differently from the way we perceive the nonsocial world, in at least the sense that, beyond relatively low-level sensory and attentional mechanisms, social perception depends on mechanisms or modes of processing whose containing-system or proper functions (or both) lie squarely within the social domain.

Delineating the social from nonsocial domains is only a start, however, for both the social world and the brain are highly complex, multilayered systems. Consider, for instance, two characteristics of the brain's functional organization illustrated by our survey of the neural systems underpinning social perception:

1. A one-to-many mapping of structure to function: A number of neural regions are engaged in multiple processes and at various points in time, and thus have multiple functions. An example is the amygdala. On the face of it, the face-, body- and biological-motion-selective regions of cortex are possible exceptions, but as we discussed, recent evidence suggests that they too may be involved in multiple processes and at different points in time.

2. A one-to-many mapping of function to structure: Functional roles are likely to be implemented by a number of different neural regions, the more so the higher the level of functional description. An ultimate aim is to provide a one-to-one mapping, that is, to uncover the specific functional contributions of individual neural structures (bearing in mind the one-to-many mapping of structure to function). With respect to their specific roles in social perception, we are getting closer to this ideal in the case of the amygdala. However, the brain and its parts can also be described at different levels of analysis; for example, the amygdala itself is composed of several different nuclei and studies are now beginning to uncover distinct roles for those nuclei in emotion perception.

Where does this leave us with respect to the questions of domain specificity and functional specialization we raised at the outset of this chapter, and the framework we suggested in Figure 21.1? On the whole, we believe that the data we have reviewed here argue strongly for domain-specific and functionally specialized aspects of information processing when it comes to social perception: information processing that would fall within quadrant 1 in Figure 21.1. However, the primary difficulty at this stage is that we simply do not know what the domain(s) of information/stimuli should be, nor what the functional specialization is that special-purpose and domain-specific processing would draw upon. Arguably, these are questions that only more data can answer, but the data will require meta-analyses and data-mining techniques to pull out the domains and the functional specializations. These are challenges for the next generation of young scientists in social cognitive neuroscience to address.

REFERENCES

Adams, R. B., Gordon, H. L., Baird, A. A., Ambady, N., & Kleck, R. E. (2003). Effects of gaze on amygdala sensitivity to anger and fear faces. *Science, 300*(5625), 1536–1536.

Adolphs, R. (2002). Recognizing emotion from facial expressions: Psychological and neurological mechanisms. *Behavioral and Cognitive Neuroscience Reviews, 1*(1), 21–62.

Adolphs, R., Damasio, H., & Tranel, D. (2002). Neural systems for recognition of emotional prosody: a 3-D lesion study. *Emotion, 2*(1), 23–51.

Adolphs, R., Damasio, H., Tranel, D., Cooper, G., & Damasio, A. R. (2000). A role for somatosensory cortices in the visual recognition of emotion as revealed by three–dimensional lesion mapping. *Journal of Neuroscience, 20*(7), 2683–2690.

Adolphs, R., Gosselin, F., Buchanan, T. W., Tranel, D., Schyns, P., & Damasio, A. R. (2005). A mechanism for impaired fear recognition after amygdala damage. *Nature, 433*(7021), 68–72.

Adolphs, R., & Spezio, M. (2006). Role of the amygdala in processing visual social stimuli. *Progress in Brain Research, 156*, 363–378.

Adolphs, R., & Tranel, D. (2003). Amygdala damage impairs emotion recognition from scenes only when they contain facial expressions. *Neuropsychologia, 41*(10), 1281–1289.

Adolphs, R., Tranel, D., & Damasio, A. R. (1998). The human amygdala in social judgment. *Nature, 393*(6684), 470–474.

Adolphs, R., Tranel, D., Damasio, H., & Damasio, A. (1994). Impaired recognition of emotion in facial expressions following bilateral damage to the human amygdala. *Nature, 372*, 669–672.

Adolphs, R., Tranel, D., Hamann, S., Young, A. W., Calder, A. J., Phelps, E. A., et al. (1999). Recognition of facial emotion in nine individuals with bilateral amygdala damage. *Neuropsychologia, 37*(10), 1111–1117.

Allen, C., Bekoff, M., & Lauder, G. (Eds.). (1998). *Nature's purposes: Analyses of function and design in biology.* Cambridge, MA: MIT Press/ Bradford Books.

Allison, T., Ginter, H., McCarthy, G., Nobre, A. C., Puce, A., Luby, M., et al. (1994a). Face recognition in human extrastriate cortex. *Journal of Neurophysiology, 71*(2), 821–825.

Allison, T., McCarthy, G., Nobre, A., Puce, A., & Belger, A. (1994b). Human extrastriate visual cortex and the perception of faces, words, numbers, and colors. *Cerebral Cortex, 4*(5), 544–554.

Allison, T., Puce, A., & McCarthy, G. (2000). Social perception from visual cues: role of the STS region. *Trends in Cognitive Sciences, 4*(7), 267–278.

Allison, T., Puce, A., Spencer, D. D., & McCarthy, G. (1999). Electrophysiological studies of human face perception. I: Potentials generated in occipitotemporal cortex by face and non-face stimuli. *Cerebral Cortex, 9*(5), 415–430.

Amaral, D. G., Behniea, H., & Kelly, J. L. (2003). Topographic organization of projections from the amygdala to the visual cortex in the macaque monkey. *Neuroscience, 118*(4), 1099–1120.

Ambady, N., Hallahan, M., & Rosenthal, R. (1995). On judging and being judged accurately in zero–acquaintance situations. *Journal of Personality and Social Psychology, 69*(3), 518–529.

Atkinson, A. P. (2007). Face processing and empathy. In T. F. D. Farrow & P. W. R. Woodruff (Eds.), *Empathy in mental illness* (pp. 360–385). Cambridge, UK: Cambridge University Press.

Atkinson, A. P., & Adolphs, A. (2005). Visual emotion perception: Mechanisms and processes. In L. F. Barrett, P. M. Niedenthal & P. Winkielman (Eds.), *Emotion and consciousness* (pp. 150–182). New York: Guilford Press.

Atkinson, A. P., Heberlein, A. S., & Adolphs, R. (2007). Spared ability to recognise fear from static and moving whole-body cues following bilateral amygdala damage. *Neuropsychologia, 45*(12), 2772–2782.

Bar, M. (2003). A cortical mechanism for triggering top-down facilitation in visual object recognition. *Journal of Cognitive Neuroscience, 15*(4), 600–609.

Bar, M., Kassam, K. S., Ghuman, A. S., Boshyan, J., Schmidt, A. M., Dale, A. M., et al. (2006a). Top–down facilitation of visual recognition. *Proceedings of the National Academy of Sciences of the United States of America, 103*(2), 449–454.

Bar, M., Neta, M., & Linz, H. (2006b). Very first impressions. *Emotion, 6*(2), 269–278.

Baylis, G. C., Rolls, E. T., & Leonard, C. M. (1985). Selectivity between faces in the responses of a population of neurons in the cortex in the superior temporal sulcus of the monkey. *Brain Research, 342*(1), 91–102.

Beauchamp, M. S. (2005). See me, hear me, touch me: multisensory integration in lateral occipital-temporal cortex. *Current Opinion in Neurobiology, 15*(2), 145–153.

Beintema, J. A., & Lappe, M. (2002). Perception of biological motion without local image motion. *Proceedings of the National Academy of Sciences, 99*(8), 5661–5663.

Bentin, S., Allison, T., Puce, A., Perez, E., & McCarthy, G. (1996). Electrophysiological studies of face perception in humans. *Journal of Cognitive Neuroscience, 8*(6), 551–565.

Bentin, S., & Deouell, L. Y. (2000). Structural encoding and identification in face processing: ERP evidence for separate mechanisms. *Cognitive Neuropsychology, 17*(1–3), 35–54.

Betts, L. R., & Wilson, H. R. (2007). fMRI adaptation in fusiform face area and occipital face area. [Abstract]. *Perception, 36*(Supplement), 145.

Blakemore, C., & Campbell, F. W. (1969). On the existence of neurones in the human visual system selectively sensitive to the orientation and size of retinal images. *The Journal of Physiology, 203*(1), 237–260.

Bonda, E., Petrides, M., Ostry, D., & Evans, A. (1996). Specific involvement of human parietal systems and the amygdala in the perception of biological motion. *Journal of Neuroscience, 16*(11), 3737–3744.

Breiter, H. C., Etcoff, N. L., Whalen, P. J., Kennedy, W. A., Rauch, S. L., Buckner, R. L., et al. (1996). Response and habituation of the human amygdala during visual processing of facial expression. *Neuron, 17*(5), 875–887.

Bruce, V., & Young, A. (1986). Understanding face recognition. *British Journal of Psychology, 77*, 305–327.

Buccino, G., Binkofski, F., Fink, G. R., Fadiga, L., Fogassi, L., Gallese, V., et al. (2001). Action observation activates premotor and parietal areas in a somatotopic manner: an fMRI study. *European Journal of Neuroscience, 13*, 400–404.

Buchanan, T. W., Tranel, D., & Adolphs, R. (2009). The human amygdala in social function. In P. W. Whalen & L. Phelps (Eds.), *The human amygdala*. New York: Oxford University Press.

Bullier, J. (2001). Integrated model of visual processing. *Brain Research Reviews, 36*(2-3), 96–107.

Buschman, T. J., & Miller, E. K. (2007). Top-down versus bottom-up control of attention in the prefrontal and posterior parietal cortices. *Science, 315*(5820), 1860–1862.

Calder, A. J., Beaver, J. D., Winston, J. S., Dolan, R. J., Jenkins, R., Eger, E., et al. (2007). Separate coding of different gaze directions in the superior temporal sulcus and inferior parietal lobule. *Current Biology, 17*(1), 20–25.

Calder, A. J., & Young, A. W. (2005). Understanding the recognition of facial identity and facial expression. *Nature Reviews Neuroscience, 6*(8), 641–651.

Calder, A. J., Young, A. W., Rowland, D., Perrett, D. I., Hodges, J. R., & Etcoff, N. L. (1996). Facial emotion recognition after bilateral amygdala damage: Differentially severe impairment of fear. *Cognitive Neuropsychology, 13*(5), 699–745.

Calvert, G. A., Bullmore, E. T., Brammer, M. J., Campbell, R., Williams, S. C. R., McGuire, P. K., et al. (1997). Activation of auditory cortex during silent lipreading. *Science, 276*(5312), 593–596.

Campbell, R., MacSweeney, M., Surguladze, S., Calvert, G., McGuire, P., Suckling, J., et al. (2001). Cortical substrates for the perception of face actions: an fMRI study of the specificity of activation for seen speech and for meaningless lower-face acts (gurning). *Cognitive Brain Research, 12*(2), 233–243.

Campbell, R., Zihl, J., Massaro, D., Munhall, K., & Cohen, M. M. (1997). Speechreading in the akinetopsic patient, L.M. *Brain, 120*, 1793–1803.

Carr, L., Iacoboni, M., Dubeau, M. C., Mazziotta, J. C., & Lenzi, G. L. (2003). Neural mechanisms of empathy in humans: a relay from neural systems for imitation to limbic areas. *Proceedings of the National Academy of Sciences, 100*(9), 5497–5502.

Castelli, F., Happe, F., Frith, U., & Frith, C. (2000). Movement and mind: a functional imaging study of perception and interpretation of complex intentional movement patterns. *Neuroimage, 12*(3), 314–325.

Chan, A. W., Peelen, M. V., & Downing, P. E. (2004). The effect of viewpoint on body representation in the extrastriate body area. *Neuroreport, 15*(15), 2407–2410.

Craig, A. D. (2002). How do you feel? Interoception: the sense of the physiological condition of the body. *Nature Reviews Neuroscience, 3*(8), 655–666.

Cummins, R. (1975). Functional analysis. *Journal of Philosophy, 72*, 741–765.

Damasio, A. R., Tranel, D., & Damasio, H. (1990). Face agnosia and the neural substrates of memory. *Annual Review of Neuroscience, 13*, 89–109.

Davidson, R. J. (1992). Anterior cerebral asymmetry and the nature of emotion. *Brain and Cognition, 20*(1), 125–151.

de Gelder, B. (2006). Towards the neurobiology of emotional body language. *Nature Reviews Neuroscience, 7*(3), 242–249.

de Gelder, B., Snyder, J., Greve, D., Gerard, G., & Hadjikhani, N. (2004). Fear fosters flight: a mechanism for fear contagion when perceiving emotion expressed by a whole body. *Proceedings of the National Academy of Sciences, 101*(47), 16701–16706.

Deffke, I., Sander, T., Heidenreich, J., Sommer, W., Curio, G., Trahms, L., et al. (2007). MEG/EEG sources of the 170-ms response to faces are co-localized in the fusiform gyrus. *Neuroimage, 35*(4), 1495–1501.

Desimone, R., Albright, T. D., Gross, C. G., & Bruce, C. (1984). Stimulus–selective properties of inferior temporal neurons in the macaque. *Journal of Neuroscience, 4*(8), 2051–2062.

Downing, P. E., Jiang, Y., Shuman, M., & Kanwisher, N. (2001). A cortical area selective for visual processing of the human body. *Science, 293*(5539), 2470–2473.

Downing, P. E., Peelen, M. V., Wiggett, A. J., & Tew, B. D. (2006). The role of the extrastriate body area in action perception. *Social Neuroscience, 1*(1), 52–62.

Downing, P. E., Wiggett, A. J., & Peelen, M. V. (2007). Functional magnetic resonance imaging investigation of overlapping lateral occipitotemporal activations using multi-voxel pattern analysis. *Journal of Neuroscience, 27*(1), 226–233.

Eimer, M. (2000). Event–related brain potentials distinguish processing stages involved in face perception and recognition. *Clinical Neurophysiology, 111*(4), 694–705.

Eimer, M., & Holmes, A. (2007). Event–related brain potential correlates of emotional face processing. *Neuropsychologia, 45*(1), 15–31.

Emery, N. J., Capitanio, J. P., Mason, W. A., Machado, C. J., Mendoza, S. P., & Amaral, D. G. (2001). The effects of bilateral lesions of the amygdala on dyadic social interactions in rhesus monkeys (Macaca mulatta). *Behavioral Neuroscience, 115*(3), 515–544.

Ewbank, M. P., Smith, W. A. P., Hancock, E. R., & Andrews, T. J. (2007). The M170 reflects a viewpoint-dependent representation for both familiar and unfamiliar faces. *Cerebral Cortex*, bhm060.

Farah, M. J., Wilson, K. D., Drain, M., & Tanaka, J. N. (1998). What is "special" about face perception? *Psychological Review, 105*(3), 482–498.

Fletcher, P. C., Happe, F., Frith, U., Baker, S. C., Dolan, R. J., Frackowiak, R. S., et al. (1995). Other minds in the brain: a functional imaging study of "theory of mind" in story comprehension. *Cognition, 57*(2), 109–128.

Fodor, J. A. (1983). *The modularity of mind.* Cambridge, MA: MIT Press/ Bradford Books.

Freese, J. L., & Amaral, D. G. (2005). The organization of projections from the amygdala to visual cortical areas TE and V1 in the macaque monkey. *The Journal of Comparative Neurology, 486*(4), 295–317.

Frith, C. D., & Frith, U. (1999). Interacting minds – A biological basis. *Science, 286*, 1692–1695.

Furey, M. L., Tanskanen, T., Beauchamp, M. S., Avikainen, S., Uutela, K., Hari, R., et al. (2006). Dissociation of face–selective cortical responses by attention. *Proceedings of the National Academy of Sciences, 103*(4), 1065–1070.

Furl, N., van Rijsbergen, N. J., Treves, A., Friston, K. J., & Dolan, R. J. (2007). Experience–dependent coding of facial expression in superior temporal sulcus. *Proceedings of the National Academy of Sciences, 104*(33), 13485–13489.

Gallagher, H. L., Happe, F., Brunswick, N., Fletcher, P. C., Frith, U., & Frith, C. D. (2000). Reading the mind in cartoons and stories: an fMRI study of 'theory of mind' in verbal and nonverbal tasks. *Neuropsychologia, 38*(1), 11–21.

Gallese, V., Keysers, C., & Rizzolatti, G. (2004). A unifying view of the basis of social cognition. *Trends in Cognitive Sciences, 8*(9), 396–403.

Gauthier, I., Anderson, A. W., Tarr, M. J., Skudlarski, P., & Gore, J. C. (1997). Levels of categorization in visual recognition studied using functional magnetic resonance imaging. *Current Biology, 7*(9), 645–651.

Gauthier, I., Behrmann, M., & Tarr, M. J. (1999). Can face recognition really be dissociated from object recognition? *Journal of Cognitive Neuroscience, 11*(4), 349–370.

Gauthier, I., Tarr, M. J., Moylan, J., Anderson, A. W., Skudlarski, P., & Gore, J. C. (2000a). Does visual subordinate–level categorisation engage the functionally defined fusiform face area? *Cognitive Neuropsychology, 17*(1-3), 143–163.

Gauthier, I., Tarr, M. J., Moylan, J., Skudlarski, P., Gore, J. C., & Anderson, A. W. (2000b). The fusiform "face area" is part of a network that processes faces at the individual level. *Journal of Cognitive Neuroscience, 12*(3), 495–504.

Giese, M. A., & Poggio, T. (2003). Neural mechanisms for the recognition of biological movements. *Nature Reviews Neuroscience, 4*(3), 179–192.

Grézes, J., Pichon, S., & de Gelder, B. (2007). Perceiving fear in dynamic body expressions. *Neuroimage, 35*(2), 959–967.

Grill–Spector, K., Knouf, N., & Kanwisher, N. (2004). The fusiform face area subserves face perception, not generic within-category identification. *Nature Neuroscience, 11*, 11.

Grosbras, M.–H., & Paus, T. (2006). Brain networks involved in viewing angry hands or faces. *Cerebral Cortex, 16*(8), 1087–1096.

Grossman, E., Donnelly, M., Price, R., Pickens, D., Morgan, V., Neighbor, G., et al. (2000). Brain areas involved in perception of biological motion. *Journal of Cognitive Neuroscience, 12*(5), 711–720.

Grossman, E. D., Battelli, L., & Pascual–Leone, A. (2005). Repetitive TMS over posterior STS disrupts perception of biological motion. *Vision Research, 45*(22), 2847–2853.

Grossman, E. D., & Blake, R. (2001). Brain activity evoked by inverted and imagined biological motion. *Vision Research, 41*(10-11), 1475–1482.

Grossman, E. D., & Blake, R. (2002). Brain areas active during visual perception of biological motion. *Neuron, 35*(6), 1167–1175.

Hadjikhani, N., & de Gelder, B. (2003). Seeing fearful body expressions activates the fusiform cortex and amygdala. *Current Biology, 13*(24), 2201–2205.

Harris, A., & Nakayama, K. (2007). Rapid face-selective adaptation of an early extrastriate component in MEG. *Cerebral Cortex, 17*(1), 63–70.

Haxby, J. V., Hoffman, E. A., & Gobbini, M. I. (2000). The distributed human neural system for face perception. *Trends in Cognitive Sciences, 4*(6), 223–233.

Heberlein, A. S., & Adolphs, R. (2004). Impaired spontaneous anthropomorphizing despite intact perception and social knowledge. *Proceedings of the National Academy of Sciences, 101*(19), 7487–7491.

Heberlein, A. S., & Adolphs, R. (2007). Neurobiology of emotion recognition: Current evidence for shared substrates. In E. Harmon-Jones & P. Winkielman (Eds.), *Social neuroscience: Integrating biological and psychological explanations of social behavior.* New York: Guilford Press.

Heberlein, A. S., Adolphs, R., Tranel, D., & Damasio, H. (2004). Cortical regions for judgments of emotions and personality traits

from point–light walkers. *Journal of Cognitive Neuroscience, 16*(7), 1143–1158.

Heberlein, A. S., & Saxe, R. R. (2005). Dissociation between emotion and personality judgments: Convergent evidence from functional neuroimaging. *Neuroimage, 28*(4), 770–777.

Heider, F., & Simmel, M. (1944). An experimental study of apparent behavior. *American Journal of Psychology, 57*, 243–259.

Henson, R. N., Goshen–Gottstein, Y., Ganel, T., Otten, L. J., Quayle, A., & Rugg, M. D. (2003). Electrophysiological and haemodynamic correlates of face perception, recognition and priming. *Cerebral Cortex, 13*(7), 793–805.

Herrmann, M. J., Ehlis, A. C., Ellgring, H., & Fallgatter, A. J. (2005a). Early stages (P100) of face perception in humans as measured with event-related potentials (ERPs). *Journal of Neural Transmission, 112*(8), 1073–1081.

Herrmann, M. J., Ehlis, A. C., Muehlberger, A., & Fallgatter, A. J. (2005b). Source localization of early stages of face processing. *Brain Topography, 18*(2), 77–85.

Herry, C., Bach, D. R., Esposito, F., Di Salle, F., Perrig, W. J., Scheffler, K., et al. (2007). Processing of temporal unpredictability in human and animal amygdala. *The Journal of Neuroscience, 27*(22), 5958–5966.

Heywood, C. A., & Cowey, A. (1992). The role of the 'face-cell' area in the discrimination and recognition of faces by monkeys. *Philosophical Transactions of the Royal Society of London B: Biological Sciences, 335*(1273), 31–37; discussion 37–38.

Hirai, M., & Hiraki, K. (2006). The relative importance of spatial versus temporal structure in the perception of biological motion: An event-related potential study. *Cognition, 99*(1), B15–B29.

Hirai, M., Senju, A., Fukushima, H., & Hiraki, K. (2005). Active processing of biological motion perception: an ERP study. *Cognitive Brain Research, 23*(2–3), 387–396.

Hirschfeld, L. A., & Gelman, S. A. (1994). Toward a topography of mind: An introduction to domain specificity. In L. A. Hirschfeld & S. A. Gelman (Eds.), *Mapping the mind: Domain specificity in cognition and culture* (pp. 3–35). Cambridge, UK: Cambridge University Press.

Hoffman, E. A., & Haxby, J. V. (2000). Distinct representations of eye gaze and identity in the distributed human neural system for face perception. *Nature Neuroscience, 3*(1), 80–84.

Hughes, H. C., Nozawa, G., & Kitterle, F. (1996). Global precedence, spatial frequency channels, and the statistics of natural images. *Journal of Cognitive Neuroscience, 8*(3), 197–230.

Humphreys, G. W., Donnelly, N., & Riddoch, M. J. (1993). Expression is computed separately from facial identity, and it is computed separately for moving and static faces: neuropsychological evidence. *Neuropsychologia, 31*(2), 173–181.

Itier, R. J., & Taylor, M. J. (2004). Effects of repetition learning on upright, inverted and contrast–reversed face processing using ERPs. *Neuroimage, 21*(4), 1518–1532.

Jellema, T., Baker, C. I., Wicker, B., & Perrett, D. I. (2000). Neural representation for the perception of the intentionality of actions. *Brain and Cognition, 44*(2), 280–302.

Jellema, T., & Perrett, D. I. (2003). Cells in monkey STS responsive to articulated body motions and consequent static posture: a case of implied motion? *Neuropsychologia, 41*(13), 1728–1737.

Jiang, X., Rosen, E., Zeffiro, T., VanMeter, J., Blanz, V., & Riesenhuber, M. (2006). Evaluation of a shape-based model of human face discrimination using fMRI and behavioral techniques. *Neuron, 50*(1), 159–172.

Jiang, Y., & He, S. (2006). Cortical responses to invisible faces: Dissociating subsystems for facial-information processing. *Current Biology, 16*(20), 2023–2029.

Johansson, G. (1973). Visual perception of biological motion and a model for its analysis. *Perception and Psychophysics, 14*(2), 201–211.

Jokisch, D., Daum, I., Suchan, B., & Troje, N. F. (2005). Structural encoding and recognition of biological motion: evidence from event-related potentials and source analysis. *Behavioural Brain Research, 157*(2), 195–204.

Jones, E. G., & Burton, H. (1976). Projection from medial pulvinar to amygdala in primates. *Brain Research, 104*(1), 142–147.

Kanwisher, N., McDermott, J., & Chun, M. M. (1997). The fusiform face area: a module in human extrastriate cortex specialized for face perception. *Journal of Neuroscience, 17*(11), 4302–4311.

Kanwisher, N., & Yovel, G. (2006). The fusiform face area: a cortical region specialized for the perception of faces. *Philosophical Transactions of the Royal Society B: Biological Sciences, 361*(1476), 2109–2128.

Kawashima, R., Sugiura, M., Kato, T., Nakamura, A., Hatano, K., Ito, K., et al. (1999). The human amygdala plays an important role in gaze monitoring. A PET study. *Brain, 122 (Pt 4)*, 779–783.

Klüver, H., & Bucy, P. C. (1939). Preliminary analysis of functions of the temporal lobes in monkeys. *Archives of Neurology and Psychiatry, 42*, 979–1000.

Krolak-Salmon, P., Henaff, M. A., Isnard, J., Tallon-Baudry, C., Guenot, M., Vighetto, A., et al. (2003). An attention modulated response to disgust in human ventral anterior insula. *Annals of Neurology, 53*(4), 446–453.

Krolak-Salmon, P., Henaff, M. A., Vighetto, A., Bertrand, O., & Mauguiere, F. (2004). Early amygdala reaction to fear spreading in occipital, temporal, and frontal cortex: A depth electrode ERP study in human. *Neuron, 42*(4), 665–676.

Lange, J., Georg, K., & Lappe, M. (2006). Visual perception of biological motion by form: A template-matching analysis. *Journal of Vision, 6*(8), 836–849.

Lange, J., & Lappe, M. (2006). A model of biological motion perception from configural form cues. *Journal of Neuroscience, 26*(11), 2894–2906.

Langlois, J. H., Kalakanis, L., Rubenstein, A. J., Larson, A., Hallam, M., & Smoot, M. (2000). Maxims or myths of beauty? A meta-analytic and theoretical review. *Psychological Bulletin, 126*(3), 390–423.

Leder, H., & Bruce, V. (2000). When inverted faces are recognized: the role of configural information in face recognition. *Quarterly Journal of Experimental Psychology, A, 53*(2), 513–536.

LeDoux, J. E. (2000). Emotion circuits in the brain. *Annual Review of Neuroscience, 23*, 155–184.

Lee, T.-W., Dolan, R. J., & Critchley, H. D. (2007). Controlling emotional expression: Behavioral and neural correlates of nonimitative emotional responses. *Cerebral Cortex, 18*(1), 104–113.

Lee, T.-W., Josephs, O., Dolan, R. J., & Critchley, H. D. (2006). Imitating expressions: emotion–specific neural substrates in facial mimicry. *Social Cognitive and Affective Neuroscience, 1*(2), 122–135.

Little, A. C., & Perrett, D. I. (2007). Using composite images to assess accuracy in personality attribution to faces. *British Journal of Psychology, 98*(1), 111–126.

Liu, J., Harris, A., & Kanwisher, N. (2002). Stages of processing in face perception: an MEG study. *Nature Neuroscience, 5*(9), 910–916.

Liu, L., & Ioannides, A. A. (2006). Spatiotemporal dynamics and connectivity pattern differences between centrally and peripherally presented faces. *Neuroimage, 31*(4), 1726–1740.

Machado, C. J., & Bachevalier, J. (2006). The impact of selective amygdala, orbital frontal cortex, or hippocampal formation lesions on established social relationships in rhesus monkeys (Macaca mulatta). *Behavioral Neuroscience, 120*(4), 761–786.

Marinkovic, K., Trebon, P., Chauvel, P., & Halgren, E. (2000). Localised face processing by the human prefrontal cortex: Face-selective intracerebral potentials and post-lesion deficits. *Cognitive Neuropsychology, 17*(1–3), 187–199.

Martin, A., & Weisberg, J. (2003). Neural foundations for understanding social and mechanical concepts. *Cognitive Neuropsychology, 20*(3–6), 575–587.

Maurer, D., O'Craven, K. M., Le Grand, R., Mondloch, C. J., Springer, M. V., Lewis, T. L., et al. (2007). Neural correlates of processing facial identity based on features versus their spacing. *Neuropsychologia, 45*(7), 1438–1451.

Mazard, A., Schiltz, C., & Rossion, B. (2006). Recovery from adaptation to facial identity is larger for upright than inverted faces in the human occipito-temporal cortex. *Neuropsychologia, 44*(6), 912–922.

McCarthy, G., Puce, A., Gore, J. C., & Allison, T. (1997). Face-specific processing in the human fusiform gyrus. *Journal of Cognitive Neuroscience, 9*(5), 605–610.

McGaugh, J. L. (2004). The amygdala modulates the consolidation of memories of emotionally arousing experiences. *Annual Review of Neuroscience, 27,* 1–28.

McKone, E., Kanwisher, N., & Duchaine, B. C. (2007). Can generic expertise explain special processing for faces? *Trends in Cognitive Sciences, 11*(1), 8–15.

McLeod, P., Dittrich, W., Driver, J., Perrett, D., & Zihl, J. (1996). Preserved and impaired detection of structure from motion by a "motion-blind" patient. *Visual Cognition, 3*(4), 363–391.

Meunier, M., Bachevalier, J., Murray, E. A., Malkova, L., & Mishkin, M. (1999). Effects of aspiration versus neurotoxic lesions of the amygdala on emotional responses in monkeys. *European Journal of Neuroscience, 11*(12), 4403–4418.

Michels, L., Lappe, M., & Vaina, L. M. (2005). Visual areas involved in the perception of human movement from dynamic form analysis. *Neuroreport, 16*(10), 1037–1041.

Millikan, R. G. (1989). In defence of proper functions. *Philosophy of Science, 56,* 288–302.

Mitchell, J. P., Macrae, N. C., & Banaji, M. R. (2005). Forming impressions of people versus inanimate objects: Social-cognitive processing in the medial prefrontal cortex. *Neuroimage, 26*(1), 251–257.

Mondloch, C. J., Le Grand, R., & Maurer, D. (2002). Configural face processing develops more slowly than featural face processing. *Perception, 31*(5), 553–566.

Morris, J. S., deBonis, M., & Dolan, R. J. (2002). Human amygdala responses to fearful eyes. *Neuroimage, 17*(1), 214–222.

Morris, J. S., DeGelder, B., Weiskrantz, L., & Dolan, R. J. (2001). Differential extrageniculostriate and amygdala responses to presentation of emotional faces in a cortically blind field. *Brain, 124*(Pt 6), 1241–1252.

Morris, J. S., Friston, K. J., Buchel, C., Frith, C. D., Young, A. W., Calder, A. J., et al. (1998). A neuromodulatory role for the human amygdala in processing emotional facial expressions. *Brain, 121,* 47–57.

Morris, J. S., Frith, C. D., Perrett, D. I., Rowland, D., Young, A. W., Calder, A. J., et al. (1996). A differential neural response in the human amygdala to fearful and happy facial expressions. *Nature, 383*(6603), 812–815.

Morris, J. S., Ohman, A., & Dolan, R. J. (1999). A subcortical pathway to the right amygdala mediating "unseen" fear. *Proceedings of the National Academy of Sciences of the United States of America, 96*(4), 1680–1685.

Oram, M. W., & Perrett, D. I. (1994). Responses of anterior superior temporal polysensory (STPa) neurons to "biological motion" stimuli. *Journal of Cognitive Neuroscience, 6*(2), 99–116.

Oram, M. W., & Perrett, D. I. (1996). Integration of form and motion in the anterior superior temporal polysensory area (STPa) of the macaque monkey. *Journal of Neurophysiology, 76*(1), 109–129.

Parry, F. M., Young, A. W., Saul, J. S., & Moss, A. (1991). Dissociable face processing impairments after brain injury. *Journal of Clinical and Experimental Neuropsychology, 13*(4), 545–558.

Pavlova, M., Birbaumer, N., & Sokolov, A. (2006). Attentional modulation of cortical neuromagnetic gamma response to biological movement. *Cerebral Cortex, 16*(3), 321–327.

Pavlova, M., Lutzenberger, W., Sokolov, A., & Birbaumer, N. (2004). Dissociable cortical processing of recognizable and non-recognizable biological movement: Analysing gamma MEG activity. *Cerebral Cortex, 14*(2), 181–188.

Pavlova, M., Lutzenberger, W., Sokolov, A. N., Birbaumer, N., & Krageloh-Mann, I. (2007). Oscillatory MEG response to human locomotion is modulated by periventricular lesions. *Neuroimage, 35*(3), 1256–1263.

Peelen, M. V., Atkinson, A. P., Andersson, F., & Vuilleumier, P. (2007). Emotional modulation of body–selective visual areas. *Social Cognitive and Affective Neuroscience, 2*(4), 274–283.

Peelen, M. V., & Downing, P. E. (2005). Selectivity for the human body in the fusiform gyrus. *Journal of Neurophysiology, 93*(1), 603–608.

Peelen, M. V., & Downing, P. E. (2007). The neural basis of visual body perception. *Nature Reviews Neuroscience, 8*(8), 636–648.

Peelen, M. V., Wiggett, A. J., & Downing, P. E. (2006). Patterns of fMRI activity dissociate overlapping functional brain areas that respond to biological motion. *Neuron, 49*(6), 815–822.

Pegna, A. J., Khateb, A., Lazeyras, F., & Seghier, M. L. (2005). Discriminating emotional faces without primary visual cortices involves the right amygdala. *Nature Neuroscience, 8*(1), 24–25.

Pelphrey, K. A., Mitchell, T. V., McKeown, M. J., Goldstein, J., Allison, T., & McCarthy, G. (2003). Brain activity evoked by the perception of human walking: Controlling for meaningful coherent motion. *Journal of Neuroscience, 23*(17), 6819–6825.

Pelphrey, K. A., Morris, J. P., Michelich, C. R., Allison, T., & McCarthy, G. (2005). Functional anatomy of biological motion perception in posterior temporal cortex: An fMRI study of eye, mouth and hand movements. *Cerebral Cortex, 15*(12), 1866–1876.

Pelphrey, K. A., Viola, R. J., & McCarthy, G. (2004). When strangers pass: Processing of mutual and averted social gaze in the superior temporal sulcus. *Psychological Science, 15*(9), 598–603.

Penton–Voak, I. S., Pound, N., Little, A. C., & Perrett, D. I. (2006). Personality judgments from natural and composite facial images: More evidence for a "kernel of truth" in social perception. *Social Cognition, 24*(5), 607–640.

Perrett, D. I., Mistlin, A. J., Chitty, A. J., Smith, P. A., Potter, D. D., Broennimann, R., et al. (1988). Specialized face processing and hemispheric asymmetry in man and monkey: evidence from single unit and reaction time studies. *Behavioural Brain Research, 29*(3), 245–258.

Perrett, D. I., Oram, M. W., Harries, M. H., Bevan, R., Hietanen, J. K., Benson, P. J., et al. (1991). Viewer-centred and object–centred coding of heads in the macaque temporal cortex. *Experimental Brain Research, 86*(1), 159–173.

Perrett, D. I., Smith, P. A., Mistlin, A. J., Chitty, A. J., Head, A. S., Potter, D. D., et al. (1985). Visual analysis of body movements by neurones in the temporal cortex of the macaque monkey: a preliminary report. *Behavioural Brain Research, 16*(2–3), 153–170.

Pessoa, L. (2005). To what extent are emotional visual stimuli processed without attention and awareness? *Current Opinion in Neurobiology, 15*(2), 188–196.

Pessoa, L., McKenna, M., Gutierrez, E., & Ungerleider, L. G. (2002). Neural processing of emotional faces requires attention. *Proceedings of the National Academy of Sciences, 99*(17), 11458–11463.

Peterson, M. P., & Rhodes, G. (Eds.). (2003). *Perception of faces, objects and scenes: Analytic and holistic processing.* Cambridge, MA: Oxford University Press.

Peuskens, H., Vanrie, J., Verfaillie, K., & Orban, G. A. (2005). Specificity of regions processing biological motion. *European Journal of Neuroscience, 21*(10), 2864–2875.

Pichon, S., de Gelder, B., & Grézes, J. (2008). Emotional modulation of visual and motor areas by dynamic body expressions of anger. *Social Neuroscience, 3*(3), 199–212.

Pinsk, M. A., DeSimone, K., Moore, T., Gross, C. G., & Kastner, S. (2005). Representations of faces and body parts in macaque temporal cortex: A functional MRI study. *Proceedings of the National Academy of Sciences of the United States of America, 102*(19), 6996–7001.

Pitcher, D., Walsh, V., Yovel, G., & Duchaine, B. (2007). TMS evidence for the involvement of the right occipital face area in early face processing. *Current Biology, 17*(18), 1568–1573.

Pobric, G., & Hamilton, A. F. (2006). Action understanding requires the left inferior frontal cortex. *Current Biology, 16*(5), 524–529.

Potanina, P. V., Pfeifer, J. H., Lieberman, M. D., & Amodio, D. M. (in prep.). Dissociable neural correlates of implicit stereotyping vs. implicit evaluation.

Pourtois, G., Peelen, M. V., Spinelli, L., Seeck, M., & Vuilleumier, P. (2007). Direct intracranial recording of body-selective responses in human extrastriate visual cortex. *Neuropsychologia, 45*(11), 2621–2625.

Pourtois, G., Sander, D., Andres, M., Grandjean, D., Reveret, L., Olivier, E., et al. (2004). Dissociable roles of the human somatosensory and superior temporal cortices for processing social face signals. *European Journal of Neuroscience, 20*(12), 3507–3515.

Puce, A., Allison, T., Bentin, S., Gore, J. C., & McCarthy, G. (1998). Temporal cortex activation in humans viewing eye and mouth movements. *Journal of Neuroscience, 18*(6), 2188–2199.

Puce, A., Allison, T., Gore, J. C., & McCarthy, G. (1995). Face–sensitive regions in human extrastriate cortex studied by functional MRI. *Journal of Neurophysiology, 74*(3), 1192–1199.

Puce, A., Allison, T., & McCarthy, G. (1999). Electrophysiological studies of human face perception. III: Effects of top–down processing on face-specific potentials. *Cerebral Cortex, 9*(5), 445–458.

Puce, A., & Perrett, D. (2003). Electrophysiology and brain imaging of biological motion. *Philosophical Transactions of the Royal Society of London, Series B: Biological Sciences, 358*(1431), 435–445.

Puce, A., Syngeniotis, A., Thompson, J. C., Abbott, D. F., Wheaton, K. J., & Castiello, U. (2003). The human temporal lobe integrates facial form and motion: evidence from fMRI and ERP studies. *Neuroimage, 19*(3), 861–869.

Reed, C. L., Stone, V. E., Grubb, J. D., & McGoldrick, J. E. (2006). Turning configural processing upside down: Part and whole body postures. *Journal of Experimental Psychology: Human Perception and Performance, 32*(1), 73–87.

Rhodes, G., Brake, S., & Atkinson, A. P. (1993). What's lost in inverted faces? *Cognition, 47*(1), 25–57.

Rhodes, G., Jeffery, L., Watson, T. L., Jaquet, E., Winkler, C., & Clifford, C. W. (2004). Orientation-contingent face aftereffects and implications for face–coding mechanisms. *Current Biology, 14*(23), 2119–2123.

Riesenhuber, M., Jarudi, I., Gilad, S., & Sinha, P. (2004). Face processing in humans is compatible with a simple shape-based model of vision. *Proceedings of the Royal Society of London, B: Biological Sciences, 271*, S448–S450.

Romanski, L. M., Giguere, M., Bates, J. F., & Goldman-Rakic, P. S. (1997). Topographic organization of medial pulvinar connections with the prefrontal cortex in the rhesus monkey. *Journal of Comparative Neurology, 379*, 313–332.

Rossion, B., Caldara, R., Seghier, M., Schuller, A. M., Lazeyras, F., & Mayer, E. (2003). A network of occipito-temporal face-sensitive areas besides the right middle fusiform gyrus is necessary for normal face processing. *Brain, 126*(Pt 11), 2381–2395.

Rotshtein, P., Geng, J. J., Driver, J., & Dolan, R. J. (2007a). Role of features and second–order spatial relations in face discrimination, face recognition, and individual face skills: Behavioral and functional magnetic resonance imaging data. *Journal of Cognitive Neuroscience, 19*(9), 1435–1452.

Rotshtein, P., Vuilleumier, P., Winston, J., Driver, J., & Dolan, R. (2007b). Distinct and convergent visual processing of high and low spatial frequency information in faces. *Cerebral Cortex, 17*(11), 2713–2724.

Santi, A., Servos, P., Vatikiotis-Bateson, E., Kuratate, T., & Munhall, K. (2003). Perceiving biological motion: Dissociating visible speech from walking. *Journal of Cognitive Neuroscience, 15*(6), 800–809.

Saxe, R. (2006a). Uniquely human social cognition. *Current Opinion in Neurobiology, 16*(2), 235–239.

Saxe, R. (2006b). Why and how to study Theory of Mind with fMRI. *Brain Research, 1079*(1), 57–65.

Saxe, R., & Powell, L. J. (2006). It's the thought that counts: Specific brain regions for one component of theory of mind. *Psychological Science, 17*(8), 692–699.

Saxe, R., & Wexler, A. (2005). Making sense of another mind: The role of the right temporo-parietal junction. *Neuropsychologia, 43*(10), 1391–1399.

Saxe, R., Xiao, D. K., Kovacs, G., Perrett, D. I., & Kanwisher, N. (2004). A region of right posterior superior temporal sulcus responds to observed intentional actions. *Neuropsychologia, 42*(11), 1435–1446.

Saygin, A. P. (2007). Superior temporal and premotor brain areas necessary for biological motion perception. *Brain, 130*(9), 2452–2461.

Saygin, A. P., Wilson, S. M., Hagler, D. J., Bates, E., & Sereno, M. I. (2004). Point–light biological motion perception activates human premotor cortex. *Journal of Neuroscience, 24*(27), 6181–6188.

Schiltz, C., & Rossion, B. (2006). Faces are represented holistically in the human occipito–temporal cortex. *Neuroimage, 32*(3), 1385–1394.

Schiltz, C., Sorger, B., Caldara, R., Ahmed, F., Mayer, E., Goebel, R., et al. (2006). Impaired face discrimination in acquired prosopagnosia is associated with abnormal response to individual faces in the right middle fusiform gyrus. *Cerebral Cortex, 16*(4), 574–586.

Schultz, R. T., Grelotti, D. J., Klin, A., Kleinman, J., Van der Gaag, C., Marois, R., et al. (2003). The role of the fusiform face area in social cognition: implications for the pathobiology of autism. *Philosophical Transactions of the Royal Society, London, B: Biological Sciences, 358*(1430), 415–427.

Schwarzlose, R. F., Baker, C. I., & Kanwisher, N. (2005). Separate face and body selectivity on the fusiform gyrus. *Journal of Neuroscience, 25*(47), 11055–11059.

Schyns, P. G., Petro, L. S., & Smith, M. L. (2007). Dynamics of visual information integration in the brain for categorizing facial expressions. *Current Biology, 17*(18), 1580–1585.

Servos, P., Osu, R., Santi, A., & Kawato, M. (2002). The neural substrates of biological motion perception: an fMRI study. *Cerebral Cortex, 12*(7), 772–782.

Smith, M. L., Cottrell, G. W., Gosselin, F., & Schyns, P. G. (2005). Transmitting and decoding facial expressions. *Psychological Science, 16*(3), 184–189.

Steeves, J. K. E., Culham, J. C., Duchaine, B. C., Pratesi, C. C., Valyear, K. F., Schindler, I., et al. (2006). The fusiform face area is not sufficient for face recognition: Evidence from a patient with dense prosopagnosia and no occipital face area. *Neuropsychologia, 44*(4), 594–609.

Sugase, Y., Yamane, S., Ueno, S., & Kawano, K. (1999). Global and fine information coded by single neurons in the temporal visual cortex. *Nature, 400*(6747), 869–873.

Sutton, S. K., & Davidson, R. J. (1997). Prefrontal brain asymmetry: A biological substrate of the behavioral approach and inhibition systems. *Psychological Science, 8*(3), 204–210.

Tanskanen, T., Nasanen, R., Montez, T., Paallysaho, J., & Hari, R. (2005). Face recognition and cortical responses show similar sensitivity to

noise spatial frequency. *Cerebral Cortex, 15*(5), 526–534.

Tanskanen, T., Nasanen, R., Ojanpaa, H., & Hari, R. (2007). Face recognition and cortical responses: Effect of stimulus duration. *Neuroimage, 35*(4), 1636–1644.

Tarr, M. J., & Gauthier, I. (2000). FFA: a flexible fusiform area for subordinate-level visual processing automatized by expertise. *Nature Neuroscience, 3*(8), 764–769.

Taylor, J. C., Wiggett, A. J., & Downing, P. E. (2007). fMRI analysis of body and body part representations in the extrastriate and fusiform body areas. *Journal of Neurophysiology*, 00012.02007.

Thierry, G., Martin, C. D., Downing, P., & Pegna, A. J. (2007). Controlling for interstimulus perceptual variance abolishes N170 face selectivity. *Nature Neuroscience, 10*(4), 505–511.

Thompson, J. C., Clarke, M., Stewart, T., & Puce, A. (2005). Configural processing of biological motion in human superior temporal sulcus. *Journal of Neuroscience, 25*(39), 9059–9066.

Thompson, J. C., Hardee, J. E., Panayiotou, A., Crewther, D., & Puce, A. (2007). Common and distinct brain activation to viewing dynamic sequences of face and hand movements. *Neuroimage, 37*(3), 966–973.

Todorov, A., Gobbini, M. I., Evans, K. K., & Haxby, J. V. (2007). Spontaneous retrieval of affective person knowledge in face perception. *Neuropsychologia, 45*(1), 163–173.

Todorov, A., Harris, L. T., & Fiske, S. T. (2006). Toward socially inspired social neuroscience. *Brain Research, 1079*(1), 76–85.

Todorov, A., Mandisodza, A. N., Goren, A., & Hall, C. C. (2005). Inferences of competence from faces predict election outcomes. *Science, 308*(5728), 1623–1626.

Todorov, A., & Uleman, J. S. (2002). Spontaneous trait inferences are bound to actors' faces: Evidence from a false recognition paradigm. *Journal of Personality and Social Psychology, 83*(5), 1051–1065.

Todorov, A., & Uleman, J. S. (2003). The efficiency of binding spontaneous trait inferences to actors' faces. *Journal of Experimental Social Psychology, 39*(6), 549–562.

Tranel, D., Gullickson, G., Koch, M., & Adolphs, R. (2006). Altered experience of emotion following bilateral amygdala damage. *Cognitive Neuropsychiatry, 11*(3).

Tsao, D. Y., Freiwald, W. A., Knutsen, T. A., Mandeville, J. B., & Tootell, R. B. H. (2003). Faces and objects in macaque cerebral cortex. *Nature Neuroscience, 6*(9), 989–995.

Tsao, D. Y., Freiwald, W. A., Tootell, R. B. H., & Livingstone, M. S. (2006). A cortical region consisting entirely of face-selective cells. *Science, 311*(5761), 670–674.

Urgesi, C., Berlucchi, G., & Aglioti, S. M. (2004). Magnetic stimulation of extrastriate body area impairs visual processing of nonfacial body parts. *Current Biology, 14*(23), 2130–2134.

Urgesi, C., Calvo–Merino, B., Haggard, P., & Aglioti, S. M. (2007a). Transcranial magnetic stimulation reveals two cortical pathways for visual body processing. *Journal of Neuroscience, 27*(30), 8023–8030.

Urgesi, C., Candidi, M., Ionta, S., & Aglioti, S. M. (2007b). Representation of body identity and body actions in extrastriate body area and ventral premotor cortex. *Nature Neuroscience, 10*(1), 30–31.

Vaina, L. M. (1994). Functional segregation of color and motion processing in the human visual cortex: Clinical evidence. *Cerebral Cortex, 4*(5), 555–572.

Vaina, L. M., Lemay, M., Bienfang, D. C., Choi, A. Y., & Nakayama, K. (1990). Intact "biological motion" and "structure from motion" perception in a patient with impaired motion mechanisms: A case study. *Visual Neuroscience, 5*(4), 353–369.

Vaina, L. M., Solomon, J., Chowdhury, S., Sinha, P., & Belliveau, J. W. (2001). Functional neuroanatomy of biological motion perception in humans. *Proceedings of the National Academy of Sciences, 98*(20), 11656–11661.

Valentine, T. (1991). A unified account of the effects of distinctiveness, inversion, and race in face recognition. *Quarterly Journal of Experimental Psychology, 43A*(2), 161–204.

van Rijn, S., Aleman, A., van Diessen, E., Berckmoes, C., Vingerhoets, G., & Kahn, R. S. (2005). What is said or how it is said makes a difference: role of the right fronto–parietal operculum in emotional prosody as revealed by repetitive TMS. *European Journal of Neuroscience, 21*(11), 3195–3200.

Vuilleumier, P. (2005). How brains beware: neural mechanisms of emotional attention. *Trends in Cognitive Sciences, 9*(12), 585–594.

Vuilleumier, P., & Driver, J. (2007). Modulation of visual processing by attention and emotion: windows on causal interactions between human brain regions. *Philosophical Transactions of the Royal Society B: Biological Sciences, 362*(1481), 837–855.

Vuilleumier, P., & Pourtois, G. (2007). Distributed and interactive brain mechanisms during emotion face perception: Evidence from functional neuroimaging. *Neuropsychologia, 45*(1), 174–194.

Vuilleumier, P., Richardson, M. P., Armony, J. L., Driver, J., & Dolan, R. J. (2004). Distant influences of amygdala lesion on visual cortical activation during emotional face processing. *Nature Neuroscience, 7*(11), 1271–1278.

Watanabe, S., Kakigi, R., & Puce, A. (2003). The spatiotemporal dynamics of the face inversion effect: A magneto- and electro-encephalographic study. *Neuroscience, 116*(3), 879–895.

Whalen, P. (1999). Fear, vigilance, and ambiguity: Initial neuroimaging studies of the human amygdala. *Current Directions in Psychological Science, 7*, 177–187.

Whalen, P. J., Kagan, J., Cook, R. G., Davis, F. C., Kim, H., Polis, S., et al. (2004). Human amygdala responsivity to masked fearful eye whites. *Science, 306*(5704), 2061–.

Whalen, P. J., Shin, L. M., McInerney, S. C., Fischer, H., Wright, C. I., & Rauch, S. L. (2001). A functional MRI study of human amygdala responses to facial expressions of fear versus anger. *Emotion, 1*(1), 70–83.

Wheaton, K. J., Thompson, J. C., Syngeniotis, A., Abbott, D. F., & Puce, A. (2004). Viewing the motion of human body parts activates different regions of premotor, temporal, and parietal cortex. *Neuroimage, 22*(1), 277–288.

Wheeler, M., & Atkinson, A. (2001). Domains, brains and evolution. In D. M. Walsh (Ed.), *Naturalism, evolution and mind*. Cambridge: Cambridge University Press.

Williams, M. A., Morris, A. P., McGlone, F., Abbott, D. F., & Mattingley, J. B. (2004). Amygdala responses to fearful and happy facial expressions under conditions of binocular suppression. *Journal of Neuroscience, 24*(12), 2898–2904.

Willis, J., & Todorov, A. (2006). First Impressions: Making up your mind after a 100-Ms exposure to a face. *Psychological Science, 17*(7), 592–598.

Winston, J. S., Henson, R. N., Fine-Goulden, M. R., & Dolan, R. J. (2004). fMRI-adaptation reveals dissociable neural representations of identity and expression in face perception. *Journal of Neurophysiology, 92*(3), 1830–1839.

Winston, J. S., O'Doherty, J., & Dolan, R. J. (2003). Common and distinct neural responses during direct and incidental processing of multiple facial emotions. *Neuroimage, 20*(1), 84–97.

Winston, J. S., Strange, B. A., O'Doherty, J., & Dolan, R. J. (2002). Automatic and intentional brain responses during evaluation of trustworthiness of faces. *Nature Neuroscience, 5*(3), 277–283.

Wright, L. (1973). Functions. *Philosophical Review, 82*, 139–168.

Young, A. W. (1998). *Face and mind.* Oxford: Oxford University Press.

Young, A. W., Newcombe, F., de Haan, E. H., Small, M., & Hay, D. C. (1993). Face perception after brain injury. Selective impairments affecting identity and expression. *Brain, 116 (Pt 4)*, 941–959.

Yovel, G., & Kanwisher, N. (2004). Face perception: Domain specific, not process specific. *Neuron, 44*(5), 889–898.

Zion-Golumbic, E., & Bentin, S. (2007). Dissociated neural mechanisms for face detection and configural encoding: Evidence from N170 and induced gamma-band oscillation effects. *Cerebral Cortex, 17*(8), 1741–1749.

CHAPTER 22

Side Bias: Cerebral Hemispheric Asymmetry in Social Cognition and Emotion Perception

Kimberley R. Savage, Joan C. Borod, and Lorraine O. Ramig

INTRODUCTION

Skilled social functioning requires the ability to accurately perceive and interpret subtle, often implicit, cues that reveal the emotions, intentions, and beliefs of other people. At the most basic level, this means having awareness that other people's representations of the world are different from one's own. At a higher level, it means having the ability to see the perspective of another person and identify their thoughts and feelings. Although some of this information is transmitted directly through verbal communication, social information is also garnered from nonverbal information, such as facial expressions, eye gaze, gestures, and body posture.

Given the importance of understanding what other people think and feel, it is not surprising that research has indicated that a number of networks in the brain are dedicated specifically to the perception and interpretation of social information (Adolphs, 2003). As the amount of research in this field grows, it is becoming increasingly evident that the two hemispheres of the brain are differentially involved in social cognitive processes and that the right hemisphere, in particular, may be biased toward the processing of social information. Support for the lateralization of social cognition comes from a variety of sources, including behavioral

paradigms and neuroimaging studies with healthy individuals, patients with brain damage, and/or "split-brain" patients (patients who have undergone a corpus callosotomy). Although results of this literature are not conclusive, they do at least point to hemispheric differences in social cognitive processes.

The goal of this chapter is to characterize the nature of the hemispheric biases in social cognition. This includes both description and discussion of the literature examining the extent of hemispheric specialization in (1) how we identify and interpret the mental states of other people, and (2) how we perceive emotion.

HISTORICAL BACKGROUND

The idea of functional asymmetries in the brain is not new. Researchers have been interested in asymmetries in the hemispheric function of the brain since the nineteenth century. Many attribute the discovery of hemispheric specialization to Paul Broca, a French physician and anatomist. In 1865, based on the postmortem examination of several aphasic patients, Broca concluded that the left hemisphere was dominant for language, thus establishing, for the first time, a functional asymmetry within the brain (for reviews, see Joynt, 1964; Springer & Deutsch, 1981).

Since Broca published his findings, research on hemispheric asymmetry has flourished as researchers have attempted to characterize the differences between the two halves of the brain within a variety of functional domains, including emotion and social cognition (the study of information processing in a social setting; Frith, 2008). For example, in the 1800s, Hughlings Jackson noted that emotional words, such as curses, were sometimes selectively spared in patients with left-hemisphere lesions, even in the presence of aphasia (Jackson, 1874, 1880). One of the first to make a direct connection between the right hemisphere and emotional processing was Charles Mills, an American neurologist. In 1912, Mills noted that patients with unilateral right-sided lesions were more likely to exhibit reduced emotional expression relative to patients with similar left-sided lesions (Mills, 1912). Although these reported connections between the right hemisphere and emotional processing were merely observational and anecdotal, they opened the door to the empirical study of the role of the right hemisphere in emotion processing and social cognition. In fact, since Mills first made these observations, research on the laterality of social cognition has blossomed.

EVIDENCE FOR HEMISPHERIC BIAS IN SOCIAL COGNITION

A substantial portion of the research in the field of social cognitive neuroscience is dedicated to identifying the brain networks responsible for facilitating our ability to "read" other people. This is not surprising, given that the ability to make accurate attributions about the emotions and mental states of other people is crucial for successful social interactions. Evidence from this research suggests that the right hemisphere may be particularly important for the processing of nonverbal social information, including facial expressions, gestures, eye gaze, and body posture. In this next section, we will review this evidence, focusing on studies of functional asymmetry in two key areas of social cognition: mental state attributions and emotional processing.

Mental State Attributions

By the age of four or five years, we human beings are aware that other people have minds that are separate from our own and we begin to develop the skills necessary to decode the mental states (e.g., thoughts, beliefs, and desires) of other people (Flavell, 1999). As mature adults, we tend to make these mental state attributions everyday, without even noticing. Often without conscious awareness, we are able to understand nonliteral speech, such as sarcasm, metaphor, and irony. We can express and comprehend humor. And we can often put ourselves in "someone else's shoes" or try to see things from another person's perspective in order to understand why they do the things they do.

The ability to attribute thoughts, beliefs, or intentions to the self and others, often referred to as "theory of mind" (ToM) (Premack & Woodruff, 1978), appears to be dissociable from other cognitive mechanisms, suggesting that it may be mediated by a dedicated cognitive system (Happé, Brownell, & Winner, 1999). In addition, it seems to have a similar developmental trajectory in different cultures, suggesting that the neural mechanisms underlying this domain may be innate (Avis & Harris, 1991; Callaghan et al., 2005; Liu, Wellman, Tardif, & Sabbagh, 2008).

Like other aspects of social cognition, ToM is likely the result of integrated activity in a network of brain regions. Research has not conclusively determined the neural mechanisms responsible for ToM, but candidate brain networks include the frontal (medial prefrontal and orbitofrontal) cortex, the cingulate cortex, the temporoparietal junction, and the amygdala (e.g., Castelli, Happé, Frith, & Frith, 2000; Costa, Torriero, Oliveri, & Caltagirone, 2008; for reviews, see Saxe & Powell, 2006; Siegal & Varley, 2002).

Although the literature contains opposing views on the functional specificity of ToM, it has been proposed that the right hemisphere may be particularly well suited for the mediation of ToM. This hypothesis is largely based on the striking deficits in ToM observed in patients with right hemisphere damage. Not only does this group consistently display deficits in emotion recognition, as described in detail later, but a number of studies have also indicated that patients with right hemisphere damage tend to have pragmatic and social impairments, which include deficits in the perception and comprehension of humor and lies, as well as difficulties with the integration of verbal and pictorial information and the correct usage of social skills (Bihrle, Brownell, Powelson, & Gardner, 1986; Bloom, Borod, Obler, & Gerstman, 1992, 1993; Borod, Rorie, et al., 2000; Brownell, Michel, Powelson, & Gardner, 1983; Brozgold et al., 1998; Happé et al., 1999; Shamay-Tsoory, Tomer, & Aharon-Peretz, 2005; Siegal, Carrington, & Radel, 1996; Winner, Brownell, Happé, Blum, & Pincus, 1998; for a review, see Happé et al., 1999).

Recognizing False Beliefs

One of the most fundamental impairments reported in patients with right-hemisphere damage (RHD) is a difficulty in attributing false beliefs to other people; that is, these patients have a hard time recognizing that other people can hold beliefs about the world that are incorrect or based on faulty information. For example, Siegal, Carrington, and Radel (1996) asked RHD and LHD patients (without significant aphasia) to complete a basic false-belief task. Participants heard short vignettes, such as "Sam is looking for his puppy. He thinks his puppy is in the kitchen, but it is really in the garage." They then were asked where the character would look for the puppy. Patients with RHD had difficulties correctly predicting where Sam would look for his pet, making significantly more errors than patients with LHD, guessing that Sam would look for his pet in the garage. However, it should be noted that the RHD group was more successful when provided with a different version of the same question ("Where will Sam look *first* for his puppy?"), designed to make implied information more explicit. No differences were found between the groups on the more explicit question. Based on this finding, Siegal and colleagues suggested that the RHD group's inability to make false-belief attributions might be due to underlying

pragmatic language deficits. This view is in line with research demonstrating that patients with RHD often fail to understand nonliteral speech and indirect requests (Bloom, Borod, Obler, & Gerstman, 1993; Foldi, 1987; Kaplan, Brownell, Jacobs, & Gardner, 1990; Winner et al., 1998) and have deficits perceiving prosodic intonation (for reviews of this literature, see Borod, Bloom, Brickman, Nakhutina, & Curko, 2002; Demaree, Everhart, Youngstrom, & Harrison, 2005; Snow, 2000).

Humor and Narrative

On its own, difficulties understanding false beliefs are not enough to explain the dramatic social deficits observed in patients with RHD, but the ability to recognize second-order false beliefs can be seen as the foundation of a number of higher order abilities. For example, the ability to appreciate humor often depends on the recognition that at least one person in a joke or cartoon holds a false belief. Not surprisingly, given their inability to successfully complete false-belief tasks, patients with RHD also show impairments in their ability to appreciate humor relative to both healthy control participants and patients with LHD (Bihrle et al., 1986; Brownell et al., 1983). For example, Happé and colleagues (1999) compared the performance of RHD patients, LHD patients, and healthy controls on a cartoon task. The cartoon task consisted of single-frame cartoons taken from popular magazines, such as the *New Yorker*. Understanding the humor in the cartoons required an understanding that at least one character in the cartoon held a false-belief. Nonmentalistic control cartoons were also administered. Successful completion of the control cartoons required the participant to make an inference about prior physical events. For an example of the cartoons used, see Figure 22.1.

Results from this study indicated that the RHD group performed significantly worse than both the LHD patients and the healthy controls on the ToM cartoon task. No difference was seen in performance on the control cartoons, suggesting that the deficits of RHD patients on this humor task were specific to the attribution of mental states.

Theory of Mind Cartoon

"I give up Robert. What does have two horns,
one eye, and creeps?"

Non-mental Cartoon

"Looks like Wesselsman's hit on
something interesting."

Figure 22.1 Examples of cartoons used in the cartoon task. Reprinted from Happé, Brownell, and Winner (1999) with permission from Elsevier.

Interestingly, research has also indicated that the pattern of errors made by patients with RHD on cartoon tasks is predictable. Specifically, patients with RHD tend to select endings that are surprising as the funniest ending, even if the surprising ending lacks coherence with the rest of the narrative. This is contrary to the pattern seen when patients with LHD make errors; LHD patients tend to select unsurprising, coherent endings (Bihrle et al., 1986). Once again, this view of how patients with RHD process humor is consistent with their difficulties comprehending nonliteral speech and establishing coherent verbal narratives (Foldi, 1987; Kaplan et al., 1990; Winner et al., 1998; cf. Bloom, Borod, Santschi-Haywood, Pick, & Obler, 1996).

Even more difficult than appreciating basic humor is the ability to distinguish ironic humor from lies. This ability is also closely related to ToM, particularly the ability to recognize second-order mental state attributions (i.e., attributions about one person's knowledge of another person's knowledge). Winner and colleagues (1998) tested the ability of adults with RHD following stroke to discriminate between lies and jokes. In this study, patients heard a number of brief stories in which one of the characters held either a true or a false belief.

For example, in one story, an employee calls out sick from work to go to a hockey game with his friends, but his boss sees him at the game. The next day at work, his boss asks if he got a lot of rest during his day off, to which the employee replies, *"Yes, and that day of bed rest cured me."* In one condition of the study, the employee *knows* that his boss saw him at the game (true belief), and, therefore, his response is intended as a self-deprecating joke. In the second condition, the employee *does not know* that his boss saw him (false belief), and, therefore, his response is an intentional lie to hide his real reason for not coming to work. The RHD group made significantly more errors than the healthy control group on this task, confirming a deficit in distinguishing lies from jokes.

Deception

Findings from the Winner et al. (1998) study are also in line with recent literature demonstrating that the right hemisphere may play a preferential role in the detection of deception. Although it has been widely shown that most people are usually no better than chance at recognizing deception based on an individual's facial expression and tone of voice (Frank & Ekman, 1997), some advantage seems to be afforded when information is processed in the right hemisphere, as opposed to the left. As with other areas of social cognition, some evidence supporting this hemispheric bias comes from brain-damaged patients. For example, Etcoff, Ekman, Magee, and Frank (2000) studied the deception detection abilities of patients with RHD and LHD and healthy controls. Patients in the RHD had a significantly lower success rate in interpreting lying cues as compared to both the LHD and healthy control groups. Subsequent research has corroborated these results (Stuss, Gallup, & Alexander, 2001).

Work with healthy control participants has further implicated the right hemisphere in deception detection (studies of other aspects of ToM in healthy control participants are discussed below). Specifically, research has shown that left-handed individuals are better at detecting deception than their right-handed counterparts, suggesting a possible right hemisphere advantage (Porter, Campbell, Stapleton, & Birt, 2002). Furthermore, dichotic listening tasks have demonstrated a left ear (i.e., right hemisphere) advantage for discriminating between true and false statements (Malcolm & Keenan, 2005).

ToM in the Healthy Individual

Data from some imaging studies with healthy controls shows increased right-hemisphere activation during ToM tasks, consistent with reports from brain-damaged patients (Baron-Cohen et al., 1994; Brunet, Sarfati, Hardy-Baylé, & Decety, 2000; Gallagher et al., 2000; Siegal & Varley, 2002). One area that is often implicated in ToM tasks is the right temporoparietal junction (RTPJ), an area of the inferior parietal cortex at the junction with the posterior temporal cortex, encompassing the supramarginal gyrus, caudal parts of the superior temporal gyrus, and dorsal-rostral parts of the occipital gyri (Decety & Lamm, 2007). The temporoparietal junction (TPJ) serves as an association cortex, receiving and integrating input from a number of areas, including the posterior temporal gyrus and the parietal cortex, as well as the thalamus, the visual and auditory cortices, the limbic system, and the prefrontal cortex (Decety & Lamm, 2007). Thus, the TPJ is in a prime position to integrate information about the environment with information about the self. Not surprisingly, this area has been implicated in several facets of self-processing, including agency and self-awareness (Blanke et al., 2005; Decety & Lamm, 2007; Jackson & Decety, 2004; Ruby & Decety, 2001; Salmon et al., 2006). Recently, the RTPJ has also been implicated in aspects of social cognition, including perspective taking and ToM. For example, in a recent string of neuroimaging studies, Saxe and her colleagues demonstrated that the RTPJ was selectively activated during the attribution of mental states (Saxe & Powell, 2006; Saxe & Wexler, 2005).

It is important to note that while studies with brain-damaged patients have consistently supported the involvement of the right hemisphere in ToM, results from functional imaging studies with healthy individuals are not as consistent or clear. For example, the functional specificity of the RTPJ has been disputed (Mitchell, 2008). Furthermore, a number of other cortical regions have been consistently identified as candidate regions for the mediation of mental-state attributions, including the medial prefrontal cortex, the superior temporal sulcus, the left temporoparietal junction, the anterior and posterior cingulate, and the amygdala (for reviews of this literature, see Adolphs, 2003; Frith & Frith, 2006). Activation in these areas has been shown bilaterally and on the left side (e.g., Castelli et al., 2000; Gallagher et al., 2000).

These conflicting findings highlight the fact that the brain must be considered as a whole. Studies of impairments in mental state attribution in brain-damaged patients in this domain imply that at least some portion of the right hemisphere is necessary for successful functioning in this domain. However, based on neuroimaging data from healthy control subjects showing involvement of both hemispheres in ToM tasks, the right hemisphere is clearly not sufficient for these processes. In line with this reasoning, some studies have shown similar ToM impairments in patients with LHD, even in the absence of RHD (e.g., Samson, Apperly, Chiavarino, & Humphreys, 2004).

Emotional Processing

Understanding what people are thinking or what their intentions or beliefs are will go a long way toward facilitating our attempts to "read" other people. However, thoughts and intentions are only part of the picture. To truly see things from another person's shoes, we also have to understand how they *feel*, or what kinds of emotions they are experiencing.

Emotion processing is a complex skill, consisting of both expression and perception. Expression and perception of emotion have been shown to be separate processes (Borod, 1993, 2000), which develop along discrete trajectories (Odom & Lemond, 1972) and are not systematically related (e.g., Borod, Koff, Perlman Lorch, & Nicholas, 1986; Borod et al., 1990; Ross, 1981).

Since the goal of this chapter is to examine functional asymmetries in how we "see" other people, we will be focusing primarily on the perceptual mode and the face, in particular. By emotion perception, we refer to the "processing, appreciation, or comprehension of the emotional aspect of a stimulus" (Borod, 1992, p. 340). Particularly relevant to our review are studies examining the perception of emotion via the facial channel (i.e., facial expressions). However, it should be noted that stimuli can also be processed through other channels of communication, including the prosodic (i.e., vocal intonation), lexical (i.e., speech content), gestural, and postural channels (Borod, 1993; Borod, Koff, Lorch, & Nicholas, 1985; Borod, Pick, et al., 2000). Evidence for hemispheric lateralization has been found in all three channels (for reviews, see Borod, 1992; Borod, Zgaljardic, Tabert, & Koff, 2001; Borod, 2002; Demaree et al., 2005). But among these three channels of communication (facial, prosodic, and lexical), the facial channel has received the most attention in the literature.

Right-Hemisphere Hypothesis

It has been proposed that the right hemisphere is dominant for emotional processing in right-handed individuals, regardless of valence (Borod, Koff, & Caron, 1983; Bryden &

Ley, 1983; Buck, 1984; Heilman, Bowers, & Valenstein, 1985). Although it is not entirely clear why the right hemisphere might be dominant for emotion, there are some likely explanations according to Borod and colleagues (Borod, 1992, 1996; Borod, Bloom, & Santschi-Haywood, 1998). First, these authors have suggested that the neuroanatomical structure of the right hemisphere makes it better suited than the left hemisphere for handling the multimodal integration necessary for emotional processing (Borod, 1996; Goldberg & Costa, 1981; Semmes, 1968). As compared to the left hemisphere, the right hemisphere has more widespread interlobular organization (Egelko et al., 1988), greater neural interconnectivity among regions (Gur et al., 1980; Thatcher, Krause, & Hrybyk, 1986; Tucker, Roth, & Bair, 1986), more overlapping axonal interconnectivity (Woodward, 1988), and more horizontal axonal connectivity (Springer & Deutsch, 1981; Woodward, 1988). Furthermore, the right hemisphere is thought to control certain nonverbal, integrative functions and capabilities that are necessary for emotional processing (particularly the perception of emotion). These functions include pattern perception, visuospatial organization, and the processing of visual imagery (Borod, 1992).

Much of the research on functional asymmetry has come from the study of patients with unilateral brain damage. In general, many of these studies provide support for the right-hemisphere hypothesis, showing that individuals with RHD perform worse on tasks requiring the identification or discrimination of emotion as compared to individuals with LHD (for reviews of this literature, see Borod, 1992; Borod et al., 1998; Demaree et al., 2005; Etcoff, 1984; Gainotti, Caltagirone, & Zoccolotti, 1993; Heilman, Blonder, Bowers, & Crucian, 2000; Kolb & Taylor, 1990; Ross, 1997). In a comprehensive review of emotional processing in patients with unilateral brain damage, Borod and colleagues (2002) reported that, overall, for facial emotion perception, the majority of the 23 studies reviewed showed support for the right-hemisphere hypothesis. Specifically, for the facial channel, 87 percent of the studies reviewed showed selective deficits in the perception of emotion among patients with RHD, whereas only 4 percent showed selective deficits in patients with LHD; 9 percent found no selective deficits.

Support for the right-hemisphere hypothesis has also come from experiments with "split-brain" patients. Split-brain patients have undergone a procedure known as "corpus callosotomy," which severs the corpus collosum, the major fiber tract connecting the left and right hemispheres. This procedure is used as a treatment for medically intractable epilepsy, as severing the corpus collosum reduces the frequency of seizures. As a result of this procedure, the two hemispheres of the brain cannot communicate with one another and, therefore, operate independently, with each hemisphere unaware of the experiences of the other (Sperry, Gazzaniga, & Bogen, 1969). This creates a unique opportunity for experimental work, because it becomes possible to restrict the presentation of visual stimuli to one hemisphere by projecting information to a single visual field. Results from studies using this methodology appear to support the right-hemisphere hypothesis. For example, Benowitz and colleagues (1983) demonstrated that split-brain patients were unable to identify facial expressions if the stimuli were presented only in the right visual field (i.e., to the left hemisphere), but had no difficulty identifying the same facial expressions when the stimuli were presented only in the left visual field (i.e., to the right hemisphere). However, other studies have failed to support the right-hemisphere hypothesis. For instance, Stone, Nisenson, Eliassen, and Gazzaniga (1996) tested the ability of a patient who had undergone a corpus callosotomy to identify and discriminate among facial emotional expressions and found no hemispheric differences in accuracy.

Additional research supporting the right-hemisphere hypothesis comes from research done while patients are undergoing the intracarotid sodium amytal procedure, often referred to as the Wada Test (Wada & Rasmussen, 2007). This procedure, which is typically used as part of the preparation for surgical treatment of epilepsy, involves the injection of an anesthetic into either the right or left internal carotid artery, the result of which is functional inactivation of one hemisphere of the brain. Ahern and colleagues (1991) asked patients to rate pictures of positive and negative facial expressions while undergoing the Wada test. Results from this study indicated that patients rated the pictures as less intense when the right hemisphere was inactivated than when the left hemisphere was inactivated, thus providing support for the right-hemisphere hypothesis.

Research investigating the laterality of facial perception has also been extended to healthy controls. In order to investigate functional asymmetry in normal adults, studies have relied on paradigms such as tachistoscopic viewing, which predominantly limits stimuli presentation to one hemisphere. Studies using tachistoscopic viewing have generally shown that individuals discriminate among emotional expressions more accurately when the information is presented in the left visual field (i.e., mediated by the right hemisphere) than when the information is presented to the right visual field (i.e., mediated by the left hemisphere; Landis, Assal, & Perret, 1979; Ley & Bryden, 1979; McKeever & Dixon, 1981; Suberi & McKeever, 1977; for review, see Borod et al., 2001).

Another common behavioral paradigm used with healthy control participants is the free-field viewing task, which often involves the use of "chimeric" faces. A chimeric face is a composite of two separate hemifaces, often an emotive hemiface and a neutral hemiface. In the free-field viewing paradigm, two mirror-image chimeric faces are presented vertically on a page and the viewer is asked to judge which of the chimeric stimuli has greater emotional intensity (Levy, Heller, Banich, & Burton, 1983). The two sets of stimuli do not differ from each other except for which side the emotive hemiface is presented on. However, healthy right-handed controls typically demonstrate a left hemiface bias, meaning that they rate the chimeric face with the emotive hemiface in the left visual field as being more intense than the chimeric face with the emotive hemiface in the right visual field (e.g., Christman & Hackworth, 1993; Luh, Rueckert,

& Levy, 1991; Moreno, Borod, Welkowitz, & Alpert, 1990). Because the right hemisphere predominantly processes stimuli viewed in the left visual field, these findings provide support for the right-hemisphere hypothesis.

Recent contributions from the neuroimaging literature have also begun to uncover evidence of a right-hemisphere bias in emotion perception. For example, studies using evoked response potentials (ERP) have shown greater right-hemisphere activity during the processing of facial emotion, as compared to activity in the left hemisphere (Kestenbaum & Nelson, 1992; Laurian, Bader, Lanares, & Oros, 1991; Vanderploeg, Brown, & Marsh, 1987). Similar results have been reported in some studies using functional magnetic resonance imaging (fMRI). Specifically, these studies have reported greater activation in regions of the right hemisphere when processing facial emotion stimuli, as compared to nonemotional facial stimuli (Narumoto, Okada, Sadato, Fukui, & Yonekura, 2001; Sato, Kochiyama, Yoshikawa, Naito, & Matsumura, 2004; for review, see Borod et al., 2001).

However, it should be noted that not all functional imaging studies have reported a right-hemisphere bias in the processing of emotion. In a meta-analysis on 65 neuroimaging studies of emotion, Wager, Phan, Liberzon, and Taylor (2003) failed to find support for the right-hemisphere hypothesis. Based on their results, the authors concluded that emotion processing is more complex and more region specific than predicted by traditional theories of lateralization.

Alternative Theoretical Models

As demonstrated by the meta-analysis conducted by Wager and colleagues (described earlier), the right-hemisphere hypothesis has garnered a lot of support, but it has not gone unchallenged. Other studies have shown valence-specific hemispheric differences in emotion processing, suggesting that each hemisphere may preferentially process certain emotions. Based on these studies, alternative models of hemispheric specialization have been developed, the most notable of which are the valence hypothesis and the approach-withdrawal model.

The Valence Hypothesis.   The valence hypothesis proposes that the right hemisphere is specialized for negative or unpleasant emotions, whereas the left hemisphere is specialized for positive or pleasant emotions, regardless of processing mode (i.e., perception or expression of emotion; Silberman & Weingartner, 1986). Alternatively, a second version of the valence hypothesis, which has been termed the "variant hypothesis" (Borod, 1992), proposes that the right hemisphere is specialized for the *perception* of emotion, regardless of valence, whereas there is differential hemispheric specialization for the *expression* or *experience* of emotion, with the right hemisphere being specialized for negative emotions and the left hemisphere being specialized for positive emotions (Borod, 1992; Bryden, 1982; Davidson, 1984; Ehrlichman, 1987; Hirschman & Safer, 1982; Sackeim et al., 1982). Although both versions of the valence hypothesis have been actively studied, we will focus on the first version, because the scope of this chapter does not allow for an examination of emotional expression.

Several studies have provided support for the valence hypothesis using emotional facial stimuli. For example, using a tachistoscope, Reuter-Lorenz and Davidson (1981) presented faces expressing sadness, happiness, anger, and disgust in either the left or right visual field and measured the time it took for participants to identify the emotion portrayed. Results from their study indicated a robust differential effect: participants responded more quickly to happy faces presented initially to the left hemisphere (i.e., right visual field) as compared to sad faces. However, when stimuli were presented to the right hemisphere (i.e., left visual field), reaction times were quicker for the sad faces as compared to happy faces. Jansari, Tranel, and Adolphs (2000) found similar results using a free-field viewing paradigm. Specifically, these authors demonstrated that participants were able to discriminate positive emotions more accurately when the stimuli were presented on the right-hand side, whereas negative emotions were more accurately discriminated on the left-hand side. For a comprehensive review of behavioral findings from the facial emotional perception literature in healthy adults in which findings are presented separately for positive and negative facial stimuli, see Borod et al. (2001).

In an interesting adaptation of the free-field viewing paradigm, researchers have also demonstrated that there are valence effects for the processing of unconscious information. Using a subliminal affective priming paradigm, Sato and Aoki (2006) presented angry facial expressions, happy facial expressions, or plain gray images briefly (25 msec) in either the left or right visual field, immediately followed by a mask stimulus. Following presentation of the emotional primes and mask, a nonsense target was displayed and participants were simply asked whether they liked or disliked the target. Participants reported liking targets less when they followed unseen negative primes (relative to positive or control primes) when the primes were presented in the left, but not right, visual field.

The Approach-Withdrawal Model. A third model that has received strong support in the literature is the approach-withdrawal model, which postulates that the left hemisphere is specialized for the processing of "approach behaviors" (e.g., happiness and anger), whereas the right hemisphere is specialized for the processing of emotions that elicit "withdrawal behaviors" (e.g., fear and disgust) (Davidson, 1984; Fox, 1991; Harmon-Jones, 2004; Harmon-Jones & Allen, 1998; Kinsbourne & Bemporad, 1984). In proposing this model, researchers have noted that the issue of valence and hemispheric specialization may have been confounded by the relationship between approach motivation and valence. Specifically, most emotions that elicit approach behaviors have a positive valence (such as happiness), whereas emotions that elicit withdrawal behaviors tend to be negative in valence (such as fear). However, there are some exceptions to this general rule. Most notably, anger typically elicits approach behavior, although it is characterized as a negative emotion (Borod, Caron, & Koff, 1981; Harmon-Jones, 2004).

Much of the research supporting the approach withdrawal model has examined asymmetrical brain activity, typically using EEG, during the *expression and experience* of emotion (for a review, see Harmon-Jones, 2004). For example, research has examined the relationship between trait affect or emotion and resting EEG (e.g., Allen, Iacono, Depue, & Arbisi, 1993; Harmon-Jones, 2004; Schaffer, Davidson, & Saron, 1983) and the relationship between resting EEG and responses to emotion-eliciting stimuli (Coan, Allen, & Harmon-Jones, 2001; Ekman & Davidson, 1993). However, at least one study examining the effects of valence on the *perception* of facial emotion has shown some support for the approach-withdrawal hypothesis. In this study, Mandal, Borod, Asthana, Mohanty, Mohanty, and Koff (1999) found that patients with RHD had specific deficits in perceiving negative and withdrawal emotions as compared to LHD patients, although there were no differences observed among groups in perceiving positive/approach emotions. Aside from this study, to our knowledge, existing research examining the approach-withdrawal hypothesis has focused on the experience or expression of emotion. Therefore, it does not directly inform our goal of understanding how we read other people and will not be described in detail in this chapter.

Social Emotions

Traditionally, research investigating hemispheric specialization for emotional processing has focused on "basic emotions," such as happiness, sadness, fear, surprise, anger, and disgust (Izard, 1971; Tamietto, Adenzato, Geminiani, & de Gelder, 2007). These emotions are generally thought to be core emotions, which are each signaled by specific facial expressions and recognized across cultures (Ekman, 1992; Izard, 1990). However, the range of human emotion clearly is not limited to these basic emotions. Rather, the range of human emotions is expansive and includes many complex emotional states, such as arrogance, jealousy, hostility, and admiration (Buck, 1988; Shaw et al., 2005; see Figure 22.2). Social emotions are less likely than basic emotions to be associated with reflexlike adaptive behaviors,

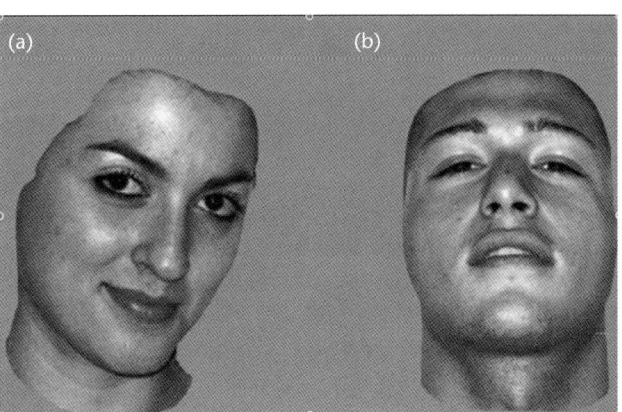

Figure 22.2. Examples of social emotion expressions: (a) flirtatiousness and (b) arrogance. Reprinted from Tamietto, Adenzato, Geminiani, and de Gelder (2007) with permission from Elsevier.

and the perception of these emotions may be more reliant on contextual cues and the ability to understand interpersonal relationships (Tamietto et al., 2007).

Very few studies have directly examined hemispheric biases in social emotions, but the few studies available have suggested that the processing of these so-called "social emotions" may show a different pattern of hemispheric asymmetry than that of basic emotions, although this evidence is not as robust as the evidence supporting hemispheric specialization in basic emotions (Ross, Homan, & Buck, 1994). For example, Ross and colleagues (1994) asked patients to recall emotional life events during the Wada test. When the right hemisphere was inactivated following injection of sodium amobarbital, most of the patients changed their affective recall as compared to their recall before the injection, substituting social emotions for more basic emotions. Based on these findings, Ross and colleagues concluded that social emotions are mediated by the left hemisphere and basic emotions mediated by the right.

Not all studies have supported this claim. For example, Shaw and colleagues (2005) found that patients with RHD were impaired in the recognition of social facial expressions, but patients with LHD were not impaired. Some other studies of the laterality of social emotions have not found clear evidence for hemispheric bias in the recognition of social emotions. A recent study by Tamietto and colleagues (2007) suggested that the processing of social emotions is best when

the hemispheres work together to decode social emotions (Tamietto et al., 2007). This particular study used the "redundant target paradigm" (Corballis, 2002; Dimond & Beaumont, 1972), a tachistoscopic viewing paradigm where facial stimuli were presented either unilaterally (i.e., to the right or left visual field) or simultaneously to both visual fields. Participants were asked to indicate whether either of the two faces shown on top were congruent (i.e., showed the same emotion) with the face shown on the bottom. Results did not show differences in response time or accuracy between the unilateral presentations. However, responses were faster and more accurate in the bilateral congruent displays as opposed to the noncongruent displays. Tamietto and colleagues (2007) interpreted their findings to mean that there was no hemispheric specialization for the perception of social emotions. Rather, both hemispheres are involved in the perception of social emotions and that simultaneous involvement of both hemispheres (i.e., hemispheric cooperation) enhances performance.

CONCLUSIONS

The goal of this chapter was to provide a summary of research on hemispheric asymmetry in mental state attribution and emotion processing (including both basic and social emotions). Overall, research continues to demonstrate the importance of the right cerebral hemisphere for social cognitive processes. The role of the right hemisphere is most apparent in studies involving patients with brain damage (i.e., the brain lesion approach) and in studies of healthy participants using behavioral paradigms, such as chimeric faces or tachistoscopic procedures. Findings in neuroimaging studies are less conclusive because activation is sometimes seen bilaterally while participants are performing tasks of social cognition.

These conflicting findings highlight the fact that the brain must be considered as a whole. Based on lesion studies, the right hemisphere appears to be necessary for engaging in mental-state attribution and emotion recognition. However, it is not *sufficient* for these processes, and therefore, deficits in social cognition may also be seen in patients with LHD (e.g., Samson et al., 2004).

This raises several interesting questions for future researchers to tackle. To what extent do the two hemispheres of the brain communicate and interact with each other? Are there certain conditions in which the coordination of processes across the hemispheres would allow the brain to operate more effectively? Also, does this communication always take place via cortical connections (i.e., corpus callosum), or are subcortical pathways in the limbic system also involved in the transfer of emotional information between hemispheres?

Researchers have already begun to consider these questions (e.g., Banich & Belger, 1990; Compton, Feigenson, & Widick, 2005; Schweinberger, Baird, Blümler, Kaufmann, & Mohr, 2003; Tamietto et al., 2007). Results from these studies demonstrate that, for the most part, interhemispheric communication becomes progressively more advantageous as task difficulty increases, suggesting that the ability to divide processing between the hemispheres reduces the work-load of each hemisphere, thereby making processing more efficient (for a review, see Hoptman & Davidson, 1994). This may explain why a right-hemispheric bias is more apparent in the perception of basic emotions, a relatively simple task, than it is in the perception of social emotions or the attribution of mental states, relatively more complex tasks.

However, to date, few studies have been conducted examining interhemispheric communication specifically in emotion processing, and results of these studies are equivocal. Two studies in this area have indicated that interhemispheric communication facilitated the processing of emotional compared to nonemotional faces (Compton et al., 2005; Tamietto et al., 2007), but a third study failed to find evidence of such an advantage (Schweinberger et al., 2003). Furthermore, none of the studies mentioned attempted to determine the mechanisms of interhemispheric communication (e.g., cortical or subcortical). Therefore, future studies are needed to clarify the role and mechanisms of interhemispheric cooperation in emotion processing. As suggested by some investigators (e.g., Hoptman & Davidson, 1994; Tamietto et al., 2007), measures of interhemispheric transfer time obtained from paradigms using event-related potentials (ERP) may be particularly important in clarifying these issues. Regardless of the paradigm used, increasing our knowledge of the role of interhemispheric cooperation in emotional and social cognitive processing will no doubt further our understanding of the social brain.

ACKNOWLEDGMENTS

This work was supported, in part, by Professional Staff Congress—City University of New York research awards 68150-00-37 & 69683-0038 to Joan C. Borod and by NIH RO1 DC 01150 to Lorraine O. Ramig.

REFERENCES

Adolphs, R. (2003). Cognitive neuroscience of human social behaviour. *Nature Reviews Neuroscience, 4*, 165–178.

Ahern, G. L., Schomer, D. L., Kleefield, J., Blume, H., Cosgrove, G. R., Weintraub, S., et al. (1991). Right hemisphere advantage for evaluating emotional facial expressions. *Cortex, 27*, 193–202.

Allen, J. J., Iacono, W. G., Depue, R. A., & Arbisi, P. (1993). Regional electroencephalographic asymmetries in bipolar seasonal affective disorder before and after exposure to bright light. *Biological Psychiatry, 33*, 642–646.

Avis, J., & Harris, P. L. (1991). Belief-desire reasoning among Baka children: Evidence for a universal conception of mind. *Child Development, 62*, 460–467.

Banich, M.T., & Belger, A. (1990). Interhemispheric interaction: How do the hemispheres divide and conquer a task? *Cortex, 26*, 77–94.

Baron-Cohen, S., Ring, H., Moriarty, J., Schmitz, B., Costa, D., & Ell, P. (1994). Recognition of mental state terms. Clinical findings in children with autism and a functional neuroimaging study of normal adults. *The British Journal of Psychiatry, 165*, 640–649.

Benowitz, L. I., Bear, D. M., Rosenthal, R., Mesalum, M. M., Zaidel, E., & Sperry, R. W. (1983). Hemispheric specialization in nonverbal communication. *Cortex, 19*, 5–11.

Bihrle, A. M., Brownell, H. H., Powelson, J. A., & Gardner, H. (1986). Comprehension of humorous and nonhumorous materials by left and right brain-damaged patients. *Brain and Cognition, 5*, 399–411.

Blanke, O., Mohr, C., Michel, C.M., Pascual-Leone, A., Brugger, P., Seeck, M., et al. (2005). Linking out-of-body experience and self processing to mental own-body imagery at the temporoparietal junction. *Journal of Neuroscience, 19*, 550–557.

Bloom, R.L., Borod, J.C., Obler, L.K., & Gerstman, L.J. (1992). Impact of emotional content on discourse production in patients with unilateral brain damage. *Brain and Language, 42*, 153–164.

Bloom, R.L., Borod, J.C., Obler, L.K., & Gerstman, L.J. (1993). Suppression and facilitation of pragmatic performance: effects of emotional content on discourse following right and left brain damage. *Journal of Speech and Hearing Research, 36*, 1227–1235.

Bloom, R.L., Borod, J.C., Santschi-Haywood, C., Pick, L.H., & Obler, L.K. (1996). Left and right hemispheric contributions to discourse coherence and cohesion. *International Journal of Neuroscience, 88*, 125–140.

Borod, J. C. (1992). Interhemispheric and intrahemispheric control of emotion: A focus on unilateral brain damage. *Journal of Consulting and Clinical Psychology, 3*, 339–348.

Borod, J. C. (1993). Emotion and the brain — Anatomy and theory: An introduction to the Special Section. *Neuropsychology, 7*, 427–432.

Borod, J. C. (1996). Emotional disorders/emotion. In J. G. Beaumont, P. Kenealy, & M. Rogers (Eds.), *The Blackwell dictionary of neuropsychology* (pp. 312–320). Oxford, England: Blackwell Publishers.

Borod, J. C. (Ed.) (2000). *The neuropsychology of emotion.* New York: Oxford University Press.

Borod, J.C., Bloom, R., Brickman, A.M., Nakhutina, L., & Curko, E. A. (2002). Emotional processing deficits in individuals with unilateral brain damage. *Applied Neuropsychology, 9*, 23–36.

Borod, J. C., Bloom, R., & Santschi–Haywood, C. (1998). Verbal aspects of emotional communication. In M. Beeman & C. Chiarello (Eds.), *Right hemisphere language comprehension: Perpsectives from cognitive neuroscience* (pp. 285–307). Mahwah, NJ: Erlbaum.

Borod, J. C., Caron, H., & Koff, E. (1981). Facial asymmetry for positive and negative expressions: Sex differences. *Neuropsychologia, 19*, 819–824.

Borod, J. C., Koff, E., & Caron, H. S. (1983). Right hemispheric specialization for the expression and appreciation of emotion: A focus on the face. In E. Perecman (Ed.), *Cognitive processing in the right hemisphere* (pp. 83–110). New York: Academic Press.

Borod, J. C., Koff, E., Lorch, M. P., & Nicholas, M. (1985). Channels of emotional expression in patients with unilateral brain damage. *Archives of Neurology, 42*, 345–348.

Borod, J. C., Koff, E., Perlman Lorch, M., & Nicholas, M. (1986). The expression and perception of facial emotion in brain-damaged patients. *Neuropsychologia, 24*, 169–180.

Borod, J. C., Pick, L. H., Hall, S., Sliwinski, M., Madigan, N., Obler, L. K., et al. (2000). Relationships among facial, prosodic, and lexical channels of emotional perceptual processing. *Cognition & Emotion, 14*, 193–211.

Borod, J.C., Rorie, K.D., Pick, L.H., Bloom, R.L., Andelman, F., Campbell, A.L., et al. (2000). Verbal pragmatics following unilateral stroke: Emotional content and valence. *Neuropsychology, 14*, 112–124.

Borod, J. C., Welkowitz, J., Alpert, M., Brozgold, A. Z., Martin, C., Peselow, E., et al. (1990). Parameters of emotional processing in neuropsychiatric disorders: Conceptual issues and a battery of tests. *Journal of Communication Disorders, 23*, 247–271.

Borod, J. C., Zgaljardic, D., Tabert, M., & Koff, E. (2001). Asymmetries of emotional perception and expression in normal adults. In G. Gainotti (Ed.), *Handbook of neuropsychology: Emotional behavior and its disorders* (pp. 181–205). Oxford, UK: Elsevier Science.

Brownell, H. H., Michel, D., Powelson, J., & Gardner, H. (1983). Surprise but not coherence: Sensitivity to verbal humor in right–hemisphere patients. *Brain and Language, 18*, 20–27.

Brozgold, A.Z., Borod, J.C., Martin, C.C., Pick, L.H., Alpert, M., & Welkowitz, J. (1998). Social functioning and facial emotional expression in neurological and psychiatric disorders. *Applied Neuropsychology, 5*, 15–23.

Brunet, E., Sarfati, Y., Hardy-Baylè, M.-C., & Decety, J. (2000). A PET investigation of the attribution of intentions with a nonverbal task. *NeuroImage, 11*, 157–166.

Bryden, M. P. (1982). *Laterality.* New York: Academic Press.

Bryden, M. P., & Ley, R. G. (1983). Right-hemispheric involvement in the perception and expression of emotion in normal humans. In K. M. Heilman & P. Satz (Eds.), *Neuropsychology of human emotion* (pp. 6–44). New York: Guilford.

Buck, R. (1984). *The communication of emotion.* New York: Guilford.

Buck, R. (1988). *Human motivation and emotion.* New York: Wiley.

Callaghan, T., Rochat, P., Lillard, A., Claux, M. L., Odden, H., Itakura, S., et al. (2005). Synchrony in the onset of mental-state reasoning. *Psychological Science, 16*, 378–384.

Castelli, F., Happé, F., Frith, U., & Frith, C. (2000). Movement and mind: A functional imaging study of perception and interpretation of complex intentional movement patterns. *Neuroimage, 12*, 314–325.

Christman, S. D., & Hackworth, M. D. (1993). Equivalent perceptual asymmetries for free viewing of positive and negative emotional expressions in chimeric faces. *Neuropsychologia, 31*, 621–624.

Coan, J. A., Allen, J. J., & Harmon-Jones, E. (2001). Voluntary facial expression and hemispheric asymmetry over the frontal cortex. *Psychophysiology, 38*, 912–925.

Compton, R. J., Feigenson, K., & Widick, P. (2005). Take it to the bridge: An interhemispheric processing advantage for emotional faces. *Cognitive Brain Research, 24*, 66–72.

Corballis, M. C. (2002). Hemispheric interactions in simple reaction time. *Neuropsychologia, 40*, 423–434.

Costa, A., Torriero, S., Oliveri, M., & Caltagirone, C. (2008). Prefrontal and temporo-parietal involvement in taking others' perspective: TMS evidence. *Behavioral Neurology, 19*, 71–74.

Davidson, R. (1984). Affect, cognition, and hemispheric specialization. In C. E. Izard, J. Kagan, & R. Zajonc (Eds.), *Emotions, cognition, and behavior* (pp. 320–365). Cambridge, England: Cambridge Press.

Decety, J., & Lamm, C. (2007). The role of the right temporoparietal junction in social interaction: How low-level computational processes contribute to meta-cognition. *Neuroscientist, 13*, 580–593.

Demaree, H. A., Everhart, D. E., Youngstrom, E. A., & Harrison, D. W. (2005). Brain lateralization of emotional processing: Historical roots and a future incorporating "dominance." *Behavioral and Cognitive Neuroscience Reviews, 4*, 3–20.

Dimond, S., & Beaumont, G. (1972). Processing in perceptual integration between and within the cerebral hemispheres. *British Journal of Psychology, 63*, 509–514.

Egelko, S., Gordon, W., Hibbard, M., Diller, L., Lieberman, A., Holliday, R., et al. (1988). Relationship among CT scans, neurological exam, and neuropsychological test performance in right-brain-damaged stroke patients. *Journal of Clinical and Experimental Neuropsychology, 10*, 539–564.

Ehrlichman, H. (1987). Hemispheric asymmetry and positive-negative affect. In D. Ottoson (Ed.), *Duality and unity of the brain: Unified functioning and specialization of the hemispheres* (pp. 194–206). New York: Plenum Press.

Ekman, P. (1992). An argument for basic emotions. *Cognition and Emotion, 6*, 169–200.

Ekman, P., & Davidson, R. J. (1993). Voluntary smiling changes regional brain activity *Psychological Science, 4*, 342–345.

Etcoff, N. L. (1984). Perceptual and conceptual organization of facial emotions: Hemispheric differences. *Brain and Cognition, 3*, 385–412.

Etcoff, N. L., Ekman, P., Magee, J. J., & Frank, M. G. (2000). Lie detection and language comprehension. *Nature, 405*, 139.

Flavell, J.H. (1999). Cognitive development: Children's knowledge about the mind. *Annual Review of Psychology, 50*, 21–45.

Foldi, N. S. (1987). Appreciation of pragmatic interpretations of indirect commands: Comparison of right and left hemisphere brain-damaged patients. *Brain and Language, 31*, 88–108.

Fox, N. A. (1991). If it's not left, it's right. *American Psychologist, 46*, 863–872.

Frank, M. G., & Ekman, P. (1997). The ability to detect deceit generalizes across different types of high-stake lies. *Journal of Personality and Social Psychology, 72*, 1429–1439.

Frith, C. D. (2008). Social cognition. *Philosophical Transactions of the Royal Society B: Biological Sciences, 363*, 2033–2039.

Frith, C. D., & Frith, U. (2006). The neural basis of mentalizing. *Neuron, 50*, 531–534.

Gainotti, G., Caltagirone, C., & Zoccolotti, P. (1993). Left/right and cortical/subcortical dichotomies in the neuropsychological study of human emotions. *Cognition & Emotion, 7*, 71–93.

Gallagher, H. L., Happé, F., Brunswick, N., Fletcher, P. C., Frith, U., & Frith, C. D. (2000). Reading the mind in cartoons and stories: An fMRI study of 'theory of mind' in verbal and nonverbal tasks. *Neuropsychologia, 38*, 11–21.

Goldberg, E., & Costa, L. D. (1981). Hemisphere differences in the acquisition and use of descriptive systems. *Brain and Language, 14*, 144–173.

Gur, R. C., Packer, I. K., Hungerbuhler, J. P., Reivich, M., Obrist, W. D., Amarnek, W. S., et al. (1980). Differences in the distribution of gray and white matter in human cerebral hemispheres. *Science, 207*, 1226–1228.

Happé, F., Brownell, H., & Winner, E. (1999). Acquired 'theory of mind' impairments following stroke. *Cognition, 70*, 211–240.

Harmon-Jones, E. (2004). Contributions from research on anger and cognitive dissonance to understanding the motivational functions of asymmetrical frontal brain activity. *Biological Psychology, 67*, 51–76.

Harmon-Jones, E., & Allen, J. J. B. (1998). Anger and frontal brain activity: EEG asymmetry consistent with approach motivation despite negative affective valence. *Journal of Personality and Social Psychology, 74*, 1310–1316.

Heilman, K. M., Blonder, L. X., Bowers, D., & Crucian, G. P. (2000). Neurological disorders and emotional dysfunction. In J. C. Borod (Ed.), *The neuropsychology of emotion* (pp. 377–402). New York: Oxford University Press.

Heilman, K. M., Bowers, D., & Valenstein, E. (1985). Emotional disorders associated with neurological diseases. In K. M. Heilman & E. Valenstein (Eds.), *Clinical neuropsychology* (pp. 377–402). New York: Oxford University Press.

Hirschman, R. S., & Safer, M. A. (1982). Hemisphere differences in perceiving positive and negative emotions. *Cortex, 18*, 569–580.

Hoptman, M. J., & Davidson, R. J. (1994). How and why do the two cerebral hemispheres interact? *Psychological Bulletin, 116*, 195–219.

Izard, C.E. (1971). *The face of emotion.* New York: Appleton-Century-Crofts.

Izard, C.E. (1990). Facial expressions and the regulation of emotion. *Journal of Personality and Social Psychology, 58*, 487–498.

Jackson, J. H. (1874). On the nature of the duality of the brain. *The Medical Press & Circular, 1*, 41–44.

Jackson, J. H. (1880). On affections of speech from disease of the brain. *Brain, 2*, 203–222.

Jackson, P.L., & Decety, J. (2004). Motor cognition: A new paradigm to investigate social interactions. *Current Opinions in Neurobiology, 14*, 1–5.

Jansari, A., Tranel, D., & Adolphs, R. (2000). A valence-specific lateral bias for discriminating emotional facial expressions in free field. *Cognition and Emotion, 14*, 341–353.

Joynt, R. J. (1964). Paul Pierre Broca: His contribution to the knowledge of aphasia. *Cortex, 1*, 206–213.

Kaplan, J. A., Brownell, H. H., Jacobs, J. R., & Gardner, H. (1990). The effects of right hemisphere damage on the pragmatic interpretation of conversational remarks. *Brain and Language, 38*, 315–333.

Kestenbaum, R., & Nelson, C. A. (1992). Neural and behavioral correlates of emotion recognition in children and adults. *Journal of Experimental Child Psychology, 54*, 1–18.

Kinsbourne, M., & Bemporad, B. (1984). Lateralization of emotion: A model and the evidence. In N. A. Fox & R. Davidson (Eds.), *The psychobiology of affective development* (pp. 259–291). Hillsdale, NJ: Erlbaum.

Kolb, B., & Taylor, L. (1990). Neocortical substrates of emotional behaviors. In N. Stein, B. Leventhal, & T. Trabasso (Eds.), *Psychological and biological approaches to emotion* (pp. 115–144). Hillsdale, NJ: Erlbaum.

Landis, T., Assal, G., & Perret, E. (1979). Opposite cerebral hemispheric superiorities for visual associative processing of emotional facial expressions and objects. *Nature, 278*, 739–740.

Laurian, S., Bader, M., Lanares, J., & Oros, L. (1991). Topography of event–related potentials elicited by visual emotional stimuli. *International Journal of Psychophysiology, 10*, 231–238.

Levy, J., Heller, W., Banich, M. T., & Burton, L. A. (1983). Asymmetry of perception in free viewing of chimeric faces. *Brain and Cognition, 2*, 404–419.

Ley, R. G., & Bryden, M. P. (1979). Hemispheric differences in processing emotions and faces. *Brain and Language, 7*, 127–138.

Liu, D., Wellman, H. M., Tardif, T., & Sabbagh, M. A. (2008). Theory of mind development in Chinese children: A meta–analysis of false–belief. *Developmental Psychology, 44*, 523–531.

Luh, K. E., Rueckert, L. M., & Levy, J. (1991). Perceptual asymmetries for free viewing of several types of chimeric stimuli. *Brain and Cognition, 16*, 83–103.

Malcolm, S. R., & Keenan, J. P. (2005). Hemispheric asymmetry and deception detection. *Laterality: Asymmetries of Body, Brain and Cognition, 10*, 131–148.

Mandal, M.K., Borod, J.C., Asthana, H.S., Mohanty, A., Mohanty, S., & Koff. E. (1999). Effects of lesion variables and emotion type on the perception of facial emotion. *Journal of Nervous and Mental Disease, 187*, 603–609.

McKeever, W. F., & Dixon, M. S. (1981). Right-hemisphere superiority for discriminating memorized from nonmemorized faces: Affective imagery, sex, and perceived emotionality effects. *Brain and Language, 12*, 246–260.

Mills, C. K. (1912). The cerebral mechanism of emotional expression. *Transactions of the College of Physicians of Philadelphia, 34*, 381–390.

Mitchell, J. P. (2008). Activity in right temporo-parietal junction is not selective for theory-of-mind. *Cerebral Cortex, 18*, 262–271.

Moreno, C. R., Borod, J. C., Welkowitz, J., & Alpert, M. (1990). Lateralization for the expression and perception of facial emotion as a function of age. *Neuropsychologia, 28*, 199–209.

Narumoto, J., Okada, T., Sadato, N., Fukui, K., & Yonekura, Y. (2001). Attention to emotion modulates fMRI activity in human right superior temporal sulcus. *Cognitive Brain Research, 12*, 225–231.

Odom, R. D., & Lemond, C. M. (1972). Developmental differences in the perception and production of facial expressions. *Child Development, 43*, 359–369.

Porter, S., Campbell, M. A., Stapleton, J., & Birt, A. R. (2002). The influence of judge, target, and stimulus characteristics on the accuracy of detecting deceit. *Canadian Journal of Behavioral Science, 34*, 172–185.

Premack, D., & Woodruff, G. (1978). Does the chimpanzee have a theory of mind? *Behavioral and Brain Sciences, 1*, 515–526.

Reuter–Lorenz, P., & Davidson, R. J. (1981). Differential contributions of the two cerebral hemispheres to the perception of happy and sad faces. *Neuropsychologia, 19*, 609–613.

Ross, E., Homan, R. W., & Buck, R. (1994). Differential hemispheric lateralization of primary and social emotions. *Neuropsychiatry, Neuropsychology, and Behavioral Neurology, 7*, 1–19.

Ross, E. D. (1981). The aprosodias. Functional-anatomic organization of the affective components of language in the right hemisphere. *Archives of Neurology, 38*, 561–569.

Ross, E. D. (1997). Right hemisphere syndromes and the neurology of emotion. In S. C. Schachter & O. Devinsky (Eds.), *Behavioral neurology and the legacy of Norman Geschwind* (pp. 183–191). Philadelphia, PA: Lippincott–Raven.

Ruby, P., & Decety, J. (2001). Effect of subjective perspective taking during simulation of action: A PET investigation of agency. *Nature Neuroscience, 4*, 546–550.

Sackeim, H. A., Greenberg, M. S., Weiman, A. L., Gur, R. C., Hungerbuhler, J. P., & Geschwind, N. (1982). Hemispheric asymmetry in the expression of positive and negative emotions: Neurologic evidence. *Archives of Neurology, 39*, 210–218.

Salmon, E., Perani, D., Herholz, K., Marique, P., Kalbe, E., Holthoff, V., et al. (2006). Neural correlates of anosognosia for cognitive impairment in Alzheimer's disease. *Human Brain Mapping, 27*, 588–597.

Samson, D., Apperly, I. A., Chiavarino, C., & Humphreys, G. W. (2004). Left temporoparietal junction is necessary for representing someone else's belief. *Nature Neuroscience, 7*, 499–500.

Sato, W., & Aoki, S. (2006). Right hemisphere dominance in processing of unconscious negative emotion. *Brain and Cognition, 62*, 261–266.

Sato, W., Kochiyama, T., Yoshikawa, S., Naito, E., & Matsumura, M. (2004). Enhanced neural activity in response to dynamic facial expressions of emotion: An fMRI study. *Cognitive Brain Research, 20*, 81–91.

Saxe, R., & Powell, L. J. (2006). It's the thought that counts: Specific brain regions for one component of theory of mind. *Psychological Science, 17,* 692–699.

Saxe, R., & Wexler, A. (2005). Making sense of another mind: The role of the right temporo–parietal junction. *Neuropsychologia, 43,* 1391–1399.

Schaffer, C. E., Davidson, R. J., & Saron, C. (1983). Frontal and parietal electroencephalogram asymmetry in depressed and nondepressed subjects. *Biological Psychiatry, 18,* 753–762.

Schweinberger, S.R., Baird, L.M., Blümler, M., Kaufmann, J.M., & Mohr, B. (2003). Interhemispheric cooperation for face recognition but not for affective facial expressions. *Neuropsychologia, 41,* 407–414.

Semmes, J. (1968). Hemispheric specialization: A possible clue to mechanism. *Neuropsychologia, 6,* 11–26.

Shamay-Tsoory, S. G., Tomer, R., & Aharon–Peretz, J. (2005). The neuroanatomical basis of understanding sarcasm and its relationship to social cognition. *Neuropsychology, 19,* 288–300.

Shaw, P., Bramham, J., Lawrence, E. J., Morris, R., Baron-Cohen, S., & David, A. S. (2005). Differential effects of lesions of the amygdala and prefrontal cortex on recognizing facial expressions of complex emotions. *Journal of Cognitive Neuroscience, 17,* 1410–1419.

Siegal, M., Carrington, J., & Radel, M. (1996). Theory of mind and pragmatic understanding following right hemisphere damage. *Brain and Language, 53,* 40–50.

Siegal, M., & Varley, R. (2002). Neural systems involved in 'theory of mind.' *Nature Reviews Neuroscience, 3,* 463–471.

Silberman, E. K., & Weingartner, H. (1986). Hemispheric lateralization of functions related to emotion. *Brain and Cognition, 5,* 322–353.

Snow, D. (2000). The emotional basis of linguistic and nonlinguistic intonation: Implications for hemispheric specialization. *Developmental Neuropsychology, 17,* 1–28.

Sperry, R. W., Gazzaniga, M. S., & Bogen, J. E. (1969). Role of the neocortical commissures. In P. J. Vinken & G. W. Bruyn (Eds.), *Handbook of clinical neurology* (Vol. IV, pp. 273–290). Amsterdam: North Holland Publishers.

Springer, S. P., & Deutsch, G. (1981). *Left brain, right brain.* New York, NY: Freeman and Company.

Stone, V. E., Nisenson, L., Eliassen, J. C., & Gazzaniga, M. S. (1996). Left hemisphere representations of emotional facial expressions. *Neuropsychologia, 34,* 23–29.

Stuss, D. T., Gallup, G. G., & Alexander, M. P. (2001). The frontal lobes are necessary for 'theory of mind.' *Brain, 124,* 279–286.

Suberi, M., & McKeever, W. F. (1977). Differential right hemispheric memory storage of emotional and non-emotional faces. *Neuropsychologia, 15,* 757–768.

Tamietto, M., Adenzato, M., Geminiani, G., & de Gelder, B. (2007). Fast recognition of social emotions takes the whole brain: Interhemispheric cooperation in the absence of cerebral asymmetry. *Neuropsychologia, 45,* 836–843.

Thatcher, R. W., Krause, P. J., & Hrybyk, M. (1986). Cortico–cortical associations and EEG coherence: A two-compartmental model. *Electroencephalography and Clinical Neurophysiology, 64,* 123–143.

Tucker, D. M., Roth, D. L., & Bair, T. B. (1986). Functional connections among cortical regions: Topography of EEG coherence. *Electroencephalography and Clinical Neurophysiology, 63,* 242–250.

Vanderploeg, R. D., Brown, W. S., & Marsh, J. T. (1987). Judgements of emotion in words and faces: ERP correlates. *International Journal of Psychophysiology, 5,* 193–205.

Wada, J., & Rasmussen, T. (2007). Intracarotid injection of sodium amytal for the lateralization of cerebral speech dominance: Experimental and clinical observations. *Journal of Neurosurgery, 106,* 1117–1133.

Wager, T. D., Phan, K. L., Liberzon, I., & Taylor, S. F. (2003). Valence, gender, and lateralization of functional brain anatomy in emotion: A meta-analysis of findings from neuroimaging. *NeuroImage, 19,* 513–531.

Winner, E., Brownell, H., Happé, F., Blum, A., & Pincus, D. (1998). Distinguishing lies from jokes: Theory of mind deficits and discourse interpretation in right hemisphere brain-damaged patients. *Brain and Language, 62,* 89–106.

Woodward, S. H. (1988). An anatomical model of hemispheric asymmetry [Abstract]. *Journal of Clinical and Experimental Neuropsychology, 10,* 68.

CHAPTER 23

Biological Motion and Multisensory Integration: The Role of the Superior Temporal Sulcus

Michael S. Beauchamp

The gaits of a drunken hooligan and an elderly woman are visually distinct, and are likely to produce different reactions in those who see them approaching on the sidewalk. What brain areas are important for making this ethologically relevant distinction? In this chapter, I will present evidence that the superior temporal sulcus (STS) is a critical brain area for processing biological motion. Evidence will also be presented showing the essential role of the STS in multisensory integration. Both biological motion and multisensory integration require combining information from different processing streams. The STS may be specialized for this computational role, and is likely to play an important role in social interactions, which often require integration of a diverse set of environmental cues.

ABOUT THE STS

About two-thirds of the human cerebral cortex is not visible on the surface of the brain but is instead buried in sulci. Other than the Sylvian fissure (also known as the lateral sulcus), the largest sulcus in the human brain is the superior temporal sulcus, averaging 39 cm^2 of tissue, about the same area as a business card (Van Essen, 2005). Figure 23.1 shows the location of the human superior temporal sulcus in an individual human brain.

BOLD FMRI STUDIES OF BIOLOGICAL MOTION PROCESSING

Blood-oxygen-level-dependent functional magnetic resonance imaging (BOLD fMRI) uses the metabolic consequences of neuronal activity to measure changes in brain activity. BOLD fMRI is a relative measure of activity: activation in a given condition can only be measured relative to some other condition. A common control condition is fixation baseline, in which subjects view a blank screen (usually with a fixation crosshairs). When human subjects view brief videos of different whole-body movements, a broad network of brain areas is more active than during fixation baseline (Fig. 23.2). Biological motion stimuli, such as videos of whole-body movements, evoke a greater volume of cortex in right hemisphere than left hemisphere, although similar areas are activated in both hemispheres. These include early areas of visual cortex (V1/V2/V3); ventral-stream visual areas important for processing visual form; dorsal-stream visual areas important for processing visual location and motion; the superior temporal sulcus (STS); the premotor cortex; and the amygdala.

Based on previous research, we can make a speculative account of the function of these different areas (Adolphs, 2003; Blake & Shiffrar, 2007; de Gelder, 2006; Haxby, Hoffman, Gobbini, 2000). Early visual areas (V1/V2)

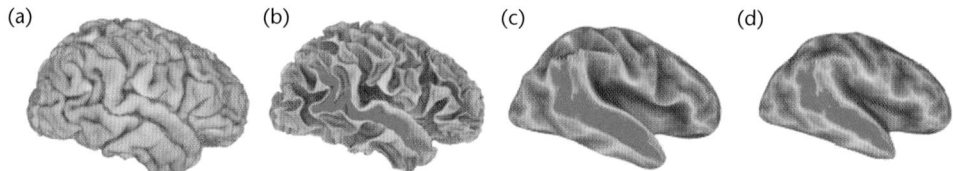

Figure 23.1 The location of the human superior temporal sulcus (STS). The right hemisphere of an individual subject is shown in four different configurations, with cortex in and near the STS shown in green. Grayscale shows sulcal depth (dark—fundus of sulci, light—crowns of gyri). These cortical surface models consist of thousands of connected triangles that form a single sheet for the entire hemisphere. In the original version (**A**), the sheet is folded to match the actual geometry of the surface of the cortex, viewed from the side as it would look if removed from the head. In the white matter version (**B**), the sheet is folded to match the geometry of the white matter that underlies the cortex. Because most cortex is buried in the depths of sulci, the sheet may be partially unfolded to allow viewing of most sulcal cortex while preserving the major sulci (**C**) or fully unfolded to form a smooth elliptical shape that reveals all sulcal cortex (**D**).

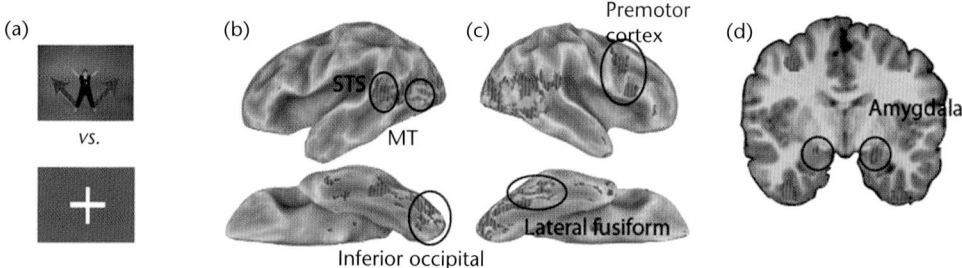

Figure 23.2 BOLD fMRI activation to videos of biological motion
A. Visual stimulus (32 different whole body movements motion *vs.* fixation). **B.** Lateral view (top) and ventral view (bottom) of left hemisphere (left) and right hemisphere (right). Colored areas show regions with a greater response to biological motion *vs.* fixation. **C.** Coronal slice showing subcortical activation in the amygdala.

analyze the visual form of the stimulus and pass the information onto higher areas, which identify the visible face and body parts, including the occipital face area and the fusiform face area and body-selective areas (Downing et al., 2006; Kanwisher and Yovel, 2006). At the same time, area MT and associated areas in lateral occipital temporal cortex process the visual motion present in the visual stimulus, extracting the direction and speed of the different moving body parts (Beauchamp et al., 2002; 2003). The superior temporal sulcus receives motion information from MT and form information from fusiform areas (Puce et al., 2001). Using this information, it computes a likely orientation and

type of movement to the visible body. Neurons in the premotor cortex create an internal simulation of the putative action in order to determine if it is physically possible and to permit imitation, if necessary (Saygin et al., 2004). In parallel, the amygdala assesses the identified action to determine whether it is threatening or otherwise emotionally valenced (Adolphs, 2009).

Because BOLD fMRI measures only relative changes in neural activity, it is always necessary to contrast two or more different stimulus conditions; in the simplest case this is a biological motion stimulus and a visual fixation baseline. Two approaches used in fMRI studies of biological motion are

1. studying the effects of different modifications to the biological motion stimulus, often using the Johannsen point light display, and
2. comparing the response to biological motion with the response to a control stimulus other than a simple fixation baseline.

ABOUT JOHANNSEN POINT-LIGHT DISPLAYS

Video clips of real biological motion contains a number of complex cues, such as form, color, and motion. Different visual areas are specialized for processing different visual stimuli, so these real video clips will activate many different areas. By simplifying visual stimuli so they contain fewer cues, we can examine which cues are most important in determining the response of different brain areas. The most common simplified biological motion stimulus are known as Johannsen displays, after the Swedish psychologist who first described them (Johansson, 1973). In the initial experiment, small Christmas tree lights were attached to the joints of an actor, who was then filmed in a dark room performing different movements. The resulting film consisted of small points of light moving with different trajectories. A single frame of the film consisted of unrecognizable points; once set in motion, the film is recognizable as a human body motion.

Because no form or color information is present in these displays, they contain fewer complex cues than real videos of biological motion. Surprisingly, viewers are able to extract a great deal of information from these unnatural displays. Behavioral studies have shown that different actions can be distinguished in as little as 200 ms (Johansson, 1977). Using only the motion cues found in point-light videos, viewers can distinguish male from female actors (Pollick, Kay, Heim, & Stringer, 2005) and recognize unique individuals (Cutting and Kozlowski, 1977; Loula, Prasad, Harber, & Shiffrar, 2005). Infants as young as three months preferentially look at point-light videos (Fox and McDaniel, 1982), suggesting that a great deal of visual experience is not necessary to interpret point-light videos.

Point-light stimuli can be easily manipulated to change the visual properties of the display. During a given motion, each joint moves with a characteristic pattern. During a jumping jack (Fig. 23.3A) the arms move mainly up and down as the legs move mainly outward and inward. In the point-light version of this motion, each marker moves with the same motion as its real joint. The simplest control version of this stimulus is simply inverting the motion so that all points are flipped in the up and down axis; viewers are impaired at recognizing inverted motion. In a more sophisticated maneuver, we have each marker move with the same motion, but we change its spatial position so that, for instance, the arm marker moves up and down in the bottom part of the display right next to the arm and leg marker. We may also change the relative phase of the joint movements. In a normal jumping jack, the arms are up while the legs are out; in a phase-scrambled jumping jack, this order would be reversed. Combining both forms of scrambling (physical position and phase order) produces an even more difficult to decode motion. Because these scrambling operations are easy to implement, it is possible to parametrically degrade motion images. For instance, adding just two extra points moving with the same motion vectors as individual joints (Fig. 23.3E). Noise points can be added to the motion until the observers are unable to distinguish them from a completely scrambed display, providing a behavioral index for acuity of biological motion perception (Cutting, Moore, & Morrison, 1988).

Motion-capture devices of the kind used in producing movie special effects can be used to digitally record the location of each joint at each time point. The digitized actions can even be mapped to nonhuman objects (like the dancing brooms in Disney's Fantasia) using commonly available animation software (Pelphrey et al., 2003). The fact that these videos are very different from normal stimuli, but produce a compelling percept of biological motion, suggests that brain regions that process biological motion, like STS, should be active when viewing point-light videos. In fact, point-light videos do strongly activate STS and premotor brain regions (Beauchamp et al., 2003; Grossman et al., 2000;

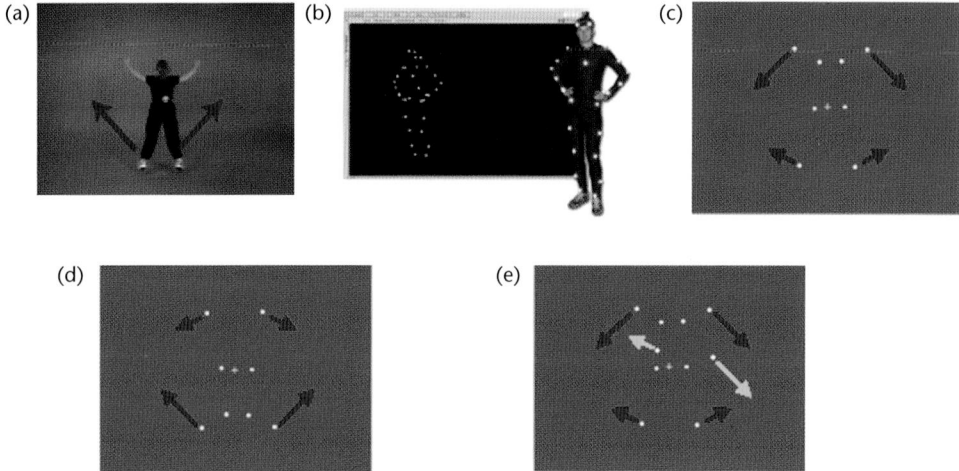

Figure 23.3 Johannsen Point-Light Displays
A. A single frame from a real video clip of a whole-body movement (jumping jack).
B. An actor in a motion capture suit and a digitized display of the marker positions.
C. A simplified point-light display of the jumping jack motion.
D. An inverted point-light jumping jack.
E. Point-light jumping jack with additional noise points (yellow arrows).

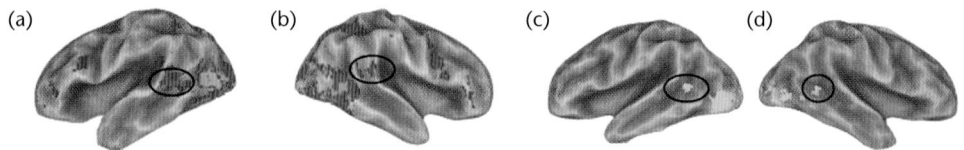

Figure 23.4 fMRI activation to point-light displays of biological motion
A. Left hemisphere brain activation in a single subject for point-light displays (12 different whole body movements) contrasted with fixation baseline.
B. Right hemisphere brain activation.
C. Left hemisphere brain activation for point-light displays (two movements, walking and running, at three different speeds) contrasted with fixation baseline.
D. Right hemisphere for activation for walking and running point-light displays.

Grossman and Blake, 2001; Saygin et al., 2004). Figure 23.4A shows brain activation maps from the same subject as in Figure 23.2, viewing point-light videos instead of real videos. A possible criticism of this result is that because the same subject viewed both real and point-light videos of similar motion, the point-light videos could have served as cues to recall the more complex information in the real video. Fig. 23.4B answers this objection by showing brain activation to point-light videos of walking and running in a subject who did not view real videos. As in Fig. 23.4A, activation is visible in the STS.

Simplified stimuli, such as point-light displays, provides valuable insight into the processing of biological motion stimuli. However, they have some important limitations. First, while they provide a strong impression of

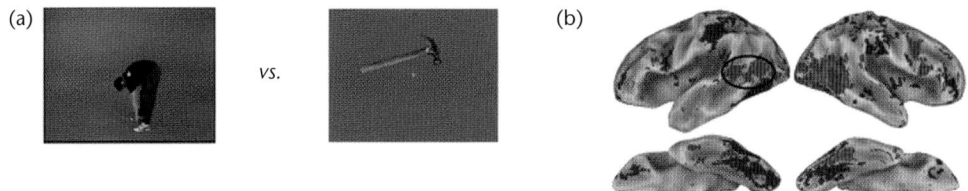

Figure 23.5 fMRI activation to videos of biological motion contrasted with videos of tools A. Stimulus (biological motion vs. tools). B. Brain areas showing greater activation to biological motion shown in orange, brain areas preferring tools shown in blue.

biological motion, the percept is quite different from that experienced when viewing real biological motion, perhaps because of their abstract nature. Although it is possible to discriminate emotions from point-light stimuli, they do not have the same degree of affective, visceral salience as when viewing real emotional video clips. This is reflecting in BOLD fMRI, where amygdala activation to point-light displays is reduced or eliminated. Even within the STS, activation to point-light displays is less than the response to real videos of the same movements, suggesting other visual cues, such as form and color, are important contributors to the STS response. Therefore, another approach is to contrast real videos of biological motion with real videos containing form, color and nonbiological motion. This approach was used by Beauchamp, Lee, Haxby, and Martin (2002) by contrasting videos of whole-body movements with videos of moving man-made manipulable objects (tools). Tools are a suitable set of control stimuli, because they move with different motions (just as human motions differ greatly) and contain form, color, and texture, but do not have the emotional valence of biological stimuli. Because visual properties of individual tools (such as color and speed of motion) differ from individual human stimuli, it is not possible to exactly match the visual properties between the different types of stimuli. To circumvent this problem, many exemplars from each category were used (28 different tools and human motions) filmed from five different viewpoints on a gray background to yield 140 unique stimuli per object category. Because a spectrum of values in each visual property were

to be sampled (for instance, hammers hammer quickly, while water pitchers pour slowly; jumping jacks are rapid while sitting motions are slower) any consistent between-category difference across all stimuli in each set would be unlikely to be due to confounding factors such as speed of motion.

As shown in Figure 23.5, regions of STS, premotor cortex, and lateral fusiform, responded more strongly to whole-body movements than to tool videos, demonstrating that these regions are specialized for processing biological motion (Beauchamp et al., 2002). Contrasting static images of bodies with static images of faces have revealed regions of lateral temporal cortex posterior to STS that prefer bodies to faces, the so-called extrastriate body area (EBA) (Downing, Jiang, Shuman, & Kanwisher, 2001). This would be a candidate area to compute the visual form of the body before passing the information to the STS. More can be learned about the mechanisms of biological motion processing in STS by examining the activation maps in response to different stimuli (Figure 23.6).

First and foremost, it is important to note that the STS shows strong responses to biological motion but also responds to other stimulus types. The STS shows significant responses to static images of bodies, as well as to static faces (Chao, Haxby, & Martin, 1999a; Chao, Martin, & Haxby, 1999b; Haxby et al., 1999; Hoffman and Haxby, 200; Kanwisher, McDermott, & Chun, 1997) and static animals (Chao et al., 1999a; Chao et al., 1999b). However, STS responded much more strongly to moving than static bodies, indicative of its important role in biological motion processing. In contrast,

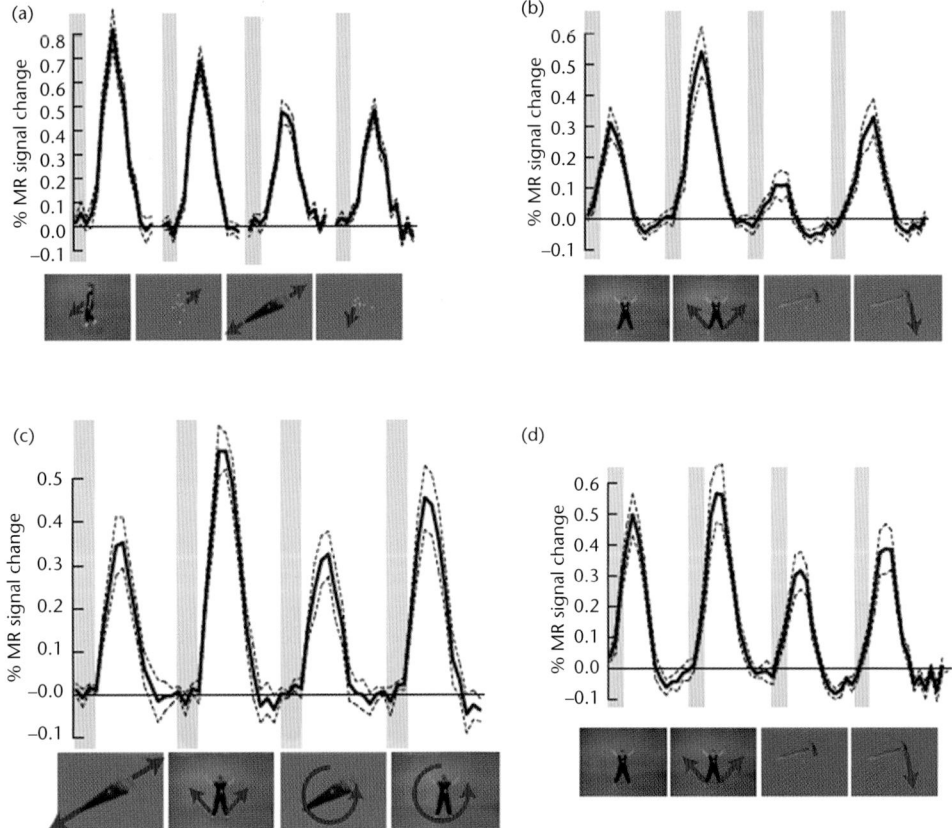

Figure 23.6 Response of the STS to different stimuli. The solid black line shows the mean response across subjects to a single stimulus presentation in the fifteen seconds following stimulus onset. The dashed lines show +– 1 SEM about the mean. The gray bars show the duration of the video stimulus (2.5 second presentations).

A. Response to real videos of moving humans, point-light displays of moving humans, real videos of moving tools, point-light displays of moving tools.

B. STS response to static pictures of humans, moving humans, static pictures of tools, moving tools.

C. STS response to naturally-moving tools, naturally-moving people, artificially moving tools, artificially moving people. The artificial movements consisted of translations or rotations generated by computer.

D. Fusiform response to static pictures of humans, moving humans, static pictures of tools, moving tools.

the fusiform responded similarly to moving and static bodies (Fig. 23.6D), suggesting that it is primarily involved in extracting the form, not the motion, of biological stimuli.

A second piece of evidence is the finding that a body moving in a realistic whole-body motion, such as a jumping jack, is a more effective activator of STS than the same still image undergoing a nonbiological motion, such as spinning around its axis. Similarly, an

animation of a robot walking and an animation of a person walking are both effective activators of STS (Pelphrey et al., 2003). One model for these responses is that STS prefers articulated movements (Beauchamp and Martin, 2007). However, animated creatures that move with many degrees of articulation do not activate STS as well as human movements (Pyles, Garcia, Hoffman, & Grossman, 2007), suggesting that it is the combination of a human figure and an articulated, biological-type movement that is the key to evoking a large response from STS. Experiments using facial stimuli also demonstrate that both form and motion are effective drivers of STS (Puce et al., 2003).

There is converging evidence that STS plays a key role in processing biological motion. Neurons in monkey STS respond to hand, eye, mouth, or body movements (Oram and Perrett, 1994). To address the necessity of STS for biological-motion perception, patients with damage to the STS must be examined. Most strokes or other diseases do not affect only the superior temporal sulcus, making it difficult to separate out impairments due to STS damage with impairments due to damage to surrounding regions. However, techniques have been adapted from functional brain mapping to measure the brain damage in each brain region and correlate it with the resulting brain damage. A recent study demonstrated that damage to both the STS and prefrontal cortex is associated with increased thresholds in detecting biological motion (Saygin, 2007).

However, the importance of STS for biological-motion processing does not mean that the STS is a module for biological motion, in the commonly accepted view of a brain area whose function is only to process biological motion. This is illustrated in the next section, in which we demonstrate that STS is equally important for a very different cognitive operation, that of multisensory integration.

MULTISENSORY INTEGRATION

In everyday life, perceptual events often occur in multiple sensory modalities at once. In our "stranger approaching" scenario, we might hear the hooligan shouting drunken obscenities. This would no doubt add additional weight on our behavioral decision about the best course of action. Most scientific investigations have focused on single modalities (frequently vision) in isolation. Recently, there has been increasing interest in studying integration across sensory modalities. While some scientists even suggest that there is no such thing as unisensory cortex (Ghazanfar and Schroeder, 2006), multisensory

responses are most prominent in specific brain regions, especially the STS (Calvert, 2001).

Speech and language related processing is one domain of meaningful stimuli in which auditory-visual integration is particularly important. Wright et al. (Wright et al., 2003) measured responses to auditory (A), visual (V), and auditory-visual (AV) animated characters speaking single words. Auditory-visual stimuli elicited a greater response than auditory or visual stimuli alone throughout the STS. Using simpler linguistic stimuli that did not contain biological motion, Van Atteveldt and colleagues (Van Atteveldt, Formisano, Goebel, & Blomert, 2004) found regions in STS that responded to both visually presented or spoken single letters. As in the Wright study, the STS response was greatest for AV stimuli. Interestingly, this multisensory enhancement was seen for congruent stimuli (i.e., visual "b" + auditory "bah") but not incongruent stimuli (e.g., "b" + "kah"). Because no behavioral task was required of the subjects in the Wright and Van Atteveldt studies, the enhanced response during AV stimulation (or congruent stimuli in the Van Atteveldt study) could be partially explained by increased attention and arousal. However, a similar result was found for synchronous vs. asynchronous AV speech in which a behavioral task was used (Macaluso et al., 2004) and for audiovisual objects with a behavioral task (Beauchamp, Lee, Argall, & Martin, 2004a). Imaging studies examining more complex speech stimuli have found that the STS is more active when the speech stimuli are spatially congruent (Callan et al., 2004), intelligible (Sekiyama, Kanno, Miura, & Sugita, 2003), or perceived as fused (Miller and D'Esposito, 2005), than when they are not. The STS has also been implicated in the McGurk effect (Callan et al., 2003; Sekiyama et al., 2003). Multisensory responses in STS are not restricted to linguistic stimuli. Even simple flashes and beeps activate STS, with greater activation when the stimuli are temporally congruent (Noesselt et al., 2007). In order to determine if auditory properties about nonbiological objects are represented in STS, Beauchamp et al. examined responses to stimuli representing animals and man-made

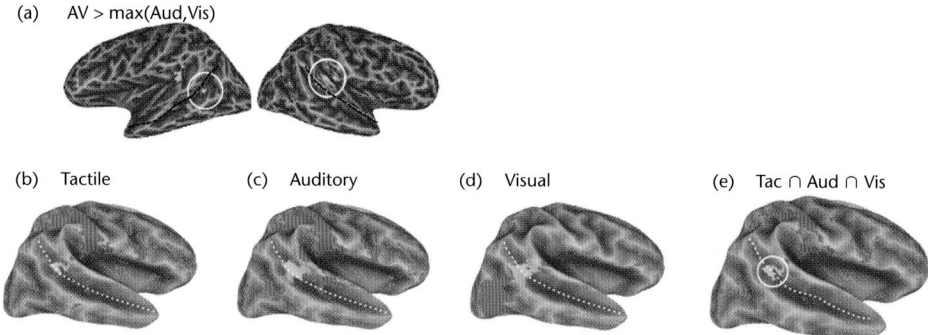

Figure 23.7 fMRI activation to multisensory stimuli.
A. Brain regions showing an enhanced response to auditory and visual stimuli presented simultaneously, compared with auditory or visual stimuli presented alone. White circle highlight the STS.
B. Brain regions responding to tactile vibrations on the hand or foot, compared with fixation baseline. Yellow color highlights activity in the STS.
C. Brain areas responding to auditory stimuli consisting of brief recordings of different sounds, both natural and artificial, compared with fixation baseline.
D. Brain areas responding to moving visual points, compared with fixation baseline.
E. Areas responding to all three sensory modalities. White circle highlights the STS.

graspable objects (tools) (Beauchamp et al., 2004a). In the first experiment, subjects were presented with static pictures or sound recordings of animals and tools, as well as scrambled auditory or visual control stimuli, and performed a one-back same/different task. STS showed strong responses to the meaningful animal/tool stimuli in both auditory and visual modalities that were greater than the responses to scrambled auditory or visual control stimuli, even though the task was equally difficult for meaningful and meaningless stimuli. In the second experiment, auditory and visual stimuli were presented in combination, and an enhanced response was observed in STS for multisensory compared with unisensory stimulation. In the third experiment, an event-related design was used in which the presentation of the sensory stimulus, consisting of videos of moving tools or recordings of the same tools, was separated in time from the behavioral decision made by the subject (selecting the name of the tool from three choices). Even for nonlinguistic, nonbiological tool stimuli, STS showed enhanced activity during AV compared with unisensory stimulus presentation.

In macaque, an important multisensory region lies along the fundus of the STS. This region was functionally defined as area STP (superior temporal polysensory) on the basis of single-cell recordings (Bruce, Desimone, & Gross, 1981) showing that neurons in this area responded to tactile, auditory, and visual stimuli. As shown in Figure 23.7, human STS also responds to touch, sound, and vision (Beauchamp, Yasar, Frye, & Ro, 2008).

WHY IS STS RESPONSIVE TO BIOLOGICAL MOTION AND MULTISENSORY INTEGRATION—A ROLE FOR COMMUNICATION

The STS stands at an anatomical crossroads. In the visual domain, it receives inputs from motion-processing areas, such as MT, and form-processing areas in ventral occipitotemporal cortex. In the multisensory domain, it sits near the intersection of visual, auditory, and somatosensory cortex. Because of its rich connectivity within and across modalities, over the course of evolution and development, STS may have been recruited to perform behavioral tasks that require integration of information.

Integrating cues from both within and across modalities is advantageous because the noise from independent observations is independent, allowing a more accurate estimate than from any one modality in isolation. A number of studies show that the brain combines different modalities is an optimal fashion to extract the maximum possible information (Alais and Burr, 2004; Ernst and Banks, 2002). Cue integration is likely to be particularly important in social interactions because social cues are frequently weak, or even ambiguous—imagine a friendly grin combined with a crushing handshake.

In support of a role for STS in social cognition, regions in and near the STS have been implicated in disorders such as autism (Hadjikhani, Joseph, Snyder, Tager-Flusberg, 2006) and complex social tasks such as theory of mind (Pelphrey, Morris, & McCarthy, 2005; Saxe, Carey, & Kanwisher, 2004). The STS responds to both dynamic and static body poses that express emotion (de Gelder, 2006; Grezes, Pichon, & deGelder, 2007; Hadjikhani and de Gelder, 2003). It is also suggestive that Wernicke's area, one of the classical language areas, is located directly adjacent to the STS in the posterior superior temporal gyrus. A related idea for the role of STS is the possibility that it is a member of the "mirror neuron" network, which may form the neural substrates for imitation (Iacoboni, 2005; Iacoboni et al., 1999). In this model, the STS could serve as a coordinator, receiving information about biological movements and forms, and the sounds or touches associated with them, in order to pass the information to motor systems which recreate the actions (Kohler et al., 2002). Imitation in nonhuman primates, facilitated by the STS, may have been an evolutionary precursor to humans' language abilities (Rizzolatti and Arbib, 1998).

An example of how biological motion and language processes interact is the McGurk effect, in which, an auditory syllable (phoneme) is perceived very differently depending on whether it is accompanied by a visual movie of a speaker pronouncing the same syllable or a different, incongruent syllable (McGurk and MacDonald, 1976). In an experiment in which TMS was delivered as subjects viewed McGurk and control stimuli, subjects were significantly less likely to report the McGurk effect

across different speakers and McGurk syllables (Beauchamp et al., 2010).

FUTURE DIRECTIONS

There is a high degree of overlap between biological motion and multisensory responses in the STS (Fig. 23.8A). However, it is not clear if the STS response to biological-motion stimuli is a by-product of the response to multisensory stimuli, or vice-versa. One possibility is that the STS serves to integrate information both within and between modalities (Fig. 23.8B). Because both multisensory and biological stimuli require a high degree of integration, both types of stimuli evoke large responses in STS.

Although fMRI is an exceedingly useful technique, it has two important problems: first, the relatively slow time course of the hemodynamic response makes it difficult to study the details of the neuronal computations underlying a cognitive operation. Second, because activation maps constructed from fMRI data are correlational, not causal, it is difficult to demonstrate unequivocally that a brain area is critical for a particular task; for instance, there is debate on whether the STS is, in fact, specialized for auditory-visual multisensory integration because it is also active in fMRI studies of other tasks (Hocking and Price, 2008).

Improved fMRI experimental designs and analysis techniques provide one way to overcome these limitations. Methods such as MR adaptation (Grill-Spector, Henson, & Martin, 2006; Krekelberg, Boynton, & van Wezel, 2006), high-resolution fMRI (Beauchamp et al., 2004b) and multivoxel pattern analysis (Norman, Polyn, Detre, & Haxby, 2006) allow for the examination of response selectivities of small populations of neurons in the STS and provide a new window into biological-motion processing and multisensory integration in the STS.

A second critical way to overcome the limitations of fMRI is to combine fMRI with other experimental methods. For instance, magnetoenchephalogaphy (MEG) and intracranial recording allow direct measurement of neuronal activity in the STS during perception of biological motion and multisensory

(a)

(b)

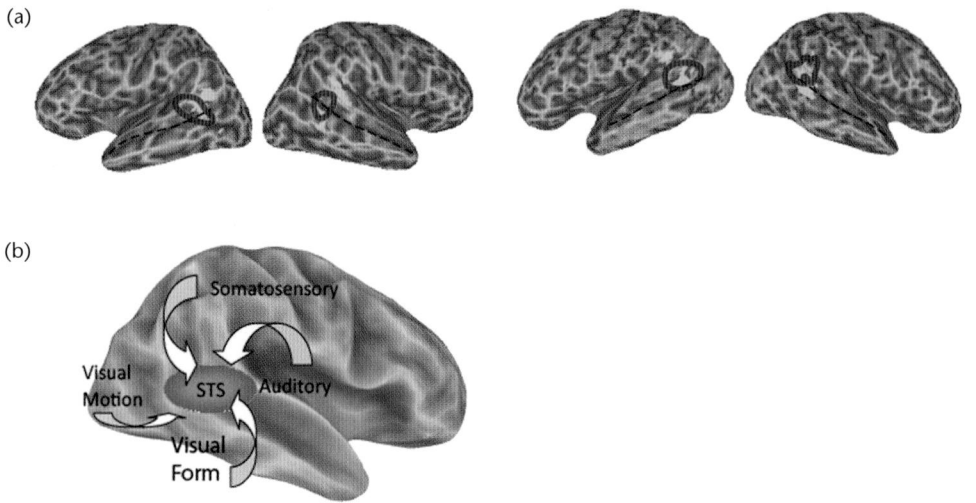

Figure 23.8. Functional diversity of STS.
A. Overlap between STS multisensory activation (yellow color shows auditory-visual responses) and
   biological motion (red outline shows preference for whole-body compared with tool movements).
B. Hypothesized inter- and intramodality integration in STS.

integration with high temporal resolution (Moran, Molholm, Reilly, & Foxe, 2008; Singh et al., 2002). Transcranial magnetic stimulation (TMS) allows activity in the normal human brain to be disrupted to demonstrate a causal link between a specific brain area and a specific behavior, such as the STS and the McGurk effect (Beauchamp et al., 2010).

ACKNOWLEDGMENTS

This research was supported in part by NSF grant 0642801.

REFERENCES

Adolphs, R. (2003). Cognitive neuroscience of human social behaviour. *Nat Rev Neurosci* 4,165–178.

Adolphs, R. (2009). The social brain: neural basis of social knowledge. *Annu Rev Psychol 60,* 693–716.

Alais, D., & Burr, D. (2004). The ventriloquist effect results from near-optimal bimodal integration. *Curr Biol 14,* 257–262.

Beauchamp, M.S., & Martin, A. (2007). Grounding object concepts in perception and action, evidence from fMRI studies of tools. *Cortex 43,* 461–468.

Beauchamp, M.S., Nath, A.R., & Pasalar, S. (2010). fMRI-Guided transcranial magnetic stimulation reveals that the superior temporal sulcus is a cortical locus of the McGurk effect. *J Neurosci 30,* 2414–2417.

Beauchamp, M.S., Lee, K.E., Haxby, J.V., & Martin, A. (2002). Parallel visual motion processing streams for manipulable objects and human movements. *Neuron 34,* 149–159.

Beauchamp, M.S., Lee, K.E., Haxby, J.V., & Martin, A. (2003). fMRI Responses to Video and Point–Light Displays of Moving Humans and Manipulable Objects. *Journal of Cognitive Neuroscience 15,* 991–1001.

Beauchamp, M.S., Lee, K.E., Argall, B.D., & Martin, A. (2004a). Integration of auditory and visual information about objects in superior temporal sulcus. *Neuron 41,* 809–823.

Beauchamp, M.S., Yasar, N.E., Frye, R.E., & Ro, T. (2008). Touch, sound and vision in human superior temporal sulcus. *Neuroimage 41,* 1011–1020.

Beauchamp, M.S., Argall, B.D., Bodurka, J., Duyn, J.H., & Martin, A. (2004b). Unraveling multisensory integration, patchy organization within human STS multisensory cortex. Nature *Neuroscience 7,* 1190–1192.

Blake, R., & Shiffrar, M. (2007). Perception of human motion. *Annu Rev Psychol 58,* 47–73.

Bruce, C., Desimone, R., & Gross, C.G. (1981). Visual properties of neurons in a polysensory area in superior temporal sulcus of the macaque. *J Neurophysiol 46*, 369–384.

Callan, D.E., Jones, J.A., Munhall, K., Callan, A.M., Kroos, C., & Vatikiotis-Bateson, E. (2003). Neural processes underlying perceptual enhancement by visual speech gestures. *Neuroreport 14*, 2213–2218.

Callan, D.E., Jones, J.A., Munhall, K., Kroos, C., Callan, A.M., & Vatikiotis-Bateson, E. (2004). Multisensory integration sites identified by perception of spatial wavelet filtered visual speech gesture information. *J Cogn Neurosci 16*, 805–816.

Calvert, G.A. (2001). Crossmodal processing in the human brain, insights from functional neuroimaging studies. *Cereb Cortex 11*, 1110–1123.

Chao, L.L., Haxby, J.V., & Martin, A. (1999a). Attribute-based neural substrates in temporal cortex for perceiving and knowing about objects. *Nat Neurosci 2*, 913–919.

Chao, L.L., Martin, A., & Haxby, J.V. (1999b) Are face-responsive regions selective only for faces? *Neuroreport 10*, 2945–2950.

Cutting, J.E., & Kozlowski, L.T. (1977). Recognising friends by their walk, gait perception without familiarity cues. *Bulletin of the Psychonomic Society 9*, 353–356.

Cutting, J.E., Moore, C., & Morrison, R. (1988). Masking the motions of human gait. Percept *Psychophys 44*, 339–347.

de Gelder, B. (2006) .Towards the neurobiology of emotional body language. *Nat Rev Neurosci 7*, 242–249.

Downing, P.E., Jiang, Y., Shuman, M., & Kanwisher, N. (2001). A cortical area selective for visual processing of the human body. *Science 293*, 2470–2473.

Downing, P.E., Chan, A.W., Peelen, M.V., Dodds, C.M., & Kanwisher, N. (2006). Domain specificity in visual cortex. *Cereb Cortex 16*, 1453–1461.

Ernst, M.O., & Banks, M.S. (2002). Humans integrate visual and haptic information in a statistically optimal fashion. *Nature 415*, 429–433.

Fox, R., McDaniel, C. (1982). The perception of biological motion by human infants. *Science 218*, 486–487.

Ghazanfar, A.A., & Schroeder, C.E. (2006). Is neocortex essentially multisensory? *Trends Cogn Sci 10*, 278–285.

Grezes, J., Pichon, S., & de Gelder, B. (2007) Perceiving fear in dynamic body expressions. *Neuroimage 35*, 959–967.

Grill-Spector, K., Henson, R., & Martin, A. (2006). Repetition and the brain, neural models of stimulus–specific effects. *Trends Cogn Sci 10*, 14–23.

Grossman, E., Donnelly, M., Price, R., Pickens, D., Morgan, V., Neighbor, G., & Blake, R. (2000). Brain areas involved in perception of biological motion. *J Cogn Neurosci 12*, 711–720.

Grossman, E.D., & Blake, R. (2001). Brain activity evoked by inverted and imagined biological motion. *Vision Res 41*, 1475–1482.

Hadjikhani, N., & de Gelder, B. (2003). Seeing fearful body expressions activates the fusiform cortex and amygdala. *Curr Biol 13*, 2201–2205.

Hadjikhani, N., Joseph, R.M., Snyder, J., & Tager-Flusberg, H. (2006). Anatomical differences in the mirror neuron system and social cognition network in autism. *Cereb Cortex 16*, 1276–1282.

Haxby, J.V., Hoffman, E.A., & Gobbini, M.I. (2000). The distributed human neural system for face perception. *Trends Cogn Sci 4*, 223–233.

Haxby, J.V., Ungerleider, L.G., Clark, V.P., Schouten, J.L., Hoffman, E.A., & Martin, A. (1999). The effect of face inversion on activity in human neural systems for face and object perception. *Neuron 22*, 189–199.

Hocking, J., & Price, C.J. (2008). The role of the posterior superior temporal sulcus in audiovisual processing. *Cereb Cortex 18*, 2439–2449.

Hoffman, E.A., & Haxby J.V. (2000). Distinct representations of eye gaze and identity in the distributed human neural system for face perception. *Nat Neurosci 3*, 80–84.

Iacoboni, M. (2005). Neural mechanisms of imitation. *Curr Opin Neurobiol 15*, 632–637.

Iacoboni, M., Woods, R..P, Brass, M., Bekkering, H., Mazziotta, J.C., & Rizzolatti, G. (1999). Cortical mechanisms of human imitation. *Science 286*, 2526–2528.

Johansson, G. (1973). Visual perception of biological motion and a model for its analysis. *Percept Psychophys 14*, 201–211.

Johansson, G. (1977). Studies on visual perception of locomotion. *Perception 6*, 365–376.

Kanwisher, N., & Yovel, G. (2006). The fusiform face area, a cortical region specialized for the perception of faces. *Philos Trans R Soc Lond B Biol Sci 361*, 2109–2128.

Kanwisher, N., McDermott, J., & Chun, M.M. (1997). The fusiform face area, a module in human extrastriate cortex specialized for face perception. *J Neurosci 17*, 4302–4311.

Kohler, E., Keysers, C., Umilta, M.A., Fogassi, L., Gallese, V., & Rizzolatti, G. (2002).Hearing sounds, understanding actions, action representation in mirror neurons. *Science 297*, 846–848.

Krekelberg, B., Boynton, G.M., & van Wezel, R.J. (2006) .Adaptation, from single cells to BOLD signals. *Trends Neurosci 29*, 250–256.

Loula, F., Prasad, S., Harber, K., & Shiffrar, M. (2005). Recognizing people from their movement. *J Exp, Psychol Hum Percept Perform 31*, 210–220.

Macaluso, E., George, N., Dolan, R., Spence, C., & Driver, J. (2004). Spatial and temporal factors during processing of audiovisual speech, a PET study. *Neuroimage 21*, 725–732.

McGurk, H., & MacDonald, J. (1976). Hearing lips and seeing voices. *Nature 264*, 746–748.

Miller, L.M., & D'Esposito, M. (2005). Perceptual fusion and stimulus coincidence in the cross–modal integration of speech. *J Neurosci 25*, 5884–5893.

Moran, R.J., Molholm, S., Reilly, R.B., & Foxe, J.J. (2008). Changes in effective connectivity of human superior parietal lobule under multisensory and unisensory stimulation. *Eur J Neurosci 27*, 2303–2312.

Noesselt, T., Rieger, J.W., Schoenfeld, M.A., Kanowski, M., Hinrichs, H., Heinze, H.J., & Driver, J. (2007). Audiovisual temporal correspondence modulates human multisensory superior temporal sulcus plus primary sensory cortices. *J Neurosci 27*, 11431–11441.

Norman, .KA., Polyn, S.M., Detre, G.J., & Haxby, J.V. (2006). Beyond mind-reading, multi-voxel pattern analysis of fMRI data. *Trends Cogn Sci 10*, 424–430.

Oram, M.W., & Perrett, D.I. (1994). Responses of anterior superior temporal polysensory (STPa) neurons to "biological motion" stimuli. *J Cogn Neurosci 6*, 99–116.

Pelphrey, K.A., Morris, J.P., & McCarthy, G. (2005). Neural basis of eye gaze processing deficits in autism. *Brain 128*, 1038–1048.

Pelphrey, K.A., Mitchell, T.V., McKeown, M.J., Goldstein, J., Allison, T., & McCarthy, G. (2003). Brain activity evoked by the perception of human walking, controlling for meaningful coherent motion. *J Neurosci 23*, 6819–6825.

Pollick, F.E., Kay, J.W., Heim, K., & Stringer, R. (2005). Gender recognition from point-light walkers. *J Exp Psychol Hum Percept Perform 31*, 1247–1265.

Puce, A., Castiello, U., Syngeniotis, A., & Abbott, D. (2001). The human STS integrates form and motion. *Neuroimage 13*, S931.

Puce, A., Syngeniotis, A., Thompson, J.C., Abbott, D.F., Wheaton, K.J., & Castiello, U. (2003). The human temporal lobe integrates facial form and motion, evidence from fMRI and ERP studies. *Neuroimage 19*, 861–869.

Pyles, J.A., Garcia, J.O., Hoffman, D.D., & Grossman, E.D. (2007). Visual perception and neural correlates of novel 'biological motion'. *Vision Res 47*, 2786–2797.

Rizzolatti, G., & Arbib, M.A. (1998). Language within our grasp. *Trends Neurosci 21*, 188–194.

Saxe, R., Carey, S., & Kanwisher, N. (2004). Understanding other minds, linking developmental psychology and functional neuroimaging. *Annu Rev Psychol 55*, 87–124.

Saygin, A.P. (2007). Superior temporal and premotor brain areas necessary for biological motion perception. *Brain 130*, 2452–2461.

Saygin, A.P., Wilson, S.M., Hagler, D.J., Jr., Bates, E., & Sereno, M.I. (2004). Point-light biological motion perception activates human premotor cortex. *J Neurosci 24*, 6181–6188.

Sekiyama, K., Kanno, I., Miura, S., & Sugita, Y. (2003). Auditory–visual speech perception examined by fMRI and PET. *Neurosci Res 47*, 277–287.

Singh, K.D., Barnes, G.R., Hillebrand, A., Forde, E.M., & Williams, A.L. (2002). Task-related changes in cortical synchronization are spatially coincident with the hemodynamic response. *Neuroimage 16*,103–114.

Van Atteveldt, N., Formisano, E., Goebel, R., & Blomert, L. (2004) .Integration of letters and speech sounds in the human brain. *Neuron 43*, 271–282.

Van Essen, D.C. (2005). A Population-Average, Landmark- and Surface-based (PALS) atlas of human cerebral cortex. *Neuroimage 28*, 635–662.

Wright, T.M., Pelphrey, K.A., Allison, T., McKeown, M.J., & McCarthy, G. (2003). Polysensory interactions along lateral temporal regions evoked by audiovisual speech. *Cereb Cortex 13*, 1034–1043.

CHAPTER 24

Specialized Brain for the Social Vision: Perspectives from Typical and Atypical Development

Teresa Farroni and Atsushi Senju

INTRODUCTION

As other authors have discussed in previous chapters, information derived from the face, and especially from the eye region, are among the most critical percepts that social vision has to deal with. It serves a number of different functions in social interaction, such as triggering a reflexive shift of an observer's visual attention (Driver et al., 1999; Friesen and Kingstone, 1998 and Hietanen, 1999), regulating turn-taking in conversation (Argyle & Cook, 1976), expressing intimacy (Kleinke, 1986, Langton et al., 2000), and inferring mental states (Baron-Cohen, 1995). Recent behavioral studies in adults have demonstrated that direct gaze can modulate other aspects of face processing. For example, perceived eye contact can affect both the speed of online gender face judgments and the accuracy of incidental recognition memory of faces (Vuilleumier et al., 2005), and performance in face memory tasks can be influenced by gaze direction both at the encoding and at the retrieval levels (Hood, Macrae, Cole-Davies, & Dias, 2003).

Cognitive neuroscience studies with adults have also revealed modulation of processing resulting from the detection of direct gaze. For example, George, Driver, & Dolan, (2001), investigated how gaze direction (direct or averted), influences face processing using a gender-recognition

task. They observed that specific regions of the fusiform gyrus yielded stronger responses to faces when these looked directly at the subject (regardless the orientation of the head). Since it has been recently shown that the fusiform response can be sensitive to recognition of individuals (Gauthier et al., 1999; George et al., 1999; Sergent, Ohta, & MacDonald, 1992), and is stronger for attended faces (Wojciulik, Kanwisher, & Driver, 1998), the authors concluded that the stronger activity found for faces with direct gaze could be interpreted in terms of enhanced attention and deeper encoding for faces with direct gaze (George et al. 2001). In addition, several electrophysiological studies with adults also found that an occipital-temporal negative peak around 170 msec after stimulus onset that is related to face processing (Bentin et al., 1996; McCarthy, Puce, Belger, & Allison, 1999) is also sensitive to eye gaze perception (Bentin et al., 1996; Puce, Smith, & Allison, 2000; Senju, Yaguchi, Tojo, & Hasegawa, 2005).

How does this specialization found in adults arise during development? The development of the brain circuitries involved in all kinds of cognitive processes depends upon the interaction of two broad factors: nature (genetic factors), and nurture (environmental influences). If we aim to understand how these factors interact to build the mature social brain network, it seems of particular importance to look at how the human brain deals with social information during infancy. The perception of faces elicits activity in distributed regions of the brain involving several cortical and subcortical structures. Different parts of this distributed neural system for face perception seem to mediate different aspects of face perception (see Haxby, Hoffman, & Gobbini, 2002 for a review). Further, in several developmental disorders (e.g., autism spectrum disorder (ASD), Williams Syndrome) aspects of social cognition and perception appear to be impaired or deviant. Studying both typical and atypical development in the same tasks, and with the same methodology, can be both mutually informative, and can help reveal underlying mechanisms of developmental change (see Cicchetti 1984, 1991; Urban, Carlson, Egeland, & Sroufe, 1991). In this chapter we will discuss and review evidence about how certain cortical regions develop their individual functionality, and become integrated components of the adult human social brain network, in both typical and atypical development. For atypical development, we will focus on ASD, since impairment in both social interaction and communication are core symptom of ASD, and thus this disorder can provide an ideal case in which the development of social vision goes atypical.

The attempt to relate brain to behavioral development in humans has been usually related to the idea of a maturation of particular regions of the brain, usually regions of cerebral cortex, to newly emerging sensory, motor, and cognitive functions. Another way to interpret the human functional brain development comes from recent evidence that suggests that some of the regions that are slowest to develop by neuroanatomical criteria show activity from shortly after birth (Johnson et al., 2001; Johnson, 2005). The idea that postnatal functional brain development, at least within the cerebral cortex, could involve a process of organizing patterns of inter-regional interactions comes from the "interactive specialization approach" (Johnson, 2001; Johnson, 2005). According to this view, the response properties of a specific region are partly determined by its patterns of connectivity to other regions,

and their patterns of activity. During postnatal development changes in the response properties of cortical regions occur as they interact and compete with each other to acquire their role in new computational abilities. From this perspective, some cortical regions may begin with poorly defined functions, and consequently are partially activated in a wide range of different contexts and tasks. During development, activity-dependent interactions between regions sharpens up the functions of regions such that their activity becomes restricted to a narrower set of circumstances (e.g., a region originally activated by a wide variety of visual objects, may come to confine its response to upright human faces). In other words, modularity (in the sense of regional specialization) is an outcome of postnatal brain development, and not a precursor to it. The onset of new behavioral competencies during infancy will, therefore, be associated with changes in activity over several regions, and not just by the onset of activity in one or more additional region(s). From this perspective, the social brain network is a product of development that can sometimes fail to emerge for a variety of reasons.

Applying the interactive-specialization approach, Johnson et al. (2005) predicted that during infancy the social brain network will not yet have clearly emerged from surrounding brain regions and networks. Furthermore, during infancy and early childhood the social brain network will emerge as a whole, and not in a region-by-region (maturation of modules) manner and that later infancy and early childhood specialization *within* the social brain network will occur with different patterns of regional activation for different tasks (e.g., eye gaze processing may become partially distinct from general face processing). Finally the atypical development, following this approach can be considered as a lack of specialization of, or within, the social brain network. The lack of specialization may account for some of the cognitive and behavioral symptoms observed in certain developmental disorders. Atypical development could also result in deviant patterns of specialization.

THE DEVELOPMENT OF FACE PROCESSING

Within cognitive neuroscience one the best-studied aspects of the social brain is the visual processing of faces. Neuroimaging studies have shown the implication of several face-sensitive regions within the social brain network, including regions of the fusiform gyrus, lateral occipital area, and superior temporal sulcus (Adolphs, 2003; Kanwisher, McDermott, & Chun, 1997); all these regions are involved in aspects of encoding/detecting facial information. In particular, the stimulus specificity of response has been most extensively studied for the fusiform face area (FFA), a region that is more activated by faces than by many other comparison stimuli including houses, textures, and hands (Kanwisher et al., 1997). Although the greater activation of the FFA to faces than to other objects has led some to propose it is a face module (Kanwisher et al., 1997), the possible specialization of this area is still under discussion. In particular, the major debate in the adult literature continues to concern whether the cortical specialization for face processing is a result of expertise with this class of stimulus, or whether cortical structures specialized for face processing result from prespecified wiring patterns.

One of the first theoretical perspectives that have tried to understand how nature/nurture interact to build the mature social brain network is a recently updated version of Johnson and Morton's (1991; Morton & Johnson 1991) two-process model (Johnson 2005). A tendency for newborns to orient to faces (CONSPEC), and an acquired specialization of cortical circuits for other aspects of face processing (CONLERN) is postulated. The authors hypothesized that CONSPEC (mainly subcortical visuo-motor pathways) served to bias the input to developing cortical circuitry over the first weeks and months of life, thus ensuring that appropriate cortical specialization occurred in response to the social and survival-relevant stimulus of faces.

Most recently, cognitive neuroscience, electrophysiological, and neuropsychological studies with adults have provided evidence for a rapid, low spatial frequency, subcortical face-detection system in adults that involves the superior colliculus, pulvinar, and amygdala (Johnson 2005) and it has been supposed that this low-level neural route for face processing in adults, could be the same system that operates in young infants, including newborns (Johnson, 2005). Since 1991 a lot of studies have been conducted on face preferences in newborns (see Johnson, 2005 for review). All of these studies found some evidence of discrimination of face-like patterns (apart from Easterbrook, Kislevsky, Hains, & Muir, 1999). At present, the Conspec notion occupies the middle ground between those who argue that face preferences in newborns are due to low-level psychophysical biases (see Simion Turati, Simion, & Zanon, 2003), and others who propose that infants' representations of faces are, in fact, richer and more complex than we supposed (Farroni et al., 2005). The behavioral data discussed by Simion and colleagues is consistent with a preference for up-down asymmetrical patterns with more elements or features being in the upper half of a bounded object or area. One of the reasons for doubting that an upper visual field bias alone is sufficient to account for newborn preferences comes from studies of the effects of phase contrast.

In a recent experiment, the effects of phase contrast on newborns' preferences for schematic and realistic face images was assessed (Farroni et al., 2005, see Figure 24.1). In these experiments newborns' preferences for upright compared to inverted configural patterns, and photographic face images, were assessed with both black elements on white (as in previous studies) and the converse. If the newborns are seeking elements or features, then phase contrast should make either no difference or possibly cause them to prefer white elements on a black background (since lighter elements are typically closer to the viewer in natural scenes). In contrast, if the purpose of the representation is to detect faces, then black elements on white should be more effective, since the eyes and mouth region are recessed into the face, and appear in shadow under natural (top-down) lighting conditions. Consistent with

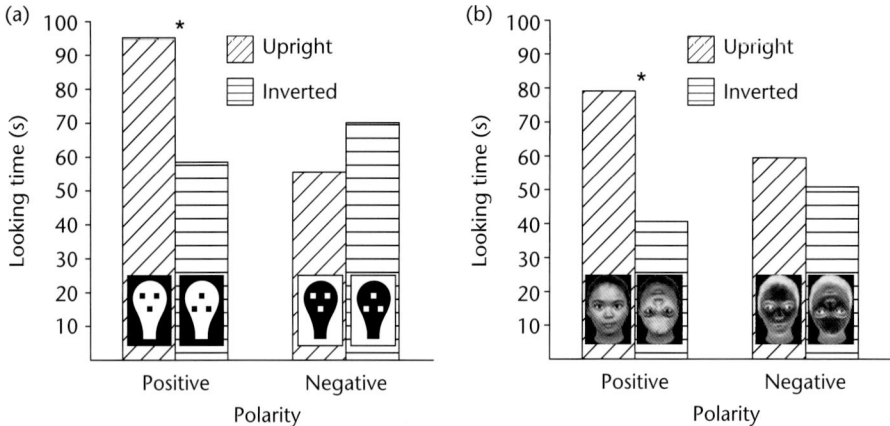

Figure 24.1 Stimuli and looking times on newborns preference for schematic (a) and realistic face (b) images with phase contrast manipulation. Significant differences are indicated by asterisks (* = P < .05). (see Farroni et al., 2005)

the latter view, we (Farroni et al., 2005) found the preference for an upright face only under conditions of black on white or when smaller dark blobs are placed inside the light elements. Infants preferred facelike configurations only when some contrast relations within the image resembled to the natural difference between the darker iris and the lighter sclera of human eyes. This was also shown to be the case with photographic images. Newborns seem to seek facelike stimuli that provide them with gaze information as well. An interpretation of these results is that newborns are responding best to surfaces/objects that have a number of indentations or holes in the upper half.

Another area that casts doubt on the "top-heavy" hypothesis is evidence taken to support the existence of complex face-processing abilities in newborns. Some empirical results include a preference for attractive faces (Slater et al. 1998, 2000), data indicating that newborns are sensitive to the presence of eyes in a face (Batki et al. 2000), and that they prefer to look at faces with direct gaze that engage them in eye contact (Farroni, Csibra, Simion, & Johnson, 2002).

According to the developing cortical areas for face processing, the interactive- specialization perspective posits that functional brain development, at least in the cerebral cortex, involves

a process of specialization in which regions go from initially having very broadly tuned functions, to having increasingly finely tuned (more specialized) functions (Johnson, 2001). A consequence of increased specialization of cortical regions is the increasingly focal patterns of cortical activation resulting from a given task demand or stimulus. By this view, some regions of cortex gradually become increasingly specialized for processing social stimuli and thus become recruited into the social brain network.

One way to investigate this question is focusing on event-related potential (ERP) studies of face processing in infancy (see de Haan, Johnson, & Halit, 2003 for review).

In adults and in children at least as young as 4 years, there is a "face-sensitive" negative deflection in the ERP, called the N170, that peaks at around 170 ms after stimulus onset and is most prominent over posterior temporal electrodes (e.g., Bentin, Allison, Puce, Perez, & McCarthy, 1996; Taylor, Edmonds, McCarthy & Allison, 2001; Taylor, McCarthy, Saliba, & Degiovanni, 1999). The N170 is of larger amplitude and longer latency to inverted compared to upright faces (Bentin et al., 1996; de Haan, Pascalis & Johnson, 2002; Eimer, 2000; George et al., 1996; Rebai, Poiroux, Bernard, & Lalonde, 2001; Taylor et al., 2001). In contrast, there is no difference in amplitude or latency of the N170 elicited by upright compared to inverted animal faces (de Haan et al., 2002) or upright compared to inverted objects (Rebai et al., 2001; Rossion et al., 2000.). These results suggest that the N170 elicited by the human face is not simply a reaction to the basic configuration of eyes-nose-mouth (since this is also present in animal faces), but is tuned more specifically to characteristics of the upright, human face.

In infants as young as 6 months, an ERP component is elicited that is of similar morphology to the adult N170 but with a longer peak latency and smaller amplitude—the N290 (de Haan et al., *2002*, Halit, de Haan, & Johnson, 2003). Recent experiments have established that this component is likely a precursor to the adult N170 (Halit et al., 2003; Halit, Csibra, Volein, & Johnson, 2004). However, at 6 months and younger, the N290 is not affected by face inversion. This is not because infants of this age cannot detect the difference between upright and inverted faces, as a longer-latency ERP component (P400) is affected by orientation. It is not until 12 months of age that a more adult-like response is seen: like adults, 12-month-olds show a larger N170/290 for inverted than upright human faces but no difference in the N170/290 to inverted and upright monkey faces (Halit, et al., 2003). These results are consistent with the idea that the infants' cortical processing of faces is initially relatively broad and poorly tuned, and only later in development becomes more specific to the upright human face. This type of change is consistent with expectations from the interactive-specialization perspective on functional brain development (see Johnson & de Haan, 1999). Further, this specialization process likely extends beyond infancy, because there are developmental changes in the characteristics of the N170 throughout childhood (Taylor et al., 1999; Taylor et al., 2001). By applying new source separation and localization methods (Richards, 2004) to the infant ERP data (Halit et al., 2003) it was possible to identify candidate cortical sources of the face-inversion effect. This analysis suggested that generators in the left and right lateral occipital area, the right FFA, and the right superior temporal sulcus (STS) discriminated between upright and inverted faces

in 3- and 12-month-olds (Johnson et al., 2005). All three cortical areas have been implicated in the core face-processing system in adults (Haxby et al., 2000), and they also generally overlap with the areas identified in the previously discussed PET study with 2-month-olds (Tzourio-Mazoyer et al., 2002).

It is important to point out that the development of the brain processes reflected in the N170/N290 continues well beyond infancy (for a review, see Taylor, Batty, & Itier, 2004). Although latency of the adult N170 is delayed by face inversion, no such effect is observed for the latency of the infant N290 at any age (de Haan et al., 2002; Halit et al., 2003). There is evidence that suggests that this latency effect is not apparent until 8 to 11 years (Taylor et al., 2004). Another important developmental finding is that while the amplitude of the adult N170 is larger to the monkey faces, infants' N290 shows the opposite pattern. A completely adult-like modulation of the amplitude of the N170 has not been reported until 13 to 14 years (Taylor et al., 2004).

THE ATYPICAL DEVELOPMENT OF FACE PROCESSING

Impaired face processing is one of the most well-documented aspects of the social cognition deficits in ASD. However, it is not clear whether individuals with ASD have a specific impairment in facial recognition: Some studies report the impairment of face recognition in ASD compared to typically developing children (Boucher & Lewis, 1992; Boucher, Lewis & Collins, 1998; Gepner, de Gelder & de Schonen, 1996; Hauck et al.,1998), but others failed to find the specific impairments (Davies, Bishop, Manstead, & Tantam, 1994; Klin, Sparrow et al., 1999; Volkmar et al;.,1989). Other studies emphasize an atypical strategy in face processing, such as a preference for feature-based processing than for configural and/or holistic processing (for a review, see Jemel, Mottron & Dawson, 2006). In this chapter, we will focus on facial orienting in individuals with ASD, and its relations with neural responses to face perception. It is because facial orienting plays a critical role in typical development of cortical specialization for face processing, as we discussed earlier. In addition, several lines of researches suggest that individuals with ASD show atypical pattern of orienting to the face, or to particular parts of the face, such as eyes or mouth.

First of all, failure to orient to the face was commonly reported in retrospective home-video analyses (Baranek, 1999; Clifford, Young, & Williamson, 2007; Maestro et al., 2005; Osterling & Dawson, 1994; Osterling, Dawson, & Munson, 2002; Werner & Dawson, 2005). In their studies, infants in their first years who later diagnosed as ASD showed less orienting to other faces than typically developing children or children who later diagnosed with other developmental disorders. In a pioneering experimental study, N. O'Conner and Hermelin (1967) used a preferential-looking paradigm with paired presentation of natural and scrambled faces, and found that children with ASD, like typically developing children, orient more to a face than a scrambled image of a face. In addition, van der Geest, Kemner, Camfferman, Verbaten, & van Engeland (2002a) used eye-tracking techniques and reported that individuals with ASD fixate more to human features than to other items in cartoonlike pictures. However, recent studies revealed atypical patterns of face orienting in ASD, such as slower orienting to the face (Sasson et al., 2007) or less gaze onto the face (Trepagnier, Sebrechts, & Peterson, 2002) in individuals with ASD. In addition, our recent study (Kikuchi et al., 2009) utilized a change-blindness paradigm and examined attention to the face and to the object. As a result, typically developing children were better at detecting the change of identity or spatial location of faces than other objects. Children with ASD, on the other hand, are equally adept at detecting change of faces as well as that of objects. These studies suggest that typically developing individuals are faster and more efficiently orient to faces than objects, but such facilitative orienting to the face is absent in individuals with ASD.

In addition to face orienting, other studies investigated whether individuals with ASD show atypical orienting to different parts of the faces, such as eyes or mouth. To the best of these

authors' knowledge, Langdell (1978) was the first to demonstrate that children with ASD, compared to typically developing children, rely less on upper part of the face. This finding has been replicated by independent studies (Joseph & Tanaka, 2003; Rutherford, Clements, & Sekular, 2007; Spezio, Adolphs, Hurley, & Piven, 2007). Eye-tracking studies also consistently found that individuals with ASD fixate less to the eyes compared to typically developing individuals (Dalton et al., 2005; Klin et al., 2002; Neumann, Spezio, Piven, & Adolphs, 2006; Pelphrey et al., 2002; Spezio, Adolphs, et al., 2007, but see also van der Geest et al., 2002b).

However, it is not clear whether it is due to the selective use of lower part of the face in individuals with ASD (Joseph & Tanaka, 2003; Spezio. Adolphs, et al., 2007), or their impairment in using upper part of the face (Rutherford et al., 2007). In some of the eye-tracking studies with static and unedited face stimuli, individuals with ASD indeed fixate more to the eyes than to the mouth (Dalton et al., 2005; Pelphrey et al., 2002; van der Geest et al., 2002b). On the other hand, individuals with ASD manifests longer fixation to the mouth than to the eyes when faces were blurred with bubble masking (Neumann et al., 2006; Spezio, Adolphs, et al., 2007) or when dynamic videotape stimuli, including conversations, were used (Klin et al., 2002; Speer, Cook, McMahon, & Clark, 2007). These mouth fixations may be based on a top-down modulation of fixation, rather than a bottom-up process (Neumann et al., 2006), perhaps in order to compensate for their impairment in dynamic and/or social processing of the face.

Such reduced eye fixation may not be specific to ASD, but shared with broader phenotypes. Dalton, Nacewicz, Alexander, & Davidson, (2007) revealed that individuals who have a sibling with ASD also show fewer fixations to the eyes than typically developing individuals. Merin, Young, Ozonoff and Rogers (2007) reported that even subgroup of 6-months-old infants with sibling with ASD show diminished eye fixations. Note that this diminished eye fixation did not predict later diagnosis of ASD (Young, Merin, Ozonoff, & Rogers, 2009). Thus it suggests that reduced eye fixation is a risk factor that can be shared by unaffected family members of ASD, not directly related to the diagnosis of ASD.

Another important issue of face orienting in ASD is that it may be related to their cortical response to the face. Until recently, both electrophysiological and neuroimaging studies reported atypical neural response to face perception in ASD. Using electrophysiological measurement, some studies found delayed latency (McPartland et al., 2004; O'Connor, Hamm, & Kirk, 2005), weaker amplitude (Bailey, Braeutigam, Jousmaki, & Swithenby, 2005; Kylliäinen, Braeutigam, Hietanen, Swithenby, & Bailey, 2006; O'Connor et al., 2005) and/or weaker lateralization (Bailey et al., 2005; Dawson et al., 2004; McPartland et al., 2004; Senju, Hasagawa, & Tojo, 2005) of face-specific components of electrophysiological response, such as N170, or its equivalents in event-related field (ERF) magnoencephalography. These studies suggest atypical cortical processing, or even atypical localization, of face-processing in individuals with ASD. On the other hand, these studies also demonstrated the face-specificity of N170 (Bailey et al., 2005; Grice et al., 2005; McPartland et al., 2004), which is inconsistent with the claim that individuals with ASD process faces in the same manner as they process objects.

Neuroimaging studies have been focused on the functioning of FFA in individuals with ASD. Early studies consistently found weaker FFA activation, or its absence, in individuals with ASD when they are discriminating identity (Schultz et al., 2000), gender (Hubl et al., 2003; Pierce et al., 2001) or facial expression (Critchley et al., 2000; Hubl et al., 2003; Piggot et al., 2004; Wang et al., 2004) of the presented faces. However, recent studies revealed that individuals with ASD do activate FFA for facial processing under careful experimental control. Hadjikhani et al. (2004, 2007) found FFA activation in ASD; they controlled participants' eye fixation by putting a 'fixation point' on top of the eye region and instructed participants to fixate on it. In addition, Dalton et al. (2005) conducted a concurrent measurement of eye-tracking and functional brain activity with fMRI, and found

that activation in the fusiform gyrus was correlated with the amount of eye fixation in individuals with ASD. These studies suggest that the lack of FFA activation in individuals with ASD found in earlier studies may be based on their reduced eye fixations.

These studies suggest that atypical face/eye orienting contribute to the atypical cortical specialization for face processing in individuals with ASD. A recent study revealed that atypical patterns of face fixation can distort FFA activation even in typically developed adults (Morris, Pelphrey & McCarthy, 2007). It is not yet clear what the neural basis of atypical face/eye orienting in ASD is, but recent studies seem to suggest that atypical functioning or subcortical structures, especially the amygdala, may contribute to it. In typical development, the amygdala is thought to play a critical role in both face orienting (Johnson, 2005) and eye orienting (Adolphs et al., 2005; Spezio, Huang, Castelli, & Adolphs, 2007b). Gliga and Csibra (2007) even claim that these are based on the same mechanism: eye orienting may guide face orienting. In addition, structural- imaging studies revealed atypical structure of the amygdala (for a review, see Brambilla, Hardan, di Nemi, Perez Soares, & Barale, 2003), as well as atypical course of its structural development (Schumann et al., 2004) in individuals with ASD. Thus it is possible that the lack of bias to orient to the face/eyes, possibly due to the atypical functioning of the amygdala, impede the fusiform gyrus to acquire adequate inputs to develop the functional specialization. Other scientists also argue that dysfunction of amygdala impede the perceived salience of the face (Schultz, 2005) or motivation to attend to the face (Dawson. Webb, & McPartland, 2005) and result in the lack of cortical specialization for face processing.

THE DEVELOPMENT OF EYE GAZE PROCESSING

In a previous section we discussed evidence pertaining to the emergence of the social brain network and suggested, based on the existing evidence, that this cortical network gradually becomes increasingly encapsulated from other cortical networks. In this section we turn to specialization within the social brain network, and focus on the processing of information about the eyes of other humans. Rather than a single region being attributed to a single function, from an interactive-specialization viewpoint, specialization within a cortical network concerns differential patterns of activation of regions.

The first investigations of the brain basis of eye gaze processing involved electrophysiological recording in monkeys. In these species, eye gaze has an important regulatory influence on social interaction, and can be used to assert dominance or submission. Perrett and colleagues (Perrett et al. 1982, 1985; 1992) studied the responses of macaque monkey's superior temporal sulcus (STS) cells to the perception of gaze direction. They observed that neurons that were most responsive to viewing a full face preferred eye contact (direct gaze), whereas cells that were tuned to the profile view of a face preferred averted gaze. These results indicated that the brain has evolved mechanisms for interpreting the direction of the eye gaze, and that these mechanisms involve the activation of specific brain regions.

The advent of functional imaging has allowed the study of the neural basis of eye gaze processing in adults. Using these methods, several authors have established that the STS is also important for eye gaze perception in humans (see Allison, Puce, & McCarthy, 2000 for review). The STS region is defined as being the region adjacent to the cortex on the surface of the superior and middle temporal gyri and adjacent to the cortex on the surface of the angular gyrus (see Figure 24.2). Figure 24.2 also shows the distribution of areas of the STS that are related to eye gaze processing, body, and actions (i.e., regions related to biological movements).

Functional imaging studies have also revealed that a network of other cortical areas is activated during the processing of eye gaze. Since the perception of eye gaze involves the detection of movement, one issue is the extent of overlap between structures involved in motion perception and those engaged in eye gaze processing. For example, the eye regions of STS are very close to the MT/V5 area, a structure known to be important for the perception of motion in general. To examine the responses of this latter region, Puce et al. (1998) ran an fMRI experiment in which participants viewed moving eyes, moving mouths, or movements of checkerboard patterns. The results of this study showed that although all three conditions activated the motion area MT/V5, only moving eyes and mouths activated the STS. These results suggest that the STS is preferentially involved in the perception of gaze direction and mouth movements, but not to nonbiological motion. A MEG study by Watanabe, Kakigi, & Puce (2001) found similar results.

Because eyes always occur within the context of a face, another issue is the extent of overlap between the brain basis of eye gaze perception and the regions activated by face processing in general. To address this question Wicker, Michel, Henaff, & Decety (1998) used PET to study the pattern of cortical activation resulting from direct (mutual) eye gaze. They contrasted four experimental conditions; a face with neutral gaze, a face with averted gaze (to the right or left), a face with direction of gaze not visible, and a control condition in which participants kept their eyes closed. The results were that in all three experimental conditions, regardless of direction of gaze, areas related to face processing were activated. These areas included the occipital pole (striate and extrastriate visual cortex) and the occipito-temporal areas, particularly in the right hemisphere. In addition to these regions, other brain regions were activated by processing direction of gaze, including the occipital part of the fusiform gyrus, the right parietal lobule, the right inferior temporal gyrus, and the middle temporal gyrus in both hemispheres. At the subcortical level there was activation in the right amygdala, the right pulvinar, and bilaterally in the middle dorsal thalamic nucleus. However, in this study no conclusive evidence for specific mutual gaze processing areas was described. This result suggests the processing of eye gaze is controlled by a distributed network of brain areas not completely independent of general face processing.

(a)

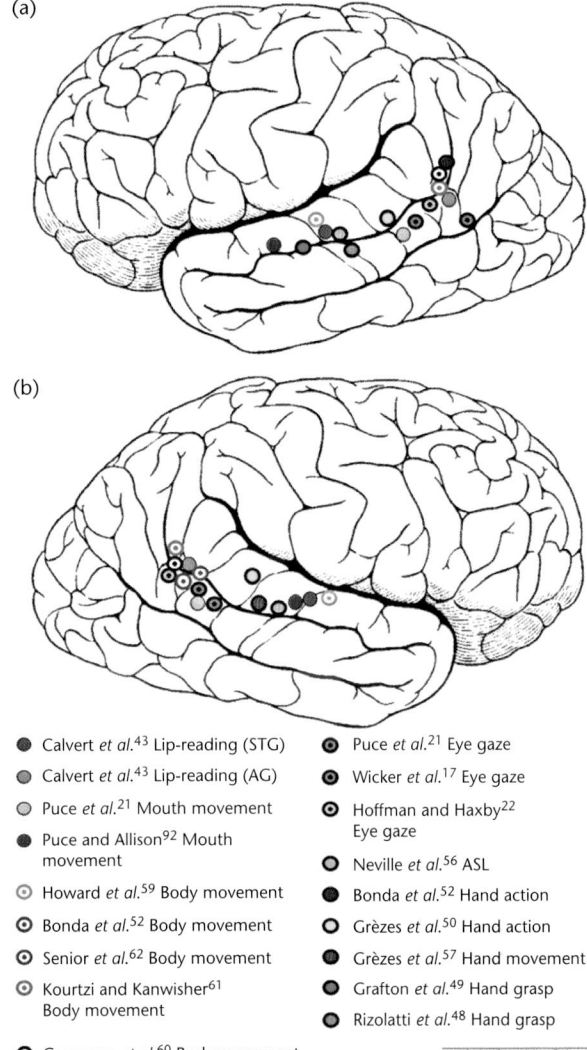

(b)

Figure 24.2 Activation of the Superior Temporal Sulcus (STS) region in the left hemisphere (a) and in the right hemisphere (b) during the perception of biological motion (from Allison et al. 2000). The references cited in the figure can be found in Allison et al., 2000.

● Calvert *et al.*[43] Lip-reading (STG)
● Calvert *et al.*[43] Lip-reading (AG)
● Puce *et al.*[21] Mouth movement
● Puce and Allison[92] Mouth movement
⊙ Howard *et al.*[59] Body movement
⊙ Bonda *et al.*[52] Body movement
⊙ Senior *et al.*[62] Body movement
⊙ Kourtzi and Kanwisher[61] Body movement
⊙ Grossman *et al.*[60] Body movement

◉ Puce *et al.*[21] Eye gaze
◉ Wicker *et al.*[17] Eye gaze
◉ Hoffman and Haxby[22] Eye gaze
○ Neville *et al.*[56] ASL
● Bonda *et al.*[52] Hand action
○ Grèzes *et al.*[50] Hand action
◐ Grèzes *et al.*[57] Hand movement
◑ Grafton *et al.*[49] Hand grasp
◑ Rizolatti *et al.*[48] Hand grasp

trends in Cognitive Sciences

In summary, results reviewed so far indicate substantial overlap between the network of regions involved in gaze processing, and those activated by motion and face processing. Going into development of eye gaze processing, by the end of their first year of life, infants appear to know that the looking behaviors of others conveys significant information. It is commonly agreed that eye gaze perception is important for mother-infant interaction, and that it provides a vital foundation for social development (e.g., Jaffe, Stern, & Peery, 1973). The two questions we address in this section are: first, at what age are infants first able to detect eye gaze direction (i.e., perceiving eye gaze); and second, when are infants able to use direction of eye gaze to influence their own behavior? (i.e., acting on eye gaze).

The significance of mutual gaze in the development of human relationships has been shown in many studies, revealing its function to provide information, to regulate adult-infant interaction, to exercise social control, and to facilitate task goals (Blass & Camp, 2001; Kleinke, 1986).

We (Farroni et al. 2002) tested healthy human newborn infants by presenting them with a pair of stimuli, one a face with eye gaze directed straight at the newborns, and the other with averted gaze. Results showed that the fixation times were significantly longer for the face with the straight gaze. Further, the number of orientations was higher with the straight gaze than with the averted gaze. These results demonstrate preferential orienting to direct eye gaze from birth. The preference is probably a result of a fast and approximate analysis of the visual input, dedicated to find socially relevant stimuli for further processing.

In order to examine the specificity of this newborn preference, we conducted two further experiments. The goal of the first of these was to ascertain whether inverting faces has any effect on gaze perception in newborns. Newborns did not show significant difference in total looking time at the straight gaze and at the averted gaze, and they did not orient more frequently to the direct gaze inverted face than to the other. These results allow us to rule out symmetry and local spatial frequency as possible explanations of the newborn effect. At least two possible types of underlying mechanism for this behavioral phenomenon remain possible. By one account, even newborns have sophisticated face processing abilities sufficient to extract gaze direction when presented in the context of a face. By an alternative account, the preferences of newborns are based on a primitive CONSPEC detector that responds to an optimal configuration of high-contrast elements. Straight-on faces with direct gaze better fit this simple template than do faces with averted gaze (see Farroni et al. 2002, 2003). To test between these hypotheses we conducted another experiment that involved similar face stimuli, but with averted head angles. We reasoned that a sophisticated face-processing system would be able to extract gaze direction even when head angle varied. In contrast, a simple CONSPEC mechanism may only produce a preference for direct gaze under conditions in which the spacing between eyes and mouth is optimal. Changing head angle will alter the relative spacing of the two eyes and mouth, and thus

may disrupt the preference seen with a straight head. In this experiment, newborns did not show significant differences in total looking time at the direct gaze and at the averted gaze, and they did not orient more frequently to the direct gaze face than to the other. The results of these experiments show that the strong preference for faces with direct gaze is dependent on the eyes being situated within the context of an upright straight-ahead face. This finding simultaneously rules out many low-level explanations of the original result, and the suggestion that newborns may have sophisticated eye gaze perception abilities. Rather, the view that newborns orient to direct gaze due to a primitive configuration detection system (such as CONSPEC) gains some credence.

In a second line of experiments, we attempted to gain converging evidence for the differential processing of direct gaze in infants, by recording event related potentials (ERPs) from the scalp as infants viewed faces. We studied 4-month-old babies with the same stimuli as those used in the previous experiment with newborns and found a difference between the two gaze directions at the time and scalp location of a known face-sensitive component of the infant ERP ("infant N170", deHaan et al. 2002). This component of the infant ERP is thought to be the equivalent of a well-studied adult face-sensitive component, and in infants is sensitive to changes in the orientation and species of a face, at least by 12 months of age (Halit et al. 2003). Thus, our conclusion from these studies is that direct eye contact enhances the perceptual processing of faces in 4-month-old infants. This suggests a fast mechanism of gaze direction analysis that may precede the full processing of faces. This hypothesis is also supported by adults' data. An fMRI study by George et al. (2001), investigated how gaze direction (direct or averted), influences face processing using a gender-recognition task. They presented a face with direct or averted gaze, and the face was either a frontal view or tilted at 45 degrees. They observed that specific regions of the fusiform gyrus yielded stronger responses to faces when these looked directly at the subject (regardless of the orientation of the head). This suggests that there may be deeper encoding of faces when gaze is directed at the observer.

In order to examine further the specificity of these eye gaze processing effects, we conducted two more ERP experiments with 4-month olds. As in the newborn experiments, it remains possible that low-level aspects of the stimuli, such as symmetry or local spatial frequency differences, could have contributed to the effects observed. Further, the importance of an upright face configuration is unknown. For these reasons we conducted a high-density ERP experiment with a group of 4-month-olds using the same inverted-face stimuli employed in the earlier newborn study. No modulation of the "infant N170" was observed in this experiment, showing that under conditions of face inversion gaze direction does not modulate face processing. The clear difference in ERP results obtained in the two experiments with 4-month-olds also allows us to rule out symmetry and local spatial frequency as contributors to the gaze effect with upright faces. A further question is whether the cortical processing of faces is modulated by gaze direction in the context of an averted head. The ability to extract gaze direction under these circumstances would suggest a more sophisticated mechanism of processing than that we observed in newborns. The results of this experiment were more complicated, but showed an effect of direct gaze on face processing when the head was angled to the left. This effect of head angle on gaze processing is remarkably consistent with reports from adults indicating that there is a left visual field (right hemisphere) bias for various aspects of face processing including gaze cueing (Ricciardelli, Ro, & Driver, 2002).

Another issue that we investigated is the ability of infants to act on eye gaze. Several studies have demonstrated that gaze cues are able to trigger an automatic and rapid shifting of the focus of the viewer's visual attention (Driver et al, 1999; Friesen & Kingstone, 1998; Langton & Bruce,1999). All these studies used variants of Posner's (1980) spatial-cueing paradigm, where a central or peripheral cue directs the attention to one of the peripheral locations. When the target appears in the same location where the cue was directed (the congruent position),

the participant is faster to look at that target compared to another target at an incongruent position relative to the previous cue. Using this paradigm Schuller and Rossion, (2001) presented a face on the screen that was first looking to the subject and then either to the right or the left. Then a target appeared, which could be in the same position where the face was looking or in the opposite position. The results with adults were that facilitation of visual processing by spatial attention is reflected in enhanced early visual evoked potentials (P1 and N1). Reflexive attention increases visual activity and speeds up the processing of visual attention. Probably, in addition to the areas discussed before, eye gaze tasks activate regions involved in covert attention such as parts of parietal cortex.

When does the ability to use eye gaze direction as an attentional cue start? Human infants start to discriminate and follow adults' direction of attention at the age of 3 or 4 months (Hood, Willen & Driver, 1998; Vecera & Johnson, 1995; Farroni et al., 2000). In a more recent study (Farroni, Massaccesi, Lai, & Johnson, 2004) we examined further the visual properties of the eyes that enable infants to follow the direction of the gaze. We tested 4-month-olds using a cueing paradigm adapted from Hood et al. (1998), and the results suggested that critical features for eye gaze cue in infants are: the movement of the pupils, and not the final direction of the pupils; the context of an upright face; and a brief preceding period of eye contact with an upright face (Farroni et al., 2000; 2004). Farroni et al. (2004) extended this finding further to show that the direction of the motion of eyes by shifting pupils can guide looking behavior in newborns as well. Specifically, we have established that newborns are (1) sensitive to direct gaze, and (2) influenced by the direction of motion of elements in an array suggesting a surprising degree of competence in the perception and processing of eye-related information by newborns, and may be an important foundation stone on which more sophisticated social cognitive abilities are later constructed.

Recently, we have examined three further aspects of the neurodevelopment of eye gaze processing. In the first of these, we have assessed whether, like older children and adults, the deeper encoding of faces when accompanied by direct gaze leads to better individual recognition (Farroni Massaccesi, Menon, & Johnson, 2007). Specifically, we habituated groups of 4-month-old infants to individual faces with either direct gaze or averted gaze. We then assessed the extent of novelty preferences in a paired comparison test between the habituated face and a novel one. Infants that had been exposed to the face with direct gaze subsequently showed a stronger novelty preference in the test, providing evidence that they had encoded the habituation face more deeply. Time to habituation did not predict novelty preference, allowing us to rule out the simpler explanation that it is the longer looking time to faces with direct gaze that determines better processing. Rather, it seems that increased covert attention to, or deeper processing of, faces with direct gaze is the likely explanation. In a second line of recent research, we have begun to investigate whether such abilities might exist in newborns. To maximize our likelihood of success, we used large schematic faces with targets located close to the stimulus head. Under such conditions, we observed that even newborns oriented preferentially to targets cued by the direction of gaze. Although this study requires replication, together with our previous results on the detection of direct (mutual) gaze, it suggests that newborns may possess the same mechanisms we have identified at 4 months of age.

Further question will be that whether such early gaze-following behaviors are based on the understanding of referential nature of the gaze (Csibra & Gergely, 2006), or on a simpler mechanism that reflexively shifts attention toward others' gaze direction (e.g., Butterworth & Jarrett, 1991; Moore & Corkum, 1994). Recent findings revealed that infants younger than 1-year-olds seem to encode the relations between gaze direction and the location of the object being looked at. Csibra and Volein (2008) found that 8-month-old infants expect the presence of an object at a hidden location targeted by adult's gaze. Johnson, Ok, & Luo, (2007) also found

that 9-month-old infants appear to encode the relations between the actor and the target of her gaze. In addition, Senju and colleagues (Senju, Johnson & Csibra, 2006; Senju, Csibra & Johnson, 2008) found that 9-month-old infants encode the relations between the gaze direction and object location, and are biased to look at the object-directed gaze. These studies suggest that by around 8 or 9 months after birth, infants have the ability to encode the relation between gaze and object, and possibly prefer to watch referential gaze.

These results indicate that the processing of eye gaze is specialized into a different pattern of activation of regions within the social brain network from the general processing of faces, along with the course of development.

ATYPICAL DEVELOPMENT OF EYE GAZE PROCESSING

Failure to develop typical mutual gaze behavior is one of the core symptoms of severe social and communicative disorders, or of autism (American Psychiatric Association, 2000; Baron-Cohen, 1995). As we reviewed earlier in this chapter, individuals with ASD fixate less to others' eyes compared to typically developing individuals (Dalton et al., 2005; Klin et al., 2002; Neumann et al., 2006; Pelphrey et al., 2002; Spezio, Adolphs et al., 2007, but see also van der Geest et al., 2002b), and rely less on the information from others' eye region for face processing (e.g., Joseph & Tanaka, 2003; Langdell, 1978; Rutherford et al., 2007; Spezio, Adolphs et al., 2007). In addition, impairment in the development of gaze following behavior is consistently reported as well (Landry & Loveland, 1988; Leekam et al, 1997; Leekman, Lopez, & Moore, 2000, Loveland & Landry, 1986; Mundy Sigman, Ungerer, & Sherman, 1986). Atypical joint attention behavior in early development, including the lack of gaze following, is also reported to be one of the best predictors of the emergence of ASD (Charman, 2003).

In this section, we will summarize atypical eye gaze processing in individuals with ASD, both in gaze direction detection (i.e., perceiving eye gaze) and in following the gaze and finding objects being looked at (i.e., acting on eye gaze).

To date, there are not many studies investigated eye contact detection in individuals with ASD, and results are (apparently) inconsistent. Some studies reported intact, or even over-represented, direct gaze processing in ASD (Elsabbagh et al., 2009; Grice et al., 2005; Kylliäinen et al., 2006; Kylliäinen & Hietanen, 2006). Grice et al. (2005) recorded EEGs from young children with autism (3.5–7 years old) and age-matched typically developing children, and found that in children with ASD, faces with direct gaze elicited larger N290 than faces with averted gaze (Figure 24.3). In contrast, N290 did not discriminate gaze direction in typically developing children. Recent study from our group replicated similar trends in

infants (6–14 months old) at high risk for ASD (Elsabbagh et al., 2009). Kylliäinen et al. (2006) recorded MEG from slightly older children with ASD (7–12 years old). In children with ASD, faces with direct gaze elicited larger MEG signal in left occipito-temporal region. In typically developing children, on the other hand, it was faces with averted gaze that elicited larger signals, in the right occipito-temporal region. In addition, Kylliäinen and Hietanen (2006) recorded skin conductance ratio (SCR) while children (7-14 years old) were watching a looming face with direct or averted gaze. Results revealed that children with ASD elicited larger SCR response for perceived direct gaze compared to averted gaze. Typically developing children did not show such preferential SCR response to perceived direct gaze. These studies suggest that perception of direct gaze recruits

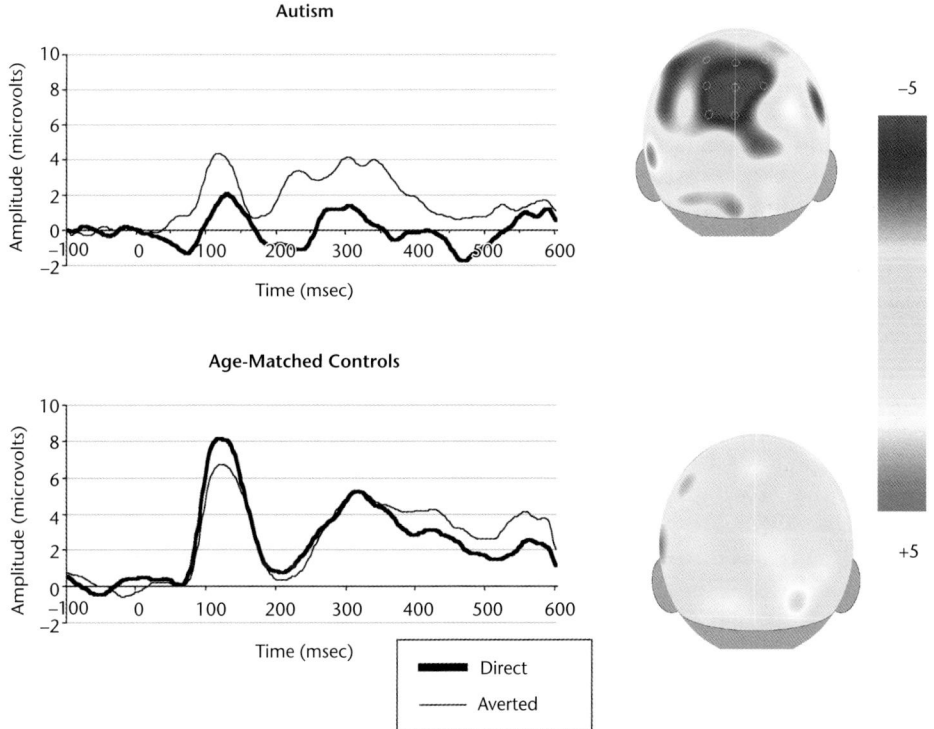

Figure 24.3 ERP waveform averaged across electrodes included in mid-line N170 channel group for direct and averted gaze a) autism group b) age matched controls and relative spherical spline interpolations for the surface distribution of the average amplitude difference obtained for direct minus averted gaze (see Grice et al. 2005).

additional neural and physiological activity in children with ASD, but not in typically developing children.

However, other studies reported the opposite findings. Senju et al. (2003, 2005a) conducted a series of behavioral studies with school age children with ASD as well as typically developing children (9–14 years old), and found that typically developing children were better at detecting direct gaze than averted gaze. In contrast, gaze direction did not affect performance of children with ASD. Senju et al. (2005b) also recorded EEGs, and found that faces with direct gaze, compared to those with averted gaze elicited larger ERP components in the bilateral occipito-temporal region. Again, ERPs did not discriminate between faces with direct and averted gaze in children with ASD. These studies suggest that direct gaze facilitates cognitive and neural processing in typically developing children, but not in children with ASD.

Why do children with ASD show sensitivities to perceived direct gaze in some studies, but not in others? One possibility is that the facial orientation of the stimuli affects direct gaze processing in ASD. In the studies that found intact, or over-represented, direct gaze processing in ASD (Grice et al., 2005; Kylliäinen et al., 2006; Kylliäinen & Hietanen, 2006) used front-view faces as the stimuli. In contrast, in the studies that found impairment in direct gaze processing in ASD (Senju et al., 2003, 2005a, 2005b), the stimuli were laterally oriented faces. These studies may suggest that the facilitative effect of perceived direct gaze in ASD is limited to those within the context of front-view faces, and is not generalized to those within laterally oriented faces. To examine this possibility, one of the authors have conducted a follow-up study (Senju et al., 2008), using the same visual search paradigm as Senju et al. (2005a) except that front-view faces, not laterally oriented faces, were used as stimuli. Results found the facilitative effect of direct gaze in the performance of ASD, as well as in typically developing children. This finding corroborates the earlier argument and suggests that eye contact of the front-view

face, but not that of the laterally averted face, facilitates face detection in individuals with ASD.

These results show a surprising remembrance with newborn's results, where the manipulation of head angle eliminated preference for direct gaze. It may even suggest that children with ASD lack the expertise to the eye gaze processing that is achieved in first few months of typical development. Further study will be required to test the developmental specialization for gaze processing in individuals with ASD.

Studies with attentional cueing paradigm generally found that individuals with ASD shift their attention toward the gaze direction just as typically developing individuals do (Kemner et al., 2006; Kylliäinen & Hietanen, 2004; Okada et al., 2003; Senju, Tojo, Dairoku, & Hasagawa, 2004; Swettenham et al., 2003; Vlaming, Stauder, van Son, & Mottron, 2005, but see also Johnson et al., 2005; Ristic et al., 2005). However, some of these studies also report the differences between individuals with ASD and typically developing individuals.

Senju et al. (2004) compared the size of the cueing effect between gaze cue and nonsocial cue (arrow), and found that the eye gaze elicits larger cueing effect than an arrow for typically developing children, but such predominance of gaze cue over arrow cue was not found in children with ASD. Vlaming et al. (2005) also compared gaze cue and arrow cue, and reported that (1) eye gaze cues were processed slower than arrow cues in typically developing adults, but processing speed did not differ between gaze and arrow cues in adults with ASD, and (2) the cueing effect for eye gaze were only significant in right, but not in left, visual field in typically developing adults, but such asymmetry was not found for eye gaze cues in adults with ASD. In addition, Ristic et al. (2005) used schematic faces as the stimuli, instead of photographic stimuli used in most of the other studies (Johnson et al., 2005, Kylliäinen & Hietanen, 2004; Okada et al., 2003; Senju et al., 2004; Swettenham et al., 2003; Vlaming et al., 2005), and found no cueing effect in ASD, except when the gaze cue is predictive (i.e., target appears to the gazed side in 80 percent of the trials). These studies suggest that the mechanism underlying gaze cueing in ASD is different from that in typically developing individuals, even though both apparently show similar behavior. Moreover, Johnson et al. (2005) examined young children with ASD (2–5 years old), as well as those with language delay and typically developing children with gaze cueing task, and found that young children with ASD do not show gaze cueing effect. This study is in line with other gaze following studies (e.g., Leekam, Hunnisett, & Moore,1998) and suggests that the development of gaze following in ASD is either delayed or divergent from that of typically developing individuals.

Although it is reported that children with ASD acquire gaze following during development, it is possible that they have difficulty in encoding the referential information from others' gazes. Previous studies have revealed that children with ASD have difficulty inferring desire of the protagonist from his/her gaze direction (Ames & Jarrold, 2007; Baron-Cohen et al., 1995). It is unlikely that this deficit comes from a general impairment in representing a goal, because children with ASD show intact goal inference in other tasks (Carpenter, Pennington, & Rogers, 2001). In addition, other studies found that children with ASD do not refer to the speaker's gaze in word learning (Baron-Cohen, Baldwin, & Crowson, 1997). These studies suggest that children with ASD have difficulty in encoding gaze-object relations and referring to others' gazes. Moreover, Pelphrey, Morris, & McCarthy, (2005) found that even adults with ASD do not encode gaze-object relations in the same manner as typically developing individuals. In their study, adults with ASD and typically developed adults observed the gaze shift of a computer-generated face. For some trials, the face looked toward a target object, but in other trials the face looked at an empty place. fMRI recording revealed that typically developed participants elicited larger activity in right superior temporal sulcus, as well as left inferior parietal sulcus, in response

to the perception of nonobject-directed gaze shift, compared to object-directed gaze shift. In participants with ASD, however, the activation in these regions did not discriminate the gaze-object relations. This study suggests that the neural substrates that encode gaze-object relations in typically developing individuals are impaired or they do not develop in the same manner as in typical development in individuals with ASD.

To summarize, these studies suggest that the processing of eye gaze is subserved by atypical neural substrates in individuals with ASD, and their characteristics of gaze processing changes with development. It may also indicate the failure to develop cortical specialization for gaze processing, and/or developing compensatory mechanism to process gaze, in individuals with ASD.

DISCUSSION

The empirical evidence we and others have gathered on the development and neural basis of face and eye gaze processing in typical and atypical developmental populations is consistent with an interactive-specialization perspective on functional brain development (Johnson & de Haan, 1999). Contrary to the view that there are innate mechanisms, interactive specialization emphasises the importance of the gradual specialization of individual regions through their emerging role within brain networks starting from a few initial predispositions (see Johnson & de Haan, 1999 for further details). Focussing on the first of these aspects of interactive specialization, we (Farroni et al. 2002) suggest that a primitive representation of high-contrast elements (such as Johnson & Morton's Conspec) would be sufficient to direct orienting in newborns toward faces with eye contact. Therefore, the more frequent orienting to the direct gaze in newborns could be mediated by the same mechanism that underlies newborns' tendency to orient to faces in general. Specifically, Johnson and Morton (1991) hypothesised that subcortical circuits supported a primitive representation of high-contrast elements relating to the location of the eyes and mouth. A face with direct gaze would better fit the spatial relation of elements in this template than one with gaze averted, suggesting that the functional role of this putative mechanism is more general than previously supposed. This primitive bias ensures a biased input of human faces with direct gaze to the infant over the first days and weeks of life.

According to the interactive-specialization view, a network as a whole becomes specialized for a particular function. Therefore, we suggest that the eye region of the STS does not develop in isolation, or in a modular fashion, but that its functionality emerges within the context of interacting regions involved in either general face processing or in motion detection. Viewed from this perspective, STS may be a region that integrates motion information with the processing of faces (and other body parts). Although STS may be active in infants, we propose that it is not yet efficiently integrating motion and face information. By this account, making eye contact with upright face fully engages face processing, which then facilitates the orienting of attention by lateral motion. At older ages, eye gaze perception becomes a fully integrated function where even static presentations of averted eyes are sufficient to facilitate gaze.

From this perspective, atypical development can involve a failure of specialization of, and within, the social brain network. Preliminary evidence relating to this hypothesis from children, as well as adults with ASD was presented and discussed. General symptoms of such a failure will include partial or complete failure to develop the modular organization characteristic of adult social cognition. It will also include the application of atypical stimulus processing to social stimuli, which may partly compensate for the lack of functional specialization in early development. Finally, we believe that it is only through studying both typical and atypical development with the same tasks and methods that progress in the comprehension of the development of social brain will be made.

REFERENCES

Adolphs, R. (2003). Cognitive neuroscience of human social behaviour. *Nature Reviews Neuroscience, 4*, 165–178.

Adolphs, R., Gosselin, F., Buchanan, T. W., Tranel, D., Schyns, P., & Damasio, A. R. (2005). A mechanism for impaired fear recognition after amygdala damage. *Nature, 433*, 68–72.

Allison, T., Puce, A. & McCarthy, G. (2000). Social perception from visual cues: role of STS region. *Trends in Cognitive Sciences, 4*, 267–278.

American Psychiatric Association (2000). *Diagnostic and statistical manual of mental disorders fourth edition: Text revision.* Washington, DC: Author.

Ames, C. S., & Jarrold, C. (2007). The problem with using eye–gaze to infer desire: A deficit of cue inference in children with autism spectrum disorder? *Journal of Autism and Developmental Disorders, 37*, 1761–1775.

Argyle, M., & Cook, M. (1976). *Gaze and Mutual Gaze.* New York: Cambridge University Press.

Bailey, A. J., Braeutigam, S., Jousmaki, V., & Swithenby, S. J. (2005). Abnormal activation of face processing systems at early and intermediate latency in individuals with autism spectrum disorder: a magnetoencephalographic study. *European Journal of Neuroscience, 21*, 2575–2585.

Baranek, G. T. (1999). Autism during infancy: a retrospective video analysis of sensory–motor and social behaviors at 9–12 months of age. *Journal of Autism and Developmental Disorders, 29*, 213–224.

Baron–Cohen, S. (1995). *Mindblindness: An essay on autism and theory of mind.* Cambridge, MA: MIT Press.

Baron–Cohen, S., Baldwin, D. A., & Crowson, M. (1997). Do children with autism use the speaker's direction of gaze strategy to crack the code of language? *Child Development, 68*, 48–57.

Baron–Cohen, S., Campbell, R., Karmiloff–Smith, A., Grant, J., & Walker, J. (1995). Are children with autism blind to the mentalistic significance of the eyes? *British Journal of Developmental Psychology, 13*, 379–398.

Batki, A., Baron–Cohen, S., Wheelwright, S., Connellan, J., & Ahluwalia, J. (2000). Is there an innate module? Evidence from human neonates. *Infant Behavior & Development, 23*, 223–229.

Bentin, S., Allison, T., Puce, A., Perez, E., & McCarthy, G. (1996). Electrophysiological studies of face perception in humans. *Journal of Cognitive Neuroscience, 8*, 551–565.

Blass, E.M. & Camp, C.A. (2001). The ontogeny of face recognition: eye contact and sweet taste induce face preference in 9– and 12–week–old human infants. *Developmental Psychology, 37*, 762–774.

Boucher, J., & Lewis, V. (1992). Unfamiliar face recognition in relatively able autistic children. *Journal of Child Psychology and Psychiatry, 33*, 843–859.

Boucher, J., Lewis, V., & Collis, G. (1998). Familiar face and voice matching and recognition in children with autism. *Journal of Child Psychology and Psychiatry, 39*, 171–181.

Brambilla, P., Hardan, A., di Nemi, S. U., Perez J., Soares, J. C., & Barale, F. (2003). Brain anatomy and development in autism: review of structural MRI studies. *Brain Research Bulletin, 61*, 557–569.

Butterworth, G. & Jarrett, N. (1991). What minds have in common is space: spatial mechanisms serving joint visual attention in infancy. *British Journal of Developmental Psychology, 9*, 55–72.

Carpenter, M., Pennington, B. F., & Rogers, S. J. (2001). Understanding of others' intentions in children with autism. *Journal of Autism and Developmental Disorders, 31*, 589–599.

Charman, T. (2003). Why is joint attention a pivotal skill in autism? *Philosophical Transactions of the Royal Society of London B: Biological Sciences, 358*, 315–324.

Cicchetti, D. (1984). The Emergence of Developmental Psychopathology. *Child Development, 55*, 1–7.

Cicchetti, D. (1991). Fractures in the crystal: Developmental Psychopathology and the emergence of the self. *Developmental Review, 11*, 271–287.

Clifford, S., Young, R., & Williamson, P. (2007). Assessing the early characteristics of autistic disorder using video analysis. *Journal of Autism and Developmental Disorders, 37*, 301–313.

Critchley, H. D., Daly, E, M., Bullmore, E. T., Williams, S. C. R., Van Amelsvoort, T., Robertson, D. M., Rowe, A., Phillips, M., McAlonan, G., Howlin, P. & Murphy, D. G. M. (2000). The functional neuroanatomy of social behavior: Changes in cerebral blood flow when people with autistic disorder process facial expressions. *Brain, 123*, 2203–2212.

Csibra, G., & Gergely, G. (2006). Social learning and social cognition: The case for pedagogy. In Y. Munakata & M. H. Johnson (Eds.), *Processes of change in brain and cognitive development. Attention and Performance XXI* (pp. 249–274). Oxford: Oxford University Press.

Csibra, G. & Volein, Á. (2008). Infants can infer the presence of hidden objects from referential gaze information. *British Journal of Developmental Psychology, 26*, 1–11.

Dalton, K. M., Nacewicz, B. M., Alexander, A. L., & Davidson, R. J. (2007). Gaze–fixation, brain activation, and amygdala volume in unaffected siblings of individuals with autism. *Biological Psychiatry, 61*, 512–520.

Dalton, K. M., Nacewicz, B. M., Johnstone, T., Schaefer, H. S., Gernsbacher, M. A., Goldsmith, H. H., Alexander, A. L., & Davidson, R. J. (2005). Gaze fixation and the neural circuitry of face processing in autism. *Nature Neuroscience, 8*, 519–526.

Dawson, G., Webb, S. J., Carver, L., Panagiotides, H., & McPartland, J. (2004). Young children with autism show atypical brain responses to fearful versus neutral facial expressions of emotion. *Developmental Science, 7*, 340–359.

Dawson, G., Webb, S. J., & McPartland, J. (2005). Understanding the nature of face processing impairment in autism: Insights from behavioral and electrophysiological studies. *Developmental Neuropsychology, 27*, 403–424.

Davies, S., Bishop, D., Manstead, A. S., & Tantam, D. (1994). Face perception in children with autism and Asperger's syndrome. *Journal of Child Psychology and Psychiatry, 35*, 1033–1057.

de Haan, M., Johnson, M. H., & Halit, H. (2003). Development of face–sensitive event–related potentials during infancy: a review. *International Journal of Psychophysiology, 51*, 45–58.

de Haan, M., Pascalis, O. & Johnson, M.H. (2002). Specialization of neural mechanisms underlying face recognition in human infants. *Journal of Cognitive Neuroscience, 14*, 199–209.

Driver, J., Davis, G., Ricciardelli, P., Kidd, P., Maxwell, E. & Baron–Cohen, S. (1999). Gaze perception triggers reflexive visuospatial orienting. *Visual Cognition, 6*, 509–540.

Eimer, M. (2000). The face-specific N170 component reflects late stages in the structural encoding of faces. *Neuroreport, 11,* 2319–2324.

Easterbrook, M.A., Kisilevsky, B.S. , Hains S.M.J., and Muir D.W., Faceness or complexity: Evidence from newborn visual tracking of face-like stimuli. *Infant Behavior and Development 22* (1999), pp. 17–35.

Farroni, T., Csibra, G., Simion, F. & Johnson, M.H. (2002). Eye contact detection in humans from birth. *Proceeding of the National Academy of Sciences U S A, 99,* 9602–9605.

Farroni, T., Johnson, M. H., Menon, E., Zulian, L., Faraguna, D., & Csibra, G. (2005). Newborns' preference for face-relevant stimuli: effects of contrast polarity. *Proceedings of National Academy of Science USA, 102*(47), 17245–17250.

Farroni, T, Mansfield, E. M. Lai C. & Johnson M. H., (2003). Motion and mutual gaze in directing infants' spatial attention. *Journal Experimental Child Psychology, 85,* 199–212.

Farroni, T., Massaccesi, S., Pividori, D., & Johnson, M. H. (2004). Gaze Following in Newborns. *Infancy, 5,* 39–60.

Farroni, T., Massaccesi, S., Menon, E., and Johnson, H.M. (2007). Direct gaze modulates face recognition in young infants. *Cognition 102 (3),* 396–404.

Farroni, T., Valenza, E., Simion, F., & Umilta, C. (2000). Configural processing at birth: evidence for perceptual organisation. *Perception, 29*(3), 355–372.

Friesen, C.K. & Kingstone, A. (1998). The eyes have it! Reflexive orienting is triggered by nonpredictive gaze. *Psychonomic Bulletin & Review, 5,* 490–495.

Gauthier, I., Tarr, M. J., Anderson, A. W., Skudlarski, P., & Gore, J. C. (1999). Activation of the middle fusiform "face area" increases with expertise in recognizing novel objects. *Nature Neuroscience, 2,* 568–573.

George, N., Driver, J. & Dolan, R.J. (2001). Seen gaze-direction modulates fusiform activity and its coupling with other brain areas during face processing. *Neuroimage, 13,* 1102–1112.

George, N., Evans, J., Fiori, N., Davidoff, J., & Renault, B. (1996). Brain events related to normal and moderately scrambled faces. *Cognitive Brain Research, 4,* 65–76.

Gepner, B., de Gelder, B., & de Schonen, S. (1996). Face processing in autistics: Evidence for a generalised deficit? *Child Neuropsychology, 2,* 123–139.

Grice, S.J., Halit, H., Farroni, T., Baron–Cohen, S., Bolton, P & Johnson, M.H. (2005). Neural Correlates of Eye–Gaze Detection in Young Children with Autism. *Cortex 3,* 277–281.

Gliga, T. & Csibra, G. (2007). Seeing the face through the eyes: A developmental perspective on face expertise. *Progress in Brain Research, 164,* 323–339.

Hadjikhani, N., Joseph, R. M., Snyder, J., Chabris, C. F., Clarka, J., Steele, S., McGrath, L., Vangel, M., Aharon, I., Feczko, E., Harris, G. J., & Tager–Flusberg, H. (2004). Activation of the fusiform gyrus when individuals with autism spectrum disorder view faces. *NeuroImage, 22,* 1141–1150.

Hadjikhani, N., Joseph, R. M., Snyder, J., & Tager–Flusberg, H. (2007). Abnormal activation of the social brain during face perception in autism. *Human Brain Mapping, 28,* 441–449.

Halit, H., Csibra, G., Volein, A., & Johnson, M. H. (2004). Face-sensitive cortical processing in early infancy. *Journal of Child Psychology and Psychiatry, 45,* 1228–1234.

Halit, H., de Haan, M. & Johnson, M.H. (2003). Cortical specialization for face processing: Face-sensitive eve–related potential components in 3 and 12 month old infants. *NeuroImage 1,* 1180–1193.

Hauck, M., Fein, D., Maltby, N., Waterhouse, L., & Feinstein, C. (1998). Memory for faces in children with autism. *Child Neuropsychology, 4,* 187–198.

Haxby, J. V., Hoffman, E. A., & Gobbini, M. I. (2000). The distributed human neural system for face perception. *Trends in Cognitive Sciences, 4*(6), 223–233.

Haxby, J.V., Hoffman, E.A. & Gobbini, M.I. (2002). Human neural systems for face recognition and social communication. *Biological Psychiatry, 51,* 59–67.

Hietanen, J. K. (1999). Does your gaze direction and head orientation shift my visual attention? *Neuroreport, 10,* 3443–3447.

Hood, B. M., Macrae, C. N., Cole-Davies, V., & Dias, M. (2003). Eye remember you: the effects of gaze direction on face recognition in children and adults. *Developmental Science, 6,* 67–71.

Hood, B. M., Willen, J.D. & Driver, J. (1998). Adult's eyes trigger shifts of visual attention in human infants. *Psychological Science, 9,* 131–134.

Hubl, D., Bolte, S., Feineis–Matthews, S., Lanfermann, H., Federspiel, A., Strik, W., Poustka, F., & Dierks, T. (2003). Functional imbalance of visual pathways indicates alternative face processing strategies in autism. *Neurology, 61*, 1232–1237.

Jaffe, J., Stern, D.N. & Peery, J.C. (1973). "Conversational" coupling of gaze behavior in prelinguistic human development. *Journal of Psycholinguistic Research, 2*, 321–329.

Jemel, B., Mottron, L., & Dawson, M. (2006). Impaired face processing in autism: fact or artifact? *Journal of Autism and Developmental Disorders, 36*, 91–106.

Johnson, M. H. (2005). Subcortical face processing. *Nature Reviews Neuroscience, 6*, 766–774.

Johnson, M.H. & de Haan, M. (1999). Developing cortical specialization for visual–cognitive function: The case of face recognition. In J.L. McClelland & R.S.Seigler(Eds.), *Mechanisms of Cognitive Development: Behavioral and Neural Perspectives*. New Jersey: Lawrence Erlbaum Associates.

Johnson, M. H. (2001). Functional brain development in humans. *Nature Reviews Neuroscience, 2*, 475–483.

Johnson, M. H., Griffin, R., Csibra, G., Halit, H., Farroni, T., de Haan, M., Tucker, L., Baron–Cohen, S., & Richards, J. (2005). The emergence of the social brain network: Evidence from typical and atypical development. *Development and Psychopathology, 17*, 599–619.

Johnson, M. H., & Morton, J. (1991). *Biology and cognitive development*. Oxford: Blackwell.

Johnson, S. C., Ok, S., & Luo, Y. (2007). The attribution of attention: Nine–month–olds' interpretation of gaze as goal–directed action. *Developmental Science, 10*, 530–537.

Joseph, R. M., & Tanaka, J. (2003). Holistic and part–based face recognition in children with autism. *Journal of Child Psychology and Psychiatry, 44*, 529–542.

Kanwisher, N., McDermott, J. & Chun, M. M. (1997). The fusiform face area: a module in human extrastriate cortex specialized for face perception. *Journal of Neuroscience, 17*, 4302–4311.

Kemner, C., Schuller, A. M., & van Engeland, H. (2006). Electrocortical reflections of face and gaze processing in children with pervasive developmental disorder. *Journal of Child Psychology and Psychiatry, 47*, 1063–1072.

Kleinke, C.L. (1986). Gaze and eye contact: a research review. *Psychological Bulletin, 100*, 78–100.

Klin, A., Jones, W., Schultz, R., Volkmar, F., & Cohen, D. (2002). Visual fixation patterns during viewing of naturalistic social situations as predictors of social competence in individuals with autism. *Archives of General Psychiatry, 59*, 809–816.

Klin, A., Sparrow, S. S., de Bildt, A., Cicchetti, D. V., Cohen, D. J. & Volkmar, F. R. (1999). A normed study of face recognition in autism and related disorders. *Journal of Autism and Developmental Disorders, 29*, 499–508.

Kylliäinen, A., Braeutigam, S., Hietanen, J. K., Swithenby, S. J., & Bailey, A. J. (2006). Face– and gaze–sensitive neural responses in children with autism: A magnetoencephalographic study. *European Journal of Neuroscience, 24*, 2679–2690.

Kylliäinen, A., & Hietanen, J. K. (2004). Attention orienting by another's gaze direction in children with autism. *Journal of Child Psychology and Psychiatry, 43*, 435–444.

Kylliäinen, A., & Hietanen, J. K. (2006). Skin conductance responses to another person's gaze in children with autism. *Journal of Autism and Developmental Disorders, 36*, 517–525.

Landry, S. H., & Loveland, K. A. (1988). Communication behaviors in autism and developmental language delay. *Journal of Child Psychology and Psychiatry, 29*, 621–634.

Langdell, T. (1978). Recognition of faces: an approach to the study of autism. *Journal of Child Psychology and Psychiatry, 19*, 255–268.

Langton, S.R.H. & Bruce, V. (1999). Reflexive visual orienting in response to the social attention of others. *Visual Cognition, 6*, 541–567.

Langton, S. R., Watt, R. J., & Bruce, V. (2000). Do the eyes have it? Cues to the direction of social attention. *Trends in Cognitive Sciences, 4*, 50–59.

Leekam, S., Baron–Cohen, S., Perrett, D., Milders, M., & Brown, S. (1997). Eye–direction detection: A dissociation between geometric and joint attention skills in autism. *British Journal of Developmental Psychology, 15*, 77–95.

Leekam, S. R., Hunnisett, E., & Moore, C. (1998). Targets and cues: Gaze–following in children with autism. *Journal of Child Psychology and Psychiatry, 39*, 951–962.

Leekam, S. R., Lopez, B., & Moore, C. (2000). Attention and joint attention in preschool children with autism. *Developmental Psychology, 26*, 261–273.

Loveland, K. A., & Landry, S. H. (1986). Joint attention and language in autism and developmental language delay. *Journal of Autism and Developmental Disorders, 16*, 335–349.

Maestro, S., Muratori, F., Cavallaro, M. C., Pecini, C., Cesari, A., Paziente, A., Stern, D., Golse, B., & Palacio-Espasa, F. (2005). How young children treat objects and people: An empirical study of the first year of life in autism. *Child Psychiatry and Human Development, 35*, 383–396.

McCarthy, G., Puce, A., Belger, A., & Allison, T. (1999). Electrophysiological studies of human face perception. II: Response properties of face–specific potentials generated in occipitotemporal cortex. *Cerebral Cortex, 9*, 431–444.

McPartland, J., Dawson, G., Webb, S. J., Panagiotides, H., & Carver, L. J. (2004). Event–related brain potentials reveal anomalies in temporal processing of faces in autism spectrum disorder. *Journal of Child Psychology and Psychiatry, 45*, 1235–1245.

Merin, N., Young, G. S., Ozonoff, S., & Rogers, S. J. (2007). Visual fixation patterns during reciprocal social interaction distinguish a subgroup of 6–month–old infants at–risk for autism from comparison infants. *Journal of Autism and Developmental Disorders, 37*, 108–121.

Moore, C. & Corkum, V. (1994). Social understanding at the end of first year of life. *Developmental Review, 14*, 19–40.

Morris, J. P., Pelphrey, K. A., & McCarthy, G. (2007). Controlled scanpath variation alters fusiform face activation. *Social Cognitive and Affective Neuroscience, 2*, 31–38.

Morton, J. & Johnson, M.H. (1991). CONSPEC and CONLERN: A two–process theory of infant face recognition. *Psychological Review, 98*, 164–181.

Mundy, P., Sigman, M., Ungerer, J., & Sherman, T. (1986). Defining the social deficits of autism: The contribution of non–verbal communication measures. *Journal of Child Psychology and Psychiatry, 27*, 657–669.

Neumann, D., Spezio, M. L., Piven, J., & Adolphs, R. (2006). Looking you in the mouth: Abnormal gaze in autism resulting from impaired top–down modulation of visual attention. *Social Cognitive and Affective Neuroscience, 1*, 194–202.

O'Connor, K., Hamm, J. P., & Kirk, I. J. (2005). The neurophysiological correlates of face processing in adults and children with Asperger's syndrome. *Brain and Cognition, 59*, 82–95.

O'Connor, N., & Hermelin, B. (1967). The selective visual attention of psychotic children. *Journal of Child Psychology and Psychiatry, 8*, 167–179.

Okada, T., Sato, W., Murai, T., Kubota, Y., & Toichi, M. (2003). Eye gaze triggers visuospatial attentional shift in individuals with autism. *Psychologia, 46*, 246–254.

Osterling, J., & Dawson, G. (1994). Early recognition of children with autism ? A study of 1st birthday home videotapes. *Journal of Autism and Developmental Disorders, 24*, 247–257.

Osterling, J. A., Dawson, G., & Munson, J. A. (2002). Early recognition of 1–year–old infants with autism spectrum disorder versus mental retardation. *Development and Psychopathology, 14*, 239–251.

Pelphrey, K. A., Morris, J. P., & McCarthy, G. (2005). Neural basis of eye gaze processing deficits in autism. *Brain, 128*, 1038–1048.

Pelphrey, K. A., Sasson, N. J., Reznick, J. S., Paul, G., Goldman, B. D., & Piven, J. (2002). Visual scanning of faces in autism. *Journal of Autism and Developmental Disorders, 32*, 249–261.

Perrett, D.I., Hietanen, J.K., Oram, M.W. & Benson, P.J. (1992). Organization and functions of cells responsive to faces in the temporal cortex. In V. Bruce, A. Cowey, A. Ellis & D. Perrett (Eds.), *Processing the facial image: Philosophical Transactions of the Royal Society of London, 335*, 1–128. Oxford University Press.

Perrett, D.I., Rolls, E.T. & Caan, W. (1982). Visual neurones responsive to faces in the monkey temporal cortex. *Experimental Brain Research, 47*, 229–238.

Perrett, D.I., Smith, P.A., Potter, D.D., Mistlin, A.J., Head, A.S., Milner, A.D. & Jeeves, M.A. (1985). Visual cells in the temporal cortex sensitive to face view and gaze direction. *Processing of the Royal Society of London, 223*, 293–317.

Pierce, K., Müller, R.–A., Ambrose, J., Allen, G., & Courchesne, E. (2001). Face processing occurs outside the fusiform 'face area' in autism: evidence from functional MRI. *Brain, 124*, 2059–2073.

Piggot, J., Kwon, H., Mobbs, D., Blasey, C., Lotspeich, L., Menon, V., Bookheimer, S., &

Reiss, A. L. (2004). Emotional attribution in high-functioning individuals with autistic spectrum disorder: a functional imaging study. *Journal of American Academy of Child and Adolescent Psychiatry, 43*, 473–480.

Posner, M.I. (1980). Orienting of attention. *Quarterly Journal of Experimental Psychology, 32*, 3–25.

Puce, A., Allison, T., Bentin, S., Gore, J.C. & McCarthy, G. (1998). Temporal cortex activation in humans viewing eye and mouth movements. *Journal of Neuroscience, 18*, 2188–2199.

Puce, A., Smith, A., & Allison, T. (2000). ERPs evoked by viewing facial movements. *Cognitive Neuropsychology, 17*, 221–239.

Rebai, M., Poiroux, S., Bernard, C., & Lalonde, R. (2001). Event-related potentials for category-specific information during passive viewing of faces and objects. *International Journal of Neuroscience, 106*, 209–226.

Ricciardelli, P., Ro, T., Driver, J. (2002). A left visual field advantage in perception of gaze direction. *Neuropsychologia, 40*, 769–777.

Richards, J. E. (2004). Recovering cortical dipole sources from scalp-recorded event-related-potentials using component analysis: Principal component analysis and independent component analysis. *International Journal of Psychophysiology, 54*, 201–220.

Ristic, J., Mottron, L., Friesen, C. K., Iarocci, G., Burack, J. A., & Kingstone, A. (2005). Eyes are special but not for everyone: The case of autism. *Cognitive Brain Research, 24*, 715–718.

Rossion, B., Gauthier, I., Tarr, M. J., Despland, P., Bruyer, R., Linotte, S., & Crommelinck, M. (2000). The N170 occipito-temporal component is delayed and enhanced to inverted faces but not to inverted objects: an electrophysiological account of face-specific processes in the human brain. *NeuroReport, 11*, 0069–0074.

Rutherford, M. D., Clements, K. A., & Sekuler, A. B. (2007). Differences in discrimination of eye and mouth displacement in autism spectrum disorders. *Vision Research, 47*, 2099–2110.

Sasson, N., Tsuchiya, N., Hurley, R., Couture, S. M., Penn, D. L., Adolphs, R., & Piven, J. (2007). Orienting to social stimuli differentiates social cognitive impairment in autism and schizophrenia. *Neuropsychologia, 45*, 2580–2588.

Schultz, R. T. (2005). Developmental deficits in social perception in autism: The role of the amygdala and fusiform face area. *International Journal of Developmental Neuroscience, 23*, 125–141.

Schuller, A.M. & Rossion, B. (2001). Spatial attention triggered by eye gaze increases and speeds up early visual activity. *Neuroreport, 12*, 2381–2386.

Schultz, R. T., Gauthier, I., Klin, A., Fulbright, R. K., Anderson, A. W., Volkmar, F., Skudlarski, P., Lacadie, C., Cohen, D. J., & Gore, J. C. (2000). Abnormal ventral temporal cortical activity during face discrimination among individuals with autism and Asperger syndrome. *Archives of General Psychiatry, 57*, 331–340.

Schumann, C. M., Hamstra, J., Goodlin-Jones, B. L., Lotspeich, L. J., Kwon, H., Buonocore, M. H., Lammers, C. R., Reiss, A. L., & Amaral, D. G. (2004). The amygdala is enlarged in children but not adolescents with autism: The hippocampus is enlarged at all ages. *Journal of Neuroscience, 24*, 6392–6401.

Senju, A., Csibra, G., & Johnson, M. H. (2008). Understanding the referential nature of looking: Infants' preference for object-directed gaze. *Cognition, 108*(2), 303–319.

Senju, A., Hasegawa, T., & Tojo, Y. (2005a). Does perceived direct gaze boost detection in adults and children with and without autism? The stare-in-the-crowd effect revisited. *Visual Cognition, 12*, 1474–1496.

Senju, A., Johnson, M. H., & Csibra, G. (2006). The development and neural basis of referential gaze perception. *Social Neuroscience, 1*, 220–234.

Senju, A., Kikuchi, Y., Hasegawa, T., Tojo, Y., & Osanai, H., (2008). Is anyone looking at me? Direct gaze detection in children with and without autism. *Brain and Cognition, 67*, 127–139.

Senju, A., Tojo, Y., Dairoku, H., & Hasegawa, T. (2004). Reflexive orienting in response to eye gaze and an arrow in children with and without autism. *Journal of Child Psychology and Psychiatry, 45*, 445–458.

Senju, A., Tojo, Y., Yaguchi, K., & Hasegawa, T. (2005b). Deviant gaze processing in children with autism: An ERP study. *Neuropsychologia, 43*, 1297–1306.

Senju, A., Yaguchi, K., Tojo, Y., & Hasegawa, T. (2003). Eye contact does not facilitate detection in children with autism. *Cognition, 89*, B43–B51.

Sergent, J., Ohta, S., & MacDonald, B. (1992). Functional neuroanatomy of face and object processing. A positron emission tomography study. *Brain, 115*, 15–36.

Slater, A., Von der Schulenburg, C., Brown, E., Badenoch, M., Butterworth, G., Parsons, S., et al. (1998). Newborn infants prefer attractive faces. *Infant Behavior and Development, 21*(2), 345–354.

Slater, A., Bremner, G., Johnson, S. P., Sherwood, P., Hayes, R., & Brown, E. (2000). Newborn Infants' Preference for Attractive Faces: The Role of Internal and External Facial Features. *Infancy, 1*(2), 265–274.

Speer, L. L., Cook, A. E., McMahon, W. M., & Clark, E. (2007). Face processing in children with autism: Effects of stimulus contents and type. *Autism, 11*, 265–277.

Spezio, M. L., Adolphs, R., Hurley, R. S., & Piven, J. (2007a). Abnormal Use of Facial Information in High–Functioning Autism. *Journal of Autism and Developmental Disorders, 37*, 929–939.

Spezio, M. L., Huang, P. Y., Castelli, F., & Adolphs, R. (2007b). Amygdala damage impairs eye contact during conversations with real people. *Journal of Neuroscience, 27*, 3994–3997.

Swettenham, J., Condie, S., Campbell, R., Milne, E., & Coleman, M. (2003). Does the perception of moving eyes trigger reflexive visual orienting in autism? *Philosophical Transactions of the Royal Society of London B: Biological Sciences, 358*, 325–334.

Taylor, M. J., Batty, M., & Itier, R. J. (2004). The faces of development: a review of early face processing over childhood. *Journal of Cognitive Neuroscience, 16*(8), 1426–1442.

Taylor, M. J., Edmonds, G. E., McCarthy, G., & Allison, T. (2001). Eyes first! Eye processing develops before face processing in children. *Neuroreport, 12*, 1671–1676.

Taylor, M. J., McCarthy, G., Saliba, E., & Degiovanni, E. (1999). ERP evidence of developmental changes in processing of faces. *Clinical Neurophysiology, 110*, 910–915.

Trepagnier, C., Sebrechts, M. M., & Peterson, R. (2002). Atypical face gaze in autism. *Cyberpsychology & Behavior, 5*, 213–217.

Turati, C, Simion, F., & Zanon, L. (2003). Newborns' perceptual categorization for closed and open geometric forms. *Infancy, 4*, 309–325.

Tzourio-Mazoyer, N., De Schonen, S., Crivello, F., Reutter, B., Aujard, Y., & Mazoyer, B. (2002). Neural Correlates of Woman Face Processing by 2-Month-Old Infants. *Neuroimage, 15*(2), 454–461.

Urban, J., Carlson, E. A., Egeland, B., & Sroufe, L. A. (1991). Patterns of individual adaptation across childhood. *Development and Psychopathology, 3*, 445–560.

Valenza, E., Simion, F., Cassia, V.M. & Umilta', C. (1996). Face preference at birth. *Journal of Experimental Psychology: Human Perception and Performance, 22*, 892–903.

van der Geest, J. N., Kemner, C., Camfferman, G., Verbaten, M. N., & van Engeland, H. (2002a). Looking at images with human figures: comparison between autistic and normal children. *Journal of Autism and Developmental Disorders, 32*, 69–75.

van der Geest, J. N., Kemner, C., Verbaten, M. N., & van Engeland, H. (2002b). Gaze behavior of children with pervasive developmental disorder toward human faces: A fixation time study. *Journal of Child Psychology and Psychiatry, 43*, 669–678.

Vecera, S.P. & Johnson, M.H. (1995). Eye gaze detection and the cortical processing of faces: Evidence from infants and adults. *Visual Cognition, 2*, 101–129.

Vlamings, P. H. J. M., Stauder, J. E., van Son, I. A. M., & Mottron, L. (2005). Atypical visual orienting to gaze– and arrow–cues in adults with high functioning autism. *Journal of Autism and Developmental Disorders, 35*, 267–277.

Volkmar, F. R., Sparrow, S. S., Rende, R. D., & Cohen, D. J. (1989). Facial perception in autism. *Journal of Child Psychology and Psychiatry, 30*, 591–598.

Vuilleumier, P., George, N., Lister, V., Armony, J., Driver, J. (2005). Effects of perceived mutual gaze and gender on face processing and recognition memory. *Visual Cognition, 12*, 85–101.

Wang, A. T., Dapretto, M., Hariri, A. R., Sigman, M., & Bookheimer, S. Y. (2004). Neural correlates of facial affect processing in children and adolescents with autism spectrum disorder. *Journal of the American Academy of Child and Adolescent Psychiatry, 43*, 481–490.

Watanabe, S., Kakigi, R. & Puce, A. (2001). Occipitotemporal activity elicited by viewing eye movements: a magnetoencephalographic study. *Neuroimage, 13,* 351–363.

Werner, E., & Dawson, G. (2005). Validation of the phenomenon of autistic regression using home videotapes. *Archives of General Psychiatry, 62,* 889–895.

Wicker, B., Michel, F., Henaff, M.A. & Decety, J. (1998). Brain regions involved in the perception of gaze: a PET study. *Neuroimage, 8,* 221–227.

Wojciulik, E., Kanwisher, N., & Driver, J. (1998). Covert visual attention modulates face–specific activity in the human fusiform gyrus: fMRI study. *Journal of Neurophysiology, 79,* 1574–1578.

Young, G. S., Merin, N., Rogers, S. J., & Ozonoff, S. (2009). Gaze behavior and affect at 6 months: predicting clinical outcomes and language development in typically developing infants and infants at risk for autism *Developmental Science, 12*(5), 798–814.

AUTHOR INDEX

Abdel-Azim, E., 220
Abdi, H., 9, 19
Abrahams, D., 164
Ackerman, J. M., 96
Adams, G., 75
Adams, R. B., 6, 7, 11, 14, 17, 92, 94, 96, 98, 99, 101, 108, 373
Adelmann, P. K., 208
Adenzato, M., 51, 59, 401, 402f
Adinolfi, A. A., 165
Adolphs, A., 377, 378
Adolphs, R., 6, 14, 65, 142, 159, 240, 254, 363, 373, 374, 374f, 375, 377, 378, 379, 381, 393, 397, 400, 409, 423, 426, 427
Aglioti, S. M., 61, 369
Aharon, I., 6, 13, 14, 19
Aharon- Peretz, J., 395
Ahlberg, C., 273
Ahlenstiel, H., 292t
Ahlfors, S. P., 55
Ahlgren, A., 218
Ahlstrom, U., 242
Ahlstrom, V., 242
Ahluwalia, J., 218, 424
Akamatsu, S., 10, 11, 188
Akbudak, E., 222
Akert, R. M., 239, 240
Akiyama, T., 123
Alais, D., 417
Albright, T. D., 366
Alexander, A. L., 426
Alexander, M. P., 397
Allard, E., 143, 144
Allen, C., 364n1
Allen, G., 278
Allen, J. J. B., 401
Alley, T. R., 5, 168, 169, 170
Allison, T., 6, 55, 119, 219, 254, 366, 370, 421, 424, 428
Allport, G. W., 37, 38, 41, 42, 229, 240, 266, 272, 322
Alpert, M., 399

Amaral, D. G., 256, 257, 375
Ambadar, Z., 11, 230, 242
Ambady, N., xxii, xxv, 6, 14, 17, 91, 94, 100, 101, 229, 230, 231, 232, 234, 235, 236, 237, 238, 253, 267, 380
Ames, C. S., 435
Amodio, D. M., 380
Anastasi, J. S., 17
Anders, S., 65, 68
Anderson, A. K., 69, 221
Anderson, A. W., 34, 53
Anderson, J. R., 128, 307
Anderson, N. D., 348
Anderson, S., 306
Andersson, F., 373
Ando, S., 113, 113n2
Andreoletti, C., 5, 7, 10
Andresen, D. R., 34
Andrews, T. J., 366
Andrzejewski, S. A., 6, 239
Angelone, B. L., 357
Angleitner, A., 237
Angstadt, M., 13
Anstis, S., 109, 110, 111, 112, 114, 116, 347, 355
Anthony, J., 292t
Aoki, S., 401
Apatow, K., 10
Apicella, C. L., 169, 170, 173f, 210
Apperly, I. A., 397
Arak, A., 173, 177
Arauz, R. M., 77
Arbib, M. A., 417
Arbisi, P., 401
Archer, D., 90, 230, 239
Argall, B. D., 415
Arguin, M., 323
Argyle, M., 54, 97, 98, 421
Arnold, D. H., 348
Aron, A., 81, 86
Aronoff, J., 12, 19, 98
Aronson, V., 164
Asch, S. E., 80

Ashby, F. G., 92
Ashmore, R. D., 5, 165, 306
Ashwin, C., 219
Assal, G. I. L., 399
Asthana, H. S., 401
Astington, J., 217
Atkinson, A. P., 95, 253, 257, 268, 363, 365, 365f, 367, 373, 374, 377, 378
Aube, J., 306
Aucoin, K., 196, 197
Austin, W., 211
Avis, J., 394
Avni-Babad, D., 236

Babad, E., 233, 236
Babcock, R. D., 165
Baccus, S. A., 348
Bachevalier, J., 372
Bachmann, T., 7
Bachoud-Lévi, A. -C., 58
Badad, E., 236
Baddeley, A. D., 9, 299
Bader, M., 400
Baier, B., 67
Bailey, A. J., 427
Bair, T. B., 398
Baird, A. A., 14, 101, 222
Baird, L. M., 403
Baker, C. I., 53, 369, 370
Baker, D., 220
Baker, R. R., 179
Bakker, T. C. M., 178
Balaban, M. T., 6
Balcetis, E., 136
Baldwin, D., 218, 435
Baltes, M. M., 136
Baltes, P. B., 136, 137
Banaji, M. R., 13, 307n1, 326, 330, 339, 380
Banaszynski, T. L., 307n1
Banich, M. T., 399, 403
Banks, M. S., 417
Bar, M., 12, 94, 98, 254, 368, 378

Barale, F., 427
Baranek, G. T., 426
Barbee, A. P., 166, 175
Barclay, A. M., 12
Barclay, C. D., 253, 266
Barclay, P., 207
Barden, C. R., 165
Bargh, J. A., xxii, 41, 42, 44, 75, 145,
    266, 272, 309
Bar-Haim, Y., 18
Barkowitz, P., 323
Barlow, H. B., xiv, xxv, 348
Barnard, M., 198
Baron, R. M., xxiv, 4, 8, 96, 167, 249
Baron-Cohen, S., xvi, 96, 98, 101, 108,
    151, 216, 218, 219, 219f, 220, 222,
    223, 242, 259, 397, 421, 424, 432,
    435
Barrett, L. F., 5
Bartlett, J., 37, 38
Bartlett, M. S., 348
Barton, R. A., 291
Bassili, J. N., 11
Bates, J. F., 373n4
Batki, A., 424
Ba'tki, A., 218
Battelli, L., 370, 418
Battistich, V. A., 19
Baudouin, J., 95
Baum, M. R., 7
Baumeister, R. F., 137, 140
Baylis, G. C., 14, 91, 368
Bayliss, A. P., 122, 126, 127
Beach, F. A., 166
Beale, J. M., 332, 335, 357
Beall, A. E., 358
Beardsworth, T., 267
Beauchamp, M. S., 372, 409, 411, 413,
    414, 415, 416, 418
Beaumont, G., 402
Beaupre, M. G., 101
Beauvois, J. -L. o., 5
Beaver, J. D., 120, 347
Becker, D. V., 7, 11, 19, 96, 98, 273
Becker, E. S., 135
Becquart, E., 307, 307n1
Behniea, H., 375
Behrman, B. W., 322
Behrmann, M., 53, 365
Beintema, J. A., 372
Bekoff, M., 364n1
Belger, A., 403
Bellis, M. A., 179
Bemporad, B., 401
Benson, P. J., 119, 340, 348
Bentin, P. G., 59
Bentin, S., 55, 95, 366, 421, 424
Bereczkai, T., 16
Berenbaum, S. A., 273
Berg, R., 187
Bergman, T., 151, 242
Berlin, L., 303
Berlucchi, G., 369
Bernard, C., 424
Bernieri, F. J., xxii, xxv, 101, 229, 233,
    234, 236

Berntson, G. G., 329
Berry, D. S., 5, 10, 11, 96, 175
Berscheid, E., 164, 165, 166
Bertamini, M., 211
Bertenthal, B. I., 250
Berthoz, S., 57
Berti, A., 67
Bertrand, O., 15
Best, D. L., 97
Best, F., 292t
Betts, L. R., 367
Beupré, M., 17
Bevan, W., 322
Beverley, K. I., 348
Bidet-Caulet, A., 15
Biek,. M., 231
Biernat, M., 270
Bihrle, A. M., 395, 396
Bindemann, M., 95, 108
Birbaumer, N., 371
Birt, A. R., 397
Bishop, D., 425
Bisiach, E., 67
Bittles, A. H., 208
Blackwell, K. C., 7, 273
Blair, I. V., 7, 10, 38, 40, 41, 42, 43, 44,
    45, 46n1, 266, 307, 308, 308n2,
    309, 310, 310n2, 313, 330
Blair, R. J., 218, 220
Blairy, S., 5, 97, 273
Blake, R., 53, 242, 250, 257, 258, 259,
    370, 371, 409, 412
Blakemore, C., 348, 368
Blanchard, F. A., 233
Blanck, P. D., 233, 234
Blandon-Gitlin, I., 17
Blank, A. L., 12
Blanke, O., 397
Blanz, V., 18, 331, 347
Blascovich, J., 341
Blass, E. M., 429
Blomert, L., 415
Blonder, L. X., 398
Bloom, R. L., 395, 396, 398
Blum, A., 395
Blumenthal, J., 7
Blümler, M., 403
Boddaert, N., 258
Bodenhausen, G.
Bodenhausen, G. V., 33, 38, 40, 41, 42,
    45, 46, 266, 306, 307, 308, 309
Boduroglu, A., 79
Bogen, J. E., 399
Boland, J. E., 79
Bond, C. F. Jr., 237, 238
Bonda, E., 251, 370
Bondar, I., 350
Bonnar, L., 34
Borkenau, P., 134, 231, 237
Bornstein, R. F., 5, 7
Borod, J. C., 393, 395, 396, 398, 399,
    400, 401
Boshyan, J., 94
Boucher, J., 425
Boudreau, L. A., 96
Bowd, C., 348

Bowen, M., 195
Bower, G. H., 307
Bower, N. J., 16
Bower, T. G. R., 16, 348
Bowers, D., 398
Bowman, N. A., 75, 78
Boyd, C. E., 323
Boynton, G. M., 355, 418
Boynton, R M., 338
Braden, V., 267
Bradley, B. P., 100
Bradley, M. M., 140
Bradshaw, M. F., 242, 253
Braeutigam, S., 427
Brain, R., 186, 187, 198
Brajkovich, G., 7, 213
Brake, S., 16, 33, 367
Brambilla, P., 427
Bratslavsky, E., 137
Bray, D., 123
Brédart, S., 307
Breiter, H. C., 373
Breitmeyer, B. G., 241
Brennan, S., 9, 348
Bressan, P., 211, 212
Brewer, M. B., 7, 10, 31, 37, 38, 40, 41,
    42, 43, 45, 46, 266, 272, 306,
    307, 308
Brickman, A. M., 395
Bridgestock, R., 172
Brigham, J. C., 9, 17, 101, 322, 323, 335
Brockbank, M., 124
Bronstad, P. M., 7, 13, 14, 18, 19, 197, 198
Brothers, L., xvi, 92, 256
Broughton, R., 96
Brown, B., 196
Brown, C. E., 96
Brown, E., 33, 34, 40
Brown, P., 96
Brown, R., 41, 42
Brown, T. D., Jr., 9
Brown, W. M., 253
Brown, W. S., 400
Brownell, H. H., 394, 395
Brownlow, S., 175, 253
Brozgold, A. Z., 395
Bruce, C., 366, 416
Bruce, V., 3, 9, 10, 16, 32, 33, 34, 35, 37,
    38, 40, 55, 91, 95, 99, 113, 122,
    123, 127, 167, 188, 191, 195, 348,
    367, 368, 431
Bruderlin, A., 253, 268
Bruner, J. S., 75, 296
Brunet, E., 219, 397
Bryden, M. P., 398, 399, 400
Buccino, G., 222, 371
Buchanan, T. W., 379
Buchel, C., 54
Buck, R., 398, 401, 402
Buckingham, G., 210, 213
Buckner, T., 267
Bucy, P. C., 372
Bullier, J., 254, 368
Bullmore, E. T., 222
Bulthoff, H. H., 188, 259
Bulthoff, I., 259

Burch, R. L., 210
Burianova, H., 141
Burley, N., 178
Burnham, D., 9
Burquest, M., 196
Burr, D., 417
Burriss, R. P., 197, 212
Burt, D. M., 95, 173, 174, 176, 196, 204, 205
Burt, P., 252
Burton, A. M., 11, 34, 95, 108, 188, 195
Burton, H., 66, 373n4
Burton, L. A., 399
Burton, M., 10, 348
Buschman, T. J., 368
Busey, T. A., 3, 354
Bushnell, I. W., 16
Buss, D. M., 19
Butterworth, G., 128, 432
Butz, D. A., 304, 335
Byatt, G., 3, 169, 348, 350, 350n1
Byrne, R. W., 92

Caan, W., 91, 331
Cabeza, R., 348
Cacioppo, J. T., 5, 63, 217, 328, 329, 341
Cacioppo, T., 6
Caldara, R., 9, 19
Calder, A. J., 3, 11, 54, 92, 95, 100, 120, 121, 127, 219, 220, 347, 368, 369, 373
Callaghan, T., 394
Callan, D. E., 415
Caltagirone, C., 394, 398
Calvert, G. A., 371, 415
Calvo, M. G., 134
Calvo-Merino, B., 369
Camfferman, G., 426
Camp, C. A., 429
Campbell, F. W., 368
Campbell, J. L., 293t
Campbell, M. A., 397
Campbell, N., 12
Campbell, R., 112, 119, 370, 371, 372
Campeau, S., 66
Campos, J., 216
Candidi, M., 369
Canli, T., 221
Cárdenas, R. A., 198
Carey, S., 9, 33, 220, 348, 417
Carlson, C., 145
Carlston, D., 307
Caron, H. S., 398, 401
Carpenter, M., 435
Carr, L., 219, 377
Carrington, J., 395, 396
Carroll, J. M., 229
Carroll, S. B., xxii
Carroo, A. W., 323
Carstensen, L. L., 134, 135, 137, 138
Carter, L. F., 323
Cartmill, M., 310
Carton, J. S., 142
Casey, J., 165
Cash, T. F., 165, 195
Cassel, A., 120

Cassinello, J., 171
Castelli, F., 219, 223, 260, 371n2, 377, 394, 397
Castelli, L., 51
Castillo, M., 117
Castles, D. L., 208, 212
Catty, S., 18, 272
Cavanagh, P., 323
Cedrone, C. C., 111
Cerella, J., 144
Chabris, C. F., 238
Chakrabarti, B., 216, 219, 222, 223
Chaminade, T., 220
Chan, A. W., 369
Chan, J., 174
Chance, J. E., 324, 348
Chandra, M., 199
Changizi, M. A., 188n2, 283, 284f, 293t
Chao, L. L., 413
Chapleau, K. M., 7, 40, 308
Chaplin, G., 188, 192
Chapman, E., 223
Charles, S. T., 134, 137
Charlesworth, W. R., 217
Charman, T., 217, 432
Chartrand, T. L., xxii
Chaudhuri, A., 125
Chauvel, P., 366
Chavajay, P., 77, 87
Chen, J. Y., 174
Cheng, Y. D., 33, 34, 35, 188
Chiao, J. Y., 96, 323
Chiao, K. W., 6
Chiavarino, C., 397
Chiroro, P., 323, 324, 325
Chiu, R. K., 165
Choe, B. Y., 350
Choi, I., 76
Choi, S., 267
Chouchourelou, A., 255f, 256, 257, 268
Chowdhry, O., 328, 329, 334
Christe, P., 174
Christensen, P. N., 212
Christman, S. D., 399
Chu, L., 90
Chua, H. F., 79
Chubb, C., 331, 354
Chun, M. M., 13, 34, 91, 350, 366, 413, 423
Ciaramitaro, V. M., 355
Cicchetti, D., 422
Cipolotti, L., 220
Clark, E., 426
Clark, J. J., 79
Clarke, A., 231
Clarke, M., 372
Clarke, T. J., 242, 253, 254
Clausen, A., 268
Clayton, N. S., xvii
Clements, K. A., 426
Clements, W., 217
Clifford, C. W. G. E., 18, 120, 331, 347, 348, 351
Cline, M. G., 109, 110, 110f, 111, 112, 114, 116
Cliord, S., 426

Cloutier, J., 6, 38, 41, 43, 46
Coan, J. A., 401
Coats, E. J., 234
Cochran, E. L., 38
Cockburn, D. M., 292t
Cohen, D., 242
Cohen, J. F., 11, 13
Cohn, J. F., 11, 230
Cole, B. L., 293t
Cole, M. G. H., 327
Cole-Davies, V., 421
Collins, M. A., 6, 7, 8, 12, 249
Collis, G., 425
Collishaw, S. M., 37
Colvin, C. R., 133, 134, 233
Colzato, L., 123
Compton, R. J., 69, 403
Condry, J., 273
Condry, S., 273
Connellan, J., 218, 424
Conner, B., 232, 253
Conway, C. A., 100
Cook, A. E., 426
Cook, M., 97, 98, 421
Corballis, M. C., 402
Cordell, L. D. H., 233
Corkum, V., 128, 432
Corneille, O., 307, 307n1
Cornwell, R. E., 197
Correa-Chavez, M., 77
Correll, J., 75, 296, 297, 304, 321, 327, 328, 329, 330, 341
Corrigan, P. W., 231
Corson, R., 199, 200
Cosmides, L., 266
Costa, A., 394
Costa, L. D., 398
Costanzo, M., 239
Cottrell, G. W., 373
Cousins, A. J., 212
Cowey, A., 63, 112, 119, 368
Cox, C. L., 195
Craig, A. D., 379
Craig, T. Y., 232
Craighero, L., 222
Craik, F. I. M., 144
Crick, N. R., 218
Crisp, R. J., 91
Critchley, H. D., 14, 95, 220, 221, 222, 377, 427
Croizet, J. -C., 195, 197
Cronin-Golomb, A., 142
Cross, J. F., 17, 323, 325
Crowson, M., 218, 435
Crozier, R. W., 278
Crucian, G. P., 398
Crupain, M. J., 13
Csibra, G., 425, 427, 432
Cuddy, A. J. C., 5, 5n2, 96
Culver, C., 17
Cummins, R., 364
Cunningham, M. R., 166, 168, 169, 170, 175, 187, 241
Curko, E. A., 395
Currier, J. D., 292t
Cuthbert, B. N., 140

Cutler, B. L., 32
Cutting, J. E., 242, 250, 253, 266, 267, 411
Cynader, M. S., 357
Czogalik, D., 90
Czyzewska, M., 17

Dahl, M., 6
Dal Martello, M. F., 204
Dalton, K. M., 135, 426, 427, 432
Daly, J., 17, 323
Daly, M., 218
Damasio, A. R., 6, 91, 220, 368, 373, 378
Damasio, H., 240, 368, 373, 377
Dane, F. C., 9
Dangerfield, C. L., 307n1
Darling, S., 169
Darwin, C., 63, 98, 187, 216, 267, 278, 287
Dasgupta, N., 42, 307n1
Daum, I., 253, 372
Davenport J. L., 100
Davey, S. L., 322
David, A. S., 220
Davidson, R. J., 98, 220, 378, 400, 401,
    403, 426
Davies, P. G., 7, 10, 75, 307, 309
Davies, S., 425
Davis, F., 198
Davis, M. H., 66, 216, 218, 241
Davis, P., 195
Dawkins, R., xxiii
Dawson, G., 426, 427
Dawson, K., 195
Dawson, M., 425
Dayagi-Mendels, M., 199
Dean, M., 11
Deaner, R. O., 6
deBonis, M., 65, 373
DeBruine, L. M., 7, 169, 170, 176, 176F,
    177, 197, 204, 207, 208, 209, 211,
    212, 213, 352
Decety, J., 6, 219, 220, 252, 397, 428
De Diego Balaguer, R., 58
Deegan, J. F., 283
Deffke, I., 366
de Gelder, B., 11, 15, 51, 53, 54, 55, 56,
    57, 58, 59, 61, 62, 63, 65, 66, 69,
    264, 268, 369, 373, 375, 376, 401,
    402f, 409, 417, 425
Degiovanni, E., 424
de Haan, M., 348, 424, 425, 435
Dehaene-Lambertz, G., 55, 59
Deichmann, R., 220
Del Boca, F., 306
Delibes, M., xxii
De Lima, A. D., 66
Demaree, H. A., 395, 398
Dench, N., 10, 34, 188, 195, 348
Deneen, N. E., 233
Dennett, D. C., xvi
Deouell, L. Y., 366
DePaulo, B. M., 11, 12, 229, 237, 238, 243
Depue, R. A., 401
Deregowski, J. B., 324
Dermer, M., 165
de Schonen, S., 425
Desimone, R., 366, 416

D'Esposito, M., 415
Detre, G. J., 418
Deutsch, G., 393, 398
Devine, P. G., 6, 42, 266, 272, 273
de Waal, F. B. M., xx, 54, 217, 222
DeWall, C. N., 5
Diamond, R., 33, 348
Dias, M., 421
DiGeronimo, K., 231
Dilthey, W., xv
DiMatteo, M. R., 90, 230
Dimberg, U., 6, 54, 61, 69, 219
Dimond, S., 402
di Nemi, S. U., 427
Dion, K. K., 164, 165
di Pellegrino, G., 127
Dittrich, W. H., 253, 257, 268
Dixon, A. R., 253
Dixon, M. A., 335
Dixon, M. S., 399
Dixon, R., 324
Dobbelsteyn, C., 192
Dobish, H., 5, 7
Dodds, C. M., 123
Dodge, K., 218
Doherty, M. J., 128
Dolan, R. J., 13, 14, 54, 61, 63, 65, 69,
    95, 220, 221, 222, 356, 368, 373,
    377, 379, 421
Donald, M. W., xxiv
Dong, C. -J., 357
Donk, M., 143
Donnelly, M., 169
Donnelly, N., 368
Doron, N. N., 66
Dovidio, J. F., 42, 96, 232, 266
Downing, P. E., 53, 54, 58, 123, 366,
    369, 376, 410, 413
Downs, A. C., 165
Doyle, T., 10, 348
Drain, M., 242, 367
Dreher, J. C., 100
Drenth, T., 90
Driscoll, D. M., 232
Driver, J., 62, 69, 95, 121, 122, 124, 356,
    368, 375, 377, 421, 431
Druen, P. B., 166
Dube, S., 323
Dubeau, M. -C., 219
Dubois, N., 5
Duchaine, B. C., 13, 365, 368
Duffy, S., 75, 76, 77, 81, 85, 86f, 87
Dufour, K. W., 171
Dufour, V., 16
Duhamel, P., 18, 347
Duke, M. P., 239
Dunamel, P., 321
Dunbar, R. I. M., xvi, 93
Duncan, B. L., 295
Duncan, L. A., 19
Dunning, D., 136
Duntley, S. Q., 188
Durham, M. D., 9
Dutta, R., 7
Dwyer, J., 322
Dziurawiec, S., 164

Dzur, C., 217

Eagly, A. H., 5, 12, 165, 358
Easterbrook, M. A., 423
Eastwood, J. D., 69
Eaton, J. L., 38
Eberhardt, J. L., 7, 10, 75, 267, 307,
    307n1, 309, 323
Ebin, V., 187, 198
Eckes, T., 306
Edgerton, R. B., 78, 87
Edmonds, G. E., 424
Edmonds, J., 250
Edwards, E. A., 188, 220
Edwards, K., 11
Edwards, M., 349, 351
Egbert, C. A., 253
Egelko, S., 398
Ehlis, A. C., 366
Ehrlichman, H., 400
Eibl-Eibesfeldt, I., 5
Eimer, M., 55, 59, 366, 375, 424
Eisenberg, N., 144
Ekman, P., 11, 93, 96, 141, 229, 267,
    268, 396, 397, 401
Elder, G. H. J., 164
Elfenbein, H. A., 17, 100, 230
Elgueta, A., 42
Eliassen, J. C., 399
Ellgring, H., 366
Ellgring, J. H., 110
Elliott, E. S., 324
Ellis, H. D., 6, 164, 324
Ellsworth, P. C., 80
Ellyson, S. L., 96
Elmehead, K., 219
Elmehed, K., 54
Elsabbagh, 433
Emde, R., 216
Emery, N. J., xvii, 90, 151, 162, 220, 372
Endo, M., 114, 324, 347
Enlow, D. H., 8, 10, 188
Enlow, D. M., 174
Enquist, M., 173, 177
Entwistle, D. R., 325
Ernst, M. O., 417
Esteves, F., 61, 69, 145, 329
Etcoff, N. L., 61, 63, 91, 94, 186, 187,
    397, 398
Eugene, F., 220
Euler, H. A., 210
Evans, A., 251, 370
Evans, K. K., 379
Evans, N., 42, 266
Everhart, D. E., 395
Ewbank, M. P., 366
Ewing, L., 348
Ewy, R., 187
Eysenck, H. J., 240

Fabes, R. A., 218
Fabiani, M., 327
Fadiga, L., 222
Fagot, B. I., 273
Fallgatter, A. J., 366
Fallman, J. L., 309, 313

Fan, J., 139
Fang, F., 120
Farah, M. J., 144, 242, 367
Farkas, L. G., 188, 195
Farrer, C., 68
Farroni, T., 124, 423, 424, 430, 431, 432, 435
Faulkner, J., 19
Fazendeiro, T., 18, 272
Fechner, G., 330
Feigenson, K., 403
Feinberg, D. R., 197, 208, 212
Feingold, A., 5, 165
Feinman, S., 325
Feldman, R. S., 240
Fellous, J. M., 5, 7, 10, 11
Fera, F., 220
Fermano, Z., 259
Fessler, D. M. T., 19
Fidopiastis, C., 267
Field, D. J., 325, 348
Field, D. T., 242, 253
Fieldman, G., 195, 196
Fine, I., 355
Fine-Goulden, M. R., 368
Fink, B., 187, 188, 196, 212
Fink, G. R., 34
Finkenauer, C., 137
Finney, D. J., 331
Fiorentini, A., 249
Fischer, M. H., 112
Fischl, B., 53
Fisher, D. L., 135
Fiske, S. T., 5, 5n2, 13, 31, 32, 37, 38, 41, 42, 43, 46, 96, 266, 267, 272, 306, 307, 307, 378
Fitzgerald, D. A., 13
Fize, D., 56
Flavell, J. H., 394
Fleck, M. S., 303
Flegr, J., 212
Fletcher, P. C., 222, 379
Flowerdew, G., 192
Flykt, A., 145
Fodor, J. A., 250, 365
Foldi, N. S., 395, 396
Folk, C. L., 145
Folstad, I., 12, 171, 174
Fonagy, P., 223
Fonlupt, P., 15, 252
Ford, C. S., 166
Ford, M. E., 165
Forkman, B., 173
Forman, S., 293t
Formisano, E., 415
Fox, E., 100, 127
Fox, N. A., 401
Fox, R., 411
Foxe, J. J., 418
Franck, N., 95
Frank, M. G., 396, 397
Frank, S. A., xiii
Franklin, M., 212
Fredrickson, B. L., 137, 139
Freese, J. L., 375

Freiwald, W. A., 349, 366
Freund, T., 309
Freyd, J. J., 252
Friedman, G. B., 234
Friedman, H., 8, 12, 19, 97, 98
Friedman, J. N. W., 233
Friesen, C. K., 122, 123, 421, 431
Friesen, W. V., 93, 96, 229, 267
Frijda, N. H., 54, 68
Frisby, J. P., 347
Frischen, A., 122, 127
Friston, K. J., 54, 223
Frith, C. D., 14, 54, 219, 220, 223, 254, 260, 377, 379, 394, 397
Frith, U., 14, 219, 220, 223, 260, 377, 379, 394, 397
Frost, P., 10, 179, 188
Frye, R. E., 416
Frykholm, G., 253, 268, 269
Fukui, K., 400
Fukushima, H., 372
Funder, D. C., 241
Fung, H., 77
Furey, M. L., 366, 368
Furl, N., 9, 17, 19, 366

Gabrieli, J. D. E., 81, 86, 221, 323
Gaertner, S. L., 232
Gailliot, M. T., 5
Gainotti, G., 398
Galati, D., 67
Gallagher, H. L., 254, 379, 397
Gallese, V., 222, 377
Gallup, G. G., 210, 397
Galton, F. J., 168
Galumbeck, C., 195
Ganel, T., 40, 43, 95
Gangestad, S. W., 12, 19, 167, 168, 171, 174, 179, 187, 188, 212, 231, 236, 238
Garcia, J. O., 414
Gardner, H., 395
Garner, M., 100, 269
Garner, W. R., 94
Garver-Apgar, C. E., 212
Gaulin, S. J. C., 210
Gauthier, I., 33, 34, 35, 53, 355, 365, 421
Gazzaniga, M. S., 123, 399
Geisler, W. S., 325
Gelman, S. A., 365
Geminiani, G., 51, 59, 61, 62, 67, 69, 401, 402f
Gemmell, A. J., 253, 268
Genero, R., 62
Geng, J. J., 368
Gentry, T. A., 357
Georg, K., 372
George, N., 421, 424, 430
Gepner, B., 425
Gerard, G., 54
Gerhart, J. C., xxii
Gerstman, L. J., 395
Gescheider, G. A., 330
Ghazanfar, A. A., 415

Ghuman, A. S., 254
Giard, M. H., 43, 45
Gibson, E. J., 4, 6, 8, 12, 13, 16, 248
Gibson, J. J., xiv, xv, 4, 14, 15, 75, 93, 109, 110, 111, 112, 248, 331
Giese, M. A., 350, 372
Gifford, R., 97
Giguere, M., 373n4
Gilad, S., 368
Gilbert, D. T., 32, 41, 42, 43, 266, 309
Gill, S., 232, 253, 270f, 271f, 272
Gillis, J. S., 236
Gleason, M. E. J., 233
Glick, P., 96
Glick, W. H., 195
Gliga, T., 55, 59, 427
Gluck, M., 33
Gobbini, M. I., 3, 33, 91, 368, 378, 409, 422
Godijn, R., 123
Goebel, R., 415
Goff, P. A., 10, 75, 267, 307
Goffaux, V., 249
Golby, A. J., 323, 328, 341
Goldberg, E., 398
Goldenfeld, N., 219, 223
Goldman-Rakic, P. S., 373n4
Goldschmidt, W., 78
Goldstein, A. G., 324, 348
Goldstein, N. E., 240
Goldstein, S. B., 268
Goldstone, R. L., 16
Gollwitzer, P. M., 145
Gomendio, M., 171
Gonin, L. -C. M. W., 187
Gonzalez-Lima, F., 220
Goodale, M. A., xv
Goodman, C. C., 296
Gordon, E., 135
Gordon, H. L., 14
Gordon, P. C., 135
Gore, J. C., 34, 53, 366
Goren, A., 229, 379
Goren, C. C., 164
Goren, D., 136, 138
Goshen-Gottstein, Y., 40, 43, 95
Gosselin, F., 9, 34, 373
Gotlib, I., 221
Goto, S. G., 85
Grabowecky, M., 9
Grady, C. L., 141
Grady, J., 172
Grafton, S., 222
Graham, J. A., 195
Graham, R., 95
Grahe, J. E., 234
Graif, M., 54
Gralewski, L., 12
Grammer, K., 171, 172, 175, 188, 196, 212
Grant, M. C., 168
Gratton, G., 327
Gray, H. M., 234
Gray, J. M., 12
Gray, S. A., 42, 307
Green, M. F., 242

Green, R., 306
Greenwald, A. G., 42
Greicius, M. D., 220
Greve, D., 54
Grèzes, J., 54, 55, 57, 268, 373, 376, 417
Grice, S. J., 427, 433, 434
Griffin, A. M., 5
Griffin, Z. M., 135
Griffiths, P. E., 220
Griffiths, R. J., 208, 309
Grill-Spector, K., 355, 368, 418
Gronlund, S. D., 145
Grosbras, M. -H., 54, 220, 376
Gross, C. G., 366, 416
Gross, J. J., 134
Gross, S. R., 322
Grossman, E. D., 53, 251, 256, 370, 371, 412, 414, 418
Grossman, M., 273
Grotpeter, J. K., 218
Grubb, J. D., 369
Grühn, D., 137, 140
Gruneberg, M. M., 9
Guerit, J. M., 65
Guez, J., 144
Gullickson, G., 379
Gunns, R. E., 253, 269
Guofeng, W., 14
Gur, R. C., 398
Gusnard, D., 222
Gutchess, A. H., 79
Gutierrez, E., 62, 373n3
Gyuris, P., 16

Hackworth, M. D., 399
Hadar, U., 54
Hadjikhani, N., 15, 53, 54, 55, 57, 65, 66, 268, 373, 376, 417, 427
Haenel, H., 292t
Hagan, R., 273
Hagel, R., 212
Haggard, P., 369
Hagit, B. L., 240
Hahn, S., 145
Haig, N. D., 324
Hains, S. M. J., 423
Haith, M. M., 110, 111, 151, 242
Halberstadt, J., 7, 18, 170, 213, 272
Halgren, E., 55, 366
Halit, H., 424, 425, 430
Hall, A., 90
Hall, C. C., 229, 379
Hall, J. A., 5, 6, 133, 134, 217, 230, 233, 234, 236, 239, 241
Hallahan, M., 232, 238, 253, 380
Halliday, T., 174
Hamalainen, M. S., 55
Hamilton, A. F., 369
Hamm, A. O., 63
Hamm, J. P., 427
Hamm, N. H., 7
Hampson, S. E., 242, 253
Hamzei, F., 222
Hancock, E. R., 366
Hancock, P. J. B., 176
Handley, I. M., 134

Happe, F., 217, 219, 223, 260, 377
Happé, F., 394, 395
Harber, K., 253, 257, 267, 268, 411
Hardan, A., 427
Hardin, C. L., 287f
Hardy-Baylè, M. -C., 219, 397
Hari, R., 55, 368
Hariri, A. R., 220, 221
Harmon-Jones, E., 98, 401
Harries, M. H., 124
Harrigan, J. A., 11, 230, 231
Harrigan, K. M., 231
Harris, A., 34, 42, 59, 366
Harris, J., 331
Harris, L. J., 13, 198
Harris, L. T., 378
Harris, M. J., 241
Harris, P. L., 217, 394
Harrison, D. W., 395
Harrison, L., 223
Hart, A. J., 327
Hasegawa, T., 95, 427
Hasher, L., 136
Hasselmo, M. E., 14, 91, 92, 95
Hatch, C. E., 164
Hatfield, E., 200, 217
Hatfield, H., 63
Hauck, M., 425
Hauk, O., 14
Havlicek, J., 212
Hawkes, L. M., 242
Haxby, J. V., 3, 13, 14, 33, 34, 35, 43, 53, 91, 92, 119, 222, 223f, 366, 368, 369, 379, 409, 411, 413, 418, 422, 425
Hay, D. C., 9
Hayes-Roth, B., 307
Hayward, W. G., 351
He, S., 120, 373
Hebb, D. A., 307
Hebb, D. O., 348
Heberlein, A. S., 19, 240, 363, 374, 375, 377, 378, 380
Heckhausen, J., 146
Hedden, T., 81, 86
Heider, F., 260, 374
Heilman, K. M., 398
Heim, K., 253, 266, 411
Heimann, H., 12
Helfrich, H., 10
Helland, S., 221
Hellawell, D., 9
Heller, W., 399
Helson, H., 348
Henaff, M. A., 428
Henderson, W. L., 232
Hendler, T., 54
Hendrick, R., 135
Henik, A., 143, 145
Henson, R. N., 366, 368, 418
Henson, R. N. A., 356
Henss, R., 10
Heptulla-Chatterjee, S., 251
Hermans, E., 100
Hermelin, B., 426
Herrmann, M. J., 366

Herry, C., 374
Hershler, O., 5
Hess, U., 5, 7, 11, 17, 92, 97, 98, 101, 273
Hewstone, M., 91, 309, 323
Heywood, C. A., 63, 112, 119, 368
Hickford, C., 175
Hietanen, J. K., 119, 122, 124, 126, 127, 127f, 340, 421, 427, 433, 434
Higgins, D. A., 218
Higgins, E. T., 75
Hildreth, E., 251
Hill, H., 10, 188, 267
Hill, K., 175, 187
Hill, R. A., 291
Hill, T., 17
Hillgarth, N., 174
Himer, W., 12
Hingston, R. W. G., 287
Hinsz, V. B., 208
Hinton, G. E., 17
Hirai, M., 371, 372
Hiraki, K., 372
Hiris, E., 248, 250
Hirschfeld, L. A., 365
Hirschman, R. S., 400
Hixon, J. G., 32, 41, 42, 43, 266, 309
Hobson, R. P., 217, 242, 257
Hochberg, J. E., 348
Hochstein, S., 5
Hocking, J., 418
Hodes, R. M., 18
Hodgins, H. S., 12
Hofer, C., 144
Hoffman, D. D., 414
Hoffman, E. A., 3, 33, 91, 119, 222, 223f, 366, 368, 409, 413, 422
Hoffman, K., 188
Hoffman, M. L., 217
Holder, J., 223
Hole, G. J., 37
Holmes, A., 375
Holmes, S. J., 164
Homan, C. P., 268
Homan, R. W., 402
Hommel, B., 123
Honekopp, J., 197
Honeyman, H., 117
Hongwanishkul, D., 141
Honig, W. K., 279
Hood, B. M., 108, 124, 421, 431
Hooker, 13
Hoptman, M. J., 403
Horner, C., 90
Horowitz, T. S., 303
Hosch, H. M., 323
Hosie, J. A., 324
Hosoya, T., 348
Hrybyk, M., 398
Huart, J., 307, 307n1
Hubert, B., 258
Hubl, D., 427
Hudson, S. M., 253, 269
Hugdahl, K., 98
Hugenberg, K., 17, 96
Hughes, H. C., 368
Huguet, P., 195, 197

Hume, D., 166
Humphrey, N. K., xvi, xx, xxiii, 51
Humphreys, G. W., 368, 397
Hunnisett, E., 435
Hupe, J. M., 254
Hurley, R. S., 426
Huss, D., 12
Hussey, T., 195, 196
Hutton, S. B., 142
Hyde, J. S., 273
Hyman, L. M., 12, 98
Hynes, C., 222
Hyönä, J., 134

Iacoboni, M., 219, 223f, 254, 417
Iacono, W. G., 401
Ida Gobbini, M., 222, 223f
Ida-Gobbini, M., 222
Ikeda, H., 242
Imada, T., 75, 78
Inhelder, B., 217
Inn, D., 348
Ioannides, A. A., 366
Ionta, S., 369
Isaacowitz, D. M., 133, 134, 135, 136,
    137, 138, 139, 140, 141, 142, 143,
    144, 146
Isen, A. M., 134
Ishai, A., 15
Ishii, K., 75, 78, 82, 84
Ishii, M., 268
Itakura, S., 87
Itier, R. J., 55, 366
Ito, T. A., 5, 6, 13, 14, 321, 327, 328, 329,
    330, 334, 340, 341, 357, 358
Iverson, A., 196
Izard, C. E., 11, 17, 401

Jablonski, N. G., 186, 188, 192
Jackson, J. H., 394
Jackson, P. L., 219, 397
Jackson, R. L., 307n1
Jacobs, A., 253, 256, 267
Jacobs, G. H., 283
Jacobs, J. R., 395
Jacoby, L. L., 297, 300, 301, 301f, 302f
Jaffe, J., 429
James, A., 335
Janowsky, J. S., 137
Jansari, A., 400
Jansson, L., 173, 177
Japee, S., 61
Jaquet, E., 347, 351, 351f, 352, 352f, 353,
    353f, 354, 355f, 356, 356n3, 357f,
    357n5, 358, 359
Jarrett, N., 128, 432
Jarrold, C., 435
Jarudi, I., 196, 368
Jeannerod, M., 256
Jeffery, L., 18, 175, 347, 348, 349, 350f, 354
Jeffries, B. J., 292t
Jellema, T., 370
Jelsone, L. M., 13
Jemel, B., 425
Jenike, M. A., 61, 63
Jenkins, C., 7, 38, 307

Jenkins, J., 111, 113
Jenkins, R., 120, 347
Jensen, A., 165
Jeun, S. S., 350
Ji, L-J., 77, 80, 81
Jiang, X., 368
Jiang, Y., 53, 369, 373, 413
Jinghan, W., 14
Joffres, M., 192
Johansson, G., 248, 250, 265, 370, 411
John, O. P., 134
Johnson, D. W., 218
Johnson, J. C., 145
Johnson, J. T., 273
Johnson, K. L., 232, 242, 253, 270, 270f,
    271f, 272, 273, 274f
Johnson, M. H., 112, 124, 128, 135,
    164, 348, 422, 423, 424, 425, 427,
    431, 432, 434, 435
Johnson, R. A., 95
Johnson, R. R., 7, 10
Johnson, S. L., 7, 309
Johnson-Frey, S., 222
Johnson, M. H., 431, 432
Johnston, A., 9
Johnston, L., 253, 267, 269
Johnston, V. S., 179, 212
Johnstone, R. A., 173
Jokisch, D., 253, 372
Jolicoeur, P., 33
Joliffe, T., 242
Jolij, J., 61
Jones, B. C., 169, 170, 172, 174, 176, 178,
    179, 196, 197, 204, 208, 212, 213, 352
Jones, D. M., 175, 187
Jones, E. G., 66, 373n4
Jones, M. E., 90
Jones, W., 242
Jonides, J., 122, 123
Joseph, R. M., 417
Josephs, O., 222, 377
Joshi, P., 329
Jouhar, A. J., 195
Jousmaki, V., 55, 427
Joynt, R. J., 393
Judd, C. M., 7, 38, 42, 46, 46n1, 75, 91,
    296, 304, 307, 308, 309, 313, 328
Jung, S. L., 350
Juslin, P. N., 11
Juth, P., 95

Kagan, J., 100
Kahn, A., 211
Kaiser, M. D., 259
Kaiser, S., 11
Kakigi, R., 55, 368, 428
Kalakanis, L., 18
Kalin, N. H., 220
Kalish, H. I., 279
Kamachi, M., 9
Kampe, K. K. W., 14
Kanda, N., 174
Kanno, I., 415
Kanwisher, N., 13, 34, 42, 53, 59, 91,
    220, 350, 355, 356, 365, 366, 367,
    368, 369, 410, 413, 417, 421, 423

Kaping, D., 18, 321, 347
Kaplan, J. A., 395, 396
Karlsson, A., 95
Karnath, H. O., 67
Karter, A. J., 12, 174
Kashy, D. A., 90
Kato, T., 348
Katra, E., 287f
Katz, B., 322
Katz, D. B., 13
Kaufmann, J. M., 403
Kawabata, H., 15
Kawamura, T., 75, 81
Kawano, K., 368
Kawashima, R., 373
Kawato, M., 371
Kay, J. W., 253, 266, 411
Kay, P., 284
Keane, J., 11
Keating, C. F., 92, 96, 175
Keele, S. W., 34
Keenan, J. P., 211, 397
Keesee, T., 304
Keightley, M. L., 141
Keil, F. C., 334, 335
Keller, H., 87
Kelly, J. L., 375
Kelly, J. R., 232
Kelly, S. W., 95
Keltner, D., 273
Kemner, C., 54, 426, 434
Kemp, R. I., 9
Kendon, A., 108
Kennedy, Q., 141
Kenner, N. M., 303
Kenny, D. A., 90
Kenrick, D. T., 7, 273
Kentridge, R. W., 63
Kersten, D., 188
Kestenbaum, R., 400
Ketay, S., 81, 86
Keysers, C., 222, 377
Khateb, A., 63, 373n4
Khera, A. V., 6
Kibler, J. L., 341
Kiefer, M., 14
Kikuchi, M., 11
Kikuchi, Y., 426
Kilcullen, R. N., 165
Killgore, W. D., 61
Kilner, J. M., 13, 95
Kim, B. S., 350
Kim, H., 159, 160, 161
Kim, J. S., 350
Kingstone, A., 122, 123, 421, 431
Kinsbourne, M., 401
Kirchner, H., 56
Kirk, I. J., 427
Kirkham, N. Z., 135
Kirschner, M. W., xxii
Kisilevsky, B. S., 423
Kisley, M. A., 140
Kitayama, S., 75, 76, 77, 78, 81, 82, 83,
    84, 85, 86f, 87
Kitterle, F., 368
Klatzky, R., 306

Kleck, R. E., 5, 6, 7, 11, 14, 92, 94, 96, 97, 98, 99, 108, 273
Kleinke, C. L., 134, 421
Klin, A., 242, 426, 432
Kling, K. C., 273
Klinnert, M., 216
Kloth, N., 59
Klüver, H., 372
Knapp, M. L., 236
Knight, G. P., 218
Knight, M., 137, 143, 144, 145
Knight, R. T., 34
Knoblich, G., 15
Knouf, N., 355, 368
Knutson, B., 5, 97
Ko, S. J., 46n1
Kobayashi, H., 112
Koch, M., 379
Kochiyama, T., 400
Koenken, G., 6
Koestner, R., 306
Koff, E., 398, 401
Kohler, E., 417
Kohshima, S., 112
Kolarz, C. M., 137
Kolb, B., 398
Kong, L., 85
Koo, J., 235, 236
Kopecky, J., 83
Kosslyn, S. M., 33, 34, 35, 143
Kozlowski, K., 198
Kozlowski, L. T., 242, 253, 266, 267, 411
Kramer, B. M., 322
Kranz, F., 15
Kraus, L. A., 241
Krause, P. J., 398
Kravitz, J., 101, 322
Krebeck, A., 250
Krebs, D., 165
Krekelberg, B., 418
Krizay, E., 357
Krolak-Salmon, P., 375
Krueger, S., 144
Kruglanski, A., 309
Krulewitz, J. E., 211
Krupp, D. B., 207, 208, 212
Kubota, J. T., 327
Kuhn, A., 16
Kühnen, U., 309
Kunda, Z., 37, 299
Kunz, P., 208
Künzler, R., 178
Kurzban, R., 266
Kveraga, K., 94, 254
Kwan, S. Y., 91
Kwas, M., 323
Kylliäinen, A., 427, 433, 434

LaBar, K. S., 13, 14, 95, 258
Labowitz, D. A., 293t
Lacruz, I., 323
Laeng, B., 35
Lagesen, K., 171
Laird, A. R., 220
Laird, J. D., 6
Lalonde, R., 424

Lamb, M. R., 34
Lambert, A. J,
Lamm, C., 397
Lamm, H., 211
Lamme, V. A., 61
Lamy, D., 18
Lanares, J., 400
Lander, K., 9
Landis, T., 112, 399
Landry, S. H., 432
Lang, P. J., 140
Langdell, T., 426
Langdon, R., 123
Lange, J., 372
Langlois, J. H., xiii, 5, 12, 18, 165, 166, 168, 187, 188, 379
Langton, S. R. H., 95, 108, 111, 113, 117, 118, 118f, 121, 122, 123, 127, 188, 431
Lanzetta, J. T., 6
Lappe, M., 369, 372
Larsen, J. T., 75, 81
Laser, P. S., 92
Lassiter, G. D., 134
Latini Corazzini, L., 59, 62
Lauder, G., 364n1
Laurian, S., 400
Lavigueur, H., 324
Lavrov, M., 267
Law, K., 135
Lawrence, A. D., 220, 221
Lawrence, E. J., 220
Law-Smith, M. J., 174
Lazeyras, F., 63, 373n4
Lea, S. E. G., 268
Leapold, D. A., 332
LeBeau, L. S., 234
Leder, H., 37, 38, 368
LeDoux, J. E., 15, 63, 66, 92, 220, 372
Ledoux, J. E., 66
Lee, A., 242, 257
Lee, F., 236
Lee, H. K., 7, 18, 96
Lee, K. E., 111, 348, 348f, 411, 413, 415
Lee, K. J., 3
Lee, M. B., 61, 63
Lee, S. W-S., 75, 78, 87
Lee, S. Y., 7
Lee, T. -W., 221, 222, 377
Lee, Y., 135
Leekam, S. R., 432, 435
Le Gal, P. M., 95
Le Grand, R., 37, 367
Lehman, D. R., 330
Leigland, L. A., 137
Leinbach, M. D., 273
Leinster, S. J., 171
Lemond, C. M., 398
Lenzi, G., 219
Leonard, C. M., 368
Leopold, D. A., 18, 331, 347, 348, 350
Lepore, L., 41, 42
Leslie, K., 222
Leu, J., 80
Levenson, R., 217
Leveque, J. -L., 195, 196

Lévesque, M., 17
Levin, D. T., 9, 307n1, 323, 326, 339, 341, 357
Levinson, S. C., 96
Levy, J., 9, 400
Levy, Y., 95
Lewicki, P., 7, 17
Lewis, M. B., 9
Lewis, P., 221
Lewis, R. S., 85
Lewis, S., 14
Lewis, V., 425
Lewis-Jones, D. I., 171
Ley, R. G., 398, 399
Liang, C. H., 77
Liberzon, I., 221, 400
Lichtey, L., 251
Liddell, B. J., 61, 66
Lieberman, M. D., 239, 241, 380
Liebich, S., 14
Liebler, A., 134, 231
Light, J., 146
Lilly, T., 233
Lin, L-M., 117
Lindsay, R. C. L., 323
Ling, J., 219
Linke, R., 66
Linkenkaer-Hansen, K., 55
Liotti, M., 220
Lippmann, W., 306
Little, A. C., 169, 170, 172, 173, 174, 176, 178, 196, 197, 208, 212, 213, 352, 354, 378
Little, W. S., 292t
Liu, C. H., 125
Liu, D., 394
Liu, J., 42, 43, 45, 59, 366, 367
Liu, L., 366
Livingston, R. W., 7, 10, 38, 40, 42, 45, 307
Livingstone, M. S., xxiv, 366
Lobmaier, J. S., 112
Locke, V., 38, 40, 42, 45
Loffler, G., 348, 349
Logan, J. S., 292t
Long, J. R., 242
Longo, L. C., 5, 165
Lopez, B., 432
Lorch, M. P., 398
Lord, C., 110, 111
Lorenceau, J., 251
Lorig, T. S., 6
Loula, F., 253, 267, 411
Loveland, K. A., 432
Lowenberg, K., 85
Lucas, P. W., 278
Ludwig, W., 171
Luevano, V. X., 12, 14
Luh, K. E., 399
Lui, L., 307
Lulenski, M. E., 34
Lundqvist, D., 5, 95, 329
Luo, J., 136
Lutzemberger, L., 61
Lutzenberger, W., 371
Lux, E., 174
Lyons, P. M., 165

Ma, Y., 273
Macaluso, E., 415
Maccoby, E., 217
MacDonald, B., 421
MacDonald, C. J., 11
Machado, C. J., 372
Macko, K. A., 92
MacLean, D., 192
MacLeod, C., 42, 100, 134, 135
MacLeod, D. I. A., 348, 349, 350, 357
MacLin, M. K., 326, 329
MacLin, O. H., 99, 321, 325, 326, 327,
    328, 329, 330, 331, 332, 334, 335,
    337, 339, 347, 348, 351, 354
Macrae, C. N., 5, 6, 17, 33, 34, 35, 36, 38,
    40, 41, 42, 43, 44f, 45, 45f, 46, 94,
    95, 96, 99, 108, 266, 272, 309, 421
Macrae, N., 306, 307, 308, 380
Madden, D. J., 143, 144, 146
Maddox, K. B., 10, 42, 307, 326
Maddux, W. W., 17
Maffei, L., 249
Magee, J. J., 397
Magnée, M. J., 54
Mahon, B. Z., 53
Makhijani, M. G., 5, 165
Malach, R., 54
Malatesta, C. Z., 17
Malcolm, S. R., 397
Malhi, G., 220
Maloney, L. T., 204, 348
Malpass, R. S., 99, 101, 322, 323, 324,
    325, 326, 327, 328, 329, 334, 339
Mandal, M. K., 401
Mandel, D. R., 330
Mandisodza, A. N., 229, 379
Maner, J. K., 5
Manis, M., 270
Manning, J. T., 171
Mannion, H., 176
Manor, B. R., 135
Manstead, A. S., 11, 425
Marcel, A. J., 67
Marey, E. J., 250
Marinkovic, K., 55, 366
Mark, L. E., 10
Mark, L. S., 10
Markus, H., 81, 86
Markus, H. R., 75, 76, 77
Marlot, C., 56
Marlowe, C. M., 165
Marlowe, F. W., 169, 210
Marr, D., xiv, 33, 35, 248
Marsh, A. A., 6, 11, 19, 98, 99, 100
Marsh, J. T., 400
Marshuetz, C., 6
Marsman, G., 90
Marsolek, C. J., 34, 35
Martin, A., 371n2, 411, 413, 414, 415, 418
Martin, C. D., 58, 366
Martin, C. L., 273
Martin, D., 33, 40, 41, 42, 43, 44f, 45f,
    46, 99, 266, 272
Martin, F., 95
Martin, W. W., 110
Martinez, A., 34

Maruyama, K., 114
Marzi, C. A., 61
Mason, M. F., 6, 34, 35, 36, 38, 108
Massaccesi, S., 431, 432
Masuda, T., 17, 79, 80
Mather, G., 242, 266, 331, 347
Mather, M., 135, 137, 138, 143, 144, 145
Mathews, A., 100, 127, 134, 135
Mathie, V. A., 92
Matsuka, T., 257, 268
Matsumura, M., 400
Matsuzawa, T., 9
Mattay, V., 220
Mattingley, J. B., 62, 69
Matts, P. J., 196
Mauer, N., 237
Maurer, D., 37, 38, 41, 348, 367
Ma Wyatt, A., 348
May, K. A., 164, 170
Mayberg, H., 220
Mayhew, J. W., 109
Mayr, U., 137
Mazard, A., 367
Mazur, A., 92, 96
Mazzi, D., 178
Mazziotta, J., 219
McArthur, L. A. K., 5, 10, 175
McArthur, L. Z., 4, 8, 10, 96, 175, 249
McBurney, D. H., 210
McCandliss, B. D., 139
McCarthy, G., 6, 13, 119, 219, 254,
    258, 366, 370, 371, 417, 421, 424,
    427, 435
McCarthy, J. E., 348
McClelland, J. L., 17
McClintock, M. K., xxiv
McClure, K. A., 326
McClure, S., 13
McDaniel, C., 411
McDermott, J., 13, 34, 91, 350, 366,
    413, 423
McGaugh, J. L., 372
McGinn, N. C., 211
McGoldrick, J. E., 369
McInerney, S. C., 61, 63
McKay, L., 273, 274f
McKeever, W. F., 399
McKenna, M., 62, 373n3
McKone, E., 13, 349, 351, 365
McLeod, P., 370
McMahon, M., 347
McMahon, W. M., 426
McPartland, J., 427
Mealey, L., 172
Meeren, H. K. M., 55, 59, 60f
Meissner, C. A., 9, 17, 101, 322, 335
Meister, M., 348
Meltzoff, A., 219
Menon, V., 220
Merikle, P. M., 69
Merin, N., 426
Mesquita, B., 76, 80
Mesulam, M. M., 6
Meunier, M., 372
Meyer, D. E., 83
Michel, D., 395

Michel, F., 428
Michelich, C. R., 6
Michels, L., 369, 371
Mignault, A., 5, 10
Mignon, A., 5
Mikels, J. A., 137, 138
Millar, N., 100
Miller, E. K., 368
Miller, L. M., 415
Miller, P. J., 11, 77
Millikan, R. G., 364
Mills, C. K., 394
Milne, E., 258
Milner, A. D., xv
Milord, J., 324
Minelli, A., 61
Mishkin, M., xv, 92
Misovich, S. J., 96
Mistlin, A. J., 95
Mitchell, J. P., 13, 380, 397
Mitroff, S. R., 303
Mitton, J. B., 168
Miura, S., 415
Miyake, K., 12
Mizokami, Y., 18, 321, 347
Mobbs, D., 220
Mogg, K., 100
Mohamedc, F. B., 211
Mohanty, A., 401
Mohanty, S., 401
Mohr, B., 403
Molholm, S., 418
Moll, J., 220
Mollaret, P., 5
Møller, A. P., 167, 171, 174, 178
Mollon, J. D., 278, 332
Mondloch, C. J., 37, 367
Monteith, 233
Montepare, J. M., 4, 5, 7, 8, 10, 11, 16,
    19, 20, 22, 25, 30, 32, 40, 44, 96,
    107, 253, 267, 268, 276, 277, 357,
    371, 375,
Moore, C., 17, 125, 242, 250, 411, 432, 435
Moore, D. G., 257
Moore, M. J., 151, 242
Moran, R. J., 418
Morant, R. B., 357
Moreno, C. R., 400
Morgan, D., 268
Morland, T., 62
Morley, T., 109
Morling, B., 76, 231
Morris, D., 287
Morris, J. P., 6, 119, 220, 258, 417, 427,
    435
Morris, J. S., 54, 61, 63, 65, 66, 373,
    373n4, 375
Morris, M. W., 77
Morris, P. E., 9
Morrison, E. R., 12
Morrison, R., 242, 250, 411
Morton, J., 164, 423, 435
Moscovitch, M., 53, 140
Moses, N. N., 307n1
Moss, A., 368
Mottron, L., 425

Mouchetant-Rostaing, Y., 43, 45
Moynihan, M., 93
Mroczek, D. K., 137
Muehlberger, A., 366
Muir, D. W., 9, 423
Mulhern, R., 195, 196
Müller, K-M., 348
Mullin, J. T., 16
Muncer, S., 219
Mundy, N. I., 278, 283
Mundy, P., 432
Munro, I. R., 188, 195
Munson, J. A., 426
Murdoch, L., 266
Murphy, F. C., 221
Murphy, N. A., 5, 133, 134, 137, 138, 141, 142, 146, 229, 233, 238
Murphy, N. M., 143
Murphy, S. T., 61, 208
Musselman, L., 168
Myowa-Yamakoshi, M., 9

Nacewicz, B. M., 426
Nagayama, R. S., 121, 127
Nagele, T., 67
Naito, E., 400
Nakayama, K., xxiv, 13, 18, 91, 366
Nakhutina, L., 395
Nalli, A., 211
Nars, F., 194n3
Narumoto, J., 400
Nasanen, R., 368
Nathan, P. J., 13
Nava, C., 96
Navarrete, C. D., 19
Naveh-Benjamin, M., 144
Navon, D., 34
Neargarder, S., 142
Neave, N., 187
Neil Macrae, C., 13
Nelson, C. A., 5, 16, 400
Nelson, C. E., 165
Nelson, H., 331
Nelson, M., 231
Nelson, T. E., 270
Nesselroade, J., 137
Neta, M., 12, 98
Neuberg, S. L., 7, 31, 37, 38, 41, 42, 43, 46, 266, 267, 272, 273, 306, 307, 308
Neufeld, P., 322
Neumann, D., 426
Ng, M., 355
Ng, W., 323
Nicholas, C. D., 34
Nicholas, M., 398
Nichols, S., 217
Nickell, E. F., 134
Nicolelis, M. A., 13
Nicolich, M., 17
Niebur, E., 135
Niedenthal, P. M., 5, 6, 61
Niendenthal, P. M., 208
Nikels, K. W., 7
Nimmo-Smith, I., 67, 221
Nisbett, R. E., 76, 77, 78, 79, 80, 87

Nisenson, L., 399
Nishimura, M., 111
Nissen, M. J., 123
Noesselt, T., 415
Norcliffe, H., 306
Norenzayan, A., 76
Norman, D. A., 299
Norman, J. F., 242
Norman, KA., 418
Norton, M. I., 5n2
Nowicki, S., 239
Nowicki, S., Jr., 142
Nozawa, G., 368
Nuechterlein, K. H., 242
Nummenmaa, L., 134
Nurmoja, M., 7

Obler, L. K., 395, 396
O'Boyle, C., 273
O'Connor, K., 427
O'Connor, N., 426
Oda, M., 348
O'Doherty, J., 13, 14, 95, 220, 379
O'Doherty, J. P., 13, 14, 95, 159, 220, 379
Odom, R. D., 398
Ogan, T., 216
Ogden, W. C., 123
O'Hara, R., 144
Ohman, A., 5, 6, 54, 61, 63, 69, 329, 373
Öhman, A., 95, 145
Ohta, S., 421
Ojanpaa, H., 368
Okada, T., 400
Okon-Singer, H., 143, 145
O'Leary, A., 347
O'Leary, V. E., 211
Oliva, A., 39, 40, 94, 99
Oliver, M. B., 307n1
Oliveri, M., 394
Olson, D., 217
Olson, E. A., 322
Olson, I. R., 6
Olson, K., 188
Oltmanns, T. F., 233
O'Malley, C., 127
Opeyo, A., 358
Oram, M. W., 119, 340, 370, 372, 415
Orban, G. A., 370
Orbelo, D., 9
O'Regan, J. K., 79
Orlikoff, R. F., 10
Oros, L., 400
Orr, S. P., 6
Osgood, C. E., 283
Osorio, D., 278, 283
Osterling, J. A., 426
Ostrove, N., 165
Ostry, D., 251, 370
Osu, R., 371
O'Toole, A. J., 3, 9, 18, 188, 331, 347
Ouston, J., 242
Oyserman, D., 75, 78, 87
Ozonoff, S., 426

Padmala, S., 62
Palermo, R., 5

Paller, K. A., 9
Palomares, F., xxii
Pandya, D. N., 254
Panter, A. T., 240
Panyavin, I. S., 210
Pape, H. C., 66
Paramo, M. F., 81
Park, B., 42, 46, 75, 296, 304, 328
Park, D. C., 79
Park, J. H., 19
Parkhurst, D., 135
Parry, F. M., 368
Pascalis, O., 9, 16, 424
Pascual-Leone, A., 370, 418
Pasupathi, M., 137
Paterson, E., 273
Paterson, H. M., 253, 268
Paterson, T., 140
Patterson, R., 348
Pauker, K., 101
Paus, T., 54, 220, 376
Pavlova, M., 371
Payne, B. K., 296, 297, 300, 301, 301f, 302f, 304
Payton, S. M., 242
Pearl, E., 196
Peelen, M. V., 53, 54, 369, 371, 372, 373, 376
Peery, J. C., 429
Pegna, A. J., 58, 63, 65, 66, 366, 373n4
Peirce, J. W., 208, 209
Peiss, K., 186
Pellicano, E., 258
Pelphrey, K. A., 6, 119, 219, 258, 370, 371, 411, 414, 417, 427, 435
Pendry, L. F., 309
Peng, K., 76, 77, 80
Pennington, B. F., 435
Penny, W., 223
Penrod, S. D., 32
Pentland. A., 325
Pentland, B., 12
Penton-Voak, I. S., 12, 172, 173, 174, 176, 179, 208, 209, 212, 378
Perez, E., 55, 421, 424
Perez, J., 427
Perlman Lorch, M., 398
Perozzo, P., 51
Perra, O., 220
Perret, D. I., 91, 156, 196
Perret, E., 399
Perrett, D. I., 13, 33, 34, 40, 92, 95, 119, 120, 121, 124, 164, 170, 172, 173, 173f, 174, 175, 176, 176f, 179, 188, 197, 204, 205, 208, 209, 212, 220, 222, 251, 254, 331, 340, 348, 366, 368, 370, 372, 378, 415, 428
Peruche, B. M., 304
Pessoa, L., 61, 62, 63, 143, 145, 373n3, 373n4
Peters, M., 12
Peterson, D. J., 329, 335
Peterson, M. P., 368
Peterson, R., 426
Petit, O., 16
Petrides, M., 251, 370

Petrie, M., 174
Petro, L. S., 373
Petty, R. E., 134, 136
Peuskens, H., 370, 371, 372
Pezdek, K., 17
Pfeifer, J. H., 380
Phan, K. L., 13, 221, 400
Phelps, E. A., 69, 321, 323, 327, 341
Phillips, A., 242
Phillips, K. C., 9
Phillips, M. L., 92
Phillips, P. J., 9
Phillips, W., 220
Phinney, R. E., 348
Piaget, J., 217
Pichon, S., 54, 268, 373, 376, 417
Pick, A. D., 38, 109, 110, 111, 112
Pick, H. L., 38
Pick, L. H., 396, 398
Pierce, J., 179
Pierce, K., 427
Pike, C. L., 175
Pike, G. E., 9
Pincus, D., 395
Pineau, P., 195, 196
Pineda, J. A., 96
Pinsk, M. A., 366
Pinto, J., 250, 253, 267
Pipingas, A., 55
Pitcairn, T. K., 12
Pitcher, D., 368
Pittenger, J. B., 10
Pittinsky, T. L., 91
Piven, J., 6, 426
Pividori, D., 431, 432
Plant, E. A., 273, 304
Platek, S. M., 210, 211, 212
Platt, M. L., 6
Platz, S. J., 323
Plutchik, R., 97
Pobric, G., 369
Poggio, T., 372
Poiroux, S., 424
Polk, T. A., 144
Pollatsek, A., 135
Pollick, F. E., 253, 257, 266, 267, 268,
    273, 274f, 411
Polyn, S. M., 418
Porter, S., 397
Posner, M. I., 34, 122, 123, 139, 431
Potanina, P. V., 380
Potter M. C., 100
Pound, N., 378
Pourtois, G., 14, 61, 63, 65, 369, 375, 377
Powell, L. J., 379, 394, 397
Powelson, J. A., 395
Power, T. G., 218
Prasad, S., 253, 267, 411
Pratt, J., 123
Pratto, F., 309
Premack, D., 92, 394
Preston, S. D, 217, 222
Price, C. J., 418
Prkachin, G. C., 37
Prodan, C., 9
Proffitt, D. R., 266

Proffitt, F., 172
Pruzan, K., 140
Puccinelli, N. M., 230, 235, 236
Puce, A., 55, 92, 119, 251, 254, 366,
    368, 370, 372, 415, 421, 424, 428
Purdie, V. J., 10, 75, 307
Purdie-Vaughns, V. J., 7, 309
Putnam, P., 100
Pyles, J. A., 414
Pylyshyn, Z., 250

Quinn, K. A., 5, 95, 96
Quinn, P. C., 16

Racinet, A., 279f
Radcliffe, R. D., 253
Radeke, M. K., 331
Radel, M., 395, 396
Radford, K., 242
Radner, M., 331
Ragas, M. C., 198
Raichle, M., 222
Raij, T., 55
Ramaswamy, J., 75, 78
Rapson, R. L., 63, 217
Rasmussen, T., 399
Rassovsky, Y., 242
Rauch, S. L., 61, 63, 100
Rayner, K., 135
Raz, M., 139
Rebai, M., 424, 425
Reber, R., 18
Redican, W. K., 93
Reed, C. L., 55, 369
Reed, S. K., 348
Regan, BC, 278
Regan, D., 348
Regard, M., 112
Regier, D. A., 137
Regier, T., 284
Reichle, E. D., 135
Reichman, V., 232, 253, 270f, 271f, 272
Reierson, G. W., 175, 177
Reilly, R. B., 418
Reis, H. T., 12
Reiss, A. L., 220
Reiss, M. J., 293t
Remington, R. W., 145
Rensink, R. A., 79
Reuter-Lorenz, P., 400
Reyes, J. A., 76, 82
Rhodes, G. E., 3, 5, 7, 8n4, 9, 12, 16, 18,
    33, 34, 35, 168, 169, 170, 172, 174,
    175, 176, 187, 188, 193, 197, 213,
    325, 331, 347, 348, 349, 350, 350f,
    350n1, 351, 352, 354, 355f, 356,
    358, 359, 367, 368
Rhodes, M. G., 17, 35
Ricciardelli, P., 121, 431
Richards, J., 425
Richardson, M. J., 267, 269
Richeson, J. A., xxii, xxv, 101, 229,
    233, 236
Richetin, J., 195, 197
Riddle, W. J. R., 12
Riddoch, M. J., 368

Riemann, R., 237
Riesenhuber, M., 368
Riggio, R. E., 12, 164, 238, 240
Righart, R., 56, 58, 268
Rime, B., 229
Rinck, M., 135
Ristic, J., 123, 434
Ritter, J. M., 165, 167
Rizzo, M., 6
Rizzolatti, G., 222, 377, 417
Ro, T., 416, 431
Roark, D. A., 9
Robbins, R., 349, 351
Roberts, A. R., 166
Roberts, S. C., 168, 212
Robertson, L. C., 34
Rockland, K. S., 254
Rogers, P. L., 90, 230
Rogers, S. J., 426, 435
Roggman, L. A., xiii, 18, 167, 168, 188
Rogoff, B., 77, 87
Rohleder, L., 90
Roldan, E. R. S., 171
Rolls, E. T., 14, 91, 220, 331, 368
Romanski, L. M., 373n4
Rorie, K. D., 395
Rosch, E. H., 18
Rose, D., 242, 254
Rosenberg, S., 5
Rosenthal, R., 11, 90, 229, 230, 231,
    233, 234, 235, 236, 238, 239, 240,
    241, 243, 380
Rosip, J. C., 239, 241
Ross, E. D., 9, 398, 402
Rossion, B., 65, 188, 249, 367, 368, 437
Roth, D. L., 398
Rotshtein, P., 54, 221, 356, 367, 368
Rottman, L., 164
Rovira, M. L., 110
Rowland, D., 204
Royzman, E. B., 137, 140
Rozin, P., 137, 140
Rubenstein, A. J., 18
Rubin, M., 91
Ruble, D. N., 273
Ruby, P., 397
Rueckert, L. M., 399
Ruffman, T., 142, 217
Rule, N. O., 6, 17
Rumelhart, D. E., 17
Runeson, S., 253, 268, 269
Rusconi, M., 69
Russell, J. A., 229
Russell, R. L., 18, 90, 186, 193, 194f,
    197, 201
Rutherford, M. D., 426
Rutter, M., 220

S., 17
S, Tessitore, A., 220
Sabbagh, M. A., 394
Sabourin, G., 92
Sackeim, H. A., 400
Sadato, N., 400
Sadler, M. S., 7, 38, 304, 307
Sadr, J., 196

Safer, M. A., 400
Sahraic, A., 66
Sai, F., 16
Saiki, J., 83
Sakreida, K., 53
Sale, B. A., 231
Salib, E. R., 6
Saliba, E., 424
Salin, P-A., 254
Salmon, E., 397
Salthouse, T. A., 136
Salyer, K., 165
Samson, D., 397, 403
Samuels, C. A., 167, 172, 187
Sanders, C., 174
Sanders, J. D., 326
Sandini, G., 249
Sandnabba, N. K., 273
Sanford, A. J., 253, 268
Sangrigoli, S., 17
Santi, A., 371
Santschi-Haywood, C., 396, 398
Sapir, E., 90
Sarfati, Y., 219, 397
Saron, C., 401
Sarty, M., 164
Sasson, N., 426
Sato, W., 11, 400, 401
Saul, J. S., 368
Savazzi, S., 61
Sawada, M., 268
Saxe, R., 220, 377, 379, 394, 397, 417
Saxe, R. R., 19, 220, 377, 379, 380, 394, 397, 417
Saygin, A. P., 254, 256, 370, 371, 412, 415
Schacter, D. L., 34
Schaefer, E. S., 97
Schafer, A., 221
Schaffer, C. E., 401
Schaller, M., 19
Scheck, B. C., 322
Scheib, J. E., 171, 172, 179
Scherer, K. R., 11, 82
Schiaratura, L., 229
Schienle, A., 221
Schiltz, C., 367, 368
Schimmack, U., 140
Schlangel, M., 143
Schmidt, S., 11
Schneider, F., 12
Schneider, S. L., 165
Schneider, W., 144
Schooler, J. W., 11, 230
Schroeder, C. E., 415
Schroeder, U., 220
Schubotz, R. I., 53
Schuller, A. M., 431, 437
Schuller, G., 17
Schulman, G. A., 273
Schultz, R. T., 242, 260, 371n2, 377, 427
Schulz, L. E., 137
Schulz, R., 146
Schumann, C. M., 427
Schwaninger, A., 112
Schwartz, C. E., 100
Schwartz, S., 62, 69

Schwarz, N., 18
Schwarzlose, R. F., 53, 369
Schweers, N., xv
Schwegler, H., 66
Schweinberger, S. R., 95, 403
Schyns, P. G., 9, 34, 38, 39, 40, 42, 43, 94, 99, 373, 375
Scutt, D., 171
Sczesny, S., 17, 309
Searcy, J., 37, 38
Sears, L., 6
Sebanz, N., 15, 253
Sebestyen, G., 96
Sebrechts, M. M., 426
Secord, P. F., 4, 322
Segall, M. H., 92, 96
Seghier, M. L., 63, 373n4
Sekiyama, K., 415
Sekuler, A. B., 426
Semmes, J., 398
Senju, A., 95, 372, 421, 427, 432, 433, 434
Sergent, J., 325, 421
Sergi, M. J., 242
Servos, P., 371
Seyama, J., 121, 127
Shallice, T., 299
Shamay-Tsoory, S. G., 395
Shapiro, P. P., 17
Shaw, P., 220, 401
Shaw, R. E., 10
Shelton, J. N., 233, 236
Shelton, S. E., 220
Shepard, R. N., 248
Shepherd, J. W., 323, 324, 325
Sherman, T., 432
Sherman-Williams, B., 299
Shi, C., 66
Shiffrar, M., 250, 251, 252, 253, 255f, 256, 257, 259, 260, 267, 268, 409, 411
Shiffrin, R. M., 144
Shih, M., 91
Shimizu, Y., 301, 302f
Shimojo, E., 152, 153f, 158
Shimojo, S., 152, 153f, 157f, 158, 158f, 159, 188n2, 283, 293t
Shimzu, Y., 300, 301f
Shin, L. M., 100
Shubel, E., 357
Shulman, G., 222
Shumake, J., 220
Shuman, M., 53, 369, 413
Siegal, M., 394, 395, 396, 397
Sigall, H., 165
Sigman, M., 432
Silberman, E. K., 400
Silberstein, R. B., 55
Sim, E. -J., 14
Simion, C., 152, 153f, 157f, 158, 158f
Simion, F., 124, 423
Simmel, M., 260, 374
Simmons, L. W., 12, 174
Simon, S. A., 13
Simons, D. J., 238
Simpson, J. A., 212, 231

Sindale, N. V., 357
Singer, S., 145
Singerman, J. D., 119, 219
Singh, D., 198
Singh, K. D., 418
Sinha, P., 113, 196, 259, 368
Sivers, H., 221
Six, B., 306
Skowbo, D., 357
Skudlarski, P., 34, 53
Skuse, D., 223
SL, W., 221
Slater, A. M., 9, 16, 187
Slaughter, V., 55
Slone, A. E., 17, 322, 323
Small, D., 221
Smilek, D., 69
Smith, A., 216, 421
Smith, D. M., 7, 273
Smith, E. E., 81
Smith, E. R., 323, 329, 330, 333
Smith, G. L., 273
Smith, J., 137
Smith, L., 9
Smith, M. L., 373
Smith, P. M., 123, 218
Smith, S. T., 348
Smith, W. A. P., 366
Smolensky, P., 17
Snodgrass, J. G., 330
Snow, D., 395
Snyder, J., 54, 417
Snyder, M., 165
Soares, J. C., 427
Sobel, D. M., 135
Sokolov, A., 371
Soler, M., 171
Solso, R. L., 348
Solwin, D., 165
Sommer, T., 139
Sommerville, J. A., 6
Sorce, J., 216
Spalding, B., 292t
Spalding, J. A. B., 292t, 293t
Speer, L. L., 426
Spelke, E. S., 242
Spencer, D. D., 366
Spencer, J., 258
Spencer, S. J., 37
Sperling, G., 252, 331
Sperry, R. W., 399
Spezio, M. L., 381, 426
Spinath, F. M., 237
Spiridon, M., 53
Sporer, S. L., 322, 327
Sprecher, S., 200
Springer, S. P., 393, 398
Squire, L. R., 34, 35
Stanley, D., 34
Stapleton, J., 397
Stark, R., 221
Steele, H., 223
Steele, M., 223
Steeves, J. K. E., 368
Stein, E., 217
Stekelenburg, J. J., 55, 59

Stenberg, G., 6
Stern, D. N., 429
Sternberg, R. J., 358
Stevenage, S. V., 4
Stevens, J. A., 252
Stevenson, L. A., 12
Steward, S. M., 293t
Stewart, T., 372
Steyvers, M., 335
Stokes, J. M., 90
Stone, V. E., 55, 369, 399
Stout, A., 250
Strange, B. A., 379
Strauss, M. S., 348
Strayer, F. F., 218
Striano, T., 11
Stringer, R., 253, 266, 411
Strom, M., 7
Stroop, J. R., 298
Sturman, D., 61
Stuss, D. T., 397
Subbarayappa, B. V., 199
Suberi, M., 399
Suchan, B., 372
Suda, K., 268
Sugase, Y., 368, 376
Sugita, Y., xxiv, 415
Sullivan, S., 142
Sumich, A., 169, 172
Surridge, A. K., 278, 283
Sutton, P., 348
Sutton, S. K., 378
Swaddle, J. P., 171, 175, 177
Swaim, G. W., 12
Swanson, J., 42
Swart, L. A., 341
Swithenby, S. J., 427
Swope, T. M., 322
Sykes, R. N., 9
Symons L. A., 111

Tabert, M., 398
Tager-Flusberg, H., 417
Takahashi, H., 221
Takemura, K., 75, 78
Talmi, D., 140
Tamaki, K., 174
Tamietto, M., 51, 54, 59, 61, 62, 62f, 64, 65, 67, 68, 69, 402, 402f, 403
Tan, S., 16, 33
Tanaka, J. N., 14, 242, 367, 426, 432
Tanaka, J. W., 331, 334, 357
Tanaka, M., 9
Tanida, S., 80
Tanke, E. D., 165
Tannen, D., 218
Tanskanen, T., 368
Tantam, D., 425
Tardif, T., 394
Tarr, M. J., 33, 34, 35, 53, 188, 365
Tassinari, G., 61
Tassinary, L. G., 232, 253, 270, 270f, 271f, 272
Tata, P., 100
Tatkow, E. P., 108
Taylor, J. C., 369, 370

Taylor, K., 16, 33
Taylor, L., 398
Taylor, M. J., 55, 366, 424, 425
Taylor, S. E., 31, 32, 221, 307
Taylor, S. F., 221, 400
Tegner, R., 67
Tessler, E., 117
Testa, J., 9
Tew, B. D., 369
Thatcher, R. W., 398
Theeuwes, J., 143
Thibault, P., 92
Thiel, D. L., 165
Thierry, G., 55, 58, 59, 366
Thomas, L. A., 321, 323, 341
Thompson, E., 328
Thompson, J. C., 371, 372
Thornhill, R., 12, 167, 168, 171, 172, 174, 175, 178, 179, 187, 188, 196
Thorpe, S. J., 56
Thunberg, M., 54, 219
Tiberghien, G., 95
Tickle-Degnen, L., 230, 235, 236
Tiddeman, B. P., 204, 205, 208
Timney, B. N., 357
Tinajero, C., 81
Tinti, C., 67
Tipper, S. P., 122, 126, 127
Tipples, J., 95, 100, 123
Todd, A. R., 101
Todd, J. T., 10
Todorov, A., 6, 90, 229, 378, 379
Todorovic, D., 114, 115f, 118
Tojo, Y., 427
Tomer, R., 395
Tomonaga, M., 9
Toner, K., 138
Tong, F., 91
Tooby, J., 266
Tooman, G. D., 233
Toosi, N., 267
Tootell, R. B. H., 366
Toriyama, R., 87
Torriero, S., 394
Towell, N. A., 9
Townsend, G., 172
Townsend, J. T., 3, 92, 95
Tranel, D., 6, 91, 240, 368, 373, 377, 378, 379, 400
Trawalter, S., 101
Trebon, P., 366
Tredoux, C. G., 323, 325
Treisman, A., 323
Tremewan, T., 168, 169
Trepagnier, C., 426
Treves, A., 356
Triandis, H. C., 87
Triplett, N., 329
Troje, N. F., xxvi, 188, 253, 266, 267, 372
Trope, Y., 299
Troscianko, T., 268
Tsao, D. Y. N., xv, xxiv, 349, 366, 368
Tsuchida, T., 174
Tsukasaki, T., 84
Tucker, D. M., 398

Tulving, E., 33
Tunstall, M. L., 268
Turk, M., 325
Turkheimer, E., 233
Turner, J., 348
Tyler, R. B., 42, 266
Tzelgov, J., 143, 145

Uchida, Y., 75, 76
Ueno, S., 368
Uhlmann, E., 42
Uleman, J. S., 378
Unger, L., 208
Ungerer, J., 432
Ungerleider, L. G., xv, 61, 62, 92, 373n3
Urcuioli, P. J., 279
Urgesi, C., 369
Urland, G. R., 5, 13, 14, 321, 327, 328, 329, 330, 341, 357, 358
Uskul, A. K., 78, 87

Vaghn, L. A., 233
Vaina, L. M., 368, 369, 370, 372
Vaish, A., 11
Vaitl, D., 221
Valen, L. V., 171
Valenstein, E., 398
Valentine, T., 3, 9, 19, 38, 41, 169, 323, 324, 325, 347, 348, 367
Vallar, G., 67
Van Atteveldt, N., 415
van den Bos, W., 13
Vanden Stock, J., 57, 58
Van den Stock, J., 268
van der Geest, J. N., 426, 432
Vanderploeg, R. D., 400
Van de Veerdonk, E., 80
van Engeland, H., 54, 426
Van Essen, D. C., 409
van Heijnsbergen, C. C., 55
van Honk, J., 100
Van Overwalle, F., 90
van Raamsdonk, M., 61, 65
van Reekum, C. M., 146
Vanrie, J., 370
van Rijn, S., 378
van Wezel, R. J., 418
van Zoest, W., 143
Varley, R., 394, 397
Vatikiotis- Bateson, E., 9
Vaughan, J., 144
Vaughn, L. S., 167
Vecera, S. P., 112, 128
Verbaten, M. N., 426
Verfaillie, K., 250, 370
Verhaeghen, P., 144
Verlut, I., 95
Vernon, P. E., 229
Verstraten, F. A. J., 331, 347
Vescio, T. K., 91
Vetter, T., 18, 188, 331, 347
Vighetti, S., 51
Vine, I., 110, 111
Viola, R. J., 119, 371
Virji-Babul, N., 252, 259
Vivekananthan, P. S., 5

Vohs, K. D., 137
Voinescu, L., 12
Voisin, J., 15
Voke, J., 292t
Volein, Á., 425, 432
Volkmar, F., 242
von Cramon, D. Y., 53
Von Cranach, M., 110
von der Twer, T., 348, 349, 350
von Grunau, M., 323
Vorobyev, M., 278
Voyvodic, J. T., 13
Vroomen, J., 61, 63, 65
Vuilleumier, P., 11, 62, 69, 373, 375, 377, 421
Vul, E., 357

Wada, J., 399
Wade, N. J., 331
Wadlinger, H. A., 136, 141
Wager, T. D., 14, 81, 221, 400
Wagner, H. L., 11
Waiter, G. D., 220
Waitt, C., 173, 287
Walden, K. J., 348
Walden, T., 216
Walk, R. D., 268
Walker, I., 42
Walker, P. M., 323, 331, 334, 357
Walsh, V., 368
Walster, E., 164, 166
Walter, B., 221
Walton, G. E., 16, 348
Walton, J. H., 10
Wartell, S. L. B., 210
Wasserman, B. H., 210
Watanabe, K., 242
Watanabe, S., 55, 368, 428
Watson, T. L., 18, 331, 347, 351
Watt, R. J., 95, 113, 125
Watts, F. N., 134, 135
Waxer, P. H., 231
Weatherhead, P. J., 171
Webb, S. J., 427
Webster, M. A., 18, 321, 325, 331, 332, 336, 337, 338, 339, 347, 348, 351, 354
Wedekind, C., 174
Wegener, D. T., 134, 136
Wehrle, T., 11
Weinberger, D. R., 220
Weineke, K., 18
Weingartner, H., 400
Weisberg, J., 371n2
Weisbuch, M., 231
Weisel, A., 240
Weisfeld, Glenn, E., 16
Weiskrantz, L., 51, 61, 63, 65, 373
Weitzel, B., 210
Welch, R. B., 331
Weldon, D. E., 324
Welkowitz, J., 400
Welling, L. L. M., 212
Wellman, H. M., 394
Wells, G. L., 322
Welsh, R. C., 79

Wenderoth, P., 348
Wenger, M. J., 3, 95
Werblin, F. S., 348
Werner, E., 426
Werner, J. S., 325, 348
Wertheimer, M., 252
West, S., 242
Westerlund, A., 16
Westhoff, C., 267
Wexler, A., 379, 397
Whalen, P. J., 61, 63, 65, 257, 373, 374
Wheaton, K. J., 55, 370, 371
Wheeler, M. E. 42, 365, 365f
Wheelwright, S., 218, 219, 223, 242, 424
White, B., 18
Whitehouse, G. H., 171
Whiten, A., 92, 217, 220
Wicker, B., 57, 219, 220, 370, 428
Wickler, W., 287
Widick, P., 403
Wiggett, A. J., 369
Wiggins, J. S., 5, 96
Wiking, S., 6
Wiley, A., 77
Wilkinson, F., 117, 348
Willadsen-Jensen, E. C., 327, 328, 329, 330, 334
Willen, J. D., 124, 431
Williams, J. E., 97
Williams, J. H. G., 220
Williams, J. M. G., 134, 135
Williams, L. E., 145
Williams, L. J., 144
Williams, L. M., 61, 66, 140
Williams, M. A., 373
Williamson, P., 426
Willis, J., 6, 90, 378
Wills, E. J., 324
Wilson, D., 242
Wilson, G., 292t
Wilson, H. R., 117, 118, 136, 138, 348, 367
Wilson, K., 230
Wilson, K. D., 367
Wilson, M., 218
Wingfield, J. C., 174
Winkielman, P., 5, 18, 272
Winner, E., 394, 395, 396
Winocur, G., 141
Winograd, C. H., 235
Winston, J. S., 13, 95, 368, 369, 373, 377, 379
Witkin, H. A., 80, 81
Wittenbrink, B., 42, 75, 296, 304, 328
Woike, B. A., 12, 98
Wojciulik, E., 421
Wolfe, J. M., 303
Wolfensteller, U., 53
Woll, S., 164
Wollaston, W. H., 116
Wong, B., 142
Wood, S., 140
Wood, W., 273
Woodruff, G., 92, 394
Woodward, A. L., 242

Wooten, B. R., 287f
Wormser, G. P., 293t
Wright, C. I., 100
Wright, D. B., 323
Wright, L., 364
Wright, T. M., 415
Wu, P. Y. K., 164
Wyer, N. A., 341

Xiaohu, P., 14
Xing, C., 140
Xing, W., 14

Yahr, J., 16
Yamagiwa, J., 151
Yamaguchi, M. K., 9
Yamane, S., 368
Yamashita, J. A., 354, 357, 358
Yantis, S., 145
Yarbus, A. L., 111
Yasar, N. E., 416
Yeagley, E., 231
Yesilova, Z., 174
Yiend, J., 100, 127
Yin, R. K., 34
Yonekura, Y., 400
Yoon, H. W., 350
Yoshikawa, S., 11, 164, 170, 400
Yoshimura, E. A., 395
Yovel, G., 9, 356, 365, 366, 367, 368, 410
Young, A. W., 3, 6, 9, 11, 16, 32, 33, 34, 35, 38, 54, 55, 91, 92, 95, 99, 167, 220, 253, 268, 367, 368, 369
Young, G. S., 426
Young, R., 426
Youngstrom, E. A., 395
Yourganov, G., 348
Yovel, G., 9, 356, 365, 366, 367, 368, 410
Yuejia, L., 14
Yuki, M., 17
Yurgelun-Todd, D. A., 61

Zacks, R. T., 136
Zahavi, A., 174
Zahn, R., 221
Zajonc, R. B., 5, 7, 18, 61, 208, 210
Zanutto, A., 211
Zárate, M. A., 323, 329, 333
Zarrinpar, A., 35
Zebrowitz, L. A., 3, 4, 5, 6, 7, 7n3, 8, 8n4, 10, 11, 12, 13, 14, 16, 18, 19, 40, 92, 94, 96, 97, 98, 174, 187, 188, 197, 240, 249, 267, 310, 330
Zebrowitz-McArthur, L. A., xxiv, 8, 10, 167, 253, 267
Zeki, S., 15
Zgaljardic, D., 398
Zhang, Q., 188n2, 283, 293t
Zhang, S., 7
Zhang, Y., 6, 13, 14
Zhao, L., 331, 354
Zion-Golumbic, E., 366
Ziv, T., 18
Zoccolotti, P., 398
Zonios, G., 282f
Zuckerman, M., 12

SUBJECT INDEX

Note: Page references followed by '*f*' and '*t*' denote figures and tables, respectively.

Above-chance accuracy, 9
Accuracy, 6
Action errors, 297–99, 298*f*, 303
Adaptive behavior
   and perceived affordances, 4–6
      accuracy and overgeneralization,
         6–8
Adaptive norm-based coding of
      identity, 347–50
   coding model, 350*f*
Adaptive processes, 347
Affective empathy, 217
Affective state
   detection of, in human movement,
      253
Affordances, xv, 4–6
   concept of, 4
   for taste, 13
African American, 306, 322
   composite faces, 325–26
   face markers, 326
   face measurements, 310–11, 311*t*
   physical features, 318
   and stereotyping, 313
   and race bias, 233, 322
Afrocentric facial features, 306–19
   category-based stereotyping,
      306–7
   defining, 310–18
   face measurements, 310–11, 311*t*
   feature-based stereotyping, 307–10,
      308*f*
   selection of, 311–12, 312–13*f*
   in stereotyping, 313–18, 314*t*, 315*f*,
      316*t*, 317*f*, 317*t*
      full mediation model, 316, 317*f*
      indirect effects, 317, 317*t*
      mediational model, 315, 315
      regression model, 315, 316*t*
Afrocentrism, 312, 313, 315, 316, 317,
      318, 319

Age
   -based social categorization, 267
   in face perception, 4–5
   and thin-slice vision, 239
Age cues, 10–11
Agents' distance, bodily expressions
      and, 54
Agent vision and social vision, 51
Age–wrinkles, 46
Aging eyes and motivated gaze
   age differences and visual attention,
      136
   age effects, debates on motivation
      of, 138–41
      age-related gaze effects and
         motivation, summary of, 141
      gaze preferences and stimuli, 141
      laboratory manipulation
         approach, 139–40
   age-related findings, motivational
      accounts of, 136–38
   motivated gaze to emotional
      stimuli, social context of,
      141–43
   information processing, motivation
      affecting, 143–46
   summary and future directions
      of, 146
   visual attention, measurement of,
      134–35
"All possible subsets" approach
   for Afrocentric features selection,
      312–13
Ambiguous race faces (AFRs), 325–26,
      328
   stimulus development, 334–39
Amygdala (AMG), 13, 14, 321
   emotional states, role of, 372–75
      facial expressions and body
         languageautism patients,

emotional body perception
   in, 57
   and fusiform face area (FFA),
      fearful bodily expressions
      in, 54
   hemodynamic response on, 59
   in personality judgment, 379
Ancient Egypt
   cosmetics usage in, 199
Anger
   and amygdala, 376
   expression, emotion recognition
      and older adults, 142
   neuroimaging, 220
   recognition, in older adults, age
      related gazing, 142
Angry faces, and hand movements,
      5–6
Animal analogies, 7n3
Anomalous face overgeneralization, 8
Anosognosia, dissociated
      consciousness phenomena,
      67–68
Anthropometric comparisons, of
      babies and adults, 10
Anxiety
   in thin-slice vision, 231
Apparent motion, 252, 253, 255–56, 255*f*
Approachability, identifying of, 378
Approach-withdrawal model, 401
Area STP (superior temporal
      polysensory), 416
Asian faces, 6
Attention
   gaze cueing of, 121–22
      overt shift of attention, 122
      shifting gaze and observer's
         covert attention, 122
      studies on, 122–25
      threat cues, 121
   role of, in attributions,, 134

Attentional capacity, 42
Attentional preferences and mood
    changes, 139, 141, 143
Attentional weighting, 16–17
"Attention control settings," 145
Attention Network Task (ANT), 139
Attention shift, gaze cascade effect
    and, 155
Attention-shifting status, gaze cueing
    and, 124, 127f
Attraction, traits associated with,
    167–77
    facial averageness, 168–70
    facial symmetry, 170–74
    secondary sexual characteristics
        and face, 174–77
Attractive face
    attractiveness, judgment of, 166–67
    vs. average face, 170
        dates, impact on, 164
        schools, preference in, 165
    cognitive processing and, 170
    concern about, 164
    in mock interviews, selection of,
        165
    negative attributes associated with,
        164–65
    short-term sexual relationship,
        perceriver's cues under, 179
Attractiveness, 12
    and body shape, 270–71, 271f
    in face perception, 4–5
    facial, 12, 187–88
Attractiveness/preference task, gaze,
    153f
Auditory attention, cultural variation
    and attention strategies,
    82–83
Auditory thin-slice impressions, vs.
    visual thin-slice impressions,
    230
Auditory-visual integration, 415
Autism, 6
    eye tracking, use of, 135
Autism spectrum disorder (ASD),
    257–59, 422, 427
    preferential-looking paradigm, 426
Autism-Spectrum Quotient, 259
Automatic categorization, 42
Automatic motivated gaze preferences,
    145–46
Average faces
    health and, 168
    vs. nonaverage faces, 168
Averaging technique, 204, 205f
    vs. transforming technique,
        comparison between, 205–6
Baby face, features of, 10
Baby-faced eye-region metrics, 11
Baby-face overgeneralization, 7–8
Beautification, 198
Behavioral importance, gaze cueing
    and, 121
Behavior and attractiveness, 164, 165
    positive attitude, 165
Biased attitudes

in thin-slice vision, 232–33
Biological-motion displays. See Point-
    light displays
Biological motion perception, 15,
    101, 248–60, 264–74, 365–69,
    370–72, 375–77, 379, 402–18,
    429
Black faces, 6
Blood, and skin color, 280–87
Blood-oxygen-level-dependent
    functional magnetic
    resonance imaging (BOLD
    fMRI)
    of biological motion, 410–11, 410f
    for measuring brain activity,
        409–10
"Bloodshot illusion," luminance
    mechanism, 113
Blue, meaning of, 283, 285f
Body decoration, 186
Body language, 52, 57–59, 57f, 63
Body perception, 369–70
Body posture, 393
Body shape
    and attractiveness, 270–71, 271f
    in sex categorization, 269–70, 270f
"Bogart Illusion," luminance
    mechanism, 113
Bonobo, xx–xxi
    vs chimpanzee, xxi
Brain, 365
    biological motion perception,
        370–72
    body perception, 369–70
    and face perception, 366–69,
        398–403
    functions, understanding of, 363
Brain-Machine-Interface, eye gaze
    and, 163
Calcarine sulcus, face-specific
    processing, 55
Camouflage, and thin-slice vision, 237
Caricature, attractiveness and facial
    averageness, 168
Categorical thinking, 42
Categorization, importance of, 41–45
Categorization and individuation, role
    of perceptual differences in,
    33–36
Category-based stereotyping, 306–7
    operation of, 308
Category-specific emotional
    modulation, 376
Caucasians
    adaptive condition, aftereffect, 352
    face markers, 326
    and race bias, 322
Cerebral asymmetry, and person
    construal, 34
Children
    with ASD, and human motion
        detection, 258
    facial resemblance of, 210–12
Chimeric face, 399
Chimpanzee, xix–xx
    vs. bonobo, xxi

Chinese faces, 352
    adaptive condition, aftereffect, 352
Coding faces, of different races
    implications of, 352–53
Cognitive abilities and social
    dimension, 51, 54
    conscious visual perception and, 65
    in HD patients, 57
Cognitive architectures, for face
    processing, 365
Cognitive changes, age-related gazing,
    138, 139
Cognitive ethology xvii
Cognitive control
    ambiguity and, 299–302, 299f, 301f
    definition of, 299
    low, conditions of, 300
    and older adults, 143–44
        divided-attention paradigms,
            use of, 144
Cognitive empathy, 217
Cognitive gating mechanism, 339–41
    and racial markers, 329
Cognitive impairment, and thin-slice
    vision, 240
"Cognitive misers," 31
Cognitive preference decision, 162. See
    also Gaze cascade effect
    and neural correlates, 162
    and preference-decision process,
        152
    robustness of, 152–55
        commercial products, gaze
            manipulation in, 155f
        face stimuli, gaze manipulation
            in, 154f
        other's gaze, sensitivity to, 154
Cognitive processing and attractive
    face, 170
Color cosmetics, 186n1
Color naming, longer latencies for,
    134–35
Color spectrum, variation in, 283, 284,
    287, 284f
Color vision. See also Social color
    vision
    reasons, 291
    as socio-emotional perception, 279
Commercial products, demonstrating
    gaze cascade effect with, 155f
Competence, identifying of, 378
Compound social cues
    in human face
        processingconclusion of,
        101–2
    current face-processing models,
        91–92
    ecological approach, 96–99
    face processing, towards new
        look at, 92–94
    introduction to, 90–91
    perceptual interference and
        integration, evidence for,
        94–96
    person-level factors, 99–101
    own-race bias as, 101

Computer graphic techniques, morphing faces by, 175
Conditional automaticity, 42
Configural cues, in body perception, 369
Congruence effects, face-body, 58–59, 61
    face–body compound stimuli, categories of, 60f
    five bilateral simultaneous stimulation (BSS), examples of, 62f
CONLERN notion, 423
Consciousness, social-evolutionary perspective on, 51–52
Conscious perception, factors influencing, 75
CONSPEC notion, 423, 430
Construal errors, 297–99, 297f
Consumer behavior, eye gaze and, 163
Containing-system sense of function, in perceptual mechanism, 364
Context, and thin-slice vision, 236–37
Context-sensitivity
    responses to facial resemblance, 210–11
Contextual cues and direct eye gaze, 111–12
Cooperation, and facial resemblance, 207–8
Cortical blindness, nonconscious perception in, 63–64
    blindsight patient and neural correlates, 64f
    superior colliculus, role of, 64
Cortical face selectivity, 366
Cosmetics, 186–201
    and beauty, 186–88
    cultural variation of, 199–200
    exaggeration of facial contrast by, 195
    exaggeration of sex differences by, 190
    and facial attractiveness, 187–88
    future of, 200–201
    manipulate biological factors of attractiveness, 195–96
    paradox of, 188
    power of, 186–87
    received style of, 194–95
    science and, 187
    as technology, 196–97, 199
    during Victorian era, 186
Cosmetic science, 197n4
Criminal behavior, future outcomes of in thin-slice vision, 234–35
Cross-cultural context, facial attractiveness, 166
    averageness preferences, cognitive explanations for, 170
    human faces, debates on attractiveness of, 169
    preference, cognitive explanations for, 173–74
        nonhuman species facial -symmetry preference, 173

sexual dimorphism, debates on attractiveness of, 175–77
    symmetry and human faces, debates on attractiveness of, 171–73
Cross-race effect, 321
    ecological explanations for, 327–29
    explanations forrace as feature, 323
    race as stimulus class, 323–27
    social theories, 322–23
    importance of, 322
Cued targets and uncued targets, 122
Cultural variation, attention strategies and
    conclusions of, 86–88
        East Asian vs. European American cultureauditory attention, 82–83
        mnemonic context effect, 85–86
        multitasking, 83
        perceptual inference, 83–84
        visual attention, 79–82
    evidence for, 75–89
        charting domains, 78–79
        European American culture, 76
        independence and interdependence, precursors of, 77–78
Deafness, and thin-slice vision, 240
"Decentering", 217
Deception, 253, 396–97
    and right-hemisphere damage (RHD), 397
Deception detection, 237, 396–97
Decision-making, and race, 296
Declarative memory modulation amygdala role in, 372–73
Decoration. See also Cosmetics
    of body, 186
    with parochial forms, 187
Deficits, facial expressions and body language, 57–58
    Huntington's disease (HD), 57–58
    prosopagnosia, 56–57
Deficit-versus optimal-processing model, 341–42
Depression, in thin-slice vision, 231–32
Depth electrode studies, in face perception, 366
Dichromats, and skin color perception, 291, 292–93t
Diet change, and face expression, 348
Differentiation, perceptual learning, 16
Direct gazes, visually mediated attention, 109
    and avert gaze, 117
    in infants, 128
    difficulties in comparing studies on, 111
Disgust and body involvement, 54
Dispersed (or D) strategy, cultural variation and perception, 77, 84

in East Asian cultures, 78
    in Guatemalan Mayan caregivers, 87
Dispositional optimism, young adults and, 136
Dissociable coding model, 352–53
Divided visual-field paradigm, 35, 36
Dominance
    and affiliation, ecological approach, 96
    in thin-slice vision, 233–34
Dot-probe paradigm, measuring visual attention, 134, 135
    with eye tracking, 138–39
    single-session attentional training using, 141
Dual process model, 3
Dynamic body-movement, 374
Dynamic facial movements, 10
East Asian cultures, attention strategy in, 76
    vs. European American culture, visual attention, 79–82
    holistic strategies of attention in, 78, 79
    interdependence of, 78
    shaming, practice of, 77
Ecological approach, 3–20, 96–99
    babyish facial appearance, 10, 96
    to visual perception, 93
Eigenfaces, 325
Electroencephalography (EEG) and fMRI
    neural correlates of attention by, 79–86
        auditory attention, 82–83
        mnemonic context effect, 85–86
        multitasking, 83
        perceptual inference, 83–84
        visual attention, 79–82
Electromyography (EMG), facial, 221
Emotional contagion, 217
Emotional expression
    and facial identity, 91
    facial maturity and babyfacedness, appearance cues related to, 11, 99
    neo-Darwinian perspectives on co-evolution of, 3
    perceptual resemblance, 97f
Emotional memory, amygdala role in, 372–73
Emotional modulation
    face, body, and biological motion, 375–77
Emotional processes, change human movement perception, 256–57
Emotional processing, 398–402
    alternate theoretical model, 400–401
    right-hemisphere hypothesis, 398–400
    social emotions, 401–2
Emotional states, perceiving and understanding of, 372
    amygdala, role of, 372–75

Emotional states, perceiving and
    understanding of, (cont.)
  emotion recognition via emotional
    contagion and simulation,
    377–78
  face, body, and biological motion,
    emotional modulation of,
    256–57, 375–77
Emotional support and cultural
    variation, 76
Emotional valence, 141
  in young and older adults, 136, 145
Emotional words, and patients with
    left-hemisphere lesions, 394
Emotion cues, 11–12
Emotion expression, facial perception,
    4, 398–402
Emotion overgeneralization, 7
Emotion perception, definition of, 398
Emotion recognition
  via emotional contagion and
    simulation, 377–78
  and older adults, 142
Emotion-recognition accuracy, 141
  young vs. older adults, 141
Emotion regulation, aging eyes and
    motivation, 137, 138, 141
  attention and feeling states, causal
    relationships between, 141
Emotions, 216
  basic, neuroimaging, 220–21
  bodily expression of, 268
  complex, neuroimaging, 221
  detection of, in human movement,
    253
  discrete, empathizing with, 221–22
  perception of, 267–68, 398–402
  sex differences on, 221
Emotion-specific facial muscle
    activity, 54
Empathizing, 216
  with discrete emotions, 221–22
    conjunctional analysis, 221–22
    whole-brain analysis, 222
  sex differences in, 217–19, 219f
Empathy, 216–23
  common and discrete neural
    substrates of, 222–23
  distribution of, 218, 219f
  empathizing, 216
  fractionating, 217
  neuroimaging, 219–20
Ethnicity, 306
  and color vision, 280
European American culture, attention
    strategy, 76
  vs. East Asian cultures, visual
    attention, 79–82
    Framed-Line Test (FLT), 81, 87
  independence in, 77
Event-related brain potentials (ERPs),
    430, 434
  definition of, 327
  prosopagnosia, 56
"Evil eye," eye gaze as, 151

Evoked response potentials (ERPs),
    400
  for face perception, 14
Executive control, 299
Executive functioning, 299
Exemplar-based model
  for perceptual learning, 324
Expertise-individuation hypothesis,
    365
Expressive behavior, 229
External stimulus environment, 8
Extrastriate body area (EBA)
  in early stage of perception, 369
  location of, 367f
  modulation of, and amygdala, 376
Extraversion, 236, 238
Eyebrow plucking, 195–96
Eyebrows, 40
  in face recognition, 24
Eye contact, perception, 421
Eye direction detection (EDD), 219–20
Eye gaze, 393
  angle of rotation, computation of,
    109
    determining direction
      ofgeometric mechanism,
      112–13
    luminance mechanism, 113–14
    social attention perception,
      neural mechanisms of, 119–21
  head orientation, influence of,
    114–19, 117f
    environment-related gaze
      direction, 114
    independent mechanisms
      account, 118
    iris location as cue, 116–17, 118
    nose angle, influence of, 117
    observer-related gaze direction,
      scleral contrast measure
      under, 115
    output, integration of, 121
    social attention cues from, 122
  iris and sclera, contrast between,
    112
  social attention perception, neural
    mechanisms of, 119–21
    superior temporal sulcus (STS)
      region, role of, 119
  studies on direction of, 109
    difficulties in comparing, 111
    thresholds and constant errors,
      109
  triadic gaze, studies on, 111
  visually mediated attention and,
    108–29
  understanding social world
    through, 108
Eye gaze, orienting mechanisms and
    preference looking, 151–63
  coevolution scenario, views on,
    162–63
  decision-making process of
    preference, gaze bias, 155–58
  display-off experiment, 158f

Fourier descriptors, 156
  peep-hole experiment, 157f
  gaze bias preceding preference,
    151, 152
  gaze cascade effect, 152–55
  introduction to, 151–52
    social-cognitive development,
      preferential looking and, 151
    "somatic precursor" hypothesis,
      152
  preference decision, neural
    correlates of, 159–61
  preference manipulation, gaze
    manipulation and, 158–59
  round-face task, use of, 159
  summary and implications of,
    161–62
Eye-gaze direction, women and, 100
Eye gaze processing
  atypical development of, 432
    in ASD patients, 432–33
    attentional cueing paradigm, 434
    fMRI recording, 435
  development of, 427–28
    adult-infant interaction, 429–30
    brain basis of, 428
    electrophysiological recordings,
      428
    in mother-infant interaction, 429
    neurodevelopment of, 431–32
Eye information, amygdala role in,
    372–73
Eye movements, 6
Eye tracking, recording gaze fixation,
    134
  and dot-probe paradigm, 138–39
  emotion recognition and older
    adults, 142
  in young and older adults, 135–36,
    137, 138
Face and body perception
  and integrated processing, 58–59
    face-body congruence effects,
      neurofunctional basis of, 59
  socialconsciousness, social vision
    to, 67–69
    affective blindsight and
      mechanism linking, 68–69
  and social vision, debates on, 52–59
    associated deficits of, 57–58
    functional neuroanatomy,
      52–54
    temporal dynamics of, 55–56
  subcortical social vision, 59–66
    cortical blindness, nonconscious
      perception in, 63–64
    nonconscious or unattended
      perception, 61–63
    subcortical social vision and
      faces, debates on, 65–66
Face coding
  of different races, 352–53
  neurons in, 352–53
  and sex, 354
  and sex selective nature, 353–55

Face detection, perceptual timeline
     for, 328*f*
Face memory tasks, 421
Face perception, 366–69, 398–402
     ecological theory of, 3–4, 3–20
     for empathy, 222, 223*f*
     system, confluence in, 19–20
Face processing
     atypical development of, 425–27
     development of, 423–25
Face processing, compound social
     cues in
     conclusion of, 101–2
     current face-processing models,
          91–92
          emotional expression and facial
               identity, 91
     ecological approach, 96–99
          babyish facial appearance, 96
          face processing, towards new look
               at, 92–94
          brain evolution and social
               factors, 93
          introduction to, 90–91
          perceptual interference and
               integration, evidence for,
               94–96
          facial clues, 96
          person-level factors, 99–101
Face-processing asymmetry, 36
Face race, and hand movements, 6
Face selectivity, and neurons, 366–67
"Face-sensitive" negative deflection
     and N170, 424–25, 427
     and N290, 425
Face-space conceptual framework, 9
Face stimuli
     demonstrating gaze cascade effect
          with, 153–54
     repeated exposures, attractiveness
          resulting by, 158–59
     structural encoding of, 367
Face traits and attraction, 167–77
     facial averageness, 168–70
          major histocompatibility
               complex (MHC), male facial
               attractiveness and, 168
          facial symmetry, 170–74
          secondary sexual characteristics
               and face, 174–77
Facial adaptation, 331–33
     creating morph, 332*f*
     neuron activity in, 331
Facial and scalp hair, in face
     recognition, 9–10
Facial attractiveness, 164–80, 187–88
     attraction, traits associated with,
          167–77
          facial averageness, 168–70
          facial symmetry, 170–74
          secondary sexual characteristics
               and face, 174–77
     facial beauty, power of, 164–67
          attractiveness, judgment of,
               166–67

social impact, 165–66, 179
facial contrast relevance to, 193–94,
     194*f*
and facial resemblance, 209
from perceiver's perspective, 197
sexual dimorphism, individual
     preferences for, 178–79
     peak fertility, 179
     perceiver attractiveness, 178
     relationship context and
          partnership status, 179
summary and conclusions of,
     179–80
Facial attributes, signaling low fitness,
     12
Facial averageness, 168–70, 180, 208–9
     and actual quality, 168
     major histocompatibility
          complex (MHC), male facial
          attractiveness and, 168
     evolutionary view of, 168
     and facial attractiveness, 196
     in human faces, debates on
          attractiveness of, 168–69
     in cross-cultural context, 169
     preference, cognitive explanations
          for, 170
Facial contrast
     exaggeration, by cosmetics, 195
     illusion, 193*f*
     perceptual relevance of, 192–93
          to attractiveness, 193–94, 194*f*
     sex differences in, 190–92
          and face shape, 191
          and skin tone, 192
Facial electromyography (EMG), 54
     subcortical social vision and faces,
          65, 66*f*
Facial expression, 216, 249, 393. *See
     also* Empathy
     and body language, 52
     in early latencies, 56
     multiple emotional expressions,
          integration of, 58–59
     upright faces, stronger responses
          in, 55
     voluntary cognitive control, 54
Facial identity, 9
Facial masculinity preference, peak
     fertility, 179
Facial muscle activity, emotion-
     specific, 54
Facial resemblance, 204–13
     of children, 210–12
     experimental evidence, 206
     and genetic relatedness, 204
     hormone-mediated preferences for,
          212, 212*f*
     methodological issues, 204–6
     in opposite-sex faces, 208–9
     and prosocial behavior, 207–10,
          207*f*
     in mating, 208–10, 209–10*f*
Facial rotation, 38, 39
Facial stimulus class, 324

Facial symmetry, 170–74, 180
     and actual quality, 171
     evolutionary view of, 171
     and facial attractiveness, 196
     in human faces, debates on, 171–73
     preference, cognitive explanations
          for, 173–74
False beliefs, recognizing of, 395
     and right-hemisphere damage
          (RHD), 395
Familiar face overgeneralization, 7
Familiarity
     cues, 8–10
     in face perception, 4–5
Fear
     conditioning, amygdala role in,
          372–73
     neuroimaging, 220
Fearful bodily expressions
     Functional MRI (fMRI) activation
          associated with, 53*f*
     fusiform cortex and amygdala,
          activation in, 54
     with happy face, integrated
          processing, 58, 61
     N170 amplitude enhanced for fear
          and VPP amplitude enhanced
          for fear, 55
Featural vs. configural information,
     37–38
Feature-based stereotyping, 307–10,
     308*f*
     Afrocentric, 308, 310n3, 313–18
     challenges for control, 309–10
     efficiency of, 309
     operation of, 308–9
Feature labeling, 190*f*
Feedback connections, and visual
     processes, 254
Femininity
     and attractiveness, 193
     and facial contrast, 192, 195
Feminized male faces, preference
     for, 176
Fertility and average face, 168
Figural aftereffects, 351
Finckism, 200
Focal attention, 242
Focused (or F) strategy, cultural
     variation and perception, 77
     as "analytic attention," 84
     in Asian cultural context, 78, 79,
          80, 86
     in independent cultures, 78
Forced-choice labeling, 374
Framed-line test (FLT), measuring
     visual attention, 81, 87
Free-field viewing task, 399
"Frequency of seeing curve," 338
Functional magnetic resonance
     imaging (fMRI)
     activation to biological motion,
          413*f*
     to multisensory stimuli, 416*f*
     to point-light displays, 412*f*

Functional magnetic resonance imaging (fMRI), (*cont.*)
   research directions, 417–18
   fearful bodily expressions and, 53*f*
   vs. invasive single-cell recording technique, gaze-direction perception, 119, 120
   with maganeto-encephalography (MEG), face-specific processing and, 55–56
   of preference-decision task and neural correlates, facial attractiveness, 159, 160*f*, 161, 162
   right-hemisphere activityin facial emotion, 400
   in split-brain patient, 35
Functional neuroanatomy, face and body perception, 52–54
   facial electromyography (EMG), 54
   fearful bodily expressions, fusiform cortex and amygdale, 54
   fusiform face area (FFA), activation in, 53, 53*f*, 54
   superior temporal sulcus (STS), activation in, 54
Functional specialization, in conceptual map, 365
Function prime, task performance as, 44*f*
Fusiform body area (FBA)
   in configural cue, 369
   in face discrimination, 368
   location of, 367*f*
   modulation of, and amygdale, 376
Fusiform face area (FFA), 13
   activation in, 53, 53*f*, 54
   and amygdale, fearful bodily expressions in, 54
   face-body congruence effects, neurofunctional basis of, 59
   in face discrimination, 368
   location of, 367*f*
   in stimulus specificity, 423
Fusiform gyrus
   in face memory, 421
   social brain network, 423
   and social stimuli, 364
Future behavior, in thin-slice vision, 234–35
Garner selective attention paradigm, face-processing literature, 94–92
Gating mechanism theory, 336
Gaze
   and human sensitivity, literature on, 162–63
   mind and body, understanding, 163
   in nonhuman species, 151
Gaze, age-related motivational states and
   age differences and visual attention, 136
   age effects, debates on motivation of, 138–41

age-related gaze effects and motivation, summary of, 141
   gaze preferences and stimuli, 141
   laboratory manipulation approach, 139–40
   age-related findings, motivational accounts of, 136–38
   information processing, motivation affecting, 143–46
   motivated gaze to emotional stimuli, social context of, 141–43
   summary and future directions of, 146
   visual attention, measurement of, 134–35
Gaze cascade effect. *See also* Cognitive preference decision
   and preference-decision process, 152
   robustness of, 152–55
     commercial products, gaze manipulation in, 155*f*
     face stimuli, gaze manipulation in, 154*f*
     other's gaze, sensitivity to, 154
Gaze-cueing
   attention of, 121–22
     overt shift of attention, 122
     shifting gaze and observer's covert attention, 122
     studies on, 122–25
     threat cues, 121
   behavioral importance and, 121
   and gaze perception, 125–27
   geometric or luminance information, effect of, 125–26, 125*f*
   on listener's attention, influence of, 128
   Median reaction times (RTs), computation of, 126
   special social-orienting response, 122–25
   stimulus onset asynchronies (SOAs), 122
Gaze direction, facial perception, 4
Gaze patterns, mood and, 136
   emotion recognition, eye tracking by, 142
   older adults, 137
Gaze perception and gaze cueing, 125–27
Gaze perception and visually mediated attention
   attention, gaze cueing of, 121–22
   conclusion of, 127–29
   gaze cueing and, 125–27
   gaze cueing, specialness about, 122–25
   brain mechanisms, involvement of, 123–24
   dedicated neural circuitry, involvement of, 124

neonates and two-month-olds, gaze-cueing behavior in, 124–25
   split-brain patient, brain mechanisms in, 123
   supporting evidence for, 124
   geometric mechanism, 112–13
   configural processing, disruption to, 113
   eye gaze, determining direction of, 112
   head orientation, contribution of, 114–19
   environment-related gaze direction, 114
   independent mechanisms account, 118
   iris location as cue, 116–17, 118
   nose angle, influence of, 117
   observer-related gaze direction, scleral contrast measure under, 115
   output, integration of, 121
   social attention cues from, 122
   luminance mechanism, 113–14
   psychophysical studies, 109–12
   social attention perception, neural mechanisms of, 119–21
   superior temporal sulcus (STS) region, role of, 119
   Theory of Mind and, 108
Gaze shift
   newborns and, 151
   preference decision-making process, 155–58
   display-off experiment, 158*f*
   Fourier descriptors, 156
   peep-hole experiment, 157*f*
Gazing patterns, 134
   and moods, 136
Geisha, 200
Gender
   in empathizing, 217–19, 219*f*
   and thin-slice vision, 239
Gender atypicality, 272
Gender stereotypes, 273
Genetic diversity, facial averageness and, 168
Genetic relatedness, and facial resemblance, 204
Geometric mechanism, 112–13
   configural processing, disruption to, 113
   eye gaze, determining direction of, 112
   minimal geometric information, luminance cue containing, 125*f*
   vs. luminance mechanism, 114
Geometric shapes, demonstrating gaze cascade effect with, 154–55
Gestures, 393
   multimodal cues, 10
Global motion processing
   and ASD observers, 258

Goal attainment expression, 4
Goal directed behavior, 15
Green, meaning of, 283, 285f
Group-based knowledge, 41
Group X Emotion Type interaction,
    emotional stimuli and age-
    related gazing, 140
Hairstyle
    perceiver attunements and face
        processing, 99
    as sex cue, 44
Hand movements, and face race, 6
Head orientation, eye gaze direction
    and, 114–19, 117f
    environment-related gaze direction,
        114
    independent mechanisms account,
        118
    iris location as cue, 116–17, 118
    nose angle, influence of, 117
    observer-related gaze direction,
        scleral contrast measure
        under, 115
    output, integration of, 121
    social attention cues from, 122
Health, and average face 168
Health practitioners, future outcomes
    of
    in thin-slice vision, 235
Hedonic Contingency Model, aging
    eyes and motivation, 136–37
Hemispheric bias
    emotional processing, 398
        alternate theoretical model,
            400–401
        right-hemisphere hypothesis,
            398–400
        social emotions, 401–2
    in social cognition, 394–97
        deception, 396–97
        false beliefs, recognizing of, 395
        humor and narrative, 395–96
        mental state attributions, 394–95
        ToM in healthy individuals, 397
Hemoglobin, 188n2
Hippocampal damage and amygdala,
    375
Hispanics
    composite faces, 325–26
    face markers, 326
Homogeneity of skin, and facial
    attractiveness, 196
Human body
    parts, visibility of, 283–84
    movement of 248–60, 264–74,
        365–69, 370–72, 375–77, 379,
        402–18, 429
Human brain. See Brain
Human face, 164
    facial averageness and, 168–69
    facial symmetry in, 171–73
    and secondary sexual
        characteristics, 175–76
Human face processing, compound
    social cues in

conclusion of, 101–2
current face-processing models,
    91–92
    emotional expression and facial
        identity, 91
    ecological approach, 96–99
        babyish facial appearance, 96
    face processing, towards new look
        at, 92–94
        brain evolution and social
            factors, 93
    introduction to, 90–91
    perceptual interference and
        integration, evidence for,
        94–96
        facial clues, 96
    person-level factors, 99–101
Human movement, 248–60, 264–74,
    365–69, 370–72
    detection of social and emotional
        information from, 253–54
    differences in visual analysis of,
        250–53
    objectification of, 248–50, 249f
        perceptionemotional processes
            change, 256–57
        social processes change, 254–56
    social behavior and detection of,
        257–59
        autism spectrum disorder
            observers, 257–59
        typical observers, 259
Human skin
    color, 278–79
        changes in, 280–81, 281f
        spectrum, 281, 282f
Humor and narrative, 395–96
    and right-hemisphere damage
        (RHD), 395–96
Huntington's disease (HD) patients, 58
    cognitive and emotional deficits
        in, 57
Identical twins, similarities in
    perception, 4
Identity
    -based processing, 37
    facial perception, 4
    perception from body motion,
        253, 267
Identity recognition, 11
Ideograms, 35
Illusion, 297, 303
Implicit Attitude Test (IAT), 326
Imprinting, perceivers' attunements,
    16
Independence and interdependence,
    cultural variation and
    attention strategies
    ecological conditions and
        subsistence
    long-term cultural traditions,
        influence of, 77–78
Individual differences, compound
    social cues, 97f
Individuation, perception of, 267

Individuation and categorization, role
    of perceptual differences in,
    33–36
Individuation hypothesis, 365
Indus Valley Civilization, cosmetics
    usage in, 199
"Infant N170," 430, 431
Inferior occipital gyrus, face-specific
    activation on, 53
Information processing and motivation,
    gaze preferences, 143
    cognitive control resources and
        older adults, 143–44
Insula, in personality judgment, 379
Intact and crossed-face targets, 45f
Integrated processing, facial
    expressions and body
    language, 58–59
    context factors, impact of, 58
    face–body compound stimuli,
        categories of, 60f
    face–body congruence effects,
        neurofunctional basis of, 59
    five bilateral simultaneous
        stimulation (BSS), examples
        of, 62f
    multiple emotional expressions, 59
Intelligence, in thin-slice vision, 233,
    237–38
Intention
    detection of, in human movement,
        253
    perception of, 268–69
Intentionality detection (ID), 219
Intentional stancexvi
"Interactive specialization approach,"
    422
    in social brain network, 422
Interactive-specialization perspective
    on functional brain development, 435
    STS role in, 435–36
Interdependent cultures
    holistic strategies of attention in,
        78, 86
    perceptual consequences and, 77
Internal states, 267
    in thin-slice vision, 231–32
International Affective Picture System
    (IAPS), emotional stimuli and
    age-related gazing, 140
Intracranial recording, 418
Intuition, 229
Invasive single-cell recording
    technique vs. functional
    imaging, gaze-direction
    perception, 119, 120
Involuntary facial mimicry, 219
Iris and sclera, contrast between, 112,
    115–16
    luminance mechanism, 113
Japan, cosmetics usage in, 200
Johansson point-light displays,
    248–60, 264–74, 365–69,
    370–72, 375–77, 379, 402–18,
    429

Joint attention, 220

Jury behavior, future outcomes in thin-slice vision, 234

Just noticeable difference (JND), 330, 331

Kin recognition, 210, 212

Koreans, in face perception, 6

Lateral displacement, eye gaze, 109, 110

and head orientation, 117

Lateral fusiform, for biological motion, 413

Lateral occipital area, social brain network, 423

Learning-disabled children, thin-slice vision of, 240

Left cerebral hemisphere (LH) versus right cerebral hemisphere (RH), 34, 35

Left frontal operculum, in personality judgment, 379

Left-hemisphere activation for "approach behaviors," 401

for positive emotions, 400–401

Lifespan literature, "motivational approach" in, 136

Lingual gyrus, face-specific processing, 55

Linking, 68–69

brain-damaged patients, studies on, 69

Listener's attention and gaze cueing, 128

Long versus short hairs as sex-specifying information, 40

Lorenz's geese, 16

Low facial expressiveness, 12

Luminance contrast, 190

Luminance mechanism, 113–14

angle of rotation measurement by, 113

extracting gaze information by, 114

no luminance information, geometric cue with, 125

M100, for facial discrimination, 367

M170, negative peak of face-selective activity, 366

Magnetoencephalography (MEG), 251–52, 418

face-specific processing and, 55

Magnification, and thin-slice vision, 238

Major histocompatibility complex (MHC), male facial attractiveness and, 168

Masculine female faces, 354

Masculine male faces, 354

Masculinity and attractiveness, 193

and facial contrast, 192

Mating, facial resemblance and, 208–10, 209–10f

Medial orbito-frontal cortex (mOFC), preference-decision task and neural correlates, 161

Meerkats xvii–xviii

Melanin, 192

Men preference for self-resembling children, 210–11

vs. women, pigmentation differences, 188–90

Menstrual cycle, and self-resemblance, 212, 212f

Mental state attributions, 394–95

in social cognition, 394

deception, 396–97

false beliefs, recognizing of, 395

humor and narrative, 395–96

ToM in healthy individuals, 397

Mesopotamia, cosmetics usage in, 199

Michelson contrast, 190

Midfusiform cortex, studies on, 53, 56

Mild cognitive impairment (MCI), individuals with, 144

Mimicking, gaze as primary basis for, 151

Mimicry and imitation, 54

"Mirror neuron" network, 417

Mnemonic context effect, cultural variation and attention strategies, 85–86

oddball paradigm, 85

Mood changes and attentional preferences, 134, 141, 143

Morph array, 335f

using Adobe Photoshop, 335

Morphing faces, 332–34

racial categorization boundaries for, 336f, 337f

and adaptation, 339f

"Motion-blind" patients, 370

Motion-capture devices, 411, 412f

Motion capture techniques, 9

Motivated concealment, 238

Motivated gaze and aging eyes, role of age differences and visual attention, 136

age effects, debates on motivation of, 138–41

age-related gaze effects and motivation, summary of, 141

gaze preferences and stimuli, 141

laboratory manipulation approach, 139–40

age-related findings, motivational accounts of, 136–38

dispositional optimism, young adults and, 136

socioemotional selectivity theory, 137

information processing, motivation affecting, 143–46

motivated gaze to emotional stimuli, social context of, 141–43

summary and future directions of, 146

visual attention, measurement of, 134–35

eye tracking and studying saccades, 135

observer-based approach, use of, 134, 135

Mouth movements, 6

Movement, definition of, 250

Movement patterns, age-related differences, 10

Müller-Lyer illusion, 297–98, 297f, 300, 334, 334f

Multidimensional scaling (MDS), for facial dimensions, 325

Multimodal cues, 10

Multisensory integration, 415–16

Multitasking, cultural variation and attention strategies, 83

Muscle movements, facial, 11

N170 as adult face-sensitive component, 430

for directed and averted gazing, 433f

and face emotions, 375

negative ERP component, 55, 59

negative peak of face-selective activity, 366

Naturalistic paradigm, aging eyes and motivation, 139

Nature, in cognitive processes, 421–22

"Navon"-type tasks, 34

N-dimensional face-space model, 324

Negative and positive stimuli, measuring visual attention, 136

in young and older adults, 137, 138, 140, 141, 142

Neo-Darwinian perspectives, face processing, 93

Neural correlates of preference decision, facial attractiveness, 159–61

extended decision–making (TED) paradigm, 161

frontal channels, EEG recording of, 159

Neural mechanisms, 12–15

Neural substrates distribution, for face perception, 13–14

Neurons in biological motion, 415

in face coding, 352–53

in face selectivity, 366–67

Neutral stimuli response, measuring visual attention, 138

Newborns eye contacts of, 435

face processing abilities of, 430

face recognition studies, 423–24

"New Look," conscious perception, 75

Night vision, 51

Nonaverage faces, distinctive aspect in, 168

Nonconscious or unattended perception, subcortical social vision, 61–63

direct "guessing" methods, use
of, 61
Nonverbal cue knowledge, and
thin-slice vision, 241
Nonverbal information. *See* Facial
expressions; Eye gaze;
Gestures; Body posture
Normal cue, gaze perception, 125*f*
Normal-looking face, 354
North Americans, mnemonic context
effect for, 85–86
Nose length dimension, 324
Novelty P300, mnemonic context
effect, 85–86
Nucleus accumbens(NAC),
preference-decision task and
neural correlates, 161
Nurture, in cognitive processes,
421–22
Objective indices, of emotions, 11
Object motion, 260
differences in visual analysis of,
250–53
and social behavior, 258–59
Object perception, 296
Object recognition, 33
Observable behavior, 236
Obstruction, and thin-slice vision,
237–38
Occipital face area (OFA), right
in facial discrimination, 368
Older adults and negativity avoidance,
stimuli response and gazing,
137, 138, 140
cognitive control, need for, 144
Operculum/insula (OP/INS),
preference-decision task and
neural correlates, 161
Optimal-processing perspective,
342
Orbital frontal cortex (ORB), 13
Orienting and preference looking,
gaze, 151–63
coevolution scenario, views on,
162–63
decision-making process of
preference, gaze bias, 155–58
display-off experiment, 158*f*
Fourier descriptors, 156
peep-hole experiment, 157*f*
gaze bias preceding preference,
151, 152
gaze cascade effect, 152–55
introduction to, 151–52
social-cognitive development,
preferential looking and, 151
"somatic precursor" hypothesis,
152
preference decision, neural
correlates of, 159–61
preference manipulation, gaze
manipulation and, 158–59
round-face task, use of, 159
summary and implications of,
161–62

Orienting mechanism, preference
decision-making process,
155–58
display-off experiment, 158*f*
Fourier descriptors, 156
peep-hole experiment, 157*f*
Overgeneralization, in perceived
affordances, 6–7
anomalous face overgeneralization,
8
baby-face overgeneralization, 7–8
emotion overgeneralization, 7
familiar face overgeneralization, 7
Own-race bias. *See* Cross-race effect
Oxygenation, modulation in, 283, 284,
287, 284*f*, 287*f*
P3 response, mnemonic context effect,
85–86
Passive encoding, 43
Patterns, influence of
proximate causes, influence of, 78
Peak fertility, sexual dimorphism, 179
People, as visual stimuli, 363
Perceived affordances
and adaptive behavior, 4–6
accuracy and overgeneralization,
6–8
and stimulus information,
commonalities, 20
Perceiver attractiveness, sexual
dimorphism, 178
Perceiver attunements
and culture, 100–101
social categorization cues, hairstyle
as, 99
threat cues, 100
Perceiver goals, 18–19
Perceivers, immobilization of, 14
Perceivers' attunements, 15, 19
adaptation, 16
attentional weighting, 16–17
differentiation, 16
imprinting, 16
perceiver goals, 18–19
prototype extraction, 18
stimulus generalization, 16, 18
unitization, 16
Perception and thought, cultural
variation influencing
interdependent cultures, perceptual
consequences and, 77
visual attention, 79–82
rod and frame
Perceptual and cognitive abilities, 51
Perceptual fluency, 272
Perceptual inference
cultural variation and attention
strategies, 83–84
and integration, evidence for,
94–96
Garner selective attention
paradigm, use of, 94–95
averted eyes vs. direct eyes, 95
Perceptual learning, 16
race as stimulus class, 323–27

Perceptual resemblance, compound
social cues, 97*f*
Personal beliefs, 42
Personal decoration, 197–98
types of, 198
cultural variation of, 199–200
Personal expectations, in thin-slice
vision, 233
Personal identity, perception of, 267
Personality, in thin-slice vision, 231
Personality disorders, in thin-slice
vision, 233
Personality traits, perceiving and
identifying of, 378–80
Person categorization, 33, 42, 46
perceptual efficiency of, 36–41
Person-perception process, 42
Phenotype matching, 204, 210
Photographic superimposing
techniques, attractiveness and
facial averageness, 168
Physical attractiveness, 164
in nonhuman species, importance
of, 167
Physical behavior, 236
Physical features
and social group categorization, 307
and traits, 307, 308*f*
Pigmentation, sex differences in,
188–90
Point-light displays, 9, 250, 251, 251f,
253, 265, 265*f*
fMRI activation to, 412*f*
Johannsen displays, 411–13, 412*f*
Point-light walker stimuli, 257
in personality judgment, 380
Popping-out faces, 323
Positive mood, age-related
motivational states and gaze,
134
Positive mood induction, measuring
visual attention, 136
Positive personality attributions,
attractive face and, 164
Positive stimuli response, measuring
visual attention, 136
in young and older adults, 137
Posterior superior temporal sulcus
(pSTS), right
in discriminating faces, 370–71
in face, hand, mouth, and leg
movements, 371
in personality judgment, 379–80
in whole body identification, 371
Posterior superior temporal sulcus
(STSp), 15, 251, 254, 256
in acoustic cues, 15
Power
and cosmetics usage, 200
in thin-slice vision, 233–34
Preference manipulation, gaze
manipulation and, 158–59
repeated exposures, attractiveness
resulting by, 158
round-face task, use of, 159

Preferential looking patterns, 138
  in children with ASD, 422, 427
  sensory-motor coordination and,
    151
Premotor cortex, for biological
  motion, 413
Present-focused goals, aging eyes and
  motivation, 137
Principal components analysis (PCA),
  19
Processing goals, 42
Profile of Nonverbal Sensitivity
  (PONS), 239
Prolonged gaze
  as threat cue, group-living primate
    species, 151, 162
Proper function, in perceptual
  mechanism, 364
Propithecus, 287
Prosocial behavior, and facial
  resemblance, 207–10, 207*f*
Prosopagnosia, 6
Prototype extraction, 18
Prototypical ideograms, 35
Psychological impairment, and thin-
  slice vision, 239–40
Psychological self, 228
Psychological states, perception of,
  267–69
Purple, meaning of, 283, 285*f*
Race, 306
  -based social categorization, 267
Race and cross-race effect, importance
  of, 322
Race-based weapon-misidentification,
  295–304
  action errors, 297–99, 299*f*
  ambiguity and cognitive control,
    299–302, 299*f*, 301*f*
    low, 300–301
    high, 301–2
  and behavior, 295
  bias, 297
  construal errors, 297–99
  implications for minimizing bias,
    304
  rare targets, 303–4
  weapon misidentification, 296–97
Race categorization
  using psychophysicsambiguous
    race faces, 334–39
Race-contingent aftereffects, 351, 353
Race-selective face coding mechanism,
  350–52
  locus of, 355–57
Race–skin-tone, 10, 46
Racial bias, 297
  in thin-slice vision, 232–33
  minimizing, 304
Racial categorization
  effect of racial markers on, 329
  stereotyping, 313, 316–19
  psychophysics to examine, 334–39
Racial markers, 321
  methodology, 329

facial adaptation, 331–33
  morphing faces, *332–34*
  psychophysical methods, 330–31
  social psychophysics, 329–30
Reaction times (RTs)
  face recognition, using TMS, in
    SSC, 378
  measuring visual attention, 134
Reading others, and social cognition,
  394, 398
Red, meaning of, 283, 285*f*
"Redundant target paradigm," 402
Reflexive or exogenous orienting, 124
Reflex-like EBL, 57*f*
Region-of-interest (ROI) analysis,
  221–22
Relationship context and partnership
  status, sexual dimorphism, 179
Relationships, in thin-slice vision, 234
Repetitive transcranial magnetic
  stimulation (rTMS) study,
  facial discrimination, 368
Right cerebral hemisphere (RH),
  versus left cerebral
  hemisphere (LH), 34, 35
Right-hemisphere activation
  in facial emotion, 400
  for negative emotions, 400–401
  in ToM, 397
  for "withdrawal behavior," 401
Right-hemisphere damage (RHD)
  in comparison with left-hemisphere
    damage (LHD), 395, 396,
    397, 402
  and deception, 396–97
  and false beliefs, 395
  and humor and narrative, 395–96
Right-hemisphere hypothesis,
  398–400
Right temporoparietal junction
  (RTPJ), in ToM, 397
Rod and frame test (RFT), 80–81, 87
Rule-out approach, emotional stimuli
  and age-related gazing,
  138–40
  versus rule-in approach, 138
Sadness, neuroimaging, 220
"Scleral contrast," luminance
  mechanism, 113, 125
Scleral contrast measures
  and head orientation, eye gaze
    direction, 115–16, 116*f*
Secondary sexual characteristics, face,
  174–77, 180
  and attractiveness, 177
  evolutionary view of, 174
  in human faces, debates on
    attractiveness of, 175–76
    male faces, 175
  male attractiveness and
    masculinity, 176–77, 175
  masculinity preferences, cognitive
    explanations for, 177
  sexual dimorphism and actual
    quality, 174

Selectivity, in conceptual map, 365
Semantic differential, 5
Separate neural mechanisms code,
  social attention perception
  and, 119–21
  superior temporal sulcus (STS)
    region, role of, 119
  stimulus-specific aftereffect, 120
Set selectivity scores, 356, 357*f*
Sex, detection of, 253, 264–74
Sex-based social categorization,
  266–67
Sex categorization
  constrains human body perception,
    269–72, 270*f*, 271*f*
  and gender stereotypes, 273, 274*f*
Sex differences
  in empathizing, 217–19, 219*f*
  and self-resembling children, 211
Sex–hairstyle, 46
Sex-specifying information, long
  versus short hairs, 40
Sex stereotypes, 273
Sexual dimorphism, 193
  individual preferences for, 178–79,
    180
    perceiver attractiveness, 178
    relationship context and
      partnership
Sexual harassment, likelihood to
  in thin-slice vision, 232
Sexuality, in thin-slice vision, 232
Sexual orientation
  detection of, in human movement,
    253
  in thin-slice vision, 232
Shape-only morph, 205, 206
Shared signal hypothesis, 94, 95–96,
  98
Shared signals, compound social cues,
  91, 94, 95, 96, 97*f*, 99, 100
Short-term sexual relationship,
  perceiver's cues under, 179
Signification, 198, 199
Simultaneous multiple regression, for
  Afrocentric features selection,
  313, 312–13*t*
Single-cell recording technique
  eye gaze direction and head
    orientation, 121
  vs. functional imaging, gaze-
    direction perception, 119, 120
Situational circumstances, compound
  social cues, 97*f*
Skin color, 278–79, 306
  and blood, 280–87, 281–82*f*,
    285–87*f*
  in face recognition, 9–10
Skin conductance ratio (SCR), 433
Social activists, and thin-slice vision,
  240
Social affordances, 4
Social attention perception, neural
  mechanisms of, 119–21
  stimulus-specific aftereffect, 120

superior temporal sulcus (STS) region, role of, 119
Social behavior, amygdala role in, 372–73
Social categorization, 264
  constrains other social judgments, 269–72
  perception of, 265–67
Social cognition, and hemispheric bias, 394
  mental state attributions, 394–95
    deception, 396–97
    false beliefs, recognizing of, 395
    humor and narrative, 395–96
    ToM in healthy individuals, 397
Social-cognitive development, preferential looking and, 151
Social-cognitive functioning, 37–38
Social cognitive misers, 46
Social color vision, 278–93
  and baring emotions, 287–89, 288–90f
  color accent, 278–80, 279f
Socialconsciousness, social vision to, 67–69
  affective blindsight and mechanism anosognosia, dissociated consciousness phenomena, 67–68
  right posterior insula, activation in, 67–68
Social constraints, on biological motion perception, 264–74
  social categorization perception, 265–67
  personal identity perception, 267
  psychological state perception, 267–69
Social context, 295, 303
  motivated gaze and emotional stimuli, 141–43
Social directional cues, gaze cueing, 124
Social emotions, 401–2, 402f
Social information, extraction of, 31
Socialized attention hypothesis, 75–89, 76f
  antecedent conditions, influence of, 76–77
  attention and perception, cultural variation in, 79–86
    auditory attention, 82–83
    mnemonic context effect, 85–86
    multitasking, 83
    perceptual inference, 83–84
    visual attention, 79–82
  conclusions of, 86–88
    attention and self, social behavior and, 87–88
    attention strategy, socialization of, 87
    self orientation in attention regulation, causal role of, 86–87
  and culture, 76–79

charting domains, 78–79
  independence and interdependence, precursors of, 77–78
focused vs. dispersed strategy, 77, 78, 79, 80, 84, 86
introduction of, 75–76
Social lives
  cognitive requirements for, xxi–xxiii
  face role in, 321
Social perception
  neural system underpinning of, 381
  thin-slice vision and, 230
Social processes
  change human movement perception, 254–56
Social psychology, 364
Social psychophysics, 329–30
Social referencing, gaze as primary basis for, 151, 162
Social stereotypes, 31, 32
Social theories, attitudes and contacts, 322–23
Social vision, face and body perception and
  and awareness, 51
  and consciousness, 51–53
  debates on, 52–59
    associated deficits of, 57–58
    functional neuroanatomy, 52–54
    temporal dynamics of, 55–56
  and integrated processing, 58–59
    face-body congruence effects, neurofunctional basis of, 59
  socialconsciousness, social vision to, 67–69
    affective blindsight and mechanism linking, 68–69
  spontaneous muscle reaction, measurement of, 54
  subcortical social vision, 59–66
    cortical blindness, nonconscious perception in, 63–64
    nonconscious or unattended perception, 61–63
    subcortical social vision and faces, debates on, 65–66
Socioemotional selectivity theory, aging eyes and motivation, 137
Sociosexuality, in thin-slice vision, 232
Sodium amobarbital, 402
Somatosensory cortex (SSC) using TMS, in face recognition, 378
Specialness, of faces, 364
Special social-orienting response, gaze cueing and, 122–25
  brain mechanisms, involvement of, 123–24
  neonates and two-month-olds, gaze-cueing behavior in, 124–25
  in split-brain patient, 123

supporting evidence for, 124
Speech-patterns, recognizing of, 370
"Split-brain" patients, 393, 399
  fMRI scans of, 35
Static body postures, 374
Static facial components, two-dimensional, 11
Static images, and expressive behavior, 229–30
Status, 179
  peak fertility, 179
Stepwise regression, for Afrocentric features selection, 313
Stereotype-based errors
  and subjective experience, 302, 302f
Stereotypes, 41
  constrains social perception, 272–74
  definition of, 32
Stereotyping
  category-based, 306–7
  feature-based, 307–10, 308f
Stimuli
  age-related motivational states and gaze, 134,, 137, 138, 140, 141
    threat detection and phobic individuals, automatic gaze motives, 145
    facial attractivenessrewarded and nonrewarded stimuli recognition, nonhuman species facial-symmetry preference, 173
Stimulus generalization, 16, 18
Stimulus information, 8, 20
  age cues, 10–11
  attractiveness, 12
  emotion cues, 11–12
  familiarity cues, 8–10
  and perceived affordances, commonalities, 20
Stimulus onset asynchronies (SOAs), gaze cueing, 122
"Stranger approaching" scenario, 415
Stroop color naming test, 298, 298f
Stroop paradigms, measuring reaction time, 134, 135
Structural encoding, of face stimuli, 367
  debate on, 367–68
Subcortical social vision, 59–66
  cortical blindness, nonconscious perception in, 63–64
  faces, debates on, 65–66
  neurological patients and normal observers, subliminal perception in, 61
  nonconscious or unattended perception, 61–63
    direct "guessing" methods, use of, 61
Subjective experience, 301–2, 302f
Subjective ratings, of emotions, 11

Subliminal perception, in neurological patients and normal observers, 61
"SuperCaucasian" faces, 356
"SuperChinese" faces, 356
Superior temporal sulcus (STS), 13
  activation during biological motion, 429*f*
  for biological motion, 409, 413
  functional diversity of, 418*f*
  gaze directions and, 119, 120
  location of, 410*f*
  in motion processing of, 367*f*, 371
  research directions, 417–18
  responses to stimuli, 414*f*
  social brain network, 423
Surprise, neuroimaging, 220
Sylvian fissure, 409
Symmetry
  attractiveness and facial averageness, 168–69, 169*f*
  evolutionary view of, 171
  in human faces, debates on attractiveness of, 171–73
    computer graphic studies, use of, 172
Sympathy, 217, 220
Tachistoscopic procedures, 402
Teacher effectiveness, future outcomes of
  in thin-slice vision, 234
Technology, definition of, 201
Temporal cortex activation, speech and nonspeech facial movements, 371
Temporal dynamics, facial expressions and body language, 55–56
  N170, negative ERP-component, 55
Test (RFT), 80–81
  auditory attention, 82–83
  conclusions of, 86–88
    attention and self, social behavior and, 87–88
    attention strategy, socialization of, 87
    self orientation in attention regulation, causal role of, 86–87
  Framed-Line Test (FLT), 81
  mnemonic context effect, 85–86
  multitasking, 83
  perceptual inference, 83–84
Test of Nonverbal Cue Knowledge (TONCK), 241
Textural cues, 10
"Theory of mind" (ToM), 217, 220, 394
  in healthy individuals, 397
  and right hemisphere damage, 394–95
The Senses Considered as Perceptual Systems (Gibson), 13
Thin-slice vision, 228–43
  vs. auditory thin-slice impressions, 230
  boundaries for, 235–38

camouflage, 237–38
size and context, 235–37
definition of, 243
domains of, 230–35
individual, factors that increase or diminish, 238–41
as social perception modality, 243
using visual peephole, 228–30
visual processes in, 241–43
Threat cues
  detection of from motion, 257
  face processing, 92, 98, 100
  perceiver attunements and face processing, 100
  prolonged gaze as, 151, 162
Threat detection and phobic individuals, automatic gaze motives, 145
Threat inhibition effect, age-related gazing, 145
Top-down perspectives, aging eyes and, 133, 146
"Top heavy" hypothesis, 424
  and newborns, 424
"Tragedy of the commons" game, 207
Trait anxiety, 100
  in thin-slice vision, 231
Trait hostility, 236
Transcranial magnetic stimulation (TMS), 418
  in SSC, in face recognition, 378
Transforming technique, 205–6, 205–6*f*, 208
  vs. averaging, comparison between, 205–6
"Trust game", 207
Trusting behavior
  and facial resemblance, 207
Trustworthiness, identifying of, 378
Two alternative forced-choice (2AFC) experiment, gaze cascade effect, 152, 160, 161*f*
  and 4AFC task, 155
Ultraviolet (UV) radiation exposure, benefits of, 192
Unconditional automaticity, 42
Unconditional category activation, concept of, 41
Unitization, perceptual learning, 16
Utilitarian Hypothesis, 323
Valenced preferences, 138, 139
  positively valenced stimuli, motivation and age-related gaze, 136–37
Valence hypothesis, 400–401
Varecia, 287
"Variant hypothesis," 400
Vision, and social world, xxiii–xxvi
Vision science
  history of, xiii–xv
  in social psychology xv–xvii
Visual ambiguity
  cognitive control and, 299–302, 299*f*, 301*f*

Visual and social aspects, face processing
  conclusion of, 101–2
  current face-processing models, 91–92
  ecological approach, 96–99
  face processing, towards new look at, 92–94
  perceptual interference and integration, evidence for, 94–96
  person-level factors, 99–101
Visual attention, cultural variation and attention strategies, 79–82
  framed-line test (FLT), 81
  rod and frame test (RFT), 80–81
Visual cues, 46n1
Visual focus, in thin-slice vision, 242–43
Visually mediated attention, gaze perception and
  attention, gaze cueing of, 121–22
  gaze cueing and, 125–27
  gaze-cueing, specialness about, 122–25
    brain mechanisms, involvement of, 123–24
    dedicated neural circuitry, involvement of, 124
    neonates and two-month-olds, gaze-cueing behavior in, 124–25
    split-brain patient, brain mechanisms in, 123
    supporting evidence for, 124
  geometric mechanism, 112–13
    configural processing, disruption to, 113
    eye gaze, determining direction of, 112
  head orientation, contribution of, 114–19
    environment-related gaze direction, 114
    independent mechanisms account, 118
    iris location as cue, 116–17, 118
    nose angle, influence of, 117
    observer-related gaze direction, scleral contrast measure under, 115
    output, integration of, 121
    social attention cues from, 122
  luminance mechanism, 113–14
  psychophysical studies, 109–12
  social attention perception, neural mechanisms of, 119–21
  superior temporal sulcus (STS) region, role of, 119
  Theory of Mind and, 108
Visual masking, in thin-slice vision, 241–42
Visual motion perception, 248
  and information over time, 252

and motion movements, 251
multiple-aperture technique,
    250–51
and neural mechanisms, 252–53
point-light technique of, 250, 251,
    251*f*
and social processes, 249
Visual perception, and social
    cognition, 363
Visual processes, 250
    in thin-slice vision, 241–43

Visual system
    role in brain xiv
    stages of xv
Vocal cues, 11
Vocal qualities, multimodal cues, 10
Walker detection, 257
Wealth, and cosmetics usage, 200
Weapon misidentification, 296–97
    and ambiguity, 299
    race-based, 295–304
Williams Syndrome, 422

Women
    attractiveness, 178
    vs. men, pigmentation differences,
        188–90
    preference in facial resemblance,
        211, 212
    thin-slice vision of, 239
Yellow, meaning of, 283, 285*f*
Youthfulness, and facial
    attractiveness, 196